INTERNATIONAL BIBLIOGRAPHY OF HISTORICAL SCIENCES

INTERNATIONALE BIBLIOGRAPHIE DER GESCHICHTSWISSENSCHAFTEN
BIBLIOGRAFIA INTERNACIONAL DE CIENCIAS HISTORICAS
BIBLIOGRAPHIE INTERNATIONALE DES SCIENCES HISTORIQUES
BIBLIOGRAFIA INTERNAZIONALE DELLE SCIENZE STORICHE

VOLUME LXVIII
1999

Edited by Massimo Mastrogregori

with the contribution of a number of scholars,
under the auspices of the
International Committee of Historical Sciences

K · G · SAUR   MÜNCHEN 2004

The IBOHS for the years 1978 to 1992 (Vol. 47 – 61) was edited by
Michel François and Michael Keul for Vol. 47/48 (1978/1979) and
Jean Glénisson and Michael Keul for Vol. 49 – 61 (1980 – 1992)
on behalf of the International Committee of Historical Sciences
and was published by K. G. Saur Munich.

Bibliographic information published by Die Deutsche Bibliothek
Die Deutsche Bibliothek lists this publication in the Deutsche Nationalbibliografie;
detailed bibliographic data is available in the Internet at http://dnb.ddb.de.

Printed on acid-free paper / Gedruckt auf säurefreiem Papier

© 2004 by K. G. Saur Verlag GmbH, München
Printed in Germany

All Rights Strictly Reserved / Alle Rechte vorbehalten
No part of this publication may be reproduced, stored in a retrieval system,
or transmitted in any form or by any means, electronic, mechanical, photocopying,
recording, or otherwise, without permission in writing from the publisher /
Jede Art der Vervielfältigung ohne Erlaubnis des Verlags ist unzulässig

Technical partner: Dr. Rainer Ostermann, München
Managing partner and technical support: Ellediemme libri dal mondo, Roma
Printed and Bound by Strauss Offsetdruck GmbH, Mörlenbach

ISSN 0074-2015
ISBN 3-598-20430-2

General editor

Massimo MASTROGREGORI, Università di Roma 'La Sapienza'

Assistant editor

Carlo COLELLA, Roma

Advisory board

Maria Tereza AMADO, Universidad de Evora
Girolamo ARNALDI, Istituto storico italiano per il Medioevo, Roma
† Yuri BESSMERTNY, Institute of General History, Russian Academy of Sciences, Moscow
† Wiesław BIEŃKOWSKI, Polska Akademia Nauk
László BIRÓ, Hungarian Academy of sciences, Budapest
Corinne BONNET, Academia Belgica, Rome
Luciano CANFORA, Università di Bari
Alejandro CATTARUZZA, University of Buenos Aires, Argentina
Anne EIDSFELDT, University of Oslo Library
Ilse FREDERIKSEN VÄHÄKYRÖ, Turku University Library, Finland
Jean GLÉNISSON, Comité International des Sciences Historiques, Paris
Kazuhiko KONDO, University of Tokyo
Mario MAZZA, Università di Roma "La Sapienza"
Vilém PREČAN, Institute of Contemporary History, Prague
Matjaz REBOLJ, Ljubljana
Jacques REVEL, Ecole des Hautes Etudes en Sciences Sociales, Paris
† Ruggiero ROMANO, Ecole des Hautes Etudes en Sciences Sociales, Paris
Gabrielle M. SPIEGEL, Johns Hopkins University, Baltimore
Martina STERCKEN, Universität Zurich
Natasa STERGAR, Ljubliana
Abdeljellil TEMIMI, Fondation Temimi, Tunis
Șerban TURCUȘ, Università di Cluj Napoca, Romania
Nenad VEKARIĆ, Dubrovnik
Bahaeddin YEDİYILDIZ, Hacettepe Universitesi, Ankara

Contributing editors

Kira E. AGEEVA, State University of Human Sciences, Moscow (*Russian historiography*)
Maria Tereza AMADO, Universidad de Evora (*Portuguese historiography*)
Vassili N. BABENKO, Russian Academy of Sciences, Moscow (*Russian Historiography*)
† Wiesław BIEŃKOWSKI, Polska Akademia Nauk (*Polish historiography*)
Wolfdieter BIHL, Institut für Geschichte, Universität Wien (*Austrian historiography*)
László BIRÓ, Hungarian Academy of sciences, Budapest (*Hungarian historiography*)
Vera BRENOVA, Institute of Contemporary History, Prague (*Czech historiography*)
Alejandro CATTARUZZA, University of Buenos Aires, Argentina (*Latin American historiography*)
Carlo COLELLA (*History by countries, History of international relations*)

Laura DE GIORGI, Università di Venezia (*Chinese historiography*)
Francesca DEVESCOVI, Istituto italiano per gli studi storici, Napoli (*History of modern culture*)
Anne EIDSFELDT, University of Oslo Library, (*Norvegian historiography*)
Ilse FREDERIKSEN VÄHÄKYRÖ, Turku University Library, Finland (*Finnish historiography*)
Anna GRUCA, Instytut Historii PAN. Pracownia Bibliografii Bieżącej (*Polish historiography*)
Alessandro GUERRA, Università di Roma 'La Sapienza' (*Modern religious history*)
Timophey GUIMON, Institute of Universal History of the Russian Academy of Sciences, Moscow (*Russian historiography*)
Libby KAHANE, The Jewish National and University Library, Jerusalem (*Historiography of Israel*)
Kazuhiko KONDO, University of Tokyo (*Japanese historiography*)
Mauro LENZI, Società Romana di Storia Patria, Roma (*Palaeography, Diplomatics, History of the book, Medieval history*)
Jean Marie MAILLEFER, Université Charles-De-Gaulle Lille 3 (*Danish and Swedish historiography*)
Massimo MASTROGREGORI, Università di Roma 'La Sapienza' (*Auxiliary sciences, General works, Modern history*)
Stjepan MATKOVIĆ, (*Croatian historiography*)
Massimo PONTESILLI, Istituto italiano per gli studi storici, Napoli (*History of modern culture*)
Matjaz REBOLJ, Ljubljana (*Slovenian historiography*)
Eszter SALGÓ, dottoranda in Storia d'Europa presso l'Universitá di Roma 'La Sapienza', Roma (*Hungarian historiography*)
Lidia SANTARELLI, Università di Roma 'La Sapienza' (*Modern Greek historiography*)
Marco SANTUCCI, Università di Roma 'La Sapienza' (*Ancient history*)
Evgeny E. SAVITSKI, Institute of Universal History of the Russian Academy of Sciences, Moscow (*Russian historiography*)
Alžbeta SEDLIAKOVÁ, (*Slovak historiography*)
A. SLIVA, Rossijskaja Akademija Nauk, Moskva (*Russian historiography*)
Natale SPINETO, Università di Milano (*History of religions*)
Natasa STERGAR, Ljubliana (*Slovenian historiography*)
Paola STIRPE, Università di Roma 'La Sapienza' (*Ancient history*)
Şerban TURCUŞ, Università di Cluj Napoca, Romania (*Romanian historiography*)
Michaela VALENTE, Università di Roma 'La Sapienza' (*Modern religious history*)
Alec VUIJLSTEKE, Academia Belgica, Rome (*Belgian historiography*)
Galina A. YANKOVSKAYA, Perm State University, Perm (*Russian historiography*)
Bahaeddin YEDİYILDIZ, Hacettepe Universitesi, Ankara (*Historiography of Turkey*)

Consulting editors

Maurice AYMARD, Maison des sciences de l'homme, Paris
Eric BRIAN, Centre Alexandre Koyré, Paris
Louis CHATELLIER, Université de Nancy II

Sten EBBESEN, University of Copenhagen
Carlo FRANCO, Università di Venezia
Olivier GUYOTJEANNIN, Ecole nationale des Chartes, Paris
Michel MORINEAU, Paris
Brian TIERNEY, Cornell University, Ithaca
Giusto TRAINA, Università di Lecce
Pietro VANNICELLI, Università di Urbino
André VAUCHEZ, Ecole Française de Rome

Special Assistant editor

Luigi Maria FRATEPIETRO, Roma
Dario IPPOLITO, Scuola superiore di studi storici, Università di San Marino

CONTENTS

	Pages
FOREWORD	XI
SCHEME	XIII
GENERAL HISTORICAL BIBLIOGRAPHIES	XIX
BIBLIOGRAPHY	1
INDEX OF NAMES	341
GEOGRAPHICAL INDEX	411

FOREWORD

The International Bibliography of Historical Sciences (I. B. O. H. S.) is a selective and descriptive bibliography, and the works it mentions, both books and articles, are arranged according to a methodical and chronological scheme originally drawn up and established by the Bibliographical Commission of the International Committee of Historical Sciences; the scheme has been revised only in details.

An exposition of the principles which were followed in the choice of works included and of the rules which were observed for their presentation in the present volume is set out below.

A. Manner of Selection.

In agreement with the wish expressed by the Bibliographical Commission of the C. I. S. H., the selection is actuated by the twin concern of preserving for the I. B. O. H. S. its character of a general bibliography comprehending the whole field of historical sciences, and of putting at the disposal of historians as also librarians the essential facts of historical production throughout the world, in one complete volume appearing annually.

In view of the multiplication of specialized bibliographies, it has in fact appeared more than ever necessary to offer to isolated scholars and even scientific establishments unable to obtain all these bibliographies the means of keeping informed, each year, of the advancement of historical science. But it was also desirable that these bibliographies be mentioned, and this has been done in two different ways: firstly, we have listed, outside the systematic inventory and immediately preceding it, the great international or national bibliographies giving the historical production of a country and in which a conspectus of works connected with this country is given; on the other hand, in the systematic inventory, at the head of each division or subdivision are mentioned general bibliographies dealing with one of the historical disciplines or particular bibliographies devoted to one question, one author or one province or state, and which find their logical position in that division or subdivision; in the latter case, the bibliographies are preceded by an asterisk (*).

In order to justify its existence as a working instrument of a high scientific standard and of international application, the I. B. O. H. S. only mentioned books or articles with a wider scope than the narrow field of local preoccupations, and rejects also reviews which are mere presentations or of courtesies. Like-wise re-editings, translations, descriptions of research which do not include new elements of information, exhibition catalogues without commentary, typed or stencilled works and works of popularization and propaganda have been normally eliminated.

On the other hand, the contributing editors have been careful to describe those works which, through slight or of apparently only local interest, make an obvious contribution to general history or to the solution of current problems; this is the case of certain reports on excavations and of articles bearing on controversial subjects touching the history of institutions or civilization; in this case, as whenever the title of an article was too vague, it has been followed whenever possible by a brief remark or by a date in brackets for the reader's orientation. Herein can be found an effort which will not fail to be useful to those who use the I. B. O. H. S., and which can be increased in future volumes without incurring the temptation to transform this essentially *selective* and *descriptive* bibliography into an analytical and critical one, this double character being in fact reserved to specialized bibliographies.

Unlike the greater number of national bibliographies, the I. B. O. H. S. does not limit the works included by any fixed date; that is to say that works connected with the most recent history find a place in it, notably those connected with international relations (P 8); at the same time the selection had to be correspondingly strictly.

By this conception, the I. O. B. H. S. keeps a physiognomy peculiar to itself; it has no tendency towards substituting for any existing bibliography, but while avoiding as far as possible a double role, it allows to be necessary that amount or overlapping which is profitable in the scholarly world.

B. Rules of Presentation.

The volume LXVIII, 1999 mentions the works published with the date: 1999. Within each division or subdivision, the works are presented in alphabetical order of their authors. Slavonic, Greek, Japanese, Hebraic and Arabic names are transcribed into Latin characters and placed according to the order of the Latin alphabet, but characters with diacritics, for instance ć, č, ś, š are considered as if ordinaries c, s. Germanic and Scandinavian names are classed according to the function of the developed value of letters of inflection: ä, ö, ø, ü become ae, oe, ue. Mc and M' are indexed as if Mac.

Anonymous or collective works are classed alphabetically according to the initial of the key word in the title, for instance: «Congress (Fourteenth) of the Learned Societies...» At the same time, in heavy type are the names of scholars who have been the object of an important biographical or historiographical study (B § 2 b) and those of Saints (G § 4, I § 13 d); in the first case, the works are indicated in the alphabetical order of the people concerned.

As it has been done for the bibliographies peculiar to a division or subdivision, the publications of texts which had their place in the alphabetical list of each division or subdivision have been extracted and transferred to the head of the alphabetical list and immediately following the list of bibliographies; these publications of texts have been distinguished by being preceded by two asterisks. Thus the reader has immediately before his eyes the bibliographies and editions of the most recent texts bearing on a particular question or period. However, concerning the texts, the procedure of two asterisks (**) has not been adopted in chapter E, F, G and H, each of which already has a division especially devoted to the texts.

When the current year has been marked by the commemoration of an important historical event, the works to which this commemoration has led are grouped separately and under a special title at the end of the subdivision where this event finds its normal place.

When a work which has been in circulation for three or four years has been the object of a review every succeeding year, only the name of the author is cited plus the essential of the title, preceded by a reference to the number of the last volume of the I. B. O. H. S. in which it was quoted; it is thus possible to follow year to year the state of the criticism which the publication of a book has provoked.

Where the «collation» of works is concerned, the unification of references to pages, plates and illustrations, etc. has been sought as far as possible by putting them into either French or English, these being the two languages which have the most words or initial letters of words of an identical meaning in common.The transferrings of works interesting for one part to a section other than their logical one, transferences indicated by «*Cf. n°*...», have been grouped at the end of each section.

In the index of names of authors and persons, the names of Classical authors, Saints and Popes are written in their Latin form.

SCHEME

GENERAL HISTORICAL BIBLIOGRAPHIES
(p. XIX-XX)

A

AUXILIARY SCIENCES
(p. 1-17)

§ 1. Palaeography. 1-22. – § 2. Diplomatics. 23-28. – § 3. History of the book (*a*. Manuscripts; *b*. Printed books). 29-141. – § 4. Chronology. 142-164. – § 5. Genealogy and family history. 165-203. – § 6. Sigillography and heraldry. 204-235. – § 7. Numismatics and metrology. 236-252.– § 8. Linguistics. 253-300. – § 9. Historical geography, travels and discoveries. 301-373. – § 10. Iconography and images. 374-409.

B

MANUALS, GENERAL WORKS AND WORKS ON LARGE PERIODS
(p. 19-58)

§ 1. Archives, libraries and museums (*a*. Archives; *b*. Libraries; *c*. Museums). 410-482. – § 2. History of historiography (*a*. General; *b*. Special studies). 483-806. – § 3. Methodology, philosophy, and teaching of history. 807-883. – § 4. Ethnology, folklore and historical anthropology. 884-926. – § 5. General history. 927-1049. – § 6. Theory of the state and of society. 1050-1109. – § 7. Constitutional and legal history. 1110-1142. – § 8. Economic and social history. 1143-1192. – § 9. History of civilization, sciences and education. 1193-1269. – § 10. History of art. 1270-1300. – § 11. History of religions (*a*. General; *b*. Special studies). 1301-1389. – § 12. History of philosophy. 1390-1409. – § 13. History of literature. 1410-1445.

C

PREHISTORY
(p. 59-63)

§ 1. General. 1446-1483. – § 2. Palaeolithic and Mesolithic. 1484-1513. – § 3. Neolithic. 1514-1525. – § 4. Bronze age. 1526-1541. – § 5. Iron age. 1542-1561.

D

THE ANCIENT EAST
(the Hellenistic States included)
(p. 65-73)

§ 1. General. 1562-1576. – § 2. The Near East. 1577-1610. – § 3. Egypt. 1611-1661. – § 4. Mesopotamia. 1662-1720. – § 5. Hittites. 1721-1743. – § 6. Jews and Semitic peoples to the end of the ancient world. 1744-1780. – § 7. Iran. 1781-1812.

E

GREEK HISTORY
(p. 75-89)

§ 1. Classical world in general. 1813-1834. – § 2. Prehellenic epoch. 1835-1853. – § 3. Sources and criticism of sources (*a*. Epigraphical sources; *b*. Literary sources). 1854-1968. – § 4. General and political history. 1969-2010. – § 5. History of law and institutions. 2011-2026. – § 6. Economic and social history. 2027-2077. – § 7. History of literature, philosophy and science (*a*. Literature; *b*. Philosophy and sciences). 2078-2177. – § 8. Religion and mythology. 2178-2215. – § 9. Archaeology and history of art. 2216-2259.

F

HISTORY OF ROME, ANCIENT ITALY AND THE ROMAN EMPIRE
(p. 91-109)

§ 1. The peoples of Italy. 2260-2279. – § 2. The Etruscans. 2280-2306. – § 3. Sources and criticism of sources. (*a*. Epigraphical sources; *b*. Literary sources). 2307-2391. – § 4. General and political history. 2392-2473. – § 5. History of law and institutions. 2474-2526. – § 6. Economic and social history. 2527-2585. – § 7. History of literature, philosophy and science (*a*. Literature; *b*. Philosophy and science). 2586-2691. – § 8. Religion and mythology. 2692-2726. – § 9. Archaeology and history of art. 2727-2788. – § 10. Late antiquity. Transformation of the Roman world. 2789-2826.

G

EARLY HISTORY OF THE CHURCH TO GREGORY THE GREAT
(p. 111-115)

§ 1. Sources. 2827-2866. – § 2. General. 2867-2876. – § 3. Special studies. 2877-2950. – § 4. Hagiography. 2951-2959.

H

BYZANTINE HISTORY
(since Justinian)
(p. 117-122)

§ 1. Sources. 2960-2975. – § 2. General. 2976-2995. – § 3. Special studies. 2996-3094.

I

HISTORY OF THE MIDDLE AGES
(p. 123-157)

§ 1. Sources and criticism of sources (*a*. Non-literary sources; *b*. Literary sources). 3095-3183. – § 2. General works. 3184-3216. – § 3. Political history (*a*. General; *b*. 476–900; *c*. 900–1300; *d*. 1300–1500). 3217-3268. – § 4. Jews. 3269-3292. – § 5. Islam. 3293-3318. – § 6. Vikings. 3319-3327. – § 7. History of law and institutions. 3328-3355. – § 8. Economic and social history. 3356-3433. – § 9. History of civilization, literature, technology and education (*a*. Civilization; *b*. Literature; *c*. Technology; *d*. Education). 3434-3633. – § 10. History of art. (*a*. General; *b*. Special studies). 3634-3682 – § 11. History of music. 3683-3696. – § 12. History of philosophy, theology and science (*a*. Sources; *b*. Studies). 3697-3757. – § 13. History of the Church and religion (*a*. General; *b*. History of the Popes; *c*. Monastic history; *d*. Hagiography; *e*. Special studies). 3758-3910. – § 14. Settlements. Place names. Town planning. 3911-3920.

K

MODERN HISTORY, GENERAL WORKS
(p. 159-212)

§ 1. General. 3921-4008. – § 2. History by countries. 4009-5257.

L

MODERN RELIGIOUS HISTORY
(p. 213-223)

§ 1. General. 5258-5317. – § 2. Roman Catholicism (*a*. General; *b*. History of the Popes; *c*. Special studies; *d*. Religious orders; *e*. Missions). 5318-5453. – § 3. Orthodox Church. 5454-5460. – § 4. Protestantism. 5461-5526. – § 5. Non-Christian religions and sects. 5527-5557.

M

HISTORY OF MODERN CULTURE
(p. 225-263)

§ 1. General. 5558-5718. – § 2. Academies and intellectual organizations. 5719-5759. – § 3. Education. 5760-5827. – § 4. The Press. 5828-5878. – § 5. Philosophy. 5879-6029. – § 6. Exact, natural, medical sciences and technique. 6030-6183. – § 7. Literature (*a*. General; *b*. Renaissance; *c*. Classicism; *d*. Romanticism and after). 6184-6381. – § 8. Art and Industrial art (*a*. General; *b*. Architecture; *c*. Sculpture, painting, etching and drawing; *d*. Decorative, popular and industrial art). 6382-6512. – § 9. Music, theatre, cinema and broadcasting. 6513-6634.

N

MODERN ECONOMIC AND SOCIAL HISTORY
(p. 265-281)

§ 1. General. 6635-6670. – § 2. Political economy. 6671-6687.– § 3. Industry, mining and transportation. 6688-6728. – § 4. Trade. 6729-6754. – § 5. Agriculture and agricultural problems. 6755-6781. – § 6. Money and finance. 6782-6820. – § 7. Demography and urban history. 6821-6860. – § 8. Social history. 6861-7035. – § 9. Working-class movement and socialism. 7036-7065.

O

MODERN LEGAL AND CONSTITUTIONAL HISTORY
(p. 283-288)

§ 1. General. 7066-7080. – § 2. History of constitutional law. 7081-7107. – § 3. Public law and institutions. 7108-7143. – § 4. Civil and penal law. 7144-7189. – § 5. International law. 7190-7202.

P

HISTORY OF INTERNATIONAL RELATIONS
(p. 289-322)

§ 1. General. 7203-7300. – § 2. History of colonization and decolonization (*a*. General; *b*. Asia; *c*. Africa; *d*. America; *e*. Oceania). 7301-7386. – § 3. From 1500 to 1789 (*a*. General; *b*. 1500–1648; *c*. 1648–1789). 7387-7451. – § 4. From 1789 to 1815. 7452-7475. – § 5. From 1815 to 1910. 7476-7538. – § 6. From 1910 to 1935. The First World War. 7539-7622. – § 7. From 1935 to 1945. The Second World War (*a*. General; *b*. Diplomacy. Economy; *c*. Military operations; *d*. Resistance). 7623-7800. – § 8. From 1945. 7801-8036.

R

ASIA
(p. 323-334)

§ 1. General. 8037-8048. – § 2. Western and central Asia. 8049-8073. – § 3. South Asia and Southeast Asia. 8074-8096. – § 4. China. 8097-8272. – § 5. Japan (before 1868). 8273-8320. – § 6. Korea. 8321-8329.

S

AFRICA
(To its colonization)
(p. 335-336)

Nᵒˢ 8330-8360.

T

AMERICA
(To its colonization)
(p. 337-338)

Nᵒˢ 8361-8386.

U

OCEANIA
(To its colonization)
(p. 339)

Nᵒˢ 8387-8393.

GENERAL HISTORICAL BIBLIOGRAPHIES

I. [Austria]. Österreichische historische Bibliographie. Austrian historical bibliography 1997. [1996. Cf. Bibl. 98, n° *I.*] Hrsg. v. Günther HÖDL u. Wolfdieter BIHL. Bearb. v. Uta HÖDL, Martha JAUERNIG u. Bettina KUTTIN. Graz, Neugebauer u. Santa Barbara, Clio, 99, 631 p. – Österreichische historische Bibliographie. Nachträge 1945–1994: Austrian historical bibliography Nachträge 1945–1994. Bearbeitet von Martha JAUERNIG, unter Mitwirkung von Bettina KUTTIN und Uta HÖDL. Graz, Wolfgang Neugebauer Verlag u. Santa Barbara, ABC-Clio, 99, 653 p.

II. [Belgium] Bibliographie de l'histoire de Belgique. Bibliografie van de geschiedenis van België 1997. [1996. Cf. Bibl. 98, n° *II.*]. Ed. par Romain VAN EENOO, Jean BOVESSE [et al.]. *Revue Belge de philologie et d'histoire – Belgisch Tijdschrift voor Filologie en Geschiedenis*, 99, 77, 2bis, [s. p

III. [Czechoslovak Republik] Bibliografie ceskych / ceskoslovenskych dejin 1918–1999 Vyber knih, sborniku a clanku vydanych v letech 1996–1999 a doplnky za roky 1990–1995. Praha, Ustav pro soud. Dejin, 99, 2 vol., 396 p., 164 p., 99, [s. p.].

IV. [Finland] ANTIN (Kirsti). Finländsk historisk litteratur 1997 i bibliografiskt urval. [1996. Cf. Bibl. 98, n° *IV.*] (La littérature historique de la Finlande. Une sélection bibliographique. 1996). *Histisk Tidskrift (Finland)*, 99, 84, p. 119-145.

V. [France] Bibliographie annuelle de l'histoire de France du Ve siècle à 1958. Année 1998. [1997. Cf. Bibl. 98, n° *V.*] Redigée par M. SONNET, B. KERIVEN et Cl. GHIATI. Paris, Ed. du C. N. R. S., 99, LXXXIII-958 p.

VI. [Germany] Historische Bibliographie. Berichtsjahr 1998 [1997. Cf. Bibl. 98, n° *VI.*] Hrsg. von der Arbeitsgemeinschaft ausseruniversitärer Forschungseinrichtungen in der Bundesrepublik Deutschland. München, Oldenbourg, 99, 920 p. – Jahresberichte für Deutsche Geschichte. Neue Folge. 50. Jahrgang 1998. Mit Nachträgen. [48. Jahrgang 1997. Cf. Bibl. 98, n° *VI.*] Hrsg. von der Berlin-Brandeburgischen Akademie der Wissenschaften. Berlin, Akademie Verlag, 99, IV-1237 p.

VII. [Great Britain] Annual bibliography of British and Irish history. Publications of 1998. [1997. Cf. Bibl. 98, n° *VII.*] Ed. by Austin GEE. Oxford, Oxford U. P., 99, XV-444 p. – Articles relating to the history of Wales published mainly in 1996. Comp. by Sean DAVIES and Peter FREEMAN. *Welsh History Review*, 99, 19, p. 576-591. – GRAHAM (T. W.). A list of articles on Scottish history published during the year 1997. *Scottish Historical Review*, 99, 78, p. 95-105. – GRANT (Alexander). A list+of essays on Scottish history published during the years 1996–1997. *Scottish Historical Review*, 99, 78, p. 106-110. – Historical research for higher degrees in the United Kingdom. Theses completed 1998. Ed. by Joyce M. HORN et Jane WINTERS. London, Institute of historical research, 99, 55 p. – Major accessions to repositories in 1997 relating to Welsh history. *Welsh History Review*, 99, 19, p. 526-532. – WINTERS (Jane), PAYANE (Annie). Historical research for higher degrees in United Kingdom: theses completed 1998, 1999, list 60-61. *Historical Research,* 99, list n. 60, 71 p.

VIII. International bibliography of historical sciences. Internationale Bibliographie der Geschichtswissenschaften. Bibliografia internacional de ciencias historicas. Bibliographie internationale des sciences historiques. Bibliografia internazionale delle scienze storiche. Vol. LXII, 1993 [Vol. LXI, 1992. Cf. Bibl. 96, n° VII.] Ed. by Massimo MASTROGREGORI with the contribution of a number of scholars. München, K. G. Saur, 99, XV-400 p.

IX. [Ireland] Writings on Irish history 1993 and 1994. Incorporating Addenda from previous years. Ed by S. WARD-PERKINS. Dublin, Irish Committee of historical sciences a. Irish historical studies, 99, [s. p.].

X. [Netherlands] VAN DER PLAAT (G. N.), DE KEUNING (M.), VAN HERWIJNEN (G.), VAN VLIET (C.). Kroniek. Lijst van de voornaamste in 1998 verschenen boeken en artikelen op het terrein van de Nederlandse geschiedenis. [1997. Cf. Bibl. 98, n° *XI.*] La Haye, Koninklijk Nederlands Historisch Genootschap, 99, 104 p.

XI. [Nigeria] AKINBODE (Rahmon O.), OLUMOROTI (Oluranti). Historical+research in Nigeria: index to articles in Journal of Historical Society of Nigeria (JHSN) and bibliography of Nigerian books and monographs on history (1956–2000 A.D.). Ibadan, Options Books and Information Services, 99, 107 p.

XII. [Norway] Norsk bokfortegnelse. Årskatalog 1998. (The Norwegian national bibliography. Catalog for 1998 [books on history]). Oslo, Nasjonalbiblioteket, 99, p. 686-692.

XIII. [Poland] Bibliografia historii polskiej za rok 1998. [1996–1997. Cf. Bibl. 98, n° *XIII.*] (Biliographie de l'histoire polonaise pour l'année 1998). Auteurs: Wojciech FRAZIK, Stefan GASIOROWSKI, Anna GRUCA, Zbigniew SOLAK. Réd. Wiesław BIENKOWSKI. Kraków, Wydawn. Profesjonalnej Szkoły Biznesu, 99, [s. p.]. (Pol. Akad. Nauk, Inst. Hist., Zakł. Bibliografii Bieżącej).

XIV. [Slovakia] SEDLIAKOVÁ (Alžbeta). Historiografia na Slovensku 1997. Výberová bibliografia. [1995. Cf. Bibl. 97, n° *XVII.*] (Historiography in Slovakia 1997. Selected Bibliography). *Historický časopis*, 99, 47, 4, p. 727-763.

XV. [Spain] Indice histórico español. Publicación semestral del centro de estudios históricos internacionales. Ed. por Pere MOLAS RIBALTA y Rosa ORTEGA CANADELL. Vol. 37, n. 111-112, 1999. [1998. Cf. Bibl. 98, n° *XVI.*] Barcelona, Publicacions de la Universitat de Barcelona, 99, 2 vol., 357 p., 352 p.

XVI. [Switzerland] Bibliographie der Schweizergeschichte. Bibliographie de l'histoire suisse. 1996. [1995. Cf. Bibl. 98, n° *XVIII.*] Bearb. v./Etablie par P. L. SURCHAT. Bern, Bibliothèque nationale suisse/Schweizerische Landesbibliothek, 99, XXVII-237 p.

General historical bibliographies. Addenda 1998

XVII. [Norway] Norsk bokfortegnelse. Årskatalog 1997. (The Norwegian national bibliography. Catalog for 1997 [books on history]). Oslo, Universitetsbiblioteket i Oslo, 98, p. 633-643. – Norske tidsskriftartikler. Årskatalog 1997. (The Norwegian Index to Periodical Articles. 1997 [articles on history]). Oslo, Universitetsbiblioteket i Oslo, 98, p. 499-530.

XVIII. [Slovakia] SEDLIAKOVÁ (Alžbeta). Historiografia na Slovensku 1996. Výberová bibliografia. [1995. Cf. Bibl. 97, n° *XVII.*] (Historiography in Slovakia 1996. Selected Bibliography). *Historický časopis*, 98, 46, 4, p. 713-762.

A

AUXILIARY SCIENCES

§ 1. Palaeography. 1-22. – § 2. Diplomatics. 23-28. – § 3. History of the book (*a*. Manuscripts; *b*. Printed books). 29-141. – § 4. Chronology. 142-164. – § 5. Genealogy and family history. 165-203. – § 6. Sigillography and heraldry. 204-235. – § 7. Numismatics and metrology. 236-252.– § 8. Linguistics. 253-300. – § 9. Historical geography, travels and discoveries. 301-373. – § 10. Iconography and images. 374-409.

§ 1. Palaeography.

* 1. BMB. Bibliografia dei manoscritti in scrittura beneventana. A cura della Scuola di specializzazione per Conservatori di beni archivistici librari della civiltà medievale, Università di Cassino. Vol. 7. [Vol. 6. Cf. Bibl. 98, n° 2.] Roma, Viella, 98, 308 p.

* 2. BOYLE (Leonard E.). Paleografia latina medievale: introduzione bibliografica. Roma, Edizioni Quasar, 99, XIV-493 p.

* 3. Bulletin codicologique, publié par le Centre International de Codicologie. [1998. Cf. Bibl. 98, n° 3.] Éd. par Pierre COCKSHAW. *Scriptorium*, 99, 53, 1-2, p. 1*-324*.

4. ALTURO I PERUCHO (Jesús). Studia in codicum fragmenta. Bellaterra i Barcelona, Universitat Autonoma de Barcelona, 99, 310 p. (ill.). (Universitat Autònoma de Barcelona. Seminari de Paleografia, Diplomàtica i Codicologia. Monografíes, 1).

5. CAVALLO (Guglielmo). Per le mani e la datazione del codice Ven. Marc. Gr. 450. *Quaderni di storia*, 99, 25, 49, p. 155-177.

6. COX (Richard A. V.). The language of the Ogam inscriptions of Scotland: contributions to the study of Ogam, Runic and Roman alphabet inscriptions in Scotland. Aberdeen, Dept. of Celtic, University of Aberdeen, 99, XVI-187 p. (ill., map). (Scottish Gaelic studies monograph series, 1).

7. DUMVILLE (David). A palaeographer's review: the insular system of scripts in the early Middle Ages. Osaka, Institute of Oriental and Occidental Studies, Kansai University, 99, X-130 p.

8. EDROIU (Nicolae). Introducere în Ştiinţele auxiliare ale Istoriei. (Introduction to the auxiliary sciences of history). Cluj-Napoca, Editura Presa Universitară Clujeană, 99, 467 p.

9. FRASCADORE (Angela). La scomunica e la scrittura: un'indagine sulla cultura grafica di notai, giudici e testimoni nella Puglia del primo Trecento. Tavarnuzze-Firenze, SISMEL-Edizioni del Galluzzo, 99, 195 p. (pl., ill.). (Millennio medievale, 13. Studi, 3).

10. FUCIC (Branko). Croatian Glagolitic epigraphy. London, Stephen Osborne, 99, 42 p. (ill.).

11. HÉBRARD (Jean), CHARTIER (Roger), PETRUCCI (Armando). Alfabetismo, escritura, sociedad. Barcelona, Gedisa Editorial, 99, 319 p. (Colección LeA, 14).

12. Inschrift und Material, Inschrift und Buchschrift. Fachtagung für mittelalterliche und neuzeitliche Epigraphik, Ingolstadt 1997. Hrsg. v. Walter KOCH und Christine STEININGER. München, Verlag der Bayerischen Akademie der Wissenschaften, 99, 250 p.-104 p. of plates (ill.). (Abhandlungen / Bayerische Akademie der Wissenschaften, Philosophisch-Historische Klasse, 117).

13. KENDRICK (Laura). Animating the letter: the figurative embodiment of writing from late antiquity to the Renaissance. Columbus, Ohio State U. P., 99, IX-326 p. (ill.).

14. Methoden der Schriftbeschreibung. Hrsg. v. Peter RÜCK. Stuttgart, Jan Thorbecke Verlag, 99, 490 p. (ill., facs.). (Historische Hilfswissenschaften, 4).

15. PRESTON (Jean F.), YEANDLE (Laetitia). English handwriting, 1400–1650: an introductory manual. Asheville, Pegasus Press, 99, XIV-98 p. (ill.). (Pegasus paperbooks).

16. RIESCO TERRERO (Angel). Introducción a la paleografía y la diplomática general. Madrid, Editorial Sintesis, 99, 366 p. (ill.). (Letras universitarias).

17. SASSOON (Rosemary). Handwriting of the twentieth century. London a. New York, Routledge, 99, 208 p. (ill.).

18. SCHNEIDER (Karin). Paläographie und Handschriftenkunde für Germanisten: eine Einführung. Tübingen, Max Niemeyer Verlag, 99, X-237 p. (ill.). (Sammlung kurzer Grammatiken germanischer Dialekte. B. Ergänzungsreihe, 8).

19. Scriptures (The) and early medieval Ireland. Proceedings of the 1993 Conference of the society for Hiberno-Latin studies on early Irish exegesis and homilectics. Ed. by Thomas O'LOUGHLIN. Turnhout, Brepols, 99, VIII-332 p. (Instrumenta patristica, 31).

20. SHIBAEV (M. A.). Opyty po istochnikovedeniiu. Drevnerusskaiaknizhnost': arkheografiia, paleografiia, kodikologiia. S.-Peterburg, Dmitrii Bulanin, 99, 250 p. (facs.).

21. WILLIMAN (Daniel), CORSANO (Karen). Tracing provenances by dictio probatoria. *Scriptorium,* 99, 53, 1, p. 124-145.

22. ZALIZNJAK (Andrej A.). Problema tozhdestva i skhodstva pocherkov v berestjanykh gramotakh. (The problem of identity and similarity of scripts in the birchbark documents of Novgorod). *In:* Velikij Novgorod v istorii srednevekovoj Evropy [Cf. n° 3216], p. 293-328.

Cf. n°s 23-28, 79, 445, 1965, 3095-3183, 3523, 8286

§ 2. Diplomatics.

23. CUBITT (Catherine). Finding the forger: an alleged decree of the 679 council of Hatfield. *English historical review,* 99, 114, 459, p. 1217-1248.

24. GARCÍA VALLE (Adela). El notariado hispánico medieval: consideraciones histórico-diplomáticas y filológicas. [Valencia], Universitat de València, Departamento de Filología Espanola, 99, 217 p. [Anejo no. 36 de la revista Cuadernos de Filología].

25. HOWLETT (D. R.). Sealed from within: self authenticating insular charters. Dublin, Four Courts Press, 99, X-110 p.

26. Papsturkunde und europäisches Urkundenwesen. Studien zu ihrer formalen und rechtlichen Kohärenz vom 11. bis 15. Jahrhundert. Hrsg. v. Peter HERDE und Hermann JAKOBS. Köln, Böhlau Verlag, 99, XI-433 p. (ill.). (Archiv für Diplomatik, Schriftgeschichte Siegelund Wappenkunde. Beiheft, 7).

27. SARADI (Heleni G.). Il sistema notarile bizantino, VI–XV secolo. Milano, Giuffré, 99, IX-325 p. (Per una storia del notariato nella civiltà europea, 4).

28. Svenskt diplomatariums huvudkartotek över medeltidsbreven. (Fichier général des chartes médiévales du Diplomatarium suédois). Stockholm, Riksarkivet, 99, CD-rom (version 1.0).

Cf. n°s 1-22, 592, 3095-3183

§ 3. History of the book.

a. *Manuscripts*

29. Abadía (La) del Sacromonte de Granada: catálogo de manuscritos. Ed. por María del Carmen CALERO PALACIOS. Granada, Universidad de Granada, 99, 391 p. (ill.). (Biblioteca Chronica nova de estudios históricos, 63).

30. Abtei (Die) Echternach, 698–1998. Hrsg. v. Michele Camillo FERRARI, Jean SCHROEDER, Henri TRAUFFLER und Jean KRIER. Luxembourg, Publications du CLUDEM, 99, 374 p. (ill., facs., maps, pl., music). (Publications du CLUDEM, 15).

31. ALVAREZ MÁRQUEZ (María del Carmen). Manuscritos localizados de Pedro Gómez Barroso y Juan de Cervantes, arzobispos de Sevilla. Alcalà de Henares, Servicio de Publicaciones, Universidad de Alcalà y Seville, Excma. Diputacion Provincial de Sevilla, 99, 302 p. (pl., ill.). (Anexos de « Signo », 3).

32. Aventure (L') des écritures. La page. Ed. par Hans-Jörg HUNZIKER, Ursula HELD et Anne ZALI. Paris, Bibliotheque nationale de France, 99, 215 p. (ill.).

33. Beute und Erbe: Spuren ungewöhnlicher Bücherwanderungen. Eine Ausstellung der Universitätsbibliothek Marburg vom 27. April bis 30. Mai 1999. Marburg, Universitätsbibliothek Marburg, 99, 246 p. (ill.). (Schriften der Universitätsbibliothek Marburg, 91).

34. BIANCHI (Simona). I manoscritti medievali della provincia di Prato. Firenze, Regione Toscana e SISMEL-Edizioni del Galluzzo, 99, XV-133 p. (ill.). (Manoscritti medievali della Toscana, 2).

35. Bilderwelt (Die) des Klosters Engelberg: das Skriptorium unter den Äbten Frowin (1143–1178), Berchtold (1178–1197), Heinrich (1197–1223). Hrsg. v. Christoph EGGENBERGER. Luzern, Diopter, 99, 187 p. (ill.).

36. British (The) Library catalogue of the Ashley manuscripts. Ed. by T. A. J. BURNETT. London, British Library, 99, 2 vol., XI-725 p. (pl., facs.).

37. Buch und Bild im Mittelalter. Hrsg. v. Marlis STÄHLI und Ulrich KNAPP. Hildesheim, Dom-Museum Hildesheim u. Gerstenberg, 99, 128 p. (ill.).

38. BURKHART (Peter). Die lateinischen und deutschen Handschriften der Universitäts-Bibliothek Leipzig. Die theologischen Handschriften (Ms 501-625). Wiesbaden, Harrassowitz, 99, 422 p. (Katalog der Handschriften der Universitäts-Bibliothek Leipzig, 5).

39. BUSCH (Lothar). Der handschriftliche Nachlass Ludwig Tiecks und die Tieck-Bestände der Staatsbibliothek zu Berlin Preussischer Kulturbesitz: Katalog. Wiesbaden, Harrassowitz, 99, 209 p. (Kataloge der Handschriftenabteilung, 5).

40. Calligrafia di Dio: la miniatura celebra la Parola. A cura di Giordana CANOVA MARIANI e Paola

FERRARO VETTORI. Modena, F. C. Panini, 99, 251 p. (ill.).

41. CALLU (Florence), ANGREMY (Annie). Catalogue des nouvelles acquisitions françaises du département des manuscrits, 1972–1986: n°s 16428-18755. Paris, Bibliothèque nationale de France, 99, XIII-590 p.

42. Care and conservation of manuscripts, 4th: proceedings of the fourth international seminar held at the University of Copenhagen 13th–14th October 1997. Ed. by Gillian FELLOWS-JENSEN and Peter SPRINGBORG. Copenhagen, The Royal Library, 99, 180 p. (ill.).

43. CLASSEN (Albrecht). The book and the magic of reading in the Middle Ages. New York, Garland Pub., 99, XLII-308 p. (ill.). (Garland reference library of the humanities, 2118).

44. COATES (Alan). English medieval books. The Reading Abbey collections from foundation to dispersal. Oxford, Clarendon Press, 99, XXI-211 p. (pl., facs.). (Oxford historical monographs).

45. Codex Biblicus Legionensis: veinte estudios. Ed. por Antonio VINAYO GONZÁLEZ y César ALVAREZ ALVAREZ. León, Real Colegiata de San Isidoro, Fundación Hullera Vasco Leonesa, Universidad de León y Ediciones Lancia, 99, 339 p. (ill.).

46. Codicum fragmenta: sul ritrovamento di antiche pergamene negli archivi di Stato di Massa e Pontremoli (secoli XII–XV). A cura di Hillel M. SERMONETA, Patrizia RADICCHI ed Ilaria ZOLESI. Pisa, Edizioni ETS, 99, 248 p. (pl., ill.).

47. Corpus catalogorum Belgii: the medieval booklists of the southern Low Countries. Counts of Flanders, Provinces of East Flanders, Antwerp and Limburg. Ed. by Jan Willem KLEIN, Benjamin VICTOR, Michel OOSTERBOSCH, Albert DEROLEZ and Wouter BRACKE. Brussel, Koninklijke Academie voor Wetenschappen, Letteren en Schone Kunsten van België, 99, 328 p. (pl.).

48. DANELLA (Patrizia). I codici greci conservati nell'Archivio di Montecassino. Montecassino, Pubblicazioni cassinesi, 99, 130 p. (pl., ill.). (Biblioteca cassinese, 1).

49. DAVIDSDOTTIR (Sigrun). Håndskriftsagens saga i politisk belysning. (Aspects politiques de l'histoire des manuscrits islandais). Odense, Odense Universitets forlag, 99, 408 p., ill. (Odense University studies in history and social sciences, 216).

50. DE SILVA Y VERASTEGUI (Soledad). La miniatura en el Monasterio de San Millán de la Cogolla: una contribución al estudio de los códices miniados en los siglos XI al XIII. Logroño, Gobierno de La Rioja, Instituto de Estudios Riojanos, 99, 331 p. (ill.).

51. DIAZ Y DIAZ (Manuel C.), MILLARES (Carlo Agustín). Corpus de códices visigóticos. 1. Estudio. 2. Album. Las Palmas de Gran Canaria, Universidad de Educación a Distancia y Centro Asociado de Las Palmas de Gran Canaria y Gobierno de Canarias, 99, 2 vol., 251 p., 317 p. (ill.).

52. FONKICH (B. L.). Grecheskie rukopisi evropeiskikh sobranii. (Manuscrits grecs dans les collections européennes). Paleograficheskie i kodikologicheskie issledovaniia, 1988–1998 gg.. Moskva, Izd-vo "Indrik", 99, 152 p.-111 p. of plates (ill.). (Rossiiskaia akademiia nauk, Institut vseobshchei istorii. Paleografiia, kodikologiia, diplomatika).

53. GAMESON (Richard). The manuscripts of early Norman England (c.1066–1130). Oxford a. New York, British Academy by Oxford U. P., 99, XVII-190 (pl., ill.).

54. GAMPER-SCHLUND (Rudolf), JUROT (Romain). Catalogue des manuscrits médiévaux conservés à Porrentruy et dans le canton du Jura. Dietikon-Zurich, Graf, 99, 160 p. (ill.).

55. GREENE (V.). Un cimetière livresque: la liste nécrologique médiévale. *Moyen Age*, 99, 105, p. 307-330.

56. Handlist of manuscripts in the National Library of Wales: MSS 21701-22852. Aberystwyth, National Library of Wales, 99, X-436 p.

57. Handschriften (Die) der Württembergischen Landesbibliothek Stuttgart. Hrsg. v. Ingeborg KREKLER. Wiesbaden, Harrassowitz, 99, XXXIV-401 p.

58. HINZ (Ulrich). Handschriftencensus Westfalen. Wiesbaden, Reichert, 99, XXXIV-483 p. (Schriften der Universitäts- und Landesbibliothek Münster, 18).

59. Historischen (Die) und philosophischen Handschriften der Codices Palatini Latini in der Vatikanischen Bibliothek (Cod. Pal. Lat. 921-1078). Hrsg. v. Dorothea WALZ, Veit PROBST und Karin ZIMMERMANN. Wiesbaden, Reichert, 99, LX-329 p. (pl., ill.). (Kataloge der Universitätsbibliothek Heidelberg, 3).

60. Iluminura (A) em Portugal: identidade e influências. Catálogo da exposiçao, 26 de Abril a 30 de Junho 1999. Ed. Maria Adelaide MIRANDA, Isabel VILARES CEPEDA, Aires Augusto NACIMENTO. Lisboa, Ministerio da Cultura e Biblioteca Nacional, 99, 391 p. (ill., facs.).

61. Imaging the early medieval Bible. Ed. by John WILLIAMS. University Park, Pennsylvania State U. P., 99, 227 p. (pl., ill.). (The Penn State series in the history of the book).

62. Jüdische Buchmalerei in Hamburg und Altona: zur Geschichte der Illumination hebräischer Handschriften im 18. Jahrhundert. Hrsg. v. Iris FISHOF, Dina HERZ, Smadar RAHVEH-KLEMKE und Andreas BRÄMER. Hamburg, H. Christians, 99, 380 p. (ill.). (Hamburger Beiträge zur Geschichte der deutschen Juden, 21).

63. KOGMAN-APPEL (Katrin). Die zweite Nürnberger und die Jehuda Haggada: jüdische Illustratoren zwischen Tradition und Fortschritt. Frankfurt, Lang, 99, 495 p. (ill.). (Judentum und Umwelt, 69).

64. Lateinische mittelalterliche Handschriften in Folio der Universitätsbibliothek Augsburg: Cod. II. 1.2 91-226. Hrsg. v. Hardo HILG. Wiesbaden, Harrassowitz, 99, 479 p. (pl., ill.). (Handschriften der Universitätsbibliothek Augsburg. Erste Reihe, Die lateinischen Handschriften, 2).

65. Lisboa, Biblioteca Nacional. Catálogo da colecçao de códices: COD. 12888-13292. Introduçao, catalogaçao e indices por Teresa FERREIRA A. S. DUARTE. Lisboa, Biblioteca Nacional, 99, 207 p. (facs.). (Bibliografias Biblioteca Nacional).

66. Manuscrits (Les) de David Aubert. Éd. par Danielle QUERUEL. Paris, Presses de l'universite de Paris-Sorbonne, 99, 100 p. (ill.). (Cultures et civilisations médiévales, 18).

67. Manuscrits et enluminures dans le monde normand (X^e–XVe siècles). Colloque de Cerisy-la-Salle (octobre 1995), actes. Éd. par Pierre BOUET et Monique DOSDAT. Caen, Presses universitaires de Caen, 99, 227 p. (ill.).

68. MAZAL (Otto). Griechisch-römische Antike. Graz, Akademische Druck- u. Verlagsanstalt, 99, 415 p. (pl., ill.). (Geschichte der Buchkultur, 1).

69. Miniatura (La) a Padova: dal Medioevo al Settecento. Catalogo della mostra, Bologna-Rovigo, 21 marzo–21 giugno 1999. A cura di Giordana CANOVA MARIANI, Giovanna BALDISSIN MOLLI e Federica TONIOLO. Modena, F. C. Panini, 99, 623 p. (ill.).

70. NASH (Susie). Between France and Flanders: manuscript illumination in Amiens in the fifteenth century. London, The British Library a. Toronto, University of Toronto Press, 99, 421 p. (ill.). (British Library studies in medieval culture).

71. NEUHEUSER (Hanns Peter). Die Handschriften des Propsteiarchivs Kempen: interdisziplinäre Beiträge. Köln, Böhlau, 99, VIII-391 p. (ill.).

72. OUY (Gilbert). Les manuscrits de l'Abbaye de Saint-Victor: catalogue établi sur la base du répertoire de Claude de Grandrue (1514). [Turnhout], Brepols, 99, 2 vol., 398 p., 636 p. (pl., ill.). (Bibliotheca Victorina, 10).

73. Papier (Le) au Moyen Âge: histoire et techniques. Actes du colloque international du Centre National de la Recherche Scientifique. Paris, Institut de France 23, 24 et 25 avril 1998. Éd. par Monique ZERDOUN BAT-YEHOUDA. Turnhout, Brepols, 99, XII-279 p. (ill.). (Publications de l'Institut de recherche et d'histoire des textes).

74. PERANI (Mauro), CAMPANINI (Saverio). I frammenti ebraici di Modena, Archivio capitolare, Archivio della Curia, e di Correggio, Archivio storico comunale: inventario e catalogo. Firenze, L.S. Olschki, 99, 130 p. (pl., ill.). (Inventari dei manoscritti delle biblioteche d'Italia, 111).

75. SANJIAN (Avedis Krikor). Medieval Armenian manuscripts at the University of California, Los Angeles. Berkeley a. London, University of California Press, 99, XXIV-382 p. (ill.). (University of California publications. Catalogs and bibliographies, 14).

76. SHAYESTEH FAR (Mahnaz). Shî'ah artistic elements in the Tîmûrid and the early Safavid periods: book illustrations and inscriptions. London, BookExtra, 99, XXV-506 p. (ill.).

77. SMEYERS (Maurits). Flemish miniatures from the 8th to the mid-16th century: the medieval world of parchment. [Turnhout], Brepols, 99, 528 p. (ill.).

78. Sources for the history of medieval books and libraries. Proceedings Groningse Codicologendagen, 9–11 October 1996. Ed. by Jos. M. M. HERMANS, Rita SCHLUSEMANN and Margriet HOOGVLIET. Groningen, Egbert Forsten, 99, XXIII-428 p. (ill., facs.). (Boekhistorische reeks, 2).

79. STOLIAROVA (L. V.). STOLJAROVA (Lubov' V.). Iz istorii knizhnoj kul'tury russkogo srednevekovogo goroda (XI–XVII vv.). (On the history of the book culture of medieval Russian town, the 11–17th centuries). Rosssijskij gos. gumanit. un-t; RAN, In-t rossijskoj istorii. Moskva, Izd-vo RGGU, 99, 174 p. (ill., bibl.).

80. STONEMAN (William P.). Dover Priory. London, British Library in association with the British Academy, 99, XVI-326 p. (pl., ill., facs.). (Corpus of British medieval library catalogues, 5).

81. Summary catalogue of Greek manuscripts in the British Library. Vol. 1. Ed. by T. S. PATTIE and S. MAC KENDRICK. London, British Library Board, 99, XXVI-469 p.

82. SZIRMAI (J. A.). The archaeology of medieval bookbinding. Aldershot, Ashgate, 99, XVI-352 p. (ill.).

83. Treasury (The) of Petrus Alamire: music and art in Flemish court manuscripts 1500–1535. Ed. by Hernbert KELLMAN and Eugeen SCHREURS. Ghent a. Amsterdam, Ludion, 99, 179 p. (ill., music, pl.).

Cf. n°s 3160, 3454

b. *Printed books*

* 84. 50 years K.G. Saur: history and bibliography, 1949–1999. Ed. by Klaus G. SAUR; history by Titus ARNU; bibliography by Andreas BRANDMAIR and Konrad KRATZSCH. München, K.G. Saur, 99, XXXI, 183 p.

* 85. ABHB. Annual bibliography of the history of the printed book and libraries. Vol. 27. [Vol. 26. Cf. Bibl. 98, n° 87.] Ed. by the Department of special collections of Koninklijke bibliotheek. The Hague, Martinus Nijhoff, 99, 628 p.

* 86. Bibliographie der Buch- und Bibliotheksgeschichte (BBB). Vol. 17. 1997 (mit Nachträgen aus den Jahren 1980 bis 1996) [Vol. 16. 1996. Cf. Bibl. 98, n° 88.] Hrsg. v. Horst MEYER. Bad Iburg, Bibliographischer Verlag Dr. Horst Meyer, 99, [s. p.].

* 87. DUMAN (Hasan). Osmanlı sâlnâmeleri ve nevsâlleri bibliyografyası ve toplu kataloğu. A bibliography and union catalogue of Ottoman year-books. Ankara, Kültür Bakanlığı, 99, 2 vol., XXVII-223 p., XVII-454 p.

* 88. Répertoire bibliographique des livres imprimés en France au XVIe siècle. T. 6. Bibliographie des livres imprimés à Lyon. Ed. par Sybille VON GÜLTLINGEN. Baden-Baden et Bouxwiller, Éditions Valentin Koerner, 99, 216 p.

* 89. Répertoire bibliographique des livres imprimés en France au XVIIe siècle. T. 24. Bourges. Ed. par Jean JENNY. Baden-Baden et Bouxwiller, Éditions Valentin Koerner, 99, 214 p.

* 90. SHENCK (David H. J.). Directory of the lithographic printers of Scotland 1820–1870. Edinburgh, Edinburgh Bibliographical Society a. Oak Knoll Press, 99, 124 p.

** 91. Catálogo das obras impressas no século XVIII: a colecção da Santa Casa da Misericórdia de Lisboa. Ed. por Júlio Caio VELOSO. Lisboa, Santa Casa da Misericórdia de Lisboa, 99, 2 vol., XLVIII-543 p.

** 92. Fonti per la storia del lavoro e dell'impresa in Italia: l'editoria d'occasione. Una bibliografia: secc. XIX e XX. A cura di Fabrizio DOLCI. Milano, Franco Angeli, 99, 624 p. (Studi e ricerche di storia dell'editoria, 4).

** 93. VAN HUISSTEDE (Peter). Dutch printer's devices, 15th–17th century: a catalogue. Nieuwkoop, De Graaf, 99, 3 vol., 1639 p. a. 1 computer laser optical disc (ill.).

---

94. Anatomie bibliologiche: saggi di storia del libro per il centenario de "La Bibliofilía". A cura di Luigi BALSAMO e Pierangelo BELLETTINI. Firenze, L.S. Olschki, 99, 632 p. (plates, ill.).

95. BABAZADAH (Shahla). Tarikh-i chap dar Iran. (History of printing in Iran). Tihran, Tahuri, 99, 269 p. (ill.).

96. BAYANI (Manijeh), CONTADINI (Anna), STANLEY (Tim). The decorated word: Qur'ans of the 17th to 19th centuries. London, Nour Foundation in association with Azimuth Editions and Oxford U. P., 99, 271 p. (Nasser D. Khalili Collection of Islamic Art, 4).

97. Bewegte (Das) Buch: Buchwesen und soziale, nationale und kulturelle Bewegungen um 1900. Hrsg. v. Mark LEHMSTEDT und Andreas HERZOG. Wiesbaden, Harrassowitz in Kommission, 99, 429 p. (ill.). (Veröffentlichungen des Leipziger Arbeitskreises zur Geschichte des Buchwesens. Schriften und Zeugnisse zur Buchgeschichte, 12).

98. Bible (The) as book: the first printed editions. Ed by Paul SAENGER and Kimberly VAN KAMPEN. London a. New Castle, The British Library a. Oak Knoll Press, 99, XII-164 p. (plates).

99. Cambridge history (The) of the book in Britain. Vol. 3. 1400–1557. Ed. by Lotte HELLINGA a. J.B. TRAPP. Cambridge, Cambridge U. P., 99, XXIV-743 p. (plates, ill.).

100. CANDAUX (Jean-Daniel), BONNANT (Georges). Le livre genevois sous l'Ancien Régime. Gèneve, Librairie Droz, 99, 362 p., (ill., facs.). (Travaux d'histoire éthico-politique, 58).

101. CHARTIER (Roger). Cultura escrita, literatura e historia. México, Fondo de Cultura Económica, 99, 271 p. – IDEM. Publishing drama in early modern Europe. London, British Library, 99, 73 p. (Panizzi Lectures 1998).

102. CONWAY (Melissa). The Diario of the printing press of San Jacopo di Ripoli (1476–1484): commentary and transcription. Firenze, Olschki, 99, VIII-366 p. (Studi della tipografia e del commercio librario, 4).

103. DOBRANSKI (Stephen B.). Milton, authorship, and the book trade. Cambridge, Cambridge U. P., 99, XIII-245 p. (ill.).

104. ESCOLAR (Hipólito). Gente del libro: autores, editores y bibliotecarios (1939–1999). Madrid, Gredos, 99, 378 p.

105. Escribir y leer en el siglo de Cervantes. Ed. por Antonio CASTILLO GÓMEZ. Barcelona, Gedisa Editorial, 99, 362 p. (ill.).

106. Fabbrica (La) del codice: materiali per la storia del libro nel Tardo Medioevo. A cura di Maria Antonietta CASAGRANDE MAZZOLI, Paola BUSONERO, Luciana DEVOTI ed Ezio ORNATO. Roma, Viella, 99, 300 p. (ill.). (I libri di Viella, 14).

107. FÜSSEL (Stephan). Gutenberg und seine Wirkung. Frankfurt am Main, Insel, 99, 140, p. (plates, ill., bibl.).

108. GONZALEZ SANCHEZ (Carlos Alberto). Los mundos del libro: medios de difusión de la cultura occidental en las Indias de los siglos XVI y XVII. Sevilla, Diputación de Sevilla y Universidad de Sevilla, 99, 260 p. (Serie Historia y geografía, 43).

109. Handbuch der Bibliographie. Begründet von Georg SCHNEIDER; völlig neu bearbeitet von Friedrich NESTLER. Stuttgart, Hiersemann, 99, XII-726 p.

110. HITZEL (Frédéric). Livres et lecture dans le monde ottoman. Aix-en-Provence, Edisud, 99, 350 p. (ill.). (Revue des mondes musulmans et de la Méditerranée, 87-88).

111. Human face (The) of the book trade: print culture and its creators. Proceedings of the 16th seminar on the British Book Trade, Edinburgh, July 1998. Ed. by Peter ISAAC a. Barry MAC KAY. Winchester a. New Castle, St. Paul's Bibliographies a. Oak Knoll Press, 99, X-228 p. (ill., bibl.) (Print networks, 3).

112. Incunabula: studies in fifteenth-century printed books presented to Lotte Hellinga. Ed. by Martin DA-

VIES. London, British Library, 99, XVIII-650 p. (ill., facs.). (The British Library studies in the history of the book).

113. INFELISE (Mario). I libri proibiti: da Gutenberg all'Encyclopédie. Roma e Bari, Laterza, 99, 153 p.

114. ISPHORDING (Eduard). Seitenansichten: Buchkunst aus deutschen Handpressen und Verlagen seit 1945. Die Sammlung des Germanischen Nationalmuseums Nürnberg. Leipzig, Faber & Faber, 99, 287 p. (ill.).

115. KALLENDORF (Craig). Virgil and the Myth of Venice: books and readers in the Italian Renaissance. New York, Oxford U. P., 99, VI-251 p.

116. KUPIEC (Gabriel). La bibliothèque politique de Gabriel Naudé. *Tumultes*, 99, 12, p. 11-29.

117. Libro, scrittura, documento della civiltà monastica e conventuale nel basso medioevo (secoli XIII-XV). Atti del Convegno di studio, Fermo, 17–19 settembre 1997. A cura di Giuseppe AVARUCCI, Gianmario BORRI e Rosa Marisa BORRACCINI VERDUCCI. Spoleto, Centro Italiano di Studi sull'Alto Medioevo, 99, XV-528 p. (ill.). (Studi e ricerche, 1).

118. Livre (Le) illustré italien au XVIe siècle: texte-image. Actes du colloque organisé par le Centre de recherche Culture et société en Italie aux XVe, XVIe et XVIIe siècles de l'Université de la Sorbonne nouvelle, 1994. Éd. par Michel PLAISANCE. Paris, Klincksieck et Publications de la Sorbonne nouvelle, 99, 316 p. (ill.). (Actes et colloques, 50).

119. LUBORSKY SAMSON (Ruth), INGRAM MORLEY (Elizabeth). A guide to English illustrated books, 1536–1603. Tempe, Medieval & Renaissance Texts & Studies, 99, 2 vol., XXXI-754 p., V-217 p. (tab., ill.). (Medieval & Renaissance texts & studies, 166).

120. MAC KENZIE (Donald Francis). Bibliography and the sociology of texts. Cambridge, Cambridge U. P., 99, 130 p.

121. MANGONI (Luisa). Pensare i libri. La casa editrice Einaudi dagli anni Trenta agli anni Sessanta. Torino, Bollati Boringhieri, 99, X-976 p.

122. MARTIN (Henri-Jean). La naissance du livre moderne. Mise en page et mise en texte du livre français (XIVe–XVIIe siècles). Paris, Ed. du Cercle de la Librairie, 99, 494 p.

123. MERKL (Ulrich). Buchmalerei in Bayern in der ersten Hälfte des 16. Jahrhunderts: Spätblüte und Endzeit einer Gattung. Regensburg, Schnell u. Steiner, 99, 589 p. (pl., ill., facs.).

124. MOLLIER (Jean-Yves). Louis Hachette. Paris, Fayard, 99, 554 p.

125. Muller dynasty (The). Vol. 1. Jan Ewoutszoon, Harmen Janszoon Muller. Vol. 2. Jan Harmenszoon Muller. Vol. 3. Production of illustrated books. Ed. by Jan Piet Filedt KOK, Harriet STROOMBERG, Ger LUIJTEN und Christiaan SCHUCKMAN. Rotterdam, Sound & Vision Interactive, 99, 3 vol., XVI-252 p., 329 p., 339 p. (ill., facs.). (Dutch & Flemish etchings, engravings and woodcuts, 1450-1700).

126. Notion (La) d'œuvres complètes. Textes présentés par Jean SGARD et Catherine VOLPILHAC-AUGER. Oxford, Voltaire Foundation, 99, 150 p.

127. RAGONE (Giovanni). Un secolo di libri: storia dall'editoria in Italia dall'unità al post-moderno. Torino, Einaudi, 99, XIV-277 p. (bibl.). (Biblioteca Einaudi, 56).

128. Reliures royales de la Renaissance, la Librairie de Fontainebleau, 1544–1570. Exposition présentée à la Galerie Mazarine de la Bibliothèque nationale de France du 26 mars au 27 juin 1999. Éd. par Marie-Pierre LAFFITTE et Fabienne LE BARS. Paris, Bibliothèque nationale de France, 99, 274 p. (ill.).

129. RHODES (Barbara J.), STREETER (William W.). Before photocopying: the art & history of mechanical copying, 1780–1938. New Castle, Oak Knoll Press a. Northampton, Heraldry Bindery, 99, VII-495 p. (ill.).

130. RICHARDSON (Brian). Printing, writers and readers in Renaissance Italy. Cambridge, Cambridge U. P., 99, XII- 220 p. (ill., pl.).

131. SEILER (R. M.). The book beautiful: Walter Pater and the House of Macmillan. London a. New Brunswick, Athlone Press, 99, XII-206 p.

132. SENNEWALD (Adolf). Deutsche Buchillustratoren im ersten Drittel des 20. Jahrhunderts: Materialien für Bibliophile. Wiesbaden, Harrassowitz, 99, 302 p. (Bibliographien. Buch, Bibliothek, Literatur, 2).

133. SERRAI (Alfredo). Storia della bibliografia. Vol. 9. Manualistica, didattica e riforme nel secolo XVIII. A cura di Vesna STUNIC. Vol. 10. Specializzazione e pragmatismo: i nuovi cardini della attività bibliografica. Roma, Bulzoni, 99, 3 vol., 886 p., 1123 p. [in 2 vol.].

134. STAUFFACHER (Jack Werner). A typographic journey: the history of the Greenwood Press and bibliography, 1934–2000. San Francisco, Book Club of California, 99, 323 p. (ill.). (Publication of the Book Club of California, 210).

135. TIMPANARO MORELLI (Maria Augusta). Autori, stampatori, librai: per una storia dell'editoria in Firenze nel secolo XVIII. Firenze, L.S. Olschki, 99, V-721 p. (bibl.). (Studi. Accademia toscana di scienze e lettere La Colombaria, 182).

136. TORTORELLI (Gianfranco). Trasformazione e sviluppo dell'editoria italiana nel secondo dopoguerra. *Risorgimento*, 99, 51, p. 235-257.

137. TYMOSHYK (Mykola). Ii velychnist knyha: istoriia vydavnychoi spravy Kyivskoho universytetu 1834-1999. (Her majesty the book: a history of publishing at the university of Kiev, 1834–1999). Kiev, Nasha kul'tura i nauka, 99, 341 p.

138. VOGEL (Sabine). Kulturtransfer in der Frühen Neuzeit. Die Vorworte der Lyoner Drucke des 16. Jahrhunderts. Tübingen, Mohr Siebeck, 99, 320 p. (Spätmittelalter und Reformation, 12).

139. WALTHER (Karl Klaus). Buch und Leser in Bamberg 1750-1850: zur Geschichte der Verlage, Buchhandlungen, Druckereien, Lesegesellschaften und Leihbibliotheken. Wiesbaden, Harrassowitz, 99, 295 p. (Beiträge zum Buch- und Bibliothekswesen, 39).

140. WEIL (Françoise). Livres interdits, livres persécutés: 1720-1770. Oxford, Voltaire Foundation, 99, 138 p. (Françoise Weil Series: Histoire du livre).

141. WHEALE (Nigel). Writing and society: literacy, print and politics in Britain, 1590-1660. London a. New York, Routledge, 99, XIV-188 p. (ill.).

Cf. n°s 426-448, 3523, 5828-5878, 6165

§ 4. Chronology.

** 142. BAUER (Volker). Repertorium territorialer Amtskalender und Amtshandbücher im Alten Reich. Adreß-, Hof-, Staatskalender und Staatshandbücher des 18. Jahrhunderts. Band 2. Heutiges Bayern und Österreich, Liechtenstein. Frankfurt am Main, Klostermann, 99, VII-609 p. (Ius Commune, Sonderhefte: Studien zur europäischen Rechtsgeschichte, 123).

143. ANSARI (Shahabuddin). A compendium of calendars: a cyclopaedia of the Christian (Julian and Gregorian) calendar, from 1 S.E. to 2500 S.E., the Muslim calendar, from 210 B.H. to 2730 A.H. Delhi, B.R. Pub. Corp. 99, IX-196 p.

144. BHATTACHERJE (Satya Bikash). Encyclopaedia of Indian events and dates. New Delhi, Sterling Publishers, 99, 4 vol., 238 p., 89 p., 56 p., 135 p.

145. BLACKBURN (Bonnie J.), HOLFORD-STREVENS (Leofranc). The Oxford companion to the year. Oxford, Oxford U. P., 99, XVII-937 p.

146. BRENDECKE (Arndt). Die Jahrhundertwenden. Eine Geschichte ihrer Wahrnehmung und Wirkung. Frankfurt am Main, Campus Verlag, 99, 428 p. – IDEM. Fin(s) de siècle und kein Ende. Wege und Irrwege der Betrachtung von Jahrhundertwenden. *Historische Zeitschrift*, 99, 268, p. 107-120.

147. COHEN (Paul A.). Time, culture, and Christian eschatology: the year 2000 in the West and the world. [Review essay]. *American historical review*, 99, 104, 5, p. 1615-1628.

148. Construire le temps: normes et usages chronologiques au moyen âge. Études réunies par Marie-Clotilde HUBERT. *Bibliothèque de l'École des chartes*, 157, 1, 99, p. 7-220. – Construire le temps: normes et usages chronologiques à l'époque moderne et contemporaine. Études réunies par Marie-Clotilde HUBERT. *Bibliothèque de l'École des chartes*, 157, 2, 99, p. 337-508.

149. DE LI (Andrés). Reportorio de los tiempos. Ed. with an introduction by Laura DELBRUGGE. Woodbridge, Tamesis, 99, 157 p. (ill.). (Colección Támesis. Serie A, Monografías, 180).

150. DE SOLAN (O.). Le réforme du calendrier dans une question quodlibétique d'Henri de Runen (1444). *Bibliothèque de l'École des chartes*, 99, 157, p. 171-220.

151. DELATOUR (J.). Noël le 15 décembre. La réception du calendrier grégorien en France (1582). *Bibliothèque de l'École des chartes*, 99, 157, p. 369-416.

152. DIERKS (Klaus). Chronology of Namibian history: from pre-historical times to independent Namibia. Windhoek, Namibia Scientific Society, 99, VI-270 p.

153. GÓMEZ PALLARÉS (Joan). Studia Chronologica: estudios sobre manuscritos latinos de cómputo. Madrid, Ediciones Clasicas, 99, XVIII-251 p. (Series Maior).

154. GREENWAY (D. E.). Dates in history: chronology and memory. *Historical research*, 99, 72, p. 127-39.

155. GUYOTJEANNIN (O.), TOCK (B.-M.). «Mos presentis patrie»: les styles de changement du millésime dans les actes français (XIe–XVIe s.). *Bibliothèque de l'École des chartes*, 99, 157, p. 41-109.

156. HENISCH (Bridget Ann). The medieval calendar year. University Park, Pennsylvania State U. P., 99, VIII-232 p.

157. HORSNELL (Malcolm John Albert). The year-names of the first dynasty of Babylon. Hamilton, McMaster U. P., 99, 2 vol., XVIII-286 p.

158. Jahrhundertwenden: Endzeit- und Zukunftvorstellungen vom 15. bis zum 20. Jahrhundert. Hrsg. v. Manfred JAKUBOWSKI-TIESSEN. Göttingen, Vandenhoeck & Ruprecht, 99, 420 p. (ill.). (Veröffentlichungen des Max-Planck-Instituts für Geschichte, 155).

159. LEDUC (Jean). Les historiens et le temps. Conceptions, problématiques, écritures. Paris, Ed. du Seuil, 99, 332 p.

160. MORA (Fabio). Fasti e schemi cronologici. La riorganizzazione annalistica del passato remoto romano. Stuttgart, Steiner, 99, 389 p.

161. MORINI (C.). «Horologium» e «dægmæl» nei manoscritti anglosassoni del computo. *Aevum*, 99, 73, p. 273-293.

162. POULLE (E.). L'horlogerie a-t-elle tué les heures inégales? *Bibliothèque de l'École des chartes*, 99, 157, p. 137-156.

163. ROSE (Lynn E.). Sun, moon, and Sothis: a study of calendars and calendar reforms in ancient Egypt. Deerfield Beach, Kronos Press, 99, XXXVI-339 p. (Osiris series, 2).

164. SARRAZIN-CANI (V.). Formes et usages du calendrier dans les almanachs parisiens au XVIIIe s. *Bibliothèque de l'École des chartes*, 99, 157, p. 417-446.

Cf. n° 3208

§ 5. Genealogy and family history.

* 165. HAWGOOD (David). Internet for genealogy. London, D. Hawgood, 99, 24 p.

* 166. LUQUE TALAVÁN (Miguel). Bibliografía española de genealogía, heráldica, nobiliaria y derecho nobiliario en Iberoamérica y Filipinas (1900–1997). Madrid, Fundación Histórica Tavera, 99, 172 p. (Documentos Tavera, 8).

* 167. TAMALIO (Raffaele). La memoria dei Gonzaga. Repertorio bibliografico gonzaghesco (1473–1999). Firenze, Olschki, 99, XVIII-310 p. (Biblioteca di bibliografia italiana, 158).

** 168. FRÆNKEL (Louis), FRÆNKEL (Henry). Genealogical tables of Jewish families: 14th–20th centuries: forgotten fragments of the history of the Frænkel family. Vol. 1. Text and indexes. Vol. 2. Genealogical tables. Ed. by Georg SIMON on behalf of The Memorial Foundation of Eva and Henry Frænkel. München, Saur, 99, 2 vol., 189 p., 10 tav.

** 169. MASTERSON (Josephine). Ireland: 1841/1851 census abstracts (Republic of Ireland). Baltimore, Genealogical Publishing Co., 99, X-138 p.

---

170. ALBORNOZ DE LÓPEZ (Teresa). Linaje, matrimonios y poder en Mérida colonial: la familia cerrada. Mérida, Grupo de Investigación sobre Historiografía de Venezuela, CDCHT. Universisdad de los Andes, 99, 91 p. (Colección Historiográfica, 2).

171. Almanach českých šlechtických rodů. (An Almanach of aristocratic families from the Bohemian Lands). Eds. Vladimír POUZAR, František LOBKOWICZ, Petr MAŠEK, Pavel R. POKORNÝ. Il. Antonín JAVORA. Praha, Martin, 99, 413 p. (ill.).

172. BAUD (Michel). Famille royale et pouvoir sous l'Ancien Empire égyptien. Le Caire, Institut français d'archéologie orientale, 99, [s. p.]. (Bibliothèque d'études, 126).

173. BINAYÁN (Narciso). Historia genealógica argentina. Buenos Aires, Emecé Editores, 99, 578 p.

174. BLAISE (S.). Un arbre de nos forêts: Maurice Barrès. *Généalogie lorraine*, 99, 111, p. 41-46.

175. BREDIN (Jean-Denis). Une singulière famille. Jacques Necker, Suzanne Necker et Germaine de Staël. Paris, Fayard, 99, 454 p.

176. Capétiens (Les): histoire et dictionnaire, 987–1328. Coordonné par François MENANT. Paris, Laffont, 99, LXXIX-1220 p. (Bouquins).

177. CARIDI (Giuseppe). I Ruffo di Calabria: secoli XIII–XIX. Reggio Calabria, Falzea, 99, 257 p.

178. CARLUER (Jean-Yves). Historiens et généalogistes: des cousins qui s'ignorent. *Revue française de généalogie*, 99, 21, 124, p. 17-323.

179. DE ALMEIDA BARATA (Carlos Eduardo), DA CUNHA BUENO (Antônio Henrique). Dicionário das famílias brasileiras. Sao Paulo, Originis-X, 99, 2 vol., CXLVI-2384 p.

180. DE BRUYN (Günter). Die Finckensteins. Eine Familie im Dienste Preußen. Berlin, Siedler, 99, 270 p.

181. DE MONTJOUVENT (Philippe). Ephéméride de la Maison de France de 1589 à 1848: Henri IV et ses descendants. Charenton, Chaney, 99, 477 p.

182. DOMBECK (Birgit), SIMON (Maria). Familienchroniken als genealogische Darstellungsmöglichkeit. T. 2. Versuch einer Typisierung. *Genealogie*, 99, 48, 1-2, p. 399-409.

183. FERGUSON (Niall). The House of Rothschild. Vol. 1. Money's prophets 1798–1848. Vol. 2. The world's banker 1849–1999. New York, Penguin, 99, 2 vol., XXI-518 p., XXX-546 p.

184. FISCHER (Wilfried Peter A.). Rekonstruktionen iranisch-germanischer Genealogien. Münster, E. Fischer, 99, [s. p.].

185. FRANCIOSI (Gennaro). Clan gentilizio e strutture monogamiche: contributo alla storia della famiglia romana. Napoli, Jovene, 99, XVI-360 p.

186. FRÜH (Dorothee). Die Genealogie als Hilfswissenschaft der Humangenetik. *Jahrbuch für Geschichte und Theorie der Biologie*, 99, 6, p. 141-162.

187. FUBINI LEUZZI (Maria). Condurre a onore: famiglia, matrimonio e assistenza dotale a Firenze in età moderna. Firenze, L. S. Olschki, 99, 312 p. (Biblioteca di storia toscana moderna e contemporanea. Studi e documenti, 46).

188. GENTA (Enrico). Genealogia, araldica, nobiltà nella storia del diritto fra finzione e realtà. *Rivista di storia del diritto italiano*, 99, 72, p. 155-176.

189. GESTRICH (Andreas). Geschichte der Familie im 19. und 20. Jahrhundert. München, R. Oldenbourg, 99, XII-150 p. (Enzyklopädie deutscher Geschichte, 50).

190. History (The) of fatherhood. Guest editor: Robert GRISWOLD. *Journal of family history*, 99, 24, 3, p. 251-390.

191. KALUS (Peter). Die Fugger in der Slowakei. Augsburg, Wissner, 99, 304 p. (Materialien zur Geschichte der Fugger, 2).

192. KLAPISCH-ZUBER (Christiane). Parrains et compères. A propos d'un «bon» rapport social (note critique). *Annales*, 99, 54, 3, p. 739-746.

193. KRÆMMER (Michæl). Den hvide klan: Absalon, hans slægt og hans tid. (Le Clan Hvide: Absalon, sa famille et son temps). København, Spektrum, 99, 197 p. (ill., tab.).

194. KRAUS (Elisabeth). Die Familie Mosse. Deutsch-jüdisches Bürgertum im 19. und 20. Jahrhundert. München, Beck, 99, 793 p.

195. NATHAN (Geoffrey S.). The family in late antiquity: the rise of Christianity and the endurance of tradition. London, Routledge, 99, XV-271 p.

196. PUPPI (Lionello). "Per li rami" dei Belli. *Studi veneziani*, 99, 38, p. 223-242.

197. RĂDULESCU (Mihai Sorin). Genealogii. (Genealogies). București, Editura Albatros, 99, 312 p.

198. ROUCHON (Olivier). L'enquête généalogique et ses usages dans la Toscane des Médicis. Un exemple pisan de 1558. *Annales*, 99, 54, 3, p. 705-738.

199. SÁNCHEZ DOMINGO (Rafael). El régimen señorial en Castilla Vieja: la casa de los Velasco. Burgos, Universidad de Burgos, 99, 226 p (Estudios y monografías, 8).

200. SCHAD (Lothar). Wer war wer? Genealogisches Lexikon. Personen, Sippen, Stämme, Orte vom Altertum bis ins ausgehende 16. Jh. Band 1. A–L. Band 2. M–Z. Eschborn, Stifts-Verl., 99, 2 vol., 649 p., 599 p.

201. Second Ordre (Le): l'idéal nobiliaire. Hommage à Ellery Schalk. Ed. par Chantal GRELL et Armand RAMIÈRE DE FORTENIER. Paris, Presses de l'Université de Paris-Sorbonne, 99, 389 p.

202. TORRES SEVILLA-QUINONES DE LEÓN (Margarita). Linajes nobiliarios en León y Castilla: siglos IX–XIII. Valladolid, Junta de Castilla y León, Consejería de Educación y Cultura, 99, 573 p.

203. VAN HOUTS (Elisabeth Maria Cornelia). History and family traditions in England and the Continent, 1000–1200. Aldershot a. Brookfield, Ashgate, 99, XIV-356 p. (Variorum collected studies series).

Cf. n°s 2556, 6871

§ 6. **Sigillography and heraldry.**

* 204. ADAMS (Alison), RAWLES (Stephen), SAUNDERS (Alison). A bibliography of French emblem books in sixteenth and seventeenth centuries. Genève, Droz, 99, XXXII-670 p.

* 205. DOGARU (Maria), MUREȘAN (Augustin). Bibliografia vexilologiei românești. (Bibliography of Romanian vexillology). Arad, Complexul Muzeal Arad, 99, 69 p.

* 206. LOPEZ POZA (S.). Los estudios sobre Emblemática: logros, perspectivas y tendencias de investigación. *Signo*, 99, 6, p. 81-95.

** 207. Brasonário da nobreza de Portugal: manuscrito anónimo do séc. XVII. Introduçao, José TEIXEIRA DA MOTA; transcriçao, Filipe FOLQUE DE MENDOÇA. Lisboa, Ediçoes Moreira & Almeida, 99, XXVI-819 p.

** 208. Libro del conosçimiento de todos los regnos et tierras et señorios que son por el mundo, et de las señales et armas que han. Ed. por María Jesús LACARRA, María del Carmen LACARRA DUCAY, Alberto MONTANER FRUTOS. Zaragoza, Institucion "Fernando el Catolico", 99, 267 p. (facs., pl., ill.)

---

209. ANDROUDIS (P.). Origine et symbolique de l'aigle bicéphale des Turcs Seldjoukides et Artuqides de l'Asie Mineure (Anatolie). *Byzantiakà*, 99, 19, p. 309-345.

210. Aspects of Renaissance and Baroque symbol theory, 1500–1700. Ed. by Peter M. DALY and John MANNING. New York, AMS Press, 99, XXII-283 p. (AMS studies in the emblem, 14).

211. Atti della Società Italiana di studi araldici. 14°–15° Convivio, Tortona 17 maggio 1997, Torino 15 novembre 1997, Pinerolo 14 novembre 1998. Torino, Società Italiana di Studi Araldici, 99, 438 p.

212. BASCAPÈ (Giacomo Carlo), DEL PIAZZO (Marcello). Insegne e simboli: araldica pubblica e privata, medievale e moderna. Con la cooperazione di Luigi BORGIA. Roma, Ministero per i beni culturali e ambientali, Ufficio centrale per i beni archivistici, 99, XVI-1064 p. (ill.). (Pubblicazioni degli archivi di Stato. Sussidi, 11).

213. BRAUNLIN (M.), NESBITT (J.). Thirteen seals and an unpublished revolt coin from an American private collection. *Byzantion*, 99, 69, p. 187-205.

214. BRUNA (D.). De l'agréable à l'utile: le bijou emblématique à la fin du Moyen Age. *Revue historique*, 99, 123, 609, p. 3-22.

215. BUBEN (Milan). Encyklopedie heraldiky. (Encyclopedia of heraldry). Praha, Libri, 99, 459 p.

216. CACUA PRADA (Antonio). Los símbolos patrios. Santafé de Bogotá, Academia Colombiana de Historia, 99, 159 p. (ill.). (Academia Colombiana de Historia, XLVII).

217. CARMONA DE LOS SANTOS (María), DESANTES FERNANDEZ (Blanca), DE ALFONSO ALONSO-MUNOYERRO (Belén). Sellos, fotografías y documentación notarial. Madrid, Ministerio de Educación y Cultura, Dirección General del Libro, Archivos y Bibliotecas, Subdirección General de los Archivos Estatales, 99, 61 p. (Escuela Iberoamericana de Archivos / Experiencias y Materiales).

218. CARMONA DE LOS SANTOS (María). Bibliografía de sigilografía española. Madrid, Ministerio de Educación y Cultura, Dirección General del Libro, Archivos y Bibliotecas, Subdirección General de los Archivos Estatales, 99, 122 p.

219. Collezione sfragistica (La): Roma, Museo nazionale del Palazzo di Venezia. A cura di Silvana BALBI DE CARO. Vol. 1. Collezione Corvisieri romana. A cura di Carla BENOCCI. Roma, Ministero per i beni e le attività culturali, Ufficio centrale per i beni archeologici, architettonici, artistici e storici, 99, 296 p. (Bollettino di numismatica. Monografia, 7.1).

220. DELMAS (Marie-Claire). Quels instruments de recherche pour les sceaux? Tradition et perspectives d'avenir. *Bibliothèque de l'Ecole de Chartes*, 99, 156, 2, p. 573-579.

221. DEUTSCH (Robert). Messages from the past: Hebrew bullae from the time of Isaiah through the destruction of the First Temple. Tel Aviv, Archaeological Center, 99, 205 p.

222. Heraldique religieuse (L'): Actes du Xe Colloque Internationale d'Heraldique, Rothenburg o. d. T. 22–27 IX 1997. Ed. par C. D. BLEISTEINER. München, Degener & Co, 99, 446 p.

223. Jesuits (The) and the emblem tradition: selected papers of the Leuven International Emblem Conference, 18–23 August, 1996. Ed. by John MANNING and Marc VAN VAECK. Turnhout, Brepols, 99, VIII-367 p. (Imago figurata, Studies, 1).

224. JÖHRENS (Gerhard). Amphorenstempel im Nationalmuseum von Athen. Zu den H. G. LOLLING aufgenommenen 'unedierten Henkelinschriften'. Mit einem Anhang: Die Amphorenstempel in der Sammlung der Abteilung Athen des Deutschen Archäologischen Instituts. Mainz, von Zabern in Komm., 99, XVIII-336 p. (tables).

225. KLIMANOV (Lev G.). Vizantijskie otrazhenija v sfragistike: Kollektsija metallicheskikh pechatej VII–XX vv. N.P. Likhacheva v Zapadnoevropejskoj sektsii Arkhiva Sankt-Peterburgskogo FIRI RAN. (The Byzantine Reflections in the Seals: N.P. Likhachev's collection of metallic seals of the 7th–20th centuries, Saint-Petersburg). Sankt-Peterburg, Aletejja, 99, 350 p. (ill., ind.). (Vizantijskaja biblioteka. Issledovanija).

226. NIJHOWNE (Jeanne). Politics, religion, and cylinder seals: a study of Mesopotamian symbolism in the second millennium B.C. Oxford, Archeopress, 99, VI-126 p. (BAR international series, 772).

227. SAVORELLI (Alessandro). Piero della Francesca e l'ultima crociata. Araldica, storia e arte tra Gotico e rinascimento. Firenze, Le Lettere, 99, 152 p. (ill.)

228. Sellos reales, de gobernadores, obispos y personajes del Paraguay del período hispano. Coordinación Beatriz GÓMEZ DE BENÍTEZ. Asunción, Archivo Nacional de Asunción, Vice Ministerio de Cultura M.E.C. y Academia Paraguaya de la Historia, 99, 68 p.

229. Siegel und Papyri: das Siegelwesen in Ägypten von römischer bis in früharabische Zeit (Exhibition: 1999: Österreichische Nationalbibliothek and Österreichische Akademie der Wissenschaften). Hrsg. v. Alexandra-Kyriaki WASSILIOU unter Mitarbeit von Hermann HARRAUER. Wien, OVG, 99, 950 p. (Nilus, 4).

230. SLIWA (Joachim). Egyptian scarabs and seal amulets from the collection of Sigmund Freud. Kraków, Polska Akademia Umiejetnosci, 99, 60 p. (Rozprawy Wydzialu Historyczno-Filozoficznego, 89).

231. STIELDORF (Andrea). Rheinische Frauensiegel: zur rechtlichen und sozialen Stellung weltlicher Frauen im 13. und 14. Jahrhundert. Köln, Böhlau, 99, VIII-708 p. (ill.). (Rheinisches Archiv, 142).

232. Studies in Byzantine sigillography. Part 6. Ed. by Nicolas OIKONOMIDES. Washington, Dumbarton Oaks Research Library and Collection, 99, IX-219 p.

233. TSITOU (Anatol'). Sfrahistyka i heral'dyka Belarusi: iliustravany kurs lektsyi. (Sphragistics and heraldry of Belarus). Minsk, RIVSh BDU, 99, 175 p.

234. VOINOT (Jacques). Les cachets à collyres dans le monde romain. Préf. de Ralph JACKSON. Montagnac, Éditions Monique Mergoil, 99, VIII-368 p. (Monographies instrumentum, 7).

235. VRTEL (Ladislav). Osem storočí slovenskej heraldiky. (Eight Centuries of the Slovak Heraldry). Martin, Vydavateľstvo Matice slovenskej, 99, 296 p. [Englische Zfassung].

Cf. n° 8278

§ 7. Numismatics and metrology.

* 236. SCHÖNERT-GEIß (Edith). Bibliographie zur antiken Numismatik Thrakiens und Moesiens. Berlin, Akademie Verlag, 99, 1710 p.

237. ALFÖLDI (Maria). Bild und Bildersprache der römischen Kaiser. Beispiele und Analysen. Mainz, von Zabern, 99, 304 p. (Abb.).

238. Arkheologiia severo-vostochnoi Azii, astroarkheologiia, paleometrologiia. (Archaeology of North-Eastern Asia, astroarchaeology, paleometrology). Otvetstvennyi redaktor A. N. ALEKSEEV. Novosibirsk, Nauka, Sibirskoe predpriiatie RAN, 99, 264 p. (ill., maps).

239. BRAND (John D.). The English coinage, 1180–1274: money, mints and exchanges. London, British Numismatic Society, 99, 92 p. (British Numismatic Society Special Publication, 1).

240. Coins, art, and chronology: essays on pre-Islamic history of the Indo-Iranian borderlands. Ed. by Michael ALRAM and Deborah E. KLIMBURG-SALTER. Wien, Vlg. d. Öst. Akad., 99, VIII-498 p. (Beiträge zur Kultur- und Geistesgeschichte Asiens, 31. Denkschriften/Österreichische Akademie der Wissenschaften, Philosophisch-Historische Klasse, 280. Veröffentlichungen der Numismatischen Kommission, 33).

241. CUNNALLY (John). Images of the illustrious. The numismatic presence in the Renaissance. Princeton, Princeton U. P., 99, XI-230 p.

242. FABIANI (Roberta). La questione delle monete SYN: per una nuova interpretazione. *Annali dell'Istituto italiano per gli Studi storici*, 99, 16, p. 87-123.

243. Fundmünzen (Die) der römischen Zeit in Ungarn. Hrsg. v. Ferenc REDO; bearb. v. Miklós BAKOS [et al.]. Band. 3. Komitat Komárom-Esztergom. Zu-

sammengestellt von Vera LÁNYI, Ferenc REDO und Melinda TORBÁGYI. Berlin, Mann u. Budapest, Archaeolingua, 99, 472 p.

244. GARIPZANOV (I. H.). The image of authority in Carolingian coinage. The image of a ruler and Roman imperial tradition. *Early Medieval Europe*, 99, 8, p. 197-218.

245. LE RIDER (Georges). Antioche de Syrie sous les Séleucides: corpus des monnaies d'or et d'argent. 1. De Séleucos 1 à Antiochos V c. 300–161. Paris, Académie des Inscriptions et belles-lettres, 99, 260 p. (Mémoires de l'Académie des inscriptions et belles-lettres. Nouvelle série, 19). – IDEM. Études d'histoire monétaire et financière du monde grec: écrits 1958–1998. Ed. par Eleni PAPAEFTHYMIOU, François DE CALLATAŸ et François QUEYREL. Athènes, Société Hellénique de Numismatique, 99, 3 vol., [s. p.]. (Bibliothèque de la Société Hellénique de Numismatique, 6. Ecole Pratique des Hautes Études. Sciences historiques et philologiques, 1. Hautes études numismatiques, 3).

246. Moneta locale, moneta straniera: Italia ed Europa, XI–XV secolo = Local coins, foreign coins: Italy and Europe, 11th–15th centuries. The second Cambridge numismatic Symposium. A cura di Lucia TRAVAINI. Milano, Società numismatica italiana, 99, 448 p. (ill., maps). (Collana di numismatica e scienze affini, 2).

247. PELLICER I BRU (Josep). Repertorio paramétrico metrológico medieval de los reinos hispánicos. Barcelona, Asociación Numismática Española, Museo Casa de la Moneda, 99, 252 p (A. Vives y Escudero, 10).

248. Rutas, ciudades y moneda en Hispania: Actas del II Encuentro Peninsular de Numismática Antigua, Porto, marzo de 1997. Coordinadores: R. M. S. CENTENO, M. P. GARCÍA-BELLIDO, G. MORA. Madrid, Centro de Estudios Históricos, Depto. de Historia Antigua y Arqueología, CSIC, 99, 476 p. (Anejos de Archivo Español de Arqueología, 20).

249. SCHWARZENBACH (Alexis). Portraits of the nation: stamps, coins and banknotes in Belgium and Switzerland, 1880–1945. Bern, Peter Lang, 99, 395 p. (European university studies. Series III, History and allied studies = Europäische Hochschulschriften. Reihe III, Geschichte und ihre Hilfswissenschaften, 847).

250. Storia mutilata (La). La dispersione dei rinvenimenti monetali in Italia. Atti dell'incontro di studio. Roma 1997. A cura di Sara SORDA. Roma, Istituto italiano di numismatica, 99, 210 p. (Studi e materiali, 6).

251. Uluslararasi nümismatik sempozyumu bildirileri = The notes of 1st. international numismatic symposium 9–10 XI. 1993 / The Turkish Nümismatik Dernegi = The Turkish Numismatic Society. İstanbul, Turkish Numismatic Society, 99, V-345 p.

252. VAN WIE (Paul D.). Image, history, and politics: the coinage of modern Europe. Lanham a. Oxford, University Press of America, 99, VIII-208 p.

Cf. n°s 374-409, 1039, 1562, 2584, 2739

§ 8. Linguistics.

* 253. TYAS (Shaun). A catalogue of the contents of Nomina: volumes 1 to 20 (1977–1997). Stamford, Paul Watkins, 99, 21 p.

** 254. LONGNON (Auguste). Les noms de lieu de la France: leur origine, leur signification, leurs transformations. Résumé des conférences de toponomastique faites à l'Ecole Pratique des Hautes Etudes, section de sciences historiques et philologiques. Paris, H. Champion, 99, XV-831 p.

** 255. ROYAL COMMISSION ON HISTORICAL MANUSCRIPTS. Guides to sources for British history, II: principal family and estate collections: family names L–W. London, The Stationery Office, 99, XIII-183 p.

256. ABELLAN PEREZ (Juan). Toponimia hispano-árabe y romance: fuentes para la historia medieval. Cádiz, Agrija Ediciones, 99, 166 p.

257. AMIGÓ I ANGLÈS (Ramon). Introducció a la recerca en toponímia i antroponímia. Barcelona, Publicacions de l'Abadia de Montserrat, 99, 228 p. (Biblioteca Serra d'Or, 222).

258. ANGELOPOULOS (Athanasios A.). He proïstorike Hellas: lexikon toponymion. Athenai, Aldebaran, 99, 517 p.

259. BERGER (Dieter). Geographische Namen in Deutschland: Herkunft und Bedeutung der Namen von Ländern, Städten, Bergen und Gewässern. Mannheim, Dudenverlag, 99, 318 p. (Duden-Taschenbücher, 25).

260. BONFANTE (Giuliano). The origin of the romance languages. Stages in the developments of Latin. Ed. by Larissa BONFANTE. Heidelberg, Universitätsverlag C. Winter, 99, XXXIII-153 p. (maps). (Bibliothek der klassischen Altertumswissenschaften, 100).

261. BOULLÓN AGRELO (Ana Isabel). Antroponimia medieval galega (ss. VIII–XII). Tübingen, M. Niemeyer, 99, VII-558 p. (Patronymica Romanica, 12).

262. BRUUN (Christer). Methodisches zu den pejorativen Spitznamen in der Antike und im Mittelalter (am Beispiel Notkers des Stammlers). *Archiv für Kulturgeschichte*, 99, 81, 2, p. 259-282.

263. CASAPULLO (Rosa). Storia della lingua italiana: il medioevo. Bologna, il Mulino, 99, 476 p. (Nuova scienza. Serie di linguistica e critica letteraria).

264. DALBERA-STEFANAGGI (Marie José). Nouvel atlas linguistique et ethnographique de la Corse. Vol. 2. Le lexique de la mer. Paris, CNRS Editions, 99, [s. p.]. (Atlas linguistiques de la France par régions).

265. DE ALMEIDA FERNANDES (A.). Toponímia portuguesa: (exame a um dicionário). Arouca, Associaçao para a Defesa da cultura Arouquense, 99, 576 p.

266. DESHAYES (Albert). Dictionnaire des noms de lieux bretons. Douarnenez, Ed. le Chasse-Marée – Ar Men, 99, 608 p.

267. DIAZ Y DIAZ (M. C.). La lengua institucional en la Hispania de los siglos VI–XI. In: Ideologie e pratiche del reimpiego nell'alto Medioevo [Cf. n° 3458], p. 435-458.

268. DONAT (Peter), REIMANN (Heike), WILLICH (Cornelia). Slawische Siedlung und Landesbau im nordwestlichen Mecklenburg. Stuttgart, F. Steiner, 99, 246 p. (Forschungen zur Geschichte und Kultur des östlichen Mitteleuropa, 8).

269. FIERRO (Alfred). Histoire et mémoire du nom des rues de Paris. Paris, Parigramme, 99, 430 p.

270. FORDANT (Laurent). Atlas des noms de famille en France. Avec la collaboration de Martine CHEVALIER et Virginie TOPCHA. Paris, Archives & Culture, 99, 190 p. (Noms de famille).

271. Fuentes toponímicas en los pergaminos condales de Cancillería del Archivo de la Corona de Aragón (S. IX–XII) y su valoración histórica. Barcelona, Publicacions de la Universitat de Barcelona, 99, 150 p. (Rubrica. Palaeographica et diplomatica studia, 6).

272. GHISALBERTI (Carlo). Nazione e lingua in Carlo Cattaneo. Lo scritto "Del nesso tra la lingua valaca e l'italiana". *Clio*, 99, 99, 35, p. 27-37.

273. GOICU (Simona). Termeni creștini în onomastica românească. (Christian terms in Romanian onomatology). Timișoara, Editura Amphora, 99, 254 p.

274. GUINOT RODRÍGUEZ (Enric). Els fundadors del Regne de València: repoblament, antroponímia i llengua a la València medieval. València, E. Climent, 99, 2 vol., [s. p.]. (Biblioteca d'estudis i investigacions, 39-40. Tres i quatre).

275. HORVÁTH (Pavel). Neuvážený návrh na zrušenie slovenskej transkripcie starých rodových mien a priezvisk. (Ill-judged proposal for the abolishment of Slovak transcription of old family names). *Historický časopis*, 99, 47, 2, p. 306-315.

276. JUUSOLA (Hannu). Linguistic peculiarities in the Aramaic magic bowl texts. Helsinki, Finnish Oriental Society, 99, 264-6 p. (Studia Orientalia, 86) (ill.).

277. KOUTRAKOU (N.). Defying the other's identity. Language of acceptance in iconoclastic Byzantium. *Byzantion*, 99, 69, 1, p. 107-118.

278. MÄKI-PETÄYS (Mari). Nomen est omen. Esimerkkejä Aleksanteri Nevskin pyhimyselämäkerran kielikuvista.(Nomen est omen. Examples of metaphor in Alexander Nevskiy's hagiography). *Faravid*, 98-99, 22-23, p.163-180. [English summary].

279. MATHIEU (Nicolas). Histoire d'un nom: les Aufidii dans la vie politique, économique et sociale du monde romain; IIe siècle avant Jésus-Christ–IIIe siècle après Jésus-Christ. Rennes, Presses universitaires de Rennes, 99, 259 p. (Collection histoire).

280. MENZER (M. J.). Ælfric's Grammar: solving the problem of the English-language text. *Neophilologus*, 99, 83, p. 637-652.

281. MLEZIVA (Štěpán). Územní změny a změny názvů obcí a osad v českých zemích od roku 1850 do současnosti ve světle právních norem. (Territorial changes and changes in names of municipalities and villages in the Czech lands since 1850 until today in the light of legal standards). *Historická geografie*, 99, 30, p. 101-118.

282. NORBERG (Dan). Manuale di latino medievale. A cura di M. OLDONI. Bibliografia aggiornata a cura di P. GARBINI. Salerno, Avagliano, 99, 256 p. (Schola salernitana. Studi e testi, 1).

283. NUNES (Naidea Nunes), KREMER (Dieter). Antroponímia primitiva da Madeira e repertório onomástico histórico da Madeira: séculos XV e XVI. Tübingen, Niemeyer, 99, VIII-705 p. (Patronymica Romanica, 13).

284. PIETRINI (S.). Il disordine del lessico e la varietà delle cose. Le denominazioni latine e romanze degli intrattenitori medievali. *Quaderni medievali*, 99, 47, p. 77-113.

285. PIVATO (Stefano). Il nome e la storia. Onomastica e religioni politiche nell'Italia contemporanea. Bologna, Il Mulino, 99, 393 p.

286. PRICOCO (Salvatore). Alcune considerazioni sul linguaggio monastico. *Cassiodorus*, 99, 5, p. 171-199.

287. Romania, Germania: die Bedeutung von Ortsnamen für die Sprachgeschichte im Grenzgebiet zweier Sprachen: Jahrespreise 1996 und 1997 der Henning-Kaufmann-Stiftung zur Förderung der deutschen Namenforschung auf sprachgeschichtlicher Grundlage. Hrsg. v. Friedhelm DEBUS; mit Beiträgen v. Friedhelm DEBUS [et al.]. Heidelberg, C. Winter, 99, 61 p. (Beiträge zur Namenforschung. Neue Folge. Beiheft, 52).

288. SANGOÏ (Jean-Claude). Forename family and society in Southwest France (XVIIIe–XIXe siècles). *History of family*, 99, 4, 3, p. 239-259.

289. SAVIO (Giulio). Monumenta onomastica romana medii aevi (X–XII sec.). Roma, Il cigno Galileo Galilei, 99, 5 vol., [s. p.].

290. SKINNER (P.). «And her name was …?» Gender and naming in medieval southern Italy. *Medieval prosopography*, 99, 20, p. 23-49.

291. Sprachgeschichte als Kulturgeschichte. Hrsg. v. Andreas GARDT, Ulrike HASS-ZUMKEHR u. Thorsten ROELCKE. Berlin, de Gruyter, 99, VIII-418 p. (Studia linguistica Germanica, 54).

292. STRID (Jan Paul). Kulturlandskapets språkliga dimension: Ortnamnen. (La dimension linguistique du paysage: la toponymie). Stockholm, Riksantikvarieämbetet, 99, 128 p. (ill.).

293. SÜMER (Faruk). Türk devletleri tarihinde sahis adlari. (Personal names of Turkic peoples). İstanbul, Türk Dünyasi Arastirmalari Vakfi, 99, 2 vol., 878 p.

294. TIMM (Erika). Matronymika im aschkenasischen Kulturbereich: ein Beitrag zur Mentalitäts- und Sozial-

geschichte der europäischen Juden. Unter Mitarbeit von Gustav Adolf BECKMANN. Tübingen, Niemeyer, 99, 67 p.

295. VERDON (L.). L'anthroponymie, un lieu pour quelle(s) mémoires(s)? L'exemple du Roussillon du Xe au XIIIe s. In: Faire mémoire: souvenir et commémoration au Moyen Age [Cf. n° 551], p. 347-368.

296. WERMICH (Jürgen). Zum Aussterben von Familiennamen. Herold-Jahrbuch, 99, 4, p. 199-212.

297. WOLFFSOHN (Michael), BRECHENMACHER (Thomas). Die Deutschen und ihre Vornamen. 200 Jahre Politik und öffentliche Meinung. München u. Zürich, Diana, 99, 463 p.

298. WRIGHT (R.). La tradución entre el Latin y el Romance en la alta edad media. Signo, 99, 6, p. 41-63.

§ 8. Addenda 1997–1999.

299. ROCHETTE (B.). Le latin dans le monde grec. Recherches sur la diffusion de la langue et des lettres latines dans les provinces hellénophones de l'Empire romain. Bruxelles, Latomus, 97, 423 p. (Latomus, 233).

300. WEIJERS (O.). Problema, une enquête. In: Roma, magistra mundi (2). Itineraria culturae medievalis. Mélanges offerts au Père L.E. Boyle à l'occasion de son 75e anniversaire. Ed. par Jacqueline HAMESSE. Louvain-la-Neuve, F.I.D.E.M., Collège Mercier, 98, p. 991-1008.

Cf. n°s 2559, 2648, 3523, 3897

§ 9. Historical geography, travels and discoveries.

* 301. CLERICI (Luca). Viaggiatori italiani in Italia 1700–1998: per una bibliografia. Milano, S. Bonnard, 99, 405 p. (L'ordine dei libri).

* 302. HERRERO MASSARI (José Manuel). Libros de viajes de los siglos XVI y XVII en España y Portugal: lectura y lectores. Madrid, Fundación Universitaria Española, 99, 222 p. (Publicaciones de la Fundación Universitaria Española. Colección Tesis "cum laude". Serie L, Literatura, 6).

* 303. WETTLAUFER (Jörg), PAVIOT (Jacques). Europäische Reiseberichte des späten Mittelaters. Eine analytische Bibliographie. Bd. 2. Französische Reiseberichte. Frankfurt, Peter Lang, 99, 270 p. (Kieler Werkstücke. Reihe D, Beiträge zur europäischen Geschichte des späten Mittelalters, 12).

** 304. Beschreibung der dreijährigen chinesischen Reise. Die russische Gesandtschaft von Moskau nach Peking 1692 bis 1695 in den Darstellungen von Eberhard Isbrand Ides und Adam Brand. Hrsg. v. Michael HUNDT. Stuttgart, Steiner, 99, VIII-364 p. (Quellen und Studien zur Geschichte des Östlichen Europa, 53).

** 305. ULFELDT (Jakob). Ruslandsrejsen 1578. (Voyage en Russie en 1578, traduit du latin). Trad. par Richard MOTT. Gentofte, Øresund, 99, 192 p.

306. ADORNO (Rolena), PAUTZ (Patrick Charles). Alvar Núñez Cabeza de Vaca: his account, his life, and the expedition of Pánfilo de Narváez. Lincoln a. London, University of Nebraska Press, 99, 3 vol., XXXV-413 p., XXXVII-428 p., XXI-476 p.

307. AGUINAGA (Hélio). A expediçao de Pedr'Álvarez, 9 de março 1500–26 de Julho de 1501: razoes e conseqüências da posse do Brasil. Rio de Janeiro, Lidador, 99, 152 p. (ill., maps).

308. BASSIN (Mark). Imperial visions: nationalist imagination and geographical expansion in the Russian Far East, 1840–1865. Cambridge, Cambridge U. P., 99, XV-329 p. (Cambridge Studies in historical geography, 29).

309. BERGER (Gottfried). Amerika im XIX. Jahrhundert: die Vereinigten Staaten im Spiegel zeitgenössischer deutschsprachiger Reiseliteratur. Wien, Molden, 99, 238 p.

310. BESSE (Jean-Marc). Les grandeurs de la terre. Essai sur les transformations du savoir géographique au XVIe siècle. Paris, [s. n.], 99, [s. p.]. [Thèse (Doctorat Histoire), Paris, Université Paris 1, 1999].

311. BIGGS (Michael). Putting the state on the map: cartography, territory, and European state formation. Comparative studies in society and history, 99, 41, p. 374-405.

312. BLUM (D.). Die europäische Entdeckungen Indiens. Diversifikation der Indienwahrnehmung in europäische Reiseberichten des XV. Jahrhunderts. Saeculum, 99, 50, p. 211-233.

313. BOGLIONE (A.). Contributo alle biografie di Giovanni e Girolamo da Verrazzano. Archivio storico italiano, 99, 157, p. 231-267.

314. BOLD (Christine). The WPA Guides: Mapping America. Jackson, University Press of Mississippi, 99, XVI-246 p.

315. BOURNE (M.). Francesco II Gonzaga and maps as palace decoration in Renaissance Mantua. Imago mundi, 99, 51, p. 51-82.

316. CALVINO (André). La création et la diffusion de la carte générale de la France par les astronomes Cassini. Archistra, 99, 183, p.123-134.

317. CARMEL (Alex), EISLER (Ejal Jakob). Der Kaiser reist ins Heilige Land. Die Palästinareise Wilhelms II. 1898. Eine illustrierte Dokumentation. Stuttgart, Berlin u. Köln, Kohlhammer, 99, 187 p.

318. Cartografía histórica iberoamericana: Cuba, Puerto Rico, Filipinas (1890–1899). Ministerio de Defensa, Secretaría General Técnica. Madrid, Ministerio de Defensa, Secretaría General Técnica, 99, 258 p.

319. CASTELNOVI (Michele). Lo spazio della geografia nel monumento della cultura italiana: l'Enciclopedia Italiana (1929–1938). Studi piacentini, 99, 26, p. 137-177.

320. CAZACU (Matei). Des femmes sur les routes de l'Orient. Le voyage à Costantinople au XIXe siècle. Genève, Georg Editeur, 99, 205 p.

321. CHARD (Chloe). Pleasure and guilt on the grand tour: travel writing and imaginative geography 1600–1830. Manchester, Manchester U. P., 99, IX-278 p.

322. CHEKIN (Leonid S.). Kartografija khristianskogo srednevekov'ja VIII–XIII vv.: Teksty, perevod, commentarij. ([Eastern Europe in] the cartography of the Christian Middle Ages: texts, transl., comment). RAN, In-t vseobshchej istorii; In-t rossijskoj istorii. Moskva, Vostochnaja literatura, 99, 366 p. (ill., bibl., ind.). (Drevneyshie istochniki po istorii Vostochnoy Evropy).

323. CLARKE (Katherine). Between geography and history. Hellenistic constructions of the Roman world. Oxford, Clarendon Press, 99, XI-407 p.

324. CONNOLY (D. K.). Imagined pilgrimage in the itinerary maps of Matthew Paris. *ArtB*, 99, 81, p. 598-622.

325. DA FONSECA (Luís Adao). Pedro Alvares Cabral, Uma Viagem. Lisboa, Edicoes Inapa, 99, 175 p. – IDEM. The discoveries and the formation of the Atlantic Ocean: 14th century–16th century. Lisboa, Comissao Nacional para as Comemoraçoes dos Descobrimentos Portugueses, 99, 149 p.

326. Danske geografiske forskere. (Les Géographes danois). Red. par Sven ILLERIS. Frederiksberg, Roskilde Universitetsforlag, 99, 478 p. (ill.).

327. DE DIJN (Rosine). Des Kaisers Frauen. Eine Reise mit Karl V. von Flandern durch Deutschland bis in die Estremadura. Mit einl. Essay v. Ferdinand SEIBT. Stuttgart, Deutsche Verlags-Anstalt, 99, 368 p.

328. DE SETA (Cesare). Vedutisti e viaggiatori in Italia tra Settecento e Ottocento. Torino, Bollati Boringhieri, 99, 172 p.

329. DELANO-SMITH (Catherine), KAIN (Roger J. P.). English maps: a history. London, British Library, 99, XIV-320 p. (British Library studies in map history, 2).

330. Discours (Les) de voyages: Afrique, Antilles. Ed. par Romuald FONKOUA. Paris, Karthala, 99, 327 p.

331. ELIASSON (Pär). Platsens blick: Vetenskapsakademien och den naturalhistoriska resan 1790–1840. (Le regard topographique: l'Académie des Sciences et le voyage naturaliste entre 1790 et 1840). Umeå, Univ., 99, 285 p. (Idéhistoriska skrifter 29). [English summary].

332. Empire and others: British encounters with indigenous peoples, 1600-1850. Ed. by Martin DAUNTON and Rick HALPERN. London, UCL Press, 99, XII-400 p.

333. Enquêtes en Méditerranée: les expéditions françaises d'Égypte, de Morée et d'Algérie. Actes de Colloque, Athènes-Nauplie, 8–10 juin 1995. Ed. par Marie-Noëlle BOURGUET, Daniel NORDMAN, Vassilis PANAYOTOPOULOS [et al.]. Athina, Institut de Recherches Néohelléniques/ F.N.R.S, 99, 349 p. (ill).

334. Entdeckung und Selbstentdeckung: die Begegnung europäischer Reisender mit dem England und Irland der Neuzeit. Hrsg. v. Otfried DANKELMANN. Frankfurt am Main, P. Lang, 99, 213 p.

335. ESAKOV (Vasilii Alekseevich). Ocherki istorii geografii v Rossii. (Essays on the history of Russian geography): XVIII–nachalo XX veka. Moskva, Editorial URSS, 99, 237 p.

336. FRIMMOVÁ (Eva). Obraz Uhorska v Bartoliniho cestopise Hodoeporicon z roku 1515. (Das Bild Ungarns in der Reisebeschreibung Hodoeporicon von Riccardo Bartolini aus dem Jahre 1515). *Historický časopis*, 99, 47, 4, p. 615-634. [Deutsche Zfassung]

337. GARCIA (José Manuel). Breve história dos descobrimentos e expansao de Portugal. Lisboa, Editorial Presença, 99, 243 p.

338. Geography and Enlightenment. Ed. by David N. LIVINGSTONE and Charles W. J. WITHERS. Chicago, University of Chicago Press, 99, VIII-455 p.

339. Giovanni Caboto e le vie dell'Atlantico settentrionale. Atti del Convegno internazionale di studi, Roma, 29 settembre–1 ottobre 1997. A cura di Marcella ARCA PETRUCCI e Simonetta CONTI. Genova, Brigati, 99, IX-579 p. (ill.). (Centro italiano per gli studi storico-geografici).

340. GNOLI (Tommaso). I papiri dell'Eufrate. Studio di geografia storica. *Mediterraneo antico*, 99, 2, p. 321-358.

341. GODLEWSKA (Anne Marie Claire). Geography unbound: French geographic science from Cassini to Humboldt. Chicago, University of Chicago Press, 99, XII-444 p.

342. GRENDI (Edoardo). Dal Grand Tour a "La passione mediterranea". *Quaderni storici*, 99, 34, p. 121-133.

343. Historical atlas of South-West England. Ed. by Roger KAIN and William RAVENHILL; cartography by Helen JONES. Exeter, University of Exeter Press, 99, 584 p.

344. IPSEN (Dorothea). Das Land der Griechen mit der Seele suchend. Die Wahrnehmung der Antike in deutschsprachigen Reiseberichten über Griechenland um die Wende zum 20. Jahrhundert. Osnabrück, Rasch, 99, 242 p. (Osnabrücker Forschungen zu Altertum und Antike-Rezeption, 2).

345. ISHIDA (Hidetaka). Régimes narratifs et récits de voyage au Japon (1890–1930). Le voyage comme «leçon des choses» de la modernisation. *Genèses*, 99, 35, p. 83-106.

346. JANIN (Valentin L.). Plany Novgoroda Velikogo XVII–XVIII vekov. (The 17th–and 18th-century city maps of Novgorod the Great: [Study and publication]). RAN, Otd. istorii. Moskva, Nauka, 99, 158 p. (ill.).

347. JELEČEK (Leoš). Environmentalizace historické geografie, historiografie a historický Land Use. (Environmentalisation of historical geography, historiography and historical land use). *Historická geografie*, 99, 30, p. 53-84.

348. KABAYAMA (Koichi). Iwanami koza sekai rekishi 12: Sogu to hakken; Ibunka eno shiya. (Iwanami world history. Vol. 12. Encounters and discoveries; the eyes to different cultures). Tokyo, Iwanami Shoten, 99, 274 p.

349. KONOVALOVA (Irina G.). Vostochnaja Evropa v sochinenii al-Idrisi. (Eastern Europe in the writing of al-Idrisi, [1154]). RAN, In-t rossijskoj istorii. Moskva, Vostochnaja literatura, 99, 254 p. (bibl., ind.). [Table of contents in English.]

350. KORDOSIS (M.). The limits of the known land (Ecumene) in the East according to Cosmas Indicopleustes. Tzinista (China) and the ocean. *Byzantion*, 99, 69, p. 99-106.

351. LARNER (John). Marco Polo and the discovery of the world. New Haven a. London, Yale U. P., 99, XIII-250 p.

352. Mensch und Landschaft in der Antike: Lexikon der historischen Geographie. Hrsg. v. Holger SONNABEND. Stuttgart, J.B. Metzler, 99, XII-660 p.

353. MEYZIE (Vincent). Tunis et Alger dans les récits de voyage française des XVIIe et XVIIIe siècles: un révélateur des mentalités européennes. *Correspondances. Bulletin de l'Institut de recherche sur le Maghreb contemporain*, 99, 57, p. 11-17.

354. Nationalising and denationalising European border regions, 1800–2000: views from geography and history. Ed. by Hans KNIPPENBERG and Jan MARKUSSE. Dordrecht a. London, Kluwer Academic, 99, XII-290 p. (GeoJournal library, 53).

355. Other side (The) of the frontier: economic explorations into Native American history. Ed. by Linda BARRINGTON. Boulder, Cumnor Hill a. Oxford, Westview, 99, XIII-301 p. (American and European economic history).

356. PICQUET (Théa). Voyages d'un florentin: Giovanni da Verrazzano (1485–1528). *Rinascimento*, 99, 50, 2, 39, p. 431-465.

357. PODOSINOV (Aleksandr V.). Ex oriente lux! Orientatsija po stranam sveta v arkhaicheskikh kul'turakh Evrasii. (Orientation on cardinal directions in archaic cultures of Eurasia). Moskva, Jazyki russkoj kul'tury, 99, 718 p. (ill., bibl.). [Eng. summary.]

358. PRO RUIZ (Juan), RIVERO (Manuel). Breve atlas de historia de España. Madrid, Alianza Editorial, 99, 1 atlas, 182 p (Alianza atlas, 15).

359. PUCCINI (Sandra). Andare lontano. Viaggi ed etnografia nel secondo ottocento. Roma, Carocci, 99, 297 p.

360. ROBIC (Marie-Claire). Traditions, courants et ruptures: pour une histoire de la géographie en tension. *In*: Histoire (L') des sciences de l'homme [Cf. n° 575], p. 159-180.

361. SAUNIER (Pierre-Yves). Qui porte l'histoire urbaine sur ses épaules? Une lecture de l'Atlas historique des villes de France. *Revue d'histoire moderne et contemporaine*, 99, 46, p. 788-796.

362. SCARGILL (David Ian). The Oxford School of Geography, 1899–1999. Oxford, Oxford U. P., 99, 46 p. (School of Geography, Oxford University, research papers, 55).

363. Seas (The) as Europe's external borders and their role in shaping a European identity. Ed. by Maria PETRICIOLI a. Antonio VARSORI. London, Lothian Foundation Press, 99, VII-289 p. [Cf. n° <choice> 7711.]

364. SERNA (Virginie). Le fleuve de papier. Visites de rivières et cartographies de fleuve (XIIIe–XVIIIe s.). *Médiévales*, 99, 36, p. 31-41.

365. SIVIGNON (M.). Cinquante ans de géographie de la Grèce, d'Élisée Reclus à Jules Sion (1883–1934). *Bullettin de correspondance hellénique*, 99, 123, p. 227-243.

366. Stari krajepisi Istre, (Knjižnica Annales majora). (Old Topographies of Istria). Ur. Darko DAROVEC. Koper, Zgodovinsko društvo za južno Primorsko, Znanstveno-raziskovalno središče Republike Slovenije: Pokrajinski muzej, 99, 292 p. (ill.).

367. SUÁREZ (Thomas). Early mapping of Southeast Asia. [S. l.], Periplus, 99, 280 p.

368. TAILLEMITE (Étienne). Marins français à la découverte du monde: De Jacques Cartier à Dumont d'Urville. Paris, Fayard, 99, 725 p.

369. TOUBERT (Pierre). De l'Antiquité tardive à la fin du Moyen Age: genèse des paysages et des terroirs méditerranéens. *Méditerranées*, 99, 18-19, p. 45-65.

370. TRAMONTANA (Salvatore). Il regno di Sicilia: uomo e natura dall'XI al XIII secolo. Torino, G. Einaudi, 99, XIII-488 p. (Biblioteca di cultura storica, 221).

371. WINTLE (Michael). Renaissance maps and the construction of the idea of Europe. *Journal of historical geography*, 99, 25, p. 137-165.

372. WYCKOFF (William). Creating Colorado: the making of a Western American landscape, 1860–1940. New Haven a. London, Yale U. P., 99, XIV-336 p.

373. YLI-JOKIPII (Pentti). Trends in Finnish geographical research at the turn of the millennium and bibliography for the 1990's. *Fennia*, 99, 178, 1, p. 151-189.

Cf. n°s 970, 3140, 4370, 6147, 6199

§ 10. Iconography and images.

* 374. Lexicon Iconographicum Mythologiae Classicae (LIMC). Index 1. Museen Sammlungen Orte; Mu-

seums Collections Sites; Musées Collections Sites; Musei Collezioni Siti. Index 2. Literarische und epigraphische Quellen zu nicht erhaltenen Werken; mythologische Namen. Literary and epigraphic sources mentioning lost works; mythological names. Sources littéraires et épigraphiques rélatives aux oeuvres perdues; noms mythologiques. Fonti letterarie ed epigrafiche delle opere perdute; nomi mitologici. Düsseldorf, Artemis Verlag, 99, 2 vol., XLIII-629 p., VI-397 p.

375. ALBERRO (Solange). El águila y la cruz: orígenes religiosos de la conciencia criolla: México, siglos XVI–XVII. México, Colegio de México, Fideicomiso Historia de las Américas, Fondo de Cultura Económica, 99, 192 p. (Sección de obras de historia. Serie Ensayos).

376. Augustine in iconography: history and legend. Ed. by Joseph C. SCHNAUBELT and Frederick VAN FLETEREN; art editor George RADAN; literary editor Joseph REINO. New York, P. Lang, 99, XXI-750 p. (Augustinian Historical Institute. Collectanea Augustiniana).

377. BAR (Virginie), BRÊME (Dominique). Dictionnaire iconologique. Les Allégories et les symboles de Ripa et Jean Baudouin. Paris, Ed. Faton, 99, 350 p.

378. Bilderverbot. Hrsg. v. Michael J. RAINER und Hans-Gerd JAN-EN. Münster u. London, Lit, 99, VIII-263 p.

379. BOROVICH (Beatriz). Los caminos de Borges: la Kábala, los mitos y los símbolos. Buenos Aires, Lumen, 99, 158 p.

380. BRIGNARDELLO (Carlos). Simbología prehispánica del paisaje. Lima, [s.n.], 99, 316 p.

381. BROWN (Cynthia J.). Allegorical design and image-making in fifteenth-century France: Alain Chartier's Joan of Arc. *French studies,* 99, 53, 4, p. 385-404.

382. BUSQUETTE-LABOUERIE (Christine). Visages et fonctions du patriciat dans l'iconographie des Grandes chroniques de France. *In*: Construction, reproduction et représentation des patriciats urbains de l'Antiquité au XXe siècle [Cf. n° 1152], p. 413-430.

383. CLOUZOT (Martine). La musique des marges. L'iconographie des animaux et des êtres hybrides musiciens dans les manuscrits enluminés du XIIe au XIVe siècle. *Cahiers de civilisation médiévale,* 99, 42, 168, p. 323-342.

384. DUHAMEL-LACOSTE (Sophie). Le règne de Louis XIV vu par l'iconographie de la diplomatie. *Revue d'histoire diplomatique,* 99, 113, 3, p. 279-290.

385. FIORENTINI (Erna). Ikonographie eines Wandels: Form und Intention von Selbstbildnis und Porträt des Bildhauers im Italien des 16. Jahrhunderts. Berlin, Tenea, 99, 228 p. (Tenea Wissenschaft).

386. HAGENOW (Elisabeth von). Bildniskommentare. Allegorisch gerahmte Herrscherbildnisse in der Graphik des Barock: Entstehung und Bedeutung. Hildesheim, Zürich u. New York, Georg Olms Verlag, 247 p. (ill.)

387. HARVEY (John). Image of the invisible. The visualization of religion in the Welsh nonconformist tradition. Cardiff, University of Wales Press, 99, XIV-218 p.

388. HUBERT (Gérard), LEDOUX-LEBARD (Guy). Napoléon, portraits contemporains, bustes et statues. Paris, Athéna, 99, 245 p. (ill.)

389. Iconographica. Mélanges offerts à Piotr Skubiszewski par ses amis, ses collègues, ses éléves. Ed. par R. FAVREAUS et M.-H. DEBIES. Poitiers, Centre d'études supérieures de civilisation médiévale, 99, XXIX-253 p. (Civilisation médiévale, 7).

390. Illustration (L'): essais d'iconographie. Actes du séminaire CNRS (GDR 712), Paris, 1993–1994. Éd. par Ségolène LE MEN et Maria Teresa CARACCIOLO. Paris, Klincksieck, 99, 421 p. (ill.). (Histoire de l'art et iconographie).

391. Images, icons and the Irish nationalist imagination 1870–1925. Ed. by Lawrence W. MAC BRIDE. Dublin, Four Courts Press, 99, 188 p. (ill.).

392. KELSALL (Malcolm Miles). Jefferson and the iconography of romanticism: folk, land, culture, and the romantic nation. Houndmills, Macmillan a. New York, St. Martin's Press, 99, IX-207 p. (Romanticism in perspective).

393. KLINGBEIL (Martin). Yahweh fighting from heaven: God as warrior and as God of heaven in the Hebrew psalter and ancient Near Eastern iconography. Fribourg, University Press a. Göttingen, Vandenhoeck & Ruprecht, 99, XII-361 p. (Orbis biblicus et orientalis, 169).

394. Law and the image: the authority of art and the aesthetics of law. Ed. by Costas DOUZINAS and Lynda NEAD. Chicago, University of Chicago Press, 99, XVI-268 p.

395. LECLERCQ-MARX (J.). Vox Dei clamat in tempestate. A propos de l'iconographie des vents et d'un groupe d'inscriptions campanaires (IXe–XIIIe s.). *Cahiers de civilisation médiévale,* 99, 42, p. 179-187.

396. LEWUILLON (Serge). Vercingétorix, ou, Le mirage d'Alésia. Bruxelles, Editions Complexe, 99, 223 p. (Questions à l'histoire).

397. LEYDI (Silvio). Sub umbra imperialis aquilae: immagini del potere e consenso politico nella Milano di Carlo V. Firenze, L. S. Olschki, 99, 334 p. (Studi e testi/Fondazione Luigi Firpo, Centro di studi sul pensiero politico, 9).

398. MANCUSO (Barbara). Il latte della virtù o dell' uso delle immagini durante la Rivoluzione francese. *Ricerche di storia dell'arte,* 99, 68, p. 68-80.

10. ICONOGRAPHY AND IMAGES

399. MARTIN (Xavier). L'image du Gaulois (et celle de sa femme) dans le miroir du Français révolutionnaire. *Revue d'histoire du droit,* 99, 77, 4, p. 463-490.

400. MEIFFRET (Laurence). Les cycles de la vie de saint Antoine ermite dans l'iconographie française et italienne du XIVe au XVIe siècle: invention des légendes et influence cultuelle dans la constitution de l'image d'un saint. Thèse Doctorat Histoire, Université Paris 1 Panthéon – Sorbonne, 1999. *Revue Mabillon*, 99, 10, p. 332-335.

401. MOFFITT (John F.). The native american «sauvage» as pictured by French romantic artists and writers. *Gazette des beaux-arts,* 99, 141, 6, 134, p. 117-130.

402. PALAZZO (Eric). L'évêque et son image: l'illustration du pontifical au Moyen Âge. Turnhout, Brepols, 99, 380 p. (ill.).

403. PANOFSKY (Erwin). Hercule à la croisée des chemins et d'autres matériaux figuratifs de l'Antiquité dans l'art plus récent. Paris, Flammarion, 99, 143 p. (ill).

404. PARSHALL (P.). The art of memory and the passion. *Art bulletin*, 99, 81, p. 456-472.

405. REVILLA (Federico). Diccionario de iconografía y simbología. Madrid, Catedra, 99, 471 p.

406. SCALLEN (C. B.). Rembrandt's reformation of a Catholic subject. The penitent and the repentant St. Jerome. *Sixteenth century journal*, 99, 30, p. 71-88.

407. Signa deorum: l'iconographie divine en Gaule romaine. Etudes réunies et publiées par Yves BURNAND et Henri LAVAGNE. Paris, De Boccard, 99, 123 p. (Gallia romana, 4).

408. WIRTH (Jean). L'image à l'époque romane. Paris, Ed. du Cerf, 99, 498 p.

409. ZEITLER (B.). Ostentatio genitalium: displays of nudity in Byzantium. *In*: Desire and denial in Byzantium [Cf. n° 1215], p. 185-201.

Cf. n° 79, 236-252, 1270-1300

B

MANUALS, GENERAL WORKS AND WORKS ON LARGE PERIODS

§ 1. Archives, libraries and museums (*a*. Archives; *b*. Libraries; *c*. Museums). 410-482. – § 2. History of historiography (*a*. General; *b*. Special studies). 483-806. – § 3. Methodology, philosophy, and teaching of history. 807-883. – § 4. Ethnology, folklore and historical anthropology. 884-926. – § 5. General history. 927-1049. – § 6. Theory of the state and of society. 1050-1109. – § 7. Constitutional and legal history. 1110-1142. – § 8. Economic and social history. 1143-1192. – § 9. History of civilization, sciences and education. 1193-1269. – § 10. History of art. 1270-1300. – § 11. History of religions (*a*. General; *b*. Special studies). 1301-1389. – § 12. History of philosophy. 1390-1409. – § 13. History of literature. 1410-1445.

§ 1. Archives, libraries and museums.

a. *Archives*

* 410. DUCLERT (Vincent). La «question archives» en France: une approche bibliographique. *Histoire et archives*, 99, 5, p. 163-177.

411. ALESSANDRONE PERONA (Ersilia). Gli archivi personali come fonte della storia contemporanea. *Contemporanea*, 99, 2, 2, p. 325-330.

412. Archives (Les) du personnel des grandes entreprises et établissements publics: un patrimoine essentiel à l'histoire sociale. Actes du Séminaire du 14 janvier 1999. *Gazette des archives*, 99, 186-187, p. 169-301.

413. Archivi televisivi e storia contemporanea: quattro esperienze europee a confronto. A cura di Luisa CIGOGNETTI, Lorenza SERVETTI e Pierre SORLIN; Istituto regionale Ferruccio Parri. Venezia, Marsilio, 99, 119 p. (Ricerche).

414. Archivistica docet. Beiträge zur Archivwissenschaft und ihres interdisziplinären Umfelds. Hrsg. v. F. BECK. Potsdam, Verlag für Berlin-Brandenburg, 99, 788 p. (Potsdamer Studien, 9).

415. CIFRES (A.). Das historische Archiv der Kongregation für die Glaubenslehre in Rom. *Historische Zeitschrift*, 99, 268, 1, p. 97-106.

416. DERRAINE (Pierre-Jacques), VEGLIA (Patrick). Les étrangers en France. Guide des sources d'archives publiques et privées, XIXe–XXe siècles. Paris, Générique – Direction des archives de France, 99, 3 vol., CXX-2408 p.

417. DUCLERT (Vincent). Les historiens et les archives. *Genèses*, 99, 36, p. 132-146.

418. GARCÍA RUIPÉREZ (Mariano), FERNÁNDEZ HIDALGO (María del Carmen). Los archivos municipales en España durante el Antiguo Régimen: regulación, conservación, organización y difusión. Cuenca, Ediciones de la Universidad de Castilla-La Mancha, 99, 303 p. (Colección Biblos, 3).

419. KOZLOV (Vladimir Petrovich). Rossiiskoe arkhivnoe delo: arkhivno-istochnikovedcheskie issledovaniia. Moskva, ROSSPEN, 99, 334 p.

420. LEMOINE (Hervé), SARMANT (Thierry). Les archives contemporaines du Service historique de l'armée de terre, 1945–1995. Pouvoir politique et autorité militaire de la décolonisation à l'ère nucléaire. *B. inst. Pierre Renouvin*, 99, 7, p. 158-182.

421. MANIGAND-CHAPLAIN (Catherine). Les sources du patrimoine industriel. Paris, CILAC inventaire général, 99, 96 p.

422. MEDING (Holger). Historical archives of the Republic of Panama. *Latin American research review*, 99, 34, 3, p. 129-142.

423. SICKINGER (James P.). Public records and archives in classical Athens. Chapel Hill a. London, University of North Carolina Press, 99, XII-274 p. (Studies in the history of Greece and Rome).

424. Sources (Les) de l'histoire de l'environnement: le XIXe siècle. Ed. par Andrée CORVOL. Paris, l'Harmattan et Institut d'Histoire moderne et contemporaine, Direction des Archives de france, 99, XX-502 p. (ill.).

425. TOFFOLETTO (Mavis). Gli archivi storici delle Comunità europee. *Contemporanea*, 99, 2, 1, p. 171-177.

Cf. nos 1687, 1706, 4985, 5033, 8049, 8286, 8303

b. *Libraries*

** 426. PALLADINI (Fiammetta). La biblioteca di Samuel Pufendorf, Catalogo dell'asta di Berlino del settembre 1697. Wiesbaden, Harrassowitz, 99, LXXIV-660 p. (Wolfenbütteler Schriften zur Geschichte des Buchwesens, 32).

427. BARBIER (Frédéric). Représentation, contrôle, identité: les pouvoirs politique et les bibliothèques centrales en Europe, XVe–XIXe siècles. *Francia*, 99, 26, 2, p. 1-22.

428. BESSONE (Tânia Maria Tavares). Palácios de destinos cruzados: bibliotecas, homens e livros no Rio de Janeiro, 1870–1920. Rio de Janeiro, Ministério da Justiça, Arquivo Nacional, 99, 240 p.

429. BIDUSSA (David). La Biblioteca Feltrinelli dall'«accumulazione originaria» alla nascita degli «Annali» (1950–1959). *Studi storici*, 99, 40, 4, p. 945-992.

430. CANFORA (Luciano). Aristotele «fondatore» della Biblioteca di Alessandria. *Quaderni di storia*, 99, 50, p. 11-21.

431. COLTMAN (Vicky). Classicism in the English library: reading classical culture in the late eighteenth and early nineteenth centuries. Oxford, Oxford U. P., 99, 16 p. (ill.).

432. DE GREGORI (Giorgio), BUTTÒ (Simonetta). Per una storia dei bibliotecari italiani del XX secolo: dizionario bio-bibliografico 1900–1990. Con la collaborazione di Giuliana ZAGRA; presentazione di Alberto PETRUCCIANI. Roma, Associazione italiana biblioteche, 99, 182 p.

433. DE GREGORI (Giorgio). Vita di un bibliotecario romano: Luigi De Gregori. Con la collaborazione di Andrea PAOLI; con i suoi diari, documenti inediti note e figure. Roma, Associazione italiana biblioteche, 99, 269 p. (ill.).

434. DEL REY FAJARDO (José). Las bibliotecas jesuíticas en la Venezuela colonial. Caracas, Academia Nacional de la Historia, 99, 2 vol., [s. p.]. (Biblioteca de la Academia Nacional de la Historia. Fuentes para la historia colonial de Venezuela, 247).

435. DÜCKERS (R.). «Claustrum sine armario sicut castrum sine armamentario». De bibliotheek van de St.-Laurentabdij te Luik in de XIIde eeuw. *Millennium*, 99, 13, p. 105-122.

436. FUMAROLI (Marc). Rhétorique et société en Europe (XVIe–XVIIe siècles). *Annuaire du Collège de France*, 99, 99, p. 563-574.

437. GARCÍA ORO (José), PORTELA SILVA (Maria José). La monarquía y los libros en el Siglo de Oro. Alcalá de Henares, Centro Internacional de Estudios Históricos "Cisneros", Universidad de Alcalá, 99, 495 p. (Centro Internacional de Estudios Históricos "Cisneros". Estudios y documentos, 1).

438. Geschichte des Bibliothekswesens in der DDR. Hrsg. v. Peter VODOSEK und Konrad MARWINSKI. Wiesbaden, Harrassowitz, 99, 196 p. (Wolfenbütteler Schriften zur Geschichte des Buchwesens, 31).

439. HANNEMA (Kiki), KLAVERSMA (Nel). Jan en Casper Luyken to boek gesteld: catalogus van de boekencollectie Van Eeghen in het Amsterdams Historisch Museum. Hilversum, Verloren, 99, 576 p. (ill.).

440. HOBSON (Anthony). Renaissance book collecting: Jean Grolier and Diego Hurtado de Mendoza, their books and bindings. Cambridge, Cambridge U. P., 99, XIX-275 p. (ill.).

441. INNOCENTI (Piero). Jakob Gråber af Hemsö nella biblioteca Palatina di Firenze: 1841–1847. *Nuovi annali scuola archiv. univ. Roma*, 99, 13, p. 141-164.

442. KOCK (Thomas). Die Buchkultur der Devotio moderna: Handschriftenproduktion, Literaturversorgung und Bibliotheksaufbau im Zeitalter des Medienwechsels. Frankfurt am Main a. New York, P. Lang, 99, 410 p. (Tradition – Reform – Innovation, 2).

443. MARION (Michel). Collections et collectionneurs de livres au XVIIIe siècle. Paris, H. Champion, 99, 570 p. (ill.). (Histoire du livre et des bibliothèques, 1).

444. MENDE (U.). Das Germanische Nationalmuseum, die Monumenta Germaniae historica und die Bibliothek der Nationalversammlung in der Frankfurter Paulskirche. Zur Vorgeschichte einer deutschen Nationalbibliothek. *Anzeiger des Germanischen Nationalmuseums*, 99, p. 203-225.

445. NEWTON (Francis). The scriptorium and library at Monte Cassino, 1058–1105. Cambridge a. New York, Cambridge U. P., 99, XXVI-421 p. (ill.). (Cambridge studies in palaeography and codicology, 7).

446. PARENT-LARDEUR (Françoise). Lire à Paris au temps de Balzac: les cabinets de lecture à Paris, 1815–1830. Paris, Ed. de l'EHESS, 99, 300 p.

447. TRANIELLO (Paolo). Una vicenda intricata. Editoria, biblioteche e controllo bibliografico in Italia. *Contemporanea*, 99, 2, p. 651-669.

448. WEISS (Valentine). Enquête sur un don récent, histoire d'une collection: le fonds Max Jacob. *Revue bibl. Nat. France*, 99, 1, p. 38-45.

b. *Libraries. Addenda 1998*

449. CANFORA (Luciano). La biblioteca del patriarca: Fozio censurato nella Francia di Mazzarino. Roma, Salerno, 98, 260 p. (ill.). (Piccoli saggi, 2).

Cf. n°s 84-141

c. Museums

** 450. DENON (Vivant). Vivant Denon, directeur des musées sous le Consulat et l'Empire: correspondance (1802–1815). Ed. par Marie-Anne DUPUY, Isabelle LE MASNE DE CHERMONT et Elaine WILLIAMSON. Paris, Editions de la Réunion des musées nationaux, 99, 2 vol., 1468 p. (Notes et documents des musées de France, 32).

451. Academies, museums and canons of art. Ed. by Gill PERRY and Colin CUNNINGHAM. New Haven a. London, Yale U. P., 99, 268 p.

452. AUERBACH (Jeffrey A.). The great exhibition of 1851: a nation of display. New Haven, Yale U. P., 99, VIII-279 p.

453. BAYER (Waltraud). Die Beute der Oktoberrevolution: Über Zerstörung, Erhaltung und Verkauf privater Kunstsammlungen in der Sowjetunion, 1917–1938. *Archiv für Kulturgeschichte*, 99, 81, 2, p. 417-442.

454. BENFOUGHAL (T.). La constitution des collections ethnographiques russes au musée de L'Homme: histoires croisées. *Cahiers slaves*, 99, 2, p. 234-275.

455. BOREAN (Linda). Appunti per una storia del collezionismo a Venezia nel Seicento: la pinacoteca di Lorenzo Dolfin. *Studi veneziani*, 99, 38, p. 259-300.

456. BURTON (Anthony). Vision & accident: the story of the Victoria and Albert Museum. London, V&A Publications, 99, 264 p.

457. Collecting native America, 1870–1960. Ed. by Shepard KRECH III and Barbara A. HAIL. Washington a. London, Smithsonian Institution Press, 99, VI-298 p.

458. Collezioni (Le) di antichità nella cultura antiquaria europea: incontro internazionale, Varsavia-Nieborów, 17–20 giugno 1996. A cura di Manuela FANO SANTI. Roma, G. Bretschneider, 99, 160-75 p. (Supplementi alla RdA, 21).

459. DEWACHTER (Michel). Du texte au signe. La pierre de Rosette et les premières collections d'antiquités égyptiennes. *Bulletin de la Société française d'Egyptologie*, 99, 146, p. 25-58.

460. DORGERLOH (Hartmut). Die Nationalgalerie in Berlin: zur Geschichte des Gebäudes auf der Museumsinsel 1841–1970. Mit einem Verzeichnis der Pläne und Entwürfe bis 1945 von Barbara GÖTZE. Berlin, Gebr. Mann, 99, 342 p. (Die Bauwerke und Kunstdenkmäler von Berlin. Beiheft, 13).

461. DUPUIS (Anne). A propos de souvenirs inédits de Denise Paulme et Michel Leiris sur la création de musée de l'Homme en 1936. *Cahiers Et. Africaines*, 99, 39, 155-156, p. 511-538.

462. GERÇEK (Ferruh). Türk müzeciliği. (La Muséologie turque). Ankara, Kültür Bakanlığı Yayımlar Dairesi Başkanlığı, 99, X-533 p.

463. HAMILTON (Christian). A quantitative history of the classical collections at the Ashmolean Museum, Oxford. Cambridge, [s. n.], 99, VI-84 p. [Thesis (M.Phil.) – University of Cambridge].

464. HEAMAN (E. A.). The inglorious arts of peace: exhibitions in Canadian society during the nineteenth century. Buffalo, University of Toronto Press, 99, VIII-412 p.

465. KLAMT (Johann-Christian). Sternwarte und Museum im Zeitalter der Aufklärung: der Mathematische Turm zu Kremsmünster (1749–1758). Mainz, von Zabern, 99, X-494 p.

466. LEE (Paula Young). The logic of the bones: architecture and the anatomical sciences at the Muséum d'histoire naturelle, Paris, 1793–1889. Chicago, K. Taylor, 99, XIII-449 p.

467. Making Early Histories in Museums. Ed. by Nick MERRIMAN. New York, Leicester U. P., 99, XII-212 p. (Making histories in museums).

468. MALEUVRE (Didier). Museum memories: history, technology, art. Stanford, Stanford U. P., 99, XII-325 p. (Cultural memory in the past).

469. MAZZOLINI (Renato). "Il sublime linguaggio della materia raccolta nei Musei". Il caso del collezionismo scientifico nel Trentino (1815–1918). *Archivio trentino*, 99, 5, 48, 1, p. 133-204.

470. MICHEL (Patrick). Mazarin, prince des collectionneurs: les collections et l'ameublement du Cardinal Mazarin (1602–1661): histoire et analyse. Paris, Réunion des musées nationaux, 99, 665 p. (Notes et documents des musées de France, 34).

471. MUSIAL (Bogdan). Bilder einer Ausstellung. Kritische Anmerkungen zur Wanderausstellung «Vernichtungskrieg. Verbrechen der Wehrmacht 1941 bis 1944». *Vierteljahrshefte für Zeitgeschichte*, 99, 47, 4, p. 563-592.

472. OLIVERO (Isabelle). L'invention de la collection: de la diffusion de la littérature et des savoirs à la formation du citoyen au XIXe siècle. Paris, Editions de la Maison des Sciences de l'Homme, 99, 335 p. (In Octavo).

473. PERROIS (Louis). Arts africains: objets, artistes et sociétés. *Historiens et geographes*, 99, 367, p. 111-128.

474. Producing the past: aspects of antiquarian culture and practice, 1700–1850. Ed. by Martin MYRONE and Lucy PELTZ. Aldershot, Ashgate, 99, XIII-214 p.

475. Spiegelbild der Welt. Anmerkungen zur Geschichte der Weltausstellungen. Hagen, Ardenku-Verl., 99, 240 p.

476. STARA (Alexandra). Lenoir, Quatremère and the hermeneutic significance of the Musée des Monuments français. Oxford, [s. n.], 99, IV-VII-260 p. [Thesis (D.Phil.) – University of Oxford].

477. TAYLOR (Brandon). Art for the nation: exhibitions and the London public 1747–2001. New Brunswick, Rutgers U. P., 99, 314 p.

478. WEST (Patricia). Domesticating history: the political origins of America's house museums. Washington, Smithsonian Institution, 99, XIII-241 p.

479. WIRTY (Emeline). Le budget des Beaux-Arts sous la Restauration (1815–1830). *Cahiers d'histoire*, 99, 44, 3, p. 399-413.

480. WÖRNER (Martin). Vergnügung und Belehrung. Volkskultur auf den Weltausstellungen 1851–1900. Münster, New York, München u. Berlin, Waxmann, 99, 345 p.

481. YANNI (Carla). Nature's museums: Victorian science and the architecture of display. Baltimore, Johns Hopkins U. P., 99, XVI-199 p.

482. ZWACH (Eva). Deutsche und englische Militärmuseen im 20. Jahrhundert: eine kulturgeschichtliche Analyse des gesellschaftlichen Umgangs mit Krieg. Münster, Lit, 99, 376 p. (Museen, Geschichte und Gegenwart, 4).

Cf. n°s 230, 914, 922, 7177

§ 2. History of historiography.

a. *General*

* 483. Bollettino di storiografia. 1999. Storici italiani del Novecento. [1997–1998. Cf. Bibl. 98, n° 510.] Dir. da Massimo MASTROGREGORI. Pisa e Roma, Istituti Editoriali e Poligrafici Internazionali, 99, 82 p. (Storiografia, supplemento critico e bibliografico, 3).

** 484. HARTOG (François), CASEVITZ (Michel). L'histoire d'Homère à Augustin. Paris, Ed. du Seuil, 99, 290 p.

485. 20 seiki no rekishika tachi 3. (Historians of the 20th century, vol. 3). Ed. by Isamu OGATA, Koichi KABAYAMA and Yoichi KIBATA. Tokyo, Tosui Shobo, 99, 415 p.

486. 50 Jahre Institut für Zeitgeschichte. Eine Bilanz. Hrsg. v. Horst MÖLLER und Udo WENGST. München, Oldenbourg, 99, XXV-598 p.

487. Alemanes (Los), el holocausto y la culpa colectiva. El debate Goldhagen. Ed. por Federico FINCHELSTEIN. Buenos Aires, EUDEBA, 99, 237 p.

488. Annalistique romaine (L'). Tome 2. L'annalistique moyenne (fragments). Ed. par Martine CHASSIGNET. Paris, Les Belles Lettres, 99, XCV-185 p.

489. Art, memory and family in Renaissance Florence. Ed. by G. CIAPPELLI and P. Lee RUBIN. Cambridge, Cambridge U. P., 99, 400 p.

490. ASSMANN (Aleida). Das Gedächtnis der Orte. *In*: Orte der Erinnerung. Denkmal, Gedenkstätte, Museum [Cf. n° 625], p. 59-78. – EADEM. Erinnerungsräume. Formen und Wandlungen des kulturellen Gedächtnisses. München, Beck, 99, 424 p. (C. H. Beck Kulturwissenschaft). – EADEM. Zeit und Tradition. Kulturelle Strategien der Dauer. Köln, Weimar u. Wien, Böhlau, 99, VI-167 p. (Beiträge zur Geschichtskultur, 15).

491. ASSMANN (Jan). Kollektives und kulturelles Gedächtins. Zur Phänomenologie und Funktion von Gegen-Erinnerung. *In*: Orte der Erinnerung. Denkmal, Gedenkstätte, Museum [Cf. n° 625], p. 13-32. – IDEM. Krypta-bewahrte und verdrängte Vergangenheit. Künstlerische und wissenschaftliche Exploration des Kulturellen Gedächtnisses. *In*: Archäologie zwischen Imagination und Wissenschaft. Anne und Patrick Poirier. Hrsg. v. Jussen BERND. Göttingen, Wallstein-Verl., 99, p. 83-99. – IDEM. Monothéisme et mémoire. Le Moïse de Freud et la tradition biblique. *Annales*, 99, 54, 5, p. 1011-1026.

492. BACZKO (Bronislaw). Los imaginarios sociales. Memorias y esperanzas colectivas. Buenos Aires, Nueva Visión, 99, 199 p.

493. BALUEV (Boris P.). Spory o sud'bakh Rossii: N.Ja. Danilevskij i ego kniga «Rossija i Evropa». (The dispute on the fortunes of Russia: Nikolay Danilevsky and his book 'Russia and Europe' [1869]). Moskva, Editorial-URSS, 99, 279 p. (bibl., ind.).

494. BEDELL (John). Memory and proof of age in England 1272–1327. *Past and present*, 99, 162, p. 3-27.

495. BENEŠ (Zdeněk). Dějiny a přítomnost. Zamyšlení nad povahou soudobých dějin. (History and the present. On the nature of contemporary history). *Soudobé dějiny*, 99, 6, 1, p. 45-54.

496. BENREKASSA (Georges). Oublier le XVIIIe siècle? *In*: Invention (L') du XIXe siècle: le XIXe siècle par lui-même (littérature, histoire, société) [Cf. n° 5642], p. 29-54.

497. BENTLEY (Michael). Modern historiography: an introduction. New York, Routledge, 99, 208 p.

498. BERGIN (Joseph). Réflexions sur un demi-siècle d'historiographie du XVIIe siècle. *XVIIe siecle*, 99, 51, 203, p. 247-259.

499. BERNARD (Mathias). La prosopographie et l'histoire politique de la France contemporaine: essai d'historiographie. *Siècles*, 99, 10, p. 47-60.

500. BESSMERTNYJ (Jurij L.). Kollizija mikro- i makropodkhodov i franzuzskaja istorifrafija 90-kh godov. (A Collision of micro- and macro-approaches in the 1990s French historiography). *In*: Istorik v poiske [Cf. n° 840], p. 10-30.

501. BETTERIDGE (Thomas). Tudor histories of the English Reformation 1530–1583. Aldershot, Ashgate, 99, VIII-246 p.

502. BIANCHI (Lorenzo). «Ad limina Petri». Spazio e memoria della Roma cristiana. Roma, Donzelli, 99, XIII-142 p.

503. BIDUSSA (David). La nuova storiografia israeliana. Note di lettura. *Rassegna mensile di Israel*, 99, 65, 2, p. 81-96.

504. BOROZNJAK (Aleksandr I.). Iskuplenie. Nuzhen li Rossii germanskij opyt preodolenija totalitarnogo proshlogo? (The Expiation: does Russia need the Germany's experience of overcoming totalitarian past? [A history of scientific and public discussions on nazism]). Concl. by H.-H. HOLTKE. Moskva, PIK, 99, 285 p. (bibl.).

505. BOSSUAT (Gérard). Des lieux de mémoire pour l'Europe unie. *Vingtième siècle. Revue d'histoire*, 99, 61, p.56-69.

506. BOSWORTH (R. J. B.). Explaining «Auschwitz» after the end of history: the case of Italy. *In*: Comparative historiography: problems and perspectives [Cf. n° 529], p. 84-99.

507. BOUZA (Fernando). Comunicación, conocimiento y memoria en la España de los siglos XVI y XVII. Salamanca, Publicaciones del Seminario de Estudios Medievales y Renacentistas, 99, 148 p.

508. BRANDWEIN (Pamela). Reconstructing reconstruction: the Supreme Court and the production of historical truth. Durham, Duke U. P., 99, XI-272 p.

509. British study (The) of politics in the twentieth century. Ed. by Jack HAYWARD, Brian BARRY and Archie BROWN. Oxford, Oxford U. P., 99, XV-511 p.

510. BRUGÈRE (Fabienne). L'histoire et les Lumières selon Cassirer. *Kairos*, 99, 14, p. 29-48.

511. BRUGUIÈRE (Marie-Bernadette). Qu'est-ce que la Grèce, vue de France au XIXe siècle? *Méditerranées*, 99, 21, p. 75-96.

512. BURGESS (Richard W.). Studies in Eusebian and Post-Eusebian chronography. With the assistance of Witold WITAKOWSKI. Stuttgart, Franz Steiner, 99, 358 p. (Historia. Einzelschriften, 135).

513. BURGUIÈRE (André). L'anthropologie historique et l'Ecole des Annales. *Cahiers du Centre de Recherches historiques*, 99, 23, p. 39-53.

514. CANFORA (Luciano). La discussione antica sulla "utilità della storia". *In*: Storiografia e poesia nella cultura medievale [Cf. n° 670], p. 119-126.

515. CANNADINE (David). On reviewing and being reviewed. *History today*, 99, 49, 3, p. 31-33.

516. CARACCIOLO (A.). La prima generazione [della rivista Quaderni storici]. *Quaderni storici*, 99, 34, 100, p. 13-29.

517. CASALI (Luciano). Autobiografie: fra storia, letteratura e antropologia. La "Banca della memoria popolare" di Pieve Santo Stefano. *Spagna contemporanea*, 99, 8, 15, p. 147-161.

518. CASINI (Simone). Un'utopia nella storia. Carlo Botta e la «Storia d'Italia dal 1789 al 1814». Roma, Bulzoni, 99, 228 p.

519. CATTARUZZA (Marina). Ordinary men? Gli storici tedeschi durante il nazionalsocialismo. *Contemporanea*, 99, 2, 2, p. 331-340.

520. CHAZAN (Mireille). L'Empire et l'histoire universelle de Sigebert de Gembloux à Jean de Saint-Victor, XIIe–XIVe siècle. Paris, Honoré Champion, 99, 784 p. (Études d'histoire médiévale, 3).

521. China and historical capitalism: genealogies of sinological knowledge. Ed. by Timothy BROOK and Gregory BLUE. Cambridge, Cambridge U. P., 99, XII-291 p. (Studies in modern capitalism = Etudes sur le capitalisme moderne).

522. CHRIST (Karl). Hellas. Griechische Geschichte und deutsche Geschichtswissenschaft. München, Beck, 99, VIII-534 p.

523. Chronicler (The) as author: studies in text and texture. Ed. by M. Patrick GRAHAM and Steven L. MAC KENZIE. Sheffield, Sheffield Academic Press, 99, 422 p. (Journal for the study of the Old Testament. Supplement series, 263).

524. CINGOLANI (Stefano Maria). "Pour remenbrer des ancessurs" ovvero Goffredo di Monmouth e Wace fra Historiae e aventures. *In*: Storiografia e poesia nella cultura medievale [Cf. n° 670], p. 81-96.

525. Classics in 19th and 20th century Cambridge: curriculum, culture and community. Ed. by Christopher STRAY. Cambridge, Cambridge Philological Society, 99, XII-176 p.

526. Claustra Alpium Iuliarum, il confine di Rapallo e il fascismo: archeologia come esempio di continuità – Claustra Alpium Iuliarum, rapalska meja in fašizem: arheologija kot primer kontinuitete. A cura di Remo BITELLI, Mitja GUŠTIN e Matej ŽUPANČIČ. Koper – Capodistria, Zgodovinsko društvo za južno Primorsko – Società storica del Litorale, 99, 157 p. (ill.). (Knjižnica Annales majora).

527. COLLA (Piero). La memoria rimossa del razzismo. La Svezia tra le due guerre. *Contemporanea*, 99, 2, 3, p. 411-434.

528. COLLINI (Stefan). English pasts: essays in history and culture. Oxford, Oxford U. P., 99, VIII-348 p.

529. Comparative historiography: problems and perspectives. Ed. by Chris LORENZ. *History and theory*, 99, 38, 1, p. 25-99. [Cf. n^{os} <choice> 506, 530, 591, 600, 606.]

530. CONRAD (Sebastian). Auf der Suche nach der verlorenen Nation. Geschichtsschreibung in Westdeutschland und Japan, 1945–1960. Göttingen, Vandenhoeck & Ruprecht, 99, 485 p. (Kritische Studien zur Geschichtswissenschaft, 134). – IDEM. What time is Japan? Problems of comparative (intercultural) historiography. *In*: Comparative historiography: problems and perspectives [Cf. n° 529], p. 67-83.

531. CROIZY-NAQUET (Catherine). Ecrire l'histoire romaine au début du XIIIe siècle: l'Histoire ancienne

jusqu'à César et les Faits des Romains. Paris, Champion, 99, 352 p. (Nouvelle Bibliothèque du Moyen âge, 53).

532. CROUZET (François). French historians and Robespierre. *Robespierre,* 99, p. 255-288.

533. DAMIAN-GRINT (Peter). The new historians of the twelfth-century Renaissance: authorising history in the vernacular revolution. Woodbridge a. Rochester, Boydell Press, 99, XII-292 p.

534. DE FRANCESCO (Antonino). L'ombra di Buonarroti. Giacobinismo e Rivoluzione francese nella storiografia italiana del dopoguerra. *Storica,* 99, 5, 15, p. 7-67.

535. DELACROIX (Christian), DOSSE (François), GARCIA (Patrick). Les courants historiques en France, XIXe–XXe siècles. Paris, A. Colin, 332 p.

536. DELOGU (Paolo). Trasformazione, estenuazione, periodizzazione. Strumenti concettuali per la fine dell'antichità. *Mediterraneo antico,* 99, 2, p. 3-17.

537. DEMÉNY (Lajos). A román történetírás önértékelése. (The self analysis of the Romanian historiography). *Historia,* 99, 7, p. 15-18.

538. DESPLAND (Michel). L'émergence des sciences de la religion. La monarchie de Juillet: un moment fondateur. Paris, L'Harmattan, 99, 598 p.

539. Deutsche Historiker im Nationalsozialismus. Hrsg. v. Winfried SCHULZE und Otto G. OEXLE. Frankfurt am Main, Fischer Taschenbuch Verlag, 99, 367 p. [Cf. n[os] <Auswahl> 569, 591, 618, 660, 676.]

540. DICKIE (M.W.). Narrative-patterns in Christian Hagiography. *Greek Roman & Byzantine studies,* 99, 40, p. 83-98.

541. DINTENFASS (Michael). Crafting historians' lives: autobiographical constructions and disciplinary discourses after the linguistic turn. *Journal of modern history,* 99, 71, 1, p. 150-165.

542. DOOLEY (Brendan Maurice). Veritas Filia Temporis: experience and belief in early modern culture. *Journal of the history of ideas,* 99, 60, 3, p. 487-504.

543. Eine offene Geschichte: Zur Kommunikativen Tradierung der nationalsozialistischen Vergangenheit. Hrsg. v. Elisabeth DOMANSKY und Harald WELZER. Tübingen, Diskord, 99, 192 p. (Studien zum Nationalsozialismus, 4).

544. Einheit der Geschichte. Studien zur Historiographie. Hrsg. v. Werner PARAVICINI und Karl F. WERNER. Stuttgart, Thorbecke, 99, 292 p. (Francia, 45).

545. Enciclopedie e scienze sociali nel XX secolo. A cura di Giuliana GEMELLI. Milano, Franco Angeli, 99, 325 p.

546. Encyclopedia of historians and historical writing. Ed. by Kelly BOYD. London, Fitzroy Dearborn, 99, 2 vol., XLIX-1562 p.

547. ERKENS (Franz R.). Moderne und Mittelalter oder Von der Relevanz des praktisch Unmöglichen. Ein Plädoyer für das historische Interesse an älteren Epochen. *Das Mittelalter,* 99, 4, 2, p. 95-122.

548. ESCH (Arnold). Der Umgang des Historikers mit seinen Quellen. Über die bleibende Notwendigkeit von Editionen. *In:* Quelleneditionen und kein Ende? [Cf. n° 637], p. 129-148.

549. EUJANIAN (Alejandro). Polémicas por la historia. El surgimiento de la crítica en la historiografía argentina 1864–1882. *Entrepasados,* 99, 8, 16, p. 9-24.

550. Fabrique (La) des héros. Ed. par Pierre CENTLIVRES, Daniel FABRE et Françoise ZONABEND. Paris, Ed. de la Maison des Sciences de l'Homme, 99, 318 p.

551. Faire mémoire: souvenir et commémoration au Moyen Age. Séminaire Sociétés, idéologies et croyances au Moyen Age. Éd. par Huguette TAVIANI-CAROZZI et Claude CAROZZI. Aix-en-Provence, Publications de l'Université de Provence, 99, 368 p. (ill., maps). [Cf. n° <sélection> 295.]

552. FOX (A.). Remembering the past in early modern England: oral and written tradition. *Transactions of the Royal Historical Society,* 99, 9, p. 233-256.

553. FREI (Norbert). Vergangenheitspolitik: die Anfänge der Bundesrepublik und die NS-Vergangenheit. München, DTV, 99, 460 p.

554. FRIER (Bruce W.). Libri annales pontificum maximorum: the origins of the annalistic tradition. Ann Arbor, University of Michigan Press, 99, XIX-345 p.

555. FROLOV (Eduard D.). Russkaja nauka ob antichnosti: Istoriograficheskie ocherki. (Studies of Antiquity in Russia: historiographical essays). Sankt-Peterburg, Izd. S.-Peterb. un-ta, 99, 542 p. (bibl., ind.).

556. GABBA (Emilio). Rec. di MARINCOLA (J.). Authority and tradition in Ancient historiography. *Athenaeum,* 99, 87, p. 321-323.

557. GALLO (L.). La «Biblioteca di storia economica» e le indagini demografiche sul mondo greco. *Quaderni di storia,* 99, 25, p. 23-46.

558. GARCIA-ARENAL (Mercedes). Historiens de l'Espagne, historiens du Maghreb au 19e siècle: comparaison des stéréotypes. *Annales,* 99, 54, 3, p. 687-704.

559. GASNAULT (Pierre). L'érudition mauriste à Saint-Germain-des-Prés. Paris, Institut d'Etudes Augustiniennes, 99, 334 p. (Etudes Augustiniennes. Moyen âge et temps modernes, 34).

560. GEBHARDT (Miriam). Das Familiengedächtnis: Erinnerung im deutsch-jüdischen Bürgertum 1890 bis 1932. Stuttgart, Franz Steiner Verlag, 99, 229 p. (Studien zur Geschichte des Alltags, 16).

561. Gedeutete Realität. Krisen, Wirklichkeiten, Interpretationen (3.–6. Jh. N. Chr.). Hrsg. v. Hartwin BRANDT. Stuttgart, Steiner, 99, 151 p. (Historia Einzelschriften, 134).

562. GERMINARIO (Francesco). L'altra memoria. L'estrema destra, Salò e la Resistenza. Torino, Bollati Boringhieri, 99, 152 p.

563. Geschichtsschreibung (Die) in Mitteleuropa. Projekte und Forschungsprobleme. Hrsg. v. J. WENTA. Toruń, Wydawnictwo Uniwersytetu M. Kopernika, 99, 338 p. (Subsidia historiographica, 1).

564. Geschichtsschreibung und politischer Wandel im 3. Jh. n. Chr.: Kolloquium zu Ehren von Karl-Ernst Petzold (Juni 1998) Anlässlich seines 80. Geburtstags. Hrsg. v. Martin ZIMMERMANN. Stuttgart, Steiner, 99, 244 p.

565. GIARRIZZO (Giuseppe). La scienza della storia: interpreti e problemi. A cura di Fulvio TESSITORE. Napoli, Liguori, 99, XV-618 p. (Domini. La cultura storica, 1).

566. GOETZ (Hans-Werner). Geschichtsschreibung und Geschichtsbewusstsein im hohen Mittelalter. Berlin, Akademie Verlag, 99, 501 p. (ill.). (Orbis mediaevalis, 1). – IDEM. Moderne Mediävistik. Stand und Perspektiven der Mittelalterforschung. Darmstadt, Primus Verlag, 99, IV-412 p. – IDEM. Vergangenheitswahrnehmung, Vergangenheitsgebrauch und Geschichtssymbolismus in der Geschichtsschreibung der Karolingerzeit. *In*: Ideologie e pratiche del reimpiego nell'alto Medioevo [Cf. n° 3458], p. p. 177-225.

567. GREATREX (J.). Prosopographical perspectives, or what can be done with five thousand monastic biographies? *Medieval prosopography*, 99, 20, p. 129-145.

568. GRIBAUDI (Gabriella). Napoli 1943. Memoria individuale e memoria collettiva. *Quaderni storici*, 99, 34, 101, p. 507-538.

569. HAAR (Ingo). "Kämpfende in Wissenschaft". Entstehung und Niedergang der völkischen Geschichtswissenschaft im Wechsel der Systeme. *In*: Deutsche Historiker im Nationalsozialismus [Cf. n° 539], p. 215-240.

570. HÄHNER (Olaf). Historische Biographik. Die Entwicklung einer geschichtswissenschaftlichen Darstellungsform von der Antike bis ins 20. Jh. Frankfurt am Main, Lang, 99, XII-289 p. (Europäische Hochschulschriften, 3, 829).

571. HANNOUM (Abdelmajid). Historiographie et légende au Maghreb: la Kâhina ou la production d'une mémoire. *Annales*, 99, 54, 3, p. 667-686.

572. HANZAL (Josef). Cesty české historiografie 1945–1989. (Wege der tschechischen Historiographie, 1945–1989). Praha, Karolinum, 99, 272 p.

573. HEUCK-ALLEN (Susan). Finding the walls of Troy: Frank Calvert and Heinrich Schliemann at Hisarlik. Berkeley, University of California Press, 99, XIII-409 p.

574. HIGMAN (B. W.). Writing West Indian histories. London, Macmillan Education, 99, XIV-289 p.

575. Histoire (L') des sciences de l'homme: trajectoires, enjeux et questions vives. Sous la dir. de Claude BLANCKAERT [et al.]. Paris, L'Harmattan, 99, 308 p. [Cf. n° <sélection> 360.].

576. Historiae Augustae colloquium Genovese. A cura di François PASCHOUD. Bari, Edipuglia, 99, 358 p. (Historiae Augustae colloquia. Nova series, 7. Munera, 13).

577. Historical perspectives on memory. Ed. by Anne OLLILA. Helsinki, Suomen Historiallinen Seura, 99, 222 p. [Cf. n° <Choice> 882.]

578. Historický ústav Akademie věd České republiky. Všeobecná a bio-bibliografická příručka. (The Institute of History, Academy of Sciences of the Czech Republic). Ed. by Miloslav POLÍVKA and Jiří MIKULEC. Praha, Historický ústav AV ČR, 99, 135 p.

579. Historiography of imperial Russia: the profession and writing of history in a multinational state. Ed. by Thomas SANDERS. Armonk, M. E. Sharpe, 99, XIV-521 p.

580. Historische Zeitschriften im internationalen Vergleich. Hrsg. v. Matthias MIDDELL. Leipzig, Akademische Verlagsgesellschaft, 99, 408 p. (Geschichtswissenschaft und Geschichtskultur im 20. Jahrhundert, 2). [Cf. n° <Auswahl> 775.]

581. HUANG (Ray). Broadening the horizons of Chinese history: discourses, syntheses, and comparisons. Armonk, M. E. Sharpe, 99, VIII-274 p. (An east gate book).

582. IBARRA ROJAS (Eugenia). Cristóbal Colón y la etnohistoria de América Central en los albores del siglo XXI. *Revista de historia de América*, 99, 124, p. 7-28.

583. IGOUNET (Valérie). Histoire du négationnisme en France. Paris, Ed. du Seuil, 99, 692 p.

584. Invention (L') de l'art roman au XIXe siècle. L'èpoque romane vue par le XIXe siècle. Actes du Colloque tenu à Issoire en 1995. R. Auvergne, 99, 553, 257 p. (ill).

585. JANJATOVIĆ (Bosiljka). U povodu 30. obljetnice izlaženja Časopisa za suvremenu povijest (1969.–1999). (On the 30th anniversary of the Journal for Contemporary History, 1969–1999). *Časopis za suvremenu povijest*, 99, 31, 3, p. 445-459.

586. JENSEN (Ola W.). Historiska forntider: en arkeologihistorisk studie över 1000- 1600-talens idéer om forntid och antikviteter. (Préhistoires historiques: les idées sur la préhistoire et les antiquités du 11e au 17e siècle. Göteborg, Institution för arkeologi, Göteborgs universitet, 99, 162 p. (GOTARC, serie C, Arkeologiska skrifter, 29).

587. KIM (S.G.). Sovremennaja nemeckaja istoriografija o vozmozhnost'jakh mikro- i makroanaliza. (Modern historiography in Germany on possibilities of micro- and macro-analysis). *In*: Istorik v poiske [Cf. n° 840], p. 64-91.

588. Kioku no katachi: Komemoreishon no bunkashi. (Forms of memory: cultural history of commemoration). Ed. by Yasunari ABE, Takashi KOSEKI [et al.]. Tokyo, Kashiwa Shobo, 99, 253 p.

589. KLEBER (Hermann). Die französischen Mémoires. Geschichte einer literarischen Gattung von den Anfängen bis zum Zeitalter Ludwigs XIV. Berlin, Erich Schmidt, 99, 382 p.

590. KLIMÓ (Árpád). La statalizzazione della storia. I tentativi di creare una nuova storia nazionale ungherese (1945-1948). *Le carte e la storia*, 99, 5, 2, p. 24-35.

591. KOCKA (Jürgen). Asymmetrical historical comparison: the case of the German Sonderweg. *In*: Comparative historiography: problems and perspectives [Cf. n° 529], p. 40-50. – IDEM. Zwischen Nationalsozialismus und Bundesrepublik. Ein Kommentar. *In*: Deutsche Historiker im Nationalsozialismus [Cf. n° 539], p. 340-357.

592. KOZLOV (Vladimir P.). Rossijskaja arkheografija kontsa XVIII–pervoj chetverti XIX veka: uchebn. posobie. (Russian archaeography [publishing primary sources] in the late 18th and the first quarter of the 19th century: a manual). Ros. gos. gumanit. un-t, Istoriko-arkhivnyj in-t. Moskva, RGGU, 99, 415 p. (bibl., ind.).

593. KURATOV (Anatolij A.). Istorija i istoriki Arkhangel'skogo Severa: Voprosy istochnikovedenija i istoriografii: Monografija. (History and historians of the Achangelsk North [Russia]: questions of source studies and historiography: a monograph). Arkhangel'sk, Pomor. gos. un-t im. M.V. Lomonosova, 99, 271 p. (bibl.).

594. KYLE CROSSLEY (Pamela). A translucent mirror: history and identity in Qing imperial ideology. Berkeley a. Los Angeles, University of California Press, 99, XIV-402 p. (A Philip E. Lilienthal Book).

595. LALOUETTE (Jacqueline). Les épithaphes: l'épigraphie funéraire et la prosopographie. *Siècles*, 99, 10, p. 61-74.

596. LAPLANCHE (François). L'histoire des religions au début de XXe siècle. *In*: Franz Cumont et la science de son temps [Cf. n° 708], p. 623-634.

597. LAURENT (Franck). Penser l'Europe avec l'histoire. La notion de civilisation européenne sous la Restauration et la monarchie de Juillet. *Romantisme*, 99, 29, 104, p. 53-68.

598. LEPETIT (Bernard). La société comme un tout: sur trois formes d'analyse de la totalité sociale. *Cahiers du Centre de recherches historiques*, 99, 23, p. 21-38.

599. LEUTERT (Sebastian), PILLER (Gudrun). Deutschschweizerische Selbstzeugnisse (1500–1800) als Quellen der Mentalitätsgeschichte. Ein Forschungsbericht. *Schweizerische Zeitschrift für Geschichte*, 99, 49, 2, p. 197-221.

600. LEVY (Daniel). The future of the past: historiographical disputes and competing memories in Germany and Israel. *In*: Comparative historiography: problems and perspectives [Cf. n° 529], p. 51-66.

601. LEWIS (Mark Edward). Writing and authority in early China. Albany, State University of New York Press, 99, VII-544 p. (SUNY Series in Chinese Philosophy and Culture).

602. Lexikon současných českých historiků. (The lexicon of contemporary Czech historians]. Eds. Jaroslav PÁNEK, Petr VOREL [et al.]. Praha, Historický ústav AV ČR, 99, 373 p.

603. LEYDESDORFF (Selma). Gender and the categories of experienced history. *Gender and history*, 99, 11, 3, p. 597-613.

604. LINDENBERG (Daniel). L'histoire au service de la théologie? La querelle des historiens israéliens. *Esprit*, 99, p. 151-165.

605. LINDNER (Rainer). Historiker und Herrschaft: Nationsbildung und Geschichtspolitik in Weissrussland im 19. und 20. Jahrhundert. München, R. Oldenbourg, 99, 536 p. (Ordnungssysteme, 5).

606. LORENZ (Chris). Comparative historiography: problems and perspectives. *In*: Comparative historiography: problems and perspectives [Cf. n° 529], p. 25-39.

607. MAREK (Jaroslav), ŠMAHEL (František). Škola Annales v zrcadle českého dějepisectví. (Die Schule der Annales im Spiegel der tschechischen Geschichtsschreibung). *Český časopis historický*, 99, 97, 1, p. 1-18.

608. MASTROGREGORI (Massimo). Storici italiani del Novecento. Appunti e osservazioni. *Storiografia* [Bollettino], 99, 3 p. 9-31.

609. Material Memories. Design and evocation. Ed. by Marius KWINT, Christopher BREWARD and Jeremy AYNSLEY. New York, Berg, 99, XIV-257 p.

610. MATKOVIĆ (Hrvoje). Hrvatska historiografije o razdoblju 1918–1945. (Croatian historiography in the 1918 and 1945 period). *Historijski zbornik*, 99, 52, p. 187-192.

611. MAZZA (Mario). Historia Fabularis: le relazioni pericolose di Clio nella tarda antichità. *In*: Storiografia e poesia nella cultura medievale [Cf. n° 670], p. 1-22.

612. Medieval (The) chronicle. Proceedings of the 1st International Conference on the Medieval Chronicle, Driebergen/Utrecht, 13–16 July 1996. Ed. by Erik KOOPER. Amsterdam a. Atlanta, Rodopi, 99, VI-299 p. (Costerus, 120).

613. Memorie (Le) della Repubblica. A cura di Leonardo PAGGI. Firenze, La nuova Italia, 99, XLII, 424 p. (Biblioteca di storia, 78).

614. MEYRAN (Régis), FABRE (Daniel). Ecrits, pratiques et faits. L'ethnologie sous le régime de Vichy. *L'homme*, 99, 150, p. 203-216.

615. MINTS (Svetlana S.). Rozhdenie kul'turologii. (The birth of culturology: [culture studies to the middle of the 19th century]). Ed. S.N. POLTORAK. Sankt-Peterburg, Nestor, 99, 266 p. (bibl.).

616. MOKHNACHEVA (Marina P.). Zhurnakistika i istoricheskaja nauka. (The press and the historical science). Vol. 2. Zhurnalistika i istoriograficheskaja traditsija v Rossii 30–70-kh gg. XIX v. (The press and the historiographical tradition in Russia, 1830–1870es.). RAN, Arkheograficheskaja komissija. Moskva, Ros. gos. gumanit. un-t, 99, 551 p. (bibl., ind.).

617. MÖLLER (Hans G.). Erinnern und Vergessen. Gegensätzliche Strukturen in Europa und China. *Saeculum*, 99, 50, 2, p. 235-246.

618. MOMMSEN (Wolfgang J.). Vom "Volkstumskampf" zur nationalsozialistischen Vernichtungspolitik in Osteuropa. Zur Rolle der deutschen Historiker unter dem Nationalsozialismus. *In*: Deutsche Historiker im Nationalsozialismus [Cf. n° 539], p. p. 183-214.

619. MOSCROP (John James). Measuring Jerusalem: the Palestine Exploration Fund and British interests in the Holy Land. London, Leicester U. P., 99, X-242 p.

620. Mythen, Geschichte(n), Identitäten. Der Kampf um die Vergangenheit. Hrsg. v. Stephan CONERMANN. Hamburg, EB-Verl., 99, 385 p. (Asien und Afrika, 2).

621. Natsional'nye istorii v sovetskom i postsovetskikh gosudarstvakh. (National histories in Soviet and Post-Soviet states). Eds. Karl AJMERMAKHER, Gennadij A. BORDJUGOV. With intr. by Falk BOMSDORF. Moskva, Airo-XX, 99, 436 p. (ill., bibl., ind.).

622. NEVEU (Bruno). Histoire religieuse et spiritualité dans [la revue] XVIIe Siècle (1949–1997). *XVIIe siècle*, 99, 51, 203, p. 261-312.

623. NEYZİ (Leyla). İstanbul'da hatırlamak ve unutmak: birey, bellek ve aidiyet. (Souvenir et oubli à İstanbul: individu, mémoire et appartenance). İstanbul, Tarih Vakfı Yurt Yayınları, 99, 221 p.

624. Origini (Alle) della cronachistica bolognese: il Chronicon Bononiense o Cronaca lolliniana. A cura di Gherardo ORTALLI. Roma, Viella, 99. 78 p.

625. Orte der Erinnerung. Denkmal, Gedenkstätte, Museum. Hrsg. v. Ulrich BORSDORF und Heinrich T. GRÜTTER. Frankfurt am Main, Campus Verlag, 99, 357 p. [Cf. n^{os} <Auswahl> 490, 491.]

626. PASSERINI (Luisa). La memoria orale: l'opera di Nuto Revelli e la sua ricezione. *Il presente e la storia*, 99, 55, p. 21-48.

627. PASTA (Renato). Dopo le «Annales»: il ritorno alla storia politica. *Risorgimento*, 99, 90, 2, p. 273-303.

628. PENE VIDARI (Gian Savino). Tendenze e prospettive dell'insegnamento della storia giuridica. *Rivista di storia del diritto italiano*, 99, 72, 72, p. 299-315.

629. Penser avec l'histoire. Présenté par Paul PATITIER. *Romantisme*, 99, 29, 104, p. 3-106.

630. PERRETT (Roy W.). History, time, and knowledge in ancient India. *History and theory*, 99, 38, 3, p. 307-321.

631. PERTICI (Roberto). Storici italiani del Novecento. *Storiografia*, 99, 3, p. 1-340. [Numero monografico].

632. POCOCK (J. G. A.). British history: the pursuit of the expanding subject. *In*: British studies into the 21st century: perspectives and practices. Ed. by Wilfrid PREST. Melbourne, Australian Scholarly Publishing, 99, p. 58-72.

633. POPKIN (Jeremy D.). Historians on the autobiographical frontier. *American historical review*, 99, 104, 3, p. 725-748.

634. PORTELLI (Alessandro). L'ordine è già stato eseguito. Roma, le Fosse Ardeatine, la memoria. Roma, Donzelli, 99, 448 p.

635. POTTER (David Stone). Literary texts and the Roman historian. London, Routledge, 99, X-218 p.

636. Presentazione e scrittura della storia: storiografia, epigrafi, monumenti: atti del Convegno di Pontignano, aprile 1996. A cura di Emilio GABBA. Como, New press, 99, 178 p. (ill.). (Biblioteca di Athenaeum, 42). [Contienuto: GABBA (Emilio). Premessa (p. 7-8). – DONADONI (Sergio). Egitto: storia e arte (p. 9-22). – MORA (Clelia). Una nuova scrittura per la storia. Iscrizioni e monumenti dell'ultimo periodo dell'Impero Ittita (p. 23-42). – LANFRANCHI (Giovanni B.). Le iscrizioni reali assire (p. 43-60). – SACCHI (Paolo). La storiografia ebraica (p. 61-76). – GNOLI (Gherardo). Presentazione della storia e identità nazionale nell'Iran antico (p. 77-99). – ASHERI (David). Erodoto e Bisitun (p. 101-116). – AVANZINI (Alessandra). La "lista degli eponimi" e l'inizio della documentazione storica dell' Arabia meridionale preislamica (p. 117-126). – PANAINO (Antonio). Cronologia e storia religiosa nell'Iran zoroastriano (p. 127-143). – INVERNIZZI (Antonio). Storia per le immagini dell'Impero partico (p. 145-153). – TROIANI (Lucio). Storiografia orientale di lingua greca (p. 155-163). – BOFFO (laura). La pietra e la memoria: storia e "Storie" nell'epigrafia dell'Oriente (p. 165-173). GABBA (Emilio). Qualche riflessione conclusiva (175-178)].

637. Quelleneditionen und kein Ende? Symposium der Monumenta Germaniae Historica und der Historischen Kommission bei der Bayerischen Akademie der Wissenschaften, München, 22./23. Mai 1998. Hrsg. v. Lothar GALL und Rudolf SCHIEFFER. München, R. Oldenbourg, 99, 150 p. [Cf. n° <Auswahl> 548.]

638. Récit et vérité. Du moyen âge au XVIe siècle. Articles réunis par M. ACCARIE et E. KOTLER. Nice, Faculté des lettres, arts et sciences humaines, 99, 141 p. (Cahiers du centre d'études médiévales de Nice, 15).

639. Reconstructing history: the emergence of a new Historical Society. Ed. by Elizabeth FOX-GENOVESE and Elisabeth LASCH-QUINN. London a. New York, Routledge, 99, XXII-377 p.

640. REEVES (Marjorie). The prophetic sense of history in medieval and renaissance Europe. Aldershot, Ashgate, 99, 306 p. (ill.). (Variorum collected studies series, 660).

641. Remembrance and denial. The case of the Armenian genocide. Ed. by Richard G. HOVANNISIAN. Detroit, Wayne State U. P., 99, 328 p.

642. RÉMOND (René). Peut-on écrire aujourd'hui encore, une histoire nationale? *In*: Finances, pouvoirs et mémoire [Cf. n° 1160], p. 819-826.

643. Renan (De) à Marrou: l'histoire du christianisme et les progrès de la méthode historique, 1863–1968. Ed. par Yves-Marie HILAIRE. Villeneuve d'Ascq, Presses universitaires du Septentrion, 99, 262 p. (Histoire et civilisations). [Cf. n° <sélection> 750.]

644. REPINA (Lorina P.). Kombinatsija mikro- i makropodkhodov v sovremennoj britanskoj i amerikanskoj istoriogrfii: neskol'ko kazusov i opyt ikh prochtenija. (Combination of micro- and macro-approaches in modern British and American historiography). *In*: Istorik v poiske [Cf. n° 840], p. 31-63.

645. Repressirovannye etnografy. (Ethnographers subjected to the repressions, [Soviet Russia, biographical articles]). Vol. 1. Ed. Daniil D. TUMARKIN. RAN, In-t etnologii i antropologii im. N.N. Miklukho-Maklaja. Moskva, Vostochnaja literatura, 99, 343 p.

646. Resistenza (La) tra storia e memoria. A cura di Nicola GALLERANO. Istituto romano per la storia d'Italia dal fascismo alla Resistenza. Milano, Mursia, 99, 415 p.

647. Resources (The) of history. Tradition, narration, and nation in South Asia. Ed. by Jackie ASSAYAG. Paris a. Pondichéry, Ecole française d'Extrême-Orient, 99, 374 p. (Etudes thématiques, 8).

648. RIIS (Carsten). En osmannisk arv: historieskrivning og religion i Bulgarien. (Un héritage ottoman: écriture de l'histoire et religion en Bulgarie). Århus, Det teologiske fakultet, Aarhus Universitet, 99, 344 p. (Rés. anglais).

649. ROMAGNANI (Gian Paolo). Fortemente moderati: intellettuali subalpini fra Sette e Ottocento. Alessandria, Edizioni dell'Orso, 99, 240 p. (Forme e percorsi della storia, 4). – IDEM. Sotto la bandiera dell'istoria: eruditi e uomini di lettere nell'Italia del Settecento. Maffei, Muratori, Tartarotti. Sommacampagna, Cierre, 99, XIV-272 p. (Università degli studi di Verona).

650. ROMANO (Ruggiero). La memoria e i modelli. *Proposte e ricerche*, 99, 22, 42, p. 7-21. – IDEM. Sobre algunos grandes temas historiográficos. *Estudios sociales*, 99, 9, 16, p. 9-19.

651. ROSENFELD (Gavriel D.). The controversy that isn't: the debate over Daniel J. Goldhagen's "Hitler's willing executioners" in comparative perspective. *Contemporary European history*, 99, 8, 2, p. 249-273.

652. ROSKIES (David G.). The Jewish search for a usable past. Bloomington, Indiana U. P., 99, XII-217 p. (Helen and Martin Schwartz lectures in Jewish studies, 1998).

653. SALMERI (Giovanni). La periodizzazione della storia romana imperiale e l'emergere del sé. *Storica*, 99, 5, 13, p. 105-124.

654. Sanctity and secularity during the modernist period. Six perspectives on hagiography around 1900. Six perspectives sur l'agiographie aux alentours de 1900. Ed. by L. BARMANN and C. TALAR. Bruxelles, Société des Bollandistes, 99, XI-199 p. [Cf. n° <choice> 700.]

655. SANTOMASSIMO (Gianpasquale). Storia e uso della storia nella guerra dei Balcani. *Passato e presente*, 99, 17, 48, p. 99-112.

656. SANTORO (Stefano). Cultura e propaganda nell'Italia fascista: l'Istituto per l'Europa Orientale. *Passato e presente*, 99, 17, 48, p. 55-78.

657. SCHAEBLER (Birgit). Coming to terms with failed revolutions: historiography in Syria, Germany and France. *Middle Eastern studies*, 99, 35, 1, p. 17-44.

658. SCHEIDEL (Walter). Professional historians of classical antiquity in the English-speaking world: a quantitative analysis. *Ancient history bulletin*, 99, 13, p. 151-156.

659. SCHUCK (G.). Theorien moderner Vergesellschaftung in den historischen Wissenschaften um 1900. Zum Entstehungszusammenhang des Sozialdisziplinierungskonzeptes im Kontext der Krisenerfahrungen der Moderne. *Historische Zeitschrift*, 99, 268, 1, p. 35-60.

660. SCHULZE (Winfried), HELM (Gerd), OTT (Thomas). Deutsche Historiker im Nationalsozialismus. Beobachtungen und Überlegungen zu einer Debatte. *In*: Deutsche Historiker im Nationalsozialismus [Cf. n° 676], p. 11-50.

661. SCHUSTER (Armin). Die Entnazifizierung in Hessen 1945–1954. Vergangenheitspolitik in der Nachkriegszeit. Wiesbaden, Historische Kommission für Nassau, 99, X-438 p. (Veröffentlichungen der Historischen Kommission für Nassau, 66; Vorgeschichte und Geschichte des Parlamentarismus in Hessen, 29).

662. SCHUSTER (Peter). Die Krise des Spätmittelalters. Zur Evidenz eines sozial- und wirtschaftsgeschichtlichen Paradigmas in der Geschichtsschreibung des 20. Jahrunderts. *Historische Zeitschrift*, 99, 269, 1, p. 19-56.

663. SHERMAN (Daniel J.). The construction of memory in interwar France. Chicago, University of Chicago Press, 99, 414 p.

664. SINGARAVÉLOU (Pierre). L'Ecole française d'Extrême-Orient ou l'institution des marges (1898–1956). Essai d'histoire sociale et politique de la science coloniale. Paris, L'Harmattan, 99, 382 p.

665. SOMMERLECHNER (Andrea). Stupor mundi? Kaiser Friedrich II, und die mittelalterliche Geschichtsschreibung. Wien, Verlag der Österreichischen Akademie der Wissenschaften, 99, 660 p. (Abb.) (Publikationen des Historischen Instituts beim Österreichischen Kulturinstitut in Rom 1, 11).

666. SPATH (Thomas). Nouvelle histoire ancienne? Sciences sociales et histoire romaine (note critique). *Annales*, 99, 54, 5, p. 1137-1156.

667. SPIEGEL (Gabrielle M.). Les débuts français de l'historiographie royale: quelques aspects inattendus. *In*: Saint-Denis et la royauté [Cf. n° 3222], p. 395-404.

668. SPINETO (Natale). Storici delle religioni italiani del '900. Notizie e osservazioni sugli studi recenti (1995–2000). *Storiografia* (Bollettino), 99, 3, p. 63-82.

669. STEINHAUF (B.). Die Wahrheit der Geschichte. Zum Status katholischer Kirchengeschichtsschreibung am Vorabend des Modernismus. Frankfurt am Main, P. Lang, 99, XI-456 p. (Bamberger theolog. Studien, 8).

670. Storiografia e poesia nella cultura medievale. Atti del Colloquio, Roma, 21–23 febbraio 1990. Roma, Istituto storico italiano per il Medioevo, 99, XI-333 p. (Nuovi studi storici, 35). [Cf. n^{os} <scelta> 514, 524, 611.]

671. TREMIL (Vladimir Guy). Censorship, access, and influence: Western sovietology in the Soviet Union. Berkeley, University of California, 99, XI-91 p.

672. TRENTER (Cecilia). Granskningens retorik och historisk vetenskap: kognitiv identitet i recensioner i dans Historisk Tidsskrift, norsk Historisk Tidsskrift och svensk Historisk Tidskrift 1965–1990. (La Rhétorique de l'évaluation et la science historique: l'identité cognitive dans les comptes rendus publiés dans la Revue Historique danoise, norvégienne et suédoise). Uppsala, Acta Universitatis Upsaliensis, Univ. Bibliotek, 99, 237 p. (Studia Historica Upsaliensia, 192). (rés. anglais).

673. Umkämpfte Vergangenheit: Geschichtsbilder, Erinnerung und Vergangenheitspolitik im internationalen Vergleich. Hrsg. v. Petra BOCK und Edgar WOLFRUM. Göttingen, Vandenhoeck & Ruprecht, 99, 304 p. (Sammlung Vandenhoeck).

674. Uses (The) and abuses of antiquity. Ed. by M. BIDDIS a. M. WYKE. Bern, Berlin, Bruxelles, Frankfurt am M., New York a. Wien, Lang, 99, 281 p. [Cf. n° <choice> 686.]

675. War and remembrance in the twentieth century. Ed. by Jay WINTER and Emmanuel SIVAN. Cambridge, Cambridge U. P., 99, VI-260 p. (Studies in the social and cultural history in modern warfare, 5).

676. WEHLER (Hans U.). Nationalsozialismus und Historiker. *In*: Deutsche Historiker im Nationalsozialismus [Cf. n° 539], p. 306-339.

677. WENDLAND (Ulrike). Biographisches Handbuch deutschsprachiger Kunsthistoriker im Exil: Leben und Werk der unter dem Nationalsozialismus verfolgten und vertriebenen Wissenschaftler. München, Saur, 99, 2 vol., 813 p.

678. Western views of Islam in medieval and early modern Europe: perception of other. Ed. by David R. BLANKS and Michael FRASSETTO. New York, St. Martin's Press, 99, VIII-235 p.

679. WOLFE (Patrick). Settler colonialism and the transformation of anthropology: the politics and poetics of an ethnographic event. London, Cassell, 99, 246 p. (Writing past colonialism series).

680. WOLFRUM (Edgar). Geschichtspolitik in der Bundesrepublik Deutschland: der Weg zur bundesrepublikanischen Erinnerung, 1948–1990. Darmstadt, Wissenschaftliche Buchgesellschaft, 99, VII-532 p.

681. WOOD (Nancy). Vectors of memory: legacies of trauma in postwar Europe. New York, Berg, 99, VII-204 p.

682. World history today. Chimera or necessity?. Conference, Leipzig, April 12–13 1998, Zentrum für Höhere Studien – Universität Leipzig. *Storia della storiografia*, 99, 35, p. 5-161.

683. Writing (The) of official military history. Ed. by Robin HIGHAM. Westport, Greenwood, 99, XII-182 p.

684. Writing national histories: Western Europe since 1800. Ed. by Stefan BERGER, Mark DONOVAN and Kevin PASSMORE. London a. New York, Routledge, 99, XIII-314 p. [Contents: Part 1. Comparative perspectives. BERGER (Stefan), DONOVAN (Mark), PASSMORE (Kevin). Apologias for the nation-state in Western Europe since 1800 (p. 3-14). – IGGERS (Georg G.). Nationalism and historiography, 1789–1996: the German example in historical perspective (p. 15-29). – STUCHTEY (Benedikt). Literature, liberty and life of the nation: British historiography from Macaulay to Trevelyan (p. 30-46). – Part 2. The age of Bourgeois revolution. CROSSLEY (Ceri). History as a principle of legitimation in France (1820–1848) (p. 49-56). – BAHNERS (Patrick). National unification and narrative unity: the case of Ranke's German History (p. 57-68). – THOM (Martin). Unity and confederation in the Italian Risorgimento: the case of Carlo Cattaneo (p. 69-82). – Part 3. The age of the masses. JONES (Stuart). Taine and the nation-state (p. 85-96). – THOMPSON (Alastair). 'Prussian in a good sense': German historians as critics of Prussian conservatism, 1890–1920 (p. 97-110). – MORETTI (Mauro). The search for a 'national' history: Italian historiographical trends following unification (p. 111-122). – Part 4. Liberal democracy and antifascism (1918–1945). SCHÖTTLER (Peter). Marc Bloch as a critic of historiographical nationalism in the interwar years (p. 125-136). – LAMBERT (Peter). From antifascist to Volkshistoriker: demos and ethnos in the political thought of Fritz Rörig, 1921–1945 (p. 137-149). – MORGAN (Philip). Reclaiming Italy? Antifascist historians and history in justice and liberty (p. 150-160). – Part 5. Fascist historiography and the nation-

state. GORDON (Bertram M.). Right-wing historiographical models in France, 1918–1945 (p. 163-175). – SCHLEIER (Hans). German historiography under National Socialism: dreams of a powerful nation-state and German Volkstum come true (p. 176-188). – CLARK (Martin). Gioacchino Volpe and fascist historiography in Italy (p. 189-202). – Part 6. The Cold War years. FREY (Hugo). Rebuilding France: Gaullist historiography, the rise-fall myth and French identity (1945–1958) (p. 205-216). – FULBROOK (Mary). Dividing the past, defining the present: historians and national identity in the two Germanies (p. 217-229). – VIVARELLI (Roberto). A neglected question: historians and the Italian national state (1945–1995). (p. 230-236). – Part 7. Contemporary trends. JACKSON (Julian). Historians and the nation in contemporary France (p. 239-251). – BERGER (Stefan). Historians and the search for national identity in the reunified Germany (p. 252-264). – LEVY (Carl). Historians and the 'First Republic' (p. 265-278). – Part 8. Conclusion. PASSMORE (Kevin), BERGER (Stefan), DONOVAN (Mark). Historians and the nation-state: some conclusions (p. 281-304)].

685. Wushinian lai Zhongguo jindai shi yanjiu zhuanji. (A special issue on fifty years of historical research on modern China). *Jindai shi yanjiu*, 99, 5, 313 p.

686. WYKE (M.). Sawdust Caesar: Mussolini, Julius Caesar, and the drama of dictatorship. *In*: Uses (The) and abuses of antiquity [Cf. n° 674], p. 167-186.

687. YONEYAMA (Lisa). Hiroshima Traces: Time, Space, and the Dialectics of Memory. Berkeley a. Los Angeles, University of California Press, 99, XIII-298 p. (Twentieth century Japan: the emrgence of a world power, 10).

688. ZABBIA (Marino). I notai e la cronachistica cittadina italiana nel Trecento. Roma, Istituto storico italiano per il Medio Evo, 99, XIII-382 p. (Nuovi studi storici, 49).

689. Zastave vihrajo: spominski dnevi in praznovanja na Slovenskem od sredine 19. stoletja do danes. (Fluttering flags: memorial days and celebrations in Slovenia from the middle of the 19th century to the present). Ur. Franc ROZMAN, Vasilij MELIK, Božo REPE, Darja KEREC v Dejan VONČINA. Ljubljana: Modrijan, 99, 181 p. (ill.).

a. *General. Addenda 1997–1998*

690. CRACCO RUGGINI (Lellia). La storiografia latina da Ammiano Marcellino a Cassiodoro (e anche più in là): documenti, relitti e fantasmi reinterpretati. *Cassiodorus*, 97, 3, p. 175-187.

691. RONCHEY (Silvia). Profilo di storia della storiografia su Bisanzio da Tillemont alle Annales. *In*: Europa medievale e mondo bizantino [Cf. Bibl. 98, n° 3534], p. 283-304.

Cf. n^{os} *382, 888, 905, 926, 1538, 1576, 1741, 1794, 1825, 1829, 1850, 1965, 2352, 2436, 2816, 2969, 2975, 2988, 2994, 3094, 3158, 3228, 3256, 3531,*

3537, 4174, 4327, 4423, 4551, 4611, 4753, 5013, 5017, 5150, 6023, 6475, 6557, 7177, 8075, 8076, 8084, 8099, 8271, 8381

b. *Special studies*

692. ARRIVO (Giorgia). Philippe **Ariès** (1914–1984). *Ricerche storiche*, 99, 29, p. 573-593.

693. BORGEAUD (Ph.), DURISCH (N.), KOLDE (A.), SOMMER (G.). La mythologie du matriarcat. L'atelier de J. J. **Bachofen**. Genève, Droz, 99, 252 p.

694. FUBINI (Riccardo). **Baronio** e la tradizione umanistica. *Cristianesimo nella storia*, 99, 20, p. 147-159.

695. DINGEL (Irene). Zwischen Orthodoxie und Aufklärung. Pierre **Bayle**s historisch-kritisches Wörterbuch im Umbruch der Epochen. *Zeitschrift für Kirchengeschichte*, 99, 110, 2, p. 229-246.

696. CHITTOLINI (Giorgio). 'L'Europa delle città' secondo Marino **Berengo**. *Storica*, 99, 5, 14, p. 105-128.

697. GRUCA (Anna). Wiesław **Bieńkowski** (1926–1999). *Biul. Bibl.i Jagiell.*, 99, 49, p. 283-285.

698. **BLOCH** (Marc). La terre et le paysan: agriculture et vie rurale aux XVIIe et XVIIIe siècle. Paris, A. Colin, 99, 608 p. – Marc **Bloch**, Historiker und Widerstandskämpfer. Hrsg. v. Peter SCHÖTTLER. Frankfurt am Main, Campus, 99, 279 p. [Cf. n° <Auswahl> 698.] – MÜLLER (Bertrand). Marc **Bloch** und die Sozialwissenschaften. *In*: Marc Bloch, Historiker und Widerstandskämpfer [Cf. n° 698], p.72-101. – SCHÖTTLER (Peter). Marc **Bloch** und Deutschland. *In*: Marc Bloch, Historiker und Widerstandskämpfer [Cf. n° 698], p. 33-71.

699. RICUPERATI (Giuseppe). Jacques-Bénigne **Bossuet** et l'histoire universelle. *Storia della storiografia*, 99, 35, p. 27-61.

700. GOICHOT (E.). H. **Brémond**. Aux frontières de l'hagiographie. *In*: Sanctity and secularity during the modernist period [Cf. n° 654], p. 67-102.

701. BLÄNKNER (Reinhard). Otto **Brunner**s Perspektivenwechsel der Verfassungshistorie im Spannungsfeld zwischen völkischem und alteuropäischem Geschichtsdenken. *In*: Alteuropa und Frühe Moderne. Deutinsmuster für das 16. bis 18. Jahrhundert aus dem Krisenbewußtsein der Weimarer Republik in Theologie, Rechts- und Geschichtswissenschaft. Hrsg. v. Luise SCHORN-SCHÜTTE. Berlin, Duncker & Humblot, 99, p.87-136.

702. GROẞE (Jürgen). Geschichte lesen oder Geschichte schreiben? Zu Jacob **Burckhardt**s Quellenlektüren. *Archiv für Kulturgeschichte*, 99, 81, 2, p. 339-370. – IDEM. Reading history: on Jacob **Burckhardt** as source-reader. *Journal of the history of ideas*, 99, 60, 3, p. 525-548. – HOWARD (Thomas Albert). Jacob **Burckhardt**, religion, and the historiography of «Crisis» and «Transition». *Journal of the history of ideas*, 99, 60, 1, p. 149-164. – MATTIOLI (Aram). Jacob **Burckhardt**s

Antisemitismus. Eine Neuinterpretation aus mentalitätsgeschichtlicher Sicht. *Schweizerische Zeitschrift für Geschichte*, 99, 49, 4, p. 496-529.

703. LECARME (Jacques). Jérôme **Carcopino**: Rome au service de Vichy. *Histoire,* 99, 232, p. 26-27.

704. HASLAM (Jonathan). The vices of integrity: E. H. **Carr**, 1892–1982. London, Verso, XIV-306 p.

705. ESCRIBANO (M. V.). Estrategias retóricas y pensamiento político en la Historia Romana de **Casio Dión**. *L'antiquité classique*, 99, 68, p. 171-189. – MURISON (C. L.). Rebellion and reconstruction. Galba to Domitian. An historical commentary on **Cassius Dio**'s Roman history. Books 64-67 (A.D. 68–96). Atlanta, Scholars Press, 99, XXI-291 p.

706. CONSTANT (Benjamin). De la religion considérée dans sa source, ses formes et ses développements, texte intégral présenté par Tzvetan TODOROV et Etienne HOFMANN. Arles, Actes Sud, 99, 1122 p.

707. SASSO (Gennaro). Benedetto **Croce** dal 1943 al 1947. *La cultura*, 99, 37, 1, p. 9-34. – SASSO (Gennaro). **Croce**, Serra e Piero Nardi. *La cultura*, 99, 37, 1, p. 143-150.

708. Franz **Cumont** et la science de son temps. Actes de la Table ronde organisée à Paris, 5–6 décembre 1997. *Mélanges de l'Ecole française de Rome. Italie Méditerranée*, 99, 111, 2, p. 501-666. [Cf. n° <sélection> 596.]

709. BARBAGALLO (Francesco). L'Italia repubblicana di Franco **De Felice**: fondamenti e categorie. *Studi storici*, 99, 40, 3, p. 681-698.

710. Renzo **De Felice**: il lavoro dello storico tra ricerca e didattica. A cura di Giovanni ALIBERTI e Giuseppe PARLATO. Milano, LED, 99, 210 p. (Colloquium).

711. BO (Carlo), DE LUCA (Giuseppe). Carteggio, 1932–1961. A cura di M. BRUSCIA. Roma, Edizioni di Storia e letteratura, 99, XX-313 p. – DE LUCA (Giuseppe), MINELLI (Fausto). Carteggio. Vol. 1. 1930–1934. A cura di Marco RONCALLI, premessa di Carlo BO. Roma, Edizioni di storia e letteratura, 99, XLI-593 p. (ill.).

712. SASSO (Gennaro). Gli esordi di Ernesto **De Martino**. Questioni preliminari. *Annali dell'Istituto Italiano per gli Studi Storici*, 99, 16, p. 671-724.

713. BORGHESI (Angela). L'officina del metodo: le lezioni del giovane De Sanctis. Firenze, La Nuova Italia, 99, IX-176 p.

714. **DE SANCTIS** (Gaetano). Alessandro Magno. Inedito a cura di Michele COCCIA. *Quaderni di storia*, 99, 50, p. 95-134.

715. SAUTEL (Jacques-Hubert). L'autorité dans la Rome royale selon **Denys d'Halicarnasse**. Aperçus sémantiques. *Revue belge de philologie et d'histoire*, 99, 77, 1, p. 77-104.

716. GUGLIELMINETTI (Marziano). Per una nuova storia della letteratura italiana: Carlo **Dionisotti**. *Rivista storica italiana*, 99, 111, 3, p. 932-946.

717. DELLE DONNE (Fulvio). Austerità espositiva e rielaborazione creatrice nel "Chronicon" di **Domenico da Gravina**. *Studi storici*, 99, 40, p. 301-314.

718. FARDON (Richard). Mary **Douglas**: an intellectual biography. London a. New York, Routledge, 99, 352 p.

719. CAPITANI (Ovidio). Ricordo di Georges **Duby** (1919–1997). *In*: Ideologie e pratiche del reimpiego nell'alto Medioevo [Cf. n° 3458], p. 49-71.

720. CAPITANI (Ovidio). Da Volpe a Morghen: riflessioni eresiologiche a proposito del centenario della nascita di Eugenio **Dupré Theseider**. *Studi medievali*, 99, 40, p. 305-321.

721. JONES (Robert Alun). The development of **Durkheim**'s social realism. Cambridge, Cambridge U. P., 99, XI-324 p. (Ideas in context, 55).

722. PARMEGGIANI (G.). Mito e spatium historicum nelle Storie di **Efeso da Cuma** (Note a Eph. FgrHist 70 T8). *Rivista storica dell'antichità*, 99, 29, p. 107-125.

723. DELLE DONNE (Fulvio). Coscienza urbana e storiografia cittadina. A proposito dell'edizione critica del "Chronicon" di **Falcone di Benevento**. *Studi storici*, 99, 40, p. 1127-1141.

724. BIDUSSA (David). L'uso pubblico della geografia. A proposito del Reno di Lucien **Febvre**. *Humanitas*, 99, 54, p. 1110-1135. – BURKE (Peter). Lucien **Febvre**, ecclesiastical historian? *Journal of ecclesiastical history*, 99, 50, p. 760-766. – MÜLLER (Bertrand). «Histoire traditionnelle» et «histoire nouvelle»: un bilan de combat de Lucien **Febvre**. *Genèses*, 99, 34, p. 132-143.

725. MONTANARI (M.). Ricordo di Vito **Fumagalli** (1938–1997). *In*: Ideologie e pratiche del reimpiego nell'alto Medioevo [Cf. n° 3458], p. 1-24.

726. CHRISTOFFERSON (Michael Scott). An antitotalitarian history of the French Revolution: François **Furet**'s Penser la Révolution française in the intellectual politics of the late 1970s. *French hist. stud.*, 99, 22, 4, p. 557-611. – HASSNER (Pierre). François **Furet** et les passions du XXᵉ siècle. *Débat*, 99, 107, 137-150. – OZOUF (Mona). François **Furet** journaliste. *Débat*, 99, 103, p. 3-27.

727. GERBI (Sandro). "Don Ferrante" e il nuovo mondo. [Su Antonello **Gerbi**]. *Nuova antologia*, 99, 134, 583, 2212, p. 200-210.

728. MANNARINO (Lia). Le mille favole degli antichi. Ebraismo e cultura europea nel pensiero religioso di Pietro **Giannone**. Firenze, Le Lettere. 99, 252 p.

729. POCOCK (J. G. A.). Barbarism and religion. Vol. 1. The Enlightenments of Edward **Gibbon**, 1737–1764. Vol. 2. Narratives of civil government. Cam-

bridge, Cambridge U. P., 99, 2 vol., XV-339 p., XIV-422 p.

730. GORSKAJA (Natal'ja A.). Boris Dmitrievich **Grekov**. With an app. containing the correspondence of Boris D. Grekov, 1905–1940. RAN, In-t rossijskoj istorii. Moskva, [s. n.], 99, 271 p, (bibl., ind.).

731. RAGGIO (O.). La storia come pratica. Omaggio a Edoardo **Grendi** (1932–1999). *Quaderni storici*, 99, 34, 100, p. 1-10.

732. VIVARELLI (Roberto). Elie **Halévy** e la Grande Guerra. *Rivista storica italiana*, 99, 111, 3, p. 756-772.

733. HERHOLT (Volker). Ludo Moritz **Hartmann**. Alte Geschichte zwischen Darwin, Marx und Mommsen. Berlin, Weißensee, 99, 187 p.

734. WHITELEY (Linda). Francis **Haskell**: a bibliography. *Saggi e memorie di storie dell'arte*, 99, 23, p. 223-274.

735. Opera (L') di Arnold H. **Heeren**. *Rivista storica italiana*, 99, 111, 3, p. 773-830. [Contiene: GABBA (Emilio). A. H. L. **Heeren**, politica e commercio: qualche riflessione (p. 773-782). – BONDÌ (Sandro Filippo). Il commercio fenicio nell'opera di Arnold H. L. **Heeren** (p. 783-797). – DE ROMANIS (Federico). Il 'südlicher Völkerverkehr' e la proprietà della terra nell' India antica nelle "Ideen" di A. H. L. **Heeren** (p. 798-808). – MARCONE (Arnaldo). La polemica di Niebuhr verso **Heeren** (p. 809-830)].

736. PETERS (E.), SIMONS (W. P.). The new **Huizinga** and the old Middle ages. *Speculum*, 99, 74, p. 587-620.

737. OSTERHAMMEL (Jürgen). Alexander von **Humboldt**: Historiker der Gesellschaft, Historiker der Natur. *Archiv für Kulturgeschichte*, 99, 81, 1, p. 105-132.

738. KASPI (André). Jules **Isaac** et les malheurs du siècle. *Coll. Hist.*, 99, 6, p. 68-71. – MOINE (Philippe). Les archives Jules Isaac. *Archives juives*, 99, 32, 1, p. 117-123.

739. CORCELLA (Aldo). Rec. di **JACOBY** (F.). Die Fragmente der griechischen Historiker continued. *Quaderni di storia*, 99, 50, p. 175-192.

740. DUCLERT (Vincent). Un engagement démocratique: **Jaurès** et la troisième affaire Dreyfus (1900–1906). *In*: Avenirs et avant-gardes en France, XIXᵉ-XXᵉ siècles. Hommage à Madeleine Rebérioux [Cf. n° 3930], p. 307-323.

741. CAZANAVE (C.). **Joinville** et La vie de saint Louis. Un historien et une œuvre multiformes. *Moyen Age*, 99, 105, 1, p. 129-136.

742. CURTA (Fl.). Hiding behind a piece of tapestry: **Jordanes** and the Slavic Venethi. *Jahrbücher für Geschichte Osteuropas*, 99, 47, p. 321-340.

743. LAMOUR (Denis). L'«autobiographie» de Flavius **Josèphe** ou le roman d'une vie. *Revue belge de philologie et d'histoire*, 99, 77, 1, p. 105-130.

744. SZCZUCHI (Lech). Stanislaw **Kot** (1885–1975). *Rivista storica italiana*, 99, 111, 1, p. 124-145.

745. Rudolf **Kötzschke** und das Seminar für Landesgeschichte und Siedlungskunde an der Universität Leipzig. Hrsg. v. Wieland HELD und Uwe SCHIRMER. Beucha, Sax-Verl. 99, 213 p. (Schriften der Rudolf-Kötzschke-Gesellschaft).

746. HINDRICHS (G.). «Empirische Historik». Traditionalität und Innovation im Geschichtskonzept Karl **Lamprechts**. *Archiv für Kulturgeschichte*, 99, 81, p. 371-395.

747. Primo **Levi** testimone e scrittore di storia. Atti del Convegno in ricordo di Primo Levi. A cura di Paolo MOMIGLIANO LEVI e Rosanna GORRIS. Firenze, Giuntina, 99, 232 p.

748. ZIMPEL (Detlef). Zur Bedeutung des Essens in der «Relatio de legatione Constantinopolitana» des **Liutprand von Cremona**. *Historische Zeitschrift*, 99, 269, 1, p. 1-18.

749. CABRINI (Anna Maria). Machiavelli e **Livio**. *Acme*, 99, 52, 3, p. 173-191. – FORSYTHE (GARY). **Livy** and early Rome. A study in historical method and judgement. Stuttgart, Steiner, 99, 147 p. – OAKLEY (S. P.). A commentary on **Livy**, Books VI-X. Oxford, Oxford U. P., 99, XXI-799 p.

750. LAPLANCHE (François). De **Loisy** à Guignebert. *In*: Renan (De) à Marrou [Cf. n° 643], 99, p. 57-72.

751. LOMBARDI (M.). Convenzioni storiografiche, moduli retorici greco-ellenistici e tradizione giudaico-cristiana nel prologo del vangelo di **Luca**. *Orpheus*, 99, 19-20, p. 326-362.

752. MOULINET (Daniel). L'art religieux du XIIIᵉ siècle en France [d'E. **Mâle**]: genèse d'un grand livre. *R. Inst. Cath. Paris,* 99, 70, p. 187-208.

753. MAZZONIS (Filippo). Thomas **Mann** e la Spagna. *Passato e presente*, 99, 17, 46, p. 207-211.

754. **MICHELET** (Jules). Correspondance générale. T. 9. 1859–1861. T. 10. 1862–1865. Textes réunis, classés et annotés par Louis LE GUILLOU. Paris, H. Champion, 99, 2 vol., 927 p., 912 p. – MITZMAN (Arthur). **Michelet** ou la subversion du passé. Quatre leçons au Collège de France. Préface de Michelle PERROT. Paris, La boutique de l'histoire éditions, 99, 214 p.

755. KELLEY (Donald R.). Writing cultural history in early modern France: Christoph **Milieu** and his project. *Renaissance quarterly*, 99, 52, p. 342-65.

756. FERRERI (Luigi). Introduzione alle lettere di Arnaldo **Momigliano** a Raffaello Morghen (1936–1971). *Storiografia*, 99, 3, p. 33-46. – GABBA (Emilio). Arnaldo **Momigliano**: pace e libertà nel mondo antico. *Rivista storica italiana*, 99, 111, 1, p. 146-154. – MOMIGLIANO (Arnaldo). Lettere a Raffaello Morghen (1936–1971). A cura di L. FERRERI. *Storiografia* (Bollettino), 99, 3, p. 47-59. – SASSO (Gennaro). Postilla semiautobiografica su lontane vicende. *Cultura*, 99, 37,

2. HISTORY OF HISTORIOGRAPHY

p. 295-312. [Arnaldo **Momigliano** e Federico Chabod]. – SASSO (Gennaro). Postilla alla "Postilla autobiografica". *Cultura*, 99, 37, p. 481-489.

757. BEHNE (Frank). Heinrich Siber und das Römische Staatsrecht von Theodor **Mommsen**: ein Beitrag zur Rezeptionsgeschichte Mommsens im 20. Jahrhundert. Hildesheim, Olms-Weidmann, 99, VIII-278 p. – REBENICH (Stefan). "Mommsen ist er niemals näher getreten". Theodor **Mommsen** und Hermann Diels. *In*: Hermann Diels (1848–1922) et la science de l'antiquité = Entretiens sur l'antiquité classique. 45. Genève, 99, p. 85-142.

758. MANCA (Sergio). La nazione organizzata. Istituzioni, gruppi sociali e Stato moderno nella storiografia di Roland **Mousnier**. *Rivista storica italiana*, 99, 111, 3, p. 847-931.

759. TAGLIAFERRI (Teodoro). Dai partiti ai tipi: sir Lewis **Namier** e la morfologia della "nazione politica" inglese del Settecento. *Archivio di storia della cultura*, 99, 12, p. 155-166.

760. BIANCHI (Lorenzo). Politique, histoire et recommencement des lettres dans l'Addition à l'histoire de Louis XI de Gabriel **Naudé**. *Corpus*, 99, 35, p. 89-115. – Gabriel **Naudé**: la politique et les mythes de l'histoire de France. Sous la dir. de Robert DAMIEN et Yves-Charles ZARKA. *Corpus*, 99, 35, 1.168 p.

761. Situating the History of Science: dialogues with Joseph **Needham**. Ed. by S. Irfan HABIB and Dhruv RAINA. New York, Oxford U. P., 99, X-358 p.

762. MÉGIER (Elisabeth). Cotidie operatur. Christus und die Geschichte in der Historia ecclesiastica des **Ordericus Vital**. *R. Mabillon*, 99, 71, 10, p. 169-204.

763. RICHÉ (P.). Frédéric **Ozanam**, historien du haut moyen âge. *RHEF*, 99, 85, p. 89-97.

764. BÄHLER (Ursula). Gaston **Paris** dreyfusard. Le savant dans la cité. Paris, CNRS Ed., 99, 232 p.

765. LYON (Bryce). Guillaume Des Marez and Henri **Pirenne**: a remarkable rapport. *Revue belge de philologie et d'histoire*, 99, 77, 4, p. 1051-1078. – MASTRUZZO (Antonino). Tra erudizione e storia sociale. Henri **Pirenne** e la paleografia. *Scrittura e civiltà*, 99, 23, p. 379-394.

766. GOERLITZ (Uta). Humanismus und Geschichtsschreibung am Mittelrhein. Das "Chronicon urbis et ecclesia Maguntinensis" des Hermannus **Piscator** OSB. Tübingen, Niemeyer, 99, XVI-525 p. (Frühe Neuzeit, 47).

767. FOULON (E.). **Polybe** et les Celtes. *Les études classiques*, 99, 68, p. 319-354.

768. VOROB'EVA (Irina G.). Professor-slavist Nil Aleksandravich **Popov**: Nauchnaja, pedagogicheskaja i obshchestvennaja dejatel'nost'. (Nil A. Popov: professor of Slavonic: his pedagogic and public activity). Tver', [s. n.], 99, 192 p. (bibl.).

769. ESIPOV (Valerij V.). Provintsial'nye spory v konste XX veka. (Disputes in Province in the Late 19th Century: [I.G. **Pryzhov**]). Vologda, Grifon, 99, 328 p. (ill., portr., bibl.).

770. BERNARD-GRIFFITHS (Simone). Le mythe romantique de Merlin dans l'oeuvre d'Edgar **Quinet**. Paris, Champion, 99, 688 p.

771. TURI (Gabriele). Politica culturale e storiografia in Ernesto **Ragionieri**. *Storia e problemi contemporanei*, 99, 12, 23, p. 169-200.

772. WERDING (Vera). Die Französische Revolution im politisch-historischen Denkes **Ranke**s und Droysens. Marburg, Tectum, 99, 2 Mikrof. u. 133 p. (Edition Wissenschaft. Reihe Geschichte, 42).

773. DUCLERT (Vincent), CANDAR (Gilles). Madeleine **Rebérioux**. Bibliographie générale (1945–1999 ...). *In*: Avenirs et avant-gardes en France, XIXe-XXe siècles. Hommage à Madeleine Rebérioux [Cf. n° 3930], p. 395-432. – VIDAL-NAQUET (Pierre). Notes pour un portrait de la citoyenne. *In*: Avenirs et avant-gardes en France, XIXe-XXe siècles. Hommage à Madeleine Rebérioux [Cf. n° 3930], p. 17-21.

774. JOUET (Valérie). Et un temps pour parler ... La communication orale sous le règne de Charles VI: le témoignage de la chronique du **Religieux de Saint-Denis**. Paris, [s. n.], 99, [s. p.]. [Thèse (Doctorat Histoire), Paris, Université Paris I, 1999].

775. CORNELIßEN (Christoph). Herausgeber in schwierigen Zeiten. Gerhard **Ritter**s Beziehungen zum "Archiv für Reformationsgeschichte" und zur "Historischen Zeitschrift" (1930–1950). *In*: Historische Zeitschriften im internationalen Vergleich [Cf. n° 580], p. 161-199.

776. GALASSO (Giuseppe). Rosario **Romeo** (1924–1987). *Journal of modern Italian studies*, 99, 4, 2, p. 256-272.

777. WIRSCHING (Andreas). Politik und Zeitgeschichte. Arthur **Rosenberg** und die Berliner Philosophische Fakultät 1914–1933. *Historische Zeitschrift*, 99, 269, 3, p. 561-602.

778. MARCONE (Arnaldo). Un inedito di M. **Rostovtzeff** sulle cause della caduta dell'impero romano. *Historia*, 99, 48, p. 254-256. – **Rostovtzeff** e l'Italia. A cura di A. MARCONE. Gubbio, Casa di Sant'Ubaldo, 25–17 maggio 1995. Napoli, Edizioni scientifiche italiane, 99, 470 p. (Pubblicazioni dell'Università degli studi di Perugia. Incontri perugini di storia della storiografia antica e sul mondo antico, 9).

779. ULIANICH (Boris). Christoph von Dohna, Christian von Anhalt e la «Istoria del Concilio Tridentino» di Paolo **Sarpi**. Paderborn, F. Schöningh, 99, p. 367-426.

780. KVÆRNDRUP (Sigurd). Tolv principper hos **Saxo**: en tolkning af Danernes bedrifter. (Douze principes chez Saxo Grammaticus: une interprétation de la

Geste des Danois). København, Multivers, 99, 358 p. (diagr.).

781. MARIANO (Marco). Lo storico nel suo labirinto: Arthur M. **Schlesinger** Jr. tra ricerca storica, impegno civile e politica. Milano, Franco Angeli, 99, 270 p.

782. PLUMPE (Werner). Gustav von **Schmoller** und der Institutionalismus: Zur Bedeutung der Historischen Schule der Nationalökonomie für die moderne Wirtschaftsgeschichtsschreibung. *Geschichte und Gesellschaft*, 99, 25, 2, p. 252-275.

783. HAMACHER (Elisabeth). Gershom **Scholem** und die allgemeine Religionsgeschichte. Berlin u. New York, de Gruyter, 99, X-358 p.

784. LORETO (Luigi). Guerra e libertà nella repubblica romana. John R. **Seeley** e le radici intellettuali della Roman Revolution di Ronald Syme. Roma, 'L'Erma' di Bretschneider, 99, XVII-169 p.

785. ALBANESE (Francesco). Emilio **Sereni**: l'ultimo degli enciclopedisti. Fonti per la storia dei protagonisti dell'Italia del Novecento. Il fondo "Emilio Sereni". *Annali dell'Istituto Alcide Cervi*, 99, 19, p. 197-245. – MORENO (Diego), RAGGIO (Osvaldo). Dalla storia del paesaggio agrario alla storia rurale. L'irrinunciabile eredità scientifica di Emilio **Sereni**. *Quaderni storici*, 99, 34, p. 89-104.

786. BOUREAU (Alain). Richard **Southern**: a landscape for a portrait. *Past and present*, 99, 165, p. 218-229.

787. ELLIOTT (J. H.). Lawrence **Stone**. *Past and present*, 99, 164, p. 3-5.

788. RÖMER (F.). Kontrastfiguren in den Annalen von **Tacitus**. *Acta Antiqua Hungarica*, 99, 39, p. 297-312.

789. SEYS (Pascale). Hippolyte **Taine** et l'avénement du naturalisme. Un intellectuel sous le Second Empire. Paris, L'Harmattan, 99, XXVI-228 p.

790. AMANN (P.). **Theopomp** und die Etrusker, *Tyche*, 99, 14, p. 3-14.

791. KENNY (Michael). Edward Palmer **Thompson**. *Political quarterly*, 99, 70, 3, p. 319-328. – RÉE (Jonathan). E. P. **Thompson** and the drama of authority. *History workshop journal*, 99, 47, p. 211-221.

792. CANFORA (Luciano). Il mistero **Tucidide**. Milano, Adelphi, 99, 138 p. – LUZZATTO (Maria Jagoda). Tzetzes lettore di **Tucidide**: note autografe sul codice Heidelberg Palatino greco 252. Bari, Dedalo, 99, 183 p. (Paradosis, 1). – NICOLAI (Roberto). Storiografia e storia: a proposito di un nuovo commento a **Tucidide**. *Rivista di filologia ed istruzione classica*, 99, 127, p. 239-251. – PAPATHOMAS (A.). **Thukydides** 6, 11, 7 – 12, 1. Identifizierung eines übersehenen Fragments (Berliner Klassikertexte IX, 121). *Rheinisches Museum*, 99, 142, p. 149-152. – POLI (S.). Le congetture di H. Estienne e di K.A. Duker al testo tucidideo. *Sileno*, 1999, 25, p. 165-196. – PORCIANI (Leone). Come si scrivono i discorsi. Su **Tucidide** I 22.1 an málist'eipeín. *Quaderni di storia*, 99, 49, p. 103-136.

793. BELL (Daniel). Alexis de **Tocqueville**: at the crossroads of history. *Tocqueville R.*, 99, 20, 2, p. 177-190.

794. REZAR (Vlado). Dubrovački humanistički historiograf Ludovik Crijević **Tuberon**. (Ludovik Crijević Tubero: humanist and historiographer from Dubrovnik). *Anali zavoda za povijesne znanosti*, 99, 37, p. 47-94.

795. Lettere 1943–1979. Leo Valiani, Franco **Venturi**. A cura di Edoardo TORTAROLO; introduzione di Giorgio VACCARINO. Firenze, La nuova Italia, 99, XXXIX-380 p. (Biblioteca di storia, 76. Dall'azionismo agli azionisti, 4).

796. SCALVINI (Barbara). Notizie intorno alla "Storia d'Italia" di Alessandro **Verri**. *Rivista storica italiana*, 99, 111, 1, p. 65-96.

797. DUCLERT (Vincent). Un devoir d'histoire: le vies de Pierre **Vidal Naquet**. *Critique*, 99, 55, 624, p. 433-444.

798. PERRODOT (Mathieu). Tribus, empires, nations: initiation au vocabulaire de l'analyse historique de Pierre **Vilar**. *Cahiers pour analyse concrète*, 99, 41-42, p. 9-20.

799. BRAGA (G.), PAGANI (I.). Bibliografia degli scritti di Gustavo **Vinay** (1912–1993). *Studi medievali*, 99, 40, 1, p. 395-440.

800. **VOLTAIRE** (François-Marie Arouet, dit). Histoire de l'empire de Russie sous Pierre le Grand. Ed. critique par Michel MERVAUD [et al.]. Oxford, Voltaire Foundation, 99, 2 vol., XXXII-1338 p.

801. **VOVELLE** (Michel). La mia strada alla storia (colloquio con Paolo BIANCHINI). *Studi storici*, 99, 40, 3, p. 657-680.

802. Max **Weber** Gesamtausgabe. Im Auftrag der Kommission für Sozial- und Wirtschaftsgeschichte der Bayerischen Akademie der Wissenschaften hrsg. v. Horst BAIER [et al.]. Abt. 1. Schriften und Reden. Band 8. Wirtschaft, Staat und Sozialpolitik. Schriften und Reden 1900–1912. Hrsg. v. Wolfgang SCHLUCHTER in Zusammenarbeit mit Peter KURTH und Birgitt MORGENBROD. Band 22. Wirtschaft und Gesellschaft. Die Wirtschaft und die gesellschaftlichen Ordnungen und Mächte. Nachlaß. Teilbande 5. Die Stadt. Hrsg. v. Wilfried NIPPEL. Tübingen, Mohr, 99, 2 vol., XVI-545 p., XXVI-389 p. – Studienausgabe der Max **Weber** Gesamtausgabe. Band I/8. Wirtschaft, Staat und Sozialpolitik. Schriften und Reden 1900–1912. Hrsg. v. Wolfgang SCHLUCHTER in Zusammenarbeit mit Peter KURTH und Birgitt MORGENBROD. Tübingen, Mohr, 99, VI-224 p. – TENBRUCK (Friedrich). Das Werk Max **Weber**s. Gesammelte Aufsätze zu Max Weber. Hrsg. v. Harald HOMANN. Tübingen, Mohr Siebeck, 99, XXIV-267 p.

803. MÖLLENDORFF (Peter von), HUSS (Bernhard). 'Und es wird gehen!' Der Briefwechsel zwischen Ulrich von **Wilamowitz-Moellendorff** und August Frickenhaus. *Quaderni di storia*, 99, 49, p. 199-236.

b. *Special studies. Addenda 1996–1998*

804. MIGLIO (Massimo). Petrarca. Una fonte della «Roma instaurata» di **Biondo Flavio**. *In*: Roma, magistra mundi (2). Itineraria culturae medievalis. Mélanges offerts au Père L. E. Boyle à l'occasion de son 75ᵉ anniversaire. Ed. par Jacqueline HAMESSE. Louvain-la-Neuve, F.I.D.E.M., Collège Mercier, 98, p. 615-625.

805. MENDEL (Maurice). Historia romana. Cahiers de collège de la main de **Montesquieu**. Louvain et Paris, Ed. Peeters, 96, XVI-262 p.

806. ANDRIVET (Patrick). **Saint-Evrémond** et l'histoire romaine. Orléans, paradigme, 98, 345 p.

Cf. n°s 1908, 1909, 1968, 2119, 2349, 2350, 2379, 2459, 2588, 2808, 3216

§ 3. **Methodology, philosophy, and teaching of history.**

807. ANKERSMIT (Frank R.). Trauma und Leiden. Eine vergessene Quelle des westlichen historischen Bewusstsein. *In*: Westliches Geschichtsdenken [Cf. n° 879], p. 127-145.

808. ASSMANN (Jan). Zeitkonstruktion und Gedächtnis als Basisfunktionen historischer Sinnbildung. Eine Reaktion auf Peter Burkes Thesen. *In*: Westliches Geschichtsdenken [Cf. n°s 819, 879], p. 81-98.

809. BASTYN (Vladimir). The Secretary General's new initiative: the reform of history teaching and the preparation of new history textbooks in the Russian Federation. Strasbourg, Council of Europe, 99, 52 p.

810. BAXMANN (Dorothee). Wissen, Kunst und Gesellschaft in der Theorie Condorcets. Stuttgart, Klett-Cotta, 99, 412 p. (Sprache und Geschichte, 25).

811. BERRY (Stephan). On the problem of laws in nature and history: a comparison. *In*: Return (The) of science: evolutionary ideas and history [Cf. n° 863], p. 121-137.

812. Beyond the cultural turn. Ed. By Lynn HUNT and Victoria BONNEL. Berkeley, University of California Press, 99, XI-350 p.

813. Biografia (La): un genere letterario in trasformazione. A cura di Cristina CASSINA e Francesco TRANIELLO. *Contemporanea*, 99, 2, 2, p. 287-306.

814. BISK (Izrail' Ja.). Razmyshlenija o prepodavanii istorii. (Reflections on teaching history). Tambov, Tsentr-Press, 99, 160 p. (ind.).

815. BODEI (Remo). La filosofia e la sua storia. Un modello in crisi. *Contemporanea*, 99, 2, 1, p. 3-14.

816. BOJTSOV (Mikhail A.). Vpered k Gerodotu. (Forward to Herodotus!) *In*: Istorik v poiske [Cf. n° 840],

p. 144-165. – GUREVICH (Aron J.). Ne «Vpered k Gerodotu!», a nazad – k anekdotam. (Not «Forward to Herodotus!» but back to funny stories). *In*: Istorik v poiske [Cf. n° 840], p. 234-239. – BOJTSOV (Mikhail A.). Vpered k Gerodotu. (Forward to Herodotus!) With a discussion, provoked by this article. *In*: Kasus [Cf. n° 844], p. 17-75.

817. BROWN (Donald E.). Human nature and history. *In*: Return (The) of science: evolutionary ideas and history [Cf. n° 863], p. 138-157.

818. BULHOF (Johannes). What if? Modality and history. *History and theory*, 99, 38, 2, p. 145-168.

819. BURKE (Peter). Erwiderung. *In*: Westliches Geschichtsdenken [Cf. n°s 808, 879], p. 305-317. – IDEM. Westliches historisches: Denken in globaler Perspektive. 10 Thesen. *In*: Westliches Geschichtsdenken [Cf. n°s 808, 879], p. 31-52.

820. CABRERA (M.A.). Linguistic approach or return to subjectivism in search of the alternative to social history. *Social history*, 99, 24, p. 74-89.

821. CARDINI (Franco). Per un'archeologia dell' esotismo e del pregiudizio. Tre casi di costruzione di Idealtypus. *Nuova rivista storica*, 99, 83, 1, p. 55-66.

822. CORBIN (Alain), FARGE (Arlette), PROCHASSON (Christophe), CHARLE (Christophe). Les historiens et la sociologie de Pierre Bourdieu. Suivi d'un débat avec Pierre Bourdieu, édité par Etienne ANHEIM. *Bulletin de la Société hist. moderne*, 99, 3-4, p. 4-27.

823. CROCE (Benedetto). L'obiezione contro le «Storie dei propri tempi». Lezione tenuta all'Istituto Italiano per gli Studi Storici nell'anno accademico 1949–1950. Torino, Centro Studi e Ricerche «Mario Pannunzio», 99, 18 p.

824. CULCLASURE (Scott P.). The past as liberation from history. Frankfurt am Main, Lang, 99, X-170 p. (Counterpoints, 63).

825. DAWSON (Doyne). Evolutionary theory and group selection: the question of warfare. *In*: Return (The) of science: evolutionary ideas and history [Cf. n° 863], p. 79-100.

826. DIAKONOFF (Igor M.). The Paths of History. New York, Cambridge U. P., 99, XI-335 p.

827. Dialog so vremenem: Al'manakh intellektual' noj istorii. (Dialogue with time: intellectual history yearbook). Vol. 1. Eds. Lorina P. REPINA, Viktorija I. UKOLOVA. RAN, In-t vseobshchej istorii. Moskva, [s. n.], 99, 368 p. [Eng. summaries]

828. DOSSE (François). L'histoire ou le temps réfléchi. Paris, Hatier, 99, 79 p.

829. DUMOULIN (Olivier). Crise de la pensée, crise de la communauté: deux crises de l'histoire au XXᵉ siècle à l'épreuve de l'histoire des sciences. *Les crises de la pensée scientifique et leur résolution historique (XVIIIᵉ–XXᵉ siècles). Raison présente*, 99, 131, p. 61-76.

830. FRACCHIA (Joseph), LEWONTIN (Richard C.). Does culture evolve? *In*: Return (The) of science: evolutionary ideas and history [Cf. n° 863], p. 52-78.

831. GALLERANO (Nicola). Le verità della storia. Scritti sull'uso pubblico del passato. Introduzione di Tommaso DETTI e Marcello FLORES. Roma, Manifesto libri, 99, 306 p.

832. GAUCHET (Marcel). L'élargissement de l'objet historique. *Le débat*, 99, 103, p. 131-147.

833. GEARY (Patrick J.). Geschichte als Erinnerung? *In*: Kontinuität und Wandel. Geschichtsbilder in verschiedenen Fächern und Kulturen. Hrsg. v. Evelyn SCHULZ und Wolfgang SONNE. Zürich, vfd Hochschulverlag AG der ETH Zürich, 99, p. 115-142.

834. Geschichtsdiskurs. Band 5. Globale Konflikte, Erinnerungsarbeit und Neueorientierungen seit 1945. Hrsg. v. Wolfgang KÜTTLER, Jörn RÜSEN und Ernst SCHULIN. Frankfurt am Main, Fischer, 99, 407 p.

835. GIL (Thomas). Kritik der klassischen Geschichtsphilosophie. Baden-Baden, Nomos, 99, 230 p.

836. GINZBURG (Carlo). Distancia y perspectiva. Dos metáforas. *Entrepasados*, 99, 8, 16, p. 99-124. – IDEM. History, rhetoric and proof. Hanover a. London, University Press of New England, 99, XV-120 p. (Menahem Stern Jerusalem lectures).

837. HARTOG (François). Für eine Archäologie des historischen Denkens. *In*: Westliches Geschichtsdenken [Cf. n° 879], p. 117-126.

838. HERY (Evelyne). Un siècle de leçons d'histoire: l'histoire enseignée en lycée de 1870 à 1970. Berlin, E. Schmidt, 99, 432 p. (ill., bibl.). (Collection "Histoire" – Rennes, France).

839. Introduzione alla storia orale. Storia, conservazione delle fonti e problemi di metodo. A cura di Cesare BERMANI. Roma, Odradek, 99, 209 p.

840. Istorik v poiske: mikro- i makropodkhody k izucheniju proshlogo: dokl. i vystupl. na konf., 5–6 oktjabrja 1998. (The historian in search: micro- and macro-approaches to studying the past: papers read at the Institute of general history conference, October 5–6, 1998). RAN, In-t vseobshchej istorii. Moskva, IVI RAN, 99, 308 p. (bibl.). [Table of contents in English; App. in French.] [Cf. nos <choice> 500, 587, 644, 816.]

841. JANEKOVIĆ-ROEMER (Zdenka). Povijesna spoznaja i metodologija povijesti u postmoderni. (The cognition of history and methodology in post-modern historiography). *Radovi zavoda za hrvatsku povijest*, 99, 32-33, p. 203-222.

842. JENKINS (Keith). Why History? Ethics and Postmodernity. London a. New York, Routledge, 99, X-232 p.

843. JORDAN (Stefan). Geschichtstheorie in der ersten Hälfte des 19. Jahrhunderts: die Schwellenzeit zwischen Pragmatismus und klassischem Historismus. Frankfurt a. New York, Campus, 99, 264 p. (Campus Forschung).

844. Kasus: Individual'noe i unikal'noe v istorii. (Casus: the individual and unique in history: [Articles]). Vol. 2 (1999). Eds. Jurij L. BESSMERTNYJ, Mikhail A. BOJTSOV. Moskva, Izd. Ros. gos. gumanit. un-ta, 99, 370 p. (bibl.). [Eng. summaries] [Cf. nos <choice> 816, 862.]

845. KITTSTEINER (Heinz D.). Kants Theorie des Geschichtszeichens. Vorläufer und Nachfahren. *In*: Geschichtszeichen. Hrsg. v. Heinz D. KITTSTEINER. Köln, Weimar u. Wien, Böhlau, 99, p. 81-115.

846. KOOY (Michael John). Romanticism and Coleridge's idea of history. *Journal of the history of ideas*, 99, 60, 4, p. 717-736.

847. KRUSE (Volker). "Geschichts- und Sozialphilosophie" oder "Wirklichkeitswissenschaft?" Die deutsche historische Soziologie und die logischen Kategorien René Königs und Max Webers. Frankfurt am Main, Suhrkamp, 99, 309 p.

848. LEPETIT (Bernard). Carnets de croquis. Sur la connaissance historique. Paris, Albin Michel, 99, 316 p.

849. MAC PHAIL (Eric). Diderot and the plot of history. *New literary history*, 99, 30, 2, p. 439-452.

850. MALI (Joseph). The reconciliation of myth: Benjamin's homage to Bachofen. *Journal of the history of ideas*, 99, 60, 1, p. 165-188.

851. MILLER (Louis). Foucault, Nietzsche, Enlightenment: some historical considerations. *Historical reflections,* 99, 25, 2, p.341-364.

852. MORLEY (Neville). Writing ancient history. London, Duckworth, 99, 175 p.

853. NEUMANN (Florian). Ars historica. Famiano Strada S.I. (1572–1649) und die Diskussion um die rhetorische Konzeption der Geschichtsschreibung in Italien. München, Diss., 99, VIII-371 p.

854. O'DALY (Gerard James Patrick). Augustine's City of God: a reader's guide. Oxford, Clarendon Press, 99, XII-323 p.

855. Odissej: Chelovek v istorii. (Odisseus: Man in History: [Articles]). 1999: Trapeza. (Meal). Ed. Aron Ja. GUREVICH. RAN, In-t vseobshchej istorii. Moskva, Nauka, 99, 340 p. (ill., bibl.). [Eng. summaries].

856. ÖZTÜRK (Mustafa). Tarih felsefesi. (La Philosophie de l'histoire). Elazığ, [s. n.], 99, 155 p.

857. PALTI (Elias). The «Metaphor of Life»: Herder's philosophy of history and uneven developments in late eighteenth-century natural sciences. *History and theory*, 99, 38, 3, p. 322-347.

858. PEÑA (Alonso). On the role of mathematical biology in contemporary historiography. *In*: Return (The) of science: evolutionary ideas and history [Cf. n° 863], p. 101-120.

859. PIHLAINEN (Kalle). Resisting history. On the ethics of narrative representation. Turku, Turku University, Cultural History, 99, 215 p.

860. POMIAN (Krzysztof). L'irréductible pluralité de l'histoire. *Débat*, 99, 104, p. 171-178.

861. RAULFF (Ulrich). Der unsichtbare Augenblick. Zeitkonzepte in der Geschichte. Göttingen, Wallstein, 99, 143 p. (Göttinger Gespräche zur Geschichtswissenschaft, 9).

862. REPINA (Lorina P.). «Personal'naja istorija»: biografija kak sredstvo istoricheskogo poznanija. ('Personal history': biography as a means of historical learning). *In*: Kasus [Cf. n° 844], p. 76-100.

863. Return (The) of science: evolutionary ideas and history. Ed. by D. Gary SHAW and Philip POMPER. *History and theory*, 99, 38, 4, p. 1-157. [Cf. n[os] <choice> 811, 817, 825, 830, 858, 867, 869, 6121.]

864. RICUPERATI (Giuseppe). Universalismo e uso pubblico della storia. *Rivista storica italiana*, 99, 111, 3, p. 685-704.

865. SADMON (Zeev W.). Die Historikerin Leni Yahil anlässlich des Erscheinens ihres Werkes "Die Shoa. Überlebenskampf und Vernichtung der europäischen Juden" in deutscher Übersetzung. *Geschichte im Westen*, 99, 14, 2, p. 210-220.

866. SENJAVSKAJA (Elena S.). Psikhologija vojny v XX veke: Istorichekij opyt Rossii. (The psychology of the war in the 20th century: historical experience of Russia). RAN, In-t rossijskoj istorii. Moskva, ROSSPEN, 99, 383 p. (ill., plates; bibl., ind.). – EADEM. Psikhologija vojny v XX veke kak istoriko-teoreticheskaja problema. (The psychology of the war in the 20th century as a theoretical problem of history). *In*: Teoreticheskie problemy istoricheskikh issledovanij [Cf. n° 871], p. 75-103. – EADEM. Psikhologija voennogo byta kak istoricheskaja problema. (The psychology of the everyday life in the war as a historical problem). *Voenno-istoricheskij arkhiv*, 99, 8, p. 203-231.

867. SHAW (David Gary). The return of science. *In*: Return (The) of science: evolutionary ideas and history [Cf. n° 863], p. 1-9.

868. Structure and agency in historical causation. *History and theory*, 99, 38, 3, p. 281-306. [Contents: LINDENFELD (David F.). Causality, chaos theory, and the end of the Weimar republic: a commentary on Henry Turner's Hitler's Thirty Days to Power. – TURNER (Henry Ashby, jr.). Human agency and impersonal determinants in historical causation: a response to David Lindenfeld].

869. STUART-FOX (Martin). Evolutionary theory of history. *In*: Return (The) of science: evolutionary ideas and history [Cf. n° 863], p. 33-51.

870. TANG (Yanfang). Language, truth, and literary interpretation: a cross-cultural examination. *Journal of the history of ideas*, 99, 60, 1, p. 1-20.

871. Teoreticheskie problemy istoricheskikh issledovanij. (Theoretical problems of historical research). Part 2: July 1999. Ed. Efim O. PIVOVAR. Moskva, [s. n.], 99, 174 p. (bibl.). (Trudy Istoricheskogo fakul'teta MGU, 8). [Table of contents in Eng.] [Cf. n° <choice> 866.]

872. TESSITORE (Fulvio). Vico, la decadenza e il ricorso. *Archivio di storia della cultura*, 99, 12, p. 3-19.

873. THADEN (Edward C.). The rise of historicism in Russia. New York, Peter Lang, 99, IX-374 p. (American University studies, series 9, 192).

874. THOMSON (Alistair). Making the most of memories: the empirical and subjective value of oral history. *Transactions of the Royal Historical Society*, 99, 6, 9, p. 291-301.

875. TOPOLSKI (Jerzy). The role of logic and aesthetics in constructing narrative wholes in historiography. *History and theory*, 99, 38, 2, p. 198-210.

876. TŘEŠTÍK (Dušan). Mysliti dějiny. (To think history). Praha, Paseka, 99, 222 p.

877. VIND (Ole). Grundtvigs historiefilosofi. (La philosophie de l'histoire de Grundtvig). København, Gyldendal, 99, 645 p. (Skrifter udg. af Grundtvig-Selskabet, 32). (rés. anglais).

878. Virtual history: alternatives and counterfactuals. Ed. by Niall FERGUSON. New York, Basic Books, 99, X-548 p.

879. Westliches Geschichtsdenken: Eine interkulturelle Debatte. Hrsg. v. Jörn RÜSEN. Göttingen, Vandenhoeck & Ruprecht, 99, 322 p. (Sammlung Vandenhoeck). [Cf. n[os] <Auswahl> 807, 808, 819, 837, 880.]

880. WHITE (Hayden). Die Verwestlichung der Weltgeschichte. *In*: Westliches Geschichtsdenken [Cf. n° 879], p. 178-190. – IDEM. Figural realism: studies in the mimesis effect. Baltimore, Johns Hopkins U. P., 99, XII-205 p.

881. ZAGORIN (Perez). History, the referent, and narrative: reflections on postmodernism now. *History and theory*, 99, 38, 1, p. 1-24.

882. ZEMON DAVIS (Natalie). Who owns history? *In*: Historical perspectives on memory [Cf. n° 577], p. 19-34.

883. ZERMEÑO PADILLA (Guillermo). Condición de subalternidad, condición posmoderna y saber histórico. ¿Hacia una nueva forma de escritura de la historia? *Historia y Grafía*, 99, 12, p. 11-48.

Cf. n° 5014

§ 4. Ethnology, folklore and historical anthropology.

* 884. VILLANUEVA (María), SERRANO (Carlos), VERA (José Luis). Cien años de antropología física en México: inventario bibliográfico. México, Instituto de

Investigaciones Antropológicas, Universidad Nacional Autónoma de México, 99, 498 p.

885. AIBABIN (A. I.). Etnicheskaia istoriia rannevizantiiskogo Kryma. (Ethnische Geschichte der frühbyzantinischen Krim). Simferopol', DAR, 99, 350 p.

886. Altsachsen (Die) im Spiegel der nationalen und internationalen Sachsenforschung: neue Forschungsergebnisse. Hrsg. v. Hans-Jürgen HÄSSLER; in Verbindung mit Ulla LUND HANSEN [et al.]. Oldenburg, Isensee, 99, 463 p. (Studien zur Sachsenforschung, 13).

887. BALZER (Marjorie Mandelstam). The tenacity of ethnicity: a Siberian saga in global perspective. Princeton a. Chichester, Princeton U. P., 99, XIV-326 p.

888. BELMONT (Nicole). Poétique du conte. Essai sur le conte de tradition orale. Paris, Gallimard, 99, 250 p.

889. BESTOR (Jane Fair). Marriage transactions in Renaissance Italy and Mauss's essay on the gift. *Past and present*, 99, 164, p. 6-46.

890. BONIFAČIĆ (Vjera). Ethnology, anthropology and cultural history of the Mediterranean: inside and outside perspectives. *Narodna umjetnost: hrvatski časopis za etnologiju i folkloristiku*, 99, 36, 1, p. 269-282.

891. BRONZINI (Giovanni Battista). Croce e le nuove prospettive per le letterature dialettali/popolari. *Lares*, 99, 65, p. 247-257.

892. BULATOVA (Angara G.). Sel'skokhozjajstvennyj kalendar' i kalendarnye obychai i obrjady narodov Dagestana. (Agricultural calendar and calendar rituals and traditions of the peoples of Dagestan, [Russia]). RAN, Dagestan. nauch, tsentr., In-t istorii, arkheologii i etnografii. Sankt-Peterburg, Peterburgskoe vosokovedenie, 99, 286 p. (ill., bibl.).

893. CENTLIVRES (Pierre), CENTLIVRES-DEMONT (Micheline). État, Islam et tribus face aux organisations internationales. Le cas de l'Afghanistan, 1978-1998. *Annales*, 99, 54, 4, p. 945-966.

894. Colonial subjects: essays on the practical history of anthropology. Ed. by Peter PELS and Oscar SALEMINK. Ann Arbor, University of Michigan Press, 99, VIII, 364 p.

895. COPPENS (Yves). Le genou de Lucy: l'histoire de l'homme et l'histoire de son histoire. Paris, O. Jacob, 99, 250 p.

896. Etiket u narodov Jugo-Vostochnoj Azii. (The Etiquette of the peoples of South-East Asia: [Articles]). Eds. Evgenija V. IVANOVA, Mikhail RESHETOV. RAN, Muzej antropologii i etnografii im. Petra Velikogo (Kunstkamera). Sankt-Peterburg, Peterburgskoe vostokovedenie, 99, 189 p. (bibl.).

897. Etničnost i povijest. (Ethnicity and history). Ed. by Emil HERŠAK. Zagreb, Institut za migracije i narodnosti, Naklada Jesenski i Turk, Hrvatsko sociološko društvo, 99, 213 p.

898. Europäischer Völkerspiegel: imagologisch-ethnographische Studien zu den Völkertafeln des frühen 18. Jahrhunderts. Hrsg. v. Franz K. STANZEL; unter Mitwirkung von Ingomar WEILER und Waldemar ZACHARASIEWICZ. Heidelberg, Universitätsverlag C. Winter, 99, 324 p.

899. FINZSCH (Norbert). Blood, ethnicity and comparative history. *In*: German and American nationalism [Cf. n° 3954], p. 453-473.

900. Frontiers and borderlands. Anthropological perspectives. Ed. by Michael RÖSLER and Tobias WENDL. Frankfurt am Main, Lang, 99, XII-239 p.

901. GRUAU (Maurice). L'homme rituel: anthropologie du rituel catholique français: essai d'une ethnologie de l'intérieur. Paris, Métailié, 99, 239 p. (Collection Traversées).

902. GUHA (Sumit). Environment and ethnicity in India, 1200-1991. Cambridge, Cambridge U. P., 99, XV-217 p. (Cambridge studies in Indian history and society, 4).

903. HAYDEN (Robert M.). Disputes and arguments amongst nomads: a caste council in India. Oxford, Oxford U. P., 99, XIV-177 p.

904. HENGARTNER (Thomas). Forschungsfeld Stadt: zur Geschichte der volkskundlichen Erforschung städtischer Lebensformen. Berlin, Reimer, 99, 373 p. (Lebensformen, 11).

905. HERMANN (Pálsson). Oral tradition and saga writing. Wien, Fassbaender, 99, 143 p. (Studia medievalia Septentrionalia, 3).

906. Human growth in the past: studies from bones and teeth. Ed. by Robert D. HOPPA and Charles M. FITZGERALD. Cambridge a. New York, Cambridge U. P., 99, XVIII-315 p. (Cambridge studies in biological and evolutionary anthropology, 25).

907. Ingrians and neighbours. Focus on the eastern Baltic Sea region. Ed. by Markku TEINONEN and Timo J. VIRTANEN. Helsinki, Finnish Literature Society, 99, 241 p. (Studia Fennica. Ethnologica, 5).

908. JAHODA (Gustav). Images of savages: ancient roots of modern prejudice in Western culture. London, Routledge, 99, XX-297 p.

909. KALOEV (Boris A.). Osetinskie istoriko-etnographicheskie etjudy. (Essays on history and ethnology of Ossets). RAN, In-t etnologii i antropologii im. N.N. Miklukho-Maklaja. Moskva, Nauka, 99, 393 p. (bibl.).

910. KARABAŞ (Seyfi). Bütüncül Türk budunbilimine doğru. (Vers l'ethnologie totale turque). İstanbul, Yapı Kredi Yayınları, 99, 551 p.

911. KEREJTOV (Ramazan Kh.). Etnicheskaja istorija nogajtsev: k probleme etnogeneticheskikh svjazej nogajtsev. (An ethnic history of Nogays: the problem

of their ethnogenesis). Karachaevo-Cherkesskij in-t gumanit. issled. Stavropol', Stavropol'serviskniga, 99, 175 p. (ill., maps, bibl.).

912. KURAKEEVA (Marija F.). Verhnekubanskie kazaki: byt, kul'tura, traditsii: XIX–nachalo XX v.: k 80-letiju repressirovannogo kazachestva. (The Cossacks of upper Kuban: their everyday life, culture, traditions, the 19th and the early 20th centuries: for the 80th anniversary of the repressions of Cossacks). Karachaevo-Cherkesskij in-t gumanit. issled., etc. Cherkessk, [s. n.], 99, 277 p. (bibl.).

913. LINKE (Uli). German bodies: race and representation after Hitler. New York a. London, Routledge, 99, XIII-274 p. (ill.).

914. MAXWELL (Anne). Colonial photography and exhibitions: representations of the 'native' and the making of European identities. London, Leicester U. P., 99, XII-243 p.

915. Odeurs et parfums. Congrès national des sociétés historiques et scientifiques, 121e, Nice, 26–31 octobre 1996, Section d'ethnologie et anthropologie françaises. Textes réunis et publiés par Danielle MUSSET et Claudine FABRE-VASSAS. Paris, Éditions du CTHS, 99, 244 p.

916. PASCHT (Arno). Ethnizität: zur Verwendung des Begriffs im wissenschaftlichen und gesellschaftlichen Diskurs: eine Einführung. München, Akademischer Verlag München, 99, 115 p. (Münchener ethnologische Abhandlungen, 21. Edition Anacon).

917. Simpozij Staroiransko podrijetlo Hrvata. (The old Iranian origin of Croats). Zagreb, Kulturni centar pri Veleposlanstvu I. R. Irana, 99, 525 p.

918. Slovensko prebivalstvo Furlanije-Julijske krajine v družbeni in zgodovinski perspektivi. (Slovene population of Friuli-Venezia Giulia; social and historical perspectives). Ur. Pavel STRANJ, Milan BUFON v Aleksej KALC. Trieste, Slovenski raziskovalni inštitut, Narodna in študijska knjižnica v Ljubljana, Znanstveni inštitut Filozofske fakultete Univerze, 99, 366 p.

919. STRAUSS (Rafael A.). Diccionario de cultura popular. Caracas, Fundación Bigott, 99, 2 vol., XXXII-1243 p.

920. TRIGG (Roger). Ideas of human nature: an historical introduction. Oxford, Blackwell Publishers, 99, VIII-216 p.

921. Urbane Welten: Referate der Österreichischen Volkskundetagung 1998 in Linz. Im Auftrag des Vereins für Volkskunde in Wien und des Österreichischen Fachverbands für Volkskunde; herausgegeben von Olaf BOCKHORN, Günter DIMT und Edith HÖRANDNER; redigiert von Andrea EULER. Wien, Selbstverlag des Vereins für Volkskunde Wien, 99, 484 p. (Buchreihe der Österreichischen Zeitschrift für Volkskunde, 16).

922. VELAY VALLANTIN (Catherine). Le Congrès International de folklore de 1937. *Annales*, 99, 54, 2, p. 481-506.

923. VERNIER (Bernard). Le visage et le nom. Contribution à l'étude des systèmes de parenté. Paris, Presses Universitaires de France, 99, 179 p. (Ethnologie).

924. Wissenschaftlicher Rassismus: Analysen einer Kontinuität in den Human- und Naturwissenschaften. Hrsg. v. Heidrun KAUPEN-HAAS und Christian SALLER. Frankfurt am Main, Campus, 99, 451 p.

925. Wörterbuch der Völkerkunde. Begründet von Walter HIRSCHBERG. Berlin, Reimer, 99, 427 p.

926. ZAGREBIN (Aleksej E.). Finny ob udmurtakh: Finskie issledovateli etnografii udmurtov XIX–pervoj poloviny XX v. (Finns studying the Udmurts: Finnish scholars of the ethnology of the Udmurts, the 19th and the 1st half of the 20th century). RAN, Ural'skoe otd., Udmurt. in-t istorii, jazyka i literatury. Izhevsk, [s. n.], 99, 182 p. (ill., bibl.). [German summary]

Cf. n[os] *357, 615, 938, 1199, 1315, 1364, 1470, 3212, 3475, 6967, 7032, 8071*

§ 5. General history.

* 927. American bibliography (The) of Slavic and East European studies for 1994. Compiled and edited by Maria GORECKI NOWAK and Aaron TREHUB; prepared at the University of Illinois at Urbana-Champaign for the American Advancement of Slavic Studies. Armonk a. London, M.E. Sharpe, 99, XXVI, 701 p.

* 928. Antisemitism: an annotated bibliography. Vol. 10-11: 1994-1995. The Vidal Sassoon International Center for the Study of Antisemitism, the Hebrew University of Jerusalem; edited by Susan Sarah COHEN. München, Saur, 99, 2 vol., XLV-1001p.

* 929. Intelligence, espionage and related topics: an annotated bibliography of serial journal and magazine scholarship, 1844–1998. Compiled by James D. CALDER. Westport a. London, Greenwood Press, 99, XXXVI-1330 p. (Bibliographies and indexes in military studies, 11).

930. ACUN (Fatma). Osmanlı'dan Türkiye Cumhuriyetine: Değişme ve Süreklilik. (Changement et continuité de l'Empire Ottoman jusqu'à la République Turque). *Hacettepe Üniversitesi Edebiyat Fakültesi Dergisi*, 99, ekim, p. 155-167.

931. ALFÖLDY (Géza). Das Imperium Romanum: ein Vorbild für das vereinte Europa? Basel, Schwabe, 99, 50 p. (Jacob-Burckhardt-Gespräche auf Castelen, 9).

932. Arad. Monografia orașului de la începuturi până la 1989. (Arad. The monograph of the town since the beginnings until 1989). Coordonatori: Ion VĂRARU, Pascu HUREZAN și Mihai POPOVICI. Prefață de Nicolae EDROIU. Arad, Editura Nigredo, 99, 459 p.

933. ARGATSKI (Velin Asenov). Voenna istoriia na Bulgariia 681–1945. (L'histoire militaire de la Bulgarie 681–1945). Veliko Turnovo, Vital, 99, 230 p.

934. Armată şi societate în spaţiul românesc. Epoca veche şi mileniul migraţiilor. (Army and society in the Romanian area. The ancient age and the millennium of migrations). Coordonator: M. DOGARU, Bucureşti, Editura Globus, 99, 210 p. (Studii de istorie militară I).

935. ARNALDI (Girolamo). Lo Stato della Chiesa nella lunga durata. *Cultura*, 99, 37, p. 197-217.

936. ARNOLD (Guy). Historical dictionary of civil wars in Africa. Lanham, Scarecrow Press, 99, XXI-377 p. (Historical dictionaries of war, revolution, and civil unrest, 12).

937. AUBERT (Alberto), SIMONCELLI (Paolo). Storia moderna: dalla formazione degli stati nazionali alle egemonie internazionali. Bari, Cacucci, 99, 922 p.

938. Avtoportret slavjanina. (The self-portrait of a Slav: the self-consciousness of the Slavs from the Middle Ages till nowadays: Articles). Eds. L. A. SOFRONOVA, T. I. CHEPĘLEVSKAJA. RAN, In-t slavjanovedenija. Moskva, Indrik, 99, 255 p. (bibl.). (Biblioteka In-ta slavjanovedenija RAN, 12).

939. BERNECKER (Walther L.). Spanische Geschichte. Vom 15. Jahrhundert bis zur Gegenwart. München, Beck, 99, 127 p.

940. BERTÉNYI (István). Magyarország rövid története. (The short history of Hungary). Budapest, Talentum, 99, 661 p.

941. BIERBRIER (M.L.). Historical dictionary of Ancient Egypt. Lanham, Scarecrow press, 99, XIX-303 p. (Historical dictionaries of ancient civilizations and historical eras, 1).

942. BOBB (F. Scott). Historical dictionary of Democratic Republic of the Congo (Zaire). Lanham a. London, Scarecrow Press, 99, XXXVIII-598 p. (African historical dictionaries, 76).

943. BURKI (Shahid Javed). Historical dictionary of Pakistan. Lanham a. London, Scarecrow Press, 99, LIII-403 p. (Asian/Oceanian historical dictionaries, 33).

944. Cambridge History (The) of the Native Peoples of the Americas. Vol. 3. South America. Part 1 and 2. Ed. by Frank SALOMON and Stuart B. SCHWARTZ. New York, Cambridge U. P., 99, 2 vol., XIV-1054 p., XIV-976 p.

945. CARDINI (Franco). Europa e Islam: storia di un malinteso. Roma e Bari, Laterza, 99, VIII-347 p.

946. CARMAGNANI (Marcello), HERNÁNDEZ CHÁVEZ (Alicia). Para una historia de América II. Los nudos. México, Fondo de Cultura Económica/El Colegio de México, 99, 2 vol., 463 p., 516 p. (ill.).

947. CASTILLO INFANTE (Fernando), FUENTES (Jordi). Diccionario histórico y biográfico de Chile. [S. l.], Chile Zig-Zag, 99, 573 p. (Colección Historia y geografía).

948. Chichukai sekaishi 3: Nettowaku no naka no Chichukai. (History of the Mediterranean world, 3. The Mediterranean in networks). Ed. by Rekishigaku Kenkyukai. Tokyo, Aoki Shoten, 99, 341 p.

949. CIACHIR (Nicolae). Basarabia voievodală românească până la sfârşitul celui de al II-lea război mondial. (Romanian Voivodal Bessarabia until the end of World War II). Bucureşti, Editura Oscar Print, 99, 152 p.

950. CSENDES (Peter). Historical dictionary of Vienna. Lanham, Scarecrow Press, 99, XXXV-258 p. (Historical dictionaries of cities of the world, 8).

951. CVIRN (Janez), SIMONITI (Vasko), ŠTIH (Peter), FRIŠ (Darko), VIDIC (Marko), BRENK, (Lan). Ilustrirana zgodovina Slovencev. (Illustrated History of Slovenes). Ljubljana, Mladinska knjiga, 99, 526 p. (Knjižnica Enciklopedije Slovenije).

952. DAVIES (Norman). The Isles: a history. New York, Oxford U. P., 99, XLII-1222 p.

953. DEHN-NIELSEN (Henning). Danmarks konger og regenter. Fra Hugleik til Margrethe 2. (Monarques et régents du Danemark. De Hugleik à Marguerite II). Lyngby, Holkenfeldt, 99, 400 p.

954. Dictionnaire de l'histoire de France. Sous la dir. scientifique de Jean-François SIRINELLI; et le conseil éditorial de Daniel COUTY. Paris, A. Colin, 99, 2 vol., XI-1712 p.

955. Dictionnaire du Moyen âge: littérature et philosophie. Paris, Encyclopaedia Universalis, 99, 868 p.

956. Dictionnaire Napoléon. Sous la dir. de Jean TULARD. Paris, Fayard, 99, 2 vol., 977 p., 1000 p.

957. DIRLMEIER (Ulf), GESTRICH (Andreas), HERRMANN (Ulrich), HINRICHS (Ernst), KLEßMANN (Christoph), REULECKE (Jürgen). Deutsche Geschichte. Stuttgart, Reclam, 99, 440 p.

958. Dizionario biografico degli italiani. Vol. 52. Gambacorta–Gelasio. Vol. 53. Gelati–Ghisalberti. Roma, Istituto della Enciclopedia Italiana, 99, 2 vol., XIX-811 p., XIX-815 p.

959. Dizionario della civiltà etrusca. A cura di Mauro CRISTOFARI. Firenze, Giunti, 99, XIII-340 p. (Ill.).

960. DOCHERTY (James C.). Historical dictionary of Australia. Lanham, Scarecrow Press, 99, XLIL-425 p. (Asian/Oceanian historical dictionaries, 32).

961. DUMONT (Georges-Henri). Histoire de la Belgique. Bruxelles, Le cri, 99, 655 p. (ill.). (Histoire).

962. Enciclopedia di Roma: dalle origini all'anno duemila. Milano, F. M. Ricci, 99, 1005 p. (ill.).

963. Encyclopedia (The) of Malaysia. Vol. 4. Early history. Ed. by Nik HASSAN SHUHAIMI NIK ABDUL RAHMAN. Singapore, Archipelago Press, 99, 144 p.

964. Entstehung (Die) der Schweiz. Von Bundesbrief 1291 zur nationalen Geschichtskultur des 20. Jh.. Hrsg. v. Josef WIGET. Schwyz, Historischer Verein d. Kantons Schwyz, 99, 176 p.

5. GENERAL HISTORY

965. FALOLA (Toyin). The history of Nigeria. London a. Westport, Greenwood Press, 99, XVIII-269 p. (Greenwood Histories of the Modern Nations Series).

966. FICHTNER (Paula S.). Historical dictionary of Austria. Lanham, Scarecrow Press, 99, XXVI-301 p. (European historical dictionary series, 36).

967. FINZSCH (Norbert), HORTON (Lois E.), HORTON (James O.). Von Benin nach Baltimore. Geschichte der African Americans. Hamburg, Hamburger Edition, 99, 672 p.

968. FISCHEL (Jack R.). Historical dictionary of the Holocaust. Lanham, Scarecrow Press, 99, XLV-321 p. (Historical dictionaries of war, revolution, and civil unrest, 10).

969. France (La) d'un siècle à l'autre: 1914–2000: dictionnaire critique. Sous la dir. de Jean-Pierre RIOUX et Jean-François SIRINELLI. Paris, Hachette Littératures, 99, 979 p.

970. Frontiers in question: Eurasian borderlands, 700–1700. Ed. by Daniel POWER a. Naomi STANDEN. New York, Macmillan Press a. a. London, St. Martin's Press, 99, XXIV-293 p. (maps). (Themes in focus).

971. GARCÍA DE CORTÁZAR (Fernando), MONTERO (Manuel). Diccionario de historia del País Vasco: A–H [i.e. A–Z]. San Sebastián, Txertoa, 99, 2 vol., [s. p.] (Collección Illargi amandrea).

972. GEISS (Imanuel). Imperien und Nationen. Zur universalistorischen Topographie von Macht und Herrschaft. *Tel Aviver Jb. für deutsche Geschichte*, 99, 28, p. 57-92.

973. GILBERT (Mark F.), NILSSON (K. Robert). Historical dictionary of modern Italy. Lanham, Scarecrow Press, 99, XXXVI-463 p. (European historical dictionaries, 34).

974. GOLDINA (Irina D.). Drevnjaja i srednevekovaja istorija udmurtskogo naroda. (Ancient and Medieval history of the Udmurt people). Izhevsk, Udmurtskij unt, 99, 464 p. (ill., bibl.).

975. GORDILLO Y ORTIZ (Octavio). Diccionario de la revolución en el estado de Chiapas (1910–1920). San Cristóbal de Las Casas, UNAM, 99, 169 p. (Universidad Nacional Autónoma de Mexico. Programa de Investigaciones Multidisciplinarias sobre Mesoamérica y el Sureste. Serie divulgación, 1).

976. GOUGH (Barry M.). Historical dictionary of Canada. Lanham, Scarecrow Press, 99, 271 p.

977. Hand (In der) des Feindes. Kriegsgefangenschaft von der Antike bis zum Zweiten Weltkrieg. Hrsg. v. Rüdiger OVERMANS. Köln u. Weimar u. Wien, Böhlau, 99, 551 p.

978. Handbuch zur deutschen Einheit: 1949–1989–1999. Hrsg. v. Werner WEIDENFELD und Karl-Rudolf KORTE. Frankfurt u. New York, Campus, 99, 895 p.

979. Historical dictionary of the 1960s. Ed. by James S. OLSON; associate editor Samuel FREEMAN. Westport a. London, Greenwood Press, 99, VIII-548 p.

980. Historical dictionary of the 1970s. Ed. by James S. OLSON. Westport a. London, Greenwood Press, 99, VIII-414 p.

981. HUGHES (Arnold), GAILEY (Harry A.). Historical dictionary of the Gambia. Lanham, Scarecrow Press, 99, XXII-231 p. (African historical dictionaries, 79).

982. Ile laboratoire (L'). Colloque de l'université de Corse, 19–21 juin 1997. Textes réunis par Anne MEISTERSHEM. Ajaccio, Ed. Alain Piazzola, 99, 459 p.

983. IVANIČ (Martin). Kratka ilustrirana zgodovina Slovencev. (Short illustrated history of Slovenes). Ljubljana, Mladinska knjiga, 99, 147 p. (ill.).

984. Iwanami koza sekai rekishi 16: shuken kokka to keimo. (Iwanami world history vol. 16. Sovereign states and Enlightenment). Ed. by Kazuhiko KONDO. Tokyo, Iwanami Shoten, 99, 266 p.

985. Iwanami koza sekai rekishi 19: Ido to imin. (Iwanami world history vol. 19. Immigration and Immigrants). Ed. by Kaoru SUGIHARA. Tokyo, Iwanami Shoten, 99, 321 p.

986. JANSON (Henrik). Till frågan om Svearikets vagga. (Le Berceau du royaume de Suède). Vara, Västergötlands hembygdsförbund, 99, 143 p. (ill.).

987. JOHNSON (Graham Edwin), PETERSON (Glen D.). Historical dictionary of Guangzhou (Canton) and Guangdong. Lanham, Scarecrow Press, 99, XLII-276 p. (Historical dictionaries of cities of the world, 6).

988. JOHNSON BARKER (Brian). A concise dictionary of the Boer War. Cape Town, Francolin, 99, 143 p. (Francolin reference).

989. Jugoslawien-Krieg (Der): Handbuch zu Vorgeschichte, Verlauf und Konsequenzen. Hrsg. v. Dunja MELCIC; im Auftrag des Ost-Westeuropäischen Kultur- und Studienzentrums, Palais Jalta. Opladen, Westdeutscher Verlag, 99, 590 p.

990. JULIÁ (Santos). Un siglo de España. Política y sociedad. Madrid, Marcial Pons Ediciones de Historia, 99, 380 p.

991. Kalaallit Nunaat. Gyldendals bog om Grønland. (Le Groenland). Red. par Bert GYNTHER et Aqigssiaq MØLLER. København, Gyldendalske Boghandel, 99, 400 p., ill., cartes.

992. KIRSCHBAUM (Stanislav J.). Historical dictionary of Slovakia. Lanham, Scarecrow Press, 99, LXXXVI-213 p. (European historical dictionaries, 31).

993. KNUTSEN (Torbjørn L.). The Rise and Fall of World Orders. New York, Manchester U. P., 99, VIII-234 p.

994. KONTLER (László). Millennium in Central Europe: a history of Hungary. Budapest, Atlantis, 99, 537 p.

995. KOSELLECK (Reinhart). Europäische Umrisse deutscher Geschichte. Heidelberg, Manutius, 99, 79 p.

996. KÜHL (Jörgen), HARDT (Nils). Danevirke. Nordens største fortidsminne. (Le Danevirke, le plus grand vestige archéologique de Scandinavie). Herning, Poul Kristensen, 99, 159 p. (ill.).

997. LE GOFF (Jacques), SCHMITT (Jean Claude), ALESSIO (Franco). Dictionnaire raisonné de l'Occident médiéval. Paris, Fayard, 99, IX-1236 p. (ill.).

998. Lexikon des Mittelalters. Bd. 10. Registerband. Hrsg. v. Charlotte BRETSCHER-GISIGER, Bettina MARQUIS und Thomas MEIER. Stuttgart, J. B. Metzler, 99, 776 coll.

999. Makedonija: Problemy istorii i kul'tury. (Macedonia: problems of history and culture: [articles]). Ed. R.P. GRISHINA. RAN, In-t slavjanovedenija. Moskva, [s. n.], 99, 370 p. (maps; bibl.).

1000. MAROLT (Janez), MIHELIČ (Darja), ŽVANUT (Maja), ROZMAN (Franc), PRUNK (Janko), KRESAL (Franc), KACIN-WOHINZ (Milica), FERENC (Tone), REPE (Božo), MIHELAČ (Jaro). Slovenci skozi čas: kronika slovenske zgodovine. (Slovenes through time: chronicle of Slovene history). Ljubljana, Mihelač, 99, 519 p.

1001. MOEGLIN (J.-M.). Nation et nationalisme du Moyen Age à l'époque moderne (France-Allemagne). *Revue historique*, 99, 123, 611, p. 537-554.

1002. MULDOON (James). Empire and order: the concept of empire, 800–1800. New York, St. Martin's Press, 99, VIII-209 p. (Studies in modern history).

1003. Nueva historia de la nación argentina. Academia Nacional de la Historia. Buenos Aires, Planeta, 99, [s. p.].

1004. OLSEN (Olaf). Da Danmark blev til: seks radioforedrag. (La Naissance du Danemark: six conférences radiophoniques). København, Fremad, 99, 107 p. (ill.).

1005. OLSEN (Rikke Agnete). Da riket var ungt. (Les Premiers siècles du royaume de Danemark). København, Fremad, 99, 364 p. (ill.). – IDEM. Konge og Adel: kroner og katastropher. (Rois et noblesse: couronnes et catastrophes). København, Fremad, 99, 114 p. (ill.).

1006. ØRSTED (Per). Danmark før Danmark: romerne og os. (Le Danemark avant le Danemark: les Romains et les Danois). København, Samleren, 99, 165 p. (ill., cartes).

1007. Osmanlı. (Les Ottomans). Edited by Güler EREN, Kemal ÇIÇEK, Cem OĞUZ. Ankara, Yeni Türkiye, 99, 12 vol., 702 p., 704 p., 704 p., 702 p., 699 p., 702 p., 703 p., 701 p., 868 p., 818 p., 738 p., 702 p.

1008. Oxford history (The) of the British Empire. General editor Wm. Roger LOUIS. Vol. 3. The nineteenth century. Ed. by Andrew PORTER, ass. ed. Alaine LOW. Vol. 4. The twentieth century. Ed. by Judith M. BROWN and Wm. Roger LOUIS, ass. ed. Alaine LOW. Vol. 5. Historiography. Ed. by Robin W. WINKS, ass. ed. Alaine LOW. Oxford a. New York, Oxford U. P., 99, 3 vol., XXII-774 p., XXVI-773 p., XXIV-731 p.

1009. PALMER (Alan). The Penguin dictionary of twentieth-century history. London, Penguin, 99, 554 p. (Penguin reference).

1010. PALUMBO-LIU (David). Asian/American: historical crossing of a racial frontier. Stanford, Stanford U. P., 99, VI-504 p.

1011. PARKER (Noel). Revolutions and history: an essay in interpretation. Malden, Blackwell, 99, VI-232 p.

1012. PERKINS (Dorothy). Encyclopedia of China: the essential reference to China, its history and culture. Chicago a. London, Fitzroy Dearborn, 99, IX-662 p. (A Roundtable press book).

1013. PIRJEVEC (Jože). Serbi, croati, sloveni: storia di tre nazioni. Bologna, Il Mulino, 99, 193 p. (Universale paperbacks Il Mulino, 296).

1014. Pomlad narodov = Volkerfrühling. Hrsg. v. Andreas MORITSCH und Tina BAHOVEC. Celovec, Mohorjeva založba, 99, 239 p. (Zgodovina brez meja = Unbegrenzte Geschichte, 6).

1015. POP (Ioan Aurel). Romanians and Romania: a brief history. Boulder, East European Monographs, 99, V-150 p. (East European monographs, 542).

1016. POPE (Stephen). The Cassell dictionary of the Napoleonic Wars. London, Cassell, 99, 572 p.

1017. PRATT (Keith), RUTT (Richard). Korea: a historical and cultural dictionary. With additional material by James HOARE. Richmond, Curzon, 99, XX-568 p. (Durham East-Asia series).

1018. PREGO (Victoria). Diccionario de la transición. Barcelona, Plaza Janés, 99, 778 p. (Así fue, 32).

1019. PRODI (Paolo). Introduzione allo studio della storia moderna. Con la collaborazione di Giancarlo ANGELOZZI e Carla PENUTI. Bologna, Il Mulino, 99, 257 p. (Strumenti storia).

1020. REDGATE (Anne Elizabeth). The Armenians. Oxford, Blackwell Publishers, 99, XVIII-331 p. (The Peoples of Europe).

1021. REINHARD (Wolfgang). Geschichte des Staatsgewalt. Eine vergleichende Verfassungsgeschichte Europas von den Anfängen bis zur Gegenwart. München, Beck, 99, 631 p.

1022. RICHTER (Karel). Češi a Němci v zrcadle dějin. Tomo 1–2. 1, Od nejstarších časů – květen 1938. 2, Květen 1938 – do dnešní doby. (Czech and German in the mirror of history. Vol. 1. From earliest times to May 1938. Vol. 2. From May 1938 to the present). Třebíč, Akcent, 99, 2 vol., 274 p., 301 p. (Fakta).

1023. RÖPKE (Ian Martin). Historical dictionary of Osaka and Kyoto. Lanham, Scarecrow Press, 99, XIII-273 p. (Historical dictionaries of cities of the world, 9).

1024. ROSENDORFER (Herbert). Deutsche Geschichte. Ein Versuch. Von den Anfängen bis zum Wormser Konkordat. München, Nyphenburger, 99, 253 p.

1025. SCHILLING (Heinz). Die neue Zeit. Vom Christenheitseuropa zum Europa der Staaten, 1250–1750. Berlin, Siedler, 99, 559 p. (Siedler Geschichte Europas, 3).

1026. SCOCOZZA (Benito), JENSEN (Grethe). Danmarks historie. Hvem, hvad og hvornær. (Histoire du Danemark. Personnages, événements, dates). København, Politiken, 99, 543 p. (ill., cartes, diagr., tab.).

1027. SKYDSBJERG (Henrik). Grønland. 20 år med hjemmestyre. (Le Groenland. Vingt ans sous le régime d'autonomie). Nuuk, Atuagkat, 99, 198 p.

1028. Spory o dějiny. Sborník kritických textů. Tomo 1–2. (Disputes over history. Essays). Ed. Miloslav BEDNÁŘ. Praha, Masarykův ústav AV ČR, 99, 2 vol., 153 p., 125 p.

1029. STALLAERTS (Robert). Historical dictionary of Belgium. Lanham, Scarecrow Press, 99, XXVIII-303 p. (European historical dictionaries, 35).

1030. Studii istorice româno-ungare. (Romanian-Hungarian historical studies). Volum editat de Lucian NĂSTASĂ, cu o prefață de Alexandru ZUB. Iași, Fundația Academică "A. D. Xenopol", 99, 400 p.

1031. SUNDHAUSSEN (Holm). Europa balcanica. Der Balkan als historischer Raum Europas. *Geschichte und Gesellschaft*, 99, 25, p. 626-653.

1032. SUSTER (Zeljan E.). Historical dictionary of the Federal Republic of Yugoslavia. Lanham, Scarecrow Press, 99, C-421 p. (European historical dictionaries, 29).

1033. SWIETOCHOWSKI (Tadeusz), COLLINS (Brian C.). Historical dictionary of Azerbaijan. Lanham, Scarecrow Press, 99, XIII-145 p. (Asian/Oceanian historical dictionaries, 31).

1034. TENENTI (Alberto). Venezia e il senso del mare: storia di un prisma culturale dal XIII al XVII secolo. Milano, Guerini, 99, 653 p. (Saggi/Istituto italiano per gli studi filosofici, 34).

1035. TILLY (Richard). Globalisierung aus historischer Sicht und das Lernen aus der Geschichte. Köln, Forschungsinstitut für Sozial- und Wirtschaftsgeschichte an der Universität Köln 99, 48 p. (Kölner Vorträge zur Sozial- und Wirtschaftsgeschichte, 41).

1036. Total War and 'Modernization.' Ed. by Yasushi YAMANOUCHI, J. Victor KOSCHMANN and Ryuichi NARITA. Ithaca, Cornell University, East Asia Program, 99, XVIII-326 p.

1037. TOWNSON (D.). A dictionary of contemporary history. London, Blackwell, 99, 448 p.

1038. VÁRKONYI (Ágnes). Századfordulóink: esszék, tanulmányok. (Our turns of the centuries: essays, studies). Budapest, Liget Mühely Alapítvány, 99, 260 p.

1039. VEKSLER (Aleksandr G.), MEL'NIKOVA (Alla S.). Rossijskaja istorija v moskovskikh kladakh. (Russian history in the treasures of Moscow, [from neolithic to 1812]). Moskva, Zhiraf, 99, 272 p. (ill., bibl.).

1040. Verstaatlichung der Welt? Europäische Staatsmodelle und außereuropäische Machtprozesse. Hrsg. v. Wolfgang REINHARD und Elisabeth MÜLLER-LUCKNER. München, Oldenbourg, 99, XVI-375 p. (Schriften des Historischen Kollegs. Kolloquien, 47). [Cf. n° <Auswahl> 3993.]

1041. Vietnam. Fra drage til tiger: Vietnams historie fra kolontiden til i dag. (Le Vietnam. Du dragon au tigre: histoire du Vietnam de l'époque coloniale jusqu'à nos jours). Red. par Peter FREDERIKSEN. Ærhus, Systime, 99, 159 p. (ill., cartes).

1042. Vilfanov zbornik: pravo, zgodovina, narod = Recht, Geschichte, Nation. Hrsg. v. Vincenc RAIŠP und Erst BRUCKMULLER. Ljubljana, Založba ZRC (ZRC SAZU), 99, 713 p. (ill.).

1043. Vostochnaja Evropa v drevnosti i srednevekov'je: kontakty, zony kontaktov i kontaktnye zony: XI chtenija pamjati V.T. Pashuto, Mat-ly konf. (Eastern Europe in Antiquity and Middle Ages: contacts, zones of contacts, contact zones: papers read at the 11th conf. dedicated to the memory of Vladimir T. Pashuto). Chief ed. Elena A. MEL'NIKOVA. RAN, In-t vseobshchej istorii. Moskva, IVI RAN, 99, 166 p. (bibl.). – Vostochnaja Evropa v istoricheskoj retrospektive: K 80-letiju V.T. Pashuto. (Eastern Europe in historical retrospective: articles devoted to the 80th anniversary of Vladimir T. Pashuto). RAN, In-t vseobshchej istorii. Moskva, Jazyki russkoj kul'tury, 99, 307 p. (8 f. ill., bibl.).

1044. WAGNER (John A.). Historical dictionary of the Elizabethan world: Britain, Ireland, Europe, and America. Chicago a. London, Fitzroy Dearborn, 99, XXXIX-392 p.

1045. War and society in the ancient and medieval worlds: Asia, the Mediterranean, Europe, and Mesoamerica. Ed. by Kurt A. RAAFLAUB and Nathan ROSENSTEIN. Cambridge, Harvard University Center for Hellenic Studies, 99,VIII-484 p. (Center for Hellenic Studies colloquia, 3). [Cf. n° <choice> 2981.]

1046. WORTZEL (Larry M.). Dictionary of contemporary Chinese military history. Westport a. London, Greenwood Press, 99, XV-334 p.

1047. YOUNG (John W.). The Longman companion to America, Russia and the Cold War, 1941–1998. New York, Addison Wesley Longman, 99, XIV-309 p. (Longman companions to history).

1048. Zakladi tisočletij: zgodovina Slovenije od neandertalcev do Slovanov. (Millennia Treasures: Slovene history from Neanderthals to Slavs). Vodja projekta Janez DULAR; avtorji besedil Dragan BOŽIČ [et al.]. Ljubljana, Modrijan, 99, 430 p.

1049. ZHANG (Yuanlin). Mao Zedongs Bezugnahme auf Clausewitz. *Archiv für Kulturgeschichte*, 99, 81, 2, p. 443-472.

Cf. n°s 593, 3921-4008, 5233, 8107, 8171, 8275, 8352

§ 6. Theory of the state and of society.

1050. 1748, l'année de l'Esprit des Lois. Ed. par Catherine LARRÈRE et Catherine VOLPILHAC-AUGER. Paris, H. Champion, 99, 191 p.

1051. ALTRICHTER (Helmut). «Offene Großbaustelle Rußland». Reflexionen über das «Schwarzbuch des Kommunismus». *Vierteljahreshefte für Zeitgeschichte*, 99, 47, 3, p. 321-362.

1052. ANTÓN MARTÍNEZ (Beatriz). Tácito en el siglo XVIII: Instrucción de príncipes de Juan de Simoni. Valladolid, Universidad de Valladolid, Secretariado de Publicaciones e Intercambio Científico, 99, 367 p. (Lingüística y filología, 34).

1053. Aspects de la pensée médiévale dans la philosophie politique moderne. Sous la direction de Yves Charles ZARKA. Paris, Presses universitaires de France, 99, 276 p. (Fondements de la politique. Série Essais).

1054. BAGNOLI (Paolo). Profilo di storia del pensiero politico italiano del Novecento. Firenze, Polistampa, 99, 195 p.

1055. BARBERIS (Mauro). Libertà. Bologna, Il Mulino, 99, 155 p. (Lessico della politica).

1056. BEALEY (Frank). The Blackwell dictionary of political science: a user's guide to its terms. Oxford, Blackwell, 99, 384 p.

1057. BLONDIAUX (Loïc), VEITL (Philippe). La carriére symbolique d'un père fondateur: André Siegfried et la science politique française après 1945. *Genéses*, 99, 37, p. 4-26.

1058. BRIGGS (Charles F.). Giles of Rome's De regimine principum: reading and writing politics at court and university, c. 1275–c. 1525. Cambridge a. New York, Cambridge U. P., 99, XIV-207 p. (ill., facs.). (Cambridge studies in palaeography and codicology, 5).

1059. BROWNING (Gary K.). Hegel and the history of political philosophy. Basingstoke, Macmillan, 99, VIII-185 p.

1060. CASTRO ALFÍN (Demetrio). La historia de las ideas politicas, contenidos y métodos. Barcelona, Institut de Ciencies Politiques i Socials, 99, 48 p. (Working paper, 168).

1061. CEDRONIO (Marina). Rivoluzioni e costituzioni in recenti approcci di storiografia e di filosofia politica. *Rivista storica italiana*, 99, 111, 2, p. 543-581.

1062. CORNELL (Saul). The other founders: antifederalism and the dissenting tradition in America, 1788–1828. Chapell Hill, University of North Carolina Press, 99, XVI-327 p.

1063. COSTA (Pietro). Civitas: storia della cittadinanza in Europa. Vol. 1. Dalla civiltà comunale al Settecento. Roma e Bari, Laterza, 99, XXIII-693 p. (Collezione storica).

1064. CUTINELLI RÈNDINA (Emanuele). Introduzione a Machiavelli. Roma e Bari, Laterza, 99, 201 p. (I filosofi, 78).

1065. DUBUISSON (M.). La permanence de la pensée politique romaine de la Renaissance à la Révolution. *Etudes classiques*, 99, 67, p. 229-238.

1066. ELÍAS DE TEJADA Y SPÍNOLA (Francisco). La tradición portuguesa: los orígenes (1140–1521) (doctrinas políticas). Madrid, Editorial Actas, Fundación Francisco Elías de Tejada, 99, 307 p (Actas/historia).

1067. Enlightenment (The). Ed. by David WILLIAMS. Cambridge, Cambridge U. P., 99, XII-529 p. (Cambridge readings in the history of political thought).

1068. Eriarvoisuus, valistuksen lupaus ja rasismi. (Inequality, the Enlightenment, and racism). Ed. by Pekka ISAKSSON and Jouko JOKISALO. Helsinki, Suomen Historiallinen Seura, 99, 180 p. (Historiallinen arkisto, 112).

1069. GOZZI (Gustavo). Democrazia e diritti. Germania: dallo Stato di diritto alla democrazia costituzionale. Roma e Bari, Laterza, 99, X-307 p. (Libri del tempo Laterza, 291).

1070. GUASCO (Maurilio). Il concetto di nazione nel cattolicesimo italiano. *Humanitas*, 99, 54, p. 229-240.

1071. Histoire de la philosophie politique. T. 1. La liberté des anciens. T. 2. Naissances de la modernité. T. 3. Lumières et romantisme. T. 4. Les critiques de la modernité politique. T. 5. Les philosophies politiques contemporaines (depuis 1945). Sous la direction de Alain RENAUT; avec la collaboration de Pierre-Henri TAVOILLOT et Patrick SAVIDAN. Paris, Calmann-Lévy, 99, 5 vol., [s. p.].

1072. HOFFMAN (Piotr). Freedom, equality, power: the ontological consequences of the political philosophies of Hobbes, Locke, and Rousseau. New York a. Frankfurt am Main, Lang, 99, XI-383 p.

1073. HUTTNER (Markus). Totalitarismus und säkulare Religionen: zur Frühgeschichte totalitarismuskritischer Begriffs- und Theoriebildung in Grossbritannien. Bonn, Bouvier, 99, 413 p. (Schriftenreihe Extremismus & Demokratie, 14).

1074. IHALAINEN (Pasi). The discourse on political pluralism in early eighteenth-century England. A conceptual study with special reference to terminology of religious origin. Helsinki, SHS, 99, 375 p. (Bibliotheca historica, 36.).

1075. IRIGOIN (Jean). Rec. di MONTESQUIEU (Charles Louis de Secondat). Considérations sur les causes de la grandeur des Romains et de leur décadence. *Quaderni di storia*, 99, 49, p. 273-274.

6. THEORY OF THE STATE AND OF SOCIETY

1076. LARKINS (Jeremy Daniel). The idea of the territorial state: discourses of political space in Renaissance Italy. London, [s. n.], 99, 333 p. [Thesis Ph.D. – London].

1077. LENCI (Mauro). Individualismo democratico e liberalismo aristocratico nel pensiero politico di Edmund Burke. Pisa, Istituti editoriali e poligrafici internazionali, 99, 258 p. (Idee e storia, 10).

1078. LESSNOFF (Michael Harry). Political philosophers of the twentieth century. Oxford, Blackwell Publishers, 99, VI-304 p.

1079. LIM (Jie-Hyun). Ilsangjuk Fascismui Kodirkki. (Reading the Fascist code in everyday life). *Contemporary criticism*, 99, 8, [s. p.].

1080. Linguaggi politici. A cura di Enrico ARTIFONI e Maria Luisa PESANTE. *Quaderni storici*, 99, 34, 102, p. 591-732. [Contiene: TODESCHINI (Giacomo). Linguaggi teologici e linguaggi amministrativi: le logiche sacre del discorso economico fra VIII e X secolo (p. 597-616). – GANDINO (Germana). Ruolo dei linguaggi e linguaggio dei ruoli: Ottone III, Silvestro II e un episodio delle relazioni tra impero e papato (p. 617-658). – GIANSANTE (Massimo). Linguaggi politici e orizzonti d'attesa a Bologna fra XIII e XIV secolo (p. 659-676). – LAMBERTINI (Roberto). La diffusione della «Politica» e la definizione di un linguaggio politico aristotelico].

1081. MAC ALEER (Graham). Giles of Rome on political authority. *Journal of the history of ideas*, 99, 60, 1, p. 21-36.

1082. MACHIAVELLI (Niccolò). Vol. 1. 1. De principatibus. Discorsi sopra la prima deca di Tito Livio (Libri I-II). Vol. 1. 2. Discorsi sopra la prima deca di Tito Livio (libro III). Dell'arte della guerra. Dalle legazioni. A cura di Rinaldo RINALDI. Torino, UTET, 99, 2 vol., 1680 p.

1083. MARTELLI (Mario). Saggio sul Principe. Roma, Salerno, 99, 299 p. (Studi e ricerche per la edizione nazionale delle opere di Niccolò Machiavelli).

1084. MARTINELLI (Alberto). Economia e società: Marx, Weber, Schumpeter, Polanyi, Parsons e Smelser. Torino, Edizioni di Comunità, 99, XII-191 p. (Territori di comunità, 11).

1085. MASTELLONE (Salvo). Storia del pensiero politico europeo: dal XV al XVIII secolo. Torino, UTET, 99, 317 p.

1086. METZGER (Jan). Die Milizarmee im klassischen Republikanismus. Die Odyssee eines militär-politischen Konzeptes von Florenz über England und Scottland nach Nordamerika (15.–18. Jahrhundert). Bern, Stuttgart u. Wien, Haupt, 99, 478 p. (St. Galler Studien zur Politikwissenschaft, 22).

1087. Millénaires, messianismes et millénarismes. Actes du Colloque de Paris, 25–26 mars 1999. Sous la dir. de Jean GAUDEMET, Bernard GUENÉE et Jean IMBERT. *Revue française d'histoire des idées politiques*, 99, 10, p. 229-444.

1088. Mondo nuovo (Il) e le virtù civili: l'epistolario di Gaetano Filangieri 1772–1788. A cura di Eugenio LO SARDO. Napoli, Fridericiana editrice universitaria, 99, 336 p. (Fridericiana historia, 5).

1089. OAKLEY (Francis). Politics and eternity: studies in the history of medieval and early modern political thought. Leiden a. Boston, Brill, 99, X-359 p. (Studies in the history of Christian thought, 92).

1090. ÖZ (Mehmet). Klasik Dönem Osmanlı Siyasi Düşüncesi: Tarihi Temeller ve Ana İlkeler. (La pensée politique ottomane à l'époque classique). *İslami Araştırmalar*, 99, 12, 1, p. 27-33.

1091. Pensiero politico (Il): idee teorie dottrine. A cura di Alberto ANDREATTA e Artemio Enzo BALDINI. Vol. 1. Età antica e Medioevo. A cura di Carlo DOLCINI [et al.]. Vol. 2. Età moderna. A cura di Alberto ANDREATTA e Artemio Enzo BALDINI. Vol. 3. Ottocento e Novecento. A cura di Gianfranco PASQUINO. 1. Saggi di Paolo BAGNOLI [et al.]. 2. Saggi di Raffaella BARITONO [et al.]. Torino, UTET, 99, 4 vol., XII-356 p., XXII-490 p., XIX-318 p., 331 p.

1092. PETRILLO (Agostino). Teoria e politica ne "La città" di Max Weber. *Materiali per una storia della cultura giuridica*, 99, 29, p. 87-143.

1093. Polis e piccolo stato tra riflessione antica e pensiero moderno: atti delle Giornate di studio 21–22 febbraio 1997, Firenze. A cura di Emilio GABBA e Aldo SCHIAVONE. Como, New Press, 99, 93 p. (Biblioteca di Athenaeum, 43). [Contiene: GABBA (Emilio). Riflessioni intorno all'idea di Polis (p. 8-14). – CAMBIANO (G.). Polis e piccolo stato in Platone e Aristotele (p. 15-31). – ASHERI (D.). Al di là di Atene e Sparta: la "polis normale" e il "terzo mondo greco" (p. 32-47). – MANNORI (L.). Il 'piccolo Stato' nel 'grande Stato'? Archetipi classici e processi di territorializzazione nell'Italia tardomedievale e protomoderna (p. 48-66). – GIARRIZZO (G.). Il piccolo Stato nell'età moderna (p. 67-75). – BAZZOLI (M.). Piccolo Stato e teoria dell'ordine internazionale nell'età moderna (p. 76-93)].

1094. Populism in Latin America. Ed. by Michael L. CONNIFF. Tuscaloosa a. London, University of Alabama Press, 99, VII-243 p.

1095. QUIN (Eckehard). Personenrechte und Widerstandsrecht in der katholischen Widerstandslehre Frankreichs und Spaniens un 1600. Berlin, Duncker & Humblot, 99, 693 p. (Beiträge zur Politischen Wissenschaft, 10).

1096. Ragion (La) di stato dopo Meinecke e Croce. Dibattito su recenti pubblicazioni. Atti del seminario internazionale di Torino, 21–22 ottobre 1994. A cura di Artemio Enzo BALDINI. Genova, Name, 99, 279 p. (Storia delle idee e delle istituzioni politiche, Medioevo e Età moderna, 2).

1097. Reception (The) of Locke's politics. Ed. by Mark GOLDIE. London, Pickering & Chatto, 99, 6 vol., LXXXVIII-369 p., 377 p., 384 p., 448 p., 385 p., 405 p.

1098. Reform in Great Britain and Germany. Ed. by T. C. W. BLANNING and Peter WENDE. Oxford, Oxford U. P., 99, 179 p. (Proceedings of the British Academy, 100).

1099. Repräsentation in Föderalismus und Korporativismus. Hrsg. v. Wilhelm BRAUNEDER und Elisabeth BERGER. Frankfurt am Main, Lang, 99, 290 p. (Rechts- und sozialwissenschaftliche Reihe, 21). [Cf. n° <Auswahl> 4122.]

1100. Rethinking Leviathan: the eighteenth-century state in Britain and Germany. Ed. by John BREWER and Eckhart HELLMUTH. London, German Historical Institute a. Oxford, Oxford U. P., 99, X-402 p. (ill.). (Studies of the German Historical Institute London).

1101. SBARBERI (Franco). L'utopia della libertà eguale. Il liberalismo sociale da Rosselli a Bobbio. Torino, Bollati Boringhieri, 99, 218 p.

1102. SCHIERA (Pierangelo). Specchi della politica. Disciplina, melanconia, socialità nell'Occidente moderno. Bologna, Il Mulino, 99, 399 p.

1103. State (The): historical and political dimensions. Ed. by Richard ENGLISH and Charles TOWNSHEND. London, Routledge, 99, IX-253 p. [Includes chapters on Ireland by Mary E. DALY and Steve BRUCE].

1104. STERNHELL (Zeev), SZNAJDER (Mario), ASHERI (Maia). Die Entstehung der faschistischen Ideologie. Von Sorel zu Mussolini. Hamburg, Hamburger Edition, 99, 409 p.

1105. Thomas Hobbes e la fondazione della politica moderna. A cura di Giuseppe SORGI. Milano, A. Giuffrè, 99, XXIII-847 p. (Collana della Facoltà / Università degli studi di Teramo. Facoltà di scienze politiche, 2).

1106. VIROLI (Maurizio). Repubblicanesimo. Roma e Bari, Laterza, 99, 127 p.

1107. WESTERMAN (Ingmar). Authority and utility: John Millar, James Mill and the politics of history, c. 1770–1836. Amsterdam, Universiteit van Amsterdam, 99, 250 p.

1108. WOLF (Eric Robert). Envisioning power: ideologies of dominance and crisis. Berkeley a. London, University of California Press, 99, XI-339 p.

1109. ZIEGLER (Charles E.). The history of Russia. Westport a. London, Greenwood Press, 99, XXII-242 p.

Cf. n°s 1462, 1818

§ 7. Constitutional and legal history.

* 1110. BLICKLE (Peter). Ordnung schaffen. Alteuropäische Rechtskultur in der Schweiz. Eine monumentale Edition. *Historische Zeitschrift*, 99, 268, 1, p. 121-136.

1111. AJELLO (Raffaele). L'esperienza critica del diritto: lineamenti storici. Vol. 1. Le radici medievali dell'attualità. Napoli, Jovene, 99, XV-417 p.

1112. ARTOLA GALLEGO (Miguel). La monarquía de España. Madrid, Alianza Editorial, 99, 641 p. (maps). (Historia y geografía ensayo).

1113. ASCHERI (Mario). Città-Stato e Comuni: qualche problema storiografico. *Le carte e la storia*, 99, 5, 1, p. 16-28.

1114. BAKER (John Hamilton). Why the history of English law has not been finished: an inaugural lecture delivered in the Law School on 14 October 1998. Cambridge, Cambridge U. P., 99, 32 p.

1115. BOURGON (Jérôme). La coutume et le droit en Chine à la fin de l'Empire. *Annales*, 99, 54, 5, p. 1073-1108.

1116. CARPINELLA (Alessandro). Voltaire e il giusnaturalismo. *Cultura*, 99, 37, p. 125-142.

1117. Dictionnaire des institutions françaises. Bruxelles, De Boeck Université, 99, 534 p.

1118. DIESTELKAMP (Bernhard). Recht und Gericht im Heiligen Römischen Reich. Frankfurt am Main, Klostermann, 99, VIII-611 p. (Ius Commune, Sonderhefte: Studien zur europäische Rechtsgeschichte, 122).

1119. DILCHER (Gerhard). Warum mittelalterliche Rechtsgeschichte heute? *Zs. der Savigny-Stiftung für Rechtsgeschichte. Germanistische Abt.*, 99, 116, p. 1-22. – IDEM. Zur Rolle der Rechtsgeschichte in einer Sozialgeschichte des 20. Jh. Überlegungen und Thesen. *Zs. für Neuere Rechtsgeschichte*, 99, 21, 3/4, p. 389-407.

1120. Droit romain, jus civile et droit français. Contributions à la Table ronde réunie à l'université de Toulouse I, du 24 au 26 septembre 1998. Sous la dir. de Jacques KRYNEN. *Et. Hist. Droit Idées pol.*, 99, 3, 472 p.

1121. DURĂ (Nicolae). Le régime de la synodalité selon la législation canonique conciliaire, du Ier millénaire. Bucureşti, Editura Ametist, 99, 1024 p.

1122. EISENHARDT (Ulrich). Deutsche Rechtsgeschichte. München, C.H. Beck, 99, XXVIII-638 p. (Grundrisse des Rechts).

1123. ELLUL (Jacques). Histoire des institutions. 1. L'Antiquité. 2. Le Moyen Age. 3. XVIe-XVIIIe siècle. 4. Le XIXe siècle. Paris, Presses Universitaires de France, 99, 4 vol., [s. p.]. (Quadrige, 274-277).

1124. FELL (A. London). Origins of legislative sovereignty and the legislative state. Vol. 5. Modern origins, developments, and perspectives against the background of "Machiavellism". Book III: Modern major "isms" (19th–20th centuries). Westport a. London, Praeger, 99, XV-502 p.

1125. GARCÌA Y GARCÌA (Antonio). En el entorno del derecho comùn. Madrid, Universidad Rey Juan Carlos, Servicio de Publicaciones, 99, 253 p.

1126. HARDIN (Russell). Liberalism, constitutionalism, and democracy. New York a. Oxford, Oxford U. P., 99, XVIII-379 p.

1127. KRAUSE (Thomas). Geschichte des Strafvollzugs. Von den Kerken des Altertums bis zur Gegenwart. Darmstadt, Primus, 99, 151 p.

1128. LABRUNA (Luigi). "Civitas, quae est constitutio populi …". Per una storia delle costituzioni. *Labeo*, 99, 45, p. 165-182.

1129. Law and literature. Ed. by Michael FREEMAN and Andrew D.E. LEWIS. Oxford a. New York, Oxford U. P., 99, XXXI-764 p. (Current legal issues, 2).

1130. MARQUARDT (Bernd). Das Römisch-Deutsche Reich als Segmentäres Verfassungssystem (1348–1806/48). Versuch zu einer neuen Verfassungstheorie auf der Grundlage der lokalen Herrschaften. Zürich, Schulthess, pp, XVII-561 p. (Zürcher Studien zur Rechtsgeschichte, 39).

1131. PADOA-SCHIOPPA (A.). Il ruolo del diritto nella genesi dello Stato moderno: modelli, strumenti, principii. *In*: Studi di storia del diritto, II. Milano, Giuffrè, 99, p. 25-77. (Università degli studi di Milano, Facoltà di giurisprudenza, Pubblicazioni dell'Istituto di storia del diritto italiano, 23).

1132. Personnalité, territorialité et droit. Actes des journées internationales de la Société d'Histoire du Droit, tenues à Bruxelles du 28 au 31 mai 1998. Éd. Jean-Marie CAUCHIES et Serge DAUCHY. Bruxelles, Facultés universitaires Saint-Luois, 99, XI-276 p. (Cahiers du Centre de Recherche en Histoire du Droit et des Istitutions, 11-12).

1133. Procedure di giustizia. A cura di Renata AGO e Simona CERUTTI. *Quaderni storici*, 99, 34, 101, p. 307-474. [Contiene: VALLERANI (Massimo). Pace e processo nel sistema giudiziario del comune di Perugia (p. 315-354). – ASCHERI (Mario). Il processo civile tra diritto comune e diritto locale: da questioni preliminari al caso della giustizia estense (p. 355-388). – AGO (Renata). Una giustizia personalizzata. I tribunali civili di Roma nel XVII secolo (p. 389-412). – CERUTTI (Simona). Fatti e fatti giudiziari. Il Consolato di commercio di Torino nel XVIII secolo (p. 413-446). – SILVESTRINI (Maria Teresa). Giustizia civile e giurisdizione. Il giudizio di possessorio in materia ecclesiastica nel Piemonte del XVIII secolo (p. 447-474)].

1134. QUAGLIONI (Diego). Machiavelli e la lingua della giurisprudenza. *Pensiero politico*, 99, 32, p. 171-185.

1135. SÁNCHEZ DE LA TORRE (Á.). Qu'en est-il de la réalité du droit? *Archives de philosophie du droit*, 99, 43, p. 13-25.

1136. SCHIERA (Pierangelo). «Bonum Commune» zwischen Mittelalter und Neuzeit. Überlegungen zur substanziellen Grundlade der modernen Politik. *Archiv für Kulturgeschichte*, 99, 81, 2, p. 283-304.

1137. SEIRING (Claudia). Fremde in der Stadt (1300–1800). Die Rechtsstellung Auswärtiger in mittelalterlichen und neuzeitlichen Quellen der deutschsprachigen Schweiz. Frankfurt am Main, Peter Lang, 99, LXXIV-380 p. (Abb.) (Europäische Hochschulschriften, Reihe II, 2566).

1138. Státnost česká a československá – tradice a kontinuita. (Die tschechische Staatlichkeit – die Tradition und Kontinuität). Ed. Pavel KLENER. Praha, Karolinum, 99, 261 p. (Acta Universitatis Carolinae. Iuridica, 1/2).

1139. Studi di storia del diritto medievale e moderno. A cura di Filippo LIOTTA. Bologna, Monduzzi, 99, 340 p.

1140. Studi in onore di Leopoldo Elia. A cura di A. PACE. Milano, Giuffrè, 99, 2 vol., LXV-1806 p.

1141. TROPER (Michel). La loi Gayssot et la constitution. *Annales*, 99, 54, 6, p. 1239-1256.

1142. YLIKANGAS (Heikki). Väkivallasta sanan valtaan. Suomalaista menneisyyttä keskiajalta nykypäiviin. (Changing bodily violence with rhetorics. The Finnish legal past from the Middle ages to the present days). Helsinki, WS, 99, 399 p. (ill., maps).

Cf. n°s 1462, 7068

§ 8. Economic and social history.

1143. Adoption et fosterage. Ed. par Mireille CORBIER. Paris, Ed. de Boccard, 99, 392 p.

1144. Agriculture in Egypt. From Pharaonic to modern times. Ed. by A.K. BOWMAN, E. ROGAN. Oxford, Oxford U. P., 99, XXVIII-427 p. (tables). [Cf. n[os] <choice> 1636, 1649, 1650, 1655, 3000.]

1145. Aktie (Von) bis Zoll. Ein historisches Lexikon des Geldes. Hrsg. v. Michael NORTH. München, Beck, 99, 467 p.

1146. ARMIERO (Marco). Ambiente e storia: indagine su alcune riviste storiche. *Società e storia*, 99, 22, p. 145-185.

1147. AVGUŠTIN (Cene). Kranj: naselbinski razvoj od prazgodovine do 20. Stoletja. (Kranj: development of the settlement from prehistoric times to the 20th century). Ljubljana, Znanstveni inštitut Filozofske fakultete, 99, 127 p. (ill.). (Razprave Filozofske fakultete. Gorenjski kraji in ljudje, 15).

1148. AVRAM (Cezar), CIOBOTEA (Dinică), JOIŢA (Virgil), OSIAC (Vladimir), PĂTROIU (Ion), PETRESCU (Ileana). Istoria comerţului în sud-vestul României. Sec. VIII–XX. (The history of trade in south-western Romania. The 8th–20th centuries). Craiova, Editura de Sud, 99, 392 p.

1149. BASINI (Gian Luigi). Storia economica dell' Europa contemporanea: aspetti e problemi. Torino, G. Giappichelli, 99, XII-254 p.

1150. BERENGO (Marino). L' Europa delle città: il volto della società urbana europea tra Medioevo ed età moderna. Torino, G. Einaudi, 99, XV-1040 p. (Biblioteca di cultura storica, 224).

1151. BIANCHINI (Marco). Introduzione: il prestigio come problema di storia della civiltà industriale. *Cheiron*, 99, 16, 31, p. 7-26.

1152. Construction, reproduction et représentation des patriciats urbains de l'Antiquité au XXe siècle. Ed. par Claude PETITFRÈRE. Tours, CEHVI, 99, 569 p. [Cf. n° <sélection> 382.]

1153. Crises, revolutions and self-sustained growth: essays in European fiscal history, 1130–1830. Ed. by Mark ORMROD, Margaret BONNEY and Richard BONNEY. Stamford, Shaun Tyas, 99, VIII-456 p. (ill., figs., tabs.).

1154. DAMELL (David), ERICSSON (Christer). Eskilstuna historia. Band 1: Forntiden och medeltiden. (Histoire de la ville d'Eskilstuna. Tome 1: Préhistoire et Moyen Age). Red. par Bror-Erik OHLSSON. Eskilstuna, Stadsarkivet, 99, 291 p. (ill.). (Årsbok. Lokalhistoriska sällskapet i norra Södermanland).

1155. Devianz, Widerstand und Herrschaftspraxis in der Vormoderne. Studien zu Konflikten im südwestdeutschen Raum (15.–18. Jahrhundert). Hrsg. v. Mark HÄBERLEIN. Konstanz, Universitätsverlag Konstanz, 99, 354 p. (Konflikte und Kultur – Historische Perspektiven, 2).

1156. Eigentum im internationalen Vergleich, 18.–20. Jahrhundert. Hrsg. v. Hannes SIEGRIST und David SUGARMAN. Göttingen, Vandenhoeck & Ruprecht, 99, 291 p. (Kritische Studien zur Geschichtswissenschaft, 130).

1157. Encountering the past in nature: essays in environmental history. Ed. by Timo MYLLYNTAUS and Mikko SAIKKU. Helsinki, Helsinki U.P., 99, 174 p. (figs, tab).

1158. Etrangers (Les) dans la ville: minorités et espace urbain du bas Moyen Âge à l'époque moderne. Éd. de Jacques BOTTIN et Donatella CALABI. Paris, Maison des sciences de l'homme, 99, VII-486 p. (ill., maps, plan).

1159. FENOALTEA (Stefano). Europe in the African mirror: the slave trade and the rise of feudalism. *Rivista di storia economica,* 99, 15, 2, p. 123-165.

1160. Finances, pouvoirs at mémoire. Mélanges offerts à Jean Favier. Ed. par Jean KERHERVÉ et Albert RIGAUDIÈRE. Paris, Fayard, 99, 838 p. [Cf. n° <sélection> 642.]

1161. Gale encyclopedia of U.S. economic history. Ed. by Thomas CARSON, associate editor Mary BONK. Detroit, Gale Group, 99, 2 vol., LVI-1250 p.

1162. GAMES (Alison). Migration and the origins of the English Atlantic world. Cambridge a. London, Harvard U.P., 99, VII-322 p. (tabs, figs).

1163. GARCÌA DELGADO (José Luis), JIMÉNEZ (Juan Carlos). Un siglo de España. La economìa. Madrid, Marcial Pons Ediciones de Historia, 99, 220 p.

1164. Gender and Japanese history. Vol. 1. Religion and customs. The body and sexuality. Vol. 2. The self and expression. Work and life. Ed. by Haruko WAKITA, Anne BOUCHY and Chizuko UENO. Osaka, Osaka U. P., 99, 2 vol., 419 p., 602 p.

1165. Geschichte der Stadt Saarbrücken. Band 1. Von den Anfängen zum industriellen Aufbruch (1860). Band 2. Von der Zeit des stürmischen Aufbruchs bis zur Gegenwart. Hrsg. Rolf WITTENBROCK. Saarbrücken, Saarbrücker Druckerei und Verlag, 99, 2 vol., 1500 p.

1166. Geschichte des Wohnens. Band I: 5000 v.Chr.– 500 n.Chr. Vorgeschichte, Frühgeschichte, Antike. Hrsg. v. W. HOEPFNER. Ludwigsburg, Wüstenrot Stiftung, Deutscher Eigenheimverein e.V. u. Stuttgart, Deutsche Verlags-Anstalt, 99, 959 p. [Cf. n^{os} <Auswahl> 1567, 1821, 1843.]

1167. GIJSBERS (Wilhelmina Maria). Kapitale ossen: de internationale handel in slachtvee in Noordwest-Europa (1300–1750). Hilversum, Verloren, 99, 661 p. (ill., maps). (N.W. Posthumus reeks, 9).

1168. Giochi (I) del prestigio. Modelli e pratiche della distinzione sociale. A cura e con introduzione di Marco BIANCHINI. *Cheiron*, 99, 16, 31, p. 3-312.

1169. Handwerk in Europa. Vom Spätmittelalter bis zur Frühen Neuzeit. Hrsg. v. Knut SCHULZ unt. Mitarb. v. Elisabeth MÜLLER-LUCKNER. München, Oldenbourg, 99, XVII-313 p. (Schriften des Historischen Kollegs, Kolloquien, 41).

1170. IŞIN (Ekrem). İstanbul'da gündelik hayat: tarih, kültür ve mekân ilişkileri üzerine toplumsal tarih denemeleri. (La vie quotidienne à Istanbul: essais d'histoire sociale sur les relations entre histoire, culture et lieu). İstanbul, Yapı Kredi Yayınları, 99, 361 p.

1171. JANEKOVIĆ ROEMER (Zdenka). Okvir slobode: dubrovačka vlastela između srednjovjekovlja i humanizma. (Horizons of liberty: Ragusian aristocracy between the Middle Ages and Renaissance). Dubrovnik, Zavod za povijesne znanosti Hrvatske akademije znanosti i umjetnosti, 99, 454 p.

1172. JANTING (Jørgen), TOLSTRUP (Tor). Kongehuset i arbejdstøjer: monarkernes indsats for dansk erhvervsliv gennem et årtusind. (La monarchie en habits de travail: l'intervention royale dans la vie économique depuis un millénaire). Viby, Jyllandspostens Erhvervsbøger, 99, 207 p. (ill.).

1173. KAUFMANN (Franz-Xaver). Kritik des neutralen Geldes. *Geschichte und Gesellschaft,* 99, 25, 2, p. 226-251.

1174. KAZGAN (Haydar). İstanbul'da suyun tarihi: İstanbul'un su sorununun tarihsel kökenleri ve Osmanlı'da yabancı su şirketleri. (Histoire de l'eau à Istanbul:

les origines historiques du problème de l'eau d'İstanbul et les associations etrangères de l'eau dans l'Empire Ottoman). İstanbul, İletişim Yayınları, 99, 167 p.

1175. KOCKA (Jürgen). Wider die Idealisierung der historischen Stadt. In: Stadtgesellschaft [Cf. n° 1187], p. 97-100.

1176. LASSEN (Eva Maria). Indefra: europeiske kvinders historie belyst ved kildetexter. (De l'intérieur: histoire des femmes européennes sous l'éclairage des sources écrites). København, Museum Tusculanum Forlag, 99, 264 p. (ill.).

1177. Marriage and rural economy: Western Europe since 1400. Ed. by Isabelle DEVOS and Liam KENNEDY. Turnhout, Brepols, 99, 292 p. (CORN, 3).

1178. MOON (David). The Russian peasantry, 1600–1930: the world the peasants made. London a. New York, Addison Wesley Longman, 99, XII-396 (fig., tabs., maps).

1179. Ó GRÁDA (Cormac). Black '47 and beyond: the great Irish famine in history, economy, and memory. Princeton, Princeton U. P., 99, XII-302 p. (The Princeton economic history of the Western world).

1180. Ökonomie der Bürgerkriege. Hrsg. v. François JEAN und Jean C. RUFIN. Hamburg, Hamburger Edition, 99, 477 p.

1181. Orders and hierarchies in late Medieval and Renaissance Europe. Ed. by Jeffrey DENTON. Basingstoke, Macmillan, 99, XII-206 p. (ill.). (Problems in focus).

1182. PAMUK (Şevket). Osmanlı İmparatorluğunda paranın tarihi. (Histoire de la monnaie dans l'Empire Ottoman). İstanbul, Tarih Vakfı Yurt Yayınları, 99, 327 p.

1183. Quellen zur Geschichte der Stadt Köln. Band 1. Antike und Mittelalter von den Anfängen bis 1396/97. Hrsg. v. Wolfgang ROSEN und Lars WIRTLER. Köln, Bachem, 99, XIV-337 p.

1184. Rise (The) of fiscal state in Europe, c. 1200–1815. Ed. by Richard BONNEY. Oxford a. New York, Oxford U. P., 99, XII-527 p.

1185. SIEGENTHALER (Hansjörg). Geschichte und Ökonomie nach der kulturalistischen Wende. *Geschichte und Gesellschaft,* 99, 25, 2, p. 276-301.

1186. Sotsial'naja istorija: Ezhegodnik, 1998/1999. (Social History: the annual, 1998/1999). Eds. Kirill M. ANDERSON, Leonid I. BORODKIN. RAN, In-t vseobshchej istorii. Moskva, ROSSPEN, 99, 354 p. (bibl.). [Eng. summaries]

1187. Stadtgesellschaft. Hrsg. v. Michael MÖNNINGER. Frankfurt am Main, Suhrkamp, 143 p. (Edition Suhrkamp, 2074). [Cf. n° <Auswahl> 1175.]

1188. Storia economica d'Italia. A cura di Pierluigi CIOCCA e Gianni TONIOLO. Vol. 1. BEVILACQUA (Piero), [et al.]. Interpretazioni. Vol. 2. BATTILOSSI (Stefano). Annali. Roma e Bari, Laterza, 99, 2 vol., XIX-419 p., VIII-713 p.

1189. Terms of labor: slavery, serfdom, and free labor. Ed. by Stanley L. ENGERMAN. Stanford, Stanford U.P., 99, IX-350 p. (tabs).

1190. Wirtschaft und Energie im Wandel der Zeit. Hrsg. v. Harald WIXFORTH. Köln, Weimar u. Wien, Böhlau, 99, 300 p.

1191. Women in business. Ed. by Mary A. YEAGER. Cheltenham a. Northampton, Edward Elgar, 99, 3 vol., XCIII-661 p., X- 465 p., XXII-691 p.

1192. YATES (Margaret). Change and continuities in rural society from the later middle ages to the sixteenth century: the contribution of west Berkshire. *Economic history review,* 52, 99, 4, p. 617-637.

Cf. n°s 165-203, 6635-6070, 8048, 8254

§ 9. History of civilization, sciences and education.

* 1193. Dictionary of the history of medicine. Ed. by Anton SEBASTIAN. New York, Parthenon, 99, VI-781 p.

* 1194. Isis, current bibliography of the history of science. Vol. 90. [Vol. 89. Cf. Bibl. 98, n° 1272.] Ed. by John NEU. *Isis,* 99 (suppl.), [s. p.].

* 1195. MAC IVER (Tom). The end of the world: an annotated bibliography. Jefferson a. London, McFarland, 99, IX-389 p.

1196. ABBATE (Janet). Inventing the Internet. Cambridge, MIT Press, 99, XIII-264 p.

1197. Ægteskabet i Norden fra Saxo til idag. (Le Mariage en Scandinavie de Saxo Grammaticus à aujourd'hui). Red. par Kari MELBU, Anu PYLKÄNEN et Bente ROSENBECK. København, Nordisk Ministerråd, 99, 224 p. (Forskningsprogrammet Norden og Europa).

1198. ALPARSLAN (Ali). Osmanlı hat sanatı tarihi. (Histoire de la calligraphie ottomane). İstanbul, Yapı Kredi Yayınları, 99, 215 p.

1199. ANDREWS (Peter A.). Felt tents and pavilions: the nomadic tradition and its interaction with princely tentage. London, Melisende, 99, 2 vol., XLI-1472 p. (Kölner ethnologische Mitteilungen. Sonderband).

1200. ARON (Cindy S.). Working at play: a history of vacations in the United States. New York, Oxford U. P., 99, XI-324 p.

1201. BELL (Rudolph M.). How to do it: guides to good living for Renaissance italians. Chicago, University of Chicago Press, 99, XIII-375 p.

1202. Beyond the limits: the concept of space in Russian history and culture. Ed. by Jeremy SMITH. Helsinki, Suomen Historiallinen Seura, 99, 276 p. (bibl.). (Studia historica, 62).

1203. BOURKE (Joanna). An intimate history of killing: face-to-face killing in twentieth-century warfare. New York, BasicBooks, 99, XXIII-509 p.

1204. BURCKHARDT (Martin). Vom Geist der Maschine. Eine Geschichte kultureller Umbrüche. Frankfurt am Main u. New York, Campus-Verlag, 99, 409 p.

1205. BURNETT (John). Liquid pleasures: a social history of drinks in modern Britain. London a. New York, Routledge, 99, VIII-254 p.

1206. Cambridge companion (The) to modern Spanish culture. Ed. by David T. GIES. Cambridge, Cambridge U. P., 99, XXIX-327 p. (Cambridge companions to culture).

1207. Cambridge companion (The) to modernism. Ed. by Michael LEVENSON. Cambridge, Cambridge U. P., 99, XVII-246 p. (Cambridge companions to literature).

1208. Cathedrals of consumption: the European department store, 1850–1939. Ed. by Geoffrey CROSSICK and Serge JAUMAIN. Aldershot, Ashgate, 99, XVII-326 p. (tabs., figs., pls.).

1209. CAVALLO (Dominick). A fiction of the past: the Sixties in American history. New York, St. Martin's Press, 99, 282 p.

1210. CLARK (William). On the table manners of academic examination. *In*: Wissenschaft als kulturelle Praxis, 1750–1900 [Cf. n° 6180], p. 33-67.

1211. Companion (A) to Hungarian studies. Ed. by László KÓSA. Budapest, Akadémiai Kiadó, 99, 509 p.

1212. Costruzione (La) dell'immagine scientifica del mondo: mutamenti della concezione dell'uomo e del cosmo dalla scoperta dell'America alla meccanica quantistica. A cura di Marco MAMONE CAPRIA. Napoli, La Città del Sole, 99, 495 p. (ill., bibl.). (Il Pensiero e la Storia, 56).

1213. Croats (The). Christianity, culture, art. Ed. by V. MARKOVIĆ and A. BADURINA. Zagreb, Ministry of Culture of the Republic of Croatia, 99, 576 p.

1214. DE ROMILLY (Jacqueline), VERNANT (Jean Pierre). Contre la mort programmée des études classiques. *Quaderni di storia*, 99, 50, p. 5-10.

1215. Desire and denial in Byzantium. Papers of the thirty-first spring symposium of Byzantine studies, (University of Sussex, Brighton, March 1997). Ed. by L. JAMES. Aldershot, Ashgate, 99, XI-220 p. [Cf. n^{os} <choice> 409, 3076, 3080.]

1216. DEVOTO (Fernando), MADERO (Marta). Historia de la vida privada en la Argentina. Buenos Aires, Taurus, 99, 3 vol., 307 p., 364 p., 321 p. (ill.). [Cf. n° <selección> 6858.]

1217. DOERING-MANTEUFFEL (Anselm). Wie westlich sind die Deutschen? Amerikanisierung und Westernisierung im 20. Jahrhundert. Göttingen, Vandenhoeck & Ruprecht, 99, 160 p. (Kleine Reiha V&R).

1218. DOSSENA (Giampaolo). Enciclopedia dei giochi. Torino, UTET, 99, 3 vol., 1399 p.

1219. Dreadful visitations: confronting natural catastrophe in the age of Enlightenment. Ed. by Alessa JOHNS. London a. New York, Routledge, 99, XXV-198 p.

1220. ELFWENDAHL (Magnus). Från kärva till kärl. Ett bidrag till vardagslivets historia i Uppsala. (Du tesson au récipient. Contribution à l'histoire de la vie quotidienne à Uppsala). Stockholm, Elfwendahl, 99, 427 p. (ill.). [English summary].

1221. EMMERSON (Richard K.). The secret. [AHR Forum: Millenniums]. *American historical review*, 99, 104, 5, p. 1603-1614.

1222. ERTUĞ TARIM (Zeynep). XVI. Yüzyıl Osmanlı Devleti'nde cülûs ve cenaze törenleri. (Les funérailles et les cérémonies d'avènement imperial). Ankara, Kültür Bakanlığı Yayımlar Dairesi Başkanlığı, 99, XI-175 p.

1223. Espacio interior (El) de América del Sur. Geografía, historia, política, cultura. Ed. por Barbara POTTHAST, Karl KOHUT y Gerd KOHLHEPP. Frankfurt am Main, Vervuert, 99, 430 p. (Americana Eystettensia. Publicaciones del Centro de Estudios Latinoamericanos de la Universidad Católica de Eichstätt, 19).

1224. Estudios sobre historia y ambiente en América. Vol. 1. Argentina, Bolivia, México, Paraguay. Ed. por Bernardo GARCÍA MARTÍNEZ y Alba GONZÁLEZ JÁCOME. México, Colegio de México, 99, VIII-296 p.

1225. Fabrication (La) du paysage. Actes du Colloque organisé par le Centre de recherche bretonne et celtique du CNRS à Brest, 12–14 mars 1998. Réunis par Gaeël MILIN. Brest, Université de Bretagne occidentale, 99, 428 p.

1226. FOLTZ (Richard C.). Religions of the Silk Road: overland trade and cultural exchange from antiquity to the fifteenth century. New York, St. Martin's Press, 99, VIII-186 p.

1227. Food in global history. Ed. by Raymond GREW. Boulder, Westview, 99, X-293 p.

1228. FOX (Robert), GUAGNINI (Anna). Laboratories, workshops, and sites: concepts and practices of research in industrial Europe, 1800–1914. Berkeley, University of California Press, 99, II-214 p. (figs., tabs).

1229. FRENKEN (Ralph). Kindheit und Autobiographie vom 14. bis 17. Jahrhundert. Psychohistorische Rekonstruktionen. Kiel, Oetker-Voges, 99, 2 vol., XII-777 p.

1230. FUSI (Juan Pablo). Un siglo de España. La cultura. Madrid, Marcial Pons Ediciones de Historia, 99, 232 p.

1231. GELBER (Steven M.). Hobbies: leisure and the culture of work in America. New York, Columbia U. P., 99, XI-374 p.

1232. GOGA (Mircea). Cultura și civilizația poporului român. Sinteze. (Culture and civilization of the Ro-

9. HISTORY OF CIVILIZATION, SCIENCES AND EDUCATION

manian people. Syntheses). Cluj-Napoca, Editura Dacia, 99, 455 p.

1233. GOLAS (Peter J.). Science and civilisation in China. Vol. 5. Chemistry and chemical technology. Part 13. Mining. New York, Cambridge U. P., 99, XXVI-538 p.

1234. HELLIE (Richard). The economy and material culture of Russia, 1600–1725. Chicago a. London, University of Chicago Press, 99, XI-672 p. (tabs., figs.).

1235. HICKETHIER (Knut). Zwischen Gutenberg-Galaxis und Bilder-Universum. Medien als neues Paradigma, Welt zu erklären. *Geschichte und Gesellschaft*, 99, 25, 1, p. 146-171.

1236. HIGONNET (Patrice). Les mythes de Paris, des Lumières au surréalisme. Leçon inaugurale du 8 janvier 1999 au Collège de France, 99, 36 p.

1237. Historical dictionary of American education. Ed. by Richard J. ALTENBAUGH. Westport, Greenwood Press, 99, XVI-499 p.

1238. HÖLSCHER (Lucian). Die Entdeckung der Zukunft. Frankfurt am Main, Fischer, 99, 262 p.

1239. Körper macht Geschichte, Geschichte macht Körper. Körpergeschichte als Sozialgeschichte. Hrsg. v. Bielefelder Graduiertenkolleg Sozialgeschichte. Bielefeld, Verlag für Regionalgeschichte, 99, 351 p.

1240. KOSTIS (K.). O mythos tou xenou ì i Pechiney stin Ellada. (The myth of the stranger or Pechiney in Greece). Athena, Ekdoseis Alexandreia, 99, [s. p.].

1241. Kriegserlebnis und Legendenbildung. Das Bild des "modernen" Krieges in Literatur, Theater, Photographie und Film. Band 1. Vor dem Ersten Weltkrieg. Der Erste Weltkrieg. Band 2. Der Zweite Weltkrieg. Westliche Perspektiven. Östliche Perspektiven. Mythen. Nachkrieg. Band 3. "Postmoderne" Kriege? Krieg auf der Bühne. Krieg auf der Leinwand. Hrsg. v. Thomas F. SCHNEIDER. Osnabrück, Rasch, 99, 3 vol., XXX-1118 p. (Krieg und Literatur).

1242. Kulturelle Reformation: Sinnformationen im Umbruch 1400–1600. Hrsg. v. Bernhard JUSSEN und Craig KOSLOFSKY. Göttingen, Vandenhoeck & Ruprecht, 99, 386 p. (Veröffentlichungen des Max-Planck-Instituts für Geschichte, 145).

1243. LANGE (Johan). Kulturplanternes indförselshistorie i Danmark. (Histoire de l'introduction des plantes cultivées au Danemark). Frederiksberg, DSR Forlag, 99, 477 p. (ill.).

1244. Learning the law: teaching and the transmission of law in England, 1150–1900. Ed. by Jonathan A. BUSH and Alain WIJFFELS. London, Hambledon Press, 99, XXV-417 p.

1245. Lettera (Per). La scrittura epistolare femminile tra archivio e tipografia, secoli XV–XVII. A cura di Gabriella ZARRI. Roma, Viella, 99, 629 p.

1246. Lettre et réflexion morale. La lettre, miroir de l'âme. Ed. par Geneviève HAROCHE-BOUZINAC. Paris, Klincksieck, 99, 195 p. (Bibliothèque de l'âge classique).

1247. LÖFGREN (Orvar). On holiday: a history of vacationing. Berkeley a. Los Angeles, University of California Press, 99, XIV-320 p. (California studies in critical human geography, 6).

1248. LOUREIRO (Rui Manuel), GRUZINSKI (Serge). Passar as fronteiras. Actos do II Colloquio Internacional sobre Mediadores Culturais, seculos XV a XVIII. Lagos, Centro de Estudios Gil Eanes, 99, 408 p.

1249. LÜCKE (Hans-Karl), LÜCKE (Susanne). Antike Mythologie: ein Handbuch. Der Mythos und seine Überlieferung in Literatur und bildender Kunst. Reinbek, Rowohlt, 99, 767 p. (Rowohlts Enzyklopädie, 55600).

1250. LUSIGNAN (S.), TARDIF (A.-I.). Des druides aux clercs: quelques lectures françaises de Jules César aux XIIIe et XIVe siècles. *Revue historique*, 99, 123, 611, p. 463-482.

1251. Memoria e memorie. Convegno internazionale di studi, Roma, 18–19 maggio 1995. A cura di L. BOLZONI, V. ERLINDO e M. MORELLI. Firenze, Olschki, 99, VI-222 p. (Studi pichiani, 6).

1252. OLDENZIEL (Ruth). Making technology masculine: men, women and modern machines in America, 1870–1945. Amsterdam, Amsterdam U. P., 99, 271 p.

1253. Oxford companion (An) to the romantic age: British culture, 1776–1832. Ed. by Iain MAC CALMAN, John MEE, Gillian RUSSELL and Clara TUITE. Oxford, Oxford U. P., 99, XIII-780 p. [Cf. n° <choice> 6138.]

1254. PANICO (Guido). Sport, cultura, società: dallo svago al professionismo. Torino, Paravia scriptorium, 99, 160 p. (Viaggi nella storia del Novecento).

1255. PFISTER (Christian). Wetternachhersage. 500 Jahre Klimavariationen und Naturkatastrophen (1496–1995). Vorw. v. Hartmut GRAßL, sowie Beiträgen v. Jürgen LUTERBACH und Heinz WANNER. Unt. Mitarb. v. Beat BRODBECK und Paul-Anthon NIELSON. Bern, Stuttgart u. Wien, Haupt, 99, 304 p.

1256. PICCIONI (Luigi). Il volto amato della Patria. Il primo movimento per la protezione della natura in Italia, 1880–1934. Camerino, Università degli Studi, 99, V-330 p.

1257. Quoi joue-t-on (A)? Pratiques et usages des jeux et jouets à travers les âges. Festival d'histoire de Montbrison, 30 septembre–2 octobre 1998, sous la présidence scientifique de Michel PASTOREAU. Montbrison, la Ville, 99, 552 p.

1258. REQUATE (Jörg). Öffentlichkeit und Medien als Gegenstände historischer Analyse. *Geschichte und Gesellschaft*, 99, 25, 1, p. 5-32.

1259. SEBASTIAN (Anton). A dictionary of the history of medicine. New York a. London, Parthenon, 99, VI-781 p.

1260. Silences and images. The social history of the classroom. Ed. by Ian GROSVENOR [et al.]. Frankfurt am Main, Lang, 99, VI-274 p. (History of schools and schooling, 7).

1261. SORCINELLI (Paolo). Gli italiani e il cibo. Dalla polenta ai cracker. Milano, Bruno Mondadori, 99, 264 p. (ill.).

1262. SPENCE (Mark David). Dispossessing the wilderness: Indian removal and the making of the national parks. New York, Oxford U. P., 99, VIII-190 p.

1263. Sport, culture et religion: les patronages catholiques (1898–1998). Actes du Colloque de Brest, 24–26 septembre 1998. Ed. par Gérard CHOLVY et Yvon TRANVOUEZ. Brest, Université de Bretagne occidentale, faculté des Lettres Victor Segalen, Centre de Recherche bretonne et celtique, 99, 383 p.

1264. Stätten des Geistes. Große Universitäten Europas von der Antike bis zur Gegenwart. Hrsg. v. Alexander DEMANDT. Köln, Weimar u. Wien, Böhlau, VIII-322 p.

1265. STÖLLER (Erich). Mythos und Aufklärung. Psychoanalystische und kulturgeschichtliche Aspekte des Themas Herrschaft. Stuttgart, Heinz, 99, 220 p. (Stuttgarter Arbeiten zur Germanistik, 367).

1266. TRAHAIR (Richard C. S.). Utopias and Utopians: an historical dictionary. London, Fitzroy Dearborn, 99, XVI-480 p.

1267. VAN LAAK (Dirk). Weisse Elefanten: Anspruch und Scheitern technischer Grossprojekte im 20. Jahrhundert. Stuttgart, Deutsche Verlags-Anstalt, 99, 304 p.

1268. Vetenskap och historia. Sju essäer. (Sept essais sur la science et l'histoire). Red. par Ingmar NILSSON. Göteborg, Institution för idé- och lärdomshistoria, Göteborgs universitet, 99, 156 p. (Arachne, 12).

1269. WEBER (Gregor). Herrscher und Traum in hellenistischer Zeit. Archiv für Kulturgeschichte, 99, 81, 1, p. 1-34.

Cf. n°s 357, 615, 913, 1287, 8340

§ 10. History of art.

* 1270. ALVAREZ CASADO (Ana Isabel). Bibliografía artística del franquismo: publicaciones periódicas entre 1936 y 1948. Madrid, Fundación Universitaria Española, 99, 515 p. (Colección Tesis doctorales "cum laude". Serie A, Arte, 2).

* 1271. BHA. Bibliography of the History of Art. Bibliographie de l'Histoire de l'Art. Vol. 9, 1-4, 1999. [Vol. 8, 1-4, 1998. Cf. Bibl. 98, n° 1346.] Ed. by Michael RINEHART a. Marise BIDEAULT. Paris, Centre National de la Recherche Scientifique a. Santa Monica, The J. Paul Getty Trust, 99, 4 vol., [s. p.].

* 1272. FORD (Robert). A blues bibliography: the international literature of an Afro-American music genre. Bromley, Paul Pelletier, 99, 800 p.

1273. ACUN (Hakkı). Manisa'da Türk devri yapıları. (Edifices de l'époque turque à Manisa). Ankara, Türk Tarih Kurumu, 99, XI-672 p.

1274. Allgemeines Künstlerlexikon. Biobibliographischer Index A–Z. Vol. 1. A–Bielitz. Vol. 2. Bielke–Danvin. Vol. 3. Danny–Gachot. München u. Leipzig, Saur, 99, 3 vol., 2460 p.

1275. Allgemeines Künstlerlexikon: die Bildenden Künstler aller Zeiten und Völker. Vol. 22. Courts–Cuccini. Vol. 23. Cuccioni–Dambsman. München u. Leipzig, Saur, 99, 2 vol., LII-580 p., LII-587 p.

1276. Vacat.

1277. Artisten und Philosophen. Wissenschafts- und Wirkungsgeschichte einer Fakultät vom 13. bis zum 19. Jahrhundert. Hrsg. v. Rainer Christoph SCHWINGES. Red. Barbara STUDER. Basel, Schwabe, 99, XI-501 p. (Veröffentlichungen der Gesellschaft für Universitäts- und Wissenschaftsgeschichte, 1).

1278. Bach Handbuch. Hrsg. v. Konrad KÜSTER. Kassel u. London, Bärenreiter, 99, X-997 p.

1279. BENGTSSON (Herman). Den höviska kuturen i Norden. En konsthistorisk undersökning. (La culture courtoise en Scandinavie. Recherches d'histoire de l'art). Stockholm, Almqvist & Wiksell, 99, 320 p. [English summary]. (Kungliga Vitterhets historie och antikvitets Akademiens handlingar. Antikvariska serien, 43).

1280. Bilder (Die) und das Wort: Zum Verstehen christlicher Kunst in Afrika und Asien. Hrsg. v. Theo SUNDERMEIER und Volker KÜSTER. Göttingen, Vandenhoeck & Ruprecht, 99, 159 p. (Studien zur Aussereuropäischen Christentumsgeschichte. Asien, Afrika, Lateinamerika, 2).

1281. BURUCUA (José). Arte, sociedad y política. Buenos Aires, Sudamericana, 99, 318 p. (ill.).

1282. Cambridge companion (The) to Beethoven. Ed. by Glenn STANLEY. Cambridge, Cambridge U. P., 99, XIII-372 p.

1283. Cambridge companion (The) to Brahms. Ed. by Michael MUSGRAVE. Cambridge, Cambridge U. P., 99, XXII-325 p.

1284. CAMPBELL (Alastair). The designer's lexicon. London, Weidenfeld & Nicolson, 99, 320 p. (ill.).

1285. Companion (The) to Irish traditional music. Ed. by Fintan VALLELY. Cork, Cork U. P., 99, 478 p.

1286. Diccionario de la música española y hispanoamericana. Director y coordinador general, Emilio CASARES RODICIO; directores adjuntos, José LÓPEZ-CALO y Ismael FERNÁNDEZ DE LA CUESTA; [edición musicológica, Instituto Complutense de Ciencias Musicales]. Madrid, Sociedad General de Autores y Editores, 99, 6 vol., L-946 p., XXXIV-1019 p., XXXIV-977 p., XXXIV-953 p., XXXIV-953p., XXXIV-1104 p.

1287. Dictionnaire des monuments d'Ile-de-France. Sous la dir. de Georges POISSON. Paris, Ed. Hervas, 99, 958 p. (ill.).

1288. ESCH (Arnold). Reimpiego dell'antico nel medioevo: la prospettiva dell'archeologo, la prospettiva dello storico. In: Ideologie e pratiche del reimpiego nell'alto Medioevo [Cf. n° 3458], p. 73-108.

1289. FLEMING (John), HONOUR (Hugh), PEVSNER (Nikolaus). The Penguin dictionary of architecture and landscape architecture. London, Penguin, 99, VII-643 p.

1290. GOCER (Asli). A hypothesis concerning the character of Islamic art. Journal of the history of ideas, 99, 60, 4, p. 683-692.

1291. HURWIT (J.M.). The Athenian Acropolis: history, mythology and archaeology from the Neolithic Era to the present. Cambridge, Cambridge University, 99, XV-384 p.

1292. JAKIČ (Ivan). Vsi slovenski gradovi: leksikon slovenske grajske zapuščine. Dopolnjeni ponatis. (All Slovene castles: a lexicon of Slovene castle heritage). Ljubljana, DZS, 99, 470 p. (ill.).

1293. JELAVICH (Peter). National Socialism, Art and Power in the 1930s. Past and present, 99, 164, p. 244-265.

1294. Mimétismes, camouflages ... Camouflage et trompe l'oeil en couleur de la nature à l'homme. Actes du Colloque du Havre, 9, 10 et 11 novembre 1998. Bulletin trimestriel de la Société géologique de Normandie et des Amis du Muséum du Havre, 99, 86, 3-4, 115 p.

1295. MORGAN (David). Protestants and pictures: religion, visual culture, and the age of American mass production. New York, Oxford U. P., 99, XIV-417 p.

1296. ROECK (Bernd). Kunstpatronage in der Frühen Neuzeit: Studien zu Kunstmarkt, Künstlern und ihren Auftraggebern in Italien und im Heiligen Römischen Reich (15.–17. Jahrhundert). Göttingen, Vandenhoeck & Ruprecht, 99, 236 p. (Sammlung Vandenhoeck).

1297. ROSSI (Leena-Maija). Taide vallassa. Politiikkakäsityksen muutoksia 1980-luvun suomalaisessa taidekeskustelussa. (Art in power. Discussion on politics and art). Helsinki, Taide, 99, 301 p. (ill.). [English summary].

1298. SCHNEIDER (Norbert). Geschichte der Landschaftsmalerei. Vom Spätmittelalter bis zur Romantik. Darmstadt, Primus, 99, 214 p.

1299. SMITH SHAWN (Michelle). American archives: gender, race, and class in visual culture. Princeton, Princeton U. P., 99, XI-299 p.

1300. STRIETER (Terry W.). Nineteenth-century European art: a topical dictionary. Westport, Greenwood Press, 99, X-300 p.

Cf. n°s 357, 408, 584, 615, 1419, 3642

§ 11. History of religions.

a. General

* 1301. Chroniques bibliographiques. Hieros, 99, 4, p. 63-91.

* 1302. Critical review of books in religion. 1998. [1997. Cf. Bibl. 98, n° 1377.] Ed. by Charles PREBISH. 99, 11, [s. p.].

* 1303. Ephemerides theologicae lovanienses. Elenchus bibliographicus. Tomus LXXV. [Tomus LXXIV. Cf. Bibl. 98, n° 1378.] Editae cura E. BRITO, L. DE FLEURQUIN, J. FAMERÉE, É. GAZIAUX, J. HAERS, A. HAQUIN, M. LAMBERIGTS, J. LUST, G. VAN BELLE, J. VERHEIDEN. Leuven, Peeters, 99, 688 p.

* 1304. Religious studies review, 99, 25, 1-4, 451 p.

* 1305. Revue d'histoire ecclésiastique. Bibliographie. Tome 94. 1999. [Tome 93, 1998. Cf. Bibl. 98 n° 1380.] Ed. par M. HAVERALS. Louvain-la-Neuve, Bureaux de la R. H. E., Bibliothèque de l'université, 98, 610*p.

1306. Approaching Religion. Part 1. Part 2. Based on Papers Read at the Symposium on Methodology in the Study of Religions Held at Åbo, Finland, on the 4th–7th August 1997. Ed. by Tore AHLBÄCK. Åbo, The Donner Institute for Research in Religious and Cultural History, 99, 2 vol., 310 p., 282 p.

1307. ARNAL (William E.). Approaches to the study of religion. Method & theory in the study of religion, 99, 11, p. 107-118.

1308. Atlas of the World's Religions. Ed. by Ninian SMART. Oxford, Oxford U. P., 99, 240 p.

1309. Bibel og historieskrivning. (La Bible et l'écriture de l'Histoire). Red. par Geert HALLBÄCK et John STRANGE. København, Museum Tusculanum Forlag, 99, 238 p. (Forum for bibelsk eksegese, 10).

1310. FABRE (Pierre-Antoine). Conversions religieuses: histoires et récits. Annales, 99, 54, 4, p. 805-812.

1311. GILL (Sam D.). Approaches to the study of religion. Method & theory in the study of religion, 99, 11, p. 119-125.

1312. LÖHR (Gebhard). In or out? The relationship between religion, philosophy, and the science of religions. Method & theory in the study of religion, 99, 11, p. 395-400.

1313. MAC CUTCHEON (Russell T.). The insider/outsider problem in the study of religion: a reader. London, New York, Cassell, 99, X-405 p.

1314. MAGNANI (Giovanni). Storia comparata delle religioni. Principi fenomenologici. Assisi, Cittadella, 99, 653 p.

1315. MASSENZIO (Marcello). Sacré et identité ethnique. Frontières et ordre du monde. Préf. de Marc AUGÉ. Paris, EHESS, 99, 183 p. (Cahiers de l'Homme).

1316. Muslim perceptions of other religions: a historical survey. Ed. by Jacques WAARDENBURG. New York, Oxford U. P., 99, XV-350 p.

1317. Pragmatics (The) of defining religion: contexts, concepts and contests. Ed. Jan G. PLATVOET and Arie L. MOLENDIJK. Leiden, Brill, 99, XVII-543 p. (Studies in the History of Religions, 84).

1318. Religion in Geschichte und Gegenwart. Hrsg. v. Hans Dieter BETZ, Don S. BROWNING, Berndt JANOWSKI und Eberhard JUNGEL. Band 2. C–E. Tübingen, Mohr, 99, LX p.-1850 col.

1319. Rol' religii v formirovanii juzhnoslav'janskikh natsij. (The role of religion in the formation of south Slavonic nations). Ed. Iskra V. CHURKINA. RAN, In-t slavjanovedenija. Moskva, Editorial-URSS, 99, 262 p.

1320. THROWER (James). Religion. The classical theories. Edinburgh, Edinburgh U. P., 99, VIII-209 p.

Cf. n°s 615, 5258-5317

b. *Special studies*

* 1321. Bibliographia franciscana. T. 21. Principaliora, complectens opera anno 1997 edita. Roma, Istituto storico dei Cappuccini, 99, 421 p. (CF. Sectio bibliographica).

* 1322. Bulletin de bibliographie biblique. N. 25. Avril 99, VI-114 p. N. 26. Juillet 99, VI-109 p. N. 27. Déc. 99, VI-142 p. [n°s 22-24. Cf. Bibl. 98, n° 1413.]

* 1323. Index Islamicus: a bibliography of books, articles and reviews on Islam and the Muslim world published in the year 1997 with additions from 1993–1996. [1996. Cf. Bibl. 98, n° 1414.] Compiled and edited by G. J. ROPER and C.H. BLEANEY. London, Bowker Saur, 99, 873 p.

* 1324. Internationale Zeitschriftenschau für Bibelwissenschaft und Grenzgebiete. International Review of Biblical Studies. Revue internationale des études bibliques. Bd. XLIV 1997-1998. [Band XLIII. Cf. Bibl. 98, n° 1415.] Düsseldorf, Patmos Verlag, 99, XV-475 p.

* 1325. Mircea Eliade. Biobibliografie. Vol. 3. Receptarea Critică. Ed. Mircea HANDOCA. Bucureşti, Editura «Jurnalul literar», 99, 432 p.

* 1326. New Testament Abstracts. Vol. 43, 99, 683 p. [Vol. 42. Cf. Bibl. 98, n° 1416.]

* 1327. NORTH (Robert). Elenchus of biblical bibliography. Vol. 11, 2, 1995. [Vol. 11, 1, 1995. Cf. Bibl. 98, n° 1417.] Roma, Ed. Istituto Pontificio Biblico, 99, 954 p.

* 1328. Old Testament Abstracts. Vol. 22, 99, 600 p. [Vol. 21. Cf. Bibl. 98, n° 1418.]

1329. ANDERSEN (Peter B.), LÜCHAU (Peter), WARBURG (Margit). Gender, profession, and non-conformal religiosity. *Journal of contemporary religion*, 14, 1999, p. 277-290.

1330. Animaux dans les religions. Animals in the religious world. *Lumen vitae*, 99, 54, p. 245-254.

1331. Annäherungen an das Heilige: Gottesliebe und Nächstenliebe in den Religionen. Edmund Weber zum 60. Geburtstag. Stuttgart, Kohlhammer, 99, 230 p.

1332. ANTES (Peter). Autonomie und Gehorsam: Zum Askese-Ideal in den Weltreligionen. *Zeitschrift für Religionswissenschaft*, 99, 7, p. 81-93.

1333. Augustinus-Lexikon. Vol. 2. Fasc. 3-4. Deus–Donatistas (Contra-). Hrsg. v. C. MAYER. Bâle, Schwabe, 99, XLIX-LII, col. 321-640.

1334. BELIER (Wouter W.). Durkheim, Mauss, classical evolutionism and the origin of religion. *Method & theory in the study of religion*, 99, 11, p. 24-46.

1335. BELLAH (Robert N.). Max Weber and world-denying love: a look at the historical sociology of religion. *Journal of the American Academy of Religion*, 99, 67, 2, p. 277-304.

1336. Born in heaven – Made on earth: the making of the cult image in the ancient Near East. Ed. by E. Michael B. DICK. Winona Lake, Eisenbrauns, 99, XII-243 p.

1337. CAMPBELL (Robert A.). Georges Bataille's surrealistic theory of religion. *Method & theory in the study of religion*, 99, 11, p. 127-142.

1338. Catholicisme hier aujourd'hui demain. Encyclopédie publiée sous le patronage de l'Institut Catholique de Lille par G. MATHON et G.H. BAUDRY. Fasc. 72. Vaudois–Victorin. Fasc. 73. Victorin–Vocation. Paris, Letouzey & Ané, 99, col. 769-1024, 1025-1280.

1339. Ciel dans les civilisations orientales (Le). Ed. par Julien RIES [et al.]. Bruxelles, Louvain-la-Neuve, Leuven, Société belge d'études orientales, 99, XXVI-258 p. (Acta orientalia belgica, 12).

1340. CIURTIN (Eugen). Mircea Eliade: Posteritatea Tratatului de Istorie a Religiilor. *Archaeus*, 99, 3, 2, p. 175-206.

1341. COLPE (Carsten). Weltdeutungen im Widerstreit. Berlin u. New York, de Gruyter, 99, XXVI-381 p. (Theologische Bibliothek Töpelmann, 100).

1342. Conscience in world religions. Ed. by Jayne HOOSE. Leominster, Herefordshire, Gracewig, Notre Dame, University of Notre Dame Press, 99, IX-199 p.

1343. DECHARNNEUX (Baudouin), NEFONTAINE (Luc). L'initiation: splendeurs et misères. Bruxelles, Labor, 99, 90 p.

1344. DI DONATO (Riccardo). I Greci selvaggi. Antropologia storica di Ernesto de Martino, Roma, Manifestolibri, 99, 231 p.

1345. DIETZSCH (Steffen), MARROQUIN (Carlos). Der Mythos als Institution und als Erkenntnisproblem: Die Durkheim-Schule und Ernst Cassirer. *Zeitschrift für Religionswissenschaft*, 99, 7, p. 25-34.

1346. Dossier: Ernesto de Martino. *Gradhiva*, 99, 26, p. 51-107.

1347. Feminism and world religions. Ed. by Arvind SHARMA and Katherine K. YOUNG. Albany, State University of New York Press, 99, X-331 p. (Mc Gill Studies in the History of Religions).

1348. FILORAMO (Giovanni). Millenarismo e New Age. Apocalisse e religiosità alternativa. Bari, Dedalo, 99, 173 p.

1349. Fine dei tempi (La). *Annali di storia dell'esegesi*, 99, 16, 1, p. 7-272.

1350. Focus on fundamentalism. *Journal for the scientific study of religion*, 99, 38, 1, p. 1-35.

1351. Genealogien zur Papstgeschichte. T. 1. T. 2. Bearb. v. Christoph WEBER, unt. Mitw. v. Michael BECKER. Stuttgart, Hiersemann, 99, CXXXII-980 p. (Päpste und Papsttum, 29).

1352. GOLD (Daniel). A tapestry of kings: Edited volumes on the growth of knowledge in religious studies. *Religion*, 99, 29, p. 243-259.

1353. GRIMES (Ronald L.). Jonathan Z. Smith's theory of ritual space. *Religion*, 29, 99, p. 261-273.

1354. HERVIEU-LEGER (Danièle). Le Pèlerin converti. La religion en mouvement. Paris, Flammarion, 99, 290 p.

1355. Historical dictionary of reformed churches. Ed. by Robert BENEDETTO, Darrell L. GUDER and Donald K. MAC KIM. Lanham, Scarecrow Press, 99, LII-508 p.

1356. JOAS (Hans). Die Soziologie und das Heilige: Schlüsseltexte der Religionssoziologie. *Merkur*, 99, 53, p. 990-998.

1357. JUSCHKA (Darlene M.). The category of gender in the study of religion. *Method & theory in the study of religion*, 99, 11, p. 77-105.

1358. KAMPPINEN (Matti). Evolutionary theory and the study of religion: Darwin's dangerous idea. *Method & theory in the study of religion*, 99, 11, p. 145-149.

1359. KÜNG (Hans). Spurensuche: die Weltreligionen auf dem Weg. München, Zürich, Piper, 99, 314 p.

1360. Lexikon für Theologie und Kirche. Achter Bd. Pearson–Samuel. Herausgegeben von Walter KASPER [et al.]. Freiburg, Basel, Roma u. Wien, Herder, 99, 1518 col.

1361. LIDEGAARD (Mads). Da danerne blev kristne. (La Conversion des Danois au Christianisme). København, Nyt nordisk forlag Arnold Busck, 99, 256 p. (ill.).

1362. MANCINI (Silvia). Postface. *In*: DE MARTINO (Ernesto). Le monde magique. Paris, Sanofi-Synthélabo, 99, p. 285-593.

1363. MARKALE (Jean). Nouveau dictionnaire de la mythologie celtique. Paris, Pygmalion, 99, 320 p.

1364. MEJTARCHIJAN (Margarita B.). Pogrebal'nyj obrjad zoroastrijtsev. (The Zoroastrians' funeral rite). RAN, In-t vostokovedenija. Sankt-Peterburg, [s. n.], 99, 242 p. (ill., bibl.). [Eng. summary]

1365. Metaphor, canon and community: Jewish, Christian and Islamic approaches. Ed. by Ralph BISSCHOPS and James FRANCIS. Bern, Berlin, Bruxelles a. Frankfurt am Main, Lang, 99, 307 p.

1366. Métissage culturel entre religions écrites et traditions orales. *Diogène*, 99, 187, p. 1-194.

1367. Mitológia és humanitás. Ed. J-G. SZILÁGYI. Budapest, Osiris Kiadó, 99, 283 p.

1368. MOLENDIJK (Arie L.). Tiele on religion. *Numen*, 99, 46, p. 237-268.

1369. MURPHY (Tim). The concept «Entwicklung» in German Religionswissenschaft: before and after Darwin. *Method & theory in the study of religion*, 99, 11, p. 8-23.

1370. Mythologie (La) du matriarcat. Ed. par Philippe BORGEAUD. Genève, Droz, 99, 254 p.

1371. Nature godsdienstig (Van). *Wereld en Zending*, 99, 28, 2, p. 1-128.

1372. New religious movements: challenge and response. Ed. by Bryan WILSON and Jamie CRESSWELL. London, New York, Routledge, 99, XVIII-284 p.

1373. OLSON (Carl). Mircea Eliade, postmodernism, and the problematic nature of representational thinking. *Method & theory in the study of religion*, 99, 11, p. 357-385.

1374. RAPPAPORT (R.A.). Ritual and religion in the making of humanity. Cambridge, Cambridge U. P., 99, XXIII-535 p. (Cambridge Studies in Social and Cultural Anthropology).

1375. Reallexikon für Antike und Christentum. Hrsg. v. Ernst DASSMANN. 148. Jünger–Iulianus I. 149-150. Iulianus I–Iustinus 2. Stuttgart, Hiersemann, 99, col. 321-480, 481-800.

1376. Religion och samhälle i det förkristna Norden. Ett symposium. (Religion et société dans la Scandinavie préchrétienne. Un Colloque). Red. par Ulf DROBIN, en collaboration avec Jens Peter SCHJØDT, Gro STEINSLAND et Preben MEULENGRACHT SØRENSEN. Odense, Odense Universitetsforlag, 99, 250 p.

1377. Religions de l'antiquité. Ed. par Yves LEHMANN. Paris, PUF, 99, 592 p.

1378. Ressembler au monde: Nouveaux documents sur la théorie du macro-microcosme dans l'antiquité orientale. Ed. par Philippe GIGNOUX. Turnhout, Brepols, 99, 194 p.

1379. Sociology and religions: an ambiguous relationship. Sociologie et religion: des relations ambiguës. Ed. by Liliane VOYÉ and Jaak BILLIET. Leuven, Leuven U. P., 99, 263 p. (KADOC Studies, 23).

1380. SPINETO (Natale). Storia delle religioni e storia del cristianesimo: un dibattito intellettuale di inizio secolo. *In*: Il cristianesimo e le diversità. Studi per Attilio Agnoletto. A cura di Remo CACITTI, Grado Giovanni MERLO e Paola VISMARA. Milano, Edizioni Biblioteca francescana, 99, p. 263-293.

1381. Syncrétismes religieux (Les) dans le monde méditerranéen antique. Actes du colloque international en l'honneur de Franz Cumont à l'occasion du cinquantième anniversaire de sa mort (Rome, Academia Belgica, 25–27 septembre 1997). Ed. par Corinne BONNET et André MOTTE. Bruxelles, Rome et Turnhout, Brepols, 99, 402 p. [Cf. n^{os} <sélection> 2284, 2692.]

1382. TARDAN-MASQUELIER (Ysé). L'hindouisme: Des origines védiques aux courants contemporains. Paris, Bayard, 99, 384 p.

1383. Theologische Realenzyklopädie. Hrsg. v. G. MÜLLER. Bd. 30. Samuel–Seele. Berlin u. New York, De Gruyter, 99, 813 p.

1384. Transformations of the inner self in ancient religions. Ed. by Jan ASSMANN and Guy G. STROUMSA. Leiden, Brill, 99, VII-437 p. (Studies in the History of Religions, 83).

1385. TURTAS (Raimondo). Storia della Chiesa in Sardegna dalle origini al duemila. Roma, Città Nuova, 99, 978 p.

1386. ULIČNÝ (Ferdinand). Problematika metodského kresťanstva na Slovensku. (Die Problematik des vom heiligen Method aus Byzanz eingeführten Christentums in der Slowakei). *Historický časopis*, 99, 47, 3, p. 349-356. [Deutsche Zfassung]

1387. WASSERSTROM (Steven M.). Religion after religion: Gershom Scholem, Mircea Eliade, and Henry Corbin at Eranos. Princeton, Princeton U. P., 99, 368 p.

1388. WIEBE (Donald). The politics of religious studies: the continuing conflict with theology in the academy. Basingstoke a. London, Macmillan, 99, XX-332 p.

1389. Wörterbuch der Mythologie. Hrsg. v. H.W. HAUSSIG und E. SCHMALZRIEDT. 1. Abteilung. Die alten Kulturvölker. 33. Stuttgart, Klett-Cotta, 99, p. 831-875.

Cf. n°s 357, 1470, 3523, 8099

§ 12. **History of philosophy.**

* 1390. Bibliografia filosofica italiana, 1997. A cura di Carlo SCALABRIN. Firenze, L. S. Olschki, 99, 223 p. (Biblioteca di Bibliografica Italiana, 155).

* 1391. Bibliography of philosophy = Bibliographie de la philosophie: a quarterly bulletin. Vol. 46, 1999. Fasc. 1-4. [Vol. 45, 1998. Cf. Bibl. 98, n° 1485.] Paris, Vrin, 99, 504 p.

* 1392. BRISSON (Luc). Platon, 1990–1995: bibliographie. Avec la collaboration de Frédéric PLIN. Paris, J. Vrin, 99, 415 p. (Tradition de la pensée classique).

* 1393. DAIBER (Hans). Bibliography of Islamic philosophy. Leiden, Brill, 99, 2 vol., [s. p.]. (Handbuch der Orientalistik. Abt. 1, Der Nähe und Mittlere Osten, 43).

* 1394. International philosophical bibliography = Répertoire bibliographique de la philosophie. Vol. 51, 1999. [Vol. 50, 1998. Cf. Bibl. 98, n° 1486.] Louvain, Ed. de l'Institut Supérieur de Philosophie, 99, [s. p.].

1395. Blackwell guide (The) to epistemology. Ed. by John GRECO and Ernest SOSA. Oxford, Blackwell Publishing, 99, IX-464 p. (Blackwell Philosophy Guides).

1396. Cambridge companion (The) to early Greek philosophy. Ed. by A. A. LONG. Cambridge, Cambridge U. P., 99, XXX-427 p. (Cambridge companions to philosophy).

1397. Cambridge companion (The) to Malebranche. Ed. by Steven NADLER. Cambridge, Cambridge U. P., 99, 352 p. (Cambridge companions to philosophy).

1398. Cambridge companion (The) to Schopenhauer. Ed. by Christopher JANAWAY. Cambridge, Cambridge U. P., 99, XIV-478 p.

1399. Companion (A) to continental philosophy. Ed. by Simon CRITCHLEY and William R. SCHROEDER. Oxford, Blackwell, 99, XV-680 p.

1400. Dictionary (The) of eighteenth-century British philosophers. Ed. by John YOLTON, John Valdimir PRICE and John STEPHENS. Bristol, Thoemmes, 99, 2 vol., XXIII-1013 p.

1401. Dictionary of existentialism. Ed. by Haim GORDON. London, Fitzroy Dearborn, 99, XII-539 p.

1402. Dictionnaire d'histoire et philosophie des sciences. Ed. par Dominique LECOURT. Paris, Presses Universitaire de France, 99, XXII-1032 p.

1403. Dictionnaire de Diderot. Sous la dir. de Roland MORTIER et Raymond TROUSSON. Paris, Champion, 99, 546 p. (Dictionnaires & références, 4).

1404. DIETHE (Carol). Historical dictionary of Nietzscheanism. Lanham a. London, Scarecrow Press, 99, XVII-265 p. (ill., plates). (Historical dictionaries of religions, philosophies, and movements, 21).

1405. *Vacat.*

1406. INWOOD (Michael James). A Heidegger dictionary. Oxford, Blackwell, 99, XVI-283 p. (Blackwell philosophers dictionaries).

1407. LANCEL (Serge). Saint Augustin. Paris, Fayard, 99, 792 p.

1408. New Fontana dictionary (The) of modern thought. Ed. by Alan BULLOCK and Stephen TROMBLEY, assistant editor Alf LAWRIE. London, Harper & Collins, 99, XXIV-933 p.

1409. NOONAN (Harold W.). Routledge philosophy guidebook to Hume on knowledge. London a. New York, Routledge, 99, 221 p.

Cf. n°s 5879-6029

§ 13. History of literature.

* 1410. Bibliografia Internazionale Dantesca 1978–1984. Firenze, Le lettere, 99, V-469 p. (Quaderni degli "Studi danteschi" fondati da Michele Barbi, 64).

* 1411. Bibliographie der deutschen Sprach- und Literaturwissenschaft. Band XXXVIII. 1998. Bearb. v. Doris MAREK und Susanne PRÖGER. Frankfurt am Main, Vittorio Klostermann, 99, XXXIV-918 p.

* 1412. Bibliographie der französischen Literaturwissenschaft. Band XXXVI. 1998. Bearb. v. Astrid KLAPP-LEHRMANN. Frankfurt am Main, Vittorio Klostermann, 99, 1077 p.

* 1413. BIGLI. Bibliografia generale della lingua e della letteratura italiana. Vol. 7, 1997. Tomi 1-2. [Vol. 6, 1996. Tomi 1-2. Cf. Bibl. 98, n° 1515.] Diretta da Enrico MALATO. Roma, Salerno, 99, 2 vol., 1168 p., 353 p. (Pubblicazioni del "Centro Pio Rajna").

* 1414. HOWARD-HILL (Trevor Howard). British literary bibliography, 1980–1989: a bibliography. Oxford, Clarendon Press, 99, 2 vol., [s. p.]. (Index to British literary bibliography, 8-9).

* 1415. LASNER (Mark Samuels). A bibliography of Enoch Soames (1862–1897). With an afterword by Margaret D. STETZ. Oxford, Rivendale, 99, 42 p.

* 1416. PÖPPEL (Hubert) SALAZAR-PÖPPEL (Amalia). Las vanguardias literarias en Bolivia, Colombia, Ecuador, Perú: bibliografía y antología crítica. Frankfurt am Main, Vervuert, 99, XXV-225 p. (Bibliografía y antología crítica de las vanguardias literarias en el mundo ibérico, 2).

* 1417. SEIFERT (Siegfried). Goethe Bibliographie, 1950 bis 1990. Unter Mitarbeit von Rosel GUTSELL und Hans-Jürgen MALLES, herausgegeben von der Stiftung Weimarer Klassik. München, K. G. Saur, 99, 3 vol., LXVI, 1565 p.

1418. American women prose writers to 1820. Ed. by Carla MULFORD, with Angela VIETTO and Amy E. WINANS. Detroit a. London, Gale Research, 99, XXX-541 p. (Dictionary of literary biography, 200).

1419. Anarchisme et création littéraire. Actes du Colloque de la Société d'histoire littéraire de la France, Paris, 28 novembre 1998. Revue d'histoire littéraire de la France, 99, 99, 3, p. 371-525.

1420. BALDERSTON (Daniel), GALLO (Gastón), HELFT (Nicolás). Borges: una enciclopedía. Barcelona y Buenos Aires, Grupo Editorial Norma, 99, 372 p.

1421. Cambridge Companion (The) to Ockham. Ed. by Paul Vincent SPADE. Cambridge, Cambridge U. P., 99, XVII-420 p. (Cambridge Companions to philosophy).

1422. Cambridge guide (The) to women's writing in English. Ed. by Lorna SAGE. Cambridge, Cambridge U. P., 99, VIII-696 p.

1423. Cambridge history (The) of medieval English literature. Ed. by David WALLACE. Cambridge, Cambridge U. P., 99, XXV-1043 p. (The New Cambridge History of English Literature).

1424. CASTRO (Silvana). Breve diccionario biográfico de autores argentinos: desde 1940. Dirección y crítica literaria, Pedro ORGAMBIDE. Buenos Aires, Ediciones Atril, 99, 237 p.

1425. Companion (A) to Shakespeare. Ed. by David Scott KASTAN. Oxford, Blackwell Publishers, 99, XII-523 p. (Blackwell companions to literature and culture, 3).

1426. DEL MORAL (Rafael). Enciclopedia de la novela española. Prólogo de Andrés AMORÓS. Barcelona, Planeta, 99, 712 p. (Enciclopedias Planeta. Serie mayor).

1427. Deutsches Literatur-Lexicon: biographisch-bibliographisches Handbuch. Ergänzungsband VI: Maag–Ryslavy. Begründet von Wilhelm KOSCH; herausgegeben von Hubert HERKOMMER (Mittelalter) und Carl Ludwig LANG (Neuzeit). Bern, K.G. Saur, 99, XIV-635 p.

1428. Don Quijote dictionary. Compiled by Tom LATHROP. Newark, Juan de la Cuesta, 99, VI-150 p. (Juan de la Cuesta Hispanic monographs. Documentación cervantina, 17).

1429. ECO (U.). Riflessioni sulle tecniche di citazione nel medioevo. In: Ideologie e pratiche del reimpiego nell'alto Medioevo [Cf. n° 3458], p. 461-484.

1430. Ecrivain (L') et son éditeur. 2e Journée du 50e Congrès de l'Association internationale des études françaises. Cahiers de l' Association internationale des Etudes françaises, 99, 51, p. 179-205.

1431. Fremde (Das): Reiseerfahrungen, Schreibformen und kulturelles Wissen. Hrsg. v. Alexander HONOLD und Klaus R. SCHERPE; unter Mitarbeit von Stephan BLESSER, Markus JOCH und Oliver SIMONS. Bern u. Oxford, P. Lang, 99, 341 p. (Zeitschrift für Germanistik. Beiheft, 2).

1432. HOFMANN (H.). Odysseus: von Homer bis zu James Joyce. In: Antike Mythen [Cf. n° 1816], p. 27-67.

1433. Late-Victorian and Edwardian British novelists. Ed. by George M. JOHNSON. Detroit a. London, Gale Research, 99, XXIII-396 p. (Dictionary of literary biography, 197).

1434. Littérature et politique: France/Allemagne. Actes du Colloque de Grenoble, 14–15 novembre 1997. Textes recueillis et préséntes par Jean SERROY. Recherches et travaux, 99, 56, 232 p.

1435. Medieval Japanese writers. Ed. by Steven D. CARTER. Detroit a. London, Gale Research, 99, XXII-378 p. (Dictionary of literary biography, 203).

1436. MUKHERJEE (Sujit). A dictionary of Indian literature. Hyderabad, Orient Longman, 99, [s. p.].

1437. Mythe (Le) d'Orphée au XIXe et au XXe siècle. Actes du Colloque de la Sorbonne organisé par Pierre BRUNEL en octobre 1998, avec la collab. de Anna-Maria BABBI et Martine BERCOT. *Revue de litterature. comparee,* 99, 73, 4, p. 445-657.

1438. Oxford companion (The) to crime and mystery writing. Editor in chief, Rosemary HERBERT; editors, Catherine AIRD and John M. REILLY; consulting editor, Susan OLEKSIW. New York a. Oxford, Oxford U. P., 99, XXIII-535 p.

1439. Paradoxe (Le) du héros ou d'Homère à Malraux. Ed. par J. DION. Nancy et Paris, de Boccard, 99, 199 p. [Cf. n^{os} <sélection> 2608, 2712, 2724.]

1440. Russian literature in the age of Pushkin and Gogol. Ed. by Christine A. RYDEL. Detroit, Gale Research, 99, XXV-432 p. (Dictionary of literary biography, 198).

1441. Search (In) of Sunjata: the mande oral epic as history, literature, and performance. Ed. by Ralph A. AUSTEN. Bloomington, Indiana U. P., 99, 349 p.

1442. SINNREICH-LEVI (Deborah M.), LAURIE (Ian S.). Literature of the French and Occitan Middle Ages: eleventh to fifteenth centuries. Detroit a. London, Gale Group, 99, XXI-440 p. (ill.). (Dictionary of literary biography, 208).

1443. STABLEFORD (Brian M.). The dictionary of science fiction places. New York, Wonderland Press, 99, 384 p.

1444. Twentieth-century American Western writers. Ed. by Richard H. CRACROFT. Detroit, Gale Research, 99, XVIII-374 p. (Dictionary of literary biography, 212).

1445. VIDAL (César). Enciclopedia del Quijote. Barcelona, Planeta, 99, 682 p. (Enciclopedias Planeta).

Cf. n°s 1826, 3523, 3642, 5017, 8099

C

PREHISTORY

§ 1. General. 1446-1483. – § 2. Palaeolithic and Mesolithic. 1484-1513. – § 3. Neolithic. 1514-1525. – § 4. Bronze age. 1526-1541. – § 5. Iron age. 1542-1561.

§ 1. General.

1446. Atti del XVII Convegno nazionale sulla preistoria-protostoria-storia della Daunia. A cura di A. GRAVINA. S. Severo, Città, 99, 461 p.

1447. BAKKER (J.A.), KRUK (J.), LANTING (A.E.), MILISAUSKAS (S.). The earliest evidence of wheeled vehicles in Europe and the Near East. *Antiquity*, 99, 73, p. 778-790.

1448. BARREIRO MARTÍNEZ (D.), VILLOCH VÁZQUEZ (V.), CRIADO BOADO (F.). El desarollo de tecnologías para la gestión del Patrimonio Arqueológico: hacia un modelo de evaluación de impacto arqueológico. *Trabajos de prehistoria*, 99, 56, 1, p. 13-26.

1449. BERROCAL (M.C.), GOITRE SAMANIEGO (J.), LEAL VALLADARES (J.G.), LÓPEZ DOMÍNGUEZ (M.). Crítica al estudio del Arte Levantino desde una perspectiva bibliométrica. *Trabajos de prehistoria*, 99, 56, 1, p. 53-75.

1450. BRADLEY (R.), FÁBREGAS VALCARCE (R.). La 'ley de la frontera': grupos rupestres galaico y esquemático y Prehistoria del Noroeste de la Península Ibérica. *Trabajos de prehistoria*, 99, 56, 1, p. 103-114.

1451. BULL (I.D.), SIMPSON (I.A.), VAN BERGEN (P.F.), EVERSHED (R.P.). Muck 'n' molecules: organic geochemical methods for detecting ancient manuring. *Antiquity*, 99, 73, p. 86-96.

1452. BUXEDA I GARRIGÓS (J.), CAU ONTIVEROS (M.A.), GRACIA ALONSO (F.). Caracterización arqueométrica de la cerámica ática del palacio-santuario de Cancho Roano (Zalamea de la Serena, Badajoz). *Trabajos de prehistoria*, 99, 56, 1, p. 157-168.

1453. CERDÀ I JUAN (D.). El vi en l'ager pollentinus i en el seu entorn. Palma de Mallorca, Consell de Mallorca, 99, 223 p.

1454. COHEN (C.). L'homme des origines. Savoirs et fictions en préhistoire. Paris, Seuil, 99, 314 p.

1455. Evrazijskaja lesostep' v epokhu metalla. (The forest-steppe zone of Eurasia in the Age of Metal). Ed. A.D. PRJAKHIN. Voronezh, Izd-vo Voronezhskogo gos. un-ta, 99, 152 p. (ill., bibl.). (Arkheologija Vostochnoevropejskoj lesostepi, 13).

1456. FRITZ (C.). La gravure dans l'art mobilier magdalénien, du geste à la représentation. Contribution de l'analyse microscopique. Paris, Éditions de la Maison des Sciences de l'Homme, 99, 217 p.

1457. GREENE (K.). V. Gordon Childe and the vocabulary of revolutionary change. *Antiquity*, 99, 73, p. 97-109.

1458. HERNANDO (A.). Percepción de la realidad y Prehistoria. Relación entre la construcción de la identidad y la complejidad socio-económica en los grupos humanos. *Trabajos de prehistoria*, 99, 56, 2, p. 19-35.

1459. HØJ (Dan). Bue og pil: fra Danmarks sten-, bronze- og jernalder. (Arc et flèche: néolithique, âges du bronze et du fer au Danemark). Broager, Danage Target, 99, 82 p. (ill.).

1460. Issledovanija po arkheologii severa Dal'nego Vostoka. (Archeological investigations of Northern Far East: [Paleolithic and Neolithic]). RAN, Dal'nevost. otd., Severo-Vost. nauch. tsentr; Severo-Vost. kompleksnyj nauch.-issled. in-t. Magadan, [s. n.], 99, 147 p. (ill., bibl.).

1461. JAMES (S.). The Atlantic Celts: ancient people or modern invention? London, British Museum, 99, 160 p. (fig.).

1462. Kompleksnye obshchestva Tsentral'noj Evrasii v III–I tys. do n.e.: Regional'nye osobennosti v svete universal'nykh modelej: Mat-ly k mezhdunar. konf. (Complex societies of central Eurasia in III–I millennia BC: regional specifics in the light of global models: materials for the conf., Aug. 25–Sept. 2). Cheljabinsk, Arkaim, [s. n.], 99, 361 p. [Text parallel in Russian and in English]

1463. LANTING (J.N.), BRINDLEY (A.L.). Fechando hueso cremado: la base científica. *Trabajos de prehistoria*, 99, 56, 2, p. 137-140.

1464. LORBLANCHET (M.). La naissance de l'art. Genèse de l'art préhistorique. Paris, Éditions Errance, 99, 304 p.

1465. MAC GLADE (J.). Arqueología dinámica no lineal y discurso histórico. *Trabajos de prehistoria*, 99, 56, 2, p. 5-18.

1466. Mégalithisme de l'Atlantique à l'Ethiopie. Ed. par J. GUILAINE. Paris, Éditions Errance, 99, 224 p.

1467. MUÑOZ IBÁÑEZ (F.J.). Algunas consideraciones sobre el inicio de la arquería prehistórica. *Trabajos de prehistoria*, 99, 56, 1, p. 27-40.

1468. ÖKSE (Tuba). Yukarı Kızılırmak havzası tunç çağları yerleşim tarihi (Siedlungsgeschichte des Oberen Kızılırmak-Gebietes von der Frühbronze- bis zur Eisenzeit). Ankara, Türk Tarih Kurumu, 99, 28 p.

1469. PIANA (E.L.), ORQUERA (L.A.). Il processo di adattamento umano nel canale Beagle (Terra del Fuoco). *Bullettino di paletnologia italiana*, 99, 90, p. 209-277.

1470. Pogrebal'nyj obrjad. Rekonstruktsija i interpretatsija drevnikh ideologicheskikh predstavlenij: Sb. st. (Funeral ritual: reconstruction and interpretation of ancient ideology: [Articles]). Moskva, Vostochnaja literatura, 99, 248 p. (ill., bibl.).

1471. Primeras etapas metalúrgica (Las) en la Península Ibérica. II. Estudios regionales. Ed. por G. DELIBES y I. MONTERO. Madrid, Instituto Universitario Ortega y Gasset, 99, 357 p.

1472. REITZ (E.J.), WING (E.S.). Zooarchaeology. Cambridge, Cambridge U. P., 99, XIX-455 p. (fig., tables).

1473. ROVIRA (S.). Una propuesta metodológica para el estudio de la metalurgia prehistórica: el caso de Gorny en la región de Kargaly (Orenburg, Rusia). *Trabajos de prehistoria*, 99, 56, 2, p. 85-113.

1474. RUGGLES (C.). Astronomy in prehistoric Britain and Ireland. New Haven & London, Yale U. P., 99, XI-286 p.

1475. STAPERT (D.), JOHANSEN (L.). Flint and pyrite: making fire in the Stone Age. *Antiquity*, 99, 73, p. 765-777.

1476. STEVENSON (C.M.), WOZNIAK (J.), HAOA (S.). Prehistoric agricultural production on Easter Island (Rapa Nui), Chile. *Antiquity*, 99, 73, p. 801-812.

1477. STONE (T.). The chaos of collapse: disintegration and reintegration of interregional systems. *Antiquity*, 99, 73, p. 110-118.

1478. THOMPSON (M.), RENFREW (C.). The catalogues of the Pitt-Rivers Museum, Farnham, Dorset. *Antiquity*, 99, 73, p. 377-393.

1479. TRÉMENT (F.). Archéologie d'un paysage. Les etangs de Saint-Blaise (Bouches-du-Rhône). Paris, Éditions de la Maison des Sciences de l'Homme, 99, 314 p. (ill., plan.pleg.).

1480. TUNZI SISTO (A.M.). Ipogei della Daunia. Preistoria di un territorio. Foggia, Grenzi editore, 319 p.

1481. UFUK (Esin). Some archaeological evindence from the Aşıklı excavations for climatic fluctuations in Central Anatolia during the early holocene 10./9. mill. B. P. (1 table, 7 figs). *Anadolu Araştırmaları*, 99, 14, 1-26.

1482. Unravelling the landscape: an inquisitive approach to archaeology. Ed. by M. BOWDEN. Stroud a. Charleston, Tempus, 99, 223 p. (fig.).

1483. World prehistory: studies in memory of Grahame Clark. Ed. by John COLES, Robert BEWLEY and Paul MELLARS. New York, Oxford U. P., 99, XIII-246 p. (Proceedings of the British Academy, 99).

Cf. n° 974

§ 2. Palaeolithic and Mesolithic.

1484. AMMERMANN (A.J.), MAC CLENNEN (C.E.), DE MIN (M.), HOUSLEY (R.). Sea-level change and the archaeology of early Venice. *Antiquity*, 99, 73, p. 303-312.

1485. ATHENS (J.S.), WARD (J.V.). The late quaternary of the Western Amazon: climate, vegetation and humans. *Antiquity*, 99, 73, p. 287-302.

1486. BARTON (R.N.E.), CURRANT (A.P.), FERNANDEZ-JALVO (Y.), FINLAYSON (J.C.), GOLDBERG (P.), MAC PHAIL (R.), PETTITT (P.B.), STRINGER (C.B.). Gibraltar Neanderthals and results of recent excavations in Gohram's, Vanguard and Ibex Caves. *Antiquity*, 99, 73, p. 13-23.

1487. BELJAEVA (E.V.). Must'erskij mir Gubskogo Ushchel'ja (Severnyj Kavkaz). [Mousterian world of the Guba-Canyon (the Northern Caucasus)]. Sankt-Peterburg, [s. n.], 99, 216 p. (ill., bibl.). (RAN, In-t istroii material'noj kul'tury. Trudy. T. 1: "Paleolit Kavkaza", 2). [Eng. summary]

1488. BUENO RAMIREZ (P.), DE BALBÍN (R.), BARROSO (R.), ALCOLEA (J. J.), VILLA (R.), MORALEDA (A.). El dolmen de Navalcán. El poblamiento megalítico en el Guadyerbas. Toledo, Instituto Provincial de Investigationes y Estudios Toledanos, 99, 136 p.

1489. BUENO RAMÍREZ (P.), DE BALBÍN BEHRMANN (R.), BARROSO BERMEJO (R.), CASADO MATEOS (A.B.), AMPARO ALDECOA QUINTANA (M.). Proyecto de excavación y restauración en dólmenes de Alcántara (Cáceres). Segunda campaña. *Trabajos de prehistoria*, 99, 56, 1, p. 131-146.

1490. CALATTINI (M.), CRESTI (G.), PALMA DI CESNOLA (A.). L'industria acheuleana di Masseria Tiberio nel Gargano. *Bullettino di paletnologia italiana*, 99, 90, p. 1-59.

1491. CALVO GÓMEZ (F.), APPELLÁNÍZ (J.M.). La forma del arte paleolítico y la estadistica. Bilbao, Universidad de Deusto, 99, 388 p. (ill.).

1492. Excavations at the lower Palaeolithic site at East Farm, Barnham, Suffolk, 1989–1994. Ed. by N. ASHTON, S.G. LEWIS and S. PARFITT. London, British Museum, 99, VII-305 p.

1493. GONÇALVES (V.S.). Reguengos de Monsaraz, territórios magalíticos. Lisboa, Câmara municipal de Reguengos de Monsaraz, 99, 151 p.

1494. HOWARD (A.J.), MACKLIN (M.G.). A generic geomorphological approach to archaeological interpretation and prospection in British river valleys: a guide for archaeologists investigating Holocene landscapes. *Antiquity*, 99, 73, p. 527-541.

1495. IAKOLEVA (L.), PINÇON (G.). Un habitat orné en abri sous-roche au Magdalénien Moyen, Angles-sur-l'Anglin (Vienne, France). *Trabajos de prehistoria*, 99, 56, 1, p. 41-52.

1496. KAISER (T.), FORENBAHER (S.). Adriatic sailors and stone knappers: Palagruža in the 3rd millennium BC. *Antiquity*, 99, 73, p. 313-324.

1497. KOL'TSOV (Lev V.), ZHILIN (Mikhail G.). Mezolit Volgo-Okskogo mezhdurech'ja (Pamjatniki butovskoj kul'tury). (The Mesolith in the Volga-Oka River Basin: the monuments of the Butov culture). Moskva, Nauka, 99, 155 p. (ill., bibl.). [Eng. summary]

1498. KUHN (S.), STINER (M.C.), GÜLEÇ (E.). Initial Upper Palaeolithic in south-central Turkey and its regional context: a preliminary report. *Antiquity*, 99, 73, p. 505-517.

1499. LEIGHTON (R.). Sicily before history: an archaeological survey from the Palaeolithic to the Iron Age. London, Duckworth, 99, VIII-312 p. (ill., tables).

1500. MORWOOD (M.J.), AZIZ (F.), NASRUDDIN, HOBBS (D.R.), O'SULLIVAN (P.), RAZA (A.). Archaeological and palaeontological research in central Flores, east Indonesia: results of fieldwork 1997–1998. *Antiquity*, 99, 73, p. 273-286.

1501. NADEL (D.), WERKER (E.). The oldest ever brush hut plant remains from Ohalo II, Jordan Valley, Israel (19000 BP). *Antiquity*, 99, 73, p. 755-764.

1502. OLÀRIA (C.). Cova Matutano (Villafamés, Castellón). Un modelo ocupacional del magdaleniense superior final en la vertiente mediterránea peninsular. Castelló, Servei d'Investigacions Arqueològiques i Preistóriques, 99, 455 p. (ill.).

1503. PAILLET (P.). Le bison dans les arts magdaléniens du Périgord. Paris, CNRS, 99, 475 p.

1504. RIPOLL LÓPEZ (S.), RIPOLL PERELLÓ (E.), COLLADO GIRALDO (H.), MAS CORNELLÁ (M.), JORDÁ PARDO (J.F.), LABORATORIO DE ESTUDIOS PALEOLÍTICOS. Maltravieso. El santuario extremeño de las manos. *Trabajos de prehistoria*, 99, 56, 2, p. 59-84.

1505. RUBINOS PÉREZ (A.), FÁBREGAS VALCARCE (R.), ALONSO MATHIAS (F.), CONCHEIRO COELLO (A.). Las fechas C-14 del castro de O Achadizo (Boiro, A Coruña): problamática de la calibración de conchas marinas. *Trabajos de prehistoria*, 99, 56, 1, p. 147-155.

1506. SÁNCHEZ MARCO (A.). Nuevas aves fósiles del yacimiento mesopleistocénico de Ambrona (Soria, España). *Trabajos de prehistoria*, 99, 56, 1, p. 115-118.

1507. SHENNAN (S.). Cost, benefit and value in the organization of early European copper production. *Antiquity*, 99, 73, p. 352-363.

1508. STINER (M.C.). Palaeolithic mollusc exploitation at Riparo Mochi (Balzi Rossi, Italy): food and ornaments from the Aurignacian through Epigravettian. *Antiquity*, 99, 73, p. 735-754.

1509. STREET (M.), TERBERGER (TH.). The last Pleniglacial and the human settlement of Central Europe: new information from the Rhineland of Wiesbaden-Igstadt. *Antiquity*, 99, 73, p. 259-272.

1510. VAQUERO (M.). Intrasite spatial organization of lithic production in the Middle Palaeolithic: the evidence of the Abric Romaní (Capellades, Spain). *Antiquity*, 99, 73, p. 493-504. – IDEM. Variabilidad de las estrategias de talla y cambio tecnológico en el Paleolítico Medio del Abric Romaní (Capellades, Barcelona). *Trabajos de prehistoria*, 99, 56, 2, p. 36-58.

1511. VOLOKITIN (Aleksandr V.), KOSINSKAJA (Lubov' L.). Mezoliticheskie zhilishcha Evropejskogo Severo-Vostoka. (Mesolithic dwellings of the European North-East). Syktyvkar, [s. n.], 99, 36 p. (ill., bibl.). (Nauchnye doklady Ural'skogo Otd. RAN, 414).

1512. WATSON (A.), KEATING (D.). Architecture and sound: an acoustic analysis of megalithic monuments in prehistoric Britain. *Antiquity*, 99, 73, p. 325-336.

1513. WEBER (S.). Seeds of urbanism: palaeoethnobotany and the Indus civilization. *Antiquity*, 99, 73, p. 813-826.

Cf. n° 1460

§ 3. Neolithic.

1514. AURENCHE (O.), KOZLOWSKI (S.K.). La naissance du Néolitique au Proche Orient. Paris, Éditions Errance, 99, 256 p.

1515. BUENO RAMÍREZ (P.), DE BALBÍN BEHRMANN (R.), BARROSO BERMEJO (R.), ROJAS RODRÍGUEZ-MALO (J.M.), VILLA GONZALEZ (R.), FÉLIX LÓPEZ (R.), ROVIRA LLORENS (S.). Neolítico y Calcolítico en Huecas (Toledo): el túmulo de Castillejo. Campaña de 1998. *Trabajos de prehistoria*, 99, 56, 2, p. 141-160.

1516. CLOSE (A.E.). Distance and decay: an uneasy relationship. *Antiquity*, 99, 73, p. 24-32.

1517. CONOLLY (J.). Technical strategies and technical change at Neolithic Çatalhöyük, Turkey. *Antiquity*, 99, 73, p. 791-800.

1518. FRIIS-HANSEN (Jan). Brugen af pil og spyd i Europas stenålder. (L'usage de la flèche et de la lance pendant l'âge de pierre en Europe). Horsholm, Dansk Jagt- og skovbrugsmuseum, 99, 48 p. (ill.). (Jagt og Skov, 1). [English summary].

1519. KOHN (M.), MITHEN (S.). Handaxes: products of sexual selection? *Antiquity*, 99, 73, p. 518-526.

1520. MASHKOUR (M.), FONTUGNE (M.), HATTE (C.). Investigations on the evolution of subsistence economy in the Qazvin Plain (Iran) from the Neolithic to the Iron Age. *Antiquity*, 99, 73, p. 65-76.

1521. MONTERO RUIZ (I.), RIHUETE HERRADA (C.), RUIZ TABOADA (A.). Precisiones sobre el enterramiento colectico neolítico de Cerro Virtud (Cuevas de Almanzora, Almería). *Trabajos de prehistoria*, 99, 56, 1, p. 119-130.

1522. MYL'NIKOVA (Ljudmila N.). Goncharstvo neoliticheskikh plemen Nizhnego Amura (po materialam poselenija Kondon-Pochta). (The pottery of the Lower Amur Neolithic tribes: the settlement of Kondon-Pochta). Novosibirsk, Izd-vo In-ta arkheologii i etnografii SO RAN, 99, 160 p. (ill., bibl. p. 83-95). [Eng. summary]

1523. POLLEX (A.). Comments on the interpretation of the so-called cattle burials of Neolithic Central Europe. *Antiquity*, 99, 73, p. 542-550.

1524. VEGAS ARAMBURU (J.I.). El enterramiento neolítico de San Juan Ante Portam Latinam. Vitoria-Gasteiz, Museo de Arqueología de Álava, 99, 129 p.

1525. ZAFRA DE LA TORRE (N.), HORNOS MATA (F.), CASTRO LÓPEZ (M.). Una macro-aldea en el origen del modo de vida campesino: Marroquíes Bajos (Jaén) c. 2500-2000 cal. ANE. *Trabajos de prehistoria*, 99, 56, 1, p. 77-102.

Cf. n°s 1039, 1460

§ 4. Bronze age.

1526. BONDIOLI (L.), MACCHIARELLI (R.), SALVADEI (L.). I resti umani ossei e dentari. *Bullettino di paletnologia italiana*, 99, 90, p. 152-159.

1527. CARANCINI (G.L.), PERONI (R.). L'età del bronzo in Italia: per la cronologia della produzione metallurgica. Perugia, Alieno, 99, 86 p. (tables, ill.).

1528. CASTRO (P.V.), CHAPMAN (R.W.), GILI (S.), LULL (V.), MICÓ (R.), RIHUETE (C.), RISCH (R.), SANAHUJA (M.E.). Agricultural production and social change in the Bronze Age of southeast Spain: the Gatas Project. *Antiquity*, 99, 73, p. 846-856.

1529. COLES (J.M.), LEACH (P.), MINNITT (S.C.), TABOR (R.), WILSON (A.S.). A later Bronze Age shield from South Cadbury, Somerset, England. *Antiquity*, 99, 73, p. 33-48.

1530. DELIBES DE CASTRO (G.), FERNÁNDEZ MANZANO (J.), FONTANEDA PÉREZ (E.), ROVIRA LLORENS (S.). Metalurgia de la Edad del Bronce en el piedemonte meridional de la Cordillera Cantábrica: la Colección Fontaneda. Valladolid, Junta de Castilla y León, 99, 209 p.

1531. FUGAZZOLA DELPINO (M. A.), PELLEGRINI (E.). Il complesso cultuale "campaniforme" di Fosso Conicchio (Viterbo). *Bullettino di paletnologia italiana*, 99, 90, p. 61-151.

1532. GARCÍA (J. F. F.). La transición del Bronce Final al Hierro I en el Sur de la Meseta Norte. Nuevos datos para su sistemazión. *Trabajos de prehistoria*, 99, 56, 2, p. 161-180.

1533. GARCÍA SANJUÁN (L.). Expressions of inequality: settlement patterns, economy and social organization in the southwest Iberian Bronze Age (c. 1700-1100 BC). *Antiquity*, 99, 73, p. 337-351.

1534. GUNEL (S.). Vorbericht über die mittel- und spätbronzezeitliche Keramik vom Liman Tepe. *Istanbuler Mitteilungen*, 99, 49, p. 41-82.

1535. KIJASHKO (Aleksej V.). Proiskhozhdenie katakombnoj kul'tury Nizhnego Podon'ja. (The origin of the lower Don catacomb culture). Volgograd, Izd-vo Volgogradskogo gos. un-ta, 99, 182 p. (ill., bibl.).

1536. MEDEROS MARTÍN (A.). La metamorfosis de Villena. Comercio de oro, estaño y sal durante el Bronce Final I entre el Atlántico y el Mediterráneo (1625-1300 AC). *Trabajos de prehistoria*, 99, 56, 2, p. 115-136.

1537. RIEHL (S.). Bronze Age environment and economy in the Troad: the archaeobotany of Kumtepe and Troy. Tübingen, Mo-Vince-Verlag, 99, XI-268 p. (ill.).

1538. Spiralens öga. Tjugo artiklar kring aktuell bronsålderforskning. (L'œil de la spirale. Vingt articles sur l'état actuel de la recherche sur l'âge du bronze). Red. par Michael OLAUSSON. Stockholm, Riksantivarieämbetet, 99, 406 p. (ill.). (Skrifter. Riksantivarieämbetet. Arkeologiska undersökningar, 25). (rés. anglais).

1539. THRANE (H.). Pots and peoples-once again. The goblets from the Bronze Age settlement at Tepe Guran, Luristan. *Iranica antiqua*, 99, 34, p. 21-40.

1540. VENTURINO GAMBARI (M.). In riva al fiume Eridano: una necropoli dell'età del Bronzo finale a Morano sul Po. Alessandria, Edizioni dell'Orso, 99, 171 p. (ill.).

1541. WEBB (J. M.), FRANKEL (D.). Characterizing the Philia faces: material culture, chronology and the origin of the Bronze Age in Cyprus. *American journal of archaeology*, 99, 103, p. 3-43.

Cf. n°s 1039, 1455, 1462

§ 5. Iron age.

1542. ANDRUKH (Svetlana I.), TOSHCHEV (Gennadij N.). Mogil'nik Mamaj-Gora. (Burial ground Mamay-Gora, [generally Scythian]) Part 1. Zaporozh'e, [s. n.], 99, 232 p. (ill., bibl.).

1543. BAHAR (H.). The Konya region in the Iron Age and its relations with Cilicia. *Anatolian studies*, 99, 49, p. 1-10.

1544. BILGI (Ö). İkiztepe in the late Iron Age. *Anatolian studies*, 99, 49, p. 27-54.

1545. BUDANOVA (Vera P.), GORSKIJ (Anton A.), ERMOLOVA (Irina E.). Velikoe pereselenie narodov: Etnopoliticheskie i sotsial'nye aspekty. (The great migration: ethno-political and social aspects). RAN, In-t rossijskoj istorii. Moskva, [s. n.], 99, 347 p. (bibl., ind.).

1546. CRESPIN (A.-S.). Between Phrygia and Cilicia: the Porsuk area and the beginning of the Iron Age. *Anatolian studies*, 99, 49, p. 61-71.

1547. FAUST (A.). Differences in family structure between cities and village in Iron Age II. *Tel Aviv*, 99, 26, p. 233-252.

1548. HANSEN (C.K.), POSTGATE (J.N.). The Bronze to Iron Age transition at Kilise Tepe. *Anatolian studies*, 99, 49, p. 111-121.

1549. HEY (G.), BAYLISS (A.), BOYLE (A.). Iron Age inhumation burials at Yarnton, Oxfordshire. *Antiquity*, 99, 73, p. 551-562.

1550. Itogi izuchenija skifskoj epokhi Altaja i sopredel'nykh territorij. (The results of Altai and neighbouring territories Scythian epoch study). Eds. Ju. F. KIRJUSHIN, A. A. TISHKIN. Barnaul, Izd-vo Altajskogo gos. un-ta, 99, 284 p. (ill., bibl.).

1551. JARVA (Eero). A look at ankles: two bronze rings from Roman Iron Age necropolis of Tervakangas (Raahe) in Northern Ostrobothnia. *Faravid*, 98-99, 22-23, p. 95-106. (ill., maps).

1552. KOLTUKHOV (Sergej G.). Ukreplenija Krymskoj Skifii. (Fortifications of the Crimean Scythia). NAN Ukrainy, Krymskij filial, In-t arkheologii. Simferopol', Sonat, 99, 221 p. (ill., bibl.).

1553. KRUTA PUPPI (L.). Le arti del fuoco dei Celti: ceramica, ferro, bronzo e vetro nella Champagne dal V al I secolo a.C. Sceaux Cedex, Kronos B.Y., 99, 148 p. (ill.).

1554. LAMBERG-KARLOVSKY (C.C.), MAGEE (P.). The Iron Age platforms at Tepe Yahya. *Iranica antiqua*, 99, 34, p. 41-52.

1555. MEDVEDEV (Aleksandr P.). Rannij zheleznyj vek lesostepnogo Podon'ja. Arkheologija i etnokul'turnaja istorija I tys. do d.e. (The early Iron Age of the Don forest-steppe region: Archaeology and ethno-cultural history, the 1st millenium B.C.). Moskva, Nauka, 99, 160 p. (ill., bibl.).

1556. MORGENROTH (U.). Southern Iberia and the Mediterranean trade-routes. *Oxford journal of archaeology*, 99, 18, p. 395-401.

1557. MYL'NIKOV (Vladimir P.). Obrabotka dereva nositeljami pazyrykskoj kul'tury. (Woodworking in Pazyryk culture, [Altai]). Novosibirsk, Izd-vo In-ta arkheologii i etnografii SO RAN, 99, 232 p. (ill., bibl. p. 45-49). [Eng. summary]

1558. RYSTEDT (E.). No words, only pictures: iconography in the transition between the Bronze Age and the Iron Age in Greece. *Opuscula Atheniensia*, 99, 24, p. 89-98.

1559. SAGONA (A.). The Bronze Age-Iron Age transition in northeast Anatolia: a view from Sos Höyük. *Anatolian studies*, 99, 49, p. 153-157.

1560. YALÇIN (Ü.). Early iron metallurgy in Anatolia. *Anatolian studies*, 99, 49, p. 177-187.

1561. YEZERSKI (I.). Burial cave distribution and the borders of the kingdom of Judah toward the end of the Iron Age. *Tel Aviv*, 99, 26, p. 253-270.

Cf. n°s 357, 974, 1039, 1043, 1455, 1462, 1566, 3149, 3215, 8070, 8071

D

THE ANCIENT EAST
(the Hellenistic states included)

§ 1. General. 1562-1576. – § 2. The Near East. 1577-1610. – § 3. Egypt. 1611-1661. – § 4. Mesopotamia. 1662-1720. – § 5. Hittites. 1721-1743. – § 6. Jews and Semitic peoples to the end of the ancient world. 1744-1780. – § 7. Iran. 1781-1812.

§ 1. General.

1562. ASCALONE (E.), PEYRONEL (L.). Typological and quantitative approach to the ancient weight system. Susa, Persian Gulf and Indus Valley from the end of the III mill. to the beginning of the II mill. BC. *Altorientalische Forschungen*, 99, 26, p. 352-376.

1563. BLÁZQUEZ (J.M.). Mitos, dioses, héroes en el Mediterráneo antiguo. Madrid, Real Academia de la Historia, 99, 382 p.

1564. BONNET (H.). On understanding syncretism (translated by J. Baines). *Orientalia*, 99, 68, p. 181-198.

1565. BRESSON (A.). Cnide à l'époque classique: la cité et ses villes. *Revue des études anciennes*, 99, 101, p. 83-114.

1566. Drevnejshie gosudarstva Vostochnoj Evropy. (The earliest states of Eastern Europe), 1996–1997 gg.: Severnoe Prichernomor'e v antichnosti: Voprosy istochnikovedenija. (The North Black sea region in antiquity: articles on criticism of sources). Ed. Aleksandr V. PODOSINOV. RAN, In-t vseobshchej istorii, In-t rossijskoj istorii. Moskva, Vostochnaja literatura, 99, 399 p. (bibl., selected bibliography on the region in antiquity, p. 373-391).

1567. KOSE (A.). Alter Orient und Ägypten. *In*: Geschichte des Wohnens [Cf. n° 1166], p. 13-85.

1568. LUND (J.). Trade patterns in the Levant from ca. 100 BC to AD 200 as reflected by the distribution of ceramic fine wares in Cyprus. *Münstersche Beiträge zur antiken Handelsgeschichte*, 99, 18, p. 1-22.

1569. MAC GINNIS (J.). Additional prebend texts from the British Museum. *Altorientalische Forschungen*, 99, 26, p. 3-12.

1570. MAISELS (C. K.). Early civilizations of the old world: the formative histories of Egypt, the Levant, Mesopotamia, India and China. London a. New York, Routledge, 99, XVI-479 p. (fig.).

1571. NAGEL (W.), BOLLWEG (J.), STROMMENGER (E.). Der 'onager' in der Antike und die Herkunft des Hausesels. *Altorientalische Forschungen*, 99, 26, p. 154-202.

1572. PARKER (K.). Early modern tales of Orient: a critical anthology. London a. New York, Routledge, 99, IX-290 p.

1573. PARKER (V.). Zum Text des Tauagalauaš-Briefes: Ahhiiaua-Frage und Textkritik. *Orientalia*, 99, 68, p. 61-83.

1574. SEIDL (U.). Orientalische Bleche in Olympia. *Zeitschrift für Assyriologie und vorderasiatische Archäologie*, 99, 89, p. 269-282.

1575. STRECK (M. P.). Texte aus Münchener Sammlungen. *Zeitschrift für Assyriologie und vorderasiatische Archäologie*, 99, 89, p. 29-35.

1576. VAN DE MIEROOP (M.). Cuneiform texts and the writing of history. London a. New York, Routledge, 99, IX-196 p.

Cf. n°s 357, 555, 1043, 8099

§ 2. The Near East.

1577. ÇILINGIROĞLU (A.), SALVINI (M.). When was the castle of Ayanis built and what is the meaning of the word 'šuri'? *Anatolian studies*, 99, 49, p. 55-60.

1578. DEN DRIESCH (A. von), PETERS (J.). Vorläufiger Bericht über die archäozoologischen Untersuchungen am Göbekli Tepe und Gürcütepe bei Urfa, Türkei. *Istanbuler Mitteilungen*, 99, 49, p. 23-39.

1579. DERIN (Z.). Potters' marks of Ayanis citadel, Van. *Anatolian studies*, 99, 49, p. 81-100.

1580. DMITRIEV (S.). Three notes on Attalid history. *Klio*, 99, 81, p. 397-411.

1581. EHRINGHAUS (H.), BÜRGLE (M.), HAIDER (P. W.), MASCH (L.), REITMAIER (Th.), RIEDMAN (N.), TOCHTERLE (U.), TORGGLER (A.). Vorläufiger Bericht über die Ausgrabung auf dem Sirkeli Höyük, Provinz Adana/ Türkei im Jahre 1997. *Istanbuler Mitteilungen*, 99, 49, p. 83-140.

1582. FAIZER (R. S.). The issue of authenticity regarding the traditions of al-Wāqidī as established in his Kitāb al-Maghāzī. *Journal of Near Eastern studies*, 99, 58, p. 97-106.

1583. FOOTE (R. M.). Frescoes and carved ivory from the Abbasid family homestead at Humeima. *Journal of Roman archaeology*, 99, 12, p. 423-428.

1584. GARRISON (M. B.), DION (P.). The seal of Ariyāramna in the Royal Ontario Museum, Toronto. *Journal of Near Eastern studies*, 99, 58, p. 1-17.

1585. HABICHT (C.). Zu griechischen Inschriften aus Kleinasien. *Epigraphica Anatolica*, 99, 31, p. 19-29.

1586. HELD (W.), BERGER (A.), HERDA (A.). Loryma in Karien. Vorbericht über die Kampagnen 1995 und 1998. *Istanbuler Mitteilungen*, 99, 49, p. 159-196.

1587. JACOBS (B.), SCHÜTTE-MAISCHATZ (A.). Statuette eines Adligen aus der nördlichen Osroëne. *Istanbuler Mitteilungen*, 99, 49, p. 431-442.

1588. JAPP (S.). Frühromische dünnwandige Hartware. *Istanbuler Mitteilungen*, 99, 49, p. 301-331.

1589. KARAMUT (I.), RUSSELL (J.). Nephelis: a recently discovered town of coastal Rough Cilicia. *Journal of Roman archaeology*, 99, 12, p. 355-371.

1590. KONRAD (M.). Research on the Roman and early Byzantine frontier in North Syria. *Journal of Roman archaeology*, 99, 12, p. 392-410.

1591. LANCELLOTTI (M.G.). Adamna, Adamma o Adamas? A proposito di Hipp. Ref. V 9,8. *Studi e materiali di storia delle religioni*, 99, 65, p. 157-179.

1592. LANG-AUINGER (C.). Die Terrakottagruppe Eros und Psyche aus dem Hanghaus in Ephesos und das Gegenstück aus Berlin – Beide aus derselben Werkstatt? *Istanbuler Mitteilungen*, 99, 49, p. 363-375.

1593. LEICK (G.). Who's who in the ancient Near East. London & New York, Routledge, 99, XX-229 p.

1594. LUTHER (A.). Das Datum des Orpheus-Mosaiks aus Urfa. *Die Welt des Orients*, 99, 30, p. 129-137. – IDEM. Die ersten Könige von Osrhoene. *Klio*, 99, 81, p. 437-454. – IDEM. Elias von Nisibis und die Chronologie der edessenischen Könige. *Klio*, 99, 81, p. 180-198.

1595. MA (J.). Antiochos III and the cities of western Asia Minor. Oxford, Oxford U. P., 99, XVII-403 p.

1596. MIETKE (G.), WESTPHALEN (S.). Basilika 3 in Kanlidivane (Kanytelis). *Istanbuler Mitteilungen*, 99, 49, p. 517-526.

1597. MÜLLER (U.). Die eisenzeitliche Stratigraphie von Lidar Höyük. *Anatolian studies*, 99, 49, p. 123-131.

1598. PARKER (A.). Northeastern Anatolia: on the periphery of empires. *Anatolian studies*, 99, 49, p. 133-141.

1599. PESCHLOW-BINDOKAT (A.). Das Straßennetz der Latmos. *In*: Stadt und Umland [Cf. n° 2257], p. 186-200.

1600. RHEIDT (K.). Ländlicher Kult und städtische Siedlung: Aizanoi in Phrygien. *In*: Stadt und Umland [Cf. n° 2257], p. 237-253.

1601. ROLLER (L. E.). Early Phrygian drawings from Gordion and the elements of Phrygian artistic style. *Anatolian studies*, 99, 49, p. 143-152.

1602. RUMSCHEID (F.). Mylasas Verteidigung: Burgen statt Stadtmauer? *In*: Stadt und Umland [Cf. n° 2257], p. 206-222.

1603. SAFRAN (J.M.). Ceremony and submission: the symbolic representation and recognition of legitimacy in tenth century al-Andalus. *Journal of Near Eastern studies*, 99, 58, p. 191-201.

1604. ŞAHIN (M.). Neue Beobachtungen zum Felsrelief von İvriz/Konya. Nicht in den Krieg, sondern zur Ernte: der Gott mit der Sichel. *Anatolian studies*, 99, 49, p. 165-176.

1605. SCHEMANN (M.). Beobachtungen an den Köpfen des sog. Psamathia-Reliefs in Berlin. *Istanbuler Mitteilungen*, 99, 49, p. 443-466.

1606. SCHIRMER (W.). Eine richtige Bergstadt? Die Bauanlagen auf dem Göllüdağ und ihre historischen Zugangswege. *In*: Stadt und Umland [Cf. n° 2257], p. 129-142.

1607. SCHMIDT (K.), DEN DRIESCH (A. von), PETERS (J.). Frühe Tier- und Menschenbilder vom Göbekli Tepe - Kampagnen 1995–1998. Ein kommentierter Katalog der Großplastik und der Reliefs. *Istanbuler Mitteilungen*, 99, 49, p. 5-21.

1608. VANDEPUT (L.), BÜYÜKKOLANCI (M.). Das Große Propylon in Kremna in Pisidien. *Istanbuler Mitteilungen*, 99, 49, p. 213-248.

1609. WULF (U.). Vom Herrensitz zur Metropole – zur Stadtenwicklung von Pergamon. *In*: Stadt und Umland [Cf. n° 2257], p. 33-49.

1610. XELLA (P.). Materiali per Adamma. Ricerche su una dea siro-anatolica. *Studi e materiali di storia delle religioni*, 99, 65, p. 19-30.

Cf. n° 8071

§ 3. Egypt.

1611. AMER (A. A. M. A.). The gateway of Ramesses IX in the temple of Amun at Karnak. Warminster, Aris & Phillips, 99, VII-43 p. (plates).

1612. AUDERHEIDE (A.C.), [et al.]. Human mummification practices at Ismant el-Kharab. *Journal of Egyptian archaeology*, 99, 85, p. 197-210.

1613. BAILEY (D. M.). A ghost palaestra at Antinoopolis. *Journal of Egyptian archaeology*, 99, 85, p. 235-239. – IDEM. Sebakh, sherds and survey. *Journal of Egyptian archaeology*, 99, 85, p. 211-218.

1614. BAINES (J.). Egyptian syncretism: Hans Bonnet's contribution. *Orientalia*, 99, 68, p. 199-214.

1615. BÁRTA (M.). The title "Priest of Heket" in the Egyptian old kingdom. *Journal of Near Eastern studies*, 99, 58, p. 107-116.

1616. BEIT-ARIEH (I.), GOPHNA (R.). The Egyptian Protodynastic (Late EB I) site at Tel Ma'ahaz: a reassessment. *Tel Aviv*, 99, 26, p. 191-207.

1617. BOGAERT (R.). Les opérations des banques de l'Égypte ptolémaique. *Ancient society*, 99, 29, p. 49-145.

1618. CIAMPINI (E. M.). La fenice, il serpente e il tempo. *Studi e materiali di storia delle religioni*, 99, 65, p. 31-40.

1619. CLAGETT (M.). Ancient Egyptian science. Vol. 3. Ancient Egyptian mathematics. Philadelphia, American Philosophical Society, 99, XII-462 p.

1620. COENEN (M.). A remarkable judgement scene in a "Document of breathing made by Isis": Papyrus Florence 3665-3666 and Papyrus Vienna 3850. *Orientalia*, 99, 68, p. 98-103.

1621. DODSON (A.). The decorative phases of the tomb of Sethos II and their historical implications. *Journal of Egyptian archaeology*, 99, 85, p. 131-142.

1622. EATON-KRASS (M.). The fate of Sennefer and Senetnay at Karnak temple and in the Valley of the Kings. *Journal of Egyptian archaeology*, 99, 85, p. 113-129.

1623. EDDY (F. W.), WENDORF (F.), [et al.]. An archaeological investigation of the central Sinai, Egypt. Niwot, University Press of Colorado/Cairo, XXI-340 p.

1624. FOURNET (J. L.). Hellénisme dans l'Égypte du VIe siècle. La bibliothèque et l'œuvre de Dioscore d'Aphrodité. Le Caire, Institut français d'archéologie orientale, 99, 2 vol., 735 p.

1625. GOUDSMIT (J.), BRANDON-JONES (D.). Mummies of olive baboons and barbary macaques in the baboon catacomb of the sacred animal necropolis at north Saqqara. *Journal of Egyptian archaeology*, 99, 85, p. 45-53.

1626. HIGGENBOTHAM (C.). The statue of Ramses III from Beth Shean. *Tel Aviv*, 99, 26, p. 225-232.

1627. IVANTCHIK (A. I.). Eine griechische Pseudo-Historie. Der Pharao Sesostris und der skytho-ägyptische Krieg. *Historia*, 99, 48, p. 395-441.

1628. JANSEN-WINKELN (K.). Gab es in der altägyptischen Geschichte eine feudalistische Epoche? *Die Welt des Orients*, 99, 30, p. 7-20.

1629. KAMRIN (J.). The Kosmos of Khnumhotep II at Beni Hasan. London a. New York, Kegan Paul International, 99, XIV-196 p.

1630. KRUSE (Th.). 'Katakrima'-Strafzahlung oder Steuer? Überlegungen zur Steuererhebung im römischen Ägypten in iulisch-claudischer Zeit anhand von P.Oxy. XLI 2971, SB XIV 11381, SPP IV p. 70-71, BGU VII 1613 und OGIS II 669. *Zeitschrift für Papyrologie und Epigraphik*, 99, 124, p. 157-190.

1631. LEAHY (A.). More fragments of the Book of the Dead of Padinemty. *Journal of Egyptian archaeology*, 99, 85, p. 230-232.

1632. LECLANT (J.), MINAULT-GOUT (A.). Fouilles et travaux en Égypte et au Soudan, 1997–1998. Première partie. *Orientalia*, 99, 68, p. 313-420.

1633. LIEVEN (A. VON). Divination in Ägypten. *Altorientalische Forschungen*, 99, 26, p. 77-126.

1634. LUNDSTRÖM (S.). Überlegungen zur ägyptischen Reichstriade ausgehend von Mittani-Brief I 74-80, 98-103 (EA 24). *Altorientalische Forschungen*, 99, 26, p. 322-351.

1635. MALAISE (M.), WINAND (J.). Grammaire raisonnée de l'égyptien classique. Liège, Université de Liège, 99, VI-866 p.

1636. MANNING (J.G.). The land-tenure regime in Ptolemaic upper Egypt. *In*: Agriculture in Egypt [Cf. n° 1144], p. 83-105.

1637. MATHIESON (I.), BETTLES (E.), DITTMER (J.), READER (C.). The National Museums of Scotland Saqqara survey project, Earth Sciences 1990–1998. *Journal of Egyptian archaeology*, 99, 85, p. 21-43.

1638. MESKELL (L.). Archaeologies of life and death. *American Journal of archaeology*, 99, 103, p. 181-199.

1639. PAMMINGER (P.). Hori, Hoherpriester des Amon. *Journal of Egyptian archaeology*, 99, 85, p. 226-230.

1640. PERDICOYIANNI-PALEOLOGU (H.). Les contrats d'apprentissage en provenance d'Oxyrhyncus. *Antiquité classique*, 99, 68, p. 150-169.

1641. PFROMMER (M.). Alexandria. Im Schatten der Pyramiden. Mainz am Rhein, Verlag Philipp von Zabern, 99, 148 p.

1642. PINCH-BROCK (L.). The real location of KV 'C'? *Journal of Egyptian archaeology*, 99, 85, p. 223-226.

1643. QUACK (J. F.). A new bilingual fragment from the British Museum (Papyrus BM EA 69574). *Journal of Egyptian archaeology*, 99, 85, p. 153-164.

1644. RAY (J. D.). The voice of authority: Papyrus Leiden I 382. *Journal of Egyptian archaeology*, 99, 85, p. 189-195.

1645. RICE (M.). Who's who in ancient Egypt. London a. New York, Routledge, 99, LXI-257 p.

1646. RIDGWAY (D.). The reabilitation of Bocchoris: notes and queries from Italy. *Journal of Egyptian archaeology*, 99, 85, p. 143-152.

1647. ROBINS (G.). The names of Hatshepsut as king. *Journal of Egyptian archaeology*, 99, 85, p. 103-112.

1648. ROSSI (C.). Note on the pyramidion found at Dahshur. *Journal of Egyptian archaeology*, 99, 85, p. 219-222.

1649. ROWLANDSON (J.). Agricultural tenancy and village society in Roman Egypt. *In*: Agriculture in Egypt [Cf. n° 1144], p. 139-158.

1650. SHARP (M.). The village of Theadelphia in the Fayyum: land and population in the second century. *In*: Agriculture in Egypt [Cf. n° 1144], p. 159-192.

1651. SHAW (I.), BUMBURRY (J.), JAMESON (R.). Emerald mining in Roman and Byzantine Egypt. *Journal of Roman archaeology*, 99, 12, p. 203-215.

1652. SOWADA (K. N.). Black-topped ware in early dynastic contexts. *Journal of Egyptian archaeology*, 99, 85, p. 85-102.

1653. SPENCER (N. A.). The epigraphic survey of Samanud. *Journal of Egyptian archaeology*, 99, 85, p. 55-83.

1654. THOMAS (S.). A saite figure of Isis in the Petrie Museum. *Journal of Egyptian archaeology*, 99, 85, p. 232-235.

1655. THOMPSON (D. J.). Irrigation and drainage in the early Ptolemaic Fayyum. *In*: Agriculture in Egypt [Cf. n° 1144], p. 107-122. – IDEM. New and old in Ptolemaic Egypt. *In*: Agriculture in Egypt [Cf. n° 1144], p. 123-138.

1656. VAN DER VLIET (J.) The church of the twelve Apostles: the earliest cathedral of Faras? *Orientalia*, 99, 68, p. 84-97.

1657. VENIT (M. S.). The Stagni painted Tomb: cultural interchange and gender differentiation in Roman Alexandria. *American Journal of archaeology*, 99, 103, p. 641-669.

1658. WATTERSON (B.). Amarna: ancient Egypt's age of revolution. Stroud a. Charleston, Tempus, 99, 160 p. (fig.).

1659. WIDMER (G.). Emphasizing and non-emphasizing second tenses in the "Myth of the Sun's Eye". *Journal of Egyptian archaeology*, 99, 85, p. 165-188.

1660. WILSON (P.), GALLORINI (C.), KIRBY (C.J.), KEMP (B.), NICHOLSON (P.T.). Fieldwork, 1998–1999: Sais, Memphis, Gebel el-Haridi, Tell el-Amarna glass project. *Journal of Egyptian archaeology*, 99, 85, p. 1-20.

1661. ZIERMANN (M.), FEUERSBACH (U.). Die ägyptische Stadt des 3. Jts. v.Chr. als Festung. *In*: Stadt und Umland [Cf. n° 2257], p. 63-89.

§ 4. Mesopotamia.

* 1662. FLEMING (D.). Chroniques bibliographiques: I. Recent works on Mari. *Revue d'assyriologie et d'archéologie orientale*, 99, 93, p. 157-174.

1663. AMIET (P.). Textes et monuments: à la recherche de concordances à propos des cachets de Bactriane. *Revue d'assyriologie et d'archéologie orientale*, 99, 93, p. 97-106.

1664. BEAL (R.). Seeking divine approval for campaign strategy. KUB 5,1-KUB 52,65. *Ktema*, 99, 24, p. 41-54.

1665. BEAULIEU (P.-A.). Un inventaire de joaillerie sacrée de l'Eanna d'Uruk. *Revue d'assyriologie et d'archéologie orientale*, 99, 93, p. 141-155.

1666. BELLI (O.). Dams, reservoirs and irrigation channels of the Van plain in the period of the Urartian kingdom. *Anatolian studies*, 99, 49, p. 11-26.

1667. BESNIER (M.-F.). La conception du jardin en Syro-Mésopotamie à partir des textes. *Ktema*, 99, 24, p. 195-212.

1668. BEST (R. M.). Noah's ark and the Ziusudra epic: Sumerian origins of the flood myth. Fort Myers, Enlil, 99, 303 p.

1669. BLOCHER (F.). Der Thronsaal Sargons II. Gestalt und Schicksal. *Altorientalische Forschungen*, 99, 26, p. 223-250.

1670. BUCHHOLZ (H. G.). Ugarit, Zypern und Ägäis: Kulturbeziehungen im zweiten Jahrtausend v. Chr. Münster, Ugarit Verlag, 99, XIII-812 p. (ill.).

1671. CANCIK-KIRSCHBAUM (E.). Nebenlinien des assyrischen Königshauses in der 2. Hälfte des 2. Jts. v. Chr. *Altorientalische Forschungen*, 99, 26, p. 210-222.

1672. COBB (P. M.). Al-Mutawakkil's Damascus: a new 'Abbāsid capital? *Journal of Near Eastern studies*, 99, 58, p. 241-257.

1673. D'ALFONSO (L.). Tarhuntašša in einem Text aus Emar. *Altorientalische Forschungen*, 99, 26, p. 314-321.

1674. DALLEY (S.). Sennacherib and Tarsus. *Anatolian studies*, 99, 49, p. 73-80.

1675. DASSOW (E. von). On writing the history of southern Mesopotamia. *Zeitschrift für Assyriologie und vorderasiatische Archäologie*, 99, 89, p. 227-246.

1676. DE GRAEF (K.). «In Cauda divinum» –(l)um dans quelques noms amorrites et accadiens. *Revue d'assyriologie et d'archéologie orientale*, 99, 93, p. 119-139.

1677. DE MARTINO (S.). Ura and the boundaries of Tarhuntašša. *Altorientalische Forschungen*, 99, 26, p. 291-300.

1678. FLÜCKIGER-HAWKER (E.). Urnamma of Ur in Sumerian literary tradition. Fribourg Switzerland, University Press u. Göttingen, Vandenhoeck & Ruprecht, 99, XVII-383 p.

1679. FRAME (G.). The inscriptions of Sargon II at Tang-I Var. *Orientalia*, 99, 68, p. 31-57.

1680. FREYDANK (H.). Zur Interpretation einer mittelassyrischen Urkunde aus Tell Chuēra. *Altorientalische Forschungen*, 99, 26, p. 207-209.

1681. GRODDEK (D.). CTH 331: Mythos vom verschwundenen Wettergott oder Aitiologie der Zerstörung Lihzinas? *Zeitschrift für Assyriologie und vorderasiatische Archäologie*, 99, 89, p. 36-49.

1682. GUICHARD (M.). Les aspects religieux de la guerre à Mari. *Revue d'assyriologie et d'archéologie orientale*, 99, 93, p. 27-48.

1683. HAAS (V.). Babylonischer Liebesgarten: Erotik und Sexualität im Alten Orient. München, Beck, 99, 208 p.

1684. HAGENBUCHNER-DRESEL (A.). Das "Fachbuch" der Erkrankungen der Altmungsorgane. *Zeitschrift für Assyriologie und vorderasiatische Archäologie*, 99, 89, p. 165-200.

1685. Hammurabi "Hoten": Kodai oriento shiryo shusei 1. (Code of Hammurabi: the compilation of historical materials in Ancient Orient, vol. 1). Trans. by Ichiro NAKATA. Tokyo, Riton, 99, 233 p.

1686. HELD (W.). Vom urartäischen Raupenhelm zum ionischen Helm. Zu einer Wangenklappe aus dem Athenaheiligtum in Milet. *Istanbuler Mitteilungen*, 99, 49, p. 141-157.

1687. KALLA (G.). Die Geschichte der Entdeckung der altbabylonischen Sippar-Archive. *Zeitschrift für Assyriologie und vorderasiatische Archäologie*, 99, 89, p. 201-226.

1688. KATZ (D.). The messager, Lulil and the cult of the dead. *Revue d'assyriologie et d'archéologie orientale*, 99, 93, p. 107-118.

1689. KOCH (J.). Die Planeten-Hypsomata in einem babylonischen Sternenkatalog. *Journal of Near Eastern studies*, 99, 58, p. 19-31.

1690. KUPPER (J.-R.). Un épisode de l'histoire du royaume d'Ašnakkum. *Revue d'assyriologie et d'archéologie orientale*, 99, 93, p. 79-90.

1691. LAFONT (B.). Sacrifices et rituels à Mari et dans la Bible. *Revue d'assyriologie et d'archéologie orientale*, 99, 93, p. 57-78.

1692. LEMAIRE (A.). Traditions amorrites et Bible: le prophétisme. *Revue d'assyriologie et d'archéologie orientale*, 99, 93, p. 49-56.

1693. LUCIANI (M.). Zur Lage Terqas in schriftlichen Quellen. *Zeitschrift für Assyriologie und vorderasiatische Archäologie*, 99, 89, p. 1-23.

1694. MARCHESI (G.). Two delivery records from Umma and related subjects. *Orientalia*, 99, 68, p. 104-113.

1695. MAYER (W. R.). Das Ritual KAR 26 mit dem Gebet "Marduk 24". *Orientalia*, 99, 68, p. 145-163.

1696. MELVILLE (Sarah C.). The role of Naquia/Zakutu in Sargonid politic. Helsinki, State Archives of Assyria, 99, 125 p.

1697. MONCHAMBERT (J.-Y.). De Korsoté à Circesium: la confluence du Khabour et de l'Euphrate de Cyrus à Justinien. *Ktema*, 99, 24, p. 225-241.

1698. MORANDI BONACOSSI (D.). Urartian bronze belts in the National Museum of Aleppo. *Zeitschrift für Assyriologie und vorderasiatische Archäologie*, 99, 89, p. 88-100.

1699. MÜLLER-KESSLER (Chr.), KESSLER (K.). Spätbabylonische Gottheiten in spätantiken mandäischen Texten. *Zeitschrift für Assyriologie und vorderasiatische Archäologie*, 99, 89, p. 65-87.

1700. NYLANDER (C.). Breaking the cup of kingship. An Elamite coup in Nineveh? *Iranica antiqua*, 99, 34, p. 71-83.

1701. PENTIUC (E.). West semitic terms in Akkadian texts from Emar. *Journal of Near Eastern studies*, 99, 58, p. 81-96.

1702. Poema (El) de Erra. Introducción, traducción del texto original acadio y notas de R. JIMÉNEZ ZAMUDIO. Madrid, Ediciones Clasicas, 99, 125 p.

1703. POLLOCK (S.). Ancient Mesopotamia: the Eden that never was. Cambridge, Cambridge U. P., 99, 272 p. (tables, fig., maps, plans).

1704. PONGRATZ-LEISTEN (B.). "Öffne den Tafelbehälter und lies ...". Neue Ansätze zum Verständnis des Literaturkonzeptes in Mesopotamien. *Die Welt des Orients*, 99, 30, p. 67-90.

1705. Prosopography (The) of the Neo-Assyrian Empire. Vol. I. Part II. B–G. Ed. by K. RADNER. Helsinki, The Neo-Assyrian Text Corpus Project, 99, IX-192 p.

1706. RADNER (K.). Ein neuassyrisches Privatarchiv der Tempelgoldschmiede von Assur. Saarbrücker, Saarbrücker Druckerei und Verlag, 99, XXII-252 p. (tables).

1707. REDFORD (D. B.). A note on the chronology of dynasty 25 and the inscriptions of Sargon II at Tang-I Var. *Orientalia*, 99, 68, p. 58-60.

1708. RUSSELL (J. M.). Some painted bricks from Nineveh, a preliminary report. *Iranica antiqua*, 99, 34, pp. 85-114. – IDEM. The writing on the wall: studies in the architectural context of late Assyrian palace inscriptions. Winona Lake, Eisenbrauns, 99, XII-348 p. (fig.).

1709. SASSMANNSHAUSEN (L.). Zur poetischen Struktur babylonischer Besitzübertragungsmonumente (Kudurru). *Die Welt des Orients*, 99, 30, p. 47-66.

1710. SEIDL (U.). Ein Monument Darius' I aus Babylon. *Zeitschrift für Assyriologie und vorderasiatische Archäologie*, 99, 89, p. 101-114.

1711. SEVIN (V.). The origins of the Urartians in the light of the Van/Karagündüz excavations. *Anatolian studies*, 99, 49, p. 159-164.

1712. SMITH (A. T.). The making of an Urartian landscape in southern Transcaucasia: a study of political architectonics. *American journal of archaeology*, 99, 103, p. 45-71.

1713. SOMMERFELD (W.). Die Texte der Akkade-Zeit, 1. Das Dijala-Gebiet: Tutub. Münster, Rhema Verlag, 99, VIII-214 p.

1714. STEINER (G.). Was bedeutet LUGAL-zu-nu.....ul-tam-li im Aleppo-Vertrag? *Altorientalische Forschungen*, 99, 26, p. 13-25.

1715. STIEHLER-ALEGRIA (G.). Greifvogel und Beute, ein kassitischer Topos. Bemerkungen zur typologischen Entwicklung eines Anzû-Imdugud-Motivs. *Altorientalische Forschungen*, 99, 26, p. 251-268.

1716. TROPPER (J.), VITA (J.-P.). Der Wettergott von Halab in Ugarit (KTU 4.728). *Altorientalische Forschungen*, 99, 26, p. 310-313.

1717. TROPPER (J.). Els Schöpfungsakt nach KTU 1.16.V.: 28-32. *Altorientalische Forschungen*, 99, 26, p. 26-32. – IDEM. Zur Etymologie von akkadisch šukênu/šuhehhunu. *Die Welt des Orients*, 99, 30, p. 91-94.

1718. VOLK (K.). Kinderkrankheiten nach der Darstellung babylonisch-assyrischer Keilschrifttexte. *Orientalia*, 99, 68, p. 1-30.

1719. ZIEGLER (N.). Le Harem du vaincu. *Revue d'assyriologie et d'archéologie orientale*, 99, 93, p. 1-26.

1720. ZÓLYOMI (G.). Directive infix and oblique object in Sumerian: an account of the history of their relationship. *Orientalia*, 99, 68, p. 215-253.

§ 5. Hittites.

1721. BECKMAN (G.). The goddess Pirinkir and her ritual from Hattuša (CTH 644). *Ktema*, 99, 24, p. 25-39.

1722. BONECHI (M.). Studies on the architectonic and topographic terms in the Ebla texts, I. *Die Welt des Orients*, 99, 30, p. 21-34.

1723. BRENTJES (B.). Das Bestattungsritual der Hethiter – ein Erbe aus den eurasischen Steppen? *Altorientalische Forschungen*, 99, 26, p. 58-76.

1724. BRYCE (T.). The kingdom of the Hittites. New York, Oxford U. P., 99, XIV-464 p.

1725. CAMPBELL (S.), CARTER (E.), HEALEY (E.), ANDERSON (S.), KENNEDY (A.), WHITCHER (S.). Emerging complexity on the Kahramanmaras plain, Turkey: the Domuztepe project, 1995–1997. *American journal of archaeology*, 99, 103, p. 395-418.

1726. CHANIOTIS (A.). Empfängerformular und Urkundenfälschung: Bemerkungen zum Urkundossier von Magnesia am Mäander. *In*: Urkunden und Urkundenformulare [Cf. n° 1743], p. 51-69.

1727. CORNIL (P.). La tradition écrite des textes magiques hittites. *Ktema*, 99, 24, p. 7-16.

1728. Corpus of hieroglyphic Luwian inscriptions. Vol. 2. Karatepe-Aslantaş. The inscriptions: facsimile edition. Ed. by H. ÇAMBEL, W. RÖLLIG and J. D. HAWKINS. Berlin a. New York, de Gruyter, 99, XXIII-99 p. (tables).

1729. CRAIG MELCHERT (G.). Hittite tuk(kan)zi- "cultivation, breeding". *Ktema*, 99, 24, p. 17-23.

1730. CZICHON (R.M.). Das Umland der hethitischen Hauptstadt Hattuša. Erste Ergebnisse eines Surveys. *In:* Stadt und Umland [Cf. n° 2257], p. 123-128.

1731. DIETRICH (M.), MEYER (W.). The Hurrian and the Hittite texts. *In:* Handbook of Ugaritic studies [Cf. n° 1734], p. 58-75.

1732. GRECO (P.). Two Umma "Messenger Texts" belonging to the University of Messina. *Zeitschrift für Assyriologie und vorderasiatische Archäologie*, 99, 89, p. 161-164.

1733. GRODDEK (D.). Fragmenta Hethitica dispersa VII/VIII. *Altorientalische Forschungen*, 99, 26, p. 33-52. – IDEM. Fragmenta Hethitica dispersa IX. *Altorientalische Forschungen*, 99, 26, p. 301-309.

1734. Handbook of Ugaritic studies. Ed. by W. G. E. WATSON and N. WYATT. Leiden, Boston a. Köln, Brill, 99, XIII-892 p. (ill.). [Cf. n.° <choice> 1731.]

1735. KHOURY (R. G.). Vielfalt und Bedeutung der Dokumente in den ersten islamischen Jahrhunderten. *In*: Urkunden und Urkundenformulare [Cf. n° 1743], p. 135-141.

1736. NEVE (P.). Hattuša. Planungskonzept und Anlage der hetthitischen Hauptstadt zur Zeit des hethitischen Großreiches. *In:* Stadt und Umland [Cf. n° 2257], p. 254-262.

1737. PARKER (V.). Reflexions on the Career of Hattušiliš III until the time of his coup d'État. *Altorientalische Forschungen*, 99, 26, p. 269-290.

1738. PETTINATO (G.). Ebla: il trionfo della burocrazia ovvero la meticolosità e rigore dei conti pubblici evidenziati dalle clausole amministrative. *In*: Urkunden und Urkundenformulare [Cf. n° 1743], p. 11-27.

1739. POPKO (M.). Nochmals zum hethitischen ^{GIŠ}halmaš(š)uitt-. *Altorientalische Forschungen*, 99, 26, p. 53-57.

1740. SICKER-AKMAN (M.). Untersuchungen zur Architektur der späthethitischen Burganlage Karatepe-Aslantaş. *Istanbuler Mitteilungen*, 99, 49, p. 529-541.

1741. UCHITEL (A.). Local versus general history in old Hittite historiography. *In*: Limits of historiography [Cf. n° 2352], p. 55-67.

1742. ÜNAL (Ahmet). Hititler – Etiler ve Anadolu uygarlıkları. (Les Hittites et les civilisations de l'Anatolie). İstanbul, Etibank, 99, 292 p.

1743. Urkunden und Urkundenformulare im klassischen Altertum und in den orientalischen Kulturen. Hrsg. v. R. G. KHOURY. Heidelberg, Winter, 99, 228 p. [Cf. n^{os} <Auswahl> 1726, 1735, 1738, 1861, 2082, 2103.]

§ 6. Jews and Semitic peoples to the end of the ancient world.

1744. BEGG (Ch.). David's conquests and officials according to Josephus. *Athenaeum*, 99, 87, p. 169-190.

1745. BEIT-ARIEH (I.). Excavation of an EB II site at Ramat Matred in the Negev Highlands. *Tel Aviv*, 99, 26, p. 76-91.

1746. Vacat.

1747. CAPRARA (M.). Nonno e gli Ebrei. Note a Par. IV 88-121. *Studi italiani di filologia classica*, 99, 17, p. 195-215.

1748. CIVIL (M.), RUBIO (G.). An Ebla incantation against insomnia and the Semiticization of Sumerian: notes on ARET 5 8b and 9. *Orientalia*, 99, 68, p. 254-266.

1749. CLAUSS (M.). Das alte Israel. Geschichte, Gesellschaft, Kultur. München, Beck, 99, 126 p.

1750. COHEN (S. J. D.). The beginnings of Jewishness: boundaries, varieties, uncertainties. Berkeley, Los Angeles a. London, University of California Press, 99, XV-426 p.

1751. COTTON (H. M.). The languages of the legal and administrative documents from the Judaean desert. *Zeitschrift für Papyrologie und Epigraphik*, 99, 125, p. 219-231.

1752. ECK (W.). The Bar Kokhba revolt: the Roman point of view. *Journal of Roman studies*, 99, 89, p. 76-89.

1753. EGAN (V.), BIKAI (P. M.). Archaeology in Jordan. *American Journal of archaeology*, 99, 103, p. 485-520.

1754. ESHEL (H.), MAGNESS (J.), SHENHAV (E.), BESONEN (J.). Interim report on Khirbet Yattir in Judea: a mosque and monastic church. *Journal of Roman archaeology*, 99, 12, p. 411-422.

1755. FALES (F. M.), MORA (C.). An international workshop on Aramaic argillary texts. *Athenaeum*, 99, 87, p. 556-565.

1756. FRIEDRICH (J.), RÖLLIG (W.), AMADASI GUZZO (M. G.), MAYER (W. R.). Phönizisch-punische Grammatik. 3. Roma, Editrice Pontificio Istituto Biblico, 99, XXXVIII-266 p.

1757. FRITZ (V.). Kinneret: excavations at Tell el-Oreimeh (Tel Kinrot). Preliminary report on the 1994–1997 seasons. *Tel Aviv*, 99, 26, p. 92-115.

1758. GROTTANELLI (Cristiano). Kings and prophets. Monarchic power, inspired leadership and sacred text in Biblical narrative. New York a. Oxford, Oxford U. P., 99, X-210 p.

1759. HENGEL (M.). Judaica, Hellenistica et Christiana. Kleine Schriften II. Tübingen, Mohr Siebeck, 99, X-466 p.

1760. HIRT (M.). L'inscription de Nazareth: nouvelle interprétation. *Zeitschrift für Papyrologie und Epigraphik*, 99, 124, p. 107-132.

1761. Jews, Christians and Polytheists in the ancient synagogue. Cultural interaction during the Graeco-Roman period. Ed. by S. FINE. London a. New York, Routledge, 99, p. XVIII-253.

1762. Jüdische Geschichte in hellenistisch-römischer Zeit. Wege der Forschung: vom alten zum neuen Schürer. Hrsg. v. A. OPPENHEIMER und E. MÜLLER-LUCKNER. München, Oldenbourg, 99, XI-275 p.

1763. LABAHN (M.). Jesus als Lebensspender. Untersuchungen zu einer Geschichte der johanneischen Tradition anhand ihrer Wundergeschichten. Berlin u. New York, de Gruyter, 99, X-559 p.

1764. LIPSCHITS (O.). The history of the Benjamin region under Babylonian rule. *Tel Aviv*, 99, 26, p. 155-190.

1765. MANSEL (K.), MARTIN-KILCHER (S.), NOBIS (G.), NOLLÉ (J.), RAKOB (F.), REDISSI (T.), SCHNEIDER (G.), SCHNURBEIN (S. von), TRIAS (G.), VATTIONI (F.), VEGAS (M.). Die deutschen Ausgrabungen in Karthago. Mainz, von Zabern, 99, XLVII-643 p. (tables).

1766. Masada VI. Yigael Yadin excavations 1963–1965, final reports. Jerusalem, Israel Exploration Society/Hebrew University of Jerusalem, 99, VIII-252 p. (ill.).

1767. MIRANDA (E.). La comunità giudaica di Hierapolis di Frigia. *Epigraphica Anatolica*, 99, 31, p. 109-156.

1768. NETZER (E.). Die Paläste der Hasmonäer und Herodes des Großen. Mainz, von Zabern, 99, 131 p.

1769. PARKER (S. T.). Brief notice on a possible early 4th-c. church at 'Aqaba, Jordan. *Journal of Roman archaeology*, 99, 12, p. 372-376.

1770. RICHTER (H.-F.). Das Liedgut am Anfang der 'jahwistischen' Urgeschichte (Fortsetzung). *Die Welt des Orients*, 99, 30, p. 95-124.

1771. ROSENFIELD (B.-Z.), MENIRAV (J.). The ancient synagogue as an economic center. *Journal of Near Eastern studies*, 99, 58, p. 259-276.

1772. SAGONA (C.). Silo or vat? Observations on the ancient textile industry in Malta and early Phoenician interests in the island. *Oxford journal of archaeology*, 99, 18, p. 23-60.

1773. SCHWEMER (D.). Vier aramäische Ostraka aus Tall Šaih Hasan. *Orientalia*, 99, 68, p. 114-121.

1774. SINGER-AVITZ (L.). Beersheba. A gateway community in southern Arabian long-distance trade in the eighth century B.C.E. *Tel Aviv*, 99, 26, p. 3-74.

1775. STRECK (M. P.). Der Gottesname "Jahwe" und das amurritische Onomastikon. *Die Welt des Orients*, 99, 30, p. 35-46.

1776. SWEENEY (D.), YASUR-LANDAU (A.). Following the path of the sea persons: the women in the Medinet Habu reliefs. *Tel Aviv*, 99, 26, p. 116-145.

1777. TEPPER (Y.). A basilica at Beth Yerah? Beth Yerah revisited. *Tel Aviv*, 99, 26, p. 271-282.

1778. VEGAS (M.). Eine archaische Keramikfüllung aus einem Haus am Kardo XIII in Karthago. *Mitteilungen des Deutschen Archäologische Instituts, Römische Abteilung*, 99, 106, p. 395-438.

1779. YANNAI (E.). New typological and technological aspects of grey burnished bowls in light of the excavation at 'Ain Assawir. *Tel Aviv*, 99, 26, p. 208-224.

1780. ZORN (J.). A note on the date of the 'Great Wall' of Tell en Nasbeh: a rejoinder. *Tel Aviv*, 99, 26, p. 146-150.

§ 7. Iran.

1781. AUGÉ (Ch.), DENTZER (J.-M.). Pétra: la cité des caravanes. Paris, Gallimard, 99, 128 p.

1782. AZARPAY (G.). In search of the Persian tiger. *Iranica antiqua*, 99, 34, p. 325-332.

1783. BADER (F.). Les grandes de l'Iliade et les Achéménids. *Révue des études grecques*, 99, 112, p. 337-382.

1784. BRENTJES (B.). Zum "Bildbestand" der achämenidischen Kunst. Gedanken zu den "Lücken" im Fundbestand altpersischer Kunst. *Altorientalische Forschungen*, 99, 26, p. 377-382.

1785. BRIANT (Pierre). L'histoire de l'empire achéménide aujourd'hui: l'historien et ses documents (commentaire de l'auteur). *Annales*, 99, 54, 5, p. 1127-1136.

1786. BURNEY (Ch.). Beyond the frontiers of empire: Iranians and their ancestors. *Iranica antiqua*, 99, 34, p. 1-20.

1787. CAGNAZZI (S.). Tradizioni su Dati, comandante persiano a Maratona. *Chiron*, 99, 29, p. 371-393.

1788. CHAUMONT (M.-L.). Histiée de Milet, le roi Darius Ier et la Sardaigne. *Quaderni di storia*, 99, 49, p. 137-156.

1789. COLE ROOT (M.). The cylinder seal from Pasargadae: of wings and wheels, date and fate. *Iranica antiqua*, 99, 34, p. 157-190.

1790. DANDAMAYER (M. A.). Achaemenid imperial policies and provincial governments. *Iranica antiqua*, 99, 34, p. 269-282.

1791. DEBORD (P.). L'Asie Mineure au IVe siècle (412–323 av. J.-Chr.): pouvoirs et enjeux politiques. Talence, Ausonius, 99, 558 p.

1792. DUSINBERRE (E. R. M.). Satrapal Sardis: Achaemenid bowls in an Achaemenid capital. *American journal of archaeology*, 99, 103, p. 73-102.

1793. DYSON (R. H.). Triangle-festoon ware reconsidered. *Iranica antiqua*, 99, 34, p. 115-144. – IDEM. The Achaemenid painted pottery of Hasanlu IIIA. *Anatolian studies*, 99, 49, p. 101-110.

1794. FLUSIN (M.). Comment les Mèdes ont raconté leur histoire: l'épopée d'Arbacès et le Médikos Logos d'Hérodote. *Ktema*, 99, 24, p. 135-145.

1795. FRANÇOIS (V.). Les Seldjoukides médiateurs des importations de céramique perse à Byzance. *Byzantinische Forschungen*, 99, 25, p. 101-110.

1796. GUO (L.). Arabic documents from the Red Sea port of Quseir in the seventh/thirteenth century, part I: Business letters. *Journal of Near Eastern studies*, 99, 58, p. 161-190.

1797. KOHL (Ph.), KROLL (S.). Notes on the fall of Horom. *Iranica antiqua*, 99, 34, p. 243-259.

1798. LERNER (J.D.). The impact of Seleucid decline on the eastern Iranian plateau. The foundations of Arsacid Parthia and Graeco-Bactria. Stuttgart, Steiner, 99, 139 p.

1799. LOYET (M.A.). Small ungulate butchery in the Islamic period at Tell Tuneinir, Syria. *Journal of Near Eastern studies*, 99, 58, p. 33-45.

1800. LUNSINGH SCHEURLEER (R.A.). Une bouterolle de fourreau. *Iranica antiqua*, 99, 34, p. 261-267.

1801. MAC DERMOT (B. C.), SCHIPPMAN (K.). Alexander's march from Susa to Persepolis. *Iranica antiqua*, 99, 34, p. 283-308.

1802. MEDVEDSKAYA (I. N.). Media and its neighbours I: the localization of Ellipi. *Iranica antiqua*, 99, 34, p. 53-70.

1803. MOUSAVY (A.). La ville de Parsa: quelques remarques sur la topographie et le système défensif de Persépolis. *Iranica antiqua*, 99, 34, p. 145-155.

1804. RAPTOU (E.). Athènes et Cypre à l'époque perse (VIe–IVe s. av. J.-Ch.). Lyons, Maison de l'Orient, 99, 304 p.

1805. ROLLINGER (R.). Zur Lokalisation von Parsu(m)a(š) in der Fārs und zu einigen Fragen der frühen persischen Geschichte. *Zeitschrift für Assyriologie und vorderasiatische Archäologie*, 99, 89, p. 115-139.

1806. SCHMITT (R.). Bemerkungen zum Schlußabschnitt von Dareios' Grabinschrift DNb. *Altorientalische Forschungen*, 99, 26, p. 127-139.

1807. SIMA (A.). Kleinasiatische Parallelen zu den altsüdarabischen Buß- und Sühneinschriften. *Altorientalische Forschungen*, 99, 26, p. 140-153.

1808. STOLPER (Matthew W.). Une «vision dure» de l'histoire achéménide (note critique). *Annales*, 99, 54, 5, p. 1109-1126. [Cf. n° 1785].

1809. SUMNER (W. M.), WHITCOMB (D.). Islamic settlement and chronology in fars: an archaeological perspective. *Iranica antiqua*, 99, 34, p. 309-324.

1810. VARGAS (P.). 'Kaspu' ginnu and the monetary reform of Darius I. *Zeitschrift für Assyriologie und vorderasiatische Archäologie*, 99, 89, p. 247-268.

1811. VOIGT (M. M.), CUYLER YOUNG JR. (T.). From Phrygian capital to Achaemenid entrepot: middle and late Phrygian Gordion. *Iranica antiqua*, 99, 34, p. 191-241.

1812. WIESEHÖFER (J.). Das frühe Persien. Geschichte eines antiken Weltreichs. München, Beck, 99, 128 p.

Cf. n°s 917, 1364

E

GREEK HISTORY

§ 1. Classical world in general. 1813-1834. – § 2. Prehellenic epoch. 1835-1853. – § 3. Sources and criticism of sources (*a*. Epigraphical sources; *b*. Literary sources). 1854-1968. – § 4. General and political history. 1969-2010. – § 5. History of law and institutions. 2011-2026. – § 6. Economic and social history. 2027-2077. – § 7. History of literature, philosophy and science (*a*. Literature; *b*. Philosophy and sciences). 2078-2177. – § 8. Religion and mythology. 2178-2215. – § 9. Archaeology and history of art. 2216-2259.

§ 1. Classical world in general.

* 1813. Année philologique (L'). Bibliographie critique et analytique de l'antiquité gréco-latine. Publiée par la Société Internationale de Bibliographie Classique. Tome LXVII, Bibliographie de l'année 1996 et compléments d'années antérieures. [Tome LXVI, 1996. Cf. Bibl. 98, n° 1937.] Paris, Les Belles Lettres, 99, LII-1446 p. – Année philologique (L'). Bibliographie critique et analytique de l'antiquité gréco-latine. Publiée par la Société Internationale de Bibliographie Classique. Tome LXVIII, Bibliographie de l'année 1997 et compléments d'années antérieures. Paris, Les Belles Lettres, 99, LVI-1277 p.

* 1814. Bibliografia topografica della colonizzazione greca in Italia e nelle isole tirreniche. Diretta da G. NENCI e G. VALLET. 15. Opere di carattere generale 1991–1995; Addenda 1977–1990. A cura di G. PANESSA. Pisa, Scuola Normale Superiore, Roma, École Française de Rome e Napoli, Centre J. Bérard, 99, XII-207 p.

1815. AMOURETTI (M.C.), RUZÉ (F.). Les sociétés grecques et la guerre à l'époque classique. Paris, Ellipse, 99, 175 p. (ill.).

1816. Antike Mythen in der europäischen Tradition. Hrsg. v. H. HOFMANN. Tübingen, Attempto Verlag, 99, 303 p. [Cf. n°s <Auswahl> 1405, 2180, 2190, 2193, 2204, 2209.]

1817. BRISSON (L.). La synthèse la plus achevée de l'hellénisme. *Révue des études grecques*, 99, 112, p. 734-739.

1818. CARTLEDGE (Paul). Democratic politics ancient and modern: from Cleisthenes to Mary Robinson. *Hermathena*, 99, 166, p. 5-29.

1819. DONIGER (W.). Splitting the difference. Gender and myth in ancient Greece and India. Chicago a. London, Chicago U. P., 99, XI-376 p.

1820. Große Gestalten der griechischen Antike. 58 historische Portraits von Homer bis Kleopatra. Hrsg. v. K. BRODERSEN. München, C.H. Beck, 99, 507 p.

1821. HOEPFNER (W.) und Mitarbeiter. Die Epoche der Griechen. *In*: Geschichte des Wohnens [Cf. n° 1166], p. 123-608.

1822. JOHNSTON (S.I.). Restless dead. Encounters between the living and the dead in ancient Greece. Berkeley, Los Angeles a. London, California U. P., 99, XXI-329 p.

1823. JOST (M.). Guerre et religion. *Pallas*, 99, 51, p. 129-139.

1824. KLOFT (H.). Mysterienkulte der Antike. Götter, Menschen, Rituale. München, Beck, 99, 127 p.

1825. MORA (F.). Storiografia greca e romana. *Dialogues d'histoire ancienne*, 99, 25, 1, p. 7-33.

1826. MUSTI (Domenico). I Telchini, le Sirene. Immaginario mediterraneo e letteratura da Omero e Callimaco al romanticismo europeo. Pisa e Roma, Istituti editoriali e poligrafici internazionali, 99, 124 p. (tables).

1827. Neue Pauly (Der). Enzyklopädie der Antike. Hrsg v. H. CANCIK und H. SCHNEIDER. Vol. 6. Iul–Lee. Vol. 7. Lef-Men. Stuttgart u. Weimar, Verlag J.B. Metzler, 99, 2 vol., 1222 p., 1268 p.

1828. Péloponnèse (Le): archéologie et histoire. Actes de la rencontre internationale de Lorient (12–15 mai 1998). Ed. par J. RENARD. Rennes, Presses universitaire de Rennes, 99, 322 p. [Cf. n° <sélection> 3047.]

1829. PETZOLD (Karl-Ernst). Geschichtsdenken und Geschichtsschreibung. Kleine Schriften zur griechischen und römischen Geschichte. Stuttgart, Steiner, 99, 629 p.

1830. POLITO (E.). Emblèmes macédoniens. Une hypothèse sur une série de boucliers de Macédoine en Numidie. *Antiquités africaines*, 99, 35, p. 39-70.

1831. POMEROY (S. B.), BURSTEIN (S. M.), DONLAN (W.), ROBERTS (J. T.). Ancient Greece: a political, social and cultural history. Oxford a. New York, Oxford U. P., 99, XXX-512 p. (ill., maps).

1832. PORCIANI (L.). Tre cronologie arcaiche: una discussione. *Athenaeum*, 99, 87, p. 539-550.

1833. RHODES (P. J.). Sparta, Thebes and autonomia. *Eirene*, 99, 35, p. 33-40.

1834. Ricordando Raffaele Cantarella. A cura di F. CONCA. Milano, Studio parole e Bologna, Cisalpino, 99, 302 p. [Cf. n^{os} <scelta> 2087, 2179, 2354, 2669.]

Cf. n°s 357, 1566

§ 2. Prehellenic epoch.

1835. ALLEN (S. H.). Finding the walls of Troy: Frank Calvert and Heinrich Schliemann at Hisarlik. Berkeley, Los Angeles a. London, University of California Press, 99, XIII-409 p. (figs., maps).

1836. BANOU (E.). New evidence on early Helladic Laconia. *Annual of the British School at Athens*, 99, 94, p. 63-79.

1837. BENZI (M.). Mycenean figurines from Iasos. *La parola del passato*, 99, 54, p. 269-282.

1838. BRYCE (T. R.). Anatolian scribes in Mycenaean Greece. *Historia*, 99, 48, p. 257-264.

1839. DANDRAU (A.). La peinture murale minoenne, I. La palette du peintre égéen et égyptien à l'Âge du Bronze. Nouvelles données analytiques. *Bulletin de correspondance hellénique*, 99, 123, p. 1-41.

1840. 'Epi ponton plazomenoi'. Simposio italiano di Studi Egei dedicato a L. Bernabò Brea e G. Pugliese Carratelli, Roma 18–20 febbraio 1998. A cura di V. LA ROSA, D. PALERMO e L. VAGNETTI. Roma e Atene, Scuola Archeologica Italiana di Atene, 99, 518 p.

1841. GÄRTNER (Th.). Klassische Vorbilder mittelalterlicher Trojaepen. Stuttgart u. Leipzig, Teubner, 99, 580 p.

1842. KNAPPETT (C.). Assessing a polity in Protopalatial Crete: the Malia-Lasithi State. *American journal of archaeology*, 99, 103, p. 615-639. – IDEM. Tradition and innovation in pottery forming technology: wheel throwing at Middle Minoan Knossos. *Annual of the British School at Athens*, 99, 94, p. 101-129.

1843. LANG (F.). Minoische, mykenische und geometrische Zeit. *In*: Geschichte des Wohnens [Cf. n° 1166], p. 85-122.

1844. MAC GILLIVRAY (J.A.). Knossos: pottery groups of the Old Palace period. London, The British School at Athens, 99, 195 p. (ill., plates).

1845. MALKIN (I.). Ulysse protocolonisateur. *Mediterraneo antico*, 99, 2, p. 243-261.

1846. MANGANI (E.). Troia. I materiali degli scavi di Heinrich Schliemann conservati nel Museo Nazionale Preistorico Etnografico "L. Pigorini". *Bullettino di paletnologia italiana*, 99, 90, p. 161-207.

1847. Minoan farmers (From) to Roman traders: sidelights on the economy of ancient Crete. Ed. by A. CHANIOTIS. Stuttgart, Franz Steiner Verlag, 99, LX-391 p. (tables, maps, figs). [Cf. n° <choice> 2528.]

1848. ROCCHETTI (L.), D'AGATA (A. L.). L'insediamento di Thronos-Kephala (antica Sybrita) e la Dark Age nella valle di Amari a Creta (XII-VII a. C.). *La parola del passato*, 99, 54, p. 209-228.

1849. SCHOEP (I.). Tablets and territories? Reconstructing late Minoan IB political geography through undeciphered documents. *American journal of archaeology*, 99, 103, p. 201-221. – IDEM. The origins of writing and administration on Crete. *Oxford journal of archaeology*, 99, 18, p. 265-276.

1850. Scritture mediterranee tra il IX e il VII secolo a.C. Atti del Seminario, Università degli Studi di Milano, Istituto di Storia Antica, 23–24 febbraio 1998. A cura di G. BAGNASCO GIANNI e F. CORDANO. Milano, Edizioni ET, 99, 159 p. [Cf. n° <scelta> 2280.]

1851. WAANDERS (F. M. J.). Studies in local case relations in Mycenaean Greek. Amsterdam, J.C. Gieben, 99, VII-134 p.

1852. WHITTAKER (J. C.). Alonia: the ethnoarchaeology of Cypriot threshing floors. *Journal of Mediterranean archaeology*, 99, 12, p. 7-25.

1853. WILSON (D. E.), DAY (P. M.). EM II B ware groups at Knossos: the 1907–1908 south front tests. *Annual of the British School at Athens*, 99, 94, p. 1-62.

§ 3. Sources and criticism of sources.

a. *Epigraphical sources*

* 1854. Bulletin épigraphique. *Révue des études grecques*, 99, 112, p. 568-714.

1855. BRODERSEN (K.), GÜNTHER (W.), SCHMITT (H. H.). Historische griechische Inschriften in Übersetzung. Vol. 3: der griechische Osten und Rom (250–1 v. Chr.). Darmstadt, Wissenschaftliche Buchgesellschaft, 99, XVIII-182 p.

1856. CHANKOWSKI (V.), DOMARADZKA (L.). Réédition de l'inscription de Pistiros et problèmes d'interprétation. *Bulletin de correspondance hellénique*, 99, 123, p. 247-258.

1857. CROWTHER (C.V.). Aus der Arbeit der "Inscriptiones Graecae" IV. Koan decrees for foreign judges. *Chiron*, 99, 29, p. 251-310.

1858. DOMARADZKA (L.). Monuments épigraphiques de Pistiros. *Bulletin de correspondance hellénique*, 99, 123, p. 347-358.

1859. GAUTHIER (Ph.). 'Symbola' athéniens et tribunaux étrangers à l'époque hellénistique. *Bulletin de correspondance hellénique*, 99, 123, p. 157-174. – IDEM. Nouvelles inscriptions de Claros: décrets d'Aigai et de Mylasa pour des juges colophoniens. *Révue des études grecques*, 99, 112, p. 1-36.

1860. GIOVANNINI (A.). Les pouvoirs d'Auguste de 27 à 23 av. J.-C. Une relecture de l'ordonnance de Kymè de l'an 27 (IK 5, n° 17). *Zeitschrift für Papyrologie und Epigraphik*, 99, 124, p. 95-106.

1861. GSCHNITZER (F.). Indirekte Beurkundung in den griechischen Inschriften. *In*: Urkunden und Urkundenformulare [Cf. n° 1743], p. 37-50.

1862. HALLOF (K.). Decretum Samium Syll.^{3} 312 redivivum. *Klio*, 99, 81, p. 392-396.

1863. HAMON (P.). Juges thasiens à Smyrne: I. Smyrna 582 complété. *Bulletin de correspondance hellénique*, 99, 123, p. 175-194.

1864. HEDRICK (C. W.). Democracy and the Athenian epigraphical habit. *Hesperia*, 99, 68, p. 387-439.

1865. JACQUEMIN (A.), MORANT (M.-J.). Inscriptions de Kadyanda. *Ktema*, 99, 24, p. 283-288.

1866. JÖRDENS (A.). IG II^2 1682 und die Baugeschichte des hellenistischen Telesterion im 4. Jh. v. Chr. *Klio*, 99, 81, p. 359-391.

1867. ŁAJTAR (A.). Greek inscriptions in Polish collections. A checklist. *Zeitschrift für Papyrologie und Epigraphik*, 99, 125, p. 147-172.

1868. LAMBERT (S. D.). IG II^2 2345, thiasoi of Herakles and the Salaminioi again. *Zeitschrift für Papyrologie und Epigraphik*, 99, 125, p. 93-130.

1869. LÓPEZ JIMENO (M^a del Amor). Nuevas tabellae defixionis Áticas. Amsterdam, Hakkert, 99, XX-488 p.

1870. MARCHETTI (P.). Révision des comptes à 'apousiai' (CID II 75-78). *Bulletin de correspondance hellénique*, 99, 123, p. 405-422.

1871. RAUSCH (M.). Miltiades, Athen und "die Rhamnusier auf Lemnos" (IG I^3 522bis). *Klio*, 99, 81, p. 7-17.

1872. SCHMIDT (D.). An unusual victory list from Keos: IG XII,5,608 and the dating of Bacchylides. *Journal of Hellenic studies*, 99, 119, p. 67-85.

1873. Sicilia epigraphica. Atti del Convegno Internazionale, Erice 15–18 ottobre 1998. A cura di M. I. GULLETTA. Pisa, Scuola Normale Superiore, 99, 2 vol., XI-600 p., 342 p. (tables).

1874. SMARCZYK (B.). Einige Bemerkungen zur Datierung der Beiträge zu Spartas Kriegkasse in IG V, 11. *Klio*, 99, 81, p. 45-67.

1875. Supplementum Epigraphicum Graecum, 1996, 46. Ed. by H. W. PLEKET, R. S. STROUD, A. CHANIOTIS and J. H. M. STRUBBE. Amsterdam, J.C. Gieben, 99, XXVII-844 p.

1876. Supplementum Epigraphicum Graecum. Consolidated index for volumes XXXVI-XLV (1986–1995). Ed. by J. H. M. STRUBBE. Amsterdam, J.C. Gieben, 99, VII-858 p.

Cf. n° 2234

b. *Literary sources*

1877. [Aeschylus] HEATH (J.). Disentangling the beast: humans and other animals in Aeschylus' Oresteia. *Journal of Hellenic studies*, 99, 119, p. 17-47.

1878. [Alcaeus] LIBERMAN (G.). Alcées, Fragments. Tomes I et II. Paris, Les Belles Lettres, 99, CXXVII-95 p., 281 p.

1879. [Alcmanes] DETTORI (E.). Alcmane, fr. 1,8 Dav.: 'agrotan'. *Rivista di filologia e istruzione classica*, 99, 127, p. 182-196.

1880. [Alexander Aetolus] MAGNELLI (E.). Alexandri Aetoli testimonia et fragmenta. Firenze, Università degli Studi di Firenze, 99, 304 p.

1881. [Apollonius Dyscolus] DALIMIER (C.). Apollonios Dyscole sur la fonction des conjonctions explétives. *Révue des études grecques*, 99, 112, p. 719-730.

1882. [Apollonius Pergaeus] FEDERSPIEL (M.). Notes linguistiques et critiques sur le livre II des Croniques d'Apollonius de Perge. *Révue des études grecques*, 99, 112, p. 409-443.

1883. [Aristophanes] DESFRAY (S.). Oracles et animaux dans les Cavaliers d'Aristophane. *Antiquité classique*, 99, 68, p. 35-56.

1884. [Aristophanes] DORATI (M.). Acqua e fuoco nella Lisistrata. *Quaderni urbinati di cultura classica*, 99, 92, p. 79-86.

1885. [Aristophanes] DORATI (M.). Ebbrezza e decisioni nella Lisistrata. *Quaderni urbinati di cultura classica*, 99, 92, p. 87-90.

1886. [Aristophanes] GIACOMONI (A.). Rito e trasgressione erotica: Aristoph. Thesm. 466 ss. *Quaderni urbinati di cultura classica*, 99, 92, p. 91-95.

1887. [Aristophanes] PERUSINO (F.). Violenza degli uomini e violenza delle donne nella Lisistrata di Aristofane. *Quaderni urbinati di cultura classica*, 99, 92, p. 71-78.

1888. [Aristophanes] SLATER (N.W.). Making the Aristophanic audience. *American journal of philology*, 99, 120, p. 351-368.

1889. [Aristophanes] SLAVITT (D.R.), BOVIE (P.). Aristophanes, 2. Wasps, Lysistrata, Frogs, The sexual congress. Aristophanes, 3. The suits, Clouds, Birds. Philadelphia, University of Pennsylvania Press, 99, 2 vol., XIV-360 p., XIV-308 p.

1890. [Aristophanes] THIEL (R.). 'Kyamotrox' in Aristoph. Eq. 41 und ein falsches Fragment aus der attischen Komödie. *Quaderni urbinati di cultura classica*, 99, 92, p. 67-69.

1891. [Arrianus] HAMMOND (N.G.L.). The meaning of Arrian, Anabasis 7.9.5. *Journal of Hellenic studies*, 99, 119, p. 166-168.

1892. [Arrianus] HAMMOND (N.G.L.). The speeches in Arrian's Indica and Anabasis. *Classical quarterly*, 99, 49, p. 238-253.

1893. [Asclepiades Bithynicus] POLITO (R.). On the life of Asclepiades of Bithynia. *Journal of Hellenic studies*, 99, 119, p. 48-66.

1894. [Asclepiades Samius, Leonidas Tarentinus] CLACK (J.). Asclepiades of Samos and Leonidas of Tarentum. The poems. Wauconda, Bolcahzy-Carducci, 99, VIII-270 p.

1895. [Callimachus] SCHMITZ (Th. A.). 'I hate all common things': the reader's role in Callimachus' Aetia prologue. *Harvard studies*, 99, 99, p. 151-178.

1896. [Corpus Hermeticum] The way of Hermes. The Corpus Hermeticum. Ed. by C. SALAMAN, D. VAN OYEN and W. D. WHARTON. The definitions of Hermes Trismegistus to Asclepius. Ed. by J.-P. MAHÉ. London, Duckworth, 99, 124 p.

1897. [Cratinus, Menander] AUSTIN (C.). From Cratinus to Menander. *Quaderni urbinati di cultura classica*, 99, 92, p. 37-47.

1898. [Demostenes, Aeschines] PAULSEN (Th.). Die parapresbeia-Reden des Demosthenes und des Aischines. Kommentar und Interpretationen zu Demosthenes, or. XIX, und Aischines, or. II. Trier, Wissenschaftlicher Verlag Trier, 99, 566 p.

1899. [Diodorus Siculus] DI VASTO (F.). 'Êthai': Diod. 21,3. *La parola del passato*, 99, 54, pp. 145-151.

1900. [Diogenes Laertius] PICCIRILLI (L.). L'Apologia del padre di Feace nella testimonianza di Diogene Laerzio. *Rivista di filologia e istruzione classica*, 99, 127, p. 129-134.

1901. DREYER (B.). Zum ersten Diadochenkrieg. Der Göteborger Arrian-Palimpsest (ms. Graec. I). *Zeitschrift für Papyrologie und Epigraphik*, 99, 125, p. 39-60.

1902. [Galenus] MAGNALDI (I.). Claudii Galeni Pergameni 'Peri psychês pathôn kai hamartematon'. Roma, Istituto Poligrafico e Zecca dello Stato, 99, LXII-131 p.

1903. [Gorgias] NOËL (M.-P.). Gorgias et l'«invention» des 'Gorgieia schemata'. *Révue des études grecques*, 99, 112, p. 193-211.

1904. [Heliodorus] ZIETHEN (G.). Heliodor's Aithiopika und die Gesandtschaften zu den Aithiopen. *Klio*, 99, 81, p. 455-490.

1905. [Hermippus] BOLLANSÉE (J.). Hermippos of Smyrna and his biographical writings. A reappraisal. Leuven, Peeters, 99, XXXVI-271 p.

1906. [Herodotus] DE VIDO (S.). Il nome del padre. *Rivista di filologia e istruzione classica*, 99, 127, p. 436-468.

1907. [Herodotus] IVANTCHIK (A.I.). Une légende sur l'origine des Scythes (Hdt. IV, 5-7) et le problème de sources du 'Scythicos logos' d'Hérodote. *Révue des études grecques*, 99, 112, p. 141-192.

1908. [Herodotus] LENFANT (D.). Peut-on se fier aux "fragments" d'historiens? L'exemple des citations d'Hérodote. *Ktema*, 99, 24, p. 103-121.

1909. [Herodotus] ROMM (J.). Herodotus. New Haven a. London, Yale U. P., 99, XV-212 p.

1910. [Herodotus] RUGGIERO (R.). Erodoto V, 49-54: esercizi di critica verbale. *Antiquité classique*, 99, 68, p. 23-33.

1911. [Hesiodus] LAURIOLA (R.). Theog. 207-210: un caso di prolessi narrativa. *Athenaeum*, 99, 87, p. 15-26.

1912. [Hesiodus] RAMIRES (G.). Serv. Auct. ad Aen. I 273, un frammento di tradizione esiodea? *Rivista di filologia e istruzione classica*, 99, 127, p. 135-138.

1913. [Hesiodus] SCHÖNBERGER (O.). Hesiod, Theogonie. Stuttgart, Reclam, 99, 165 p.

1914. [Hesiodus] WASHBOURNE (R.). Hesiod's smile-loving, member-loving Aphrodite. *La parola del passato*, 99, 54, p. 135-145.

1915. [Hippocrates] ANASTASSIOU (A.), IRMER (D.). Index Hippocraticus. Supplement. Göttingen, Vandenhoeck & Ruprecht, 99, XXXIII-75 p.

1916. [Hippocrates] DILLER (H.), MÜLLER (C.W.). Hippocrates, Über die Umwelt. Berlin, Akademie Verlag, 99, 101 p.

1917. [Hippocrates] MARZULLO (B.). Il "dolore" in Ippocrate. *Quaderni urbinati di cultura classica*, 99, 92, p. 123-128.

1918. [Hippocrates, Nicander] OIKONOMAKOS (K.). Les Alexipharmaques et le Corpus hippocratique, Nicandre lecteur d'Hippocrate (?). *Révue des études grecques*, 99, 112, p. 238-252.

1919. [Homerus] BRACCESI (L.), ROSSIGNOLI (B.). Gli Eubei, l'Adriatico e la geografia nell'Odissea. *Rivista di filologia e istruzione classica*, 99, 127, pp. 176-181.

1920. [Homerus] LUNDON (J.). 'Homeros philotechnos' nel contesto degli scoli bT ad A 149 b e bT a Λ 102 a. *Athenaeum*, 99, 87, p. 5-13.

1921. [Homerus] MACKIE (C. J.). Scamander and the rivers of Hades in Homer. *American journal of philology*, 99, 120, p. 485-501.

1922. [Homerus] PIZZOCARO (M.). Il canto nuovo di Femio. Le origini dell'epos storico. *Quaderni urbinati di cultura classica*, 99, 90, p. 7-33.

1923. [Homerus] SCALERA MAC LINTOCK (G.). Magia e contromagia nel canto X dell'Odissea. *La parola del passato*, 99, 54, p. 5-16.

1924. [Homerus] SOMVILLE (P.). Cadavres exquis. *Kernos*, 99, 12, p. 73-83.

1925. [Ion] PICCIRILLI (L.). Cimone in Ione di Chio. *Quaderni di storia*, 99, 49, p. 267-271.

1926. [Isocrates] DUŠANIĆ (S.). Isocrates, the Chian intellectuals, and the political context of the Euthydemus. *Journal of Hellenic studies*, 99, 119, p. 1-16.

1927. [Isocrates, Aristoteles] LOMBARDI (M.). Un'eco dell'Anonimo di Giamblico (Vorsokr. 89,7, 1-9 D.-K.) nell'Aeropagitico di Isocrate e nella Politica di Aristotele. *Rivista di filologia e istruzione classica*, 99, 127, pp. 263-281.

1928. LUNDON (J.). L'avverbio 'philotechnos' nel contesto di tre scoli tragici. *Athenaeum*, 99, 87, p. 507-514.

1929. [Menander] FRANCO (C.). Dai Sicioni di Menandro al mercato di Mylasa. *La parola del passato*, 99, 54, p. 261-268.

1930. [Nonnus] FRANGOULIS (H.). Nonnos de Panopolis. Les Dionysiaques. Tome XIII: chant XXXVII. Texte établi et traduit par H.. Paris, Belles Lettres, 99, XII, 191 p.

1931. [Nonnus] SIMON (B.). Nonnos de Panopolis. Les Dionysiaques. Tome XIV, chants XXXVIII-XL. Paris, Les Belles Lettres, 99, XII-317 p.

1932. [Pausanias] KENDRICK PRITCHETT (W.). Pausania Periegetes, II. Amsterdam, Gieben, 99, VIII-355 p.

1933. [Pausanias] KNOEPFLER (D.). Pausanias à Rome en l'an 148? *Révue des études grecques*, 99, 112, p. 485-509.

1934. [Pindarus] CALVANI MARIOTTI (G.). 'Hoi proupomnematisamenoi' negli scoli a Pindaro. *Athenaeum*, 99, 87, p. 51-56.

1935. [Pindarus, Sophocles, Aristophanes] CATENACCI (C.). 'Aponemein'/"leggere" (Pind. Isthm. 2, 47; Soph. fr. 144 Radt; Arist. Av. 1289). *Quaderni urbinati di cultura classica*, 99, 91, p. 49-61.

1936. [Pindarus] NEGRI (M.). Per un'interpretazione di Pindaro, fr. 26 Mähler. *Athenaeum*, 99, 87, p. 279-290.

1937. [Pindarus] SEVIERI (R.). Rimozione collettiva e riabilitazione individuale: Tebe dopo le guerre persiane nella prima Istmica di Pindaro. *Quaderni urbinati di cultura classica*, 99, 91, p. 35-48.

1938. [Pindarus] STRAUSS CLAY (J.). Pindar's sympotic epinicia. *Quaderni urbinati di cultura classica*, 99, 91, p. 25-34.

1939. [Plato] BECHTLE (G.). The anonymous commentary on Plato's Parmenides. Bern, Stuttgart u. Wien, Verlag Paul Haupt, 99, 285 p.

1940. [Plato] BLÖSSNER (N.). Musenrede und "geometrische Zahl": ein Beispiel platonischer Dialoggestaltung ("Politeia" VIII 545c8-547a7). Mainz, Akademie der Wissenschaften und der Literatur u. Stuttgart, Steiner, 99, 194 p.

1941. [Plato] HEITSCH (E.). Grenzen philologischer Echtskritik: Bemerkungen zum "Grossen Hippias". Mainz, Akademie der Wissenschaften und der Literatur u. Stuttgart, Steiner, 99, 40 p.

1942. [Plato] LISI (F.). Platon, Diálogos. VIII: Leyes (libros I-VI). IX: Leyes (libros VII-XII). Madrid, Gredos, 99, 2 vol., 502 p., 363 p.

1943. [Plato] MANCINI (S.). Un insegnamento segreto (Plat. Phaed. 62b). *Quaderni urbinati di cultura classica*, 99, 90, p. 153-168.

1944. [Plato] ROBIN (L.), MOREAU (J.). Platon, Gorgias, Ménon. Paris, Gallimard, 99, LXXXI-201 p.

1945. [Plutarchus] VAN DER STOCKT (L.). A Plutarchan hypomnema on self-love. *American journal of philology*, 99, 120, p. 575-599.

1946. [Plotinus] O'MEARA (D.). Plotin: Traité 51. Paris, Les Éditions du Cerf, 99, 191 p.

1947. [Polybius] BIRASCHI (A.M.). La fondazione di Iasos fra mito e storia. A proposito di Polibio XVI 12,2. *La parola del passato*, 99, 54, p. 250-260.

1948. [Posidonius] KIDD (I.G.). Posidonius. Vol. III, The translations of the fragments. Cambridge, Cambridge U. P., 99, XVI-414 p.

1949. [Protagoras] MANUWALD (B.). Protagoras. Göttingen, Vandenhoeck&Ruprecht, 99, 495 p.

1950. [Ps. Andocides] GAZZANO (F.). Pseudo-Andocide: Contro Alcibiade. Genova, Il nuovo melangolo, 99, CX-177 p.

1951. [Ps. Longinus] BILLAULT (A.). Les jugements de goût dans le traité Du sublime. *Révue des études grecques*, 99, 112, p. 212-233.

1952. [Ps. Lucianus] WHITMARSH (T.). Greek and Roman in dialogue: the pseudo-Lucianic Nero. *Journal of Hellenic studies*, 99, 119, p. 142-160.

1953. [Rhetorica ad Alexandrum] CHIRON (P.). Observations sur le lexique de la Rhétorique à Alexandre. *Ktema*, 99, 24, p. 313-340.

1954. [Sappho] MARTINELLI TEMPESTA (S.). Nota a Saffo, fr. 16, 12-13 V. (P.Oxy. 1231). *Quaderni urbinati di cultura classica*, 99, 91, p. 7-14.

1955. [Scholia Homerica] FUCECCHI (Marco). 'Cavalli al pascolo' nella notte di Eurialo e Niso. Rovesciamento e reimpiego di uno scolio omerico nell'Eneide (con una appendice su Stazio). *Rivista di filologia e di istruzione classica*, 99, 127, p. 206-222.

1956. [Sophocles] BLAISE (F.). Une polémique tragique: le seconde volet de l'Ajax de Sophocle. *Révue des études grecques*, 99, 112, p. 383-408.

1957. [Sophocles] BOWMAN (L.). Prophecy and authority in the Trachiniai. *American journal of philology*, 99, 120, p. 335-350.

1958. [Sophocles] CARAWAN (E.). The edict of Oedipus (Oedipus tyrannus 223-251). *American journal of philology*, 99, 120, p. 187-222.

1959. [Sophocles] DAVIDSON (J.). Sophocles, Trachiniae 100-101. *Athenaeum*, 99, 87, p. 533-539.

1960. [Sophocles] GOLDER (H.), PEVEAR (R.). Sophocles: Aias (Ajax). New York a. Oxford, Oxford U. P., 99, X-100 p.

1961. [Sophocles] PATTONI (M. P.). Sofocle Edipo a Colono 1293. *Rivista di filologia e istruzione classica*, 99, 127, p. 257-262.

1962. [Sophocles] Sophocles revisited. Essays presented to Sir H. Lloyd-Jones. Ed. by J. GRIFFIN. Oxford, U. P., 99, X-343 p.

1963. [Stobaeus] PICCIONE (R. M.). Caratterizzazione dei lemmi nell'Anthologion di G. Stobeo. Questioni di metodo. *Rivista di filologia e istruzione classica*, 99, 127, pp. 139-175.

1964. [Strabo] BIFFI (N.). L'Africa di Strabone. Libro XVII della Geografia. Introduzione, testo e commento. Modugno, Edizioni del Sud, 99, 450 p.

1965. Sulla tradizione dei testi greci. *Quaderni di storia*, 99, 50, p. 47-94. [Contiene: IRIGOIN (Jean). La transmission des textes grecs de l'auteur à l'éditeur d'aujourd'hui (p. 49-56). – CANFORA (Luciano). De la quête de l'archétype à l'histoire des textes. Note brève sur la critique à la française (p. 57-60). – JACOB (Christian). Du livre au texte: pour une histoire comparée des philologies (p. 61-94)].

1966. [Theocritus] GARCÍA TEIJEIRO (M.). Il secondo Idillio di Teocrito. *Quaderni urbinati di cultura classica*, 99, 90, p. 71-86.

1967. [Theocritus] HUNTER (R.). Theocritus. A selection. Idills 1, 3, 4, 6, 7, 10, 11 and 13. Cambridge, Cambridge U. P., 99, XI-308 p.

1968. [Thucydides] WINTON (R. I.). Thucydides I 22,1. *Athenaeum*, 99, 87, p. 527-533.

Cf. n°ˢ 2078-2177

§ 4. General and political history.

1969. ALONSO TRONCOSO (V.). 395–390/89 a.C., Atenas contra Esparta: ¿de qué guerra hablamos? *Athenaeum*, 99, 87, p. 57-77.

1970. ASHLEY (J. R.). The Macedonian empire. The era of warfare under Philip II and Alexander the Great, 359–323 B.C. Jefferson a. London, McFarland & Co., 99, X-486 p. (maps).

1971. Aspirazione al consenso e azione politica in alcuni contesti di fine V sec. a.C.: il caso di Alcibiade. Seminario interdisciplinare Cattedre di Storia greca e di Epigrafia greca. Chieti, 12-13 marzo 1997. A cura di E. LUPPINO MANES. Alessandria, Edizioni dell'Orso, 99, 108 p.

1972. BERNAND (André). Guerre et violence dans la Grèce antique. Paris, Hachette-Littératures, 99, 452 p. (Histoires).

1973. BILIK (R.). Hippias von Elis als Quelle von Diodors Bericht über den elisch-spartanischen Krieg? *Ancient society*, 99, 29, p. 21-47.

1974. BLACKWELL (C. W.). In the absence of Alexander. Harpalus and the failure of Macedonian authority. New York, Peter Lang, 99, 185 p.

1975. Colonisation grecque (La) en Méditerranée Occidentale. Actes de la rencontre scientifique en hommage à Georges Vallet organisée par le Centre J. Bérard, École Française de Rome, l'Istituto Orientale et l'Università degli Studi di Napoli 'Federico II': Rome-Naples 15–18 novembre 1995. Roma, École Française de Rome, 99, VI-446 p. (ill.). [Cf. n°ˢ <sélection> 2267, 2279.]

1976. CONSOLO LANGHER (S.). Tessaglia, Calcidica e Focide nella politica di Filippo II (dalla politica espansionistica al disegno panellenico). *Athenaeum*, 99, 87, p. 191-200.

1977. COPPOLA (A.). Fra Alessandro e gli Eneadi, da Tiberio a Traiano. *Athenaeum*, 99, 87, p. 447-456.

1978. CORSTEN (Th.). Vom Stamm zum Bund. Gründung und territoriale Organisation griechischer Bundesstaaten. München, Oberhummer Gesellschaft e.V., 99, 271 p.

1979. DANY (O.). Akarnanien im Hellenismus: Geschichte und Völkerrecht in Nordwestgriechenland. München, Beck, 99, XII-363 p.

1980. DUPLOUY (A.). L'utilisation de la figure de Crésus dans l'idéologie aristocratique athénienne. Solon, Alcméon, Miltiade et le dernier roi de Lydie. *Antiquité classique*, 99, 68, p. 1-22.

1981. FALKNER (C.). Sparta and Lepreon in the Archidamic war (Thuc. 5.31.2-5). *Historia*, 99, 48, p. 385-394.

1982. FAUBER (C. M.). Deconstructing 375–371 BC: towards an unified chronology. *Athenaeum*, 99, 87, p. 481-506.

1983. FORSDYKE (S.). From aristocratic to democratic ideology and back again: the Trasybulus anecdote in Herodotus' Histories and Aristotle' Politics. *Classical philology*, 99, 94, p. 361-372.

1984. GREENWALT (W.). Why Pella? *Historia*, 99, 48, p. 158-183.

1985. GRIBBLE (D.). Alcibiades and Athens. A study in literary presentation. Oxford, Clarendon Press, 99, XII-304 p.

1986. GYOMLAY (Gyula). A görögök története a római hódítás koráig. (The history of the Greek until the age of the Roman conquest). Szeged, Szekszárdi Nyomda, 99, 691 p.

1987. HEFTNER (H.). Die Rede für Polystratos ([Lysias] XX) als Zeugnis für den oligarchischen Umsturz von 411 v.Chr. in Athen. *Klio*, 99, 81, p. 68-94.

1988. JANNENS (E.). Thucydide I 23 ou la démistification de la guerre. *Ancient society*, 99, 29, p. 5-19.

1989. JEHNE (M.). Formen der thebanischen Hegemonialpolitik zwischen Leuktra und Chaironeia (371–338 v. Chr.). *Klio*, 99, 81, p. 317-358.

1990. JOHNSTONE (S.). Disputes and democracy: the consequences of litigation in ancient Athens. Austin, University of Texas Press, 99, XIV-207 p.

1991. KALLET (L.). The diseased body politic, Athenian public finance and the massacre at Mykalessos (Thucydides 7.27-29). *American journal of philology*, 99, 120, p. 223-244.

1992. LEPPIN (H.). Argos. Eine griechische Demokratie der fünften Jahrhunderts v. Chr. *Ktema*, 99, 24, p. 297-312. – IDEM. Thukydides und die Verfassung der Polis. Ein Vertrag zur politischen Ideengeschichte des 5. Jahrhunderts v.Chr. Berlin, Akademie Verlag, 99, 253 p.

1993. LÉVY (E.). La Sparte d'Hérodote. *Ktema*, 99, 24, p. 123-134.

1994. MAC GLEW (J.F.). Politics on the margins: the athenian Hetaireiai in 415 B.C. *Historia*, 99, 48, p. 1-22.

1995. MASTROCINQUE (A.). Studi sulle guerre mitridatiche. Stuttgart, Steiner, 99, 128 p.

1996. MOSSÉ (C.). Politique et société en Grèce ancienne: le "modèle" athénien. Paris, Flammarion, 99, 242 p.

1997. MUELLER (H.F.). Ephialtes accusator: a case study in anecdotal history and ideology. *Athenaeum*, 99, 87, p. 425-445.

1998. PAL'TSEVA (Larisa A.). Iz istorii arkhaicheskoj Gretsii: Megary i megarskie kolonii. (From the history of archaic Greece: Megars and their colonies). Sankt-Peterburgskij gos. un-t. Sankt-Peterburg, Izd. S.-Peterb. un-ta, 99, 302 p. (maps, ind.).

1999. PERRIN-SAMINADAYAR (É.). Les succès de la diplomatie athénienne de 229 à 168 av. J.-C. *Révue des études grecques*, 99, 112, p. 444-462.

2000. PETZOLD (Karl-Ernst). Die Freiheit der Griechen und die Politik der nova sapientia. *Historia*, 99, 48, p. 61-93.

2001. PICCIRILLI (L.). I 'symbouloi' spartani. *Quaderni di storia*, 99, 49, p. 261-265.

2002. RAUSCH (M.). Isonomia in Athen. Veränderungen des öffentlichen Lebens vom Sturz der Tyrannis bis zur zweiten Perserabwehr. Frankfurt am Main, Berlin, New York, Paris u. Wien, Lang, 99, XIII-416 p.

2003. RUZICKA (S.). Glos, son of Tamos, and the end of the Cypriot war. *Historia*, 99, 48, p. 23-43.

2004. SALVIAT (F.). Le roi Kersobleptès, Maronée, Apollonia, Thasos, Pistiros et l'histoire d'Hérodote. *Bulletin de correspondance hellénique*, 99, 123, p. 259-273.

2005. SCHULZ (R.). Militärische Revolution und politischer Wandel. Das Schicksal Griechenlands im 4. Jahrhundert v. Chr.. *Historische Zeitschrift*, 99, 268, 2, p. 281-310.

2006. SMITH (A. C.). Eurymedon and the evolution of political personifications in the early classical period. *Journal of Hellenic studies*, 99, 119, p. 128-141.

2007. VICKERS (M.). Alcibiades and Melos: Thucydides 5.84-116. *Historia*, 99, 48, p. 265-281.

2008. WEBER (G.). The Hellenistic rulers and their poets. Silencing dangerous critics? *Ancient society*, 99, 29, p. 147-174.

2009. WELWEI (K. W.). Das klassische Athen. Demokratie und Machtpolitik im 5. und 4. Jahrhundert. Germany, Primus Verlag, 99, VIII-468 p.

2010. WYLIE (G.). Pyrrhus polemistes. *Latomus*, 99, 58, p. 298-313.

§ 5. History of law and institutions.

2011. BOËLDIEU-TREVET (J.). Commandement et institutions dans les cités grecques à l'époque classique. *Pallas*, 99, 51, p. 81-104.

2012. COBETTO CHIGGIA (P.). L'adozione ad Atene in epoca classica. Alessandria, Ed. dell'Orso, 99, VI-371 p.

2013. D'ANGOUR (A.J.). Archinus, Eucleides and the reform of the Athenian alphabet. *Bulletin of the Institut of Classical Studies*, 99, 43, p. 109-130.

2014. DARMEZIN (L.). Les affranchissements par consécration en Béotie et dans le monde grec hellénistique. Nancy, Association pour la Diffusion de la Recherche sur l'Antiquité, 99, 314 p.

2015. GASTALDI (V.). El juicio de Orestes: 'prodikasia' y 'zetesis'. *Faventia*, 99, 21, p. 29-35.

2016. HAMMOND (N. G. L.). The role of the epistates in Macedonian contexts. *Annual of the British School at Athens*, 99, 94, p. 369-375.

2017. HAUDE (R.). Alphabet und Demokratie. *Saeculum*, 99, 50, p. 1-28.

2018. MARCACCINI (C.). Spunti per una nuova interpretazione della figura del basileus in Grecia arcaica. *Athenaeum*, 99, 87, p. 395-424.

2019. MARI (M.). Le 'primizie di uomini' ad Apollo delfico. Indagine su un rito greco. *Mediterraneo antico*, 99, 2, p. 263-320.

2020. MEIER (M.). Kleomenes I., Damaratos und das spartanische Ephorat. *Göttinger Forum für Altertumswissenschaft*, 99, 2, p. 89-108.

2021. NIGHTINGALE (A.W.). Plato's lawcode in context: rule by written law in Athens and Magnesia. *Classical quarterly*, 99, 49, p. 100-122.

2022. O'NEIL (J.L.). Political trials under Alexander the Great and his successors. *Antichthon*, 99, 33, p. 28-47.

2023. PERE-NOGUES (S.). Mercenaires et mercenariat d'Occident: réflexions sur le développement du mercenariat en Sicile. *Pallas*, 99, 51, p. 105-127.

2024. ROY (J.). Polis and oikos in classical Athens. *Greece and Rome*, 99, 46, p. 1-17.

2025. SORDI (Marta). Fazioni e congiure nel mondo antico. Milano, Vita e Pensiero, 99, VII-335 p.

2026. VIRGILIO (Biagio). Lancia, diadema e porpora: il re e la regalità ellenistica. Pisa, Istituti editoriali e poligrafici internazionali, 99, 196 p.

Cf. n° 2481

§ 6. Economic and social history.

2027. AULT (B.A.). "Koprones" and oil presses at Halieis: interactions of town and country and the integration of domestic and regional economics. *Hesperia*, 99, 68, p. 549-573.

2028. BRAVO (B.), CHANKOWSKI (A.S.). Cités et emporia dans le commerce avec les barbares, à la lumière du document dit à tort «inscription de Pistiros». *Bulletin de correspondance hellénique*, 99, 123, p. 275-317.

2029. BULTRIGHINI (U.). Elementi di dinamismo nell'economia greca tra VI e IV secolo. L'eccezione e la regola. Alessandria, Edizioni dell'Orso, 99, 176 p.

2030. COLLIN BOUFFIER (S.). La pisciculture dans le monde grec. État de la question. *Mélanges de l'École Française de Rome*, 99, 111, p. 37-50.

2031. COOPER (J. M.). Reason and emotion. Essay on ancient moral psychology and ethical theory. Princeton, Princeton U. P., 99, XVI-588 p.

2032. CORVISIER (J.-N.). Guerre et démographie en Grèce à la période classique. *Pallas*, 99, 51, p. 57-79.

2033. COSTABILE (F.). 'Katadesmoi'. *Mitteilungen des deutschen archäologischen Institutes (Athenische Abteilung)*, 99, 114, p. 87-104.

2034. D'AGOSTINO (B.). 'Oinops pontos'. Il mare come alterità nella percezione arcaica. *Mélanges de l'École Française de Rome*, 99, 111, p. 107-117.

2035. Demografia, sistemi agrari, regimi alimentari nel mondo antico. Atti del Convegno Internazionale di Studi (Parma 17–19 ottobre 1997). A cura di Domenico VERA. Bari, Edipuglia, 99, 398 p. [Cf. n^{os} <scelta> 2529, 2535, 2545, 2572, 2899.]

2036. DETTENHOFER (M. H.). Praxagoras Programm. Eine politische Deutung von Aristophanes' Ekklesiazusai als Beitrag zur inneren Geschichte Athens im 4. Jahrhundert v. Chr. *Klio*, 99, 81, p. 95-111.

2037. DILLON (M. P. J.). Post-nuptial sacrifices on Kos (Segre, ED 178) and ancient Greek marriage rites. *Zeitschrift für Papyrologie und Epigraphik*, 99, 124, p. 63-80.

2038. DUCREY (P.). Prisonniers de guerre en Grèce antique: 1968-1999. *Pallas*, 99, 51, p. 9-23.

2039. DUNN (F. M.). The council's solar calendar. *American journal of philology*, 99, 120, p. 369-380.

2040. FAGAN (G. G.). Gifts of gymnasia: a test case for reading quasi-technical jargon in Latin inscriptions. *Zeitschrift für Papyrologie und Epigraphik*, 99, 124, p. 263-275.

2041. FERNOUX (H.-L.). Guerres, cités et mondes indigènes du Pont-Euxin et de la Propontide aux Ve et IVe siècles av.J.-C. *Pallas*, 99, 51, p. 173-204.

2042. FLASHAR (M.). Panhellenische Feste und die Asyl – Parameter lokaler Identitätsstiftung in Klaros und Kolophon [Klaros-Studien III]. *Klio*, 99, 81, p. 412-436.

2043. FORTE (F.). Storia del pensiero dell'economia pubblica. 1. Il pensiero antico greco-romano e cristiano. Milano, Giuffrè, 99, XII-562 p.

2044. GARLAN (Y.). Guerre et économie en Grèce ancienne. Paris, Éd. La Découverte, 99, 225 p.

2045. GIZEWSKI (C.). Die Lehre des Aristoteles von der 'Widerlegung der Sophismen' und die Struktur der Öffentlichkeit in der Polis. *Klio*, 99, 81, p. 112-130.

2046. HALLOF (K.). Der samische Kalender. *Chiron*, 99, 29, p. 193-204.

2047. HARRISON (C.M.). Triremes at rest: on the beach or in the water? *Journal of Hellenic studies*, 99, 119, p. 168-171.

2048. HINDLEY (C.). Xenophon on male love. *Classical quarterly*, 99, 49, p. 74-99.

2049. ITO (Tadashi). Girisha kodai no tochi jijo. (Conditions of land in ancient Greece). Tokyo, Taga Shuppan, 99, 436 p.

2050. JACQUES-RIMASSA (P.). Les représentations de la musique, divertissement du 'symposion' grec, dans les céramiques attique et italiote (440-300). *Revue des études anciennes*, 99, 101, p. 37-63.

2051. JÖHRENS (G.). Kerameikos: griechische Amphorenstempel spätklassischer und hellenistischer Zeit. *Mitteilungen des deutschen archäologischen Institutes (Athenische Abteilung)*, 99, 114, p. 157-170.

2052. JONES (N. F.). The associations of classical Athens: the response to democracy. New York a. Oxford, Oxford U. P., 99, XVIII-345 p.

2053. KAIMIO (M.). The citizenship of the theatremakers in Athens. *Würzburger Jahrbücher für Altertumswissenschaft*, 99, 23, p. 43-61.

2054. KENNELL (N. M.). Age categories and chronology in the Hellenistic Theseia. *Phoenix*, 99, 53, p. 249-262.

2055. KURKE (L.). Coins, bodies, games and gold. The politics of meaning in archaic Greece. Princeton, Princeton U. P., 99, XXI-384 p.

2056. LANDELS (J. G.). Music in ancient Greece and Rome. London a. New York, Routledge, 99, XII-296 p.

2057. LAWALL (M. L.). Studies in Hellenistic Ilion: transport amphoras from the Lower City. *Studia Troica*, 99, 9, p. 187-224.

2058. LEGUILLOUX (M.). Sacrifices et repas publics dans le sanctuaire de Poséidon à Ténos: les analyses archéozoologiques. *Bulletin de correspondance hellénique*, 99, 123, p. 423-455.

2059. LOOMIS (W. T.). Wages, welfare costs and inflation in classical Athens. Ann Arbor, The University of Michigan Press, 99, XVII-403 p.

2060. LOUKOPOULOU (L.). Sur le statut et l'importance de l''emporion' de Pistiros. *Bulletin de correspondance hellénique*, 99, 123, p. 359-371.

2061. MUSTI (Domenico). Nuove riflessioni sui Nikephoria pergameni e Diodoro Pasparo. *Rivista di filologia e istruzione classica*, 99, 127, pp. 325-333.

2062. NOEL (D.). Les Anthestéries et le vin. *Kernos*, 99, 12, p. 125-152.

2063. OGDEN (D.). Polygamy, prostitutes and death. The Hellenistic dynasties. London, Duckworth, 99, XXXIV-317 p. (figs.).

2064. PALACZYK (M.). Die Zusatzstempel («secondary stamps») der rhodischen Amphoren. *Jahreshefte der Österreichischen Archäologischen Institutes in Wien*, 99, 68, p. 59-103.

2065. PALEOTHODOROS (D.). Pisistrate et Dionysos: mythes et réalités de l'érudition moderne. *Les études classiques*, 99, 67, p. 321-340.

2066. PICARD (O.). Le commerce de l'argent dans la charte de Pistiros. *Bulletin de correspondance hellénique*, 99, 123, p. 331-346.

2067. PRITCHARD (D. M.). Fool's gold and silver: reflections on the evidentiary status of finely painted Attic pottery. *Antichthon*, 99, 33, p. 1-27.

2068. ROSENBERGER (V.). Die Ökonomie der Pythia oder: wirtschaftliche Aspekte griechischer Orakel. *Laverna*, 99, 10, p. 153-164.

2069. ROSIVACH (V. J.). Enslaving barbaroi and the Athenian ideology of slavery. *Historia*, 99, 48, p. 129-157.

2070. RUMSCHEID (F.). Vom Wachsen antiker Säulenwälder: zu Projektierung und Finanzierung antiker Bauten in Westkleinasien und anderswo. *Jahrbuch des Deutschen Archäologischen Instituts*, 99, 114, p. 19-63.

2071. SCHACHTER (A.). The Nyktophylaxia of Delos. *Journal of Hellenic studies*, 99, 119, p. 172-174.

2072. SCHMIDT (S. G.). Eine Gruppe nordägäischer Transportamphoren. *Mitteilungen des deutschen archäologischen Institutes (Athenische Abteilung)*, 99, 114, p. 143-156.

2073. SCHMITZ (W.). Nachbarschaft und Dorfgemeinschaft im archaischen und klassischen Griechenland. *Historische Zeitschrift*, 99, 268, 3, p. 561-598.

2074. SCHOFIELD (M.). Saving the city: philosopher-kings and other classical paradigms. London a. New York, Routledge, 99, X-242 p.

2075. STANČIČ (Z.), SLAPŠAK (B.). The Greek field system at Pharos: a metric analysis. *Revue des études anciennes*, 99, 101, p. 115-124.

2076. STANLEY (P. V.). The economic reforms of Solon. St. Katharinen, Scripta Mercaturae Verlag, 99, III-329 p.

2077. VINOKUROV (Nikolaj I.). Vinodelie antichnogo Bospora. (The wine-making of Ancient Bosporian Kingdom). Mosk. gos. ped. un-t. Moskva, [s. n.], 99, 191 p. (ill., bibl.). [Eng. preface and summary]

§ 7. History of literature, philosophy and science.

a. *Literature*

2078. ASHBY (C.). Classical Greek theatre: new views of an old subject. Iowa City, University of Iowa Press, 99, XIX-191 p. (figs.).

2079. AUBRIOT (D.). Imago Iliadis. Le bouclier d'Achille et la poésie de l'Iliade. *Kernos*, 99, 12, p. 9-56.

2080. BELLONI (L.), CITTI (V.), DE FINIS (L.). Dalla lirica al teatro: nel ricordo di Mario Untersteiner (1899–1999). Trento, Università degli Studi di Trento, 99, 451 p.

2081. BETA (S.). La 'parola inutile' nella commedia antica. *Quaderni urbinati di cultura classica*, 99, 92, p. 49-66.

2082. BOMMELAER (J.-F.). Traces de l'épigraphie delphique dans le texte de Pausanias. *In*: Urkunden und Urkundenformulare [Cf. n° 1743], p. 83-93.

2083. BONNECHER (P.). «La 'machaira' était disimulée dans le 'kanoûn'»: quelques interrogations. *Revue des études anciennes*, 99, 101, p. 21-35.

2084. BOUVIER (D.). La mémoire et la mort dans l'épopée homérique. *Kernos*, 99, 12, p. 57-71.

2085. BRUNET (Ph.). Les dactyles lyriques de la tragédie. *Révue des études grecques*, 99, 112, p. 127-140.

2086. CALAME (C.). Tempo del racconto e tempo del rito nella poesia greca: Bacchilide tra mito, storia e culto. *Quaderni urbinati di cultura classica*, 99, 91, p. 63-83.

2087. CAVALLI (M.). Le Rane di Aristofane: modelli tradizionali nell'agone tra Eschilo ed Euripide. *In*: Ricordando Raffaele Cantarella [Cf. n° 1834], p. 83-105.

2088. CLARKE KOSAK (J.). Therapeutic touch and Sophokles' Philoktetes. *Harvard studies*, 99, 99, p. 93-134.

2089. COLVIN (S.). Dialect in Aristophanes. The politics of language in ancient Greek literature. Oxford, Clarendon Press, 99, XII-347 p.

2090. Comedia (La) griega y su influencia en la literatura española. Ed. por J. A. LÓPEZ FÉREZ. Madrid, Ediciones Clásicas, 99, VIII-490 p.

2091. CUSSET (C.). La Muse dans la Bibliothèque. Réécriture et intertexualité dans la poésie alexandrine. Paris, CNRS éditions, 99, 424 p.

2092. DEAN ANDERSON (R.). Glossary of Greek rhetorical terms connected to methods of argumentation, figures and tropes from Anaximenes to Quintilian. Leuven, Peeters, 99, 130 p.

2093. DUFF (T.). Plutarch's Lives. Exploring virtue and vice. Oxford, Clarendon Press, 99, XX-423 p.

2094. Epic traditions in the contemporary world: the poetic of community. Ed. by M.J. BESSINGER, J. TYLUS and S. WOFFORD. Berkeley a. Los Angeles a. London, University of California Press, 99, X-314 p. [Cf. n° <choice> 2117.]

2095. ERBSE (H.). Über Pindars Umgang mit dem Mythos. *Hermes*, 99, 127, p. 13-32.

2096. FRANCO (Carlo). Il romanzo di Alessandro. Con appendice: la recensio vetusta e i suoi testimoni orientali. La versione armena. A cura di G. TRAINA. La versione siriaca. A cura di C. A. CIANCAGLINI. *Quaderni di storia*, 99, 49, p. 45-102.

2097. GERBER (D.E.). Greek elegiac poetry: from the seventh to the fifth centuries B.C. Cambridge a. London, Harvard U. P., 99, X-493 p. – IDEM. Greek iambic poetry: from the seventh to the fifth centuries B.C. Cambridge a. London, Harvard U. P., 99, VIII-551 p.

2098. GIANNISI (Phoebé). La profondeur et l'itinéraire dans l'Odyssée. *Quaderni di storia*, 99, 50, p. 135-144.

2099. GOWARD (B.). Telling tragedy. Narrative technique in Aeschylus, Sophocles and Euripides. London, Duckworth, 99, VI-214 p.

2100. GUEZ (J.-Ph.). Du rêve homérique au rêve posthomérique. *Antiquité classique*, 99, 68, p. 81-98.

2101. HUMMEL (P.). "Traduction photographique" ou "traduction microscopique": la tradition pindarique vue par J.J. Schwickert (1879). *Antiquité classique*, 99, 68, p. 135-147. – IDEM. L'épithète pindarique. Étude historique et philologique. Bern, Peter Lang, 99, 676 p.

2102. HUSS (B.). The dancing Sokrates and the laughing Xenophon or the other Symposium. *American journal of philology*, 99, 120, p. 381-409.

2103. JACQUEMIN (A.). Le rèdacteur et le lapicide: 'barbouillage dialectal' et repentirs dans les inscriptions de Delphes. *In*: Urkunden und Urkundenformulare [Cf. n° 2103], p. 71-80.

2104. JAY-ROBERT (G.). Essai d'interprétation du sens du substantif 'hosiê' dans l'Odyssée et dans les Hymnes Homériques. *Revue des études anciennes*, 99, 101, p. 5-20.

2105. LADA-RICHARDS (I.). Initiating Dionysus: ritual and theatre in Aristophanes' Frogs. Oxford, Clarendon Press, 99, XXIV-387 p.

2106. LAMBIN (G.). L'épopée: genèse d'un genre littéraire en Grèce. Rennes, Presses Universitaires de Rennes, 99, 223 p. – IDEM. Sur les origines du roman grec. *Antiquité classique*, 99, 68, p. 57-80.

2107. LAVECCHIA (S.), MARTINELLI (M. C.). P.Oxy. XXXV 2736. Quattro fragmenta dubia di Pindaro. *Zeitschrift für Papyrologie und Epigraphik*, 99, 125, p. 1-24.

2108. LOUDEN (B.). The Odyssey: structure, narration and meaning. Baltimore a. London, The Johns Hopkins U. P., 99, XX-182 p.

2109. MAC CLURE (L.). Spoken like a woman. Speech and gender in Athenian drama. Princeton, Princeton Univesity Press, 99, VIII-203 p.

2110. MAIULLARI (F.). L'interpretazione anamorfica dell'Edipo Re. Una nuova lettura della tragedia sofoclea. Pisa e Roma, Istituti editoriali e poligrafici internazionali, 99, XIX-482 p.

2111. MAZZARA (G.). Gorgia. La retorica del verosimile. Sankt Augustin, Academia Verlag, 99, IX-261 p.

2112. MILES FOLEY (J.). Homer's traditional art. University Park, Pennsylvania State U. P., 99, XVIII-363 p.

2113. MONTANARI (O.). I pesci di pregio nella Vita di Delizie di Archestrato di Gela. *Mélanges de l'École Française de Rome*, 99, 111, p. 67-77.

2114. MOOIJ-VALK (S.). Arrianus en Alexander. *Lampas* 32, 99, p. 25-43.

2115. MORRISON (J. V.). Homeric darkness patterns and manipulation of death scenes in the 'Iliad'. *Hermes*, 99, 127, p. 129-144.

2116. MOST (G. W.). Two problems in the third stasimon of Euripides' Medea. *Classical philology*, 99, 94, p. 20-35.

2117. MURNAGHAN (S.). The poetics of loss in Greek epic. *In*: Epic traditions [Cf. n° 2094], p. 203-220.

2118. NENCI (F.), ARATA (L.). Eschilo. Le Coefore. Fra genos e polis. La scelta di Oreste. Bologna, Cappelli editore, 99, 338 p.

2119. NESSELRATH (H.-G.). Dodona, Siwa und Herodot: ein Testfall für den Vater der Geschichte. *Museum Helveticum*, 99, 56, p. 1-14.

2120. OGUIBENINE (B.). Stratégie de l'aède homérique et sacrifice du poète védique. Essai de comparaison des pratiques du langage religieux. *Ktema*, 99, 24, p. 55-84.

2121. PARK POE (J.). Entrances, exits, and the structure of Aristophanic comedy. *Hermes*, 99, 127, p. 189-207.

2122. PIETSCH (C.). Die Argonautika des Apollonios von Rhodos. Untersuchungen zum Problem der einheitlichen Konzeption des Inhalts. Stuttgart, Steiner, 99, 307 p.

2123. PINTO (Pasquale Massimo). Demostene, Contro Androzione (XXII) 72: khoiniký. *Quaderni di storia*, 99, 50, p. 145-156.

2124. PÖTSCHNER (W.). Nochmals Solons Musenelegie. *Acta antiqua Academiae Scientiarum Hungaricae*, 99, 39, p. 261-274.

2125. RIU (X.). Dionysism and Comedy. Lanham, Boulder, New York a. Oxford, Rowman & Littlefield, 99, X-293 p.

2126. ROISMAN (H. M.). Nothing is as it seems: the tragedy of the implicit in Euripides' Hippolytus. Lanham, Boulder, New York a. Oxford, Rowman & Littlefield, 99, XVI-213 p.

2127. SAMIR (K.). La version arabe melkite du Roman d'Alexandre du Pseudo-Callisthène. *Byzantinische Forschungen*, 99, 25, p. 55-82.

2128. SCHIAPPA (E.). The beginnings of rhetorical theory in classical Greece. New Haven a. London, Yale U. P., 99, X-230 p.

2129. SCHMIDT THOMAS (S.). Plutarque et les barbares. La rhétorique d'une image. Louvain et Namur, Peeters-Société des Études Classiques, 99, IX-374 p.

2130. SCHRÖDER (S.). Geschichte und Theorie der Gattung Paian. Eine kritische Untersuchung mit einem Ausblick auf Behandlung und Auffassung der lyrischen Gattungen bei den alexandrinischen Philologen. Stuttgart u. Leipzig, B.G. Teubner, 99, XV-172 p.

2131. SCODEL (R.). Credible impossibilities. Conventions and strategies of verisimilitude in Homer and Greek tragedy. Stuttgart u. Leipzig, B.G. Teubner, 99, 216 p.

2132. SERRA (G.). La fine di re Edipo. *Quaderni di storia*, 99, 49, p. 5-44.

2133. Signs of orality. The oral tradition and its influence in the Greek and Roman world. Ed. by E. A. MACKAY. Leiden, Boston a. Köln, Brill, 99, X-261 p. (plates, figs).

2134. SOUTO (F.). La crítica musical en la Comedia griega antigua. *Minerva*, 99, 13, p. 87-101.

2135. SPINA (Luigi). Chiamare le cose col loro nome: a proposito di Tucidide III 82,4. *Quaderni di storia*, 99, 49, p. 247-260.

2136. SULTAN (N.). Exile and the poetics of loss in Greek tradition. Lanham, Rowman & Littlefield, 99, XIII-137 p.

2137. TRAVIS (R.). Allegory and the tragic chorus in Sophocles Oedipus at Colonus. Lanham, Boulder a. New York a. Oxford, Rowman & Littlefield, 99, XII-243 p.

2138. UDWIN (V. M.). Between two armies: the place of the duel in epic culture. Leiden, Boston a. Köln, Brill, 99, X-235 p.

2139. VISA-ONDARÇUHU (V.). L'image de l'athlète d'Homère à la fin du Ve siècle avant J.-C. Paris, Les Belles Lettres, 99, 453 p. (figs.).

2140. WARTELLE (A.). La poèsie grecque et sa traduction. *Révue des études grecques*, 99, 112, p. 234-237.

2141. WÖHRLE (G.). Telemachs Reise. Väter und Söhne in Iliad und Odyssee oder ein Beitrag zur Erforschung der Männlichkeitsideologie in der homerischen Welt. Göttingen, Vandenhoeck & Ruprecht, 99, 170 p.

2142. YATROMANOLAKIS (D.). Alexandrian Sappho revisited. *Harvard studies*, 99, 99, p. 179-195.

2143. ZEVI (F.). Dionigi e il valore dell'archeologia. *In*: Epigrafia e territorio [Cf. n° 2319], p. 286-293.

Cf. n°s 1566, 1877-1968

b. *Philosophy and sciences*

2144. CERRI (G.). La poesia di Parmenide. *Quaderni urbinati di cultura classica*, 99, 92, p. 7-27.

2145. Corpus dei papiri filosofici greci e latini (CPF). Testi e lessico nei papiri di cultura greca e latina. Parte I: Autori noti. Vol. 1, 3 (Nicolaus Damascenus–Platonis fragmenta); (Platonis testimonia–Zeno Tarsensis). Firenze, Olschki, 99, 2 vol., LXXXI-480 p., 481-895 p.

2146. DESTRÉE (P.). Platon et Leibniz, lecteurs d'Anaxagore. Note sur le sens de la finalité naturelle en philosophie grecque. *Antiquité classique*, 99, 68, p. 119-133.

2147. Fragende (Der) Sokrates. Hrsg. v. K. PESTALOZZI. Stuttgart u. Leipzig, B.G. Teubner, 99, XII-316 p.

2148. FRANK (M.). Untersuchungen zu den Politika des Aristoteles. Frankfurt am Main, Berlin, New York, Paris u. Wien, Lang, 99, 183 p.

2149. Geschichte der Mathematik und der Naturwissenschaften in der Antike. Vol. 1. Biologie. Hrsg. v. G. WÖHRLE. Stuttgart, Franz Steiner, 99, 284 p.

2150. GIGANTE (Marcello). 'Kepos' e 'Peripatos'. Contributo alla storia dell'aristotelismo antico. Napoli, Bibliopolis, 99, 159 p.

2151. GIULIANO (F.M.). Per una interpretazione letteraria di Platone: questioni di metodologia ermeneutica. *Elenchos*, 99, 20, p. 309-344.

2152. Histoire de la philosophie: idées, doctrines. 1. La philosophie païenne (du VIe siècle av. J.-C. au IIIe siècle apr. J.-C.). Ed. par F. CHÂTELET. Paris, Hachette, 99, 283 p.

2153. IOPPOLO (A. M.). Socrate e la conoscenza delle cose d'amore. *Elenchos*, 99, 20, p. 53-74.

2154. KERSTING (W.). Platons «Staat». Darmstadt, Wissenschaftliche Buchgesellschaft, 99, X-341 p.

2155. LARFOUILLOUX (J.). Sculpture et philosophies: perspectives philosophiques occidentales sur la sculpture et ses techniques de Socrate à Hegel. Paris, Éd. Arguments, 99, 432 p.

2156. LAURENTI (R.). Empedocle. Napoli, M. D'Auria, 99, 502 p.

2157. LEFEBVRE (R.). Les paradoxes du rapport 'phôs'/'phantasia'. *Revue des études anciennes*, 99, 101, p. 65-81.

2158. LOMBARD (J.). Platon et la médecine: le corps affaibli et l'âme attristée. Paris et Montréal, L'Harmattan, 99, 149 p.

2159. LONGO (O.). Simbiogenesi empedoclea. *Quaderni urbinati di cultura classica*, 99, 90, p. 129-152.

2160. MARBACK (R.). Plato's dream of sophistry. Columbia, University of South Carolina Press, 99, XII-163 p.

2161. MOURAVIEV (S. N.). Hèraclite d'Éphèse. La tradition antique et médiévale. Témoignages et citations. I. D'Épicharme à Philon d'Alexandrie. Sankt Augustin, Academia Verlag, 99, XXIII-269 p.

2162. NEHAMAS (A.). Virtues of authenticity. Essays on Plato and Socrates. Princeton, Princeton U. P., 99, XXXVI-372 p.

2163. NETZ (R.). Proclus' division of the mathematical proposition into parts: how and why was it formulated? *Classical quarterly*, 99, 49, p. 282-303. – IDEM. The shaping of deduction in Greek mathematics. A study in cognitive history. Cambridge, Cambridge U. P., 99, XVIII-331 p.

2164. NEWMYER (S. T.). Speaking of beasts: the Stoics and Plutarch on animal reason and the modern case against animals. *Quaderni urbinati di cultura classica*, 99, 92, p. 99-110.

2165. NOTOMI (N.). The unity of Plato's "Sophist": between the sophist and the philosopher. Cambridge, Cambridge U. P., 99, XXII-346 p.

2166. PALMER (J.A.) Plato's reception of Parmenides. Oxford, Clarendon Press, 99, XIII-294 p.

2167. PAPATHANASSIOU (M.). Historia Alexandri Magni: astronomy, astrology and tradition. *Dialogues d'histoire ancienne*, 99, 25, 2, p. 113-126.

2168. PAPAZIAN (M. B.). Stoic ontology and the reality of time. *Ancient philosophy*, 99, 19, p. 105-119.

2169. Proceedings of the Boston Area Colloquium in Ancient Philosophy. Ed. by J.J. CLEARY and G.M. GURTLER. Leiden, Boston a. Köln, Brill, 99, XVIII-291 p.

2170. PUGLIESE CARRATELLI (Giovanni). 'Monas mnemosyne, dekas pistis mneme'. *La parola del passato*, 99, 54, p. 186-192.

2171. RIHLL (T. E.). Greek Science. Oxford, Oxford U. P., 99, 163 p. (Greece and Rome, New Surveys, 29).

2172. SAUVANET (P.). Le rhytme grec: d'Héraclite à Aristote. Paris, Presses Universitaires de France, 99, 127 p.

2173. SHIELDS (C.). Order in multiplicity: homonymy in the philosophy of Aristotle. Oxford, Clarendon Press, 99, XIV-290 p.

2174. STARKE (D.). Geschichte der Naturwissenschaften: erste Anfänge. Thun, Deutsch, 99, 213 p.

2175. THESLEFF (H.). Studies in Plato's two-level model. Helsinki, Societas scientiarum Fennica, 99, VII-143 p.

2176. Topics in Stoic philosophy. Ed. by K. IERODIAKONOU. Oxford, Clarendon Press, 99, 259 p.

2177. Traditions of Platonism. Essays in honour of John Dillon. Ed. by J. J. CLEARY. Aldershot, Ashgate, 99, XXV-416 p.

Cf. n°s 1877-1968

§ 8. Religion and mythology.

2178. Ancient Greek hero cult. Proceedings of the Fifth international Seminar on ancient Greek cult, organized by the Department of Classical Archaeology and Ancient History, Göteborg University 21–23 April 1995. Ed. by R. HÄGG. Stockholm, Paul Aströms Förlag, 99, 207 p. (figs.).

2179. ARRIGONI (G.). Perseo contro Dioniso a Lerna. *In*: Ricordando Raffaele Cantarella [Cf. n° 1834], p. 9-70.

2180. BURKERT (W.). Antiker Mythos. Begriff und Funktion. *In*: Antike Mythen [Cf. n° 1816], p. 11-26.

2181. CASADIO (G.). Eudemo di Rodi: un pioniere della storia delle religioni tra oriente e occidente. *Wiener Studien*, 112, 99, p. 39-54. – IDEM. Il vino dell'anima. Storia del culto di Dioniso a Corinto, Sicione, Trezene. Roma, Il calamo, 99, p. 231.

2182. CLARKE (M.). Flesch and spirit in the songs of Homer. A study of words and myths. Oxford, Clarendon Press, 99, XV-378 p.

2183. CURTY (O.). La parenté légendaire à l'époque hellénistique. Précisions méthodologiques. *Kernos*, 99, 12, p. 167-194.

2184. DAMASKOS (D.). Untersuchungen zu hellenistischen Kultbildern. Stuttgart, Steiner, 99, XIV-363 p.

2185. DESHOURS (N.). Les Messéniens, le règlement des mystères et la consultation de l'oracle d'Apollon Pythéen à Argos. *Révue des études grecques*, 99, 112, p. 463-484.

2186. FRANÇOISE DE ROGUIN (C.). Apollon Lykeios dans la tragédie: dieu protecteur, dieu tueur, "dieu de l'initiation". *Kernos*, 99, 12, p. 99-123.

2187. GENTILE (L.). L'epiteto 'katagogis' e l'uso del verbo 'katago' in ambito religioso. *Rivista di filologia e istruzione classica*, 99, 127, pp. 334-343.

2188. GIORDANO (M.). La parola efficace. Maledizioni, giuramenti e benedizioni nella Grecia arcaica. Pisa e Roma, Istituti Editoriali e Poligrafici Internazionali, 99, 70 p.

2189. HAGL (H.). Das "officium" des Synesios für Heimat und Reich: Ein Leben im Spannungsverhältnis zwischen Heidentum und Christentum. *Klio*, 99, 81, p. 199-217.

2190. HOFMANN (H.). Orpheus. *In*: Antike Mythen [Cf. n° 1816], p. 153-198.

2191. HOLT (F. L.). Thundering Zeus: the making of Hellenistic Bactria. Berkeley a. Los Angeles a. London, University of California Press, 99, XVIII-221 p.

2192. JOUANNA (J.). Le trône, les fleurs, le char et la puissance d'Aphrodite. *Révue des études grecques*, 99, 112, p. 99-126.

2193. KANNNICHT (R.). Pandora. *In*: Antike Mythen [Cf. n° 1816], p. 127-151.

2194. MAGGI (S.). Diomede a Ravenna? *Athenaeum*, 99, 87, p. 551-555.

2195. MAHE (M.). Le pythagorisme d'Italie du Sud vu par Tite-Live. *Ktema*, 99, 24, p. 147-157.

2196. MORANT (M.-J.). Mains levée, mains supines, à propos d'une base funéraire da Kadyanda (Lycie). *Ktema*, 99, 24, p. 289-294.

2197. MOREAU (A.). Mythes grecs I. Origines. Montpellier, Université Paul-Valéry, Séminaire d'Étude des mentalités antiques, Publ. de la recherche, 99, 264 p.

2198. Mythe grec (Le) dans l'Italie antique: fonction et image: actes du colloque international organisé par l'École française de Rome, l'Istituto italiano per gli studi filosofici (Naples) et l'UMR 126 du CNRS (Archéologies d'Orient et d'Occident), Rome, 14–16 novembre 1996. Ed. par Françoise-Hélène MASSA-PAIRAULT. Roma, École française de Rome, 99, 670 p. (ill., maps). (Collection de l'Ecole française de Rome, 253). [Cf. n°ˢ <sélection> 2270, 2271, 2277, 2286, 2292, 2294, 2298, 2717.]

2199. Plutarco, Dioniso y el vino. Actas del VI Simposio Español sobre Plutarco (Cadiz 14–16 de mayo de 1998), Sociedad Española de plutarquistas (sección de la International Plutarch Society). Ed. por J. G. MONTES CALA, M. SÁNCHEZ ORTIZ DE LANDALUCE y R. J. GALLÍ CEIUDO. Madrid, Edicciones Clasicas, 99, p. X-540.

2200. POSTLETHWAITE (N.). The date of Zeus Kretagenes. *Kernos*, 99, 12, p. 85-98.

2201. PRICE (Simon). Religions of the Ancient Greeks. Cambridge, Cambridge U. P., 99, XII-217 p.

2202. QUANTIN (F.). Aspects épirotes de la vie religieuse antique. *Révue des études grecques*, 99, 112, p. 61-98.

2203. RUDHARDT (J.). Thémis et les Hôrai. Recherche sur les divinités grecques de la justice et de la paix. Genève, Droz, 99, 167 p.

2204. SCHMIDT (E. A.). Achill. *In*: Antike Mythen [Cf. n° 1816], p. 91-125.

2205. Sibille e linguaggi oracolari: mito, storia, tradizione. Atti del Convegno Internazionale di Studi Macerata-Norcia 20–24 settembre 1994, Università degli Studi di Macerata 1998. A cura di I. CHIRASSI E T. SEPPILLI. Pisa-Roma, Istituti Editoriali e Poligrafici Internazionali, 99, 822 p.

2206. SINEUX (P.). Le péan d'Isyllos: forme et finalités d'un chant religieux dans le culte d'Asklépios à Épidaure. *Kernos*, 99, 12, p. 153-166.

2207. STRID (O.). Die Dryoper. Eine Untersuchung der Überlieferung. Uppsala, Uppsala U. P., 99, 126 p.

2208. SUCEVEANU (A.). Le "Grand Dieu" d'Histria. *Ktema*, 99, 24, p. 271-281.

2209. SZLEZÁK (Th. A.). Ödipus nach Sophokles. *In*: Antike Mythen [Cf. n° 1816], p. 199-220.

2210. USTINOVA (Y.). The supreme gods of the Bosporan kingdom. Celestial Aphrodite and the most high god. Leiden, Brill, 99, 321 p. (plates).

2211. VAN LIEFFERINGE (C.). La théurgie: des Oracles chaldaïques à Proclus. Liège, Centre International d'Étude de la Religion Grecque Antique, 99, 320 p.

2212. VAN NUFFELEN (P.). Le culte des souverains hellénistiques, le gui de la religion grecque. *Ancient society*, 99, 29, p. 175-189.

2213. VENTURI BERNARDINI (I.). Le epiclesi di Atena in Omero. *Studi e materiali di storia delle religioni*, 99, 65, p. 41-97.

2214. WOLFF (C.). L'enlèvement de Charité: fiction complète. *Révue des études grecques*, 99, 112, p. 253-258.

2215. Zwischen Krise und Alltag. Antike Religionen im Mittelmeerraum. Conflit und normalité. Religions anciennes dans l'espace méditerranéen. Hrsg. v. C. BATSCH, U. EGELHAAF-GAISER und R. STEPPER. Stuttgart, Franz Steiner Verlag, 99, 287 p. (figs.). [Cf. n^{os} <Auswahl> 2698, 2716, 2718, 2719, 2721, 2726, 2877, 2929.]

§ 9. Archaeology and history of art.

2216. ANDREUSSI (M.). Per uno studio dello sviluppo urbanistico di Iasos. *La parola del passato*, 99, 54, p. 414-418.

2217. ANGIOLILLO (S.). A proposito di una lamina in bronzo con auriga vincitore. *La parola del passato*, 99, 54, p. 360-372.

2218. Archéomatériaux: marbres et autres roches. Asmosia IV. Actes de la IVe conférence internationale de l'Association pour l'étude des marbres et autres roches utilisés dans le passé, Bordeaux-Talence 9–13 octobre 1995. Ed. par M. SCHVOERER. Bordeaux, Pr. Universitaires de Bordeaux, 99, 368 p. (ill.).

2219. BALDONI (D.). Tre placche di cintura in bronzo da Iasos. *La parola del passato*, 99, 54, p. 401-410.

2220. BASCH (L.). Un modèle de navire chypriote du VIe siècle av. J.-C. trouvé en mer au large d'Amathonte. *Bulletin de correspondance hellénique*, 99, 123, p. 43-64.

2221. BEJOR (G.). Vie colonnate; paesaggi urbani nel mondo antico. Roma, Giorgio Bretschneider, 99, 143 p. (maps, figs.).

2222. BERNS (Ch.), MERT (H.). Architekturfragmente aus der Nekropole von Stratonikeia. *Istanbuler Mitteilungen*, 99, 49, p. 197-212.

2223. BERTI (F.). Precisazioni su uno scutulatum iasio. *La parola del passato*, 99, 54, p. 333-342.

2224. BLOEDOW (E. F.). The mourning/sinnende Athena: the story behind the relief. *Athenaeum*, 99, 87, p. 27-50.

2225. BOMMELAER (J.-F.). Sur le paysage antique de Delphes. *Ktema*, 99, 24, p. 213-224.

2226. BONIFACIO (R.). Osservazioni su alcune statuette votive del Thesmophorion di Iasos. *La parola del passato*, 99, 54, p. 304-315.

2227. BOSNAKOV (K.). Identification archéologique et historique de l'emporion de Pistiros en Thrace. *Bulletin de correspondance hellénique*, 99, 123, p. 319-329.

2228. BRUN (J. P.). Laudatissimum fuit antiquitus in Delo insula. La maison 1B du Quartier du stade et la production des parfums à Délos. *Bulletin de correspondance hellénique*, 99, 123, p. 87-155.

2229. BRUNET (M.). Territoires des cités grecques. Actes de la Table Ronde International organisée par l'École Française d'Athènes 31 octobre–3 novembre 1991. Paris, De Boccard, 99, 432 p.

2230. DONATI (L.). Sull'Heroon di Iasos. *La parola del passato*, 99, 54, p. 316-332.

2231. FABRICIUS (J.). Die hellenistischen Totenmahlreliefs. Grabrepräsentation und Wertvorstellungen in ostgriechischen Städten. München, Pfeil, 99, 384 p.

2232. FOURRIER (S.). Petite plastique chypriote de Délos. *Bulletin de correspondance hellénique*, 99, 123, p. 373-388.

2233. GRACH (Nonna L.). Nekropol' Nimfeja. (The Necropolis of Nymphaion). Sankt-Peterburg, Nauka, 99, 328 p. (ill., bibl. p. 8-10). [Eng. summary]

2234. GÜNEL (Sevinç). Panaztepe II: M.Ö.2. Bine tarihlendirilen Panaztepe seramiğinin Batı Anadolu ve Ege Arkeolojisindeki yeri ve önemi. [Die Keramik von Panaztepe und ihre Bedeutung für Westkleinasien und die Ägäis im 2. Jahrtausend]. Ankara, Türk Tarih Kurumu, 99, 271 p.

2235. HALM-TISSERANT (M.). Le paysage sacré dans la peinture de vases grecques. *Ktema*, 99, 24, p. 243-250.

2236. HOFFELNER (K.), WALTER-KARYDI (E.). Das Apollon-Heiligtum. Tempel, Altäre, Temenosmauer, Thearion. Mainz, von Zabern, 99, 190 p.

2237. HUBER (K.). Le ceramiche attiche a figure rosse. Bari, Edipuglia, 99, 188 p.

2238. JOHANNOWSKY (W.). Note sullo sviluppo urbanistico di Iasos. *La parola del passato*, 99, 54, p. 283-288.

2239. KARAGEORGHIS (J.). The coroplastic art of ancient Cyprus. V. The Cypro-Archaic period small female figurines. Nicosia, The A.G. Leventis Foundation, 99, XXXIII-341 p.

2240. 'Koina'. Miscellanea di studi archeologici in onore di Piero Orlandini. A cura di M. CASTOLDI. Milano, Edizioni Et, 99, 490 p. (ill.).

2241. LANDOLFI (M.). Thymiateria a Iasos di Caria: il tipo persepolitano. *La parola del passato*, 99, 54, p. 289-303.

2242. MARZOLFF (P.). Zentrum und Peripherie im Wandel der Besiedlungsstruktur an der Bucht von Iolkos. In: Stadt und Umland [Cf. n° 2257], p. 168-185.

2243. MILLER (M. C.). Reexamining transvestitism in archaic and classical Athens: the Zewadski Stamnos. *American journal of archaeology*, 99, 103, p. 223-253.

2244. MYLONAS SHEAR (I.). Maidens in Greek architecture: the origin of the «Caryatids». *Bulletin de correspondance hellénique*, 99, 123, p. 65-85. – IDEM. The western approach to the Athenian akropolis. *Journal of Hellenic studies*, 99, 119, p. 86-127.

2245. PARAPETTI (R.). Due capitelli dal Bouleuterion di Iasos. *La parola del passato*, 99, 54, p. 354-359.

2246. PLANTZOS (D.). Hellenistic engraved gems. Oxford, Clarendon Press, 99, XV-148 p.

9. ARCHAEOLOGY AND HISTORY OF ART

2247. PRÊTRE (C.). Le matériel votif à Délos. Exposition et conservation. *Bulletin de correspondance hellénique*, 99, 123, p. 389-396.

2248. Proceedings of the XVth international congress of classical archaeology, Amsterdam, July 12–17, 1998. Classical archaeology towards the third millennium: reflections and perspectives. Ed. by R. F. DOCTER and E. M. MOORMAN. Amsterdam, Allard Pierson Stichting, Publication department, 99, 2 vol., XVII-469 p., [s. p.]. (tables).

2249. PROST (F.). La statue cultuelle d'Apollon à Délos. *Révue des études grecques*, 99, 112, p. 37-60.

2250. RAUTMAN (M. L.), NEFF (H.), GOMEZ (B.), VAUGHAN (S.), GLASCOCK (M. D.). Amphoras and rooftiles from Late Roman Cyprus: a compositional study of calcareous ceramics from Kalavasos-Kopetra. *Journal of Roman archaeology*, 99, 12, p. 377-391.

2251. ROMUALDI (A.). Antefisse fittili da Iasos. *La parola del passato*, 99, 54, p. 343-353.

2252. SÄFLUND (G.). Myter i marmor. Grekiska konstwerk i romerska museer. (Myths in marble. Greek art in Roman museums). Jonsered, P. Aström, 99, 77 p. (figs.).

2253. SCHNEIDER (W.J.). Eine Polemik Polemons in den Propyläen. Ein Votivgemälde des Alkibiades – Kontext und Rezeption. *Klio*, 99, 81, p. 18-44.

2254. SCHWARZER (H.). Untersuchungen zum hellenistischen Herrscherkult in Pergamon. *Istanbuler Mitteilungen*, 99, 49, p. 249-300.

2255. Siponto antica. A cura di M. MAZZEI e M. TORELLI. Foggia, Grenzi, 99, 512 p. [Cf. n° <scelta> 2320.]

2256. Sparta in Laconia: the archaeology of a city and its countryside. Proceedings of the 19th British Museum Classical Colloquium. Ed. by W. G. CAVANAGH and S. E. C. WALKER. London, British School at Athens, 99, 171 p. (fig.).

2257. Stadt und Umland. Neue Ergebnisse der archäologischen Bau- und Siedlungsforschung. Bauforschungskolloquium in Berlin vom 7. bis 10 Mai 1997 veranstaltet vom Architektur-Referat des DAI. Hrsg. v. E. L. SCHWANDNER und K. RHEIDT. Mainz, von Zabern, 99, X-293 p. [Cf. n[os] <Auswahl> 1599, 1600, 1602, 1606, 1609, 1661, 1730, 1736, 2242.]

2258. VALAVANIS (P.). Hysplex. The starting mechanism in ancient stadia. A contribution to ancient Greek technology. Berkeley, Los Angeles a. London, University of California Press, 99, XVIII-183 p. (ills.).

2259. WARLAND (D.). Que représente la fresque de la paroi Ouest de la tombe "du plongeur" de Posidonia? *Kernos*, 99, 12, p. 195-206.

Cf. n°s 1566, 2744

F

HISTORY OF ROME, ANCIENT ITALY AND THE ROMAN EMPIRE

§ 1. The peoples of Italy. 2260-2279. – § 2. The Etruscans. 2280-2306. – § 3. Sources and criticism of sources. (*a*. Epigraphical sources; *b*. Literary sources). 2307-2391. – § 4. General and political history. 2392-2473. – § 5. History of law and institutions. 2474-2526. – § 6. Economic and social history. 2527-2585. – § 7. History of literature, philosophy and science (*a*. Literature; *b*. Philosophy and science). 2586-2691. – § 8. Religion and mythology. 2692-2726. – § 9. Archaeology and history of art. 2727-2788. – § 10. Late antiquity. Transformation of the Roman world. 2789-2826.

§ 1. The peoples of Italy.

2260. ANGELELLI (C.), FALZONE (S.). Considerazioni sull'occupazione protostorica dell'area sud-occidentale del Palatino. *Journal of Roman archaeology*, 99, 12, p. 5-32.

2261. BALDAROTTA (Donatella). La configurazione etnica dei Latini tra Lavinium, Ardea e Satricum. *Studi romani*, 99, 47, 3-4, p. 261-269.

2262. BENUCCI (Franco). Moneta e sacrificio nel mondo italico. *La parola del passato*, 99, 54, p. 81-134. – IDEM. Victimarum probatio e origine dell'uso monetario nell'Italia antica. *La parola del passato*, 99, 54, p. 161-185.

2263. BRUNI (S.). I confini del territorio della polis pisana in età arcaica. Una proposta. *Athenaeum*, 99, 87, 1, p. 243-266 (ill.).

2264. CAPPELLETTI (L.). Il giuramento degli Italici sulle monete del 90 a. C. *Zeitschrift für Papyrologie und Epigraphik*, 99, p. 85-92.

2265. CÀSSOLA GUIDA (Paola). Lineamenti delle culture altoadriatiche tra Bronzo finale e prima età del Ferro. *In*: Protostoria e storia del 'Venetorum angulus' [Cf. n° 2274], p. 47-72 (carte).

2266. DE MARINIS (R. C.). Il confine occidentale del mondo proto-veneto/paleo-veneto dal bronzo finale alle invasioni galliche del 338 a.C. *In*: Protostoria e storia del 'Venetorum angulus' [Cf. n° 2274], p. 511-564.

2267. GRECO (Emanuele). Siculi ed Enotri: tra analogie e differenze. *In*: Colonisation grecque (La) en Méditerranée occidentale [Cf. n° 1975], p. 281-292.

2268. LO PORTO (Felice Gino). Corredi di tombe daunie da Minervino Murge. Roma, Giorgio Bretschneider, 99, 53-115 p. (ill., tav.).

2269. MARTINEZ-PINNA (Jorge). Caton y la tesis griega sobre los Aborigines. *Athenaeum*, 99, 87, 1, p. 93-109.

2270. MAZZEI (M.). Committenza e mito. Esempi dalla Puglia settentrionale. *In*: Mythe grecque (Le) dans l'Italie antique [Cf. n° 2198], p. 467-483.

2271. MENICHETTI (M.). Una città e le sue immagini: la mitologia delle ciste prenestine. *In*: Mythe grecque (Le) dans l'Italie antique [Cf. n° 2198], p. 485-510.

2272. MUSTI (Domenico). Ausonia terra 1-2. *Rivista di cultura classica e medievale*, 99, 41, 2, p. 167-172.

2273. PAGLIARA (A.). Ausonia terra. *Rivista di cultura classica e medievale*, 99, 41, 2, p. 173-199.

2274. Protostoria e storia del 'Venetorum angulus'. Atti del XX convegno di studi etruschi ed italici Portogruaro, Quarto d'Altino, Este e Adria, 16–19 ottobre 1996). A cura di Orazio PAOLETTI e Luisa TAMAGNO PERNA. Pisa e Roma, Istituti editoriali e poligrafici internazionali, 99, 664 p. (ill., tav.). [Cf. n[os] <scelta> 2265, 2266, 2278, 2283, 2297, 2303.]

2275. RAWLINGS (L.). Condottieri and clansmen. *In*: Organised crime in antiquity [Cf. n° 2569], p. 97-127.

2276. RICCARDI (A.). Forme ideali e materiali della romanizzazione della Peucezia. *In*: Bitonto e la Puglia tra tardoantico e regno normanno [Cf. n° 2789], p. 29-49.

2277. TAGLIENTE (M.). Immagini e mito nel mondo indigeno della Puglia e della Basilicata. *In*: Mythe grecque (Le) dans l'Italie antique [Cf. n° 2198], p. 423-433.

2278. ZANINI (A.). Rapporti tra Veneto ed area medio-tirrenica nel bronzo finale. Nuovi contributi per la definizione del problema. *In*: Protostoria e storia del 'Venetorum angulus' [Cf. n° 2274], p. 307-343.

2279. ZEVI (Fausto). Siculi e troiani. Roma e la propaganda greca nel V secolo a.C. *In*: Colonisation grecque (La) en Méditerranée occidentale [Cf. n° 1975], p. 315-343.

§ 2. The Etruscans.

2280. BAGNASCO GIANNI (Giovanna). L'acquisizione della scrittura in Etruria: materiali a confronto per la ricostruzione del quadro storico e culturale. *In*: Scritture mediterranee tra il IX e il VII secolo a.C. [Cf. n° 1850], p. 85-106 (ill.).

2281. BARBIERI (G.). Materiali etruscoromani da Viterbo. Corredi funerari inediti dalla località San Nicolao. *Opuscula Romana*, 99, 24, p. 7-61.

2282. BECKER (Marshall J.). Etruscan gold dental appliances: three newly 'discovered' examples. *American Journal of Archaeology*, 99, 103, 1, p. 103-111.

2283. BENELLI (E.). La romanizzazione attraverso l'epigrafia: il Veneto e il modello etrusco. *In*: Protostoria e storia del 'Venetorum angulus' [Cf. n° 2274], p. 651-664.

2284. BRIQUEL (D.). De l'Occident à l'Orient: l'évolution de la religion étrusque dans l'antiquité tardive. *In*: Syncrétismes religieux (Les) dans le monde méditerranéen antique [Cf. n° 1381], p. 337-356.

2285. CAGIANELLI (C.). Bronzi a figura umana. Città del Vaticano, Direzione Generale dei Monumenti, Musei e Gallerie Pontificie, 99, 342 p.

2286. CERCHIAI (L.). La rappresentazione di Teseo sulle stele felsinee. *In*: Mythe grecque (Le) dans l'Italie antique [Cf. n° 2198], p. 353-365.

2287. COLONNA (G.), BACKE-FORSBERG (Y.). Le iscrizioni del 'sacello' del ponte di San Giovenale. Etruscan inscriptions and graffiti from the bridge at San Giovenale. *Opuscula Romana*, 99, 24, p. 63-81.

2288. Corpus speculorum Etruscorum. Italia, V. Viterbo, Museo archeologico nazionale. A cura di Gabriella BARBIERI e Lorenzo GALEOTTI. Roma, 'L'Erma' di Bretschneider, 99, 209 p. 156 (tav.).

2289. D'AGOSTINO (Bruno), CERCHIAI (Luca). Il mare, la morte, l'amore. Gli Etruschi, i Greci e l'immagine. Roma, Donzelli, 99, XXXVI-220 p. (ill.).

2290. DE ANGELIS (F.). Tragedie familiari. Miti greci nell'arte sepolcrale etrusca. *In*: Spiegel (Im) des Mythos [Cf. n° 2720], p. 53-66.

2291. GALLUCCIO (F.). Volterra etrusca alla luce delle nuove scoperte. *Opuscula Romana*, 99, 24, p. 83-98.

2292. GRAN-AYMERICH (J.). Images et mythes sur les vases noirs d'Étrurie (VIIIe–VIe siècle av. J.-C.). *In*:

Mythe grecque (Le) dans l'Italie antique [Cf. n° 2198], p. 382-404.

2293. JURGEIT (F.). Die etruskischen und italischen Bronzen sowie Gegenstände aus Eisen, Blei und Leder im Badischen Landesmuseum Karlsruhe. Band 1. Text. Band 2. Tafeln. Pisa u. Roma, Istituti editoriali poligrafici internazionali, 99, 2 vol., XXXII-657, XIV-348 p.

2294. KRAUSKOPF (I.). Interesse privato nel mito. Il caso degli scarabei etruschi. *In*: Mythe grecque (Le) dans l'Italie antique [Cf. n° 2198], p. 405-421.

2295. LEHOËRFF (Anne). Le travail en laboratoire au service de l'histoire de l'artisanat métallurgique du début du premier millénaire avant notre ère en Italie. Quelques résultats sur des mobiliers de Tarquinia, Veio, et des collections villanoviennes britanniques. *Mélanges de l'Ecole française de Rome. Antiquité*, 99, 111, 2, p. 787-846.

2296. MARCHESINI (Simona). Etrusco Śatri. *La parola del passato*, 99, 54, p. 17-47.

2297. MARZATICO (F.). Apporti etrusco-italici nell'area retica. *In*: Protostoria e storia del 'Venetorum angulus' [Cf. n° 2274], p. 475-484.

2298. MASSA-PAIRAULT (F.-H.). Mythe et identité politique. L'Étrurie du IVe siècle à l'époque hellénistique. *In*: Mythe grecque (Le) dans l'Italie antique [Cf. n° 2198]. p. 521-554.

2299. MEURANT (A.). Les jumeaux mythiques de Pérouse. *Latomus*, 99, 58, p. 269-275.

2300. NIELSEN (M.). Common tombs for women in Etruria: buried matriarchies? *In*: Female networks and the public sphere in Roman society [Cf. n° 2541], p. 65-136.

2301. PASQUINUCCI (Marinella), MENCHELLI (Simonetta). The landscape and economy of the territories of Pisae and Volaterrae (coastal North Etruria). *Journal of Roman archaeology*, 99, 12, p. 123-141.

2302. PRAYON (F.). Individualporträts in der etruskischen Kunst? *In*: Antike Porträts [Cf. n° 2728], p. 85-90.

2303. SASSATELLI (G.). Nuovi dati epigrafici e il ruolo degli Etruschi nei rapporti con l'Italia nord-orientale. *In*: Protostoria e storia del 'Venetorum angulus' [Cf. n° 2274], p. 453-474.

2304. SHEPHERD (Elizabet J.). Populonia, un mosaico e l'iconografia del naufragio. *Mélanges de l'Ecole française de Rome. Antiquité*, 99, 111, 1, p. 119-144.

2305. STEINBAUER (Dieter H.). Neues Handbuch des Etruskischen. St. Katharinen, Scripta Mercaturae Verlag, 99, IX-519 p. (Subsidia Classica, 1).

2306. WARDEN (P. G.), THOMAS (M. L.), GALLOWAY (J.). The Etruscan settlement of Poggio Colla (1995–98 excavations). *Journal of Roman archaeology*, 99, 12, p. 231-246.

§ 3. Sources and criticism of sources.

a. *Epigraphical sources*

* 2307. Année épigraphique 1996 (L'). Ed. par Mireille CORBIER, Patrick LE ROUX et Sylvie DARDAINE. Paris, Presses universitaires de France, 99, 784 p.

2308. ALFÖLDY (Géza). Die Inschriften des Jüngeren Plinius und seine Mission in der Provinz Pontus et Bithynia. *Acta antiqua Academiae scientiarum Hungaricae*, 99, 39, p. 21-44.

2309. Atti dell'XI Congresso Internazionale di Epigrafia Greca e Latina (Roma, 18–24 Settembre 1997). Vol. I. Vol. II. Roma, Quasar, 99, 889, 797 p. (ill.). [Cf. n^{os} <scelta> 2329, 2963.]

2310. Auxilia epigraphica. Volumen I: Inscriptiones Britanniae. Hrsg. v. Manfred HAINZMANN und Peter SCHUBERT. Berlin u. New York, de Gruyter, 99, CD-ROM

2311. BRUUN (Ch.). Imperial procuratores and dispensatores: new discoveries. *Chiron*, 99, 29, p. 29-42.

2312. CALDELLI (Maria Letizia). La dédicace de l'amphitéâtre de Metz. *Mélanges de l'Ecole française de Rome. Antiquité*, 99, 111, 2, p. 919-925.

2313. CAMODECA (G.). Un nuovo decreto decurionale puteolano con concessione di superficies agli Augustali e le entrate cittadine da solarium. *In*: Capitolo (Il) delle entrate nelle finanze municipali in occidente e in oriente [Cf. n° 2534], p. 1-23.

2314. CECAMORE (Claudia). Faustinae aedemque decernerent (SHA, Marcus, 26). Les fragments 69-70 de la Forma Urbis et la première dédicace du temple de la Vigna Barberini. *Mélanges de l'Ecole française de Rome. Antiquité*, 99, 111, 1, p. 311-349.

2315. CHELOTTI (M.). Iscrizioni monumentali latine di Venosa e Lucera. *In*: Epigrafia e territorio [Cf. n° 2319], p. 17-36.

2316. DE LIGHT (L.). Studies in legal and agrarian history I: the inscription from Henchir-Mettich and the Lex Manciana. *Ancient society*, 98-99, 29, p.219-239.

2317. DI STEFANO MANZELLA (Ivan). Avidum mare nautis. Un naufragio nel porto di Odessus e altre iscrizioni. *Mélanges de l'Ecole française de Rome. Antiquité*, 99, 111, 1, p. 79-106.

2318. ECK (W.). Zur Einleitung. Römische Provinzialadministration und die Erkenntnismöglichkeiten der epigraphischen Überlieferung. *In*: Lokale Autonomie und römische Ordnungsmacht in den Kaiserzeitlichen Provinzen vom 1.–3. Jahrhundert [Cf. n° 2428], p. 1-15.

2319. Epigrafia e territorio. Politica e società. Temi di antichità romane. A cura di Mario PANI. Bari, Edipuglia, 99, 300 p. [Cf. n^{os} <scelta> 2143, 2315, 2401, 2410, 2443, 2511, 2548.]

2320. FOLCANDO (E.). Le iscrizioni romane. *In*: Siponto Antica [Cf. n° 2255], p. 437-451.

2321. GAMBERALE (Leopoldo). In margine a CIL IX 955: una nota di metrica epigrafica. *Rivista di filologia e di istruzione classica*, 99, 127, p. 469-479.

2322. GONZÁLES (Julián). Tacitus, Germanicus, Piso, and the Tabula Siarensis. *American journal of philology*, 99, 120, p. 123-142.

2323. HERMON (Ella). Le Lapis Satricanus et la colonisation militaire au début de la République. *Mélanges de l'Ecole française de Rome. Antiquité*, 99, 111, 2, p. 847-881.

2324. Inscripțiile antice din Dacia și Scythia Minor. Inscripțiile Daciei Romane. (Ancient Inscriptions in Dacia and Scythia Minor. Inscriptions in Roman Dacia). Vol. III. Dacia Superior. 6. Apulum – Instrumentum Domesticum. Adunate, însoțite de comentarii și indice, traduse de Cloșca L. BĂLUȚĂ. București, Editura Academiei Române, 99, 276 p.

2325. KRUMSCHWITZ (P.). Römische Werbeinschriften. *Gymnasium*, 99, 106, p. 231-253.

2326. LEPELLEY (C.). Témoignages épigraphiques sur le contrôle des finances municipales par les gouverneurs à partir du règne de Dioclétien. *In*: Capitolo (Il) delle entrate nelle finanze municipali in Occidente e in Oriente [Cf. n° 2534], p. 235-247.

2327. PÉREZ RIVERA (J. M.), DEL HOYO CALLEJA (J.), BERNAL CASASOLA (D.). Epígrafe inédito hallado en Ceuta. Acerca del estatuto jurídico-administrativo de Septem fratres. *Latomus*, 99, 58, p. 839-849.

2328. PRIETO (A.). Index de la esclavitud en Barcino según las fuentes epigraphicas: la mujer. *In*: Femmes-esclaves [Cf. n° 2542], p. 331-342.

2329. SOLIN (H.). Epigrafia repubblicana. Bilancio, novità, prospettive. *In*: Atti dell'XI Congresso internazionale di epigrafia greca e latina (Roma, 18–24 settembre 1997) [Cf. n° 2329], p. 379-404.

2330. SUERBAUM (W.). Schwierigkeiten bei der Lektüre des SC de Cn. Pisone patre durch die Zeitgenossen um 20 n. Chr., durch Tacitus und durch heutige Leser. *Zeitschrift für Papyrologie und Epigraphik*, 99, 128, p. 213-234.

2331. Tabula Siarensis. Edición, traducción y comentario. Ed por A. SÁNCHEZ-OSTIZ. Pamplona, Ediciones Universidad de Navarra, 99, XXIV-486 p.

2332. Tabulae Pompeianae Sulpiciorum (TPSulp.). Edizione critica dell'archivio puteolano dei Sulpicii. A cura di Giuseppe CAMODECA, Roma, Quasar, 99, VII-437, p. (ill.).

2333. VERVAET (F. J.). CIL IX 3426: a new light on Corbulo's career, with special reference to his official mandate in the East from AD 55 to AD 63. *Latomus*, 99, 58, p. 574-599.

Cf. n° 1566

b. *Literary sources*

2334. [Ammianus Marcellinus] Ammiani Marcellini Rerum gestarum libri qui supersunt. Hrsg. v. Wolfgang SEYFARTH, Liselotte JACOB-KARAU und Ilse ULMANN. Volumen 1. Libri XIV-XXV. Volumen 2. Libri XXVI-XXXI. Stuttgart u. Leipzig, Teubner, 99, L-380 p., 248 p.

2335. [Ammianus Marcellinus] AMMIEN MARCELLIN. Histoire. Tome VI. Livres XXIX-XXXI. Index général. Ed. par Guy SABBAH et Laurent ANGLIVIEL DE LA BEAUMELLE. Paris, Les Belles Lettres, 99, LXVI-371 p. (maps). (Collection des universités de France).

2336. [Ammianus Marcellinus] WIEBER-SCARIOT (Anja). Zwischen Polemik und Panegyrik. Frauen des Kaiserhauses und Herrscherinnen des Ostens in den Res gestae des Ammianus Marcellinus. Trier, Wissenschaftlicher Verlag Trier, 99, 464 p.

2337. [Ammianus Marcellinus] ZARINI (V.). Histoire panégyrique et poésie: trois éloges de Rome l'éternelle autour de l'an 400 (Ammien Marcellin, Claudien, Rutilius Namatianus). *Ktema*, 99, 24, p. 167-179.

2338. [Cassius Dio] DE BLOIS (L.). The perception of Emperor and Empire in Cassius Dio's Roman history. *Ancient society*, 98-99, 29, p. 267-281.

2339. [Catullus] CATULLUS. Catullus, the shorter poems. Ed. by John GODWIN. Warminster, Aris & Phillips, 99, XII-223 p.

2340. [Catullus] Catullus' Epithalamia. Translation and commentary. Part II. Catullus 62 – hexametric nuptial song. Ed. by T. RYAN and M. JOHNSON. *Classicum*, 99, 25, p. 22-27.

2341. [Celsus] CORNELIO CELSO (A.). La chirurgia (Libri VII e VIII del De medicina). A cura di Innocenzo MAZZINI. Macerata, Pisa e Roma, Istituti editoriali e poligrafici internazionali, 99, 383 p.

2342. [Celsus] SCHULZE (Christian). Aulus Cornelius Celsus. Arzt oder Laie? Autor, Konzept und Adressaten der De medicina libri octo. Trier, Wissenschaftlicher Verlag Trier, 99, 188 p.

2343. [Cicero] DRUMMOND (A.). Furorem incredibilem biennio ante conceptum (Cicero, pro Sulla 67). *Rheinisches Museum*, 99, 142, p. 296-308.

2344. [Cicero] DUBUISSON (M.). Quid pragmatikón: «nouvelle d'intérêt pratique» ou «nouvelle du Forum»? (Cic., Att. XIV, 3). *Latomus*, 99, 58, p. 95-98.

2345. [Cicero] GRILLI (A.). La costituzione romana in Cicerone. *Atene e Roma*, 99, 4, p. 44-52.

2346. [Claudianus] FELGENTREU (Fritz). Claudians praefationes. Bedingungen, Beschreibungen und Wirkungen einer poetischen Kleinform. Stuttgart u. Leipzig, Teubner, 99, X-263 p.

2347. [Curtius Rufus] MAC KECHNIE (Paul). Manipulation of themes in Quintus Curtius Rufus Book 10. *Historia* 99, 48, p. 44-60.

2348. [Dionysius Halicarnassensis] DENYS D'HALICARNASSE. Les antiquités romaines. Livre III. Ed. par Jacques-Hubert SAUTEL. Paris, Les Belles Lettres, 99, XXVII-183 p.

2349. [Eusebius] EUSEBIUS. Life of Constantine. Ed. by Averil CAMERON and Stuart G. HALL. Oxford, Clarendon Press, 99, XVII-395 p.

2350. [Eutropius] EUTROPE. Abrégé d'histoire romaine. Ed. par Joseph HELLEGOUARC'H. Paris, Les Belles Lettres, 99, LXXXV-274 p.

2351. [Fronto] VAN DEN HOUT (Michel P. J.). A commentary on the letters of M. Cornelius Fronto. Leiden, Boston, a. Köln, Brill, 99, XI-725 p.

2352. Limits of historiography (The). Genre and narrative in ancient historical texts. Ed. by Christina SHUTTLEWORTH KRAUS. Leiden, Boston a. Köln, Brill, 99, XI-363 p. (Mnemosyne, Supplements, 191). [Cf. n[os] <choice> 1741, 2353, 2373, 2378.]

2353. [Livius] JAEGER (M.). Guiding metaphor and narrative point of view in Livy's Ab urbe condita. *In*: Limits of historiography (The) [Cf. n° 2352], p. 169-195.

2354. [Lucanus] CAVAJONI (G. A.). Catone in Lucano 9, 509 s. Sic concitus ira / excussit galeam suffecitque omnibus unda. *In*: Ricordando Raffaele Cantarella [Cf. n° 1834], p. 71-82.

2355. [Ovidius] DAVIS (P. J.). Ovid's Amores: a political reading. *Classical philology*, 99, 94, p. 431-449.

2356. [Ovidius] OVID. Metamorphoses IX-XII. Ed. by D. E. HILL. Warminster, Aris & Phillips, 99, VII-230 p.

2357. [Ovidius] Ovidian transformations. Essays on the Metamorphoses and its reception. Ed. by Philip HARDIE, Alessandro BARCHIESI a. Stephen HINDS. Cambridge, Cambridge philological society, 99, 336 p. (Cambridge philological society, suppl. 23)

2358. [Ovidius] PUBLIUS OVIDIUS NASO. Heroides. A cura di Pierpaolo FORNARO. Alessandria, Edizioni dell'Orso, 99, 424 p.

2359. [Ovidius] PUBLIUS OVIDUS NASO. Liebesgedichte. Amores. Lateinisch-deutsch. Hrsg. v. Niklas HOLZBERG. Düsseldorf u. Zürich, Artemis & Winkler, 99, 294 p.

2360. [Ovidius] WEINLICH (Barbara). Ovids Amores. Gedichtfolge und Handlungsablauf. Stuttgart u. Leipzig, Teubner, 99, 295 p.

2361. [Petronius]. FOCARDI (G.). Claudio e Trimalchione: due personaggi a confronto? *Invigilata lucernis*, 99, 21, p. 149-166.

2362. [Plautus] CECCARELLI (Lucio). Plauto, Poenulus 266 e una presunta variante manoscritta attestata da Giovanni Battista Pio. *Rivista di filologia e di istruzione classica*, 99, 127, p. 306-324.

2363. [Plautus] Studien zu Plautus'Amphitruo. Hrsg. v. Thomas BAIER. Tübingen, Narr, 99, 243 p.

2364. [Plinius Maior] GAILLARD-SEUX (P.). Le «sang de basilic» chez Pline l'Ancien (N. H., XXIX, 66): résine de genévrier ou hématite? *L'Antiquité classique*, 99, 68, p. 227-238.

2365. [Plinius Maior] TAUTZ (Burkhard). Das Bild des Kaisers Augustus in der Naturalis Historia des Plinius. Trier, Wissenschaftlicher Verlag Trier, 99, 445 p.

2366. [Propertius] BOLDRER (Francesca). L'elegia di Vertumno (Properzio 4.2). Introduzione, testo critico, traduzione e commento. Amsterdam, Hakkert, 99, 167 p. (Supplementi di Lexis, 4)

2367. [Pseudo-Aurelius Victor] PSEUDO-AURELIUS VICTOR. Abrégé des Césars. Ed. par Michel FESTY. Paris, Les Belles Lettres, 99, 302 p. (Collection des universités de France).

2368. [Pseudo-Caesar] PSEUDO-CÉSAR. Guerre d'Espagne. Ed. par Nicole DIOURON. Paris, Les Belles Lettres, 99, CIX-196 p. (maps) (Collection des universités de France).

2369. [Quintilianus] STRAMAGLIA (Antonio). I gemelli malati: un caso di vivisezione. Cassino, Edizioni dell'università degli studi di Cassino, 99, 194 p. (Declamazioni maggiori, 8).

2370. [Sallustius] FUNARI (R.) La ricerca del verum storico nelle monografie di Sallustio: procedimenti linguistici e forme narrative. *Fontes*, 99, 2, p. 155-208.

2371. [Seneca] LUCIO ANNEO SENECA. La follia di Ercole. A cura di Elena ROSSI. Milano, RCS Libri, 99, 177 p.

2372. [Seneca]. SENECA. Hercules furens. Einleitung, Text, Übersetzung und Kommentar. Hrsg. v. Margarethe BILLERBECK. Leiden u. Boston u. Köln, Brill, 99, XXIX-727 p.

2373. SHUTTLEWORTH KRAUS (Christina). Jugurthine disorder. In: Limits of historiography (The) [Cf. n° 2352], p. 217-247.

2374. [Tacitus] ASH (Rh.). Ordering anarchy. Armies and leaders in Tacitus' Histories. London, Duckworth, 99, X-246 p.

2375. [Tacitus] DAMON (Cynthia). The trial of Cn. Piso in Tacitus' Annals and the Senatus Consultum de Cn. Pisone patre: new light on narrative technique. *American journal of philology*, 99, 120, p. 143-162.

2376. [Tacitus] KEITEL (Elizabeth). The non-appearance of the Phoenix at Tacitus Annals 6.28. *American journal of philology*, 99, 120, p. 429-442.

2377. [Tacitus] LEBEK (W. D.). Das Senatus consultum de Cn. Pisone patre und Tacitus. *Zeitschrift für Papyrologie und Epigraphik*, 99, 128, p. 183-211.

2378. [Tacitus] LEVENE (D. S.). Tacitus' Histories and the theory of deliberative oratory. In: Limits of historiography (The) [Cf. n° 2352], p. 197-216.

2379. [Tacitus] MARINCOLA (J.). Tacitus' prefaces and the decline of imperial historiography. *Latomus*, 99, 58, p. 391-404.

2380. [Tacitus] PAGÁN (V. E.). Beyound Teutoburg: transgression and transformation in Tacitus, Annales 1.61-62. *Classical philology*, 99, 94, p. 302-320.

2381. [Tacitus] TACITUS. Germania. Ed. by J. R. RIVES. Oxford, Clarendon Press, 99, X-346 p. (maps)

2382. [Tacitus] TACITUS. Germany. Germania. Ed. by Herbert W. BENARIO. Warminster, Aris & Phillips, 99, IV-123 p.

2383. [Tacitus] TALBERT (Richard J. A.). Tacitus and the Senatus Consultum de Cn. Pisone Patre. *American journal of philology*, 99, 120, p. 89-97.

2384. [Terentius] TERENCE. Eunuchus. Ed. by J. BARSBY. Cambridge, Cambridge U. P., 99, VIII-336 p.

2385. [Valerius Flaccus] MANUWALD (Gesine). Die Cyzicus-Episode und ihre Funktion in den Argonautica des Valerius Flaccus. Göttingen, Vandenhoeck & Ruprecht, 99, 292 p. (Hypomnemata, 127).

2386. [Varro] VARRON. Satires Ménippées. Vol. 13: Thitonus-E Saturis incertis. Ed. Par J.-P. CEBE. Paris, de Boccard et Rome, 'L'Erma' di Bretschneider 99, p. XIX-XXXIII-2033-2228. (Collection de l'Ecole Française de Rome, 9).

2387. [Velleius Paterculus] VELLEIO PATERCOLO. I due libri al console Marco Vinicio. Introduzione, testo e traduzione. A cura di Maria ELEFANTE, Napoli, Loffredo, 99, 230 p.

2388. [Vergilius] REGGI (G.). Catone, Varrone, Virgilio e i paesaggi agrari dell'Italia romana. *Atene e Roma*, 99, 44, p. 130-146.

2389. [Vergilius] VIRGIL. Eclogues, Georgics, Aeneid I-VI. With an english translation. Ed. by H. RUSHTON FAIRCLOUGH a. G. P. GOOLD. Cambridge a. London, Harvard U. P., 99, X-597 p.

2390. [Vitellius L.] GALIMBERTI (Alessandro). I Commentarii di L. Vitellio e la fonte romana del XVIII libro delle Antichità giudaiche di Flavio Giuseppe. *Historia*, 99, 48, p. 224-234.

2391. [Vitruvius] VITRUVE. De l'architecture. Livre II. Ed. par Louis CALLEBAT, Pierre GROS et Catherine JACQUEMARD. Paris, Les Belles Lettres, 99, LXVI-191 p.

Cf. n^{os} *2586-2691, 2808*

§ 4. General and political history.

* 2392. Bulletin analytique d'histoire romaine. Vol. 8. [Vol. 7. Cf. Bibl. 98, n° 2513.] Strasbourg, Université des Sciences humaines de Strasbourg, 99, 579 p.

* 2393. HINARD (F.). Rome. Des origines à la fin de la République. *Revue historique*, 99, 123, 612, p. 833-858.

2394. ALDRETE (Gregory S.). Gestures and acclamations in ancient Rome. Baltimore a. London, The Johns Hopkins U. P., 99, XXV-227 p.

2395. ANASTASIADIS (Vasilis I.). Inventing a kakoétheuma: a propagandist attack against P. Rutilius Rufus. *La parola del passato*, 99, 54, p. 48-68.

2396. BALL (W). Rome in the East. The transformation of an empire. London a. New York, Routledge, 99, XIX-523 p.

2397. BIRD (H. W.). Mocking Marius Maximus. *Latomus*, 99, 58, p. 850-860.

2398. BOUET (Alain). Campus et juventus dans les agglomérations secondaires des provinces occidentales. *Revue des études anciennes*, 99, 101, p. 461-486.

2399. BURGERS (P.). The role and function of senatorial debate. The case of the reign of Tiberius AD 14–37. *Latomus*, 99, 58, p. 564-573.

2400. CHRISTOL (M.). L'ascension de l'ordre équestre. Un thème historiographique et sa réalité. *In*: Ordre équestre (L') [Cf. n° 2568], p. 613-628. – IDEM. La municipalisation de la Gaule Narbonnaise. *In*: Cités, municipes, colonies [Cf. n° 2484], p. 1-27.

2401. COSI (R.). Rapporti di sodalitas e degenerazione politica a Roma. *In*: Epigrafia e territorio [Cf. n° 2319], p. 181-204.

2402. DE FILIPPIS CAPPAI (CH.). In Britannico exercitu nihil irarum. Le legioni di Britannia nell'anno 68–69 d. Cr. *Bollettino di studi latini*, 99, 29, p. 125-135.

2403. DEMOUGIN (S.). L'ordre équestre en Asie mineure. Histoire d'une romanisation. *In*: Ordre équestre (L') [Cf. n° 2568], p. 579-612. – IDEM. Les vétérans dans la Gaule Belgique et la Germanie inférieure. *In*: Cités, municipes, colonies [Cf. n° 2484], p. 355-380.

2404. DI VITA (Antonino). Das antike Libyen. Vergessene Stätten des römischen Imperiums. Köln, Könemann, 99, 249 p.

2405. DONDIN-PAYRE (M.). Magistratures et administration municipale dans les Trois Gaules. *In*: Cités, municipes, colonies [Cf. n° 2484], p. 127-230.

2406. DRUMMOND (Andrew). Tribunes and tribunician programmes in 63 B.C. *Athenaeum*, 99, 87, 1, p. 121-167.

2407. ECK (Werner). L'Italia nell'impero romano. Stato e amministrazione in epoca imperiale. Bari, Edipuglia, 99, 353 p.

2408. ELIODORO (Savino). Città di frontiera nell'impero romano. Forme della romanizzazione da Augusto ai Severi. Bari Edipuglia, 99, 278 p. (Abb.).

2409. ÉVRARD (É.). Sénèque et l'enfermement. *In*: Carcer [Cf. n° 2481], p. 179-190.

2410. FIORE (D.). La felicitas del principe in Plinio il Giovane. *In*: Epigrafia e territorio [Cf. n° 2319], p. 205-226.

2411. FITTSCHEN (Klaus). Prinzenbildnisse antoninischer Zeit. Mainz, von Zabern, 99, XXVIII-156 p. (Beiträge zur Erschließung hellenistischer und kaiserzeitlicher Skulptur und Architektur, 18).

2412. FREYBERGER (Bert). Südgallien im I. Jahrhundert v. Chr. Phasen, Konsequenzen und Grenzen römischer Eroberung (125–27/22 v. Chr.). Stuttgart, Steiner, 99, 317 p.

2413. GABBA (Emilio), FORABOSCHI (Daniele), MANTOVANI (Dario), LO CASCIO (Elio), TROIANI (Lucio). Introduzione alla storia di Roma. Milano, LED, 99, 663 p.

2414. GALSTERER (H.). Kolonisation im Rheinland. *In*: Cités, municipes, colonies [Cf. n° 2484], p. 251-269. – IDEM. Statthalter und Stadt im Gerichtswesen der westlichen Provinzen. *In*: Lokale Autonomie und römische Ordnungsmacht in den Kaiserzeitlichen Provinzen vom 1.–3. Jahrhundert [Cf. n° 2428], p. 243-256.

2415. GASCOU (Jacques). César a-t-il fondé une colonie à Vienne? *Mélanges de l'Ecole française de Rome. Antiquité*, 99, 111, 1, p. 157-165.

2416. HAMDOUNE (Christine). Les auxilia externa africains des armées romaines (IIIe siècle av. J.-C.–IVe siècle apr. J.-C.). Montpellier, Université Paul-Valéry, 99, 277 p.

2417. HENNING (Dirk). Periclitans res publica. Kaisertum und Eliten in der Krise des weströmischen Reiches 454/5-493 n. Chr. Stuttgart, Steiner, 99, 362 p.

2418. HOWARTH (Randell S.). Rome, the Italians and the land. *Historia*, 99, 48, p. 282-300.

2419. HUSAR (Adrian). Celți și germani în Dacia romană. (Celts and Germans in Roman Dacia). Editura Presa Universitară Clujeană, Cluj Napoca, 99, III-290 p.

2420. KERNEIS (S.). La Bretagne rhénane. Note sur les établissements brétons dans les Champs Décumates. *Latomus*, 99, 58, p. 357-390.

2421. KOLOBOV (Aleksandr V.). Rimskie legiony vne polej srazhenij (Epokha rannej imperii): Uchebn. posobie po spetskursu. (Roman legions outside the battle-fields: the early empire: a manual). Permskij gos. un-t. Perm', [s. n.], 99, 127 p. (bibl.).

2422. LAFON (X.). Les îles de la mer tyrrhénienne: entre palais et prisons sous les Julio-Claudiens. *In*: Carcer [Cf. n° 2481], p. 149-161.

2423. LEPELLEY (C.). Du triomphe à la disparition. Le destin de l'ordre équestre de Dioclétien à Théodose. *In*: Ordre équestre (L') [Cf. n° 2568], p. 629-646.

2424. LEPPIN (Hartmut). Constantius II. und das Heidentum. *Athenaeum*, 99, 87, 2, p. 457-480.

2425. LEVICK (Barbara). Vespasian. London a. New York, Routledge, 99, 310 p.

2426. LIMONIER (Fabien). Rome et la destruction de Carthage: un crime gratuit? *Revue des études anciennes*, 99, 101, 3-4, p. 405-411.

4. GENERAL AND POLITICAL HISTORY

2427. LIOU-GILLE (Bernadette). César, 'flamen Dialis destinatus'. *Revue des études anciennes*, 99, 101, 3-4, p. 433-459.

2428. Lokale Autonomie und römische Ordnungsmacht in den Kaiserzeitlichen Provinzen vom 1.–3. Jahrhundert. Hrsg. v. W. ECK und E. MÜLLER-LUCKNER. München, Oldenbourg, 99, IX-327 p. [Cf. n^os <Auswahl> 2318, 2414, 2437, 2471, 2561.]

2429. LOLLI (M.). La celeritas principis fra tattica militare e necessità politica nei Panegyrici Latini. *Latomus*, 99, 58, p. 620-625.

2430. MALOSSE (Pierre-Louis). Qu'est donc allé faire Constant 1er en Bretagne pendant l'hiver 343? *Historia*, 99, 48, p. 465-476.

2431. MAROTTA (Valerio). Liturgia del potere. Documenti di nomina e cerimonie di investitura fra principato e tardo impero romano. Napoli, Loffredo, 99, 185 p.

2432. MARSHALL (A. M.). Atticus and the eastern sojourn. *Latomus*, 99, 58, p. 56-68.

2433. MASSELLI (G. M.). La leggenda dei 'Decii': un percorso fra storia, religione e magia. *Aufidus*, 99, 39, p. 7-37.

2434. MATTERN (Susan P.). Rome and the enemy. Imperial strategy in the principate. Berkeley, Los Angeles a. London, California U. P., 99, XVIII-259 p.

2435. MAUSE (M.). Augustus: "Friedensfürst" in einer unruhigen Zeit. *Klio*, 99, 81, 1, p. 142-155.

2436. MELLOR (R.). The Roman historians. New York a. London, Routledge, 99, X-212 p.

2437. MITCHELL (St.). The administration of Roman Asia from 133 BC to AD 250. *In*: Lokale Autonomie und römische Ordnungsmacht in den Kaiserzeitlichen Provinzen vom 1.–3. Jahrhundert [Cf. n° 2428], p. 17-46.

2438. MÓCSY (András). Katonák Pannóniában. (Soldiers in Pannonia). *Historia*, 99, 5-6, p. 8-10.

2439. MOLINA VIDAL (J.). Vinculaciones entre Apulia y el área de influencia de Cathago Nova en época tardo-republicana. *Latomus*, 99, 58, p. 509-524.

2440. MOSIG-WALBURG (Karin). Zur Schlacht bei Singara. *Historia*, 99, 48, p. 330-384.

2441. MOURITSEN (Henrik). Electoral campaigning in Pompeii: a reconsideration. *Athenaeum*, 99, 87, 2, p. 515-523.

2442. ÖSTENBERG (I.). Demostrating the conquest of the world. The procession of peoples and rivers on the shield of Aeneas and the triple triumph of Octavian in 29 B.C. (Aen. 8.722-728). *Opuscula Romana*, 99, 24, p. 115-162.

2443. PANI (M.). L'Italia, Roma e la fine della democrazia antica. *In*: Epigrafia e territorio [Cf. n° 2319], p. 227-249.

2444. PARKER (N.). The romanisation of Ino. (Fasti, 6, 475-550). *Latomus*, 99, 58, p. 336-347.

2445. PISO (I.). Les chevaliers romains dans l'armée impériale et les implications de l'imperium. *In*: Ordre équestre (L') [Cf. n° 2568], p. 321-350.

2446. PORTMANN (Werner). Die politische Krise zwischen den Kaisern Constantius II. und Constans. *Historia*, 99, 48, p. 301-329.

2447. POTTER (D. S.). Political theory in the Senatus Consultum Pisonianum. *American journal of philology*, 99, 120, p. 65-88.

2448. QUETIN (L.). Lucius Cornelius Sylla: de la scène politique à la scène lyrique. *Bulletin de l'Association Guillaume Budé*, 99, 4, p. 435-462.

2449. Roman frontier studies. Proceedings of the XVIIth International Congress of Roman frontier studies. Zalău 1999. Edited by Nicolae GUDEA. Zalău, 99, XVII-953 p.

2450. ROMANO (C. C.). I sodales nell'età di Traiano e di Adriano. *Patavium*, 99, 14, p. 45-62.

2451. ROTH (J. P.). The logistics of the Roman army at war (264 BC–AD 235). Leiden, Brill, 99, XXI-399 p. (figs.).

2452. SAAVEDRA-GUERRERO (M. D.). El elogio de las virtues patronales en los municipios de la Italia altoimperial. *L'Antiquité classique*, 99, 68, p. 191-209.

2453. SABLAYROLLES (R.). Fastigium equestre. Les grandes préfectures équestres. *In*: Ordre équestre (L') [Cf. n° 2568], p. 351-389.

2454. SANTALUCIA (B.). La carcerazione di Nevio. *In*: Carcer [Cf. n° 2481], p. 27-39.

2455. SCHNEIDER (W.). Tarnrede und Anklage: Caelius' anticaesarische Selbstcharakterisierung Arruntanum me Catonem (Cicero, fam. 8, 17). *Latomus*, 99, 58, p. 77-94.

2456. SEAGER (R.). Roman policy on the Rhine and the Danube in Ammianus. *Classical quarterly*, 99, 49, p. 579-605.

2457. SHIMADA (Makoto). Korosseumu kara yomu roma teikoku. (The Roman Empire as seen from Colosseum). Tokyo, Kodansha, 99, 262 p.

2458. SION-JENKIS (Karin). Entre république et principat: reflexions sur la théorie de la constitution mixte à l'époque impériale. *Revue des études anciennes*, 99, 101, 3-4, p. 413-425.

2459. SMITH (R.). Telling tales: Ammianus' narrative of the Persian expedition of Julian. *In*: Late Roman world (The) and its historians [Cf. n° 2809], p. 89-104.

2460. STICHEL (Rudolf H. W.). Fortuna Redux, Pompeius und die Goten: Bemerkungen zu einem wenig beachteten Säulenmonument Kostantinopels. *Istanbuler Mitteilungen*, 99, 49, p. 467-492.

2461. TANTILLO (Ignazio). L'ideologia imperiale tra centro e periferie. A proposito di un 'elogio' di Costantino da Augusta Traiana in Tracia. *Rivista di filologia e di istruzione classica*, 99, 127, p. 73-95.

2462. TATUM (M. Jeffrey). The patrician tribune Publius Clodius Pulcher. Chapel Hill a. London, North Carolina U. P., 99, 365 p.

2463. TAUSEND (Klaus). Bemerkungen zum Wandeleneinfall des Jahres 271. *Historia*, 99, 48, p. 119-127.

2464. TEXIER (Yves). La question de Gergovie. Essai sur un problème de localisation. Bruxelles, *Latomus*, 99, 417 p.

2465. TORELLI (Mario). Tota Italia. Essays in the cultural formation of Roman Italy. Oxford, Clarendon Press, 99, XV-191 p.

2466. VANOTTI (Gabriella). Roma polis hellenis, Roma polis tyrrhenis. Riflessioni sul tema. *Mélanges de l'Ecole française de Rome. Antiquité*, 99, 111, 1, p. 217-255.

2467. VEYNE (Paul). L'identité grecque devant Rome et l'empereur. *Revue des études grecques*, 99, 112, p. 510-567.

2468. WATSON (A.). Aurelian and the third century. London a. New York, Routledge, 99, XVI-303 p. (maps.).

2469. WEIR (R.). Nero and the Herakles frieze at Delphi. *Bulletin de correspondance hellénique*, 99, 123, p. 397-404.

2470. WIEDEMANN (Th.). Valerius Asiaticus and the regime of Vitellius. *Philologus*, 99, 143, p. 323-335.

2471. WOLFF (H.). 'Administrative Einheiten' in den Nordprovinzen und ihre Beziehungen zu römischen Funktionsträgern. *In*: Lokale Autonomie und römische Ordnungsmacht in den Kaiserzeitlichen Provinzen vom 1.–3. Jahrhundert [Cf. n° 2428], p. 47-60.

2472. YAKOBSON (Alexander). Elections and electioneering in Rome. A study in the political system of the late republic. Stuttgart, Steiner, 99, 151 p.

2473. YAVETZ (Zvi). Tiberio. Dalla finzione alla pazzia. Con un'appendice su Tacito. Il trauma della tirannia. Bari, Edipuglia, 99, 143 p.

Cf. n°s 666, 1545

§ 5. History of law and institutions.

2474. AUBERT (J.-J.). La gestion des collegia: aspects juridiques, économiques et sociaux. *Cahiers du Centre Gustave Glotz*, Paris, de Boccard, 99, 10, p. 49-69.

2475. AVRAM (Alexandru). Der Vertrag zwischen Rom und Kallatis. Ein Beitrag zum römischen Völkerrecht. Amsterdam, Hakkert, 99, VI-165 p.

2476. BAUMAN (R. A.). Human rights in ancient Rome. London a. New York, Routledge, 99, XIII-193 p.

2477. BODEL (John). Punishing Piso. *American journal of philology*, 99, 120, p. 43-63.

2478. BRADFORD (Churchill J.). Ex qua quod vellent facerent: Roman magistrates' authority over praeda and manubiae. *Transactions of the American philological association*, 99, 129, p. 85-116.

2479. BRINGMANN (Klaus). Ein Dekret des Kaisergerichts. Bemerkungen zu P. Oxy. XLVII 3361. *Klio*, 99, 81, 2, 491-495.

2480. BUTI (I.). Si serva servo quasi dotem dederit. Matrimoni servili e dote. *Index*, 99, 27, p. 127-140.

2481. Carcer. Prison et privation de la liberté dans l'antiquité classique. Actes du colloque (Strasbourg, 5–6 decembre 1997). Ed. par Cécile BERTRAND-DAGENBACH, Alain CHAUVOT, Michel MATTER et Jean-Marie SALAMITO. Paris, de Boccard, 99, 250 p. [Cf. n°s <sélection> 2409, 2422, 2454, 2483, 2503, 2931.]

2482. CASCIONE (Cosimo). Tresviri capitales. Storia di una magistratura minore. Napoli, Editoriale scientifica, 99, VII-328 p.

2483. CHAUVOT (A.). La détention sous Tibère. *In*: Carcer [Cf. n° 2481], p. 163-177.

2484. Cités, municipes, colonies. Les processus de municipalisation en Gaule et en Germanie sous le Haut Empire romain. Ed. par Monique DONDIN-PAYRE et Marie-Thérése RAEPSAET-CHARLIER. Paris, Publications de la Sorbonne, 99, 485 p. [Cf. n°s <sélection> 2400, 2403, 2405, 2414, 2492, 2512, 2718, 2723.]

2485. COPPOLA (Giovanna). Studi sulla pro herede gestio. II: La valutazione dell'animus nel 'gerere pro herede'. Milano, Giuffrè, 99, 392 p. (Pubblicazioni della Facoltà di Giurisprudenza della università di Messina, 199).

2486. CORBIER (Mireille). Lois, normes, pratiques individuelles et collectives: la petite enfance à Rome. *Annales*, 99, 54, 6, p. 1257-1290.

2487. Corpus der römischen Rechtsquellen zur antiken Sklaverei (CRRS). Prolegomena. Teil I. Die Begründung des Sklavenstatus nach ius gentium und ius civile. Hrsg. v. J. Michael RAINER, Elisabeth HERRMANN-OTTO und Hans WIELING. Stuttgart, Steiner, 99, IX-74 p., XII-167 p.

2488. Corpus iuris civilis. Text und Übersetzung. III: Digesten 11–20. Hrsg. v. O. BEHRENDS, R. KNÜTEL, B. KUPISCH und H. H. SEILER. Heidelberg, Müller Verlag, 99, XVIII-661 p.

2489. D'AMATI (L.). Pater ab hostibus captus e status dei discendenti nei giuristi romani. *Index*, 99, 27, p. 55-85.

2490. DAMON (Cynthia), TAKÁCS (Sarolta). The Senatus Consultum de Cn. Pisone patre (special issue): Introduction. *American journal of philology*, 99, 120, p. 1-12.

2491. DAMON (Cynthia).The Senatus Consultum de Cn. Pisone patre. *American journal of philology*, 99, 120, p. 13-42 (plates).

5. HISTORY OF LAW AND INSTITUTIONS

2492. DENIAUX (É.). Viducasses et Unelles. Recherches sur la municipalisation de l'Ouest de la Gaule. *In*: Cités, municipes, colonies [Cf. n° 2484], p. 231-249.

2493. FLOWER (Harriet I.). Piso in Chicago: a commentary on the APA/AIA joint seminar on the Senatus Consultum de Cn. Pisone Patre. *American journal of philology*, 99, 120, p. 99-115.

2494. FORNI (Giovanni). Le tribù romane. I. Tribules. II. C-I. Roma, Giorgio Bretschneider, 99, p. 291-751.

2495. GAMAUF (Richard). Ad statuam licet confugere. Untersuchungen zum Asylrecht im römischen Prinzipat. Frankfurt am Main, Berlin, Bern, New York, Paris u. Wien, Lang, 99, XVII-257 p.

2496. GENOVESE (Mario). Gli interventi edittali di Verre in materia di decime sicule. Milano, Giuffrè, 99, 496 p.

2497. HACKL (H.). Il processo civile nelle province. *In*: Ordinamenti giudiziari (Gli) di Roma imperiale [Cf. n° 2510], p. 299-318.

2498. HARRIES (J.). Constructing the judge: judicial accountability and the culture of criticism in late antiquity. *In*: Constructing identities in late antiquity [Cf. n° 2794], p. 214-233.

2499. HUMM (M.). Le Comitium du forum romain et la réforme des tribus d'Appius Claudius Caecus. *Mélanges de l'École Française de Rome. Antiquités*, 99, 111, p. 625-694.

2500. JOHNSTON (David). Roman law in context. Cambridge, Cambridge U. P., 99, IX-153 p.

2501. LAMBERTI (F.). Fideicommissa libertas ancillae data. *In*: Femmes-esclaves [Cf. n° 2542], p. 369-390.

2502. LITEWSKI (Wieslaw). Die Ablehnung (recusatio) des Richters im römischen Recht. *Revue d'histoire du droit*, 99, 67, 1-2, p. 39-56.

2503. LOVATO (Andrea). Poena sine provocatione? *In*: Carcer [Cf. n° 2481], p. 41-56.

2504. LOVISI (Claire). Contribution à l'étude de la peine de mort sous la république romaine (509–149 av. J.-C.). Paris, de Boccard, 99, 393 p.

2505. MAC GINN (Thomas A.J.). The social policy of Emperor Constantine in Codex Theodosianus 4,6,3. *Revue d'histoire du droit*, 99, 47, 1-2, p. 57-73.

2506. MASI DORIA (C.). Libertinitas e successione gentilizia. *Index*, 99, 27, p. 251-300.

2507. MILLAR (Fergus). The Greek East and Roman law: the dossier of M. Cn. Licinius Rufinus. *Journal of Roman studies*, 99, 89, p. 90-108.

2508. NICOLET (Claude). Le Monumentum Ephesenum, la loi Terentia Cassia et les dîmes d'Asie. *Mélanges de l'Ecole française de Rome. Antiquité*, 99, 111, 1, p. 191-215.

2509. NOORDRAVEN (Bert). Die Fiduzia im römischen Recht. Amsterdam, Gieben, 99, VII-386 p.

2510. Ordinamenti giudiziari (Gli) di Roma imperiale. Princeps e procedure dalle leggi Giulie ad Adriano. Atti del convegno internazionale di diritto romano e del III Premio romanistico 'G. Boulvert' (Copanello, 5–8 giugno 1996). A cura di Francesco MILAZZO. Napoli, Roma e Milano, Edizioni scientifiche italiane, 99, 517 p. [Cf. n^{os} <scelta> 2497, 2517, 2518, 2520.]

2511. PIGNATELLI (A.). La lex Licinia de sumptu minuendo. *In*: Epigrafia e territorio [Cf. n° 2319], p. 251-262.

2512. RAEPSAET-CHARLIER (M.-Th.). Les institutions municipales dans les Germanies sous le Haut Empire: bilan et questions. *In*: Cités, municipes, colonies [Cf. n° 2484], p. 271-352.

2513. RIGGSBY (A. M.). Crime and community in Ciceronian Rome. Austin, University of Texas Press, 99, XVI-249 p.

2514. ROTH (Hans-Jörg). Alfeni Digesta. Eine spätrepublikanische Juristenschrift. Berlin, Duncker & Humblot, 99, 211 p.

2515. RYAN (Frank). A mysterious Memmius and his missing magistracies. *Klio*, 99, 81, 1, p. 131-141.

2516. SMADJA (E.). L'affranchissement des femmes esclaves à Rome. *In*: Femmes-esclaves [Cf. n° 2542], p. 355-368.

2517. SPAGNUOLO VIGORITA (T.). La giurisdizione fiscale tra Augusto e Adriano. *In*: Ordinamenti giudiziari (Gli) di Roma imperiale [Cf. n° 2510], p. 449-484.

2518. STEIN (P.). Procedure giudiziali e politica nel primo impero. *In*: Ordinamenti giudiziari (Gli) di Roma imperiale [Cf. n° 2510], p. 21-35.

2519. STORCHI MARINO (A.). Restaurazione dei mores e controllo della mobilità sociale a Roma nel I sec. d.C.: il senatusconsultum Claudianum de poena feminarum quae servis coniungerentur. *In*: Femmes-esclaves [Cf. n° 2542], p. 391-426.

2520. TALAMANCA (M.). Il riordinamento augusteo del processo privato. *In*: Ordinamenti giudiziari (Gli) di Roma imperiale [Cf. n° 2510], p. 63-260.

2521. TONDO (S.). Aspetti della usucapione in diritto romano. *Index*, 99, 27, p. 345-358.

2522. TRANNOY-COLTELLONI (Michèle). La place des sénateurs au cirque: une réforme de l'empereur Claude. *Revue des études anciennes*, 99, 101, 3-4, p. 487-498.

2523. VINCENTI (U.). La presunzione muciana e la connessione con il divieto di donazione tra coniugi. *Index*, 99, 27 p. 451-469.

2524. WEISHAUPT (Arnd). Die lex Voconia. Köln u. Weimar, Böhlau, 99, VIII-188 p.

2525. WESTBROOK (Raymond). Vitae necisque potestas. *Historia*, 99, 48, p. 203-223.

2526. WINTERLING (Aloys). Aula Caesaris. Studien zur Institutionalisierung des römischen Kaiserhofes in der Zeit von Augustus bis Commodus (31 v. Chr.–192 n. Chr.). München, Oldenbourg, 99, X, 271 p.

§ 6. Economic and social history.

2527. ANDREAU (Jean). Banking and business in the Roman world. Cambridge, Cambridge U. P., 99, XIX-176 p. – IDEM. Intérêts non agricoles des chevaliers romains (IIe siècle av. J.-C.–III siècle ap. J.-C.). *In*: Ordre équestre (L') [Cf. n° 2568], p. 271-290.

2528. BALDWIN BOWSKY (M. W.). The business of being Roman: the prosopographical evidence. *In*: Minoan farmers (From) to Roman traders [Cf. n° 1847], p. 303-347.

2529. BANDELLI (G.). La popolazione della Cisalpina dalle invasioni galliche alla guerra sociale. *In*: Demografia, sistemi agrari, regimi alimentari nel mondo antico [Cf. n° 2035], p. 189-215.

2530. BARRETT (Anthony A.). Agrippina. Sex, power, and politics in the early empire. London, Routledge, 99, 330 p.

2531. BEACHAM (R. C.). Spectacle entertainments of early imperial Rome. New Haven a. London, Yale U. P., 99, 306 p. (ill.).

2532. BEARD (M.). The erotics of rape: Livy, Ovid and the Sabine women. *In*: Female networks and the public sphere in Roman society [Cf. n° 2541], p. 1-10.

2533. BRIANDE-PONSART (C.). Une évérgesie modeste: les combats de boxe dans quelques cités d'Afrique proconsulaire pendant l'Empire. *Antiquités africaines*, 99, 35, p. 135-149.

2534. Capitolo (Il) delle entrate nelle finanze municipali in Occidente e in Oriente. Actes de la Xe rencontre franco-italienne sur l'épigraphie du monde romain (Rome, École française de Rome et Università di Roma 'La Sapienza', 27–29 mai 1996). Paris, de Boccard et Roma, 'L'Erma' di Bretschneider, 99, IX-330 p. (Collection de l'École française de Rome, 256). [Cf. n[os] <scelta> 2313, 2326, 2544, 2549, 2550, 2560, 2562.]

2535. CARLSEN (J.). Gli alimenta imperiali e privati in Italia: ideologia ed economia. *In*: Demografia, sistemi agrari, regimi alimentari nel mondo antico [Cf. n° 2035], p. 271-288.

2536. DEVIJVER (H.). Les relations sociales des chevaliers romains. *In*: Ordre équestre (L') [Cf. n° 2568], p. 237-269.

2537. DI PAOLA (Lucietta). Viaggi, trasporti e istituzioni. Studi sul cursus publicus. Messina, Dipartimento di Scienze dell'antichità dell'università degli studi di Messina, 99, 163 p.

2538. ECK (W.). Ordo equitum Romanorum, ordo libertorum. Freigelassene und ihre Nachkommen im römischen Ritterstand. *In*: Ordre équestre (L') [Cf. n° 2568], p. 5-29.

2539. ERDKAMP (P.). Agriculture underemployment, and the cost of rural labour in the Roman world. *Classical quarterly*, 99, 49, p. 556-572.

2540. ERKELENZ (D.). Cicero, pro Flacco 55-59. Zur Finanzierung von Statthalterfesten in der Frühphase des Koinon von Asia. *Chiron*, 99, 29, p. 43-57.

2541. Female networks and the public sphere in Roman society. Ed. by P. SETÄLÄ and L. SAVUNEN. Roma, Institutum Romanum Finlandiae, 99, 139 p. [Cf. n[os] <choice> 2300, 2532, 2703.]

2542. Femmes-esclaves. Modèles d'interpretation anthropologique, économique, juridique. Atti del XXI colloquio internazionale Girea (Lacco Ameno e Ischia, 27–29 ottobre 1994). A cura di Francesca REDUZZI MEROLA e Alfredina STORCHI MARINO. Napoli, Jovene, 99, VII-426 p. (Diáphora, 9). [Cf. n[os] <sélection> 2328, 2501, 2516, 2519, 2546, 2558, 2580.]

2543. FLEMMING (Rebecca). Quae corpore quaestum facit: the sexual economy of female prostitution in the Roman empire. *Journal of Roman studies*, 99, 89, p. 38-61.

2544. FRANCE (J.). Les revenus douaniers des communautés municipales dans le monde romain (république et haut-empire). *In*: Capitolo (Il) delle entrate nelle finanze municipali in occidente e in oriente [Cf. n° 2534], p. 95-113.

2545. GARNSEY (G). Malnutrizione e produttività agricola nel mediterraneo antico. *In*: Demografia, sistemi agrari, regimi alimentari nel mondo antico [Cf. n° 2035], p. 11-23.

2546. GARRIDO-HORY (M.). Femmes, femmes-esclaves et processus de feminisation dans les oeuvres de Martial et Juvénal. *In*: Femmes-esclaves [Cf. n° 2542], p. 303-313.

2547. GASCOU (J.). Un municeps et patronus pagi de Thugga. *Antiquités africaines*, 99, 35, p. 71-75.

2548. GIARDINA (Andrea). Dionigi di Alicarnasso e gli strani Greci di Roma. *In*: Epigrafia e territorio [Cf. n° 2319], p. 277-285.

2549. GREGORI (G. L.). Nomina transcripticia e praedia subsignata: debiti, ipoteche e finanze locali a Trebula Suffenatium. *In*: Capitolo (Il) delle entrate nelle finanze municipali in occidente e in oriente [Cf. n° 2534], p. 25-39.

2550. GRELLE (F.). I munera civilia e le finanze cittadine. *In*: Capitolo (Il) delle entrate nelle finanze municipali in occidente e in oriente [Cf. n° 2534], p. 137-153.

2551. GRÜNEWALD (Thomas). Räuber, Rebellen, Rivalen, Rächer. Studien zu latrones im römischen Reich. Stuttgart, Steiner, 99, X-269 p.

2552. HAGENDORN (Andrea). Die Villa rustica von Großsachsen, Gem. Hirschberg, Rhein-Neckar-Kreis. Ein römischer Gutshof im Spiegel seiner zentralen Gebäude. Stuttgart, Theiss, 99, 245 p.

2553. HARRIS (W. V.). Demography, geography and the sources of Roman slaves. *Journal of Roman studies*, 99, 89, p. 62-75.

2554. HEMELRIJK (Emily A.). Matrona docta. Educated women in the Roman elite from Cornelia to Julia Domna. London a. New York, Routledge, 99, XVI-382 p.

2555. HOLDER (P. A.). Exercitus pius fidelis: the army of Germania inferior in AD 89. *Zeitschrift für Papyrologie und Epigraphik*, 99, 128, p. 237-250.

2556. HÖLKESKAMP (K.-J.). Römische gentes und griechische Genealogien. *In*: Rezeption und Identität [Cf. n° 2574], p. 3-21.

2557. HOLLANDER (D. B.). The management of the mint in the late Roman republic. *Ancient history bulletin*, 99, 13, p. 14-27.

2558. KOLENDO (J.). Sithonum gentes femina dominantur. Liberté, esclavage et pouvoir exercé par une femme d'après la Germanie de Tacite. *In*: Femmes-esclaves [Cf. n° 2542], p. 315-322.

2559. KUNST (Christiane). Identität und Unsterblichkeit: Zur Bedeutung des römischen Personennamens. *Klio*, 99, 81, 1, p. 156-179.

2560. LE ROUX (P.). Vectigalia et revenus des cités en Hispanie au haut-empire. *In*: Capitolo (Il) delle entrate nelle finanze municipali in occidente e in oriente [Cf. n° 2534], p. 155-173.

2561. LO CASCIO (E.). Census provinciale, imposizione fiscale e amministrazioni cittadine nel principato. *In*: Lokale Autonomie und römische Ordnungsmacht in den Kaiserzeitlichen Provinzen vom 1.–3. Jahrhundert [Cf. n° 2428], p. 197-211.

2562. MAGIONCALDA (A.). Donazioni private a fini perpetui destinate alle città. Esempi dalla documentazione latina in età imperiale. *In*: Capitolo (Il) delle entrate nelle finanze municipali in occidente e in oriente [Cf. n° 2534], p. 175-216.

2563. MANCUSO (M. A.). Il rapporto padri e figli nella prima deca di Tito Livio. *Latomus*, 99, 58, p. 109-120.

2564. MENCACCI (F.). Päderastie und lesbische Liebe. Die Ursprünge zweier sexueller Verhaltensweisen und der Unterschied der Geschlechter in Rom. *In*: Rezeption und Identität [Cf. n° 2574], p. 60-80.

2565. MROZEWICZ (L.). Munizipalgesellschaft und römische Ritter. Das Beispiel der Nordprovinzen des römischen Reiches. *In*: Ordre équestre (L') [Cf. n° 2568], p. 31-78.

2566. NONNIS (D.). Attività imprenditoriali e classi dirigenti nell'età repubblicana. Tre città campione. *Cahiers du Centre Gustave Glotz*. Paris, de Boccard, 99, 10, p. 71-109.

2567. Onomasticon provinciarum Europae Latinarum (OPEL). Vol. II. Cabalicius-Ixus. Hrsg. v. András MÓCSY, Reinhardo FELDMANN, Elizabetha MARTON SZILÁGYI und Barnabás LÖRINCZ. Wien, Forschungsgesellschaft Wiener Stadtarchäologie, 99, 232 p.

2568. Ordre équestre (L'). Histoire d'une aristocratie (IIe siècle av. J.-C.–IIIe siècle ap. J.-C.). Actes du colloque international organisé par Ségolène DEMOUGIN, Hubert DEVIJVER et Marie-Thérèse RAPSAET-CHARLIER (Bruxelles et Leuven, 5–7 octobre 1995). Paris, de Boccard et Rome, École française de Rome et 'L'Erma' di Bretschneider, 99, 694 p. [Cf. n^{os} <sélection> 2400, 2403, 2423, 2445, 2453, 2527, 2536, 2538, 2565, 2571, 2576.]

2569. Organised crime in antiquity. Ed. by K. HOPWOOD. London, Duckworth, 99, XVI-278 p. [Cf. n° <choice> 2275.]

2570. PAPI (Emanuele). Ad delenimenta vitiorum (Tac. Agr. 21). Il balneum nelle dimore di Roma dall' età repubblicana al I secolo d.C. *Mélanges de l'Ecole française de Rome. Antiquité*, 99, 111, 2, p. 695-728.

2571. RAPSAET-CHARLIER (M.-Th.). Matrones equestres. La parenté féminine de l'ordre équestre. *In*: Ordre équestre (L') [Cf. n° 2568], p. 215-236.

2572. REMESAL RODRÍGUEZ (J.). Politica e regimi alimentari nel principato di Augusto: il ruolo dello stato nella dieta di Roma e dell'esercito. *In*: Demografia, sistemi agrari, regimi alimentari nel mondo antico [Cf. n° 2035], p. 247-271.

2573. REVILLA CALVO (V.). Viticultura y actividades complementarias en el fundus: el ejemplo de la Hispania Tarraconensis. *Latomus*, 99, 58, p. 30-55.

2574. Rezeption und Identität. Die kulturelle Auseinandersetzung Roms mit Griechenland als europäisches Paradigma. Hrsg. v. Gregor VOGT-SPIRA, Bettina ROMMEL und Immanuel MUSÄUS. Stuttgart, Steiner, 99, IX-410 p. [Cf. n^{os} <Auswahl> 2556, 2564, 2628, 2631, 2634, 2642, 2656, 2663, 2678, 2711.]

2575. SALMON (Pierre). La limitation des naissances dans la societé romaine. Bruxelles, *Latomus*, 99, 103 p.

2576. SCHEID (J.), GRANINO CECERE (M. G.). Les sacerdoces publics équestres. *In*: Ordre équestre (L') [Cf. n° 2568], p. 79-189.

2577. SCHEIDEL (W.). Emperors, aristocrats, and the grim reaper: towards a demographic profile of the Roman élite. *Classical quarterly*, 99, 49, p. 254-281.

2578. ŠKEGRO (Ante). Gospodarstvo rimske provincije Dalmacije. (Economy of the Roman province of Dalmatia). Zagreb, Hrvatski studiji, 99, 441 p.

2579. TABORELLI (L.). Una tecnica vetraria di artigianato artistico tra l'oriente mediterraneo e il cuore dell'impero. *Latomus*, 99, 58, p. 139-149.

2580. TAČEVA (M.). Les femmes-esclaves et affranchies dans les provinces Moesia Inferior et Thracia. *In*: Femmes-esclaves [Cf. n° 2542], p. 323-330.

2581. TARPIN (M.). Oppida ui capta, uici incensi. Les mots latins de la ville. *Latomus*, 99, 58, p. 279-297

2582. WILLIAMS (Craig A.). Roman homosexuality. Ideologies of masculinity in Classical antiquity. New York a. Oxford, Oxford U. P., 99, 395 p.

2583. WOLFF (Catherine). Comment devient-on brigand? *Revue des études anciennes*, 99, 101, 3-4, p. 393-403.

2584. WOLTERS (Reinhard). Nummi signati. Untersuchungen zur römischen Münzprägung und Geldwirtschaft. München, Beck, 99, 475 p. (Taf.).

2585. ZIOLKOWSKI (Adam). La scomparsa della clientela arcaica: un'ipotesi. *Athenaeum*, 99, 87, 2, p. 369-382.

§ 7. **History of literature, philosophy and science.**

a. *Literature*

2586. ADAMS (J. N.). The poets of Bu Njem: language, culture and the centurionate. *Journal of Roman studies*, 99, 89, p. 109-134.

2587. Antike Rhetorik und ihre Rezeption. Symposion zu Ehren von Professor Dr. Carl Joachim Classen D. Litt. Oxon. (Göttingen, am 21. und 22. November 1998). Hrsg. v. Siegmar DÖPP. Stuttgart, Steiner, 99, 181 p. [Cf. n[os] <auswahl> 2644, 2674.]

2588. ARETINI (Paola). Ch. G. Heyne e la geografia infernale nel VI libro dell'Eneide. *Quaderni di storia*, 99, 49, p. 179-198.

2589. ARONEN (J.). Perché il verso saturnio fu chiamato 'saturnio'? *In*: Imago antiquitatis [Cf. n° 2705], p. 53-72.

2590. Aspects of the language of Latin poetry. Ed. by J. N. ADAMS and R. G. MAYER. Oxford, Oxford U. P., 99, VIII-447 p.

2591. AUHAGEN (Ulrike). Der Monolog bei Ovid. Tübingen, Narr, 99, 244 p.

2592. BELL (A. J. E.). The popular poetics and politics of the Aeneid. *Transactions of the American philological association*, 99, 129, p. 263-279.

2593. BRACCHI (Remo). Turdus e i suoi corrispondenti: l'uccello 'che cova nel fango inaridito'. *Athenaeum*, 99, 87, 1, p. 79-92.

2594. BUISEL (M. D.). Discurso mítico y discurso histórico en la IV Égloga de Virgilio. *Auster*, 99, 4, p. 41-62.

2595. CAGNIART (P.). Le soldat et l'armée dans le théâtre de Plaute. L'antimilitarisme de Plaute. *Latomus*, 99, 58, p. 753-779.

2596. CALBOLI (G.). Il giudizio di Quintiliano su Seneca. *In*: Seneca nella coscienza dell'Europa [Cf. n° 2659], p. 19-57.

2597. CANFORA (Luciano). Rec. di ORAZIO. Enciclopedia oraziana. *Quaderni di storia*, 99, 49, p. 275-278.

2598. CIRILLO (O.). Spunti di poetica tibulliana. Tra idillio ed epigramma alessandrino. *Bollettino di studi latini*, 99, 29, p. 44-62.

2599. CLAASSEN (Jo-Marie). Displaced persons. The literature of exile from Cicero to Boethius. London, Duckworth, 99, VIII-352 p.

2600. CONNORS (C.). Rereading the Arbiter: arbitrium and verse in the Satyrica and in 'Petronius redivivus'. *In*: Latin fiction [Cf. n° 2633], p. 64-77.

2601. COURTNEY (Edward). Archaic Latin prose. Atlanta, Scholars, 99, 164 p.

2602. CRESCI-MARRONE (Giovannella). Orazio, Munazio Planco e il 'vecchio del mare'. *Athenaeum*, 99, 87, 1, p. 111-120.

2603. D'ANGOUR (Armand J.). Ad Unguem. *American journal of philology*, 99, 120, p. 411-427.

2604. DANESI MARIONI (G.). Andromaca e Astianatte. Riscrittura senecana di due personaggi tragici. *Bollettino di studi latini*, 99, 29, p. 477-496.

2605. DANGEL (J.). Parole et écriture chez les Latins: approche stylistique. *Latomus*, 99, 58, p. 3-29.

2606. DAVIES (P.). Instructing the emperor: Ovid, Tristia 2. *Latomus*, 99, 58, p. 799-809.

2607. DE SIMONE (Carlo). Latino Mercurius < *Mercu-sio-s e gli aggettivi di classificazione in -(ā)rius < -(ā)sio-s. *Rivista di filologia e di istruzione classica*, 99, 127, p. 385-425.

2608. DION (J.). L'idéal héroïque et l'écriture d'ombre chez Virgile et Properce. *In*: Paradoxe (Le) du héros ou d'Homère à Malraux (Le) [Cf. n° 1439], p. 109-130.

2609. DRINKWATER (J. F.). Re-dating Ausonius' war poetry. *American journal of philology*, 99, 120, p. 443-452.

2610. EDWARDS (M. J.). The role of Hercules in Valerius Flaccus. *Latomus*, 99, 58, p. 150-163.

2611. Élégie et épopée dans la poésie ovidienne (Héroïdes et Amours). Hommage à Simone Viarre (15–16 mai 1998). Ed. par Jacqueline FABRE-SERRIS et Alain DEREMETZ. Villeneuve d'Ascq (nord), Université Charles-de-Gaulle-Lille 3, 99, 168 p. [Cf. n[os] <sélection> 2629, 2667.]

2612. FANTHAM (ELAINE). Fighting words: Turnus at bay in the latin council (Aeneid 11.234-446). *American journal of philology*, 99, 120, p. 259-280.

2613. FÖGEN (Th.). Spracheinstellungen und Sprachnormbewußtsein bei Cicero. *Glotta*, 99, 75, p. 1-33.

2614. FRANCHET D'ESPEREY (Sylvie). Conflit, violence et non-violence dans la Thébaide de Stace. Paris, Les Belles Lettres, 99, 445 p.

7. HISTORY OF LITERATURE, PHILOSOPHY AND SCIENCE

2615. FRANGOULIDIS (Stavros). Scaena feralium nuptiarum: wedding imagery in Apuleius' tale of Charite (Met. 8.1-14). *American journal of philology*, 99, 120, p. 601-619.

2616. FREYBURGER-GALLAND (Marie L.). Les rêves chez Dion Cassius. *Revue des études anciennes*, 99, 101, 3-4, p. 533-545.

2617. *Vacat.*

2618. FUZIER (H.). La biche transpercée par Hercule avait-elle des pieds d'airain? (À propos de Virgile, Én. VI, 802). *Latomus*, 99, 58, p. 99-108.

2619. GAMBERALE (L.). L'amicizia delusa: una lettura del carme 38 di Catullo. *Invigilata lucernis*, 99, 21, p. 167-182.

2620. GIBSON (Bruce). Ovid on reading: reading Ovid. Reception in Ovid Tristia II. *Journal of Roman studies*, 99, 89, p. 19-37.

2621. GIBSON (R. K.). Aeneas as hospes in Vergil, Aeneid 1 and 4. *Classical quarterly*, 99, 49, p. 184-202.

2622. GOGA (S.). Encolpe et l'enfermement. *Latomus*, 99, 58, p. 816-819.

2623. GREBE (Sabine). Martianus Capella, 'De nuptiis Philologiae et Mercurii'. Darstellung der Sieben Freien Künste und ihrer Beziehungen zueinander. Stuttgart u. Leipzig, Teubner, 99, 939 p.

2624. GREWING (F.). Mundus inversus: Fiktion und Wirklichkeit in Martials Büchern XIII und XIV. *Prometheus*, 99, 25, p. 259-281.

2625. HOFFMANN (Manfred). Statius, Thebais 12, 312-463. Einleitung, Übersetzung, Kommentar. Göttingen, Duehrkohp & Radicke, 99, 99 p.

2626. HUBER-REBENICH (Gerlinde). Metamorphosen der 'Metamorphosen'. Ovids Verwandlungssagen in der textbegleitenden Druckgraphik. Rudolstadt u. Jena, Hain, 99, 64 p.

2627. Interpretare Lucano. Miscellanea di studi. A cura di Paolo ESPOSITO e Luciano NICASTRI. Napoli, Arte tipografica, 99, 504 p.

2628. JOCELYN (H. D.). Code-switching in the comoedia palliata. *In*: Rezeption und Identität [Cf. n° 2574], p. 169-195.

2629. JOLIVET (J.-Ch.). La dispute d'Ovide et des Alexandrins ou Briséis grammatikotate: trois problèmes homériques et une quaestio ovidiana dans la troisième Héroïde. *In*: Élégie et épopée dans la poésie ovidienne (Héroïdes et Amours) [Cf. n° 2611], p. 15-39.

2630. LA BUA (Giuseppe). L'inno nella letteratura poetica latina. San Severo, Gerni editori, 99, XVI-537 p.

2631. LAHUSEN (G.). Griechisches Pathos und römische Dignitas. Zu Formen bildlicher Selbstdarstellung der römischen Aristokratie in republikanischer Zeit. *In*: Rezeption und Identität [Cf. n° 2574], p. 196-222.

2632. LAIGNEAU (Sylvie). La femme et l'amour chez Catulle et les Élégiaques augustéens. Bruxelles, Latomus, 99, 420 p. (Collection Latomus 249).

2633. Latin fiction. The Latin novel in context. Ed. by Heinz HOFMANN. London a. New York, Routledge, 99, 277 p. [Cf. n^{os} <choice> 2600, 2640, 2653, 2658.]

2634. LEFÈVRE (E.). Catulls Alexandrinisches Programm (C. 1-3). *In*: Rezeption und Identität [Cf. n° 2574], p. 225-239. – IDEM. Terenz' und Apollodors Hecyra. München, Beck, 99, 204 p. (Zetemata, 101).

2635. LIEBERG (G.). Formale und inhaltliche Analyse von Properz III, 12. *Latomus*, 99, 58, p. 785-798.

2636. LLEWELYN (Morgan). Patterns of redemption in Virgil's Georgics. Cambridge, Cambridge U. P., 99, X-255 p.

2637. LÖFSTEDT (B.). Nochmals zum Vokativ von Deus. *Latomus*, 99, 58, p. 276-278.

2638. LUCIFORA (Rosa Maria). Voci politiche in Properzio 'erotico'. Ideologia e progetto elegiaco in II,16 e III,11. Bari, Edipuglia, 99, 131 p.

2639. MASO (STEFANO). Lo sguardo della verità. Cinque studi su Seneca. Padova, Il Poligrafo, 99, 187 p.

2640. MASON (H. J.). The Metamorphoses of Apuleius and its Greek sources. *In*: Latin fiction [Cf. n° 2633], p. 103-112.

2641. MAUGER-PLICHON (B.). Maximianus: un mystérieux poète. *Bulletin de l'Association Guillaume Budé*, 99, 4, p. 369-387.

2642. MAZZOLI (G.). Seneca, Roma e il paradigma greco. *In*: Rezeption und Identität [Cf. n° 2574], p. 289-298.

2643. MONDA (Salvatore). Fragm. poet. Lat. inc. 59 Blänsdorf. *Rivista di filologia e di istruzione classica*, 99, 127, p. 291-305.

2644. NICKAU (K.). Peripateticorum consuetudo. Zu Cic. Tusc. 2,9, 1528. *In*: Antike Rhetorik und ihre Rezeption [Cf. n° 2587], p. 15-28.

2645. PACKMAN (Z. M.). Feminine role designations in the comedies of Plautus. *American journal of philology*, 99, 120, p. 245-258.

2646. PARSONS (J.). A new approach to the Saturnian verse and its relation to Latin prosody. *Transactions of the American philological association*, 99, 129, p. 117-137.

2647. PERUTELLI (Alessandro). L'Orpheus di Lucano. *Rivista di filologia e di istruzione classica*, 99, 127, p. 47-72.

2648. POCCETTI (Paolo), POLI (Diego), SANTINI (Carlo). Una storia della lingua latina. Formazione, usi, comunicazione. Roma, Carocci, 99, 431 p.

2649. RECKFORD (Kenneth J.). Only a wet dream? Hope and skepticism in Horace, Satire 1.5. *American journal of philology*, 99, 120, p. 525-554.

2650. RIPOLL (François). Silius Italicus et Valérius Flaccus. *Revue des études anciennes*, 99, 101, 3-4, p. 499-521.

2651. RUTLEDGE (Steven H.). Delatores and the tradition of violence in Roman oratory. *American journal of philology*, 99, 120, p. 555-573.

2652. RYAN (F. X.). The chronological arrangement of Cicero, Brutus 239-242. *Latomus*, 99, 58, p. 525-533.

2653. SANDY (G. N.). The tale of Cupid and Psyche. *In*: Latin fiction [Cf. n° 2633], p. 126-138.

2654. SANTINI (P.). Vista annebbiata e viaggio difficile: la griglia figurativa del De vita beata di Seneca. *Invigilata lucernis*, 99, 21, p. 357-369.

2655. SCHENK (Peter). Studien zur poetischen Kunst des Valerius Flaccus. Beobachtungen zur Ausgestaltung des Kriegsthemas in den Argonautica. München, Beck, 99, 405 p. (Zetemata, 102).

2656. SCHERBERG (B.). Milde Väter in den Komödien des Terenz. Dichten im Zeichen des Philhellenismus. *In*: Rezeption und Identität [Cf. n° 2574], p. 135-148.

2657. SCHIESARO (Alessandro). Bere tranquilli: Seneca, Tieste 452 (e Fedra 208). *Rivista di filologia e di istruzione classica*, 99, 127, p. 197-205.

2658. SCHUMATE (N.). Apuleius' Metamorphoses: the inserted tales. *In*: Latin fiction [Cf. n° 2633], p. 113-125.

2659. Seneca nella coscienza dell'Europa. A cura di Ivano DIONIGI. Milano, Mondadori, 99, XXXII-460 p. [Cf. n° <scelta> 2596.]

2660. SKLENÁŘ (R.). Nihilistic cosmology and Catonian ethics in Lucan's Bellum civile. *American journal of philology*, 99, 120, p. 281-296.

2661. SMITH (Rebekah M.). Deception and sacrifice in Aeneid 2.1-249. *American journal of philology*, 99, 120, p. 503-523.

2662. SMITH (St. C.). Remembering the enemy: narrative, focalisation, and Vergil's portrait of Achilles. *Transactions of the American philological association*, 99, 129, p. 22-261.

2663. STAHL (H.-P.). Griechenhetze in Vergils Aeneis: Roms Rache für Troja. *In*: Rezeption und Identität [Cf. n° 2574], p. 249-273.

2664. STOVER (T. J.). Placata posse omnia mente tueri: "Demythologizing" the Plague in Lucretius. *Latomus*, 99, 58, p. 69-76.

2665. SUERBAUM (Werner). Vergils Aeneis. Epos zwischen Geschichte und Gegenwart. Stuttgart, Reclam, 99, 425 p.

2666. THOMAS (R. F.). Reading Virgil and his texts. Studies in intertextuality. Ann Arbor, Michigan U. P., 99, 351 p.

2667. TRONCHET (G.). La nuit obscure des Amours: la tradition épique et sa traduction élégiaque. *In*: Élégie et épopée dans la poésie ovidienne (Héroïdes et Amours) [Cf. n° 2611], p. 85-126.

2668. URECH (H. J.). Hoher und niederer Stil in den Satiren Juvenals. Untersuchung zur Stilhöhe von Wörtern und Wendungen und inhaltliche Interpretation von Passagen mit auffälligen Stilwechseln. Bern, Berlin, Bruxelles, Frankfurt am Main, New York u. Wien, Lang, 99, 322 p.

2669. VINCHESI (M. A.). Alcune considerazioni sul caso di Dafni nel XIV libro delle Guerre puniche di Silio Italico. *In*: Ricordando Raffaele Cantarella [Cf. n° 1834], p. 247-255.

2670. VITALE (Maria T.). Alcuni rimedi testuali all' Aegritudo Perdicae. *Athenaeum*, 99, 87, 1, p. 215-242.

2671. VONS (J.). «Il est des parfums sauvages comme l'odeur du désert». Étude du vocabulaire des parfums chez Pline l'Ancien. *Latomus*, 99, 58, p. 820-838.

2672. WARDLE (David). The preface to Valerius Maximus: a note. *Athenaeum*, 99, 87, 2, p. 523-525.

2673. WATSON (P.). Martial on the wedding of Stella and Violentilla. *Latomus*, 99, 58, p. 348-356.

2674. WENSKUS (O.). 'Gespräche' unter Freunden. Rhetorik als Briefthema bei Cicero und Plinius. *In*: Antike Rhetorik und ihre Rezeption [Cf. n° 2587], p. 29-40.

2675. WHEELER (Stephen M.). A discourse of wonders. Audiences and performances in Ovid's Metamorphoses. Philadelphia, Pennsylvania U. P., 99, X-272 p.

2676. WOOTTON (G. E.). A mask of Attis. Oscilla as evidence for a theme of pantomime. *Latomus*, 99, 58, p. 314-335.

2677. ZAINA (E.). Nota a Catulo 68, 70-72. *Latomus*, 99, 58, p. 780-784.

2678. ZIMMERMANN (B.). Cicero und die Griechen. *In*: Rezeption und Identität [Cf. n° 2574], p. 240-248.

2679. ZWIERLEIN (Otto). Die Ovid- und Vergil-Revision in Tiberischer Zeit. Band 1. Prolegomena. Berlin u. New York, de Gruyter, 99, XV-685 p.

Cf. n^{os} *1566, 2334-2391, 2881*

b. *Philosophy and science*

2680. ALBRECHT (M. von). Seneca über sich selbst. Sprache und Stil im Dienste der praktischen Philosophie. *Acta antiqua Academiae scientiarum Hungaricae*, 99, 39, p. 9-20.

2681. ALLISON (J.). Tacitus' Dialogus and Plato's Symposium. *Hermes*, 99, 127, p. 479-492.

2682. AMATO (Eugenio). Un aspetto della polemica antiepicurea in età imperiale: Dione Crisostomo, Lucrezio e la teoria della generazione spontanea. Salerno, Helios editrice, 99, 33 p.

2683. Ancient histories of medicine. Essays in medical doxography and historiography in Classical antiquity. Ed. by P. J. VAN DER EIJK. Leiden, Boston a Cologne, Brill, 99, VIII-537 p.

2684. COURRENT (M.). Équilibre et changement dans le De architectura de Vitruve: mécanique et chimie du monde appliquées à l'architecture. *Latomus*, 99, 58, p. 534-563.

2685. FRANZ (M.). Von Gorgias bis Lukrez. Antike Ästhetik und Poetik als vergleichende Zeichentheorie. Berlin, Akademie Verlag, 99, XVI-680 p. (ills.).

2686. GALINSKY (K.). El discurso de Pitágoras en las Metamorphosis de Ovidio. *Auster*, 99, 4, p. 21-40.

2687. HEALY (J. F.). Pliny the Elder on science and technology. Oxford, Oxford U. P., 99, XV-467 p.

2688. LEONHARDT (Jürgen). Ciceros Kritik der Philosophenschulen. München, Beck, 99, 229 p. (Zetemata, 103).

2689. REGEN (F.). Il De deo Socratis di Apuleio. *Maia*, 99, 51, p. 429-456.

2690. SCHÖNEGG (Beat). Senecas epistulae morales als philosophisches Kunstwerk. Bern, Berlin, Frankfurt am Main, New York, Paris u. Wien, Lang, 99, 260 p.

2691. SCHRIJVERS (P. H.). Lucrèce et les sciences de la vie. Leiden, Brill, 99, 231 p.

Cf. n°s 2334-2391

§ 8. Religion and mythology.

2692. ARCE (J.). Los funerales romanos: problemas y perspectivas. *In*: Syncrétismes religieux (Les) dans le monde méditerranéen antique [Cf. n° 1381], p. 323-336.

2693. BELLEMORE (Jane). Josephus, Pompey and the Jews. *Historia*, 99, 48, p. 94-118.

2694. BOSWORTH (Brian). Augustus, the Res gestae and hellenistic theories of apotheosis. *Journal of Roman studies*, 99, 89, p. 1-18.

2695. CALLOT (Jean-Jacques). Recherches sur les cultes en Cyrénaïque durant le haut-empire romain. Nancy, A.D.R.A. et Paris, de Boccard, 99, 364 p.

2696. CLAUSS (Manfred). Kaiser und Gott. Herrscherkult im römischen Reich. Stuttgart u. Leipzig, Teubner, 99, 597 p.

2697. COLEMAN (K.). Mythological figures as spokepersons in Statius' Silvae. *In*: Spiegel (Im) des Mythos [Cf. n° 2720], p. 67-80.

2698. CRIPPA (S.). Entre vocalité et écriture: les voix de la Sibylle et les rites vocaux de magiciens. *In*: Zwischen Krise und Alltag [Cf. n° 2215], p. 95-110.

2699. FAUTH (Wolfgang). Carmen magicum. Das Thema der Magie in der Dichtung der römischen Kaiserzeit. Frankfurt am Main, Lang, 99, 217 p.

2700. GIOVINI (M.). Il De somnio tra elegia ed epica: una rivisitazione onirica del mito di Cerere e Fame. *Maia*, 99, 51, p. 279-193.

2701. GROTTANELLI (Cristiano). Ideologie del sacrificio umano: Roma e Cartagine. *Archiv für Religionsgeschichte*, 99, 1, p. 41-60.

2702. GURY (F.). Caligula entre les Castores. *In*: Imago antiquitatis [Cf. n° 2705], p. 265-280.

2703. HÄNNINEN (M.-L.). The dream of Caecilia Metella: aspects of inspiration and authority in late republican Rome religion. *In*: Female networks and the public sphere in Roman society [Cf. n° 2541], p. 39-52.

2704. HOPKINS (Keith). A world full of Gods. Pagans, Jews and Christians in the Roman empire. London, Weidenfeld & Nicolson, 99, VIII-402 p.

2705. Imago antiquitatis. Religions et iconographie du monde romain. Mélanges offerts à Robert TURCAN. Ed. par Nicole BLANC et André BUISSON. Paris, de Boccard, 99, 443 p. [Cf. n^{os} <sélection> 2589, 2702, 2714.]

2706. IRBY-MASSIE (Georgia). Military religion in Roman Britain. Leiden, Brill, 99, 408 p. (Mnemosyne, suppl. 199).

2707. JACOBS (Bruno). Die Herkunft und Entstehung der römischen Mithrasmysterien. Überlegungen zur Rolle des Stifters und zu den astronomischen Hintergründen der Kultlegende. Konstanz, UVK Universitätsverl. Konstanz, 99, 84 p.

2708. KLEDT (A.). Der Mythos von Demeter in der Deutung des Firmicus Maternus. *Latomus*, 99, 58, p. 626-634.

2709. MAYER (M.). Aproximación a la religión cívica en Hispania bajo los Flavios. *Ktema*, 99, 24, p. 341-345.

2710. MÉTHY (Nicole). Deus exsuperantissimus: une divinité nouvelle? À propos de quelques passages d' Apulée. *L'Antiquité classique*, 99, 68, p. 99-117. – EADEM. Le personnage d'Isis dans l'oeuvre d'Apulée: essai d'interpretation. *Revue des études anciennes*, 99, 101, 1-2, p. 125-142.

2711. PETACCIA (R.). Der griechische Mythos in der republikanischen Tragödie Roms. Aitiologische Tendenzen in Ennius' Telephus. *In*: Rezeption und Identität [Cf. n° 2574], p. 155-168.

2712. POUTHIER (P.). Réflexions sur quelques héros de la légende et de l'histoire de Rome. *In*: Paradoxe (Le) du héros ou d'Homère à Malraux (Le) [Cf. n° 1439], p. 87-94.

2713. REBILLARD (Éric). Église et sépulture dans l'Antiquité tardive (Occident latin, 3e–6e siècles). *Annales*, 99, 54, 5, p. 1027-1046. – IDEM. La «conversion» de l'Empire romain selon Peter Brown (note critique). *Annales*, 99, 54, 4, p. 813-824.

2714. REBUFFAT (R.). Auguste et les Dinosaures. *In*: Imago antiquitatis [Cf. n° 2705], p. 371-381.

2715. RIVES (J. B.). The decree of Decius and the religion of empire. *Journal of Roman studies*, 99, 89, p. 135-154.

2716. SAUER (V.). Religiöses als Argument im politischen Alltag der späten römischen Republik: Skizze eines Dissertationsvorhabens. *In*: Zwischen Krise und Alltag [Cf. n° 2215], p. 187-196.

2717. SAURON (G.). Légende noire et mythe de l'âge d'or. Les pôles complémentaires de la mystification augustéenne. *In*: Mythe grecque (Le) dans l'Italie antique [Cf. n° 2198]. p. 593-625.

2718. SCHEID (John). Aspects religieux de la municipalisation. Quelques réflexions générales. *In*: Cités, municipes, colonies [Cf. n° 2484], p. 381-423. – IDEM. 'Livres' sacerdotaux et érudition: l'exemple des chapelles des Argées. *In*: Zwischen Krise und Alltag [Cf. n° 2215], p. 161-170.

2719. SEBAÏ (M.). La vie religieuse en Afrique proconsulaire sous le haut-empire: l'exemple de la cité de Thugga. Premières observations. *In*: Zwischen Krise und Alltag [Cf. n° 2215], p. 81-94

2720. Spiegel (Im) des Mythos: Bilderwelt und Lebenswelt (Lo specchio del Mito: immaginario e realtà). Symposium (Rom, 19.–20. Februar 1998). Hrsg. v. Francesco DE ANGELI und Susanne MUTH. Wiesbaden, Reichert, 156 p. (ill., maps, plans). [Cf. n[os] <Auswahl> 2290, 2697.]

2721. STEPPER (R.). Der Oberpontifikat von Caesar bis Nerva: zwischen Tradition und Innovation. *In*: Zwischen Krise und Alltag [Cf. n° 2215], p. 171-185.

2722. STRAMAGLIA (Antonio). Res inauditae, incredulae. Storie di fantasmi nel mondo greco-latino. Bari, Levante editori, 99, 552 p.

2723. VAN ANDRINGA (W.). Prêtrises et cités dans les Trois Gaules et les Germanies au Haut Empire. *In*: Cités, municipes, colonies [Cf. n° 2484], p. 425-446.

2724. VOGT-SPIRA (G.). La Tyché du héros ou l'individu et la contingence: un concept paradoxale? L' exemple de la Fortune de César. *In*: Paradoxe (Le) du héros ou d'Homère à Malraux [Cf. n° 1439], p. 95-107.

2725. ZIOLKOWSKI (A.). Ritual cleaning-up of the city: from the Lupercalia to the Argei. *Ancient society*, 98-99, 29, p. 191-218.

2726. ZOGRAFOU (A.). L'énigme de la triple Hécate: de l'entre deux à la triplicité. *In*: Zwischen Krise und Alltag [Cf. n° 2215], p. 57-79.

§ 9. Archaeology and history of art.

2727. Antenor. Miscellanea di studi di archeologia, I. A cura di M. L. BASSANI e A. R. GHIOTTO, Padova, Bottega d'Erasmo e Aldo Ausilio editore in Padova, 99, 155 p. [Cf. n[os] <scelta> 2735, 2748, 2765.]

2728. Antike Portraits. Zum Gedächtnis von Helga von Heintze. Hrsg. v. Hans von STEUBEN. Möhnesee-Wamel, Bibliopolis, 99, 328 p. (Taf.). [Cf. n[os] <Auswahl> 2302, 2745, 2754, 2777.]

2729. BARDILL (Jonathan). The golden gate in Constantinople: a triumphal arch of Theodosius I. *American journal of archaeology*, 99, 103, 4, p. 671-696.

2730. BARTMAN (E.). Portraits of Livia: imaging the imperial woman in Augustan Rome. Cambridge, Cambridge U. P., 99, XXIV-242 p. (ill.).

2731. BAUER (F. A.), HEINZELMANN (M.). The Constantinian bishop's church at Ostia: preliminary report on the 1998 season. *Journal of Roman archaeology*, 99, 12, p. 342-354.

2732. BROISE (Henri), THEBERT (Yvon). Élagabal et le complexe religieux de la Vigna Barberini. Heliogabalium in Palatino monte iuxta aedes imperatorias consecrauit eique templum fecit (HA, Ant. Heliog., III, 4). *Mélanges de l'Ecole française de Rome. Antiquité*, 99, 111, 2, p. 729-747.

2733. CAPRINO (Catia). Rinvenimenti a Villa Adriana (Tivoli). Roma, Giorgio Bretschneider, 99, 47 p. (ill.).

2734. CHRISTENSEN (J.). Vindicating Vitruvius on the subject of perspective. *Journal of Hellenic studies*, 99, 119, p. 161-166.

2735. COLPO (I.). La raffigurazione delle ville nell'arte di I secolo d.C. come excerptum della pittura romana di paesaggio. *In*: Antenor [Cf. n° 2727], p. 47-70.

2736. Constructions of the classical body. Ed. by James I. PORTER. Ann Arbor, University of Michigan Press, 99, 397 p. (ill.).

2737. COOL (H. E. M.), BAXTER (M. J.). Peeling the onion: an approach to comparing vessel glass assemblages. *Journal of Roman archaeology*, 99, 12, p. 72-100.

2738. Corpus signorum imperii Romani. Corpus des sculptures du monde romain. Pologne. Vol. III. Fasc. 2. Les sculptures mythologiques et décoratives dans les colléctions polonaises. Ed. par Tomasz MIKOCKI, Sabina GRZEGRZOLKA, Krystyna MOCZULSKA et Janusz A. OSTROWSKI. Warszawa, Institut d'archéologie, Université de Varsovie, 99, 120 p. (ill., tables).

2739. DE CALLATAŸ (François), VAN HEESCH (Johan). Greek and Roman coins from the du Chastel collection. London, Spink, 99, XIX-162 p. (ill.). (Coin cabinet of the royal library of Belgium).

2740. DE CALLATAŸ-VAN DER MERSCH (Colette). Vitruve, l'architecte du Panthéon. Leuven, Peeters, 99, 127 p.

2741. DENIAUX (Élizabeth). Découverte d'un nouveau milliaire de la Via Egnatia à Apollonia (Albanie). *Mélanges de l'Ecole française de Rome. Antiquité*, 99, 111, 1, p. 167-189.

2742. DUNBABIN (Katherine M. D.). Mosaics of the Greek and Roman world. Cambridge, Cambridge U. P., 99, XXII, 357 p.

2743. ECK (W.), FOERSTER (G.). Ein Triumphbogen für Hadrian im Tal von Beth Shean bei Tel Shalem. *Journal of Roman archaeology*, 99, 12, p. 294-313

2744. Eye expanded (The). Life and the arts in Grecoroman antiquity. Ed. by F. B. TITCHENER and R. F. MOORTON. Berkeley, Los Angeles a. London, University of California Press, 99, XIII-294 p. (ill.).

2745. FEJFER (J.). What is a private Roman portrait? *In*: Antike Portraits [Cf. n° 2728], p. 137-148.

2746. FILGES (Axel). Marmorstatuetten aus Kleinasien. Zu Ikonographie, Funktion und Produktion antoninischer, severischer und späterer Idealplastik. *Istanbuler Mitteilungen*, 99, 49, p. 377-430.

2747. FISHWICK (D.). The "temple of Augustus" at Tarraco. *Latomus*, 99, 58, p. 121-137.

2748. GHIOTTO (A. R.). Ornatissimi lacus, munera nymphaea. Le fontane monumentali pubbliche di Roma nella loro evoluzione lessicale. *In*: Antenor [Cf. n° 2727], p. 71-90.

2749. GIANFROTTA (Piero A.). Archeologia subacquea e testimonianze di pesca. *Mélanges de l'Ecole française de Rome. Antiquité*, 99, 111, 1, p. 9-36.

2750. HAALEBOS (J. K.), WILLEMS (W. J. H.). Recent research on the limes in the Netherlands. *Journal of Roman archaeology*, 99, 12, p. 247-262.

2751. JACOBSON (David M.), WILSON JONES (M.). The annexe of 'Temple of Venus' at Baiae: an exercise in Roman geometrical planning. *Journal of Roman archaeology*, 99, 12, p. 57-71.

2752. KAUFMANN-HEINIMANN (Annemarie). Eighteen new pieces from the late Roman silver treasure of Kaiseraugst: first notice. *Journal of Roman archaeology*, 99, 12, p.333-341.

2753. KING (Anthony). Diet in the Roman world: a regional inter-site comparison of the mammal bones. *Journal of Roman archaeology*, 99, 12, p. 168-202.

2754. KOCH (G.). Produktion auf Vorrat oder Anfertigung auf besonderen Auftrag? Überlegungen zu stadtrömischen frühchristlichen Sarkophagen der vorkonstantinischen und konstantinischen Zeit. *In*: Antike Portraits [Cf. n° 2728], p. 303-316.

2755. LANCASTER (Lynne). Building Trajan's Column. *American journal of archaeology*, 99, 103, 3, p. 419-439.

2756. Lexicon Topographicum urbis Romae. A cura di Eva Margareta STEINBY. Vol. IV: P–S. Roma, Quasar, 99, 520 p. (ill.).

2757. LILJENSTOLPE (P.). Superimposed orders: the use of the architectural orders in multistoreyed structures of the Roman imperial era. *Opuscula Romana*, 99, 24, p. 117-154.

2758. LING (Roger). Stuccowork and painting in Roman Italy. Aldershot, Brookfield, Singapore a. Sydney, Ashgate, 99, IX-372 p. (Abb.).

2759. MARCO-SIMÓN (F.). Ambivalencia icónica y persuasión ideológica: las monedas de Juliano con representación del toro. *Athenaeum*, 99, 87, 1, p. 201-214.

2760. MARINESCU-NICOLAJSEN (Liliana). La colonne Trajane: le tryptique de la victoire. Contribution à une nouvelle interprétation de la scène IX. *Mélanges de l'Ecole française de Rome. Antiquité*, 99, 111, 1, p. 273-310.

2761. MEYER (Katharina Eleonore). Axial peristyle houses in the Western empire. *Journal of Roman archaeology*, 99, 12, p. 101-121.

2762. MIERSE (W. E.). Temples and towns in Roman Iberia. The social and architectural dynamics of sanctuary designs from the third century B.C. to the third century A.D. Berkeley, Los Angeles a. London, University of California Press, 99, XXIII-346 p. (figs.).

2763. Mills-bakeries of Ostia (The). Description and interpretation. Ed. by Jan Theo BAKKER. Amsterdam, Gieben, 99, V-217 p. (Abb., Taf.).

2764. MORAND (Isabelle). La structure des mosaïques romaines et ses rapports avec la pensée grecque. *Revue des études anciennes*, 99, 101, 1-2, p. 143-159

2765. NOVELLO (M.). Echi di cultura classica nei contorniati a soggetto epico. *In*: Antenor [Cf. n° 2727], p. 91-120.

2766. PASQUALINI (Anna). Note sull'ubicazione del Latiar. *Mélanges de l'Ecole française de Rome. Antiquité*, 99, 111, 2, p. 779-786.

2767. PAVOLINI (Carlo). I resti romani sotto la chiesa dei SS. Nereo e Achilleo a Roma. Una rilettura archeologica. *Mélanges de l'Ecole française de Rome. Antiquité*, 99, 111, 1, p. 405-448.

2768. PEKÁRY (Irene). Repertorium der hellenistischen und römischen Schiffsdarstellungen. Münster, 99, VIII-448 p.

2769. PETERSE (Kees). Steinfachwerk in Pompeji. Bautechnik und Architektur. Mit einem Beitrag von Ineke JOOSTEN. Amsterdam, Gieben, 99, XI, 182 p. (Abb., Taf.).

2770. PIRSON (Felix). Mietwohnungen in Pompeji und Herkulaneum. Untersuchungen zur Architektur, zum Wohnen und zur Sozial- und Wirtschaftsgeschichte der Vesuvstädte. München, Pfeil, 99, 287 p. (Abb., Taf.).

2771. POULLE (Bruno). Le théâtre de Marcellus et la sphère. *Mélanges de l'Ecole française de Rome. Antiquité*, 99, 111, 1, p. 257-272.

2772. RAECK (Wulf). Untersuchungen zur Vorgängerbebauung des Trajaneums von Pergamon I: Überblick. Obere Hangstufe. *Istanbuler Mitteilungen*, 99, 49, p. 333-361.

2773. REHREN (T.), KRAUS (K.). Cupel and crucible: the refining of debased silver in the Colonia Ulpia Traiana, Xanten. *Journal of Roman archaeology*, 99, 12, p. 263-272.

2774. RIZZO (Giorgio), VILLEDIEU (Françoise), VITALE (Micaela). Mobilier de tombes des VIe–VIIe siècles mises au jour sur le Palatin (Rome, Vigna Barberini). *Mélanges de l'Ecole française de Rome. Antiquité*, 99, 111, 1, p. 351-403.

2775. ROYO (Manuel). Domus imperatoriae. Topographie, formation et imaginaire des palais impériaux du Palatin (IIe siècle av. J.-C.–Ier siècle ap. J.-C.). Roma, 'L'Erma' di Bretschneider et Paris, de Boccard, 99, 436 p. (ill., tables).

2776. RUSTICO (Letizia). Peschiere romane. *Mélanges de l'Ecole française de Rome. Antiquité*, 99, 111, 1, p. 51-66.

2777. SCHÄFER (Th.). Felicior Augusto, melior Traiano! Das Bildnis des Konstantin in New York. *In*: Antike Portraits [Cf. n° 2728], p. 295-302.

2778. SCHMID (Stephan G.). Decline or prosperity at Roman Eretria? Industry, purple dye works, public buildings, and gravestones. *Journal of Roman archaeology*, 99, 12, p. 273-293.

2779. SKUPINSKA-LØVSET (Ilona). Portraiture in Roman Syria. A study in social and regional differentiation within the art of portraiture. Łódź, Wydawnictwo uniwersytetu Łódzkiego, 99, 280 p. (ill.).

2780. SPERLING (Gert). Das Pantheon in Rom. Abbild und Maß des Kosmos. Neuried, Ars una Verlag, 99, 362 p. (Abb.).

2781. STERN (Marianne E.). Roman glassblowing in a cultural context. *American Journal of archaeology*, 99, 103, 3, p. 441-484.

2782. TREGGIARI (Susan). The upper-class house as symbol and focus of emotion in Cicero. *Journal of Roman Archaeology*, 99, 12, p. 33-56.

2783. TREVISANATO (A.). Architetture difensive romane: spazialità e simbolismi. *Patavium*, 99, 13, p. 63-81.

2784. TURCAN (Robert). Messages d'outre-tombe. L'iconographie des sarcophages romains. Paris, de Boccard, 99, 195 p.

2785. UYTTERHOEVEN (Inge). The forum of Aesernia: a development Sketch. *Ancient society*, 98-99, 29, p. 241-266.

2786. VANIT (Marjorie S.). The Stagni painted tomb: cultural interchange and gender differentiation in roman Alexandria. *American journal of archaeology*, 99, 103, 4, p. 641-669.

2787. VILLEDIEU (Françoise), VELTRI (Patrizia). Les soutènements nord-ouest et nord de la terrasse de la Vigna Barberini (Palatin). *Mélanges de l'Ecole française de Rome. Antiquité*, 99, 111, 2, p. 749-778.

2788. WILSON (Andrew). Deliveries extra urbem: aqueducts and the countryside. *Journal of Roman archaeology*, 99, 12, p. 314-331.

Cf. n° 1566

§ 10. Late antiquity. Transformation of the Roman world.

2789. Bitonto e la Puglia tra tardoantico e regno normanno. Atti del convegno (Bitonto, 15–17 ottobre 1998). A cura di C. S. FIORIELLO. Bari, Edipuglia, 99, 340 p. [Cf. n^{os} <scelta> 2276, 2822.]

2790. BRECHT (Stephanie). Die römische Reichskrise von ihrem Ausbruch bis zu ihrem Höhepunkt in der Darstellung byzantinischer Autoren. Rahden u. Westf, Leidorf, 99, 300 p.

2791. CAMERON (A.). The antiquity of the Symmachi. *Historia*, 99, 48, p. 477-505.

2792. CHRISTOL (M.). Le métier d'empereur et ses représentations à la fin du IIIe et au début du IVe siècle. *Cahiers du Centre Gustave Glotz*, 99, 10, p. 355-368.

2793. CLOVER (Frank M.). A game of the Bluff: the fate of Sicily after A.D. 476. *Historia*, 99, 48, p. 235-244.

2794. Constructing identities in Late antiquity. Ed. by Richard MILES. London a. New York, Routledge, 99, 262 p. (ill.). [Cf. n^{os} <choice> 2498, 2798, 2803, 2819, 2838, 2909.]

2795. COOPER (Kate). The virgin and the bride. Idealized womanhood in Late antiquity. Cambridge a. London, Harvard U. P., 99, 180 p.

2796. DRIJVERS (J. W.). Ammianus Marcellinus' image of Arsaces and early Parthian history. *In*: Late Roman world (The) and its historians [Cf. n° 2809], p. 193-206.

2797. East and west: modes of communication. Proceedings of the first plenary conference at Merida. Ed. by Euangelos K. CHRYSOS and I. N. WOOD. Leiden a. Boston, Brill, 99, XIV-288 p. (pl., ill.). (Transformation of the Roman world, 5).

2798. EASTERLING (P.), MILES (R.). Dramatic identities: tragedy in Late antiquity. *In*: Constructing identities in Late antiquity [Cf. n° 2794], p. 95-111.

2799. FREDE (M.). Monotheism and pagan philosophy in later antiquity. *In*: Pagan monotheism in Late antiquity [Cf. n° 2814], p. 41-67.

2800. GIARDINA (A.). Esplosione di tardoantico. *Studi storici*, 99, 40, p. 157-180.

2801. GRANT (M.). The collapse and recovery of the Roman empire. London a. New York, Routledge, 99, XVIII-121 p. (ill.)

2802. HARRIES (Jill). Law and empire in the Late antiquity. Cambridge, Cambridge U. P., 99, IX-235 p.

2803. HEATHER (P.). Ammianus of Jovian: history and literature. *In*: Late Roman world (The) and its historians [Cf. n° 2809], p. 105-116. – IDEM. The barbarian in Late antiquity: image, reality, and transformation. *In*: Constructing identities in late antiquity [Cf. n° 2794], p. 234-258.

2804. HEIJMANS (Marc). La topographie de la ville d'Arles durant l'antiquité tardive. *Journal of Roman archaeology*, 99, 12, p. 143-167.

2805. HUNT (D.). The outsider inside: Ammianus on the rebellion of Silvanus. *In*: Late Roman world (The) and its historians [Cf. n° 2809], p. 51-63.

2806. Idea (The) and ideal of the town between Late Antiquity and the early Middle Ages. Ed. by G. P. BROGIOLO and Bryan WARD-PERKINS. Leiden, Boston a. Köln, Brill, 99, XVI-265 p. (ill., plans). (The Transformation of the Roman World. Volume 4.). [Cf. n^{os} <choice> 3005, 3032.]

2807. KLEIN (Richard). Roma versa per aevum. Ausgewählte Schriften zur heidnischen und christlichen Spätantike. Hildesheim, Zürich u. New York, Olms, 99, XX-687 p.

2808. Late antiquity. A guide to the postclassical world. Ed. by G. W. BOWERSOCK, P. BROWN and O. GRABAR. London, Harvard UP a. Belknap press, 99, 832 p.

2809. Late Roman world (The) and its historians. Interpreting Ammianus Marcellinus. Ed. by Jan Willem DRIJVERS and David HUNT. London a. New York, Routledge, 99, XII-243 p. [Cf. n^{os} <choice> 2459, 2796, 2803, 2805, 2810.]

2810. LENSSEN (J.). The Persian invasion of 359: presentation by suppression in Ammianus Marcellinus' Res Gestae 18.4.1-18.6.7. *In*: Late Roman world (The) and its historians [Cf. n° 2809], p. 40-50.

2811. MACKAY (Ch. S.). Lactantius and the succession to Diocletian. *Classical philology*, 99, 94, p. 198-209.

2812. Memoria del passato, urgenza del futuro: il mondo romano fra V e VII secolo. Atti delle VI Giornate di studio sull'età romanobarbarica, Benevento, 18–20 giugno 1998. A cura di Marcello ROTILI. Napoli, Arte tipografica, 99, 296 p. (ill.).

2813. MITCHELL (St.). The cult of theos hypsistos between Pagans, Jews, and Christians. *In*: Pagan monotheism in Late antiquity [Cf. n° 2814], p. 81-148.

2814. Pagan monotheism in Late antiquity. Ed. by P. ATHANASSIADI and M. FREDE. Oxford, Clarendon Press, 99, 211 p. [Cf. n^{os} <choice> 2799, 2813.]

2815. Prosopographie chrétienne du Bas-Empire. Dir. par Charles PIETRI et Luce PIETRI. T. 2. Prosopographie de l'Italie chrétienne (313–604). Vol. 1. A–K. Par Janine DESMULLIEZ [et al.]. Roma, Ecole française de Rome, 99, XL-1226 p.

2816. Prospettive sul tardoantico. Atti del convegno di Pavia, 27–28 novembre 1997. A cura di Giancarlo MAZZOLI e Fabio GASTI. Como, New Press, 99, 174 p. (Biblioteca di Athenaeum, 41).

2817. Rezeption der hellenistischen Philosophie in der Spätantike. Akten der I. Tagung der Karl und Gertrud-Abel-Stiftung (Trier, 22.–25. September 1997). Hrsg. v. T. FUHRER, M. ERLER und K. SCHLAPBACH. Stuttgart, Steiner, 99, 316 p. [Cf. n^{os} <Auswahl> 2828, 2830, 2837, 2839, 2841, 2922, 2923.]

2818. SMITH (R. R. R.). Late antique portraits in a public context; honorific statuary at Aphrodisias in Caria, A.D. 300–600. *Journal of Roman studies*, 99, 89, p. 155-189.

2819. STEWART (P.). The destruction of statues in Late antiquity. *In*: Constructing identities in Late antiquity [Cf. n n° 2794], p. 159-189.

2820. VERA (Domenico). Massa fundorum. Forme della grande proprietà e poteri della città in Italia fra Costantino e Gregorio Magno. *Mélanges de l'Ecole française de Rome. Antiquité*, 99, 111, 2, p. 991-1025.

2821. Visigoths (The) from the migration period to the seventh century: an ethnographic approach. Ed. by P. HEATHER. Woodbridge, The Boydell Press, 99, 563 p.

2822. VOLPE (G.). Aspetti della geografia economica della Puglia nei secoli III–VII d.C. *In*: Bitonto e la Puglia tra tardoantico e regno normanno [Cf. n° 2789], p. 87-99.

2823. WELLS (Peter S.). The barbarians speak. How the conquered peoples shaped Roman Europe. Princeton, Princeton U. P., 99, XII-335 p.

2824. WILLIAMS (S.), FRIELL (G.). The Rome that did not fall: the survival of the East in the fifth century. London a. New York, Routledge, 99, XII-282 p. (ill., maps)

2825. WITSCHEL (Christian). Krise – Rezession – Stagnation? Der Westen des römischen Reiches im 3. Jahrhundert n.Chr. Frankfurt am Main, Clauss, 99, 421 p.

§ 10. Addenda 1998.

2826. MAZZA (Mario). Di Ellenismo, Oriente e Tarda Antichità. Considerazioni a margine di un saggio (e di un convegno). *Mediterraneo antico*, 98, 1, p. 141-170.

Cf. n°s 536, 2827-2959, 3195, 3197, 3198, 3212, 3837

G

EARLY HISTORY OF THE CHURCH TO GREGORY THE GREAT

§ 1. Sources. 2827-2866. – § 2. General. 2867-2876. – § 3. Special studies. 2877-2950. – § 4. Hagiography. 2951-2959.

§ 1. Sources.

2827. [Alcimus Avitus] ARWEILER (A.). Die Imitation antiker und spätantiker Literatur in der Dichtung 'De spiritalis historiae gestis' des Alcimus Avitus. Mit einem Kommentar zu Avit. Carm. 4,429-540 und 5,526-703. Berlin u. New York, de Gruyter, 99, 384 p.

2828. [Arnobius] FÖLLINGER (S.). Aggression und Adaptation: Zur Rolle philosophischer Theorien in Arnobius' apologetischer Argumentation. *In*: Rezeption der hellenistischen Philosophie in der Spätantike [Cf. n° 2817], p. 13-31.

2829. [Augustinus] Augustine's City of God. A reader's guide. Ed. by Gerard O'DALY. Oxford, Clarendon Press, 99, XII-323 p.

2830. [Augustinus] BETTETINI (M.). Ai limiti della materia, tra neoplatonismo e cristianesimo. Per una lettura del De musica di Agostino di Ippona. *In*: Rezeption der hellenistischen Philosophie in der Spätantike [Cf. n° 2817], p. 123-138

2831. [Augustinus] BOCHET (I.). Une nouvelle lecture du Liber ad Honoratum d'Augustin (=epist. 140). *Revue des études augustiniennes*, 99, 45, p. 353-361.

2832. [Augustinus] CLARK (E. A.). Rewriting early Christian history: Augustin's representation of Monica. *In*: Portraits of spiritual authority [Cf. n° 2872], p. 3-23.

2833. [Augustinus] DOIGNON (J.). Fragments de l'Hortensius chez Augustin à récupérer ou à invalider. *Latomus*, 99, 58, p. 164-171.

2834. [Augustinus] DOLBEAU (F.). Un second manuscrit complet du Sermo contra Pelagium d'Augustin. *Revue des études augustiniennes*, 99, 45, p. 353-361.

2835. [Augustinus] DUVAL (Y.-M.). La correspondance entre Augustin et Pélage. *Revue des études augustiniennes*, 99, 45, p. 363-384.

2836. [Augustinus] ELFASSI (J.). Le sermon 150 de saint Augustin. Édition critique et tentative de datation. *Revue des études augustiniennes*, 99, 45, p. 21-50.

2837. [Augustinus] FUHRER (Th.). Zum wahrnehmungstheoretischen Hintergrund von Augustins Glaubensbegriff. *In*: Rezeption der hellenistischen Philosophie in der Spätantike [Cf. n° 2817], p. 191-211.

2838. [Augustinus] HARRISON (S.). Autobiographical identity and philosophical past in Augustine's dialogue De libero arbitrio. *In*: Constructing identities in late antiquity [Cf. n° 2794], p. 133-158.

2839. [Augustinus] HARWARDT (H.). Die Glücksfrage der Stoa in Augustins De beata vita: Übernahme und Anwendung stoischer Argumentationsmuster. *In*: Rezeption der hellenistischen Philosophie in der Spätantike [Cf. n° 2817], p. 153-171.

2840. [Augustinus] PIERI (B.). Retorica, conversione, introversione. Su alcuni aspetti dello stile di Agostino. *Bollettino di studi latini*, 99, 29, p. 523-540.

2841. [Augustinus] SCHLAPBACH (K.). Ciceronisches und Neuplatonisches in den Proömien von Augustin, Contra Academicos 1 und 2. *In*: Rezeption der hellenistischen Philosophie in der Spätantike [Cf. n° 2817], p. 139-151.

2842. [Augustinus] TOUBOULIC (A.-I.). Les valeurs d'ordo et leur réception chez Saint Augustin. *Revue des études augustiniennes*, 99, 45, p. 295-334.

2843. [Augustinus] WURM (A.). 'Nec vocemini magistri'. Die Funktion von Confessiones IX 6,14. *Revue des études augustiniennes*, 99, 45, p. 277-293.

2844. [Dracontius] STELLA (F.). Innovazioni lessicali delle 'Laudes Dei' di Dracorizio fra latinità tardo antica e medievale. *Invigilata lucernis*, 99, 21, p. 417-444.

2845. [Epictetus] BOTER (Gerard). The Encheiridion of Epictetus and its three Christian adaptations. Transmission and critical editions. Leiden, Boston a. Köln, Brill, 99, XVIII-446 p.

2846. [Flavius Josephus] PRESTEL (P.). Die Erprobung des Abraham. Zur Gestaltung der Aqedah bei Flavius Josephus. *Wort und Dienst*, 99, 25, p. 93-112.

2847. [Gregorius Nyssenus] GREGOR VON NYSSA. Oratio consolatoria in Pulcheriam. Hrsg. v. Ulrike GANTZ. Basel, Schwabe & Co, 99, 315 p.

2848. GUADALAJARA-MEDINA (J.), JIMÉNEZ-CALVENTE (T.). Un opúsculo latino sobre el Anticristo. *Minerva*, 99, 13, p. 179-200.

2849. [Hieronymus] ADKIN (Neil). Jerome on Tertullian: Epist. LVIII 10,1. *Athenaeum*, 99, 87, 2, p. 383-394.

2850. [Hieronymus] ADKIN (Neil). Jerome's vow 'never to reread the classics': some observations. *Revue des études anciennes*, 99, 101, 1-2, p. 161-167.

2851. [Hieronymus] ADKIN (Neil). Sallust, Hist. frg. II, 64 and Jerome's commentary on Zechariah. *Latomus*, 99, 58, p. 635-639.

2852. [Hieronymus] Commentaires de Jérôme sur le prophète Isaie. Livres XVI–XVII. Ed. par R. GRYSON et C. GABRIEL. Freiburg, Herder, 99, 1617-1991 p.

2853. [Hieronymus] RATTI (S.). La Chronique de Jérôme: opus tumultuarium? *Latomus*, 99, 58, p. 861-871.

2854. [Johannes Philoponos] FLADERER (Ludwig). De opificio mundi. Spätantikes Sprachdenken und christliche Exegese. Stuttgart u. Leipzig, Teubner, 99, 419 p.

2855. [Minucius Felix] INGREMEAU (Ch.). Minucius Felix et ses 'sources': le travail de l'écrivain. *Revue des études augustiniennes*, 99, 45, p. 3-20.

2856. Neutestamentliche Apokryphen in deutscher Übersetzung. Band 1. Evangelien. Band 2. Apostolisches, Apokalypsen und Verwandtes. Hrsg v. Wilhelm SCHNEEMELCHER. Tübingen, Mohr, 99, p. 98.

2857. [Paulinus Nolanus] NAZZARO (A. V.). Il proemio della Laus sancti Iohannis (Carm. VI) di Paolino di Nola. *Vichiana*, 99, 4 ser., 1, p. 45-61.

2858. [Paulinus Nolanus] TROUT (D. E.). Paulinus of Nola. Life, letters and poems. Berkeley, Los Angeles a. London, California UP, 99, XV-326 p.

2859. [Pelagius] THEIR (SEBASTIAN). Kirche bei Pelagius. Berlin u. New York, IX-358 p. (Patristische Texte und Studien, 50).

2860. SANNA (D.). L'epigrafia paleocristiana della Sardegna: Theodor Mommsen e la condanna delle 'falsae'. *In*: Sardegna paleocristiana (La) tra Eusebio e Gregorio Magno [Cf. n° 2932], p. 405-435.

2861. [Tertullianus] Chronica Tertullianea et Cyprianea 1975–1994. Bibliographie critique de la première littérature latine chrétienne. Ed. par René BRAUN, Frédéric CHAPOT, Simone DELEANI, François DOLBEAU, Jean-Claude FREDOUILLE et Pierre PETITMENGIN. Paris, Institut d'Études augustiniennes, 99, XII-629 p.

2862. [Tertullianus] WELLSTEIN (Matthias). Nova verba in Tertullianus Schriften gegen die Häretiker aus montanistischer Zeit. Stuttgart u. Leipzig, Teubner, 99, 351 p.

2863. [Test. nov.] PROSTMEIER (Ferdinand R.). Der Barnabasbrief. Übersetzt und erklärt. Göttingen, Vandenhoeck & Ruprecht, 99, 648 p. (Kommentar zu Apostolischen Vätern, 8).

2864. [Test. Vet.] BERGES (U.). Die Armen im Buch Jesaja. Ein Beitrag zur Literaturgeschichte des AT. *Biblica*, 99, 80, p. 153-177.

2865. [Test. Vet.] WEITZMANN (M. P.). The syriac version of the Old Testament: an introduction. Cambridge UP, 99, XV-357 p.

2866. [Test. Vet] BALTZER (Klaus). Deutero-Jesaja. Kommentar zum Alten Testament. Gütersloh, Gütersloher Verlagshaus, 99, 680 p.

§ 2. General.

2867. Apologetics in the Roman empire. Pagans, Jews, and Christians. Ed. by Mark EDWARDS, Martin GOODMAN and Simon PRICE. Oxford, Oxford U. P., 99, X-315 p.

2868. AVALOS (Hector). Health care and the rise of Christianity. Peabody, Hendrickson, 99, IX-166 p.

2869. DASSMANN (Ernst). Kirchengeschichte. 2, 2. Theologie und innerkirchliches Leben bis zum Ausgang der Spätantike. Stuttgart, Kohlhammer, 99, 272 p.

2870. GNILKA (Joachim). Die frühen Christen: Ursprünge und Anfang der Kirche. Freiburg im Breisgau, Herder Verlag, 99, 348 p.

2871. Lexicon der christlichen Antike. Hrsg. v. Johannes B. BAUER und Manfred HUTTER. Stuttgart, Kröner, 99, XXXI-387 p.

2872. Portraits of spiritual authority. Religious power in early Christianity. Byzantium and the Christian Orient. Ed. by J. W. DRIJVERS and J. W. WATT. Leiden, Boston a. Köln, Brill, 99, 227 p. [Cf. n^os <choice> 2832, 2891, 2942, 2959, 3034.]

2873. RIZZO (Francesco Paolo). La chiesa dei primi secoli. Lineamenti storici. Bari, Edipuglia, 99, 252 p.

2874. SAWYER (John F. A.). Sacred languages and sacred texts. London a. New York, Routledge, 99, 190 p. (Religion in the first Christian centuries).

2875. SPEYER (Wolfgang). Frühes Christentum im antiken Strahlungsfeld. Tübingen, Mohr, 99, X-303 p. (Kleine Schriften, 2). (Wissenschaftliche Untersuchungen zum Neuen Testament, 116).

2876. ZAGER (Werner). Jesus und die frühchristliche Verkündingung: historische Rückfragen nach den Anfängen. Vluyn, Neukirchener Verlag, 99, XI-143 p.

Cf. n° 2713

§ 3. Special studies.

2877. BARCELÓ (P.). Warum Christus? Überlegungen zu Constantins Entscheidung für das Christentum. *In*: Zwischen Krise und Alltag [Cf. n° 2215], p. 255-269.

2878. BAUSENHART (Guido). Das Amt in der Kirche: eine not-wendende Neubestimmung. Freiburg im Breisgau, Herder Verlag, 99, 402 p.

2879. BEALE (G. K.). Peace and mercy upon the Isreael of God. The Old Testament background of Galatians 6, 16b. *Biblica*, 99, 80, p. 204-223.

2880. BERNARD (Charles André). Mystère trinitaire et transformation en Dieu. *Gregorianum*, 99, 80, 3, p. 441-467.

2881. BRENK (Frederick E.). Clothed in purple light. Studies in Vergil and in Latin literature, including aspects of philosophy, religion, magic, Judaism, and the New Testament background. Stuttgart, Steiner, 99, 256 p.

2882. BRENNECKE (Hanns Christoph). Wie man einen Heiligen politisch instrumentalisiert: der Heilige Simeon Stylites und die Synode von Chalkedon. *In*: Theologie und Kultur [Cf. n° 2939], p. 237-260.

2883. CAMPIONE (Ada), NUZZO (Donatella). La Daunia alle origini cristiane. Bari, Edipuglia, 99, 147 p.

2884. CLARK (Elisabeth A.). Reading renunciation. Ascetism and scripture in early Christianity. Princeton, Princeton U. P., 99, XIII-420 p.

2885. COLOMBO (Arrigo). Il diavolo. Genesi, storia, orrori di un mito cristiano che avversa la società di giustizia. Bari, Dedalo, 99, 222 p.

2886. DAL COVOLO (E.). Il 'capovolgimento' dei rapporti tra la chiesa e l'impero nel secolo di Sant'Eusebio di Vercelli. *In*: Sardegna paleocristiana (La) tra Eusebio e Gregorio Magno [Cf. n° 2932], p. 137-152.

2887. DE CHURRUCA (Juan). Actitud del cristianismo ante el Imperio Romano. Albolote, Comares, 99, 121 p.

2888. DE VOS (Craig Steven). Church and community conflicts: the relationships of Thessalonian, Corinthian and Philippian churches with their wider civic communities. Atlanta, Scholars Press, 99, X-332 p.

2889. DEGÓRSKI (Bazyli). Uno schizzo di escatologia paleocristiana. *Vox Patrum*, 99, 19, p. 427-453.

2890. DI BERNARDINO (Angelo). Christianity on the road. *Augustinianum*, 99, 39, 2, p. 231-244.

2891. DRIJVERS (J. W.). Promoting Jerusalem: Cyril and the true cross. *In*: Portraits of spiritual authority [Cf. n° 2872], p. 79-95.

2892. DUVAL (Noël). L'église V (des Saints-Gervais-Protais-et-Tryphon) à Sbeitla (Sufetula), Tunisie. Recherches 1954–1963. *Mélanges de l'Ecole française de Rome. Antiquité*, 99, 111, 2, p. 927-989.

2893. ESCRIBANO (María Victoria). El Edicto de Tésalonica (CTh 16, 1, 2. 380.) y Teodosio: norma antiarriana y declaración programática. *Cassiodorus*, 99, 5, p. 35-64.

2894. EVANS (C. A.). Jesus' self-designation 'The son of man' and the recognition of his divinity. *In*: Trinity (The) [Cf. n° 2943], p. 29-47.

2895. EVENEPOEL (W.). Ambrose vs. Symmachus: Christians and Pagans in AD 384. *Ancient society*, 98-99, 29, p. 283-306.

2896. FAIVRE (Alexandre). Les premiers laïcs: lorsque l'Église naissait au monde. Strasbourg, du Signe, 99, 323 p. (cartes).

2897. FINZI (C.). Il pensiero politico dell'età eusebiana. *In*: Sardegna paleocristiana (La) tra Eusebio e Gregorio Magno [Cf. n° 2932], p. 153-167.

2898. FLACH (Dieter). Die römischen Christenverfolgungen. Gründe und Hintergründe. *Historia*, 99, 48, p. 442-464.

2899. FORLIN PATRUCCO (M.). Cristianesimo, monachesimo, demografia. *In*: Demografia, sistemi agrari, regimi alimentari nel mondo antico [Cf. n° 2035], p. 289-307.

2900. GASTONI (L.). La battaglia antiariana di Lucifero e il suo coinvolgimento in alcuni scismi del tempo. *In*: Sardegna paleocristiana (La) tra Eusebio e Gregorio Magno [Cf. n° 2932], p. 169-185.

2901. GIL (L.). El ceremonial de la palabra imperativa: de los Evangelios al exorcismo cristiano. *Cuadernos de filología clásica*, 99, 9, p. 163-183.

2902. GRÉGOIRE (R.). Agiografia e storiografia nella 'Vita antiqua' di Eusebio di Vercelli. *In*: Sardegna paleocristiana (La) tra Eusebio e Gregorio Magno [Cf. n° 2932], p. 187-200.

2903. GRELOT (Pierre). Corps et sang du Christ en gloire: enquête dogmatique. Paris, du Cerf, 99, 180 p.

2904. GROSSI (V.). La questione della 'predestinazione' nell'agostinismo di Fulgenzio da Ruspe (Cagliari 502–523). *In*: Sardegna paleocristiana (La) tra Eusebio e Gregorio Magno [Cf. n° 2932], p. 201-225.

2905. HANNAH (Darrell D.). Isaiah's vision in the "Ascension of Isaiah" and the early church. *Journal of theological studies*, 99, 50, 1, p. 80-101. – IDEM. Michael and Christ. Michael traditions and angel Christology in early Christianity. Tübingen, Mohr, 99, XIV-289 p. – IDEM. The ascension of Isaiah and docetic christology. *Vigiliae Christianae*, 99, 51, p. 165-196.

2906. HARVEY (Paul B.). Scripta velut fulgura percurrentia. *Athenaeum*, 99, 87, 1, p. 267-279.

2907. HEIM (F.). Solstice d'hiver, solstice d'été dans la prédication chrétienne du Ve siècle. Le dialogue des évêques avec le paganisme, de Zénon de Vérone à saint Léon. *Latomus*, 99, 58, p. 640-660.

2908. HEISER (Lothar). Mosaike und Hymnen: frühes Christentum in Syrien und Palästina. St. Ottilien, EOS Verlag, 99, 756 p. (ill.)

2909. JAMES (P.). Prudentius' Psychomachia: the Christian arena and the politics of display. *In*: Constructing identities in late antiquity [Cf. n° 2794], p. 70-94.

2910. JENSEN (Robin M.). The economy of the Trinity at the creation of Adam and Eve. *Journal of early Christian studies*, 99, 7, 4, p. 527-546.

2911. JOHNSON (Maxwell E.). The rites of Christian initiation: their evolution and interpretation. Collegeville, Liturgical Press, 99, XXII-414 p.

2912. LABAHN (M.). Between tradition and literary art. The use of the miracle tradition in the Fourth Gospel. *Biblica*, 99, 80, p. 178-203.

2913. LANCEL (Serge). Le proconsul Anullinus et la grande persécution en Afrique en 303-304 ap. J.-C.: nouveux documents. *Comptes rendus de l'Académie des inscriptions et belles-lettres*, 99, 3, p. 1013-1022.

2914. LEFTOW (B.). Anti social trinitarianism. *In*: Trinity (The) [Cf. n° 2943], p. 203-249.

2915. LOPEZ (David Andrew). Killing Sisara: salvation, apocalypse and apologetic in pre-constantinian Christianity (AD 135–312). New Haven, [s. n.], 99, 399 p. [Ph. d. Thesis, Yale University]

2916. MASTINO (A.). La Sardegna cristiana in età tardoantica. *In*: Sardegna paleocristiana (La) tra Eusebio e Gregorio Magno [Cf. n° 2932], p. 263-307.

2917. MAC LEOD (Frederick G.). The image of God in the antiochene tradition. Washington, Catholic University of America Press, 99, XI-276 p.

2918. MEHLHAUSEN (Joachim). Vestigia Verbi. Aufsätze zur Geschichte der evangelischen Theologie. Berlin u. New York, de Gruyter, 99, X-574 p. (Arbeiten zur Kirchengeschichte, 72).

2919. MENKE (K.-H.). Fleisch geworden aus Maria: die Geschichte Israels und der Marienglaube der Kirche. Regensburg, Pustet, 99, 187 p.

2920. MÜHLSTEDT (Corinna). Die christlichen Ursymbole: wie sie entstanden, was sie bedeuten, was sie uns heute sagen. Freiburg im Breisgau, Herder Verlag, 99, 205 p. (ill.)

2921. NORELLI (Enrico). Profetismo e profeti cristiani nella "Ascensione di Isaia". *Rivista di storia e letteratura religiosa*, 99, 35, 2, p. 362-376.

2922. OPSOMER (J.), STEEL (C.). Evil without a cause. Proclus' doctrine on the origin of evil, and its antecedents in hellenistic philosophy. *In*: Rezeption der hellenistischen Philosophie in der Spätantike [Cf. n° 2817], p. 229-260.

2923. OSER-GROTE (C.). Virtus Romana und Virtus Christiana. Die Rezeption und Transformation eines römischen Wertbegriffs bei Prudentius. *In*: Rezeption der hellenistischen Philosophie in der Spätantike [Cf. n° 2817], p. 213-228.

2924. PESCE (M.), DESTRO (A.). La lavanda dei piedi in Gv. 13,1-20, il Romanzo di Esopo e i Saturnalia di Macrobio. *Biblica*, 99, 80, p. 240-249.

2925. PETINOS (Ch.). L'Église de Chypre entre Constantinopel et Antioche (IVe–Ve siècle). *Byzantinische Forschungen*, 99, 25, p. 131-142.

2926. PORTER (Stanley E.). The Paul of Acts. Essays in literary criticism, rhetoric, and theology. Tübingen, Mohr, 99, 230 p.

2927. RAMELLI (Ilaria). Annotazioni sulle origini del cristianesimo in Sicilia. *Rivista di storia della chiesa in Italia*, 99, 53, 1, p. 1-15.

2928. RECCHIA (V.). Le vedove nella letteratura istituzionale nell'antico cristianesimo e nella tipologia biblica. *Invigilata lucernis*, 99, 21, p. 303-332.

2929. RIEMER (U.). Flavius Clemens – vom römischen Konsul zum christlichen Märtyrer. *In*: Zwischen Krise und Alltag [Cf. n° 2215], p. 243-253.

2930. RUNIA (D. T.). Philo of Alexandria and the Greek hairesis-model. *Vigiliae Christianae*, 99, 53, p. 117-147.

2931. SALAMITO (J.-M.). Synaichmalotoi: les 'compagnons de captivité' de l'apôtre Paul. *In*: Carcer [Cf. n° 2481], p. 191-210.

2932. Sardegna paleocristiana (La) tra Eusebio e Gregorio Magno. Atti del convegno nazionale di studi (Cagliari, 10–12 ottobre 1996). A cura di Attilio MASTINO, Giovanna SOTGIU e Natalina SPACCAPELO. Cagliari, Università degli studi di Cagliari, Pontificia Facoltà teologica dela Sardegna e Università degli studi di Sassari, 99, XIV-542 p. [Cf. n^{os} <scelta> 2860, 2886, 2897, 2900, 2902, 2904, 2916, 2944.]

2933. SILLETT (Helen Marie). Culture of controversy: the christological disputes of the early fifth century. Berkeley, [s. n.], 99, 197 p. [Diss., University of California].

2934. STERLING (G. E.). 'The School of sacred laws': the social setting of Philo's treatises. *Vigiliae Christianae*, 99, 53, p. 148-164.

2935. STEUBEN (Hans von). Wahrheit und Bekenntnis. Lichtoffenbarungen in antiker und christlicher Zeit. Möhnesee, Bibliopolis, 99, 188 p.

2936. STROUMSA (Guy G.). Barbarian philosophy. The religious revolution of early Christianity. Tübingen, Mohr, 99, XII-345 p.

2937. SYNEK (Eva Maria). Der Frauendiakonat der Alten Kirche und seine Rezeption durch die orthodoxen Kirchen: Lösungsansätze für die katholische Ordinationsdiskussion? *Ostkirchliche Studien*, 99, 48, p. 3-21.

2938. TEJA (Ramón). Los concilios en el cristianismo antiguo. Madrid, del Orto, 99, 94 p. (Biblioteca de las religiones, 4)

2939. Theologie und Kultur. Geschichten einer Wechselbeziehung. Festschrift zum einhundertfünfzigjährigen Bestehen des Lehrstuhls für Christliche Archäologie und Kirchliche Kunst an der Humboldt-Universität zu

Berlin. Hrsg. v. Gerlinde STROHMAIER-WIEDERANDERS. Halle, Gursky, 99, 261 p. [Cf. n° <Auswahl> 2882.]

2940. THÜMMEL (Hans Georg). Die Memorien für Petrus und Paulus in Rom: die archäologischen Denkmäler und die literarische Tradition. Berlin u. New York, de Gruyter, 99, X-102 p. (Abb.)

2941. TRÄNKLE (H.). Der Brunnen im Atrium der Petersbasilika und der Zeitpunkt von Prudentius' Romaufenthalt. *Zeitschrift für antikes Christentum*, 99, 3, p. 97-112.

2942. TREVETT (Ch.). Spiritual authority and the 'heretical' woman: Firmilian's word to the church in Carthage. *In*: Portraits of spiritual authority [Cf. n° 2872], p. 45-62.

2943. Trinity (The). An interdisciplinary symposium on the trinity. Ed. by Stephen DAVIS, Daniel KENDALL and Gerald O'COLLINS. Oxford, Oxford UP, 99, XXVIII-393 p. [Cf. n[os] <choice> 2894, 2914.]

2944. TURTAS (R.). Gregorio Magno e la Sardegna: gli informatori del pontefice. *In*: Sardegna paleocristiana (La) tra Eusebio e Gregorio Magno [Cf. n° 2932], p. 497-513.

2945. VEYNE (P.). Païens et chrétiens devant la gladiature. *Mélanges de l'Ecole française de Rome. Antiquité*, 99, 111, 2, p. 883-917.

2946. VOGT (Hermann Josef). Monarchianismus im 2. Jahrhundert. *Theologische Quartalschrift*, 99, 179, 4, p. 237-259.

2947. WALDMANN (Helmut). Petrus und die Kirche. Petri Versuchung (Mat. 16: 'Weiche von mir, Satan! ... Was nützt es dem Menschen ...') und der Kampf der Kirche mit dem Kaisertum um die Weltherrschaft. Tübingen, Verlag der Tübinger Gesellschaft, 99, 249 p.

2948. WATSON (A.). Jesus and the adulteress. *Biblica*, 99, 80, p. 1-21

2949. WHEATLEY (Alan Brent). The use and transformation of patronage in early Christianity from Jesus of Nazareth to Paul of Samosata. Los Angeles, [s. n.], 99, 338 p. [Ph. D. Thesis, University California at Los Angeles (UCLA)]

2950. WYPUSTEK (A.). Un aspect ignoré des persécutions des chrétiens dans l'antiquité: les accusations de magie érotique imputées aux chrétiens aux IIe et IIe siècles. *Jahrbuch für Antike und Christentum*, 99, 42, p. 50-71.

Cf. n° 3523

§ 4. Hagiography.

2951. CRACCO RUGGINI (Lellia). Prêtre et fonctionnaire: l'essor d'un modèle épiscopal aux IVe-Ve siècles. *Antiquité tardive*, 99, 7, p. 175-186.

2952. HÄGG (T.). Photius as a reader of hagiography: selection and criticism. *Dumbarton Oaks papers*, 99, 53, p. 43-58.

2953. KEY FOWDEN (Elizabeth). The barbarian plain. Saint **Sergius** between Rome and Iran. Berkeley, Los Angeles a. London, University of California Press, 99, XIX-227 p.

2954. KRUEGER (D.). Hagiography as an ascetic practice in the early Christian East. *Journal of religion*, 99, 79, p. 216-232.

2955. LOZITO (Vito). Agiografia, magia, superstizione. Bari, Levante editori, 99, 329 p.

2956. ORSELLI (A. M.). Modelli di santità e modelli agiografici nell'Occidente latino. *Augustinianum*, 99, 39, 1, p. 169-185.

2957. VIEROW (H.). Feminine and masculine voices in the Passion of Saints **Perpetua** and **Felicitas**. *Latomus*, 99, 58, p. 600-619.

2958. WALTER (Christopher). **Theodore**, archetype of the warrior saint. *Revue des études byzantines*, 99, 57, p. 163-210 (ill.).

2959. WILLIAMS (R.). Troubled breasts: the holy body in hagiography. *In*: Portraits of spiritual authority [Cf. n° 2872], p. 63-78.

H

BYZANTINE HISTORY
(since Justinian)

---

§ 1. Sources. 2960-2975. – § 2. General. 2976-2995. – § 3. Special studies. 2996-3094.

§ 1. Sources.

2960. [Damascius] DAMASCIUS. The philosophical history. Ed. by Polymnia ATHANASSIADI. Athens, Apamea cultural association a. Oxford, Oxbow books, 99, 403 p.

2961. [Eudocia] Homerocentones Eudociae Augustae. Hrsg. v. M. D. USHER. Stuttgart u. Leipzig, Teubner, 99, XII-114 p.

2962. [Eusebius] BURGESS (R. W.), WITAKOWSKI (W.). Studies in Eusebian and post-Eusebian chronography. I: The chronici canones of Eusebius of Caesarea: structure, content, and chronology, AD 282–325. II: The continuatio antiochiensis Eusebii: A chronicle of Antioch and the Roman Near East during the reigns of Costantine and Constantius II, AD 325–350. Stuttgart, Steiner, 358 p.

2963. FEISSEL (Denis). Les inscriptions des premiers siècles byzantins (330–641). Documents d'histoire sociale et religieuse. *In*: Atti dell'XI Congresso Internazionale di Epigrafia Greca e Latina [Cf. n° 2309], p. 577-589.

2964. GENTILE (R.). Tipologia della rappresentazione dei Turchi in fonti bizantine dei secc. XI–XII. *Byzantinische Forschungen*, 99, 25, p. 305-324.

2965. [Georgius Pachymeres]. Relations historiques. Tome 3. Livres VII-IX. Tome 4. Livres X-XIII. Ed. par A. FAILLER. Paris, Institut Français d'Études Byzantines, 99, p. 1-305, p. 306-727.

2966. [Gregoras Nicephorus]. Explicatio in Librum Synesii "de insomniis". Scholia cum glossis. A cura di P. PIETROSANTI e G. GUIDORIZZI. Bari, Levante editori, 99, LXXXII-135 p.

2967. KÖNIG (I.). Aus der Zeit Theoderichs des Großen. Einleitung, Text, Übersetzung und Kommentar einer anonymen Quelle. Darmstadt, Wiss. Buchgesellschaft, 99, X-270 p.

2968. Lessico Suda (II) e la memoria del passato a Bisanzio. Atti della giornata di studio (Milano, 29 aprile 1998). A cura di G. ZECCHINI. Bari, Edipuglia, 99, 161 p. [Cf. n° <scelta> 3094.]

2969. LJUBARSKIJ (Jakov N.). Vizantijskie istoriki i pisateli. (Byzantine historians and writers: [a collection of his articles]). Sankt-Peterburg, Aletejja, 99, 381 p. (bibl., bibl. of works of Ja.N. LJUBARSKIJ). (Vizantijskaja biblioteka. Issledovanija). [Text partly in Eng.].

2970. [Procopius] KISLINGER (E.), STATHAKOOULOS (D.). Pest und Perserkriege bei Prokop. Chronologische Überlegungen zum Geschehen 540-545. *Byzantion*, 99, 69, p. 76-98.

2971. [Pseudo-Chrysostomus] WHEALEY (A.). Sermo pseudoprophetis of Pseudo-Chrysostom. A homily from Antioch under early Islamic rule. *Byzantion*, 99, 69, 1, p. 178-186.

2972. [Severinus Boethius]. Anicii Manlii Severini Boethii De consolatione philosophiae. Traduction grecque de Maxime Planude. Ed. par Manolis PAPATHOMOPOULOS. Athens, The Academy of Athens, Paris, Vrin et Bruxelles, Édition Ousia, 99, LXXX, 162 p.

2973. SMITH OLE (L.). Byzantine Achilleid. The Naples version. Introduction, critical edition and commentary. Ed. by Panagiotis A. AGAPITOS and Karin HULT. Wien, Verlag der Österreichischen Akademie der Wissenschaften, 99, XII-232 p. (Wiener Byzantinische Studien, 21)

2974. [Theophilos Korydaleus] KARPOZILU (M.). The epistolarion of Theophilos Korydaleus. *Hellenica*, 99, 49, p. 289-303.

2975. YANNOPOULOS (P. A.). L'Asie et l'Europe dans les premiers croniqueurs byzantins. *Byzantinische Forschungen*, 99, 25, p. 293-304.

Cf. n°ˢ 225, 1566, 2790, 3140

§ 2. General.

* 2976. Byzantinische Zeitschrift. Bibliographie. Vol. 92. [Vol. 91. Cf. Bibl. 98, n° 3107.] Hrsg. v. Peter SCHREINER. Stuttgart u. Leipzig, Teubner, 99, [s. p.] (Taf.).

2977. ANTONOPOULOS (P.). Byzantine diplomacy before 1000 A.D. *East Central Europe*, 99, 26, 2, p. 1-13.

2978. Arte (L') di Bisanzio e l'Italia al tempo dei Paleologi. 1261–1453. A cura di A. IACOBINI e M. DELLA VALLE. Roma, Nuova Argos Edizioni, 99, 395 p. [Cf. n^os <scelta> 3015, 3017, 3053.]

2979. Byzance et l'hellénisme: l'identité grecque au Moyen Âge. Actes du Congrès International (Trieste 1–3 octobre 1997. Ed. par P. ODORICO. Paris, de Boccard, 99, 202 p. [Cf. n^os <sélection> 3009, 3035, 3050.]

2980. Byzanz und Ostmitteleuropa 950–1453. Beiträge einer table ronde des XIX International Congress of Byzantine Studies (Copenhagen 1996). Hrsg. v. G. PRINZING und M. SALAMON. Wiesbaden, Harrassowitz, 99, XI-222 p. (Taf.). [Cf. n^os <Auswahl> 3026, 3042, 3061, 3073, 3075.]

2981. HALDON (J.). The Byzantine world. *In*: War and society in the ancient and medieval worlds [Cf. n° 1045], p. 241-270. – IDEM. Warfare, state and society in the Byzantine world 565-1204. London, UCL Press, 99, X-389 p.

2982. KARABELIAS (Ev.). Monde byzantin. *Revue historique de droit français et étranger*, 99, 77, p. 373-450.

2983. KAZHDAN (A.). A history of Byzantine literature (650–850). Athen, The National Hellenic Research Foundation. Institute for for Byzantine Research, 99, XVIII-447 p.

2984. LILIE (Ralph-Johannes). Byzanz. Geschichte des oströmischen Reiches; 326–1453. München, Beck, 99, 127 p.

2985. MUNTEAN (V. V.). Bizantinologie, I. Arhiepiscopia Timișoarei, Editura Învierea, 99, 212 p.

2986. NEZU (Yukio). Bizantsu gen'ei no sekaiteikoku. (Byzantine Empire: the illusional world empire). Tokyo, Kondansha, 99, 294 p.

2987. Roman and Byzantine Near East (The). Volume 2. Some recent archeological research. Ed by J. H. HUMPHREY. Portsmouth, Rhode Island, 99, 224 p. (*Journal of Roman archaeology*. Supplementary series, 31).

2988. Rukopisnoe nasledie russkikh vizantinistov v arkhivakh Sankt-Peterburga. (Manuscript Heritage of Russian Byzantinists in the Archives of Saint-Petersburg: [essays on Saint-Petersburg byzantinists; their unpublished works]). Ed. I. P. MEDVEDEV. RAN, In-t rossijskoj istorii, S.-Peterb. filial.; Arkhiv RAN. Sankt-Peterburg, Dmitry Bulanin, 99, 631 p. (ill., ind.).

2989. SHOJU (Keitaro). Bizantsu teikoku shi. (History of the Byzantine Empire). Tokyo, Tokai University Press, 99, 1227 p.

2990. Studienhandbuch Östliches Europa. Band 1. Geschichte Ostmittel- und Südeuropas. Hrsg. v. H. ROTH. Köln, Böhlau, 99, IX-560 p.

2991. Tarihte güney-doğu Avrupa: Balkanolojinin dünü bugünü ve sorunlari. (South east Europe in history: the past, the present and the problems of balkanology). Ankara, Ankara Üniversitesi Basemevi, 99, V-139 p. [Cf. n° <choice> 3252.]

2992. Text and tradition. Studies in Greek history and historiography in honor of Mortimer Chambers. Ed. by R. MELLOR and L. TRITLE. Claremont, Regina Books, 99, XL-382 p. [Cf. n° <choice> 3044.]

2993. Vizantija mezhdu Vostokom i Zapadom: Opyt istoricheskoj kharakteristiki. (Byzantium between East and West: [Articles]). Ed. Gennadij G. LITAVRIN. Sankt-Peterburg, Aletejja, 99, 538 p. (bibl.).

2994. Vizantijskaja tsivilizatsija v osveshchenii rossijskikh uchenykh, 1894–1927. (Byzantine civilization as studied by Russian Scholars, 1894–1927). Comp. Petr I. ZHAVORONKOV, Gennadij G. LITAVRIN. RAN, Otd. istorii, In-t vseobshchej istorii. Moskva, Ladomir, 99, 252 p. (bibl. incl). – Vizantijskaja tsivilizatsija v osveshchenii rossijskikh uchenykh, 1947–1991. (Byzantine civilization as studied by Russian scholars, 1847–1991). Comp. Petr I. ZHAVORONKOV, Gennadij G. LITAVRIN. RAN, Otd. istorii, In-t vseobshchej istorii. Moskva, Ladomir, 99, 800 p. (ill., bibl.).

2995. Vizantijskij vremennik = BYZANTINA XPONIKA. (Byzantine Review). Vol. 58 (83). Ed. Gennadij G. LITAVRIN. RAN, In-t vseobshchej istorii. Moskva, Nauka, 99, 311 p. [Articles in Russian and English.]

§ 3. Special studies.

2996. AFIGENOV (D.). Imperial repentance: the solemn procession in Costantinople on March 11, 843. *Eranos*, 99, 97, p. 1-10. – IDEM. The date of Georgios Monachos reconsidered. *Byzantinische Zeitschrift*, 99, 92, p. 437-447.

2997. AGAPITOS (Panagiotis A.). Dreams and the spatial aesthetics of narrative presentation in Livistros and Rhodamne. *Dumbarton Oaks papers*, 99, 53, p. 111-147.

2998. AMATO (E.). Appunti per la fortuna di Favorino a Bisanzio (con un'appendice sulla Probalneis). *Revue des études grecques*, 99, 112, p. 259-269.

2999. BACHRACH (B. S.). The siege of Antioch: a study in military demography. *War in history*, 99, 6, p. 127-146.

3000. BANAJI (J.). Agrarian history and the labour organisation of Byzantine large estates. *In*: Agriculture in Egypt [Cf. n° 1144], p. 193-216.

3. SPECIAL STUDIES

3001. BARDILL (Jonathan). The great palace of the Byzantine emperors and the Walker Trust excavations. *Journal of Roman archaeology*, 99, 12, p. 217-230.

3002. BERGER (A.). Die Häfen von Byzanz und Konstantinopel. *In*: Griechenland und das Meer [Cf. n° 3029], p. 111-118.

3003. BERTO (L. A.). La Venetia tra Franchi e Bizantini. Considerazioni sulle fonti. *Studi veneziani*, 99, 38, p. 189-202.

3004. BOEL (G). La mort de Digénis Akritis dans le roman et dans les chants. *Byzantion*, 99, 69, p. 24-57.

3005. BRANDES (W.). Byzantine cities in the seventh and eighth centuries – different sources, different histories? *In*: Idea (The) and ideal of the town between Late Antiquity and the Early Middle Ages [Cf. n° 2806], p. 25-57. – IDEM. Das 'Meer' als Motiv in der byzantinischen apokaliptischen Literatur. *In*: Griechenland und das Meer [Cf. n° 3029], p. 119-131.

3006. BRAVO GARCÍA (A.). Bizancio y España. Hitos en una relación de siglos. *In*: Grecia en España [Cf. n° 3028], p. 45-56. – IDEM. Una frontera no es sólo política: Bizancio y el Islam. *In*: Fronteras religiosas entre Roma, Bizancio, Damasco y Toledo (siglos V–VIII) [Cf. n° 3023], p. 65-96.

3007. BREDENKAMP (F.). The Doranites family of the 14th century Byzantine Empire of Trebizond. *Byzantiaka*, 99, 19, p. 243-248.

3008. BRUBAKER (Leslie). Vision and meaning in ninth-century Byzantium: image as exegesis in the homilies of Gregory of Nazianzus. Cambridge a. New York, Cambridge U. P., 99, XXIII-489 p. (Cambridge studies in palaeography and codicology, 6). (pl., ill., facsi.).

3009. BURGARELLA (F.). L'identità dei Bizantini di periferia: i Greci di Calabria. *In*: Byzance et l'hellénisme: l'identité grecque au Moyen Âge [Cf. n° 2979], p. 131-157.

3010. CANDAU (J. M.). Una muestra de ascetismo pagano. Parámetros de la propaganda política en el Misópogon de Juliano el Apóstata. *Byzantinische Zeitschrift*, 92, 99, p. 21-32.

3011. BURGESS (R. W.). The dates of the first sieges of Nisibis and the death of James of Nisibis. *Byzantion*, 99, 69, 1, p. 7-17.

3012. CARILE (A.). Efeso da polis a kastron. *In*: Efeso paleocristiana e bizantina – Frühchristliches und byzantinisches Ephesos [Cf. n° 3020], p. 133-145. – IDEM. Il Caucaso visto da Bisanzio e Bisanzio vista dal Caucaso. *Byzantinische Forschungen*, 99, 25, p. 165-180.

3013. CONNOR (C.). The epigram in the church of Hagios Polyeuktos in Constantinople and its Byzantine response. *Byzantion*, 99, 69, 2, p. 479-527.

3014. COSENTINO (S.). Il ceto dei viri honesti (hoi aidésimoi andres) nell'Italia tardoantica e bizantina. *Bizantinistica*, 99, 2, 1, p. 13-50.

3015. DE MAFFEI (F.). Uno sguardo sull'arte bizantina al tempo dei Paleologi. *In*: Arte (L') di Bisanzio e l'Italia al tempo dei Paleologi [Cf. n° 2978], p. 11-34.

3016. DEDEYAN (G.). Le rôle des Arméniens en Syrie du nord pendant la reconquête byzantine (vers 945–1031). *Byzantinische Forschungen*, 99, 25, p. 249-284.

3017. DELLA VALLE (M.). Costantinopoli e Tessalonica al tempo di Anna Paleologina. *In*: Arte (L') di Bisanzio e l'Italia al tempo dei Paleologi [Cf. n° 2978], p. 125-142 (ill.).

3018. DUCELLIER (A.). L'"abandon" de l'Asie par Byzance: du sens des mots à la réalité des choses. *Byzantinische Forschungen*, 99, 25, p. 13-46.

3019. DUDEK (J.). "Cala Ziemia Dyrracheńska" pod panowaniem bizantyńskim w latach 1005–1205 ("The whole land Dyrrachium" under Byzantine rule between 1005 and 1205). Zielona Góra, Wyższa Szkoła Pedagogiczna, 99, 196 p.

3020. Efeso paleocristiana e bizantina – Frühchristliches und byzantinisches Ephesos. Referate des vom 22. bis 24. Februar 1996 im Historischen Institut beim Österreichischen Kulturinstitut in Rom durchgeführten internationalen Kongresses aus Anlaß des 100-jährigen Jubiläums der österreichischen Ausgrabungen in Ephesos. Hrsg. v. R. PILLINGER, O. KRESTEN, F. KRINZINGER und E. RUSSO. Wien, Verlag der Österreichischen Akademie der Wissenschaften, 99, 145 p. [Cf. n° <Auswahl> 3012.]

3021. EICKHOFF (E.). Kaiser Otto III. Die erste Jahrtausendwende und die Entfatung Europas. Stuttgart, Klett-Cotta, 99, 481 p.

3022. FATOUROS (G.). Bessarion und Libanios. Ein typischer Fall byzantinischer Mimesis. *Jahrbuch der Österreichischen Byzantinistik*, 99, 49, p. 191-204.

3023. Fronteras religiosas entre Roma, Bizancio, Damasco y Toledo (siglos V–VIII). Ed. por S. MONTERO. *'Ilu. Revista de ciencias de las religiones* (Cuadernos), 99, 2, [s. p.]. [Cf. n° <selección> 3006.]

3024. GARLAND (L.). Basil II as humorist. *Byzantion*, 99, 69, p. 321-343. – IDEM. Stephen Hagiochristophorites: logothete tou genikou 1182/3–1185. *Byzantion*, 99, 69, p. 18-23.

3025. GARZYA (A.). La réception du monde antique chez les écrivains byzantins. *Koinonía*, 99, 23, 2, p. 5-13. – IDEM. Scienza e coscienza nella pratica medica dell'antichità tardiva e bizantina. Conferenze per la tre giorni della cultura a Napoli (26–28 marzo 1999). Napoli, Società nazionale di scienze, lettere e arti in Napoli, 99, p. 7-27.

3026. GOLDSTEIN (I.). Byzantine rule in Dalmatia in the 12th century. *In*: Byzanz und Ostmitteleuropa 950–1453 [Cf. n° 2980], p. 97-125.

3027. GRANDOLINI (S.). Didimo e la classificazione della poesia lirica. *Giornale italiano di filologia*, 99, 51, p. 1-22.

3028. Grecia en España. España en Grecia. Hacia una historia de la cultura mediterránea. Primer Congreso Internacional (Atenas, 14–17 diciembre 1996). Ed. por A. N. ZAHAREAS y Y. ADREADIS. Madrid, Ediciones Clásicas, 99, 361 p. (ill.). [Cf. n° <selección> 3006.]

3029. Griechenland und das Meer. Beiträge eines Symposions (Frankfurt, Dezember 1996). Hrsg. v. Evangelos CHRYSOS. Mannheim, Mohnesee, 99, 221 p. (ill.) [Cf. n^{os} <Auswahl> 3002, 3005, 3039, 3040, 3063, 3065, 3066, 3081.]

3030. GULDENTOPS (G.). Tyche ontgoddelijkt. Themistius over het toeval en het lot (Tyche desacralised. Themistius on chance and luck). *Tijdschrift voor filosofie*, 99, 61, p. 311-336.

3031. GÜNTHER (H.-Ch.). Andronikos Kallistos und das Studium griechischer Dichtertexte. *Eikasmós*, 99, 10, p. 315-334.

3032. HALDON (John). The idea of the town in the Byzantine empire. *In*: Idea (The) and ideal of the town between late Antiquity and the early Middle Ages [Cf. n° 2806], p. 1-23.

3033. HANNICK (Christian). Exégèse, typologie et rhétorique dans l'hymnographie byzantine. *Dumbarton Oaks papers*, 99, 53, p. 207-218. (ill.).

3034. HATLIE (P.). Spiritual authority and monasticism in Constantinople during the dark ages. *In*: Portraits of spiritual authority (650–800) [Cf. n° 2872], p. 195-222.

3035. HERSANT (Y.). Un Hellène chez les Latins: Georges Gémiste Pléthon. *In*: Byzance et l'hellénisme: l'identité grecque au Moyen Âge [Cf. n° 2979], p. 121-130.

3036. HINTERBERGER (M.). Autobiographische Traditionen in Byzanz. Wien, Verlag der Österreichischen Akademie der Wissenschaften, 99, 415 p.

3037. HIRANO (T.). Yoanisu Rokusei Kandakujinosu Tei (1357–1354) chika no Bizantsu Teikoku ni okeru Ryoudobunkatsu niyoru Touchitaisei. (Das Herrschaftssystem durch die Territorialteilung im byzantinischen Reich unter der Herrschaft von Johannes VI. Kantakuzenos, 1347–1354). *Toh Kai Sigaku*, 99, 33, p. 43-73.

3038. KALDELLIS (A.). The argument of Psellos' Chronographia. Leiden, Boston a. Köln, Brill, 99, IX-223 p. – IDEM. The historical and religious views of Agathias: a reinterpretation. *Byzantion*, 99, 69, p. 206-252.

3039. KODER (J.). Aspekte der Thalassokratia der Byzantiner in der Ägäis. *In*: Griechenland und das Meer [Cf. n° 3029], p. 101-109.

3040. KOLIAS (T. G.). Die byzantinische Kriegsmarine. Ihre Bedeutung im Verteidigungssystem von Byzanz. *In*: Griechenland und das Meer [Cf. n° 3029], p. 133-139.

3041. KORDOSIS (M.). The sea route from China to ta-Ch'in (Roman-early Byzantine state) according to the Chinese sources. *Byzantinische Forschungen*, 99, 25, p. 47-54.

3042. KRISTÓ (G.). Konstantinos Porphyrogennetos über die Landnahme der Ungarn. *In*: Byzanz und Ostmitteleuropa 950–1453 [Cf. n° 2980], p. 13-22.

3043. KÜLZER (Andreas). Disputationes Graecae contra Iudaeos. Untersuchungen zur byzantinischen antijüdischen Dialogliteratur und ihrem Judenbild. Stuttgart u. Leipzig, Teubner, 99, 440 p. (Byzantinische Archiv, 18).

3044. LANGDON (J.). The image of thirteenth-century Anatolian Byzantine Basileis as warriors. *In*: Text and tradition [Cf. n° 2992], p. 303-328.

3045. LAUXTERMANN (Marc D.). The spring of rhythm. An essay on the political verse and other Byzantine metres. Wien, Verlag der Öserreichischen Akademie der Wissenschaften, 99, 105 p.

3046. LESZKA (M. J.). Uzurpacje w cesarstwie bizantyńskim w okresie od IV do połowy IX wieku. (Usurpations in the Byzantine Empire from the 4th to the middle of the 9th century). Łódź, Uniwersytet Łódzki, 99, 149 p.

3047. LIMOUSIN (Eric). L'administration byzantine du Péloponnèse (X^e–XIIe siècle). *In*: Péloponnèse (Le) [Cf. n° 1828], p. 295-307. – IDEM. Les lettrés en société, Phílos bíos ou Politikós bíos. *Byzantion*, 99, 69, p. 344-365.

3048. LITTLEWOOD (A. R.). The byzantine letter of consolation in the Macedonian and Komnenian Periods. *Dumbarton Oaks papers*, 99, 53, p. 20-41.

3049. MAGUIRE (Henry).The profane aesthetic in Byzantine art and literature. *Dumbarton Oaks papers*, 99, 53, p. 189-205. (ill.)

3050. MALTESE (E.-V.). Letteratura bizantina e identità greca. Un appunto sulle traduzioni a Bisanzio. *In*: Byzance et l'hellénisme: l'identité grecque au Moyen Âge [Cf. n° 2979], p. 183-196.

3051. MANIATIS (George C.). Organization, market structure, and modus operandi of the private silk industry in tenth-century Byzantium. *Dumbarton Oaks papers*, 99, 53, p. 263-332.

3052. MARAVAL (Pierre). L'empereur Justinien. Paris, Presses universitaires de France, 99, 127 p.

3053. MARINI CLARELLI (M. V.). Personificazioni, metafore e allegorie nell'arte paleologa. *In*: Arte (L') di Bisanzio e l'Italia al tempo dei Paleologi [Cf. n° 2978], p. 55-67.

3054. MARTIN (Ch.). Non-reductive arguments from impossible hypotheses in Boethius and Philoponus. *Oxford studies in ancient philosophy*, 99, 17, p. 279-302.

3055. MEDVEDEV (I. P.). The fall of Constantinople in fifteenth-century Greek and Italian humanistic writings. *Bysantinska Sällskapet, Bulletin*, 99, 17, p. 5-14.

3056. MICHELUCCI (Maurizio). Lucerne tardo-antiche e protobizantine da Iasos. *La parola del passato*, 99, 54, p. 373-392.

3057. MÜLLER (A. E). Das Testament des Romanos I. Lakapenos. *Byzantinische Zeitschrift*, 99, 92, p. 68-73.

3058. NIKOLOV (S.). Building the tower of Babel. Michael III, Photius and Basil I and the Byzantine approval for the use of the Slavic liturgy and alphabet in the late ninth century. *Starobălgarska literatura*, 99, 31, p. 41-53.

3059. NYSTAZOPOULOU-PELEKIDOU (M.). Byzance et l'Europe ou Byzance en Europe? *Byzantiaka*, 99, 19, p. 53-63.

3060. OHTSUKI (Y.). Bizantsu Teikoku Zaisei to Kisin. Maria no Isan to Ibiron Syuh Doh In. (Die byzantinischen Staatsfinanzen und die Schenkung. Das Erbe von Maria und das Kloster Iviron). *Hitotsubasi Ronsoh*, 99, 122, 4, p. 506-526.

3061. OLAJOS (Th.). Contribution à l'histoire des rapports entre Constantin Monomaque et le roi hongrois Andrè Ier. *In*: Byzanz und Ostmitteleuropa 950–1453 [Cf. n° 2980], p. 85-95.

3062. PANTELIĆ (B.). Applied geometrical plannig and proportions in the church of Hagia Sophia in Istanbul. *Istanbuler Mitteilungen*, 99, 49, p. 493-515.

3063. PAPAGIANNI (E.). Formes d'entreprises maritimes des Constantinopolitains à la fin du XIVe siècle. *In*: Griechenland und das Meer [Cf. n° 3029], p. 179-184.

3064. PARMEGGIANI (A.). Le funzioni amministrative del principato di Acaia. *Bizantinistica*, 99, 2, 1, p. 91-108.

3065. PITSAKIS (C. G.). À propos des monostères-armateurs à Byzance: les origines athonites. *In*: Griechenland und das Meer [Cf. n° 3029], p. 151-164.

3066. PRINZING (G.). Zur Intensität der byzantinischen Fern-Handelsschiffahrt des 12. Jahrhunderts im Mittelmeer. *In*: Griechenland und das Meer [Cf. n° 3029], p. 141-150.

3067. RICHARD (J.). Byzance et les Mongols. *Byzantinische Forschungen*, 99, 25, p. 83-100.

3068. RIGO (A.). La "Cronaca delle Meteore". La storia dei monasteri della Tessaglia tra XIII e XVI secolo. Firenze, Olschki, 99, 232 p. (Orientalia Veneziana, 8)

3069. Satira bizantina (La) dei secoli XI–XV. Il patriota, Caridemo, Timarione, Christoforo di Mitilene, Michele Psello, Teodoro Prodromo, Carmi ptocoprodromici, Michele Haplucheir, Giovanni Catrara, Mazaris, La messa del glabro, Sinassario del venerabile asino. A cura di R. ROMANO. Torino, UTET, 99, 690 p.

3070. SCHNEIDER (J.). La poésie didactique à Byzance: Nicétas d'Héraclée. *Bulletin Budé*, 99, 4, p. 388-423.

3071. SCHREINER (P.). Bilancio pubblico, agricoltura e commercio a Bisanzio nella seconda metà del XII secolo. *In*: Venedig und die Weltwirtschaft um 1200 [Cf. n° 3089], p. 177-189.

3072. SEVCENKO (Nancy P.). The vita icon and the painter as hagiographer. *Dumbarton Oaks papers*, 99, 53, p. 149-165.

3073. SHEPARD (J.). Byzantium and the Steppe-Nomads: the Hungarian dimension. *In*: Byzanz und Ostmitteleuropa 950-1453 [Cf. n° 2980], p. 55-83.

3074. STAVRIDU-ZAFRAKA (A.). The empire of Thessaloniki (1224–1242). Political ideology and reality. *Byzantiaka*, 99, 19, p. 213-222.

3075. STEPHENSON (P.). Political authority in Dalmatia during the reign of Manuel I Comnenus (1143–1180). *In*: Byzanz und Ostmitteleuropa 950-1453 [Cf. n° 2980], p. 127-150.

3076. STOLTE (B.). Desires denied: marriage, adultery and divorce in early Byzantine law. *In*: Desire and denial in Byzantium [Cf. n° 1215], p. 77-86.

3077. STONE (A. F.). The grand hetaireiarch John Doukas. The career of a Twelfth-century soldier and diplomat. *Byzantion*, 99, 69, 1, p. 145-164.

3078. TALBOT (Alice-Mary). Epigrams in context: metrical inscriptions on art and architecture of the Palaiologan Era. *Dumbarton Oaks papers*, 99, 53, p. 75-90.

3079. THIEL (R.). Simplikios und das Ende der neuplatonischen Schule in Athen. Stuttgart, Steiner, 99, 59 p.

3080. TOUGHER (Sh.). Michael III. and Basil the Macedonian: just good friends? *In*: Desire and denial in Byzantium [Cf. n° 1215], p. 149-158.

3081. TROIANOS (Sp. N.). Die Novellen Leons VI. über die 'epochai' und ihre Nachwirkung. *In*: Griechenland und das Meer [Cf. n° 3029], p. 165-169.

3082. UTHEMANN (K.-H.). Kaiser Justinian als Kirchenpolitiker und Theologe. *Augustinianum*, 99, 39, 1, p. 5-83.

3083. VALLEJO GIRVÉS (M.). Byzantine Spain and the African exarchate: an administrative perspective. *Jahrbuch der Österreichischen Byzantinistik*, 99, 49, p. 13-23.

3084. VAN DER WAL (N.). Les termes techniques grecs dans la langue des juristes byzantins. *Subseciva Groningana. Studies in Roman and Byzantine law*, 99, 6, p.127-141.

3085. VAN DIETEN (J.-L.). Eustathios von Thessalonike und Niketas Choniates über des Geschehen im Jahre nach dem Tod Manuels I. Komnenos. *Jahrbuch der Österreichischen Byzantinistik*, 99, 49, p. 101-112.

3086. VANDERHEYDE (C.). Un motif sculpté insolite sure les piliers de templa. *Byzantion*, 99, 69, 1, p. 165-177.

3087. VANDERSPOEL (J.). Correspondence and correspondents of Julius Julianus. *Byzantion*, 99, 69, 2, p. 396-478.

3088. VASSIS (I.). Ein unediertes Gedicht anläßlich des Todes von Theodora, erster Gemahlin des Despotes Konstantinos (XI.) Palaiologos. *Jahrbuch der Österreichischen Byzantinistik*, 99, 49, p. 181-189.

3089. Venedig und die Weltwirtschaft um 1200. Hrsg. v. Wolfgang von STROMER. Stuttgart, Thorbecke, 99, VIII-269 p. (Centro tedesco di studi veneziani. Studi, 7). [Cf. n° <Auswahl> 3071.]

3090. VESPIGNANI (G.). Considerazioni sulla figura della donna di spettacolo a Bisanzio nella tarda antichità. *Bizantinistica*, 99, 2, 1, p. 1-12.

3091. VINSON (M.). The life of Theodora and the rhetoric of the Byzantine bride show. *Jahrbuch der Österreichischen Byzantinistik*, 99, 49, p. 31-60.

3092. WEBB (Ruth). The aesthetics of sacred space: narrative, metaphor and motion in ekphraseis of church buildings. *Dumbarton Oaks papers*, 99, 53, p. 59-74.

3093. YUZBASHIAN (Karen). L'Arménie et les Arméniens vus par Byzance. *Byzantinische Forschungen*, 99, 25, p. 189-202.

3094. ZECCHINI (G.). La storia romana nella Suda. *In*: Lessico Suda (II) e la memoria del passato a Bisanzio [Cf. n° 2968], p. 75-88.

Cf. n°s 1545, 2952, 3158, 3496, 3523

I

HISTORY OF THE MIDDLE AGES

§ 1. Sources and criticism of sources (*a.* Non-literary sources; *b.* Literary sources). 3095-3183. – § 2. General works. 3184-3216. – § 3. Political history (*a.* General; *b.* 476–900; *c.* 900–1300; *d.* 1300–1500). 3217-3268. – § 4. Jews. 3269-3292. – § 5. Islam. 3293-3318. – § 6. Vikings. 3319-3327. – § 7. History of law and institutions. 3328-3355. – § 8. Economic and social history. 3356-3433. – § 9. History of civilization, literature, technology and education (*a.* Civilization; *b.* Literature; *c.* Technology; *d.* Education). 3434-3633. – § 10. History of art. (*a.* General; *b.* Special studies). 3634-3682 – § 11. History of music. 3683-3696. – § 12. History of philosophy, theology and science (*a.* Sources; *b.* Studies). 3697-3757. – § 13. History of the Church and religion (*a.* General; *b.* History of the Popes; *c.* Monastic history; *d.* Hagiography; *e.* Special studies). 3758-3910. – § 14. Settlements. Place names. Town planning. 3911-3920.

§ 1. Sources and criticism of sources.

a. *Non-literary sources*

* 3095. FRANCOVICH (Riccardo). L'archeologia in Toscana fra alto e basso medioevo: una rassegna bibliografica. *Archivio storico italiano*, 99, 157, 579, p. 131-176.

** 3096. KEATS-ROHAN (K. S. B.). Domesday people: a prosopography of persons occurring in English documents, 1066–1166. Vol. 1. I. Domesday book. Woodbridge, Boydell Press, 99, VII-563 p. (map).

** 3097. Slovensko očami cudzincov.: Vzácne správy o histórii nášho územia od 6. do 10. storočia, tak ako sa javia v písomnostiach prevažne cudzieho pôvodu. Pramene k dejinám Slovenska a Slovákov. Zv. 2. (The precious reports about history of our territory from 6th to 10th century as they appear in the documents of mostly foreign origin. Sources for the history of Slovakia and Slovaks. Vol. 2). Aut. Richard MARSINA, Ján STEINHÜBEL, Ján LUKAČKA, Ján PAULINY. Ed. Pavel DVOŘÁK. Bratislava, Literárne a informačné centrum vo vydavateľstve Rak Budmerice 99, 311 p.

3098. Acta vectigalia Regni Navarrae: documentos financieros para el estudio de la Hacienda Real de Navarra. Serie I, Comptos Reales, Registros. Tomo 1. Registros de Teobaldo II, 1259, 1266. Ed. por Juan CARRASCO, Fermin MIRANDA GARCÍA, Eloisa RAMÍREZ VAQUERO. Tomo 2,1. Registros de la Casa de Francia. 1280, 1282, 1283. Ed. por Juan CARRASCO y Pascual TAMBURRI. Tomo 2,2. Registros de la casa de Francia, Felipe I el Hermoso: 1284, 1285, 1286, 1287. Ed. por Juan CARRASCO y Pascual TAMBURRI. Pamplona, Gobierno de Navarra, Departamento de Economia y Hacienda, 99, 3 vol., 420 p., 414 p., 418 p.

3099. Actes des évêques de Limoges des origines à 1197. Éd. par Jean BECQUET. Paris, CNRS, 99, 234 p. (Documents, études et répertoires (Institut de recherche et d'histoire des textes, 56).

3100. ALVERED (Zeth). Gregers Matssons kostbok för Stegeborg 1487–1492. Uppsala, Svenska Fornskriftsallskapet, 99, 314 p. (Samlingar utgivna av Svenska Fornskriftsällskapet. Serie 1, Svenska skrifter, 83).

3101. Antico inventario (L') delle pergamene del Monastero dei SS. Severino e Sossio. Archivio di Stato di Napoli, Monasteri soppressi, vol. 1788. A cura di Rosaria PILONE. Roma, Istituto Storico Italiano per il Medio Evo, 99, 4 vol., XVI-2172 p. (Fonti per la storia dell'Italia Medievale. III. Regesta chartarum, 48-51).

3102. Armburgh (The) papers. The Brokholes inheritance in Warwickshire, Hertfordshire, and Essex, c.1417–c.1453: Chetham's Manuscript Mun. E.6.10 (4). Ed. by Christine CARPENTER. Woodbridge, Boydell Press, 99, VIIII-214 p.

3103. Atti del podestà di Lio Mazor. A cura di Elsheikh Mahmoud SALEM. Venezia, Istituto veneto di scienze, lettere ed arti, 99, VIII-105 p. (Memorie. Classe di scienze morali, lettere ed arti, 86).

3104. Ausias March: colección documental. Ed. por Jesús VILLALMANZO CAMENO. Valencia, Institucio Alfons el Magnanim, 99, 506 p. (facs.). (Arxius i documents, 23).

3105. BASAÑEZ VILALLUENCA (Maria Blanca). Las morerías aragonesas durante el reinado de Jaime II. Catálogo de la documentatión de la Cancilleria Real. Vol. 1. 1291–1310. Teruel, Instituto de Estudios Turolenses, Centro de Estudios Mudéjares, 99, 502 p. (Serie Estudios Mudéjares).

3106. Carte (Le) del decimo secolo nell'Archivio arcivescovile di Ravenna: 900–957. A cura di Ruggero BENERICETTI. Ravenna, Società di studi ravennati, 99, XXXVI-268 p. (Biblioteca di "Ravenna studi e ricerche", 2).

3107. Cartulaire de Saint-Sernin de Toulouse. Éd par Pierre GERARD et Thérèse GERARD. Toulouse, Amis des Archives de la Haute-Garonne, 99, 4 vol., 1696 p. (maps)

3108. Cartulary (The) of Chatteris Abbey. Ed. by Claire BREAY. Woodbridge, Boydell Press, 99, X-479 p. (ill.).

3109. Chartae (The) of the Carthusian general chapter 1475–1503: MS. Grande Chartreuse 1 Cart. 14. Ed. by John P. H. CLARK. Salzburg, Institut fur Anglistik und Amerikanistik, Universität Salzburg, 99, VIII-107 p. (Analecta Cartusiana, 100, 31).

3110. Charters (The) of King David I: the written acts of David I, king of Scots, 1124–1153, and of his son, Henry earl of Notrhumberland, 1139–1152. Ed. by Geoffrey W. S. BARROW. Woodbridge, Boydell Press, 99, XIII-186 p. (pl.).

3111. CODIPHIS: catálogo de colecciones diplomáticas hispano-lusas de época medieval. Ed. por José Angel GARCÍA DE CORTÁZAR, José Antonio MUNITA y Luis Javier FORTÚN. Santander, Fundacion Marcelino Botin, 99, 2 vol., 604 p., 628 p. (Historia y documentos. Instrumentos para la investigación, 6.5.1-2).

3112. Colección diplomática medieval do Arquivo da Catedral de Mondonedo. Ed. por Enrique CAL PARDO. Santiago de Compostela, Consello da Cultura Galega, Ponencia de Patrimonio Historico, 99, 594 p.

3113. Colección documental de Pedro I de Castilla (1350–1369). 1360–1369, Indices. Ed. por Luis Vicente DÍAZ MARTÍN. Valladolid, Junta de Castilla y Leon, Consejeria de Educacion y Cultura, 99, 378 p. (Documentos para la historia de Castilla y León).

3114. Colección documental del Archivo de la Catedral de León. Actas capitulares. Ed. por Vicente A. ALVAREZ PALENZUELA. Tomo 1. 1376–1399. Leon, Centro de Estudios e Investigación "San Isidoro", 99, XVII-515 p. (Colección fuentes y estudios de historia leonesa, 76).

3115. Colección documental del Archivo Histórico de Bilbao. Ed. por Javier ENRÍQUEZ FERNÁNDEZ, Concepción HIDALGO DE CISNEROS AMESTOY y Adela MARTÍNEZ LAHIDALGA. Tomo 1. 1300–1473. Tomo 2. 1473–1500. Donostia, Eusko Ikaskuntza, 99, 2 vol., III-863 p. (Fuentes documentales medievales del País Vasco, 90, 95).

3116. Colección documental del monasterio de Santa María de Otero de las Duenas. Ed. por José Antonio FERNÁNDEZ FLÓREZ y Marta HERRERO DE LA FUENTE. Leon, Centro de Estudios e Investigación "San Isidoro", 99, 507 p. (Fuentes y estudios de historia leonesa, 73).

3117. Corpus des inscriptions de la France médiévale. Vol. 20. Côte-d'Or. Éd. par Robert FAVREAU, Jean MICHAUD et Bernadette MORA, Paris, CNRS, 99, IX-137 p. (pl., ill., maps).

3118. Corpus of Anglo-Saxon stone scripture. Vol. 5. Lincolnshire. Ed. by Paul EVERSON and David STOCKER. New York a. Oxford, Oxford U. P. for the British Academy, 99, XVIII-510 p.

3119. Corpus vitrearum Medii Aevi. Deutschland. Bd. 3, t. 2. Die mittelalterlichen Glasmalereien in Frankfurt und im Rhein-Main-Gebiet. Hrsg. v. Daniel HESS. Berlin, Deutscher Verlag fur Kunstwissenschaft, 99, 471 p. (ill.).

3120. Curia regis rolls of the reign of Henry III, preserved in the Public Record Office. Vol. 18. 27 to 30, Henry III (1243–1254). Ed. by Paul BRAND. Woodbridge, Boydell Press and Public Record Office, 99, XXIV-490 p.

3121. DE MINICIS (Elisabetta). Temi e metodi di archeologia medievale: ricerche sul territorio, la città, l'edilizia. Roma, Bonsignori, 99, 254 p. (ill.). (Civitates, 1).

3122. DEKÓWNA (Maria), ZOLL-ADAMIKOWA (Helena), NOSEK (E. M.). The early Mediaeval hoard: from Zawada Lanckoronska (Upper Vistula River). Warsaw, Institute of Archaeology and Ethnology, Polish Academy of Sciences, 99, 132 p. (ill.).

3123. Deutsche Inschriften. Terminologie zur Schriftbeschreibung. Erarbeitet von den Mitarbeitern der Inschriftenkommissionen der Akademien der Wissenschaften in Berlin in Deutschland und Österreich. Wiesbaden, Reichert, 99, 101 p. (ill., taf.).

3124. Deutschen Inschriften (Die). Bd. 47. (Heidelberger Reihe, Bd. 13.). Die Inschriften des Landkreises Böblingen. Gesammelt und bearbeitet von Anneliese SEELIGER-ZEISS. Bd. 49. (Mainzer Reihe, Bd. 6.). Die Inschriften der Stadt Darmstadt und der Landkreise Darmstadt-Dieburg und Gross-Gerau. Gesammelt und bearbeitet von Sebastian SCHOLZ. Wiesbaden, L. Reichert, 99, 2 vol., XLVI-346 p., XLVII-317 p. (taf.).

3125. Documenti (I) dell'Archivio capitolare di Vicenza (1083–1259). A cura di Franco SCARMONCINI, con la collaborazione di Francesca LOMASTRO e Gian Maria VARANINI. Roma, Viella, 99, XLVIII-379 p. (ill.). (Fonti per la storia della Terraferma veneta, 15).

3126. EGGERT (Wolfgang). Dokumente zur Geschichte des Deutschen Reiches und seiner Verfassung, 1331–1335. Teil. 2. 1332. Hannover, Hahnsche Buchhandlung, 99, VII-pp. 121-270 (Monumenta Germaniae Historica. Constitutiones et acta publica imperatorum et regum, 6/2).

1. SOURCES AND CRITICISM OF SOURCES

3127. English episcopal acta. London, 1076–1187. Ed. by Falko NEININGER. Oxford, Published for the British Academy by Oxford U. P., 99, LXXX-215 p. (pl., ill., facs.).

3128. Fasti ecclesiae Anglicanae, 1066–1300. York. Ed. by John LE NEVE and Diana E. GREENWAY. London, University of London, School of Advanced Study, Institute of Historical Research, 99, XXXV-151 p.

3129. Fasti ecclesiae Gallicanae. Répertoire prosopographique des évêques, dignitaires et chanoines des diocèses de France de 1200 à 1500. Diocese de Besançon. Éd. par Henri HOURS. Turnhout, Brepols, 99, XII-307 p. (ill., map, plans).

3130. FOSSIER (Robert). Sources de l'histoire économique et sociale du Moyen Age. Turnhout, Brepols, 99, 408 p.

3131. GASTON COUNT OF FOIX. Le Livre de chasse de Gaston Phébus (XIVe siècle). Paris, Bibliothèque nationale de France, 99, 1 CD-ROM (Collection Bibliothèque nationale de France: sources).

3132. GIPPIUS (Aleksej A.). K kharakteristike novgorodskogo vladychnogo letopisanija XII–XIV vv. (On the annalistic-writing of the archbishops of Novgorod, from tte 12th to the 14th century). *In*: Velikij Novgorod v istorii srednevekovoj Evropy [Cf. n° 3216], p. 345-364.

3133. HAWARD (Birkin). Suffolk medieval church roof carvings: an exploratory photographic survey with notes. Ipswich, Suffolk Institute of Archaeology and History, 99, 191 p. (ill.).

3134. Index verborum de la documentación medieval leonesa. Monasterio de Sahagun (857–1300). Ed. por José María FERNÁNDEZ CATÓN. Leon, Centro de Estudios e Investigación "San Isidoro", 99, 2 vol., 544 p., 512 p. (Colección fuentes y estudios de historia leonesa, 80).

3135. KRÜGER (Klaus). Corpus der mittelalterlichen Grabdenkmäler in Lübeck, Schleswig, Holstein und Lauenburg (1100–1600). Stuttgart, J. Thorbecke, 99, 1196 p. (ill., maps). (Kieler historische Studien, 40).

3136. LETTS (John B.). Smoke blackened thatch: a unique source of late medieval plant remains from southern England. London, Ancient Monuments Laboratory, English Heritage a. Reading, Department of Agricultural Botany and Rural History Centre, University of Reading, 99, 62 p. (ill.).

3137. Libro de acuerdos del Concejo de Avilés (1479–1492). Estudio y transcripción. Ed. por Covadonga CIENFUEGOS ÁLVAREZ. Oviedo, Real Instituto de Estudios Asturianos, 99, 226 p. (Fuentes y estudios de historia de Asturias, 17).

3138. Livro Preto. Cartulário da Sé de Coimbra. Texto integral. Director e coordenador editorial Manuel Augusto RODRIGUES, director científico cónego Avelino de Jesus DA COSTA. Coimbra, Arquivo da Universidade de Coimbra, 99, CCL-1429 p. (pl., maps, ill., facs).

3139. LOPETEGUI (Guadalupe). Estudio lingüístico de la documentación latina de la cancillería de Sancho VI de Navarra. Vitoria, Instituto de Ciencias de la Antiguedad, Servicio Editorial, Universidad del Pais Vasco, 99, 292 p. (Veleia. Anejos. Series minor, 12).

3140. MEL'NIKOVA (Elena A.), PODOSINOV (Aleksandr V.), BIBIKOV (Mikhail V), [et al.]. Drevnjaja Rus' v svete zarubezhnykh istochnikov. (Old Rus' in the foreign sources [Classical, Byzantine, Oriental, West European and Old Norse sources for the history of Eastern Europe to the 13th century]). Ed. Elena A. MEL'NIKOVA. Moskva, Logos, 99, 606 p. (bibl., ind.).

3141. OBERSTE (Jörg). Die Dokumente der Klösterlichen Visitationen. Turnhout, Brepols, 99, 153 p. (ill.). (Typologie des sources du Moyen Age occidental, 80).

3142. Original papal documents in England and Wales from the accession of Pope Innocent III to the death of Pope Benedict XI (1198–1304). Ed. by Jane E. SAYERS. Oxford, Clarendon Press, 99, CXV-678 p. (ill.).

3143. Part-Dieu (The) chartae. Ed. by John P. H. CLARK. Salzburg, Institut fur Anglistik und Amerikanistik, Universität Salzburg, 99, XX-86 p. (facs.). (Analecta Cartusiana,100, 33).

3144. Pergamene (Le) della Basilica di S. Vittore di Varese. Vol. 2. 1204–1260. A cura di Luisa ZAGNI. Milano, Università degli studi, 99, XXIV-595 p. (Pergamene milanesi dei secoli XII e XIII, 13).

3145. Pergamene (Le) dell'archivio arcivescovile di Taranto. Vol. 1/2. 1083–1258. A cura di Francesco MAGISTRALE. Lecce, Congedo, 99, IX-213 p. (Università degli studi di Lecce, Dipartimento di studi storici dal Medioevo all'età contemporanea. Fonti medievali e moderne per la storia di Terra d'Otranto, 30).

3146. Pergamins (Els) de l'arxiu comtal de Barcelona de Ramon Borrell a Ramon Berenguer I. Dir. Josep M. SALRACH I MARÉS i Gaspar FELIU. Coord. M. Josepa ARNALL i Ignasi J. BAIGES. Barcelona, Fundacio Noguera, 99, 3 vol., 1660 p. (Col.lecció Diplomataris, 18-20).

3147. Probate inventories of the York diocese, 1350–1500. Ed. by Philip Michael STELL and Louise HAMPSON. [York, York Minster Library], 99, 589 p.

3148. Processo (Il) Avogari (Treviso, 1314–1315). A cura di Giampaolo CAGNIN, con la collaborazione di Diego QUAGLIONI. Roma, Viella, 99, CXVI-712 p. (ill.). (Fonti per la storia della Terraferma veneta, 14).

3149. Rannesrednevekovye drevnosti Severnoj Rusi i ee sosedej: k 70-letiju A.N. Kirpichnikova. (Early medieval antiquities of the Northern Rus' and its neighbours: to the 70th anniversary of Anatolij N Kirpichnikov). RAN, In-t istorii material'noj kul'tury. Sankt-Peterburg, [s. n.], 99, 256 p. (ill., bibl.). [Articles in Russian, English etc.].

3150. Registrum Octaviani alias Liber Niger. The register of Octavian de Palatio, archbishop of Armagh, 1478–1513. Ed. by Mario Alberto SUGHI. Dublin, Irish Manuscripts Commission, 99, 2 vol., XCIX-145 p., 893 p.

3151. Répertoire des microfilms de cartulaires français consultables à l'I.R.H.T., Section de Diplomatique. Éd. par Caroline BOURLET et Muriel GOUGEROT. Orleans, Institut de Recherche et d'Histoire des Textes, 99, VI-327 p.

3152. Repertorio degli statuti comunali emiliani e romagnoli, secc. XII–XVI. A cura di Augusto VASINA. Vol. 3. Indici analitici. A cura di Enrico ANGIOLINI. Roma, Istituto storico italiano per il Medio Evo, 157 p. (Fonti per la storia dell'Italia medievale. IV. Subsidia, 6/3).

3153. SALICRÚ I LLUCH (Roser). Documents per a la història de Granada del Regnat d'Alfons el Magnànim (1417–1458). Barcelona, CSIC, Institució Milà i Fontanals, Departament d'estudis medievals, 99, 573 p. (tab.). (Anejos de Anuario de Estudios medievales. Collección de Monografías del Departamento de Estudios medievales del CSIC en barcelona, 37).

3154. Statuta antiqua Communis Collis vallis Else (1307–1407). A cura di Renzo NINCI e Mario ASCHERI. Roma, Istituto Storico Italiano per il Medio Evo, 99, 2 vol., XXXVII-742 p. (Fonti per la storia dell'Italia Medievale. I. Antiquitates, 10).

3155. STEIN (Henri). Catalogue des actes de Charles le Téméraire, 1467–1477. Mit einem Anhang: Urkunden und Mandate Karls von Burgund, Grafen von Charolais, 1433–1467. Bearb. von Sonja DÜNNEBEIL, Vorwort von Werner PARAVICINI. Sigmaringen, Jan Thorbecke, 99, XXXII-883 p.

3156. THÉVENAZ (Clémence). Ecrire pour gérer les comptes de la commune de Villeneuve autour de 1300. Lausanne, Université de Lausanne, 99, 425 p. (Cahiers lausannois d'histoire médiévale, 24).

3157. TOPHINKE (Doris). Handelstexte: zur Textualität und Typik kaufmännischer Rechnungsbücher im Hanseraum des 14. und 15. Jahrhunderts. Tübingen, Narr, 99, 285 p. (Script Oralia, 114).

3158. TVOROGOV (O.V.), DAVYDOVA (S.A.). Letopisets Ellinskij i Rimskij. ('The Chronicle Hellenic and Roman': [a 15th-century Russian compilation on the world history]). Vol. 1. Teksty (The texts). RAN, In-t russkoj literatury (Pushkinskij dom). Sankt-Peterburg, Dmitry Bulanin, 99, 540 p.

3159. WELCH (Martin G.), GUIDO (Margaret). The glass beads of Anglo-Saxon England c. AD 400–700: a preliminary visual classification of the more definitive and diagnostic types. Suffolk a. Rochester, Boydell Press for the Society of Antiquaries of London, 99, 361 p. (pl., ill.). (Reports of the Research Committee of the Society of Antiquaries of London, 56).

Cf. n°s 1-28

b. *Literary sources*

** 3160. KNJAZEVSKAJA (O.A.), KOROBENKO (L.A.), DOGRAMADZHIEVA (E.P.). Savvina kniga: Drevneslavjanskaja rukopis' XI, XI–XII i kontsa XIII veka. (Savvina kniga: an Old Slavonic manuscript written in the 11th, the 11–12th and the late 13th century). Ed. Ol'ga A. KNJAZEVSKAJA. Vol. 1: "Rukopis'. Tekst. Kommentarii. Issledovanie (Facsimile of the MS., transcription, commentary, introduction)". Moskva, Indrik, 99, 704 p.

3161. ACADEMIA ALFONSO X EL SABIO. Crónica de Alfonso X según el Ms. II/2777 de la Biblioteca del Palacio Real, Madrid. Ed. por Manuel GONZÁLEZ JIMÉNEZ y María Antonia CARMONA RUIZ. Murcia, Real, 99, 292 p.

3162. ADEMAR DE CHABANNES. Ademari Cabannensis Chronicon. Éd. par P. BOURGAIN. Turnhout, Brepols, 99, CXVI-392 p. (Corpus christianorum, 129. Ademari Cabannensis opera omnia, 1).

3163. ALFONSO FERNÁNDEZ DE PALENCIA. Gesta hispaniensia ex annalibus suorum dierum collecta. Ed. Robert Brian TATE y Jeremy LAWRANCE. Madrid, Real Academia de la Historia, 99, 2 vol., 643 p.

3164. BONCOMPAGNO DA SIGNA. L'assedio di Ancona. Liber de obsidiones Ancone. A cura di Paolo GARBINI. Roma, Viella, 99, 177 p. (I libri di Viella, 19).

3165. Chronicle (The) of Zuqnin, parts III and IV: A.D. 488–775. Ed. by Amir HARRAK. Toronto, Pontifical Institute of Mediaeval Studies, 99, XVI-388 p. (maps). (Mediaeval sources in translation, 36).

3166. COCHRANE (Lydia G.), CHARTIER (Roger), CAVALLO (Guglielmo). A history of reading in the West. Cambridge, Polity Press in association with Blackwell Publishers, 99, VIII-478 p.

3167. DEUTINGER (Roman). Rahewin von Freising. Ein Gelehrter des 12. Jahrhunderts. Hannover, Hahnsche Buchhandlung, 99, XVII-317 (Monumenta Germaniae Historica. Schriften, 47).

3168. Felice et divoto ad Terrasancta viagio facto per Roberto De Sancto Severino: 1458–1459. A cura di Mario CAVAGLIA e Alda ROSSEBASTIANO. Alessandria, Edizioni dell'Orso, 99, 353 p. (tav., ill.). (Oltramare, 9).

3169. Gesta Hungarorum. The deeds of the Hungarians. Ed. by László VESZPRÉMY, Simon KÉZAI, Jeno SZUCS and Frank SCHAER. Budapest a. New York, Central European U. P., 99, CII-235 p. (ill., maps, facs., geneal. tab.). (Central European medieval texts).

3170. Gesta Karoli Magni ad Carcassonam et Narbonam. Untersuchungen und Neueedition von Christian HEITZMANN. Tavarnuzze, SISMEL-Edizioni del Galluzzo, 99, CXXIV-117 p. (Il millennio medievale, 11).

3171. GONZÁLES DE CLAVIJO (Ruy). Viaggio a Samarcanda, 1403–1406. Un ambasciatore spagnolo alla corte di Tamerlano. A cura di Paola BOCCARDI STORONI. Roma, Viella, 99, 285 p. (ill.). (I libri di Viella, 18).

3172. GUICCIARDINI (Francesco). Compendio della Cronica di Froissart. A cura di Paolo MORENO. Bologna, Commissione per i testi di lingua, 99, LXXXIV-166 p. (Collezione di opere inedite o rare, 153).

3173. Libello de Constantino Magno eiusque matre Helena. La nascita di Costantino tra storia e leggenda. A cura di Giulietta GIANGRASSO. Tavernuzze, SISMEL – Edizioni del Galluzzo, 99, XLI-99 p. (Per verba. Testi mediolatini con traduzione, 13).

3174. MALASPINA (Saba). Chronik. Hrsg. v. Walter KOLLER und August NITSCHKE. Hannover, Hahnsche Buchhandlung, 99, X-430 p. (Monumenta Germaniae Historica. Scriptores, 35).

3175. MARTINUS POLONUS. The chronicles of Rome: an edition of the Middle English Chronicle of popes and emperors and the Lollard chronicle. Ed. by Dan EMBREE. Woodbridge, Boydell Press, 99, X-310 p. (facs.). (Medieval chronicles, 1).

3176. MOROSINI (Andrea). Morosini (The) codex. Ed. by Michele Pietro GHEZZO, John R. MELVILLE-JONES and Andrea RIZZI. Vol. 1. To the death of Andrea Dandolo (1354). Padova, Unipress, 99, XXI, 151 p. (Archivio del litorale adriatico, 3).

3177. Ordine et officij de casa de lo illustrissimo signor duca de Urbino [Cod. Urb. lat. 1248]. A cura di John E. LAW, Allen J. GRIECO e Sabine EICHE. Urbino, Accademia Raffaello, 99, 145 p. (pl., ill.).

3178. POLO (Marco). Il 'Milione' veneto: ms. CM 211 della Biblioteca civica di Padova. A cura di Alvaro BARBIERI, Alvise ANDREOSE, Marina MAURO e Lorenzo RENZI. Venezia, Marsilio, 99, 310 p. (Medioevo veneto).

3179. Prüfeninger (Die) Vita Bischof Ottos I. von Bamberg nach der Fassung des Grossen Österreichischen Legendars. Hrsg. v. Jürgen PETERSOHN. Hannover, Hahnsche Buchhandlung, 99, 174 p. (Monumenta Germaniae historica, Scriptores rerum Germanicarum in usum scholarum separatim editi, 71).

3180. RODERICUS XIMENIUS DE RADA. Opera omnia. Ed. por Juan A. ESTÉVEZ SOLA y Juan FERNÁNDEZ VALVERDE. Turnholti, Brepols, 99, 508 p. (Corpus Christianorum. Continuatio Mediaevalis, 72C).

3181. SALIMBENE DE ADAM. Cronica. Vol. 2. 1250-1287. Ed. G. SCALIA. Turnholti, Brepols, 99, 565 p. (Corpus Christianorum. Continuatio Mediaevalis, 125A).

3182. Summa bonorum. Eine deutsche Exempelsammlung aus dem 15. Jahrhundert nach Stephan von Bourbon. Hrsg. v. Susanne BAUMGARTE. Berlin, Erich Schmidt Verlag, 99, 330 p. (Texte des späten Mittelalters und der frühen Neuzeit, 40).

3183. WILLIAM OF MALMESBURY. Gesta regum Anglorum. The history of the English kings. Ed. by R. A. B. MYNORS, Rodney M. THOMSON and Michael WINTERBOTTOM. Oxford, Clarendon Press, 99, XLVII-496 p. (Oxford medieval texts) [Parallel texts in Latin and English].

Cf. n°s 1-28, 3130, 3256, 3503-3617

§ 2. General works.

* 3184. Bibliographie annuelle du Moyen-Âge tardif. Auteurs et textes latin. T. 9. [T. 8. Cf. Bibl. 98, n° 3324.] Rassemblée et compilée à la section latine de l'Institut de recherche et d'histoire des textes. Coordination et rédaction de Jean-Pierre ROTHSCHILD, co-rédaction Frédéric DUVAL, avec la collaboration de Pascale BARMON, Christine GEORGELIN et Patrice SICARD. Paris et Turnhout, Brepols, 99, X-669 p.

* 3185. International Medieval Bibliography (450-1500). T. 32. Part 1. January–June 1998. Part 2. July–December 1998. [T. 31, part 1 and 2. Cf. Bibl. 98, n° 3326.] Ed. by Alan MURRAY. Leeds, International Medieval Institute, University of Leeds a. Turnhout, Brepols, 99, 2 vol., [s. p.].

* 3186. Medioevo latino. Bollettino bibliografico della cultura europea da Boezio a Erasmo (secc. VI–XV). Vol. 20. [Vol. 19. Cf. Bibl. 98, n° 3327.] A cura di Claudio LEONARDI e Lucia PINELLI. Firenze, SISMEL – Edizioni del Galluzzo, 99, XXXVIII-1178 p.

3187. Anglija i Uel' s v period pozdnego srednevekov'ja. (England and Wales in the late Middle Ages: [articles]). Ed. Evgenij V. KUZNETSOV. Arzamas, Izd. Arzamas. ped. in-ta, 99, 178 p. (ill., maps; bibl., ind.).

3188. AOYAMA (Yoshinobu). Sei ibutsu no sekai: Chusei yoroppa no shinsho fukei. (The world of Relics: a scenery of images in Medieval Europe). Tokyo, Yamakawa Shuppansha, 99, 272 p.

3189. Autour de Marguerite d'Écosse: reines, princesses et dames du XVe siècle. Actes du colloque de Thouars (23 et 24 mai 1997). Éd. par Geneviève CONTAMINE et Philippe CONTAMINE. Paris, H. Champion, 99, 262 p. (pl., ill.). (Études d'histoire médiévale, 4).

3190. BARTHÉLEMY (Dominique). L'an mil et la paix de Dieu. La France chrétienne et féodale, 900-1060. Fayard, 99, 637 p. (maps, tab.).

3191. BUR (Michel). Le château. Turnhout, Brepols, 99, 165 p. (ill.). (Typologie des sources du Moyen Âge occidental, 79).

3192. Circle (The) of war in the Middle Ages. Essays on medieval military and naval history. Ed. by L. J. Andrew VILLALON and Donald J. KAGAY. Woodbridge, a. Rochester, The Boydell Press, 99, XIV-185 p. (ill., maps). (Warfare in history).

3193. CLANCHY (M. T.). Abelard: a medieval life. Oxford, Blackwell Publishers, 99, XIII-416 p. (ill., maps).

3194. FRANCE (John). Western warfare in the age of the Crusades, 1000–1300. London, UCL Press, 99, XV-327 p. (ill., maps). (Warfare and history).

3195. HEATHER (P. J.). The Visigoths from the migration period to the seventh century: an ethnographic perspective. Woodbridge a. Rochester, Boydell Press a. San Marino, Center for Interdisciplinary Research on Social Stress, 99, 563 p. (ill.). (Studies in historical archaeoethnology, 4).

3196. IKEGAMI (Shunichi). Romanesuku sekai-ron. (The romanesque world). Nagoya, University of Nagoya Press, 99, 578 p.

3197. KNIGHT (Jeremy). The end of antiquity: archaeology, society and religion AD 235–700. Stroud, Tempus, 99, 224 p. (ill., maps, plans).

3198. KÖLZER (Theo). Merowingerstudien. Bd. 2. Hannover, Hahnsche Buchhandlung, 99, XXXIII-174 p. (Studien und Texte).

3199. Krieg (Der) im Mittelalter und in der Frühen Neuzeit: Gründe, Begründungen, Bilder, Bräuche, Recht. Wiesbaden, Reichert Verlag, 99, XIX-454 p. (ill.). (Imagines Medii Aevi. Interdisziplinäre Beiträge zur Mittelalterforschung, 3).

3200. Lexikon des Mittelalters. Bd. 4. Erzkanzler bis Hiddensee. Bd. 5. Hiera-Mittel bis Lukanien. Stuttgart, J. B. Metzler, 99, 2 vol., VIII-2220 p.

3201. MAN (John). Atlas of the year 1000. London, Penguin, 99, 144 p. (ill., maps).

3202. Mezzogiorno (Il) normanno-svevo visto dall'Europa e dal mondo mediterraneo: atti delle tredicesime giornate normanno-sveve, Bari, 21–24 ottobre 1997. A cura di Giosuè MUSCA. Bari, Edizioni Dedalo, 99, 372 p. (Centro di studi normanno-svevi, Università degli studi di Bari. Atti, 13).

3203. Mittelalter und frühe Neuzeit. Übergänge, Umbrüche und Neuansätze. Hrsg. v. Walter HAUG. Tübingen, Niemeyer, 99, IX-585 p. (ill.). (Fortuna vitrea, 16).

3204. Mitteleuropäisches Städtewesen in Mittelalter und Frühneuzeit: Edith Ennen gewidmet. Hrsg. v. Wilhelm JANSSEN und Margret WENSKY. Köln, Böhlau, 99, X-284 p. (tab., maps, ill.).

3205. NEUMÜLLERS-KLAUSER (Renate). Res medii aevi: kleines Lexikon der Mittelalterkunde. Wiesbaden, Harrassowitz, 99, VII-317 p. (ill.).

3206. New (The) Cambridge medieval history. 900–1024. Ed. by Timothy REUTER. 1198–1300. Ed. by David ABULAFIA. 1300–1415. Ed. by Jones MICHAEL. Cambridge, Cambridge U. P., 3 vol., 99, XXV-863 p., XXIII-1045 p., XXX-1110 p. (pl., ill.).

3207. NICHOLAS (David). The transformation of Europe 1300–1600. London a. New York, Arnold a. Oxford U. P., 99, VI-486 p. (maps). (The Arnold history of Europe).

3208. Pace (The) of change: studies in early-medieval chronology. Ed. by Karen NIELSEN HØILUND, John HINES and Frank SIEGMUND. Oxford, Oxbow Books, 99, X-194 p. (ill., maps). (Cardiff studies in archaeology).

3209. PICCINNI (Gabriella). I mille anni del Medioevo. Milano, B. Mondadori, 99, XVI-463 p. (pl., ill.). (Sintesi).

3210. Problem i västsvensk medeltid. (La question de la Suède occidentale au Moyen Age). Red. par Lennart ANDERSSON PALM. Göteborg, Humanistiska fakulteten, Univ., 99, 95 p. (Västsvensk kultur i samhällsutveckling genom tiderna. Rapport 9).

3211. RESTON (James). The last apocalypse: Europe at the year 1000 A.D. New York a. London, Doubleday, 99, 299 p. (pl., ill., maps).

3212. SCHEIBELREITER (Georg). Die barbarische Gesellschaft: Mentalitätsgeschichte der europäischen Achsenzeit, 5.–8. Jahrhundert. Darmstadt, Primus, 99, 661 p. (map).

3213. SEE (Klaus von). Europa und der Norden im Mittelalter. Heidelberg, C. Winter, 99, 452 p. (ill.).

3214. TOMITA (Norimasa). Doitsu chusei minzoku koso shiron: Barutokai shuhen ni miru ibunkaken no sesshoku. (History of conflicts among peoples in medieval Germany: encounters with worlds of different culture around the Baltic Sea). Tokyo, Azekura Shobo, 99, 250 p.

3215. VASIL'EV (Mikhail A.). Jazychestvo vostochnykh slavjan nakanune kreshchenija Rusi: Religioznomifologicheskoe vzaimodejstvie s iranskim mirom. Jazycheskaja reforma knjazja Vladimira. (The Paganism of the eastern Slavs on the eve of Baptism of Rus': Religious and mythological interrelations with the Iranian Worlds. The Pagan reform of Prince Vladimir I). RAN, In-t slavjanovedenija. Moskva, Indrik, 99, 325 p. (bibl.).

3216. Velikij Novgorod v istorii srednevekovoj Evropy: K 70-letiju V.L. Janina. (Novgorod the Great in medieval European history: articles, devoted to the 70th anniversary of Valentin L. Yanin). Eds.: A.A. GIPPIUS, A.A. KHOROSHEV, E.N. NOSOV. Moskovskij gos. un-t im. M.V. Lomonosova, Istor. f-t. Moskva, Russkie slovari, 99, 466 p. (ill., plates; maps; bibl. incl). [Cf. n[os] <choice> 22, 3132.] A1: Zaliznjak; I1: Gippius]

Cf. n°s 357, 370, 998, 1043, 974, 1039, 3140, 3914

§ 3. Political history.

a. General

3217. BOUREAU (Alain). Les moines anglais et la construction du politique (début du 13e siècle). Annales, 99, 54, 3, p. 637-666.

3218. ČAPLOVIČ (Dušan). The Slavs and the beginnings of early-medieval Central Europe. Human affairs, 99, 9, 1, p. 28-43.

3219. EDROIU (Nicolae). Procesul de constituire a formațiunilor statale pe teritoriul României (secolele VIII–XI). (The emergence of state entities on Ro mania's territory. The 8th–11th centuries). Cluj-Napoca, Editura Presa Universitară Clujeană, 99, 209 p. (Bibliotheca Historica, X).

3220. LUKÁCS (Antal). Țara Făgărașului în evul mediu (secolele XIII–XVI). (Făgăraș land in the Middle Ages. The 13th–16th Centuries). București, Editura Enciclopedică, 99, 220 p.

3221. PAPACOSTEA (Serban). Geneza statului în evul mediu românesc: studii critice. Bucuresti, Corint, 99, 294 p. (Istorie).

3222. Saint-Denis et la royauté. Études offerts à Bernard Guenée, Membre de l'Institut. Éd par Françoise AUTRAND, Claude GAUVARD et Jean-Marie MOEGLIN. Paris, Publications de la Sorbonne, 99, 814 p. (tabl., ill.). (Série Histoire ancienne et médiévale, 59). [Cf. n° <sélection> 667.]

3223. Serviteurs (Les) de l'état au moyen âge. Association des historiens médiévistes de l'enseignement supérieur public. Paris, Publications de la Sorbonne, 99, 308 p. (Publications de la Sorbonne. Série Histoire ancienne et médiévale, 57).

3224. SETTIA (Aldo A.). Proteggere e dominare: fortificazioni e popolamento nell'Italia medievale. Roma, Viella, 99, 445 p. (I libri di Viella, 13).

3225. SUNDBERG (Ulf). Medeltidens svenska krig. (Les guerres suédoises du Moyen Age). Stockholm, Hjalmarson & Högberg, 99, 458 p. (ill.).

b. *476–900*

3226. DARK (K. R.). Civitas to kingdom: British political continuity 300–800. London, Leicester U. P., 99, XIV-322 p. (ill., maps). (Studies in the early history of Britain).

3227. HARRISON (Dick). Krigarnas och helgonens tid: Västeuropas historia 400–800 e.Kr. Stockholm, Prisma, 99, 592 p. (ill., maps).

3228. LUDWIG (Uwe). Transalpine Beziehungen der Karolingerzeit im Spiegel der Memorialüberlieferung. Hannover, Hahnsche Buchhandlung, 99, XXXIII-309 p. (Monumenta Germaniae Historica. Schriften und Texte, 25).

3229. NELSON (Janet L.). Rulers and ruling families in early medieval Europe: Alfred, Charles the Bald, and others. Aldershot a. Brookfield, Ashgate, 99, XII-[332] p. (map). (Variorum collected studies series, 657).

3230. NERLICH (Daniel). Diplomatische Gesandtschaften zwischen Ost- und Westkaisern, 756–1002. Bern, Peter Lang, 99, 337 p. (tab.). (Geist und Wert der Zeiten, 92).

3231. PEARSON LYNNE ROPER (Kathy). Conflicting loyalties in early medieval Bavaria: a view of sociopolitical interaction, 680-900. Aldershot a. Brookfield, Ashgate, 99, XIII-247 p.

Cf. n°s 1545, 3215

c. *900–1300*

* 3232. SEIBERT (H.). Heinrich der Löwe und die Welfen. Ein Jubiläum und sein Ertrag für die Forschung [Literaturbericht]. *Historische Zeitschrift*, 99, 268, 2, p. 375-406.

3233. DE VRIES (Kelly). The Norwegian invasion of England in 1066. Woodbridge, Boydell, 99, XII-322 p. (tab., maps). (Warfare in History).

3234. Hellere fanden sælv end Erik på tronen! Konfliten mellem Jens Grand og Erik Menved 1294-1302: en oversættelse af procesakterne med indledning og suppleret med andre kilder. (Plutôt le diable lui-même qu'Eric sur le trône! Le conflit entre l'archevêque Jens Grand et le roi Eric Menved de Danemark, 1294–1302: traduction des actes du procès, précédée d'une introduction et complétée par d'autres sources). Af Benedite FONNESBESCH-WULFF [et al.]. Odense, Odense Universitetsforlag, 99, 260 p. (ill.). (Odense University Studies in History and Social Sciences, 214).

3235. Ich, Ulrich von Liechtenstein: Literatur und Politik im Mittelalter. Akten der Akademie Friesach "Stadt und Kultur im Mittelalter", Friesach (Kärnten), 2.–6. September 1996. Hrsg. v. Franz Viktor SPECHTLER und Barbara MAIER. Klagenfurt, Wieser, 99, 509 p. (ill., maps). (Schriftenreihe der Akademie Friesach, 5).

3236. KIESEWETTER (Andreas). Die Anfänge der Regierung König Karls II. von Anjou (1278–1295): das Königreich Neapel, die Grafschaft Provence und der Mittelmeerraum zu Ausgang des 13. Jahrhunderts. Husum, Matthiesen Verlag, 99, 650 p. (Historische Studien, 451).

3237. Konrad von Wettin und seine Zeit. Protokoll der Wissenschaftlichen Konferenz anlässlich des 900. Geburtstags Konrads von Wettin im Burggymnasium Wettin am 18. und 19. Juli 1998. Wettin, J. Stekovics, 99, 176 p. (ill., maps). (Beiträge zur Regional- und Landeskultur Sachsen-Anhalts).

3238. KRISTÓ (Gyula). A XI. Század története. (The history of the XI century). Szeged, Szekszárdi Nyomda, 99, 182 p.

3239. LOUD (G. A.). Conquerors and chrchmen in Norman Italy. Aldershot a. Brookfield, Ashgate, 99, XII-314 p. (Variorum collected studies series, 658).

3240. MAILLEFER (Jean-Marie). Chevaliers et princes allemands en Suède et en Finland à l'époque des Folkungar (1250–1363). Bern, Peter Lang, 99, 444 p. (maps, tab.). (Kieler Werkstücke. D. Beiträge zur europäischen Geschichte des späten Mittelalters, 10).

3241. MIKA (Sándor). A hûbériség és a keresztes hadjáratok kora. (The age of the feudalism and of the crusades). Szeged, Szekszárdi Nyomda, 99, 650 p.

3242. Negotiating secular and ecclesiastical power: Western Europe in the Central Middle Ages. Ed. by Arnoud-Jan A. BIJSTERVELD, Henk TEUNIS and Andrew WAREHAM. Turnhout, Brepols, 99, XX-196 p. (ill.). (International medieval research, 6).

3243. RICHARD (Jean). The Crusades, c.1071–c.1291. Cambridge, Cambridge U. P., 99, XIV-516 p. (maps). (Cambridge medieval textbooks).

3244. THORAU (P.). Der Krieg und das Geld. Ritter und Söldner in den Heeren Kaiser Friedrichs II. *Historische Zeitschrift*, 99, 268, 3, p. 599-634.

3245. TURNER (Ralph V.), HEISER (Richard R.). The reign of Richard Lionheart: ruler of the Angevin Empire, 1189–1199. Harlow, Longman, 99, 292 p. (The medieval world).

d. *1300–1500*

3246. ANDREESCU (Mihail M.). Puterea domniei în Țara Românească și Moldova în secolele XIV–XVI. (The strength of rulership in Wallachia and Moldavia in the 14th–16th centuries). București, Editura "Nicolae Bălcescu", 99, 364 p.

3247. Arras et la diplomatie européenne XVᵉ–XVIᵉ siècles. Éd. par Denis CLAUZEL, Charles GIRY-DELOISON et Christophe LEDUC. Arras, Artois Presses Université, 99, 428 p. (pl., ill., maps). (Histoire). [Cf. nᵒˢ <sélection> 7409, 7413, 7417.]

3248. BEVERLEY (Tessa). Diplomacy and elites: Venetian ambassadors, 1454–1494. Leicester, Centre for the Study of Diplomacy, 99, 30 p. (Diplomatic Studies Programme discussion papers, 51).

3249. BLOCKMANS (Wim), PREVENIER (Walter). The promised lands: the Low Countries under Burgundian rule, 1369–1530. Philadelphia, University of Pennsylvania Press, 99, XIII-285 p. (ill.). (The Middle Age series).

3250. BOFFA (Serge). L'expédition d'octobre 1407 dirigée par Antoine duc de Brabant contre Renaud IV, duc de Juliers et de Gueldre. *Revue belge de philologie et d'histoire*, 99, 77, 2, p. 299-328.

3251. Cavalieri di San Giovanni e territorio: la Liguria tra Provenza e Lombardia nei secoli XIII–XVII. Atti del Convegno, Genova, Imperia, Cervo, 11–14 settembre 1997. A cura di Josepha COSTA RESTAGNO. Bordighera, Istituto internazionale di studi liguri, Sezione Ingauna, 99, 588 p. (ill.). (Istituto internazionale di studi liguri. Atti dei convegni, 2).

3252. CHRISTENSEN (St. T.). From fuga simulata to the armed sultanic redoubt. Reflections on the south east European impact on Ottoman battle tactics (Fourteenth to sixteenth centuries). *In*: Tarihte güney-doğu Avrupa: Balkanolojinin dünü bugünü ve sorunlari – South east Europe in history: the past, the present and the problems of balkanology [Cf. nᵒ 2991], p. 45-61.

3253. COHN (Samuel Jr.). Creating the Florentine state. Peasants and rebellion, 1348–1434. Cambridge, Cambridge U. P., 99, XIII-308 p. (graph., tab.).

3254. GODDING (Philippe). Le Conseil de Bramant sous le règne de Philippe le Bon (1430–1467). Bruxelles, Académie royale de Belgique, Classe de Lettres, 99, 610 p. (tab.). (Mémoires de la Classe des Lettres, coll. in 8°, 19).

3255. GRIFFITHS (Gordon). The justification of Florentine foreign policy offered by Leonardo Bruni in his public letters, 1428–1444, based on documents from the Florentine and Venetian archives. Istituto Storico Italiano per il Medio Evo, 99, 188 p. (Nuovi studi storici, 47).

3256. GUENÉE (Bernard). Un roi et son historien. Vingt études sur le régne de Charles IV et la Chronique du Religieux de Saint-Denis. Paris, De Boccard, 99, 538 p. (ill.). (Mémoires de l'Académie des Inscriptions et Belles-Lettres, 18).

3257. HERGERMÖLLER (Bernd-Ulrich). Cogor adversum te. Drei Studien zum literarisch-theologischen Profil Karls IV un seiner Kanzlei. Warendolf, Fahlbuch Verlag, 99, LVIII-501 p. (Studien zu den Luxemburgern und ihrer Zeit, 7).

3258. Höfe und Hofordnungen 1200–1600. 5. Symposium der Residenzen-Kommission der Akademie der Wissenschaften in Göttingen, veranstaltet gemeinsam mit dem Deutschen Historischen Institut Paris und dem Staatsarchiv Sigmaringen, Sigmaringen, 5. bis 8. Oktober 1996. Hrsg. v. Holger KRUSE und Werner PARAVICINI. Sigmaringen, Thorbecke, 99, 560 p. (ill.). (Residenzenforschung, 10).

3259. JÄSCHKE (Kurt-Ulrich). Europa und das römisch-deutsche Reich um 1300. Stuttgart, W. Kohlhammer, 99, VII-187 p. (maps).

3260. LUTTRELL (Anthony). The Hospitaller State on Rhodes and its Western provinces, 1306–1462. Aldershook, Ashgate, 99, X-340 p. (tab., ill.). (Variorum collected studies series, 655).

3261. MAZZONI (Vieri), SALVESTRINI (Francesco). Strategie politiche e interessi economici nei rapporti tra la Parte Guelfa e il Comune di Firenze. La confisca patrimoniale ai «ribelli» di San Miniato (ca. 1368–ca. 1400). *Archivio storico italiano*, 99, 157, 579, p. 3-62.

3262. PELLEGRINI (Marco). Congiure di Romagna: Lorenzo de' Medici e il duplice tirannicidio a Forlì e a Faenza nel 1488. Firenze, L. S. Olschki, 99, 190 p. (Biblioteca storica toscana, 35).

3263. REHBERG (Andreas). Kirche und Macht im römischen Trecento. Die Colonna und ihre Klientel auf dem kurialen Pfründenmarkt (1278–1378). Tübingen, Niemeyer, 99, X-658 p. (tab., maps, graph.). (Bibliothek des deutschen historischen Instituts in Rom, 88).

3264. Richard II: the art of kingship. Ed. by Antony GOODMAN and James GILLESPIE. Oxford a. New York, Clarendon Press a. Oxford U. P., 99, XII-299 p.

3265. SETTIA (Aldo A.). Gli «Insegnamenti» di Teodoro di Monferrato e la prassi bellica in Italia all'inizio del Trecento. *Archivio storico italiano*, 99, 157, 582, p. 667-990.

3266. SUMPTION (Jonathan). The Hundred Years' War. Vol. 2. Trial by fire. Philadelphia, University of Pennsylvania Press, 99, XII-680 p. (ill.).

3267. TAYLOR (Craig). Sir John Fortescue and the French polemical treatises of the Hundred Years War. *English historical review*, 99, 114, 455, p. 112-129.

3268. Wars (The) of Edward III. Sources et interpretations. Ed. by Clifford J. RODGES. Woodbridge, Boydell, 99, XXVII-384 p. (maps). (Warfare in history).

Cf. n° 3187

§ 4. Jews.

3269. ALCOLOUMBRE (Thierry). Maïmonide et le problème de la personne. Paris, J. Vrin, 99, 183 p. (Etudes de philosophie médiévale, 77).

3270. ASSIS YOM (Tov), KAPLAN (Yosef). Dor gerush Sefarad: kovets ma'amarim. Jews and Conversos at the time of the expulsion. Yerushalayim, Merkaz Zalman Shazar le-toldot Yisra'el, 99, 322-171 p.

3271. BAREKET (Elinoar). Fustat on the Nile: the Jewish elite in medieval Egypt. Leiden, Brill, 99, XVI-295 p. (pl., ill.). (Medieval Mediterranean, 24).

3272. Brûlement (Le) du Talmud à Paris 1242–1244. Éd. par Renè-Samuel SIRAT, Elie NICOLAS et Gilbert DAHAN. Paris, Editions du Cerf, 99, 256 p. (Nouvelle Gallia Judaïca).

3273. COHEN (Jeremy). Living letters of the law: ideas of the Jew in medieval Christianity. Berkeley a. London, University of California Press, 99, X-451 p. (S. Mark Taper Foundation imprint in Jewish studies).

3274. DAHAN (Gilbert). Les intellectuels chrétiens et les juifs au Moyen Âge. Paris, Editions du Cerf, 99, 637 p. (Patrimoines).

3275. FRIEDMAN MORDECHAI (Akiva). Heker ha-Genizah le-ahar me'ah shanah. Tel-'Aviv, Universitat Tel-'Aviv, 99, XXXII-428 p. (port., facs.). (Te'uda: the Chaim Rosenberg school of Jewish Studies research series, 15).

3276. FRUCHTMAN (Maya). Dikduke piyut: 'iyunim ba-shitah ha-dikdukit-ha-parshanit bi-Yeme-ha-benayim 'al-pi 'Sefer 'arugat ha-bo'sem' le-R. Avraham Ben-'Azri'el. (Unique grammatical approach in medieval commentary of piyyutim: linguistic studies in 'Sefer Arugath ha-bo'sem'). Be'er-Sheva', Hotsa'at ha-sefarim shel Universitat Ben-Guryon ba-Negev, 99, 154 p.

3277. GLICK (Leonard B.). Abraham's heirs: Jews and Christians in medieval Europe. Syracuse, Syracuse U. P., 99, XIV-323 p. (maps).

3278. GOLDIN (Simha). Juifs et juifs convertis au Moyen Age: «es-tu encore mon frère ?». *Annales*, 99, 54, 4, p. 851-874.

3279. HERSHON (Cyril P.). Faith and controversy: the Jews of mediaeval Languedoc. Birmingham, A.I.E.O., 99, 418 p. (ill.). (Association internationale d'études occitanes, 7).

3280. Juden und Christen zur Zeit der Kreuzzüge. Hrsg. v. Alfred HAVERKAMP. Sigmaringen, Thorbecke, 99, 372 p. (Vorträge und Forschungen, 47).

3281. LANGERMANN (Y. Tzvi). The Jews and the sciences in the Middle Ages. Aldershot a. Brookfield, Ashgate, 99, VIII-334 p. (ill.). (Variorum collected studies series, 624).

3282. LIPTON (Sara). Images of intolerance: the representation of Jews and Judaism in the Bible moralisée. Berkeley a. University of California Press, 99, XVI-241 p. (ill.). (The S. Mark Taper Foundation imprint in Jewish studies).

3283. MAGIN (Christine). Wie es umb der iuden recht stet. Der Status der Juden in spätmittelalterlichen deutschen Rechtbüchern. Göttingen, Wallenstein, 99, 462 p.

3284. MELAMMED LEVINE (Renée). Heretics or daughters of Israel? The crypto-Jewish women of Castile. New York a. Oxford, Oxford U. P., 99, VI-256 p.

3285. MELLINKOFF (Ruth). Antisemitic hate signs in Hebrew illuminated manuscripts from medieval Germany. Jerusalem, Center for Jewish Art, The Hebrew University of Jerusalem, 99, 158 p. (ill.).

3286. MIRONES LOZANO (Eunate). Los judíos del Reino de Navarra en la crisis del siglo XV, 1425–1479. Pamplona, Gobierno de Navarra, Departamento de Educación y Cultura, 99, 261 p. (ill.). (Serie Historia, 99).

3287. PARELLO (Vincent). Les judéo-convers, Tolède, XVe–XVIe siècles: de l'exclusion à l'intégration. Paris, L'Harmattan, 99, 271 p. (ill.). (Collection Recherches et documents. Espagne).

3288. RICH ABAD (Anna). La comunitat jueva de Barcelona entre 1348 i 1391 a través de la documació notarial. Barcelona, Fundacio Noguera, 99, 452 p. (Col.lecció Estudis, 21).

3289. RUBIN (Miri). Gentile tales: the narrative assault on late medieval Jews. New Haven a. London, Yale U. P., 99, XIII-266 p. (ill., maps).

3290. Studies in Jewish manuscripts. Ed. by Jopseph DAN and Klaus HERRMANN. Tübingen, Mohr Siebeck, 99, XV-254 p. (ill.). (Texts and studies in medieval and early modern Judaism, 14).

3291. TALMAGE (Frank), WALFISH (Barry). Apples of gold in settings of silver: studies in medieval Jewish exegesis and polemics. Toronto, Pontifical Institute of Mediaeval Studies, 99, XV-447 p. (Papers in mediaeval studies, 14).

3292. TOBI (Joseph), ROSOVSKY (Murray). The Jews of Yemen: studies in their history and culture. Leiden a. Boston, Brill, 99, X-301 p. (Etudes sur le judaïsme médiéval, 21).

§ 5. Islam.

3293. AYALON (David). Eunuchs, caliphs and sultans: a study in power relationships. Jerusalem, Magnes Press a. The Hebrew University, 99, XI-376 p.

3294. BEHRENS-ABOUSEIF (Doris). Beauty in Arabic culture. Princeton, Markus Wiener, 99, VIII-220 p. (ill.). (Princeton series on the Middle East).

3295. BERG (Herbert). The development of exegesis in early Islam: the authenticity of Muslim literature from the formative period. Richmond, Curzon, 99, 288 p. (Curzon studies in the Qur'an).

3296. BLANKS (David R.), FRASSETTO (Michael). Western views of Islam in medieval and early modern Europe: perception of other. Basingstoke, Macmillan, 99, VIII-235 p.

3297. BRETT (Michael). Ibn Khaldun and the medieval Maghrib. Aldershot, Ashgate, 99, [s. p.]. (map). (Variorum collected studies series, 627).

3298. CRONE (Patricia), MOREH (Shmuel). The book of strangers: mediaeval Arabic graffiti on the theme of nostalgia. Princeton, Markus Wiener, 99, 196 p. (Princeton series on the Middle East).

3299. DEMIRALP (Yekta). Erken dönem Osmanli medreseleri, 1300–1500. Ankara, Kultur Bakanligi, 99, XI-334 p. (ill.). (T.C. Kültür Bakanligi yayinlari, 2209, Yayimlar Dairesi Baskanligi Osmanli eserleri dizisi, 4).

3300. DUPRET (Baudouin). L'historicité de la norme. Du positivisme de l'islamologie juridique à l'anthropologie de la norme islamique. *Annales*, 99, 54, 1, p. 169-196.

3301. ECHEVARRIA (Ana). The fortress of faith: the attitude towards Muslims in fifteenth century Spain. Leiden a. Boston, Brill, 99, VI-254 p. (Medieval Iberian Peninsula. Texts and studies, 12).

3302. Editing Islamic manuscripts on science: proceedings of the Fourth Conference of Al-Furqan Islamic Heritage Foundation 29th–30th November 1997. Ed. by Yusuf IBISH. London, Al-Furqan Islamic Heritage Foundation, 99, XIX-241 p. (ill.). (Publication, 42).

3303. ELAD (Amikam). Medieval Jerusalem and Islamic worship: holy places, ceremonies, pilgrimage. Leiden a. New York, E.J. Brill, 99, VII-196 p. (maps). (Islamic history and civilization. Studies and texts, 8).

3304. GIL'ADI (Avner). Infants, parents and wet nurses: medieval Islamic views on breastfeeding and their social implications. Leiden a. Boston, Brill, 99, X-191 p. (ill.). (Islamic history and civilization. Studies and texts, 25).

3305. HAWTING (G. R.). The idea of idolatry and the emergence of Islam: from polemic to history. Cambridge, Cambridge U. P., 99, XVII-168 p. (Cambridge studies in Islamic civilization).

3306. Heritage (The) of Sufism. Vol. 1. Classical Persian Sufism from its origins to Rumi (700–1300). Ed. by Leonard LEWISOHN. Oxford, Oneworld, 99, 3 vol., XLII-662 p. (ill.).

3307. HILLENBRAND (Carole). The crusades: Islamic perspectives. Edinburgh, Edinburgh U. P., 99, LVI-648 p. (pl., ill., maps).

3308. JENKINS (Everett). The Muslim diaspora: a comprehensive reference to the spread of Islam in Asia, Africa, Europe, and the Americas. Vol. 1. 570–1550. Vol. 2. 1500–1799. Jefferson a. London, McFarland, 99, 2 vol., XII-425 p.

3309. KOCHIN (Michael S.). Weeds: cultivating the imagination in medieval Arabic political philosophy. *Journal of the history of ideas*, 99, 60, 3, p. 399-416.

3310. KUBAN (Doğan). Divriği mucizesi: Selçuklular çağında islam bezeme sanatı üzerine bir deneme. (Le Miracle de Divriği: un essai sur l'art ornemental islamique à l'époque des Séldjoukides). İstanbul, Yapı-Kredi Yayınları, 99, 225 p.

3311. LEV (Yaacov). Saladin in Egypt. Leiden, Brill, 99, XV-214 p. (Medieval Mediterranean, 21).

3312. Religion and culture in medieval Islam. Ed. by Richard G. HOVANNISIAN and Georges SABAGH. Cambridge, Cambridge U. P., 99, VIII-119 p. (ill.). (Giorgio Levi Della Vida conferences, 14).

3313. RUBIN (Uri). Between Bible and Qur'an: the children of Israel and the Islamic self-image. Princeton, Darwin Press, 99, XIV-318 p. (Studies in late antiquity and early Islam, 17).

3314. RÜHRDANZ (Karin), MILSTEIN (Rachel), SCHMITZ (Barbara). Stories of the prophets: illustrated manuscripts of Qisas al-Anbiya'. Costa Mesa, Mazda Publishers, 99, VIII-248 p. (ill., pl.). (Islamic art and architecture, 8).

3315. STROUMSA (Sarah). Freethinkers of medieval Islam: Ibn al-Rawandi, Abu Bakr al-Razi and their impact on Islamic thought. Leiden a. Boston, Brill, 99, XI-261 p. (Islamic philosophy, theology, and science, 35).

3316. SUVOROVA (Anna A.). Musul'manskie svjatye Juzhnoj Azii XI–XV vekov. (Muslim Saints of South Asia, 11th–15th century). RAN, In-t vostokovedenija. Moskva, [s. n.], 99, 280 p. (8 f. ill., bibl.; ind.). [Eng. summary].

3317. TOELLE (Heidi). Le Coran revisité: le feu, l'eau, l'air et la terre. Damas, Institut français d'études arabes de Damas, 99, 288 p. (Publications de l'I.F.E.A.D, 175).

3318. Women in the medieval Islamic world: power, patronage and piety. Ed. by Gavin R. G. HAMBLY. Basingstoke, Macmillan, 99, 566 p. (The new Middle Ages, 6).

Cf. n°s 349, 3140

§ 6. Vikings.

3319. CLARK (Philip). Weapons and warfare in the Viking age. Stroud, Tempus, 99, 176 p. (ill.).

3320. DU BOIS (Thomas A.). Nordic religions in the Viking Age. Philadelphia, University of Pennsylvania Press, 99, X-271 p. (ill., map)

3321. GÖRANSSON (Eva-Marie Y.). Bilder av kvinnor och kvinnlighet: genus och kroppsspråk under övergången till kristendomen. Stockholm, Elanders Gotab, 99, 332 p. (ill.). (Stockholm studies in archaeology, 18).

3322. LARSSON (Mats G.). Vikinger i Österled. (Les Vikings sur la route de l'est). Stockholm, Månpocket, 99, 508 p. (ill.). – IDEM. Vinland det goda: nordbornas färder till Amerika under vikingatiden. Stockholm, Atlantis, 99, 183 p. (ill., maps).

3323. OWEN (Olwyn), DALLAND (Magnar). Scar: a Viking boat burial on Sanday, Orkney. East Linton, Tuckwell, 99, 180 p. (ill.).

3324. PEEL (Christine). Guta saga: the history of the Gotlanders. London, Viking Society for Northern Research and University College London, 99, LX-97 p. (il., facs., maps). (Text series, 12).

3325. ROSS CLUNIES (Margaret). From Iceland to Norway: essential rites of passage for an early Icelandic skald. Berlin, Verlag für Wissenschaft und Bildung und der Herausgeber, 99, 72 p. (Alvíssmál. Forschungen zur mittelalterlichen Kultur Skandinaviens. Sonderdruck, 9).

3326. SELLEVOLD (Berit J.). Picts and Vikings at Westness: anthropological investigations of the skeletal material from the cemetery at Westness, Rousay, Orkney Islands. Oslo, Norsk institutt for kulturminneforskning, 99, 62 p. (ill., map). (NIKU fagrapport, 10).

3327. SIGURÐSSON (Jón Viðar). Chieftains and power in the Icelandic Commonwealth. Odense, Odense U. P., 99, 255 p. (maps). (The Viking collection, 12).

Cf. n°s 3140, 3149

§ 7. History of law and institutions.

* 3328. Catalogo della raccolta di statuti: consuetudini, leggi, decreti, ordini e privilegi dei comuni, delle associazioni e degli enti locali dal Medioevo alla fine del secolo XVIII. Vol. 8. T-U. A cura di Sandro BULGARELLI, Alessandra CASAMASSIMA e Giuseppe PIERANGELI; prefazione di Aldo MASULLO; introduzione di Gian Savino PENE VIDARI. Biblioteca del Senato della Republica. Roma, Tip. del Senato e Firenze, L. S. Olschki, 99, XCVIII-259 p.

* 3329. KÉRY (Lotte). Canonical collections of the early Middle Ages (ca. 400–1140): a bibliographical guide to the manuscripts and literature. Washington, Catholic University of America Press, 99, XXXV-311 p. (History of medieval canon law).

** 3330. GUARNERIUS IURISPERTISSIMUS. Liber divinarum sententiarum. A cura di Giuseppe MAZZANTI. Spoleto, Centro italiano di studi sull'alto Medioevo, 99, XIV-375 p. (Testi, studi, strumenti, 14).

** 3331. KOS (Dušan). Statut mesta Ptuja 1513. (Statute of the Town of Ptuj). Ptuj, Zgodovinski arhiv a. Ljubljana, Znanstveno raziskovalni center Slovenske akademije znanosti in umetnosti, 99, 267 p. (ill.). (Publikacije Zgodovinskega arhiva Ptuj, Viri, 3).

** 3332. WULFSTAN (Archbishop of York). Canon law collection. Ed. by James E. CROSS and Andrew HAMER. Rochester, D.S. Brewer, 99, X-183 p. (Anglo-Saxon texts, 1).

** 3333. ZIMIN (Aleksandr A.). Pravda Russkaja. (Pravda Russkaja: [the earliest Russian law code]). With a reconstructed text of two versions of Pravda Russkaja, p. 357-380; a list of MSS., p. 381-387. Ed. Valentin L. JANIN. Min. justitsii RF, Ros. pravovaja akademija; RAN, In-t rossijskoj istorii; Feder. arkhivnaja sluzhba Rossii, Ros. gos. arkhiv drevnikh aktov. Moskva, Drevlekhranilishche, 99, 422 p. (bibl.; ind.).

3334. ANDREOLLI (Bruno). Contadini su terre di signori. Studi sulla contrattualistica agraria nell'Italia medievale. Bologna, CLUEB, 99, 425 p. (Biblioteca di storia agraria medievale, 16).

3335. BARRAQUÉ (Jean-Pierre). Le Martinet d'Orthez (textes médiévaux inédits): violence, pactes et pouvoir judiciaire en Béarn à la fin du Moyen Âge. Biarritz, Atlantica, 99, 309 p.

3336. CHARLES-EDWARDS (T. M.). The early mediaeval Gaelic lawyer. Cambridge, Department of Anglo-Saxon, Norse and Celtic, University of Cambridge, 99, 73 p. (Quiggin pamphlets on the sources of mediaeval Gaelic history, 4).

3337. CORTESE (Ennio). Scritti. A cura di Italo BIROCCHI e Ugo PETRONIO. Spoleto, Centro italiano di studi sull'alto Medioevo, 99, 2 vol., XV-1544 p. (Collectanea, 10).

3338. HEIRBAUT (Dirk). The fief-rente: a new evaluation, based on Flemish sources (1000–1305). Revue d'histoire du droit, 99, 67, 1-2, p. 1-37.

3339. IBHLER GREIFFEN (N. von). Die Rezeption des lombardischen Lehensrechts und sein Einfluss auf das mittelalterliche Lehenswesen. Bern, Peter Lang, 99, 396 p. (Europäische Hochschulschriften. Reihe 3, 820).

3340. KÖBLER (Gerhard). Liber Exquisiti Xenii. Lexikon frühmittelalterlicher Rechtswörter für Freunde frühmittelalterlicher Rechtsgeschichte. Gießen, Arbeit zur Rechts und Sprachwissenschaft Verlag, 99 XIV-331 p. (Arbeiten zur Rechts und Sprachwissenschaft, 46).

3341. MADERO (Marta). Façons de croire. Les témoins et le juge dans l'œuvre juridique d'Alphonse X le Sage, roi de Castille. *Annales*, 99, 54, 1, p. 197-218.

3342. MANCUSO (Fulvio). Exprimere causam in sententia: ricerche sul principio di motivazione della sentenza nell'età del diritto comune classico. Milano, A. Giuffré, 99, XVIII-272 p.

3343. MARGETIĆ (Lujo), APOSTOLOVA MARŠAVELSKI (Magdalena). Hrvatsko srednjovjekovno pravo. (Croatian medieval law). Zagreb, Narodne novine, 99, 324 p.

3344. MODZELEWSKI (Karol). Culte et justice. Lieux d'assemblée des tribus germaniques et slaves. *Annales*, 99, 54, 3, p. 615-636.

3345. Nordic perspectives on medieval canon law. Papers from a workshop held at the University of Helsinki on 29 March 1998. Ed. by Mia KORPIOLA. [Helsinki], Matthias Calonius Society, 99, X-167 p. (Publications of Matthias Calonius Society, 2).

3346. O'BRIEN (Bruce R.). God's peace and king's peace: the laws of Edward the Confessor. Philadelphia, University of Pennsylvania Press, 99, XV-305 p. (map). (Middle Ages series).

3347. PARISOLI (Luca). Volontarismo e diritto soggettivo: la nascita medievale di una teoria dei diritti nella scolastica francescana. Roma, Istituto storico dei Cappuccini, 99, 192 p. (Bibliotheca seraphico-capuccina, 58).

3348. SHATZMILLER (Joseph). Justice et injustice au début du XIVe siècle. L'enquête sur l'archevêque d'Aix et sa renonciation en 1318. Texte de l'enquête éd. par Frédéric CHARTRAIN. Roma, École française de Rome, 99, X-302 p. (tab.). (Sources et documents d'histoire du Moyen Âge, 2).

3349. SOETERMEER (Frank). Livres et juristes au Moyen Âge. Goldbach, Keip, 99, XIII-431 p. (Bibliotheca Eruditorum, 26).

3350. SORRENTINO (Tommaso). Storia del processo penale: dall'ordalia all'inquisizione. Soveria Mannelli, Rubbettino, 99, 212 p.

3351. Specula principum. A cura di Angela DE BENEDICTIS con la collaborazione di Annamaria PISAPIA. Frankfurt am Main, Klostermann, 99, XXVIII-289 p. (Ius Commune. Sonderheft, 117).

3352. STOCLET (Alain J.). Immunes ab omni teloneo. Étude de diplomatique, de philologie et d'histoire sur l'exemption de tonlieux au haut Moyen Âge et spécialement sur la Praeceptio de navibus. Bruxelles et Roma, Institut historique belge de Rome, 99, 576 p. (tab., graph., ill.). (Bibliothèque de l'Institut historique belge de Rome, 45).

3353. STORTI STORCHI (Claudia). Intorno ai costituti pisani della legge e dell'uso (secolo XII). Napoli, Liguori, 99, 180 p. (Europa mediterranea. Quaderni, 13).

3354. VALLONE (Giancarlo). Le istituzioni feudali dell'Italia meridionale tra Medioevo ed Antico Regime. L'area salentina. Roma, Viella, 99, 270 p. (Ius nostrum. Studi e testi pubblicati dall'Istituto di storia del diritto italiano dell'Università di Roma "La Sapienza").

3355. WORMALD (Patrick). Legal culture in the early medieval West. Law as text, image and experience. London a. Rio Grande, Hambledon Press, 99, XXII-401 p. – IDEM. The making of English law: king Alfred to the twelfth century. Vol. 1. Legislation and its limits. Oxford, Blackwell, 99, 574 p.

Cf. n° 3152

§ 8. Economic and social history.

* 3356. COLEMAN (E.). The state of research. The Italian communes. Recent work and current trends. *Journal of medieval history*, 99, 25, p. 373-397.

** 3357. Gregers Mattsons kostbok for Stegeborg 1487–1492 utgiven med kommentarer och register. (Le Livre des comptes de Greger Mattsson pour le ravitaillement de Stegeborg, 1487–1492, édité avec des commentaires et un index). Ed. par Zeth ALVERED. Uppsala, Svenska fornskriftsällskapet, 99, 314 p. (ill.).

3358. AKASAKA (Shunichi). Kami ni tou: Chusei ni okeru chitsujo, seigi, shimpan. (Judicium dei: the medieval social order and justice). Kyoto, Sagano Shuppan, 99, 277 p.

3359. ÁLVAREZ BORGE (Ignacio). Communidades locales y transformaciones sociales en la Alta Edad Media. Hampshire (Wessex) y el sur de Castilla, un estudio comparativo. Logroño, Universidad de La Rioja, Servicio de Publicaciones, 99, 198 p. (Biblioteca de Investigación, 25).

3360. Archéologie des espaces agraires méditerranéens au Moyen âge. Actes du colloque de Murcie (Espagne) tenu du 8 au 12 mai 1992. Ed. por Andrés BAZZANA. Rome, École française de Rome et Madrid, Casa de Velázquez et Murcie, Ayuntamiento de Murcia, 99, 496 p. (ill., maps). (Collection de l'Ecole française de Rome, 105).

3361. Aristocratic women in medieval France. Ed. by Theodore EVERGATES. Philadelphia, University of Pennsylvania Press, 99, 272 p. (geneal. tables, maps). (The Middle Ages series).

3362. ASENJO GONZÁLEZ (Maria). Espacio y sociedad en la Soria medieval, siglos XIII-XV. Soria, Ediciones de la Excma-Diputación provincial de Soria, 99, 607 p. (maps, tab., graph.).

3363. Authority and community in the Middle Ages. Ed. by Rhiannon PURDIE, Donald MOWBRAY and Ian WEI. Stroud, Sutton, 99, XVIII-186 p. (ill.).

3364. BALDWIN (John W.). Aristocratic life in medieval France. The romances of Jean Renart and Ger bert de Montreuil, 1190–1230. Baltimore a. London, Johns Hopkins U. P., 99, XVII-359 p.

3365. BARDSLEY (Sandy). Women's work reconsidered: gender and wage differentiation in late Medieval England. *Past and present*, 99, 165, p. 3-29.

3366. BENNETT (Judith M.). A medieval life: Cecilia Penifader of Brigstock, c. 1295–1344. Boston a. London, McGraw-Hill College, 99, X-147 p. (ill., maps).

3367. CARDON (Dominique). La draperie au Moyen Age. Essor d'une grande industrie européenne. Paris, CNRS Editions, 99, 661 p.

3368. CASTAGNETTI (Andrea). Fra i vassalli: marchesi, conti, capitanei, cittadini e rurali (dalla documentazione del Capitolo della cattedrale di Verona: secoli X–metà XII). Verona, Libreria universitaria editrice, 99, 259 p.

3369. Castrum 5. Archéologie des espaces agraires méditerranéens au Moyen Âge. Actes du Colloque de Murcie (Espagne) tenu du 8 au 12 mai 1992. Éd. André BAZZANA. Madrid, Casa de Velázquez et Roma, École française de Rome et Murcia, Ayuntamiento de Murcia, 99, 496 p. (maps, ill., graph.). (Collection de l'École française de Rome, 105 – Collection de la Casa de Velázquez, 55).

3370. COURTENAY (William J.). Parisian scholars in early fourtheen century: a social portrait. Cambridge, Cambridge U. P., 99, XIX-284 p. (tab., maps).

3371. DE ROOVER (Raymond Adrien). Money, banking and credit in medieval Bruges. Italian merchant bankers, Lombards and money-changers: a study in the origins of banking. London, Routledge, 99, XVII-420 p. (pl., ill.). (The emergence of international business, 1200–1800, 2).

3372. DERVILLE (Alain). L'agriculture du Nord au Moyen Âge (Artois, Cambrésis, Flandre wallonne). Villeneuve d'Ascq, Presses Universitaires du Septentrion, 99, 332 p. (tab., graph., maps). (Histoire et civilisation).

3373. DOLLINGER (Philippe). The German Hansa. London, Routledge, 99, XXII-474 p. (ill., maps). (The emergence of international business, 1200–1800, 1).

3374. DUARTE (Luís Miguel). Justiça e criminalidade no Portugal medievo (1459–1481). Coimbra, Fundaçao Calouste Gulbenkian, Fundacao para a Ciencia e a Tecnologia, Ministerio da Ciencia e da Tecnologia, 99, 750 p. (Textos universitários de ciências sociais e humanas).

3375. ELSØE JENSEN (Jørgen). Danmarks middelalderlige byplaner. Bd 6. Syd- og Vestsjælland. (Plans de villes médiévales au Danemark. Tome 6: Sjælland du sud et de l'ouest). København, Dansk Komité for Byhistorie, Skov – og Naturstyrelsen, Odense, Universitetsforlag, 99, 190 p. (ill.).

3376. Expansió catalana (L') a la Mediterrània a la baixa Edad Mitjana. Acters del Séminaire/Seminari organitzat per la Casa de Velázquez (Madrid) i la Institució Milà i Fontanals (CSIC, Barcelona), celebrat a Barcelona el 20 d'abril de 1998. Ed. Maria Teresa FERRE I MALLOL i Damien COULON. Barcelone, CSIC, Institució Milà i Fontanals, Departament d'estudis medievals, 99, IX-208 p. (Anejos de Anuario de Estudios medievales. Collección de Monografías del Departamento de Estudios medievales del CSIC en barcelona, 36).

3377. Femmes et pouvoirs des femmes à Byzance et en Occident (VIe–XIe siècles). Colloque international organisé les 28, 29 et 30 mars 1996 à Bruxelles et Villeneuve d'Ascq. Éd. par Stéphane LEBECQ. Villeneuve d'Ascq, Centre de recherche sur l'histoire de l'Europe du Nord-Ouest, Université Charles de Gaulle-Lille 3, 99, 256 p. (ill., maps). (Centre de recherche sur l'histoire de l'Europe du Nord-Ouest, 19).

3378. Fiscalité (La) des villes au Moyen Âge (Occident méditerranéen). Vol. 2. Les systèmes fiscaux. Éd. par Denis MENJOT et Manuel SANCHEZ MARTINEZ. Toulouse, Privat, 99, 540 p. (tab., maps, graph.).

3379. Fondations et oeuvres charitables au Moyen Âge. Actes du 121e Congrès national des sociétés historiques et scientifiques, section d'histoire médiévale et de philologie, Nice, 26–31 octobre 1998. Éd. de Jean DUFOUR et Henri PLATELLE. Paris, Éditions du C. T. H. S., 99, 338 p. (maps, tab., ill.).

3380. FOSSIER (Robert). L'histoire économique et sociale du Moyen âge occidental: questions, sources, documents commentés. Turnhout, Brepols, 99, 408 p. (ill., maps). (L'atelier du médiéviste, 6).

3381. GANE (Robert). Le chapitre de Notre-Dame de Paris au XIVe siècle: étude sociale d'un groupe canonial. Éd. par Claudine BILLOT. Saint-Étienne, Université de Saint-Étienne, 99, 432 p. (pl., tab.). (Centre européen de recherches sur les congrégation et les ordres religieux. Travaux et recherches, 12).

3382. GERMAIN (René). La France centrale médiévale. Pouvoir, peuplement, société, économie, culture. Saint-Étienne, Publications de l'Université, 99, 323 p. (Centre interdisciplinaire d'études et de recherches sur les structures régionales).

3383. GRDINA (Igor), ŠTIH (Peter). Spomini Helene Kottanner: ženski glas iz srednjega veka. (Helena Kottanner's memoirs: a woman's voice from the Middle Ages). Ljubljana, Nova revija, 99, 124 p. (Zbirka Korenine).

3384. Haec sunt statuta: le corporazioni medievali nelle miniature bolognesi. Rocca di Vignola, 27 marzo–11 luglio 1999. A cura di Massimo MEDICA. Modena, F.C. Panini, 99, 211 p. (ill.).

3385. HARVEY (Margaret). The English in Rome, 1362–1420: portrait of an expatriate community. New York, Cambridge U. P., 99, [XIII]-278 p. (maps). (Cambridge studies in medieval life and thought).

3386. HOCQUET (Jean-Claude). Denaro, navi e mercanti a Venezia 1200–1600. Roma, Il veltro, 99, 342 p.

3387. HUNT (Ediwin S.), MURRAY (James M.). A history of business in medieval Europe, 1200–1550. Cambridge, Cambridge U. P., 99, IX-277 p. (Cambridge Medieval Textbooks).

3388. JELASKA (Zdravka). Trogirska srednjovjekovna obitelj (XIII.–XIV. stoljeće). (The medieval family in Trogir, 13th–14th Century). Povijesni priloz, 99, 18, p. 9-52.

3389. KOCH (Matthias). Siedlung und Landschaft vor den Toren von Bordeaux: die Pfarreien Begles und Villenave d'Ornon im Mittelalter und in der frühen Neuzeit. Bonn, Bouvier, 99, 659 p. (ill.). (Pariser historische Studien, 48).

3390. KUSMAN (David). Jean de Mirabello dit van Haelen (ca. 1280–1333). Haute finance et Lombards en Brabant dans le premier tiers du XIVe siècle. Revue belge de philologie et d'histoire, 99, 77, 4, p. 843-931.

3391. LEMESLE (Bruno). La société aristocratique dans le Haut-Maine (XIe–XIIe siècles). Rennes, Presses Universitaires de Rennes, 99, 315 p. (maps, graph., tab., ill.). (Histoire).

3392. LOUD (G. A.). Coinage, wealth and plunder in the age of Robert Guiscard. English historical review, 99, 114, 458, p. 815-843.

3393. MANANCHIKOVA (Nelli P.). Dubrovnik XIII–pervoj poloviny XV veka: Problemy torgovly. (Dubrovnik in the 13th–the 1st half of the 15th century: problems of trade). Voronezh, Izd. Voronezh. un-ta, 99, 207 p. (ill., bibl.).

3394. MARSHALL (Richard K.). The local merchants of Prato: small entrepreneurs in the late medieval economy. Baltimore a. London, Johns Hopkins U. P., 99, XIX-191 p. (The Johns Hopkins University studies in historical and political science, 117th).

3395. Martinet (Le) d'Orthez: violence, pactes et pouvoir judiciaire en Béarn à la fin du Moyen Âge. Éd. par Jean Pierre BARRAQUÉ. Biarritz, Atlantica, 99, 309 p. (maps).

3396. MATE (Mavis E.). Women in medieval English society. Cambridge a. New York, Cambridge U. P., 99, 114 p. (New studies in economic and social history, 39).

3397. Medieval crime and social control. Ed. by Barbara A. HANAWALT and David WALLACE. Minneapolis a. London, University of Minnesota Press, 99, XVI-259 p. (Medieval cultures, 16).

3398. MEIKLE (Maureen M.), EWAN (Elizabeth). Women in Scotland, c.1100–c.1750. East Linton, Tuckwell Press, 99, XXX-272 p. (pl., ill.).

3399. MORIMOTO (Yoshiki). Pour une étude à l'échelle européenne. A propos d'un ouvrage récent sur la formation du manoir anglais. Revue belge de philologie et d'histoire, 99, 77, 4, p. 1079-1091.

3400. MYRDAL (Janken). Det svenska jordbrukets historia. Band 2. Jordbruket under feodalismen 1000–1700. (Histoire de l'agriculture suédoise. Tome 2. L'Agriculture à l'époque du féodalisme). Stockholm, Natur och Kultur / LT i samarbete med Nordiska Museet, 99, 407 p. (ill.).

3401. NICHOLAS (David), PREVENIER (Walter). Gentse stadts- en beljuwsrekeningen (1365–1376). Bruxelles, Académie royale de Belgique, 99, XXX-539 p. (Commission royale d'Histoire, Coll. in 4°).

3402. Niveaux (Les) de vie au Moyen Âge: mesures, perceptions et représentations. Actes du colloque international de Spa, 21–25 octobre 1998. Éd. par Jean-Pierre SOSSON. Louvain-la-Neuve, Academia-Bruylant, 99, 462 p.

3403. OLIVEIRA (Luís Filipe). A casa dos Coutinhos. Linhagem, espaço e poder (1360–1452). Cascais, Patrimonia Historica, 99, 257 p.

3404. ÖZ (Mehmet). Some notes on the changes in the early Ottoman society from the 14th to the late 15th century. Hacettepe Üniversitesi Edebiyat Fakültesi Dergisi, 99, p. 33-42.

3405. PANERO (Francesco). Schiavi servi e villani nell'Italia medievale. Torino, Paravia, 99, 483 p. (Le testimonianze del passato. Fonti e studi, 11).

3406. PASTOR (Reyna). Transacciones sin mercado: instituciones, propiedad y redes sociales en la Galicia monástica 1200–1300. Madrid, Consejo Superior de Investigaciones Cientificas, 99, 251 p. (pl., ill.). (Biblioteca de historia, 36).

3407. REDON (Odile). Lo spazio di una città. Siena e la Toscana meridionale (secoli XIII–XIV). Roma, Viella, 99, 304 p. (I libri di Viella, 17).

3408. REXROTH (Frank). Das Milieu der Nacht. Obrigkeit und Randgruppen im spätmittelalterlichen London. Göttingen, Vandenhoeck und Ruprecht, 99, 450 p. (ill., pl.). (Veröffentlichungen des Max-Planck-Instituts für Geschichte, 153).

3409. RIDYARD (Susan J.). Chivalry, knighthood, and war in the Middle Ages. Sewanee, University of the South Press, 99, 218 p. (Sewanee medieval studies, 9).

3410. RJABOVA (Tat'jana B.). Zhenshchina v istorii zapadnoevropejskogo srednevekov'ja. (Woman in the West European Middle Ages). Ivanovskij gos. un-t. Ivanovo, Junona, 99, 211 p. (bibl.).

3411. ROSENWEIN (Barbara H.). Negotiating space: power, restraint, and privileges of immunity in early medieval Europe. Manchester, Manchester U. P., 99, XXII-267 p. (ill., maps).

3412. SAKAGUCHI (Kokichi). Chusei no ningenkan to rekishi. (Images of human and history in medieval world: Franciscus, Joachim, Bonaventura). Tokyo, Sobunsha, 99, 343 p.

3413. SAUNIER (Annie). "Le pauvre malade" dans le cadre hospitalier médiéval: France du Nord, vers 1300–1500. Paris, Arguments, 99, II-286 p. (ill., maps).

3414. Sermoneta e i Caetani. Dinamiche politiche, sociali e culturali di un territorio tra medioevo ed età moderna. Atti del convegno della Fondazione Camillo Caetani, Roma-Sermoneta, 16–19 giugno 1993. A cura di Luigi FIORANI. Roma, L'Erma di Bretschneider, 99, 701 p. (ill.). (Pubblicazioni della Fondazione Camillo Caetani. Studi e documenti d'archivio, 9).

3415. Showing status: representation of social positions in the late Middle Ages. Ed. by Willem Pieter BLOCKMANS and A. JANSE. Turnhout, Brepols, 99, VII-491 p. (ill.). (Medieval texts and cultures of Northern Europe, 2).

3416. SINGMAN (Jeffrey L.). Daily life in medieval Europe. Westport a. London, Greenwood Press, 99, XIX-268 p. (ill.). (Daily life through history).

3417. Sociétés méridionales (Les) à l'âge féodal (Espagne, Italie et sud de la France, X^e–XIIIe siècles). Hommage à Pierre Bonnassie. Textes réunis par Hélène DÉBAX. Toulouse, Univ. Toulouse-Le Mirail, 99, 433 p.

3418. *Vacat.*

3419. SUTHERLAND (Elizabeth). Five Euphemias: women in medieval Scotland, 1200–1420. London, Constable, 99, 282 p. (pl., ill., tab., maps).

3420. SWABEY (Fiona). Medieval gentlewoman: life in a widow's household in the later Middle Ages. Stroud, Sutton, 99, XI-210 p. (ill.)

3421. SWANSON (Heather). Medieval British towns. London, St. Martin's Press a. Macmillan, 99, 161 p. (map). (Social history in perspective).

3422. TAMBURRI BARIAIN (Pascual). Spagnoli a Bologna (1299–1330). Organizzazione e identità di una comunità studentesca. *Rivista storica italiana*, 99, 111, 1, p. 155-219.

3423. Tempi e spazi di vita femminile tra medioevo ed età moderna. A cura di Silvana SEIDEL MENCHI, Anne SCHUTTE JACOBSON e Thomas KUEHN. Bologna, Il mulino, 99, 577 p. (ill.). (Annali dell'Istituto storico italo-germanico. Quaderno, 51).

3424. TOGNETTI (Sergio). Il banco Cambini: affari e mercati di una compagnia mercantile-bancaria nella Firenze del XV secolo. Firenze, L. S. Olschki, 99, IX-398 p. (Biblioteca storica toscana. Serie I, 37). – IDEM. Problemi di vettovagliamento cittadino e misure di politica annonaria a Firenze nel XV secolo (1430–1500). *Archivio storico italiano*, 99, 157, 581, p. 419-452.

3425. Transferts (Les) patrimoniaux en Europe occidentale, VIIIe–Xe siècle (I). Actes de la table ronde de Rome, 6, 7 et 8 mai 1999. Éd. par Françoise BOUGARD et Régine LE JAN. *Melanges de l'École fraçaise de Rome. Moyen Âge*, 111, 99, 2, p. 487-972.

3426. UNDERHILL (Frances A.). For her good estate: the life of Elizabeth de Burgh. Basingstoke, Macmillan Press, 99, IX-221 p. (New Middle Ages).

3427. UNGER (Richard W.). Feeding Low Countries: the grain trade in the fifteenth century. *Revue belge de philologie et d'histoire*, 99, 77, 2, p. 329-358.

3428. VAN BAVEL (B. J. P.), THEON (Erik). Land productivity and agro-systems in the North Sea area, middle ages-20th century: elements for comparison. Turnhout, Brepols, 99, 382 p. (CORN publication series).

3429. VAN BAVEL (B. J. P.). Transitie en continuïteit: de bezitsverhoudingen en de plattelandseconomie in het westelijke gedeelte van het Gelderse rivierengebied, ca. 1300–ca. 1570. Hilversum, Verloren, 99, 720 p. (maps). (Werken Gelre, 52).

3430. WEBER (Andreas Otto). Studien zum Weinbau der altbayerischen Kloster im Mittelalter: Altbayern, österreichischer Donauraum, Südtirol. Stuttgart, Steiner, 99, 477 p. (taf., ill.). (Vierteljahrschrift für Sozial- und Wirtschsftgeschichte. Beihefte, 141).

3431. WETTLAUFER (Jörg). Das Herrenrecht der ersten Nacht. Hochzeit, Herrschaft und Heiratsins im Mittelalter und in der frühen Neuzeit. Frankfurt u. New York, Campus Verlag, 99, 430 p. (ill.). (Campus historische Studien, 27).

3432. WHEELER (Bonnie). Listening to Heloise: the voice of a twelfth-century woman. Basingstoke, Macmillan, 99, XXII-394 p. (The new Middle Ages).

3433. WILLIS (Sherry L.), REID (James D.). Life in the middle: psychological and social development in middle age. San Diego a. London, Academic Press, 99, XVII-304 p. (ill.).

Cf. n° 1039

§ 9. History of civilization, literature, technology and education.

a. Civilisation

* 3434. MOSTERT (Marco). A bibliography of works on medieval communication. *In*: New approaches to medieval communication [Cf. n° 3481], p. p. 193-318.

* 3435. RIBÉMONT (Bernard). Repères bibliographiques sur les encyclopédies médiévales de l'Occident latin (XIIe–XVe siècles). *Cahiers de recherches médiévales*, 99, 6, p. 99-110.

* 3436. SKUBISZEWSKI (Piotr), DEBIÈS (Marie-Hélène), CORRE (K.). Bibliographie 1999. *Cahiers de civilisation médiévale*, 99, 42, 168 B, 310 p.

3437. AALBÆCK-NIELSEN (Kai). Kærlighed i middelalderen. (L'amour au Moyen Age). København, Gyldendal, 99, 310 p. (ill.).

3438. Anima e corpo nella cultura medievale. Atti del V Convegno di studi della Società per lo studio del pensiero medievale, Venezia, 25–28 settembre 1995. A cura di Carla CASAGRANDE e Silvana VECCHIO. Tavarnuzze, SISMEL – Edizioni del Galluzzo, 99, XIII-332 p. (ill.). (Millennio medievale, 15. Atti di convegni, 3).

3439. Animal (L') exemplaire au Moyen Âge, V^e–XVe siècle. Éd. par Jacques BERLIOZ et Marie-Anne POLO DE BEAULIEU. Rennes, Presses Universitaires de Rennes, 99, 333 p. (tab.). (Histoire).

3440. BOISSELLIER (Stéphane). Naissance d'une identité portugaise. La vie rurale entre Tage et Guadiana, de l'Islam à la Reconquête (X^e–XIVe siècles). Lisboa, Imprensa Nacional, Casa de Moeda, 99, 707 p. (ill., maps, graph.). (Estudos Gerais, Série Universitária).

3441. Britain and Ireland, 900–1300: insular responses to medieval European change. Ed. by Brendan SMITH. Cambridge a. New York, Cambridge U. P., 99, XV-283 p.

3442. CAROZZI (Claude), TAVIANI CAROZZI (Huguette). La fin des temps. Terreurs et prophéties au Moyen Âge. Paris, Flammarion, 99, 248 p. (Champs, 446).

3443. Christians, Muslims, and Jews in medieval and early modern Spain: interaction and cultural change. Ed. by Mark D. MEYERSON and Edward D. ENGLISH. Notre Dame, University of Notre Dame Press, 99, XXI-322 p. (map). (Notre Dame conferences in medieval studies, 8).

3444. CONDE (Manuel Sílvio). Horizontes do Portugal medieval: estudos históricos. Carnaxide, Patrimonia, 99, 404 p. (ill., maps). (Patrimonia historica, Estudos).

3445. COWELL (Andrew). At play in the tavern: signs, coins, and bodies in the Middle Ages. Ann Arbor, University of Michigan Press, 99, 270 p. (Stylus).

3446. Crossing boundaries: issues of cultural and individual identity in the Middle Ages and the Renaissance. Ed. by Sally MAC KEE. Turnhout, Brepols, 99, XII-283 p. (ill., ports, music). (Arizona studies in the Middle Ages and the Renaissance, 3).

3447. Dagliv i Danmarks middelalder: en arkeologisk kulturhistorie. (La Vie quotidienne au Moyen Age au Danemark: une histoire de la civilisation d'après les données archéologiques). Red. par Else RŒSDAHL. København, Nordisk Forlag, 99, 420 p. (ill.).

3448. Death and dying in the Middle Ages. Ed. by Edelgard E. DU BRUCK and Barbara I. GUSICK. New York a. Canterbury, Peter Lang, 99, XI-515 p. (ill.). (Studies in the humanities, 45).

3449. Discursos y representaciones en la Edad Media. Actas de las VI Jornadas Medievales. Ed. por Concepción COMPANY, Lillian von der WALDE MOHENO y Aurelio GONZÁLEZ. Mexico, Universidad Nacional Autonoma de Mexico, El Colegio de Mexico, 99, X-601 p. (ill.). (Publicaciones de Medievalia, 22).

3450. EPP (Verena). Amicitia: zur Geschichte personaler, sozialer, politischer und geistlicher Beziehungen im frühen Mittelalter. Stuttgart, A. Hiersemann, 99, VI-362 p. (Monographien zur Geschichte des Mittelalters, 44).

3451. Fiestas, juegos y espectáculos en la España medieval. Actas del VII Curso de Cultura Medieval, celebrado en Aguilar de Campoo (Palencia) del 18 al 21 de septiembre de 1995. Ed. por Miguel Angel GARCÍA GUINEA. Madrid, Ediciones Polifemo y Aguilar de Campoo, Fundacion Sta. Maria la Real, Centro de Estudios del Romanico, 99, 278 p. (ill.).

3452. FREEDMAN (Paul H.). Images of the medieval peasant. Stanford, Stanford U. P., 99, XVI-459 p. (ill.). (Figurae).

3453. Friendship in medieval Europe. Ed. by Julian HASELDINE. Stroud, Sutton, 99, 320 p.

3454. GARCÍA DÍAZ (Isabel). La escritura en Cartagena en el siglo XV. Murcia, Ayuntamiento de Cartagena y Real Academia Alfonso X el Sabio, 99, 155 p. (ill., facs.).

3455. GATTO (Ludovico). Medioevo quotidiano: motivi e modelli di vita. Roma, Editori Riuniti, 99, 279 p. (Biblioteca di storia).

3456. GOUGUENHEIM (Sylvain). Les fausses terreurs de l'an Mil: attente de la fin des temps ou approfondissement de la foi. Paris, Picard, 99, 231 p.

3457. HASSIG (Debra). The mark of the beast: the medieval bestiary in art, life, and literature. New York a. London, Garland, 99, XXI-219 p. (ill.). (Garland medieval casebooks, 22).

3458. Ideologie e pratiche del reimpiego nell'alto Medioevo. Centro italiano di studi sull'alto Medioevo, XLVI Settimana di studio, Spoleto 16–21 aprile 1998. Spoleto, Centro italiano di studi sull'alto Medioevo, 99, 2 vol., XIV-1114 p. (pl., ill.). (Atti delle Settimane di studio, 46). [Cf. n[os] <scelta> 267, 566, 719, 725, 1288, 1429, 3912.]

3459. Images (Les) dans les sociétés médiévales: pour une histoire comparèe. Actes du colloque international organisé par l'Institut historique belge de Rome, en collaboration avec l'École française de Rome et l'Université libre de Bruxelles (Rome, Academia Belgica, 19–20 huin 1998). Éd. par Jean-Marie SANSTERRE et Jean-Claude SCHMITT. Bruxelles, Academia Belgica, 99, 279 p. (Bulletin de l'Institut historique belge de Rome, 69).

3460. Imaginaire (L') du sabbat. Édition critique des textes les plus anciens (1430 c.–1440 c.). Éd. par Martine OSTORERO, Agostino PARAVICINI BAGLIANI et Katherine UTZ TREMP. Lausanne, Université de Lausanne, Section d'Histoire, 99, 571 p. (ill., maps). (Cahiers lausannois d'Historie médiévale, 26).

3461. KATIČIĆ (Radoslav). Literatur- und Geistesgeschichte des kroatischen Frühmittelalters. Wien,

Österreichischen Akademie der Wissenschaften, 99, VIII-655 p. (Schriften der Balkan-Kommission. Philologische Abteilung, 40).

3462. Kunst und Kultur der Karolingerzeit. Karl der Grosse und Papst Leo III. in Paderborn. Beiträge zum Katalog der Ausstellung, Paderborn 1999. Hrsg. v. Christoph STIEGEMANN und Matthias WEMHOFF. Mainz, P. von Zabern, 99, X-744 p. (ill., facs., maps, music, plans).

3463. LA GUARDIA (David). The iconography of power: the French nouvelle at the end of the Middle Ages. Newark a. London, University of Delaware Press, Associated University Presses, 99, 178 p.

3464. LE GOFF (Jacques). Un autre Moyen âge. Paris, Gallimard, 99, 1372 p. (ill.). (Quarto).

3465. LECOUTEUX (Claude). Chasses fantastiques et cohortes de la nuit au Moyen Âge. Paris, Imago, 99, 242 p. (ill.).

3466. LECUPRE-DESJARDIN (E.). Les lumières de la ville: recherches sur l'utilisation de la lumière dans les cérémonies bourguignonnes (XIVe–XVe siècle). *Revue historique*, 99, 123, 609, p. 23-44.

3467. LOCHRIE (Karma). Covert operations: the medieval uses of secrecy. Philadelphia, University of Pennsylvania Press, 99, 292 p. (Middle Ages series).

3468. LUTTERBACH (Hubertus). Sexualität im Mittelalter: eine Kulturstudie anhand von Bussbüchern des 6. bis 12. Jahrhunderts. Köln u. Wien, Böhlau, 99, IX-299 p. (Beihefte zum Archiv für Kulturgeschichte, 43).

3469. Magie et illusion au moyen âge. Aix-en-Provence, CUER MA, Université de Provence, Centre d'Aix, 99, 634 p. (ill.). (Sénéfiance, 42).

3470. Man (The) of many devices, who wandered full many ways. Festschrift in honor of János M. Bak. Ed. by Marcell SEBOK and Balazs NAGY. Budapest, Central European U. P., 99, XVII-708 p. (ill.).

3471. Medieval and Renaissance Venice. Ed. by Donald E. QUELLER, Ellen E. KITTELL and Thomas F. MADDEN. Urbana, University of Illinois Press, 99, VIII-345 p. (ill.).

3472. MENUGE (Noël James), LEWIS (Katherine J.), PHILLIPS (Kim M.). Young medieval women. Stroud, Sutton, 99, XX-202 p. (ill.)

3473. Micrologus. Natura, scienze e società medievali / Nature, sciences and medieval societies, Vol. 7. Il cadavere / The corpse. Tavernelle, SISMEL, Edizioni del Galluzzo, 99, 552 p. (ill.).

3474. Middelalderens Danmark: kultur og samfund fra troskifte til reformation. (Le Danemark médiéval: culture et société de la conversion à la Réforme). Red. par Per INGESMAN. København, Gad, 99, 375 p. (ill.).

3475. MIKHAJLOVA (Tat'jana A.). Irlandskoe predanie o Suibne Bezumnom, ili vzgljad iz XII veka v VII. (The Irish legend of Buile Suibne: a look from the 12th to the 7th century; [with a Russian transl. of Buile Suibne, p. 357-422]). Moskovskij gos. un-t im. M.V. Lomonosova, Filol. f-t. Moskva, Izd-vo Mosk. un-ta, 99, 423 p. (ill., bibl.; ind.).

3476. MITCHELL (Linda Elizabeth). Women in medieval Western European culture. New York a. London, Garland, 99, XIV-408 p. (ill., facs., ports). (Garland reference library of the humanities, 2007).

3477. MOISL (Hermann). Lordship and tradition in barbarian Europe. Lewiston a. Lampeter, E. Mellen Press, 99, XV-203 p. (Studies in classics, 10).

3478. MURRAY (Alexander). Suicide in the Middle Ages. Vol. 1. The violent against themselves. Oxford, Oxford U. P., 99, XXIII-485 p.

3479. MURRAY (Jacqueline). Conflicted identities and multiple masculinities: men in the medieval West. New York a. London, Garland, 99, XX-308 p. (ill.). (Garland medieval casebooks).

3480. MUZZARELLI (Maria Giuseppina). Guardaroba medievale: vesti e società dal XIII al XVI secolo. Bologna, Il Mulino, 99, 380 p. (Saggi, 503).

3481. New approaches to medieval communication. Ed. by Marco MOSTERT. Turnhout, Brepols, 99, VIII-318 p. (ill., map). (Utrecht studies in medieval literacy, 1). [Cf. n° <choice> 3434.]

3482. NICOLLE (David), MAC BRIDE (Angus). Armies of medieval Russia, 750–1250. Oxford, Osprey Military, 99, 48 p. (ill., maps). (Men-at-arms series, 333).

3483. Queer Iberia: sexualities, cultures, and crossings from the Middle Ages to the Renaissance. Ed. by Josiah BLACKMORE and Gregory S. HUTCHESON. Durham a. London, Duke U. P., 99, VIII-478 p. (Series Q).

3484. Rano doba hrvatske kulture. (Croatia in the early middle ages: a cultural survey). Ed. Ivan SUPIČIĆ. Zagreb, Hrvatska akademija znanosti i umjetnosti, 99, 633 p.

3485. RICHÉ (Pierre). Les grandeurs de l'an mille. Paris, Bartillat, 99, 367 p. (ill.)

3486. RICHTER (Michael). Ireland and her neighbours in the seventh century. Dublin, Four Courts Press, 99, 256 p.

3487. SCHULER (Stefan). Vitruv im Mittelalter. Die Rezeption von De Architectura von der Antike bis in die frühe Neuzeit. Köln, Böhlau, 99, IX-463 (ill.). (Pictura et poesis. Interdisziplinäre Studien zum Verhältnis von Literatur und Kunst, 12).

3488. Seanchas. Studies in early and medieval Irish archaeology, history and literature in honour of Francis J. Byrne. Ed. by Alfred P. SMYTH. Dublin, Four Courts Press, 99, XXII-478 p. (ill., maps).

3489. SHEPARD (Laurie). Courting power. Persuasion and politics in the early thirteenth century. New York a. London, Garland, 99, XXII-240 p. (Garland reference library of the humanities, 2095).

3490. SMITH (Brendan). Colonisation and conquest in medieval Ireland. The English in Louth, 1170–1330. Cambridge, Cambridge U. P., 99, XVI-189 p. (maps). (Cambridge studies in medieval life and thought, 42).

3491. STANNARD (Jerry), KAY (Richard), STANNARD (Katherine E.). Herbs and herbalism in the Middle Ages and Renaissance. Aldershot, Ashgate, 99, XVI-322 p. (ill.). (Variorum collected studies series, 650).

3492. SUPICIC (Ivo). Croatia in the early Middle Ages: a cultural survey. London, Philip Wilson, 99, 633 p. (ill., maps). (Croatia and Europe, 1).

3493. SWANSON (R. N.). The twelfth-century Renaissance. Manchester, Manchester U. P., 99, IX-240 p. (ill., facs.).

3494. THEUWS (F.), ROYMANS (Nico). Land and ancestors: cultural dynamics in the Urnfield period and the Middle Ages in the southern Netherlands. Amsterdam, Amsterdam U. P., 99, 399 p. (plan). (Amsterdam archaeological studies, 4).

3495. Thirteenth century England. Proceedings of the seventh conference held at St. Aidan's College, Durham, September 1997. Ed. by R. H. BRITNELL, Michael PRESTWICH and Robin FRAME. Woodbridge, Boydell Press, 99, XI-254 p.

3496. THOMSON (Francis J.). The reception of Byzantine culture in mediaeval Russia. Aldershot, Ashgate, 99, XXII-390 p. (Variorum collected studies series, 590).

3497. ULEWICZ (Tadeusz). Iter Romano-Italicum Polonorum, Czyli, O zwiazkach umyslowo-kulturalnych Polski z Wlochami w wiekach srednich i renesansie. Krakow, Universitas, 99, 311 p. (ill.).

3498. VAN DEUSEN (Nancy). The place of the Psalms in the intellectual culture in the Middle Ages. Albany, State University of New York, 99, XV-220 p. (ill.). (SUNY series in medieval studies).

3499. VAN HOUTS (Elisabeth M. C.). Memory and gender in medieval Europe, 900–1200. Toronto a. Buffalo, University of Toronto Press, 99, XII-196 p.ù

3500. WILENTZ (Sean). Rites of power: symbolism, ritual and politics since the Middle Ages. Philadelphia, University of Pennsylvania Press, 99, X-344 p. (ill.).

3501. WILHELM-SCHAFFER (Irmgard). Gottes Beamter und Spielmann des Teufels: der Tod in Spätmittelalter und Früher Neuzeit. Köln, Böhlau, 99, X-436 p. (ill.).

3502. WILLIAMS (David). Deformed discours. The function of the monster in mediaeval thought and literature. Exeter, University of Exeter Press, 99, XII-392 p. (ill.).

Cf. n°s 79, 349, 494, 5293

b. *Literature*

* 3503. KLINGEBIEL (Kathrin). Bibliographie linquistique (1983–1997) de l'ancien occitan. Birmingham, Association internationale d'Étude occitanes a. University of Birmingham, III-296 p. (Association internationale d'Études occitanes, 8).

** 3504. CHAUCER (Geoffrey). The romaunt of the rose. Ed. by Charles DAHLBERG. Norman, University of Oklahoma Press, 99, XXIV-343 p. (A variorum edition of the works of Geoffrey Chaucer, 7).

** 3505. Electronic Beowulf. Ed. by Andrew PRESCOTT and Kevin S. KIERNAN. London, British Library a. Ann Arbor, University of Michigan Press, 99, 2 CD-ROM.

** 3506. GUY OF AMIENS. The Carmen de Hastingae proelio. Ed. by Frank BARLOW. Oxford, Clarendon Press, 99, XCI-55 p. (ill., maps). (Oxford medieval texts).

** 3507. HOCCLEVE (Thomas). Complaint and Dialogue. Ed. by J. A. BURROW. Oxford, Published for the Early English Text Society by the Oxford U. P., 99, LXX-140 p. (ill.). (Early English Text Society, 313).

** 3508. Math uab Mathonwy: text from the diplomatic edition of the White Book of Rhydderch, by J. GWENOGVRYN EVANS. Ed. by Patrick K. FORD. Belmont, Ford & Bailie Publishers, 99, XXXI-71 p. (ill.).

** 3509. Mocedades (Las) de Rodrigo: estudios críticos, manuscrito y edición. Ed. por Matthew BAILEY. London, King's College London, Centre for Late Antique & Medieval Studies, 99, IX-216 p. (pl.) (King's College London medieval studies, 15).

** 3510. Passion catalane-occitane. Éd. par Aileen Ann MACDONALD. Geneve, Droz, 99, 367 p. (Textes littéraires français, 518) [Bibliothèque nationale, Paris, Fr. nouv. acq. 4232, folios 19-76].

** 3511. PÉREZ GONZÀLEZ (Maurilio). G. Manetti y la traducción en el siglo XV: edición crítica del "Apologeticus", libro V. León, Ediciones Universidad de León, 99, 151 p.

** 3512. PETRARCA (Francesco). De sui ipsius et multorum ignorantia / Della mia ignoranza e di quella di molti altri. A cura di Enrico FENZI. Milano, Mursia, 99, 541 p. (GUM).

** 3513. PHILIPPE DE RÉMI SIRE DE BEAUMANOIR. Le roman de la manekine. Éd. par Barbara SARGENT-BAUR NELSON. Amsterdam and Atlanta, Rodopi B.V., 99, 675 p. (pl., ill.). (Faux titre, 159).

** 3514. RAIMON VIDAL. IL Castia-Gilos e i testi lirici. A cura di Giuseppe TAVIANI. Milano, Luni, 99, 153 p. (Biblioteca medievale, 57).

** 3515. RAUNER (Erwin). Petrarca-Handschriften in Tschechien und in der Slowakischen Republik. Padova, Antenore, 99, XIV-676 p. (Censimento dei codici petrarcheschi, 12).

** 3516. Roman (Le) de Renart: branche XX et dernière (Renard empereur). Éd. de Félix LECOY, d'après la copie de Cangé. Paris, Champion, 99, 160 p. (Classiques français du Moyen Âge, 132).

** 3517. Roman (Le) de Tristan en prose. Tome 2. De la folie du Lancelot au départ de Tristan pour la Pentecôte du Graal. Version du ms. 757 de la B.N.F. Éd. Noëlle LABORDERIE et Thierry DELCOURT. Paris, Publications de la Sorbonne, 99, 814 p. (tab., ill.). (Classiques français du Moyen Âge, 133).

** 3518. Sidrak and Bokkus. A parallel-text edition from Bodleian Library, MS Laud Misc. 559 and British Library, MS Lansdowne 793. Ed. by T. L. BURTON. Vol. 2. Books 3.-4, commentary, appendices, glossary, index. Oxford a. New York, Published for the Early English Text Society by the Oxford U. P., 99, 4 vol., pp. 496-941 (ill.). (Early English Text Society, 311-312).

** 3519. STEIN (Elisabeth). Clericus in speculo: Studien zur lateinischen Verssatire des 12. und 13. Jahrhunderts und Erstedition des "Speculum prelatorum". Leiden a. Boston, Brill, 99, VIII-405 p. (Mittellateinische Studien und Texte, 25).

** 3520. VERBIJ-SCHILLINGS (Jeanne). Het Haagse handschrift van heraut Beyeren: Hs. Den Haag, Koninklijke Bibliotheek, 131 G 37. Hilversum, Verloren, 99, 273 p. (ill., facs.). (Middeleeuwse verzamelhandschriften uit de Nederlanden, 6).

3521. ADMYTE II: Archivo digital de manuscritos y textos españoles. Ed. por Aurora MARTÍN DE SANTA OLALLA, Angel Moreno GÓMEZ, Francisco Marcos MARTÍN, John J. NITTI, Gerardo MEIRO y Charles FAULHABER. Madrid, Micronet, 99, 2 CD-ROM.

3522. AICHHOLZER (Doris). Wildu machen ayn guet essen ... Drei mittelhochdeutschen Kochbücher: Erstedition, Übersetzung, Kommentar. Bern, Peter Lang, 88, 454 p. (ill.). (Wiener Arbeiten zur germanischen Altertumskunde und Philologie, 35).

3523. ALEKSEEV (Anatolij A.). Tekstologija slavjanskoj Biblii. (Textgeschichte der slavischen Bibel. Text history of the Slavonic Bible). Russische Akademie der Wissenschaften, In-t für russische Literatur (Puškinskij Dom). Köln, Weimar u. Wien, Böhlau u. S.-Peterburg, Dmitrij Bulanin, 99, 254 p. (ind.; bibl.). (Bausteine zur slavischen Philologie und Kulturgeschichte, 24). [Eng. summary.]

3524. Arabye (From) to Engelond. Medieval studies in honour of Mahmoud A. Manzalaoui on his 75th birthday. Ed. by Auguste Elfriede Christa CANITZ and Gernot R. WIELAND. Ottawa, University of Ottawa Press, 99, VIII-307 p. (Actexpress).

3525. ASTELL (Ann W.). Political allegory in late medieval England. Ithaca a. London, Cornell U. P., 99, XII-218 p.

3526. Ausiàs March i el món cultural del segle XV. Ed. por Rafael ALEMANY. Alicante, Universidad de Alicante, Institut Interuniversitari de Filologia Valenciana, 99, 379 p. (Symposia philologica, 1).

3527. BARIL (Agnès). Raoul de Cambrai: chanson de geste du XIIe siècle (d'après l'édition de Sarah Kay). Commentaire grammatical et philologique des laisses 39 à 131, vers 629 à 2478. Paris, Ellipses, 99, 235 p. (C.A.P.E.S.. Agrégation lettres).

3528. BARRON (W. R. J.). The Arthur of the English: the Arthurian legend in medieval English life and literature. Cardiff, University of Wales Press, 99, XVII-395 p. (Arthurian literature in the Middle Ages, 2).

3529. BAUMGARTNER (Emamnuelle), HARF-LANCNER (Laurence). Raoul de Cambrai: l'impossibile révolte. Paris, Champion, 99, 192 p. (Unichamps, 83).

3530. BAZELMANS (Jos). By weapons made worthy: lords, retainers and their relationship in Beowulf. Amsterdam, Amsterdam U. P., 99, XIII-206 p. (ill.). (Amsterdam archaeological studies, 5).

3531. BERSCHIN (Walter). Biographie und Epochenstil im lateinischen Mittelalter. Bd. 1. Ottonische Biographie: das hohe Mittelalter, 920–1220 n. Chr. Stuttgart, A. Hiersemann, 99, XIII-272 p. (Quellen und Untersuchungen zur lateinischen Philologie des Mittelalters, 12/1).

3532. BERTOLUCCI PIZZORUSSO (Valeria), ALVAR (Carlos), ASPERTI (Stefano). Le letterature medievali romanze d'area iberica. Roma e Bari, Laterza, 99, 519 p. (Storia delle letterature medievali romanze / Manuali Laterza, 109).

3533. Bilingual (A) edition of the Love songs of Bernart de Ventadorn in Occitan and English: sugar and salt. Ed. by Ronnie APTER and Mark HERMAN. Lewiston a. Lampeter, E. Mellen Press, 99, XVII-307 p. (Studies in mediaeval literature, 17).

3534. BLANCHARD (Joël), QUEREUIL (Michel). Lexique de Christine de Pizan. Paris, Klincksiek, 99, V-401 p. (Matériaux pour le Dictionnaire du Moyen Français, DMF, 5).

3535. Body (The) and the soul in medieval literature. The J.A.W. Bennett Memorial Lectures, 10th series, Perugia 1998. Ed. by Piero BOITANI and Anna TORTI. Cambridge, D.S. Brewer, 99, XII-211 p. (The J.A.W. Bennett memorial lectures, 10).

3536. BOULTON BARRY MAC CANN (Maureen), DEAN (Ruth J.). Anglo-Norman literature: a guide to texts and manuscripts. Anglo-Norman Text Society, 99, XVIII-553 p. (Anglo-Norman Text Society occasional publications series, 3) [Expands on VISING (Johan), Anglo-Norman language and literature London, Oxford U. P., 1923].

3537. BOUTET (Dominique). Formes littéraires et conscience historique aux origines de la littérature française (1100–1250). Paris, Presses universitaires de France, 99, 295 p. (Moyen Age).

3538. BRANDT (Rüdiger). Grundkurs germanistische Mediävistik/Literaturwissenschaft: eine Einführung. München, Fink, 99, 318 p. (ill.). (UTB für Wissenschaft. Uni-Taschenbücher, 2071).

3539. BROWN-GRANT (Rosalind). Christine de Pizan and the moral defence of women: reading beyond gender. Cambridge, Cambridge U. P., 99, XIV-224 p. (Cambridge studies in medieval literature, 40).

3540. BRUNO PAGNAMENTA (Roberta). Il Decameron. L'ambiguità come strategia narrativa. Ravenna, Longo, 99, 162 p. (Memoria del tempo, 14)

3541. BRYAN (Elizabeth J.). Collaborative meaning in medieval scribal culture: the Otho Layamon. Ann Arbor, University of Michigan Press, 99, XVIII-238 p. (Editorial theory and literary criticism).

3542. Chaucer in perspective: Middle English essays in honour of Norman Blake. Ed. by Geoffrey LESTER. Sheffield, Sheffield Academic Press, 99, 406 p. (ill.).

3543. Chaucer's French contemporaries: the poetrys/poetics of self and tradition. Ed. by R. Barton PALMER. New York, AMS Press, 99, XXXI-360 p. (Georgia state literary studies, 10).

3544. CIRKOVIC (Sima M.), MIHALJCIC (Rade). Leksikon srpskog srednjeg veka. Beograd, Knowledge, 99, XI-832 p. (ill.).

3545. COHEN (Jeffrey Jerome). Of giants: sex, monsters, and the Middle Ages. Minneapolis a. London, University of Minnesota Press, 99, XX-235 p. (ill.). (Medieval cultures, 17).

3546. CONDREN (Edward I.). Chaucer and the energy of creation: the design and the organization of the Canterbury tales. Gainesville, University Press of Florida, 99, 295 p. (ill.).

3547. DAIBER (Andreas). Bekannte Helden in neuen Gewändern? Intertextuelles Erzählen im "Biterolf und Dietleib" sowie am Beispiel Keies und Gaweins in "Lanzelet", "Wigalois" und der "Crone". Frankfurt am Main, Peter Lang, 1999, 99, 288 p. (Mikrokosmos, 53).

3548. Dictionnaire de l'occitan médiéval. Fasc. 2. Acceptat–adenan. Tübingen, Niemeyer, 99, pp. 81-160.

3549. Dictionnaire de l'occitan médiéval. Supplément bibliographique. Éd. par la Commission scientifique du DAO/DAG. Tübingen, Niemeyer, 99, 74 p.

3550. DIETL (Cora). Minnerede, Roman und historia. Der Wilhelm von Österreich Johanns von Würzburg. Tübingen, Niemeyer, 99, VIII-429 p. (ill.). (Hermanea, germanistische Forschungen, 87).

3551. Drama and the community: people and plays in medieval Europe. Ed. by Alan HINDLEY. Turnhout, Brepols, 99, XI-294 p. (ill.). (Medieval texts and cultures of Northern Europe, 1).

3552. DUFFELL (Martin J.). Modern metrical theory and the verso de arte mayor. London, Department of Hispanic Studies, Queen Mary and Westfield College, 99, 104 p. (ill.). (Papers of the Medieval Hispanic Research Seminar, 10).

3553. EHLER (Christine). Verschriftung und Verschriftlichung des Altenglischen: eine methodisch-exemplarische Untersuchung. Frankfurt am Main, P. Lang, 99, 217 p. (ill.). (Neue Studien zur Anglistik und Amerikanistik,76).

3554. FAIVRE D'ARCIER (Bernard). Les farces: moyen âge et renaissance. Paris, Imprimerie Nationale, 99, 553 p. (La salamandre).

3555. FENZI (Enrico). La canzone d'amore di Guido Cavalcanti e i suoi antichi commenti. Genova, Il melangolo, 99, 300 p. (Opuscula, 95).

3556. FIELD (Rosalind). Tradition and transformation in medieval romance. Rochester, D.S. Brewer, 99, XV-172 p.

3557. FINCKH (Ruth). Minor mundus homo. Studien zur Mikrokosmos-Idee in der mittelalterlichen Literatur. Göttingen, Vandenhoeck & Ruprecht, 99, 475 p. (ill.). (Palaestra, 306).

3558. FINKE (Laurie A.). Women's writing in English. Medieval England. London a. New York, Longman, 99, X-251 p. (Women's writing in English).

3559. FOSTER (Edward E.). Understanding Chaucer's intellectual and interpretative world: nominalist fiction. Lewiston a. Lampeter, Edwin Mellen Press, 99, VII-234 p. (Studies in British literature, 41).

3560. FRECHE (Katharina). Von zweier vrouwen bagen wart vil manic helt verlorn: Untersuchungen zur Geschlechterkonstruktion in der mittelalterlichen Nibelungendichtung. Trier, WVT Wissenschaftlicher Verlag Trier, 99, 236 p. (Literatur, Imagination, Realität, 21).

3561. GASSER (Karen M.). Resolution of the debate in the medieval poem, The owl and the nightingale. Lewiston a. Lampeter, E. Mellen Press, 99, X-152 p. (Studies in mediaeval literature,18).

3562. Genere "tenzone" (II) nelle letterature romanze delle origini. Atti del convegno internazionale, Losanna, 13–15 novembre 1997. A cura di Antonio STÄUBLE e Matteo PEDRONI. Ravenna, Longo, 99, 412 p. (Memoria del tempo, 15).

3563. Geschichte der deutschen Literatur von den Anfängen bis zum Beginn der Neuzeit. Hrsg. v. Joachim HEINZLE. Teil 1. L. Peter JOHNSON. Die höfische Literatur der Blütezeit (1160/70–1220/30). Tübingen, Max Niemeyer, 99, XI-465 p.

3564. GREEN (Richard Firth). A crisis of truth: literature and law in Ricardian England. Philadelphia, University of Pennsylvania Press, 99, XVI-496 p. (Middle Ages series).

3565. HAYE (Thomas). Oratio: mittelalterliche Redekunst in lateinischer Sprache. Leiden a. Boston, Brill, 99, VIII-340 p. (Mittellateinische Studien und Texte, 27).

3566. HEMECKER (Wilhelm). Handschrift. Wien, Paul Zsolnay, 99, 138 p. (ill.). (Österreichische Nationalbibliothek. Profile, Magazin des Österreichischen Literaturarchivs, 4).

3567. Historij (Die) von Diocleciano in Abbildungen aus dem Codex 407 des Wiener Schottenstifts. Hrsg. v. Ralf-Henning STEINMETZ. Goppingen, Kummerle Verlag, 99, 20 p. (pl.). (Litterae, 118).

3568. HROTSVITA. Théâtre. Éd. par Monique GOULLET. Paris, Les Belles Lettres, 99, CXXXVIII-301 p. (Auteurs latins du Moyen Âge).

3569. HÜLK (Walburga). Schrift-Spuren von Subjektivität. Lektüren literarischer Texte des französischen Mittelalters. Tübingen, Niemeyer, 99, V-231 p. (Beihefte zur Zeitschrift für romanische Philologie, 297).

3570. Index (The) of Middle English prose. Manuscripts in Lambeth Palace Library, including those formerly in Sion College Library. Ed. by V. M. O'MARA and O. S. PICKERING. Manuscripts in the National Library of Wales (Llyfrgell Genedlaethol Cymru), Aberystwyth. Ed. by C. William MARX. Cambridge, D.S. Brewer, 99, 2 vol., XXVII-133 p., XXVII-100 p.

3571. JAEGER (C. Stephen). Ennobling love: in search of a lost sensibility. Philadelphia, University of Pennsylvania Press, 99, XI-311 p. (The Middle Ages series).

3572. JANSSON (Sven Bertil). Den levande balladen. Medeltida ballad i svensk tradition. (La Ballade vivante. Les Ballades médiévales dans la tradition suédoise). Stockholm, Prisma, 99, 271 p. (ill.).

3573. KELLY (Douglas). The conspiracy of allusion: description, rewriting, and authorship from Macrobius to medieval romance. Leiden a. Boston, Brill, 99, XIV-313 p. (Studies in the history of Christian thought, 97).

3574. KIMMELMAN (Burt). The poetics of authorship in the later Middle Ages: the emergence of the modern literary persona. New York, Peter Lang, 99, 288 p. (Studies in the humanities, 21).

3575. KOBIALKA (Michal). This is my body: representational practices in the early Middle Ages. Ann Arbor, University of Michigan Press, 99, VIII-313 p.

3576. LANGBEHN REGULA (Rohland de). La unidad genérica de la novela sentimental española de los siglos XV y XVI. London, Department of Hispanic Studies, Queen Mary and Westfield College, 99, 111 p. (Papers of the Medieval Hispanic Research Seminar, 17).

3577. LECLANCHE (Jean-Luc). Concordancier e Raoul de Cambrai. Paris, Champion, 99, 1 CD-ROM.

3578. LEE (Alvin A.). Gold-Hall and earth-dragon: Beowulf as metaphor. Toronto, Buffalo and London, University of Toronto Press, 99, XI-280 p.

3579. LEES (Clare A.). Tradition and belief: religious writing in late Anglo-Saxon England. Minneapolis a. London, University of Minnesota Press, 99, XVII-195 p. (Medieval cultures, 19).

3580. LENDINARA (Patrizia). Anglo-Saxon glosses and glossaries. Aldershot a. Brookfield, Ashgate, 99, XV-410 p. (pl., ill.). (Variorum collected studies series, 622).

3581. LOGIE (Philippe). L'Eneas, une traduction au risque de l'invention. Paris, Champion, 99, 512 p. (Nouvelle bibliothèque du Moyen Âge, 48).

3582. LÓPEZ-RÍOS (Santiago). Salvajes y razas monstruosas en la literatura castellana medieval. Madrid, Fundacion Universitaria Española, 99, 258 p. (Colección Tesis doctorales "cum laude.". Serie L, Literatura, 7).

3583. MALATO (Enrico). Dante. Roma, Salerno, 99, 420 p. (Sestante, 1).

3584. Medioevo romanzo e orientale. Il viaggio dei testi. III Colloquio internazionale, Venezia, 10–13 ottobre 1996. Atti a cura di Antonio PIOLETTI e Francesca RIZZO NERVO. Soveria Mannelli, Rubbettino, 99, IX-622 p. (ill.).

3585. MÉNARD (Philippe). De Chrétien de Troyes au Tristan en prose. Études sur les roman de la Table ronde. Genève, Droz, 99, 176 p. (Pulications romanes et françaises, 224).

3586. MERCERON (Jacques). Le message et sa fiction. La communication par messages dans la littérature française des XIIe et XIIIe siècles. Berkeley, University of California Press, 99, XVI-399 p. (University of California publication in modern philology, 128).

3587. Mittelalter: neue Wege durch einen alten Kontinent. Hrsg. v. Jan-Dirk MÜLLER und Horst WENZEL. Stuttgart, S. Hirzel, 99, 379 p. (ill.).

3588. MOSTEIRO LOUZAO (Manuel). Las conjunciones de causa en castellano medieval. Origen, evolución y otros usos. [Santiago de Compostela], Universidade de Santiago de Compostela, 99, 277 p. (ill.). (Verba. Anejo, 45).

3589. MÜLLER (Catherine M.). Marguerite Porete et Marguerite d'Oingt de l'autre côté du miroir. New York, P. Lang, 99, XVI-213 p. (Currents in comparative Romance languages and literatures, 72).

3590. MUSCATINE (Charles). Medieval literature, style, and culture. Essays. Columbia, University of South Carolina Press, 99, IX-252 p.

3591. NABERT (Nathalie). Les réseaux d'alliance en diplomatie aux XIVe et XVe siècles. Études de sémantique. Paris, Champion, 99, 581 p. (Bibliothèque de Grammaire et de Linguistique, 7).

3592. Natur und Kultur in der deutschen Literatur des Mittelalters. Colloquium Exetre 1997. Hrsg. v. Frank FURBERTH, Ulrike ZITZLSPERGER, Alan ROBERTSHAW und Gerhard WOLF. Tübingen, Niemeyer, 99, VIII-297 p. (ill.).

3593. NEVILLE (Jennifer). Representations of the natural world in Old English poetry. Cambridge a. New York, Cambridge U. P., 99, X-224 p. (Cambridge studies in Anglo-Saxon England, 27).

3594. NILES (John D.). Homo Narrans. The poetics and anthropology of oral literatur. Philadelphia, University of Pennsylvania Press, 99, IX-280 p.

3595. Norse Romance. Vol. 1. The Tristan legend. Vol. 2. The knights of the Round Table. Vol. 3. Hærra Ivan. Ed. by Marianne E. KALINKE. Woodbridge a. Rochester, Boydell and Brewer, 99, X-294 p., V-329 p., VI-313 p.

3596. OBERMEIER (Anita). The history and anatomy of auctorial self-criticism in the European Middle Ages. Amsterdam, Rodopi, 99, 314 p. (ill., facs.). (Internationale Forschungen zur allgemeinen und vergleichenden Literaturwissenschaft, 32).

3597. Opusculum fabularum: die Fabelsammlung der Berliner Handschrift Theol. lat. fol. 142. Hrsg. v. Christina MECKELBORG und Bernd SCHNEIDER. Leiden, Brill, 99, VII-237 p. (Mittellateinische Studien und Texte, 26)

3598. PENSOM (Roger). Aucassin et Nicolete: the poetry of gender and growing up in the French Middle Ages. Bern, Peter Lang, 99, 160 p.

3599. Rereading allegory. Essays in memory of Daniel Poirion. Ed. by Noah D. GUYNN and Sahar AMER. New Haven a. London, Yale U. P., 99, 263 p. (ill.). (Yale French studies, 95).

3600. REVOL (Thierry). Représentations du sacré dans les textes dramatiques des XIe–XIIIe siècles en France. Paris, Champion, 99, 577 p. (Nouvelle bibliothèque du Moyen Age, 51).

3601. Rhetorical (The) poetics of the Middle Ages: reconstructive polyphony. Essays in honor of Robert O. Payne. Ed. by Deborah M. SINNREICH-LEVI and John M. HILL. Madison, Fairleigh Dickinson, U. P., 99, 304 p.

3602. ROSSI (Aldo). Da Dante a Leonardo: un percorso di originali. Tavarnuzze, SISMEL – Edizioni del Galluzzo, 99, LXXXIV-430 p. (ill.). (Biblioteche e archivi, 4).

3603. SANTINA (Mary Arlene). The tournament and literature. Literary representations of the medieval tournament in old French works, 1150–1226. New York, Peter Lang, 99, 197 p. (tab.). (Studies in the Humanities. Literature, Politics, Society, 49).

3604. Schwierige Frauen – schwierige Männer in der Literatur des Mittelalters. Hrsg. v. Aloïs M. HAAS und Ingrid KASTEN. Bern, Peter Lang, 99, 326 p. (ill.).

3605. Scriptorium Alfonsí (El): de los Libros de Astrología a las "Cantigas de Santa María". Ed. por Jesús MONTOYA MARTÍNEZ y Ana DOMÍNGUEZ RODRÍGUEZ. Madrid, Editorial Complutense, 99, XII-359 p. (ill.). (Cursos de verano de El Escorial).

3606. Spazio (Lo) letterario del Medioevo. A cura di Piero BOITANI, Mario MANCINI e Alberto VÀRVARO. Vol. 1/1. La produzione del testo. Roma, Salerno, 99, 653 p. (ill.).

3607. SPOERRI (Bettina). Der Tod als Text und Signum. Der literarische Todesdiskurs in geistlichdidaktischen Texten des Mittelalters. Bern, Peter Lang, 99, 345 p. (Deutsche Literatur von den Anfängen bis 1700, 27).

3608. Text and gloss: studies in insular learning and literature presented to Joseph Donovan Pheifer. Ed. by Helen CONRAD-O'BRIAIN, Anne Marie D'ARCY and V. J. SCATTERGOOD. Dublin, Four Courts Press, 99, 214 p. (ill.).

3609. TONELLI (Natascia). Varietà sintattica e costanti retoriche nei sonetti dei Rerum vulgarium fragmenta. Firenze, L. S. Olschki, 99, 228 p.

3610. Tristan und Isolt im Spätmittelalter. Vorträge eines interdisziplinären Symposiums vom 3. bis 8. Juni 1996 an der Justus-Liebig-Universität Giessen. Hrsg. v. Xenja von ERTZDORFF und Rudolf SCHULZ. Amsterdam u. Atlanta, Rodopi, 99, 590 p. (ill.). (Chloe, 29).

3611. UDWIN (Victor Morris). Between two armies. The place of the duel in epic culture. Leiden a. Boston, E.J. Brill, 99, X-235 p. (Davis medieval texts and studies, 10).

3612. UHL (Patrice). La constellation poétique du non-sens au Moyen Age: onze études sur la poésie fatrasique et ses environs. Paris et Saint-Denis de La Réunion, Université de la Réunion, Centre de recherches littéraires et historiques, et l'Harmattan, 99, 186 p. (Collection Poétiques).

3613. UTZ (Richard J.), POSTER (Carol). Discourses of power: grammar and rhetoric in the Middle Ages. Evanston, Northwestern U. P., 99, 151 p. (Disputatio: an international transdisciplinary journal of the late Middle Ages, 4).

3614. Villon at Oxford: the drama of the text. Proceedings of the Conference held at St. Hilda's College Oxford, march 1996. Ed. by Michael FREEMAN and Jane H. M. TAYLOR. Amsterdam, Rodopi, 99, VI-391 p. (Faux titre, 165).

3615. WARNKE (Ingo). Wege zur Kultursprache: die Polyfunktionalisierung des Deutschen im juridischen Diskurs (1200–1800). Berlin, W. de Gruyter, 99, XV-467 p. (ill., maps). (Studia linguistica Germanica, 52).

3616. WOGAN-BROWNE (Jocelyn). The idea of the vernacular: an anthology of Middle English literary theory, 1280–1520. Exeter, University of Exeter Press, 99, 524 p. (Exeter medieval English texts and studies).

3617. WYLY (Bryan Weston). Figures of authority in the Old English 'Exodus'. Heidelberg, Universitätsverlag C. Winter, 99, XV-327 p. (Anglistische Forschungen, 262).

Cf. n°s 79, 349, 494, 3160-3183, 3642, 5293

c. Technology

3618. HYLAND (Ann). The horse in the Middle Ages. Stroud, Sutton, 99, XII-180 p. (ill.).

3619. Liber (Le) accipitrum de Grimaldus, un traité d'autourserie du haut Moyen Âge. Éd. par An SMETS. Nogent-le-Roi, J. Laget, 99, 187 p. (ill.). (Bibliotheca cynegetica).

3620. SWEETMAN (David). Medieval castles of Ireland. Cork, Collins Press, 99, 218 p. (ill.).

d. *Education*

3621. Artes im Mittelalter. Humboldt-Universität zu Berlin, 24–27 Feb. 1997. Hrsg. v. Ursula SCHAEFER. Berlin, Akademie Verlag, 99, X-409 p. (ill.).

3622. BEAUNE (C.). Education et culture du début du XIIe siècle au milieu du XVe siècle. Paris, SEDES, 99, 366 p. (Regards sur l'histoire. Histoire médiévale, 131).

3623. BIANCHI (Luca). Censure et liberté intellectuelle à l'Université de Paris, XIIIe–XIVe siècles. Paris, Les belles lettres, 99, 382 p. (L'âne d'or).

3624. COBBAN (Alan B.). English university life in the Middle Ages. London, UCL Press, 99, XV-264 p. (ill., facs.).

3625. Former, enseigner, éduquer dans l'Occident médiéval (1100–1450). Textes et documents. Éd. par Patrick GILLI. [Paris], SEDES, 99, 2 vol., 278 p., 310 p. (Regards sur l'histoire. Histoire médiévale, 133).

3626. GENET (Jean-Philippe). La mutation de l'éducation et de la culture médiévales: Occident chrétien, XIIe siècle-milieu du XVe siècle. Paris, Seli Arslan, 99, 2 vol., 568 p. (Histoire, cultures et sociétés).

3627. LUFF (Robert). Wissensvermittlung im europäischen mittelalter: "Imago-mundi"-werke und ihre prologe. Tübingen, Max Niemeyer, 99, X-586 p. (ill.). (Texte und Textgeschichte, 47).

3628. LUSIGNAN (Serge). "Verité garde le roy": la construction d'une identité universitaire en France, XIIIe–XVe siècle. Paris, Publications de la Sorbonne, 99, 332 p. (Histoire ancienne e médiévale, 55).

3629. O'LOUGHLIN (Thomas). Teachers and codebreakers: the Latin Genesis tradition, 430–800. Steenbrugis, In Abbatia S. Petri a. Turnhout, Brepols, 99, XVIII-376 p. (Instrumenta patristica, 35).

3630. POLO DE BEAULIEU (Marie-Anne). Education, prédication et cultures au Moyen Age: essais sur Jean Gobi le Jeune ([d.] 1350). Lyon, Centre interuniversitaire d'histoire et d'archélogie médiévales et Presses universitaires de Lyon, 99, 237 p. (ill.). (Collection d'histoire et d'archéologie médiévales, 4).

3631. RICHÉ (P.). Ecoles et enseignement dans le haut moyen âge. Fin du Ve siècle–milieu du XIe siècle. Paris, Picard, 99, 472 p.

3632. VERGER (Jacques). Les universités au Moyen Âge. Paris, PUF, 99, 226 (Quadrige, 228).

3633. WAGNER (Wolfgang Eric). Universitätsstift und Kollegium in Prag, Wien und Heidelberg. Eine vergleichende Untersuchung spätmittelalterlicher Stiftungen im Spannungsfeld von Herrschaft und Genossenschaft. Berlin, Akademie Verlag, 99, 450 p. (tab., ill.). (Europa im Mittelalter, 2).

Cf. n°s 79, 349, 494, 5293

§ 10. **History of art.**

a. *General*

3634. ARCHER (Lucy), SMITH (Edwin). Architecture in Britain and Ireland, 600–1500. London, Harvill, 99, X-467p. (ill., maps).

3635. ERLANDE-BRANDENBURG (Alain). De pierre, d'or et de feu: la création artistique au Moyen Âge, IVe–XIIIe siècle. Paris, Fayard, 99, 350 p.

3636. HERRIN (Judith). A medieval miscellany. London, Weidenfeld & Nicolson a. Facsimile Editions, 99, 207 p. (ill.).

3637. Pierre, lumière, couleur. Etudes d'histoire de l'art du Moyen Age en l'honneur d'Anne Prache. Ed. par Fabienne JOUBERT et Dany SANDRON. Paris, Presses de l'Université Paris Sorbonne, 99, 534 p.

3638. RECHT (Roland). Le croire et le voir. L'art des cathédrales (XIIe–XVe siècle). Paris, Gallimard, 99, 446 p. (Bibliothèques des Histoires).

Cf. n° 1288

b. *Special studies*

3639. Ab Aquilone. Nordic studies in honour and memory of Leonard E. Boyle, O.P. Ed. by Marie-Louise RODÉN. Stockholm, Svenska Riskarkivet, 99, 272 p. (ill.). (Suecoromana. Studia artis historiae Instituti Romani Regni Sueciae, 6).

3640. AKTUĞ-KOLAY (İlknur). Batı Anadolu 14. yüzyıl beylikler mimarisinde yapım teknikleri. (Techniques de construction dans l'architécture des Beylicats au XIVe siècle en Anatolie occidental). Ankara, Atatürk Kültür Merkezi, 99, 163 p.

3641. ALTISAPAN (Erol). Ortaçağ'da Eskişehir ve çevresinde Türk sanatı: 11.–15. yüzyıllar Türk mimarisi (L'Art turc au moyen âge à Eskişehir et à ses alentoures: l'architecture turque aux XIe et XVe siècles). Eskişehir, Anadolu Üniversitesi Edebiyat Fakültesi, 99, 265 p.

3642. Boccaccio visualizzato. Narrare per parole e per immagini fra Medioevo e Rinascimento. A cura di Vittore BRANCA. Vol. 1. Saggi generali con una prospettiva dal barocco a oggi. Vol. 2. Opere d'arte d'origine italiana. Vol. 3. Opere d'arte d'origine francese, fiamminga, inglese, spagnola, tedesca. Torino, G. Einaudi, 99, 3 vol., XVI-261 p., 383 p., 366 p. (ill.). (Biblioteca di storia dell'arte, 30).

3643. BORASO (Stefano). Brunelleschi 1420: il paradigma prospettico di Filippo di ser Brunellesco: il "caso" delle tavole sperimentali ottico-prospettiche. Padova, Edizioni Libreria Progetto, 99, 80 p. (ill.).

3644. CHRISTE (Yves). Jugements derniers. [La Pierre-qui-Vire (Yonne)], Zodiaque, 99, 371 p. (ill.). (Les formes de la nuit, 12).

3645. CORLEY (Brigitte). Painting and patronage in Cologne, 1300–1500. London, Harvey Miller, 99, 342 p. (pl., ill.).

3646. DAVY (Christian), GIRAUD (Patrice). La peinture murale romane dans les Pays de la Loire: l'indicible et le ruban plissé. Laval, Societe d'Archeologie et d'Histoire de la Mayenne (SAHM), 99, XV-397 p. (ill.). (Mayenne, Archéologie, histoire. Supplément 10).

3647. Drevnosti Pskova: arkheologija, istorija, arkhitektura: k jubileju I.K. Labutinoj. (The antiquities of Pskov: archaeology, history, architecture: to the anniversary of Inga K. Labutina). Ed. Valentin V. SEDOV. Pskov, [s. n.], 99, 305 p. (ill., bibl.).

3648. EMERY (Anthony). Greater medieval houses of England and Wales 1300–1500. East Anglia, Central England and Wales. Cambridge, Cambridge U. P., 99, XV-724 p. (ill.).

3649. GANDOLFO (Francesco). La scultura normanno-sveva in Campania: botteghe e modelli. Roma e Bari, Laterza, 99, XII-154 p. (Centro europeo di studi normanni. Fonti e studi, 9).

3650. GEDDES (J.). Medieval decorative ironwork in England. London, Society of Antiquaries of London, 99, XV-411 p. (ill., maps). (Reports of the Research Committee of the Society of Antiquaries of London, 59).

3651. GEL'MAN (E. I.). Glazurovannaia keramika i farfor srednevekovykh pamiatnikov Primor'ia. (Middle Age glazed pottery and porcelain in Primorye). Vladivostok, Institut istorii, arkheologii i etnografii, Narodov Dal'nego Vostoka DVO RAN, 99, 221 p.

3652. Gotische Architektur in Spanien. Akten des Kolloquiums der Carl Justi-Vereinigung and des Kunstgeschichtlichen Seminars der Universität Göttingen, Göttingen, 4.–6. Februar 1994 / La arquitectura gótica en España. Actas del Coloquio de la Carl Justi-Vereinigung y del Seminario de Historia del Arte de la Universidad de Gotinga, Gotinga, del 4 al 6 de febrero de 1994. Hrsg. von Christian FREIGANG, unter Mitarbeit von Cristina María STIGLMAYR. Frankfurt am Main, Vervuert u. Madrid, Iberoamericana, 99, 426 p. (ill.). (Ars Iberica).

3653. HARBISON (Peter). The golden age of Irish art: the medieval achievement, 600–1200. New York, Thames and Hudson, 99, 368 p. (ill., map).

3654. HOHLER BERGENDAHL (Erla). Norwegian stave church sculpture. Vol. 1. Analytical Survey. Vol. 2. Studies, Plates. Oslo a. Oxford, Scandinavian U. P., 99, 2 vol., 265 p., 335 p. (ill.). (Medieval art in Norway).

3655. Humanismus (Der) der Architektur in Florenz: Filippo Brunelleschi und Michelozzo di Bartolomeo. Im Auftrag der Berliner Renaissance-Gesellschaft herausgegeben von Wolfgang von LÖHNEYSEN. Hildesheim, Weidmann, 99, 135 p. (ill.). (Spolia Berolinensia, 15).

3656. INCERTI (Manuela). Il disegno della luce nell' architettura cistercense: allineamenti astronomici nelle abbazie di Chiaravalle della Colomba, Fontevivo e San Martino de' Bocci. Firenze, Certosa Cultura, 99, 224 p. (ill., tav.).

3657. Italy and the Low Countries, artistic relations: the fifteenth century. Proceedings of the symposium held at Museum Catharijneconvent, Utrecht, 14 March 1994. Ed. by Victor M. SCHMIDT. Firenze, Centro Di, 99, 108 p. (ill.). (Italia e i Paesi Bassi / Istituto universitario olandese di storia dell'arte, 4).

3658. KOSHI (Koichi). Die frühmittelalterlichen Wandmalereien der St. Georgskirche zu Oberzell auf der Bodenseeinsel Reichenau. 1. Textband. 2. Tafelband. Berlin, Deutscher Verlag fur Kunstwissenschaft, 99, 381 p., 192 p. (ill.). (Denkmäler deutscher Kunst).

3659. LEWIS (John M.). The medieval tiles of Wales. Cardiff, National Museum of Wales, 99, IX-274 p. (ill.).

3660. Leon Battista Alberti: architettura e cultura: atti del convegno internazionale, Mantova, 16–19 novembre 1994. Firenze, L. S. Olschki, 99, XII-386 p. (Miscellanea / Accademia nazionale virgiliana di scienze lettere e arti, 7).

3661. LIDEN (Anna). Olav den Helige i medeltida bildkonst: legendmotiv och attribut. (Saint Olaf dans l'art médiéval: motifs légendaires et attributs). Stockholm, Almqvist & Wiksell, 99, 432 p. (ill.). (rés. anglais).

3662. MAC ALEER (J. Philip). Rochester cathedral, 604–1540. An architectural history. Toronto, Buffalo a. London, University of Toronto Press, 99, XXIV-314 p. (ill., pl.).

3663. Medieval Cyprus. Studies in art, architecture, and history in memory of Doula Mouriki. Ed. by Nancy SEVCENKO PATTERSON and Christopher Frederick MOSS. Princeton, Dept. of Art and Archaeology, Princeton University in association with Princeton U. P., 99, XXVIII-306 p. (pl., ill., facs., map).

3664. MERBACK (Mitchell B.). The thief, the cross, and the wheel. Pain and the spectacle of punishment in medieval and Renaissance Europe. London, Reaktion Books, 99, 351 p. (ill.). (Picturing history).

3665. NOACK-HALEY (Sabine), ARBEITER (Achim). Christliche Denkmäler des frühen Mittelalters: vom 8. bis ins 11. Jahrhundert. Mainz, P. von Zabern, 99, X-581-140 p. (pl., ill., maps, plans). (Hispania antiqua).

3666. PAULI (Tatjana). Piero della Francesca. Il compasso e il pennello: l'anima razionale del Quattrocento italiano. Milano, Leonardo arte, 99, 143 p. (ill.). (ArtBook, 13).

3667. Peindre à Auxerre au Moyen Âge, IXe–XIVe siècles. 10 ans de recherche à l'abbaye Saint-Germain d'Auxerre et à la cathédrale Saint-Étienne d'Au xerre. Éd. par Christian SAPIN. Auxerre et Paris, Centre d'études médiévales - Éditions du CTHS, 99, 312 p. (ill., tab. graph.). (Mémoires de la Section d'Archéologie et d'Histoire de l'Art, 7).

3668. PERTICI (Petra). Condottieri senesi e la Rotta di San Romano di Paolo Uccello. Archivio storico italiano, 99, 157, 581, p. 537-562.

3669. PICKLES (Christopher). Texts and monuments: a study of ten Anglo-Saxon churches of the pre-Viking period. Oxford, Archaeopress, 99, IX-316 p. (ill, maps, plans). (BAR British series, 277).

3670. RUBIN LEE (Patricia), WRIGHT (Alison). Renaissance Florence: the art of the 1470s. London, National Gallery Publications, distributed by Yale U. P., 99, 360 p. (ill.).

3671. RUDOLPH (Conrad). In the beginning: theories and images of creation in the Northern Europe in the twelfth century. Art history, 99, 22, 1, p. 3-55.

3672. RUSU (Adrian Andrei), HUREZAN (George Pascu). Cetăţi medievale în judeţul Arad. (Medieval castles in Arad county). Arad, Complexul Muzeal, 99, 127 p.

3673. SAYAN (Yüksel). Türkmenistan'daki mimari eserler (XI–XVI. yüzyıl). (Les édifices architécturaux en Türkmenistan aux XIe et XVIe siècles). Ankara, Kültür Bakanlığı Yayımlar Dairesi Başkanlığı, 99, XV-510 p.

3674. SCHWALL-HOUMMADY (Christine). Bilderzählung im 15. Jahrhundert: Boccaccios Decamerone in Frankreich. Frankfurt am Main, Peter Lang, 99, 457 p. (ill.). (Europäische Hochschulschriften. Reihe 28, Kunstgeschichte / Publications Universitaires Européenes. Sér. 28, Histoire de l'art / European University Studies. Ser. 28, History of art, 338).

3675. Splendeur (La) des Rolin: un mécénat privé à la cour de Bourgogne. Société éduenne des lettres, sciences et arts, table ronde, 27–28 février 1995. Éd. par Brigitte MAURICE-CHABARD. Paris, Picard, 99, 327 p. (ill.).

3676. ŠTIH (Peter). Ustoličevanje koroških vojvod: najstarejša upodobitev 1480. (Enthronement of Carinthian Dukes: the oldest depiction from 1480). Ljubljana, Slovenska knjiga, 99, [s. p.]. (Monumenta Slovenica, 9).

3677. STROO (Cyriel). The Flemish primitives. Catalogue of early Netherlandish painting in the Royal Museums of Fine Arts of Belgium: the Dirk Bouts, Petrus Christus, Hans Memling and Hugo van der Goes groups. Bruxelles, Brepols, 99, 313 p. (ill.).

3678. Tessuti, oreficerie, miniature in Liguria: XIII–XV secolo. Atti del Convegno internazionale di studi, Genova-Bordighera, 22–25 maggio 1997. A cura di A. R. CALDERONI MASETTI, C. DI FABIO e M. MARCENARO. Bordighera, 99, 454 p. (ill.).

3679. Thesaurus Coloniensis: Beiträge zur mittelalterlichen Kunstgeschichte Kölns. Festschrift für Anton von Euw. Hrsg. v. Hiltrud WESTERMANN-ANGERHAUSEN, Wolfgang SCHMITZ und Ulrich KRINGS. Koln, SH-Verlag, 99, 376 p. (ill.). (Veröffentlichungen des Kölnischen Geschichtsvereins e.V, 41).

3680. Tilman Riemenschneider, master sculptor of the late Middle Ages. Ed. by Julien CHAPUIS and Michael BAXANDALL. Washington, National Gallery of Art, 99, 352 p. (ill., maps).

3681. TOTEV (Totiu). The ceramic icon in medieval Bulgaria. Sofia, St. Kliment Ohridski U. P., Prof. Marin Drinov Academic Pub. House, PENSOFT Publishers, 99, 155 p., XCIX p. of plates (ill.).

3682. VARTY (Kenneth). Reynard, Renart, Reinaert and other foxes in medieval England: the iconographic evidence. A study of the illustrating of Fox lore and Reynard the Fox stories in England during the Middle Ages, followed by a brief survey of their fortunes in post-medieval times. Amsterdam, Amsterdam U. P., 99, 353 p. (ill.).

Cf. n°s 357, 3459, 3462, 3844

§ 11. History of music.

** 3683. Manuscrits (Les) du processionnal. Vol. 1: Autriche à Espagne. Éd. par Michel HUGLO. München, G. Henle, 99, LXXV-322 p. (Répertoire international des sources musicales = Internationales Quellenlexikon der Musik = International inventory of musical sources. B, XIV).

3684. Antiphonaire (Un) cistercien pour le sanctoral, XIIe siècle: Paris, Bibliothèque Nationale de France, nouvelles acquisitions latines 1412. Éd. par Claire MAÎTRE. Paris, Editions du CTHS, 99, 1 score, xi-202 ff.-75 p. [Facsim.].

3685. BOETHIUS. De institutione musica: MSS Avranches, Bibliothèque Municipale, 236, 237. Ed. by Alma SANTOSUOSSO COLK. Ottawa, The Institute of Mediaeval Music, 99, CIX-97 p. (facs.). (Publications of mediaeval musical manuscripts = Veröffentlichungen mittelalterlicher Musikhandschriften, 24/1).

3686. Codice (Il) J.II.9, Torino, Biblioteca nazionale universitaria. A cura di Isabella FRAGALÀ DATA e Karl KÜGLE. Lucca, Libreria musicale italiana, 99, 117 p. (facs., pl., ill.). (Ars nova, 4).

3687. Early medieval chants from Nonantola. Vol. 1. Ordinary chants and tropes. Ed. by James BORDERS. Vol. 2. Proper chants and tropes. Ed. by James BORDERS. Vol 3. Processional chants. Ed. by James BORDERS. Vol. 4. Sequences. Ed. by Lance W. BRUNNER. Madison, A-R Editions, 99, LXXXIV-85 p., LXXII-83 p., LXXIV-152 p., LXX-78 p. (facsims, music). (Recent researches in the music of the Middle Ages and early Renaissance, 30-33).

3688. Editorial (An) transnotation of the manuscript Cappella sistina 51, Biblioteca Apostolica Vaticana, Città del Vaticano, Liber missarum. Ed. by Rex EAKINS.

Ottawa, Institute of Mediaeval Music, 99, 1 score (facs.). (Gesamtausgaben / Collected works, 17/1).

3689. FLYNN (William T.). Medieval music as medieval exegesis. Lanham a. London, Scarecrow Press, 99, XXII-271 p. (ill., music). (Studies in liturgical musicology, 8).

3690. GUIDO D'AREZZO. Regule rithmice, Prologus in antiphonarium, and Epistola ad Michahelem: a critical text and translation with an introduction, annotations, indices, and new manuscript inventories. Ed. by Dolores PESCE. Ottawa, Institute of Mediaeval Music, 99, VII-615 p. (pl., ill.). (Wissenschaftliche Abhandlungen, 73).

3691. HIGGINS (Paula). Antoine Busnoys: method, meaning, and context in late medieval music. Oxford, Clarendon Press, 99, XXII-599 p. (ill.).

3692. MARTINI (Johannes), MOOHAN (Elaine), STEIB (Murray). Masses. Madison, A-R Editions, 99, 2 score, 257 p., 305 p. (facs.). (Recent researches in the music of the Middle Ages and early Renaissance, 34-35).

3693. MÄRZ (Christoph). Die weltlichen Lieder des Mönchs von Salzburg: Texte und Melodien. Tübingen, Niemeyer, 99, X-569 p. (pl., facs.). (Münchener Texte und Untersuchungen zur deutschen Literatur des Mittelalters, 114).

3694. MATHIESEN (Thomas J.). Apollo's lyre: Greek music and music theory in antiquity and the Middle Ages. Lincoln a. London, University of Nebraska Press, 99, XV-806 p. (ill., maps, music). (Publications of the Center for the History of Music Theory and Literature, 2).

3695. PETROVIC (Danica), PETIJEVIC (Tamara). Hilandarski ktitori u pravoslavnom pojanju. (The founders of Hilandar in Orthodox chant). Beograd, Muzikoloski Institut, 99, 247 p., 1 CD (ill., music).

3696. TORKEWITZ (Dieter). Das älteste Dokument zur Entstehung der abendländischen Mehrstimmigkeit: eine Handschrift aus Werden an der Ruhr: das Düsseldorfer Fragment. Stuttgart, Franz Steiner, 99, 131 p. (pl., ill.). (Beihefte zum Archiv für Musikwissenschaft, 44).

§ 12. **History of philosophy, theology and science.**

a. *Sources*

3697. ALFONSO-GOLDFARB (Ana Maria). Livro do tesouro de Alexandre: um estudo de hermética árabe na officina da história da ciência. Petropolis, Editora Vozes, 99, 292 p.

3698. ANZULEWICZ (Henryk). De forma resultante in speculo: die theologische Relevanz des Bildbegriffs und des Spiegelbildmodells in den Frühwerken des Albertus Magnus. Eine textkritische und begriffsgeschichtliche Untersuchung. Münster, Aschendorff, 99, 2 vol., IX-356 p., VII-330 p. (ill.). (Beiträge zur Geschichte der Philosophie und Theologie des Mittelalters, 53).

3699. BRACEGIRDLE (John). John Bracegirdle's Psychopharmacon: a translation of Boethius' De consolatione philosophiae (MS BL additional 11401). Ed. by Noel Harold KAYLOR and Jason Edward STREED. Tempe, Arizona Center for Medieval and Renaissance Studies, Arizona State University, 99, 172 p. (Medieval and Renaissance texts and studies, 200).

3700. CICERI (Antonio). Petri Iohannis Olivi opera: censimento dei manoscritti. Grottaferrata, Editiones Collegii S. Bonaventurae ad Claras Aquas, 99, 248 p. (Collectio Oliviana, 1).

3701. FRAETERS (Veerle). Gods gouden thesaurus: het Middelnederlandse handschrift wenen, ÖNB, 2372, in de alchemistische traditie. Leuven, Peeters, 99, XII-359 p. (Antwerpse studies over Nederlandse literatuurgeschiedenis, 3).

3702. GIOACCHINO DA FIORE. Trattati sui quattro vangeli. A cura di Claudio LEONARDI, Gian Luca PODESTÀ e Letizia PELLEGRINI. Roma, Viella, 9, XXXI-270 p. (Centro internazionale di Studi Gioachimiti. Opere di Gioacchino da Fiore: testi e strumenti, 11).

3703. GUILLELMUS DE CONCHIS. Opera omnia. Tomus II. Glosae super Boetius. Ed. L. NAUTA. Turnhout, Brepols, 99, CXLI-384 p. (Corpus christianorum continuatio mediaevalis, 158).

3704. IOANNES SCOTUS ERIUGENA. Periphyseon. Ed. A. E. JEAUNEAU. Liber Tertius. Turnhout, Brepols, 99, XL-695 p. (Corpus christianorum continuatio mediaevalis, 163).

3705. MARTIN LE FRANC. L'Estrif de Fortune et Vertu. Éd. par Peter F. DEMBOWSKI. Gèneve, Droz, 99, LX-402 p.

3706. Medicina antiqua. Codex Vindobonensis 93, Vienna, Österreichische Nationalbibliothek. Ed. by Peter Murray JONES. Codicological analysis and commentary by Franz UNTERKIRCHER. London, Harvey Miller Publishers, 99, 161 leaves, 63 p. (ill., facs.). (Manuscripts in miniature, 4) [Adapted from the commentary volume of the original facsimile edition published by Akademische Druck und Verlagsanstalt, Graz, 1972].

3707. OTLOH VON ST. EMMERAM. Liber de temptatione cuiusdam monachi. Untersuchung, kritische Edition und Übersetzung. Hrsg. v. Sabine GÄBE. Bern, Peter Lang, 99, 384 p. (Lateinische Sprache und Literatur des Mittelalters, 29).

3708. PLATINA (Bartolomeo). De falso et vero bono. A cura di Maria Grazia BLASIO. Roma, Edizioni di storia e letetratura, 99, CXLIV-138 p. (ill.). (Edizione nazionale dei testi umanistici, 3).

3709. POTAMIUS EPISCOPUS OLISPONENSIS. Opera omnia. Altercatio ecclesiae et synagogae. Ed. ab Martino CONTI. Turnhout, Brepols, 99, 277 p, (ill.). (Corpus Christianorum, Series Latina, 69A).

3710. Suppletio defectuum, Book I. Alexander Neckam on plants, birds and animals: a supplement to the Laus sapientie divine. Ed. by Christopher James MAC DONOUGH. Tavarnuzze, SISMEL – Edizioni del Galluzzo, 99, LXXXVI-184 p. (Per verba, 12).

3711. Testamentum (Il) alchemico attribuito a Raimondo Lullo: edizione del testo latino e catalano dal manoscritto Oxford, Corpus Christi College, 244. A cura di Michela PEREIRA e Barbara SPAGGIARI. Tavarnuzze, Sismel – Edizioni del Galluzzo, 99, CLXIV-631 p. (Millennio medievale, 14).

3712. THOMAS DE CHOBHAM. Summa de commendatione virtutum et extirpatione vitiorum. Ed. by Franco MORENZONI. Concordance. Turnhout, Brepols, 99, 75 p., 9 microfiches (Corpus Christianorum, Instrumenta lexicologica Latina. Series A, Formae, 102).

b. *Studies*

* 3713. KALUZA (Zénon). Bulletin d'histoire des doctrines médiévales. Les XIVe et XVe siècles. *Revue des sciences philosophiques et théologiques,* 99, 83, 2, p. 355-376.

* 3714. WEBER (Edouard-Henri). Bulletin d'histoire des doctrines médiévales. De saint Anselme à Maître Eckart (II). *Revue des sciences philosophiques et théologiques,* 99, 83, 2, p. 315-353.

3715. ADAMS MAC CORD (Marilyn). What sort of human nature? Medieval philosophy and the systematics of Christology. Milwaukee, Marquette U. P., 99, 120 p. (The Aquinas lecture).

3716. Aristotle's animals in the Middle Ages and Renaissance. Ed. by Carlos G. STEEL, Guy GULDENTOPS and Pieter BEULLENS. Leuven, Leuven U. P., 99, 408 p. (ill.). (Mediaevalia Lovaniensia. Studia, 27).

3717. BARBELLION (frère Stéphane-Marie). Les preuves de l'existence de Dieu: pour une relecture des cinq voies de saint Thomas d'Aquin. Paris, Cerf, 99, 471 p.

3718. BARRAQUÉ (Jean Pierre), LEROY (Béatrice). Des écrits pour les rois: en Espagne médiévale, la réflexion politique, d'Isidore de Séville aux rois catholiques. Limoges, Presses universitaires de Limoges, 99, 185 p. (ill.).

3719. BOUREAU (Alain). Théologie, science et censure au XIIIe siècle. Le cas de Jean Peckham. Paris, Belles Lettres, 99, 376 p.

3720. BOWLIN (John). Contingency and fortune in Aquinas' ethics. Cambridge, Cambridge U. P., 99, 272 p. (Cambridge Studies in Religion and Critical Thought, 6).

3721. CROSS (Richard). Duns Scotus. New York a. Oxford, Oxford U. P., 99, XXI-250 p. (Great medieval thinkers).

3722. D'ACUNTO (Nicolangelo). I laici nella chiesa e nella società secondo Pier Damiani: ceti dominanti e riforma ecclesiastica nel secolo XI. Roma, Istituto storico italiano per il Medio Evo, 99, XXIII-476 p. (Nuovi studi storici, 50).

3723. DAHAN (Gilbert). L'exégèse chrétienne de la Bible en Occident médiéval, XIIe–XIVe siècle. Paris, Les Editions du Cerf, 99, 486 p. (pl., ill.). (Patrimoines. Christianisme).

3724. DAVENPORT (Anne Ashley). Measure of a different greatness: the intensive infinite, 1250–1650. Leiden, Brill, 99, XV-438 p. (Studien und Texte zur Geistesgeschichte des Mittelalters, 67).

3725. DELL'ANNA (Giuseppe). Dies critici: la teoria della ciclicità delle patologie nel XIV secolo. Vol. 1. Dies et crises. Vol. 2. Textus. Galatina, Congedo, 99, 2 vol., 391 p., 330 p.

3726. EGGINTON (William). On Dante, hyperspheres, and the curvature of the medieval cosmos. *Journal of the history of ideas,* 99, 60, 2, p. 195-216.

3727. ELLIOTT (Dyan). Fallen bodies: pollution, sexuality, and demonology in the Middle Ages. Philadelphia, University of Pennsylvania Press, 99, XII-300 p. (The Middle Ages series).

3728. GINSBERG (Warren). Dante's aesthetics of being. Ann Arbor, University of Michigan Press, 99, IX-175 p.

3729. GLAZE (Florence Eliza). The perforated wall: the ownership and circulation of medical books in medieval Europe, ca. 800–1200. Ann Arbor, University of Michigan Press, 99, XII-365 p.

3730. HORST (Ulrich). Bischöfe und Ordensleute: Cura principalis animarum und via perfectionis in der Ekklesiologie des hl. Thomas von Aquin. Berlin, Akademie Verlag, 99, 200 p.

3731. IANNELLA (Cecilia). Giordano da Pisa: etica urbana e forme della società. Pisa, ETS, 99, 254 p. (Studi medioevali, 8).

3732. KEMPSHALL (M. S.). The common good in late medieval political thought: moral goodness and material benefit. Oxford a. New York, Clarendon Press a. Oxford U. P., 99, VIII-401p. (ill.).

3733. KOPECKÝ (Milan). Jan Milíč z Kroměříže a Jan z Jenštejna. Zd'ar nad Sazavou, Cisterciana Sarensis, 99, 96 p. (ill.).

3734. KRUSE (Britta-Juliane). "Die Arznei ist Goldes wert". Mittelalterliche Frauenrezepte. Berlin, W. de Gruyter, 99, VII-414 p. (pl., ill., facs.).

3735. LAARMANN (Matthias). Deus, primum cognitum: die Lehre von Gott als dem Ersterkannten des menschlichen Intellekts bei Heinrich von Gent (gest. 1293). Münster, Aschendorff, 99, XII-528 p. (ill.). (Beiträge zur Geschichte der Philosophie und Theologie des Mittelalters, 52).

3736. LAGERLUND (Henrik). Modal syllogistics in the middle ages. Uppsala, Uppsala University, 99, XV-297 p.

3737. LEWIS (Sue). Astrology and Juan de Mena's Laberinto de fortuna. London, Department of Hispanic Studies, Queen Mary and Westfield College, 99, 78 p. (ill.). (Papers of the medieval Hispanic research seminar, 21).

3738. LONG (R. James), O'CARROLL (Maura). The life and works of Richard Fishacre, OP: prolegomena to the edition of his commentary on the Sentences. München, Verlag der Bayerischen Akademie der Wissenschaften, 99, 235 p. (Veröffentlichungen der Kommission für die Herausgabe Ungedruckter Texte aus der Mittelalterlichen Geisteswelt, 21).

3739. LÖSER (Freimut). Meister Eckhart in Melk: studien zum redaktor Lienhart Peuger. Mit einer edition des traktats "Von der sel wirdichait und aigenschafft". Tübingen, Max Niemeyer, 99, IX-604 p. (facs., ill.). (Texte und Textgeschichte, 48).

3740. MAURER (Armand A.). The philosophy of William of Ockham in the light of its principles. Toronto, Pontifical Institute of Mediaeval Studies, 99, X-590 p. (Studies and texts, 133).

3741. Medieval analyses in language and cognition. Acts of the symposium "The Copenhagen School of Medieval Philosophy, January 10-13, 1996", organized by the Royal Danish Academy of Sciences and Letters and the Institute for Greek and Latin, University of Copenhagen. Ed. by Russel L. FRIEDMAN and Sten EBBESEN. Copenhagen, Det Kongelige Danske Videnskabernes Selskab, 99, 563 p. (Historisk-filosofiske Meddelelser [Det Kongelige Danske Videnskabernes Selskab], 77).

3742. NOUZILLE (Philippe), BOULNOIS (Olivier). Expériénce de Dieu et théologie monastique au XIIe siecle: étude sur les sermons d'Aelred de Rievaulx. Paris, Editions du Cerf, 99, 331 p. (Philosophie et théologie).

3743. O'MEARA (D. J.). The structure of being and the search for the good. Essays on ancient and early medieval platonism. Aldershot, Ashgate, 99, 318 p. (Variorum collected studies series, 629).

3744. PARK (Seung-Chan). Die Rezeption der mittelalterlichen Sprachphilosophie in der Theologie des Thomas von Aquin: mit besonderer Berücksichtigung der Analogie. Boston, Brill, 99, X-524 p. (Studien und Texte zur Geistesgeschichte des Mittelalters, 65).

3745. RAWCLIFFE (Carole). Medicine for the soul. The life, death and resurrection of an English medieval hospital: St Giles's, Norwich, c.1249-1550. Stroud, Sutton, 99, XVIII-334 p. (pl., ill.).

3746. REYNOLDS (Philip Lyndon). Food and the body: some peculiar questions in high medieval theology. Leiden a. Boston, Brill, 99, XIV-458 p. (Studien und Texte zur Geistesgeschichte des Mittelalters, 69).

3747. ROUGÉ (Matthieu). Doctrine et experience de l'Eucharistie chez Guillaume de Saint-Thierry. Paris, Beauchesne, 99, XI-339 p. (Théologie historique, 111).

3748. SHOGIMEN (Takashi). The relationship between theology and canon law: another context of political thought in the early fourteenth century. Journal of the history of ideas, 99, 60, 3, p. 417-432.

3749. STANNARD (Jerry). Pristina medicamenta: ancient and medieval medical botany. Aldershot, Ashgate, 99, XX-[324] p. (Variorum collected studies series, 646).

3750. TEDOLDI (Fabio Massimo). La dottrina dei cinque sensi spirituali in San Bonaventura. Roma, Pontificium Athenaeum Antonianum, 99, 371 p. (Theses ad lauream, 365).

3751. THIHER (Allen). Revels in madness: insanity in medicine and literature. Ann Arbor, University of Michigan Press, 99, 354 p. (Corporealities).

3752. THIJSSEN (J. M. M. H.), BRAAKHUIS (H. A. G.). The commentary tradition on Aristotle's De generatione et corruptione: ancient, medieval, and early modern. Turnhout, Brepols, 99, 238 p. (Studia artistarum. Études sur la Faculté des arts dans les universités médiévales, 7).

3753. TÖPFER (Bernhard). Urzustand und Sündenfall in der mittelalterlichen Gesellschafts- und Staatstheorie. Stuttgart, A. Hiersemann, 99,VIII-642 p. (Monographien zur Geschichte des Mittelalters, 45).

3754. TROTTMANN (Christian). Théologie et noétique au XIIIe siècle: à la recherche d'un statut. Paris, Librairie philosophique J. Vrin, 99, 224 p. (Etudes de philosophie médiévale, 78).

3755. WILLIAMS (A. N.). The ground of union: deification in Aquinas and Palamas. New York a. Oxford, Oxford U. P., 99, 222 p.

3756. ZAHNER (Paul). Die Fülle des Heils in der Endlichkeit der Geschichte: Bonaventuras Theologie als Antwort auf die franziskanischen Joachiten. Werl, D.-Coelde-Verlag, 99, 315 p. (ill.). (Franziskanische Forschungen, 41).

3757. ZECHIEL-ECKES (Klaus). Florus von Lyon als Kirchenpolitiker und Publizist: Studien zur Persönlichkeit eines karolingischen "Intellektuellen" am Beispiel der Auseinandersetzung mit Amalarius (835–838) und des Prädestinationsstreits (851–855). Stuttgart, Thorbecke, 99, XXX-265 p. (Quellen und Forschungen zum Recht im Mittelalter, 8).

Cf. n° 1080

§ 13. History of the Church and religion.

a. *General*

* 3758. CHRISTINE DE PIZAN. Epistre Othea. Éd. par Gabriella PARUSSA. Géneve, Librairie Droz, 99, 539 p.

* 3759. GONZALO DE BERCEO. I miracoli di Nostra Signora. A cura di Giuseppe TAVANI. Alessandria, Edizioni Dell'Orso, 99, 344 p. (Gli Orsatti. Testi dell'altro Medioevo, 5).

** 3760. FABRI (Felix). Die Sionpilger. Hrsg. v. Wieland CARLS. Berlin, Erich Schmidt Verlag, 99, 596 p. (ill.). (Texte des späten Mittelalters und der frühen Neuzeit, 39).

** 3761. FERRARI (Michele Camillo). Il Liber sanctae crucis di Rabano Mauro. Testo, immagine, contesto. Bern, Peter Lang, 99, XIX-519 p. (tabb., ill.). (Lateinische Sprache und Literatur des Mittelalters, 30).

** 3762. JEAN TINCTOR. Invectives contre la secte de vauderie. Éd. de Émile VAN BALBERGHE et Frédéric DUVAL. Tournai, Archives du Chapitre cathédral et Louvain-la-Neuve, Université catholique de Louvain, 99, 137 p. (Tournai. Art et Histoire, 14).

** 3763. Repertorium Poenitentiariae Germanicum. Teil. 2. Verzeichnis der in den Supplikenregistern der Pönitentiariae Nikolaus' V. vorkommenden Personen, Kirchen und Orte des Deutschen Reiches, 1447–1455. Hrsg. v. Ludwig SCHMUGGE, Krystyna BUKOWSKA, Alessandra MOSCIATTI und Hildegard SCHNEIDER-SCHMUGGE. Tübingen, Niemeyer, 99, XXIX-364 p. (ill.).

** 3764. XIMENIUS (Rodericus de Rada). Opera omnia. Historiae minores; Dialogus libri vite. Ed. Juan A. ESTÉVEZ SOLA y Juan FERNÁNDEZ VALVERDE. Turnhout, Brepols, 99, 508 p. (Corpus Christianorum. Continuatio Mediaevalis, 72C).

3765. AKTAN (Ali). Memlûk-Haçlı münasebetleri. (Relations entre le Sultanat Mamelouk et les croisés). *Belleten*, 99, 53, 237, p. 411-452.

3766. BROOKE (Christopher). Churches and churchmen in medieval Europe. London, Hambledon Press, 99, XVIII-329 p.

3767. EDWARDS (John). The Spanish Inquisition. Stroud, Tempus, 99, 160 p. (pl., ill., map, ports).

3768. HYLSON-SMITH (Kenneth). Christianity in England from Roman times to the Reformation. London, SCM, 99, XXII-384 p.

3769. JANSEN LUDWIG (Katherine). The making of the Magdalen: preaching and popular devotion in the later Middle Ages. Princeton, Princeton U. P., 99, XIII-389 p.

3770. Last things: death and the Apocalypse in the Middle Ages. Ed. by Caroline WALKER BYNUM and Paul FREEDMAN. Philadelphia, University of Pennsylvania Press, 99, VIII-363 p. (ill.). (The Middle Ages series).

3771. Life and thought in the northern church, c.1100–c.1700: essays in honour of Claire Cross. Ed. by Diana WOOD. Woodbridge, Boydell Press, 99, XIV-595 p. (ill.). (Studies in church history. Subsidia, 12).

3772. Medieval (The) church: universities, heresy, and the religious life. Essays in honour of Gordon Leff. Ed. by R. B. DOBSON and Peter BILLER. Woodbridge, Published for the Ecclesiastical History Society by the Boydell Press, 99, XVII-362 p. (Studies in church history. Subsidia, 11).

3773. Mirror (The) of simple souls. Ed. by J. C. MARLER, Edmund COLLEDGE, Judith GRANT and Marguerite PORETE. Notre Dame, University of Notre Dame Press, 99, LXXXVII-209 p. (Notre Dame texts in medieval culture, 6).

3774. MOREY (James H). Book and verse: a guide to Middle English biblical literature. Urbana, University of Illinois Press, 99, XVIII-428 (Illinois medieval studies).

3775. OLD (Hughes Oliphant). The reading and preaching of the Scriptures in the worship of the Christian Church. Grand Rapids a. Cambridge, Eerdmans Publishing, 99, XVIII-646 p.

3776. Pagan (The) Middle Ages. Woodbridge a. Rochester, Boydell Press, 99, 160 p.

3777. PARTNER (Peter). The First millennium: the birth of Christianity to the Crusades. London, Granada Media, 99, 191 p. (ill.).

3778. Pfaffen und Laien, ein mittelalterlicher Antagonismus? Freiburger Colloquium 1996. Hrsg. v. Eckart Conrad LUTZ und Ernst TREMP. Freiburg, Universitätsverlag, 99, 261 p. (ill.). (Scrinium Friburgense, 10).

3779. REYNOLDS (Roger E.). Clerical orders in the early Middle Ages: duties and ordination. Aldershot a. Brookfield, Ashgate, 99, X-334 p. (ill.). (Variorum collected studies series, 670). – IDEM. Clerics in the early Middle Ages: hierarchy and image. Aldershot a. Brookfield, Ashgate, 99, VIII-334 p. (ill.). (Variorum collected studies series, 669).

3780. SÁNCHEZ SÁNCHEZ (Manuel Ambrosio). Un sermonario castellano medieval: el MS. 1854 de la Biblioteca Universitaria de Salamanca. Salamanca, Ediciones Universidad de Salamanca, 99, 2 vol., 881 p. (ill.). (Textos recuperados, 19).

3781. SCHMIDT (Hans-Joachim). Kirche, Staat, Nation: Raumgliederung der Kirche im mittelalterlichen Europa. Weimar, Hermann Böhlaus Nachfolger, 99, 580 p. (maps). (Forschungen zur mittelalterlichen Geschichte, 37).

3782. SUYDAM (Mary A.), ZIEGLER (Joanna E.). Performance and transformation: new approaches to late medieval spirituality. Basingstoke, Macmillan, 99, XXI-361 p. (ill.).

3783. Sveriges kyrkohistoria. Band 2. Hög-och senmedeltid. (Histoire ecclésiastique de la Suède. Tome 2. Moyen Age central et bas Moyen Age). Red. par Sven Erik PERNLER. Stockholm, Verbum, 99, 311 p. (ill.).

3784. VALLÉE (Gérard). The shaping of Christianity: the history and literature of its formative centuries (100–800). New York, Paulist Press, 99, VIII-265 p. (map.).

3785. VIOLANTE (Cinzio). Chiesa feudale e riforme in Occidente, secc. X–XII: introduzione a un tema storiografico. Spoleto, Centro italiano di studi sull'alto Medioevo, 99, XI-171 p. (Studi, 9).

3786. Vita Religiosa im Mittelalter: Festschrift für Kaspar Elm zum 70. Geburtstag. Hrsg. v. Franz J. FELTEN und Stephanie HAARLÄNDER. Berlin, Duncker & Humblot, 99, XIX-985 p. (ill., map). (Berliner historische Studien, Bd. 31. Ordensstudien, 13).

Cf. n° 5293

b. History of the Popes

3787. CAROCCI (Sandro). Il nepotismo nel medioevo. Papi, cardinali e famiglie nobili. Roma, Viella, 99, 240 p. (La corte dei papi, 4).

3788. HACK (Achim Thomas). Das Empfangszeremoniell bei mittelalterlichen Papst-Kaiser-Treffen. Köln, Böhlau, 99, XII-799 p. (ill.). (Forschungen zur Kaiser- und Papstgeschichte des Mittelalters, 18).

3789. JØRGENSEN (Torstein), SALETNICH (Gastone). Letters to the Pope: Norwegian relations to the Holy See in the late Middle Ages. Stavanger, Misjonshogskolens, 99, 168 p. (ill.).

3790. PÁSZTOR (Edith). Onus apostolicae sedis. Curia romana e cardinalato nei secoli XI–XV. A cura di L. GATTO, S. DI MATTIA SPIRITO, A. COCCI e A. MARINI. Roma, Sintesi informazione, 99, XXIV-426 p.

3791. PEREIRA PAGÁN (Begona). El Papa Luna: Benedicto XIII. Madrid, Alderaban, 99, 319 p. (ill.). (Colección El legado de la historia, 18).

c. Monastic history

* 3792. AYMES (Elisabeth). Bulletin d'histoire bénédictine, 13, 4. Revue bénédictine, 99, 109, 1-2, p. 233-328.

* 3793. Bulletin de spiritualité monastique. Collectanea cisterciensia., 97, 59, 1, p. 127-160; 2, 161-198; 3, p. 199-240; 4, p. 241-280; 98, 60, 1, p. 281-292; 2, p. 293-330; 3, p. 331-364; 4, p. 365-398; 99, 61, 1, p. 399-444; 2, p. 445-484; 3, p. 485-522.

3794. Abbazia (L') di Staffarda e l'irradiazione cistercense nel Piemonte meridionale. Atti del Convegno, Abbazia di Staffarda-Revello, sabato 17 e domenica 18 ottobre 1998. A cura di Rinaldo COMBA e Grado G. MERLO. Cuneo, Società per gli studi storici, archeologici ed artistici della provincia di Cuneo, 99, 430 p. (Storia e storiografia, 21).

3795. BERGER (Jutta Maria). Die Geschichte der Gastfreundschaft im hochmittelalterlichen Mönchtum: die Cistercienser. Berlin, Akademie Verlag, 99, 437 p.

3796. BERMAN (Constance H.). The Cistercian evolution: the invention of a religious order in twelfth-century Europe. Philadelphia, University of Pennsylvania Press, 99, XXIV-382 p. (ill., maps, plans, geneal. tabl.). (The Middle Ages series).

3797. BORELLI (Laura). Il francescanesimo femminile a Lucca nei secoli XIII e XIV: il Monastero di Gattaiola. Lucca, Accademia lucchese di scienze lettere ed arti, 99, 196 p. (ill.). (Studi e testi, 63).

3798. BOURGEOIS (Ginette), DOUZOU (Alain). Une aventure spirituelle dans le Rouergue méridional au Moyen Age: ermites et cisterciens à Silvanès (1120–1477). Paris, Editions du Cerf, 99, 255 p. (Histoire).

3799. BÜRKLE (Susanne). Literatur im Kloster: historische Funktion und rhetorische Legitimation frauenmystischer Texte des 14. Jahrhunderts. Tübingen, Francke, 99, 368 p. (Bibliotheca Germanica, 38).

3800. BURTON (Janet E.). The monastic order in Yorkshire, 1069–1215. Cambridge a. New York, Cambridge U. P., 99, ZIZ-352 p. (maps). (Cambridge studies in medieval life and thought).

3801. CABY (Cécile). De l'érémitisme rural au monachisme urbain: les camaldules en Italie à la fin du Moyen Âge. Rome, École française de Rome, 99, 885 p. (Bibliothèque des écoles françaises d'Athènes et de Rome, 350).

3802. COWDREY (H. E. J.). The Crusades and Latin monasticism, 11th–12th centuries. Aldershot a. Brookfield, Ashgate, 99, X-274 p. (Variorum collected studies series, 662).

3803. DALARUN (Jacques). François d'Assise ou le pouvoir en question. Principes et modalités du gouvernement dans l'ordre des Frères mineurs. Bruxelles, De Boeck Unievrsité, 99, 153 p. (Bibliothèque du Moyen Age, 15).

3804. Etica e politica: le teorie dei frati mendicanti nel Due e Trecento. Atti del XXVI Convegno internazionale, Assisi 15–17 ottobre 1998. Spoleto, Centro italiano di studi sull'Alto Medioevo, 99, 318 p. (Atti dei convegni della Società internazionale di studi francescani e del Centro interuniversitario di studi francescani, 9).

3805. GRETSCH (Mechthild). The intellectual foundations of the English Benedictine reform. Cambridge a. New York, Cambridge U. P., 99, XII-471 p. (Cambridge studies in Anglo-Saxon England, 25).

3806. HINDSLEY (Leonard P.). The mystics of Engelthal: writings from a medieval monastery. Basingstoke, Macmillan, 99, 240 p.

3807. IOTSALD VON SAINT-CLAUDE. Vita des Abtes Odilo von Cluny. Hrsg. v. Iohannes STAUB. Hannover, Hahnsche Buchhandlung, 99, VIII-366 p. (Monumenta Germaniae Historica. Scriptores rerum Germanicarum in usum scholarum separatim editi, 68). – STAUB (Iohannes). Studien zu Iotsald Vita des Abtes Odilo von Cluny. Hannover, Hahnsche Buchhandlung, 99, XIII-98 p. (ill.). (Monumenta Germaniae Historica. Studien und Texte, 24).

3808. JONES (John D.), HERVAEUS (Natalis). The poverty of Christ and the apostles. Toronto, Pontifical

Institute of Mediaeval Studies, 99, VI-174 p. (Studies in medieval moral teaching, 2).

3809. KURZAWA (Frédéric). Les moines irlandais dans la Lorraine médiévale. Metz, Editions Serpenoise, 99, 223 p.

3810. LEHMIJORI-GARDNER (Maiju). Wordly saints: social interaction of Dominican penitent women in Italy, 1200–1500. Helsinki, Suomen Historialinen Seura, 99, 189 p. (Bibliotheca Historica, 35).

3811. MAGNANI SOARES-CHRISTEN (Eliana). Monastères et aristocratie en Provence milieu X^e–début XIIe siècle. Münster, Lit, 99, XIX-610 p. (maps). (Vita regularis, 10).

3812. Mendicants, military orders, and regionalism in medieval Europe. Ed. by Jürgen SARNOWSKY. Aldershot, Ashgate, 99, XIV-334 p. (ill.).

3813. Monachesimo (Il) italiano nell'età comunale. Atti del IV Convegno di studi storici sull'Italia benedettina, Abbazia di S. Giacomo Maggiore, Pontida (Bergamo), 3-6 settembre 1995. A cura di F. G. TROLESE. Cesena, Badia di Santa Maria del Monte, 99, VIII-817 p. (ill.). (Italia benedettina, 16).

3814. Monasteries and society in medieval Britain. Proceedings of the 1994 Harlaxton Symposium. Ed. by Benjamin THOMPSON. Stamford, Paul Watkins, 99, XII-368 p. (pl., ill., maps). (Harlaxton medieval studies, 6).

3815. Monastero (Il) di Rifreddo e il monachesimo cistercense femminile nell'Italia occidentale (secoli XII–XIV). Atti del Convegno, Staffarda-Rifreddo, sabato 18 e domenica 19 maggio 1999. A cura di Rinaldo COMBA. Cuneo, Società per gli studi storici, archeologici ed artistici della provincia di Cuneo, 99, 365 p. (Storia e storiografia, 22).

3816. MONTESANO (Marina). "Supra acque et supra ad vento": "superstizioni", maleficia e incantamenta nei predicatori francescani osservanti (Italia, sec. XV). Roma, Istituto storico italiano per il Medio Evo, 99, XX-224 p. (Nuovi studi storici, 46).

3817. MULCHAHEY (Marian Michèle). First the bow is bent in study: Dominican education before 1350. Toronto, Pontifical Institute of Medieval Studies, 99, XXII-618 p. (Studies and texts, 132).

3818. OBERSTE (Jörg), MELVILLE (Gert). Die Bettelorden im Aufbau: Beiträge zu Institutionalisierungsprozessen im mittelalterlichen Religiosentum. Münster, Lit, 99, IX-668 p. (Vita regularis, 11).

3819. Ordre (L') de Cîteaux dans l'espace rhônalpin. Actes du Colloque, 1er août 1998, La Vacherie. Cahiers de Léoncel, 99, 15, p. 5-128.

3820. Ordre (L') de Cîteaux en Vivarais (1098–1998). Actes du Colloque organisé par la Revue du Vivarais à Vals-les-Bains [Ardèche] en octobre 1998. Revue du Vivarais, 99, 103, 737-738, 288 p.

3821. OTTONELLO (Piero). L'esordio cistercense in Italia: il mito del deserto, fra poteri feudali e nuove istituzioni comunali (1120-1250). Genova, ECIG, 99, 238 p. (ill., map, plans). (Collana Dimensione Europa).

3822. PARISSE (Michel). La vie de Jean, abbé de Gorze. Paris, Picard, 99, 166 p. (facs.).

3823. PICASSO (Giorgio). Tra umanesimo e devotio: studi di storia monastica raccolti per il 50° di professione dell'autore. A cura di Mauro TAGLIABUE, Giuseppe MOTTA, Giancarlo ANDENNA. Milano, Vita e pensiero, 99, XXVI-228 p. (Scienze storiche, 67).

3824. Pratique et sacré dans le espace monastiques au Moyen Âge et à l'époque moderne. Actes du Colloque de Liessies-Maubeuge, 26–28 septembre 1997. Addendum. Éd. par Philippe RACINET. Amiens et Lille, CAHMER – CREDHIR, 99, 114 p. (ill., maps). (Histoire médiévale et archéologie, 9).

3825. RILEY-SMITH (Jonathan). Hospitallers: the history of the order of St. John. London, Hambledon, 99, VII-151 p. (ill., maps, pl.).

3826. ROTH (Christoph). Literatur und Klosterreform: die Bibliothek der Benediktiner von St. Mang zu Füssen im 15. Jahrhundert. Tübingen, Niemeyer, 99, VIII-438 p. (ill.). (Studia Augustana, 10).

3827. ROWLANDS (Kenneth). The friars: a history of the British medieval friars. Lewes, The Book Guild, 99, XIV-377 p. (pl., ill.).

3828. RÜFFER (Jens). Orbis Cisterciensis: zur Geschichte der monastischen ästhetischen Kultur im 12. Jahrhundert. Berlin, Lukas, 99, 507 p. (ill.). (Studien zur Geschichte, Kunst und Kultur der Zisterzienser, 6).

3829. Schriftlichkeit und Lebenspraxis im Mittelalter: Erfassen, Bewahren, Verändern. Akten des Internationalen Kolloquiums 8 –10. Juni 1995. Hrsg. v. Hagen KELLER, Christel MEIER und Thomas SCHARFF. München, W. Fink, 99, VI-361 p. (pl., ill.). (Münstersche Mittelalter-Schriften, 76).

3830. SELWOOD (Dominic). Knights of the cloister: Templars and Hospitallers in Central-Southern Occitania, c.1100–c.1300. Woodbridge, Boydell, 99, XVII-261 p. (ill., map).

3831. SUGIZAKI (Taiichiro). 12 seiki no shudoin to shakai. (Monasteries and society in the twelfth century). Tokyo, Hara Shobo, 99, 312 p.

Cf. n°s 3475, 3656

d. *Hagiography*

* 3832. DOLBEAU (François). Les travaux français sur l'hagiographie médiolatine (1968–1998). *Hagiographica*, 99, 6, p. 23-68.

* 3833. Studi agiografici (Gli) sul Medioevo negli ultimi trenta anni in Europa. Relazioni del Convegno (Firenze, 27–28 febbraio 1998). *Hagiographica*, 99, 6, p. 1-152.

3834. ASHLEY (Kathleen M.), SHEINGORN (Pamela). Writing faith: text, sign, and history in the Miracles of Sainte Foy. Chicago, University of Chicago Press, 99, X-205 p. (ill.).

3835. BRUINS (Clara). **Chiara d'Assisi** come altera Maria. Le miniature della vita di Santa Chiara nel Manoscritto Thennenbach-4 di Karlsruhe. Roma, Istituto Storico dei Cappuccini, 99, 50 p. e 38 tavole (ill.). (Iconographia franciscana, 12).

3836. CANNON (Joanna), VAUCHEZ (André). **Margherita of Cortona** and the Lorenzetti. Sienese art and the cult of a holy woman in medieval Tuscany. University Park, The Pennsylvania State U. P., 99, XV-275 p. (ill., maps).

3837. Cult (The) of saints in late antiquity and the Middle Ages: essays on the contribution of Peter Brown. Ed. by James HOWARD-JOHNSTON and Paul Antony HAYWARD. Oxford, Oxford U. P., 99, X-298 p.

3838. DEGL'INNOCENTI (Antonella). Un leggendario fiorentino del XIV secolo. Tavarnuzze, SISMEL – Edizioni del Galluzzo, 99, XLI-120 p. (Millennio medievale. Testi, 5).

3839. Fonctions sociales et politiques du culte des saints dans les sociétés de rite grec et latin au Moyen Âge et à l'époque moderne: approche comparative. Éd. par M. V. DMITRIEV et Marek DERWICH. Wroclaw, Larhcor, 99, 484 p. (ill.). (Opera ad historiam monasticam spectantia. Series I, 3).

3840. GAUTIER DE COINCI. La Vie de sainte **Christine**, édition critique d'après le ms f. fr. 817 de la Bibliothèque nationale de France par Olivier COLLET. Genève, Droz, 99, XXIII-179 p.

3841. Gendered voices: medieval saints and their interpreters. Ed. by Catherine M. MOONEY. Philadelphia, University of Pennsylvania Press, 99, XIII-276 p. (Middle Ages series).

3842. GÉRARD (Michèle). Les Cris des la Sainte. Corps et écriture dans la tradition latine et romane des vies de saintes. Paris, Champion, 99, 232 p. (Essais sur le Moyen Âge, 18).

3843. IKEGAMI (Keiko). Barlaam and Josaphat: a transcription of MS Egerton 876 with notes, glossary, and comparative study of the Middle English and Japanese versions. New York, AMS Press, 99, XVI-243 p. (AMS studies in the Middle Ages, 21).

3844. Images of St **Francis of Assisi** in painting, stone and glass from the earliest images to ca. 1320 in Italy: a catalogue. Ed. by William R. COOK. Firenze, Leo S. Olschki a. Perth, Department of Italian, University of W. Australia, 99, 316 p. (ill.). (Italian medieval and Renaissance studies, 7).

3845. MORRIS (Bridget). St. **Birgitta** of Sweden. Woodbridge, Boydell Press, 99, XI-202 p. (ill., maps). (Studies in medieval mysticism, 1).

3846. Pellegrinaggi e itinerari dei santi nel Mezzogiorno medievale. A cura di Giovanni VITOLO. Napoli, Liguori, 99, VIII-284 p. (ill.). (Europa mediterranea).

3847. POPPENBORG (Annette). Das Leben der heiligen **Katharina von Siena**: Untersuchung und Edition einer mittelniederdeutschen Legendenhandschrift. Bielefeld, Verlag fur Regionalgeschichte, 99, 143 p. (ill.). (Westfälische Beiträge zur niederdeutschen Philologie, 9).

3848. Reliques (Les). Objects, cultes, symboles. Actes du Colloque international de l'Université du Littoral-Côte d'Opale (Boulogne-sur-Mer), 4–6 septembre 1997. Éd. Edina BOZÓKY et Anne-Marie HELVÉTIUS. Turnhout, Brepols, 99, 336 p. (tab., ill., pl., maps). (Hagiologia. Études sur la sainteté en Occident, 1).

3849. RIDYARD (Susan J.). Earthly love, spiritual love, love of the saints. Sewanee, University of the South Press, 99, 316 p. (Sewanee medieval studies, 8).

3850. SILVAS (Anna). **Jutta** and **Hildegard**: the biographical sources. University Park, Pennsylvania State U. P., 99, XXVII-299 p. (ill., tab., maps). (Brepols medieval women series).

3851. STOUCK (Mary-Ann). Medieval saints: a reader. Peterborough a. Orchard Park, Broadview Press, 99, XXIII-637 p. (ill.). (Readings in medieval civilizations and cultures, 4).

3852. Treasury (The) of Saint **Francis of Assisi**. Ed. by Laurence B. KANTER and Giovanni MORELLO. Milano, Electa, 99, 221 p. (ill.).

3853. Vita Sancti **Liudgeri** (Die): Vollständige Faksimile-Ausgabe der Handschrift Ms. theol. lat. fol. 323 der Staatsbibliothek zu Berlin-Preussischer Kulturbesitz: Text, Übersetzung und Kommentar, Forschungsbeiträge. Hrsg. v. Eckhard FREISE und Mechthild BLACK. Graz, Akademische Druck- u. Verlagsanstalt u. Bielefeld, Verlag für Regionalgeschichte, 99, 202 p. (Codices selecti phototypice impressi, 95).

Cf. n° 79

e. Special studies

** 3854. CARNIER (Marc). Parochies en bidplaatsen in het Bisdom Terwaan vóór 1300: een repertorium van de parochies van de dekenijen Veurne en Ieper en een overzicht van alle bidplaatsen van het bisdom. Bruxelles, Archives generales du Royaume, 99, 421 p. (Studia, 78).

** 3855. FRANCHI (Antonino). Ascoli pontificia. Vol. 2. Dal 1244 al 1300. Regesti a cura di Laura CIOTTI. Ascoli Piceno, Istituto superiore di studi medioevali "Cecco d'Ascoli,", 99, 313 p. (Testi e documenti, 4).

** 3856. GIOACCHINO DA FIORE. Commento a una profezia ignota. A cura di Matthias KAUP. Roma, Viella, 99, 198 p. (Centro internazionale di studi gioachimiti. Opere di Gioacchino da Fiore, testi e strumenti, 10).

13. HISTORY OF THE CHURCH AND RELIGION

** 3857. LUTHER (Martin). Verlegung des Alcoran (1442) [German translation of] RICOLDUS DE MONTECRUCIS, Confutatio alcorani (1300). Wurzburg, Echter Verlag, 99, 339 p.

3858. ABBOTT (Christopher). Julian of Norwich: autobiography and theology. Woodbridge a. Rochester, D.S. Brewer, 99, XIV-197 p. (Studies in medieval mysticism, 2).

3859. ALBERT (Bat-Sheva). Le pélerinage à l'époque carolingienne. Bruxelles, Nauwelaerts et Louvain-la-Neuve, College Erasme, VIII-462 p. (maps). (Bibliothèque de la Revue d'Histoire ecclésiastique, 82).

3860. ANDREWS (Frances). The early Humiliati. Cambridge a. New York, Cambridge U. P., 99, XI-353 p. (Cambridge studies in medieval life and thought).

3861. Angèle de Foligno: le dossier. Rome, December 1-2, 1995. Éd. par Giulia BARONE et Jacques DALARUN. Rome, École française de Rome, 99, 433 p. (pl., ill.). (Collection de l'École française de Rome, 255).

3862. BAUERSCHMIDT (Frederick Christian). Julian of Norwich and the mystical body politic of Christ. Notre Dame a. London, University of Notre Dame Press, 99, XII-290 p. (Studies in spirituality and theology, 5).

3863. BEUTIN (Wolfgang). Anima: Untersuchungen zur Frauenmystik des Mittelalters. Frankfurt am Main, P. Lang, 99, 261 p. (Bremer Beiträge zur Literatur- und Ideengeschichte, 29).

3864. BYER (Glenn). Charlemagne and baptism: a study of responses to the circular letter of 811/812. San Francisco, London a. Bethsaida, International Scholars, 99, 264 p.

3865. CAROZZI (Claude). Apocalypse et salut dans le Christianisme ancien et médiéval. Paris, Aubier, 99, 230 p. (Collection historique).

3866. Chrétienté (La) latine et les Slaves orientaux. Éd. par V. VODOFF. *Revue des études slaves*, 70, 2, 99, pp. 1-256.

3867. Church (The) in medieval York: records edited in honour of Professor Barrie Dobson. Ed. by David M. SMITH. [York], University of York, Borthwick Institute of Historical Research, 99, VIII-168 p. (map). (Borthwick texts and calendars, 24).

3868. Condamnation (La) parisienne de 1277: nouvelle édition du texte latin, traduction, introduction et commentaire. Éd. par David PICHÉ et Claude LAFLEUR. Paris, J. Vrin, 99, 351 p. (Sic et non).

3869. CURZEL (Emanuele). Le pievi trentine. Trasformazioni e continuità nell'organizzazione territoriale della cura d'anime dalle origini al XIII secolo (studio introduttivo e schede). Bologna, Edizioni Dehoniane, 99, XI-387 p. (tab., maps, pl.). (ITC-isr Centro per le scienze religiose in Trento. Serie maior, 5).

3870. DE EPALZA (Miguel). Jesús entre judíos, cristianos y musulmanes hispanos (siglos VI–XVII). Granada, Universidad de Granada, 99, 290 p. (Biblioteca Chronica nova de estudios históricos, 59).

3871. DE MIRAMON (Charles). Embrasser l'état monastique à l'âge adulte (1050–1200). Etude sur la conversion tardive. *Annales*, 99, 54, 4, p. 825-850. – IDEM. Les "donnés" au Moyen Âge: une forme de vie religieuse laïque v. 1180–v. 1500. Paris, Cerf, 99, 486 p. (ill.). (Histoire).

3872. DINZELBACHER (Peter). Die letzten Dinge: Himmel, Hölle, Fegefeuer im Mittelalter. Freiburg, Basel u. Wien, Herder, 99, 213 p. (ill.). (Herder-Spektrum, 4715).

3873. DOR (Pierre). Les reliquaires de la passion en France du Ve au XVe siècle. Amiens, CAHMER, 99, 248 p. (ill., tab.). (Histoire médiévale et archéologie, 10).

3874. DRISCOLL (Michael). Alcuin et la pénitence à l'époque carolingienne. Münster, Aschendorff, 99, VII-237 p. (ill.). (Liturgiewissenschaftliche Quellen und Forschungen, 81).

3875. DUPRÉ (José). Catharisme et chrétienté: la pensée dualiste dans le destin de l'Europe. Chancelade, La Clavellerie, 99, 559 p. (ill.).

3876. EBERSPERGER (Birgit). Die angelsachsischen Handschriften in den Pariser Bibliotheken: mit einer Edition von Aelfrics Kirchweihhomilie aus der Handschrift Paris, BN, lat. 943. Heidelberg, Winter, 99, XII-314 p. (Anglistische Forschungen, 261).

3877. Évangile et évangélisme: XIIe–XIIIe siècle. Toulouse, Privat, 99, 384 p. (pl., ill.). (Cahiers de Fanjeaux, 34).

3878. Felix Fabri, die Sionpilger. Hrsg. v. Carls WIELAND. Berlin, E. Schmidt, 99, 596 p. (ill., facs.). (Texte des späten Mittelalters und der frühen Neuzeit, 39).

3879. FLEMING (Martha H.). The late medieval Pope prophecies: the Genus nequam group. Tempe, Arizona Center for Medieval and Renaissance Studies, 99, XI-207 p. (ill.). (Medieval and Renaissance Texts and Studies, 204).

3880. FLORI (Jean). Pierre l'Ermite et la première croisade. Paris, Fayard, 99, 647 p. (maps).

3881. GARSOIAN (Nina G.). Church and culture in early medieval Armenia. Brookfield, Ashgate, 99, X-372 p. (ill.). (Variorum collected studies series, 648).

3882. GÓRECKA (Marzena). Das Bild Mariens in der Deutschen Mystik des Mittelalters. Bern, P. Lang, 99, 654 s. (ill.). (Deutsche Literatur von den Anfängen bis 1700, 29).

3883. HAMILTON (Bernard). Crusaders, Cathars, and the holy places. Aldershot a. Brookfield, Ashgate, 99, XI-320 p. (Variorum collected studies series, 656).

3884. KERR (Berenice M.). Religious life for women, c.1100–c.1350: Fontevraud in England. Oxford,

Clarendon Press, 99, XIX-299 p. (ill.). (Oxford historical monographs).

3885. KUROKAWA (Tomobumi). Roshia kirisutokyoshi: Dochaku to fukuju to fukkatsu. (History of Christianity in Russia: the natives, obedience and revival). Tokyo, Kyobunkan, 99, 254 p.

3886. LAUWERS (Michel). Le cimetière dans le Moyen Age latin. Lieu sacré, saint et religieux. *Annales*, 99, 54, 5, p. 1047-1072.

3887. LEFF (Gordon). Heresy in the later Middle Ages: the relation of heterodoxy to dissent, c. 1250-c. 1450. Manchester, Manchester U. P., 99, X-800 p.

3888. MAYER (Johannes G.). Die "Vulgata"-Fassung der Predigten Johannes Taulers: von der handschriftlichen Überlieferung des 14. Jahrhunderts bis zu den ersten Drucken. Würzburg, Konigshausen & Neumann, 99, XVI-296 p. (Texte und Wissen, 1).

3889. Medieval (The) mystical tradition: England, Ireland and Wales. Ed. by Marion GLASSCOE. Cambridge, Brewer, 99, 268 p.

3890. Milano 1300. I processi inquisitoriali contro le devote e i devoti di santa Guglielma. A cura di Marina BENEDETTI e Grado Giovanni MERLO. Milano, Libri Scheiwiller, 99, 319 p. (ill.). (Milano medievale, 2).

3891. MODESTIN (Georg). Le diable chez l'évêque: chasse aux sorciers dans le diocèse de Lausanne (vers 1460). Lausanne, Universite de Lausanne, 99, 403 p. (ill. maps). (Cahiers lausannois d'histoire médiévale, 25).

3892. MORÉE (Peter C. A.). Preaching in fourteenth-century Bohemia: the life and ideas of Milicius de Chremsir and his significance in the historiography of Bohemia. Slavkov, EMAN, 99, 290 p.

3893. New trends in feminine spirituality: the holy women of Liège and their impact. Ed. by Jocelyn WOGAN-BROWNE, Lesley JOHNSON and Juliette DOR. Turnhout, Brepols, 99, XII-350 p. (pl., maps). (Medieval women: texts and contexts, 2).

3894. Origini (Alle) della parrocchia rurale, IV-VIII sec. Atti della giornata tematica dei seminari di Archeologia Cristiana, École Francaise de Rome, 19 marzo 1998. A cura di Philippe PERGOLA e Palmira Maria BARBINI. Citta del Vaticano, Pontificio istituto di archeologia cristiana, 99, 640 p.

3895. PINI (Antonio Ivan). Città, chiesa e culti civici in Bologna medievale. Bologna, CLUEB, 99, 343 p. (ill.). (Biblioteca di storia urbana medievale, 12).

3896. Prédication (La) sur un mode dissident: laïcs, femmes, hérétiques (XIe–XIVe). Actes du 9e colloque du Centre d'Études cathares René Nelli, Coniza, 26–30 août. Éd. par Beverly M. KIENZLE. Carcassonne, Centre d'Études cathares René Nelli, Maison des Mémoires, 99, 175 p. (Heresis. Thématique, 1).

3897. PUHL (Roland W. L.). Die Gaue und Grafschaften des frühen Mittelalters im Saar-Mosel-Raum. Philologisch-onomastische Studien zur frühmittelalterlichen Raumorganisation anhand der Raumnamen und der mit ihnen spezifizierten Ortsnamen. Saarbrücken, Saarbrücker Druckerei und Verlag, 99, XVII-609 p. (maps). (Beiträge zur Sprache im Saar-Mosel-Raum).

3898. REHBERG (Andreas). Die Kanoniker von S. Giovanni in Laterano und S. Maria Maggiore im 14. Jahrhundert. Eine Prosopographie. Tübingen, Niemeyer, 99, VIII-565 p. (tab., graph.). (Bibliothek des DHI in Rome, 89).

3899. ROMANELLO (Paola R.). Il labirinto della storia: la logica delle tentazioni diaboliche in Otlone di Sant'Emmerano. Bergamo, Lubrina, 99, 158 p. (Quodlibet, 11).

3900. RUSCONI (Roberto). Profezia e profeti alla fine del Medioevo. Roma, Viella, 99, 349 p. (Centro internazionale di studi gioachimiti, Opere di Gioacchino da Fiore, testi e strumenti, 9).

3901. Savonarola e la mistica. Atti del quarto Seminario di studi, Firenze, 22 maggio 1998. A cura di Giancarlo GARFAGNINI. Firenze, SISMEL edizioni del Galluzzo, 99, XIV-79 p. (Savonarola e la Toscana, 10).

3902. STAFFORD (Pauline). Queens, nunneries and reforming churchmen: gender, religious status and reform in tenth- and eleventh-century England. *Past and present*, 99, 163, p. 3-35.

3903. SUYDAM (Mary A.), ZIEGLER (Joanna E.). Performance and transformation: a three-dimensional approach to medieval devotional and ecstatic texts. Basingstoke, Macmillan, 99, 304 p.

3904. TARAYRE (Michel). La Vierge et le miracle. Le Speculum historiale de Vincent de Beauvais. Paris, Champion, 99, 222 p. (ill.).

3905. TURCUŞ (Şerban). The Council of Lyon II. Its effect in Central-Eastern Europe. *Transylvanian review*, 99, 8, 1, p. 132-147; 99, 8, 2, p. 54-66.

3906. URRY (William). Thomas Becket: his last days. Ed. by Peter A. ROWE. Stroud, Sutton, 99, XV-192 p. (ill.)

3907. VAUCHEZ (André). Saints, prophètes et visionnaires: le pouvoir surnaturel au Moyen Age. Paris, Albin Michel, 99, 275 p. (Bibliothèque Albin Michel. Histoire).

3908. VOADEN (Rosalynn). God's words, women's voices: the discernment of spirits in the writing of late-medieval women visionaries. Suffolk a. Rochester, York Medieval Press, 99, 204 p.

3909. WEBSTER (Jill R.). Carmel in medieval Catalonia. Leiden a. Boston, Brill, 99, XVII-200 p. (The medieval Mediterranean, 23).

3910. ZAMBON (Francesco). La cena segreta: trattati e rituali catari. Milano, Adelphi, 99, 471 p. (Biblioteca Adelphi, 332).

Cf. n°s 3215, 3523

§ 14. Settlements. Place names. Town planning.

3911. BESTEMAN (J. C.). The excavations at Wijnaldum: reports on Frisia in Roman and Medieval times. Rotterdam a. Brookfield, A.A. Balkema, 99, VIII-343 p. (ill., maps).

3912. ERMINI PANI (L.). Il recupero dell'altura nell'alto medioevo. *In*: Ideologie e pratiche del reimpiego nell'alto Medioevo [Cf. n° 3458], p. 613-664.

3913. FABRICIUS (Hanne). Københavns topografiske udvikling indtil 1300. (The topographical development of Copenhagen until 1300). København, Kongelige nordiske oldskriftselskab, 99, 283 p. (ill., maps, plans). (Aarbøger for nordisk oldkyndighed og historie, 1998).

3914. Gorod v srednevekovoj tsivilizatsii Evropy. (Town in Medieval civilization of Europe). Ed. Ada A. SVANIDZE. RAN, In-t vseobshchej istorii. Vol. 1. Fenomen srednevekovogo urbanizma. (The phenomenon of Medieval urbanism). Vol. 2. Zhizn' goroda i dejatel'nost' gorozhan. (Town's life and townsmen's activities). Moskva, Nauka, 99, 2 vol., 390 p., 344 p. (ill., bibl., geogr. ind.).

3915. Habitat (L') dispersé dans l'Europe médiévale et moderne: actes des XVIIIe Journées internationales d'histoire de l'Abbaye de Flaran, 15–17 septembre 1996. Éd. par Benoît CURSENTE. Toulouse, Presses universitaires du Mirail, 99, 292 p. (ill., maps). (Flaran, 18).

3916. Maritime topography and the medieval town. Papers from the 5th international conference on waterfront archaeology in Copenhagen 14–16th May 1998. Ed. by Birthe L CLAUSEN and Jan BILL. Copenhagen, National Museum of denmark, Dept. of Danish Collections, 99, 261 p. (ill., maps). (Publications from the National Museum. Studies in archaeology and history, 4).

3917. NØRGÅRD JØRGENSEN (Anne). Waffen und Gräber: typologische und chronologische Studien zu skandinavischen Waffengräbern 520/30 bis 900 n. Chr. Kobenhavn, Det Kongelige Nordiske oldskriftselskab, 99, 417 p. (ill.). (Nordiske fortidsminder. Serie B, 17).

3918. VERHULST (Adriaan E.). The rise of cities in north-west Europe. Cambridge, Cambridge U. P. a. Paris, Editions de la Maison des Sciences de l'Homme, 99, XI-174 p. (ill., maps, plans). (Themes in international urban history, 4).

3919. WOLF (Peter). Bilder und Vorstellungen vom Mittelalter: Regensburger Stadtchroniken der frühen Neuzeit. Tübingen, M. Niemeyer, 99, VII-456 p. (Frühe Neuzeit, 49).

3920. WOOLGAR (C. M.). The great household in late medieval England. New Haven a. London, Yale U. P., 99, IX-254 p. (maps, ill.),

Cf. n°s 248-294, 346, 3204, 3647

K

MODERN HISTORY, GENERAL WORKS

§ 1. General. 3921-4008. – § 2. History by countries. 4009-5257.

§ 1. General.

* 3921. Bibliographie zur Geschichte Ost- und Westpreußen 1995. Bearb. v. Eligiusz JANUS und Urszula ZABORSKA. Marburg, Verlag Herder-Institut, 99, XLIX-220 p. (Bibliographien zur Geschichte und Landeskunde Ostmitteleuropas, 23).

* 3922. BRACHER (Karl Dietrich), SCHWARZ (Hans-Peter), MÖLLER (Horst). Bibliographie zur Zeitgeschichte. *Vierteljahrshefte für Zeitgeschichte,* 99, 47, p. 5-159. [46, 1998. Cf. Bibl. 98, n° 4140.]

3923. 1848 – Revolution in Europa. Verlauf, politische Programme, Folgen und Wirkungen. Hrsg. v. Heiner TIMMERMANN. Berlin, Duncker & Humblot, 99, 557 p. (Dokumente und Schrifte der Europäischen Akademie Otzenhausen, 87). – 1848. Scene da una rivoluzione europea. A cura di Heinz-Gerhard HAUPT e Simonetta SOLDANI. *Passato e presente,* 99, 17, 46, p. 5-211. – Ideologie del 1848 e mutamento sociale. A cura di Mirella LARIZZA LOLLI. Fondazione Luigi Firpo, Centro di Studi sul Pensiero Politico, Atti del Convegno Internazionale del 20 marzo 1998. Firenze, L. S. Olschki, p. 5-214. – LANGEWIESCHE (Dieter). 1848: ein Epochenjahr in der deutschen Geschichte? *Geschichte und Gesellschaft,* 99, 25, 4, p. 613-625.

3924. 350e anniversaire du traités de Westphalie, 1648–1998: une genèse de l'Europe, une société à reconstruire. Actes du Colloque international, Strasbourg, 15–17 octobre 1998. textes présentés par Jean-Pierre KINTZ et Georges LIVET. Strasbourg, Presses Universitaires de Strasbourg, 99, 644 p.[Cf. n[os] <sélection> 7442, 7447.]

3925. ADELMAN (Jeremy), ARON (Stephen). From borderlands to borders: empires, nation-states and the peoples in between in north American history. *American historical review,* 99, 104, 3, p. 814. – Responses [to Jeremy ADELMAN and Stephen ARON 'From borderlands to borders'. Forum essay]. *American historical review,* 99, 104, 4, p. 1221-1239. [Contents: Introduction. – HAEFELI (Evan). A note on the use of North American borderlands, p. 1222-1225. – SCHMIDT-NOWARA (Christopher Ebert). Borders and borderlands of interpretation, p. 1226-1228. – WUNDER (John R.), HÄMÄLÄINEN (Pekka). Of lethal places and lethal essays, p. 1229-1334. – ADELMAN (Jeremy), ARON (Stephen). Of lively exchanges and larger perspectives, p. 1235-1239].

3926. AGOSTI (Aldo). Bandiere rosse. Un profilo storico dei comunismi europei. Roma, Editori Riuniti, 99, 367 p.

3927. APPLEGATE (Celia). A Europe of regions: reflections on the historiography of sub-national places in modern times. *In*: Bringing regionalism back to history [Cf. n° 3938], p. 1157-1182.

3928. ARMITAGE (David). Greater Britain: a useful category of historical analysis? *In*: New British history (The) in Atlantic perspective [Cf. n° 3985], p. 427-445.

3929. ASCH (R. G.). Kriegsfinanzierung, Staatsbildung und ständische Ordnung in Westeuropa im 17. und 18. Jahrhundert. *Historische Zeitschrift,* 99, 268, 3, p. 635-672.

3930. Avenirs et avant-gardes en France, XIXe–XXe siècles. Hommage à Madeleine Rebérioux. Sous la dir. de Vincent DUCLERT, Rémi FABRE et Patrick FRIDENSON. Paris, Ed. la Découverte, 99, 439 p. [Cf. n[os] <sélection> 740, 773.]

3931. Avtoritarnye rezhimy v Tsentral'noj i Vostochnoj Evrope (1917–1990-e gody). (Authoritarian regimes in central and eastern Europe, 1917–1990s: [Papers presented in a Russian-Hungarian conference, September 1994]). Ed. Tofik M. ISLAMOV, Aleksandr S. STYKALIN; RAN, In-t slavjanovedenija. Moskva, [s. n.], 99, 237 p. (Tsentral'noevropejskie issledovanija, 1).

3932. BENIGNO (Francesco). Specchi della rivoluzione. Conflitto e identità politica nell'Europa moderna. Roma, Donzelli, 99, XVIII-302 p. (Saggi: storia e scienze sociali).

3933. BERGGREN (Lena). Nationell upplysning: drag i den svenska antisemitismens idéhistoria. (Lumières nationales: aspects de l'histoire de l'antisémitisme suédois). Stockholm, Carlsson, 99, 427 p., ill. (rés. anglais).

3934. Beyond binary histories: re-imagining Eurasia to c.1830. Ed. by Victor LIEBERMAN. Ann Arbor, University of Michigan Press, 99, 325 p. [Contents: LIEBERMAN (Victor). Transcending East-West dichotomies: state and culture formation in six ostensibly disparate areas. – BERRY (Mary Elizabeth). Was early modern Japan culturally integrated? – MOORE (R. I.). The birth of Europe as a Eurasian phenomenon. – COLLINS (James B.). State building in early modern Europe: the case of France. – KIVELSON (Valerie). Merciful father, impersonal state: Russian autocracy in comparative perspective. – WHITMORE (John K.). Literati culture and integration in Dai Viet, c.1430–c.1840. – WYATT (David K.). Southeast Asia "inside out," 1300–1800. – CAREY (Peter). Civilization on loan: the making of an upstart polity: Mataram and its successors, 1600–1830. – SUBRAHMANYAN (Sanjay). Connected histories: notes towards a reconfiguration of early modern Eurasia].

3935. BIHARI (Péter). Polgári társadalmak és nemzetállamok 1776–1870. (Civil societies and nation states 1776–1870). [S. l.], [s. n.], 99, 294 p.

3936. BOIS (Jean-Pierre). L'Europe à l'époque moderne: origines, utopie et réalités de l'idée d'Europe, XVIe–XVIIIe siècle. Paris, Armand Colin, 99, 352 p.

3937. BRACEWELL (W.). The End of Yugoslavia and new national histories. *European history quarterly*, 99, 29, 1, p. 149-156.

3938. Bringing regionalism back to history. *American historical review*, 99, 104, 4, p. 1156-1220. [Cf. n° <choice> 3927.]

3939. Chelovek epokhi prosveshchenija. (L'homme du siècle des Lumières). Ed. G. S. KUCHERENKO. RAN, Nauch. sovet po istorii mirovoj kul'tury; RAN, In-t vseobshchej istorii. Moskva, Nauka, 99, 223 p. (bibl.).

3940. Ciudadanía política y formación de las naciones: perspectivas históricas de América Latina. Comp. por Hilda SABATO. México, Fondo de Cultura Económica/ El Colegio de México, 99, 450 p.

3941. Collective identities in Central Europe in modern times. Ed. Moritz CSÁKY, Elena MANNOVÁ. Bratislava, Institute of History of the Slovak Academy of Sciences, 99, 216 p.

3942. Crossing boundaries: comparative history of Black people in diaspora. Ed. by Darlene CLARK HINE and Jacqueline MAC LEOD. Bloomington, Indiana U. P., 99, XXV-491 p. (Blacks in the diaspora).

3943. Demonizing the other: antisemitism, racism, and xenophobia. Ed. by Robert S. WISTRICH. Amsterdam, Harwood Academic, 99, X-373 p. (ill.). (Studies in anisemitism, 4). [Cf. n° <choice> 4407.]

3944. Deutsche Geschichte im Osten Europas. Galizien, Bukowina, Moldau. Hrsg. Isabel RÖSKAU-RYDEL. Berlin, Siedler, 99, 543 p.

3945. Discours européen (Le) dans les revues allemandes (1933–1939) = Der Europadiskurs in den deutschen Zeitschriften (1933–1939). Hrsg. v. Michel GRUNEWALD in Zusammenarbeit mit Hans Manfred BOCK. Bern, Berlin u. New York, P. Lang, 99, XI-479 p. (Université de Metz. Centre d'étude des périodiques de langue allemande. Convergences, 11).

3946. DUCHHARDT (Heinz). Perspektivenwechsel. Das Alte Reich als politischer Organismus. *Historische Zeitschrift*, 99, 268, 3, p. 673-680.

3947. Emancipácia Židov – antisemitizmus – prenasledovanie v Nemecku, Rakúsko-Uhorsku, v českých zemiach a na Slovensku. (Judenemanzipation – Antisemitismus – Verfolgung in Deutschland, Österreich-Ungarn, den Böhmischen Ländern und in der Slowakei.) Ed. Jörg K. HOENSCH, Stanislav BIMAN, L'ubomír LIPTÁK. Bratislava, Veda 99, 211 p.

3948. Emancipation (The) of Catholics, Jews and Protestants. Minorities and the Nation State in nineteenth century Europe. Ed. by Rainer LIEDTKE and Stephan WENDEHORST. Manchester a. New York, Manchester U.P., 99, X-223 p.

3949. Europa nie prowincjonalna: przemiany na ziemiach wschodnich dawnej Rzeczypospolitej (Bialorus, Litwa, Lotwa, Ukraina, wschodnie pogranicze III Rzeczypospolitej Polskiej) w latach 1772–1999 = Nonprovincial Europe: changes on the Eastern territories of the former Polish Republic (Belarus, Latvia, Lithuania, Ukraine, Eastern borderland of the III Republic) in 1772–1999. Praca zbiorowa pod redakcja Krzysztofa JASIEWICZA. Warszawa, Instytut Studiów Politycznych PAN, 99, 1495 p. (Biblioteka Poetycka Wydawnictwa a5, 36).

3950. Europa: en svårfångad historia. (L'Europe: une histoire difficile à saisir). Red. par Hans Åke PERSSON et Fredrik LINDSTRÖM. Lund, Studentlitteratur et Malmö, Malmö U. P., 99, 218 p. (ill., cartes).

3951. Europe (L') et la Méditerranée. Stratégie et itinéraires politiques et culturels en Méditerranée, France et Italie, XIXe–XXe siècles. Un approche comparative. Actes du Colloque de Nancy-Malzéville, 4–6 septembre 1997. Paris, l'Harmattan et Nancy, Presses universitaires de Nancy, 99, 340 p. [Cf. n°s <sélection> 7343, 7357, 7590.]

3952. Europe rhénane (L') et l'Europe centrale. Dynamique et mutations. Actes du Colloque tenu à l'université de Metz, 11–13 mars 1998, en hommage à François Reitel. *Mosella*, 99, 24, 1-2, p. 15-319.

3953. Explaining European dominance. [Review essays]. *American historical review*, 99, 104, 4, p. 1240-1257. [Contents: Introduction. – MOKYR (Joel). Eurocentricity triumphant, p. 1241-1246. – GUY (Donna J.). The morality of economic history and the immorality of imperialism, p. 1247-1252. – TILLY (Charles). A grand tour of exotic landes, p. 1253-1257.]

3954. German and American nationalism: a comparative perspective. Ed. by Hartmut LEHMANN and Hermann WELLENREUTHER. New York, Berg, 99, VII-534 p. [Cf. n° <Choice> 899.]

3955. GOULD (Eliga H.). A virtual nation: greater Britain and the imperial legacy of the American revolution. *In*: New British history (The) in Atlantic perspective [Cf. n° 3985], p. 476-489.

3956. GRAZIOSI (Andrea). Dai Balcani agli Urali: l'Europa orientale nella storia contemporanea. Roma, Donzelli, 99, V-120 p. (Saggi. Storia e scienze sociali).

3957. HOFF (J.). The American century: from Sarajevo to Sarajevo. *In*: American century (The): a roundtable. Part I [Cf. n° 7215], p. 285-319.

3958. HÖSCH (E.). Geschichte der Balkanländer: von der Frühzeit bis zur Gegenwart. München, Beck, 99, 382 p.

3959. Ibero-Amerika v mirovom tsivilizatsionnom protsesse. (Ibero-America in the world civilization process: [a 'round table']). *Latinskaja Amerika*, Moskva, 99, 35, 5-6, p. 103-106; 7-8, p. 138-148; 9, p. 91-105; 11, p. 50-57.

3960. Identities: Nations, Provinces and Regions, 1550–1900. Proceedings of the III Anglo-Spanish historical studies seminar held at the University of East Anglia, 25–26 October 1996. Ed. by Isabel BURDIEL and James CASEY. Norwich, School of History, University of East Anglia, 99, 210 p.

3961. Imágenes e imaginarios nacionales en el Ultramar español. Ed. por Consuelo NARANJO OROVIO y Carlos SERRANO. Madrid, Casa de Velázquez, 99, 391 p. (Colección Tierra Nueva e Cielo Nuevo, 37).

3962. International communism and the Communist International, 1919–1943. Ed. by Tim REES and Andrew THORPE. Manchester, Manchester U. P., 99, X-323 p.

3963. JUSTER (Susan). Demagogues or mystagogues? Gender and the language of prophecy in the age of democratic revolutions. [AHR Forum: Millenniums]. *American historical review*, 99, 104, 5, p. 1560-1581.

3964. KAELBLE (Hartmut). Der historische Vergleich. Eine Einführung zum 19. und 20. Jh. Frankfurt am Main, Campus, 99, 183 p.

3965. KALNIKOV (A.) Balkanite prez pogleda na Evropa. (Le Balkans à travers le coup d'oeil de l'Europe). Sofija, [s. n.], 99, [s. p.].

3966. KEMP (Walter A.). Nationalism and Communism in Eastern Europe and the Soviet Union. A basic contradiction? London a. New York, St. Martin's Press, 99, XV-292 p.

3967. KREHM (William). Democracies and tyrannies of the Caribbean in the 1940's. Toronto, Lugus, 99, XIX-244 p.

3968. KŘEN (Jan). Interpretace národních, středoevropských a evropských dějin. Více otázek než odpovědí. (An interpretation of national, Central European, and European histories. More questions than answers]. *Soudobé dějiny*, 99, 6, 4, p. 488-513.

3969. Krisen des 17. Jahrhunderts: Interdisziplinäre Perspektiven. Hrsg. v. Manfred JAKUBOWSKI-TIESSEN. Göttingen, Vandenhoeck & Ruprecht, 99, 126 p. (Sammlung Vandenhoeck).

3970. LANDSMAN (Ned C.). Nation, migration and the province in the first British Empire: Scotland and the Americas, 1600–1800. *American historical review*, 99, 104, p. 463-475.

3971. LIEBICH (André). Counting and classifying minorities. *In*: Socialisme, cultures, histoire: itinéraires et représentations: mélanges offerts à Miklós Molnár [Cf. n° 5701], p. 189-207.

3972. LIM (Jie-Hyun). Minjokjoouineun Banyukida. (Nationalism beyond nationalism: neither national nihilism nor mythic present). Seoul, Sonamoo, 99, [s. p.].

3973. LIU (Tien-lung). The chameleon state: global culture and policy shifts in Britain and Germany, 1914-1933. New York a. Oxford, Berghahn Books, 99, XV-171 p. (tab., figs).

3974. LOVEMAN (Brian). For la Patria: politics and the armed forces in Latin America. Wilmington, Scholarly Resources, 99, XXVII-331 p. (Latina American Silhouettes. Studies in history and culture).

3975. MAC KERCHER (B.J.C.). Transition of power: Britain's loss of global pre-eminence to the United States, 1930-1945. Cambridge, Cambridge U.P., XII-402 p. (tabs).

3976. MAZOWER (Mark). Dark Continent: Europe's Twentieth Century. New York, Alfred A. Knopf, 99, XVI-487 p.

3977. Međunarodni znanstveni skup «Jugoistočna Europa 1918–1995». (An international symposium Southeastern Europe 1918–1995). Zagreb, Hrvatska matica iseljenika, 99, 341 p.

3978. Mensch (Der) des 19. Jahrhunderts. Hrsg. v. Ute FREVERT und Heinz-Gerhard HAUPT. Frankfurt am Main u. New York, Campus, 99, 373 p.

3979. MILLER (Nicola). In the shadow of the state: intellectuals and the quest for national identity in twentieth-century Spanish America. London, Verso, 99, IX-342 p.

3980. Národnostní menšiny a jejich sociální pozice ve střední Evropě: sborník z mezinárodní vědecké konference konané ve dnech 5.–6. 10. 1999 ve Slezském ústavu Slezského zemského muzea v Opavě. (National minorities and their social positions in Central Europe).Ed. by Jana MACHAČOVÁ and Jiří MATĚJČEK. Opava, Slezský ústav Slezského zemského muzea v Opavě, 99, 294 p. [Cf. n° <choice> 4227.]

3981. Nation and Nationalism in the West. Ed. by the Korean Society for Western History. Seoul, Kachi, 99, [s. p.].

3982. Nation and religion: perspectives on Europe and Asia. Ed. by Peter VAN DER VEER and Hartmut LEHMANN. Princeton, Princeton U. P., 99, VI-231 p.

3983. Nationalism, Labour and Ethnicity 1870–1939. Ed. by Stefan BERGER and Angel SMITH. Manchester, Manchester U. P., 99, XII-292 p. [Cf. n° <choice> 4943.]

3984. Nationalismus und Nationalbewegungen in Europa 1914–1945. Hrsg. v. Heiner TIMMERMANN. Berlin, Duncker & Humblot, 99 580 p.

3985. New British history (The) in Atlantic perspective. American historical review, 99, 104, p. 426-500. [Cf. n[os] <choice> 3928, 3955, 3986, 3990.]

3986. OHLMEYER (Jane). Seventeenth-century Ireland and the new British and Atlantic histories. In: New British history (The) in Atlantic perspective [Cf. n° 3985], p. 446-462.

3987. Opposing fascism: community, authority and resistance in Europe. Ed. by Tim KIRK and Anthony MAC ELLIGOTT. Cambridge, Cambridge U. P.s, 99, IX-246 p.

3988. PANAYI (Panikos). Outsiders: a history of European minorities. London, Hambledon Press, 99, XII-208 p. (maps).

3989. PAVLOWITCH (Stevan Kosta). A history of the Balkans, 1804–1945. London, Longman, 99, VIII-375 p.

3990. POCOCK (J. G. A.). The new British history in Atlantic perspective: an antipodean commentary. In: New British history (The) in Atlantic perspective [Cf. n° 3985], p. 490-500.

3991. POZHARSKAJA (Svetlana P.), NAMAZOVA (Alla S.). Obshchie tendentsii razvitija Evropy v XIX–nachale XX v. (General tendencies of the development of Europe, the 19th and the early 20th centuries). Novaja i novejshaja istorija, 99, 47, 4, p. 51-60.

3992. PROCACCI (Giuliano). Storia del mondo contemporaneo. Vol. 1. Da Sarajevo a Hiroshima. Roma, Editori Riuniti, 99, 331 p.

3993. REINHARD (Wolfgang). Geschichte der Staatsgewalt und europäische Expansion. In: Verstaatlichung der Welt? [Cf. n° 1040], p.317-356.

3994. Revolution and revolutionaries: guerrilla movements in Latin America. Ed. by Daniel CASTRO. Wilmington, SR Books, 99, XXXVII-236 p. (Jaguar books on Latin America, 17).

3995. Revolutions (The) of 1989. Ed. by Vladimir TISMANEANU. New York, Routledge, 99, X-270 p. (Rewriting Histories).

3996. ROESLER (Jörg). Der Anschluß von Staaten in der modernen Geschichte. Eine Untersuchung aus aktuellem Anlaß. Frankfurt am Main, Lang, 99, 378 p.

3997. SAVICKÝ (Ivan). Osudová setkání. Češi v Rusku a Rusové v Čechách. 1914–1938. (Schicksalsbegegnungen. Tschechen in Russland und Russen in Tschechien in den Jahren 1914–1938). Praha, Academia, 99, 271 p. (photogr.).

3998. Second printemps (Le) des Nations. Sous la dir. de Wanda DRESSLER. Bruxelles, Editions Bruylant, 99, 452 p.

3999. SOSKICE (David). Globalisierung und institutionelle Divergenz: Die USA und Deutschland im Vergleich. Geschichte und Gesellschaft, 99, 25, 2, p. 201-225.

4000. Stalinisme et nazisme: histoire et mémoire comparées. Sous la dir. de Henry ROUSSO. Bruxelles, Ed. Complexe, 99, 387 p. (Histoire du temps présent). [Cf. n° <sélection> 4407.]

4001. SUTER (Andreas). Nationalstaat und die «Tradition der Erfindung». Vergleichende Überlegungen. Geschichte und Gesellschaft, 99, 25, 3, p. 480-503.

4002. THIEDEKE (Johnny). Magten, æren og døden. Kampen om Norden 1563–1720. (Le pouvoir, l'honneur et la mort. La lutte pour la domination sur la Scandinavie de 1563 à 1720). Valby, Pantheon, 99, 96 p. (ill.).

4003. Totalitarismus: sechs Vorträge über Gehalt und Reichweite eines klassischen Konzepts der Diktaturforschung. Hrsg. von Klaus-Dietmar HENKE. Dresden, Hannah-Arendt-Inst. für Totalitarismusforschung, 99, 94 p. (Schriftenreihe: Berichte und Studien / Hannah-Arendt-Institut für Totalitarismusforschung). [Cf. n° <Auswahl> 4407.]

4004. VAN CREVELD (Martin). The rise and decline of the state. New York, Cambridge U. P., 99, VIII-439 p.

4005. Vynútený rozchod. Vyhnanie a vysídlenie z Československa 1938–1947 v porovnaní s Poľskom, Maďarskom a Juhosláviou. (Erzwungene Trennung. Vertreibungen und Aussiedlungen in und aus Tschechoslowakei 1938–1947 im Vergleich mit Polen, Ungarn und Jugoslawien). [Zost.]: Detlef BRANDES, Edita IVANIČKOVÁ, Jiří PEŠEK. Bratislava, Veda vydavateľstvo Slovenskej akadémie vied, 99, 259 p.

4006. Widening, deepening and acceleration. The European Economic Community 1957–1963. Ed. by Anne DEIGHTON and Alan S. MILWARD. Baden-Baden, Nomos, 99, 360 p. (Veröffentlichungen der Historiker-Verbindungsgruppe bei der Kommission der Europäischen Gemeinschaften = Publications du Groupe de Liaison des Professeurs d' Histoire Contemporaines aupres, 7). [Cf. n° <choice> 8017.]

4007. WILLIS (Michael). Democracy and the state, 1830–1945. Cambridge, Cambridge U. P., 99, VI-122 p. (Cambridge perspectives in history).

4008. WINKLER (Heinrich August). Triumph des Zufalls? Zu einem Versuch, das 20. Jahrhundert als das «deutsche Jahrhundert» zu porträtieren. *Historische Zeitschrift*, 99, 268, p. 681-688.

Cf. n°s 927-1049, 1051, 1070, 1319, 4551, 4990, 5018, 5150, 5310, 5332, 5553, 5653, 6557, 7203-7300, 7822

§ 2. History by countries.

Afghanistan

4009. Afghanistan in Geschichte und Gegenwart: Beiträge zur Afghanistanforschung. Hrsg. v. Conrad J. SCHETTER and Almut WIELAND-KARIMI. Frankfurt, IKO, 99, 176 p. (ill). (Schriftenreihe der Mediothek für Afghanistan, 1).

4010. BAKSHI (Gagan Deep). Afghanistan: the first fault-line war. New Delhi, Lancer a. London, Spantech & Lancer, 99, 194 p.

4011. BRADSHER (Henry St. Amant). Afghan communism and Soviet intervention. Oxford, Oxford U. P., 99, XVIII-443 p.

4012. GIUSTOZZI (Antonio). War, politics and society in Afghanistan, 1978–1992. London, C. Hurst, 99, XIV-320 p.

4013. GOHARI (M. J.). The Taliban: ascent to power. Oxford, Oxford Logos Society, 99, XIII-161 p.

4014. KORGUN (Viktor Grigor'evich). Afganistan: politika i politiki. Moskva, IV RAN, 99, 139 p.

4015. MATINUDDIN (Kamal). The Taliban phenomenon: Afghanistan, 1994–1997: with an afterword covering major events since 1997. Oxford, Oxford U. P., 99, XVIII-298 p. (Oxford Pakistan paperbacks).

4016. NAWID (Senzil K.). Religious response to social change in Afghanistan, 1919–1929: King Aman-Allah and the Afghan Ulama. Costa Mesca, Mazda Publishers, 99, XXI-278 p.

4017. PAHLAVAN (Changiz). Afghanistan: 'asr-i Mujahidin va bar'amadan-i Taliban. (Afghanistan, the era of Mujahedeen and the rise of Taliban). Tihran, Nashr-i Qatrah, 99, 493 p.

Cf. n° 893

Albania

4018. CABANES (Pierre), CABANES (Bruno). Passions albanaises: de Berisha au Kosovo, Paris, O. Jacob, 99, 280 p.

4019. FISCHER (Bernd Jürgen). Albania at war, 1939–1945. West Lafayette, Purdue U. P., 99, XV-338 p. (Central European studies).

4020. KOLA (Paulin). Albania, its isolation and the Albanian national question: with particular emphasis on Kosova: 1941–1992. London, [s. n.], 99, [s. p.]. (Ph. D. thesis, University of London).

4021. O'DONNELL (James Salibur). A coming of age: Albania under Enver Hoxha. Boulder, East European Monographs, 99, 266 p. (East European monographs, 517).

4022. PRIFTI (Peter R.). Remote Albania: the politics of isolationism. Tiranë, Onufri, 99, 251 p.

4023. VICKERS (Miranda). The Albanians: a modern history. London, I.B. Tauris, 99, X-282 p.

Algeria

4024. 1989 en Algérie: rupture tragique ou rupture féconde. Sous la dir. de Najib REDOUANE et Yamina MOKADDEM. Toronto, Les Éditions La Source, 99, 259 p. (Agora, 1).

4025. Algérie 1830–1962. Sous la dir. de Jeanne CAUSSÉ et de Bruno DE CESSOLÉ; préface de Bruno ÉTIENNE. Paris, Maisonneuve & Larose, 99, 582 p. (Les trésors retrouvés de la Revue des deux mondes).

4026. BENRABAH (Mohamed). Langue et pouvoir en Algérie: histoire d'un traumatisme linguistique. Paris, Séguier, 99, 350 p. (Les Colonnes d'Hercule).

4027. Dissident Algeria. Guest ed. Danielle MARX-SCOURAS. Indiana, Indiana U. P. in cooperation with the Ohio State University, 99, 243 p. (Research in African literatures, 99, 30, 3).

4028. HADJADJ (Djillali). Corruption et démocratie en Algérie. Paris, La Dispute, 99, 313 p.

4029. LANDA (V.G.). Istorija Alzhira, XX vek. (A history of Algeria, the 20th century). RAN, In-t vostokovedenija. Moskva, [s. n.], 99, 308 p. (bibl., ind.). (Istorija stran Vostoka, XX vek).

4030. LAREMONT (Ricardo René). Islam and the politics of resistance in Algeria, 1783–1992. Trenton, Africa World Press, 99, 291 p.

4031. MELASUO (Tuomo). Algerian poliittinen kehitys 1800–luvulta vapautussotaan 1954. Tampere, Rauhan- ja konfliktintutkimuskeskus TAPRI, Yhteiskuntatieteiden tutkimuslaitos, Tampereen Yliopisto, 99, 554 p. (TAPRI Rauhan- ja konfliktintutkimuskeskus Tutkimuksia, 85).

4032. MSELLATI (Henri). Les juifs d'Algérie sous le régime de Vichy: 10 juillet 1940–3 novembre 1943. Préface de Benjamin STORA. Paris, L'Harmattan, 99, 302 p. (Collection histoire et perspectives méditerranéennes).

4033. Radios et télévision au temps des «événements d'Algérie», 1954–1962. Sous la direction de Michèle DE BUSSIERRE, Cécile MÉADEL et Caroline ULMANN-MAURIAT; préface de Jean-Noël JEANNENEY. Paris, L'Harmattan, 99, 298 p. (ill.). (Collection Communication et civilisation).

4034. SALGON (Jean-Michel). Violences ambiguës: aspects du conflit armé en Algérie. Avec la collaboration de Mohand KHELLIL et Roger TEBIB. Paris, Centre des hautes études sur l'Afrique et l'Asie modernes (CHEAM), 99, 126 p.

4035. SOUKEHAL (Rabah). L'écrivain de langue française et les pouvoirs en Algérie. Paris, L'Harmattan, 99, 201 p. (Collection Histoire et perspectives méditerranéennes).

4036. TURPIN (Frédéric). Le Mouvement Républicain Populaire et l'avenir de l'Algérie (1948-1962). *Revue d'histoire diplomatique*, 99, 113, 2, p. 171-204.

Angola

4037. FERREIRA (Manuel Ennes). A indústria em tempo de guerra: Angola, 1975-91. Prefácio de Adelino TORRES. Lisboa, Ediçoes Cosmos, Instituto da Defesa Nacional, 99, XXXVIII-581 p. (ill). (Atena, 5).

4038. KHAZANOV (Anatolij M.). Istorija Angoly v novoe i novejshee vremja (do 1975). (Modern and recent history of Angola, to 1975). RAN, In-t vostokovedenija, etc. Moskva, [s. n.], 99, 390 p.

Argentina

* 4039. DE DOMÍNGUEZ SOLER (Susana T. P.). Urquiza: bibliografía. Buenos Aires, Instituto Urquiza de Estudios Históricos, 99, 492 p.

4040. ABÓS (Álvaro). Delitos ejemplares: historias de la corrupción argentina, 1810-1997. Buenos Aires, Grupo Editorial Norma, 99, 284 p. (Colección Biografías y documentos).

4041. ADELMAN (Jeremy). Republic of capital: Buenos Aires and the legal transformation of the Atlantic world. Stanford, Stanford U. P., 99, X-376 p.

4042. Argentina (La) en el siglo XX. Ed. por Carlos ALTAMIRANO. Buenos Aires, Ariel, 99, 307 p.

4043. CRAMER (Gisela). Argentinien im Schatten des Zweiten Weltkriegs: Probleme der Wirtschaftspolitik und der Übergang zur Ära Perón. Stuttgart, Franz Steiner Verlag, 99, X-395 p.

4044. FANEL (Luis). La alternativa ausente: crisis y ruptura política en Argentina (1945-1998). Buenos Aires, Dirple Ediciones, 99, 313 p.

4045. GAMBINI (Hugo). Historia del peronismo. Buenos Aires, Planeta, 99, [s. n.].

4046. GAY (Luis). El Partido Laborista en la Argentina. Edición a cargo de Juan Carlos TORRE. Buenos Aires, Editorial Biblos, Fundación Simon Rodríguez, 99, 216 p. (Cuadernos Simón Rodríguez, 39).

4047. GONZÁLEZ BERNALDO DE QUIRÓS (Pilar). Civilité et politique: aux origines de la nation argentine. Les sociabilités à Buenos Aires, 1829-1862. Paris, Publications de la Sorbonne, 99, 382 p. (ill.). (Publications de la Sorbonne. Série internationale, 58).

4048. GORBATO (Viviana). Montoneros: soldados de Menem. Soldados de Duhalde? Buenos Aires, Sudamericana, 99, 431 p. (ill.)

4049. Historias de caudillos argentinos. Estudio preliminar de Tulio HALPERIN DONGHI; edición de Jorge LAFFORGUE. Buenos Aires, Aguilar, Altea, Taurus, Alfaguara, 99, 422 p.

4050. IRIGOIN (María Alejandra). Del dominio autocrático al de la negociación. Las razones económicas del renacimiento de la política en Buenos Aires en la década de 1850. *Anuario IEHS*, 99, 14, p. 195-229.

4051. KINDGARD (Adriana). Los sectores conservadores de Jujuy ante el fenómeno peronista (1943-1948). *Estudios Sociales*, 99, 9, 16, p. 77-94.

4052. LETTIERI (Alberto). Una experiencia republicana en Buenos Aires, 1852-1861. *Desarrollo económico*, 99, 39, 154, p. 72-91.

4053. Liberalismo, Estado y orden burgués (1852-1880). Dir. por Marta BONAUDO. Buenos Aires, Sudamericana, 99, 605 p. (ill.).

4054. LVOVICH (Daniel). La imagen del enemigo y sus transformaciones en La Nueva República (1928-1931). *Entrepasados*, 99, 9, 17, p. 49-71.

4055. MAC GEE DEUTSCH (Sandra). Las Derechas: the Extreme Right in Argentina, Brazil, and Chile 1890-1939. Stanford, Stanford U. P., 99, XV-491 p.

4056. MARCHAK (M. Patricia), MARCHAK (William). God's assassins: state terrorism in Argentina in the 1970s. Montreal, McGill-Queen's U. P., 99, X-393 p.

4057. MEDING (Holger M.). La ruta de los nazis en tiempos de Perón. Buenos Aires, Emecé, 99, 430 p.

4058. PÁEZ (Carlos). La roca de Sísifo: apostillas a la historia política argentina del siglo XX. Buenos Aires, Editorial Biblos, 99, 135 p. (Colección Ensayos y propuestas, 1).

4059. Primacía (La) de la política: Lanusse, Perón y la Nueva Izquierda en tiempos del GAN. Ed. por Alfredo PUCCIARELLI. Buenos Aires, Eudeba, 99, 393 p. (Estudios de sociología).

4060. RUIZ MORENO (Isidoro J.). Alianza contra Rosas: Paz-Ferré-Rivera-López. Buenos Aires, Academia Nacional de la Historia, 99, 240 p.

4061. SCARZANELLA (Eugenia). Italiani malagente: immigrazione, criminalità, razzismo in Argentina, 1890-1940. Milano, F. Angeli, 99, 207 p. (ill.). (Storia, 249).

4062. SENÉN GONZÁLEZ (Santiago), BOSOER (Fabian). El sindicalismo en tiempos de Menem: los ministros de trabajo en la primera presidencia de Menem: sindicalismo y estado (1989-1995). Introducción de Juan Carlos TORRE; balance crítico de una década por Hiroshi MATSUSHITA. Buenos Aires, Corregidor, 99, 204 p.

4063. SMOLENSKY (Eleonora M.), VIGEVANI JARACH (Vera). Tantas voces, una historia: italianos judíos en la

2. HISTORY BY COUNTRIES

Argentina, 1938–1948. Buenos Aires, Temas Grupo Editorial, 99, 336 p.

4064. TCACH (César). Gobernabilidad, poder y transición en Argentina. *Secuencia*, 99, 44, p. 9-36.

4065. ZANATTA (Loris). Perón y el mito de la nación católica: Iglesia y Ejército en los orígenes del peronismo 1943–1946. Buenos Aires, Editorial Sudamericana, 99, 452 p.

Armenia

4066. CHALABIAN (Antranig). Armenia after the coming of Islam. Southfield, A. Chalabian, 99, 608 p. (ill.).

4067. MASIH (Joseph R.), KRIKORIAN (Robert O.). Armenia: at the crossroads. Amsterdam, Harwood Academic, 99, XXXIII-142 p. (Postcommunist states and nations).

Cf. n° 7483

Australia

4068. Australian century (The): political struggle in the building of a nation. Ed. and introduced by Robert MANNE. Melbourne, Text Publishing, 99, 333 p.

4069. GARE (Deborah). Dating Australia's independence. National sovereignty and the 1986 Australia Acts. *Australian historical studies*, 99, 30, 113, p. 251-266.

4070. GREY (Jeffrey). A military history of Australia. Cambridge, Cambridge U. P., 99, XI-300 p.

4071. MACINTYRE (Stuart). A concise history of Australia. Cambridge, Cambridge U. P., 99, XIII-320 p. (ill.). (Cambridge concise histories).

4072. WAHLERT (Glenn). The Other Enemy? Australian Soldiers and the Military Police. New York, Oxford U. P., 99, VIII-208 p. (Australian Army history series).

Austria (Austria-Hungary)

** 4073. Protokolle des Kabinettsrates der Provisorischen Regierung Karl Renner 1945. Herausgegeben von der Österreichischen Gesellschaft für historische Quellenstudien. Band 2. "Right or wrong – my country!" Protokolle des Kabinettsrates 17. Juli bis 5. September 1945. Hrsg. v. Gertrude ENDERLE-BURCEL und Rudolf JERÁBEK. Horn, Berger, 99, LXII-551 p.

4074. BÖHMER (Peter). Wer konnte, griff zu: "arisierte" Güter und NS-Vermögen im Krauland-Ministerium (1945–1949). Wien, Böhlau, 99, XXXVI-226 p.

4075. DUBIN (Lois C.). The port Jews of Habsburg Trieste: absolutist politics and enlightenment culture. Stanford, Stanford U. P., 99, XI-335 p. (Stanford studies in Jewish history and culture).

4076. Hispania-Austria II. Die Epoche Philipps II. (1556–1598). Hrsg. v. Friedrich EDELMAYER. Wien,

Verlag für Geschichte und Politik u. München, Oldenbourg, 99, 349 p.

4077. HOCHEDLINGER (Michael). Mars ennobled: the ascent of the military and the creation of a military nobility in mid-eighteenth-century Austria. *German history*, 99, 17, 2, p. 141-176.

4078. IOVEVSKA (Mariana). Balkanskite provintsii na Khabsburgskata durzhava: granitsi i administrativno upravlenie ot kraia na X vek do 1918 g (Les provinces balkaniques de l'Etat des Habsbourgs). Veliko Turnovo, Izd. "PIK", 99, 255 p. (ill.). (Biblioteka "Historica").

4079. KLUETING (Harm). Das Reich und Österreich 1648–1740. Münster, Hamburg u. London, Lit, 99, III-129 p. (Historia profana et ecclesiastica, 11).

4080. KOHLER (Alfred). Karl V. 1500–1558. Eine Biographie. München, Beck, 99, 424 p.

4081. KÖSTER (Burkhard). Military und Eisenbahn in der Habsburgermonarchie 1825–1859. München, Oldenbourg, 99, VII-335 p. (Militärgeschichtliche Studien, 37).

4082. NOFLATSCHER (Heinz). Räte und Herrscher: politische Eliten und den Habsburgerhöfen der Österreichischen Länder, 1480–1530. Mainz, Verlag Philipp von Zabern, 99, XI-495 p. (Veröffentlichungen des Instituts für Europäische Geschichte Mainz, 161).

4083. RUMPLER (Helmut). Rakúska ríšska rada a prechod ku konštitucionalizmu v rokoch 1859–1867. (Der österreichische Reichsrat und der Durchbruch zum Konstitutionalismus 1859–1867). *Historický časopis*, 99, 47, 2, p. 202-210. [Deutsche Zfassung].

4084. SCHMID (Gerhard). Österreich im Aufbruch: die österreichische Sozialdemokratie in der Ära Kreisky (1970–1983). Mit einem Vorwort von Heinz FISCHER. Innsbruck, Studien Verlag, 99, 366 p. (ill.).

4085. SIGMUND (Anna Maria). Die verschollenen Tagebücher Franz Joseph. Köln, Weimar u. Wien, Böhlau, 99, 216 p.

4086. Venezia e l'Austria. A cura di Gino BENZONI e Gaetano COZZI. Venezia, Marsilio, 99, VIII-494 p. (Saggi Marsilio. Presente storico, 9).

4087. Vivat Lissa! Die Wiederkehr des Löwen. Hrsg. v. Alexander Sixtus von REDEN. Wien, Schroll, 99, 191 p. (ill., maps, ports).

4088. WIESFLECKER (Hermann). Österreich im Zeitalter Maximilians I. Die Vereinigung der Länder zum frühmodernen Staat. Der Aufstieg zur Weltmacht. Wien, Verlag für Geschichte und Politik u. München, Oldenbourg, 99, 558 p.

4089. WINKELBAUER (Thomas). Fürst und Fürstendiener. Gundaker von Liechtenstein, ein österreichischer Aristokrat des konfessionellen Zeitalters. Wien u. München, Oldenbourg, 99, 656 p. (Mitteilungen des Instituts für Österreichische Geschichtsforschung, 34).

4090. ZEHETBAUER (Ernst). Die "Einjährigen" in der alten Armee: das Reserveoffizierssystem Österreich-Ungarns 1868–1914. Osnabrück, Biblio, 99, XII-191 p. (ill.). (Militärgeschichte und Wehrwissenschaften, 4).

Cf. n°s 4867, 5655, 5716

Belarus

4091. Antysavetskiia rukhi u Belarusi: 1944–1956: davednik. (Antisoviet movements in Belarus, 1944–1956: a dictionary). Ed. by Aleh DZIARNOVICH. Minsk, Arkhiŭ Naiuoushae Historyi, 99, 190 p

Cf. n°s 4816, 5293

Belgique

4092. BEERTEN (Wilfried), [et al.]. Le rassemblement des progressistes, 1944–1976. Bruxelles, De Boeck Université, 99, 248 p. (Pol-his).

4093. BOEHME (Olivier). Revolutie van rechts en intellectuelen in Vlaanderen tijdens het interbellum: ideeënhistorische bijdragen. Leuven, Acco, 99, [s. p.].

4094. DERUETTE (Serge), MERCKX (Kris). La vie en rose: réalités de l'histoire du parti socialiste en Belgique. Bruxelles, EPO, 99, 144 p.

4095. DOMS (Frédéric). "Chrétien, souviens-toi de Namur". Une menace pour l'élargissement du PLP-PVV? (Octobre 1964–mai 1965). *Revue belge d'histoire contemporaine*, 99, 29, 3-4, p. 337-384.

4096. DUMONT (Wouter). Fenomenologie van de massamanifestaties in België in de jaren dertig. *Revue belge d'histoire contemporaine*, 99, 29, 1-2, p. 145-226.

4097. GUBIN (Eliane). Du politique au politique. Parcours du feminisme belge (1830–1914). *In*: Fabrics of feminism [Cf. n° 6909], p. 370-382.

4098. LAUREYS (Véronique), [et al.]. L'histoire du Sénat de Belgique: de 1831 à 1995. Bruxelles, Racine, 99, 470 p.

4099. LETON (André), MIROIR (André). Les conflits communautaires en Belgique. Paris, Presses universitaires de France, 99, 366 p. (Perspectives internationales).

4100. Pays (Un) si tranquille: la violence en Belgique au XIXe siècle. Ed. par Ginette KURGAN-VAN HENTENRYK. Bruxelles, Editions de l'Université de Bruxelles, 99, 252 p. (ill.). (Faculté de philosophie et lettres, 107).

4101. PIRARD (Joseph). L'extension du rôle de l'Etat en Belgique aux XIXe et XXe siècles. Bruxelles, Académie royale de Belgique, 99, 878 p. (ill.). (Histoire quantitative et développement de la Belgique aux XIXe et XXe siècles. VII. L'argent et le pouvoir, 2).

4102. SCHANDEVYL (Eva). Een bijdrage tot de studie van het intellectuele veld in Belgie: communistische intellectuelen tijdens de Koude Oorlog (1945–1956). *Revue belge de philologie et d'histoire*, 99, 77, 4, p. 1003-1049.

4103. WITTE (Els), VAN VELTHOVEN (Harry). Language and politics: the Belgian case study in a historical perspective. Brussels, VUB U. P., 99, 239 p. (ill.). (Balans, 12).

Cf. n° 4867

Bolivia

** 4104. Documentos para la historia de la guerra civil, 1898–1899. Sucre, Gobierno Municipal de Sucre, 99, 180 p.

4105. Bolivia en el siglo XX: la formación de la Bolivia contemporánea. Ed. por Fernando CAMPERO PRUDENCIO. La Paz: Harvard Club de Bolivia, 99, XXIV-634 p.

4106. IBÁÑEZ ROJO (Enrique). La política desde el socavón: el movimiento obrero en la historia de Bolivia, 1940–1970. Madrid, Entinema, 99, 94 p. (Serie Con-textos de ciencias sociales, 5).

4107. LAVAUD (Jean-Pierre). La dictature empêchée: la grève de la faim des femmes de mineurs, Bolivie, 1977–1978. Paris, CNRS, 99, 200 p. (ill.). (Amériques-pays ibériques).

4108. PONCE SANGINÉS (Carlos), MONTANO DURÁN (Ana María). La revolución federal de 1898–1899: su cruento desenlace y la frustración ideológica. La Paz, Librería Editorial «Juventud», 99, 175 p. (ill., maps).

Cf. n° 6613

Bosnia

4109. IMAMOVIC (Enver). Historija bosanske vojske. Sarajevo, Art 7, 99, 325 p. (Edicija Bosanski korijeni).

4110. IMAMOVIC (Mustafa). Historija drzave i prava Bosne i Hercegovine. (History of state and right of Bosnia-Herzegovina). Sarajevo, M. Imamovic, 99, 445 p.

4111. WEINE (Stevan M.). When history is a nightmare: lives and memories of ethnic cleansing in Bosnia-Herzegovina. New Brunswick a. London, Rutgers U. P., 99, XIV-259 p. (ill.).

Cf. n° 4811

Brazil

** 4112. ALVES FILHO (Ivan). Brasil, 500 anos em documentos. Rio de Janeiro, MAUAD, 99, 653 p.

4113. BARMAN (Roderick J.). Citizen emperor: Pedro II and the making of Brazil, 1825–1891. Stanford, Stanford U. P., 99, XVIII-548 p.

4114. BARRETO DE SOUZA (Adriana). O Exército na consolidaçao do Império: um estudo histórico sobre a política militar conservadora. Rio de Janeiro, Ministério da Justiça, Arquivo Nacional, 99, 191 p. (Prêmio Arquivo Nacional de Pesquisa, 12).

4115. BERBEL (Márcia Regina). A naçao como artefato: deputados do Brasil nas Cortes Portuguesas, 1821–1822. Sao Paulo, Editora Hucitec, 99, 206 p. (Coleçao Estudos históricos, 36).

4116. BERTONHA (Joao Fábio). Sob a sombra de Mussolini: os italianos de Sao Paulo e a luta contra o fascismo, 1919–1945. Sao Paulo, FAPESP, Annablume, 99, 313 p. (ill.).

4117. BIEBER (Judy). Power, patronage, and political violence: state building on a Brazilian frontier, 1822–1889. Lincoln, University of Nebraska Press, 99, IX-253 p. (ill., map).

4118. Brazil reader (The): history, culture, politics. Ed. by Robert M. LEVINE and John J. CROCITTI. London, Latin America Bureau, 99, X-527 p. (Latin America readers).

4119. CERQUEIRA FILHO (Gisáleo), GIZIENE (Neder). Ecos da Segunda Republica e da Guerra Civil Espanhola no Brasil. *Tempo*, 99, 4, 8, p. 89-109.

4120. COSTA COUTO (Ronaldo). Memória viva do regime militar: Brasil, 1964–1985. Rio de Janeiro, Editora Record, 99, 391 p.

4121. DE AQUINO (Maria Aparecida). Censura, imprensa, Estado autoritário (1968–1978): o exercício cotidiano da dominaçao e da resistência, O Estado de Sao Paulo e Movimento. Bauru, EDUSC, 99, 269 p (ill). (Coleçao História).

4122. DE REZENDE MARTINS (Estevão). The Brazilian Federal parliament and the State parliaments in the republican history 1891–1988. *In*: Repräsentation in Föderalismus und Korporativismus [Cf. n° 1099], p. 71-100.

4123. DUARTE (Adriano Luiz). Cidadania e exclusao: Brasil 1937–1945. Florianópolis, Editora da UFSC, 99, 341 p.

4124. FAUSTO (Boris). A concise history of Brazil. Cambridge, Cambridge U. P., 99, XI-362 p.

4125. FERREIRA (Tito Lívio), DE ANDRADA E SILVA (Raul), COSTA SANTOS TAPAJÓS (Vicente). La independencia y la vida política y social del Brasil. Caracas, Asuntos Culturales de la OEA, Universidad Simon Bolivar, 99, 347 p. (ill.). (Historia general de América, 27-1. Período nacional).

4126. FERREIRA DOS SANTOS (Estilaque). A monarquia no Brasil: o pensamento político da independência. Vitória, EDUFES, 99, 335 p. (Coleçao CEG publicaçoes, 4).

4127. FERREIRA PERAZZO (Priscila). O perigo alemao e a repressao policial no Estado Novo. Sao Paulo, Governo do Estado de Sao Paulo, Secretaria de Estado da Cultura, Departamento de Museus e Arquivos, Divisao de Arquivo do Estado, 99, 278 p. (ill., some col.). (Coleçao Teses e monografias, 1).

4128. GOERTZEL (Ted G.). Fernando Henrique Cardoso: reinventing democracy in Brazil. Boulder a. London, Lynne Rienner Publishers, 99, XII-219 p.

4129. KINGSTONE (Peter R.). Crafting coalitions for reform: business preferences, political institutions, and neoliberal reform in Brazil. University Park, Penn State U. P., 99, XXVII-284 p.

4130. LEITE LINHARES (Maria Yedda), TEIXEIRA DA SILVA (Francisco Carlos). Terra prometida: uma história da questao agrária no Brasil. Rio de Janeiro, Editora Campus, 99, XVII-211p. (ill., map).

4131. LEVINE (Robert M.). The history of Brazil. Westport a. London, Greenwood Press, 99, XVIII-208 p. (Greenwood histories of the modern nations).

4132. MACLEAN (Iain S.). Opting for democracy? Liberation theology and the struggle for democracy in Brazil. New York, Peter Lang, 99, XV-264 p. (Studies in religion, politics, and public life, 2).

4133. MALERBA (Jurandir). O Brasil imperial, 1808–1889; panorama da história do Brasil no século XIX. Maringá, Eduem, 99, 192 p. (ill.).

4134. MANSUR BARATA (Alexandre). Luzes e sombras: a açao da Maçonaria brasileira (1870–1910). Campinas, Editora da Unicamp/Centro de Memória-Unicamp, 99, 199 p. (ill., maps). (Coleçao Tempo & memória, 14).

4135. Repensando o Estado Novo. Org.: Dulce PANDOLFI. Rio de Janeiro, Editora FGV, 99, 345 p. (Brasil 500 anos).

4136. ROLLO GONCALVES (José). Escavando o chao da futilidade: colunas socias, fontes para o estudio de elites locais. *Revista de história regional*, 99, 4, 2, p. 25-42.

4137. SKIDMORE (Thomas E.). Brazil: five centuries of change. Oxford, Oxford U. P., 99, XIV-254 p. (ill). (Latin American histories).

4138. TOMATIS PETERSEN (Aurea), PEDROSO (Elizabeth M.K.), ULRICH (Maria Alayde). Política brasileira: regimes, partidos e grupos de pressao. Porto Alegre, EDIPUCRS, 99, 128 p.

4139. WITTER (José Sebastiao). República, política e partido. Prefácio de José SOUZA MARTINS. Bauru, EDUSC, 99, 255 p. (ill.). (Essência. História).

Cf. n°s 4055, 4829

Brunei Darussalam

4140. HORTON (A. V. M.). A biographical dictionary of Negara Brunei Darussalam: (1841–1998). Bordesley, A. M. V. Horton, 99, 2 vol., XXX-1120 p.

Bulgaria

4141. 120 godini izpulnitelna vlast v Bulgarija: nauchna konferentsiia, Sofiia, 6–7 iuli 1999 godina. (120 ans de pouvoir exécutif en Bulgarie). Redaktsionna kolegiia Georgi MARKOV (otgovoren redaktor) [et al.].

Sofija, Izdatelska kushta "Gutenberg", 99, 329 p. [Cf. n°s <sélection> 4145, 4150, 4154, 7744, 8011.]

4142. BKP, Kominternut i makedonskiiat vupros, 1917-1946. (Le PCB, le Komintern et le problème macédonien, 1917-1946). T. 5. Sustaviteli Tsocho BILIARSKI i Iva BURILKOVA. Sofiia, Glavno upravlenie na arkhivite, 99 683 p. (Arkhivite govoriat, 5).

4143. DAFINOV (Zdravko). Bezvremieto na komunizma: spomeni, dnevnitsi, pisma. C. 2. 1969-1989. (Le communisme sans époque. P. 2. 1969-1989. Mémoires, journaux, letters). Sofiia, Izdatelska kushta "Rodina", 99, 2 vol., [s. p.]. (Treto pokolenie, 4).

4144. DASKALOV (Doncho). Politicheski ubijstva v novata istorija na Bulgarija. (Assassinats politiques dans l'histoire moderne de la Bulgarie). Sofiia, Izdatelska kushta "Petur Beron", 99, 272 p.

4145. GREBENAROV (A.). Bulgarskite pravitelstva i nacionalnijat vupros sled Purvata svetovna vojna. (Les gouvernements bulgares et le problème national après la Première guerre mondiale). In: 120 godini izpulnitelna vlast v Bulgarija [Cf. n° 4141], p. 211-224.

4146. GRUNCHAROV (Mikhail). Chorbadzhiistvoto i bulgarskoto obshtestvo prez vuzrazhdaneto. (La classe des «tchorbadjis» [des notables] dans la société bulgare pendant la Renaissance). Sofiia, Univ. izd-vo "Sv. Kliment Okhridski", 99, 221 p.

4147. IOSIFOV (Kalin). Totalitarizmut v bulgarskoto selo: khronika na nasilieto (Le totalitarisme dans le village bulgare. Chronique de la violence). Sofiia, UI "Sv. Kliment Okhridski", 99, 164 p. (ill.).

4148. KOSEV (Konstantin Dimitrov), DOINOV (Stefan). Vuzkresenieto na Bulgariia prez 1878 g. (L'insurrection de la Bulgarie en 1878). Sofiia, Universitetsko izdatelstvo "Sv. Kliment Okhridski", 99, 408 p.

4149. KUMANOV (Milen), NIKOLOVA (Tania). Politicheski partii, organizatsii i dvizheniia v Bulgariia i tekhnite lideri, 1879-1999: kratuk spravochnik. (Partis, organisations et mouvements politiques en Bulgarie et leurs leaders aux années 1879-1999. Manuel bref de références). Sofiia, Ariadna, 99, 272 p.

4150. MARKOV (G.). Voennite b izpulnitelnata vlast. (Les militaires dans le pouvoir exécutiv). In: 120 godini izpulnitelna vlast v Bulgarija [Cf. n° 4141], p. 104-115.

4151. Österreich, Österreich-Ungarn und die Entwicklung der Bulgarischen Eliten, 1815-1918: Materialien der Ersten Wissenschaftlichen Tagung der Bilateralen Arbeitsgruppe Österreich und Bulgarien. Hrsg. v. Milčo LALKOV, Harald HEPPNER und Rumjana PREŠLENOVA. Sofija, Akademieverlag "Prof. Marin Drinov", 99, 127 p.

4152. PETROV (Liudmil Kirilov). Voennata ikonomika na Bulgariia: 1919-1945. (L'economie militaire de la Bulgarie 1919-1945). Sofiia, Universitetsko izdatelstvo "Stopanstvo", 99, 147 p.

4153. STATELOVA (Elena), GRUNCHAROV (Stoicho). Istoriia na Bulgariia v tri toma. T. 3. Istoriia na nova Bulgariia 1878-1944. (Histoire de la Bulgarie. T. 3. Histoire de la nouvelle Bulgarie. 1878-1944). Sofiia, Anubis, 99, 648 p.

4154. STOJANOVA (V.). Bulgarskata pravoslavia curkva i izpulnitelnata vlast (1919-1953). (L'église bulgare orthodoxe et le pouvoir exécutif, 1919-1953). In: 120 godini izpulnitelna vlast v Bulgarija [Cf. n° 4141], p. 125-136.

4155. Voices from the Gulag: life and death in communist Bulgaria. Compiled and edited by Tzvetan TODOROV. University Park, Pennsylvania State U. P., 99, 10-178 p.

Burkina Faso

4156. Burkina Faso, cent ans d'histoire, 1895-1995: actes du premier colloque international sur l'histoire du Burkina, Ouagadougou, 12-17 décembre 1996. Sous la direction de Yénouyaga Georges MADIÉGA et Oumarou NAO. Paris, Editions Karthala-P.U.O., 99, 2 vol., XX-2202 p. (ill.). (Collection "Hommes et sociétés").

Burundi

4157. BIRABUZA (André). Le mal burundais, ou, l'involution historique d'une vieille nation. Bujumbura, Editions de La Renaissance, 99, 174 p.

Cambodia

4158. CHANDLER (David). Voices from S-21: terror and history in Pol Pot's secret prison. Berkeley a. Los Angeles, University of California Press, 99, XIII-238 p. (A Philip E. Lilienthal book).

4159. MOSJAKOV (Dmitrij V.). Sotsial'no-politicheskoe razvitie Kambodzhi v XX veke. Derevnja i vlast'. (Social and political development of Cambodia in the 20th century: peasants and power). RAN, In-t vostokovedenija. Moskva, [s. n.], 99, 269 p. (bibl.). [Eng. summary]

Canada

4160. AMYOT (Éric). Le Québec entre Pétain et de Gaulle: Vichy, la France Libre et les Canadiens Français 1940-1945. Saint-Laurent, Fides, 99, 365 p.

4161. BICKERTON (James), GAGNON (Alain-G.), SMITH (Patrick J.). Ties that bind: parties and voters in Canada. Don Mills a. Oxford, Oxford U. P., 99, 251 p.

4162. Capitale éphémère (Une): Montréal et les événements tragiques de 1849. Textes réunis et présentés par Gaston DESCHÊNES. Sillery, Éditions du Septentrion, 99, 160 p. (ill., portr.). (Cahiers du Septentrion, 13).

4163. CODIGNOLA (Luca), BRUTI LIBERATI (Luigi). Storia del Canada: dalle origini ai giorni nostri. Milano, Bompiani, 99, 814 p. (maps). (Storia paperback).

4164. LAHAISE (Robert), VALLERAND (Noël). La Nouvelle-France, 1524–1760. Outremont, Lanctôt, 99, 334 p. (ill.).

4165. PRINCIPE (Angelo). The darkest side of the Fascist years: the Italian-Canadian press, 1920–1942. Toronto, Guernica, 99, 272 p. (plates, ill.). (Essay series, 40).

4166. ROBINSON (Daniel J.). The measure of democracy: polling, market research, and public life, 1930–1945. Toronto a. London, University of Toronto Press, 99, IX-252 p. (plates, ill.).

4167. SMITH (David Edward). The Republican option in Canada, past and present. Toronto a. London, University of Toronto Press, 99, 352 p.

4168. TRUDEL (Marcel). Le régime militaire et la disparition de la Nouvelle-France, 1759–1764. Montréal, Fides, 99, X-612 p. (maps). (Histoire de la Nouvelle-France, 10).

Chile

4169. ENSALACO (Mark). Chile under Pinochet: recovering the truth. Philadelphia, University of Pennsylvania Press, 99, XV-280 p.

4170. FUENTES WENDLING (Manuel). Memoria secretas de Patria y Libertad: y algunas confesiones sobre la guerra fría en Chile. Santiago de Chile, Grupo Grijalbo Mondadori, 99, 397 p. (Hojas nuevas).

4171. Historia contemporánea de Chile. Coordinadores Gabriel SALAZAR y Julio PINTO. Santiago, LOM, 99, [s. p.]. (Serie Historia).

4172. KURTZ (Marcus J.). Chile's neo-liberal revolution: incremental decisions and structural transformation, 1973–1989. *Journal of Latin American studies*, 99, 31, 2, p. 399-427.

4173. LÓPEZ TOBAR (Mario). El 11 en la mira de un Hawker Hunter: las operaciones y blancos aéreos de septiembre de 1973. Santiago, Sudamericana, 99, 145 p. (ill.). (Colección Tribuna libre).

4174. Manifiesto de historiadores. Compiladores Sergio GREZ TOSO y Gabriel SALAZAR VERGARA. Santiago de Chile, LOM Ediciones, 99, 117 p. (Libros del ciudadano).

4175. MANNS (Patricio). Chile: una dictadura militar permanente, 1811–1999. Santiago, Sudamericana, 99, 219 p. (Colección Tribuna libre).

4176. MORALES GORLERI (Claudio). El rey de la Patagonia: Orellie Antoine I, rey de Araucanía y Patagonia. Buenos Aires, Planeta, 99, 256 p. (ill.).

4177. Para recuperar la memoria histórica: Frei, Allende y Pinochet. Santiago, Ediciones Chile América-CESOC, 99, 479 p. [Contents: MOULIAN (Luis). Balance historiográfico. – VITALE (Luis). El primer gobierno DC: Eduardo Frei Montalva. – VITALE (Luis). El gobierno de Salvador Allende. – VITALE (Luis). Gobierno de Pinochet y de las FF.AA. como institución. – VITALE (Luis). Algunos criterios teórico-metodológicos. – AVENDANO PAVEZ (Octavio). Los campesinos del Valle Central en el Chile de la post reforma agraria. – PALESTRO (Sandra). Las mujeres en las últimas tres décadas. – SALAS (Verónica). Rasgos históricos del movimiento de pobladores. – CRUZ SALAS (Luis). Estado, partidos y movimiento obrero. – PIWONKA (Gonzalo). Los derechos humanos en los gobiernos de Frei Montalva, Allende y Pinochet].

4178. POLLACK (Marcelo). The new Right in Chile, 1973–1997. Basingstoke, Macmillan Press, 99, VII-235 p.

4179. SATER (William F.), HERWIG (Holger H.). The grand illusion: the Prussianization of the Chilean army. Lincoln a. London, University of Nebraska Press, 99, 247 p. (ill.). (Studies in war, society, and the military).

4180. VALENZUELA UGARTE (Renato). Bernardo O'Higgins: el estado de Chile y el poder naval en la independencia de los países del sur de América. Santiago de Chile, Editorial Andrés Bello, 99, 321 p. (ill., maps).

4181. VILLABLANCA Z (Hernán). Estructuración sociopolítica y desarrollo capitalista en Chile, 1820–1900. Santiago, Bravo y Allende Editores, 99, 187 p. (Colección de ciencias sociales).

4182. WILDE (Alexander). Irruptions of memory: expressive politics in Chile's transition to democracy. *Journal of Latin American studies*, 99, 31, 2, p. 473-500.

Cf. n° 4055

China

Cf. n°ˢ 8097-8272

Colombia

4183. APPELBAUM (Nancy). Whitening the region: Caucano mediation and «Antioqueño Colonization» in nineteenth-century Colombia. *Hispanic American historical review*, 99, 79, 4, p. 631-668.

4184. Armas (De las) a la política. Prólogo de Daniel PÉCAUT; compiladores, Ricardo PENARANDA y Javier GUERRERO BARÓN. Universidad Nacional de Colombia. Instituto de Estudios Políticos y Relaciones Internacionales. Santafé de Bogotá, IEPRI, 99, XXVI-333 p. (Sociología y política. Académica).

4185. ARTEAGA HERNÁNDEZ (Manuel), ARTEAGA CARVAJAL (Jaime). Historia política de Colombia. Santafé de Bogotá, Planeta Colombiana Editorial, 99, 480 p. (Línea del horizonte).

4186. Carlos Lleras Restrepo: aportes al periodismo, clientelismo y corrupción, modernización del Estado, Pacto Andino. Compilador Otto MORALES BENÍTEZ. Santafé de Bogotá, Fundación Universidad Central, 99, 277 p.

4187. Guerra (La) y la paz en la segunda mitad del siglo XX en Colombia. Ed. par Raúl ALAMEDA OSPINA. Santa Fe de Bogotá, Academia Colombiana de Ciencias Económicas y Ecoe Ediciones, 99, XII-268 p. (maps). (Colección Controversia).

4188. MARTÍNEZ CARRENO (Aída). La Guerra de los Mil Días: testimonios de sus protagonistas. Santafé de Bogotá, Planeta, 99, 232 p. (ill.). (Línea del horizonte).

4189. RAUSCH (Jane M.). Colombia: territorial rule and the Llanos frontier. Gainesville, University Press of Florida, 99, XI-285 p.

Congo

** 4190. GUEVARA (Ernesto 'Che'). Che in Africa: Che Guevara's Congo diary. Ed. by William GÁLVEZ. Melbourne, Ocean, 99, 307 p. (ill.).

4191. KOULA (Yitzhak). La démocratie congolaise "brûlée" au pétrole. Préface de François-Xavier VERSCHAVE. Paris, L'Harmattan, 99, 219 p. (Collection "Points de vue")

4192. MAKOUTA-MBOUKOU (Jean Pierre). La destruction de Brazzaville, ou, La démocratie guillotinée. Paris, L'Harmattan, 99, 181 p.

4193. O'BALLANCE (Edgar). The Congo-Zaire experience, 1960–1998. Basingstoke, Macmillan, 99, XXV-205 p.

4194. VELLUT (Jean-Luc). Prestige et pauvreté de l'histoire nationale. A propos d'une histoire nationale du Congo. *Revue belge de philologie et d'histoire*, 99, 77, 2, p. 480-517.

Costa Rica

4195. BOTEY SOBRADO (Ana María). Costa Rica: estado, economía, sociedad y cultura desde las sociedades autóctonas hasta 1914. San José, Editorial de la Universidad de Costa Rica, Cátedra Historia de las Instituciones de Costa Rica, 99, 530 p. (ill., maps).

4196. EVANS (Sterling). The green republic: a conservation history of Costa Rica. Austin, University of Texas Press, 99, XVI-317 p. (ill., maps).

4197. MOLINA (Iván), LEHOUCQ (Fabrice). Urnas de lo inesperado: fraude electoral y lucha política en Costa Rica (1901–1948). San José, Editorial de la Universidad de Costa Rica, 99, 216 p.

4198. OBREGÓN (Clotilde María). Nuestros gobernantes: verdades del pasado para comprender el futuro. San José, Editorial de la Universidad de Costa Rica, 99, 151 p.

Croatia

4199. BILANDŽIĆ (Dušan). Hrvatska moderna povijest. (Croatian contemporary history). Zagreb, Golden marketing, 99, 835 p.

4200. BUDAK (Neven). Hrvatski identitet i ranosrednjovjekovno kraljevstvo. (The Croatian identity and the early medieval kingdom). *Historijski zbornik*, 99, 52, p. 121-126.

4201. KATIČIĆ (Radoslav). Pitanje o podrijetlu Hrvata u hrvatskome intelektualnom diskurzu danas. (The issue of the origin of the Croats in the present Croatian intellectual discourse). *Historijski zbornik*, 99, 52, p. 117-120.

4202. MATKOVIĆ (Hrvoje). Povijest Hrvatske seljačke stranke. (History of the Croatian Peasant Party). Zagreb, Naklada Pavičić, 99, 532 p.

4203. MOAČANIN (Nenad). Hrvati pod vlašću Osmanskog carstva do 1791. godine – preispitivanja. (The Croats under the rule of Ottoman Empire until 1791). Zagreb, Matica Hrvatska, [s. p.].

4204. RADELIĆ (Zdenko). Božidar Magovac. S Radićem između Mačeka i Hebranga, 1908.–1955. (Božidar Magovac. With Radić between Maček and Hebrang, 1908–1955). Zagreb, Hrvatski institut za povijest, 99, 261 p. (Biblioteka Hrvatska povjesnica. Monografije i studije, III/8).

Cuba

4205. FERRER (Ada). Insurgent Cuba: race, nation, and revolution, 1868–1898. Chapel Hill a. London, University of North Carolina Press, 99, XI-273 p.

4206. HIDALGO DE PAZ (Ibrahím). Cuba, 1895–1898: contradicciones y disoluciones. La Habana, Centro de Estudios Martianos, Centro de Investigación y Desarrollo de la Cultura Cubana Juan Marinello, 99, XII-361 p.

4207. LE RIVEREND (Julio). Breve historia de Cuba. La Habana, Editorial de Ciencias Sociales, 99, VI-141 p. (ill., maps).

4208. LOSADA ALVAREZ (Abel). Cuba: población y economía entre la independencia y la revolución. Vigo, Universidade de Vigo, Servicio de Publicaciones, 99, 408 p. (Monografías da Universidade de Vigo. Serie Humanidades e ciencias xurídico-sociais, 20).

4209. PÉREZ (Louis A. jr.). On becoming Cuban: identity, nationality and culture. Chapel Hill a. London, University of North Carolina Press, 99, 505 p.

Cyprus

4210. DODD (Clement H.). A historical overview. *In*: Cyprus: the need for new perspectives. Ed. by Clement H. DODD. Huntingdon, Eothen Press, 99, p. 1-15.

4211. Questione cipriota (La): la storia e il diritto. A cura di Augusto SINAGRA e Claudio ZANGHI. Milano, Giuffrè, 99, XVIII-213 p.

4212. STEFANIDIS (Ioannis D.). Isle of discord: nationalism, imperialism and the making of the Cyprus problem. New York, New York U. P., 99, XVI-315 p.

2. HISTORY BY COUNTRIES

Czech Republic (Czechoslovakia)

** 4213. Židovské matriky. HBMa 1784–1949 (1960). (The registers of the Jewish population of Czechoslovakia). Ed. by Lenka MATUŠÍKOVÁ. Praha, Státní ústřední archiv, 99, 325 p. (Inventáře a katalogy fondů Státního ústředního archivu v Praze).

4214. BABIČKA (Vácslav). Únor 1948 a katolická církev. (Februar 1948 und die katholische Kirche). *Paginae historiae*, 99, 7, p. 277-294.

4215. BARTEČEK (Ivo). Československý antifašistický exil německého jazyka v Mexiku. Studie a dokumenty. (Das tschechoslowakische antifaschistische Exil der deutschen Sprache in Mexiko. Studien und Dokumente). Olomouc, Centrum pro československá exilová studia FFUP, 99, 102 p.

4216. BENČÍK (Antonín), PAULÍK (Jan), PECKA (Jindřich). Vojenské otázky československé reformy 1967–1970. Srpen 1968–květen 1971. (Military aspects of the Czechoslovak Reforms, 1967–1970). Brno, Doplněk, 99, 387 p. (Prameny k dějinám československé krize v letech 1967–1970, 6/2).

4217. BENČÍK (Antonín). Kauza generála V. Prchlíka. (The Case of General V. Prchlík). *Přísně tajné!*, 99, 3, p. 132-142.

4218. BROKLOVÁ (Eva). Politická kultura německých aktivistických stran v Československu 1918–1938. (The political culture of the German activist parties in Czechoslovakia, 1918–1938). Praha, Karolinum, 99, p. 144-148.

4219. Československo 1918–1938. Osudy demokracie ve střední Evropě. Sborník z mezinárodní konference. Tomo 1-2. [Czechoslovakia 1918–1938. The fate of democracy in Central Europe. Conference proceedings]. Eds. Jaroslav VALENTA, Emil VORÁČEK, Josef HARNA. Praha, Historický ústav AV ČR, 99, 2 vol., 682 p. [Cf. n° <choice> 7547.]

4220. CUHRA (Jaroslav). Církevní politika KSČ a státu v letech 1969–1972. (Communist policy towards the churches in Czechoslovakia, 1969–1972]. Praha, Ústav pro soudobé dějiny AV ČR, 99, 107 p. (Sešity Ústavu pro soudobé dějiny AV ČR, 32).

4221. Democratic Revolution (The) in Czechoslovakia. Its precondition, course, and immediate repercussions, 1987–1989. A chronology of events and a compendium of declassified documents. Briefing book for an international conference, Prague, 14–16 October 1999. Ed. by Vilém PREČAN with Derek PATON. Praha, National Security Archive, 99, 382 p.

4222. DRÁPALA (Milan). Zavržení liberalismu v Čechách a Helena Koželuhová. K ideologickému profilu poválečné republiky (1945–1948). (The rejection of liberalism in the Bohemian Lands and Helena Koželuhová. An ideological profile of the post-war Republic, 1945–1948). *Soudobé dějiny*, 99, 6, 1, p. 7-44.

4223. HARNA (Josef). Reakce české a slovenské veřejnosti na nástup Milana Hodži do čela československé vlády. (The reaction of Czech and Slovak public on Milan Hodža's appointement as the premier of new Czechoslovak Government). *Moderní dějiny*, 99, 7, p. 53-63.

4224. HERNOVÁ (Šárka). Sociální struktura národnostních menšin České republiky a její vývojové tendence po roce 1945 (Němci, Poláci, Slováci). (Die Sozialstruktur der nationalen Minderheiten in der Tschechischen Republik und ihre Entwicklungstendenz nach dem Jahre 1945 – Deutsche, Polen, Slowaken). *Slezský sborník*, 99, 97, 3/4, p. 181-200.

4225. Hilsnerova aféra a česká společnost 1899–1999. Sborník přednášek. (The Hilsner Affair and Czech society, 1899–1999: Conference proceedings). Ed. by Miloš POJAR and Leo PAVLÁT. Praha, Židovské muzeum, 99, 223 p.

4226. HLUŠIČKOVÁ (Růžena). Kladsko a Československo v letech 1945–1947. Studie a dokumenty. (Das Glatzgebiet und die Tschechoslowakei in den Jahren 1945–1947). Hradec Králové, Pedagogická fakulta VŠP, 99, 171 p. (Kladský sborník. Suppl., 1).

4227. JIRÁNEK (Tomáš). Začleňování německé menšiny do hospodářství meziválečného Československa. (Die Eingliederung der deutschen Minderheit in der Tschechoslowakei und die Wirtschaft der Zwischenkriegszeit). *In:* Národnostní menšiny a jejich sociální pozice ve střední Evropě [Cf. n° 3980], p. 124-132.

4228. KAPLAN (Karel). Nebezpečná bezpečnost. Státní bezpečnost 1948–1956. (Gefährliche Sicherheit. Staatssicherheit 1945–1956). Brno, Doplněk, 99, 289 p. (Knihy, dokumenty).

4229. KLÍMA (Jan). Kladsko po první světové válce a v období Výmarské republiky (1918–1933). (Das Glatzgebiet nach dem Ersten Weltkrieg und während der Weimarer Republik, 1918–1933). *Kladský sborník*, 99, 3, p. 115-136.

4230. KLÍPA (Bohumír). Konec mise vládního vojska v Itálii. (The end of the mission of the government force in Italy). *Historie a vojenství*, 99, 48, 4, p. 782-813. – IDEM. Vyslání vládního vojska do Itálie. (The Government Forces in Italy). *Historie a vojenství*, 99, 48, 3, p. 564-591.

4231. KOKOŠKA (Stanislav). Československé vojenské zpravodajství v roce 1938. (Czechoslovak military intelligence in 1938). *Sborník Vojenské akademie v Brně. Ser. C-D*, 99, 2, p. 97-103.

4232. KOUDELKA (František). Zasedání ÚV KSČ a obsazení nejvyšších funkcí v KSČ 1986–1989. (Tagung der ZK KPTsch und Bezetzung der höchsten Funktionen in der KPTsch 1986–1989). Praha, Ústav pro soudobé dějiny AV ČR, 99, 56 p. (Materiály, studie, dokumenty, 13).

4233. KRACIK (Jörg). Die Politik des deutschen Aktivismus in der Tschechoslowakei, 1920–1938. Frankfurt am Main, P. Lang, 99, 462 p. (Europäische Hochschulschriften. Reihe III, Geschichte und ihre Hilfswissenschaften, 833).

4234. KREJČOVÁ (Helena). K některým problémům židovské menšiny a českého antisemitismu po roce 1945. (Concerning some aspects of the Jewish minority and Czech antisemitism). *In:* Židé v české a polské občanské společnosti. Ed. by Jerzy TOMASZEWSKI and Jaroslav VALENTA. Praha, Univerzita Karlova, Filozofická fakulta, 99, p. 65-77. – EADEM. Specifické předpoklady antisemitismu a protižidovské aktivity v Protektorátu Čechy a Morava. (Special prerequisities of antisemitism and anti-Jewish activity in the Protectorate of Bohemia and Moravia). *In:* Emancipácia Židov – antisemitizmus – pronasledovanie v Nemecku, Rakúsko-Uhorsku, v českých zemiach a na Slovensku. Ed. J. K. HOENSCH. Bratislava, Veda, 99, p. 147-161.

4235. KŘESŤAN (Jiří). Dilemata židovské politiky v českých zemích v letech 1933-1938. (Die Dilemmata der jüdischen Politik in den tschechischen Ländern in den Jahren 1933-1938). *Paginae historiae*, 99, 7, p. 189-205.

4236. KUKLÍK (Jan). Programový vývoj Československé sociálně demokratické strany dělnické za první republiky. (The development of the platform of the Czechoslovak Social Party during the first Czechoslovak Republic). *In:* Současný stav a perspektivy zkoumání politických stran na našem území. Ed. Pavel MAREK. Olomouc, [s. n.], 99, p. 64-79.

4237. LUKES (Igor). Der Fall Slánský. Eine Exilorganisation und das Ende des tschechoslowakischen Kommunistenführers 1952. *Vierteljahrshefte für Zeitgeschichte*, 99, 47, 4, p. 459-502.

4238. LUTZ (Annabelle). Dissidenten und Bürgerbewegung: ein Vergleich zwischen DDR und Tschechoslowakei. Frankfurt, Campus, 99, 182 p. (Campus Forschung, 795).

4239. MALÝ (Karel), [et al.]. Dějiny českého a československého práva do roku 1945. (A history of Bohemia and Czechoslovakia law up to 1945). Praha, Linde, 99, 572 p. (photogr., maps).

4240. MAŇÁK (Jiří). Vývoj početního stavu a sociálního složení KSČ v letech 1948-1968. (The Czechoslovak Communist Party. Changes in the number of members and social composition, 1948-1968). *Soudobé dějiny*, 99, 6, 4, p. 460-478.

4241. MĚCHÝŘ (Jan). Velký převrat či snad revoluce sametová. Několik informací, poznámek a komentářů o naší takřečené něžné revoluci a jejich osudech 1989-1992. (Great Change or perhaps a 'revolution of velvet'. Information, remarks, and commentary about our so-called 'gentle revolution' and its consequences, 1989-1992]. Praha, Progetto, 99, 359 p.

4242. MILLER (Daniel E.). Forging political compromise: Antonín Švehla and the Czechoslovak Republican Party, 1918-1933. Pittsburgh, University of Pittsburgh Press, XV-323 p.

4243. OTÁHAL (Milan), VANĚK (Miroslav). Sto studentských revolucí. Studenti v období pádu komunismu. Životopisná vyprávění. (A hundred student revolutions. Students during the collapse of Communism. Biographical narratives). Praha, Lidové noviny, 99, 859 p. (photogr.).

4244. OTÁHAL (Milan). Podíl tvůrčí inteligence na pádu komunismu. (The share of the intelligentsia in the fall of Communism). Brno, Doplněk, 99, 161 p.

4245. PASÁK (Tomáš). Český fašismus 1922-1945 a kolaborace 1939-1945. (Czech Fascism 1922-1945 and collaboration 1939-1945). Ed. Jana PASÁKOVÁ. Praha, Práh, 99, 486 p. (photogr.).

4246. PEČÍNKA (Pavel). Pod rudou vlajkou proti KSČ. Osudy radikální levice v Československu. (Unter der rote Fahne gegen die KPTsch. Schicksale der radikalen Linken in der Tschechoslowakei). Brno, Doplněk, 99, 134 p.

4247. PERNES (Jiří), POTMĚŠILOVÁ (Jarmila). Od demokratického socialismu k demokracii. Skleněná kulička. Nekomunistická socialistická opozice v Brně v letech 1968-1972. (Von demokratischer Sozialismus zur Demokratie). Brno, Barrister & Principal, 99, 215 p. (Vědecké studie).

4248. PREČAN (Vilém). Delegace Slovenské národní rady v Londýně (říjen–listopad 1944). Nové dokumenty. (Delegation of the Slovak National Council in London, October–November 1944. New documents). *Československá historická ročenka 1999*, 99, p. 159-291.

4249. PROKŠ (Petr). Politické programy Československanské a Československé sociálně demokratické strany dělnické 1878-1948. (Political programmes of the Czechoslavonic and the Czechoslovak Social Democrat Party of Labour, 1878-1948). Praha, Historický ústav AV ČR, 99, 283 p. (Edice politických programů, 2).

4250. RENNER (Jan). Československá strana lidová 1945-1948. (The Czechoslovak People's Party, 1945-1948). Brno, Prius, 99, 101 p. (Prameny a studie k dějinám československého exilu 1948-1989, 1).

4251. Rozpadu Česko-Slovenska (od) do uznání československé prozatímní vlády 1939-1940. Zápisy ze zasedání Československého národního výboru 1939-1940. (From the break-up of Czecho-Slovakia to the recognition of the Czechoslovak Provisional Government, 1939-1940. Minutes from the sessions of the Czechoslovak National Committee, 1939-1940). Ed. by Jan KUKLÍK, Jan NĚMEČEK, Helena NOVÁČKOVÁ and Ivan ŠŤOVÍČEK. Praha, Ústav mezinárodních vztahů, 99, 349 p. (Dokumenty československé zahraniční politiky).

4252. SUK (Jiří), CUHRA (Jaroslav), KOUDELKA (František). Chronologie zániku komunistického režimu v Československu 1985-1990. (The end of the Communist regime in Czechoslovakia, 1985-1990. A chronology). Praha, Ústav pro soudobé dějiny AV ČR, 99, 143 p. (Sešity Ústavu pro soudobé dějiny AV ČR, 33).

4253. SUK (Jiří). K prosazení kandidatury Václava Havla na úřad prezidenta v prosinci 1989. Dokumenty a svědectví. (Archieving the candidacy of Václav Havel for the office of President, December 1989. Three documents and two testimonies]. *Soudobé dějiny*, 99, 6, 2/3, p. 346-369.

4254. Svobodu (Za) a demokracii. Tomo 1. Odpor proti komunistické moci. (Für die Freiheit und Demokratie. Band 1. Der Widerstand gegen die kommunistische Macht). Hrsg. v. Jaroslav CUHRA und Václav VEBER. Praha, Karolinum, 99, 333 p.

4255. VONDROVÁ (Jitka), NAVRÁTIL (Jaromír), MORAVEC (Jan). Komunistická strana Československa. Pokus o reformu (říjen 1967–květen 1968). (The Communist Party of Czechoslovakia, 1967–1968). Praha, Ústav pro soudobé dějiny AV ČR, 99, 580 s. (Prameny k dějinám československé krize 1967–1970, 9/1).

Cf. n°s 7646, 7788, 7962

Denmark

4256. BJØRN (Claus). Kampen om grundloven. (Le combat pour la Constitution). København, Fremad, 99, 135 p., (ill.).

4257. DAVIDSEN (Leif), LINDHARDT (Karsten). Østfronten: danskere i krig. (Le Front de l'est: les Danois en guerre). København, Høst, 99, 160 p. (ill.).

4258. DEHN-NIELSEN (Henning). Christian 8: konge af Danmark, konge af Norge. (Christian VIII: roi de Danemark, roi de Norvège). København, Sesam, 99, 216 p. (ill.).

4259. FINK (Troels). Båndene bandt: forbindelsen over Kongeåen 1864-1914. (Des Liens nous rattachaient: les relations par delà la frontière de la Kongeå). Aabenraa, Institut for grænseregionsforskning, 99, 2 vol., 397 p., 339 p. (ill.).

4260. FRIISBERG (Claus). Demokratiets triumf: den første Junigrundlov. (Le Triomphe de la démocratie: la première Constitution de Juin). Varde, Vestjysk Kulturforlag, 99, 318 p. (ill.). – IDEM. Revolution over Danmark: borgerskabets revolution marts 1848. (Révolution au Danemark: la révolution bourgeoise de mars 1848). Varde, Vestjysk Kulturforlag, 99, 184 p. (ill.).

4261. GØTZ (Heidi Inger). Skyggeprinsen: Jørgen af Danmark 1653–1708. (Le Prince fantôme: George de Danemark 1653–1708). [Vordingborg], Attika, 99, 268 p. (ill.).

4262. HARLANG (Christian), LYNGE (Aqqaluk), NIELSEN (Henrik Karl). Retten til Thulelandet. (Les Droits sur la région de Thulé). København, Dike ApS, 99, 208 p. (ill.).

4263. HERBORG (Mette), MICHAELSEN (Per). Ugræs: danske STASI kontakter. (Mauvaises herbes: les contacts danois de la STASI). Lyngby, Holkenfeldt, 99, 288 p. (ill.).

4264. JAEGER (Nils). Det historiske svigt: Socialdemokratiet og venstre fløjen i den kolde krig. (La trahison historique: la Social-démocratie et son aile gauche pendant la guerre froide). København, Gyldendal, 99, 198 p.

4265. KARPANTSCHOF (René). Nynazismen og dens modstandere i Danmark: politiske bevægelser i internationale rammer 1980–1998. (Le Néonazisme et ses opposants au Danemark: mouvements politiques dans des cadres internationaux). Esbjerg, Sydjysk Universitetsforlag, 99, 204 p.

4266. LAURIDSEN (John T.). Krig, købmænd og kongemakt; og andre 1600-tals studier. (Guerre, marchands et pouvoir royal; et autres études sur le 17e siècle). København, Det Kongelige Bibliotek, Museum Tusculanums Forlag, 99, 333 p. (Danish humanist texts and studies, 20).

4267. LAURSEN (Johnny Nørgaard), OLESEN (Thorsten Borring). Et nordisk alternativ til Europa?: samspillet mellem Danmarks nordiske og europæiske politik 1945–1999. (Une alternative nordique à l'Europe? Le jeu entre les politiques nordique et européenne du Danemark de 1945 à 1999). Århus, Systime, 99, 50 p. (Rådet for europæisk politik, 1999:2).

4268. SØNDBERG (Olaf). Den danske revolution 1830–1866. (La Révolution danoise 1830–1866). Århus, Systime, 99, 160 p. (ill.).

4269. STOKHOLM BANKE (Cecilie Felicia). Den sociale ingeniørskunst i Danmark: familie, stat og politik fra 1900 til 1945. (L'art de l'ingénieur social au Danemark: famille, Etat et politique de 1900 à 1945). Roskilde, Roskilde universitet, Institut for historie og samfundsforhold, 99, 192 p.

Dominican Republic

4270. CASSÁ (Roberto). Los orígenes del Movimiento 14 de Junio. Santo Domingo, Editoria Universitaria, 99, 370 p. (Publicaciones de la Universidad Autónoma de Santo Domingo, 1, 925. Colección Historia y sociedad, 93. La izquierda dominicana, 1).

4271. GRULLÓN (Sandino). Historia de las elecciones en la República Dominicana, desde 1913 a 1998: nombres, sucesos, estadísticas. Santo Domingo, [s. n.], 99, 630 p.

4272. HORNGREN (Myriam). Dominican Republic: women's political and social participation since Beijing. London, [s. n.], 53 p. [Thesis (M.A.) – Institute of Latin American Studies, School of Advanced Study, University of London, 1999].

4273. JIMÉNEZ POLANCO (Jacqueline). Los partidos políticos en la República Dominicana: actividad electoral y desarrollo organizativo. Santo Domingo, Editora Centenario, 99, XVI-593 p.

4274. MOYA PONS (Frank). Breve historia contemporánea de la República Dominicana. México, Fondo de Cultura Económica, 99, 270 p. (Colección popular, 567).

4275. Política, identidad y pensamiento social en la República Dominicana (siglos XIX y XX). Ed. por Raymundo GONZÁLEZ [et al.]. Madrid, Doce Calles, Academia de Ciencias de Dominicana, 99, 300 p. (Colección Antilia).

Ecuador

4276. DÍAZ CUEVA (Miguel), JURADO NOBOA (Fernando). Alfaro y su tiempo. Quito, Fundación Cultural del Ecuador, 99, 315 p. (ill.). (Colección SAG, 118. Serie Alfarada, 6).

Egypt

4277. DORAN (Michael Scott). Pan-Arabism before Nasser: Egyptian power politics and the Palestine Question. New York a. Oxford, Oxford U. P., 99, X-230 p. (Studies in Middle Eastern history).

4278. SULLIVAN (Denis Joseph), ABED-KOTOB (Sana). Islam in contemporary Egypt: civil society vs. the State. Boulder, L. Rienner, 99, XI-159 p.

4279. TROUTT POWELL (Eve Marie). Colonized colonizers: Egyptian nationalists and the issue of the Sudan, 1875 to 1919. Ann Arbor, UMI Dissertation Services, 99, 253 p.

El Salvador

4280. LAURIA-SANTIAGO (Aldo A.). Land, community, and revolt in late-nineteenth-century Indian Izalco, El Salvador. *Hispanic American historical review*, 99, 79, 3, p. 495-534.

4281. MONTOBBIO (Manuel). La metamorfosis de pulgarcito: transición política y proceso de paz en El Salvador. Pról. de Alvaro DE SOTO. Barcelona, Icaria, 99, 383 p. (Antrazyt, 130. Paz y conflictos).

Estonia

4282. ALENIUS (Kari). «Die Jugend Estlands wird ... ihren Teil zur Neuen Ordnung beitragen ...» Viron nuorisotyö saksalaismiehityksen aikana, 1941–1944. (Estonian youth movements under German occupation, 1941–1944). *Faravid*, 98-99, 22-23, p. 373-401. (ill.). [English summary].

Ethiopia

** 4283. EVALET (André). De Ménélik à Mengistu: un suisse en Éthiopie. Témoignage recueilli et annoté par Micheline FONTOLLIET HONORÉ. Genève, Musée d'ethnographie, 99, 162 p. (ill., maps, ports.). (Collection Sources et témoignages).

4284. DONHAM (Donald Lewis). Marxist modern: an ethnographic history of the Ethiopian revolution. Berkeley, University of California Press a. Oxford, J. Currey, 99, XXVI-236 p. (ill., maps).

4285. HAMMOND (Jenny). Fire from the ashes: a chronicle of the revolution in Tigray, Ethiopia, 1975–1991. Lawrenceville, Red Sea Press, 99, XXII-456 p. (ill., maps).

4286. VESTAL (Theodore M.). Ethiopia: a post-Cold War African state. Westport, Praeger, 99, XIX-229 p. (ill.).

Finland

4287. GRÖNLUND (Kimmo). Kontext, valsystem och aktivitet. Den politiska omgivningens betydelse för valdeltagandet i Stobritannien och Finland 1918–1999. (Political context, electoral systems and the voter activity. The influence of political context in voter activity in Great Britain and Finland, 1918–1999). Åbo. Åbo akademis förlag, 99, 326 p. [English summary].

4288. HENTILÄ (Seppo), JUSSILA (Osmo), NEVAKIVI (Jukka). Histoire politique de la Finlande: XIXe–XXe siècle. Paris, Fayard, 99, 522 p.

4289. JUSSILA (Osmo), HENTILÄ (Seppo), NEVAKIVI (Jukka). From Grand Duchy to a modern state: a political history of Finland since 1809. London, Hurst & Co., 99, XIV-383 p.

4290. MORGAN (K.), SAARELA (T.). Northern underground revisited: Finnish Reds and the origins of British communism. *European history quarterly*, 99, 29, 2, p. 179-216.

4291. Power and bureaucracy in Finland, 1809–1998. Ed. by Jorma SELOVUORI. Helsinki, Prime Minister's Office, 99, 241 p. (ill., maps).

Cf. n°s 926, 5133, 7681

France

* 4292. MAYAUD (Jean-Luc). 1848 et la Seconde République: 50 années de recherche. Bibliographie, 1948-1997 (suite). *Revue d'histoire du XIXe siecle*, 99, 18, p. 161-168.

** 4293. CAMBACERES (Jean-Jacques Régis). Mémoires inédites. Tome 1. la Révolution, le Consulat. Tome 2. L'Empire. Préface de Jean TULARD. Présentation et notes de Laurence CHATEL DE BRANCION. Paris, Perrin, 99, 2 vol., 792 p., 533 p.

** 4294. Corse (La) aux rapports. Préface et introduction de Gabriel Xavier CULIOLI. Ajaccio, Editions DCL, 99, 442 p.

** 4295. Journal d'un ligueur Parisien: des barricades à la levée du siège de Paris par Henri IV, 1588-1590. Ed. par Xavier LE PERSON. Genève, Droz, 99, 214 p. (Travaux d'Humanisme et Renaissance, 332).

** 4296. Trois autobiographies communistes. Présentées par Stéphane COURTOIS. *Debat*, 99, 107, p. 162-177.

4297. ANGEL (Jacques). Drancy: les premiers moi. Témoignage. *Revue d'histoire de la Shoah. Le monde juif*, 99, 165, p. 185-207.

4298. Année 1947 (L'). Sous la dir. de Serge BERNSTEIN et Pierre MILZA. Paris, Presses de la Fondation nationale des sciences politiques, 99, 531 p.

4299. ANTONMATTEI (Pierre). Léon Gambetta: héraut de la République. Paris, Michalon, 99, 608 p. (ill.).

4300. APRILE (Sylvie). «La prison agrandie». La pratique de l'internement aux lendemains du coup d'Etat du 2 décembre 1851. *Revue d'histoire moderne et contemporaine,* 99, 46, p. 658-679.

4301. ARDAILLOU (Pierre). Les républicains du Havre au XIXe siècle (1815–1889). Roue, Publications des Universités de Rouen et du Havre. 99, 452 p.

4302. BAILEY (C.R.). Monarchic survivors in France's Revolutionary government: the slow eclipse of Ministers of the Interior, 1793–1794. *European history quarterly,* 99, 29, 3, p. 381-417.

4303. BARBICHE (Bernard). Les institutions de la monarchie française à l'époque moderne: XVIe–XVIIIe siècle. Paris, Presses universitaires de France, 99, XI-430 p. (Collection Premier cycle).

4304. BERNSTEIN (Serge), MILZA (Pierre). Histoire de la France au XXe siècle. Tome 3. 1945–1958. Bruxelles, Editions Complexe, 99, 337 p. (Historiques, 123).

4305. BERTIN-MAGHIT (Jean-Pierre). Encadrer et contrôler: le documentaire de propagande sous l'Occupation. *Vingtième siècle. Revue d'histoire,* 99, 63, p. 23-49.

4306. BETHOUART (Bruno). Des syndicalistes chrétiens en politique (1944–1962). De la Libération à la Ve République. Villeneuve d'Ascq, Presses univ. Septentrion, 99, 323 p.

4307. BLACK (Jeremy). From Louis XIV to Napoleon. The fate of a great power. London, UCL Press, 99, XVI-287 p.

4308. BOLTANSKI (Ariane). Le pouvoir en partage. Les litiges entre le duc de Nevers et le gouvernement monarchique (1614–1617). *Revue d'histoire moderne et contemporaine,* 99, 46, p. 117-145.

4309. BOSWELL (Laird). Franco-Alsatian conflict and the crisis of national sentiment during the Phoney war. *Journal of modern history.* 99, 71, 3, p. 552-584.

4310. BRACONNIER (Céline). Braconnage sur terres d'Etat. Les inscriptions politiques séditieuses dans le Paris de l'après-Commune (1872–1885). *Genèses,* 99, 35, p. 103-130.

4311. BRUNET (Jean-Paul). Police contre FLN: le drame d'octobre 1961. Paris, Flammarion, 99, 345 p.

4312. CARON (Vicki). Uneasy Asylum: France and the Jewish refugee crisis, 1933–1942. Stanford, Stanford U. P., 99, XI-605 p. (Stanford studies in Jewish history and culture).

4313. CHAFFEL (Alain). Les communistes de la Drôme de la Libération au printemps 1981: de l'euphorie à la désillusion. Paris, L'Harmattan, 99, 323 p. (maps).

4314. DARD (Olivier). L'armée française face à l'Organisation armée secrète (OAS). *In*: Militaires en République 1870–1962. Les officiers, le pouvoir et la vie politique en France [Cf. n° 4366], p. 687-699.

4315. DAVIES (Peter). The National Front in France: ideology, discourse and power. London a. New York, Routledge, 99, VIII-278 p.

4316. DE LA GORCE (Paul Marie). De Gaulle. Paris, Perrin, 99, 1406 p.

4317. DECLAIR (Edward G.). Politics on the fringe: the people, policies, and organization of the French National Front. Durham, Duke U. P., 99, XIV-261 p.

4318. DESCIMON (Robert). Autopsie du massacre de l'Hôtel de Ville (4 juillet 1652). Paris et la «Fronde des Princes». *Annales,* 99, 54, 2, p. 319-352.

4319. DI RIENZO (Eugenio). Marc-Antoine Jullien de Paris (1789–1848). Una biografia politica. Napoli, Guida, 99, 346 p.

4320. Directoire (Du) au Consulat. Vol. 1. Le lien politique local dans la Grand Nation. Actes des Tables rondes de Valenciennes et de Lille. Ed. par J. BERNET, Jean-Pierre JESSENNE et Hervé LEUWERS. Lille, CRHENO-Université de Lille III, 99, 336 p.

4321. DREYFUS-ARMAND (Geneviève). L'exil des républicains espagnols en France, de la guerre civile à la mort de Franco. Paris, Albin Michel, 99, 457 p.

4322. DU CHASTEL (Pierre). Deux sermons funèbres prononcez ès obsèques de François Premier de ce nom. Ed. critique par Pascale Chiron. Genève, Droz, 99, XXXIX-105 p.

4323. DUBOST (Jean-François), SAHLINS (Peter). Et si on faisait payer les étrangers? Louis XIV, les immigrés et quelques autres. Paris, Flammarion, 99, 475 p.

4324. DUHAMEL (Morvan). Communistes et Front populaire: sur l'origine du «document Ercoli». *Cahiers d'histoire sociale,* 99, 12, p. 67-76.

4325. EBEL (Edouard). Les préfets et le maintien de l'ordre public, en France, au XIXe siècle. Paris, Documentation française, 99, 265 p. (La sécurité aujourd'hui).

4326. ECKARD (Michels). Deutsche in der Fremdenlegion, 1870–1965. Mythen und Realitäten. Paderborn, München, Wien u. Zürich, Schöning, 99, 362 p.

4327. EL GAMMAL (Jean). Histoire politique de la France de 1814 à 1870. Paris, Nathan, 99, 248 p. (Fac. Histoire). – IDEM. Politique et poids du passé dans la France "fin de siècle". Limoges, PULIM, 99, 789 p.

4328. Elites et pouvoirs locaux. La France du Sud-Est sous la Troisième République. Ed. par Bruno DUMONS et Gilles POLLET. Actes des Journées d'études, Lyon 21 et 22 mars 1996. Lyon, Presses universitaire Lyon, 99, 530 p.

4329. Ere Barthou (L'). Actes du Colloque de Strasbourg, organisé par le Centre d'études germaniques de Strasbourg et l'Univ. Paris IV en octobre 1999. *Revue* d'Europe centrale, 99, 7, 2, p. 1-145. [Cf. n^os <sélection> 7605, 7613.]

4330. FINLEY-CROSWHITE (S. Annette). Henry IV and the towns: the pursuit of legitimacy in French urban society, 1589–1610. Cambridge, Cambridge U. P., 99, XIV-219 p. (Cambridge studies in ealy modern history).

4331. French colonial empire and the Popular Front: hope and disillusion. Ed. by Tony CHAFER and Amanda SACKUR. Basingstoke, Macmillan Press, 99, [s. p.].

4332. French émigrés in Europe and the struggle against revolution, 1789–1814. Ed. by Kirsty CARPENTER and Philip MANSEL. Houndmills, Macmillan Press a. New York, St. Martin's Press, 99, XXII-236 p.

4333. French history since Napoleon. Ed. by Martin S. ALEXANDER. London, Arnold a. New York, Oxford U. P., 99, 434 p.

4334. French Revolution sourcebook (The). Ed. by John HARDMAN. London, Arnold, 99, XVII-261p

4335. GATTAZ (Yvon), SIMONNOT (Philippe). Mitterrand et les patrons 1981–1986. Paris, Fayard, 99, 325 p.

4336. GEMIE (Sharif). French revolutions, 1815–1914: an introduction. Edinburgh, Edinburgh U. P., 99, VIII-257 p.

4337. GÉRARD (Alain). "Par principe d'humanité …": la Terreur et la Vendée. Paris, Fayard, 99, 589 p.

4338. GONJO (Yasuo). Furansu shihon shugi to chuo ginko: Furansu ginko kindaika no rekishi. (French capitalism and the Central Bank: modernization of the Bank of France, 1930–1958). Tokyo, University of Tokyo Press, 99, 518 p.

4339. GORUPPI (Tiziana). Intellettuali e potere nella Francia dell'Ottocento. Paris, H. Champion, 99, 199 p. (Textes et études-domaine français, 35).

4340. GOTTERI (Nicole). Claude Petiet, ministre de la Guerre, intendant général de la Grande Armée et ses fils Alexandre, Auguste et Sylvain. Le devenir de la condition militaire de la fin de l'Ancien Régime au second Empire 1749–1868. Paris, Kronos, 99, 420 p.

4341. GRAND (Philippe). Le fichier juif: un malaise (réponse au rapport Rémond remis au Premier ministre le 3 juillet 1996). Revue d'histoire de la Shoah. Le monde juif, 99, 167, p. 53-101.

4342. GUÉRAICHE (William). Les femmes et la République: essai sur la répartition du pouvoir de 1943 à 1979. Paris, Les Editions de L'Atelier, 99, 304 p.

4343. Guerres et occupations dans le Sud Est parisien, XVIIIe–XXe siècles. Actes du Colloque de Clio 94, 24 octobre 1998. Clio 94, 99, 17, p. 87-265.

4344. HAUSER (Claude). Un réseau intellectuel franco-suisse en action sous Vichy. Relations internationales, 99, 97, p. 39-54.

4345. HEMMERDINGER (Bertrand). Quelques éclaircissements sur le règne de Napoleon III. Quaderni di storia, 99, 49, p. 237-246.

4346. HUSTON GOODFELLOW (Samuel). Between the Swastika and the Cross of Lorraine: Fascisms in interwar Alsace. DeKalb, Norther Illinois U. P., 99, VIII-230 p.

4347. IRASTORZA (Pascal). Le guêpier corse: de l'assassinat du préfet Erignac à l'arrestation du préfet Bonnet. Paris, Fayard, 99, 263 p. (ill.).

4348. Istorii evropejskogo parlamentarizma (Iz): Frantsija. (From the history of European parliamentarism: France: [articles]). Ed. Svetlana P. POZHARSKAJA. RAN, In-t vseobshchej istorii. Moskva, [s. n.], 99, 130 p. (bibl.).

4349. JOANA (Jean). Pratiques politiques des députés français au XIXe siècle: du dilettante au spécialiste. Paris, L'Harmattan, 99, 311 p. (Collection Logiques et politiques).

4350. JOHNSON (Martin Phillip). The Dreyfus affair: honour and politics in the Belle Époque. Basingstoke, Macmillan, 99, XI-171 p. (European history in perspective).

4351. KANINSKAJA (Galina N.). Radikaly i radikalizm v poslevoennoj Frantsii: respublikanskaja partija radikalov i radikal-sotsialistov v gody IV i V respublik. (Les radicaux et le radicalisme en France après la Guerre: la Partie républicaine des radicaux et des Radicaux-socialistes sous la IVe et Ve Republiques). Moskva, Nauka, 99, 239 p. (bibl.). [Resumé français]

4352. KOREMAN (Megan). The expectation of justice: France 1944–1946. Durham, Duke U. P., 99, 340 p.

4353. KREUZER (Marcus). Money, votes and political leverage: explaining the electoral performance of liberals in interwar France and Germay. Social science history, 99, 23, 2, p. 211-240.

4354. LANDAU (Philippe-E.). Les Juifs de France et la Grande Guerre: un patriotisme républicain 1914–1941. Préface de Jean-Jacques BECKER. Paris, CNRS editions, 99, 293 p. (ill.). (CNRS histoire).

4355. Länderbericht Frankreich: Geschichte, Politik, Wirtschaft, Gesellschaft. Hrsg. v. Marieluise CHRISTADLER und Henrik UTERWEDDE. Bonn, Bundeszentrale für politische Bildung, 99, 672 p. (ill.). (Schriftenreihe, 360).

4356. LAROULANDIE (Fabrice). La France des années 1940: de la défaite au relèvement. Paris, Ellipses, 99, 319 p.

4357. LENTZ (Thierry). Dictionnaire des ministres de Napoléon. Dictionnaire analytique statistique et comparé des trente-deux ministres de Napoléon. Préf. de Jean TULARD. Paris, Christian / Jas, 99, 211 p. (ill.).

4358. MAC PHAIL (Helen). The long silence: civilian life under the German occupation of Northern France, 1914–1918. New York, I. B. Tauris, 99, X-235 p.

4359. MAILLARD (Alain). La communauté des égaux: le communisme néo-babouviste dans la France des années 1840. Paris, Kime, 99, 352 p. (Le sens de l'histoire).

4360. MANIGAND (Anne), DULPHY (Christine). L'opinion publique française face à l'élection européenne de juin 1979. *Journal of European integration history*, 99, 5, 1, p. 23-40.

4361. MARGADANT (Jo Burr). Gender, vice, and the political imaginary in nineteenth-century France: reinterpreting the failure of the July monarchy, 1830–1848. *American historical review*, 99, 104, 5, p. 1461-1496.

4362. MARTIN (Benjamin F.). France and the Après Guerre 1918–1924: illusions and disillusionment. Baton Rouge, Louisiana State U. P., 99, XII-278 p.

4363. MARTIN (Jean-Clément) Contre-Révolution, révolution et nation en France, 1789–1799. Paris, Ed. du Seuil, 99, 226 p.

4364. MARTINEZ (Gilles). Comment les liberaux sont arrivés à Vichy. Etude d'un parcours paradoxal. *Revue d'histoire moderne et contemporaine*, 99, 46, p. 571-590.

4365. MASSART (Alexis). L'Union pour la démocratie française (UDF). Paris, L'Harmattan, 99, 369 p. (ill.). (Logiques politiques).

4366. Militaires en République 1870–1962. Les officiers, le pouvoir et la vie politique en France. Ed. par O. FORCADE, E. DUHAMEL et P. VIAL. Paris, Publications de la Sorbonne, 99, 734 p. [Cf. n^{os} <sélection> 4314, 8017.]

4367. NAKANO (Takao). Puragu gai no jumintachi: Furansu kindai no jutaku, minshu, kokka. (Inhabitants of the Prague Quarters: habitation, people, state of contemporary France). Tokyo, Yamakawa Shuppansha, 99, 329 p.

4368. NAVET-BOURON (Françoise). Démocraties occidentales et bouleversements de l'histoire: France. Paris, Sedes, 99, 139 p. (Regards sur l'histoire. Histoire contemporaine, 137).

4369. NOIRIEL (Gérard). Les origines républicaines de Vichy. Paris, Hachette Littératures, 99, 335 p. (Collection Histoires).

4370. NORDMAN (Daniel). Frontières de France. De l'espace au territoire XVIe–XIXe siècles. Paris, Gallimard, 99, 644 p. (Bibliothèque des histoires).

4371. PASSMORE (Kevin). «Planting the tricolor in the citadels of communism»: women's social action in the Croix de feu and Parti social français. *Journal of modern history*. 99, 71, 4, p. 814-851.

4372. PETITEAU (Natalie). Napoléon de la mythologie à l'histoire. Paris, Ed. du Seuil, 99, 442 p.

4373. POULLE (Yvonne). La France à l'heure allemande. *Bibliothèque de l'École des Chartes*, 99, 157, p. 493-502.

4374. POZNANSKI (Renée). La création du Centre de documentation juive contemporaine en France (avril 1943). *Vingtième siècle. Revue d'histoire*, 99, 63, p. 51-63.

4375. Quatrième République (La): des témoins pour l'histoire, 1947–1997: actes du colloque tenu au Sénat les 21 et 22 novembre 1997. Ed. par Agnès CALLU et Patricia GILLET; sous la direction de Jean-Jacques BECKER. Paris, H. Champion, 99, 253 p. (Histoire et archives. Hors-série, 3).

4376. REBÈRIOUX (Madeleine). De l'affaire Dreyfus à la citoyenneté sociale: l'itinéraire vers la «justice sociale» parcourou par la Ligue des droits de l'Homme. *Raison Présente*, 99, 130, p. 91-107. – EADEM. Parcours engagés dans la France contemporaine. Paris, Belin, 99, 542 p. (Socio-histoires).

4377. Robespierre. Ed. by Colin HAYDON and William DOYLE. Cambridge, New York a. Melbourne, Cambridge U. P., 99, X-292 p.

4378. SABATIER (Gérard). Versailles ou la figure du roi. Paris, Albin Michel, 99, 702 p. p. (ill.)

4379. SLUHOVSKY (Moshe). La mobilisation des saints dans la Fronde parisienne d'après les mazarinades. *Annales*, 99, 54, 2, p. 353-374.

4380. THALMANN (Rita). Gleichschaltung in Frankreich, 1940–1944. Hambourg, Europäische Verlagsanstalt u. Rotbuch Verlag, 99, 355 p.

4381. THOMAS (Jean-Paul). Les effectifs du Parti social français. *Vingtième siècle. Revue d'histoire*, 99, 62, p. 61-84.

4382. TOMBS (Robert). The Paris Commune 1871. London a. New York, Routledge, 99, VII-244 p.

4383. TYRSENKO (Andrej V.). Fel'jany: U istokov frantsuzskogo liberalizma. (Felians: at the source of French liberalism). Moskva, Izd. Mosk. un-ta, 99, 126 p. (plates; bibl.). (Trudy Istor. f-ta Moskovskogo gos. un-ta im. M.V. Lomonosova, 6; Ser. 2, 2).

4384. VERHEYDE (Philippe). Les mauvais comptes de Vichy: l'aryanisation des entreprises juives. Préface de Michel MARGAIRAZ. Paris, Perrin, 99, 564 p. (Collection terre d'histoire).

4385. Voter, élire pendant la Révolution française, 1789–1799: guide pour la recherche. Par Serge ABERDAM [et al.]; préface de Marcel MORABITO. Paris, Editions du CTHS, 99, 484 p. (Mémoires et documents, 52).

Cf. n°s 88, 89, 499, 3951, 4518, 4519, 5560, 5643, 5674, 5766, 5794, 5842, 5843, 6028, 7429, 7475, 7974

Gabon

Cf. n° 7948

Germany

** 4386. Akten der Reichskanzlei. Hrsg. für die Historische Kommission bei der Bayerischen Akademie der Wissenschaft von Hans Günter HOCKERTS, für das Bundesarchiv von Friedrich P. KAHLENBERG. Die Regierung Hitler: 1933–1945. 2. 1934/1935. Bearb. v. Friedrich HARTMANNSGRUBER. 1. August 1934–Mai 1935: Dokumente Nr. 1-168. 2. Juni 1935–Dezember 1935: Dokumente Nr. 169-286. München, Oldenbourg, 99, 2 vol., CII-610 p., 652 p.

** 4387. Deutsche Reichstagsakten: Reichsversammlungen 1556–1662. Der Kurfürstentag zu Frankfurt 1558 und der Reichstag zu Augsburg 1559. Teilbände 1-3. Bearb. v. Josef LEEB; Bayerischen Akademie der Wissenschaften Historische Kommission. Göttingen, Vandenhoeck & Ruprecht, 99, 3 vol., VI-XIV-2134 p.

** 4388. Dienstkalender (Der) Heinrich Himmlers 1941/42. Im Auftrag der Forschungsstelle für Zeitgeschichte in Hamburg bearbeitet, kommentiert und eingeleitet von Peter WITTE [et al.]; mit einem Vorwort von Uwe LOHALM und Wolfgang SCHEFFLER. Hamburg, Christians, 99, 789 p. (ill.). (Hamburger Beiträge zur Sozial- und Zeitgeschichte. Quellen, 3).

** 4389. GORBACHEV (Mikhail S.). Wie es war: die deutsche Wiedervereinigung. Berlin, Ullstein, 99, 222 p.

** 4390. Häber-Protokolle (Die): Schlaglichter der SED-Westpolitik, 1973–1985. Hrsg. v. Detlef NAKATH und Gerd-Rüdiger STEPHAN. Berlin, Dietz, 99, 480 p.

** 4391. Nationalliberalismus in der Weimarer Republik: die Führungsgremien der Deutschen Volkspartei, 1918–1933. T. 1. 1918–1925. T. 2. 1926–1933 Bearb. v. Eberhard KOLB und Ludwig RICHTER. Dusseldorf, Droste, 99, 2 vol., 1405 p. (ill.). (Quellen zur Geschichte des Parlamentarismus und der politischen Parteien. Dritte Reihe, Weimarer Republik, 9).

** 4392. Parlamentarische Rat (Der) 1948–1949. Akten und Protokolle. Band 12. Ausschuß für Finanzfragen. Bearb. v. Michael F. FELDKAMP und Inez MÜLLER. München, Boldt bei Oldenbourg, 99, LXIII-595 p.

** 4393. Protokolle (Die) des Preußischen Staatsministeriums 1817–1934/38. Hrsg. v. J. KOCKA u. W. NEUGEBAUER. Band 10. 14. Juli 1909 bis 11. November 1918. Bearbeitet von Reinhold ZILCH. Band 7. 8. Januar 1879 bis 19. März 1890. Bearbeitet von Hartwin SPENKUCH. Hildesheim, Olms-Weidmann, 99, 2 vol., [s. p.]. (Acta Borussica, 1. Reihe).

** 4394. Quellen zur Aktienrechtsreform der Weimarer Republik, (1926–1931). Hrsg. v. Werner SCHUBERT; mit einem Vorwort von Peter HOMMELHOFF und Werner SCHUBERT; eingeleitet und herausgegeben von Werner SCHUBERT. Frankfurt am Main, P. Lang, 99, 2 vol., 1118 p.

** 4395. Sitzungsprotokolle (Die) des Magistrats der Stadt Berlin, 1945–1946. Vol. 2. 1946. Hrsg. v. Dieter HANAUSKE. Berlin, Berlin Verlag, 99, 1160 p. (Schriftenreihe des Landesarchivs Berlin, 2).

4396. 50 Jahre DDR: der Alltag der DDR, erzählt in Fotografien aus dem Archiv des ADN; mit den Originalbildunterschriften. Mit Texten von Helga KÖNIGSDORF und Walter HEILIG; herausgegeben und kommentiert von Günther DROMMER. Berlin, Schwarzkopf und Schwarzkopf, 99, 317 p.

4397. 80 Jahre Weimarer Reichsverfassung: was ist geblieben? Hrsg. v. Eberhard EICHENHOFER. Tübingen, Mohr Siebeck, 99, 230 p.

4398. After the wall: Eastern Germany since 1989. Ed. by Patricia Jo SMITH. Boulder, Westview Press, 99, XVI-350 p. (Eastern Europe after communism).

4399. ALBES (Andreas). Die Behandlung der Republikaner in der Presse. Frankfurt am Main, Peter Lang, 99, 194 p.

4400. ALBRECHT (Thomas). Für eine wehrhafte Demokratie: Albert Grzesinski und die preußische Politik in der Weimarer Republik. Bonn, J. H. W. Dietz, 99, 383 p. (Forschungsinstitut der Friedrich-Ebert-Stiftung, Reihe: Politik- und Gesellschaftsgeschichte, 51).

4401. ALLINSON (Mark). Politics and popular opinion in East Germany 1945–1968. Manchester a. New York, Manchester U. P., 99, 178 p.

4402. AUERBACH (Thomas). Einsatzkommandos an der unsichtbaren Front: Terror- und Sabotagevorbereitungen des MfS gegen die Bundesrepublik Deutschland. Mit einem Vorwort von Ehrhart NEUBERG. Berlin, C. Links, 99, 192 p. (Analysen und Dokumente, 17).

4403. BADSTÜBNER (Rolf). Vom "Reich" zum doppelten Deutschland: Gesellschaft und Politik im Umbruch. Berlin, K. Dietz, 99, 557 p.

4404. BARTH (Erwin). Joseph Goebbels und die Formierung des Führer-Mythos 1917 bis 1934. Erlangen u. Jena, Palm & Enke, 99, 253 p. (Erlanger Studien, 119).

4405. BRANDT (Harm-Hinrich). Deutsche Geschichte 1850–1870. Entscheidung über die Nation. Stuttgart, Berlin u. Köln, Kohlhammer, 99, 273 p.

4406. BREY (Hans-Michael). Doppelstaat DDR: Menschenrechtsverletzungen der Deutschen Volkspolizei. Frankfurt am Main, P. Lang, 99, 387 p. (Europäische Hochschulschriften. Reihe XXXI, Politikwissenschaft, 384).

4407. BURRIN (Philippe). Charisme et radicalisme dans le régime nazi. In: Stalinisme et nazisme: histoire et mémoire comparées [Cf. n° 4000], 79-95. – IDEM. La violence congénitale du nazisme. In: Stalinisme et nazisme: histoire et mémoire comparées [Cf. n° 4000] 129-142. – IDEM. Nazi antisemitism: animalization and demonization. In: Demonizing the other: antisemitism, racism, and xenophobia [Cf. n° 3943], p. 223-235. – IDEM. Régime nazi et société allemande: les prismes de l'acceptation. In: Stalinisme et nazisme: histoire et mémoire comparées [Cf. n° 4000], p. 185-198. – IDEM. Totalitarismus und Gewalt: die Physiognomie des Nazismus. In: Totalitarismus: sechs Vorträge über Gehalt und Reichweite eines klassischen Konzepts der Diktaturforschung [Cf. n° 4003], p. 27-37.

2. HISTORY BY COUNTRIES

4408. BUTZER (Hermann). Diäten und Freifahrt im Deutschen Reichstag: der Weg zum Entschädigungsgesetz von 1906 und die Nachwirkung dieser Regelung bis in die Zeit des Grundgesetzes. Dusseldorf, Droste, 99, 515 p. (ill., ports). (Beiträge zur Geschichte des Parlamentarismus und der politischen Parteien, 116).

4409. CHOI (Sung-Wan). Von der Dissidenz zur Opposition: die politisch alternativen Gruppen in der DDR von 1978 bis 1989. Köln, Wissenschaft und Politk, 99, 238 p. (Bibliothek Wissenschaft und Politik, 56).

4410. Datenhandbuch zur Geschichte des Deutschen Bundestages 1949 bis 1999: Gesamtausgabe in drei Bänden. Band 1. Kapitel 1-6. Band 2. Kapitel 7-13. Band 3. Kapitel 14-36. Verfasser Peter SCHINDLER; Germany Bundestag Wissenschaftliche Dienste. Baden-Baden, Nomos, 99, 3 vol. [s. p.].

4411. DAUKS (Klaus-Peter). Die DDR-Gesellschaft und ihre Revolution: zur historischen Logik eines staatlichen Zerfalls sowie der Weg zur deutschen Einheit. Aachen, Shaker, 99, 499 p. (Berichte aus der Politik).

4412. DDR (Die). Erinnerung an einen untergegangenen Staat. Hrsg. v. Heiner TIMMERMANN. Berlin, Duncker & Humblot, 99, 592 p. (ill.). (Dokumente und Schriften der Europäischen Akademie Otzenhausen, 88).

4413. DDR (Die): Politik und Ideologie als Instrument. Hrsg. v. Heiner TIMMERMANN. Berlin, Duncker & Humblot, 99, 894 p. (Dokumente und Schriften der Europäischen Akademie Otzenhausen, 86).

4414. DELACOR (Regina M.). «Auslieferung auf Verlangen»? Der deutsch-französische Waffenstillstandsvertrag 1940 und das Schicksal der sozialdemokratischen Exilpolitiker Rudolf Breitscheid und Rudolf Hilferding. *Vierteljahrshefte für Zeitgeschichte*, 99, 47, 2, p. 217-242.

4415. DEMM (Eberhard). Von der Weimarer Republik zur Bundesrepublik: der politische Weg Alfred Webers 1920-1958. Dusseldorf, Droste, 99, XIII-584 p. (ill.). (Schriften des Bundesarchivs, 51).

4416. Demokratie in Deutschland: Chancen und Gefährdungen im 19. und 20. Jahrhundert: historische Essays. Festschrift für Heinrich August Winkler. Hrsg. v. Wolther von KIESERITZKY und Klaus-Peter SICK. München, C.H. Beck, 99, 438 p.

4417. Deutsche Geschichte in Osteuropa. Pommern. Hrsg. v. Werner BUCHHOLZ. Berlin, Siedler, 99, 575 p.

4418. DÖNHOFF (Marion). Deutschland, deine Kanzler: die Geschichte der Bundesrepublik 1949-1999. München, Siedler, 99, 364 p.

4419. DUBIEL (Helmut). Niemand ist frei von der Geschichte: das nationalsozialistische Herrschaft in den Debatten des Deutschen Bundestages. München, C. Hanser, 99, 303 p.

4420. Federal Republic of Germany (The) at fifty: at the end of a century of turmoil. Ed. by Peter MERKL. Basingstoke, Macmillan, 99, XV-373 p. (ill.).

4421. Fenomén holocaust. (The Holocaust phenomenon. Conference proceedings). Praha, Památník Terezín, 99, 178 p. (photogr.).

4422. FEST (Joachim C.). Speer: eine Biographie. Berlin, Alexander Fest, 99, 539 p. (ill.).

4423. FOX (Thomas C.). Stated memory: East Germany and the Holocaust. Rochester, Camden House, 99, VI-177 p. (ill.). (Studies in German literature, linguistics, and culture).

4424. GERLACH (Stefanie Virginia). Staat und Kirche in der DDR: war die DDR ein totalitäres System? Frankfurt am Main, P. Lang, 99, XI-255 p. (ill.). (Beiträge zur Politikwissenschaft, 75).

4425. Geschichte Schlesiens. Band 3. Preußisch-Schlesien 1740–1945. Österreichisch-Schlesien 1740–1918/45. Im Auftrag der Historischen Kommission für Schlesien in Verb. mit Konrad FUCHS u. Hubert UNVERRICHT herausgegeben von Josef Joachim MENZEL. Stuttgart, Thorbecke, 99, XIV-768 p.

4426. GOEDDE (P.). From villains to victims: fraternization and the feminization of Germany, 1945–1947. *Diplomatic history*, 99, 23, 1, p. 1-20.

4427. GÖRTEMAKER (Manfred). Geschichte der Bundesrepublick Deutschland: von der Gründung bis zur Gegenwart. München, Beck, 99, 915 p.

4428. GOTTHARD (Axel). Säulen des Reiches. Die Kurfürsten im frühneuzeitlichen Reichsverband. Teilbände 1. Der Kurverein. Kurfürstentage und Reichspolitik. Teilbande 2. Wahlen. Der Kampf um die kurfürstliche "Präeminenz". Husum, Matthiesen, 99, 902 p. (Historischen Studien, 457/1-2).

4429. Grenzen der Vereinigung. Die geteilte Vergangenheit im geeinten Deutschland. Hrsg. v. Martin SABROW. Leipzig, Akademische Verlagsanstalt, 99, 86 p. (Helmstedter Colloquien, 1). [Cf. n° <Auswahl> 4447.]

4430. GRIEDER (Peter). The East German leadership, 1946–1973: conflict and crisis. Manchester, Manchester U. P., 99, X-243 p.

4431. GROH (Dieter). Emanzipation und Integration: Beiträge zur Sozial- und Politikgeschichte der deutschen Arbeiterbewegung und des 2. Reiches. Konstanz, UVK Universitätsverlag Konstanz, 99, 576 p.

4432. GRUCHMANN (Lothar). Ludendorffs «prophetischer» Brief an Hindenburg vom Januar/Februar 1933. Eine Legende. *Vierteljahrshefte für Zeitgeschichte*, 99, 47, 4, p. 559-562.

4433. HAUNFELDER (Bernd). Reichstagsabgeordnete der Deutschen Zentrumspartei 1871–1933: biographisches Handbuch und historische Photographien. Düsseldorf, Droste, 99, 425 p. (ill.). (Photodokumente zur Geschichte des Parlamentarismus und der politischen Parteien, 4).

4434. HEIL (Johannes). Deutsch-jüdische Geschichte, ihre Grenzen und die Grenzen ihrer Synthesen. Anmerkungen zu neueren Erscheinungen. *Historische Zeitschrift*, 99, 269, 3, p. 653-680.

4435. Helden, Täter und Verräter: Studien zum DDR-Antifaschismus. Hrsg. v. Annette LEO und Peter REIF-SPIREK. Berlin, Metropol, 99, 232 p. (ill.).

4436. HOFFMANN (Uwe). Die NPD: Entwicklung, Ideologie und Struktur. Frankfurt am Main, Peter Lang, 99, 496 p. (Europäische Hochschulschriften. Reihe 31, Politikwissenschaft, 396).

4437. HÜTTNER (Martin). Anschauungen und Auffassungen der deutschen Gewerkschaftspresse in der Darstellung und Beurteilung des italienischen Faschismus und des Nationalsozialismus 1925–1933. Berlin, Copy Team, 99, 105 p.

4438. IZEKI (Tadahisa). Das Erbe der Runden Tische in Ostdeutschland: Bürgerorientiere Foren in und nach der Wendezeit. Frankfurt am Main, P. Lang, 99, 191 p.

4439. JANSEN (Christine). Selbstbewußtes oder gefügiges Parlament? Abgeordnetendiäten und Berufspolitiker in den deutschen Staaten des 19. Jahrhunderts. *Geschichte und Gesellschaft*, 99, 25, 1, p. 33-65.

4440. JOHNSON (Eric A.). Nazi terror: the Gestapo, Jews, and ordinary Germans. New York, Basic Books, 99, XX-636 p.

4441. Justiz im Dienst der Parteiherrschaft: Rechtspraxis und Staatssicherheit in der DDR. Hrsg. v. Clemens VOLLNAHLS und Roger ENGELMANN. Berlin, Links, 99, 574 p. (Analysen und Dokumente, 16).

4442. KAISER (Carl-Christian), KESSEL (Wolfgang). Deutscher Bundestag 1949–1999, Debatte und Entscheidung, Konsens und Konflikt: Bilder und Texte. Hrsg. vom Germany Bundestag. München, Olzog, 99, 480 p. (ill).

4443. KEVAL (Susanna). Die schwierige Erinnerung: deutsche Widerstanskämpfer über die Verfolgung und Vernichtung der Juden. Frankfurt am Main, Campus Verlag, 99, 291 p.

4444. KLÖNNE (Arno), BUTENSCHÖN (Rainer), SPOO (Eckart). Der lange Abschied vom Sozialismus: eine Jahrhundertbilanz der SPD. Hamburg, VSA-Verlag, 99, 223 p.

4445. KNABE (Hubertus). Die unterwanderte Republik: Stasi im Westen. Berlin, Propyläen, 99, 590 p.

4446. KNOPF (Volker), MARTENS (Stefan). Görings Reich. Selbstinszenierungen in Carinhall. Berlin, Links, 99, 196 p.

4447. KOCKA (Jürgen). Die DDR – eine moderne Diktatur? Überlegungen zur Begriffswahl. *In*: Geschichte und Emanzipation. Festschrift für Reinhard Rürup. Hrsg. v. Michael GRÜTTNER. Frankfurt am Main, Campus Verlag, 99, p. 540-550. – IDEM. Vereinigungskrise? *In*: Grenzen der Vereinigung [Cf. n° 4429], p. 9-24.

4448. KRANENPOHL (Uwe). Mächtig oder machtlos? Kleine Fraktionen im Deutschen Bundestag 1949 bis 1994. Wiesbaden, Westdeutscher Vlg, 99, 427 p. (ill.). (Studien zur Sozialwissenschaft, 205).

4449. KUNZE (Gerhard). Grenzerfahrungen: Kontakte und Verhandlungen zwischen dem Land Berlin und der DDR 1949–1989. Berlin, Akademie, 99, 502 p. (Studien des Forschungsverbundes SED-Staat an der Freien Universität Berlin).

4450. KVISTAD (Gregg Owen). The rise and demise of German statism: loyalty and political membership. Providence a. Oxford, Berghahn Books, 99, 264 p.

4451. LEHNERT (Detlef). Die Weimarer Republik: Parteienstaat und Massengesellschaft. Stuttgart, Reclam, 99, 398 p. (ill.). (Universal-Bibliothek, 17018).

4452. LEIBY (Richard A.). The unification of Germany, 1989–1990. Westport a. London, Greenwood Press, 99, XXI-197 p. (ill.). (Greenwood Press guides to historic events of the twentieth century).

4453. LENSING (Helmut). Die Wahlen zum Reichstag und zum Preußischen Abgeordnetenhaus im Emsland und der Grafschaft Bentheim 1867 bis 1918. Parteiensystem und politische Auseinandersetzung im Wahlkreis Ludwig Windthorsts während des Kaiserreichs. Sögel, Emsländische Landschaft für die Landkreise Emsland und Graftschaft Bentheim, 99, 615 p. (Emsland/Bentheim. Beiträge zur Geschichte, 15).

4454. MAC DONOUGH (Frank). Hitler and Nazi Germany. Cambridge, Cambridge U. P., 99, VII-152 p. (Cambridge perspectives in history).

4455. Macht und Zeitkritik: Festschrift für Hans-Peter Schwarz zum 65. Geburtstag. Hrsg. v. Peter R. WEILEMANN, Hanns Jürgen KÜSTERS und Günter BUCHSTAB. Paderborn, Schöningh, 99, XIV-853 p. (Studien zur Politik, 34). [Cf. n° <Auswahl> 7874.]

4456. MALLMANN (Klaus-Michael). Gehorsame Parteisoldaten oder eigensinnige Akteure? Die Weimarer Kommunisten in der Kontroverse. Eine Erwiderung. *Vierteljahrshefte für Zeitgeschichte*, 99, 47, 3, p. 401-416.

4457. Materialien der Enquete-Kommission "Überwindung der Folgen der SED-Diktatur im Prozeß der deutschen Einheit". Hrsg. v. Deutschen Bundestag. Baden-Baden, Nomos, 99, 14 vol., 13508 p. (13. Wahlperiode des Deutschen Bundestages).

4458. MAURER (Michael). Kirche, Staat und Gesellschaft im 17. und 18. Jahrhundert. München, Oldenbourg, 99, IX-150 p. (Enzyklopädie deutscher Geschichte, 51).

4459. MELZER (Ralf). Konflikt und Anpassung: Freimaurerei in der Weimarer Republik und im "Dritten Reich". Hrsg. v. Anton PELINKA und Helmut REINALTER. Wien, Braumuller, 99, XII-332 p. (ill.). (Vergleichende Gesellschaftsgeschichte und politische Ideengeschichte der Neuzeit, 13).

4460. MEYER (Beate). "Jüdische Mischlinge": Rassenpolitik und Verfolgungserfahrung 1933–1945. Hamburg, Dolling und Galitz, 99, 494 p. (Studien zur jüdischen Geschichte, 6).

4461. MOMMSEN (Hans). Von Weimar nach Auschwitz: zur Geschichte Deutschlands in der Weltkriegsepoche: ausgewählte Aufsätze. Mit einer Würdigung von Ian KERSHAW. Stuttgart, Deutsche Verlags-Anstalt, 99, 439 p.

4462. MONTEATH (P.). Organizing antifascism: the obscure history of the VVN [Vereinigung der Verfolgten des Naziregimes]. *European history quarterly*, 99, 29, 2, p. 289-303.

4463. MÜLLER (Alfred Lorenz). Imperialist ambitions in «Vormärz» and revolutionary Germany: the agitation for German settlement colonies overseas, 1840–1849. *German history*, 99, 17, 3, p. 346-368.

4464. MUSIAL (Bogdan). Deutsche Zivilverwaltung und Judenverfolgung im Generalgouvernement: eine Fallstudie zum Distrikt Lublin 1939–1944. Wiesbaden, Harrassowitz, 99, X-435 p. (ill). (Niemiecki Instytut Historyczny w Warszawie. Quellen und Studien, 8).

4465. Nationale Minderheiten und staatliche Minderheitenpolitik in Deutschland im 19. Jahrhundert. Hrsg. v. Hans-Henning HAHN und Peter KUNZE. Berlin, Akademie Verlag, 99, 212 p.

4466. NOTHNAGLE (Alan L.). Building the East German myth: historical mythology and youth propaganda in the German Democratic Republic, 1945–1989. Ann Arbor, University of Michigan Press, 99, 208 p. (Social history, popular culture, and politics in Germany).

4467. Opposition in der DDR von den 70er Jahren bis zum Zusammenbruch der SED-Herrschaft. Hrsg. v. Eberhard KUHRT; in Verbindung mit Hannsjörg F. BUCK und Gunter HOLZWEISSIG; im Auftrag des Bundesministerium des Innern. Opladen, Leske-Budrich, 99, XVI-845 p. (ill.). (Am Ende des realen Sozialismus, 3).

4468. ORTH (Karin). Das System der nationalsozialistischen Konzentrationslager: eine politische Organisationsgeschichte. Hamburg, Hamburger Edition, 99, 395 p.

4469. Parler des camps, penser les génocides. Ed. par Catherine COQUIO. Paris, Albin Michel, 99, 680 p.

4470. Parteien im Wandel: vom Kaiserreich zur Weimarer Republik: Rekrutierung – Qualifizierung – Karrieren. Hrsg. v. Jürgen KOCKA, Heinrich August WINKLER und Dieter DOWE. München, R. Oldenbourg Verlag, 99, 410 p. (Schriftenreihe der Stiftung Reichspräsident-Friedrich-Ebert-Gedenkstätte, 7).

4471. Pazifistische Offiziere in Deutschland 1871–1933. Hrsg. v. Wolfram WETTE; unter Mitwirkung von Helmut DONAT. Bremen, Donat, 99, 431 p. (Schriftenreihe Geschichte und Frieden, 10).

4472. PETÕ (Andrea). A náci haláltáborok. (The Nazi concentration camps). *Rubicon*, 99, 5-6, p. 89-94.

4473. PFAHL-TRAUGHBER (Armin). Rechtsextremismus in der Bundesrepublik. München, Beck, 99, 123 p. (C.H. Beck Wissen in der Beck'schen Reihe, 2112).

4474. POTTHOFF (Heinrich). Im Schatten der Mauer: Deutschlandpolitik 1961 bis 1990. Berlin, Propylaen, 99, 448 p.

4475. PYTA (Wolfgang). Konstitutionelle Demokratie statt monarchischer Restauration. Die verfassungspolitische Konzeption Schleichers in der Weimarer Staatskrise. *Vierteljahrshefte für Zeitgeschichte*, 99, 47, 3, p. 417-442.

4476. RAICO (Ralph). Die Partei der Freiheit. Studien zur Geschichte des deutschen Liberalismus. Mit ein. Einf. v. Christian WATRIN. Übers. u. bearb. v. Jörg Guido HÜLSMANN, Gabriele BARTEL und Pia WEIß. Stuttgart, Lucius, 99, XIV-298 p. (Schriften zur Wirtschaftspolitik, 7).

4477. RANDERS-PEHRSONS (Justine). Germans and the Revolution of 1848–1849. New York, Peter Lang, 99, XII-586 p.

4478. REINBOLD (Wolfgang). Mythenbildungen und Nationalismus: "Deutsche Jakobiner" zwischen Revolution und Reaktion (1789–1800). Bern, P. Lang, 99, 319 p. (Freiburger Studien zur frühen Neuzeit, 3).

4479. Revolution (Die) hat Konjunktur: soziale Bewegung, Alltag und Politik in der Revolution von 1848/49. Zusammengestellt und bearbeitet von Margarete LORINSER und Roland LUDWIG. Münster, Westfälisches Dampfboot, 99, 272 p. (ill.).

4480. Revolution und Transformation in der DDR 1989/90. Hrsg. v. Günther HEYDEMANN, Gunther MAI und Werner MÜLLER. Berlin, Duncker & Humblot, 99, 706 p. (Schriftenreihe der Gesellschaft für Deutschlandforschung e.V, 73).

4481. RÖDDER (Andreas). Reflexionen über das Ende der Weimarer Republik. Die Präsidialkabinette 1930–1932/33. Krisenmanagement oder Restaurationsstrategie? *Vierteljahrshefte für Zeitgeschichte*, 99, 47, 1, p. 87-102.

4482. ROHRMOSER (Günter). Kampf um die Mitte: der moderne Konservativismus nach dem Scheitern der Ideologien. München, Olzog, 99, 352 p.

4483. ROSTISLAVLEVA (Natal'ja V.). Zarozhdenie liberalizma v Germanii: Karl fon Rottek. (The birth of liberalism in Germany: Karl von Rotteck). Ros. gos. gumanit. un-t. Moskva, [s. n.], 99, 141 p. (bibl.).

4484. SABROW (Martin). Die verdrängte Verschwörung: der Rathenau-Mord und die deutsche Gegenrevolution. Frankfurt am Main, Fischer Taschenbuch Verlag, 9, 276 p. (ill.).

4485. SANDER (Peter). Die «Euthanasie»-Akten im Bundesarchiv. Zur Geschichte eines lange verschollenen Bestandes. *Vierteljahrshefte für Zeitgeschichte*, 99, 47, 3, p. 385-400.

4486. SCHEIL (Stefan). Die Entwicklung des politischen Antisemitismus in Deutschland zwischen 1881 und 1912: eine wahlgeschichtliche Untersuchung. Berlin, Duncker & Humblot, 99, 400 p. (maps). (Beiträge zur politischen Wissenschaft, 107).

4487. SCHILDT (Axel). Ankunft im Westen: ein Essay zur Erfolgsgeschichte der Bundesrepublik. Frankfurt am Main, S. Fischer, 99, 223 p.

4488. SCHMÄDEKE (Jürgen), BAHAR (Alexander), KUGEL (Wilfried). Der Reichstagsbrand in neuem Licht. *Historische Zeitschrift*, 99, 269, 3, p. 603-652.

4489. SCHMIDT (Georg). Geschichte des Alten Reiches. Staat und Nation in der Frühen Neuzeit 1495–1806. München, Beck, 99, 459 p.

4490. SCHOLTYSECK (Joachim). Robert Bosch und der liberale Widerstand gegen Hitler 1933–1945. München, Beck, 99, 749 p.

4491. SCHÖNHOVEN (Klaus). Aufbruch in die sozialliberale Ära. Zur Bedeutung der 60er Jahre in der Geschichte der Bundesrepublik. *Geschichte und Gesellschaft*, 99, 25, 1, p. 123-145.

4492. SCHWEIZER (Katja). Täter und Opfer in der DDR: Vergangenheitsbewältigung nach der zweiten deutschen Diktatur. Münster, Lit, 99, XXXI-255 p. (Studien zur DDR-Gesellschaft, 4).

4493. SENDLER (Bernhard). Die Führung in den Koalitions- und Präsidialkabinetten der Weimarer Republik. Berlin, Koster, 99, 679-LII p. (Wissenschaftliche Schriftenreihe Geschichte, 7).

4494. STACKELBERG (Roderick). Hitler's Germany. Origins, interpretations, legacies. London a. New York, Routledge, 99, 307 p.

4495. STAMBOLIS (Barbara). Nationalisierung trotz Ultramontanisierung oder: «Alles für Deutschland. Deutschland aber für Christus». Mentalitätsleitende Wertorientierung deutscher Katholiken im 19. und 20. Jahrhundert. *Historische Zeitschrift*, 99, 269, 1, p. 57-98.

4496. STEGMANN (Dirk). Politische Radikalisierung in der Provinz: Lageberichte und Stärkemeldungen der Politischen Polizei und der Regierungspräsidenten für Osthannover 1922–1933. Hannover, Hahnsche Buchhandl., 99, 488 p. (Veröffentlichungen der Historischen Kommission für Niedersachsen und Bremen. XXXV, Quellen und Untersuchungen zur allgemeinen Geschichte Niedersachsens in der Neuzeit, 16).

4497. STELLA (Aldo). Il "Bauernführer" Michael Gaismair e l'utopia di un repubblicanesimo popolare. Bologna, Il Mulino, 99, 340 p. (Annali dell'Istituto storico italo-germanico, Monografie, 33).

4498. STEPANOVA (Veronika V.). Politicheskaja bor' ba v Prussii v 60-e gody XIX veka: Znachenie i posledstvija dlja germanskoj istorii. (The political struggle in Prussia in the 1860es: its significance and consequences for the German history). Mosk. gor. otkr. ped. un-t. Moskva, RITs «Al'fa» MGOPU, 99, 287 p. (bibl.).

4499. STERNBURG (Wilhelm von). Deutsche Republiken: Scheitern und Triumph der Demokratie. München, C. Bertelsmann, 99, 543 p. (ill.).

4500. STOLLBERG-RILINGER (Barbara). Vormünder des Volkes? Konzepte landständischer Repräsentation in der Spätphase des Alten Reiches. Berlin, Duncker & Humblot, 99, 370 p. (Historische Forschungen, 64).

4501. STÖVER (Bernd). Der Fall Otto John. Neue Dokumente zu den Aussagen des deutschen Geheimdienstchefs gegenüber MfS und KGB. *Vierteljahrshefte für Zeitgeschichte*, 99, 47, 1, p. 103-136.

4502. SÜSS (Walter). Staatssicherheit am Ende: warum es den Mächtigen nicht gelang, 1989 eine Revolution zu verhindern. Berlin, Ch. Links, 99, 815 p. (Analysen und Dokumente, 15).

4503. SZEJNMANN (Claus-Christian W.). Nazism in central Germany: the brownshirts in red' Saxony. New York a. Oxford, Berghahn Books, 99, XXIV-312 p. (ill.). (Monographs in German history, 4).

4504. Third Reich (The). The essential readings. Ed. by Christian LEITZ. Oxford a. Malden, Blackwell, 99, XII-307 p.

4505. TOBER (Holger J.). Deutscher Liberalismus und Sozialpolitik in der Ära des Wilhelminismus: Anschauungen der liberalen Parteien im parlamentarischen Entscheidungsprozess und in der öffentlichen Diskussion. Husum, Matthiesen Verlag, 99, 477 p. (Historische Studien, 460).

4506. TURK (Eleanor L.). The history of Germany. Westport a. London, Greenwood Press, 99, XXII-231 p. (Greenwood histories of the modern nations).

4507. ULLMANN (Hans-Peter). Politik im deutschen Kaiserreich 1871–1918. München, R. Oldenbourg, 99, VIII-150 p. (Enzyklopädie deutscher Geschichte, 52).

4508. VAN MELIS (Damian). Entnazifizierung in Mecklenburg-Vorpommern. Herrschaft und Verwaltung 1945–1948. München, Oldenbourg, 99, VI-364 p. (Studien zur Zeitgeschichte, 56).

4509. WACHSMANN (Nikolaus). «Annihilation through labor»: the killing of state prisoners in the Third Reich. *Journal of modern history*. 99, 71, 3, p. 624-659.

4510. WALTER (Dirk). Antisemitische Kriminalität und Gewalt: Judenfeindschaft in der Weimarer Republik. Bonn, Dietz, 99, 349 p. (ill.).

4511. Weg in den Untergang: der innere Zerfall der DDR. Hrsg. v. Konrad Hugo JARAUSCH und Martin SABROW. Gottingen, Vandenhoeck & Ruprecht, 99, 280 p. (Sammlung Vandenhoeck).

4512. Wehrmacht (Die): Mythos und Realität. Im Auftrag des Militärgeschichtlichen Forschungsamtes, herausgegeben von Rolf-Dieter MÜLLER und Hans-Erich VOLKMANN. München, Oldenbourg, 99, XIII-1318 p. (ill.). [Cf. n[os] <Auswahl> 7787, 7795.]

4513. Wehrmacht und Vernichtungspolitik: Militär im nationalsozialistischen System. Hrsg. v. Karl Heinrich POHL. Göttingen, Vandenhoeck & Ruprecht, 99, 175 p. (Sammlung Vandenhoeck).

4514. Widerstand und Opposition in der DDR. Hrsg. v. Klaus-DIETMAR, Peter STEINBACH und Johannes TUCHEL. Köln, Böhlau, 99, 376 p. (ill.). (Schriften des Hannah-Arendt-Instituts für Totalitarismusforschung, 9).

4515. Wiedervereinigte Deutschland (Das), eine erweiterte oder eine neue Bundesrepublik? Hrsg. v. Karl ECKART und Jesse ECKHARD. Berlin, Duncker & Humblot, 99, 154 p. (Schriftenreihe der Gesellschaft für Deutschlandforschung e.V., 71).

4516. WIELAND (Lothar). Die Verteidigungslüge. Pazifisten in der deutsche Sozialdemokratie 1914–1918. Bremen, Donat, 99, 312 p. (Schriftenreihe Geschichte und Frieden, 9).

4517. Willensmenschen: Über deutsche Offiziere. Hrsg. v. Ursula BREYMAYER, Bernd ULRICH und Karin WIELAND. Frankfurt am Main, Fischer Taschenbuch, 99, 239 p.

4518. WINKLER (Heinrich August). Demokratie oder Bürgerkrieg. Die russische Oktoberrevolution als Problem der deutschen Sozialdemokraten und der französischen Sozialisten. *Vierteljahrshefte für Zeitgeschichte*, 99, 47, 1, p. 1-24.

4519. WIRSCHING (Andreas). Vom Weltkrieg zum Bürgerkrieg? Politischer Extremismus in Deutschland und Frankreich 1918–1933/39: Berlin und Paris im Vergleich. München, Oldenbourg, 99, X-702 p. (Quellen und Darstellungen zur Zeitgeschichte, 40).

4520. ZIEGLER (Dieter). Die Verdrängung der Juden aus der Dresdner Bank 1933–1938. *Vierteljahrshefte für Zeitgeschichte*, 99, 47, 2, p. 187-216.

Cf. n^{os} *504, 543, 4238, 4353, 4867, 5016, 5141, 5490, 5570, 5589, 5627, 5628, 5631, 5647, 5680, 5689, 5694, 5695, 5766, 5795, 5804, 5830, 5858, 5876, 6068, 6090, 7082, 7089, 7573, 7682, 7691, 7798*

Ghana

4521. LENZIN (René). Afrika macht oder bricht einen Mann: Sozialers Verhalten und politische Einschätzung einer Kolonialgesellschaft am Beispiel der Schweizer in Ghana, 1945–1966. Basel, Basler Afrika Bibliographien, 99, 272 p.

4522. RATHBONE (Richard). Nkrumah and the chiefs: the politics of chieftaincy in Ghana, 1951–1960. Oxford, J. Currey a. Athens, Ohio U. P., 99, XI-176 p. (ill.). (West African series).

Great Britain

** 4523. Letters (The) of Sir Walter Raleigh. Ed. by Agnes LATHAM and Joyce YOUINGS. Exeter, University of Exeter Press, 99, LXIII-403 p.

** 4524. Parliament and politics in the age of Churchill and Attlee: the Headlam diaries, 1935–1951. Ed. by Stuart BALL. Cambridge, Cambridge U. P. for the Royal Historical Society, 99, [s. p.]. (Camden fifth series, 14).

** 4525. Struggle (The) for sovereignty: seventeenth-century English political tracts. Ed. with intr. by Joyce Lee MALCOM. Indianapolis, Liberty Fund, 99, 2 vol., LXIV-1085 p.

4526. ADAMO (Pietro). La città e gli idoli: politica e religione in Inghilterra 1524–1572. Milano, UNICOPLI, 99, 395 p. (Early modern, 10).

4527. AOKI (Yasushi). Yuryoku Jentori no joken: 18seikimatsu Igirisu Safoku shu no ichijirei. (To be a leading gentry: Sir Charles Davers and Suffolk voluntary subscription, 1782). *Shien*, 99, 60, 1, p. 138-151.

4528. BARANGER (Denis). Parlementarisme des origines: essai sur les conditions de formation d'un exécutif responsable en Angleterre, des années 1740 au début de l'âge victorien. Préf. de Stéphane RIALS. Paris, Presses Universitaires de France, 99, 408 p. (Léviathan).

4529. BLACK (Jeremy). Britain as a military power, 1688–1815. London, Philadelphia, UCL Press, 99, VIII-332 p.

4530. BROOKSHIRE (J. H.). «Speak for England», act for England: Labour's leadership and British national security under the threat of war in the late 1930s. *European history quarterly*, 99, 29, 2, p. 251-287.

4531. CARLIN (Norah). The causes of the English Civil War. Oxford a. Malden, Blackwell Publishers, 99, IX-188 p. (Historical Association studies).

4532. CHADWICK (Andrew). Augmenting democracy: political movements and constitutional reform during the rise of Labour, 1900–1924. Aldershot, Ashgate, 99, XI-285 p.

4533. Chartist legacy (The). Ed. by Owen ASHTON, Robert FRYSON and Stephen ROBERTS. Rendlesham, Merlin Press, 99, XVI-297 p.

4534. COLE (Mary Hill). The portable queen: Elizabeth I and the politics of ceremony. Amherst, University of Massachusetts Press, 99, X-277 p. (map). (Massachusetts studies in early modern culture).

4535. CURRY (John Court). The security service 1908–1945: the official history. Introduction by Christopher ANDREW. Kew, Public Record Office, 99, 442 p. (ill., ports.).

4536. DAVIS (John). A history of Britain, 1885–1939. Basingstoke a. New York, Macmillan, 99, X-300 p. (British studies series).

4537. DELL (Edmund). A strange eventful history: Democratic Socialism in Britain. London, HarperCollins, 99, XV-623 p., (ill.).

4538. DEVINE (Thomas Martin). The Scottish nation, 1700–2000. London, Allen Lane, 99, XXIII-695 p.

4539. DONNELLY (Mark). Britain in the Second World War. London a. New York, Routledge, 99, XIV-124 p.

4540. FRASER (William Hamish). Scottish popular politics: from radicalism to Labour. Edinburgh, Polygon at Edinburgh, 99, 224 p.

4541. GOODARE (Julian). State and society in early modern Scotland. Oxford, Oxford U. P., 99, XV-366 p.

4542. GRAHAM (Jenny). The nation, the law, and the king: reform politics in England, 1789–1799. Lanham a. Oxford, University Press of America, 99, 2 vol., [s. p.].

4543. HAMMER (Paul E. J.). The polarisation of Elizabethan politics: the political career of Robert Devereux, 2nd Earl of Essex, 1585–1597. Cambridge a. New York, Cambridge U. P., 99, XVIII-446 p. (ill., ports.).

4544. HARMER (Harry J. P.). The Longman companion to the Labour Party, 1900–1998. Harlow, Addison Wesley Longman, 99, X-323 p. (Longman companions to history).

4545. HIRST (Derek). England in conflict, 1603–1660: kingdom, community, commonwealth. London a. New York, Oxford U. P., 99, VII-359 p.

4546. HOPKINS (A. G.). Viewpoint: back to the future: from national history to imperial history. *Past and present*, 99, 164, p. 198-243.

4547. «Igirisu» de arukoto: Identity tankyu no rekishi. (Being «British»: historical searches for the identity). Ed. by Akihiro SASHI. Tokyo, Tosui Shobo, 99, 232 p.

4548. JONES (David Martin). Conscience and allegiance in seventeenth century England: the political significance of oaths and engagements. Rochester a. Woodbridge, University of Rochester Press, 99, VIII-340 p. (ill.).

4549. JOYCE (Peter). Realignment of the left? A history of the relationship between the Liberal Democrat and Labour Parties. London, Macmillan, 99, VII-346 p.

4550. KANAZAWA (Shusaku). Kindai Eikoku ni okeru nampasen ryakudatsu: Chiiki kyodotai to zenkoku shakai. (Wrecking in modern England, from the mid-eighteenth century to the mid-nineteenth century: local community and national society). *Seiyo Shigaku*, 99, 193, p. 1-22.

4551. KIDD (Colin). British identities before nationalism. Ethnicity and nationhood in the Atlantic world, 1600–1800. Cambridge, Cambridge U. P., 99, VIII-302 p.

4552. KINGSLEY KENT (Susan). Gender and power in Britain 1640–1990. London, Routledge, 99, XII-364 p. (ill.).

4553. LOPATIN (Nancy D.). Political unions, popular politics and the great Reform Act of 1832. Basingstoke a. New York, Macmillan Press, 99, XII-236 p. (Studies in modern history).

4554. MAC GURK (John). The Tudor monarchies, 1485–1603. Cambridge a. New York, Cambridge U. P., 99, IV-124 p. (ill.). (Cambridge perspectives in history).

4555. MARSHALL (Alan). The age of faction: court politics, 1660–1702. Manchester, Manchester U. P., 99, VI-234 p. (New frontiers in history).

4556. Modern Britain since 1906: a reader. Ed. by Keith LAYBOURN. London a. New York, I.B. Tauris, 99, IX-254 p. (Tauris history readers).

4557. New British history (The): founding a modern state 1603–1715. Ed. by Glenn BURGESS. London, Tauris, 99, VI-331 p.

4558. PODVINTSEV (Oleg B.). Shagajushchie ne v nogu: Iz istorii politicheskoj bor'by v stane britanskikh konservatorov vo vtoroj-tret'ej chetverti XX stoletija. (From the history of political struggle in the camp of the British conservatives, 2nd and 3rd quarters of the 20th century). Perm', Izd. Perm. un-ta, 99, 147 p. (bibl.).

4559. Radicalism and revolution in Britain, 1775–1848: essays in honour of Malcolm I. Thomis. Ed. by Michael T. DAVIS. New York, St. Martin's Press, 99, 242 p.

4560. Remembering Cable Street: fascism and antifascism in British society. Ed. Tony KUSHNER and Nadia VALMAN. London a. Portland, Vallentine Mitchell, 99, 288 p. (Parkes-Wiener series on Jewish studies).

4561. RENTON (David). Fascism, anti-fascism and Britain in the 1940s. Basingstoke, Macmillan, 99, 224 p.

4562. RIDDELL (Neil). Labour in crisis: the second Labour government 1929–1931. Manchester a. New York, Manchester U. P., 99, XI-276 p.

4563. RUGGIERO (John). Neville Chamberlain and British rearmament: pride, prejudice, and politics. Westport a. London, Greenwood Press, 99, 251 p. (ill.). (Contributions to the study of world history, 71).

4564. Scotland and the Great War. Ed. by Catriona M. M. MACDONALD and E. W. MAC FARLAND. East Lothian, Tuckwell Press, 99, 200 p.

4565. SHAGAN (Ethan H.). Protector Somerset and the 1549 rebellions: new sources and new perspectives. *English historical review*, 99, 114, 455, p. 34-63.

4566. SMART (Nick). The national government, 1931–1940. Basingstoke a. New York, Macmillan Press, 99, VII-279 p. (British studies series).

4567. SMITH (David Lawrence). The Stuart parliaments, 1603–1689. London a. New York, Arnold, 99, XI-260 p. (Reconstructions in early modern history).

4568. STEWART (Graham). Burying Caesar: Churchill, Chamberlain and the battle for the Tory Party. London, Weidenfeld & Nicolson, 99, 533 p.

4569. TAMURA (Hideo). Kuromuweru to Igirisu kakumei. (Cromwell and the Revolution). Ageo, University of Seigakuin Press, 99, 314 p.

4570. TAYLOR (Philip M.). British propaganda in the twentieth century: selling democracy. Edinburgh, Edinburgh U. P., 99, XI-276 p. (International communications).

4571. THOMAS (Paul). Authority and disorder in Tudor times, 1485–1603. Cambridge a. New York, Cambridge U. P., 99, V-122 p. (ill.). (Cambridge perspectives in history).

4572. THOMPSON (J. Lee). Politicians, the press, and propaganda: Lord Northcliffe and the Great War, 1914-1919. Kent, Kent State U. P., 99, [s. p.].

4573. TOMITA (Rie). Sukottorando kinsei shakai no seiritsu 1560–1625: Shukyo kaikaku, shukenka, dokun rengo no jidai. (Scotland in the reformation, centralization and regal union: brighter and darker impacts of modernization on Scottish society, 1560–1625). *Seiyo Shigaku*, 98, 189, p. 1-24.

4574. TURNER (Michael J.). British politics in an age of reform. Manchester a. New York, Manchester U. P., 99, X-230 p. (New frontiers in history).

4575. WALTER (John). Understanding popular violence in the English Revolution: the Colchester plunderers. Cambridge, Cambridge U.P., 99, XI-357 p.

4576. WEIL (Rachel Judith). Political passions: gender, the family and political argument in England, 1680–1714. Manchester a. New York, Manchester U. P., 99, IX-262 p. (Politics, culture, and society in early modern Britain).

4577. YAMAMOTO (Shintaro). Ingurando shukyo kaikaku to Chantori no kaisan: Koventori no jirei kara. (English reformation and dissolution of Chantries: a case study of Coventry). *Seiyo Shigaku*, 99, 194, p. 1-22.

4578. ZOOK (Melinda S.). Radical whigs and conspiratorial politics in late Stuart England. University Park, Pennsylvania State U. P., 99, XXI-234 p. (ill.).

Cf. n^{os} *99, 528, 1008, 1244, 1253, 1400, 3187, 4287, 4290, 4665, 4679, 5206, 5216, 5604, 5634, 5658, 5661, 5663, 5664, 5670, 5684, 5695, 5700, 5777, 5835, 5891, 6519, 7089, 7610*

Greece

4579. BOESCHOTEN (R.). Perasame pollès mporès koritsi mou. (We have been through a lot of hard times, my child). Athens, Plethron, 99, [s. p.].

4580. DANFORTH (L. M.). I Makedonikì diamachi. O ethnikismos se enan iperethinikò kosmo. (The Macedonian dispute. Nationalism in a over-ethnic world). Athens, Alexandreia, 99, [s. p.].

4581. GARDIKA-ALEXANDROPOULOU (Katerina). Prostasia kai engyeseis: stadia kai mythoi tes hellenikes ethnikes holokleroses (1821–1920). (Protection and guarantees: stages and myths of the Greek national unification). Thessalonike, Vanias, 99, 166 p.

4582. Griechenland: Politik und Perspektiven. Hrsg. v. Bernd RILL. München, Hanns-Seidel-Stiftung, Akademie für Politik und Zeitgeschehen, 99, 165 p. (Argumente und Materialien zum Zeitgeschehen, 11).

4583. Istoria tis Elladas tou 20ou aiona, Oi aparches. 1900–1922. (History of Greece in the 20th century. The outset. 1900–1922). Ed. by Ch. CHATZIOSIPH. [S. l.], Bibliorama, 99, [s. p.].

4584. KOLIOPOULOS (John S.). Plundered Loyalties: World War II and Civil War in Greek West Macedonia. Foreword by C. M. WOODHOUSE. New York, New York U. P., 99, XXVIII-304 p.

4585. KOURVETARIS (Yorgos A.). Studies on modern Greek society and politics. Boulder, East European Monographs, 99, XII-424 p. (ill.). (East European monographs, 534).

4586. LAMPROPOULO (D.). Graphontas apò ti philakì. Opseis tis upokeimenikotitas ton politikòn kratoumenòn 1947–1960. (Writing from prison. Aspects of subjectivity of political prisoners 1947–1960). Athena, Nephele, 99, [s. p.].

4587. Ottoman Greeks in the Age of Nationalism. Politics, economy, and society in the nineteenth century. Ed. by Dimitri GONDICAS and Charles ISSAWI. Princeton, Darwin Press, 99, XIII-229 p.

4588. SFIKAS (T. D.). A tale of parallel lives: the second Greek republic and the second Spanish republic, 1924–1936. *European history quarterly*, 99, 29, 2, p. 217-250.

Guatemala

4589. MELANDER (Veronica). The hour of God? People in Guatemala confronting political evangelicalism and counterinsurgency (1976–1990). Uppsala, Uppsala University Library, 99, 328 p. (Studia missionalia Upsaliensia, 71).

4590. ROSADA-GRANADOS (Héctor Roberto). Soldados en el poder: proyecto militar en Guatemala, 1944–1990. Amsterdam, Thela Thesis, 99, 280 p. (Thela Latin America series).

Guyana

4591. ST. PIERRE (Maurice). Anatomy of resistance: anti-colonialism in Guyana 1823–1966. New York, Macmillan, 99, X-214 p. (Warwick University Caribbean studies).

Haiti

4592. BERNARDIN (Ernst A.). Histoire économique et sociale d'Haïti de 1804 à nos jours: (l'État complice et la faillite d'un système). Haïti, Institut national d'administration, de gestion et des hautes études internationales, 99, 239 p. (ill.). (Collection "Les classiques de l'Université", 3).

4593. DE VERGER (Jean-Claude). La lutte des Noirs de Saint-Domingue pour la liberté et l'indépendence en Haïti. Saint-Léonard, Éditions Les 5 Continents, 99, 480 p.

4594. ETIENNE (Sauveur Pierre). Haïti: misère de la démocratie. Préface de François HOUTART. Port-au-Prince, CRESFED et Paris, L'Harmattan, 99, 292 p.

4595. JEAN (Jean-Claude), MAESSCHALCK (Marc). Transition politique en Haïti: radiographie du pouvoir Lavalas. Paris, L'Harmattan, 99, 206 p. (Collection "Sociétés africaines et diaspora").

4596. MARTIN (Ian). Haiti: international force or national compromise? *Journal of Latin American studies*, 99, 31, 3, p. 711-734.

4597. MOÏSE (Claude). Le pouvoir législatif dans le système politique haïtien: un aperçu historique. Montréal, Éditions du CIDIHCA, 99, 180 p. (ill., ports).

Honduras

** 4598. Documentos para la historia de Honduras. Selección y notas de Roberto SOSA. Tegucigalpa, Imágen y Palabra, 99, [s. p.].

4599. BARAHONA (Marvin). La influencia de los Estados Unidos en Honduras, 1900–1954: del tratado de 1907 a la huelga bananera de 1954. [S. l.], M.A. Barahona, 99, 229 p. (ill., maps). [Thesis (Ph.D.)-Katholieke Universteit Nijmegen, 1999].

4600. GARCÍA LAGUARDIA (Jorge Mario). Honduras: evolución político constitucional, 1824–1936. México, Universidad Nacional Autónoma de México y Guatemala, Corte de Constitucionalidad de Guatemala, 99, 95 p. (Cuadernos constitucionales México-Centroamérica, 34).

Hungary

4601. BOROS (Zsuzsa), SZABÓ (Dániel). Parlamentarizmus Magyarországon 1867–1944. (Parliamentarianism in Hungary 1867–1944). Budapest, Korona, 99, 354 p.

4602. CSÁSZÁR (Gyula). A rendszerváltozás autonómiája. (The autonomy of the change of system). Szeged, Szekszárd Séd, 99, 299 p.

4603. CSIZMADIA (Ervin). Két liberalizmus Magyarországon. (Two liberalism in Hungary). Budapest, Századvég, 99, 259 p.

4604. DIÓSZEGI (István). A Ferenc Józsefi kor: Magyarország története 1849–1919. (The history of Hungary 1849–1918). Budapest, Vince K, 99, 194 p.

4605. FRANK (Tibor). Ethnicity, propaganda, mythmaking: studies on Hungarian connections to Britain and America 1848–1945. Budapest, Akadémiai, Kiadó, 99, 391 p. (ill.).

4606. GUNST (Péter). Polgárosodás és szabadság: Magyarország a XIX. Században. (Civilisation and freedom: Hungary in the XIX century). Budapest, Nemzeti Tankkönyvkiadó, 99, 311 p.

4607. HAJDU (Tibor). Tisztikar és középosztály 1850–1914: Ferenc József magyar tisztjei. (The regiment of officers and the middle class 1850–1914: Ferenc József's Hungarian officers). Budapest, Historia MTA Tört.tud Int, 99, 360 p.

4608. Hungarian Revolution (The) and War of Independence, 1848–1849: a military history. Ed. by Gábor BONA. Boulder, Social Science Monographs, 99, VIII-586 p. (maps). (War and society in East Central Europe, 35. Atlantic studies on scoiety in change, 93. East European monographs, 535).

4609. LAKATOS (Pál). Bûnünk és bajunk Trianon. (Our sin and our problem, Trianon). Miskolc, Felsõmagyarország, 99, 357 p.

4610. MARK (James A.). An oral history of the 1956 generation: the relationship of the individual towards the State in early communist Hungary. Oxford, [s. n.], 99, 87 p. [Thesis (M.Phil.) – University of Oxford, 1999].

4611. NYYSSÖNEN (Heino). The presence of the past in politics: '1956' after 1956 in Hungary. Jyväskylä, SoPhi, 99, 305 p.

4612. RAINER (János M.). Nagy Imre. Politikai életrajz. (Imre Nagy. Politische Biographie). Vol. 2. 1953-1958. Budapest, 1956-os Intézet, 99, 486 p.

4613. RANKI (Vera). The politics of inclusion and exclusion: Jews and nationalism in Hungary. New York, Holmes & Meier, 99, XVIII-269 p.

4614. ROMAN (Eric). The Stalin years in Hungary. Lewiston, Edwin Mellen Press, 99, 449 p. (Studies in Russian history, 2).

4615. ROMSICS (Ignác). Bethlen István: politikai önéletrajz. (István Bethlen: political curriculum vitae). 2. kiadás. Budapest, Osiris, 99, 520 p.

4616. TÖKÉCZKY (László). Történelem, eszmék, politika. (History, theories, politics). Szentendre, Kairos, 99, 361 p.

4617. Ungarische Revolution (Die) von 1848/49: vergleichende Aspekte der Revolutionen in Ungarn und Deutschland. Hrsg. v. Holger FISCHER. Hamburg, Krämer, 99, 198 p. (Beiträge zur deutschen und europäischen Geschichte, 27).

4618. VÁRKONYI (Ágnes). A királyi Magyarország 1541–1686. (The kingdom of Hungary 1541–1686). Budapest, Vince K, 99, 207 p.

Cf. n°s 4087, 4090

Iceland

4619. HANNIBALSSON (Arnór). Moskvulínan: Kommúnistaflokkur Íslands og Komintern: Halldór Laxness og Sovétríkin. Reykjavík, Nýja Bókafélagid, 99, 326 p. (ill.).

India

** 4620. Documents of the communist movement in India. Vol. 1. 1917–1928. Vol. 2. Meerut conspiracy case (1929). Vol. 3. 1929–1938. Vol. 4. 1939–1943. Vol. 5. 1944–1948. Vol. 6. 1949–1951. Vol. 7. 1952–1956. Vol. 8. 1957–1961. Vol. 9. 1962–1963. Vol. 10-A. 1964 (pt. 1). Vol. 10-B. 1964 (pt. 2). Vol. 11. 1965–1967. Vol. 12. 1968. Vol. 13. 1969. Vol. 14. 1970. Vol. 15. 1971–1972. Vol. 16. 1973–1974. Vol. 17. 1975–1977. Vol. 18. 1978–1979. Vol. 19. 1980–1981. Vol. 20. 1982–1983. Vol. 21. 1984–1986. Vol. 22. 1987–1988. Vol. 23. 1989–1991. Vol. 24. 1992–1993. Vol. 25. 1994–1996. Vol. 26. 1997–1998. Chief editor Jyoti BASU. Calcutta, National Book Agency, 99, 26 vol., [s. p.].

** 4621. NEHRU (Jawaharlal). Selected works of Jawaharlal Nehru. Ser. 2. Vol. 24. 1 October 1953–31 January 1954. Vol. 25. 1 February 1954–31 May 1954. Ed. by Ravinder KUMAR and H. Y. Sharada PRASAD; general editor S. GOPAL. Delhi: Jawaharlal Nehru Memorial Fund, 99, 2 vol., 736 p., 610 p. (ill., ports.).

** 4622. Towards freedom: documents on the movement for independence in India, 1938. Ed. by Basudev CHATTERJI. New Delhi a. Oxford, Oxford U. P., 99, 3 vol., [s. p.]. (ill.).

4623. BAYLY (Susan). The new Cambridge history of India. Vol. 4. Part 3. Caste, society and politics in India from the eighteenth century to the modern age. Cambridge, Cambridge U. P., 99, XI-421 p. (ill., maps, port.).

4624. BLOM HANSEN (Thomas). The Saffron wave. Democracy and Hindu nationalism in modern India. Princeton, Princeton U. P., 99, 293 p.

4625. CHANDRA (Bipan), MUKHERJEE (Aditya), MUKHERJEE (Mridula). India after independence. New Delhi, Penguin Books, 99, X-549 p.

4626. CHATTERJEE (Indrani). Gender, Slavery and Law in Colonial India. New York, Oxford U. P., 99, XII-286 p.

4627. CHATTERJEE (Partha). The Partha Chatterjee omnibus: comprising Nationalist thought and the colonial world, The nation and its fragments, A possible India. New Delhi a. Oxford, Oxford U. P., 99, 3 vol., X-181 p., 282 p., 301 p.

4628. CHAUDHURI (Dipak Kumar). The political agents and the native raj: conflict, concilliation and progress: Tripura between 1871 to 1890. New Delhi, Mittal, 99, XX-296 p. (maps).

4629. DADVAR (Abolghasem). Iranians in Mughal politics and society, 1606–1658. New Delhi, Gyan Pub. House, 99, 439 p. (ill.).

4630. DATTA (Pradip Kumar). Carving blocs: communal ideology in early twentieth-century Bengal. New York, Oxford U. P., 99, 312 p.

4631. HARRISON (Mark). Climates and constitutions: health, race, environment and British imperialism in India 1600–1850. New York, Oxford U. P., 99, XII-263 p.

4632. JACKSON (Peter). The Delhi Sultanate: a political and military history. New York, Cambridge U. P., 99, XX-367 p.

4633. MAHAJAN (Sucheta). Independence and partition: the erosion of colonial power in India. Thousand Oaks, Sage Publications, 99, 425 p. (Sage series in modern Indian history, 1).

4634. Nation-building in India: culture, power and society. Ed. by Anand KUMAR. London, Sangam, 99, XVI-301 p.

4635. PERKOVICH (George). India's nuclear bomb: the impact on global proliferation. Berkeley a. London, University of California Press, 99, XIII-597 p. (plates, ill., map).

4636. POUCHEPADASS (Jacques). Champaran and Gandhi: planters, peasants, and Gandhian politics. New Delhi a. New York, Oxford U. P., 99, XXII, 277 p. (ill.). (French studies in South Asian culture and society).

4637. RAY (Raka). Fields of protest: women's movements in India. Minneapolis a. London, University of Minnesota Press, 99, XIII-217 p. (Social movements, protest, and contention, 8).

4638. Region and partition: Bengal, Punjab and the partition of the subcontinent. Ed. by Ian TALBOT and Gurharpal SINGH. Oxford a. New York, Oxford U. P., 99, VIII-407 p.

4639. SETH (Sanjay). Rewriting histories of nationalism: the politics of «Moderate Nationalism» in India, 1870–1905. *American historical review*, 99, 104, 1, p. 95-116.

4640. SINGH (Gurharpal). Ethnic conflict in India: a case-study of Punjab. New York, St. Martin's Press, 99, XV-231 p.

4641. SIVARAMAKRISHNAN (K.). Modern forests: statemaking and environmental change in colonial eastern India. Stanford, Stanford U.P., 99, XXVII-341 p. (figs,tabs).

4642. State intervention and popular response: Western India in the nineteenth century. Ed. by Mariam DOSSAL and Ruby MALONI. Mumbai, Popular Prakashan, 99, XXIII-242 p.

4643. TANWAR (Raghuvendra). Politics of sharing power: the Punjab Unionist Party 1923–1947. New Delhi, Manohar, 99, 215 p.

4644. ZAKARIA (Rafiq). Gandhi and the break-up of India. Mumbai, Bharatiya Vidya Bhavan, 99, XII-304 p. (plates, ill.). (Bhavan's book university).

Cf. n°s 5850, 7330

Indonesia

4645. DROOGLEVER (P. J.), SCHOUTEN (M. J. B.). Het einde in zicht: stemmen uit het laatste jaar van Nederlands-Indië. Den Haag, Instituut voor Nederlandse Geschiedenis, 99, 167 p. (ill., ports). (Horizonreeks).

4646. Indonesia beyond Suharto: polity, economy, society, transition. Ed. by Donald K. EMMERSON. Armonk a. London, M.E. Sharpe, 99, XXVIII-395 p. (ill.).

4647. KAHIN (Audrey R.). Rebellion to integration: West Sumatra and the Indonesian polity, 1926–1998. Amsterdam, Amsterdam U. P., 99, 368 p.

4648. SURYADINATA (Leo). Interpreting Indonesian politics. Singapore, Times Academic Press, 99, VIII-264 p.

4649. TOER (Pramoedya Ananta), TOER (Koesalah Soebagyo), KAMIL (Ediati). Kronik revolusi Indonesia. Jakarta, KPG (Kepustakaan Populer Gramedia) bekerjasama dengan Yayasan Adikarya IKAPI dan The Ford Foundation, 99, [s. p.].

Iraq

4650. AL-JUMAILY (Qassam Kh). Irak ve Kemalizm hareketi, 1919–1923. Düzenleyerek yayima hazirlayan, Izzet ÖZTOPRAK. Ankara, Atatürk Kültür, Dil ve Tarih Yüksek Kurumu, Atatürk Arastirma Merkezi, 99, X-201 p.

4651. ÇETİNSAYA (Gökhan). Ottoman Iraq in the Tanzimat period. Some political, social and economic aspects. *Hacettepe Üniversitesi Edebiyat Fakültesi Dergisi*, 99, ekim, p. 105-114.

4652. EFRATI (Noga). Productive or reproductive? The roles of Iraqi women during the Iraq-Iran War. *Middle Eastern studies*, 99, 35, 2, p. 27-44.

4653. FUCCARO (Nelida). Communalism and the State in Iraq: the Yazidi Kurds, c.1869–1940. *Middle Eastern studies*, 99, 35, 2, p. 1-26.

Iran

** 4654. Asnadi az intikhabat-i Majlis-i Shura-yi Milli dar dawrah-i Pahlavi-i avval. (Documents on parliamentary elections during the reign of Pahlavi). Idarah-i Kull-i Arshiv, Asnad va Muzah, Daftar-i Ra'is-i Jumhur; zir-i nazar-i shura-yi 'ilmi: Ya'qub AZHAND [et al]. Tihran, Sazman-i Chap va Intisharat, Vizarat-i Farhang va Irshad-i Islami, 99, XX-249 p. (ill.). (Majmuʻah-'i asnad-i tarikhi. Siyasat, 2).

** 4655. Guzarish'ha-yi nazmiyah az mahallat-i Tihran: raputr-i vaqayiʻ-i mukhtalifah-i mahallat-i dar al-khilafah. [Police (Nazmiya) reports of Tehran districts]. Sazman-i Asnad-i Milli-i Iran, Pizhuhishkadah-i Asnad; bih kushish, Insiyah Shaykh RIZA'I, Shahla AZARI. Tihran, Intisharat-i Sazman-i Asnad-i Milli-i Iran, 99, 2 vol., XVI-852 p. (ill., map).

4656. BEHROOZ (Maziar). Rebels with a cause: the failure of the left in Iran. London a. New York, I.B.Tauris Publishers, 99, XV-256 p. (plates).

4657. CHELKOWSKI (Peter J.), DABASHI (Hamid). Staging a revolution: the art of persuasion in the Islamic Republic of Iran. New York, New York U. P., 99, 312 p. (ill.).

4658. DJALILI (Mohammad-Reza). L'armée et la politique: le cas de l'Iran. *CEMOTI: cahiers d'études sur la Méditerranée orientale et le monde turco-iranien*, 99, 27, p. 95-113. – IDEM. Une approche géopolitique: [l'Iran]. *Géopolitique*, 99, 64, p. 57-64.

4659. EBRAHIMNEJAD (Hormoz). Pouvoir et succession en Iran: les premiers Qâjâr, 1726–1834. Paris, L'Harmattan, Société d'histoire de l'Orient, 99, 332 p. (ill.). (Moyen Orient et Océan Indien. XVIe–XIXe s, 12).

4660. KASHANI-SABET (Firoozeh). Frontier fictions: shaping the Iranian nation, 1804–1946. Princeton, Princeton U. P., 99, XVIII-304 p. (ill.).

4661. KEDDIE (Nikki R.), GHAFFARY (Farrokh). Qajar Iran and the rise of Reza Khan, 1796–1925. Costa Mesa, Tauris Academic Studies, Mazda Publishers, 99, VIII-134 p. (ill., map).

4662. MOLAJANI (Akbar). Sociologie politique de la révolution iranienne de 1979. Paris, L'Harmattan, 99, 319 p. (Collection Comprendre le Moyen-Orient).

Ireland

** 4663. Correspondence (The) of Myles Dillon, 1922–1925: Irish-German relation and Celtic studies. Ed. by Joachim FISCHER and John DILLON. Dublin, Four Courts Press, 99, 298 p. (ill.).

** 4664. Last days (The) of Dublin Castle: the Mark Sturgis diaries. Ed. by Michael A. HOPKINSON. Ballsbridge, Irish Academic Press, 99, X-278 p. (ill.).

4665. BARBERIS (Peter), MAC HUGH (John), TYLDESLEY (Mike). Encyclopedia of British and Irish political organisations: parties, groups and movements of the twentieth century. New York, Pinter, 99, 544 p.

4666. CLARKE (Aidan). Prelude to restoration in Ireland: the end of the Commonwealth, 1659–1660. Cambridge, Cambridge U. P., 99, XII-376 p.

4667. CRONIN (Mike). Sport and Nationalism in Ireland: Gaelic Games, Soccer and Irish Identity since 1884. Portland, Four Courts Press, 99, 214 p.

4668. GEOGHEGAN (Patrick M.). The Irish Act of Union: a study in high politics, 1798–1801. Dublin, Gill & Macmillan, 99, XII-290 p.

4669. GRAY (Peter). Famine, land and politics: British government and Irish society, 1843–1850. Dublin, Irish Academic Press, 99, IX-384 p. (ill.).

4670. HELLE (Andreas). Ulster: Die blockierte Nation. Nordirlands Protestanten zwischen britischer Identität und irischem Regionalismus (1868–1922). Frankfurt am Main u. New York, Campus, 430 p. (Campus Historische Studien, 24).

4671. Ireland in the 1930s: new perspectives. Ed. by Joost AUGUSTEIJN. Dublin, Four Courts Press, 99, 170 p. (ill.).

4672. IRVIN (Cynthia L.). Militant nationalism: between movement and party in Ireland and the Basque Country. Minneapolis a. London, University of Minnesota Press, 99, XVII-281 p.

4673. JACKSON (Alvin). Ireland 1798–1998: politics and war. Oxford a. Malden, Blackwell Publishers, 99, XII-507 p. (ill.).

4674. LAFFAN (Michael). The resurrection of Ireland: the Sinn Féin Party, 1916–1923. Cambridge a. New York, Cambridge U. P., 99, XVII-512 p. (ill.).

4675. MAUME (Patrick). The long gestation: Irish nationalist life, 1891–1918. Dublin, Gill & Macmillan, 99, 340 p.

4676. Ó SIOCHRÚ (Mícheál). Confederate Ireland 1642–1649: a constitutional and political analysis. Dublin a. Portland, Four Courts Press, 99, 295 p.

4677. O'BRIEN (Brendan). The long war: the IRA and Sinn Féin. Syracuse, Syracuse U. P., 99, 445 p. (ill.). (Irish studies).

4678. O'HALPIN (Eunan). Defending Ireland: the Irish state and its enemies since 1922. Oxford a. New York, Oxford U. P., 99, XVI-382 p.

4679. PEARCE (Edward). Lines of most resistance: the Lords, the Tories and Ireland, 1886–1914. London, Little Brown, 99, 535 p (ill.).

4680. Political ideology in Ireland, 1541–1641. Ed. by Hiram MORGAN. Dublin, Four Courts, 99, 256 p.

4681. Politics and performance in contemporary Northern Ireland. Ed. by John P. HARRINGTON and Elizabeth J. MITCHELL. Amherst, University of Massachusetts Press, 99, VI-234 p.

4682. RAFFERTY (Oliver P.). The church, the state and the Fenian threat, 1861–1875. Houndmills, Macmillan, 99, XVIII-229 p.

4683. REGAN (John M.). The Irish counter-revolution, 1921–1936: Treatyite politics and settlement in independent Ireland. Dublin, Gill & Macmillan, 99, XVI-475 p.

4684. ROSE (Peter). How the troubles came to Northern Ireland. New York, St Martin's Press, 99, XX-216 p.

4685. TAYLOR (Peter). Loyalists: war and peace in Northern Ireland. New York, TV Books, 99, VIII, 278 p.

4686. TOWNSHEND (Charles). Ireland: the 20th century. London a. New York, Oxford U. P., 99, XIII-281 p.

Cf. n°s 5643, 5855

Israel

4687. FIRRO (Kais M.). The Druzes in the Jewish state: a brief history. Leiden a. Boston, Brill, 99, VIII-266 p. (Social, economic, and political studies of the Middle East and Asia, 64).

4688. Israel's transition from community to state. Ed by Efraim KARSH. London, Frank Cass, 99, VI-253 p. (Israel affairs, 1, 4).

4689. KRIEGEL (Maurice). Nation et religion. Aux origines des «néomessianismes» dans l'Israël aujourd'hui. *Annales*, 99, 54, 1, p. 3-28.

4690. KRUPP (Michael). Die Geschichte des Staates Israel: von der Gründung bis heute. Gütersloh, Gütersloher Verl.-Haus, 99, 240 p. (Gütersloher Taschenbücher, 730).

4691. PRIOR (Michael). Zionism and the state of Israel: a moral inquiry. New York, Routledge, 99, XV-291 p.

4692. SPRINZAK (Ehud). Brother against brother: violence and extremism in Israeli politics from Altalena to the Rabin assassination. New York, Free Press, 99, XII-366 p.

4693. THOMAS (Gordon). Gideon's spies: the secret history of the Mossad. London, Macmillan, 99, 354 p.

Cf. n°s 4905, 5535, 7258

Italy

** 4694. BUONACCORSI (Biagio). Diario dall'anno 1498 all'anno 1512 e altri scritti. A cura di Enrico NICOLINI. Roma, Istituto storico italiano per il Medio Evo, 99, XXXVI-441 p. (Fonti per la storia dell'Italia medievale. Antiquitates, 12).

** 4695. Carteggio universale di Cosimo I de' Medici: Archivio di Stato di Firenze: inventario. Vol. 10. 1558–1561. A cura di Irene COTTA e Orsola GORI. Firenze, Giunta regionale toscana e La nuova Italia, 99, 495 p. (Toscana-Beni librari, 9).

** 4696. CUOCO (Vincenzo). Saggio storico sulla rivoluzione di Napoli. Introduzione di Pasquale VILLANI. Milano, Biblioteca universale Rizzoli, 99, 395 p. (BUR, L, 1258).

** 4697. Epistolario (L') di un re. Carlo Alberto a Maria di Robilant 1827–1844. A cura di Isabella MASSABÒ RICCI. Torino, UTET, 99, 144 p.

** 4698. Epistolario di Quintino Sella. Vol. 5. 1875–1878. Roma, Archivio Guido Izzi, Istituto per la Storia del Risorgimento italiano, 99, 822 p. (Istituto per la Storia del Risorgimento italiano. Fonti, 87).

** 4699. Inedito (Un) di Benedetto Croce del settembre 1943. A cura di Emanuele CUTINELLI RÈNDINA. *Nuova antologia*, 99, 134, 582, 2209, p. 5-9.

** 4700. Manifesti (I) della Federazione milanese del Partito comunista italiano (1956–1984): inventario. A cura di Stefano TWARDZIK. Roma, Ministero per i beni culturali e ambientali, Ufficio centrale per i beni archivistici, 99, 349 p. (Pubblicazioni degli archivi di Stato. Strumenti, 140).

** 4701. SANTARELLI (Enzo). Mezzogiorno 1943–1944: uno sbandato nel Regno del Sud. Milano, Feltrinelli, 99, 164 p. (Universale economica, 1528).

4702. 150mo anniversario della rivoluzione del 1848 in Sicilia: Convegno di studi, Palermo, 25–26–27 marzo 1998. Atti a cura di Massimo GANCI e Rosa SCAGLIONE GUCCIONE. Palermo, Società siciliana di storia patria, 99, 414 p. (ill.). (*Archivio storico siciliano*, 99, 4, 25).

4703. ADORNI (Daniela). Francesco Crispi: un progetto di governo. Firenze, Olschki, 99, XXIX-438 p. (Storia. Facoltà di lettere filosofia. Fondo di studi Parini-Chirio, Università degli studi di Torino, 1).

4704. After the war: violence, justice, continuity and renewal in Italian society: papers given at the Contemporary history Conference, 'After the War was Over', University of Sussex, July 1996. Ed. by Jonathan DUNNAGE. Market Harborough, Troubador, 99, 100 p.

4705. Antifascismo e società italiana, 1926–1940. A cura di Leonardo RAPONE. Milano, UNICOPLI, 99, 247 p. (Questioni di storia contemporanea, 10).

4706. Archivi, territori, poteri in area estense (secc. XVI–XVIII). A cura di Euride FREGNI. Roma, Bulzoni, 99, 510 p. (Biblioteca del Cinquecento, 92).

4707. ASTUTO (Giuseppe). Crispi e lo stato d'assedio in Sicilia. Milano, A. Giuffré, 99, VIII-371 p. (Pubblicazioni della Facoltà di scienze politiche/Università di Catania, 4).

4708. BÁRÁNDI (Gergely). Velence fénykora: a Velencei Köztársaság államberendezkedésének kialakulása és kora. (The golden age of Venice: The birth and the period of the state system of the Venice Republic). Budapest, Scolar, 99, 212 p.

4709. BARBAGALLO (Francesco). Il potere della camorra (1973–1998). Torino, Einaudi, 99, XVI-208 p.

4710. BARTOCCI (Enzo). Le politiche sociali nell'Italia liberale, 1861–1919. Roma, Donzelli, 99, 332 p. (Welfare Books).

4711. BELARDELLI (Giovanni), CAFAGNA (Luciano), GALLI DELLA LOGGIA (Ernesto), SABBATUCCI (Giovanni). Miti e storia dell'Italia unita. Bologna, Il Mulino, 99, 229 p.

4712. BENIGNO (Francesco). Lotta politica e sbocco rivoluzionario: riflessioni sul caso di Messina (1647–1678). *Storica*, 99, 5, 13, p. 7-36.

4713. CADONI (Giorgio). Lotte politiche e riforme istituzionali a Firenze tra il 1494 e il 1502. Roma, Istituto storico italiano per il Medio Evo, 99, 268 p. (Fonti per la storia dell'Italia medievale. Subsidia, 7).

4714. CAMMARANO (Fulvio). Storia politica dell'Italia liberale: l'età del liberalismo classico, 1861–1901. Roma, Laterza, 99, XIV-551 p. (Quadrante Laterza, 105).

4715. CANNISTRARO (Philip V.). Blackshirts in Little Italy: Italian Americans and fascism, 1921–1929. West Lafayette, Bordighera, 99, 124 p.

4716. CANOSA (Romano). Storia dell'epurazione in Italia: le sanzioni contro il fascismo, 1943–1948. Milano, Baldini & Castoldi, 99, X-465 p. (I saggi, 130).

4717. CARFAGNA (Luciano). Cavour. Bologna, Il Mulino, 99, 227 p.

4718. CARUSI (Paolo). Superare il trasformismo: il primo ministero di Rudinì e la questione dei partiti nuovi. Roma, Studium, 99, 320 p. (La cultura, 74).

4719. CAVERA (Giovanni). Il Ministro Tambroni, primo "governo del Presidente". La crisi dell'estate 1960 nelle carte Gronchi. *Nuova storia contemporanea*, 99, 3, 3, p. 85-112.

4720. Ceti dirigenti (I) in Firenze dal gonfalonierato di giustizia a vita all'avvento del ducato. Comitato di studi sulla storia dei ceti dirigenti in Toscana: atti del 7. Convegno, Firenze, 19–20 settembre 1997. A cura di Elisabetta INSABATO; introduzione di Riccardo FUBINI. Lecce, Conte, 99, 350 p. (Attraverso la storia, 6).

4721. CEVA (Lucio). Storia delle forze armate in Italia. Torino, UTET libreria, 99, XIV-555 p.

4722. CIOTTA (Grazia), ZOLETTO (Silvia). Antifascisti padovani, 1925–1943. Vicenza, Neri Pozza, 99, 307 p. (Fonti e studi per la storia del Veneto contemporaneo, 7).

4723. COOK (Paul J.). Ugo La Malfa. Bologna, Il Mulino, 99, 367 p.

4724. CORTESI (Luigi). Le origini del PCI: studi e interventi sulla storia del comunismo in Italia. Milano, F. Angeli, 99, 439 p. (Storia, 243).

4725. CROUZET-PAVAN (Élisabeth). Venise triomphante. Les horizons d'un mythe. Paris, Albin Michel, 99, 428 p.

4726. DAHL (Ottar). Syndicalism, fascism and postfascism in Italy, 1900–1950. Oslo, Solum Forlag, 99, 179 p.

4727. DAL LAGO (Paola). Verso il regime totalitario: il plebiscito fascista del 1929. Padova CLEUP Editrice, 99, 195 p.

4728. DE FELICE (Franco). La questione della nazione repubblicana. Prefazione di Leonardo PAGGI. Roma e Bari, Laterza, 99, XXVI-254 p. (Percorsi, 2).

4729. DE ROSA (Gabriele). La storia che non passa. Diario politico 1968–1989. A cura di Sara DEMOFONTI. Soveria Mannelli, Rubbettino, 99, 470 p.

4730. DOGLIANI (Patrizia). L'Italia fascista 1922–1940. Milano, Sansoni, 99, 440 p.

4731. DONDI (Mirco). La lunga liberazione. Giustizia e violenza nel dopoguerra italiano. Roma, Editori Riuniti, 99, 275 p.

4732. FARON (Olivier). The history of modern and contemporary Italy: made in France (from the late 1970s to the late 1990s). *Journal of modern Italian studies*, 99, 4, 3, p. 416-440.

4733. FIORENTINO (Carlo M.). All'ombra di Pietro: la Chiesa cattolica e lo spionaggio fascista in Vaticano, 1929–1939. Firenze, Casa editrice le lettere, 99, 254 p. (Saggi, 21).

4734. Fondazione (La) della Repubblica: modelli e immaginario repubblicani in Emilia e Romagna negli anni della Costituente. A cura di Mariuccia SALVIATI. Milano, F. Angeli, 99, 661 p. (La società moderna e contemporanea. Analisi e contributi, 70).

4735. FOSCHI (Enrico). La massoneria nella storia politica d'Italia: dalle origini al primo governo a guida massonica ed alla politica della Loggia Universo. Roma, Gangemi, 99, 527 p. (Società e parlamento, 5).

4736. FRANCIA (Enrico). Le baionette intelligenti. La Guardia Nazionale nell'Italia liberale (1848–1876). Bologna, Il Mulino, 99, p. 260

4737. FRANZINELLI (Mimmo). I tentacoli dell'Ovra: agenti, collaboratori e vittime della polizia politica fascista. Torino, Bollati Boringhieri, 99, XIX-746 p. (ill.). (Nuova cultura, 69).

4738. GAGLIANI (Dianella). Brigate nere: Mussolini e la militarizzazione del Partito fascista repubblicano. Torino, Bollati Boringhieri, 99, XIV-305 p.

4739. GALASSO (Giuseppe). Aspetti della storia del Regno di Napoli sotto Filippo II. *Annali dell'Istituto italiano per gli studi storici*, 99, 16, p. 201-242.

4740. GANAPINI (Luigi). La repubblica delle camicie nere. I combattenti, i politici, gli amministratori, i socializzatori. Milano, Garzanti, 99, 518 p.

4741. GENTILE (Emilio). Il mito dello Stato nuovo: dal radicalismo nazionale al fascismo. Roma e Bari, Laterza, 99, XXIV-286 p. (Biblioteca universale Laterza, 510).

4742. GENTILONI SILVERI (Umberto). Conservatori senza partito: un tentativo fallito nell'Italia giolittiana. Roma, Studium, 99, XVIII-257 p. (La cultura, 75).

4743. Giangirolamo II Acquaviva: un barone meridionale nella crisi del Seicento: dai memoriali di Paolo Antonio di Tarsia. A cura di Angelantonio SPAGNOLETTI e Giuseppe PATISSO; presentazione di Francesco TATEO. Galatina, Congedo, 99, XIV-287 p. (ill.). (Biblioteca di cultura pugliese, 127).

4744. GIARRIZZO (Giuseppe). Alla corte dei Moncada (secoli XVI–XVII). *Annali di storia moderna e contemporanea*, 99, 5, p. 429-436.

4745. Giovanni Amendola tra etica e politica. Atti del Convegno di Studio. Montecatini Terme, 25–27 ottobre 1996. Pistoia, C.R.T., 99, 313 p. (Studi e ricerche / Istituto storico provinciale della Resistenza di Pistoia, 2).

4746. GRACCI (Angiolo). La rivoluzione negata: il filo rosso della rivoluzione italiana: memoria storica e riflessioni politiche nel bicentenario 1799–1999. Prefazione di Guido D'AGOSTINO. Napoli, La Città del sole, 99, 292 p.

4747. Gramsci a Roma, Togliatti a Mosca: il carteggio del 1926. A cura di Chiara DANIELE, con un saggio di Giuseppe VACCA. Torino, Einaudi, 99, L-503 p. (Gli struzzi, 505).

4748. Granducato (Il) di Toscana e i Lorena nel secolo XVIII. Incontro internazionale di Studio, Firenze, 22–24 settembre 1994. A cura di Alessandra CONTINI e Maria Grazia PARRI. Firenze, L. S. Olschki, 99, IX-678 p. (Biblioteca storica toscana. Sezione di storia del Risorgimento, 26). [Cf. n[os] <scelta> 4777, 4788.]

4749. HAYWOOD (Geoffrey A.). Failure of a dream: Sidney Sonnino and the rise and fall of liberal Italy 1847–1922. Firenze, L.S. Olschki, 99, VII-573 p. (Studi / Fondazione Luigi Einaudi, 35).

4750. ISNENGHI (Mario). La tragedia necessaria. Da Caporetto all'Otto settembre. Bologna, Il Mulino, 99, 145 p.

4751. Italia (L') altra: il Mezzogiorno dall'unità ai giorni nostri. A cura di Camillo DANEO. Milano, UNICOPLI, 99, 143 p. (Questioni di storia contemporanea, 9).

4752. Italia: origini, aspetti e problemi di una identità nazionale. Testi di L. CASTELFRANCHI, F. DELLA PERUTA, A. DE MADDALENA, E. GABBA, C. GALLICO, M. GALLUZZI, E. N. GIRARDI, G. MICHELI, A. PADOA-SCHIOPPA, E. RICCOMINI e M. VITALE. Milano, Istituto Lombardo di Scienze e Lettere, 99, 232 p.

4753. Italian fascism: history, memory and representation. Ed. by R. J. B. BOSWORTH and Patrizia DOGLIANI. New York, St. Martin's, 99, VIII-245 p.

4754. KROLL (Thomas). Die Revolte des Patriziats: der toskanische Adelsliberalismus im Risorgimento. Tübingen, Niemeyer, 99, XII-510 p. (Bibliothek des Deutschen Historischen Instituts in Rom, 90).

4755. LA ROVERE (Luca). Fascist groups in Italian universities: an organization at the service of the totalitarian state. *Journal of contemporary History*, 99, 34, p. 457-475.

4756. LA SALVIA (Sergio). La rivoluzione e i partiti. Il movimento democratico nella crisi dell'unità nazionale. Vol. 1. Roma, Archivio Guido Izzi, Istituto per la storia del Risorgimento italiano, 99, 442 p. (Memorie, 43).

4757. LEPRE (Aurelio). La storia della repubblica di Mussolini. Salò: il tempo dell'odio e della violenza. Milano, Mondadori, 99, 353 p. – IDEM. Storia della prima Repubblica: l'Italia dal 1943 al 1998. Bologna, Il Mulino, 99, 414 p. (Biblioteca storica).

4758. MANGANELLI (Giorgio). Contributo critico allo studio delle dottrine politiche del '600 italiano. A cura di Paolo NAPOLI; introduzione di Giorgio AGAMBEN. Macerata, Quodlibet, 99, 116 p. (Quodlibet, 26).

4759. MARTUCCI (Roberto). L'invenzione dell'Italia unita: 1855–1864. Milano, Sansoni, 99, 507 p. (Storie d'Italia Sansoni).

4760. MILZA (Pierre). Mussolini. Paris, Fayard, 99, VII-985 p.

4761. MONTANARI (Mario). Politica e strategia in cento anni di guerre italiane. Vol. 2. Il periodo liberale. 1. Le guerre d'Africa. Roma, Stato maggiore dell'esercito, Ufficio storico, 99, 496 p.

4762. MOSELEY (Ray). Mussolini's shadow: the double life of Count Galeazzo Ciano. New Haven a. London, Yale U. P., 99, X-302 p. (ill.).

4763. NEGRI (Guglielmo). Istituzioni e politica: governi, parlamento e magistratura nell'Italia repubblicana. Con la collaborazione di Barbara CARUSO e Luca TENTONI. Firenze, Felice Le Monnier, 99, 384 p. (Quaderni di storia).

4764. OMEZZOLI (Tullio). Prefetti e fascismo nella provincia d'Aosta 1926–1945. Aosta, Istituto storico della Resistenza in Valle d'Aosta, Le château, 99, 303 p. (ill.). (Cahiers d'histoire, 4).

4765. PÉCOUT (Gilles). Il lungo Risorgimento. La nascita dell'Italia contemporanea (1770–1922). Milano, Mondadori, 99, 463 p.

4766. Piemonte (Il) alle soglie del 1848. A cura di Umberto LEVRA. Torino, Comitato di Torino dell'Istituto per la storia del Risorgimento Italiano, Torino, 99, XXXI-853 p.

4767. Politica e cultura nell'età di Carlo Emanuele I: Torino, Parigi, Madrid. Convegno internazionale di studi, Torino, 21–24 febbraio 1995. A cura di Mariarosa MASOERO, Sergio MAMINO e Claudio ROSSO. Firenze, L. S. Olschki, 99, V-625 p. (Storia. Facoltà di lettere e filosofia, Fondo di studi Parini-Chirio, Università degli studi di Torino, 2).

4768. PONS (Silvio). L'impossibile egemonia. L'URSS, il Pci e le origini della guerra fredda (1943–1948). Roma, Carocci, 99, 240 p.

4769. PRETO (Paolo). Ideali unitari e indipendentistici dei "giacobini" veneti. Società e storia, 99, 22, p. 617-645.

4770. PUGLIESE (Stanislao G.). Carlo Rosselli: socialist heretic and antifascist exile. Cambridge, Harvard U. P., 99, XII-309 p.

4771. Razza e fascismo: la persecuzione contro gli ebrei in Toscana, 1938–1943. Vol. 1. Saggi. Vol. 2. Documenti. A cura di Enzo COLLOTTI. Roma, Carocci e Firenze, Regione Toscana, Giunta regionale, 99, 2 vol., 602 p., 199 p.

4772. Repubblica Romana (La) nel movimento europeo tra il 1848 e il 1849. Atti del Convegno Internazionale di Studi (Roma, 30 giugno–1 luglio 1999 – Biblioteca della Camera dei Deputati). A cura di Ester CAPUZZO. Rassegna storica del Risorgimento, 99, 86, p. 153-396.

4773. RICCI (Aldo G.). Il compromesso costituente: 2 giugno 1946–18 aprile 1948: le radici del consociativismo. Prefazione di Aldo A. MOLA. Foggia, Bastogi, 99, 286 p. (Collana del Centro europeo Giovanni Giolitti per lo studio dello Stato, 1).

4774. RIDOLFI (Maurizio). Interessi e passioni. Storia dei partiti politici italiani tra l'Europa e il Mediterraneo. Milano, Mondadori, 99, XVI-486 p.

4775. RIVA (Valerio). Oro da Mosca: i finanziamenti sovietici al PCI dalla rivoluzione d'Ottobre al crollo dell'URSS. In collaborazione con Francesco BIGAZZI; con 240 documenti inediti degli archivi moscoviti. Milano, Mondadori, 99, 879 p. (Le scie).

4776. ROBERTS (David D.). Giovanni Gentile e la politica italiana. A cura di Mario CORSI. Pisa, ETS, 99, 110 p. (Scuola superiore di studi universitari e di perfezionamento S. Anna).

4777. ROSA (Mario). Il "Cuore del re": l'Institution d'un prince del giansenista Duguet. In: Granducato (Il) di Toscana e i Lorena nel secolo XVIII [Cf. n° 4748], p. 385-416.

4778. SALVADORI (Massimo). La sinistra nella storia italiana. Roma e Bari, Laterza, 99, XV-246 p.

4779. SANGALLI (Maurizio). Cultura, politica e religione nella Repubblica di Venezia tra Cinque e Seicento: gesuiti e somaschi a Venezia: memoria presentata dal s.c. Gino BENZONI. Venezia, Istituto Veneto di Scienze, Lettere ed Arti, 99, IX-495 p. (Memorie, 84).

4780. SARACENO (Pietro). I magistrati italiani tra fascismo e Repubblica. Brevi considerazioni su un'epurazione necessaria ma impossibile. Clio, 99, 35, p. 65-109.

4781. SCIUTI RUSSI (Vittorio). Inquisizione, politica e giustizia nella Sicilia di Filippo II. Rivista storica italiana, 99, 111, 1, p. 37-64.

4782. SECHI (Salvatore). Truman, la politica dei sacrifici e l'apparato militare del PCI. Nuova storia contemporanea, 99, 3, 6, p. 55-94.

4783. STABILE (Francesco Michele). I Consoli di Dio. Vescovi e politica in Sicilia (1953–1963). Caltanissetta e Roma, Sciascia, 99, 514 p.

4784. Storia d'Italia. Vol. 6. L'Italia contemporanea: dal 1963 a oggi. A cura di Giovanni SABBATUCCI e Vittorio VIDOTTO. Roma e Bari, Laterza, 99, XV-780 p. (Storia e società).

4785. Storia di Torino. Vol. 9. Gli anni della Republica. A cura di Nicola TRANFAGLIA. Torino, Einaudi, 99, XVII-909 p. (ill.).

4786. TURI (Gabriele). Viva Maria: riforme, rivoluzione e insorgenze in Toscana (1790–1799). Bologna, Il Mulino, 99, 367 p. (Saggi, 508).

4787. VALIANI (Leo). Gramsci, Rosselli e il problema della rivoluzione italiana. *Nuova antologia*, 99, 134, 582, 2210, p. 43-57.

4788. VERGA (Marcello). Il Granducato di Toscana tra Sei e Settecento. *In*: Granducato (Il) di Toscana e i Lorena nel secolo XVIII [Cf. n° 4748], p. 3-33.

4789. VERUCCI (Guido). La chiesa cattolica in Italia dall'unità a oggi: 1861-1998. Roma e Bari, Laterza, V-147 p.

4790. WOLLER (Hans). Rom, 28. Oktober 1922: die faschistische Herausforderung. München, Dt. Taschenbuch-Verl., 99, 279 p.

Cf. n°s 92, 613, 3951, 4116, 4165, 5066, 5341, 5598, 5627, 5631, 5641, 5760, 5779, 5894, 6626, 6654, 8001

Jamaica

** 4791. INGRAM (Kenneth E.N.). Manuscript sources for the history of the West Indies: with special reference to Jamaica in the National Library of Jamaica and supplementary sources in the West Indies, North America, the United Kingdom and elsewhere. Kingston, University of the West Indies Press, 99, XXII-566 p.

4792. HART (Richard). Towards decolonisation: political, labour and economic developments in Jamaica 1938-1945. Barbados, Canoe Press, University of the West Indies, 99, XXII-329 p. (ill.). (UWI Press political history series, 3).

Japan

4793. ANDO (Satoshi). Okubo Toshimichi to mingyo shorei. (Okubo Toshimichi and his industrialization policy), Tokyo, Ochanomizu Shobo, 99, 333 p.

4794. DICKINSON (Frederick R.). War and national reinvention: Japan in the Great War, 1914-1919. Cambridge, Harvard University Asia Center, 99, XVIII-363 p. (Harvard East Asian monographs, 177).

4795. DOWER (John W.). Embracing defeat: Japan in the aftermath of World War II. London, Allen Lane, 99, 676 p.

4796. HOYE (Timothy). Japanese politics: fixed and floating worlds. Upper Saddle River, Prentice Hall, 99, XVII-233 p.

4797. ITO (Yukio). Rikkenkokka no kakuritsu to Ito Hirobumi: Naisei to gaiko 1889-1898. (Ito Hirobumi and the formation of the Japanese constitutional state 1889-1898). Tokyo, Yoshikawa Kobunkan, 99, 349 p.

4798. Japan's war economy. Ed. by Erich PAUER. London a. New York, Routledge, 99, XV-208 p. (Routledge studies in the growth economies of Asia, 21).

4799. MASS (Jeffrey P.). Yoritomo and the founding of the First Bakufu: the origins of dual government in Japan. Stanford, Stanford U. P., 99, XIII-278 p.

4800. MOLOD'JAKOV (Valerij E.). Konservativnaja revoljutsija v Japonii: ideologija i politika. (The conservative revolution in Japan: ideology and politics, [1868–1941]). Moskva, Vostochnaja literatura, 99, 320 p. (bibl., ind.). [Eng. summary]

4801. MURASE (Shinichi). Senkyoho kaisei mondai to Ito shinto. (Election law revisions during the second Yamagata government and the formation of ITO Hirobumi's new political party). *Shigaku Zasshi*, 99, 108, 11, p.1-37.

4802. TAKAO (Yasuo). National integration and local power in Japan. Aldershot, Ashgate, 99, X-259 p.

4803. YAMADA (Eiko). Meiji seito ron shi. (The history of controversy over the political party in Meiji Japan). Tokyo, Sobunsha, 99, 275 p.

Cf. n°s 8273-8320

Jordan

4804. BOULBY (Marion). The Muslim Brotherhood and the kings of Jordan, 1945–1993. Foreword by John O. VOLL. Atlanta, Scholars Press, 99, XIX-169 p. (South Florida-Rochester-Saint Louis studies on religion and the social order, 18).

4805. LUNT (James D.). The Arab Legion. London, Constable, 99, XVIII-178 p. (ill., maps, ports).

4806. ROGAN (Eugene L.). Frontiers of the state in the late Ottoman Empire: Transjordan, 1850–1921. Cambridge, Cambridge U. P., 99, XIV-274 p. (ill.). (Cambridge Middle East studies).

Kazakhstan

4807. EROFEEVA (I.V.). Khan Abulkhair: Polkovodets, pravitel' i politik. (Khan Abulkhair: a warrior, a ruler and a politician, [the 18th century]). Almaaty, Sanat, 99, 335 p. (Istorija Kazakhstana: Issledovanija, dokumenty).

Kenya

4808. KYLE (Keith). The politics of the independence of Kenya. New York, St. Martin's Press, 99, XVIII-258 p. (Contemporary history in context).

Korea

Cf. n°s 8321-8329

Kuwait

4809. BELTRAME (Stefano). Storia del Kuwait: gli arabi, il petrolio, l'Occidente. Padova, CEDAM, 99, XIV-332 p. (ill.). (Università degli studi di Padova, Dipartimento di studi internazionali, 9).

Latvia

4810. STROHM (Klauspeter). Die kurländische Frage (1700–1763): eine Studie zur Mächtepolitik im Ancien Régime. Berlin, Dissertation.de, 99, IV-404 p. [Thesis (doctoral) – Universität des Saarlandes, 1999].

Lebanon

4811. BIEBER (Florian). Bosnien-Herzegowina und der Libanon im Vergleich: Historische Entwicklung und Politisches System vor dem Bürgerkrieg Sinzheim, Pro Universitate, 99, 239 p.

4812. Women and war in Lebanon. Ed. by Lamia RUSTUM SHEHADEH. Gainesville, University Press of Florida, 99, XVI-363 p).

Liberia

4813. FRENKEL' (Matvej Ju.). Istorija Liberii v novoe i novejshee vremja. (Modern and recent history of Liberia). RAN, In-t Afriki. Moskva, Vostochnaja literatura, 99, 302 p. (bibl., ind.). (Istorija stran Afriki). [Eng. summary]

Libya

4814. EGORIN (Anatolij Z.). Istorija Livii, XX vek. (A history of Libya, the 20th century). RAN, In-t vostokovedenija. Moskva, [s. n.], 99, 562 p. (bibl., ind.). [Eng. summary]

Lithuania

4815. BUCHOWSKI (Krzysztof). Polacy w niepodległym państwie litewskim 1918–1940. (Polen in unabhängigem Litauen 1918–1940). Białystok, Uniw. w Białymstoku, 99, 322 p. (Instytut Hist. Uniw. w Białymstoku).

4816. FAJNHAUZ (David). 1863, Litwa i Bialorus. Warszawa, Wydawn. NERITON, Instytut Historii PAN, 99, 357 p.

Macedonia

4817. KHADŽINIKOLOVA (Elena). Bulgarite v Iuzhna Makedoniia: 70-te godini na XIX vek. (Les bulgares en Macédonie du sud, les années 70 du XIXe s.). Sofiia, "Nauka i izkustvo", 99, 153 p.

4818. SZOBRIES (Torsten). Sprachliche Aspekte des nation-building in Mazedonien: die kommunistische Presse in Vardar-Mazedonien (1940–1943). Stuttgart, F. Steiner, 99, 251 p. (Studien zur modernen Geschichte, 53).

Madagascar

4819. Madagascar 1947: la tragédie oubliée. Colloque AFASPA des 9–11 octobre 1997, Université Paris VIII-Saint Denis. Actes rassemblés par Francis ARZALIER et Jean SURET-CANALE. Paris, Temps des Cerises Ed., 99, 250 p.

Malawi

4820. MULUZI (Bakili) [et al.]. Democracy with a price: the history of Malawi since 1900. Oxford, Heinemann Educational Publishers, 99, XII-212 p. (ill.).

Malta

4821. FRENDO (Henry). The origins of Maltese statehood: a case study of decolonization in the Mediterranean. San Gwann, PEG, 99, 728 p. (ill.).

Mexico

4822. ALANÍS ENCISO (Fernando Saúl). El primer programma bracero y el gobierno de México, 1917–1918. san Luis Potosí, El Collegio de San Luis. 99, 119 p.

4823. CÁRDENAS GUTIÉRREZ (Salvador). La construcción del imaginario social «república representativa» en la folletería mexicana (1856–1861). *Historia mexicana*, 99, 48, 191, p. 523-566.

4824. CHOWNING (Margaret). Wealth and power in provincial Mexico: Michoacán from the late colony to the Revolution. Stanford, Stanford U. P., 99, XIV-477 p.

4825. Conservadurismo mexicano (El) en el siglo XIX (1810–1910). Ed. por Humberto MORALES y William FOWLER. Puebla, Benemérita Universidad Autónoma de Puebla y Gobierno del Estado de Puebla y St Andrews, University of St Andrews, 99, 335 p.

4826. Construcción de la legitimidad política en México en el siglo XIX. Coor. Brian CONNAUGHTON HANLEY, Carlos ILLADES y Sonia PÉREZ TOLEDO. Zamora, El Colegio de Michoacán y México, Universidad Autónoma Metropolitana-Iztapalapa, Universidad Nacional Autónoma de México, Instituto de Investigaciones Históricas, El Colegio de México, 99, 535 p. (Colección Memorias / El Colegio de Michoacán).

4827. DUCEY (Michael T.). Village, nation, and constitution: insurgent politics in Papantla, Veracruz, 1810–1821. *Hispanic American historical review*, 99, 79, 3, p. 463-493.

4828. ESPARZA MARTÍNEZ (Bernardino). Crisis democrática en los partidos políticos. Mexico, Cárdenas Editor Distribuidor, 99, XLIII-474 p.

4829. FRÓES DA FONSECA (María). La construcción de la patria por el discurso científico: México y Bracil (1770–1830). *Secuencia*, 99, 45, p. 5-26.

4830. GUERRA MANZO (Enrique). Poder regional y mediación política en el Bajo Zamorano (1936–1940). *Historia mexicana*, 99, 49, 192, p. 95-134.

4831. GUTIÉRREZ (Natividad). Nationalist myths and ethnic identities: indigenous intellectuals and the Mexican State. Lincoln, University of Nebraska Press, 99, XVII-242 p.

4832. HAMNETT (Brian). A concise history of Mexico. Cambridge, Cambridge U. P., 99, XV-336 p.

4833. HEATH (Jonathan). Mexico and the sexeñio curse: presidential successions and economic crises in Modern Mexico. Washington, CSIS Press, 99, XVII-124 p.

4834. HENDERSON (Peter V. N.). In the absence of Don Porfirio: Francisco León de la Barra and the Mexican Revolution. Wilmington, SR Books, 99, XIII-338 p.

4835. MACÍAS GONZÁLEZ (Víctor). El caso de una beldad asesina: la construcción narrativa, los concursos de belleza y el mito nacional posrrevolucionario (1921–1931). *Historia y grafía,* 99, 13, p. 113-154.

4836. MACÍAS RICHAR (Carlos). El territorio de Quintana Roo. Tentativas de colonización y control militar en la selva maya (1888–1902). *Historia mexicana,* 99, 49, 192, p. 5-54.

4837. MINNA STERN (Alexandra). Buildings, boundaries, and blood: medicalization and nation-building on the U.S.-Mexico border, 1910–1930. *Hispanic American historical review,* 99, 79, 1, p. 41-82.

4838. MORRIS (Stephen D.). Reforming the nation: Mexican nationalism in context. *Journal of Latin American studies,* 99, 31, 2, p. 363-397.

4839. NIBLO (Stephen R.). Mexico in the 1940s: modernity, politics, and corruption. Wilmington, Scholarly Resources, 99, XXV-408 p. (Latin American silhouettes: studies in history and culture).

4840. OTERO (Gerardo). Farewell to the peasantry? Political class formation in rural Mexico. Boulder a. Oxford, Westview Press, 99, XII-186 p.

4841. Pueblos indios (Los) y el parteaguas de la independencia de México. Coord. Manuel FERRER MUNOZ. México, Instituto de Investigaciones Jurídicas, Universidad Nacional Autónoma de México, 99, 362 p. (Serie Doctrina jurídica, 2).

4842. PURNELL (Jennie). Popular movements and state formation in revolutionary Mexico: the 'Agraristas' and 'Cristeros' of Michoacán. Durham a. London, Duke U. P., 99, X-271 p.

4843. Rebellion in Chiapas: an historical reader. Compilation, translations, and introductory material by John WOMACK, Jr. New York, New Press, 99, XVII-372 p.

4844. Recepción y transformación del liberalismo en México: homenaje al profesor Charles A. Hale. Coord. Josefina Zoraida VÁZQUEZ. México, Colegio de México, Centro de Estudios Históricos, 99, 109 p.

4845. REYNOSO (Víctor). México: gobernabilidad y normalidad electoral, 1988–1998. *Secuencia,* 99, 44, p. 97-136.

4846. SOARES ROBLES (Laura). El bandidaje en el Estado de México durante el primer gobierno de Mariano Riva Palacio (1849–1852). *Secuencia,* 99, 45, p. 27-62.

4847. Sombra (A la) de la primera República federal: el Estado de México, 1824–1835. Comp. María del Pilar IRACHETA CENECORTA y Diana BIRRICHAGA GARDIDA. Zinacantepec, El Colegio Mexiquense, 99, 370 p.

4848. THOMSON (Guy P. C.), LAFRANCE (David G.). Patriotism, politics, and popular liberalism in nineteenth-century Mexico: Juan Francisco Lucas and the Puebla Sierra. Wilmington, SR Books, 99, XVIII-420 p.

Cf. n°s 4918, 4923, 5621

Mongolia

4849. BARKMANN (Udo B.). Geschichte der Mongolei, oder, Die "Mongolische Frage": die Mongolen auf ihrem Weg zum eigenen Nationalstaat. Bonn, Bouvier, 99, 422 p.

4850. Mongolia in the twentieth century: landlocked cosmopolitan. Ed. by Stephen KOTKIN and Bruce A. ELLEMAN. Armonk, M. E. Sharpe, 99, XX-313 p.

4851. ROSHCHIN (Sergej K.). Politicheskaja istorija Mongolii (1921–1940 gg.). (A political history of Mongolia, 1921–1940). RAN, In-t vostokovedenija. Moskva, [s. n.], 99, 327 p. (bibl.; ind.).

Cf. n° 8050

Montenegro

4852. PEJOVIC (Cedomir). Komunisticka Partija Jugoslavije u Crnoj Gori, 1919–1941. (The Communist Party of Yugoslavia in Montenegro). Podgorica, CID, 99, 509 p. (Biblioteka Posebna izdanja).

Morocco

4853. DEROGY (Jacques), PLOQUIN (Frédéric). Ils ont tué Ben Barka. Avec la collaboration de Renée DEROGY WEITZMANN. Paris, Fayard, 99, 455 p. (ill.).

4854. LAFUENTE (Gilles). La politique berbère de la France et le nationalisme marocain. Paris, L'Harmattan, 99, 401 p. (Histoire et perspectives méditerranéennes).

4855. MOUHTADI (Najib). Pouvoir et religion au Maroc: essai d'histoire politique de la Zaouia. Casablanca, Eddif, 99, 193 p. (ill.).

4856. PENNELL (C. R.). Morocco since 1830: a history. London, Hurst, 99, XXXIV-442 p. (ill.).

4857. RIVET (Daniel). Le Maroc de Lyautey à Mohammed V: le double visage du protectorat. Paris, Denoël, 99, 461 p. (Aventure coloniale de la France).

4858. Shadow (In the) of the Sultan: culture, power, and politics in Morocco. Ed. by Rahma BOURQIA and Susan GILSON MILLER. Cambridge, Harvard Center for Middle Eastern Studies, 99, XI-331 p. (Harvard Middle Eastern monographs, 31).

Mozambique

4859. EBATA (Joanne Michi). The transition from war to peace: politics, political space and the peace process industry in Mozambique, 1992–1995. London, [s. n.], 99, 333 p. [Thesis (Ph. D.) - London, LSE 1999].

4860. MOSCA (Joao). A experiência "socialista" em Moçambique (1975-1986). Lisboa, Instituto Piaget, 99, 188 p. (Estudos e documentos, 4).

4861. SCHAFER (Jessica). Soldiers at peace: the post-war politics of demobilised soldiers in Mozambique, 1975-1996. Oxford, [s. n.], 99, 368-XLII p. [Thesis (D.Phil.) - University of Oxford, 1999].

Namibia

4862. EMMETT (Tony). Popular resistance and the roots of nationalism in Namibia, 1915-1966. Basel, Schlettwein, 99, XXII-389 p. (Basel Namibia Studies, 4).

4863. FISCH (Maria). The secessionist movement in the Caprivi: a historical perspective. Windhoek, Namibia Scientific Society, 99, 48 p. (ill., maps).

4864. GEWALD (Jan Bart). Herero heroes: a sociopolitical history of the Herero of Namibia, 1890-1923. Oxford, James Currey a. Athens, Ohio U. P. a. Cape Town, David Philip, 99, X-310 p.

4865. HEARN (Roger). UN peacekeeping in action: the Namibian experience. Commack, Nova Science Publishers, 99, XIV-272 p.

4866. KRÜGER (Gesine). Kriegsbewältigung und Geschichtsbewußtsein: Realität, Deutung und Verarbeitung des deutschen Kolonialkriegs in Namibia 1904 bis 1907. Göttingen, Vandenhoeck & Ruprecht, 99, 344 p. (Kritische Studien zur Geschichtswissenschaft, 133).

Netherlands

4867. EVANS (Ellen Lovell). The cross and the ballot: Catholic political parties in Germany, Switzerland, Austria, Belgium and the Netherlands, 1785-1985. Boston, Humanities, 99, X-301 p. (Studies in Central European histories).

4868. GANS (Evelien). De kleine verschillen die het leven uitmaken: een historische studie naar joodse sociaal-democraten en socialistisch-zionisten in Nederland. Amsterdam, Vassallucci, 99, 1027 p.

4869. HERRERO SÁNCHEZ (Manuel). Las Provincias Unidas y la monarquía hispánica (1588-1702). Madrid, Arco Libros, 99, 96 p. (Cuadernos de historia, 72).

4870. HOOKER (Mark T.). The history of Holland. Westport a. London, Greenwood, 99, XXI-236 p. (Greenwood histories of the modern nations).

4871. ORLOW (D.). A difficult relationship of unequal relatives: the Dutch NSB and Nazi Germany, 1933-1940. *European history quarterly*, 99, 29, 3, p. 349-380.

4872. SCHUTTE (G. J.). Oranje in de achttiende eeuw. Amsterdam, Buijten & Schipperheijn, 99, 160 p. (ill.).

4873. VAN DER LAARSE (Rob). A nation of notables: class politics and religion in the Netherlands in the nineteenth century. Salford, University of Salford, European Studies Research Institute, 99, 135 p. (Working papers in contemporary history & politics. Occasional paper series, 3).

4874. VAN NIEROP (Henk F. K.). Het verraad van het Noorderkwartier: oorlog, terreur en recht in de Nederlandse Opstand. Amsterdam, B. Bakker, 99, 343 p.

4875. VAN RAAK (R.). Een conservative camarilla op het loo. Gerrit Jan Mulder en het conservatisme in Nederland. *Theoretische geschiedenis*, 99, 26, 1, p. 103-120.

Nicaragua

4876. CLOSE (David). Nicaragua: the Chamorro years. Boulder, a. London, Lynne Rienner Publishers, 99, IX-243 p.

4877. HORTON (Lynn). Peasants in arms. War and Peace in the mountains of Nicaragua, 1979-1994. Athens, Ohio University Center for International Studies, 99, XIX-372 p. (Latin America Series, 30).

4878. KINLOCH TIJERINO (Frances). Nicaragua: identidad y cultura política (1821-1858). Managua, Edición Biblioteca "Dr. Roberto Incer Barquero", 99, XVI-387 p.

4879. Undermining (The) of the Sandinista revolution. Ed. by Gary PREVOST and Harry E. VANDEN. Basingstoke, Macmillan Press, 99, XIV-226 p.

Niger

4880. GRÉGOIRE (Emmanuel). Touaregs du Niger, le destin d'un mythe. Préface d'Edmond Bernus. Paris, Editions Karthala, 99, 339 p. (ill.). (Collection "Hommes et sociétés").

Nigeria

4881. FLINT (John E.). 'Managing nationalism': the Colonial Office and Nnamdi Azikiwe, 1932-1943. *In*: Statecraft (The) of British imperialism [Cf. n° 7318], p. 143-158.

4882. LINDSAY (Lisa A.). Domesticity and difference: male breadwinners, working women and colonial citizenship in the 1945 Nigerian general strike. *American historical review*, 99, 104, 3, p. 783-812.

4883. MOMOH (Abubakar), Adejumobi (Said). The Nigerian military and the crisis of democratic transition: a study in the monopoly of power. Lagos, Civil Liberties Organisation, 99, XVI-304 p.

Norway

4884. BERGKVAN (Øystein). Egne hjem-bevegelsen i Norge 1900-1920: tradisjon eller nye strømminger. Oslo, Universitetet i Oslo, 99, 202 p. (ill.).

4885. Deutschland-Norwegen: die lange Geschichte. Hrsg. v. Jarle SIMENSEN unter Mitwirkung von Ole GRIMMES, Rolf HOBSON und Einhart LORENZ. Oslo, Tano Aschehoug, 99, 228 p.

4886. DYRVIK (Ståle). Norsk historie 1625–1814: vegar til sjølvstende. Oslo, Samlaget, 99, 305 p. (Norsk historie, 3).

4887. FURRE (Berge). Norsk historie 1914–2000: frå vokstervisse til framtidstvil. Oslo, Samlaget, 99, 616 p. (ill.). (Norsk historie, 6).

4888. HOLTSMARK (Sven G.). Avmaktens diplomati: DDR i Norge, 1949–1973. Oslo, Den norske historiske forening, 99, 382 p. (HIFOs skriftserie, 3).

4889. NERBØVIK (Jostein). Norsk historie 1860–1914: eit bondesamfunn i oppbrot. Oslo, Samlaget, 99, 296 p. (Norsk historie, 5).

4890. PRYSER (Tore). Norsk historie 1814–1860: frå standssamfunn mot klassesamfunn. Oslo, Samlaget, 99, 316 p. (ill.). (Norsk historie, 4).

4891. SJÖSTEDT (Charlotta). I skuggen av ett hjälteland: svenska frivilliga för det ockuperade Norge. (Dans l'ombre d'un pays héroïque: les volontaires suédois pour la Norvège occupée). Stockholm, Hjalmarson & Högberg, 99, 292 p. (ill.).

Oman

4892. OWTRAM (Francis Carey). Oman and the West: state formation in Oman since 1920. London, [s. n.], 99, 378 p. [Thesis (Ph.D.) – London, London School of Economics and Political Science Department of International History, 1999].

Pakistan

** 4893. JINNAH (Mahomed Ali). Pakistan at last: 26 July–14 August 1947. Ed. in chief Z.H. ZAIDI. Islamabad, Quaid-i-Azam Papers Project, Cabinet Division, Government of Pakistan, 99, LXX-568 p. (Quaid-i-Azam Mohammad Ali Jinnah papers, series 1, 4)

4894. AHMED (Feroz). Ethnicity and politics in Pakistan. Karachi a. Oxford, Oxford U. P., 99, XXII-294 p.

4895. CLOUGHLEY (Brian). A history of the Pakistan army. Wars and insurrections. Karachi, Oxford U. P., 99, [s. p.].

4896. QALB-I-ABID (S.). Jinnah: Second World War and the Pakistan movement. Multan, Beacon Books, 99, 386 p.

Palestine

4897. ABOU DAOUD. Palestine: de Jérusalem à Munich. Avec la collaboration de Gilles DU JONCHAY; présenté par Jacqueline RAOUL-DUVAL. Paris, A. Carrière, 99, 741 p. (ill.).

4898. DE VRIES (David). Ide'alizm u-byurokratyah: shorsheha shel Hefah ha-adumah. (Idealism and bureaucracy in 1920's Palestine). Tel-Aviv, ha-Kibuts hame'uhad, 99, 380 p (ill.).

4899. LAURENS (Henry). La question de Palestine. T. 1. 1799–1922. L'invention de la Terre sainte. Paris, Fayard, 99, 720 p.

4900. RUBIN (Barry M.). The transformation of Palestinian politics: from revolution to State-building. Cambridge a. London, Harvard U. P., 99, XI-288 p.

4901. SAYIGH (Yazid Yusuf). Armed struggle and the search for state: the Palestinian national movement, 1949–1993. Oxford, Oxford U. P., 99, 800 p.

4902. SHAMIR (Ronen). The colonies of law: colonialism, Zionism, and law in early mandate Palestine. Cambridge, Cambridge U. P., 99, 308 p. (Cambridge studies in law and society).

4903. SHEPHERD (Naomi). Ploughing sand: British rule in Palestine, 1917–1948. London, John Murray, 99, X-290 p.

4904. SICKER (Martin). Reshaping Palestine: from Muhammad Ali to the British Mandate, 1831–1922. Westport, Praeger, 99, XI-187 p.

4905. TZUR (Eli). The silent pact: anti-communist co-operation between the Jewish leadership and the British administration in Palestine. *Middle Eastern studies*, 99, 35, 2, p. 103-131.

Cf. n°s 7258, 7326, 7333, 7568

Panama

4906. BELUCHE (Olmedo). Estado, nación, y clases sociales en Panamá: la constitución del estado nacional a través de las contradicciones sociales históricas. Panamá, Editorial Portobelo, Librería El Campus, 99, 177 p. (Pequeno formato, 115. Historia, política, sociología).

4907. CAMBRA (José). De la dictadura a la invasión: análisis del procéso político, 1984–1990. Panamá. Editorial Portobelo, Librería El Campus, 99, 143 p. (Pequeño formato, 119. Historia, politíca, sociología).

Paraguay

4908. CABELLO SARUBBI (Oscar). Storia del Paraguay. Roma, Vecchiarelli, 99, 169 p.

4909. PANGRAZIO (Miguel Angel). Historia política del Paraguay. Asunción, Intercontinental Editora, 99, [s. p.].

Peru

* 4910. BENNETT (John M.). Sendero Luminoso in context: an annotated bibliography. Lanham, Scarecrow Press a. Folkestone, Shelwing Ltd, 99, IX-229 p.

4911. BULLICK (Lucie). Pouvoir militaire et société au Pérou aux XIXe et XXe siècles. Paris, Publications de la Sorbonne, 99, 350 p. (ill.). (Homme et société, 26).

4912. CAHILL (David Patrick). Violencia, represión y rebelión en el sur andino: la sublevación de Túpac Amaru y sus consecuencias. Lima, IEP, 99, 20 p. (Instituto de Estudios Peruanos. Documento de trabajo, 105. Serie Historia, 17).

4913. CONTRERAS (Carlos), CUETO (Marcos). Historia del Perú contemporáneo. Lima, Red Para el Desarrollo de las Ciencias Sociales en el Perú, 99, 312 p. (Serie Estudios históricos, 27).

4914. GORRITI ELLENBOGEN (Gustavo). The Shining Path: a history of the millenarian war in Peru. With an introduction, by Robin KIRK. Chapel Hill a. London, University of North Carolina Press, 99, XXIII-290 p. (Latin America in translation).

4915. HAYA DE LA TORRE DE LA ROSA (Agustin). Estado y sociedad en el Perú contemporáneo: neoliberalismo autoritario de fin de siglo. Lima, A. Haya, 99, 304 p. [Thesis (Ph. D.) – Nijmegen, Katholieke Universiteit Nijmegen, 1999].

4916. KLARÉN (Peter Flindell). Peru: society and nationhood in the Andes. New York a. Oxford, Oxford U. P., 99, XVI-494 p. (Latin American histories).

4917. LEIBNER (Gerardo). El mito del socialismo indígena en Mariátegui. Lima. Pontificia Universidad Católica del Perú, Fondo Editorial, 99, 261 p.

4918. LORA CAM (Jorge). El Ezln [Ejército Zapatista de Liberación Nacional] y Sendero Luminoso: radicalismo de izquierda y confrontación político-militar en América Latina. Puebla, Benemérita Universidad Autónoma de Puebla. Dirección General de Fomento Editorial, 99, 448 p.

4919. LYNCH (Nicolás). Una tragedia sin héroes: la derrota de los partidos y el origen de los independientes: Perú 1980–1992. Lima, Universidad Nacional Mayor de San Marcos, Fondo Editorial, 99, 274 p.

4920. MAC EVOY (Carmen). Forjando la nación: ensayos sobre historia republicana. Lima, Pontificia Universidad Católica del Perú y Sewanee, University of the South, 99, XXIV-503 p.

4921. MARTÍNEZ RIAZA (Ascensión). Política regional y gobierno de la Amazonia peruana. Loreto, 1883–1914. *Histórica*, 99, 23, 2, p. 97-118.

4922. Perú (El) en el siglo XVIII: la Era Borbónica. Ed. por Scarlett O'PHELAN GODOY. Lima, Pontificia Universidad Católica del Perú, Instituto Riva-Agüero, 99, 449 p. (Publicación del Instituto Riva-Agüero, 179).

4923. SOARES (Gabriela Pellegrino), COLOMBO (Sylvia). Reforma liberal e lutas camponesas na América Latina: México e Peru nas últimas décadas do século XIX e princípios do XX. Sao Paulo, Humanitas, FFLCH/USP, 99, 122 p. (Textos de apoio. História, 3).

4924. STAVIG (Ward). The World of Túpac Amaru: Conflict, Community, and Identity in Colonial Peru. Lincoln, University of Nebraska Press, 99, XXXIV-348 p.

4925. WALKER (Charles F.). Smoldering ashes: Cuzco and the creation of Republican Peru, 1780–1840. Durham a. London, Duke U. P., 99, XIII-330 p.

Philippines

4926. Dominicans (The) and the Philippine revolution, 1896–1903. Collected and edited with introductions and notes by Fidel VILLARROEL. Manila, University of Santo Tomas Pub. House, 99, LV-452 p.

4927. KINTANAR (Galileo C.), MILITANTE (Pacifico V.). Lost in time: from birth to obsolescence, the Communist Party of the Philippines. Book 1. 1930-1972. Ed. by J. Augustus Y. DE LA PAZ. Quezon City, Truth and Justice Foundation, 290 p.

4928. MOJARES (Resil B.). The war against the Americans: resistance and collaboration in Cebu, 1899–1906. Quezon City, Ateneo de Manila U. P., 99, 250 p. (ill., maps).

4929. Philippine presidents: 100 years. Quezon City, Philippine Historical Association, 99, XVI-398 p. (plates, ill., ports.).

4930. Politics and Governance theory and practice in the Philippine context. Introduction by Lydia N. YU-JOSE. Manila, Dept. of Political Science, Ateneo de Manila University, 99, V-343 p.

Poland

4931. ASH (Timothy Garton). The Polish revolution. Solidarity. London, Penguin, 99, XV, 439 p.

4932. AUGUSTYNIAK (Urszula). Wazowie i "królowie rodacy". Studium władzy królewskiej w Rzeczypospolitej XVII wieku. (Wasalinie und "einheimische Könige". Ein Studium der königlichen Macht in der Republik Polen im XVII. Jahrhundert). Warszawa, Semper, 99, 254 p.

4933. BABIS (Maria). Hymnu polskiego obraz własny. (Des polnischen Nationalliedes Eigenbild). Gdańsk, Wydaw. Gdańskie, 99, 332 p.

4934. BENECKE (Werner). Die Ostgebiete der Zweiten Polnischen Republik. Staatsmacht und öffentliche Ordnung in einer Minderheitenregion 1918–1939. Köln, Böhlau, 99, VII-321 p. (ill.). (Beiträge zur Geschichte Osteuropas, 29).

4935. Białobrzegi. Studia i szkice z dziejów miasta. (Białobrzegi. Studien und Grundrisse zur Geschichte der Stadt). Pod red. Reginy RENZ. Radom, Białobrzeskie Tow. Nauk., 99, 562 p.

4936. BIEGALSKI (Bogdan). Organizacje podziemne na Środkowym Nadodrzu w latach 1945–1954. (Die Untergrundorganisationen in dem mittleren Oder-Gebiet in den Jahren 1945–1954). Zielona Góra, Lubuskie Tow. Nauk., 99, 294 p.

4937. BOGUCKA (Maria). Historia Polski do 1864 roku. (Geschichte Polens bis 1864). Wrocław, Zakł. Nar. im. Ossolińskich, 99, 377 p.

4938. BORZYSZKOWSKI (Józef). Gdańsk i Pomorze w XIX i XX wieku. Szkice z dziejów i kultury regionu. (Danzig und Pommern im XIX. und XX. Jahrhundert. Grundrisse der Geschichte und Kultur der Region). Gdańsk, Uniw. Gdański, 99, 370 p. (Niw. Gdański, Gdańskie Tow. Nauk.).

4939. CHUMIŃSKI (Jędrzej). Ruch zawodowy w Polsce w warunkach kształtującego się systemu totalitarnego 1944-1956. (Die Berufs-Bewegung in Polen angesichts des sich entfaltenden totalitären Systems 1944-1956). Wrocław, Wydaw. Akad. Ekonom. Im. Oskara Langego, 99, 428 p.

4940. FIJAŁKOWSKI (Paweł). Żydzi w województwie łęczyckim i rawskim w XV–XVIII w. (Juden in den Wojewodschaften Łęczyca und Rawa Mazowiecka von dem XV. bis zum XVIII. Jh). Warszawa, Żydowski Inst. Hist., 99, 166 p.

4941. HASS (Ludwik). Wolnomularze polscy w kraju i na świecie 1821-1999. Słownik biograficzny. (Die polnischen Freimaurer im Inland und weltweit. Biographisches Nachschlagewerk). Warszawa, Rytm, 99, 660 p.

4942. KENNEY (Padraic). The gender of resistance in communist Poland. *American historical review*, 99, 104, 2, p. 399-425.

4943. LIM (Jie-Hyun). Labour and the national question in Poland. *In*: Nationalism, Labour and Ethnicity 1870-1939 [Cf. n° 3983], [s. p.].

4944. MAZEK (Dorota). Kuratela nad osobami chorymi psychicznie w Rzeczypospolitej w drugiej połowie XVIII w. *Przeg. Hist.,* 99, 90, 2, p. 131-149.

4945. MIERNIK (Grzegorz). Opór chłopów wobec kolektywizacji w województwie kieleckim 1948-1956. (Die Auflehnung des Bauerntums gegen Kollektivierung in der Wojewodschaft Kielce 1948-1956). Kielce, Takt, 99, 414 p. (Prace Instytutu Historii WSP w Kielcach, 16).

4946. MOLENDA (Jan). Chłopi, naród, niepodległość. Kształtowanie się postaw narodowych i obywatelskich chłopów w Galicji i Królestwie Polskim w przededniu odrodzenia Polski. (Bauern, Volk, Unabhängigkeit. Die Gestaltung der nationalen und der bürgerlichen Haltung des Bauerntums in Galizien und im Königreich Polen knapp vor der Renaissance Polens). Warszawa, Neriton, Inst. Historii PAN, 99, 366 p.

4947. MYŚLIWSKI (Grzegorz). Człowiek średniowiecza wobec czasu i przestrzeni. Mazowsze od XII do połowy XVI wieku. (Der Mensch des Mittelalters im Angesicht der Zeit und des Raumes. Masowien von dem XII. bis zur Hälfte des XVI. Jahrunderts). Warszawa, Wydaw. Krupski i S-ka, 99, 462 p.

4948. PORTER (Brian A.). Democracy and discipline in late nineteenth-century Poland. *Journal of modern history*. 99, 71, 2, p. 346-393.

4949. RAMOTOWSKA (Franciszka). "Tajemne" państwo polskie w Powstaniu Styczniowym 1863-1864. Struktura organizacyjna. (Der polnische "Geheim-Staat" während des Januaraufstandes 1863-1864. Organisatorische Struktur). Warszawa, DiG, 99, 727 p. (Naczelna Dyrekcja Archiwów Państ.).

4950. SCHER-ZEMBITSKA (Lydia). Stanislas Ier: un roi fantasque. Paris, CNRS éditions, 99, 239 p.

4951. STACHURA (Peter D.). Poland in the twentieth century. New York, St. Martin's Press, 99, XV-180 p.

4952. Stalinism in Poland, 1944-1956: Selected Papers from the Fifth World Congress of Central and East European Studies, Warsaw, 1995. Ed. by A. KEMP-WELCH. New York, St. Martin's Press, 99, XIV-163 p.

4953. STĘPKA (Stanisław). Chłopi wobec wydarzeń politycznych w Polsce (1956-1959). (Das Bauerntum angesichts der politischen Ereignisse in Polen, 1956-1959). Warszawa, Wydaw. Szkoły Gł. Gospodarstwa Wiejskiego, 99, 195 p. (Rozprawy Naukowe i Monografie, 220).

4954. SZWAGRZYK (Krzysztof). Winni? Niewinni? Dolnośląskie podziemie niepodległościowe (1945-1956) w świetle dokumentów. (Schuldig? Frei von Schuld? Niederschlesiens geheime Freiheitsbewegungen [1945-1956] in Anbetracht der Dokumente). Wrocław, Zarząd Gł. Stow. Społ.-Kombatanckiego „Wolność i Niezawosłość", 99, 430 p. (Biblioteka Zeszytów Historycznych WiN-u).

4955. TONINI (Carla). Operazione Madagascar. La questione ebraica in Polonia 1918-1968. Bologna, Clueb, 99, 274 p.

4956. WANDYCZ (Piotr Stefan). Z Piłsudskim i Sikorskim. August Zalewski minister spraw zagranicznych w latach 1926-1932 i 1939-1941. (Mit Piłsudski und Sikorski. August Zalewski Minister für auswärtige Angelegenheiten in den Jahren 1926-1932 und 1939-1941). Warszawa, Wydaw. Sejmowe, 99, 262 p.

4957. WAŻNIEWSKI (Władysław). Stosunek władz państwowych do Kościoła katolickiego w Polsce 1956-1970. (Das Verhältnis der staatlichen Behörden zur katholischen Kirche in Polen 1956-1970). Siedlce, IH AP, 99, 297 p. (Inst. Historii Akad. Podlaskiej, Lud. Tow. Kult. Oddz. W Siedlcach).

Cf. n°s 5003, 5293, 7646

Portugal

4958. BERNARDO (Manuel). Equívocos e realidades: Portugal, 1974-1975. Prefácio pelo Paulo VALLADA. Lisboa, Nova Arrancada, 99, 2 vol., [s. p.] (ill.).

4959. CLIJSTERS (Edi). Portugal 1974: a non-violent revolution: causes, course and consequences of the "Revolution of Carnations", confronted with theoretical definitions of revolution. San Domenico, European University Institute, Badia Fiesolana, 99, 255 p.

4960. COSTA PINTO (Antonio). Come muore una democrazia. Il caso del Portogallo (1917-1926). *Nuova storia contemporanea*, 99, 3, 4, p. 79-102.

4961. MALERBA (Jurandir). Instituições da monarquia portuguesa decisivas na fundação do Império do Brasil. *Luso-Brazilian review*, 99, 39, 1, p. 33-48.

4962. Marcelismo (Do) ao fim do império. Coordenaçao J.M. BRANDAO DE BRITO. Lisboa, Notícias, 99, 303 p. (Revoluçao e democracia, 1).

4963. PEÑA RODRÍGUEZ (Alberto). Galicia, Franco y Salazar: la emigración gallega en Portugal y el intercambio ideológico entre el Franquismo y el Salazarismo (1936-1939). Vigo, Universidade de Vigo, 99, 167 p. (ill.). (Monografías da Universidade de Vigo. Serie Humanidades e ciencias xurídico-sociais, 18).

4964. PINTO (António Costa). The Blue Shirts: Portuguese fascists and the new state. Boulder, Social Science Monographs, 99, XV-271 p.

4965. Portugal e a transiçao para a democracia: 1974-1976: I Curso Livre de História Contemporânea, Lisboa, 23 a 28 de novembro de 1998. Organizado pela Fundaçao Máro Soares e Instituto de História Contemporânea da Universidade Nova de Lisboa; coordenaçao científica de Fernando ROSAS. Lisboa, Ediçoes Colibri, 99, 371 p.

Cf. n°s 91, 4115

Puerto Rico

4966. NAVARRO GARCÍA (Jesús Raúl). Puerto Rico a la sombra de la independencia continental (fronteras ideológicas y políticas en el Caribe, 1815-1840). Sevilla, Escuela de Estudios Hispano-Americanos y San Juan, Centro de Estudios Avanzados de Puerto Rico y el Caribe, 99, 307 p.

Romania

4967. BÁTHORY (Ludovic). Societățile carbonifere și sistemul economic și politic al României (1919-1929). (Carbon processing societies and Romania's economic and political system. 1919-1929). Cluj-Napoca, Editura Presa Universitară Clujeană, 99, 273 p.

4968. CHIRTOAGĂ (Ion). Din istoria Moldovei de sud-est până în anii 30 ai secolului al XIX-lea. (From the history of south-west Moldavia until the thirties of the 19th century). Chișinău, Editura Museum, 99, 236 p.

4969. CIOBANU (Veniamin). Carol al XII-lea și românii. (Charles XII and the Romanians). București, Editura Domus, 99, 319 p.

4970. DELETANT (Dennis). Communist terror in Romania: Gheorghiu-Dej and the police State 1948-1965. New York, St. Martin's Press, 99, XII-351 p.

4971. HITCHINS (Keith). A nation affirmed: the Romanian national movement in Transylvania, 1860-1914. București, Enciclopaedic Publishing House, 99, 407 p.

4972. IORDACHE (Anastasie). Originile și constituirea Partidului Conservator din România. (Le origini e la costituzione del Partito Conservatore di Romania).

București, Paideia, 99, 271 p. (Colecția Paideia Științe. Seria Istorie).

4973. Istoria României. Transilvania. (History of Romania. Transylvania). Vol. II (1867-1947). Coordonator: Anton DRĂGOESCU. Cluj-Napoca, Editura "George Barițiu", 99, 1644 p.

4974. LOSONCZI (Terezia), MOLDOVAN (Ioan). Revoluția de la 1848-1849 în Scaunul Mureș și împrejurimi. (The 1848-1849 revolution in the seat of Mureș and its surroundings). Târgu Mureș, Editura Tipomur, 99, 102 p.

4975. MAIER (Lothar). Terra e nazione: rivoluzionari e contadini del 1848 rumeno. *Passato e presente*, 99, 17, 46, p. 53-74.

4976. NICOLENCO (Viorica). Extrema dreaptă în Basarabia (1923-1940). (The far right in Bessarabia. 1923-1940). Chișinău, Editura Civitas, 99, 112 p.

4977. PERIE (Dorin). De Roemeense liberalen en het liberalisme: een geschiedenis van Roemenië (1918-1947). Amsterdam, D. Perie, 99, 324 p.

4978. PETRENCU (Anatol). România și Basarabia în anii celui de al doilea război mondial. (Romania and Bessarabia in the years of World War II). Chișinău, Editura Epigraf, 99, 175 p.

4979. PLATON (Gheorghe). Geneza revoluției române de la 1848. Introducere în istoria modernă a românilor. (The genesis of the 1848 Romanian revolution. Introduction to the modern history of the Romanians). Iași, Editura Universității "Al. I. Cuza", 99, 356 p.

4980. RENGGLI (F.). La communisation de la Roumanie (1944-1947). *Relations internationales*, 99, 97, p. 91-106.

4981. ROMAN (Andreia). Le populisme quarante-huitard: dans les principautés roumaines. București, Éd. de la Fondation culturelle roumaine, 99, 247 p.

4982. SCURTU (Ioan), BUZATU (Gh.). Istoria românilor în secolul XX. 1918-1948. (The Romanians' history in the 20th century. 1918-1948). București, Editura Paideia, 99, 712 p.

4983. SORANI (Alessandro Vittorio). La vicenda elettorale della Guardia di Ferro (1927-1938). *Ricerche storiche*, 99, 29, p. 595-609.

4984. SORIN (Antohi). Imaginaire culturel et réalité politique dans la Roumanie moderne. Le stigmate et l'utopie. Traduit du roumain par Claude KARNOOUH et Mona ANTOHI. Paris et Montréal, L'Harmattan, 99, [s. p.].

Russia (USSR)

* 4985. KONDAKOVA (Irina A.). Otkrytyj arkhiv: Spravochnik opublikovannykh dokumentov po istorii Rossii XX veka iz gosudarstvennykh i semejnykh arkhivov (po otechestvennoj periodike i al'manakham, 1985-1996 gg.). (A guide to the sources of Russian 20th-century history from the state and private archives

published in Russian periodicals and yearbooks in 1985–1996). 2nd ed., corrected and supplemented. Moskva, ROSSPEN, 99, 303 p. (ind.).

* 4986. RAZDORSKIJ (A.I.). Obshchie pechatnye spiski dolzhnostnykh lits gubernij i oblastej Rossijskoj imperii (1841–1908): Bibliograficheskij ukazatel'. (General printed lists of officials of the provinces and regions of the Russian Empire, 1841–1908: A bibliography). Sankt-Peterburg, Dmitry Bulanin, 99, 94 p.

** 4987. GAL'PERINA (Bella D.). Sovet ministrov Rossijskoj imperii v gody Pervoj mirovoj vojny. Bumagi A.N. Jakhontova (Zapisi zasedanij i perepiska). (The Council of Ministers of the Russian Empire during the First World War. Papers of A.N. Yakhontov: Records of the meetings and correspondence). RAN, In-t rossijskoj istorii. Sankt-Peterburg, Dmitry Bulanin, 99, 560 p. (ind.).

** 4988. KUDRJAVTSEV (Ivan I.). Kronshtadtskaja tragedija 1921 g.: Dokumenty. (The tragedy of Kronschtadt, 1921: Documents). Vol. 1-2. Moskva, ROSSPEN, 99, 688, 672 p.

** 4989. KUMANEV (Georgij A.). Rjadom so Stalinym: Otkrovennye svidetel'stva: Vstrechi, besedy, interv'ju, dokumenty. (Near Stalin: meetings, conversations, interviews, documents). RAN, In-t rossijskoj istorii. Moskva, Bylina, 99, 446 p. (ill., portr.).

** 4990. Politicheskaja istorija russkoj emigratsii, 1920–1940: Dokumenty i materialy. (Political history of the Russian emigration, 1920–1940: documents and materials). Ed. Aleksandr F. KISELEV. Moskva, VLADOS, 99, 776 p. (bibl.).

4991. ANAN'ICH (Boris V.), GANELIN (Rafail Sh.). Sergej Jul'evich Vitte i ego vremja. (Sergey Witte [1849–1915] and his time). RAN, In-t rossijskoj istorii. Sankt-Peterburg, Dmitry Bulanin, 99, 430 p. (ill., bibl., ind.).

4992. ANISIMOV (Evgenij V.). Dyba i knut: politicheskij sysk i russkoe obshchestvo XVIII v. (Political detection and the Russian society in the 18th century). Moskva, Novoe literaturnoe obozrenie, 99, 719 p. (ill., portr.; plates; bibl.). (Historia Rossika).

4993. BEBESI (György). A fekete század: az orosz szélsőjobb kialakulása és története a századelőn. (The black century: the birth and the story of the Russian extreme right). Budapest, M. Rusziszisztikai Int., 99, 331 p.

4994. BENVENUTI (Francesco). Storia della Russia contemporanea 1853–1996. Roma e Bari, Laterza, 99, XV-359 p. (Quadrante Laterza, 100).

4995. BORODIN (Anatolij P.). Gosudarstvennyj sovet Rossii (1906–1917). (The State Council of Russia, 1906–1915). Kirov, Vjatka, 99, 368 p.

4996. DEVLET (Nadir). Rusya Türklerinin Milli Mücadele tarihi. (1905–1917). (Histoire de la guerre nationale des turcs de Russie). Ankara, Türk Tarih Kurumu, 99, 347 p.

4997. DIXON (Simon M.). The modernisation of Russia 1676–1825. Cambridge, Cambridge U. P., 99, XVII-267 p. (New approaches to European history).

4998. Evrei i russkaja revoljutsija: materialy i issledovanija. (The Jews and the Russian Revolution: materials and studies). Ed. Oleg V. BUDNITSKIJ. Moskva a. Ierusalim, Gesharim, 99, 479 p. (ill., portr.; bibl., ind.).

4999. FAGGIONATO (Raffaella). Michail Speranskij e Aleksandr Golicyn: il riformismo rosacrociano nella Russia di Alessandro I. *Rivista storica italiana*, 99, 111, 2, p. 423-475.

5000. FITZPATRICK (Sheila). Everyday Stalinism: ordinary life in extraordinary times: Soviet Russia in the 1930s. New York a. Oxford, Oxford U. P., 99, X-288 p.

5001. GEIFMAN (Anna). Entangled in Terror: The Azef Affair and the Russian Revolution. Wilmington, Scholarly Resources, 99, X-247 p.

5002. GETTY (J. Arch), NAUMOV (Oleg V.). The road to terror: Stalin and the self-destruction of the Bolsheviks, 1932–1939. New Haven a. London, Yale U. P., 99, XXVII-635 p. (Annals of Communism).

5003. GORIZONTOV (Leonid E.). Paradoksy rossijskoj politiki: poljaki v Rossii i russkie v Pol'she (XIX–nachalo XX v.). (Paradoxes of the policy of Russia: Polish in Russia and Russians in Poland, the 19th and the early 20th centuries). RAN, In-t slavjanovedenija. Moskva, Indrik, 99, 270 p. (bibl., ind.).

5004. HUTCHINSON (John F.). Late imperial Russia, 1890–1917. London a. New York, Longman, 99, 134 p.

5005. IVANOV (Anatolij E.). Studenchestvo Rossii kontsa XIX–nachala XX veka: Sotsial'no-istoricheskaja sud'ba. (Students in Russia in the late 19th and the early 20th centuries: their social and historical fortune). RAN, In-t rossijskoj istorii. Moskva, ROSSPEN, 99, 415 p. (bibl., ind.). [Eng. summary]

5006. IVKIN (Vladimir I.). Gosudarstvennaja vlast' SSSR: Vysshie organy vlasti i upravlenija i ikh rukovoditeli, 1923–1991: Istoriko-biograficheskij spravochnik. (The state power of the USSR: the higher institutions and their heads, 1923–1991: a historical and biographical guide). Moskva, ROSSPEN, 99, 639 p. (ind.).

5007. JAROV (Sergej V.). Gorozhanin kak politik: Revoljutsija, voennyj kommunizm i NEP glazami petrogradtsev. (Townsman as politician: revolution, war communism and NEP through the eyes of the inhabitants of Petrograd). With documents in app. Ed. Valerij A. SHISHKIN. RAN, In-t rossijskoj istorii, S.-Peterb. f-l. Sankt-Peterburg, Dmitry Bulanin, 99, 319 p. – IDEM. Krest'janin kak politik: Krest'janstvo Severo-Zapada Rossii v 1918–1919 gg.: Politicheskoe myshlenie i massovyj protest. (Peasant as a politician: the peasantry of the north-west of Russia in 1918–1919: political thinking and mass protest). With documents in app. Ed. Valerij A. SHISHKIN. RAN, In-t rossijskoj istorii, S.-Peterb. f-l. Sankt-Peterburg, Dmitry Bulanin, 99, 168 p. – IDEM. Proletarij kak politik: Politicheskaja psikhologija rabochikh Petrograda v 1917–1923 gg. (Proletarian as a politician: political psychology of the workers of Petrograd, 1917–1923). Ed. Valerij A. SHISHKIN. RAN, In-t rossijskoj istorii, S.-Peterb. f-l. Sankt-Peterburg, Dmitry Bulanin, 99, 223 p. (bibl.).

5008. KAGAN (Frederick W.). The military reforms of Nicholas I: the origins of the modern Russian Army. New York, St. Martin's Press, 99, XII-337 p.

5009. KAL'MINA (Lilija V.), KURAS (Leonid V.). Evrejskaja obshchina v Zapadnom Zabajkal'e (60-e gody XIX veka–fevral' 1917 g.). (The Jewish community of Western Transbaikalia, 1860es–February 1917). In-t mongolovedenija, buddologii i tibetologii BNTs SO RAN. Ulan-Ude, Izd. BNTs SO RAN, 99, 171 p. (bibl.).

5010. KATZER (Nikolaus). Die Weisse Bewegung in Russland: Herrschaftsbildung, praktische Politik und politische Programmatik im Bürgerkrieg. Köln, Böhlau, 99, 612 p. (ill., maps). (Beiträge zur Geschichte Osteuropas, 28).

5011. LIEBICH (André). The Mensheviks. *In*: Russia under the last tsar: opposition and subversion 1894–1917 [Cf. n° 5021], p. 19-33.

5012. LJAMINA (Ekaterina E.), SAMOVER (Nalal'ja V.). «Bednyj Zhozef»: zhizn' i smert' Iosifa Viel'gorskogo: opyt biografii cheloveka 1830-kh godov. ('Poor Joseph': life and death of Joseph Viielgorsky: a biography of a man of the 1830es). Moskva, Jazyki russkoj kul'tury, 99, 559 p. (bibl.). (Studia Historica. Series minor).

5013. MALYSHEVA (Svetlana Ju.). Rossijskoe vremennoe pravitel'stvo 1917 goda. Otechestvennaja istoriografija 20-kh–serediny 60-kh godov. (The Russian provisional governement of 1917 in the Russian historiography, 1920–the middle of the 1960es). Kazan', Kheter, 99, 168 p. (bibl.).

5014. MARASINOVA (Elena N.). Psikhologija elity rossijskogo dvorjanstva poslednej treti XVIII veka (Po materialam perepiski). (The psychology of the elite of the Russian late 18th-century nobility: a study of letters). RAN, In-t rossijskoj istorii. Moskva, ROSSPEN, 99, 301 p. (8 f. ill., bibl., ind.).

5015. Men'sheviki v 1918 godu. Otv. red.: Ziva GALILI, Al'bert Pavlovich NENAROKOV; otv. sost. Dmitrii Borisovich PAVLOV. Moskva, ROSSPEN, 99, 797 p. (Men'sheviki v bol'shevistskoi Rossii, 1918–1924. Politicheskie partii Rossii, Konets XIX-pervaia tret' XX veka).

5016. Nakazannyj narod: po materialam konferentsii «Repressii protiv rossijskikh nemtsev». (A punished people: papers of the conf. «Repressions against Germans in Russia», 18–20 November, 1998). Goethe-Institut; O-vo 'Memorial'. Moskva, Zven'ja, 99, 287 p. (bibl.). [German summary]

5017. ORLOV (Igor' B.). Novaja ekonomicheskaja politika: istorija, opyt, problemy. (The New Economic Policy, [NEP, Russia, 1920es]: history, experience, problems). Ed. Vitalij S. LEL'CHUK. Gos. un-t gumanit. nauk, In-t istorii. Moskva, GUGN, 99, 193 p. (bibl.).

5018. PIVOVAR (Efim O.) [et al.]. Rossija v izgnanii: Sud'by rossijskikh emigrantov za rubezhom. (Russia in exile: fortunes of Russian emigrants abroad, [1920–1940es]). RAN, In-t vseobshchej istorii; Moskovskij gos. un-t im. M.V. Lomonosova, Ist. f-t. Moskva, [s. n.], 99, 457 p.

5019. Politics and Society under the Bolsheviks: selected papers from the Fifth World Congress of Central and East European Studies, Warsaw, 1995. Ed. by Kevin MAC DERMOTT and John MORISON. New York, St. Martin's Press, 99, XVIII-302 p.

5020. ROMANO (Andrea). Contadini in uniforme: l'Armata rossa e la collettivizzazione delle campagne nell'URSS. Firenze, L. S. Olschki, 99, XIV-250 p. (Storia/Facoltà di lettere e filosofia, Fondo di studi Parini-Chirio, Università degli studi di Torino, 3).

5021. Russia under the last Tsar: opposition and subversion 1894–1917. Ed. by Anna GEIFMAN. Malden, Blackwell, 99, VIII-310 p. [Cf. n° <choice> 5011.]

5022. SHIELDS KOLLMANN (Nancy). By honor bound: State and society in early modern Russia. Ithaca, Cornell U. P., 99, XIII-296 p.

5023. SKORKIN (Konstantin V.), PETROV (Nikita V.). Kto rukovodil NKVD, 1934–1941: Spravochnik. (Who managed the Peoples Commissariat of Internal Affairs (NKVD), 1934–1941: a guide). Eds. N.G. OKHOTIN, A.B. ROGINSKIJ. O-vo «Memorial». Moskva, Zven'ja, 99, 303 p. (portr.).

5024. SMITH (Jeremy). The Bolsheviks and the National Question, 1917–1923. New York, St. Martin's Press, 99, XVII-281 p. (Studies in Russia and East Europe).

5025. SMOLIN (Anatolij V.). Beloe dvizhenie na Severo-Zapade Rossii, 1918–1920 gg. (The White Movement in the North-West of Russia, 1918–1920). Sankt-Peterburg, Dmitry Bulanin, 99, 439 p. (ind.).

5026. WOLFF (David). To the Harbin station: the liberal alternative in Russian Manchuria, 1898–1914. Stanford, Stanford U. P., 99, XIV-255 p.

5027. ZUBKOVA (Elena). Die sowjetische Gesellschaft nach dem Krieg. Lage und Stimmung der Bevölkerung 1945/1946. *Vierteljahrshefte für Zeitgeschichte*, 99, 47, 3, p. 363-384.

Cf. n°s 346, 419, 493, 504, 555, 616, 621, 645, 730, 768, 769, 866, 892, 909, 911, 912, 926, 1202, 4807, 5242, 5343, 5454, 5457, 5458, 5460, 5566, 5616, 5622, 5693, 5717, 5859, 6018, 6023, 6207, 6395, 6396, 6397, 6487, 6668, 6702, 6791, 6947, 6961, 7037, 7211, 7287, 7374, 7392, 7429, 7475, 7476, 7509, 7533, 7544, 7546, 7573, 7596, 7611, 7681, 7755, 7822, 7887, 8098

São Tomé and Príncipe

5028. SEIBERT (Gerhard). Comrades, clients and cousins: colonialism, socialism and democratization in São Tomé and Príncipe. Leiden, Leiden University, Research School of Asian, African and Amerindian Studies, 99, XIV-465 p.

Saudi Arabia

5029. PFULLMANN (Uwe). Ibn Saud, König zwischen Tradition und Fortschritt. Berlin, Edition Ost, 99, 466 p.

Senegal

5030. COULIBALY (Abdou Latif). Le Sénégal à l'épreuve de la démocratie, ou, L'histoire du Parti socialiste de la naissance à nos jours: enquête sur 50 ans de lutte et de complots au sein de l'élite socialiste. Paris, L'Harmattan, 99, 252 p. (Etudes africaines).

Sierra Leone

5031. CONTEH-MORGAN (Earl), DIXON-FYLE (Mac). Sierra Leone at the end of the twentieth century: history, politics and society. New York, Peter Lang, 99, XVI-75 p.

Slovakia

** 5032. November 1989 a Slovensko. Chronológia a dokumenty (1985–1990). (Der November 1989 und Slowakei. Die Chronologie und Quellen, 1985–1990). Ed. Jozef ŽATKULIAK. Koeditor Viera HLAVOVÁ, Alžbeta SEDLIAKOVÁ, Michal ŠTEFANSKÝ. Bratislava, Nadácia Milana Šimečku - Historický ústav Slovenskej akadémie vied, 99, 622 p. [Cf. n° <Auswahl> 7962.]

** 5033. Sprievodca po slovenských archívoch. A Guide to the Slovak Archives. Ed. Zuzana KOLLÁROVÁ, Jozef HANUS. Prešov, Universum 99, 200 p.

5034. BAKKE (Elisabeth). Čechoslovakizmus v školských učebniciach. (Der Tschechoslowakismus in den Schulbücher, 1918–1938). *Historický časopis*, 99, 47, 2, p. 233-252.

5035. BARNOVSKÝ (Michal). Legalizácia gréckokatolíckej cirkvi v Československu roku 1968. (Die Legalisation der griechisch-katholischen Kirche in der Tschechoslowakei im Jahre 1968). *Historický časopis*, 99, 47, 3, p. 447-465. [Deutsche Zfassung].

5036. BYSTRICKÝ (Valerián). Zasadnutie Slovenského snemu 14. marca 1939. (Das Tagen Slowakischer Versammlung am 14. März 1939). *Historický časopis*, 99, 47, 1, p. 105-114.

5037. ĎURKOVÁ (Mária). Podpoľanie a najstaršie dejiny Detvy. (Das Waldwiesengebiet und die älteste Geschichte von Detva). *Historický časopis*, 99, 47, 3, s. 383-403. [Deutsche Zfassung].

5038. FALISOVÁ (Anna). Zdravotníctvo na Slovensku v medzivojnovom období. (Das Gesundheitswesen in der Slowakei) Bratislava, Veda vydavateľstvo Slovenskej akadémie vied, 99, 203 p.

5039. Formy a obsah vzdelanosti v historickom procese. Ed. Viliam ČIČAJ. Bratislava, Veda vydavateľstvo Slovenskej akadémie vied, 99, 187 p.

5040. GRAUS (Igor). Zápas Banskej Bystrice s vedením Turzovsko-fuggerovského mediarskeho podniku o správu bratstva Božieho tela. (Das Ringen der Stadt Banská Bystrica [Neusohl] mit der Leitung des Thurso-Fuggerischen Kupferhandels um die Verwaltung der Bruderschaft Corporis Christi der Bergleute). *Historický časopis*, 99, 47, 2, p. 173-185. [Deutsche Zfassung].

5041. HOLEC (Roman). Snahy o ústrednú slovenskú banku pred prvou svetovou vojnou. (Die Bestrebungen um eine slowakische Zentralbank vor dem ersten Weltkrieg). *Historický časopis*, 99, 47, 2, p. 211-231. [Deutsche Zfassung].

5042. HOMZA (Martin). Pokus o interpretáciu úlohy kňažnej Adelaidy v uhorsko-poľskej kronike. (Der Versuch einer Interpretation der Rolle von Fürstin Adelaide in der ungarisch-polnischen Chronik). *Historický časopis*, 99, 47, 3, s. 357-382. [Deutsche Zfassung].

5043. KOWALSKÁ (Eva). Otázka intolerancie po vydaní tolerančného patentu. (Intoleranz nach dem Erlass der Toleranzpatentes). *Historický časopis*, 99, 47, 2, p. 187-201. [Deutsche Zfassung].

5044. Kronika Slovenska. Zv. 2. (Chronik der Slowakei). Ed. Dušan KOVÁČ. Bratislava, Fortuna Print, 99, 608 p.

5045. LENGYELOVÁ (Tünde). Hospodárske pomery v zemepanských mestách na Slovensku v 16.–17. storočí. (Die Wirtschaftlichen verhältnisse in den Marktflecken der Slowakei im 16.–17. Jahrhundert). *Historický časopis*, 99, 47, 3, p. 404-419. [Deutsche Zfassung].

5046. LIPTÁK (Ľubomír). Storočie dlhšie ako sto rokov. O dejinách a historiografii. (Le siècle plus long que cent ans. Sur l'histoire et l'historiographie.) Ed. Ivan KAMENEC. Bratislava, Kalligram, 99, 353 p.

5047. LONDÁK (Miroslav). Otázky industrializácie Slovenska (1945–1960). (Die Fragen der Industrialisierung der Slowakei, 1945–1960). Bratislava, Veda vydavateľstvo Slovenskej akadémie vied 99, 149 p.

5048. MICHÁLEK (Slavomír). Rada slobodného Československa 1948–1960. (Der Rat der freien Tschechoslowakei 1948–1960). *Historický časopis*, 99, 47, 3, p. 432-446. [Deutsche Zfassung].

5049. NURMI (Ismo). Slovakia. A Playground for nationalism and national identity. Manifestations of the national identity of the Slovaks 1918–1920. Helsinki, SHS, 99, 202 p. (Bibliotheca historica, 42). (maps).

5050. PAVLENKO (Mykola). Politika Československa k internovaným ukrajinským vojakom v rokoch 1919–1923. (Die Politik der Tschechoslowakei zu den internierten ukrainischen Soldaten in den Jahren 1919–

1923). *Historický časopis*, 99, 47, 1, p. 56-68. [Deutsche Zfassung]

5051. PEŠEK (Jan), BARNOVSKÝ (Michal). Pod kuratelou moci. Cirkvi na Slovensku v rokoch 1953–1970. (Under the power's custody. Churches in Slovakia in the years 1953–1970). Bratislava, Veda, 99, 292 p. [Eng. Summary].

5052. PEŠEK (Jan). Slovenská evanjelická cirkev augsburského vyznania pod «dohľadom» štátu (1953–1970). (Die slowakische evangelische Kirche augsburger Glaubens unter der Aufsicht des Staates, 1953–1970). *Historický časopis*, 99, 47, 4, p. 635-653. [Deutsche Zfassung]. – IDEM. Štát a rímskokatolícka cirkev na Slovensku v období prvej krízy totalitného režimu (1953–1957). (Der Staat und die römisch-katholische Kirche in der Slowakei im Zeitabschnitt der ersten Krise des Totalitären Regimes, 1953–1957). *Historický časopis*, 99, 47, 1, p. 70-87. [Deutsche Zfassung].

5053. PODRIMAVSKÝ (Milan). Slovaks in the conditions of the Hungarian state at the beginning of the twentieth century. *Human affairs*, 99, 9, 1, p. 44-52.

5054. Priekopníci vedy a techniky na Slovensku. Diel 3. (Die Wegbereiter der Wissenschaft und der Technik in der Slowakei. Band 3.) Ed. Ján TIBENSKÝ, Ondrej PÖSS, Miroslav Tibor MOROVICS. Bratislava, Academic Electronic Press v spolupráci s Pro Historia 99, 417 p.

5055. Reprezentačný biografický lexikón Slovenska. Ed. Augustín MAŤOVČÍK, Pavol PARENIČKA, Margita ĎUROVČÍKOVÁ, Zdenko ĎURIŠKA. Martin, Matica slovenská, 99, 384 p.

5056. ŠUTAJ (Štefan). Občianske politické strany na Slovensku v rokoch 1944–1948. (Die bürgerliche politische Parteien in der Slowakei in Jahren 1944–1948). Bratislava, Veda vydavateľstvo Slovenskej akadémie vied, 99, 308 p. [Eng. Summary].

5057. ŠVORC (Peter). Prouhorské integračné snahy na území Slovenska na konci roku 1918. (Die proungarischen Integrationsbestrebungen in der Slowakei am Ende des Jahres 1918). *Historický časopis*, 99, 47, 1, p. 44-54. [Deutsche Zfassung].

Cf. n°s 7646, 7736, 7742

Slovenia

* 5058. ARNEŽ (Janez A.). Slovenski tisk v begunskih taboriščih v Avstriji: 1945–1949. (Slovene publications in Austrian refugee camps). Ljubljana, Studia Slovenica, 99, 350 p. (Studia Slovenica, 20).

* 5059. KURNJEK (Branko), MAUČEC (Marjan), MOZETIČ (Iztok). Dnevno časopisje o duhovniških procesih na Slovenskem 1945–1953. (Daily Newspapers on Slovene trials against priests between 1945 and 1953). Ljubljana, Inštitut za zgodovino Cerkve pri Teološki fakulteti, 99, 776 p. (Acta Ecclesiastica Sloveniae, 21).

** 5060. GRANDA (Stane). Prva odločitev Slovencev za Slovenijo: dokumenti z uvodno študijo in osnovnimi pojasnili. (First decision of Slovenes for Slovenia: documents with introduction and essential explanations). Ljubljana, Nova revija, 99, 592 p. (ill.). (Zbirka Korenine).

5061. KERNEL (Davor). Slovenska narodna zavest od zedinjene do samostojne Slovenije: (1848–1991). (Slovene national consciousness from united to independent Slovenia: 1848–1991). Pivka, Društvo za krajevno zgodovino in kulturo Lipa, 99, 39 p. (ill.).

5062. MIKOLA (Milko). Zaplembe premoženja v Sloveniji 1943–1952 (Property confiscations in Slovenia 1943–1952). Celje, Zgodovinski arhiv, 99, 304 p. (ill.). (Publikacije Zgodovinskega arhiva v Celju, Študije, 3).

5063. Množične smrti na Slovenskem: zbornik referatov. (Mass deaths in Slovenia: a collection of papers). Ur. Stane GRANDA, Barbara ŠATEJ. Ljubljana, Zveza zgodovinskih društev Slovenije, 99, 320 p., (ill.).

5064. PENIČ (Lojze), ŽNIDARIČ (Marjan), ŠVAJNCER (Janez J.). Severovzhodna Slovenija v bojih za svobodo. (Northeastern Slovenia in the fight for freedom). Ljubljana, Glavni odbor ZZB NOB Slovenije, Komisija za informativno, propagandno in promocijsko dejavnost, 99, 67 p. (ill.).

5065. Preteklost sodobnosti: izbrana poglavja slovenske novejše zgodovine. (The past of the present: selected chapters of more recent Slovene history). Ur. Zdenko ČEPIČ. Pijava Gorica, Aristoteles Žlahtič v Ljubljana, Inštitut za novejšo zgodovino, 99, 198 p. (ill.).

5066. TROHA (Nevenka). Komu Trst: Slovenci in Italijani med dvema državama. (Whose will Trieste be: Slovenes and Italians between two States). Ljubljana, Modrijan, 99, 327 p. (ill.).

Somalia

5067. TRIPODI (Paolo). Back to the Horn: Italian administration and Somalia's troubled independence. *International journal of African historical studies*, 99, 32, 2, p. 359-380. – IDEM. The colonial legacy in Somalia: Rome and Mogadishu from colonial administration to operation Restore Hope. London, Macmillan Press, 99, XIV-219 p.

South Africa

5068. BARBER (James). South Africa in the twentieth century: a political history. In search of a nation state. Oxford, Blackwell Publishers, 99, XI-332 p. (History of the contemporary world).

5069. GRUNDLINGH (Albert). The king's afrikaners? Enlistment and ethnic identity in the Union of South Africa's defence force during the Second World War, 1939–1945. *Journal of African history*, 99, 40, 3, p. 351-365.

5070. HALISI (C. R. D.). Black political thought in the making of South African democracy. Bloomington, Indiana U. P., 99, XXI-198 p.

5071. NASSON (Bill). The South African War 1899–1902. New York, Oxford U. P. a. London, Arnold, 99, XVI-304 p. (Modern wars).

5072. STIFF (Peter). The silent war: South African Recce operations 1969–1994. Alberton, Galago Publishing Ltd., 99, 608 p. (ill., maps).

5073. ZACARIAS (Agostino). Security and the state in Southern Africa. London, Tauris, Academic Studies, 99, XX-275 p.

Spain

5074. ALEXANDER (Robert Jackson). The anarchists in the Spanish Civil War. London, Janus, 99, 2 vol., [s. p.].

5075. BAENA DEL ALCÁZAR (Mariano). Elites y conjuntos de poder en España (1939–1992): un estudio cuantitativo sobre parlamento, gobierno y administración y gran empresa. Madrid, Tecnos, 99, 756 p. (Colección Semilla y surco. Serie de Ciencia política).

5076. BATALLA I GALIMANY (Ramon). Els casinos republicans: política, cultura i esbarjo: El Casino de Rubí, 1884-1939. Barcelona, Publicacions de l'Abadia de Montserrat, Ajuntament de Rubi, 99, 316 p. (Biblioteca Serra d'or, 225).

5077. BOLAÑOS MEJÍAS (Carmen). El reinado de Amadeo de Saboya y la monarquía constitucional. Madrid, Universidad Nacional de Educacion a Distancia, 99, 341 p. (Varia).

5078. CAZORLA-SÁNCHEZ (Antonio). Dictatorship from below: local politics in the making of the Francoist state, 1937–1948. *Journal of modern history*. 99, 71, 4, p. 882-901.

5079. CHUECA INTXUSTA (Josu). El nacionalismo Vasco en Navarra (1931–1936). Bilbao, Universidad del Pais Vasco, Servicio Editorial, 99, 440 p. (maps). (Historia contemporánea, 18).

5080. CLEMENTE (José Carlos). Seis estudios sobre el Carlismo. Madrid, Huerga & Fierro Editores, 99, 172 p. (ill.). (Ensayo, 24).

5081. CORDERO OLIVERO (Immaculada), LEMUS LOPEZ (Encarnación). La malla de cristal: actividad política y vida de las comunistas andaluzas en la clandestinidad de los años Cuarenta. *Spagna contemporanea*, 99, 8, 16, p. 101-120.

5082. Crisis española (La) de fin de siglo y la generación del 98: actas del Simposio Internacional, Barcelona, noviembre de 1998. Ed. por Antonio VILANOVA y Adolfo SOTELO VÁZQUEZ. Barcelona, Universitat de Barcelona, 99, 397 p.

5083. DEL MAR POZO (Andres M.), BRASTER (J. F.). The rebirth of the 'Spanish Race': the state, nationalism, and education in Spain, 1875–1931. *European history quarterly*, 99, 29, 1, p. 75-107.

5084. ELORZA (Antonio), BIZCARRONDO (Marta). Queridos camaradas: la Internacional Comunista y España, 1919–1939. Barcelona, Planeta, 99, 532 p. (ill., facsims., ports). (La España plural).

5085. España, nación de naciones? I Jornades Jaume Vicens Vives. Organizadas conjuntamente por la Asociación de Historia Contemporánea y la Universitat de Girona. Ed. por Anna M. GARCIA ROVIRA. Madrid, Marcial Pons y Asociacion de Historia Contemporanea, 99, 206 p. (ill.). (Ayer, 35).

5086. ESPINO LÓPEZ (Antonio). Cataluña durante el reinado de Carlos II: política y guerra en la frontera catalana, 1679–1697. Bellaterra, Universitat Autonoma de Barcelona, 99, 417 p. (Manuscrits, 5 Spanish).

5087. Felipe II y el Mediterráneo. Congreso Internacional, Barcelona, 23 a 27 de noviembre de 1998. Vol. 1. Los recursos humanos y materiales. Vol. 2. Los grupos sociales. Vol. 3-4. La monarquía y los reinos. Coor. Ernest BELENGUER CEBRIÀ. Madrid, Sociedad Estatal para la Conmemoración de los Centenarios de Felipe II y Carlos V, 99, 4 vol., [s. p.]. (ill., maps).

5088. Franquismo (El): visiones y balances. Ed. por Roque MORENO FONSERET y Francisco SEVILLANO CALERO. Alicante, Universidad de Alicante, 99, 368 p. (maps). (Publicaciones de la Universidad de Alicante).

5089. GARCÍA (Hernán David). Aristocracia y señorío en la España de Felipe II: la casa de Arcos. Granada, Universidad de Granada, Ayuntamiento de San Fernando, Ayuntamiento de Marchena, 99, 317 p. (ill.). (Biblioteca Chronica nova de estudios históricos, 62).

5090. GILMOUR (John). Life under and after Franco: the contrasting fortunes of the right and extreme right in Spain since the Civil war. Bristol, Department of Hispanic, Portuguese and Latin American Studies, University of Bristol, 99, 21 p. (Occasional papers series, 31).

5091. GÓMEZ URDÁNEZ (Gracia). Salustiano de Olózaga: élites políticas en el liberalismo español (1805–1843). Prólogo de Juan-Sisinio PÉREZ GARZÓN. Logrono, Universidad de La Rioja, 99, 276 p. (ill.). (Biblioteca de investigación, 26).

5092. GONZÁLEZ CALLEJA (Eduardo). El Máuser y el sufragio: orden público, subversión y violencia política en la crisis de la Restauración (1917–1931). Madrid, Consejo Superior de Investigaciones Cientificas, 99, 719 p. (ill.). (Biblioteca de historia, 37).

5093. GOODMAN (D.). Armadas in an age of scarce resources: struggling to maintain the fleet in seventeenth-century Spain. *Journal of European economic history*, 99, 28, 1, p. 49-76.

5094. HEROLD-SCHMIDT (Hedwig). Gesundheit und Parlamentarismus in Spanien: die Politik der Cortes und die öffentliche Gesundheitsfürsorge in der Restaurationszeit (1876–1923). Husum, Matthiesen Verlag, 99, 640 p. (ill.). (Historische Studien, 458).

5095. HOPKIN (Jonathan). Party formation and democratic transition in Spain: the creation and collapse of the Union of the Democratic Centre. Basingstoke, Macmillan, 99, XI-289 p.

5096. LARIO (Ángeles). El Rey, piloto sin brújula: la Corona y el sistema político de la Restauración (1875–1902). Prólogo de Javier TUSELL. Madrid, Biblioteca Nueva, Universidad Nacional de Educación a Distancia, 99, 540 p. (ill., ports). (Colección Historia Biblioteca Nueva).

5097. LUIS (J. P.). La croissance ambiguë du Léviathan dans l'Europe du XIXe siècle: l'exemple de la rationalisation de l'Etat espagnol. Revue historique, 99, 123, 611, p. 483-506.

5098. MACKAY (Ruth). The limits of royal authority: resistance and obedience in seventeenth-century Castile. Cambridge a. New York, Cambridge U. P., 99, XII-193 p. (Cambridge studies in early modern history).

5099. MALCOLM (Alistair). Don Luis de Haro and the political elite of the Spanish monarchy in the mid-seventeenth century. Oxford, [s. n.], 99, VIII-308 p. [Thesis (D.Phil.) – University of Oxford, Faculty of Modern History].

5100. MALUQUER DE MOTES (Jordi). España en la crisis de 1898: de la gran depresión a la modernización económica del siglo XX. Barcelona, Peninsula, 99, 233 p. (Historia, ciencia, sociedad, 287).

5101. MANENT (Albert). De 1936 a 1975: estudis sobre la guerra civil i el franquisme. Barcelona, Publicacions de l'Abadia de Montserrat, 99, 214 p. (Biblioteca Serra d'Or, 220).

5102. MARTÍ GILABERT (Francisco). Amadeo de Saboya y la política religiosa. Pamplona, EUNSA, Ediciones Universidad de Navarra, 99, 154 p. (Colección Historia de la Iglesia, 31).

5103. MILHOU (Alain). Pouvoir royal et absolutisme dans l'Espagne du XVIe siècle. Toulouse, Presses Universitaire du Mirail, 99, 137 p. (Anejos de Criticón, 13).

5104. MOA (Pío). Los orígenes de la guerra civil española. Madrid, Encuentro Ediciones, 99, 447 p. (Ensayos. Historia).

5105. NÚÑEZ SEIXAS (Xosé M.). Los nacionalismos en la España contemporánea (siglos XIX y XX). Barcelona, Hipotesi, 99, 176 p. (Historia contemporánea).

5106. PAYNE (Stanley G.). Fascism in Spain, 1923–1977. Madison, University of Wisconsin Press, 99, XII-601 p. (ill.).

5107. Polémica (Una) y una generación, razón histórica de 1898: actas del Congreso "1898, Pensamiento Político, Jurídico y Filosófico: Balance de un Centenario", León, 10–13 de noviembre de 1998. Coor. por Salvador RUS RUFINO y Javier ZAMORA BONILLA. León, Universidad de León, 99, 399 p.

5108. PONCE ALBERCA (Julio). Política, instituciones y provincias: la Diputación de Sevilla durante la dictadura de Primo de Rivera y la II^a República, 1923–1936. Sevilla, Diputación de Sevilla, 99, 783 p. (ill.). (Publicaciones de la Excma. Diputación Provincial de Sevilla. Sección Historia, 51).

5109. PRESTON (Paul). Las tres Españas del 36. Barcelona, Plaza & Janes, 99, 509 p. (ill.). (Historia viva).

5110. Primer franquismo (El) (1936–1959). Ed. por Glicerio SÁNCHEZ RECIO. Madrid, Marcial Pons, 99, 218 p. (Ayer, 33).

5111. PUIGSECH FARRÀS (Josep). Las relaciones entre la internacional comunista y el PSUC durante el conflicto de 1936–1939. Spagna contemporanea, 99, 8, 15, p. 53-68.

5112. REDONDO (Gonzalo). Política, cultura y sociedad en la España de Franco, 1939–1975. T. 1. La configuración del Estado español, nacional y católico (1939–1947). Barañáin, EUNSA, 99, 1143 p.

5113. RICHARDS (M.). Falange, autarky and crisis: the Barcelona general strike of 1951. European history quarterly, 99, 29, 4, p. 543-585.

5114. RODRÍGUEZ RANZ (José Antonio), DE PABLO (Santiago), MEES (Ludger). El péndulo patriótico: historia del Partido Nacionalista Vasco. Vol. 1. 1895–1936. Vol. 2. 1936–1979. Barcelona, Crítica, 99, 2 vol., [s. p.]. (ill). (Contrastes).

5115. ROMERO SALVADÓ (Francisco J.). Twentieth-century Spain: politics and society in Spain, 1898–1998. Houndmills, Macmillan, 99, XVIII-219 p. (European history in perspective).

5116. STORM (Eric). Het perspectief van de vooruitgang: denken over politiek in het Spaanse fin de siècle 1890–1914: proefschrift /te verdedigen ... door. Baarn, Agora, 99, 480 p. (ill).

5117. STORRS (C.). Disaster at Darien (1698–1900)? The persistence of Spanish Imperial power on the eve of the demise of the Spanish Habsburgs. European history quarterly, 99, 29, 1, p. 5-38.

5118. THOMÀS (Joan Maria). Lo que fue la Falange. La Falange y los falangistas de José Antonio, Hedilla y la Unificación. Franco y el fin de la Falange Española de las JONS. Barcelona, Plaza & Janes, 99, 366 p. (Así fue, 31).

5119. VILANOVA I VILA-ABADAL (Francesc). Repressió política i coacció econòmica: les responsabilitats polítiques de republicans i conservadors catalans a la postguerra (1939-1942). Pròleg d'Angel GARCÍA I FONTANET. Barcelona, Publicacions de l'Abadia de Montserrat, 99, XIV-515 p. (Biblioteca Abat Oliba, 216).

Cf. n°s 4588, 4672, 5605

Sri Lanka

5120. AMARASINGHE (Y. Ranjith). Revolutionary idealism and parliamentary politics: a study of Trotskyism in Sri Lanka. Colombo, Social Scientists Association, 99, IV-337 p.

5121. Creating Peace in Sri Lanka: Civil War and Reconciliation. Ed. by Robert I. ROTBERG. Washington, Brookings Institution, World Peace Foundation a. Belfer Center for Svience and International Affairs, 99, IX-218 p.

5122. GUNASINGAM (Murugar). Sri Lankan Tamil nationalism: a study of its origins. Sydney, MV Publications, 99, XII-246 p.

5123. History and politics: millenial perspectives; essays in honour of Kingsley de Silva. Ed. by Gerald PEIRIS and S.W.R. de A. SAMARASINGHE. Colombo, Law and Society Trust, 99, XXXVI-542 p.

5124. KRISHNA (Sankaran). Postcolonial insecurities: India, Sri Lanka and the question of nationhood. Minneapolis a. London, University of Minnesota Press, 99, XXXVIII-316 p. (Borderlines, 15).

5125. WILSON (Alfred Jeyaratnam). Sri Lankan Tamil nationalism: its origins and development in the nineteenth and twentieth centuries. Vancouver, UBC Press, 99, [s. p.].

Sweden

5126. CANTERA CARLAMAGNO (Marcos). Sverige och spanska inbördeskriget. (La Suède et la Guerre d'Espagne). Lund, Historiska Media, 99, 151 p.

5127. DAHL (Ann-Sofie). Svenskarna och NATO. (Les Suédois et l'OTAN). Stockholm, Timbro, 99, 283 p.

5128. EKENGREN (Ann Marie). Av hänsyn till folkrätten? Svensk erkännande politik 1945–1995. (Par égard pour le droit international? La politique suédoise de reconnaissance de 1945 à 1995). Stockholm, Nerenius & Santérus, 99, 341 p. (Göteborg studies of politics, 63).

5129. ERICSON (Lars). Medborgare i vapen: värnplikten i Sverige under två sekel. (Citoyens en armes: deux siècles de service militaire en Suède). Lund, Historiska Media, 99, 312 p. (ill.).

5130. FRICK (Lennart W.), ROSANDER (Lars). Det vakande ögat. (L'Œil vigilant [Histoire des services secrets suédois]). Lund, Historiska Media, 99, 317 p. (ill.).

5131. HÖJELID (Stefan). Politiskt beslutsfattande och EMU: slå till eller vänta och se. (Décision politique et Union Monétaire européenne: se décider vite ou attendre et voir). Lund, Studentlitteratur, 99, 322 p.

5132. HOLMBERG (Åke). Göteborgs handels- och sjöfartstidnings syn på kolonialismens sammanbrott i Asien och Afrika 1946–1965: ett bidrag till den svenska omvärldsbildens historia. (La Vision de l'effondrement du colonialisme en Asie et en Afrique dans le journal Göteborgs handels- och sjöfartstidning: contribution à l'histoire de la perception du monde extérieur en Suède). Göteborg, Kungliga Vetenskaps- och Vitterhetssamhället, 99, 117 p. (ill.). (Acta Regia Societatis scientiarum et litterarum Gothoburgiensis, Humaniora). (rés. anglais).

5133. Hotade landet (Det) och det skyddade. Sverige och Finland från 1500-talet till våra dagar. (Le Pays menacé et le pays protégé: la Suède et la Finlande du 16e siècle à nos jours). Red. par Tapani SUOMINEN et Anders BJÖRNSSON. Stockholm, Atlantis, 99, 250 p.

5134. HÜBINETTE (Staffan). Nykterhetsrörelsen, nazismen och demokratin: nykterhetsrörelsen och kampen för demokratin 1930–1945. (Le mouvement de tempérance, le nazisme et la démocratie: le mouvement de tempérance et le combat pour la démocratie entre 1930 et 1945). Stockholm, Sober, 99, 237 p. (ill.).

5135. LINDKVIST (Anna). Jorden åt folket. Folket åt jorden. Nationalförening mot emigrationen 1908–1925. (La terre au peuple. Des gens pour la terre. L'association nationale suédoise contre l'émigration, 1908–1925). Umeå, Institut för historiska studier, Umeå univ., 99, 44 p. (diagr.).

5136. SNICKARE (Mårten). Enväldets riter: kungliga fester och ceremonier i gestaltning av Nicodemus Tessin den yngre. (Rites de la monarchie absolue: fêtes et cérémonies d'après les représentations de Nicodème Tessin le Jeune). Stockholm, Raster, 99, 254 p. (ill.). [English summary].

5137. WALLERFELT (Bengt). Si vis pacem, para bellum. Svensk säkerhetspolitik och krigsplanering 1945–1975. (La politique suédoise de sécurité et la planification militaire entre 1945 et 1975). Stockholm, Probus, 99, 214 p. (ill.).

Cf. n° 4892

Switzerland

5138. Conservatisme, réformisme et contestation: aux origines de la Révolution neuchâteloise de 1848. Textes réunis et publiés par Philippe HENRY. Neuchâtel, Institut d'histoire, Université de Neuchâtel, 99, 209 p. (ill.). (Cahiers de l'Institut d'histoire, 6).

5139. DROZ (Laurent). L'antisémitisme au quotidien: l'emploi d'un tampon «J» dans les administrations fédérales et vaudoises entre 1936 et 1940. *Schweizerische Zeitschrift für Geschichte*, 99, 49, 3, p. 353-370.

5140. DU BOIS (Pierre). Un communiste suisse à Shanghai en 1932: Jean Vincent et l'affaire Ruegg. *In*: Socialisme, cultures, histoire: itinéraires et représentations: mélanges offerts à Miklós Molnár [Cf. n° 5701], p. 119-134.

5141. HETTLING (Manfred). Politische Bürgerlichkeit: der Bürger zwischen Individualität und Vergesellschaftung in Deutschland und der Schweiz von 1860 bis 1918. Göttingen, Vandenhoeck und Ruprecht, 99, XI-424 p. (Bürgertum, 13).

5142. Innerschweiz (Die) im frühen Bundesstaat (1848–1874): gesellschaftsgeschichtliche Annäherungen. Hrsg. v. Alexandra BINNENKADE und Aram MATTIOLI. Zürich, Chronos, 99, 248 p. (ill.) (Clio Lucernensis, 6).

5143. KOLLER (Guido). Der J-Stempel auf schweizerischen Formularen. *Schweizerische Zeitschrift für Geschichte*, 99, 49, 3, p. 371

5144. KÖNIG (M.). H.-U. Jost, Politik und Wirtschaft im Krieg. Die Schweiz 1938-1948. *Schweizerische Zeitschrift für Geschichte*, 99, 49, 2, p. 264-267. – KREIS (Georg). H.-U. Jost, Politik und Wirtschaft im Krieg. Die Schweiz 1938-1948. *Schweizerische Zeitschrift für Geschichte*, 99, 49, 2, p. 268-272.

5145. PALLUEL-GUILLARD (André). L'aigle et la croix: Genève et la Savoie, 1798-1815. Yens sur Morges, Cabédita, 99, 662 p. (Collection Archives vivantes).

5146. SCHECK (Raffael). Swiss funding for the early Nazi movement: motivation, context, and continuities. *Journal of modern history*. 99, 71, 4, p. 793-813.

5147. SCHMIDLIN (Antonia). Eine andere Schweiz: Helferinnen, Kriegskinder und Humanitäre Politik 1933–1942. Zürich, Chronos, 99, 432 p. (ill., maps).

5148. SPIRA (Henry). L'attitude de la Suisse envers les réfugiés juifs 1939-1945. [Zeugnisse / Témoignages]. *Schweizerische Zeitschrift für Geschichte*, 99, 49, 2, p. 273-279.

5149. Switzerland and war. Ed. by Joy CHARNLEY and Malcolm PENDER. Bern a. New York, P. Lang, 99, 128 p. (Occasional papers in Swiss studies, 2).

5150. ZIMMER (Oliver). Forging the Swiss nation, 1760-1939: popular memory, patriotic invention, and competing conceptions of nationhood. London, [s. n.], 99, 357 p. [Thesis (Ph. D.) – London, LSE, 1999].

Cf. n[os] 4867, 5818

Syria

5151. FREITAG (Ulrike). In search of 'historical correctness': the Ba'th Party in Syria. *Middle Eastern studies*, 99, 35, 1, p. 1-16.

5152. Modern Syria: from Ottoman rule to pivotal role in the Middle East. Ed. by Moshe MA'OZ, Joseph GINAT, and Onn WINCKLER. Brighton Sussex Academic Press, 99, XVIII-307 p. (ill.).

5153. QUILLIAM (Neil). Syria and the new world order. Reading, Ithaca Press, 99, X-292 p. (ill.). (Durham Middle East monographs series).

Tajikistan

5154. NOURZHANOV (Kirill). Tajikistan: the history of an ethnic state. London, C. Hurst, 99, 256 p.

Tanzania

5155. LUDWIG (Frieder). Church and State in Tanzania: aspects of changing relationships, 1961–1994. Leiden a. Boston, Brill, 99, XIV-285 p. (Studies of religion in Africa, 21).

Thailand

5156. GREENE (Stephen Lyon Wakeman). Absolute dreams: Thai government under Rama VI, 1910–1925. Foreword by David WYATT. Bangkok, White Lotus Press, 99, XVI-224 p.

Trinidad and Tobago

5157. REGIS (Louis). The political calypso: true opposition in Trinidad and Tobago, 1962–1987. Gainesville, University Press of Florida a. Barbados, Press University of the West Indies, 99, XIII-277 p.

Turkey

* 5158. LACINER (Sedat). A short English bibliography on Turkey: history, politics, international relations and political economy books, articles, chapters, on Turkey in English language. London, International Academics Association, 99, 123 p.

** 5159. ATIF (Mehmed). Kaşgar tarihi: bâis-i hayret ahvâl-i garibesi. (Histoire de Kachgar). Edited by İsmail AKA, Vehbi GÜNAY et Cahit TELLI. Kırıkkale, Eysi Kitap ve Yayın, 99, 381 p.

** 5160. GÜZEL (Abdurrahman). Kaygusuz Abdal (Alâeddin Gaybî) menâkıbnâmesi. (Livre des vertus de Kaygusuz Abdal). Ankara, Türk Tarih Kurumu, 99, XII-181 p.

** 5161. GÜZEL (Abdurrahman). Abdal Mûsâ velâyetnâmesi. (Le Livre de sainteté d'Abdal Musa). Ankara, Türk Tarih Kurumu, 99, XV-222 p.

** 5162. KILIÇ (Davut). Osmanlı idaresindeki Ermeniler arasında dini ve siyasi mücadeleler. (Les disputes religieuses et politiques entre les Arméniens sous l'administration ottomane). Elazığ, 99, 307 p.

** 5163. MUSTAFA HATTI EFENDI. Viyana sefaretnamesi. (Livre de l'ambassade de Vienne). Edited by Ali İbrahim SAVAŞ. Ankara, Türk Tarih Kurumu, 99, 86 p.

** 5164. Osmanlı ormancılığı ile ilgili belgeler – I. Documents on Ottoman forestry - I. Edited by Eftal ŞÜKRÜ BATMAZ, Bekir KOÇ, İsmail ÇETINKAYA. Ankara, Orman Bakanlığı, 99, 241 p.

5165. CARMONT (Pascal). Les Amiras: seigneurs de l'Arménie ottomane. Préface de Bernard DORIN. Paris, Salvator, 99, 190 p.

5166. GÜNAY (Ünver). Toplumsal değişme, tasavvuf, tarikatlar ve Türkiye. (Changement social, mysticisme musulman, ordres religieux et Turquie). Kayseri, Erciyes Üniversitesi, 99, 324 p.

5167. İÇDUYGU (Ahmet), ÇOLAK (Yilmaz), SOYARIK (Nalan). What is the matter with citizenship? A Turkish debate. *In*: Seventy-five years of the Turkish Republic [Cf. n° 5175], p. 187-208

2. HISTORY BY COUNTRIES

5168. KARABELIAS (Gerassimos). The evolution of civil-military relations in post-war Turkey, 1980–1995. In: Seventy-five years of the Turkish Republic [Cf. n° 5175], p. 152-186.

5169. KURŞUN (Zekeriya). Basra Körfezi'nde Bir Arap Aşireti: Acman Urbanı (1820–1913). (Un Tribu arab au Golfe de Basra: Acman Urbanı). *Belleten*, 99, 53, 236, p. 123-164.

5170. MANGO (Andrew). Atatürk and the Kurds. In: Seventy-five years of the Turkish Republic [Cf. n° 5175], p. 1-25.

5171. MURPHEY (Rhoads). Ottoman Warfare, 1500–1700. New Brunswick, Rutgers U. P., 99, XXII-278 p.

5172. OCAK (Ahmet Yaşar). Türkler, Türkiye ve İslam: yaklaşım, yöntem ve yorum denemeleri. (Turcs, Turquie et Islam: Essais de rapprochement, de méthodologie et d'interprétation). İstanbul, İletişim, 99, 190 p.

5173. OKUMUŞ (Ejder). Türkiye'nin laikleşme serüveninde tanzimat (Tanzimat dans le processus de laicisation de la Turquie). İstanbul, İnsan, 99, 576 p.

5174. PIREH BABI (Loghman). Nationalism and social classes. The case of Kurdish nationalism in Turkey. Helsinki, L. Pireh Babi, 99, 192 p.

5175. Seventy-five years of the Turkish Republic. Ed. by Sylvia KEDOURIE. *Middle Eastern studies*, 99, 35, 4, p. 1-234. [Cf. n^{os} <choice> 5167, 5168, 5170, 5177, 5178, 7218, 7890, 8032.]

5176. TURFAN (Mehmed Naim). Rise of the young Turks: politics, the military and Ottoman collapse. London, I. B. Tauris, 99, XIX-490 p.

5177. YILMAZ (Suhnaz). An Ottoman warrior abroad: Enver Pasa as an expatriate. In: Seventy-five years of the Turkish Republic [Cf. n° 5175], p. 40-69.

5178. ZÜRCHER (Erik-Jan). Kosovo revisited: Sultan Resad's Macedonian journey of June 1911. In: Seventy-five years of the Turkish Republic [Cf. n° 5175], p. 26-39.

Cf. n°s 4806, 7287, 8073

Uganda

5179. KAHLCKE (Jan). Politische Kommunikation in Uganda. Hamburg, Institut fur Afrika-Kunde, 99, 233 p. (ill., map). (Arbeiten aus dem Institut für Afrika-Kunde, 104).

Ukraine

5180. ABRAMSON (Henry). A prayer for the government: Ukrainians and Jews in revolutionary times, 1917–1920. Cambridge, Harvard Ukrainian Research Institute, 99, XIX-255 p.

5181. NAHAYLO (Bohdan). The Ukrainian resurgence. Buffalo, University of Toronto Press, 99, XIX-608 p.

Cf. n° 5293

United States of America (USA)

** 5182. Major problems in American military history: documents and essays. Ed. by John Whiteclay CHAMBERS II and G. Kurt PIEHLER. Boston, Houghton Mifflin, 99, XX-488 p. (Major problems in American history series).

** 5183. Papers (The) of Benjamin Franklin. Vol. 35. May 1 through October 31, 1781. Ed. by Barbara B. OBERG; Ellen R. COHN and Jonathan R. DULL, senior associate editors; Karen DUVAL, associate editor; Leslie J. LINDENAUER and Kate M. OHNO, assistant editors; Claude A. LOPEZ, consulting editor. New Haven a. London, Yale U. P., LXVI-742 p. (ill.).

5184. ADAMS (Willi Paul). Die USA vor 1900. München, Oldenbourg, 99, XIV-294 p. (Oldenbourg Grundriß der Geschichte, 28).

5185. American party battle (The): election campaign pamphlets, 1828–1876. Vol. 1: 1828–1854. Edited with an introduction by Joel H. SILBEY. Cambridge a. London, Harvard U. P., 99, XXIV-284 p.

5186. BILLINGSLEY (William J.). Communists on Campus: race, politics, and the public university in Sixties North Carolina. Athens, University of Georgia Press, 99, XVI-308 p.

5187. BRADLEY (Patricia). Slavery, propaganda, and the American Revolution. Jackson, University Press of Mississipi, 99, XXIV-184 p.

5188. BUSH (Rod). We are not what we seem: Black Nationalism and class struggle in the American century. New York, New York U. P., 99, XIII-315 p.

5189. Capitalismo (Il), il west e la storia ambientale. Conversazione con Donald WORSTER. *Meridiana*, 99, 36, p. 179-198.

5190. COGLIANO (Francis D.). Revolutionary America, 1763–1815: a political history. London, Routledge, 99, X-275 p.

5191. COWGER (Thomas W.). The National Congress of American Indians: the founding years. Lincoln, University of Nebraska Press, 99, XIII-217 p.

5192. FINNEGAN (Margaret). Selling suffrage: consumer culture and votes for women. New York, Columbia U. P., 99, XII-222 p. (Popular cultures, everyday lives).

5193. GARBUZOV (V.N.). «Rejganovskaja revolutsija»: Teorija i praktika amerikanskogo konservatizma, 1981–1988. ('The Reagan Revolution': theory and practice of American conservatism, 1981–1988). Ros. gos. ped. un-t im. A.I. Gertsena; Pskovskij gos.ped. in-t im. S.M. Kirova. Sankt-Peterburg a. Pskov, [s. n.], 99, 554 p. (ill., bibl.). [Eng. summary]

5194. GARSON (Robert A.), KIDD (Stuart S.). The Roosevelt years: new perspective on American history, 1933–1945. Edinburgh, Edinburgh U.P., 99, VIII-207 p.

5195. GARY (Brett). The nervous liberals: propaganda anxieties from World War I to the Cold War. New York, Columbia U. P., 99, XII-323 p. (Columbia studies in contemporary American history).

5196. GRASSO (Christopher). A speaking aristocracy: transforming public discourse in eighteenth-century Connecticut. Chapel Hill, University of North Carolina Press, in association with the Omohundro Institute of Early American History and Culture, Williamsburg, 99, VIII-511 p.

5197. GROCE (W. Todd). Mountain rebels: East Tennessee Confederates and the Civil War, 1860-1870. Knoxville, University of Tennessee Press, 99, XVIII-218 p.

5198. Guerrillas, Unionists, and violence on the Confederate home front. Ed. by Daniel E. SUTHERLAND. Fayetteville, University of Arkansas Press, 99, VIII-250 p.

5199. HIMMEL (Kelly F.). The conquest of the Karankawas and the Tonkawas, 1821-1859. College Station, Texas A&M U. P., 99, XVI-192 p. (Elma Dill Russel Spencer series in the west and southwest, 20).

5200. HOLT (Michael F.). The rise and fall of the American Whig Party: Jacksonian politics and the onset of the Civil War. New York, Oxford U. P., 99, XVIII-1248 p.

5201. HUNT (Andrew E.). The turning: a history of Vietnam veterans against the War. New York, New York U. P., 99, XI-259 p.

5202. JEFFREYS-JONES (Rhodri). Peace now! American society and the ending of the Vietnam War. New Haven a. London, Yale U. P., 99, IX-808 p.

5203. JOHNSON (Robert). Washington, 20. Januar 1961: der amerikanische Traum. München, Dt. Taschenbuch-Verl., 99, 315 p.

5204. JONES (Howard). Abraham Lincoln and a new birth of freedom: the Union and Slavery in the diplomacy of the Civil War. Lincoln, University of Nebraska Press, 99, XII-236 p.

5205. KENNEDY (David). Freedom from fear: the American people in depression and War, 1929-1945. New York, Oxford U. P., 99, XVII-936 p. (Oxford history of the United States, 9).

5206. KING (Desmond S.) In the name of liberalism: illiberal social policy in the USA and Britain. Oxford a. New York, Oxford U. P., 99, XIII-340 p.

5207. KLATCH (Rebecca E.). A generation divided: the New Left, the New Right, and the 1960s. Berkeley a. Los Angeles, University of California Press, XIV-386 p.

5208. LEIBIGER (Stuart). Founding friendship: George Washington, James Madison, and the creation of the American Republic. Chalottesville, University Press of Virginia, 99, X-284 p.

5209. Liberal tradition (The) in American politics: reassessing the legacy of American liberalism. Ed. by David F. ERICSON and Louisa BERTCH GREEN. New York a. London, Routledge, 99, IX-269 p.

5210. MINTZ (Max M.). Seeds of Empire: the American Revolutionary conquest of the Iroquois. New York, New York U. P., 99, XI-231 p. (World of War).

5211. Native Americans and the Early Republic. Ed. by Frederick E. HOXIE, Ronald HOFFMAN and Peter J. ALBERT. Charlottesville, University Press of Virginia for the United States Capitol Historical ociety, 99, XI-370 p. (Perspectives on the American Revolution).

5212. NEELY (Mark E., Jr.). Southern Rights: political prisoners and the myth of Confederate Constitutionalism. Chalottesville, University Press of Virginia, 99, VII-212 p. (A nation divided: new studies in Civil War history).

5213. ODOM (William O.). After the trenches: the transformation of U.S. Army doctrine, 1918-1939. College Station, Texas A&M U. P., 99, 282 p. (Texas A&M University Military Series, 64).

5214. O'LEARY (Cecilia Elizabeth). To die for: the paradox of American patriotism. Princeton, Princeton U. P., 99, XIII-365 p.

5215. PEARLMAN (Michael D.). Warmaking and American democracy: the struggle over military strategy, 1700 to the present. Lawrence, University Press of Kansas, 99, IX-441 p. (Modern war studies).

5216. PHILLIPS (Kevin P.). The cousins' wars: religion, politics, and the triumph of Anglo-America. New York, Basic Books, 99, XXVIII-707 p. (maps).

5217. PURVIS SANSON (Jerry). Louisiana during World War II: politics and society, 1939-1945. Baton Rouge, Louisiana State U. P., 99, XII-323 p.

5218. REAGAN (Patrick D.). Designing a New America: the origins of New Deal Planning, 1890-1943. Amherst, University of Massachusetts Press, 99, XII-362 p. (Political development of the American nation: studies in politics and history).

5219. SIMONELLI (Frederick J.). American Fuehrer: George Lincoln Rockwell and the American Nazi Party. Urbana a. Chicago, University of Illinois Press, 99, XI-206 p.

5220. SKEEN (C. Edward). Citizen soldiers in the War of 1812. Lexington, University Press of Kentucky, 99, 229 p.

5221. STRONG (Douglas M.). Perfectionist politics: abolitionism and the religious tensions of American democracy. Syracuse, Syracuse U. P., 99, XIII-263 p. (Religion and politics).

5222. Taking stock: American government in the twentieth century. Ed. by Morton KELLER and R. Shep MELNICK. New York, Cambridge U. P. a. Washington, Woodrow Wilson Center Press, 99, X-330 p. (Woodrow Wilson Center Series).

5223. TATE (Michael L.). The Frontier Army in the settlement of the West. Norman, University of Oklahoma Press, 99, XX-454 p.

5224. WALLACE (Anthony F. C.). Jefferson and the Indians: the tragic fate of the first Americans. Cambridge, Harvard U. P., 99, IX-394 p.

5225. WALMSLEY (Andrew Stephen). Thomas Hutchinson and the origins of the American Revolution. New York, New York U. P., 99, XVII-207 p. (The American social experience series, 38).

Cf. n°s 1062, 4715, 5621, 5672, 5716, 5729, 5730, 5846, 7375, 7476, 7598, 7887

Uruguay

** 5226. HOOD (Thomas Samuel). El consul británico en Montevideo y la independencia del Uruguay: selección de los informes de Thomas Samuel Hood (1824–1829). Ed. por José Pedro BARRÁN, Ana FREGA y Mónica NICOLIELLO. Montevideo, Universidad de la República, Facultad de Humanidades y Ciencias de la Educación, Departamento de Historia del Uruguay, 99, 176 p.

5227. SCHRÖTER (Bernd). Die Entstehung einer Grenzregion: Wirtschaft, Gesellschaft und Politik im kolonialen Uruguay 1725–1811. Köln, Böhlau, 99, XXII-581 p. (Lateinamerikanische Forschungen, 28).

Venezuela

5228. BRAVO (Manuel J.). Militarismo y política en Venezuela, 1945–1958. Caracas, Fondo Editorial de la Universidad Pedagógica Experimental Libertador, 99, 300 p.

5229. BUXTON (Julia Dianne). The Venezuela party system 1988–1995 with reference to the rise and decline of Radical Cause. London, [s. n.], 99, 340 p. [Thesis (Ph. D.) – London, LSE, 1999].

5230. CAPRILES AYALA (Carlos). Vida y muerte de la democracia: López Contreras y Medina Angaria vs. Rómulo Betancourt y Pérez Jiménez. Caracas, Consorcio de Ediciones Capriles, 99, 276 p.

5231. ELLNER (Steve). Obstacles to the consolidation of the Venezuelan neighbourhood movement: national and local cleavages. *Journal of Latin American studies*, 99, 31, 1, p. 75-97.

5232. IBARRA (Daniel E.). Las articulaciones políticas de una revolución conservadora: el comportamiento político de la élite venezolana en la transición a la república. Mérida, FUNDARTE, Alcaldía de Caracas, 99, 133 p. (Colección Delta, 69).

5233. LANGUE (Frédérique). Histoire du Venezuela: de la conquête à nos jours. Paris, L'Harmattan, 99, 397 p.

5234. LÓPEZ (Frank). La fenomenología del poder en Venezuela: el Estado, la universidad y la industria: el nacimiento de la economía, la administración y las relaciones industriales en Venezuela. Valencia, Ediciones Universidad de Carabobo, 99, 227 p. (Colección Pensamiento universitario).

5235. LUQUE (Guillermo). Educación, estado y nación: una historia política de la educación oficial venezolana, 1928–1958. Caracas, Universidad Central de Venezuela, Consejo de Desarrollo Científico y Humanístico, 99, 464 p. (Colección Estudios).

Vietnam

5236. CATTON (Philip E.). Counter-insurgency and nation building: the strategic Hamlet programme in South Vietnam, 1961–1963. *International history review*, 99, 21, 4, p. 918-940.

5237. PRÔČKOVÁ (Florentína). Vietnam a krajiny juhovýchodnej Ázie v povojnovom období. (Vietnam und die Länder im südöstlichen Asien im Nachkriegszeitabschnitt). *Historický časopis*, 99, 47, 1, p. 88-104.

5238. SINGH (Sudhir Kumar). NLF and the Communist movement in Vietnam. New Delhi, National Book Organisation, 99, XII-208 p.

5239. TAYLOR (Sandra C.). Vietnamese women at war: fighting for Ho Chi Minh and the revolution. Lawrence, University Press of Kansas, 99, X-170 p. (Modern war studies).

5240. Transforming Asian socialism: China and Vietnam compared. Ed. by Anita CHAN, Benedict J. KERKVLIET and Jonathan UNGER. St Leonards, Allen & Unwin a. Canberra, Dept. of International Relations, RSPAS, ANU, 99, 240 p. (Studies in world affairs, 20).

Yugoslavia

** 5241. Former Yugoslavia through documents: from its dissolution to the peace settlement. Ed. by Snezana TRIFUNOVSKA. The Hague a. London, Martinus Nijhoff Publishers, 99, XLVII-1346 p.

5242. ARSEN'EV (Aleksej B.). U izluchiny Dunaja: Ocherk zhizni i dejatel'nosti russkikh v Novom Sadu. (Near the bend of Danube: life and activities of Russians in Novi Sad). M., Russkij put', 99, 254 p. (bibl.).

5243. Balkankrieg: die Zerstörung Jugoslawiens. Hrsg. v. Hannes HOFBAUER. Wien, Promedia, 99, 263 p. (map). (Brennpunkt Osteuropa).

5244. BATAKOVIĆ (Dušan). L'influence française sur la formation de la démocratie parlementaire en Serbie. *In*: France (La) et la Serbie du congrès de Berlin à la crise de juillet 1914 [Cf. n° 7500], p. 17-44.

5245. DIZDAREVIC (Raif). Od smrti Tita do smrti Jugoslavije. (Dalla morte di Tito alla morte della Jugoslavia). Izbor i komentari, Stefano BIANCHINI, Aziz HADZIHASANOVIC. Sarajevo, OKO, 99, 459 p. (Biblioteka Svjedok).

5246. Gender politics in the Western Balkans: women and society in Yugoslavia and the Yugoslav successor states. Ed. by Sabrina P. RAMET. University

Park, Pennsylvania State U. P., 99, 343 p. (Post-Communist cultural studies).

5247. GORDY (Eric D.). The culture of power in Serbia: nationalism and the destruction of alternatives. University Park, Pennsylvania State U. P., 99, 230 p. (ill.). (Post-Communist cultural studies series).

5248. JAKIR (Aleksandar). Dalmatien zwischen den Weltkriegen, Agrarische und urbane Lebenswelt und das Scheitern der jugoslawischen Integration. München, Oldenbourg, 99, 534 p. (Südosteuropäische Arbeiten, 104).

5249. JOVIC (Dejan). The breakdown of elite ideological consensus: the prelude to the disintegration of Yugoslavia (1974–1990). London, [s. n.], 99, 378 p. [Ph.D. thesis (London School of Economics and Political Science Department of Government) 1999].

5250. Jugoslovenska drzava 1918–1998: zbornik radova sa naucnog skupa. (Yugoslav state 1918–1998). Redakcioni odbor Vlado STRUGAR [et al.]; odgovorni urednik Đorđe O. PILJEVIC. Beograd, Institut za savremenu istoriju, 99, 902 p. (Posebna izdanja).

5251. LAKIC (Goran). Ogledi iz istorije Jugoslavije. Podgorica, Univerzitet Crne Gore, 99, 313 p.

5252. LALKOV (Milčo). Jugoslavija (1918–1992). Dramatičnijat put na edna državna ideja. (La Yougoslavie, 1918–1992. La voie dramatique d'une idée d'Etat). Sofija, «Daniela Ubenova», 99, 263 p.

5253. MEIER (Viktor). Yugoslavia: a history of its demise. London a. New York, Routledge, 99, XVII-279 p.

5254. MOON (Paul). Milosevic, Yugoslavia, and the Kosovo crisis: a concise history. Palmerston North, Campus Press, 99, 418 p.

5255. PERICA (Vjekoslav). Dva spomenika jedne ere. Političke konotacije izgradnje pravoslavne crkve i katoličke konkatedrale u Splitu 1971.–1991. (Memorials of an era: the politics of church rebuilding in the former Yugoslavia. The case of constructions of an Orthodox church and Catholic cathedral in Split during late communism and pre-war crisis, 1971–1991). Časopis za suvremenu povijest, 99, 31, 1, p. 93-126.

5256. PRIFTI (Peter R.). Confrontation in Kosovo: the Albanian-Serb struggle, 1969–1999. Boulder, East European Monographs a. Chichester, Wiley, 99, 300 p. (East European monographs, 537).

5257. THOMPSON (Mark). Forging war: the media in Serbia, Croatia, Bosnia and Hercegovina. Luton, University of Luton Press, 99, XVI-388 p.

Cf. n°s 1319, 3937, 4852

L

MODERN RELIGIOUS HISTORY

§ 1. General. 5258-5317. – § 2. Roman Catholicism (*a*. General; *b*. History of the Popes; *c*. Special studies; *d*. Religious orders; *e*. Missions). 5318-5453. – § 3. Orthodox Church. 5454-5460. – § 4. Protestantism. 5461-5526. – § 5. Non-Christian religions and sects. 5527-5557.

§ 1. General.

** 5258. BARTOLOMÉ DE LAS CASAS. Cristianismo y defensa del indio americano. Ed. por F. F. BUEY. Madrid, Libros de la Cataratta, 99, 155 p. (Colección clásicos del pensamento critico, 5).

** 5259. ERASMUS. De libero arbitrio diatribe sive collation; Hyperapistes. Ed. Charles TRINKAUS. Toronto, University of Toronto Press, 99, CVI-331 p.

** 5260. SCALIGER (Jules-César). Orationes duae contra Erasmum. Par Michel MAGNIEN. Genève, Droz, 99, 552 p.

5261. Abolitionism and American religion. Edited with introduction by John R. MAC KIVIGAN New York. London, Garland, 99 XVI-408 p.

5262. ADAMO (Pietro). La libertà dei santi: fallibilismo e tolleranza nella Rivoluzione inglese 1640–1649. Milano, Angeli, 99, 408 p.

5263. African American religious history: a documentary witness. Ed. by Milton C. SERNETT. Durham a. London, Duke U. P., 99, X-595 p.

5264. Amérique (L') du nord française dans les archives religieuses de Rome 1600–1922: guide de recherche. Sous la direction de Pierre HURTUBISE [et al.]. Québec, Editions de l'IQRC, 99, XI-202 p.

5265. ANDRÉS GALLEGO (José). Iglesia en la España contemporanea. Madrid, Encuentro, 1999, 2 vol., 141 p., 150 p.

5266. Atheismus im Mittelalter und in der Renaissance. Hrsg. v. Friedrich NIEWÖHNER und Olaf PLUTA.Wiesbaden, Harrassowitz, 99, VI-372 p.

5267. BALOGH (Margit), GERGELY (Jenö). Az egyházak "államosítása". (The «nationalisation» of the Churches). *Historia*, 99, 2, p. 7-11.

5268. BERG MURRE (H. L.). American board and the Eastern Churches: the «Nestorian Mission» (1844–1846). *Orientalia christiana*, 99, 65, p. 117-138.

5269. BOSL (Katharina). Die Sklavenbefreiung in Brasilien, eine soziale Frage für die Kirche? Die Katholische Kirche und das Ende der Sklaverei in der Kaffeeprovinz São Paulo, 1871–1888. Stuttgart, Heinz, 99, 366 p.

5270. BRIAN (Isabelle), LE GALL (Jean-Marie). La vie religieuse en France XVIe–XVIIIe siècle. Paris, Sedes, 99, 192 p.

5271. Cattolici, ebrei ed evangelici nella guerra: vita religiosa e società 1939–1945. A cura di Bartolo GARIGLIO e Riccardo MARCHIS. Milano, Franco Angeli, 99, 355 p.

5272. CENTINO (Angel M.). Relaciones entre el gobierno, la iglesia católica y los otros cultos (1989–1998). Buenos Aires, Editorial Dunken, 99, 107 p.

5273. COLLISON (Patrick). Religion Society and the historians. *Journal of religious history*, 99, 23, p. 149-167.

5274. Controversial Concordats: the Vatican's relations with Napoleon, Mussolini, and Hitler. Edited by Frank J. COPPA. Washington, Catholic University of America Press, 99, VIII-248 p.

5275. CRAYCRAFT (Kenneth R.). The American myth of religious freedom. Dallas, Spence Pub, 99, XI-202 p.

5276. Crises de l'image religieuse. Krisen religiöser Kunst. De Nicée à Vatican II. Ed. par Olivier CHRISTIN et Dario GAMBONI. Paris, Éditions de la Maison des sciences de l'homme, 99, VI-337 p.

5277. CROSS (Claire). Church and people: England 1450–1660. Oxford, Blackwell, 99, 258 p.

5278. DE FREDE (Carlo). Religiosità e cultura nel Cinquecento italiano. Bologna, Il Mulino, 99, 488 p.

5279. DELORIA (Vine). For this land. Writings on religion in America. New York, Routledge, 99, VII-311 p.

5280. Démocratie dans les Églises. Anglicanisme, catholicisme, ortodoxie, protestantisme. Ed. par J. BAUBÉROT, J. FAMERÉE, R. T. GREENACRE et J. GUEIT. Bruxelles, Lumen Vitae, 99, 103 p.

5281. Drei Konfessionen in einer Region. Beiträge zur Geschichte der Konfessionalisierung im Herzogtum Berg vom 16. bis 18. Jahrhundert. Hrsg. v. Burkhard DIETZ und Stefan EHRENPREIS. Köln, Rheinland-Verlag, 99, VII-550 p.

5282. Early modern skepticism and the origins of toleration. Ed. by Alan LEVINE. Lanham, Lexington Books, 99, VIII-282 p.

5283. Education (The) of a Christian society: humanism and the emancipation of Catholics, Jews and Protestants: minorities and the nation state in nineteenth-century Europe. Ed. by Rainer LIEDTKE. Manchester, Manchester U. P., 99, X-223 p.

5284. FAIX (Gerhard). Gabriel Biel und die Brüder vom Gemeinsamen Leben. Quellen und Untersuchungen zu Verfassung und Selbstverständnis des oberdeutschen Generalkapitels. Tübingen, Mohr, 99, XII-423 p.

5285. Felekezetek és identitás Közép-Európában az újkorban. (Churches and identity in Central Europe in the modern age). Szerk: ILLÉS PÁL Attila. Budapest, Magyar Egyh.tört Enciklopédia Munkaközösség, 99, 358 p.

5286. Fonti ecclesiastiche per la storia sociale e religiosa d'Europa XV–XVIII secolo. A cura di Cecilia NUBOLA e Angelo TURCHINI, Bologna, il Mulino, 99, 530 p. («Annali dell'Istituto storico italo-germanico. Quaderno», 50). [Cf. n° <scelta> 5387.]

5287. GIBSON (Marion). Reading witchcraft. Stories of early English witches. New York, Routledge, 99, 242 p.

5288. Grandi problemi (I) della storiografia civile e religiosa. Atti dell'XI Convegno di studio dell'Associazione italiana dei professori di storia della Chiesa (Roma, 2–5 settembre 1997). A cura di Giacomo MARTINA e Ugo DOVERE. Roma, Edizioni Dehoniane – Associazione italiana dei professori di storia della Chiesa, 99, 354 p. [Cf. n° <scelta> 5332.]

5289. GREGORY (Brad). Salvation at stake: Christian martyrdom in early modern Europe. Cambridge, Cambridge U. P., 99, 528p.

5290. JOHNSON (Dale A.). The Changing shape of English nonconformity, 1825–1925. Cambridge, Cambridge U. P., 99, 258 p.

5291. Konfessionalisierung in Ostmitteleuropa: Wirkungen des religiösen Wandels im 16. und 17. Jahrhundert in Staat, Gesellschaft und Kultur. Hrsg. von Joachim BAHLCKE und Arno STROHMEYER. Stuttgart, Steiner, 99, 439 p.

5292. Konversionen im Mittelalter und in der Frühneuzeit. Hrsg. von Friedrich NIEWÖHNER und Fidel RÄDLE. Hildesheim, Olms, 99, VII-216 p.

5293. KORZO (Margarita A.). Obraz cheloveka v propovedi XVII veka. (Image of human being in the 17th-century sermon: [a comparative study of Catholic and Orthodox sermons of the Polish state]). RAN, In-t filosofii. Sankt-Peterburg, [s. n.], 99, 189 p. (bibl.).

5294. LARSEN (Timothy). Friends of religious equality. Nonconformist politics in mid-Victorian England. Woodbridge, Boydell, 99, 309 p.

5295. LYON (Eileen Groth). Politicians in the pulpit. Christian radicalism in Britain from the fall of the Bastille to the disintegration of Chartism. Aldershot, Ashgate, 99, X-280 p.

5296. MAZUR (Eric Michael). The Americanization of religious minorities: confronting the constitutional order. Baltimore-London, Johns Hopkins University Press, 99, XXVI-196 p.

5297. Miracoli. Dai segni alla storia. A cura di Sofia BOESCH GAJANO e Marilena MODICA. Roma, Viella, 99, 253 p.

5298. MONOD (Paul K.). The Power of kings. Monarchy and religion in Europe 1589-1715. New Haven a. London, Yale U. P., 99, X-417 p.

5299. Occult (The) in early modern Europe. Ed. by P. G. MAXWELL STUART. Basingstoke, Macmillan, 99, XV-241 p.

5300. Origines (Les) historiques du statut des confessions religieuses dans les pays de l'Union Européenne. Sous la direction de Brigitte BASDEVANT-GAUDEMET. Paris, Presses Universitaires de France, 99, IX-254 p.

5301. Patristik (Die) in der Bibelexegese des 16. Jahrhunderts. Ed. Davic C. STEINMETZ, Wiesbaden, Harrassowitz, 99, 267 p.

5302. PERKINS (Mary Anne). Nation and word, 1770–1850. Religious and metaphysical language in European national consciousness. Aldershot, Ashgate, 99, XIX-370 p.

5303. Perspectives on American religion and culture. Ed. by Peter J. WILLIAMS. Oxford, Blackwell, 99, XII-418 p.

5304. PODLES (Leon J.). The church impotent. The feminization of Christianity. Dallas, Spence publishing, 99, [s.p.]

5305. Politics (The) of ritual kinship. Confraternities and social order in early modern Italy. Ed. by N. TERPSTRA. Cambridge, Cambridge U. P., 99, XI-317 p. (Cambridge studies in Italian history and culture).

5306. Politics (The) of toleration: tolerance and intolerance in modern life. Ed. by Susan MENDUS. Edinburgh, Edinburgh U. P., 99, XII-155 p.

5307. POOLE (Christine). Radical religion from Shakespeare to Milton: figures of nonconformity in early modern England. Cambridge, Cambridge U. P., 99, 272 p.

5308. Religion and the American Civil War. Edited by Randall M. MILLER and Charles REGAN WILSON. New York, Cambridge U. P., 99, 436p.

5309. Religious toleration. "The variety of rites" from Cyrus to Defoe. Ed. by John Christian LAURSEN. Basingstoke, Macmillan, 99, XX-252p.

5310. RÉMOND (René). L'anticléricalisme en France de 1815 à nos jours. Paris, Fayard, 99, X-420 p. – IDEM. La secolarizzazione: religione e società nell'Europa contemporanea. Roma, Laterza, 99, VIII-323 p. (Fare l'Europa).

5311. Reunionsgespräche (Die) im Niedersachsen des 17. Jahrhunderts: Rojas y Spinola, Molan, Leibniz. Hrsg. v. Hans OTTE. Göttingen, Vandenhoeck und Ruprecht, 99, 258 p.

5312. ROSA (Mario). Settecento religioso. Politica della ragione e religione del cuore. Venezia, Marsilio, 99, 312 p.

5313. SATTER (Beryl). Each mind a kingdom. American women, sexual purity, and the New Thought movement, 1875-1920. Berkeley a. London, University of California Press 99, XII-382 p.

5314. SCHMIEDL (Joachim). Das Konzil und die Orden. Krise und Erneuerung des gottgeweihten Lebens. Vallendar-Schönstatt, Patris Verlag, 99, 644 p.

5315. Tolérance (La). Quatrième centenaire de l'édit de Nantes. Colloque international de Nantes (mai 1998). Ed. par Guy SAUPIN, Rémi FABRE et Marcel LAUNAY. Rennes, Presses universitaires de Rennes et Centre de Recherche sur l'histoire du monde atlantique, 99, 520 p.

5316. WACHTEL (Nathan). Francisco Maldonado de Silva. «Le ciel face à face». *Annales*, 99, 54, 4, p. 895-914.

5317. Zeichen (Im) der Krise. Religiosität im Europa des 17. Jahrhunderts Hrsg. von Hartmut LEHMANN und Anne-Charlotte TREPP. Göttingen, Vandenhoeck & Ruprecht, 99, 645p.

Cf. n°s 1301-1320, 4789, 5609

§ 2. Roman Catholicism.

a. *General*

* 5318. Bibliografia [di storia della Chiesa in Italia]. Revisione e coordinamento di Giorgio PICASSO e Salvatore PALESE. *Rivista di storia della Chiesa in Italia*, 99, 53, 1-2, p. 257-321, p. 599-717. [52, Cf. Bibl. 98, n° 5358.]

* 5319. Bibliografia Historiae Pontificiae. A cura di Johan ICKX. *Archivum historiae pontificiae*, 99, 37, p. 233-534. [36, Cf. Bibl. 98, n° 5359.]

* 5320. DEGLER-SPENGLER (Brigitte). Helvetia Sacra. Arbeitsbericht 1998. [Forschungsbericht / Bulletin critique]. *Schweizerische Zeitschrift für Geschichte*, 99, 49, 2, p. 249-252.

** 5321. Acta nuntiaturae Polonae. Moderatore Henrico Damiano WOJTYSKA. Vol. 9. Vincentius Lauro (1572–1578). 2. (1-10-1574/30-6-1578). Ediderunt Miroslau KOROLKO et Lucianus OLECH. Vol. 57. Achilles Ratti (1918–1921). 5. (1-5-1919/31-7-1919). Edidit Stalislaus WILK. Roma, [s. n.], 99, 2 vol., X-406 p., XIII-547 p.

** 5322. GIANFRANCESCO PICO DELLA MIRANDOLA. Vita Hieronymi Savonarolae A cura di E. SCHISTO, Firenze, Olschki, 99, 211 p.

5323. ALBERT (Marcel). Die katholische Kirche in Frankreich in der vierten und fünften Republik. Roma u. Freiburg, Herder, 99, 245 p.

5324. BENZONI (Gino). Di un dialogo trentino e di San Carlo. *Studi veneziani*, 99, 38, p. 37-54.

5325. BIRELEY (Robert). The refashioning of Catholicism 1450–1700: a reassessment of the counter reformation. Washington, Catholic University of America Press a. Basingstoke, Macmillan, 99, VII-231 p.

5326. Counter-Reformation (The). The essential readings. Ed. by David M. LUEBKE. Oxford a. Malden, Blackwell, 99, 234 p.

5327. GILLIS (Chester). Roman Catholicism in America. New York, Columbia U. P., 99, X-365 p.

5328. GILMONT (Jean-Francois). Charter l'édit de Nantes aujourd'hui (1598–1998). *Revue d'histoire écclesiastique*, 99, 94, p. 913-920.

5329. Kirche und Katholizismus seit 1945. Band 2. Ostmittel-, Ost- und Südosteuropa. Albanien – Baltische Staaten – Bosnien-Herzegowina – Bulgarien – Jugoslawien – Kroatien – Mazedonien – Polen – Rumänien, Slowakei, Slowenien – Sowietunion/GUS – Tschechien – Ukraine – Ungarn. Hrsg. v. Erwin GATZ. Paderborn, München, Wien u. Zürich, Schöning, 283 p.

5330. KRETSCHMAR (Georg). Das bischöfliche Amt: kirchengeschichtliche und ökumenische Studien zur Frage des kirchlichen Amtes. Hrsg. v. Dorothea von WENDEBOURG. Göttingen, Vandenhoeck & Ruprecht, 99, 355 p.

5331. MAC MANNERS (John). Church and society in eighteenth-century France. Vol. 1. The clerical establishment and its social ramifications. Vol. 2. The religion of the people and the politics of religion. Oxford, Oxford U. P., 99, 2 vol., XVIII-817 p., XIV-866 p.

5332. MICCOLI (Giovanni). Chiesa Cattolica, «questione ebraica» e antisemitismo fra Ottocento e Novecento nella recente storiografia. Linee di ricerca e problemi aperti. *In*: Grandi problemi (I) della storiografia civile e religiosa [Cf. n° 5288], p. 323-354.

5333. MISSALLA (Heinrich). Für Gott, Führer und Vaterland: die Verstrickung der katholischen Seelsorge in Hitlers Krieg. München, Kösel, 99, 239 p.

5334. MULLETT (Michael A.). The Catholic Reformation. London, Routledge, 99, XI-258 p.

5335. PROSPERI (Adriano). Scienza e immaginazione teologica nel Seicento: il battesimo e le origini dell'individuo. *Quaderni storici*, 99, 34, p. 173-198

5336. QUANTIN (Jean-Louis). Le catholicisme classique et les Pères de l'Eglise. Un retour aux sources (1669-1713). Paris, IEA, 99, 672 p.

5337. RAMSEY (Ann W.). Liturgy, politics, and salvation: the Catholic league in Paris and the nature of Catholic reform, 1540-1630. Rochester, University of Rochester Press, 99, XIII-447 p.

5338. REEKEN (Dietmar von). Kirchen im Umbruch zur Moderne: Milieubildungsprozesse im nordwestdeutschen Protestantismus 1849-1914. Gütersloh, Gütersloher, 99, 405 p.

5339. Storia del Concilio Vaticano II. La chiesa come comunione. Il terzo periodo e la terza intersessione (settembre 1964-settembre 1965). A cura di Giuseppe ALBERIGO, Bologna, il Mulino, 99, 503 p.

5340. THIEDE (Simone). Der Dialog zwischen Religionen und säkularen Weltanschauungen: dargestellt am Beispiel des christlich-marxistischen Dialogs in der DDR. Frankfurt am Main, Lang, 99, 311 p.

5341. TOKAREVA (Evgenija S.). Fashizm, tserkov' i katolicheskoe dvizhenie v Italii, 1922-1943 gg. (The Fascism, the Church and the Catholic movement in Italy, 1922-1943). Ed. Irina V. GRIGOR'EVA. RAN, In-t vseobshchej istorii. Moskva, [s. n.], 99, 365 p. (ind.).

5342. TOUCHEFEU (Yves). L'antiquité et le christianisme dans la pensée de Jean-Jacques Rousseau. Oxford, Voltaire foundation, 99, XI-704 p.

5343. TSIMBAEVA (Ekaterina N.). Russkij katolitsizm: Zabytoe proshloe russkogo liberalizma. (Russian catholicism: a forgotten past of Russian liberalism, [19th century]). Moskva, Editorial-URSS, 99, 183 p. (ill., portr.; bibl.; ind.).

5344. WANEGFFELEN (Thierry). Une difficile fidélité: catholique malgré le Concile en France, XVIe et XVIIe siècles. Paris, P.U.F., 99, 226p.

5345. ZOVATTO (Pietro). Cultura cattolica rosminiana tra '800 e '900. Trieste, Parnaso, 99, 684 p.

Cf. n°s 415, 3901, 5255, 5665

b. *History of the Popes*

5346. AUBERT (Alberto). Paolo IV. Politica, inquisizione e storiografia. Firenze, Le Lettere, 99, 245 p.

5347. LAY (Benny). Affari dei papi: storia di cardinali, nobiluomini e faccendieri nella Roma dell'Ottocento. Roma e Bari, Laterza, 99, VII-253 p.

5348. MENNITI IPPOLITO (Antonio). Il tramonto della curia nepotista: papi, nipoti e burocrazia curiale tra XVI e XVII secolo. Roma, Viella, 99, 190 p.

5349. MENOZZI (Daniele). I papi del Novecento. Firenze, Giunti, 99, 127 p.

5350. MONSAGRATI (Giuseppe). Pio IX, lo Stato della Chiesa e l'avvio delle riforme. *Rassegna storica toscana*, 99, 45, p. 215-39.

5351. Papes et papauté au XVIIIe siècle. VI colloque franco-italien. Etudes réunis par Philippe KOEPPEL. Paris, Champion, 99, 317 p.

5352. POLLARD (John F.). The unknown pope. Benedict XV (1914-1922) and the pursuit of peace. London, Geoffrey Chapman, 99, XV-240 p.

5353. RUMI (Giorgio). Benedetto XV e il sistema delle relazioni internazionali. *Studium*, 99, 95, p. 61-74.

5354. SCHWAIGER (Georg). Papsttum und Päpste im 20. Jahrhundert: von Leo XIII. zu Johannes Paul II. München, Verlag C.H. Beck, 99, 543 p.

5355. TEDDE (Emma). Angelo Roncalli e l'accentramento romano dell'«Oeuvre de la propagation de la foi». *Rivista di storia della chiesa in Italia*, 99, 53, p. 83-108.

c. *Special studies*

* 5356. MORACCINI (M.). Don Lorenzo Milani nei mass media. Catalogo bibliografico 1950-1957. Milano, Jaca Book, 99, 333 p.

** 5357. DENZINGER (Heinrich). Kompendium der Glaubensbekenntnisse und kirchlichen Lehrentscheidungen. Hrsg. v. Peter HÜNERMANN. Freiburg im Breisgau, Herder, 99, XXVII-1756 p.

** 5358. STURZO (Luigi), VAUSSARD (Maurice). Carteggio 1917-1958 A cura di Enrico SERRA. Postfazione di Gabriele DE ROSA. Roma, Gangemi, 99, 157 p.

5359. ABAD (R.). Un indice de déchristianisation? L'évolution de la consommation de viande à Paris en carême sous l'Ancien Régime. *Revue historique*, 99, 123, 610, p. 237-276.

5360. ALBERIGO (Giuseppe). Il Concilio Vaticano II e le trasformazioni culturali in Europa. *Cristianesimo nella storia*, 99, 20, 2, p. 383-405.

5361. ALTERMATT (Urs). Katholizismus und Antisemitismus: Mentalitäten, Kontinuitäten, Ambivalenzen. Zur Kulturgeschichte der Schweiz, 1918-1945. Frauenfeld, Verlag Huber, 99, 414 p.

5362. ANTOINE (Charles). Guerre froide et Eglise catholique: l'Amérique latine. Paris, Ed. du Cerf, 354 p.

5363. AYLLÓN (Fernando). El Tribunal de la Inquisición: de la leyenda a la historia. Lima, Ediciones del Congreso, 99, XIX- 686 p.

5364. Beato (Il) Guido Maria Conforti arcivescovo-vescovo di Parma: omelie e lettere a clero e popolo, capitolo cattedrale e proposta di compromesso, attività catechistica: 1917. A cura di Franco TEODORI. Città del Vaticano, 99, 409 p.

5365. BERGIN (Joseph). The Counter-Reformation Church and its bishops. *Past and present*, 99, 165, p. 30-73.

5366. BINDE (Per). Bodies of vital matter: notions of life forces and transcendence in traditional Southern Italy. Göteborg, AUG, 99, 300 p.

5367. BLASCHKE (Olaf). Katholizismus und Antisemitismus in Deutschen Kaiserreich. Göttingen, Vandenhoeck & Ruprecht, 99, 447 p. (Kritische Studien zur Geschichtswissenschaft, 122).

5368. BOHÁČ (Zdeněk). Atlas církevních dějin českých zemí 1918–1999. (An atlas of the history of the Church in the Bohemian Lands). Kostelní Vydří, Karmelitánské nakladatelství, 99, 175 p. (maps).

5369. BONZON (Anne). L'esprit de clocher: prêtres et paroisses dans le diocèse de Beauvais (1535–1650). Préf. de Marc VENARD. Paris, Ed. du Cerf, 99, 527 p. (Histoire religieuse de la France, 14).

5370. BORJA DE MEDINA (Francisco). Blas Valera y la dialectica «exclusión-integración del otro». *Archivum historicum societatis Iesu*, 99, 88, 136, p. 229-268.

5371. BOVA (Vincenzo). Democrazie cristiane: cattolici e politica nell'Italia che cambia. Soveria Mannelli, Rubbettino, 99, 116 p.

5372. BOWEN (Geraint). Welsh recusant writings. Cardiff, University of Wales press, 99, 87 p.

5373. BROCKMANN (Thomas). Die Konzilsfrage in den Flug- und Streitschriften des deutschen Sprachraumes 1518–1563. Göttingen, Vendenhoeck & Ruprecht, 99, 762 p.

5374. BURGALETA (C). José de Acosta (1540–1600). His life and thought. Chicago, Loyola Press, 99, p.

5375. BUSIN (Valérie). La correspondance de Girolamo di Vecchi, internonce aux Pays-Bas (1656–1665). Bruxelles, Inst. Historique Belge de Rome, 99, 515 p.

5376. CASELLA (M.). Clero e politica in Italia (1942–1948). Congedo, Galatina, 99, 342 p. – IDEM. Il Giuramento anti-modernista del 1910 a Perugia. *Rassegna storica del Risorgimento*, 99, 86, p. 249-286.

5377. CATTO (Michela). Le monache di S. Chiara in Udine e fra Paolo Sarpi: tra consuetudine e ragione di Stato nel consulto del 1609. *Studi veneziani*, 99, 38, p. 243-257.

5378. CEYSSENS (Lucien). L'antijansénisme à la cour de Madrid au tournant des XVIIe–XVIIIe siècles. *Revue d'histoire ecclésiastique*, 99, 94, p. 15-29.

5379. CHENEAUX (Philippe). Entre Maurras et Maritain: une génération intellectuelle catholique (1920–1930). Paris, Cerf, 99, 262 p.

5380. CICCARELLI (Silvia). Notizie su un monaco giacobino. Documenti inediti dell'Archivio diocesano di Siena. *Ricerche storiche*, 99, 29, 1, p. 89-113.

5381. CLEMENT (Jean-Louis). Les évêques au temps de Vichy: loyalisme sans inféodation. Les relations entre l'Eglise et l'Etat de 1940 à 1944. Paris, Beauchesne, 99, 279 p.

5382. Clero (Il) giacobino. Documenti inediti. A cura di Alfonso PEPE. Napoli, Procaccini, 99, 2 vol., 382 p., 326 p.

5383. COHN (S. K.). Piety and religious practice in the rural dependencies of Renaissance Florence. *English historical review*, 99, 114, 459, p. 1121-1142.

5384. DALL'OLIO (Guido). Eretici e inquisitori nella Bologna del Cinquecento. Bologna, Istituto per la storia di Bologna, 99, VIII-479 p.

5385. DEAN (Carolyn). Inka bodies and the Body of Christ. Corpus Christi in Colonial Cuzco, Peru. Durham, Duke U. P., 99, 288 p.

5386. Deutsche und polnische Christen: Erfahrungen unter zwei Diktaturen. Hrsg. v. Martin GRESCHAT. Stuttgart u. Berlin, Kohlhammer, 99, 201 p.

5387. DONATI (Cl.). Curie, tribunali, cancellerie episcopali in Italia durante i secoli dell'età moderna: percorsi di ricerca. *In*: Fonti ecclesiastiche per la storia sociale e religiosa d'Europa XV–XVIII secolo [Cf. n° 5286], p. 213-229.

5388. DUNI (Matteo). Tra religione e magia. Storia del prete modenese Guglielmo Campana. Firenze, Olschki, 99, XI-351 p.

5389. EISENSTADT (S. N.). Fundamentalism, sectarianism and revolution: the Jacobin dimension of modernity. Cambridge, Cambridge U. P., 99, XVI-280.

5390. ELOY GUTIÉRREZ (Jesús). Información sobre el fascismo en el diario católico La Religión (1923–1938). Caracas, Fondo Editorial 60 Años, 99, 171 p.

5391. ERNST (Germana). Ancora sugli ultimi scritti politici di Campanella. I. Gli inediti "Discorsi ai principi" in favore del papato; II. Gli Avvertimenti a Venezia del 1636. *Bruniana & Campanelliana*, 99, 7, p. 131-153; p. 447-465.

5392. FAGGI (Paola). Pubblicazioni italiane di Bartolomé De Las Casas nel XVII secolo: l'operazione editoriale e l'operazione culturale. *Ricerche storiche*, 99, 29, 1, p. 33-57

5393. FASANO (Jacopo). Tra fede e politica. Niccolò Tommaseo e i cattolici francesi negli anni del «primo esilio» (1834–1839). *Rivista di storia e letteratura religiosa*, 99, 35, 1, p. 71-117.

5394. Federico Ozanam e il suo tempo. A cura di Claudia FRANCESCHINI. Bologna, il Mulino, 99, 238 p.

5395. Figures du théologico-politique. Ed. par Emmanuel CATTIN et Laurent JAFFRO. Paris, Vrin, 99, 263 p.

5396. FONTANA (Paolo). Celebrando Caterina. Santa Caterina Fieschi Adorno e il suo culto nella Genova barocca. Genova, Marietti 1820, 99, 282 p.

5397. FRAGNITO (Gigliola). Girolamo Savonarola e la censura ecclesiastica. *Rivista di storia e letteratura religiosa*, 99, 35, 3, p. 501-529

5398. GARUTI (Adriano). Primato del Vescovo di Roma e dialogo cattolico luterano. *Antonianum*, 99, 74, p. 379-430; p. 587-626.

5399. Giovanni Crisostomo Trombelli (1697–1794) e i canonici regolari del SS. Salvatore. A cura di Maria Gioia TAVONI e Gabriella ZARRI. Modena, Zucchi, 99, XIV-293 p.

5400. GÓMEZ MOVELLÁN (Antonio). La iglesia católica y otras religiones en la España de hoy. Madrid, Vosa, 99, 141 p.

5401. Gran (Il) disegno di Rosmini: origine, fortuna e profezia delle Cinque piaghe della Santa Chiesa. A cura di Massimo MARCOCCHI e Fulvio DE GIORGI. Milano, Vita e Pensiero, 99, 300 p.

5402. GRECO (Gaetano). La chiesa in Italia nell'età moderna. Roma e Bari, Laterza, 99, XI-342 p.

5403. GUASCO (Maurilio). Politica e religione nel Novecento italiano. Momenti e figure. Torino, Il Segnalibro, 99, 344 p.

5404. HEINEMAN (Kenneth J.). A catholic New Deal: religion and reform in depression Pittsburgh. Pittsburgh, Pennsylvania State University Press, 99, [s. p.].

5405. Iter Germanicum: Deutschland und die reformierte Kirche in Ungarn im 16.–17. Jahrhundert. Hrsg. v. András SZABÓ. Budapest, Kálvin K., 99, 243 p.

5406. KAMMERLOHER-LIS (Stephanie). Die Entstehung des Gesetzes über die religiöse Kindererziehung vom 15. Juli 1921. Frankfurt am Main, Lang. 99, 276 p.

5407. KURZMEYER (Roman). Viereck und Kosmos. Künstler, Lebensreformer, Okkultisten, Spiritisten in Amden 1901–1912: Max Nopper, Josua Klein, Fidus, Otto Meyer-Amden. Wien u. New York, Edition Voldemeer, 99, 258 p.

5408. LAPORTE (Christian). L'affaire de Louvain, 1960–1968. Bruxelles, De Boeck, 99, 333 p.

5409. LARSSON (Olle). Biskopen visiterar: Den kyrkliga överhetens möte med lokalsamhället 1650–1760. (The Bishop's visit: the encounter of Church authorities with the local community, 1650–1760). Växjö, Stiftshistoriska Sällskap, 99, 351 p.

5410. LEIGHTON (C.D.A.). Hutchinsonianism: a Counter-Enlightenment reform movement. *Journal of religious history*, 99, 23, p. 168-184

5411. LETTIERI (Gaetano). Il metodo della grazia. Pascal e l'ermeneutica giansenista di Agostino. Roma, Edizioni Dehoniane, 99, 472 p.

5412. LIŠKA (Ondřej). Církev v podzemí a společenství Koinótés. (Geheimkirche und die Gemeinschaft 'Koinótés'). Brno, Sursum, 99, 201 p.

5413. LOSITO (Giacomo). Cristianesimo e modernità. Studio sulla formazione del personalismo di Laberthonniére 1880–1893. Napoli, Città del sole, 99, 459 p.

5414. LUXMOORE (Jonathan), BABIUCH (Jolanta). The Vatican and the red flag: the struggle for the soul of Eastern Europe. London, Geoffrey Chapman, 99, XVI-351 p.

5415. MANFREDI (Angelo). Vescovi, clero e cura pastorale. Studi sulla diocesi di Parma alla fine dell'Ottocento. Roma, Pontificia università gregoriana, 99, 774 p.

5416. MELLINGHOFF-BOURGERIE (Viviane). François de Sales. Un homme de lettres spirituelles. Genève, Droz, 99, 535 p.

5417. NARDON (Franco). Benandanti e inquisitori nel Friuli del Seicento. Prefazione di Andrea DEL COL. Trieste, Edizioni Università di Trieste e Montereale Valcellina, Centro Studi Storici "Menocchio", 99, 254 p. (Inquisizione e società, 1).

5418. ORABONA (Luciano). Domenico Zelo vescovo di Aversa nel secondo Ottocento. Chiesa, cultura e società politica. Napoli, Edizioni scientifiche italiane, 99, 407 p.

5419. ORLANDI (Giuseppe). S. Alfonso vescovo e i religiosi. *Spicilegium historicum Congregationis Ssmi Redemptoris*, 99, 47, p. 243-278.

5420. OSSA (Manuel). Iglesia evangélicas y derechos humanos en tiempos de dictadura. La confraternidad cristiana de iglesias 1981–1989. Santiago, Medellin, 99, 137 p.

5421. OVIEDO (Luís). Los errores históricos de la Iglesia en el contexto del debate apologético: el arrepentimiento eclesial. *Antonianum*, 99, 74, p. 307-354.

5422. PASAMAR LÁZARO (José Enrique). Los familiares del Santo Oficio en el distrito inquisitorial de Aragón. Zaragoza, Instituto "Fernando el Católico", 99, 200 p.

5423. PASTORELLI (Sabrina). Roma 1825: aspetti organizzativi e riflessi dell'ultimo grande giubileo celebrato al tempo del Papa-re. *Studi storici Luigi Simeoni. Istituto per gli studi storici veronesi*, 99, 49, p. 329-378.

5424. PLUM (Claus Munk). Martyrkirken: den katolske kirke i Japan. (L'Eglise martyre: l'église catholique au Japon). Lyngby, Dansk historisk håndbogsforlag, 99, 504 p. (ill., cartes).

5425. PROSPERI (Adriano). America e Apocalisse e altri saggi. Pisa e Roma, Istituti editoriali poligrafici internazionali, 99, 406 p. – IDEM. Anime in trappola. Confessione e censura ecclesiastica all'Università di Pisa tra '500 e '600. *Belfagor*, 99, 54, p. 257-287.

5426. RIVELLI (Marco Aurelio). L'arcivescovo del genocidio. Milano, Kaos, 99, 292 p.

5427. SCARAMELLA (Pierroberto). L'Inquisizione romana e i Valdesi di Calabria: 1554–1703. Napoli, Editoriale Scientifica, 99, 268 p.

5428. Studia Borromaica 13. Saggi e documenti di storia religiosa e civile della prima età moderna. Milano, Biblioteca ambrosiana, 99, 337 p.

5429. TRONCANELLI (Fabio). La spada e la croce: Guillén Lombardo e l'inquisizione in Messico. Roma, Salerno, 99, 405 p.

d. Religious orders

* 5430. Bibliographie sur l'Histoire de la Compagnie de Jésus. [Cf. Bibl. 98, n° 5454.] Ed. Par. Nicoletta BASILOTTA et László POLGÁR. *Archivum historicum societatis Iesu*, 99, 88, 136, p. 315-496.

** 5431. MAC COOG (Thomas). Robert Parsons and Claudio Acquaviva: Correspondence. *Archivum historicum societatis Iesu*, 99, 88, 135, p. 79-182.

5432. AGUIRRE BELTRÁN (Cristina). La expulsión de los jesuitas y la ocupación de sus bienes. Puebla, Universidad Autónoma de Puebla, 99, 234 p.

5433. CAEIRO (José). História da expulsão da Companhia de Jesus da Província de Portugal (séc. XVIII), Lisboa, Editorial Verbo, 99, [s. p.].

5434. CORRY (Emmet). Researching a Franciscan identità in the church: rules and constitutions influencing the history of the Franciscan brother of Brooklyn. *Analecta Tertii Ordinis regularis*, 99, 30, p. 229-269.

5435. DE ANDRADE SILVA (Antenor). Brasil: os Salesianos na tebaida. Uma história que durou 20 anos (1902–1922). *Ricerche storiche salesiane*, 99, 18, p. 259-288.

5436. FABRE (Pierre-Antoine). La conversion infinie des conversos. Des «nouveaux-chrétiens» dans la Compagnie de Jésus au 16ᵉ siècle. *Annales*, 99, 54, 4, p. 875-894.

5437. GARRIDO (Pablo María). La Virge de la fe: doctrina y piedad marianas entre los carmelitas españoles de los siglos XVI y XVII. Roma, Edizioni carmelitane, 99, 428 p.

5438. Jesuits (The): cultures, sciences, and the arts 1540–1773. Ed. by John W. O'MALLEY [et al.]. Buffalo, University of Toronto Press, 99, XX-722 p.

5439. LÓPEZ MARTINEZ (Antonio Luis). Il patrimonio rústico de los jesuitas en España. Una aproximación. *Hispania*, 99, 59, 3, p. 925-954

5440. LORENZO GARCÍA (Santiago). La expulsión de los Jesuitas de Filipinas. Alicante, Universidad de Alicante, 99, 330 p. (maps). (Publicaciones de la Universidad de Alicante).

5441. RIVERA GARCÍA (Antonio). La política del cielo: clericalismo jesuita y estado moderno. Hildesheim, Olms, 99, 177 p.

5442. SPRINGER (Klaus-Bernward). Die deutschen Dominikaner in Widerstand und Anpassung während der Reformationszeit. Berlin, Akademie, 99, VIII-492 p. (Quellen und Forschungen zur Geschichte des Dominikanerordens, 8).

Cf. n° 6148

e. Missions

** 5443. Lähetystyö ja ekumenia arkistojen valossa. Kristillisen lähetystyön ja ekumeenisen toiminnan arkistolähteitä Suomessa 1800- ja 1900-luvulla. (Missionsarbetet och ekumenin i arkivens ljus – Archives on the missions and ecumenical activities in Finland). Toim. Ed. Mirja HÄRKÖNEN [et al.]. Helsinki, SKS, 99, 332 p. (Suomen Kirkkohist. Seuran Toim., 182). [Svensk Resumé, English summary].

5444. ABAD PEREZ (Antolín), SÁNCHEZ FUERTES (Cayetano). Descalcez franciscana en España, hispanoamérica y Estremo oriente. Síntesis histórica, geográfica y bibliográfica. *Archivo ibero-americano*, 99, 59, 234, p. 457-788.

5445. Africans meeting missionaries. Ed. by Derek PETERSON and Jean ALLMAN. *Journal of religious history*, 99, 23, p. 1-128.

5446. BETTI (Claudio Maria). Missioni e colonie in Africa Orientale. Roma, Studium, 99, VII-313 p.

5447. BUTTURINI (Emilio). Le missioni cattoliche in Cina tra le due guerre mondiali: osservazioni sul metodo moderno di evangelizzazione di padre Paolo Manna. Bologna, Emi, 99, 334.

5448. GISONDI (Francesco Antonio). Michele Ruggeri s.j.: missionario in Cina, primo sinologo europeo e poeta cinese (Spinazzola 1543–Salerno 1607). Milano, Jaca Book, 99, 173 p.

5449. MOFFA (Claudio). La chiesa e le «nazioni potenti». Uno scontro dentro Propaganda Fide sulle missioni in Africa in alcune lettere inedite di Comboni. *Studi Piacentini*, 99, 24-25, p. 123-139.

5450. PALOMERO (Esteban J.). La obra educativa de los jesuitas en Puebla 1578–1945. México City, Universidad Iberoamericana, 99, 431 p.

5451. SOUTH (Malcolm H.). The Jesuits and the joint mission to England during 1580–1581. Lewiston, Mellen Press, 99, XVI-172p.

5452. WOBESER (Gisela Von). Vida eterna y preocupaciones terrenales. Las capellanías de misas en Nueva España, 1700–1821. Mexico City, UNAM, 99, 183 p.

5453. ŽUPANOV (Ines G.). Disputed mission: Jesuit experiments and Brahmanical knowledge in seventeenth-century India. New York, Oxford U. P., 99, XIII-277 p.

Cf. n° 7440

§ 3. Orthodox Church.

5454. CHUMACHENKO (Tat'jana A.). Gosudarstvo, pravoslavnaja tserkov' i verujushchie, 1941-1961. (The state, the Russian Orthodox Church and the faithful, 1941-1961). Assots. issled. ros. o-va XX v. Moskva, AIRO-XX, 99, 248 p. (bibl.; ind.). (Pervaja monografija).

5455. Religionspolitik zwischen Cäsaropapismus und Atheismus. Staat und Kirche in Rußland von 1825 bis zum Ende der Sowjetunion. Hrsg. v. Peter KOSLOWSKI. München, Fink, 99, XI-173 p.

5456. SCHEIDEGGER (Gabriele). Endzeit: Russland am Ende des 17. Jahrhunderts. Bern u. New York, Peter Lang, 99, 409 p.

5457. SHKAROVSKIJ (Mikhail V.). Obnovlencheskoe dvizhenie v Russkoj Pravoslavnoj Tserkvi XX veka. (The Renovationist movement [Obnovlentsy] in the Russian Orthodox Church in the 20th century). With documents in app. Sankt-Peterburg, Nestor, 99, 100 p.

5458. VASIL'EVA (Ol'ga Ju.). Russkaja Pravoslavnaja Tserkov' v politike Sovetskogo gosudarstva v 1943-1948 gg. (The Russian Orthodox Church in the policy of the Soviet state, 1943-1948). RAN, In-t rossijskoj istorii. Moskva, [s. n.], 99, 213 p. (ind.).

5459. War (At) with the church. Religious dissent in seventeenth-century Russia. Ed. by Georg Bernhard MICHELS. Stanford, Stanford U. P.. 99, X-354 p.

5460. ZYRJANOV (Pavel N.). Russkie monastyri i monashestvo v XIX i nachale XX veka. (The monasteries and monks of Russia in the 19th and the early 20th centuries). RAN, In-t rossijskoj istorii. Moskva, Russkoe slovo, 99, 311 p. (ill., portr., plates, ind.).

Cf. n°s 3839, 4154

§ 4. Protestantism.

* 5461. Archiv für Reformationsgeschichte. Beiheft Literaturbericht 1999. *Archiv für Reformationsgeschichte*, 99, 28, 310 p.

* 5462. ARNOLD (M.). Les recherches récentes sur les débuts de la Réformation. *Bulletin de la Société d'histoire du Protestantisme français*, 99, 145, p. 485-508.

* 5463. BOUDIN (Hugh Robert). Bibliografie van het Belgisch protestantisme. Bibliographie du protestantisme belge: 1781-1996. Bruxelles, PRODOC Uitgaven, 99, XXXIV-1065 p.

* 5464. BRADY (Thomas A., jr.). New studies on the Protestant Reformation. *Journal of modern history*, 99, 71, 2, p. 431-444.

* 5465. CALVIN (Jean). Commentarius in Epistola ad Romanos, ediderunt T. H. L. PARKER et D.C. PARKER. Genève, Droz, 99, LXXXII-356 p.

** 5466. LUTHER (Martin). Oeuvres. Edition publiée sous la direction de Marc LIENHARD et Matthieu ARNOLD. Paris, Gallimard, 99, [s. p.].

** 5467. REUCHLIN (Johannes). Briefwechsel. Hrsg. v. d. Heidelberger Akademie der Wissenschaft in Zusammenarb. mit der Stadt Pforzheim. Band 1. 1477-1505. Unt. Mitw. v. Stefan RHEIN bearb. v. Mathias DALL'ASTA und Gerald DÖRNER. Stuttgart, Fromann u. Bad Cannstatt, Holzboog, 99, LXV-505 p.

** 5468. VALDÈS (Juan de). Diálogo de la lengua. Por Antonio QUILIS. Madrid, Ediciones Libertarias, 99, 250 p.

5469. AMBROSINI (Federica). Storie di patrizi e di eresia nella Venezia del Cinquecento. Milano, Franco Angeli, 99, 352 p.

5470. AUDISIO (G). The Waldensian dissent, persecution and survival, 1170-1570. Cambridge, Cambridge U. P., 99, 360 p.

5471. BALDINI (Artemio E.). Tre inediti di Francesco Pucci al cardinal nipote e a Gregorio XIV alla vigilia del suo 'rientro' a Roma. *Rinascimento*, 99, 39, p. 157-223.

5472. BIAGIONI (Mario). Incontri italo svizzeri nell' Europa del tardo Cinquecento. Francesco Pucci e Samuel Huber. *Rivista storica italiana*, 99, 111, p. 363-422.

5473. BURNS (Arthur). The Diocesan Revival in the Church of England, c. 1800-1870. Oxford, Clarendon Press, 99, XIV-344 p. (Oxford historical monographs).

5474. CACCAMO (Domenico). Eretici italiani in Moravia, Polonia, Transilvania (1558-1611): studi e documenti. Firenze, Le Lettere, 99, XIV-286 p.

5475. CARAVALE (Giorgio). Inediti di Francesco Pucci presso l'archivio del Sant'Uffizio. *Il pensiero politico*, 99, 22, p. 69-82.

5476. CARTA (Paolo). Nunziature ed eresia nel Cinquecento. Nuovi documenti sul processo e la condanna di Francesco Pucci (1592-1597). Padova, Cedam, 99, XI-237 p.

5477. CHIARINI (Franco). Storia delle chiese metodiste in Italia (1859-1915). Torino, Claudiana, 99, 160 p.

5478. COOPER (James F.). Tenacious of their liberties: the Congregationalists in colonial Massachusetts. Oxford, Oxford U. P., 99, VIII-282 p.

5479. COZZI (Gaetano). Scoperta dell'anabattismo: lo stupore ammirato di Gregorio Barbarigo ambasciatore veneto. *Studi veneziani*, 99, 38, p. 55-77.

5480. DE LANGE (Albert). L'importanza della politica religiosa nell'asilo dei valdesi in Germania (1699) nei territori luterani. *Bollettino della società di studi valdesi*, 99, 185, p. 27-60.

5481. DE MATTEI (Roberto). A sinistra di Lutero. Sette e movimenti religiosi nell'Europa del Cinquecento. Roma, Città Nuova, 99, 215 p.

5482. DEMING (James C.). Religion and identity in Modern France: the modernization of the Protestant community in Languedoc, 1815–1848. Lanham, University Press of America, 99, XXI-237 p.

5483. DIPPEL (Stewart). The professionalization of the English Church from 1560 to 1700: ambassadors for Christ. Lewiston, Mellen Press, 99, X-252 p.

5484. Edit (L') de Nantes: sa gènese, son application en Languedoc. Actes du Colloque organisé le 15 mai 1998 par la ville de Montpellier. Sous la dir. de Arlette JOUANNA et de Michel PÉRONNET. *Bulletin historique de la ville de Montpellier*, 99, 51, 159 p.

5485. ELWOOD (Christopher). The body broken: the Calvinist doctrine of the eucharist and the symbolization of power in sixteenth-century France. Oxford, Oxford U. P., 99, XII-251 p. (Oxford studies in historical theology).

5486. FIX (Andrew). Fallen Angels. Balthasar Bekker, spirit belief, and confessionalism in the seventeenth century Dutch republic. Dordrecht, Kluwer Academic Publ., 99, 175 p.

5487. FLEGEL (Christoph). Die lutherische Kirche in der Kurpfalz von 1648 bis 1716. Mainz, von Zabern, 99, VII-568 p. (Veröffentlichungen des Instituts für Europäische Geschichte Mainz, Abt. Abendländische Religionsgeschichte, 175).

5488. FLETCHER (Brian H.). Anglicanism and nationalism in Australia, 1901–1962. *Journal of religious history*, 99, 23, p. 215-233.

5489. GRANE (Leif). Reformationsstudien. Beiträge zu Luther und zur dänischen Reformation. Hrsg. v. Rolf DECOT. Mainz, von Zabern, 99, VIII-261 p. (Veröffentlichungen des Instituts für Europäische Geschichte Mainz, Abt. Abendländische Geschichte, 49).

5490. HANKE (Christian). Die Deutschlandpolitik der Evangelischen Kirche in Deutschland von 1945 bis 1990: eine politikwissenschaftliche Untersuchung unter besonderer Berücksichtigung des kirchlichen Demokratie-, Gesellschafts- und Staatsverständnisses. Berlin, Duncker & Humblot, 99, 519 p. (Schriftenreihe der Gesellschaft für Deutschlandforschung, 68).

5491. HELMER (C.). The trinity and Martin Luther. A study on the relationship between genre, language and the trinity in Luther's works (1523–1546). Mainz am Rhein, Zabern, 99, XII-296 p.

5492. KIEFNER (Theo). L'editto di Nantes e i Valdesi. *Bollettino storico-bibliografico subalpino*, 99, 97, p. 203-244.

5493. KUPERUS (Tracy). State, civil society and apartheid in South Africa. An examination of Dutch reformed church-state relations. Basingstoke, Macmillan, 99, XVIII-211 p.

5494. LEPPIN (Volker). Antichrist und Jüngster Taf: das Profil apokalyptischer Flugschriftenpublizistik im deutschen Luthertum 1548–1618. Gütersloh, Gütersloher Verlag, 99, 394 p.

5495. LIENHARD (Marc). Martin Luther: la passion de Dieu. Paris, Bayard, 99, 334 p.

5496. LÖFFLER (Ulrich). Lissabons Fall, Europas Schrecken. Die Deutung des Erdebens von Lissabon im deutschsprachigen Protestantismus des 18. Jahrhundert. Berlin u. New York, De Gruyter, 99, 721 p.

5497. *Vacat.*

5498. MAC KEE (Elsie Anne). Katharina Schütz Zell. Leiden, Brill, 99, 2 vol., [s. p.].

5499. MAGDELAINE (Michelle). Exil et voyage. Le Refugé huguenot et l'errance. *In*: Mobilitäten = Mobilités [Cf. n° 6962], p. 105-114.

5500. MARCHETTI (Valerio). I simulacri delle parole e il lavoro dell'eresia: ricerca sulle origini del socinianesimo. Bologna, Cisec, 99, 254 p. – IDEM. Saggi di storia della chiesa evangelica tedesca tra il XVII e XVIII secolo. Bologna, Cisec, 99, 262 p.

5501. MARIUS (R.). Martin Luther, The Christian between God and Death. Cambridge a. London, Belknap Press of Harvard U. P., 99, XV-542 p.

5502. MEIER (Martin Gernot). Systembruch und Neuordnung. Reformation und Konfessionsbildung in den Markgraftümern Brandenburg-Ansbach-Kulmbach; 1520–1594; Religionspolitik, Kirche, Gesellschaft. Frankfurt am Main, Lang, 99, 457 p.

5503. MEISTAD (Tore). Martin Luther and John Wesley on the Sermon on the Mount. Lanham, Scarecrow press, 99, XVI-356.

5504. MONTER (William). Judging the French Reformation: heresy trials by sixteenth-century Parlements. Cambridge, Harvard U. P., 99, 336 p.

5505. MÜLLER (Denis). L'éthique protestante dans la crise de la modernité: généalogie, critique, reconstruction. Paris, Éd. du Cerf, 99, 369 p.

5506. OLSCHEWSKI (Ursula). Erneueung der Kirche durch Bildung und Belehrung des Volkes. Der Beitrag der Dortmunder Humanisten Jacob Schoepper zur Formung der Frömmigkeit in der frühen Neuzeit. Münster, Aschendorf, 99, VIII-348 p. (Reformationsgeschichtliche Studien und Texte, 141).

5507. PARINETTO (Luciano). La rivolta del diavolo: Lutero, Müntzer e la rivolta dei contadini in Germania e altri saggi. Sant'Arcangelo di Romagna, Rusconi, 99, 239 p.

5508. POLLMANN (Judith). Religious Choice in the Dutch Republic. The reformation of Arnoldus Buchelius (1565–1641). Manchester, University Press, 99, 288 p.

5509. RAMBEAUD (Pascal). La Rochelle, fidèle et rebelle. Paris, Croit vif, 99, 153 p.

5510. Reformation in Britain and the Netherlands: papers delivered to the Anglo-Dutch Historical Conference, 1997. Edited by N. SCOTT AMOS. Aldershot, Ashgate, 99, XII-274 p.

5511. Reformation, revolt and Civil War in France and the Netherlands 1555–1585. Ed. by Philip BENEDICT. Amsterdam, Koninklijke Nederlandse Akademie van Wetenschappen, 99, VII-298 p.

5512. RUPPEL (Karl August). Theologie und Wirtschaft. Konzepte protestantischer Wirtschaftsethik zwischen Aufklärung und Industrialisierung. Hildesheim u. New York, G. Olms Verlag, 99, X-368 p.

5513. SAUER (Thomas). Westorientierung im deutschen Protestantismus? Vorstellung und Tätigkeit der Kronberger Kreises. München, Oldenbourg, 99, 326 p. (Ordnungssysteme. Studien zur Ideengeschichte der Neuzeit, 2).

5514. SCHÖLLKOPF (Wolfgang). Johann Reinhard Hedinger (1664–1704), württembergischer Pietist und kirchlicher Praktiker zwischen Spener und den Separatisten. Göttingen, Vandenhoeck und Ruprecht, 99, 232 p.

5515. SINGH (Brijraj). The First Protestant missionary to India, Bartholomaeus Ziegenbalg 1683–1719. Cambridge, Cambridge U. P., 99, 204 p.

5516. SOMMER (Wolfgang). Politik, Theologie und Frömmigkeit im Luthertum der frühen Neuzeit: ausgewählte Aufsätze. Göttingen, Vandenhoeck und Ruprecht, 99, 317 p.

5517. STEVENSON (William). Sovereign Grace. The place and significance of Christian Freedom in John Calvin's political thought. New York, New York U. P., 99, 200 p.

5518. Sveriges kyrkohistoria. Band 3. Reformationstid. (Histoire ecclésiastique de la Suède. Tome 3. L'Epoque de la Réforme). Red. par Åke ANDREN. Stockholm, Verbum, 99, 360 p. (ill.).

5519. TAYLOR (Larissa Juliet). Heresy and Orthodoxy in sixteenth-century Paris. François Le Picart and the beginnings of the Catholic Reformation. Leiden, Brill, 99, XVIII-334 p.

5520. THUESEN (Peter J.). In discordance with the Scriptures: American Protestant battles over translating the Bible. New York, Oxford U. P., 99, XI-238 p.

5521. VAN DEN BERG (Johannes). Religious currents and cross-currents: essays on early modern Protestantism and the Protestant Enlightenment. Ed. by Jan BRUIJN. Leiden, Brill, 99, XIII-284 p.

5522. Vie (La) intellectuelle aux Refuges protestants. Par Jens HAESELER et Antony MAC KENNA. Paris, Champion, 99, 363 p.

5523. WANDEL (Lee Palmer). Voracious idols and violent hands. Iconoclasm in Reformation Zurich, Strasbourg and Basel. Cambridge, Cambridge U. P., 99, XII-205 p.

5524. WIEDEN (Susanne bei der). Luthers Predigten des Jahres 1522: Untersuchungen zu ihrer Überlieferung. Köln, Böhlau, 99, X-475 p.

5525. YATES (Nigel). Anglican ritualism in Victorian Britain: 1830–1910. Oxford, Oxford U. P., 99, XIV-455 p.

5526. Z'GRAGGEN (Bruno). Tyrannenmord im Toggenburg. Fürstäbtische Herrschaft und protestantischer Widerstand um 1600. Zürich, Chronos, 99, 439 p.

Cf. n°s 5994, 6853

§ 5. Non-Christian religions and sects.

** 5527. Processi del S. Uffizio di Venezia contro ebrei e giudaizzanti. Vol. 14. Indici generali. A cura di Pier Cesare IOLY ZORATTINI. Firenze, L. S. Olschki, 99, 417 p. (Fontes S. Officii Venetiarum ad res Iudaicas spectantes).

5528. American Buddhism: methods and findings in recent scholarship. Eds. by Duncan Ryūken WILLIAMS and Christer S. QUEEN. Richmond, Curzon Press, 99, XXXVII-329 p.

5529. ARMANI (Barbara). L'identità sfidata: gli ebrei fuori dal ghetto. Storica, 99, 5, 15, p. 69-103.

5530. BESALEL (Yusuf). Osmanlı ve Türk yahudileri. (Les Juifs turco-ottomans). İstanbul, Gözlem Gazetecilik Basın ve Yayın A.Ş., 99, 320 p.

5531. Bibliotheca dissidentium. Répertoire des nonconformistes religieux des XVIe et XVIIe s. Ed. par André SÉGUENNY en collab. avec Jean ROTT. Vol. 20. Dissidents russes. 2. Matvej Baškin, le starec Artemij. Par Mikhail V. DMITRIEV. Baden Baden, Bouxwiller, V. Koerner, 99, 179 p. (Bibliotheca bibliographica Aureliana, 169).

5532. CASINI (Fabio). Santa sede e Shoah. Considerazioni sul documento vaticano del 16 marzo 1998. Studi senesi, 99, 111, 3, p. 203-277

5533. CASSUTO (P.). Spinoza hébraïsant. L'hebreu dans le «Tractatus theologico-politicus» et le «Compendium grammatices linguae hebreae». Leuven, Peeters, 99, VIII-361 p.

5534. DALL'OLIO (Guido). Ebrei, papi, vescovi e inquisitori a Bologna alla metà del Cinquecento. Le premesse dell'espulsione del 1569. Annali dell'Istituto storico italo-germanico in Trento, 99, 25, p. 153-204.

5535. GASRATJAN (Svetlana M.). Istorija i ideologija evrejskogo religioznogo dvizhenija XIX–XX vv.: Iz predystorii Gosudarstva Izrail'. (History and ideology of Jewish religious movement, 19th–20th centuries: on the prehistory of the state of Israel). RAN, In-t vostokovedenija. Moskva, [s. n.], 99, 237 p. (bibl.). [Eng. summary]

5536. GORDIEJEW (Paul Benjamin). Voices of Yugoslav Jewry. Albany, State University of New York Press, 99, XVI-479 p. (SUNY series in anthropology and Judaic studies).

5537. GUOLO (Renzo). Avanguardie della fede: l'islamismo tra ideologia e politica. Milano, Guerini, 99, 143 p.

5538. HAGEMANN (Ludwig). Christentum contra Islam: eine Geschichte gescheiterter Beziehungen. Darmstadt, Buchges, 99, XIV-156 p.

5539. HAWTING (G.R.). The idea of idolatry and the emergence of Islam: from polemic to history. Cambridge, Cambridge U. P., 99, XVII-168 p.

5540. HELLER (Marvin J.). Printing the Talmud: a history of the individual treatises printed from 1700 to 1750. Leiden, Brill, 99, XIV-390 p. (ill.). (Brill's series in Jewish studies, 21).

5541. JALIMAM (Salih). Historija bosanskih bogomila. (History of Bosnian Bogomiles). Tuzla, IPP Hamidovic, 99, 315 p.

5542. JOHANSON (Baber). Contingency in a sacred law: legal and ethical norm in the Muslim Fiqh. Leyden, Boston a. Köln, Brill, 99, 521 p.

5543. Judenvertreibungen in Mittelalter und früher Neuzeit. Hrsg. Friedhelm BURGARD. Hannover Hahnsche Buchhandlung, 99, VI-276 p.

5544. KATZBURG (Nathaniel). Fejezetek az újkori zsidó történelemből Magyarországon. (Chapters from the modern Jewish history in Hungary). Ford: ÁCS Gábor. Budapest, MTA Judaisztikai Kutatócsoport, Osiris, 99, 244 p.

5545. Konstruktion (Die) der Nation gegen die Juden. Hrsg. v. Peter ALTER [et al.]. München, Fink, 99, 290 p.

5546. LITVINSKII (Boris Anatol'evich). Die Geschichte des Buddhismus in Ostturkestan. Wiesbaden, Harrassowitz, 99, X-130 p. (Studies in Oriental religions, 44).

5547. MOSTYN (Trevor). A history of censorship in Islamic societies. London, Saqui, 99, 240 p.

5548. MURATA (Yasuho). Shinbutsu-bunri no chihoteki tenkai. (The separation of Shintoism and Buddhism in modern Japanese provinces). Tokyo, Yoshikawa Kobunkan, 99, 311 p.

5549. NOMURA (Mari). Uin no yudayajin: 19 seiki matsu kara Horokosuto zenya made. (Jews in Vienna: from the end of nineteenth century to the eve of the Holocaust). Tokyo, Ochanomizu Shobo, 99, 455 p.

5550. OVERMYER (Daniel L.). Precious volumes. An introduction to Chinese sectarian scriptures from the sixteenth and seventeenth centuries. Cambridge, Harvard U. P., 99, XI-444 p.

5551. SALVADORI (Roberto G.). 1799. Gli ebrei italiani nella bufera antigiacobina. Firenze, Giuntina, 99, 123 p.

5552. Turkish Islam and Europe: Europe and Christianity as reflected in Turkish Muslim discourse and Turkish Muslim life in the diaspora; papers of the Istanbul workshop. October 1996. Ed. by Günter SEUFERT. Stuttgart, Steiner, 99, 352 p.

5553. Two nations: British and German Jews in comparative perspective. Ed. by Michael BRENNER, Rainer LIEDTKE and David RECHTER. Coordinated by Werner MOSSE. Tübingen, Mohr Siebeck, 99, IX-504 p. (Schriftenreihe wissenschaftlicher Abhandlungen des Leo Baeck Instituts, 60).

5554. UBEROI (J.P.S.). Religion, civil society and the State. A study of Sikhism. Oxford, Oxford U. P., 99, XVII-166 p.

5555. VITAL (David). A people apart. The Jews in Europe, 1789–1939. Oxford, Oxford U. P., 99, XVIII-944 p.

5556. WADUD-MUHSIN (Amina). Qur'an and woman: reading the sacred text from a woman's perspective. Oxford, Oxford U. P., 99, XXVI-118 p.

5557. YAMAGUCHI (Teruomi). Meiji kokka to shukyo. (Religion and the State in Meiji Japan). Tokyo, University of Tokyo Press, 99, 376 p.

Cf. n°s 62, 63, 3287, 3947, 4225, 4421, 4469, 5009, 5680, 6842, 6884, 8050, 8350

M

HISTORY OF MODERN CULTURE

§ 1. General. 5558-5718. – § 2. Academies and intellectual organizations. 5719-5759. – § 3. Education. 5760-5827. – § 4. The Press. 5828-5878. – § 5. Philosophy. 5879-6029. – § 6. Exact, natural, medical sciences and technique. 6030-6183. – § 7. Literature (*a.* General; *b.* Renaissance; *c.* Classicism; *d.* Romanticism and after). 6184-6381. – § 8. Art and Industrial art (*a.* General; *b.* Architecture; *c.* Sculpture, painting, etching and drawing; *d.* Decorative, popular and industrial art). 6382-6512. – § 9. Music, theatre, cinema and broadcasting. 6513-6634.

§ 1. General.

* 5558. Bibliografia degli scritti di Eugenio Garin: 1929–1999. Roma e Bari, Laterza, 99, 308 p.

* 5559. Bibliografia italiana di studi sull'Umanesimo e il Rinascimento. 1997. [1996. Cf. Bibl. 98, n° 5582.] Firenze, Olschki, 99, [s. p.]. (Rinascimento, XXXVII. Supplemento).

* 5560. Bibliographie de l'histoire des politiques culturelles: France, XIXe–XXe siècles. Ed. par Philippe POIRRIER. Paris, Comité d'histoire du Ministère de la culture, 99, 221 p. (Comité d'histoire du Ministère de la culture: Travaux et documents, 9).

* 5561. Bibliographie internationale de l'Humanisme et de la Renaissance. Vol. 31, 1995. Genève, Droz, 99, LX-442 p.

* 5562. Festivals and ceremonies: a bibliography of works relating to court, civic and religious festivals in Europe, 1500–1800. Ed. by Helen WATANABE-O'KELLY and Anne SIMON. London a. New York, Mansell, 99, XIX-533 p.

* 5563. Gemeinsame Haus (Das) – Fundgrube Europa: Bibliographie zur europäische Kulturgeschichte. Hrsg. v. Wulf KÖPKE und Bernd SCHMELZ, Bonn, Holos, 99, 428 p.

* 5564. KRAUS (Hans-Christof). Gegenaufklärung, Spätromantik, Konservatismus. Zu einigen neueren Veröffentlichungen. *Historische Zeitschrift*, 99, 269, 2, p. 371-413.

* 5565. Siècle (Le) des Lumières. Bibliographie chronologique. T. 18. 1776–1778. T. 19. 1779–1781. Ed. par Pierre M. CONLON. Genève, Droz, 99, 2 vol., XXXV-582 p., XXXI-631 p.

** 5566. ARTIZOV (Andrej V.), NAUMOV (Oleg V.). Vlast' i khudozhestvennaja intelligentsija: Documenty TsK RKP(b), VChK-OGPU-NKVD o kul'turnoj politike, 1917–1953 gg. (The power and the artistic intelligentsia in Russia, 1917–1953: documents). Moskva, Mezhdunar. fond. 'Demokratija', 99, 869 p. (ind.). (Rossija. XX vek. Dokumenty).

** 5567. BRAMANTI (Vanni). Lettere inedite di Jacopo Nardi. *Archivio storico italiano*, 99, 157, 579, p. 101-130.

** 5568. Edizione nazionale del carteggio di L. A. Muratori. A cura del Centro di studi muratoriani, Modena. Vol. 10. 1. Carteggio con G. Domenico Brichieri Colombi. A cura di Fabio MARRI e Barbara PAPAZZONI. Vol. 28. Carteggi con Mansi ... Marmi. A cura di Corrado VIOLA. Firenze, L. S. Olschki, 99, 2 vol., 494 p., 585 p.

** 5569. LOCK (F. P.). Unpublished Burke letters (II), 1765–1797. *English historical review*, 99, 114, 457, p. 636-657.

5570. ALBRECHT (Clemens), BEHRMANN (Günter C.), BOCK (Michael), HOMANN (Harald), TENBRUCK (Friedrich H.). Die intellektuelle Gründung der Bundesrepublik. Eine Wirkungsgeschichte der Frankfurter Schule. Frankfurt a. M., Campus Verlag, 99, 649 p.

5571. Alger 1860–1939: le modèle ambigu du triomphe colonial. Dir. par Jean-Jacques JORDI et Jean-Louis PLANCHE. Paris, Autrement, 99, 231 p. (ill.). (Collection Mémoires, 55). – Alger 1940–1962: une ville en guerres. Dir. par Jean-Jacques JORDI et Guy PERVILLÉ, Paris, Autrement, 99, 261 p. (ill.). (Collection Mémoires, 56).

5572. ALMOND (Philip C.). Adam and Eve in seventeenth-century thought. New York a. Cambridge, Cambridge U. P., 99, IX-240 p. (bibl.).

5573. ALTER (Stephen G.). Darwinism and the linguistic image: language, race, and natural theology in the ninenteenth century. Baltimore, Johns Hopkins U. P., 99, XIII-193 p.

5574. AMANN (Wilhelm). "Die stille Arbeit des Geschmacks": Die Kategorie des Geschmacks in der Ästhetik Schillers und in den Debatten der Aufklärung. Würzburg, Königshausen & Neumann, 99, 338 p. (Epistemata. Reihe Literaturwissenschaft, 268).

5575. Américains (Les) et la France (1917–1947). Engagements et représentations. Actes du Colloque organisé à Reims, 22–23 mai 1997. Paris, Maisonneueve & Larose, 99, 262 p.

5576. Anonymat et clandestinité aux XVIIe et XVIIIe siècles. Actes de la Journée de Créteil du 11 juin 1999. *Lettre clandestine*, 99, 8, p. 13-138.

5577. Antisémitisme (L') de plume, 1940–1944. Etudes et documents. Ed. par Pierre-André TAGUIEFF. Paris, Berg International, 99, 618 p.

5578. ARSLAN (Mehmet). Türk edebiyatında manzum surnameler: Osmanlı saray düğünleri ve şenlikler. (Livres en vers des réjouissances publiques dans la littérature turque: les noces et les festins impériaux ottomans). Ankara, Atatürk Araştırma Merkezi, 99, X-837 p.

5579. BADINTER (Elisabeth). Les passions intellectuelles. I. Désirs de gloire (1735–1751). Paris, Fayard, 99, 545 p.

5580. BATTISTA (Anna). La Germania di Tacito nella Francia illuminista. Urbino, Quattroventi, 99, 68 p.

5581. BEALE (Marjorie A.). The modernist enterprise: French elites and the threat of modernity, 1900–1940. Stanford, Stanford U. P., 99, IX-231 p.

5582. BECKER (Ernst Wolfgang). Zeit der Revolution! Revolution der Zeit? Zeiterfahrungen in Deutschland in der Ära der Revolutionen, 1789–1848/49. Göttingen, Vandenhoeck & Ruprecht, 99, 396 p. (Kritische Studien der Geschichtswissenschaft, 129).

5583. BENTIVEGNA (Giuseppe). Dal riformismo muratoriano alle filosofie del Risorgimento: contributi alla storia intellettuale della Sicilia. Napoli, Guida, 99, 348 p.

5584. BENZONI (Gino). Da palazzo Ducale. Studi sul Quattro-Settecento veneto. Venezia, Marsilio, 99, [s. p.].

5585. BERKOWITZ (Peter). Virtue and the making of modern liberalism. Princeton, Princeton U. P., 99, XVIII-235 p.

5586. BOLLENBECK (Georg). Tradition, Avantgarde, Reaktion. Deutsche Kontroversen um die kulturelle Moderne 1880–1945. Frankfurt am Main, Fischer, 99, 463 p.

5587. BROMER (Stephen Eric). Ideas in action: political tradition in the twentieth century. Lanham, Rowman and Littlefield, 99, X-349 p.

5588. BROOKS (Jeffrey). Thank you, comrade Stalin! Soviet public culture from the Revolution to the Cold War. Princeton, Princeton U. P., 99, XX-319 p.

5589. BURGDORF (Wolfgang). "Chimäre Europa". Antieuropäische Diskurse in Deutschland (1648–1999). Bochum, Wikler, 99, 267 p. (Herausforderung historisch-politische Analysen, 7).

5590. BURKE (Peter). Il Rinascimento europeo: centri e periferie. Roma, Laterza, 99, X-414 p. (Fare l'Europa).

5591. CANDLER HAYES (Julie). Reading the French Enlightenment: system and subversion. Cambridge, Cambridge U. P., 99, X-243 p. (Cambridge studies in French, 60).

5592. CARTOSIO (Bruno). Da New York a Santa Fe: terra, culture native, artisti e scrittori nel Sudovest, 1846–1930. Firenze, Giunti, 99, 383 p. (Saggi Giunti).

5593. CATANO (Gonzalo). Historia, sociología y política: ensayos de sociología e historia de las ideas. Santafé de Bogotá, Plaza & Janés Editores, 99, 282 p. (Serie Educación y cultura).

5594. CELENZA (Christopher S.). Renaissance Humanism and the Papal Curia: Lapo da Castiglionchio the Younger's De curiae commodis. Ann Arbor, University of Michigan Press, 99, XIV-244 p. (Papers and monographs of the American Academy in Rome, 31).

5595. CHARLE (Christophe). Paris métropole culturelle. Essai de comparaison avec Berlin (1880–1920). *Mélanges de l'École française de Rome. Italie Méditerranée*, 99, 111, 1, p. 455-476.

5596. CLARK (T. J.). Farewell to an idea: episodes from a history of modernism. New Haven a. London, Yale U. P., 99, VII-451 p.

5597. CLEMENS (Detlev). The 'Bavarian Mussolini' and his 'Beerhall Putsch': British images of Adolf Hitler, 1920–1924. *English historical review*, 99, 114, 455, p. 64-84.

5598. COFRANCESCO (Dino). Intellettuali e potere: capitoli di storia della cultura italiana del Novecento. Genova, Name, 99, 251 p. (Teoria politica).

5599. COHEN (Evelyne). Paris dans l'imaginaire national de l'entre-deux-guerres. Paris, Publ. de la Sorbonne, 99, 398 p.

5600. Cold War propaganda in the 1950s. Ed. by Gary D. RAWNSLEY. Basingstoke, Macmillan, 99, XI-246 p.

5601. COLISH (Marcia L.). Republicanism, religion, and Machiavelli's Savonarolan moment. *In*: Machiavelli and religion: a reappraisal [Cf. n° 5665], p. 597-616.

5602. COMBE (Sonia). Une société sous surveillance. Les intellectuels et la Stasi. Paris, Albin Michel, 99, 264 p.

5603. CORBIN (Annalies). The material culture of steamboat passengers: archaeological evidence from the Missouri river. New York a. London, Kluwer Academic a. Plenum Publishers, 99, XVII-237 p. (ill., bibl.).

5604. CROMARTIE (Alan). The constitutionalist revolution: the transformation of political culture in early Stuart England. *Past & present*, 99, n. 163, p. 76-120.

5605. Culture and the State in Spain 1550–1850. Ed. by Tom LEWIS and Francisco J. SÁNCHEZ. New York a. London, Garland, 99, XXIII-305 p.

5606. DART (Gregory). Rousseau, Robespierre and English romanticism. Cambridge, Cambridge U. P., 99, XI-288 p.

5607. DATTA (Venita). Birth of national icon: the literary avant-garde and the origins of the intellectual in France. Albany, State University of New York Press, 99, XII-327 p.

5608. DONNERT (Erich). Katharina II. in ihrem Verhältnis zur Aufklärung, Freimaurerei und gesellschaftskritischen Literatur in Rußland. *Archiv für Kulturgeschichte*, 99, 81, 1, p. 81-104.

5609. DOOLEY (Brendan Maurice). De bonne main: les pourvoyeurs de nouvelles à Rome au 17e siècle. *Annales*, 99, 54, 6, p. 1317-1344. – IDEM. The social history of skepticism: experience and doubt in early modern culture. Baltimore a. London, Johns Hopkins U. P., 99, VIII-213 p. (Johns Hopkins University studies in historical and political science, 117th, 2).

5610. DUCLERT (Vincent). Les intellectuels, l'antisémitisme et l'affaire Dreyfus en France. *Revue des études juives*, 9958, 1-2, p.105-211.

5611. DUSO (Giuseppe). La logica del potere. Storia concettuale come filosofia politica. Roma e Bari, Laterza, 99, VII-231 p. (Biblioteca di cultura moderna, 1147).

5612. ESGUERRA (Jorge Cañizares). New world, new stars: patriotic astrology and the invention of Indian and Creole bodies in colonial Spanish America, 1600–1650. *American historical review*, 99, 104, 1, p. 33-68.

5613. Europäische Jahrhundertwende: Wissenschaften, Literatur und Kunst um 1900. Hrsg. v. Ulrich MÖLK. Göttingen, Wallstein, 99, 327 p. (ill.).

5614. European culture in the Great War. The arts, entertainment and propaganda, 1914–1918. Ed. by Aviel ROSHWALD and Richard STITES. Cambridge, Cambridge U. P., 99, 430 p.

5615. Expédition (L') d'Egypte, une entreprise des Lumières, 1789–1801. Paris, Académie des Sciences, 99, 436 p.

5616. FEDOSOVA (El'mira P.). Rossija i Pribaltika: Kul'turnyj dialog, vtoraja polovina XIX–nachalo XX veka. (Russia and the Baltic Lands: a culture dialogue, the 2nd half of the 19th and the early 20th centuries). RAN, In-t rossijskoj istorii. Moskva, [s. n.], 99, 211 p. (bibl.; ind.).

5617. FIGAL (Gerald). Civilization and monsters: spirits of modernity in Meiji Japan. Durham, Duke U. P., 99, XI-290 p (Asia-Pacific: culture, politics, and society; studies of East Asian Institute, Columbia University).

5618. Figura (La) e l'opera di Raffaele Mattioli. Milano, Ricciardi, 99, 311 p. [relazioni presentate ai convegni tenuti a Vasto nel 1980 e 1996].

5619. FONTANA (Benedetto). Love of country and love of god: the political uses of religion in Machiavelli. *In*: Machiavelli and religion: a reappraisal [Cf. n° 5665], p. 639-658.

5620. FORSSMAN (Erik). Goethezeit: über die Entstehung des bürgerlichen Kunstverständnisses. München, Deutscher Kunstverlag, 99, 318 p. (ill.).

5621. FOX (Claire F.). The fence and the river: culture and politics at the U.S.-Mexico border. Minneapolis a. London, University of Minnesota Press, 99, X-188 p. (ill., bibl.). (Cultural studies of the Americas, 1).

5622. FRANK (Stephen P.). Crime, cultural conflict, and justice in rural Russia, 1856–1914. Berkeley a. London, University of California Press, 99, XXII-352 p. (Studies on the history of society and culture, 31).

5623. FUMAROLI (Marc). La querelle des Anciens et des Modernes. Sans vainqueurs ni vaincus. *Débat*, 99, 104, p. 73-88.

5624. Gabriel Naudé: la politique et les mythes de l'histoire de France. Sous la direction de Robert DAMIEN et Yves-Charles ZARKA. Paris, Centre d'Etudes d'Histoire de la Philosophie moderne et contemporaine, Université Paris X, 99, 202 p. (Corpus: revue de philosophie, 35).

5625. GARDEY (Delphine). Mécaniser l'écriture et photographier la parole. Des utopies au monde du bureau, histoires de genre et de techniques. *Annales*, 99, 54, 3, p. 587-614.

5626. GEERKEN (John H.). Machiavelli's Moses and renaissance politics. *In*: Machiavelli and religion: a reappraisal [Cf. n° 5665], p. 579-596.

5627. Gelehrsamkeit in Deutschland und Italien im 18. Jahrhundert. Hrsg. v. Giorgio CUSATELLI. Tübingen, Niemeyer, 99, XV-312 p. (Hallesche Beiträge zur Europäischen Aufklärung).

5628. Gelehrte Gesellschaften im mitteldeutschen Raum (1650–1820). Hrsg. v. Detlef DÖRING und Kurt NOWAK. Leipzig u. Stuttgart, Verlag der Sächsischen Akademie der Wissenschaften u. In Kommission bei S. Hirzel, 99, 238 p. (ill.). (Abhandlungen der Sächsischen Akademie der Wissenschaften zu Leipzig, Philologisch-Historische Klasse, 76).

5629. GERBI (Sandro). Tempi di malafede. Una storia italiana tra fascismo e dopoguerra. Guido Piovene ed Eugenio Colorni. Torino, Einaudi, 99, 308 p.

5630. GLAAB (Manuela). Deutschlandpolitik in der öffentlichen Meinung: Einstellungen und Regierungspolitik in der Bundesrepublik Deutschland 1949-1990. Opladen, Leske - Budrich, 99, 431 p. (ill.).

5631. Glückseligkeit (Die) des gemeinen Wesens: Wege der Ideen zwischen Italien und Deutschland im Zeitalter der Aufklärung. Hrsg. v. Fabio MARRI und Maria LIEBER. Frankfurt am Main u. New York, Lang, 99, 230 p. (ill.). (Italien in Geschichte und Gegenwart, 14).

5632. GÓMEZ ACUÑA (Luis). Ideología y política en José de la Riva Aguero y Osma. *Histórica*, 99, 23, 1, p. 79-109.

5633. GONZÁLEZ GAVIOLA (Horacio). Restos pampeanos: ciencia, ensayo y política en la cultura argentina del siglo XX. Buenos Aires, Colihue, 99, 435 p. (Serie mayor. Punaladas).

5634. GOUK (Penelope). Music, science, and natural magic in seventeenth-century England. New Haven a. London, Yale U. P., 99, XII-308 p.

5635. GRAY (Edward G.). New World Babel: languages and nations in early America. Princeton, Princeton U. P., 99, XIV-185 p. (ill., bibl.).

5636. GROEBNER (Valentin). Körpergeschichte politisch. Montaigne und die Ordnungen der Natur in den französischen Religionskriegen 1572-1592. *Historische Zeitschrift*, 99, 269, 2, p. 281-304.

5637. GUINERET (Hervé). Clausewitz et la guerre. Paris, Presses Universitaires de France, 99, 136 p. (Philosophies, 118).

5638. HARRISON (Dick). I skuggan av Cathay: Västeuropéers möte med Asien 1400-1600. (A l'ombre de Cathay: la rencontre de l'Occident avec l'Asie, 1400-1600). Lund, Historiska media, 99, 274 p.

5639. HODGES (Donald Clark). The literate communist: 150 years of the Communist Manifesto. New York, Peter Lang, 99, VI-216 p. (bibl.). (Major Concepts in Politics and Political Theory, 16).

5640. Idées politiques au temps de Saint-Simon. Journée d'etudes organisée par la société de Saint-Simon, Paris 13 mars 1999. *Cahiers Saint-Simon*, 99, 27, p. 1-59.

5641. Intellectuels européens (Les) et la campagne d'Italie, 1796-1798. Ed. par Jean-Paul BARBE et Roland BERNECKER. Münster, Nodus Publikationes, 99, 236 p.

5642. Invention (L') du XIXe siècle: le XIXe siècle par lui-même (littérature, histoire, société). Ed. par Alain CORBIN. Parigi, Klincksieck et Presses de la Sorbonne nouvelle, 99, XIII-383 p. (Bibliothèque du XIXe siècle). [Cf. n° <sélection> 496.]

5643. Ireland and the French Enlightenment, 1700-1800. Ed. by Graham GARGETT and Geraldine SHERIDAN. New York, St. Martin's Press, 99, XVII-293 p.

5644. Järnbur eller frigörelse? Studier i moderniseringen av Sverige. (Mise en cage ou libération? Etudes sur la modernisation de la Suède). Red. par Gösta ARVASTSON. Lund, Studentlitteratur, 99, 146 p.

5645. JENKINS (Philip). The Cold War at home: the Red Scare in Pennsylvania, 1945-1960. Chapell Hill, University of North Carolina Press, 99, XIV-271 p.

5646. JESSEPH (Douglas M.). Squaring the circle. The war between Hobbes and Wallis. Chicago, University of Chicago Press, 99, XIV-419 p.

5647. JONES (William Jervis). Images of language: six essays on German attitudes to European languages from 1500 to 1800. Amsterdam a. Philadelphia, John Benjamins, X-297 p. (Studies in the history of the language sciences, 89).

5648. KAMMEN (Michael G.). American culture, American tastes: social change and the 20th century. New York, BasicBooks, 99, XIX-320 p. (ill.).

5649. KLEINGELD (Pauline). Six varieties of cosmopolitanism in late eighteenth-century Germany. *Journal of the history of ideas*, 99, 60, 3, p. 505-524.

5650. KNAPÍK (Jiří). Kdo je kdo v kulturní politice 1948-1953. Biografický heslář stranických funkcionářů, svazových pracovníků, redaktorů. (Who is who in cultural policy in Czechoslovakia, 1948-1953). Opava, J. Knapík, 99, 55 p.

5651. KRAMER (Hilton). The twilight of the intellectuals: culture and politics in the era of the Cold War. Chicago, Ivan R. Dee, 99, XX-363 p.

5652. Kul'tura Vozrozhdenija i vlast': Sb. st. (The culture of the Renaissance and the power: articles). Ed. Lidija M. BRAGINA. Moskva, Nauka, 99, 223 p. (ill., bibl.).

5653. Kul'turnaja politika v stranakh Tsentral'noj i Vosotchnoj Evropy, 1920-1950-e gody. (Cultural policy in the countries of Central and Eastern Europe, 1920-1950es). Ed. A. S. STYKALIN. RAN, In-t slavjanovedenija. Moskva, [s. n.], 99, 161 p. (bibl.). (Vlast' i intelligentsija, 3).

5654. Kultur, Identität, Europa. Über die Schwierigkeiten und Möglichkeiten einer Konstruktion. Hrsg. v. Reinhold VIEHOFF und Rien T. SEGERS. Frankfurt am Main, Suhrkamp, 99, 441 p. (Suhrkamp Taschenbuch Wissenschaft, 1330).

5655. Kunst und Kultur in Österreich: das 20. Jahrhundert. Hrsg. v. Barbara DENSCHER. Wien, C. Brandstätter, 99, 320 p. (ill.).

5656. LARIZZA LOLLI (Mirella). Bandiera verde contro bandiera rossa. Auguste Comte e gli inizi della Société positiviste (1848-1852). Bologna, Il Mulino, 99, 602 p.

5657. LEE (Robert G). Orientals: Asian Americans in popular culture. Philadelphia, Temple U. P., 99, 288 p. (Asian American history and culture).

5658. LEVINE (Joseph M.). Between the ancients and the moderns: baroque culture in restoration England. New Haven, Yale U. P., 99, XIV-279 p. (ill.).

5659. LITCHFIELD (R. Burr). Un mercante fiorentino alla corte dei Medici. Le "Memorie" di Roberto di Roberto Pepi (1572–1634). *Archivio storico italiano*, 99, 157, 582, p. 727-782.

5660. LIUCCI (Raffaele). La tentazione della «casa in collina». Il disimpegno degli intellettuali nella guerra civile italiana (1943–1945). Milano, UNICOPLI, 99, 204 p.

5661. LLASERA (Margaret). Représentation scientifique et images poétiques en Angleterre au XVIIe siècle. À la recherche de l'invisible. Paris, CNRS et ENS Éditions, 99, 300 p.

5662. LLUCH (Ernest). Las Españas vencidas del siglo XVIII. Claroscuros de la Ilustración. Barcelona, Crítica, 99, 252 p.

5663. LÖSCH (Doris). Property, order und civil war. Zum Diskurs über Eigentum in England 1580–1649. Berlin, Bodenheim, 99, 319 p.

5664. MAC LAREN (Anne N.). Political culture in the reign of Elizabeth I: Queen and Commonwealth 1558–1585. New York a. Cambridge, Cambridge U. P., 99, IX-272 p. (bibl.). (Ideas in context).

5665. Machiavelli and religion: a reappraisal. *Journal of the history of ideas*, 99, 60, 4, p. 579-682. [Cf. n^{os} <choice> 5601, 5619, 5626, 5676, 5677.]

5666. MAILLARD (Jean-François), KECSKEMÉTI (Judit), MAGNIEN (Catherine), PORTALIER (Monique). La France des humanistes. Turnhout, Brepols, 99, LII-598 p.

5667. MATĚJČEK (Jiří). Stav výzkumu kulturního vývoje českých zemí v 19. století. Přehled za léta 1945–1998. (Bericht über den Forschungsstand der kulturellen Entwicklung der böhmischen Länder im 19. Jahrhundert. Übersicht für die Jahre 1945–1998]. *Slezský sborník*, 99, 97, 3/4, p. 251-264.

5668. MAUGER (Gérard), POLIAK (Claude F.), PUDAL (Bernard). Histoires de lecteurs. Paris, Nathan, 99, 446 p. (Essais et recherches).

5669. MELLEY (Timothy). Empire of conspiracy: the culture of paranoia in postwar America. Ithaca, Cornell U. P., 99, 239 p.

5670. METHA (Uday Singh). Liberalism and empire: a study in nineteenth-century british liberal thought. Chicago, University of Chicago Press, 99, XII-237 p.

5671. Mexico's new cultural history ¿Una Lucha Libre? *Hispanic American historical review*, 99, 79, 2, p. 203-383. [Contents: DEANS-SMITH (Susan), JOSEPH (Gilbert M.). The arena of dispute. – VAN YOUNG (Eric). The new cultural history comes to old Mexico. – FRENCH (William E.). Imagining and the cultural history of nineteenth-century Mexico. – VAUGHAN (Mary Kay). Cultural approaches to peasant politics in the Mexican revolution. – HABER (Stephen). Anything goes: Mexico's «new» cultural history. – MALLON (Florencia E.). Time on the wheel: cycles of revisionism and the «new cultural History». – MIGDEN SOCOLOW (Susan). Putting the «cult» in culture. – LOMNITZ (Claudio). Barbarians at the gate? A few remarks on the politics of the «new cultural history of Mexico»]

5672. MILICH (Klaus J.). Die frühe Postmoderne. Geschichte eines europäisch-amerikanischen Kulturkonflikts. Frankfurt a. M. Campus Verlag, 99, 241 p. (Nordamerikastudien, 6).

5673. Monde (Les) des Lumières. Ed. par Vincenzo FERRONE et Daniel ROCHE. Paris, Fayard, 99, 610 p.

5674. MOULINIER (Pierre). Les politiques publiques de la culture en France. Paris, Presses Universitaires de France, 99, 127 p. (Que sais-je?).

5675. Multiculturalisme (Le) et l'histoire des relations internationales du 18e siècle à nos jours. Ed. par Pierre SAVARD et Brunello VIGEZZI. Milano, UNICOPLI, 99, LXXX-541 p. (Università degli studi di Milano. Centro per gli studi di politica estera e opinione pubblica. Commission d'histoire des relationes internationale).

5676. NAJEMY (John M.). Papirius and the chickens, or Machiavelli on the necessity of interpreting religion. *In*: Machiavelli and religion: a reappraisal [Cf. n° 5665], p. 659-682.

5677. NEDERMAN (Cary J.). Amazing grace: fortune, god, and free will in Machiavelli's thought. *In*: Machiavelli and religion: a reappraisal [Cf. n° 5665], p. 617-638.

5678. NELLES (Paul). Histoire du savoir et bibliographie critique chez Naudé: le cas de la magie. *Corpus*, 99, 35, p. 117-132.

5679. Northern humanism in European context, 1469–1625: from the 'Adwert Academy' to Ubbo Emmius. Papers from a conference held at the University of Groningen on 11–12 April 1996. Ed by Fokke AKKERMAN, Arjo J. VANDERJAGT and Arend Hendrik VAN DER LAAN. Leiden a. Boston, Brill, 99, XI-373 p. (bibl.). (Brill's studies in intellectual history, 94).

5680. NOVICK (Peter). The Holocaust in American life. Boston, Houghton Mifflin, 99, 373 p.

5681. Origini (Le) della modernità. Vol. 1. Linguaggi e saperi tra XV e XVI secolo. Vol. 2. Linguaggi e saperi nel XVII secolo. Atti del Seminario, Le architetture del pensiero, Bologna, 1994. A cura di Walter TEGA. Firenze, L. S. Olschki, 99, 2 vol., VIII-197, V-226 p. (ill.). (Pansophia, 1-2).

5682. OSTRANDER (Gilman M.). Republic of Letters: the american intellectual community, 1776–1865. Madison, Madison House, 99, XVI-379 p.

5683. OTIS (Laura). Membranes: metaphors of invasion in nineteenth-century literature, science, and politics. Baltimore, Johns Hopkins U. P., 99, X-210 p. (bibl.).

5684. PASSERINI (Luisa). Europe in love, love in Europe: imagination and politics in Britain between the wars. London a. New York, 99, VIII-358 p. (ill.).

5685. PEARL (Jonathan L.). The crime of crimes: demonology and politics in France, 1560–1620. Waterloo, Wilfrid Laurier U. P., 99, VIII-181 p.

5686. Port-Royal et les mémoires. Actes du Colloque organisé par la Société des Amis de Port-Royal à Port-Royal-des-Champs les 17 et 18 septembre 1998. *Chronique du Port-Royal*, 99, 48, p. 7-248.

5687. PROCHASSON (Christophe). Paris 1900. Essai d'histoire culturelle. Paris, Calmann-Lévy, 99, 348 p.

5688. Race and the production of modern American nationalism. Ed. by Reynolds J. SCOTT-CHILDRESS. New York a. London, Garland Pub, 99, XXIV-391 p. (ill., bibl.). (Wellesley studies in critical theory, literary history, and culture, 18).

5689. ROHKRÄMER (Thomas). Eine andere Moderne? Zivilisationskritik, Natur und Technik in Deutschland 1880-1933. Paderborn u. München u. Wien u. Zürich, Schöningh, 99, 402 p.

5690. Roman presences: receptions of Rome in European culture, 1789-1945. Ed. by Catharine EDWARDS. New York, Cambridge U. P., 99, 279 p.

5691. ROWLEY (David G.). «Redeemer empire»: Russian millenarianism. [AHR Forum: Millenniums]. *American historical review*, 99, 104, 5, p. 1582-1602.

5692. RUDNITSKAJA (Evgenija L.). Poisk puti: Russkaja mysl' posle 14 dekabrja 1825 goda. (Searching the way: Russian thought after the 14th of December, 1825). Moskva, Editorial-URSS, 99, 271 p. (bibl., ind.).

5693. Ruskin and the dawn of the modern. Ed. by Dinah BIRCH. Oxford, Oxford U. P., 99, XI-194 p. [Cf. n^{os} <choice> 6130, 6177.]

5694. SCHILDT (Axel). Zwischen Abendland und Amerika: Studien zur westdeutschen Ideenlandschaft der 50er Jahre. München, R. Oldenbourg, 99, 242 p. (Ordnungssysteme, 4).

5695. SCHWARZ (Angela). Der Schlüssel zur modernen Welt. Wissenschaftspopularisierung in Großbritannien und Deutschland im Übergang zur Moderne (ca. 1870–1914). Stuttgart, Steiner, 99, 423 p.

5696. SCOTT (William B.), RUTKOFF (Peter M.). New York modern: the arts and the city. Baltimore, Johns Hopkins U. P., 99, XX-448 p.

5697. Shaping the Superman: Fascist body as political icon – Aryan Fascism. Ed. by J. A. MANGAN. Portland, Frank Cass, 99, XIII-215 p. (Sport in the global society).

5698. SHAPIRO (Barbara J.). A culture of fact: England, 1550–1720. Ithaca, Cornell U. P., 99, X-284 p.

5699. SHAVER (Robert). Rational egoism: a selective and critical history. New York a. Cambridge, Cambridge U. P., 99, XII-162 p.

5700. SMUTS (Robert Malcolm). Culture and power in England, 1585–1685. Social history in perspective. Basingstoke, Macmillan, 99, XI-201 p. (ill.).

5701. Socialisme, cultures, histoire: itinéraires et représentations: mélanges offerts à Miklós Molnár. Berne, P. Lang, 99, [s. p.]. [Cf. n^{os} <sélection> 3971, 5140, 7689.]

5702. *Vacat*.

5703. SPIES (Hans-Bernd). Achim von Arnim als Rezensent der memoiren Casanovas. *Archiv für Kulturgeschichte*, 99, 81, 2, p. 305-312.

5704. Stadt (Die) als Moloch? Das Land als Kraftquell? Wahrnehmungen und Wirkungen der Großstädte um 1900. Hrsg. v. Clemens ZIMMERMANN und Jürgen REULECKE. Basel, Boston u. Berlin, Birkhäuser, 99, 165 p. (Stadtforschung aktuelle, 76).

5705. TAROT (Camille). De Durkheim à Mauss, l'invention du symbolique: sociologie et sciences des religions. Paris, La Découverte, 99, 710 p. (Recherches. Serie Bibliotheque du M.A.U.S.S).

5706. TURCUŞ (Veronica). Alexandru Marcu (1894–1954) şi cultura italiană în România interbelică (Profil bio-bibliografic). [Alexandru Marcu (1894–1954) and Italian culture in interwar Romania. Bio-bibliographical sketch]. Cluj-Napoca, Editura Presa Universitară Clujeană, 99, 456 p. (Bibliotheca Bibliologica, 14).

5707. VALENTE (Michaela). Bodin in Italia. La 'Démonomanie des sorciers' e le vicende della sua traduzione. Firenze, CET, 1999, 226 p.

5708. Vier Besatzungsmächte (Die) und die Kultur in Berlin 1945-1949. Hrsg. v. Hans-Martin HINZ, Cyril BUFFET, Bernard GENTON und Pierre JARDIN. Leipzig, Leipziger Universitätsverlag, 99, 212 p.

5709. VILLARI (Lucio). Romanticismo e tempo dell' industria. Letteratura, libertà e macchine nell'Italia dell'Ottocento. Roma, Donzelli, 99, 100 p.

5710. Visiones de fin de siglo. Ed. por Raymond CARR. Madrid, Suma de Letras, 99, 320 p.

5711. WARREN (Frank A.). Noble Abstractions. American liberal intellectuals and World War II. Columbus, Ohio State U. P., 99, XXII-316 p.

5712. WEINER (Amir). Nature, nurture, and memory in a socialist utopia: delineating the Soviet socio-ethnic body in the age of socialism. *American historical review*, 99, 104, 4, p. 1114-1155.

5713. WHITFIELD (Stephen J.). In search of American Jewish culture. Hanover a. London, Brandeis U. P., 99, XVI-307 p. (bibl.). (Brandeis series in American Jewish history, culture, and life).

5714. WILSON (W. Daniel). Das Goethe-Tabu. Protest und Menschenrechte im klassischen Weimar. München, Deutscher Taschenbuch Verlag, 99, 413 p.

5715. Wonders, marvels, and monsters in early modern culture. Ed. by Peter G. PLATT. Newark a. London, University of Delaware Press a. Associated University Presses, 99, 341 p. (ill.). [Contents. MIROLLO (James V.). The aesthetics of the marvelous: the wondrous work of art in a wondrous world. – SUMMERS (David). Pandora's crown: on wonder, imitation, and mechanism in Western art. – DASTON (Lorraine). Marvelous facts and miraculous evidence in early modern Europe. – GREENBLATT (Stephen). Introduction to marvelous possessions. – LAKE PRESCOTT (Anne). Rabelaisian (non)wonders and Renaissance polemics. – PERRY LONG (Kathleen). Sexual dissonance: early modern scientific accounts of hermaphrodites. – KAY (Dennis). Who says "miracles are past"? Some Jacobean Marvels and the margins of the known. – BURNS (William E.). The king's two monstrous bodies: John Bulwer and the English revolution. – SPIRES (Margaret). The true face of philosophy as magical object: the limits of wisdom and the constitution of the (super)natural in Montaigne's essays 1.26 and 1.27. – BISHOP (Tom). "Come, let me clutch thee": Macbeth and the marvelous text. – KINGSLEY (Margery). Interpreting providence: the politics of Jermiad in restoration polemic. – MUSGRAVE (William R.). The politics of the monstrous in Burke and Kant. – BIESTER (James). Fancy's images: wit, the sublime, and rise of aestheticism.].

5716. World War (From) to Waldheim: culture and politics in Austria and the United States. Ed. by David F. GOOD and Ruth WODAK. New York a. Oxford, Berghahn Books, 99, VIII-248 p. (bibl.).

5717. ZEZINA (Marija R.). Sovetskaja khudozhestvennaja intelligentsija i vlast' v 1950-e-60-e gody. (The artistic intelligentsia and the power in Soviet Russia in the 1950s and the 1960s). Moskovskij gos. un-t im. M.V. Lomonosova, Ist. f-t. Moskva, Dialog-MGU, 99, 398 p. (bibl., ind.).

§ 1. Addenda 1998.

* 5718. Czasopismo prawno-historyczne. Bibliografia zawartości za lata 1948–1998. *Czasopismo Prawno-historyczne*, 98, 50, 2, 167 p.

Cf. n°s 871, 912, 938, 5014, 5379, 5505, 5994, 6395, 6947, 7852

§ 2. Academies and intellectual organizations.

** 5719. BARVÍKOVÁ (Hana), JANDEROVÁ (Helena), PODANÝ (Václav). Fondy Archivu Akademie věd České republiky. (Fonds des Archivs der Akademie der Wissenschaften). Praha, Archiv Akademie věd ČR, 99, 361 p. (photogr.). (Práce z dějin Akademie věd, Ser.B, 13).

** 5720. Giornale della gloriosissima Accademia Ricovrata. Verbali delle adunanze accademiche dal 1599 al 1694. A cura di Antonio GAMBA e Lucia ROSSETTI. Vicenza, Edizioni LINT, 99, XXI-540 p. (Accademia galileiana di scienze, lettere ed arti in Padova. Atti, documenti e testi, 1).

5721. ARTEM'EVA (Tat'iana Vladimirovna). Filosofiia v Peterburgskoi akademii nauk XVIII veka. (Philosophy at the Petersburg Academy of Sciences in the 18th century). Sankt-Peterburg, Sankt-Peterburgskii Tsentr istorii idei, 99, 182 p. (bibl.).

5722. BARROWMAN (Rachel). Victoria University of Wellington, 1899–1999: a history. Wellington, Victoria U. P., 99, 432 p. (ill.).

5723. BENEDETIČ (Ana). Poti do univerze: 1848–1898-1909-1919. (Paths to the university: 1848–1898-1909–1919). Ljubljana, Studia humanitatis, 99, 297-67 p. (ill.). (Studia humanitatis, Apes, Posebna izd.).

5724. BOOCKMANN (Harmut). Wissen und Widerstand: Geschichte der deutschen Universität. Berlin, Siedler, 99, 287 p. (ill.).

5725. BRIZZI (Gian Paolo). Les universités européennes à l'époque moderne: premières synthèses. *Histoire de l'éducation*, 99, 81, p. 23-34.

5726. CIARDI (Marco). La fine dei privilegi: scienze fisiche, tecnologia e istituzioni scientifiche sabaude nel Risorgimento. Firenze, L. S. Olschki, 99, 349 p. (bibl.).

5727. DOCHERTY (Thomas). Criticism and modernity: aesthetics, literature, and nations in Europe and its academies. Oxford, Oxford U. P., 99, VI-248 p.

5728. DONATO (Maria Pia). Accademie e accademismi in una capitale particolare. Il caso di Roma. *Mélanges de l'École française de Rome. Italie et Méditerranée*, 99, 111, p. 415-430.

5729. DOWNS (Donald Alexander). Cornell '69: liberalism and the crisis of the American university. Ithaca a. London, Cornell U. P., 99, X-359 p. (ill.).

5730. ELLSWORTH (Mary Ellen). A history of the Connecticut Academy of Arts and Sciences 1799–1999. New Haven, Connecticut Academy of Arts and Sciences, 99, X-254 p. (ill.). (Transactions of the Connecticut Academy of Arts and Sciences, 55).

5731. FAHRENBACH (Sabine), WIEDEMANN (Peter). From four-bed clinic to modern eye hospital: ophthalmology in Leipzig, 1820-1996. *Survey of ophthalmology*, 99, 44, 3, p. 253-266.

5732. FELLMANN (Dorothea). Das Gymnasium Montanum in Köln 1550–1798. Zur Geschichte der Artes-Fakultät der alten Kölner Universität. Köln, Weimar u. Wien, Böhlau, 99, VII-349 p. (Studien zur Geschichte der Universität in Köln, 15).

5733. FREEDMAN (Joseph S.). Philosophy and the arts in Central Europe, 1500–1700: teaching and texts at schools and universities. Aldershot, Ashgate, 99, 384 p.

5734. HART (Darryl G.). The university gets religion: religious studies in American higher education since 1870. Baltimore, Johns Hopkins U. P., 99, p. (bibl.).

5735. HIRAISHI (Naoaki). Fukuzawa Yukichi no senryaku-koso: Bummeiron no gairyaku ki made wo chushin ni. (Strategies for Japan's civilization and the roles assigned to intellectuals: a case study of Fukuzawa Yukichi). *Shakaikagaku Kenkyu*, 99, 51, 1, p. 63-102.

5736. HORN (Michiel). Academic freedom in Canada: a history. Buffalo, University of Toronto Press, 99, XV-446 p.

5737. JESSEN (Ralph). Akademische Elite und kommunistische Diktatur: die ostdeutsche Hochschullehrerschaft in der Ulbricht-Ära. Göttingen, Vandenhoeck & Ruprecht, 99, 551 p. (Kritische Studien zur Geschichtswissenschaft, 135).

5738. KELLEY (Brooks Mather). Yale: a history. New Haven a. London, Yale U. P., 99, 608 p.

5739. KLUXEN (Andrea M.). Die Geschichte der Kunstakademie in Nürnberg 1662-1998. *Jahrbuch für fränkische Landesforschung*, 99, n. 59, p.167-207.

5740. Königlich Preussische Akademie (Die) der Wissenschaften zu Berlin im Kaiserreich. Hrsg. v. Jürgen KOCKA; unt. Mitarb. v. Rainer HOHLFELD und Peter Th. WALTHER. Berlin, Akademie Verlag, 99, XVIII-486 p. (Interdisziplinäre Arbeitsgruppen, Forschungsberichte, 7).

5741. KRAHNKE (Holger). Reformtheorien zwischen Revolution und Restauration. Die gesamte Politik an der Universität Göttingen im ersten Drittel des 19. Jahrhunderts. Frankfurt am Main, Berlin u. Bern, Lang, 99, 650 p. (Europäische Hochschulschriften, Rh. 3: Geschichte und ihre Hilfswissenschaften, 830).

5742. LEWIS (John L.). 125 Years: The Physical Society & The Institute of Physics. Bristol, Institute of Physics Publishing, 99, XIV-243 pp. (ill., figs., tables, apps.).

5743. MAC CARTNEY (Donal). UCD: a national idea. The history of University College, Dublin. Dublin, Gill & Macmillan, 99, XXII-488 p. (ill.).

5744. PELLERIN (Denys). Histoire de l'Académie nationale de chirurgie. *Chirurgie*, 99, 124, 2, p. 201-209.

5745. PLEHN (Gottfried). Fritz-Haber-Institut der Max-Planck-Gesellschaft. München, Max-Planck-Gesellschaft, 99, 180 p. (ill.). (Berichte und Mitteilungen der Max-Planck-Gesellschaft zur Förderung der Wissenschaften, 1).

5746. PYENSON (Lewis), SHEETS-PYENSON (Susan). Servants of nature: a history of scientific institutions, enterprises and sensibilities. London, HarperCollins, 99, XIV-496 p., (ill.).

5747. Queen's College (From) to National University: essays towards an academic history of QCG/UCG/NUI, Galway. Ed. by Tadhg FOLEY. Dublin, Four Courts, 99, XII-440 p. (ill.).

5748. RABE (Carsten). Alma Mater Leopoldina. Kolleg und Universität der Jesuiten in Breslau 1638-1811. Köln, Weimar u. Wien, Böhlau, 99, X-605 p. (Neue Forschungen zur Schlesischen Geschichte, 7).

5749. ROCHE (Daniel). Trois académies parisiennes et leur rôle dans les relations culturelles et sociales au XVIIIe siècle. *Mélanges de l'École française de Rome. Italie et Méditerranée*, 99, 111, 1, p. 395-414.

5750. ROUSSEAU (George S.), HAYCOCK (David). Voices calling for reform: the Royal Society in the mid-eighteenth century: Martin Folkes, John Hill, and William Stukeley. *History of science*, 99, 37, 4, p. 377-406.

5751. RUSU (Dorina N.). Membrii Academiei Române 1866-1999. Dicţionar. (Members of the Romanian Academy. Dictionary). Cuvânt înainte de Eugen SIMION. Bucureşti, Editura Academiei Române, 99, 637 p.

5752. Slovenski študenti in Univerza: 1941-1945. (Slovene university students and the University: 1941-1945). Ur. Ana BENEDETIČ. Ljubljana, Univerza, Zveza združenj borcev in udeležencev NOB, 99, 467 p. (ill.).

5753. SOARES (Joseph A.). The decline of privilege: the modernization of Oxford University. Stanford, Stanford U. P., 99, XI-322 p. (ill., bibl.).

5754. TURI (Gabriele). Le Accademie nell'Italia fascista. *Belfagor*, 99, 54, p. 403-424.

5755. Universités et institutions universitaires européennes au XVIIIe siècle. Entre modernisation et tradition. Actes du colloque international organisé par le Centre Interdisciplinaire Bordelais d'Etudes des Lumières (2-4 octobre 1997). Ed. par François CADILHON, Jean MONDOT et Jacques VERGER. Talence, Presses Universitaires de Bordeaux, 99, 280 p.

5756. University and Society. A history of Cluj higher education in the 20th century. Ed. by Vasile PUŞCAŞ. Cluj-Napoca, Editura Presa Universitară Clujeană, 99, 477 p.

5757. VERGA (Marcello). Per una storia della accademie di Palermo nel XVIII secolo. Dal «letterato» al professore universitario. *Archivio storico italiano*, 99, 157, 581, p. 453-536.

5758. WARTENWEILER (David). Civil society and academic debate in Russia 1905-1914. Oxford, Clarendon Press, 99, X-252 p.

5759. ZAMORA VICENTE (Alonso). Historia de la Real Academia Española. Madrid, Espasa, 99, 659 p.

Cf. n°s 419, 578, 5760-5827

§ 3. Education.

* 5760. Educazione e istituzioni scolastiche nell'Italia moderna: testi e documenti. A cura di Roberto SANI. Milano, I.S.U. Universita cattolica, 99, 822 p.

* 5761. HAVELANGE (Isabelle), DAYEN (Daniel), DURAND (Isabelle), RAMOS (Carmine). Bibliographie d'histoire de l'éducation française. Titres parus au cours de l'année 1995 et suppléments des années antérieures. Titres parus au cours de l'année 1996 et suppléments des années antérieures. *History of education*, 99, 83-84, 366 p.

* 5762. Maria-Montessori-Bibliographie 1896-1996: internationale Bibliographie der Schriften und der Forschungsliteratur. Hrsg. v. Winfried BÖHM. Bad Heilbrunn, Klinkhardt, 99, 527 p.

5763. Alphabetisierung und Literalisierung in Deutschland in der Frühen Neuzeit. Hrsg. v. Hans Erich BÖDEKER und Ernst HINRICHS. Tübingen, M. Niemeyer, 99, VI-366 p. (ill.). (Wolfenbütteler Studien zur Aufklärung, 26).

5764. ARNOT (Madeleine), DAVID (Miriam), WEINER (Gaby). Closing the gender gap: postwar education and social change. Cambridge, Polity, 99, XII-191 p.

5765. Bambine (Le) nella storia dell'educazione. A cura di Simonetta ULIVIERI. Roma e Bari, Laterza, 99, VI-370 p. (ill.).

5766. BENDICK (Rainer). Kriegserwartung und Kriegserfahrung: der Erste Weltkrieg in deutschen und französischen Schulgeschichtsbüchern (1900–1939/45). Pfaffenweiler, Centaurus-Verlagsgesellschaft, 99, VIII-508 p. (Reihe Geschichtswissenschaft, 46).

5767. BOSNA (Ernesto). Lotte e contrasti per l'alfabetizzazione delle popolazioni meridionali prima e dopo l'unità. Bari, Cacucci, 99, 197 p.

5768. CACOUAULT (Marlaine). Différenciation des carrières entre les hommes et les femmes dans l'enseignement du second degré. *Cahiers du Centre Henri Aigueperse*, 99, 25, 390 p.

5769. CARON (Jean-Claude). A l'école de la violence: châtiments et sévices dans l'institution scolaire au XIXe siècle. Paris, Aubier, 99, 337 p.

5770. Cattolici, educazione e trasformazioni socioculturali in Italia tra Otto e Novecento. A cura di Luciano PAZZAGLIA. Brescia, La scuola, 99, 718 p.

5771. CHÂTELET (Anne-Marie). La naissance de l'architecture scolaire, les écoles élémentaires parisiennes de 1870 à 1940. Paris, Champion, Bibliothèque de l'Ecole des Hautes Etudes, Sciences historiques et philosophiques, Hautes Etudes d'histoire contemporaine, 99, 448 p.

5772. CORBI (Enrico Maria), SARRACINO (Vincenzo). Storia della scuola e delle istituzioni educative (1830-1999). La cultura della formazione. Napoli, Liguori, 99, 159 p.

5773. CORBI (Enrico Maria), STROLLO (Maria Rosaria). L' istruzione a Napoli dal 1806 al 1860: politica scolastica e organizzazione didattica. Lecce, Pensa multimedia, 99, 193 p.

5774. DE GIORGI (Fulvio). Cattolici ed educazione tra Restaurazione e Risorgimento: ordini religiosi, antigesuitismo e pedagogia nei processi di modernizzazione. Milano, I.S.U. Universita cattolica, 99, 341 p.

5775. DROSTE (Thomas). Die Historie der Geistigbehindertenversorgung unter dem Einfluss der Psychiatrie seit dem 19. Jahrhundert: eine kritische Analyse neuerer Entpsychiatrisierungsprogramme und geistigbehindertenpädagogischer Reformkonzepte. Münster u. London, Lit, 99, 216 p. (bibl.). (Forum Behindertenpädagogik, 2).

5776. Ecole maternelle (L') en Europe: 19e–20e. siecles. Ed. par Jean-Noel LUC. Paris, Institut national de recherche pedagogique. Service d'histoire de l'éducation, 99, 239 p.

5777. Education (The) of a Christian society: humanism and the Reformation in Britain and the Netherlands. Papers delivered to the Thirteenth Anglo-Dutch Historical Conference, 1997. Ed. by N. Scott AMOS, Andrew PETTEGREE, and Henk VAN NIEROP. Aldershot a. Brookfield, Ashgate, 99, XII-274 p. (ill., bibl.). (St. Andrews studies in Reformation history). [Contents. PETTEGREE (Andrew). Humanism and the Reformation in Britain and the Netherlands. – REX (Richard). The role of English humanists in the Reformation up to 1559. – TILMANS (Karin). From institutio to educatio: the origin of political education in the Habsburg Netherlands. – BERNARD (George). The piety of Henry VIII. – WALKER (Greg). Dialogue, resistance and accommodation: conservative literary responses to the Henrician Reformation. – BRADSHAW (Christopher J.). The exile literature of the early Reformation: "obedience to God and the King". – VELDMAN (Ilja M.). Religious propaganda in sixteenth-century Netherlandish prints and drawings. – BOSTOEN (Karel). Reformation, Counter-Reformation and literary propaganda in the Low Countries in the sixteenth century: the case of Brother Cornelis. – MARNEF (Guido). The dynamics of Reformed militancy in the Low Countries: the wonderyear. – DAWSON (Jane). Clan, kin and Kirk: the Campbells and the Scottish Reformation. – BERGSMA (Wiebe). The intellectual and cultural context of the Reformation in the Northern Netherlands.].

5778. Educazione (L') dei figli. Vol. 1. LORÈ (Biagio). L'antichità. Vol. 4. PANCERA (Carlo). Il Settecento. Firenze, La nuova Italia, 99, 2 vol., XIX-460 p., XV-475 p. (Biblioteca di scienze dell'educazione, 24).

5779. Educazione e pedagogia in Italia nell'età della guerra fredda: 1948–1989. A cura di Enzo CATARSI, Nando FILOGRASSO, Angela GIALLONGO. Trieste, Edizioni Goliardiche, 99, 370 p.

5780. Eglise, éducation, Lumières: histoires culturelles de la France, 1500–1830: en l'honneur de Jean Quéniart. Ed. par Alain CROIX, André LESPAGNOL et Georges PROVOST. Rennes, Presses universitaires de Rennes, 99, 507 p. (ill., plates). (Collection "Histoire").

5781. Erziehungsreform und Gesellschaftsinitiative in Preussen 1798–1840. Hrsg. v. Hanno SCHMITT und Frank TOSCH. Berlin, Weidler, 99, 187 p. (ill., bibl.). (Bildungs- und kulturgeschichtliche Beiträge für Berlin und Brandenburg, 1).

5782. EVREN (Nazif). Osmanlı eğitim sisteminden Cumhuriyet'e. (Les système d'éducation de l'Empire Ottoman à la République Turque). Ankara, 99, 153 p.

5783. Familia y educación en Iberoamérica. Ed. por Pilar GONZALBO AIZPURU. México, Centro de Estudios Históricos, Colegio de México, 99, 385 p.

5784. Femmes savantes, savoirs des femmes: du crepuscule de la Renaissance à l'aube des Lumières: actes du Colloque de Chantilly, 22–24 septembre 1995. Ed. par Colette NATIVEL. Genève, Librairie Droz, 99, 268 p.

5785. FRIEDRICH (Margret). "Ein Paradies ist uns verschlossen ...": zur Geschichte der schulischen Mädchenerziehung in Österreich im "langen" 19. Jahrhundert. Wien, Böhlau, 99, 438 p. (Veröffentlichungen der Kommission für Neuere Geschichte Österreiches, 89).

5786. FUHRMANN (Manfred). Der europäische Bildungskanon des bürgerlichen Zeitalters. Frankfurt a. M., Insel, 99, 219 p. (ill., bibl.).

5787. Geschichte der DDR und deutsche Einheit: Analyse von Lehrplänen und Unterrichtswerken für Geschichte und Sozialkunde. Hrsg. v. Günter BUCHSTAB. Schwalbach/Ts., Wochenschau-Verlag, 99, VI-288 p. (Studien zu Politik und Wissenschaft).

5788. GREVET (R.). L'enseignement charitable en France: essor et crise d'adaptation (milieu XVIIe–fin XVIIe siècle). *Revue historique*, 99, 123, 610, p. 277-306.

5789. HAZAREESINGH (Sudhir). The Société d' Instruction Républicaine and the propagation of civic republicanism in provincial and rural France, 1870–1877. *Journal of modern history*, 99, 71, 2, p. 271-307.

5790. History (The) of physical education & sport from European perspectives. Ed by Arnd KRUGER a. Else TRANGBAEK. Copenhagen, European Committee for the History of Sport, 99, 288 p. (ill.).

5791. History education in Scotland: into the new millennium. Ed. by Peter HILLIS. Edinburgh, John Donald, 99, X-173 p.

5792. HIZLI (Mefail). Mahkeme sicillerine göre Osmanlı klasik döneminde ilköğretim ve Bursa sıbyan mektepleri. (L'enseignement primaire à Bursa à l'époque classique ottomane d'après les registres du cadi). Bursa, Uludağ Üniversitesi, 99, 186 p.

5793. HOLMES (Larry Eugene). Stalin's school: Moscow's model School No. 25, 1931–1937. Pittsburgh, University of Pittsburgh Press, 99, X-228 p. (ill.).

5794. JACQUET-FRANCILLON (François). Instituteurs avant la République. La profession d'instituteur et ses représentation de la Monarchie de Juillet au Second Empire. Villeneuve d'Ascq, Presses Universitaires du Septentrion, 99, 318 p.

5795. KITOWSKI (Karin), WULF (Rüdiger). Die Liebe zu Volk und Vaterland: Erziehung zum Staatsbürger in der Weimarer Republik. Dortmund, Westfälisches Schulmuseum der Stadt Dortmund, 99, 133 p. (ill., map). (Schriftenreihe des Westfälischen Schulmuseums Dortmund, 5).

5796. KNOTTNERUS (J. David), VAN DE POEL-KNOTTNERUS (Frédérique). The social worlds of male and female children in the nineteenth century French educational system: youth, rituals and elites. Lewiston a. Lampeter, Edwin Mellen Press, 99, IV-155 p. (Mellen studies in education, 46).

5797. LAURENT (Stéphane). Les arts appliqués en France: genèse d'un enseignement. Paris, Éditions du C.T.H.S, 99, 684 p. (ill.). (Format, 34).

5798. LEIGHT (Robert L.), RINEHART (Alice Duffy). Country school memories: an oral history of one-room schooling. Westport a. London, Greenwood Press, 99, XII-154 p. (ill.). (Contributions to the study of education, 74).

5799. LEINWATHER (Thomas). Landwirtschaftliches Schulwesen in Österreich: Rechtfertigungsstrategien und pädagogisches Denken in der zweiten Hälfte des 20. Jahrhunderts. Wien, WUV-Universitätsverlag, 99, 398 p. (ill.). (Dissertationen der Universität Wien, 48).

5800. MAC GRATH (Michael). The Catholic church and Catholic schools in Northern Ireland: the price of faith. Dublin a. Portland, Irish Academic Press, 99, 208 p.

5801. MAC LEAN (David). Education and empire: naval tradition and England's elite schooling. London, British Academic Press, 99, VIII-184 p.

5802. MARTIN (Jane). Women and the politics of schooling in Victorian and Edwardian England. London, Leicester U. P., 99, VII-167 p. (Women, power, and politics).

5803. När studenten blev modern: Uppsala studenter 1600–1850. (Quand l'étudiant devint moderne: les étudiants d'Uppsala de 1600 à 1850). Red. par Henrik ÅGREN. Uppsala, Historiska institutionen, Univ., 99, 93 p. (ill.). (Opuscula historica Upsaliensia, 23).

5804. Neuer Anfang (Ein): politische Jugend- und Erwachsenenbildung in der westdeutschen Nachkriegsgesellschaft. Hrsg. v. Paul CIUPKE, Franz-Josef JELICH. Essen, Klartext, 99, 280 p. (ill.).

5805. NEVALA (Arto). Korkeakoulutuksen kasvu, lohkoutuminen ja eriarvoisuus Suomessa. (Growth, fragmentation and inequality in higher education in Finland). Helsinki, SHS, 99, 274 p. (Bibliotheca historica, 43). [English summary].

5806. NYHOLM (Peter). "Vår uppgift är den högsta i lifvet ...." Studier i den finlandssvenska folkskollärarkåren 1871–1971. ("Unsere Aufgabe ist die grösste im Leben ..." Eine Studie über die der schwedischsprachige Lehrerschaft in Finnland von 1871 bis 1971, gesehen aus einer pädagogisch-geschichtlichen und ausbildungssoziologischen Perspektive). Åbo, Åbo akademi förlag, 99, 288 p. [Deutsche Zfassung].

5807. PARTINGTON (Geoffrey). Teacher education in England and Wales [1945–1999]. London Institute of Economic Affairs, 99, 163 p. (Studies in Education, 8).

5808. PLANK (Angelika). Akademischer und schulischer Elementarzeichenunterricht im 18. Jahrhundert. Frankfurt am Main, P. Lang, 99, 358 p. (ill., bibl.).

5809. PLOSZAJSKA (Teresa). Geographical education, empire and citizenship: geographical teaching and learning in English schools, 1870–1944. Liverpool, Liverpool Hope University College, Department of Environmental and Biological Studies, 99, IV-298 p. (ill., maps). (Historical geography research series, 35).

5810. POUCET (Bruno). Enseigner la philosophie. Histoire d'une discipline scolaire, 1860–1990. Paris, CNRS Ed., 99, 438 p.

5811. PRUNERI (fabio). La politica scolastica del Partito Comunista italiano dalle origini al 1955. Brescia, La scuola, 99, 535 p. (Paedagogica).

5812. RENOUARD (Alfred). Histoire de l'Ecole supérieure de commerce de Paris. Paris, Raymons Castells Ed., 99, 315 p.

5813. Restauration (Zwischen) und Innovation: Bildungsreformen in Ost und West nach 1945. Hrsg. v. Manfred HEINEMANN. Köln, Böhlau, 99, IX-339 p. (Bildung und Erziehung, Beiheft 9).

5814. ROGGERO (Marina). L'alfabeto conquistato: apprendere e insegnare nell'Italia tra Sette e Ottocento. Bologna, Il Mulino, 99, 322 p. (ill., bibl.). (Saggi, 494).

5815. RUIZ ORTEGA (Manuel). La escuela gratuita de diseño de Barcelona, 1775–1808. Barcelona, Biblioteca de Catalunya, 99, 450 p. (ill.). (Unitat gràfica, 14).

5816. SANDERSON (Michael). Education and economic decline in Britain, 1870 to the 1990s. Cambridge, Cambridge U. P., 99, VIII-124 p.

5817. SANTAMAITA (Saverio). Storia della scuola: dalla scuola al sistema formativo. Milano, B. Mondadori, 99, XVII-189 p. (Scienze dell'educazione).

5818. Schule (Eine) für die Demokratie: zur Entwicklung der Volksschule in der Schweiz im 19. Jahrhundert. Hrsg. v. Lucien CRIBLEZ. Bern u. Berlin u. Bruxelles, P. Lang, 99, 471 p. (Explorationen, 27).

5819. SCHWEGMAN (Marjan). Maria Montessori. Bologna, Il Mulino, 99, 136 p.

5820. SCOTTO DI LUZIO (Adolfo). Il liceo classico. Bologna, Il Mulino, 99, 179 p.

5821. Scuola, intellettuali e identità nazionale nel pensiero di Antonio Gramsci. A cura di Lorenzo CAPITANI e Roberto VILLA. Roma, Gamberetti, 99, 151 p. (Per Gramsci, 2).

5822. SEZER (Ayten). Atatürk döneminde yabancı okullar (1923–1938). (Ecoles étrangères au temps d'Atatürk). Ankara, Türk Tarih Kurumu, 99, 154 p. – IDEM. Osmanlı'dan Cumhuriyet'e Misyonerlerin Türkiye'deki Eğitim ve Öğretim Faaliyetleri. (Les activités éducatives des missionnaires en Turquie de l'époque ottomane à la République). *Hacettepe Üniversitesi Edebiyat Fakültesi Dergisi*, 99, ekim, p. 169-183.

5823. SUTEAU (Marc). Une ville et ses écoles. Nantes, 1830–1940. Rennes, Presses Universitaires de Rennes, 99, 254 p.

5824. TANCK DE ESTRADA (Dorothy). Pueblos de indios y educación en el México Colonial, 1750–1821. México, El Colegio de México, Centro de Estudios Históricos, 99, 665 p.

5825. THOMPSON MAC CANDLESS (Amy). The past in the present: women's higher education in the twentieth-century American South. Tuscaloosa a. London, University of Alabama Press, 99, X-389 p. (ill.).

5826. VALLENTIN (Rudolf). Wilhelm von Humboldts Bildungs- und Erziehungskonzept: eine politisch motivierte Gegenposition zum Utilitarismus der Aufklärungspädagogik. München, R. Hampp, 99, 244 p. (bibl.). (Profession, 15).

5827. Women's education in early modern Europe: a history, 1500–1800. Ed. by Barbara J. WHITEHEAD. New York, Garland Publishing, 99, XVI-260 p.

Cf. n°s 809, 1263, 5005, 5406, 5719-5759

§ 4. The Press.

* 5828. Authorized press (The) in Vichy and German-occupied France, 1940–1944: a bibliography. Compiled by Donna EVLETH. Westport a. London, Greenwood Press, 99, VIII-234 p. (Bibliographies and indexes in world history, 48).

** 5829. FELTRINELLI (Carlo). Senior service. Milano, Feltrinelli, 99, 431 p.

** 5830. NS-Presseanweisungen der Vorkriegszeit. Edition und Dokumentation. Bd. 6. 1938. Vol. 1-4. Hrsg. v. Karen PETER und Claudia BARTELS. München, K.G. Saur, 99, 4 vol., 1494 p.

5831. Almanach (Von) bis Zeitung. Ein Handbuch der Medien in Deutschland 1700–1800. Hrsg. v. Ernst FISCHER, Wilhem HAEFS und York-Gothar MIX. München, Beck, 99, 448 p.

5832. ANDRZEJEWSKI (Marek), RINKLAKE (Hubert). "To live, you have to be well-informed". Erich Brost: Danzig editor, man of resistance, publisher and editor-in-chief of the "Westdeutsche Allgemeine Zeitung". Warsaw, Institute of History, Polish Academy of Science, 99, 246 p.

5833. ATTWOOD (Lynne). Creating the New Soviet Woman: women's magazines as engineers of female identity, 1922–1953. New York, St. Martin's Press in association with the Centre for Russian and East European Studies, University of Birmingham, 99, V-213 p. (Studies in Russian and East European history and society).

5834. AUZA (Néstor Tomás). La literatura periodistica porteña del siglo XIX: de caseros a la organización nacional. Buenos Aires, Editorial Confluencia, 99, 271 p.

5835. BARKER (Hannah). Newspapers, politics and English society, 1695–1855. New York, Longman, 99, 248 p. (Themes in British social history).

5836. BEZZEL (Irmgard). Leonhard Heussler (1548–1597): ein vielseitiger Nürnberger Drucker und geschickter Verbreiter von Neuigkeitsberichten. Wiesbaden, Harrassowitz, 99, VI-199 p. (ill.). (Buchwissenschaftliche Beiträge aus dem Deutschen Bucharchiv München, 62).

5837. CASTELLI (Alberto). Periodici antifascisti pubblicati in Francia tra il 1929 e il 1934 conservati presso la Biblioteca della Fondazione G. G. Feltrinelli. *Storia in Lombardia*, 99, 19, 2, p. 141-167; 99, 19, 3, p. 119-152.

5838. COWARD (John M.). The Newspaper Indian: native American identity in the press, 1820–1990. Urbana a. Chicago, University of Illinois Press, 99, VIII-244 p. (The history of communication).

5839. Cuando opinar es actuar: revistas argentinas del siglo XX. Ed. por Noemí GIRBAL-BLACHA y Diana QUATTROCCHI-WOISSON. Buenos Aires, Academia Nacional de la Historia, 99, 544 p. (bibl.).

5840. DİZMAN (İbrahim). Türkiye'nin ilk köy gazetesi Güzel Ordu ve Bilal Köyden. (Le Premier journal villageois de la Turquie et son fondateur Bilal Köyden). Ankara, Kültür Bakanlığı, 99, XV-104 p.

5841. DOUGLAS (George H.). The golden age of the newspaper. Westport a. London, Greenwood Press, 99, XIII-300 p. (ill.). (The history of American journalism, 3).

5842. FEYEL (Gilles). La presse en France des origines à 1944: histoire politique et matérielle. Paris, Ellipses, 99, 192 p. (Infocom).

5843. Gazettes et information politique sous l'Ancien Régime. Actes du colloque tenu à Lyon, 5–7 juin 1997, organisé par le Centre d'études du XVIIIe siècle et l'Institut français de presse. Ed. par Henri DURANTON et Pierre RÉTAT. Saint-Etienne, Publications de l'université de Saint-Etienne, 99, 443 p. (Lire le dix-huitième siècle).

5844. Geschäft mit Wort und Meinung: Medienunternehmer seit dem 18. Jahrhundert. Hrsg. v. Günther SCHULZ. München, H. Boldt, 99, 385 p. (ill.). (Deutsche Führungsschichten in der Neuzeit, 22).

5845. GIENOW-HECHT (J. C. E.). Art is democracy and democracy is art: culture, propaganda, and the Neue Zeitung in Germany, 1944–1947. *Diplomatic history*, 99, 23, 1, p. 21-43.

5846. HARRIS (Brayton). Blue & gray in black & white: newspapers of the Civil War. Washington a. London, Brassey's, 99, 365 p. (ill.).

5847. HORSTBØLL (Henrik). Menigmands medie: det folkelige bogtryk i Danmark 1500–1840: en kulturhistorisk undersøgelse. (Common man's media: popular press in Denmark 1500–1840: a culture history research). København, Kongelige bibliotek og Museum Tusculanums forlag, 99, 791 p. (ill.). (Danish humanist texts and studies, 19).

5848. HUGUET (Josep). Cornuts i pagar el beure: el discurs anticatalà a la premsa espanyola. Antologia a cura de Rosa M. CASSÀ; pròleg de Salvador CARDÚS. Barcelona, Columna, 99, 314 p. (Columna assaig, 27).

5849. HUNTZICKER (William). The popular press, 1833–1865. Westport a. London, Greenwood Press, 99, XII-210 p. (The history of American journalism, 3).

5850. JAGANNATHAN (N. S.). Independence and the Indian press: heirs to a great tradition. Delhi, Konark Publishers, 99, XXI-157 p. (bibl.).

5851. JEANDILLOU (Jean-François). Le tribunal des lettres: Nodier et les Questions de littérature légale. *Revue d'histoire littéraire de la France*, 99, 99, 1, p. 57-74.

5852. KAUL (Chandrika). Press and empire: the London press, government news management and India, circa 1900–1922. Oxford, [s. n.], 99, 242 p. [Thesis (D. Phil.) – University of Oxford, Faculty of Modern History]. (Nuffield College theses).

5853. KRUIP (Gudrun). Das "Welt"-"Bild" des Axel Springer Verlags: Journalismus zwischen westlichen Werten und deutschen Denktraditionen. München, R. Oldenbourg, 99, 311 p. (Gudrun Kruip Series. Ordnungssysteme, 3).

5854. KURZWEG (Martina). Presse zwischen Staat und Gesellschaft. Die Zeitungslandschaft in Rheinland-Westfalen (1770–1819). Paderborn, Schöningh, 99, XI-462 p. (Forschungen zur Regionalgeschichte, 32).

5855. LEGG (Marie-Louise). Newspapers and nationalism: the Irish provincial press, 1850–1882. Dublin, Four Courts Press, 99, 238 p. (tabs.).

5856. LEPRI (Sergio), ARBITRIO (Francesco), CULTRERA (Giuseppe). Informazione e potere in un secolo di storia italiana: l'Agenzia Stefani da Cavour a Mussolini. Firenze, Le Monnier, 99, IX-248 p. (Quaderni della Nuova antologia, 67).

5857. Lesekultur: populäre Lesestoffe von Gutenberg bis zum Internet. Hrsg. v. Petra BOHNSACK und Hans-Friedrich FOLTIN. Marburg, Universitätsbibliothek Marburg, 99. 289 p. (Schriften der Universitätsbibliothek Marburg, 93).

5858. LIPP (Michael). Bildpropaganda im Dritten Reich: die Illustrationen in den Zeitschriften unter der nationalsozialistischen Diktatur in Deutschland. Publisher. St. Katharinen, Scripta Mercaturae Verlag, 99, IV-139 p. (ill.).

5859. LOVELL (Stephen). The Russian reading revolution: print culture in the Soviet and post-Soviet eras. Basingstoke, Macmillan, 99, 240 p. (ill.). (Studies in Russia and East Europe).

5860. Making the news: modernity and the mass press in nineteenth-century France. Ed. by Dean DE LA MOTTE and Jeannene M. PRZYBLYSKI. Amherst, University of Massachusetts Press, 99, VII-386 p. (ill., bibl.). (Studies in print culture and the history of the book).

5861. MARTEN-FINNIS (Susanne), VALENCIA (Heather). Sprachinseln: jiddische Publizistik in London, Wilna und Berlin 1880–1930. Köln, Böhlau, 99, 144 p. (ill.). (Lebenswelten osteuropäischer Juden, 4).

5862. MARTIN (L.). De l'anarchisme à l'affairisme: les deux compagnies d'Eugène Merle, homme de presse (1884–1946). *Revue historique*, 99, 123, 612, p. 789-808.

5863. MASTORÍDIS (Klímis). Casting the greek newspaper: a study of the morphology of the Ephemeris from its origins to the introduction of mechanical setting. Thessaloniki, Elliniká Filologhiká ke Istoriká Arkhía [Hellenic Literary and Historical Archive], 99, XIX-453 p.

5864. "Mosaik" und "Einheit" (Zwischen): Zeitschriften in der DDR. Hrsg. v. Simone BARCK, Martina LANGERMANN und Siegfried LOKATIS. Berlin, Ch. Links, 99, 751 p. (ill., bibl.).

5865. MOUREAU (François). Répertoire des nouvelles à la main: dictionnaire de la presse manuscrite clandestine, XVIe–XVIIIe siècle. Oxford, Voltaire Foundation, 99, XLVIII-517 p.

5866. PARVIN (Nasir al-Din). Tarikh-i ruznamah'nigari-i Iraniyan va digar Parsi'nivisan. (History of journalism in the Persian-speaking world). Tihran, Markaz-i Nashr-i Danishgahi, 99, [s. p.]. (Markaz-i Nashr-i Danishgahi, 893, Tarikh, 28).

5867. PATRON (Sylvie). Critique, 1946–1996: une encyclopédie de l'esprit moderne. Paris, IMEC, 99, 459 p. (Collection L'édition contemporaine).

5868. PONDER (Stephen). Managing the press: origins of the media presidency, 1897–1933. New York, St. Martin's Press, 99, XVIII-233 p.

5869. Press and politics in Hong Kong: case studies from 1967 to 1997. Ed. by Clement Y. K. SO and Joseph MAN CHAN. Hong Kong, The Chinese University of Hong Kong, 99, IX-539 p. (Hong Kong Institute of Asia-Pacific Studies, 48).

5870. SALMAN (Jeroen). Populair drukwerk in de Gouden Eeuw: de almanak als lectuur en handelswaar. Zutphen, Walburg, 99, 495 p. (ill., bibl., computer disk).

5871. SALMINEN (Esko). The silenced media: the propaganda war between Russia and the West in Northern Europe. New York, St. Martin's, 99, XII-198 p.

5872. SCERBINSKIS (Valters). The image of Finland in Latvian periodicals 1919–1929. *Faravid*, 98-99, 22-23, p. 343-357.

5873. THING (Morten). Pornografiens historie i Danmark. (Histoire de la pornographie au Danemark). København, Aschehoug, 99, 256 p. (ill.).

5874. Transmission (The) of culture in Western Europe, 1750–1850: papers celebrating the bicentenary of the foundation of the Bibliothèque britannique (1796–1815) in Geneva. Ed. by David BICKERTON and Judith PROUD. Bern a. New York, P. Lang, 99, 264 p. (ill.).

5875. VAN DE PLASSE (Jan). Kroniek van de Nederlandse dagbladpers. Amsterdam, Cramwinckel, 99, 144 p.

5876. Voix conservatrices et réactionnaires dans les périodiques allemands de la Révolution française à la Restauration. Ed. par Pierre-André BOIS, Raymond HEITZ et Roland KREBS. Bern, Peter Lang, 99, XVI-431 p. (bibl.). (Convergences, 13).

5877. *Vacat.*

5878. WILLIAMS HEDGEPETH (Julie). The significance of the printed word in early America: colonists' thoughts on the role of the press. Westport, Greenwood Press, 99, 208 p. (Contributions to the study of mass media and communications, 55).

Cf. n°s 84-141, 616

§ 5. Philosophy.

* 5879. Bibliographie 1998–1999 (arrêtée au 1er octobre 1999). *R. Montesquieu*, 99, 3, p. 126-134.

* 5880. Bulletin cartésien, 27. Bibliographie pour l'année 1996. *Archive de philosophie*, 99, 62, 1, p. 1-80.

* 5881. Bulletin de bibliographie spinoziste. Bibliographie pour l'année 1998. *Archive de philosophie*, 99, 62, 4, p. 1-44.

* 5882. Bulletin de littérature hégélienne, 12. *Archive de philosophie*, 99, 62, 3, p. 1-43.

* 5883. Bulletin Hobbes. Bibliographie critique international des études hobbesiennes pour l'année 1997. *Archive de philosophie*, 99, 62, 2, p. 1-67.

* 5884. Edmund Husserl bibliography. Ed. by Steven SPILEERS. Dordrecht a. London, Kluwer Academic Publishers, 99, VI-450 p.

* 5885. Kant-Bibliographie 1945–1990. Hrsg. v. Margit RUFFIN. Frankfurt a. M., Vittorio Klosterman, 99, IX-976 p.

* 5886. NORDQUIST (Joan). Paul Ricoeur: a bibliography. Santa Cruz, Reference and Research Services, 99, 68 p. (Social theory: a bibliographic series, 53).

** 5887. BAYLE (Pierre). Correspondance 1662–1674. Oxford, Voltaire Foundation, 99, vol. I. XIV-432 p. (Critical edition).

** 5888. FICHTE (Johann Gottlieb). Nachgelassene Schriften 1810–1812. Hrsg. v. Reinhard LAUTH, Erich FUCHS, Peter K. SCHNEIDER und Ives RADRIZZANI. Stuttgart, Fromman-Holzboog, 99, XII-464 p. (Gesamtausgabe der Bayerischen Akademie der Wissenschaften, II, 12).

** 5889. FINK (Eugen), PATOČKA (Jan). Briefe und Dokumente. Hrsg. v. Michael HEITZ und Bernhard NESSLER. Freiburg u. München u. Prag, Verlag Alber, 99, 190 p. (Orbis Phoenomenologicus, 2. Quellen, 1).

** 5890. PATOČKA (Jan). Texte, Dokumente, Bibliographie. Hrsg. v. Ludger HAGEDORN und Hans REINER

SEPP. Freiburg u. München u. Prag, Verlag Alber, 99, 786 p. (Orbis Phoenomenologicus, 2. Quellen, 2).

5891. ADSHEAD (Samuel Adrian Miles). The philosophy of religion in nineteenth-century England and beyond. Basingstoke, Macmillan, 99, 274 p.

5892. ALTHAUS (Horst), KALINOWSKI (Isabelle). Hegel, naissance d'une philosophie: une biographie intellectuelle. Paris, Ed. du Seuil, 99, 600 p. (ill.).

5893. ANSTEY (Peter). Boyle on occasionalism: an unexamined source. *Journal of the history of ideas*, 99, 60, 1, p. 57-82.

5894. Antonio Gramsci e le tradizioni politiche dell' Emilia-Romagna. A cura dell'Istituto Gramsci, Sezione Emilia-Romagna. Introduzione di Renato ZANGHERI. Bologna, CLUEB, 99, 129 p. (Collana Istituto Gramsci Emilia-Romagna, 99/3).

5895. APPEL (Fredrick). Nietzsche contra democracy. Ithaca, Cornell U. P., 99, XV-174 p.

5896. ARIEW (Roger). Descartes and the last scholastics. Ithaca, Cornell U. P., 99, XII-230 p.

5897. Atomisme (L') aux XVIIe et XVIIIe siècles: journée d'études organisée le dimanche 26 octobre 1997, à la Sorbonne par le Centre d'histoire des systèmes de pensée moderne. Ed. par Jean SALEM. Paris, Publications de la Sorbonne, 186 p. (Publications de la Sorbonne. Série Philosophie, 4).

5898. BALMÈS (François). Ce que Lacan dit de l'être (1953–1960). Paris, PUF, 99, 214 p. (Bibliothèque du Collège international de Philosophie).

5899. BÄR (Jochen). Sprachreflexion der deutschen Frühromantik: Konzepte zwischen Universalpoesie und grammatischen Kosmopolitismus. Berlin u. New York, Walter de Gruyter, 99, IX-582 p. (Studia Linguistica Germanica, 50).

5900. BARDOUT (Jean-Christophe). Malebranche et la métaphysique. Paris, PUF, 99, 316 p. (Épiméthée. Essais philosophique).

5901. BENZ (Hubert). Individualität und Subjektivität. Interpretationstendenzen in der Cusanus-Forschung und das Selbstverständnis des Nikolaus von Kues. Münster, Aschendorff Verlag, 99, XX-470 p. (Buchreihe der Cusanus. Gesellschaft, XIII).

5902. BERTOLONI MELI (Domenico). Caroline, Leibniz, and Clarke. *Journal of the history of ideas*, 99, 60, 3, p. 469-486.

5903. BESSIRE (François). La Bible dans la correspondance de Voltaire. Oxford, Voltaire Foundation, 99, 346 p.

5904. BILLOUET (Pierre). Foucault. Paris, Belles lettres, 99, 220 p. (Figures du savoir, 16).

5905. Biografia intellettuale (La) di René Descartes attraverso la Correspondance. Atti del Convegno Descartes et l'Europe savante, Perugia 7–10 ott. 1996. A cura di Jean-Robert ARMOGATHE, Giulia BELGIOIOSO e Carlo VINTI. Napoli, Vivarium, 99, XIV-740 p. (Biblioteca Europea. Istituto Italiano per gli Studi Filosofici, 16).

5906. BLATTNER (William D.). Heidegger's temporal idealism. New York a. Cambridge, Cambridge U. P., 99, XVII-325 p. (Modern European Philosohpy).

5907. BLINDOW (Felix). Carl Schmitts Reichsordnung. Strategie für einen europäischen Großraum. Berlin, Akademie, 99, 202 p.

5908. BOM (Klaas). De ruimte van het hart. Kennen en willen in de antropologie van Blaise Pascal. Assen, van Gorcum, 99, 251 p.

5909. BONK (Sigmund). Abschied von der Anima mundi: die britische Philosophie im Vorfeld der Industriellen Revolution. Freiburg, Alber, 99, 607 p. (bibl.). (Alber-Reihe Philosophie).

5910. BRECKMAN (Warren). Marx, the young Hegelians, and the origins of radical social theory: dethroning the self. Cambridge, Cambridge U. P., 99, XII-335 p. (bibl.). (Modern European philosophy).

5911. BREDEKAMP (Horst). Thomas Hobbes visuelle Strategien. Der Leviathan: Urbild des modernen Staates. Berlin, Akademie Verlag, 99, 264 p. (ill.). (Acta humaniora).

5912. BROWN (Vivienne). The «Figure» of god and the limits to liberalism: a rereading of Locke's essay and two treatises. *Journal of the history of ideas*, 99, 60, 1, p. 83-100.

5913. BUBLITZ (Hannelore). Foucaults Archäologie des kulturellen Unbewussten: zum Wissensarchiv und Wissensbegehren moderner Gesellschaften. Frankfurt a. New York, Campus Verlag, 99, 327 p. (bibl.).

5914. BUSTARRET (Claire). Les papiers de Montesquieu: une approche codicologique du fonds de La Brède. *R. Montesquieu*, 99, 3, p. 179-187.

5915. Classical american pragmatism. Its contemporary vitality. Ed. by Sandra B. ROSENTHAL. Chicago, University of Illinois Press, 99, XII-263 p.

5916. CLATTERBAUGH (Kenneth C.). The causation debate in modern philosophy, 1637–1739. New York a. London, Routledge, 99, XI-239 p. (bibl.).

5917. COBDEN (Paul). Das endliche Selbst. Identität (und Differenz) zwischen Hegels 'Phänomenologie des Geistes' und Heideggers 'Sein und Zeit'. Würzburg, Königshausen und Neumann. 99, 211 p.

5918. CONNIFF (James). Edmund Burke and his critics: the case of Mary Wollstonecraft. *Journal of the history of ideas*, 99, 60, 2, p. 299-318.

5919. COOK (Harold John). Bernard Mandeville and the therapy of «The Clever Politician». *Journal of the history of ideas*, 99, 60, 1, p. 101-124.

5920. COOPER (Laurence D.). Rousseau, nature, and the problem of the good life. University Park, Pennsylvania State U. P., 99, IV-223 p. (ill.).

5921. COUDREUSE (Anne). Le goût des larmes au XVIIIe siècle. Paris, Presses universitaires de France, 99, 313 p. (Ecriture).

5922. COVER (Jan Arthur), O'LEARY-HAWTHORNE (John). Substance and individuation in Leibniz. Cambridge, Cambridge U. P., 99, X-307 p.

5923. CRISTOFOLINI (Paolo). Vico "pagano" e "barbaro". *Bollettino del centro di studi vichiani*, 99, 28-29, p. 71-90.

5924. CROCE (Benedetto), MATURI (Sebastiano). Carteggio Benedetto Croce – Sebastiano Maturi (1898–1915). Introduzione e note a cura F. RIZZO. Soveria Mannelli, Rubettino, 99, 269 p.

5925. CROCE (Benedetto), NOVATI (Francesco). Carteggio Croce-Novati. A cura di Alberto BRAMBILLA. Bologna, Il Mulino, 99, XIV-160 p.

5926. D'AMICO (Robert). Contemporary continental philosohy. Boulder, Westview Press, 99, XI-267 p. (Dimensions of Philosophy Series).

5927. DAULER WILSON (Margaret). Ideas and mechanism. Essays on early modern philosophy. Princeton, Princeton U. P., 99, XX-524 p.

5928. DE MIRANDA (Girolamo). "Nihil decisum fuit". Il Sant'Ufficio e la Scienza nuova di Vico: un'irrealizzata edizione patavina tra l'imprimatur del 1725 e quello del 1730. *Bollettino del centro di studi vichiani*, 99, 28-29, p. 5-69.

5929. DE ROSA (Gabriele). Rosmini, gli "indiani" e Tocqueville. *Ricerche di storia sociale e religiosa*, 99, 28, 56, p. 240-249.

5930. DEL NEGRO (Piero). Erasmo da Rotterdam all'Università di Padova (1508). *Quaderni per la storia dell'Università di Padova*, 99, 32, p.133-144.

5931. DENDLE (Peter). Hume's Dialogues and Paradise Lost. *Journal of the history of ideas*, 99, 60, 2, p. 257-276.

5932. DEPREZ (Stanislas). Mircea Eliade: la philosophie du sacré. Paris et Montréal, l'Harmattan, 99, 156 p. (Ouverture Philosophique).

5933. Descartes et la Renaissance. Actes du Colloque International de Tour, 22–24 mars 1996. Ed. par Emmanuel FAYE. Paris, Honoré Champion Éditeur, 99, 453 p.

5934. Deux Cartésiens: la polémique entre Antoine Arnauld et Nicolas Malebranche. Ed. par Denis MOREAU. Paris, J. Vrin, 99, 353 p. (Bibliothèque d'histoire de la philosophie).

5935. DI MARCO (Giuseppe Antonio). Thomas Hobbes nel decisionismo giuridico di Carl Schmitt. Napoli, Guida, 99, 871 p.

5936. Diderot, philosophie, matérialisme. Communications au Colloque de la Sorbonne, printemps 1999. Ed. par André TOSEL. *Recherches sur Diderot et sur l'Encyclopédie*, 99, 26, 244 p.

5937. DÖRING (Detlef). Die Philosophie Gottfried Wilhelm Leibniz' und die Leipziger Aufklärung in der ersten Hälfte des 18. Jahrhunderts. Stuttgart, S. Hirzel, 99, 188 p. (ill.). (Abhandlungen der Sächsischen Akademie der Wissenschaften zu Leipzig. Philologisch-Historische Klasse, 75, 4).

5938. D'ORSI (Angelo). Lo studente che non divenne "dottore". Gramsci all'Università di Torino. *Studi storici*, 99, 40, p. 39-75.

5939. DUMOUCHEL (Daniel). Kant et la genèse de la subjectivité esthétique. Esthétique et philosophie avant la «Critique de la faculté de juger». Paris, Vrin, 99, 306 p. (Bibliothèque d'histoire de la philosophie).

5940. EWERTOWSKI (Jörg). Die Freiheit des Anfangs und das Gesetz des Werdens. Zur Metaphorik von Mangel und Fülle in F. W. J. Schellings Prinzip des Schöpferischen. Stuttgart, Frommann-Holzboog, 99, 444 p. (Spekulation und Erfahrung. Texte und Untersuchungen zum Deutschen Idealismus, II, 35).

5941. FERRARI ZUMBINI (Massimo). Untergänge und Morgenröten. Nietzsche – Spengler – Antisemitismus. Würzburg, Könighausen und Neumann, 99, 217 p. (Studien zur Literatur- und Kulturgeschichte, 14).

5942. Fichte Entlassung. Der Atheismusstreit vor 200 Jahren. Hrsg. v. Klaus-M. KODALLE und Martin OHST. Würzburg, Konigshaufen und Neumann. 99, 226 p. (Kritisches Jahrbuch der Philosophie, 4).

5943. Filosofi del diritto contemporanei. A cura di Gianfrancesco ZANETTI. Milano, R. Cortina, 99, XXVII-314 p. (Testi studi e ricerche di scienze giuridiche).

5944. Filosofia pratica (La) tra metafisica e antropologia nell'età di Wolff e Vico. Atti del Convegno internazionale, Napoli, 2–5 aprile 1997. A cura di Giuseppe CACCIATORE. Napoli, Guida, 99, XVII, 521 p.

5945. FINK (Hilary L.). Bergson and Russian modernism, 1900–1930. Evaston, Northwestern U. P., 99, XVIII-169.

5946. FISCHBACH (Frank). Du commencement en philosophie. Étude sur Hegel et Schelling. Paris, Librairie philosophique J.Vrin, 99, 386 p. (Bibliothèque d'histoire de la philosophie).

5947. FOWLER (Colin F.). Descartes on the human soul. Philosophie and the demands of Christian doctrine. Dordrecht a. Boston a. London, Kluwer Academic Publisher, 99, XIII-438 p. (International archives of the history of ideas, 160).

5948. FRANCO (Paul). Hegel's philosophy of freedom. New Haven a. London, Yale U. P., 99, XVIII- 391 p.

5949. FULTON (Ann). Apostels of Sartre: existialism in America, 1945–1963. Evaston, Northwestern U. P., 99, VIII-163 p. (bibl.).

5950. GATTI (Hilary). Giordano Bruno and Renaissance science. Ithaca a. London, Cornell U. P., 99, 257 p. (bibl.).

5951. GERHARDT (Volker), MEHRING (Reinhard), RINDERT (Jona). Berliner Geist: eine Geschichte der Berliner Universitätsphilosophie bis 1946. Mit einem Ausblick auf die Gegenwart der Humboldt-Universität. Berlin, Akademie Verlag, 99, 337 p.

5952. German philosophy since Kant. Ed. by Anthony O'HEAR. Cambridge, Cambridge U. P., 99, VI-445 p. (Royal Institute of philosophy supplement).

5953. Giambattista Vico nel suo tempo e nel nostro. A cura di Mario AGRIMI. Napoli, CUEN, 99, 709 p. (Laboratorio, 34).

5954. GLAUSER (Richard). Berkeley et les philosophes du XVIIe siècle: perception et scepticisme. Sprimont, Mardaga, 99, 352 p. (Philosophie et langage).

5955. GODDARD (Jean-Christophe). La philosophie fichtéenne de la vie. Le transcendental et la pathologie. Paris, Librairie philosophique J.Vrin, 99, 239 p. (Bibliothèque d'histoire de la philosophie).

5956. GÖDDE (Günter). Traditionslinien des "Unbewussten": Schopenhauer, Nietzsche, Freud. Tübingen, Edition Diskord, 99, 655 p. (ill.).

5957. GOUDRIAAN (Aza). Philosophische Gotteserkenntnis bei Suárez und Descartes im Zusammenhang mit der niederländischen reformierten Theologie und Philosophie des 17. Jahrhunderts, Leiden, Brill, 99, X-327 p.

5958. Gramsci e il Novecento. A cura di Giuseppe VACCA. Roma, Carocci, 99, p. 9-381. (Fondazione Istituto Gramsci, Annale 1997/IX, 1).

5959. GRISWOLD (Charles L.). Adam Smith and the virtues of Enlightenment. Cambridge, Cambridge U. P., 99, XIV-412 p. (Modern european philosophy).

5960. GROULT (Martine). D'Alembert et la mécanique de la vérité dans l'Encyclopédie. Paris, Champion, 99, 504 p. (bibl.). (Dix-huitièmes siècles, 34).

5961. HACOHEN (Malachi Haim). Dilemmas of cosmopolitanism: Karl Popper, Jewish identity, and «Central European Culture». *Journal of modern history*, 99, 71, 1, p. 105-149.

5962. HARRISON (Peter). Prophecy, early modern apologetics, and Hume's argument against miracles. *Journal of the history of ideas*, 99, 60, 2, p. 241-256.

5963. HEIDER (Placidus Bernhard). Jürgen Habermas und Dieter Henrich. Neue Perspektiven auf Identität und Wirklichkeit. Freiburg i. B. u. München, Verlag K. Alber, 99, 166 p. (Alber Reihe Philosophie).

5964. HENTGES (Gudrun). Schattenseiten der Aufklärung: die Darstellung von Juden und "Wilden" in philosophischen Schriften des 18. und 19. Jahrhunderts. Schwalbach, Wochenschau, 99, 298 p.

5965. HERB (Karlfriedrich). Bürgerliche Freiheit. Politische Philosophie von Hobbes bis Constant. Freiburg u. München, 99, 243 p. (Praktische Philosophie, 61).

5966. HERZ (Dietmar). Die wohlerwogene Republik. Das Konstitutionelle Denken des politisch-philosophischen Liberalismus. Paderborn, Verlag Ferdinand Schöning, 99, 400 p.

5967. Interférences et transformations dans la philosophie française et autrichienne (Mach, Poincaré, Duhem, Boltzmann). Paris, Kimé, 99, 244 p. [*Philosophia scientiae*, 99, 3, 2].

5968. JOLLEY (Nicholas). Locke: his philosophical thought. Oxford, Oxford U. P., 99, VIII-233 p.

5969. KATER (Thomas). Politik, Recht, Geschichte. Zur Einheit der politischen Philosophie Immanuel Kants. Würzburg, Königshaufen und Neumann. 99, 195 p.

5970. KELLER (Pierre). Husserl and Heidegger on human experience. Cambridge, Cambridge U. P., 99, 261 p.

5971. KNATZ (Lothar). Geschichte-Kunst-Mythos. Schellings Philosophie und die Perspektive einer philosophischen Mythostheorie. Würzburg, Königshausen und Neumann, 99, 352 p.

5972. KOZU (Kunio). Bewusstsein und Wissenschaft. Zu Hegels Nürnberger Systemkonzeption. Frankfurt a. M., Peter Lang, 99, XI-122 p. (Hegeliana, 10).

5973. LACKEY (Michael). Killing god, liberating the «subject»: Nietzsche and post-God freedom. *Journal of the history of ideas*, 99, 60, 4, p. 737-757.

5974. LAUBE (Martin). Im Bann der Sprache. Die analytische Religionsphilosophie im 20. Jahrhundert. Berlin u. New York, 99, 498 p. (Theologische Bibliothek Topelmann, 85).

5975. LAUGIER (Sandra). Recommencer la philosophie: la philosophie américaine aujourd'hui. Paris, PUF, 99, 221 p. (Intervention philosophique).

5976. LE RIDER (Jacques). Nietzsche en France: de la fin du XIXe siècle au temps présent. Paris, Presses universitaires de France, 99, VII-279 p. (Perspectives germaniques).

5977. LECA-TSIOMIS (Marie). Ecrire l'Encyclopédie: Diderot. De l'usage des dictionnaires à la grammaire philosophique. Oxford, Voltaire Foundation, 99, XII-528 p. (Studies on Voltaire and the eighteenth century, 375).

5978. Lexicon Philosophicum. Quaderni di terminologia filosofica e storia delle idee. Vol. X. Firenze, Leo S. Olschki, 99, VIII-208 p. (Lessico intellettuale europeo, 75). [Contiene: ADAMO (G.). Tra lessicografia e terminologia. – BIANCHI (M. L.). Paracelso e l'immaginazione. – LAMARRA (A.). La traduzione latina della «Monadologie». – MUCCILLO (M.). L'utopia del Doni. – PALAIA (R.). Motivi leibniziani nella voce 'Liberté' dell'«Encyclopedie». – PIMPINELLA (P.). Ragione e sensibilità nelle poetiche critiche di Gottsched e Breitinger e nell'estetica di Baumgarten. – SPINOSA (G.). Il

5. PHILOSOPHY

senso secondo il Tommaseo. – TOTARO (P.). Libri e circolazione libraria nelle lettere di Antonio Magliabechi a corrispondenti olandesi. – VENEZIANI (M.). Il sincretismo filosofico di J.B. Du Hamel.]. – Lessico filosofico dei secoli XVII e XVIII. A cura di Marta FATTORI e Massimo Luigi BIANCHI. L.S. Olschki, 99, 252 p. (ill.). (Lessico intellettuale europeo, 76).

5979. LINSKY (Bernard). Russel's metaphysical logic. Stanford, CSLI, 99, VII-150 p. (CSLI Lecture notes, 101).

5980. LOMONACO (Fabrizio). Tolleranza e libertà di coscienza. Filosofia, diritto e storia tra Leida e Napoli nel secolo XVIII. Napoli, Liguori, 99, XIV-247 p.

5981. LUNTLEY (Michael). Conteporary philosophy of thought: truth, world, content. Oxford, Blackwell, 99, XII-398 p.

5982. MACDONALD (Bradley J.). William Morris and the aesthetic constitution of politics. Lanham, a. Oxford, Lexington Books, 99, XIX-175 p. (bibl.).

5983. MARCONI (Diego). La filosofia del linguaggio: da Frege ai nostri giorni. Torino, UTET libreria, 99, VI-140 p.

5984. MARTINICH (Aloysius P.). Hobbes: a biography. Cambridge, Cambridge U. P., 99, XVI-390 p.

5985. MASULLO (Paolo Augusto). L'intersoggettivita della persona: Husserl, Scheler, Guardini, Weizsäcker. Napoli, Loffredo, 99, 143 p.

5986. MAZZOTTA (Giuseppe). The new map of the world: the poetic philosophy of Giambattista Vico. Princeton, Princeton U. P., 99, XVIII-267 p. (bibl.).

5987. MONTAVONT (Anne). De la passivité dans la phénoménologie de Husserl. Paris, PUF, 99, 294 p. (Épiméthée).

5988. NADLER (Steven). Spinoza: a life. New York a. Cambridge, Cambridge U. P., 99, XIII-408 p. (bibl.).

5989. Novecento (Il). A cura di Pietro ROSSI e Carlo Augusto VIANO. Roma, Laterza, 99, 1258 p. (ill.). (Storia della filosofia, 6).

5990. PAINTER (Mark A.). The depravity of wisdom: The Protestant Reformation and the disengagement of knowledge from virtue in modern philosophy. Aldershot, Ahsgate, 99, 136 p.

5991. PEKACZ (Jolanta T.). The Salonnières and the Philosophies in old regime France: the authority of aesthetic judgment. *Journal of the history of ideas*, 99, 60, 2, p. 277-298.

5992. Philosophen des 17. Jahrhunderts: eine Einführung. Hrsg. v. Lothar KREIMENDAHL. Darmstadt, Primus Verlag, 99, VI-267 p.

5993. Philosophy (The) of Rawls. A collection of essays. Ed. by Henry S. RICHARDSON and Paul J. WEITHMAN. New York a. London, Garland Publishing, 99, 5 vol., XIV-312 p., XV-332 p., XIII-312 p., XIV-341 p., XVI-366 p.

5994. Pierre Bayle, citoyen du monde: de l'enfant du Carla à l'auteur du Dictionnaire: actes du Colloque du Carla-Bayle (13–15 septembre 1996). Ed. par Hubert BOST et Philippe DE ROBERT. Paris, Champion, 99, 379 p. (Vie des Huguenots, 4).

5995. PIN (Corrado). "Natum ad encyclopaediam": osservazioni sul Sarpi scienziato e filosofo dopo l'edizione integrale dei "Pensieri". *Rivista storica italiana*, 99, 111, 2, p. 582-612.

5996. Politics, philosophy, terror: essays on the thought of Hannah Arendt. Ed. by Dana VILLA. Princeton, Princeton U. P., 99, X-266 p.

5997. POOLE (Randall Allen). The neo-idealist reception of Kant in the Moscow psychological society. *Journal of the history of ideas*, 99, 60, 2, p. 319-344.

5998. PREDIERI (Alberto). La guerra, il nemico, l'amico, il partigiano: Ernst Jünger e Carl Schmitt. Firenze, La nuova Italia, 99, 118 p.

5999. Prispevki z Mednarodne konference Peter Pavel Vergerij ml., polemični mislec v Evropi 16. stoletja ob 500. letnici rojstva, Koper, 1.–2. oktober 1998 = Contributi dal Convegno internazionale Pier Paolo Vergerio il giovane, un polemista attraverso l'Europa del Cinquecento nel V centenario della nascita, Capodistria 1–2 ottobre 1998 = Contributions from the International Scientific Meeting Peter Paul Vergerius, Jr., Controversial thinker of the 16th Century Europe on 500th anniversary of his birth, Koper, 1–2 October 1998. Ur. Darko DAROVEC. Koper, Zgodovinsko društvo za južno Primorsko: = Societa storica del Litorale, Znanstveno-raziskovalno središče Republike Slovenije = Centro di ricerche scientifiche della Republica di Slovenia = Science and Research Centre of the Republic of Slovenia, 99, 279 p. (ill.). (Acta Histriae, 8, = letn. 7, leto 1999, 2).

6000. RAPIC (Smail). Erkenntnis und Sprachgebrauch: Lichtenberg und der englische Empirismus. Göttingen, Wallstein, 99, 326 p. (Lichtenberg-Studien, 8).

6001. REALE (Mario). L'interpretazione crociana di Marx tra il «canone» e il «paragone ellittico». *La cultura*, 99, 37, 2, p. 219-264.

6002. RILEY (Patrick). Leibniz's political and moral philosophy in the Novissima Sinica, 1699–1999. *Journal of the history of ideas*, 99, 60, 2, p. 217-240.

6003. RÖMPP (Georg). Ethik des Selbsbewusstseins. Der Andere in der idealistischen Grundlegung der Philosophie: Kant, Fichte, Schelling, Hegel. Berlin, Duncker und Humblot, 99, 308 p. (Philosophische Schriften, 31).

6004. Rosmini e la problematica politico-sociale dell'Europa del 2000. Atti del Convegno tenuto a Bolzano nel 1997. A cura di Danilo CASTELLANO. Napoli, Edizioni scientifiche italiane, 99, 223 p. (Institut international d'études européennes Antonio Rosmini).

6005. ROSSI (Paolo). Le sterminate antichità e nuovi saggi vichiani. Firenze, La nuova Italia, 99, XXIV-545 p. (Biblioteca di cultura, 246. Storie di idee, 7). – IDEM.

Un altro presente: saggi sulla storia della filosofia. Bologna, Il mulino, 99, 290 p.

6006. Rousseau visité, Rousseau visiteur: les dernières années (1770-1778). Actes du Colloque de Geneve, 21-22 juin 1996. Ed. par Jacques BRECHTOLD et Michel PORRET. *Annales de la Société Jean-Jacques Rousseau*, 99, n. 42, 532 p.

6007. ROUSSET (Bernard). Geulincx entre Descartes et Spinoza. Paris, Librairie philosophique J.Vrin, 99, 219 p. (Bibliothèque d'histoire de la philosophie).

6008. RUMI (Giorgio). Gioberti. Bologna, Il Mulino, 99, 111 p.

6009. SCHEUERMAN (William E.). Carl Schmitt: the end of law. Lanham, Rowman & Littlefield, 99, XI-345 p.

6010. SCHMALTZ (Tad M.). What has Cartesianism to do with Jansenism? *Journal of the history of ideas*, 99, 60, 1, p. 37-56.

6011. SCHNEIDER (Ulrich Johannes). Philosophie und Universität: Historisierung der Vernunft im 19. Jahrhundert. Hamburg, Meiner, 99, X-405 p. (ill.).

6012. SEGISSEMENT (Marie-José Pernin). Nietzsche et Schopenhauer: encore et toujours la prédestination. Paris, L'Harmattan, 99, 511 p. (La philosophie en commun).

6013. SPREMBERG (Heinz). Zur Aktualität der Ästhetik Immanuel Kants: ein Versuch zu Kants ästhetischer Urteilstheorie mit Blick auf Wittgenstein und Sibley. Frankfurt am Main a. New York, P. Lang, 99, X-370 p. (bibl.). (Europäische Hochschulschriften. Philosophie, 580).

6014. STAVRAKAKIS (Yannis). Lacan and the political. London a. New York, Routledge, 99, X-188 p. (Thinking the political).

6015. Stoïcisme (Le) au XVIe et au XVIIe siècle: le retour des philosophies antiques à l'Age classique. Ed. par Pierre-François MOREAU. Paris, A. Michel, 99, 363 p. (Bibliothèque Albin Michel des idées, 1).

6016. SWEET (Dennis). The birth of The Birth of Tragedy. *Journal of the history of ideas*, 99, 60, 2, p. 345-360.

6017. TAVER (Katja V.). Johan Gottlieb Fichtes Wissenschaftslehre 1810. Versuch einer Exegese. Amsterdam u. Atlanta, Rodopi, 99, XVIII- 395 p. (Fichte-Studien, Supplementa, 12).

6018. TIKHONOVA (Elena Ju.). V.G. Belinskij v spore so slavjanofilami. (Vissarion Belinsky disputing with the Slavophils: [Russia, 1830–1840es]). RAN, In-t rossijskoj istorii. Moskva, Editorial-URSS, 99, 130 p.

6019. TILLIETTE (Xavier). Schelling. Biographie. Paris, Calmann-Lévy, 99, 497 p. (La vie des philosophes).

6020. TIMMERMANS (Benôit). The originality of Descartes's conception of analysis as discovery. *Journal of the history of ideas*, 99, 60, 3, p. 433-448.

6021. TOMASONI (Francesco). La modernità e il fine della storia: il dibattito sull'ebraismo da Kant ai giovani hegeliani. Brescia, Morcelliana, 99, 248 p.

6022. TORTAROLO (Edoardo). L'illuminismo: ragioni e dubbi della modernità. Roma, Carocci, 99, 283 p. (ill.). (Studi superiori. Storia, 378).

6023. TVARDOVSKAJA (Valentina A.), ITENBERG (Boris S.). Russkie i Karl Marks: Vybor ili sud'ba? (The Russians and Karl Marx: choice or fortune? Attitudes toward Karl Marx in the 19th-century Russia). RAN, In-t rossijskoj istorii. Moskva, Editorial-URSS, 99, 215 p. (ind.).

6024. VACCA (Giuseppe). Appuntamenti con Gramsci: introduzione allo studio dei Quaderni dal carcere. Roma, Carocci, 99, 254 p. (Studi superiori, 374). – IDEM. Sraffa come fonte di notizie per la biografia di Gramsci. *Studi storici*, 99, 40, p. 5-37.

6025. VIEWEG (Klaus). Philosophie des Remis. Der junge Hegel und das 'Gespenst des Skeptizismum'. München, W. Fink Verlag, 99, 267 p. (Jena-Sophia. Studien und Editionen sum deutschen Idealismus und zur Frühromantik, II, 4).

6026. WESTERHOFF (Jan C.). Poeta Calculans: Harsdörffer, Leibniz, and the mathesis universalis. *Journal of the history of ideas*, 99, 60, 3, p. 449-468.

6027. WILSON (Fred). The logic and methodology of science in early modern thought. Toronto, University of Toronto Press, 99, XXIV-608 p. (bibl.).

6028. WOLF (Kurt). Religionsphilosophie in Frankreich. Der 'ganz Andere' und die personale Struktur der Welt. München, Wilhelm Fink Verlag, 99, 216 p.

6029. WOOD (Allen W.). Kant's ethical thought. Cambridge, Cambridge U. P., 99, XXIV-436 p.

Cf. n°s 802, 1050-1109, 1390-1409, 5342, 5391, 5574

§ 6. Exact, natural, medical sciences and technique.

* 6030. Bibliographia physico-mathematica hispanica, 1475–1900. Vol. 1. Libros y folletos, 1475–1600. Ed. par Víctor NAVARRO BROTÓNS. Valencia, Universitat de València-C.S.I.C.: Instituto de Historia de la Ciencia y Documentación "López Pinero", 99, 374 p. (Cuadernos Valencianos de Historia de la Medicina y de la Ciencia. Serie C, Repertorios Bio-bibliográficos, 56).

* 6031. JACKSON (Myles). Labor, skills, and practices in the scientific enterprise: recent works in the cultural history of science. *Journal of modern history*, 99, 71, 4, p. 902-913.

* 6032. Rousseau et la chimie. Repères bibliographiques. *Corpus*, 99, n. 36, p. 201-206.

** 6033. BAGLIVI (Giorgio). Carteggio (1679–1704). Conservato nella Waller Collection presso la University Library «Carolina Rediviva» di Uppsala. A cura di A. TOSCANO. Firenze, Leo S. Olschki, 99, 372 p. (ill.). (Archivio della corrispondenza degli scienziati italiani, 14). – Carteggi di Giorgio Baglivi: fondi Osler Magliabechi (1677–1706): lettere della Osler collection, Osler library della McGill university; fondo Magliabechi della Biblioteca nazionale di Firenze. A cura di Federico DI TROCCHIO, Gabriella GUERRIERI e Ennio DE SIMONE. Lecce, Milella, 99, 335 p.

** 6034. Correspondence (The) of Charles Darwin. Vol. 11. 1863. Ed. by Frederick BURKHARDT. Cambridge, Cambridge U. P., 99, XXXIX-1038 p.

** 6035. Correspondence (The) of Michael Faraday. Volume 4, January 1849–October 1855, Letters 2146-3032. Ed. by Frank A. J. L. JAMES. London, Institution of Electrical Engineers, 1999, LXIV-1003 pp. (ill., bibl.).

6036. ADAMS (Stephen B.), BUTLER (Orville R.). Manifacturing the future: a history of Western Electric. Cambridge a. New York, Cambridge U. P., 99, XII-270 p.

6037. American astronomical society's first century (The). Ed. by David H. DE VORKIN. Washington, American Institute of Phisics, 99, XII-350 p. (ill., tables).

6038. ASFOUR (Amal). Hogarth's post-Newtonian universe. *Journal of the history of ideas*, 99, 60, 4, p. 693-716.

6039. BACHMANN (Manuel), HOFMEIER (Thomas). Geheimnisse der Alchemie. Basel, Schwabe, 99, 271 p. (ill.).

6040. BALDO CEOLIN (Massimilla). Galileo e la scienza sperimentale. *Nuncius*, 99, 14, p. 443-454.

6041. BALDWIN (Peter). Contagion and the State in Europe, 1830–1930. New York, Cambridge U. P., 99, XIII-581 p.

6042. BARLES (Sabine). La ville délétère: médecins et ingénieurs dans l'espace urbain (XVIIIe–XXe siècles). Seyssel, Champ Vallon, 99, 373 p. (Milieux).

6043. BAYAT (Ali Haydar). Osmanlı Devleti'nde hekimbaşılık kurumu ve hekimbaşılar. (Institution du médecin en chef et les médecins en chef dans l'Etat Ottoman). Ankara, Atatürk Araştırma Merkezi, 99, X-213 p.

6044. BEDINI (Silvio A.). Patrons, artisans, and instruments of science, 1600–1750. Aldershots, Ashgate, 99, XIV-336 p. (ill., figs., tables). (Variorum Collected Studies Series, 635).

6045. Beiträge zur Astronomiegeschichte. Hrsg. v. Wolfgang R. DICK und Jürgen HAMEL. Frankfurt a. M., Verlag Harri Deutsch, 99, 225 p. (ill.). (Acta Historica Astronomiae, 5).

6046. BELLER (Maria). Quantum dialogue: the making of a revolution. Chicago, University of Chicago Press, 99, XVI-365 p.

6047. BEYER (Robert T.). Sounds of our times. Two hundred years of acoustic. New York, AIP-Springer, 99, XVI-444 p. (ill.).

6048. BLISS (Katherine). The science of redemption: syphilis, sexual promiscuity, and reformism in revolutionary Mexico City. *Hispanic American historical review*, 99, 79, 1, p. 1-40.

6049. BUSINO (Giovanni). Il dibattito sulla scienza nelle ricerche recenti. Dal "Programma forte" alle controversie dell'"affare Sokal". *Rivista storica italiana*, 99, 111, 3, p. 706-755.

6050. CAMPBELL (Mary Baine). Wonder and science: imagining worlds in early modern Europe. Ithaca, Cornell U. P., 99, XIV-366 p.

6051. CAPSHEW (James H.). Psychologists on the march: science, practice, and professional identity in America, 1929–1969. New York, Cambridge U. P., 99, XII-276 p. (Cambridge studies in the history of psychology).

6052. Catching up with the vision: essays on the occasion of the 75th anniversary of the founding of the History of Science Society. Ed. by Margaret W. ROSSITER. Chicago University of Chicago Press, 99, 359 p. (ill.). (Supplement to ISIS, vol. 90).

6053. CATON (Donald). What a blessing she had chloroform: the medical and social response to the pain of childbirth from 1800 to the present. New Haven, Yale U. P., 99, XVI-288 p. (ill.).

6054. ÇEÇEN (Kazım). İstanbul'un Osmanlı dönemi suyolları. (Aqueducs d'İstanbul à l'époque de l'Empire ottoman). İstanbul, İSKİ, 99, 336 p. – IDEM. Osmanlı İmparatorluğunun doruğu: 16. yüzyıl teknolojisi. (Sommet de l'Empire Ottoman: la technologie du XVIe siècle). İstanbul, İSKİ, 99, 349 p.

6055. CHAPUIS (Olivier). A la mer comme au ciel. Bontemps-Beaupré et la naissance de l'hydrographie moderne (1700–1850). Paris, Presses Université Paris – Sorbonne, 99, 1060 p.

6056. CHAUVEAU (Sophie). L'invention pharmaceutique. La pharmacie française entre l'Etat et la société au XXe siècle. Paris, Institut d'édition Sanofi-Synthélabo, 99, 720 p. (Les empêcheurs de penser en rond).

6057. Chemistry, society and environment: a new history of the British chemical industry. Ed. by Colin Archibald RUSSEL. Cambridge, Royal Society of Chemistry, 99, 320 p.

6058. CREASE (Robert P.). Making physics: a biography of Brookhaven National Laboratory, 1946–1972. Chicago a. London, University of Chicago Press, 99, XII-434 p. (ill., app., bibl.).

6059. Crises (Les) de la pensée scientifique et leur résolution historique (XVIIIe–XXe siècles). Journée d'études tenue à l'Univesité de Rouen, le 7 janvier 1998. *Raison présente*, 99, 131, p. 5-118.

6060. CURTIS (Charles W.). Pioneers of representation theory: Frobenius, Burnside, Schur and Brauer. Providence, American Mathematical Society, 99, XVI-287 p. (History of Mathematics, 15). (ill., app., bibl.).

6061. DARMON (Pierre). L'homme et les microbes, XVIIe-XXe siècles. Paris, Fayard, 99, 592 p.

6062. Darwinismo (El) en España e Iberoamérica. Ed. por Thomas F. GLICK, Rosaura RUIZ y Miguel Angel PUIG-SAMPER. Mexico y Madrid, Universidad Nacional Autónoma de México y Consejo Superior de Investigaciones Científicas, Ediciones Code Calles, 99, 333 p. (Colección Actas).

6063. DEPOVERE (Paul). La classification périodique des éléments: la merveille fondamentale de l'univers. Paris et Bruxelles, De Boeck, 99, 129 p. (ill.).

6064. Deutsch-ungarische Beziehungen in Naturwissenschaft und Technik nach dem Zweiten Weltkrieg. Hrsg. v. Holger FISCHER. München, R. Oldenbourg, 99, 555 p. (ill.). [Contents: FISCHER (Holger). Wissenschaftspolitik und internationale Wissenschaftsbeziehungen in Ungarn nach dem Zweiten Weltkrieg. – BIEGELBAUER (Peter). Drei Transformationen: Die Forschungs- und Technologiepolitik Ungarns seit dem Zweiten Weltkrieg. – FISCHER (Holger). Die deutschungarischen Wissenschaftsbeziehungen nach dem Zweiten Weltkrieg: Programme, Strukturen, Entwicklungen. – GÖBEL (Wolfgang). Zur Zusammenarbeit der Akademie der Wissenschaften der DDR mit der Ungarischen Akademie der Wissenschaften und anderen wissenschaftlichen Einrichtungen in Ungarn in der Zeit von 1955 bis 1990. – LAST (Bärbel), SCHAEFER (Hans-Dieter). Wissenschaftsbeziehungen zwischen der DDR und der Volksrepublik Ungarn am Beispiel der Hochschulbeziehungen. – SZÖGI (László). Ungarisch-deutsche Beziehungen auf dem Gebiet des technischen Hochschulwesens 1945–1989: Die deutschen Beziehungen der Budapester Technischen Universität. – PALLÓ (Gábor). Deutsch-ungarische Beziehungen in den Naturwissenschaften in der Periode des Stalinismus. – WOLF-SCHMIDT (Gudrun). Deutsch-ungarische Beziehungen in der Astronomie und Astrophysik. – JESZENSZKY (Sándor). Ungarisch-deutsche Beziehungen auf dem Gebiet der Elektrotechnik zwischen 1945 und 1995: Fallstudie zur Zusammenarbeit der deutschen Firma Siemens mit ungarischen elektrotechnischen Unternehmen. – DIENEL (Hans-Liudger). Die deutsch-ungarische Zusammenarbeit im Nutzfahrzeugbau, 1945–1995: ein vergleichende Betrachtung industrieller Kooperationen in RGW und durch bilaterale Abkommen zwischen Ungarn und den beiden deutschen Staaten. – ENDREI (Walter). Kontakte deutscher und ungarische technischer Museen nach 1945. – VÁMOS (Eva). Deutsch-ungarische Wechselbeziehungen im Rahmen der internationalen Industriemessen. – Verzeichnis der Autoren].

6065. DUPONT (Jean-Claude). Histoire de la neurotransmission. Paris, Presses Universitaire de France, 99, VIII-305 p. (Science, Histoire ed Société).

6066. DUSEK (Val). The holistic inspiration of physics: the underground history of electromagnetic theory. New Brunswick, Rutgers U. P., 99, X-387 p. (bibl.).

6067. Ecce cortex: Beiträge zur Geschichte des modernen Gehirns. Hrsg. v. Michael HAGNER. Göttingen, Wallstein, 99, 352 p. (ill., app.).

6068. Entstehung (Die) der synthetischen Theorie: Beiträge zur Geschichte der Evolutionsbiologie in Deutschland, 1930–1950. Hrsg. v. Thomas JUNKER und Eve-Marie ENGELS. Berlin, Verlag für Wissenschaft unf Bildung, 99, 380 p. (figs., tables, app.). (Verhandlungen zur Geschichte und Theorie der Biologie, 2).

6069. EPPLE (Moritz). Die Entstehung der Knotentheorie: Kontexte und Konstruktionen einer modernen mathematischen Theorie. Braunschweig, Friedrich Vieweg & Sohn, 99, XVI-449 p.

6070. FAHLBUSCH (Michael). Wissenschaft im Dienst der nationalsozialistischen Politik? Die "Volksdeutschen Forschungsgemeinschaften" von 1931–1945. Baden-Baden, Nomos Verlagsgesellschaft, 99, 887 p. (ill., maps).

6071. FERREIRÓS (José). Labyrinth of thought: a history of set theory and its role in modern mathematics. Boston, Birkhäuser, 99, 464 p.

6072. FIEDEWALD (Michael). Der Computer als Werkzeug und Medium: die geistigen und technischen Wurzeln des Personalcomputer. Berlin, Verlag für Geschichte der Naturwissenschaften und Technik, 99, 497 p. (Aachener Beiträge zur Wissenschafts- und Technikgeschichte, 3). (ill., fig., tables, bibl.).

6073. FISCHER (D.). Les étudiants, la tuberculose et le sanatorium, de la Libération à la fin des années cinquante. *Revue historique*, 99, 123, 612, p. 809-832.

6074. Francesco Redi: un protagonista della scienza moderna: documenti, esperimenti, immagini. A cura di Walter BERNARDI e Luigi GUERRINI. Firenze, L. S. Olschki, 99, XI-388 p. (Biblioteca di Nuncius, 33).

6075. FRENCH (Roger). Dissection and vivisection in the European Renaissance. Aldershot, Ashgate, 99, IX-289 p.

6076. FRUTON (Joseph). Proteins, enzymes, genes: the interplay of chemistry and biology. New Haven a. London, Yale U. P., 99, XII-783 p. (ill., bibl.).

6077. GARBER (Elizabeth). The language of physics: the calculus and the development of theoretical physics in Europe, 1750–1914. Boston, Birkhäuser, 99, XIX-399 p.

6078. GARFINKEL (Simson L.). Architects of the information society: thirty-five years of the laboratory of computer science at MIT. Cambridge a. London, MIT Press, 99, XII-72 p. (ill.).

6079. Géométrie, atomisme et vide dans l'école de Galilée. Ed. par Egidio FESTA, Vincent JULLIEN et

Maurizio TORRINI. Firenze et Fontenay et Saint-Cloud, Istituto e museo di storia della scienza et ENS éd., 99, 335 p. (fig., bibl.).

6080. GILMAN (Sander L.). Making the body beautiful: a cultural history of aesthetic surgery. Princeton, Princeton U. P., 99, XII-396 p. (ill.).

6081. Girolamo Cardano: le opere, le fonti, la vita. A cura di Marialuisa BALDI e Guido CANZIANI. Milano, F. Angeli, 99, 589 p. (Filosofia e scienza nel Cinquecento e nel Seicento. Studi, 50).

6082. GIUDICE (Franco). Luce e visione. Thomas Hobbes e la scienza dell'ottica. Firenze, Leo S. Olschki, 99, X-182 p. (Biblioteca di «Nuncius», 35).

6083. GOLDT (Verena). Zentralbegriffe der Elektrizitätsforschung im 17. und 18. Jahrhundert. Frankfurt a. M., Lang, 99, 237 p. (Germanistische Arbeiten zu Sprache und Kulturgeschichte, 36).

6084. GÖRS (Britta). Chemischer Atomismus: Anwendung, Veränderung, Alternativen im deutschsprachigen Raum in der zweiten Hälfte des 19. Jahrhunderts. Berlin, ERS Verlag, 99, 240 p. (Berliner Beiträge zur Geschichte der Naturwissenschaften und der Technik, 23).

6085. GOVE (Harry E.). From Hiroshima to the iceman: the development and applications of accelerator mass spectrometry. Bristol, Institut of Physics Publishing, 99, XIV-226 p. (ill.).

6086. GRAFTON (Anthony). Cardano's cosmos: the worlds and works of a Renaissance astrologer. Cambridge, Harvard U. P., 99, XII-284 p.

6087. GRAY (Richard (T.). Physiognomik im Spannungsfeld zwischen Humanismus und Rassismus: Johann Caspar Lavater und Carl Gustav Carus. *Archiv für Kulturgeschichte*, 99, 81, 2, p. 313

6088. GREGORY KOHLSTEDT (Sally), SOKAL (Michael M.), LEWENSTEIN (Bruce V.). The establishment of science in America: 150 Years of the American Association for the Advancement of Science. Foreword by Stephen Jay GOULD. New Brunswick, Rutgers U. P., 99, XIV-236 p.

6089. GUICCIARDINI (Niccolò). Reading the Principia: the debate on Newton's mathematical methods for natural philosophy from 1687 to 1736. Cambridge, Cambridge U. P., 99, V-285 p.

6090. HAMMERSTEIN (Notker). Die deutsche Forschungsgemeinschaft in der Weimarer Republik und im Dritten Reich: Wissenschaftspolitik in Republik und Diktatur 1920–1945. München, C.H. Beck, 99, 582 p. (ill.).

6091. HAMOU (Philippe). La mutation du visible. Essai sur la portée épistémologique des instruments d'optique au XVIIe siècle. Vol. I. Du Sidereus nuncius de Galilée à la Dioptrique cartésienne. Villeneuve d'Ascq, Presses universitarion du septentrion, 99, 320 p. (bibl.).

6092. Histories of sexually transmitted diseases and HIV/AIDS in Subsaharan Africa. Ed. by Philip W. SETEL, Milton LEWIS and Maryinez LYONS. Westport a. London, Greenwood Press, 99, VI-267 p. (maps, tables, bibl.). (Contributions in Medical Studies, 44).

6093. History (A) of science in the Netherland. Ed. by Klaas VAN BERKEL, Albert VAN HELDEN and Lodewijk PALM. Leiden, Brill, 99, XXVIII-659 p. (ill., bibl.).

6094. HOCHKIRCHEN (Thomas). Die Axiomatisierung der Wahrsacheinlichkeitsrechnung und ihre Kontexte. Von Hilberts sechstem Problem zu Kolmogoroff Grundbegriffen. Göttingen, Vandenhoeck, 99, 398 p.

6095. HOLMBERG (Gustav). Reaching for the stars: studies in the history of Swedish stellar and nebular astronomy, 1860–1960. Lund, Ugglan, 99, 243 p. (Lund studies in the history of science and ideas, 13).

6096. HÖVEL (Gerlinde). Qualitates vegetabilium, vires medicamentorum, und oeconomicus usus plantarum bei Carl von Linné. Erste Versuche einer zielgerichteten Forschung nach Arznei- und Nutzpflanzen auf wissenschaftlicher Grundlage. Stuttgart, Deutscher Apotheker-Verlag, 99, X-452 p. (ill., tables, apps., bibl.). (Braunschweiger Veröffentlichung zur Geschichte der Pharmazie und der Naturwissenschaften, 42).

6097. HOWES (Ruth H.), HERZENBERG (Caroline L.). Their day in the sun: women of the Manhattan Project. Philadelphia, Temple U. P., 99, VIII-264 p. (Labor and Social Change).

6098. IHSANOĞLU (Ekmeleddin), ŞEŞEN (Ramazan), İZGİ (Cevat). Osmanlı matematik literatürü tarihi. (Histoire de la littérature mathématique ottomane). İstanbul, IRCICA, 99, 2 vol., CXII-349 p., 370 p.

6099. IHSANOĞLU (Ekmeleddin). Suriye'de modern Osmanlı sağlık müesseseleri, hastahaneler ve Şam Tıp Fakültesi. (Institutions sanitaires ottomanes, hôpitaux et faculté de médecine de Damas en Syrie). Ankara, Türk Tarih Kurumu, 99, IX-150 p.

6100. Inventing maternity: politics, science, and literature, 1650–1865. Ed. by Susan C. GREENFIELD and Carol BARASH. Lexington, Univerity of Kentucky Press, 99, VIII-274 p.

6101. JESSEPH (Douglas M.). The decline and fall of Hobbesian geometry. *Studies in history and philosophy of science*, 99, 30, 3, p. 425-453.

6102. JONES (Ross). The master potter and the rejected pots: eugenic legislation in Victoria, 1918–1939. *Australian historical studies*, 99, 30, 112, p. 319-342.

6103. JOUTSIVUO (Timo). Scholastic tradition and humanist innovation. The concept of Neutrum in Renaissance medicine. Helsinki, Finnish Academy of Science and Letters, 99, 288 p. (A. Acad. Scie. Fennicae, Ser. Humaniora, 303). (ill.).

6104. KOCHHAR (R.K.). Science in British India. *Indian journal of history of science*, 99, 34, 4, p. 317-46.

6105. KOERNER (Lisbet). Linnaeus: nature and nation. Cambridge, Harvard U. P., 99, VIII-297 p.

6106. KRAGH (Helge). Quantum generations: a history of physics in the twentieth century. Princeton, Princeton U. P., 99, 512 p.

6107. LAGRÉE (Michel). La bénédiction de Prométhée. Religion et technologie XIXe–XXe siècle. Préf. de Jean DELUMEAU. Paris, Fayard, 438 p.

6108. LINDBORG (Rolf). Ånden i naturen: naturfilosofen og eksperimentalfysikern Hans Christian Ørsted. (L'Esprit dans la Nature: H. C. Ørsted, philosophe de la nature et physicien). København, Gyldendal, 99, 216 p., ill. (rés. anglais).

6109. LINDEMANN (Mary). Medicine and society in early modern Europe. Cambridge, Cambridge U. P., 99, 240 p. (New approaches to European history).

6110. LOW (Morris), NAKAYAMA (Shigeru), YOSHIOKA (Hitoshi). Science, technology and society in contemporary Japan. Cambridge, Cambridge U. P., 99, XIV-226 p. (ill., tables, bibl.). (Contemporary Japanese society).

6111. MAEHLE (Andreas-Holger). Drugs on trial: experimental pharmacology and therapeutic innovation in the eighteenth century. Amsterdam, Rodopi, 99, 376 p. (Clio Medica, 53).

6112. MAIOCCHI (Roberto). Scienza italiana e razzismo fascista. Firenze, La nuova Italia, 338 p.

6113. MARIN (Brigitte). Pratiche terapeutiche, perizie medico-legali: nuovi approcci di storia della medicina. *Studi storici*, 99, 40, p. 629-641.

6114. MATTILA (Markku). Kansamme parhaaksi. Rotuhygienia Suomessa vuoden 1935 sterilointilakiin asti. (In our nation's best interest. Eugenics in Finland until the promulgation of the sterilization law of 1935.) Helsinki, SHS, 99, 435 p. (Bibliotheca historica, 44). [English summary].

6115. MIDELFORT (H. C. Eric). A history of madness in sixteenth-century Germany. Cambridge, Cambridge U. P., 99, XVI-438 p.

6116. Modernización difficil (La): Henri Pittier en Venezuela, 1920–1950. Ed. por Jolanda TEXERA ARNAL. Caracas, Fundación Polar, 99, 704 p. (ill., tables,).

6117. MONMONIER (Mark). Air apparent: how meteorologists learned to map, predict, and dramatize weather. Chicago a. London, University of Chicago Press, 99, XIV-309 p. (ill., figs., tables. app.).

6118. MONNAIS-ROUSSELOT (Laurence). Médecine et colonisation: l'aventure indochinoise, 1860–1939. Paris, CNRS Edition, 99, 489 p. (ill., fig. tables, app., bibl.). (CNRS Histoire).

6119. MONTENEGRO (Angelo). Tipografi e cultura scientifica a Lodi (1840–1915). *Ricerche storiche*, 99, 29, p. p. 361-417.

6120. MOSCHOVITIS (Christos J. P.), POOLE (Hilary), SCHUYLER (Tami), SENFT (Theresa M.). History of the Internet: a chronology, 1843 to the present. Santa Barbara a. Oxford, ABC-Clio, 99, VIII-312 p. (ill.).

6121. NACCACHE (Albert F. H.). A brief history of evolution. *In*: Return (The) of science: evolutionary ideas and history [Cf. n° 863], p.10-32.

6122. NADDEO (Barbara Ann). The science of man as the science of society. Medical anthropology in the Kingdom of Naples (1760–1790). *Annali dell'istituto italiano per gli studi storici*, 99, 16, p. 287-321.

6123. Nascita (La) della pediatria e dell'ostetricia tra XVIII e XX secolo (a Firenze e altrove). Seminario presso l'Istituto degli Innocenti, Firenze (26–28 novembre 1998). A cura di Carlo A. CORSINI e Lucia SANDRI. *Bollettino di demografia storica*, 99, 30-31, p. 5-184.

6124. Natural dyestuffs and industrial culture in Europe, 1750–1880. Ed. by Robert FOX and Agustì NIETO-GALAN. Canton, Science History Pubblication, 99, XXIX-354 p. (ill., tables, app.). (European Studies in Science History and the Arts, 2).

6125. Natural particulars: nature and the disciplines in Renaissance Europe. Papers from a workshop held at Dibner Institute for the History of Science and Technology, May 5–6, 1995. Ed by Anthony GRAFTON and Nancy SIRAISI. Cambridge a. London, MIT Press, 99, XI-426 p. (ill.). (Dibner Institute studies in the history of science and technology). [Contents: COPENHAVER (Brian P.). Number, shape and meaning in Pico's Christian Cabala: the upright Tsade, the closed Mem and the gaping jaws of Azazel. – HANKINS (James). The study of the Timaeus of early Renaissance Italy. – ALLEN (Michael J. B.). Marsilio Ficino: daemonic mathematics and the hypotenuse of the spirit. – DEITZ (Luc.) Space, light and soul in Francesco Patrizi's Nova de universis philosophia (1591). – BLAIR (Ann). The Problemata as a natural philosophical genre. – MONFASANI (John). The pseudo-Aristotelian problemata and Aristotle's De animalibus in the Renaissance. – MUGNAI CARRARA (Daniela). Epistemological problems in Giovanni Mainardi's commentary on Galen's Ars parva. – NUTTON (Vivian). "A diet for barbarians": introducing Renaissance medicine to tudor England. – CRISCIANI (Chiara). From the laboratory to the library: alchemy according to Guglielmo Fabri. – NEWMAN (William). The homunculus and his forebears: wonders of art and nature. – PARK (Katharine). Natural particulars: medical epistemology, practice and the literature of healing springs. – FINDLEN (Paula). The formation of a scientific community: natural history in sixteenth-century Italy. – DACOSTA KAUFMANN (Thomas). Empiricism and community in early modern science and art: some comments on baths, plants and courts.].

6126. Newton and religion: context, nature, and influence. Ed. by James E. FORCE and Richard H. POPKIN. Dordrecht a. London, Kluwer Academic, 99, XVII-325 p. (International archives of the history of ideas, 161).

6127. Nome (Nel) della razza. Il razzismo nella storia d'Italia (1870–1945). A cura di Alberto BURGIO. Bologna, Il Mulino, 99, 565 p.

6128. "Nützliche Künste": Kultur- und Sozialgeschichte der Technik im 18. Jahrhundert. Hrsg. v. Ulrich TROITZSCH. Münster, Waxmann, 99, 279 p. (ill.). (Cottbuser Studien zur Geschichte von Technik, Arbeit und Umwelt, 13).

6129. NYE (Mary Jo). Before big science: the pursuit of modern chemistry and physics, 1800–1940. Cambridge a. London, Harvard U. P., 99, XVIII-282 p. (ill.).

6130. O'GORMAN (Francis). Ruskin's science of the 1870s: science, education, and the nation. *In:* Ruskin and the dawn of modern [Cf. n° 5693] p. 35-55.

6131. OJA (Linda). Varken Gud eller natur: synen på magi i 1600- och 1700-talets Sverige. (Ni dieu ni la nature: la conception de la magie dans la Suède des 17ᵉ et 18ᵉ siècles). Eslöv, B. Östlings bokförlag Symposion, 99, 382 p. (tab.).

6132. OSSOLA (Carlo). "Piazzette" e "caraffe": 'Metafisica' galileana. *Nuncius,* 99, 14, p. 423-441.

6133. PALSKY (Gilles). Le code des couleurs dans les cartes géologiques du XIXᵉ siècle. *Bulletin Comm. Française de cartographie,* 99, 159, p. 63-70.

6134. PEARD (Julian G.). Race, place, and medicine: the idea of the Tropics in nineteenth-century Brazilian medicine. Durham a. London, Duke U. P., 99, X-315 p. (bibl.).

6135. PHILLIPS (Gervase). Longbow and hackbutt: weapons technology and technology transfer in early modern England. *Technology and culture,* 99, 40, 3, p. 576-593.

6136. PICARD (Jean-François). La fondation Rockefeller et la recherche médicale. Paris, PUF, 99, XII-244 p. (Science, histoire et société).

6137. POGLIANO (Claudio). Bachi, polli e grani. Appunti sulla ricezione della genetica in Italia (1900–1953). *Nuncius,* 99, 14, p. 133-168.

6138. PORTER (Roy Sydney). Medicine [British culture, 1776–1832]. *In:* Oxford companion (An) to the romantic age [Cf. n° 1253], p. 170-178.

6139. PRAKASH (Gyan). Another reason: science and the imagination of modern India. Princeton, Princeton U. P., 99, XIII-304 p.

6140. Psychiatrie im Nationalsozialismus. Die Bayerischen Heil- und Pflegeanstalten zwischen 1933 und 1945. Hrsg. v. Michael von CRANACH und Hans Ludwig SIEMEN. München, Oldenbourg, 99, 508 p.

6141. Race, science, and medicine, 1700–1960. Ed. by Waltraud ERNST and Bernhard HARRIS. London, Routledge, 99, IX-300 p. (ill.). (Studies in the social history of medicine).

6142. RANDLES (William G. L.). The unmaking of the medieval Christian cosmos, 1500–1760: from solid heavens to boundless aether. Aldershot, Ashgate, 99, XV-274 p. (ill., bibl.).

6143. Repräsentationsformen in den biologischen Wissenschaften. Hrsg. v. Armin GEUS, Thomas JUNKER, Hans-Jörg RHEINBERGER, Christa RIEDL-DORN und Michael WEINGARTEN. Berlin, Verlag für Wissenschaft und Bildung, 99, 321 p. (ill.), (Verhandlungen zur Geschichte und Theorie der Biologie, 3).

6144. RASMUSSEN (Leif). Rockefeller Foundation, Carlsbergfondet og dansk medicinsk biologi i mellemkrigsårene: virkninger for forskning og undervisning gennem det 20. århundrede. *Dansk medicinhistorisk årbog,* 99, 27, p. 65-79. (bibl.).

6145. REYNOLDS (Moira Davison). American women scientists: 23 inspiring biographies, 1900–2000. Jefferson a. London, McFarland, 99, IX-149 p.

6146. RICCI (S.). I Lincei: l'invenzione della mediazione accademica. Nuova scienza, religione, vita civile. *In*: Sciences et religions de Copernic à Galilée (1540–1610) [Cf. n° 6157], p. 205-234.

6147. RICE (Tony). Voyages of discovery: three centuries of natural history exploration. London a. New York, Natural History Museum a. Potter, 99, 335 p. (ill., bibl.).

6148. ROMANO (Antonella). La contre-réforme mathématique: constitution et diffusion d'une culture mathématique jésuite à la Renaissance (1540–1640). Roma, Ecole française de Rome, 99, XII-691 p. (Befar, 306). – EADEM [en coll. avec P.-A. FABRE]. Les jésuites dans le monde moderne. Nouvelles approaches historiographiques. *Revue de synthèse,* 99, 4, [s. p.].

6149. ROSENFELD (Louis). Four centuries of clinical chemistry. Amsterdam, Gordon & Breach, 99, XVI-562 p. (ill., bibl.).

6150. SABUNCUOĞLU (Şerafeddin). Mücerreb-nâme (ilk Türkçe deneysel tıp eseri – 1468). [Livre des éprouvés (Le Premier ouvrage expérimental turc en médecine – 1468)]. Ed. par İlter UZEL et Kenan SÜREVEN. Ankara, Atatürk Kültür Merkezi, 99, XIII-188 p.

6151. SÁNCHEZ RON (José Manuel). Cincel, martillo y piedra: historia de la ciencia en España (siglos XIX y XX). Madrid, Taurus, 99, 468 p. (plates, ill.). (Pensamiento).

6152. SAUERTEIG (Lutz). Krankheit, Sexualität, Gesellschaft. Geschlechtskrankheiten und Gesundheitspolitik in Deutschland im 19. und frühen 20. Jahrhundert. Stuttgart, Steiner, 99, 542 p. (Medizin, Gesellschaft und Geschichte, 12).

6153. Science under socialism: East Germany in comparative perspective. Ed. by Kristie MACRAKIS and Dieter HOFFMANN. Cambridge, Harvard U. P., 99, XIV-380 p.

6154. Science, technology and political change: proceedings of the XXth International Congress of History of Science (Liège, 20-26 July 1997). Ed by Dieter

HOFFMANN, Benoît SEVERYNS and Raymond G. STOKES. Turnhout, Brepols, 99, 5 vol., [s. p.]. [Partial contents: Vol. 1. Science, technology and political change. Ed. by Dieter HOFFMANN, Benoît SEVERYNS and Raymond G. STOKES. – Vol. 2. Between the natural and the artificial: dyestuffs and medicines. Ed. by Gérard EMPTOZ and Patricia Elena ACEVES PASTRANA. – Vol. 3. Fundamental changes in cellular biology in the 20th century: biology of development, chemistry and physics in the life sciences. Ed. by Charles GALPERIN, Scott F. GILBERT and Brigitte HOPPE. – Vol. 4. The spread of the scientific revolution in the European periphery, Latin America and East Asia. Ed. by Celina A. LÉRTORA MENDOZA, Efthymios NICOLAÏDIS and Jan VANDERSMISSEN. – Vol. 5. Science, technology and industry in the Ottoman world. Ed. by Ekmeleddin IHSANOĞLU, Ahmed DJEBBAR and Feza GÜNERGUN]. (De diversis artibus, 41-45).

6155. Sciences (The) in Enlightened Europe. Ed. William CLARK, Jan GOLINSKI and Simon SCHAFFER. Chicago, University of Chicago Press, 99, XI-466 p.

6156. Sciences (The) in the European periphery during the Enlightenment. Ed by Kostas GAVROGLU. Dordrecht a. London, Kluwer Academic, 99, XI-224 p. (ill.). (Archimedes: new studies in the history and philosophy of science and technology, 2).

6157. Sciences et religions de Copernic à Galilée (1540–1610). Actes du colloque international, Rome 12–14 déc. 1996. Ed. par Maurizio TORRINI. Rome, École Français de Rome, 99, 550 p. [Cf. n° <sélection> 6146.]

6158. Short history (A) of neurology: the British contributions, 1660–1910. Ed. by F. Clifford ROSE. Oxford, Butterworth-Heinemann, 99, IX-282 p.

6159. STEWART (John). "The battle for health": a political history of the socialist medical association, 1930-1951. Aldershot, Ashgate, 99, VIII-259 p. (bibl.). (History of Medicine in Context).

6160. SUMMERS (William C.). Félix d'Herelle and the origins of molecolar biology. New Haven, Yale U. P., 99, XII-230 p. (ill., bibl.).

6161. Takiyüddin. Takîyüddîn'in optik kitabı: ışığın niteliği ve görmenin oluşumu = Kitâbu nûr-i hadakati'l-ebsâr ve nûr-i hadîkati'l-enzâr. (Le Livre de l'optique de Takiyüddin: essence de la lumière et formation de la vision). Ed. by Hüseyin Gazi TOPDEMİR. Ankara, Kültür Bakanlığı Yayımlar Dairesi Başkanlığı, 99, XVI-367 p.

6162. Technologies of Landscape: from reaping to recycling. Ed. by David E. NYE. Amherst, University of Massachussets Press, 99, XI-292 p.

6163. TERRY (Jennifer). An American obsession: science, medicine, and homosexuality in modern society. Chicago, University of Chicago Press, 99, XIV-537 p.

6164. THAGARD (Paul). How scientists explain disease. Princeton, Princeton U. P., 99, XVIII-263 p. (figs. tables, bibl.).

6165. TORTORELLI (Gianfranco). La produzione scientifica della casa editrice Zanichelli dalle origini agli inizi del Novecento. *Ricerche storiche*, 99, 29, p. 229-255.

6166. UIMONEN (Minna.) Hermostumisen aikakausi. Neuroosit 1800- ja 1900-lukujen vaihteen suomalaisessa lääketieteessä. (The age of nervousness. The neuroses in the late nineteenth and the early twentieth century Finnish medicine.) Helsinki, SHS, 99, 217 p. (Bibliotheca historica, 50). [English summary].

6167. VASCONI (Paola). Sistema delle scienze naturali e unità della conoscenza nell'ultimo Kant. Firenze, Leo S. Olschki, 99, XX-148 p. (bibl.). (Biblioteca di storia della scienza, 42).

6168. Věda v Československu v letech 1945–1953. Sborník z konference. (Science and scholarship in Czechoslovakia, 1945–1953). Ed. by Blanka ZILYNSKÁ and Petr SVOBODNÝ. Praha, Karolinum, 99, 563 p.

6169. Vetenskapsbärarna – Naturvetenskapen i det svenska samhället, 1880–1950. Ed. by Sven WIDHALM. Hedemora, Gidlunds förlag, 99, 368 p.

6170. VEYRASSAT (Béatrice). Mobilité et développement technique. Le rôle des migrations de savoir-faire dans la formation de systèmes nationaux d'innovation (Etats-Unies et Suisse, XIXe siècle). *In*: Mobilitäten = Mobilités [Cf. n° 6962], p. 132-137.

6171. Visions of technology: a century of vital debate about machines, systems, and the human world. Ed. by Richard RHODES. New York a. London, Simon & Schuster, 99, 394 p. (ill., maps). (The Sloan technology series).

6172. WALKER (Brett L.). The early modern Japanese state and Ainu vaccinations: redefining the body politic 1799-1868. *Past and present*, 99, 163, p. 121-160.

6173. WANG (Jessica). American science in an age of anxiety: scientists, anticommunism and the Cold War. Chapel Hill a. London, 99, XVI-376 p. (ill., bibl.).

6174. Water-supply and public health engineering. Ed. by Denis SMITH. Aldershot, Ashgate, 99, XXXIV-393 p. (ill., tables). (Studies in the History of Civil Engineering).

6175. WATTS (Sheldon). British development policies and malaria in India 1897–c.1929. *Past and present*, 99, 165, p. 141-181.

6176. WEINER (Dora B.). Comprendre et soigner: Philippe Pinel (1745–1826), la médecine de l'esprit. Paris, Fayard, 99, 479 p. (Penser la médecine).

6177. WELTMAN (Sharon Aronofsky). Myth and gender in Ruskin's science. *In*: Ruskin and the dawn of modern [Cf. n° 5693] p. 153-73.

6178. WHITAKER (Ewen A.). Mapping and naming the moon: a history of Lunar cartography and nomenclature. New York, Cambridge U. P., 99, XX-242 p. (ill., tables, app.).

6179. WINE (Humphey). Quelques aspects de l'interaction entre la science, la technique et les beaux-arts. *XVIIIe siècle*, 99, 31, p. 107-122.

6180. Wissenschaft als kulturelle Praxis, 1750–1900. Hrsg. v. Hans Erich BÖDEKER, Peter Hans REILL und Jürgen SCHLUMBOHM. Göttingen, Vandenhoeck & Ruprecht, 99, 423 p. (ill.). (Veröffentlichungen des Max-Planck-Instituts für Geschichte, 154). [Cf. n° <Auswahl> 1210.]

6181. WRÅKBERG (Urban). Vetenskapens vikingatåg: perspektiv på svenska polarforskning 1860–1930. (Les expéditions vikings de la science: la recherche polaire suédoise, 1860–1930). Stockholm, Centrum för vetenskapshistoria, Kungliga Vetenskapsakademien, 99, 260 p. (Bidrag till Kungliga Svenska Vetenskapsakademiens historia, 30). [English summary].

6182. ZIK (Yaakov). Galileo and the telescope. The status of theoretical and practical knowledge and techniques of measurement and experimentation in the development of the instrument. *Nuncius*, 99, 14, p. 31-67.

§ 6. Addenda 1998.

6183. Journals and history of science. Ed. by Marco BERETTA, Claudio POGLIANO and Pietro REDONDI. Firenze, L. S. Olschki, 98, VII-268 (Biblioteca di Nuncius).

Cf. n°s 3724, 6824

§ 7. Literature.

a. General

6184. BEEBEE (Thomas O.). Epistolary fiction in Europe 1500–1850. Cambridge, Cambridge U. P., 99, X-278 p.

6185. BERNARD (Veronika). Das emotionale Moment der Veränderung. Stadt als Dichtung. Bonn, Bouvier, 99, 630 p. (Abhandlungen zur Kunst-, Musik- und Literaturwissenschaft, 402).

6186. BERTONE (Giorgio). Lo sguardo escluso. L'idea di paesaggio nella letteratura occidentale. Novara, Interlinea, 99, 271 p.

6187. CEDERNA (Camilla Maria). Imposture littéraire et stratégies politiques: "Le conseil d'Egypte" des Lumières siciliennes à Leonardo Sciascia. Paris, Champion, 239 p.

6188. CLÉMENT (Bruno). Le lecteur et son modèle. Paris, PUF, 99, 273 p.

6189. DAINOTTO (Roberto M.). Place in literature. Regions, cultures, communities. Ithaca, Cornell U. P., 99, 178 p.

6190. DONOVAN (Josephine). Women and the rise of the novel 1405–1726. New York, St. Martin's Press, 99, XIII-176 p.

6191. FRASER (Russell). Singing masters: poets in English 1500 to the present. Ann Arbor, University of Michigan Press, 99, VIII-261 p.

6192. GALLINARO (Ilaria). I castelli dell'anima. Architetture della ragione e del cuore nella letteratura italiana. Firenze, Olschki, 99, 316 p.

6193. GARNIER (Bruno). Pour une poétique de la traduction. L' "Hécube" d'Euripide en France, de la traduction humaniste à la tragédie classique. Paris, L'Harmattan, 99, 271 p.

6194. GUTHKE (Karl S.). The gender of death. A cultural history in art and literature. Cambridge, Cambridge U. P., 99, XII-297 p.

6195. HAYNES (Roslynn). Seeking the centre. The Australian desert in literature, art and film. Cambridge, Cambridge U. P., 99, XVI-347 p.

6196. HEINRICH (Hans). Zur Geschichte des Libertin in der englischen Literatur. Verführer auf der Insel. Heidelberg, Winter, 99, 277 p.

6197. Image (The) of manhood in early modern literature: viewing the male. Ed. by Andrew P. WILLIAMS. Westport a. London, Greenwood Press, 99, XV-196 p. (bibl.). (Contributions to the study of world literature, 95).

6198. Lost worlds and mad elephants: literature, science and technology, 1700–1990. Ed. by Elmar SCHENKEL and Stefan WELZ. Berlin, Galda-Wilch Verlag, 99, 371 p. (Leipzig explorations in literature and culture, 2).

6199. MAC LEOD (Bruce). The geography of empire in English literature, 1580–1745. Cambridge, Cambridge U. P., 99, XII-284 p.

6200. MANLOVE (Colin). The fantasy literature of England. Houndmills, Basingstoke and London, Macmillan, 99, VI-222 p.

6201. Mario Sansone critico e storico della letteratura italiana. Cinquant'anni di ricerca didattica. Atti del convegno, 25–27 febbraio 1998. A cura di Francesco TATEO. Roma e Bari, Laterza, 99, 244 p. (Percorsi, 9).

6202. MELLIER (Denis). L'écriture de l'excès. Fiction fantastique et poétique de la terreur. Paris, Champion, 99, 479 p.

6203. MONTELLA (Luigi). Seguendo d'amor le tracce. Studi di letteratura italiana dal Cinquecento all'Ottocento. Salerno, EdiSud, 99, 192 p. (Civiltà letteraria italiana. Profili-Saggi-Testi, 15).

6204. Opera (L') del silenzio. A cura di Daniela DE AGOSTINI e Pietro MONTANI. Fasano, Schena Editore, 99, 607 p.

6205. Problématique des genres, problèmes du roman. Ed. par Jean BESSIÈRE et Gilles PHILIPPE. Paris, Champion, 99, 279 p.

6206. Royaume de fémynie. Pouvoirs, contraintes, espaces de liberté des femmes de la Renaissance à la

Fronde. Ed. par Kathleen WILSON-CHEVALIER et Eliane VIENNOT. Paris, Champion, 99, 300 p.

6207. TARTAKOVSKIJ (Andrej G.). A.S. Pushkin i A.N. Radishchev: Zametki istochnikoveda. (A.S. Puskin and A.N. Radishchev: notes of a primary source scholar). *Otechestvennaja istorija*, 99, 47, 1, p. 64-131; 2, p. 142-170.

6208. Writers and heroines: essays on women in French literature. Ed. by Shirley JONES DAY. Bern, Peter Lang, 99, 177 p.

Cf. n°s 79, 938

b. *Renaissance*

* 6209. Anuario bibliográfico cervantino 3: 1998. Ed. por Eduardo URBINA. Alcalá de Henares, Centro de Estudios Cervantinos, 99, 259 p.

** 6210. DE VALOIS (Marguerite). Mémoires et autre écrits, 1576–1614. Ed. par Eliane VIENNOT. Paris, Champion, 99, 372 p.

** 6211. MINUTOLO (Ceccarella). Lettere. A cura di Raffaele MORABITO. Napoli, Edizioni Scientifiche Italiane, 99, 107 p. (Istituto nazionale di studi sul Rinascimento meridionale, Studi XI).

6212. AUB (Max). De Max Aub a Cervantes. Segorbe, Fundación Max Aub, Alcalá de Henares, Universidad de Alcalá y Valladolid, Casa Cervantes, 99, 148 p.

6213. BRADEN (Gordon). Petrarchan love and the continental Renaissance. New Haven a. London, Yale U. P., 99, XVIII-198 p.

6214. Cambridge history (The) of literary criticism. Vol. 3. The Renaissance. Ed. by Glyn P. NORTON Cambridge, Cambridge U. P., 99, XXIV-758 p. (bibl.)

6215. CATTY (Jocelyn). Writing rape, writing women in early modern England: unbridled speech. Basingstoke, Macmillan and New York, St. Martin's Press, 99, IX-276 p.

6216. Cervantes y la puesta en escena de la sociedad de su tiempo. Actas del Coloquio de Montreal, 1997. Coord. de Catherine POUPENEY-HART, Alfredo HERMENEGILDO y César OLIVA. Murcia, Universidad de Murcia, 99, 231 p.

6217. COSSUTTA (Fabio). Itinerarium in mentis ac salutis: gli "Amorum libri" di Matteo Maria Boiardo. Roma, Bulzoni, 99, 312 p. (Athenaeum, 20).

6218. DUBROW (Heather). Shakesperare and domestic loss: forms of deprivation, mourning and recuperation. Cambridge, Cambridge U. P., 99, XIII-242 p. (Cambridge studies in Renaissance literature and culture, 32).

6219. Eighth International colloquium of the Asociación de Cervantistas: El Toboso, April 23–26, 1998: selected papers. [S. l.], Cervantes Society of America,

99, [s. p.]. (Cervantes: bulletin of the Cervantes Society of America, [Special issue], 19, 2).

6220. Erscheinungsformen des Sonetts. Hrsg. v. Theo STEMMLER und Stefan HORLACHER. Tübingen, Narr, 99, 309 p. (Kolloquium der Forschungstelle für europäische Lyrik, 10).

6221. Italia e Boemia nella cornice del Rinascimento europeo. A cura di Sante GRACIOTTI. Firenze, Olschki, 99, XIII-411 p. (Civiltà veneziana. Studi, 49).

6222. Italian studies in Shakespeare and his contemporaries. Ed. by Michele MARRAPODI e Giorgio MELCHIORI. Newark a. Cranbury, University of Delaware Press, 99, 299 p. (bibl.)

6223. LANGER (Ullrich). Vertu du discours, discours de la vertu. Littérature et philosophie morale au XVIe siècle en France. Genève, Droz, 99, 202 p. (Cahiers d'Humanisme et Renaissance, 55).

6224. LONGO (Nicola). Letteratura e lettere. Indagini nell'epistolografia cinquecentesca. Roma, Bulzoni, 99, 146 p. (Biblioteca del Cinquecento, 86).

6225. Malinconia ed allegrezza nel Rinascimento. A cura di Luisa ROTONDI SECCHI TARUGI. Milano, Nuovi Orizzonti, 99, 576 p.

6226. MAREK (Heidi). Vom leidenden Ixion getrösteten Narziss. Der antike Mythos im Werk von Pontus de Tyard. Frankfurt, V. Klostermann, 99, 599 p. (Analecta Romanica, 59).

6227. MARTIN-JACQUEMIER (Myriam). L'âge d'or du mythe de Babel, 1480–1600. De la conscience de l'alterité à la naissance de la modernité. Mont-de-Marson, Editions Inter Universitaires, 99, 342 p.

6228. Nicodemus Frischlin (1547–1590). Hrsg. v. Sabine HOLTZ und Dieter MERTENS. Stuttgart, Frommann-Holzboog, 99, 618 p.

6229. PAOLI (Michel). L'idée de nature chez Léon Battista Alberti (1404–1472). Paris, Champion, 99, 286 p. (Centre d'études franco-italiennes. Centro di studi franco-italiani. Université de Turin et de Savoie. Università di Torino e della Savoia, 29).

6230. Pilgrimage for love: essays in early modern literature in honor of Josephine A. Roberts. Ed. by Sigrid KING. Tempe, Arizona Center for Medieval and Renaissance studies, 99, XIX-276 p. (Medieval and Renaissance texts and studies, 213).

6231. POSNER (David M.). The performance of nobility in early modern literature. Cambridge, Cambridge U. P., 99, X-272 p. (Cambridge studies in Renaissance literature and culture, 33).

6232. PRANDI (Stefano). Scritture al crocevia. Il dialogo letterario nei secc. XV e XVI. Vercelli, Mercurio, 99, 328 p.

6233. RAHMSDORF (Sabine). Stadt und Architektur in literarischen Utopien der frühen Neuzeit. Heidelberg,

Winter, 99, 345 p. (Beiträge zur neueren Literaturgeschichte, 168).

6234. SARNELLI (Mauro). "Col discreto pennel d'alta eloquenza". "Meraviglioso" e "classico" nella tragedia (e tragicommedia) italiana del Cinque-Seicento. Roma, Aracne, 99, XXXIX-219 p.

6235. SCHOLL (Sabine). Die Welt als Ausland. Zur Literatur zwischen den Kulturen, Wien, Sonderzahl, 99, 158 p.

6236. SLIWA (Krzysztof). Documentos de Miguel de Cervantes Saavedra. Pamplona, Ediciones Universidad de Navarra, 99, 423 p. (Números anejos de RILCE, 31).

6237. Tiers (Le) livre. Actes du colloque de Rome de 5 mars 1996. Ed. par Franco GIACONE. Genève, Droz, 99, 140 p. (Etudes rabélaisiennes, 37).

6238. Umanesimo e culture nazionali europee. Testimonianze letterarie dei secoli XV–XVI. A cura di Francesco TATEO. Palermo, Palumbo, 99, 304 p. (Bibliotheca, 17).

6239. Where are we now in Shakespearean studies? Ed. by William R. ELTON and John MUCCIOLO. Aldershot, Ashgate, 99, XV-381 p. (The Shakespearean international yearbook, 1).

6240. Women's writing in the French Renaissance. Proceedings of fifth Cambridge French Renaissance Colloquium, 7–9 July 1997. Ed. by Philip FORD and Gillian JONDORF. Genève, Droz, 99, XII-243 p.

6241. WOODS (Susanne). Lanyer: a Renaissance woman poet. London a. New York, Oxford U. P., 99, XIV-192 p.

c. *Classicism*

* 6242. LOSADA GOYA (José Manuel). Bibliographie critique de la littérature espagnole en France au XVIIe siècle. Présence et influence. Genève, Droz, 99, XXII-671 p. (Travaux du Grand Siècle, 9).

6243. CABANI (Maria Cristina). La pianella di Scarpinello. Tassoni e la nascita dell'eroicomico. Lucca, Pacini Fazzi, 99, 314 p.

6244. CAMERINO (Giuseppe Antonio). Alfieri e il linguaggio della tragedia. Verso, stile, topoi. Napoli, Liguori, 99, XII-296 p. (Collana di testi e critica, 35).

6245. CANEPA (Nancy). From court to forest: Giambattista Basile's Lo cunto de li cunti and the birth of the literary fairy tale. Detroit, Wayne State U. P., 99, 333 p.

6246. Delitto (Il) narrato al popolo. A cura di Roberto De Romanis e Rosamaria Loretelli. Palermo, Sellerio, 99, 283 p. (Nuovo Prisma, 12).

6247. DOHM (Burkhard). Poetische Alchimie. Öffnung zur Sinnlichkeit in der Hohelied- und Bibeldichtung von der protestantischen Barockmystik bis zum Pietismus. Tübingen, Niemeyer, 99, 470 p. (Studien zur deutschen Literatur, 154)

6248. Figures à l'italienne: métaphores, équivoques et pointes dans la littérature maniériste et baroque. Ed. par Danielle Boillet et Alain Godard. Paris, Université Paris III Sorbonne Nouvelle, 99, X-343 p. (Centre Interuniversitaire de recherche sur la Renaissance italienne, 23).

6249. GARDINER (Ellen). Regulating readers: gender and literary criticism in the eighteenth century novel. Newark, University of Delaware Press and London, Associated Universities Presses, 99, 198 p.

6250. GRANDE (Nathalie). Stratégies de romancières. De Clélie à La Princesse de Clèves (1654–1678). Paris, Champion, 99, 497 p.

6251. GREWE (Astrid). Vertu im Sprachgebrauch Corneilles und seiner Zeit. Heidelberg, Winter, 99, 321 p.

6252. GRUNDY (Isobel). Lady Mary Wortley Montagu: comet of Enlightenment. Oxford, Oxford U. P., 99, XXIV-680.

6253. HAMMOND (Paul). Dryden and the traces of classical Rome. Oxford, Clarendon Press, 99, XII-306 p.

6254. HUPPERT (George). The style of Paris. Renaissance origins of the French Enlightenment. Bloomington, Indiana U. P., 99, 146 p.

6255. IRLAM (Shaun). Elations: the poetics of enthusiasm in eighteenth century Britain. Stanford, Stanford U. P., 99, VIII-284 p.

6256. KÄMMER (Harold). "Nur um Himmels willen keine Satyren ...". Deutsche Satire und Satiretheorie des 18. Jahrhunderts im Kontext von Anglophilie, Swift-Rezeption und ästhetischer Theorie. Heidelberg, Winter, 99, VII-353 p. (Probleme der Dichtung, 27).

6257. KELLEK (Edwige). Poétique de la mort dans la nouvelle classique (1660–1680). Paris, Champion, 99, 544 p. (Varia, 26).

6258. Literatur (Die) des 17. Jahrhunderts. Hrsg. v. Albert Meier. München u. Wien, Hanser, 99, 776 p. (Hanser Sozialgeschichte der deutschen Literatur vom 16. Jahrhundert bis zur Gegenwart, 2).

6259. LONDON (April). Women and property in the eighteenth century English novel. Cambridge, Cambridge U. P., 99, X-262 p.

6260. MAÎTRE (Myriam). Les Précieuses. Naissance des femmes de lettres en France au XVIIe siècle. Paris, Champion, 99, 799 p. (Lumière classique, 25).

6261. MANDER (Jenny). Circles of learning: narratology and the eighteenth century French novel. Oxford, Voltaire Foundation, 99, 232 p. (Studies on Voltaire and the eighteenth century, 366).

6262. MESSENGER (Ann). Woman and poet in the eighteenth century: the life of Mary Whateley Darwall (1738–1825). New York, AMS Press, 99, XIV-274 p. (AMS sudies in the eighteenth century, 27).

6263. MICHIE (Allen). Richardson and Fielding: the dynamics of a critical rivalry. Lewisburg, Bucknell U. P., 264 p.

6264. MONTADON (Alain). Le roman au XVIIIe siècle en Europe. Paris, PUF, 99, 534 p.

6265. MÜNSTER (Reinhold). Friedrich von Hagedorn. Dichter und Philosoph der fröhlichen Aufklärung. München, Iudicium, 99, XVIII-390 p.

6266. NEPOTE-DESMARRES (Fanny). La Fontaine. Fables. Paris, PUF, 99, 124 p.

6267. NEUKIRCHEN (Thomas). Inscriptio. Rhetorik und Poetik der scharfsinnigen Inschrift im Zeitalter des Barok. Tübingen, Niemeyer, 99, VI-298 p. (Studien zur deutschen Literatur, 152).

6268. NOACK (Lothar). Christian Hoffmann von Hoffmannwaldau (1616–1679). Leben und Werk. Tübingen, Niemeyer, 99, XIII-542 p. (Frühe Neuzeit, 51).

6269. NORBROOK (David). Writing the English Republic: poetry, rhetoric and politics, 1627–1660. Cambridge, Cambridge U. P., 99, XIV-510 p.

6270. PAULIN (Roger). Der Fall Wilhelm Jerusalem: zum Selbstmordproblem zwischen Aufklärung und Empfindsamkeit. Göttingen u. Wolfenbüttel, Wallstein u. Lessing-Akademie, 99, 167 p. (ill.). (Kleine Schriften zur Aufklärung, 6).

6271. PAUTLER (Stefan). Jakob Michael Reinhold Lenz. Pietistische Weltdeutung und bürgerliche Sozialreform im Sturm und Drang. Gütersloh, Gütersloher Verlaghaus, 99, 514 p. (Religiöse Kulturen der Moderne, 8).

6272. PETER (Emanuel). Geselligkeiten. Literatur, Gruppenbildung und kultureller Wandel im 18. Jahrhundert. Tübingen, Niemeyer, 99, VII-359 p. (Studien zur deutschen Literatur, 153).

6273. Pietro Verri e il suo tempo. Atti del convegno, Milano 9–11 ottobre 1997. A cura di Carlo Capra. Milano, Cisalpino-Istituto editoriale universitario, 99, 2 vol., 1140 p. (Quaderni di Acme, 35).

6274. POST (Jonathan F. S.). English lyric poet: the early seventeenth century. London a. New York, Routledge, 99, XVIII-324 p.

6275. ROBIC-DE BAECQUE (Sylvie). Le salut par l'excès. Jean-Pierre Camus (1584–1652), la poétique d'un évêque romancier. Paris, Champion, 99, 453 p. (Lumière classique, 23).

6276. SABA (Guido). Théophile de Viau: un poète rebelle. Paris, PUF, 99, XIX-232 p.

6277. SELLIER (Philippe). Port-Royal et la littérature. 1. Pascal. Paris, Champion, 99, 356 p.

6278. SERMAIN (Jean-Paul). Le singe de don Quichotte. Marivaux, Cervantes et le roman postcritique. Oxford, Voltaire Foundation, 99, 288 p. (Studies on Voltaire, 368).

6279. SHELL (Alison). Catholicism, controversy and the English literary imagination, 1558–1660. Cambridge, Cambridge U. P., 99, XII-316 p.

6280. SOSSO (Paola). Jean-Jacques Rousseau. Imagination, illusions, chimères. Paris, Champion, 99, 272 p.

6281. VAN ELSLANDE (Jean-Pierre). L'imaginaire pastoral du XVIIe siècle, 1600–1650. Paris, PUF, 99, 211 p.

6282. VENTURO (David F.). Johnson the poet: the career of Samuel Johnson. London, Associated Universities Presses, 99, 336 p.

6283. VERWIEBE (Barbara Katharina Maria). Tempora et mores. Untersuchungen zu den französischen Übersetzungen der Annalen des Tacitus im 16. und 17. Jahrhundert. Bonn, Romantischer Verlag, 99, 223 p.

6284. WOLF (Thomas). Pustkuchen und Goethe. Tübingen, Niemeyer, 99, IX-448 p. (Untersuchungen zur deutschen Literaturgeschichte, 101).

6285. ZIMMERMANN (Harro). Aufklärung und Erfahrungswandel. Studien zur deutschen Literaturgeschichte des späten 18. Jahrhunderts. Göttingen, Wallstein, 99, 383 p.

Cf. n° 5014

d. *Romanticism and after*

* 6286. BEUGNOT (Bernard), MARTEL (Jacinthe), VECK (Bernard). Francis Ponge. Paris et Roma, Memini, 99, 270 p. (Bibliographie des écrivains français, 18).

* 6287. Bibliographie stendhalienne générale. Ed. par Victor DEL LITTO et Emanuel KANCEFF. Vol. 1. Moncalieri, CIRVI, 498 p.

* 6288. JANSSEN-ZIMMERMANN (Antje) KASPER (Elke). Grenzenlos: Literatur zwischen Ost und West von 1949 bis 1989: eine Bibliographie. Frankfurt am Main, P. Lang, 99, 736 p. (Literarhistorische Untersuchungen, 32).

* 6289. MORTELETTE (Yann). José Maria de Heredia. Paris et Roma, Memini, 99, 220 p. (Bibliographie des écrivains français, 19).

* 6290. RIEDEL (Nicolai). Uwe Johnson – Bibliographie. 1959–1998. Stuttgart u. Weimar, Metzler, 99, 600 p. (Personalbibliographien zur neueren deutschen Literatur, 3).

** 6291. TEJA LEOPARDI (Teresa). Lettere agli amici pisani. A cura di Alessandro PANAJIA e Mario CURRELI. Pisa, ETS, 99, 186 p.

6292. 19. Jahrhundert Roman. Hrsg.v. Friederich WOLFZETTEL. Tübingen, Stauffenburg Verlag, 99, 287 p.

6293. ADINOLFI (Pierangela). Passione e virtù. L'idea di felicità nella prima stagione del Romanticismo francese. Alessandria, Edizioni dell'Orso, 99, 412 p.

6294. BARDINI (Marco). Elsa Morante. Italiana. Di professione, poeta. Pisa, Nistri-Lischi, 99, 778 p.

6295. BECKER (Pia). Bildkompositorische Techniken als gestatendes Prinzip des Erzählens in Marcel Proust "A la recherche du temps perdu". Bonn, Romantischer Verlag, 99, 177 p.

6296. BENNET (Andrew). Romantic poets and the culture of posterity. Cambridge, Cambridge U. P., 99, XIV-268 p. (Cambridge studies in Romanticism, 35).

6297. BERGER (Albert). Josef Weinheber, 1892–1945. Leben und Werk – Leben im Werk. Salzburg, Otto Müller, 99, 367 p.

6298. BERNDT (Franke). Anamnesis. Studien zur Topik der Erinnerung in der erzählenden Literatur zwischen 1800 und 1900. Tübingen, Niemeyer, 99, VI-528 p. (Hermaea, 89).

6299. British novelists since 1960. Third series. Ed. by Merritt MOSELEY. Detroit, Gale Group, 99, XIX-387 p. (Dictionary of literary biography, 207).

6300. CARDUCCI (Nicola). Storia intellettuale di Carlo Levi. Lecce, Pensa Multimedia Editore, 99, 300 p.

6301. COLLECOTT (Diana). H.D. [Hilda Doolittle] and the sapphic Modernism, 1910–1950. Cambridge, Cambridge U. P., 99, XIV-350 p.

6302. CONTORBIA (Franco). Montale, Genova, il Modernismo e altri saggi montaliani. Bologna, Pendragon, 99, 175 p.

6303. CORCORAN (Neil). Poets of modern Ireland: text, context, intertext. Cardiff, University of Wales Press, 99, XIV-224 p.

6304. COUSSEAU (Anne). Poétique de l'enfance chez Marguerite Duras. Genève, Droz, 99, 462 p.

6305. CRAIG (Gordon A.). Theodor Fontane: literature and history in the Bismarck Reich. New York, Oxford U. P., 99, XIII-232 p.

6306. D'ALESSIO (Carlo). Il poema necessario. Poesia e orfismo in Dino Campana e Arturo Onofri. Roma, Bulzoni, 99, 242 p.

6307. DI BIASE (Carmine). Giovanni Papini. L'anima intera. Napoli e Roma, Edizioni Scientifiche Italiane, 99, 320 p.

6308. "Difficile musa" (La) di Aldo Palazzeschi. Indagini, accertamenti testuali, carte inedite. A cura di Gino TELLINI. Studi italiani, 99, IX, 1-2, p. 344.

6309. DOWNS (Catherine M.). Becoming modern. Willa Cather's journalism. Selinsgrove, Susquehanna U. P., 99, 176 p.

6310. DROUIN (Michel). Gide et l'affaire Dreyfus. Quelques remarques. Bulletin des amis d'André Gide, 99, 32, 27, 124, p. 341-432.

6311. Else Lasker-Schüler. Ansichten und Perspektiven. Views and reviews. Hrsg. v. Ernst SCHÜRER und Sonja HEDGEPETH. Tübingen, Francke, 99, 299 p.

6312. Emile Vehraeren et l'Europe. Revue belge de philologie et d'histoire, 99, 77, 3, p. 689-794.

6313. Ernst Toller und die Weimarer Republik. Hrsg. v. Stefan NEUHAUS, Rolf SELBMANN und Thorsten UNGER. Würzburg, Königshausen & Neumann, 99, 271 p. (Schriften der Ernst Toller Gesellschaft, 1).

6314. FORDERER (Christof). Ich – Eklipsen. Doppelgänger in der Literatur seit 1800. Stuttgart u. Weimar, Metzler, 99, 284 p.

6315. Fragile Republik: Thomas Mann und Nachkriegsdeutschland. Hrsg. v. Stephan STACHORSKI. Frankfurt am Main, Fischer Taschenbuch Verlag, 99, 239 p.

6316. GEISLER-SZMULEWICZ (Anne). Le mythe de Pygmalion au XIXe siècle. Pour une approche de la coalescence des mythes. Paris, Champion, 99, 418 p. (Romantisme et modernités, 24).

6317. GILLOOLY (Eileen). Smile of discontent: humor, gender and nineteenth century British fiction. Chicago, University of Chicago Press, 99, VIII-290 p.

6318. Giuseppe Tomasi di Lampedusa. Cento anni dalla nascita, quaranta dal "Gattopardo". Atti del convegno, Palermo, 12–14 dicembre 1996. A cura di Francesco ORLANDO. Palermo, Assessorato alla cultura, 99, 257 p.

6319. GLEASON (William A.). The leisure ethic: work and play in American literature, 1840–1940. Stanford, Stanford U. P., 99, XVIII-466 p.

6320. GODARD (Henri). Louis Guilloux romancier de la condition humaine. Paris, Gallimard, 99, 421 p.

6321. Goethe - ein letztes Universalgenie? Hrsg. v. Sebastian DONAT und Hendrik BIRUS. Göttingen, Wallstein, 99, 144 p.

6322. Goethe im sozialen und kulturellen Gefüge seiner Zeit. Hrsg. v. Jürgen VOSS. Bonn, Bouvier, 99, 187 p. (Pariser Historische Studien, 51).

6323. Goethe trifft den gemeinen Mann. Alltagswahrnehmungen eines Genies. Hrsg. v. Marina MORITZ. Köln, Weimar u. Wien, Böhlau, 255 p.

6324. GORUPP (Tiziana). Intellettuali e potere nella Francia dell'Ottocento. Paris, Champion, 99, 199 p. (Centre d'études franco-italiennes. Universités de Turin et de Savoie. Textes et études – Domaine français, 35).

6325. Gothic-fantastic (The) in nineteenth-century Russian literature. Ed. by Neil CORNWELL. Amsterdam a. Atlanta, Rodopi, 99, 293 p. (Studies in slavic literature and poetics, 33).

6326. HARTLEIB-MONNET (Karin). Zwischen Literatur und Politik. Die Wochenzeitung Vendredi 1935–1938. Frankfurt am Main, Peter Lang, 99, 282 p.

6327. HOBSON (Christopher Z.). The chained boy: Orc and Blake's idea of Revolution. Lewisburg, Bucknell U. P. and London, Associated Universities Presses, 99, 412 p.

6328. HUGO (Leon). Edwardian Shaw: the writer and his age. Houndmills, Basingstoke and London, Macmillan, 99, XIV-308 p.

6329. Italien in Deutschland, Deutschland in Italian. Die deutsch-italienischen Wechselbeziehungen in der Belletristik des 20. Jahrhundert. Hrsg. v. Anna COMI und Alexandra PONTZEN. Berlin, Erich Schmidt Verlag, 99, 404 p.

6330. JAPP (Uwe). Die Komödie der Romantik. Typologie und Überblick. Tübingen, Niemeyer, 99, XIV-138 p. (Untersuchungen zur deutschen Literaturgeschichte, 100).

6331. KALIFA (Dominique). Usages du faux. Faits divers et romans criminels au 19e siècle. *Annales*, 99, 54, 6, p. 1345-1362.

6332. KAYE (Peter). Dostoevskij and English Modernism, 1900–1930. Cambridge, Cambridge U. P., 99, VIII-248 p.

6333. KNIGHTS (Ben). Writing masculinities: male narrative in twentieth century fiction. Houndmills, Basingstoke and London, Macmillan, 99, VIII-256 p.

6334. KRIPPENDORFF (Ekkehart). Goethe. Politik gegen den Zeitgeist. Frankfurt am Main u. Leipzig, Insel, 99, 232 p.

6335. LALOUETTE (J.). L'affaire Dreyfus dans le roman français. *Revue historiques*, 99, 123, 611, p. 555-576.

6336. LE RIDER (Jacques). Campagne de France en 1792. Parallèle entre Chateaubriand et Goethe. *Revue germanique internationale*, 1999, 12, p. 211-227.

6337. Leopardi e l'età romantica. Atti del convegno internazionale, Padova-Venezia, maggio 1998. A cura di Mario Andrea RIGONI. Venezia, Marsilio, 99, X-458 p.

6338. LESTRINGANT (Frank). Musset. Paris, Flammarion, 99, 796 p.

6339. LLOYD (Rosemary). Mallarmé: the poet and his circle. Ithaca, Cornell U. P., 99, 257 p.

6340. MAC CANN (Andrew). Cultural politics in the 1790's: literature, radicalism and the public sphere. Basingstoke, Macmillan, 99, XI-226 p. (ill.). (Romanticism in perspective: texts, cultures, histories).

6341. MAC CULLOUGH (Kate). Regions of identity: the construction of America in women's fiction, 1885–1914. Stanford, Stanford U. P., 99, VIII-362 p.

6342. MARCUS (Sharon). Apartament stories. City and home in nineteenth century. Berkeley, University of California Press, 99, 313 p.

6343. MAYER (Hans). Goethe. Ein Versuch über den Erfolg. Hrsg. v. Inge JENS. Frankfurt am Main, Suhrkamp, 99, 448 p.

6344. MELMOUX-MONTAUBIN (Marie-Françoise). Le roman d'art dans la seconde moitié du XIXe siècle. Paris, Klincksieck, 99, 302 p.

6345. MIGHALL (Robert). A geography of Victorian Gothic: mapping history's nightmares. Oxford, Oxford U. P., 99, XXVI-312 p.

6346. MILNES (Tim). Eclipsing art: method and metaphysics in Coleridge's Biographia Literaria. *Journal of the history of ideas*, 99, 60, 1, p. 125-148.

6347. PALEY (Morton D.). Portraits of Coleridge. New York a. Oxford, Oxford U. P., 99, XVII-171 p.

6348. PELLINI (Pierluigi). Generi, ideologie, dettagli. Sul "Capolavoro sconosciuto" di Balzac. Lecce, Manni, 99, 128 p.

6349. PICHOIS (Claude), BRUNET (Alain). Colette. Paris, Editions de Fallois, 99, 603 p.

6350. Pirandello e le Avanguardie. Atti del 35° Convegno internazionale di studi pirandelliani. A cura di Enzo LAURETTA. Agrigento, Centro Nazionale di Studi Pirandelliani, 99, 321 p.

6351. POLACCO (Marina). Gli amori, le beffe e la tragedia. Storia del Pirandello narratore (1894–1908). Lucca, Pacini Fazzi, 99, 199 p.

6352. Prosper Mérimée écrivain, archéologue, historien. Ed. par Antonia FONYI. Genève, Droz, 99, 266 p.

6353. RAJAN (Balachandra). Under Western eyes: India from Milton to Macaulay. Durham, Duke U. P., 99, X-268 p.

6354. REIZBAUM (Marilyn). James Joyce's Judaic other. Stanford, Stanford U. P., 99, X-194 p.

6355. ROMAN (Myriam). Victor Hugo et le roman philosophique. Du "drame dans les faits" au "drame dans les idées". Paris, Champion, 99, 830 p.

6356. RYAN (Judith). Rilke, Modernism and poetic tradition. Cambridge, Cambridge U. P., 99, 256 p.

6357. SANDERS (Andrew). Dickens and the spirit of the age. Oxford, Clarendon Press, 99, VIII-198 p.

6358. SAPIRO (Gisèle). La guerre des écrivains. 1940–1953. Paris, Fayard, 99, 807 p.

6359. SCANLAN (James Patrick). The case against rational egoism in Dostoevsky's Notes from Underground. *Journal of the history of ideas*, 99, 60, 3, p. 549-568.

6360. SCARAFFIA (Giuseppe). Il bel tenebroso: l'uomo fatale nella letteratura del XIX secolo. Palermo, Sellerio, 99, 152 p.

6361. SCHUBERT (Dietrich). "Jetzt wohin?" Heinrich Heine in seinen verhinderten und errichteten Denkmälern. Köln, Weimar u. Wien, Böhlau, 99, 380 p. (Beiträge zur Geschichtskultur, 17).

6362. SCHULZE (Stefan). Die Selbstreflexion der Kunst bei Baudelaire. Eine literaturgeschichtliche Untersuchung. Heidelberg, Winter, 99, 316 p.

6363. SILLARS (Stuart). Structure and dissolution in English writing, 1910–1920. Houndmills, Basingstoke and London, Macmillan, 99, VIII-216 p.

6364. SMITH (Richard Cándida). Mallarmé's children: symbolism and the renewal of experience. Berkeley a. Los Angeles, University of California Press, 99, XXIV-304 p.

6365. SNYDER (Katherine V.). Bachelors, manhood and the novel 1850–1925. Cambridge, Cambridge U. P., 99, X-286 p.

6366. TALATTOF (Kamran). The politics of writing in Iran: a history of modern Persian literature. Syracuse, Syracuse U. P., 99, XI-250 p.

6367. TAYLOR (Anya). Bacchus in Romantic England: writers and drink, 1780–1830. New York, St. Martin's Press, 99, XI-264 p.

6368. THORMÄHLEN (Marianne). The Brontës and religion. Cambridge, Cambridge U. P., 99, X-288 p.

6369. VAN DEN BERG (Hubert). Avantgarde und Anarchismus. Dada in Zürich und Berlin. Heidelberg, Winter, 99, 509 p.

6370. VERDAGUER (Pierre). La sédution policière. Signes de croissance d'un genre mineur: Pierre Magnan, Daniel Pennac et quelques autres. Birmingham, Summa Publications, 99, 315 p.

6371. Verlaine e gli altri. Verlaine et les autres. A cura di Maria Luisa PREMUDA PEROSA. Pisa, ETS, 99, 174 p. (Collana di memorie e atti di convegni, 9).

6372. VILLA (Angela Ida). Neoidealismo e rinascenza latina tra Otto e Novecento. La cerchia di Sergio Corazzini. Poeti dimenticati e riviste del crepuscolarismo romano (1903–1907). Milano, Edizioni Universitarie di Lettere, Economia, Diritto, 99, 852 p.

6373. VIOLANTE PICON (Isabel). Une oeuvre originale de poésie. Giuseppe Ungaretti traducteur. Paris, Presses de l'Université de Paris-Sorbonne, 99, 348 p.

6374. WAGNER (Michæl F.). Det polytekniske gennembrud: romantikkens teknologiske konstruktion 1780–1850. (La percée polytechnique: la construction technologique du romantisme de 1780 à 1850). Århus, Aarhus universitetsforlag, 99, 500 p., tab.. (rés. anglais).

6375. WALDRON (Mary). Jane Austen and the fiction of her time. Cambridge, Cambridge U. P., 99, X-194 p.

6376. WANNING (Frank). Gedankenexperimente. Wissenschaft und Roman im Frankreich des 19. Jahrhunderts. Tübingen, Niemeyer, 99, 287 p.

6377. WHALEN (Terence). Edgar Allan Poe and the masses: the political economy of literature in antebellum America. Princeton, Princeton U. P., 99, X-328 p.

6378. WHITTAKER (Jason). William Blake and the myths of Britain. Houndmills, Basingstoke and London, Macmillan, 99, X-216 p.

6379. WILSON (W. Daniel). "Unterirdische Gänge": Goethe, Freimaurerei und Politik. Göttingen, Wallstein, 99, 276 p.

6380. YOUNG (Arlene). Culture, class and gender in the Victorian novel: gentlemen, gents and working women. Houndmills, Basingstoke and London, Macmillan, 99, VIII-228 p.

6381. ZARD (Philippe). La fiction de l'Occident: Thomas Mann, Franz Kafka, Albert Cohen. Paris, PUF, 99, 330 p.

Cf. n°s 4027, 4035

§ 8. Art and Industrial art.

a. *General*

6382. ANDREWS (Malcolm). Landscape and Western art. Oxford, Oxford U. P., 99, 248 p. (ill.).

6383. BAILEY (Gauvin). Art in the Jesuit mission in Asia and Latin America 1542–1773. Toronto, University of Toronto Press, 99, 310 p.

6384. BLAKE (Jody). Le tumulte noir. Modernist art and popular entertainement in Jazz age Paris, 1900–1930. University Park, The Pennsylvania State U. P., 99, 207 p. (ill.).

6385. BRETTELL (Richard). Modern art, 1851–1929. Capitalism and représentation. Oxford, Oxford U. P., 99, 258 p. (ill.).

6386. CHAUDONNERET (Marie-Claude). L'Etat et les artistes. De la Restauration à la monarchie de Juillet (1815–1833). Paris, Flammarion, 99, 272 p. (bibl.).

6387. CHEDEAU (Catherine). Les arts à Dijon au XVIe siècle. Les débuts de la Renaissance 1494–1551. Aix-en-Provence, Publications de l'Université de Provence, 99, 2 vol., 386 p., 286 p. (ill.).

6388. CORN (Wanda M.). The great American thing. Modern art and national identity 1915–1935. Berkeley, University of California Press, 99, 448 p. (ill.).

6389. CRARY (Jonathan). Suspensions of perception: attention, spectacle and moderne culture. Cambridge, MIT Press, 99, 397 p. (ill.).

6390. DAY-HICKMANN (Barbara Ann). Napoleonic art. Nationalism and the spirit of rebellion in France (1815–1845). Newark, University of Delaware Press, 99, 176 p. (bibl., ill.).

6391. DILLENBERGER (John). Images and relics: theological perceptions and visual images in sixteenth century Europe. New York a. Oxford, Oxford U. P., 99, 248 p. (ill.).

6392. HAZAN (Olga). Le mythe du progrès artistique. Montréal, Les presses de l'Université de Montréal, 99, 454 p. (ill.).

6393. HERKLOTZ (Ingo). Cassiano dal Pozzo und die Archaeologie des 17. Jahrhunderts. München, Hirmer Verlag, 99, 439 p. (Römische Forschungen der Bibliotheca Hertziana, 28).

6394. Italian culture in northern Europe in the eighteenth century. Ed. by West SHEARER. Cambridge, Cambridge U. P., 99, XIV-238 p. (ill.).

6395. KHACHATUROV (Sergej V.). "Goticheskij vkus" v russkoj khudozhestvennoj kul'ture XVIII veka. (The 'Gothic Taste' in the Russian artistic culture of the 2nd half of the 18th century). RAN, In-t iskusstvoznanija MK RF. Moskva, Progress-Traditsija, 99, 184 p. (ill., bibl.). [Eng. summary].

6396. LEJKIND (Oleg L.), MAKHROV (Kirill D.), SEVERJUKHIN (Dmitrij Ja). Khudozhniki russkogo zarubezh'ja, 1917–1939: biograficheskij slovar'. (Russian artists abroad, 1917–1939: a biographical guide). Sankt-Peterburg, Notabene, 99, 715 p. (ill., bibl.). [Eng. and French summaries].

6397. MANIN (Vitalij S.). Iskusstvo v rezervatsii: khudozhestvennaja zhizn' Rossii 1917–1941 gg. (Art in a reservation: artistic life of Russia in 1917–1941). Moskva, Editorial-URSS, 99, 263 p. (ill., bibl.).

6398. MICHELS (Karen). Transplantierte Kunstwissenschaft. Deutschsprachige Kunstgeschichte im amerikanischen Exil. Berlin, Akademie Verlag, 99, 255 p. (ill.).

6399. MUSACCHIO (Jacqueline-Marie). The art and ritual of childbirth in Renaissance Italy. New Haven a. London, Yale U. P., 99, 212 p. (ill.).

6400. PUGLISI (Catherine R.). Francesco Albani. New Haven a. London, Yale U. P., 99, 244 p. (ill.).

6401. RANDALL (Catherine). Building codes. The aesthetics of Calvinism in early modern Europe. Philadelphia, University of Pennsylvania Press, 99, 288 p. (ill.).

6402. SELLES (Narcís). Art, política i societat: en la derogació del franquisme. Gauses, Llibres del Segle, 99, 274 p. (ill.). (Col.lecció Rosa d'Infern, 2).

6403. Storia delle arti in Toscana. A cura di Carlo SISI. Firenze, Edifir Edizioni, 99, 303 p. (ill.).

6404. TALVACCHIA (Bette). Taking positions. On the erotic in Renaissance culture. Princeton, Princeton U. P., 99, XIII-303 p. (ill.).

6405. TESTA (Fausto). Winckelmann e l'invenzione della storia dell'arte. I modelli e la mimesi. Bologna, Minerva Edizioni, 99, 409 p. (ill.).

6406. VENTURELLI (Roberto). La corte farnesiana di Parma (1560–1570). Programmazione artistica e identità culturale. Roma, Bulzoni, 99, 192 p. (ill.). (Biblioteca del Cinquecento, 94).

6407. WOHL (Hellmut). The aesthetics of Renaissance art. A reconsideration of style. Cambridge, Cambridge U. P., 99, 376 p. (ill.).

Cf. n° 7177

b. *Architecture*

6408. Architettura (L') dell'Eclettismo. La diffusione e l'emigrazione di artisti italiani nel Nuovo Mondo. A cura di Loretta MOZZONI e Stefano SANTINI. Napoli, Liguori, 99, 306 p.

6409. BABELON (Jean-Pierre), CHAMBLAS-PLOTON (Mic). Jardins à la française. Paris, Imprimerie nationale, 298 p. (ill.).

6410. BLAU (Eve). The architecture of red Vienna. Cambridge, MIT Press, 99, XVIII-509 p.

6411. BONA (Andrea). Gustavo Giovannoni e la "sezione architettura" dell'Enciclopedia Italiana: le ragioni storiche, il sapere e gli strumenti tecnici di una nuova professione. *Ricerche storiche*, 99, 29, p. 331-360.

6412. BRADFORD LANDAU (Sarah), CONDIT (Carl W.). Rise of the New York skyscraper, 1865–1913. New Haven a. London, Yale U. P., 99, 478 p.

6413. CHARLES (Corinne). Stalles sculptées du XVe siècle. Genève et le duché de Savoia. Paris, Picard, 99, 285 p. (ill.).

6414. CLEARY (Richard). The place royale and urban design in the Ancien Régime. Cambridge, Cambridge U. P., 99, 300 p. (ill.).

6415. COOPER (Nicholas). Houses of the gentry 1480–1680. London a. New Haven, Yale U. P., 99, 370 p. (ill.).

6416. FONTANA (Vincenzo). Profilo di architettura italiana nel Novecento. Venezia, Marsilio, 99, 434 p.

6417. FREESTONE (Robert). Preserving Sydney's built heritage in the early twentieth century. *Australian historical studies*, 99, 30, 112, p. 44-60.

6418. GARRIDO MORENO (Antonio). El arquitecto Rafael Gonzàlez-Villar. A Coruña, Diputación Provincial da Coruña, 99, 430 p. (ill.).

6419. HERZOG (Lawrence Arthur). From Aztec to high tech: architecture and landscape across the Mexico-United States border. Baltimore, Johns Hopkins U. P., 99, XIV-241 p. (Creating the North American landscape).

6420. JOKILEHTO (Jukka). A history of architecture conservation. Oxford a. Woburn, Butterworth Heinemann, 99, 359 p. (ill.).

6421. KIEFER (Marcus). Emblematische Strukturen in Stein: Vignolas Palazzo Bocchi in Bologna. Freiburg, Rombach, 99, 107 p. (ill.). (Rombach Wissenschaften. Reihe Quellen zur Kunst, 10).

6422. Kostantin S. Mel'nikov e la costruzione di Mosca. A cura di Mario FOSSO e Maurizio MERIGGI. Milano, Skira, 99, 311 p. (ill.).

6423. LAIRD (Mark). The flowering of the landscape garden. English pleasure grounds 1720–1800. Philadelphia, The University of Pennsylvania Press, 99, 446 p. (ill.).

6424. LEE (Pamela M.). Object to be destroyed: the work of Gordon Matta-Clark. Cambridge, MIT press, 99, 280 p. (ill.).

8. ART AND INDUSTRIAL ART

6425. LORCH (Ingomar). Die Kirchenfassade in Italien von 1450 bis 1527. Die Grundlagen durch Leon Battista Alberti und die Weiterentwicklung des basilikalen Fassadenspiegels bis zum Sacco di Roma. Hildesheim, Zürich u. New York, Georg Olms Verlag, 99, 211 p. (ill.).

6426. LOYER (François). Histoire de l'architecture française, de la Révolution à nos jours. Paris, Mengès, 99, 498 p. (ill.).

6427. Memoria (La), il tempo, la storia nel giardino italiano fra '800 e '900. A cura di Vincenzo CAZZATO. Roma, Istituto Poligrafico e Zecca dello Stato – Libreria dello Stato, 99, 518 p. (ill.).

6428. MICHELL (George), ZEBROWSKI (Mark). Art and architecture of the Deccan Sultanates. Cambridge, Cambridge U. P., 99, XXI-297 p. (ill.). (The new Cambridge history of India, I, 7).

6429. MIHELIČ (Breda), BRATE (Tadej). Industrijska arhitektura v Ljubljani od srede 19. stoletja do konca prve svetovne vojne: (I. faza). (Industrial Architecture in Ljubljana from the Middle of the 19th Century to the End of WWI). Ljubljana, Urbanistični inštitut Republike Slovenije, 99, 73 p.

6430. MONNIER (Gérard). Les grandes dates de l'architecture en Europe de 1830 à nos jours. Paris, PUF, 99, 126 p.

6431. MORDAUNT CROOK (Joseph). The rise of the nouveau riches: style and status in Victorian and Edwardian architecture. London, John Murray, 99, 368 p. (ill.).

6432. MOWL (Timothy), EARNSHAW (Brian). An insular Rococo: architecture, politics and society in Ireland and England, 1710-1770. London, Reaktion Books, 99, 358 p. (ill.).

6433. NICOLOSO (Paolo). Gli architetti di Mussolini. Scuole e sindacato, architetti e massoni, professori e politici negli anni del regime. Milano, F. Angeli, 99, 239 p. (Storia dell'architettura e delle città).

6434. NORTHROP MOORE (Jerrold). F. L. Griggs: the architecture of dreams. Oxford, Clarendon Press, 99, 209 p. (ill.).

6435. PACE (Sergio). Un eclettismo conveniente. L'architettura delle banche in Europa e in Italia 1788–1925. Milano, Franco Angeli, 99, 221 p. (ill.).

6436. PAYNE (Alina A.). The architectural treatise in the Italian Renaissance: architectural invention, ornament and literary culture. Cambridge, Cambridge U. P., 99, 343 p. (ill.).

6437. SANCHEZ GARCIA (Jesús Angel). Mariñán. Pazo de los Sentidos. A Coruña, Diputación Provincial da Coruña, 99, 290 p. (ill.).

6438. SCARROCCHIA (Sandro). Albert Speer e Marcello Piacentini. L'architettura del totalitarismo negli anni trenta. Milano, Skira, 99, 420 p. (ill.).

6439. SIMPSON (Pamela H.). Cheap, quick, and easy: imitative architectural materials, 1870–1930. Knoxville, University of Tennessee Press, 99, XII-215 p.

6440. TOURNIKIOTIS (Panayotis). The historiography of modern architecture. Cambridge, MIT Press, 99, 343 p.

6441. ZISKIN (Rochelle). The Place Vendôme. Architecture and social mobility in eighteenth century Paris. Cambridge, Cambridge U. P., 99, 224 p. (ill.).

c. *Sculpture, painting, etching and drawing*

** 6442. DELACROIX (Eugène). Souvenirs d'un voyage dans le Maroc. Ed. par Laure BEAUMONT-MAILLET, Barthélémy JOBERT et Sophie JOIN-LAMBERT. Paris, Gallimard, 99, 192 p.

** 6443. Lettres d'Ingres à Marcotte d'Argenteuil. Ed. par Daniel TERNOIS. Paris, Société de l'histoire de l'art français, 99, 266 p.

6444. BAJOU (Valérie). Monsieur Ingres. Paris, Adam Biro, 99, 383 p. (ill.).

6445. BAMBACH (Carmen C.). Drawing and painting in the Italian Renaissance workshop: theory and practice 1300–1600. Cambridge, Cambridge U. P., 99, 548 p. (ill.).

6446. BARTOLI (Roberta). Biagio d'Antonio. Milano, Federico Motta Editore, 99, 272 p. (ill.).

6447. BONNAFOUX (Denise). Images d'Espagne en France au détour d'un siècle. Aix-en-Provence, Publications de l'Université de Provence, 99, 463 p. (ill.).

6448. CAIN HUNGERFORD (Constance). Ernest Meissonier: master in his genre. Cambridge, Cambridge U. P., 99, 276 p. (ill.).

6449. CARANFA (Angelo). Camille Claudel. A sculpture of interior solitude. London, Associated Universities Presses, 99, 214 p. (ill.).

6450. CROCKETT (Dennis). German Post-Expressionism: the art of the great disorder 1918-1924. University Park, The Pennsylvania State U. P., 99, 215 p. (ill.).

6451. CURTIS (Pénélope). Sculpture 1900–1945, after Rodin. Oxford, Oxford U. P., 99, 286 p. (ill.).

6452. DABAKIS (Melissa). Visualizing labor in American sculpture: monuments, manliness, and the work ethic, 1880–1935. New York, Cambridge U. P., 99, XVI-296 p. (Cambridge studies in American visual culture).

6453. DWYER (Britta C.). Anna Klumpke. A turn of the century painter and her world. Boston, Northeastern U. P., 99, 222 p. (ill.).

6454. EVANS (Dorinda). The genius of Gilbert Stuart. Princeton, Princeton U. P., 99, XIX-177 p. (ill.).

6455. Frederic Leighton: antiquity, Renaissance, modernity. Ed. by Tim BARRINGER and Elizabeth

PRETTEJOHN. New Haven a. London, Yale U. P., 99, 384 p. (ill.). (Studies in British art, 5).

6456. GARIBALDI (Vittoria), BIGANTI (Tiziana). Beato Angelico e Benozzo Gozzoli: artisti del Rinascimento a Perugia. Milano, Silvana editoriale, 99, 151 p. (ill.).

6457. GOTTDANG (Andrea). Venedigs antike Helden: die Darstellung der antiken Geschichte in der venezianischen Malerei von 1680 bis 1760. München u. Berlin, Deutscher Kunstverlag, 99, 288 p. (ill.).

6458. HALL (Marcia B.). After Raphael. Painting in central Italy in the sixteenth century. Cambridge, Cambridge U. P., 99, 350 p. (ill.).

6459. HEISE (Brigitte). Johann Friedrich Overbeck. Das künstlerische Werk und seine literarischen und autobiographischen Quellen. Köln, Böhlau, 99, 310 p. (ill.).

6460. HELAS (Philine). Lebende Bilder in der italienischen Festkultur des 15. Jahrhunderts. Berlin, Akademie Verlag, 99, 326 p. (ill.).

6461. HOLMES (Megan). Fra Filippo Lippi. The Carmelite painter. London a. New Haven, Yale U. P., 99, 301 p. (ill.).

6462. JACOBS (Alain). Laurent Delvaux 1696–1778. Paris, Arthena, 99, 600 p. (ill.).

6463. KAMMEN (Michael). Robert Gwathmey. The life and art of a passionate observer. Chapel Hill a. London, University of North Carolina, 99, 240 p. (ill.).

6464. KASELOW (Gerhild). Die Schaulust am Exotischen Tier. Studien zur Darstellung des zoologischen Gartens in der Malerei des 19. und 20. Jahrhunderts. Hildesheim, Zürich u. New York, Georg Olms Verlag, 99, 336 p. (ill.).

6465. KAVALER (Ethan Matt). Pieter Bruegel: parables of order and enterprise. Cambridge, Cambridge U. P., 99, 403 p. (ill.).

6466. LAMBERT (Gisèle). Les premières gravures italiennes: Quattrocento – début du Cinquecento. Paris, Bibliothèque nationale de France, 99, 449 p. (ill.).

6467. LAMBOURNE (Lionel). Victorian painting. London, Phaidon Press, 99, 512 p. (bibl., ill.).

6468. LAYER-BURCHARTH (Ewa). Necklines: the art of Jacques-Louis David after the Terror. New Haven, Yale U. P., 99, 400 p. (ill.).

6469. LÖCHER (Kurt). Barthel Beham. Ein Maler aus dem Dürerkreis. München u. Berlin, Deutscher Kunstverlag, 99, 260 p. (ill.).

6470. MAC CORMICK EDWARDS (Lee). Herkomer. A Victorian artist. Aldershot, Ashgate, 99, 159 p. (ill.).

6471. MARANI (Pietro). Leonardo, una carriera di pittore. Milano, Federico Motta Editore, 99, 384 p. (ill.).

6472. MARSH (Jan). Dante Gabriele Rossetti: painter and poet. London, Weidenfeld & Nicolson, 99, 592 p. (ill.).

6473. MYSSOK (Johannes). Bildhauerische Konzeption und plastisches Modell in der Renaissance. Münster, Rhema, 99, 432 p. (ill.). (Beiträge zur Kunstgeschichte des Mittelalters und der Renaissance, 8).

6474. O'BRIAN (John). Ruthless hedonism: the American reception of Matisse. Chicago, University of Chicago Press, 99, 284 p. (ill.).

6475. OGONOVSZKY-STEFFENS (Judith). La peinture monumentale d'histoire dans les édifices civils en Belgique (1830-1914). Bruxelles, Académie royale de Belgique – Classe des Beaux-Arts, 99, 432 p. (ill.).

6476. Pittura (La) in Liguria. Il Cinquecento. A cura di Elena PARMA. Genova, Banca Carige – Fondazione Cassa di Risparmio di Genova e Imperia, 99, 445 p. (ill.).

6477. POESCHEL (Sabine). Alexander Maximus. Das Bildprogramm des Appartamento Borgia im Vatikan. Weimar, VDG, 99, 422 p. (ill.).

6478. PRESSLY (William). The French Revolution as blasphemy. Johan Zoffany's paintings of the Massacre at Paris, august 10, 1792. Berkeley, University of California Press, 99, 212 p. (ill.).

6479. PROMEY (Sally). Painting religion: John Singer Sargent's "Triumph of religion" at the Boston Public Library. Princeton, Princeton U. P., 99, 365 p. (ill.).

6480. ROSENTHAL (Michael). The art of Thomas Gainsborough. New Haven, Yale U. P., 99, 312 p. (ill.).

6481. SCHALLERT (Regine). Studien zu Vincenzo de Rossi. Die frühen und mittleren Werke (1536–1561). Hildesheim, Zürich u. New York, Georg Olms Verlag, 99, 560 p. (ill.). (Studien zur Kunstgeschichte, 124).

6482. SCHAMA (Simon). Rembrandt's eyes. New York, Alfred A. Knopf, 99, 728 p. (ill.).

6483. STEENSMA (Susanna). Otto Marseus van Schrieck. Leben und Werk. Hildesheim, Zürich u. New York, Georg Olms Verlag, 99, 420 p. (ill.).

6484. URREA (Jesús). Gregorio Fernández 1576–1636. Valladolid, Fundación Santander Central Hispano, 99, 167 p. (ill.).

6485. VERGARA (Alexander). Rubens and his Spanish patrons. Cambridge, Cambridge U. P., 99, 278 p. (ill.).

6486. WARD BISSEL (Roger). Artemisia Gentileschi and the authority of art. University Park, Pennsylvania State U. P., 99, XXIV-447 p. (ill.).

6487. ZOLOTONOSOV (Mikhail N.). Glyptokratoz: Issledovanie nemogo diskursa: Annotirovannyj katalog sadovo-parkovoj skul'ptury stalinskogo vremeni. (A study of a silent discourse: a catalogue of the landscape sculpture of Stalin's time). Sankt-Peterburg, INAPRESS, 99, 205 p. (ill., bibl.). (Kabinet: kartiny mira).

6488. ZWEITE (Armin). Barnett Newmann: paintings, sculptures, works on papers. Ostfildern, Hatje Cantz Publishers, 99, 336 p. (ill.).

d. *Decorative, popular and industrial art*

* 6489. ROOSENS (Laurent), SALU (Luc). History of photography: a bibliography of books. Vol. 4. London, Mansell, 449 p.

6490. BARIŞTA (Orçun). Osmanlı İmparatorluğu dönemi Türk işlemeleri. (Les broderies turques à l'époque de l'Empire Ottoman). Ankara, Kültür Bakanlığı Yayımlar Dairesi Başkanlığı, 99, VIII-265 p.

6491. BOSONI (Giampiero), NULLI (Andrea). L'epopea del treno. Milano, Mondadori, 99, 190 p. (ill.).

6492. BRUNNER (Michael). Die Illustrierung von Dantes Divina Commedia in der Zeit der Dante-Debatte (1570–1600). München u. Berlin, Deutscher Kunstverlag, 99, 372 p. (ill.). (Kunstwissenschaftliche Studien, 80).

6493. Colonising camera (The): photographs in the making of Namibian history. Ed. by Wolfram HARTMANN, Jeremy SILVESTER and Patricia HAYES. Cape Town, University of Cape Town Press a. Athens, Ohio U. P., 99, VII-220 p. (ill.).

6494. D'OENCH (Ellen). "Copper into gold". Prints by John Raphael Smith 1751–1812. New Haven a. London, Yale U. P., 99, 300 p. (ill.).

6495. DELMARCEL (Guy). La tapisserie flamande. Paris, Imprimerie nationale du XVe au XVIIIe siècle, 99, 384 p. (ill.).

6496. FUHRING (Peter). Juste-Aurèle Meissonnier. Un génie du Rococo 1695–1750. Torino, Umberto Allemandi, 99, 2 vol., 520 p. (ill.).

6497. Global fun. Kunst und Design von Mondrian/ Gehry/Versace and friends. Hrsg. v. Susanne ANNA. Ostfildern, Hatje Cantz Publishers, 99, 140 p. (ill.).

6498. GRIFFIN (Leonard). Clarice Cliff. The art of bizarre. London, Pavilion, 99, 224 p. (ill.).

6499. Gubbio (The) studiolo and its conservation. Vol. 1. Federico da Montefeltro's palace at Gubbio and its studiolo. Ed. by Olga RAGGIO. Vol. 2. Italian Renaissance intarsia and the conservation of the Gubbio studiolo. Ed. by Antoine WILMERING. New York, Metroplitan Museum of Art, 99, 2 vol., 222 p., 270 p.

6500. HARROD (Tanya). The crafts in Britain in the 20th century. New Haven a. London, Yale U. P., 99, 496 p. (ill.).

6501. HILLS (Paul A.). Venetian colour: marble, mosaic, painting and glass, 1250–1550. New Haven, Yale U. P., 99, 247 p. (bibl., ill.).

6502. LAURENT (Stéphane). Chronologie du design. Paris, Flammarion, 99, 240 p. (ill.).

6503. PURCELL (Katherine). Falize: a dynasty of jewellers. London, Thames and Hudson, 99, 320 p. (ill.).

6504. REGENER (Susanne). Fotographische Erfassung: zur Geschichte medialer Konstruktionen des Kriminellen. München, W. Fink, 99, 355 p.

6505. RICHARDS (Sarah). Eighteenth century ceramics: products for a civilised society. Manchester, Manchester U. P., 99, 236 p. (ill.).

6506. RICHEMOND (Stéphene). Terres cuites orientalistes et africanistes 1860–1940. Paris, Les éditions de l'Amateur, 99, 240 p. (ill.).

6507. SIEBEL (Ernst). Der grossbürgerliche Salon 1850–1918. Geselligkeit und Wohnkultur. Berlin, Dietrich Reimer Verlag, 99, 301 p. (ill.).

6508. Tapisserie (La) au XVIIe siècle et les collections européennes. Actes du colloque international de Chambord, octobre 1996. Ed. par Catherine ARMINJON et Nicole DE REYNIÈS. Paris, Editions du Patrimoine, 99, 205 p. (Cahiers du Patrimoine, 57).

6509. VÉLEZ (Pilar). Masriera jewellery. 200 years of history. Barcelona, Ambit, 184 p. (ill.).

6510. VENTURELLI (Paola). Glossario e documenti per la gioielleria milanese (1459–1631). Milano, La Nuova Italia, 99, 204 p. (ill.).

6511. WEBER SOROS (Susan). The secular furniture of Edward William Godwin. New Haven, Yale U. P., 99, 300 p. (ill.).

6512. YOUNG (Hilary). English porcelain 1745–1795: its makers, design, marketing and consumption. London, Victoria and Albert Museum, 99, 229 p. (ill.).

Cf. n° 131

§ 9. Music, theatre, cinema and broadcasting.

** 6513. SHIRER (William Lawrence). "This is Berlin": radio broadcasts from Nazi Germany. Introduction by John KEEGAN. Woodstock, Overlook Press, 99, XII-405 p. (ill.).

6514. ALBANO (Lucilla). Il secolo della regia: la figura e il ruolo del regista nel cinema. Venezia, Marsilio, 99, 313 p.

6515. ALEOTTI (Paolo). La Hollywood dell'era pulp: dalle prime riviste pulp al cinema di Tarantino. Roma, Editori Riuniti, 99, 271 p. (ill.).

6516. ANANIA (Francesca). Davanti allo schermo: storia del pubblico televisivo. Roma, Carocci, 99, 151 p. (Ricerche, 10).

6517. Appassionatamente: il mélo nel cinema italiano. A cura di Orio CALDIRON e Stefano DELLA CASA. Torino, Lindau, 99, 197 p.

6518. ASTINGTON (John H.). English court theatre, 1558–1642. Cambridge, Cambridge U. P., 99, XIV-293. (ill.).

6519. BAMFORD (Kenton). Distorted images: British national identity and film in the 1920s. London, I. B. Tauris, 99, XII-227 p. (ill.).

6520. BERNHARD (Nancy E.). U.S. television news and Cold War propaganda, 1947–1960. New York,

Cambridge U. P., 99, 245 p. (Cambridge studies in the history of mass communications).

6521. BIRDWELL (Michael E.). Celluloid soldiers: the Warner Bros. Campaign against Nazism. New York, New York U. P., 99, XXI-226 p.

6522. BLAME (Christopher B.). Decolonizing the stage. Theatrical syncretism and Post-Colonial drama. Oxford, Clarendon Press, 99, XIV-304 p. (ill.).

6523. BOTTONI (Luciano). Storia del teatro italiano, 1900–1945. Bologna, Il Mulino, 99, 212 p.

6524. BOURQUI (Claude). La Commedia dell'arte. Introduction au théâtre professionel italien entre le XVIe et le XVIIIe siècle. Paris, SEDES, 99, 160 p.

6525. BRANGER (Jean-Christophe). Manon de Jules Massenet ou le crépuscule de l'opéra comique. Metz, Editions Serpenoises, 99, 505 p.

6526. Breve storia del cinema: guida al cinema mondiale dalle origini ai nostri giorni. A cura di Massimo MOSCATI. Milano, Bompiani, 99, 477 p.

6527. BROJAN (Matjaž). Začetki radia na Slovenskem. (Beginnings of Slovene radio). Ljubljana, Modrijan v Radio 3 Slovenija, 99, 112 p. (ill.).

6528. BURATTELLI (Claudia). Spettacoli di corte a Mantova tra Cinque e Seicento. Firenze, Le Lettere, 99, 278 p.

6529. Cambridge companion (The) to American women playwrights. Ed. by Brenda MURPHY. Cambridge, Cambridge U. P., 99, XXXVIII-285 p. (ill.).

6530. Cambridge history (The) of American theatre. Vol. 2. 1870 to 1945. Ed. by Dan B. WILMETH and Christopher BIGSBY. Cambridge, Cambridge U. P., 99, XVIII-590 p. (ill.).

6531. CARTWRIGHT (Ken). Theatre and humanism: English drama in the sixteenth century. Cambridge, Cambridge U. P., 99, X-321 p.

6532. CAVE (Richard)-SHAFER (Elizabeth)-WOLLAND (Brian). Ben Johnson and theatre. London, Routledge, 99, XIV-223 p. (ill.).

6533. Cinema and urban culture in Shanghai, 1922–1943. Ed. by Yingjin ZHANG. Stanford, Stanford U. P., 99, XVI-369 p.

6534. COLLIER (Simon). Carlos Gardel. Su vida, su música, su época. Buenos Aires, Sudamericana, 99, 341 p.

6535. COLVIN (Sarah). The rhetorical feminine: gender and Orient on the German Stage, 1647–1742. Oxford, Clarendon Press, 99, X-332 p.

6536. Comedia (La) española y el teatro europeo del siglo XVII. Ed. por Henry W. SULLIVAN, Raul A. GALOPPE and Mahlon L. STOUTZ. Rochester, Boydell and Brewer, 99, X-193 p. (Colección Tamesis, 164).

6537. CROWTHER (Victor). The Oratorio in Bologna (1650–1730). Oxford, Oxford U. P., 99, 208 p.

6538. DAUGEVILLE (Sylvie). Le théâtre change et représente. Lecture critique des oeuvres dramatiques du Marquis de Sade. Paris, Champion, 99, 735 p. (Les Dix-huitièmes siècles, 29).

6539. DEFA: East German cinema, 1946–1992. Ed. by Seán ALLAN and John SANDFORD. New York, Berghahn Books, 99, X-328 p. (ill., bibl.).

6540. DOHERTY (Thomas). Pre-Code Hollywood: sex, immorality, and insurrection in American cinema, 1930–1934. New York, Columbia U. P., 99, XIII-430 p.

6541. DORIVAL (Jérôme). La cantate française au XVIIIe siècle. Paris, PUF, 99, 128 p. (Que sais-je? 3476).

6542. Driven into paradise: the musical migration from Nazi Germany to the United States. Ed. by Reinhold BRINKMANN and Christoph WOLFF. Berkeley a. Los Angeles, University of California Press, 99, XIII-373 p.

6543. Echo (L') du siècle: dictionnaire historique de la radio et de la télévision en France. Sous la dir. de Jean-Noël JEANNENEY. Paris, Hachette et Issy-les-Moulineaux, Arte, 99, 600 p.

6544. Economie (L') du dialogue dans l'ancien théâtre européen. Ed. par Jean-Pierre BORDIER. Paris, Champion, 99, 228 p.

6545. FALLETTI CRUCIANI (Clelia). Il teatro in Italia. 2. Cinquecento e Seicento. Roma, Studium, 99, 409 p.

6546. FAZIO (Mara). François Joseph Talma, primo divo. Teatro e storia fra Rivoluzione, Impero e Restaurazione. Milano, Leonardo arte, 99, 383 p.

6547. "Film Europe" and "Film America": cinema, commerce and cultural exchange, 1920–1939. Ed. by Andrew HIGSON and Richard MALTBY. Exeter, University of Exeter Press, 99, 406 p.

6548. First World War (The) and popular cinema: 1914 to the present. Ed. by Michael PARIS. Edinburgh, Edinburgh U. P., 1999. XV-267 p.

6549. FOOT (John). Cinema and the city. Milan and Luchino Visconti's "Rocco and his brothers" (1960). *Journal of modern Italian studies*, 99, 4, 2, p. 209-235. – IDEM. Mass cultures, popular culture and the working class in Milan, 1950–1970. *Social history*, 99, 24, p. 134-157. – IDEM. Television and the city: the impact of television in Milan, 1954–1960. *Contemporary European history*, 99, 8, 3, p. 379-394.

6550. FRANTZ (Pierre), SAJOUS D'ORIA (Michèle). Le siècle des théâtres. Salles et scenes en France 1748–1807. Paris, Bibliothèque historique de la ville de Paris, 99, 200 p. (ill.).

6551. FULCHER (Jane F.). French culture politics & music. From the Dreyfus affair to the First World War. Oxford, Oxford U. P., 99, XII-291 p.

6552. GAUTHIER (Christophe). La passion du cinéma. Cinéphiles, ciné-clubs et salles spécialisées à Paris de 1920 à 1929. Paris, Association française de recherche sur l'histoire du cinéma - Ecole des Chartes, 99, 392 p. (bibl., ill.). (Mémoires et documents de l'Ecole des Chartes, 56).

6553. GENTON (François). Des beautés plus hardies. Le théâtre allemand dans la France de l'Ancien Régime (1750–1789). Paris, Les éditions Suger-Université de Paris VIII, 99, 358 p.

6554. GIACOVELLI (Enrico). Non ci resta che ridere: una storia del cinema comico italiano. Torino, Lindau, 99, 195 p.

6555. GRAHAM-JONES (Jean). Exorcising history: Argentine theater under dictatorship. Lewisburg, Bucknell U. P., 99, 259 p.

6556. GRANDE (Troni Y.). Marlowian tragedy: the play of dilation. Lewisburg, Bucknell U. P., 99, 221 p.

6557. GREENE (Naomi). Landscapes of loss. The national past in postwar French cinema. Princeton, Princeton U. P., 99, 234 p.

6558. GYGER (Alison). Civilising the colonies: pioneering opera in Australia. Sydney, Pellinor, 99, 285 p. (ill.).

6559. HAGHIGHAT (Mamad), SABOURAUD (Frédéric). Histoire du cinéma iranien, 1900–1999. Paris, Cinéma du réel, Bibliothèque publique d'information, Centre Georges Pompidou, 99, 247 p. (ill.).

6560. HARLEY (John). Orlando Gibbons and the Gibbons family of musicians. Aldershot, Ashgate, 99, 263 p.

6561. HARRAN (Don). Salomone Rossi. Jewish musician in late Renaissance Mantua. Oxford, Oxford U. P., 99, X-320 p.

6562. HARTMANN (Günther). Karg-Elerts Harmonologik. Vorstufen und Stellungnahmen. Bonn, Orpheus Verlag, 99, 493 p. (Orpheus-Schriftenreihe zu Grundfragen der Musik, 95).

6563. History (A) of Russian theatre. Ed. by Robert LEACH and Victor BOROVSKY. Cambridge, Cambridge U. P., 99, XV-446 p. (ill.).

6564. HOLGUÍN (Sandie). Taming the seventh art: the battle for cultural unity on the cinematographic front during Spain's second republic, 1931–1936. *Journal of modern history*, 99, 71, 4, p. 852-881.

6565. HOWARD (James). Stanley Kubrick companion. London, Batsford, 99, 190 p.

6566. HOWLAND KENNEY (William). Recorded music in American life: the phonograph and popular memory, 1890–1945. New York, Oxford U. P., 99, XIX-258 p.

6567. HUEBNER (Steven). French opera at the fin de siècle: Wagnerism, nationalism and style. Oxford, Oxford U. P., 99, XVIII-526 p. (ill.).

6568. Intorno a Monteverdi. A cura di Maria CARACI VELA e Rodobaldo TIBALDI. Lucca, Libreria Musicale Italiana, 99, XIII-543 p.

6569. KERSHAW (Baz). The radical in performance: between Brecht and Baudrillard. London, Routledge, 99, XIV-252 p.

6570. KIERNAN (Pauline). Staging Shakespeare at the New Globe. Houndmills, Basingstoke and London Macmillan, 99, XIV-176 p.

6571. KÜHNL-KINEL (Agnieszka). Marcel Marceau: contribution à l'étude de l'art du mime. Lille, Presses Universitaires du Septentrion, 99, 333 p.

6572. LA POLLA (Franco). L'età dell'occhio. Il cinema e la cultura americana. Torino, Lindau, 99, 276 p.

6573. LANZA (Federica). La donna nel cinema maghrebino. Roma, Bulzoni, 99, 134 p.

6574. LEAFSTEDT (Carl S.). Inside Bluebeard's Castle. Music and drama in Béla Bartók's opera. Oxford, Oxford U. P., 99, VIII-246 p.

6575. LEINWAND (Theodore B.). Theatre, finance and society in early modern England. Cambridge, Cambridge U. P., 99, XII-199 p. (Cambridge studies in Renaissance literature and culture, 31).

6576. LIOGIER (H.). Le cinéma français en Espagne (1939–1975). *Relations internationales*, 99, 97, p. 23-38.

6577. LOACKER (Armin). Anschluß im 3/4 Takt. Filmproduktion und Filmpolitik in Österreich, 1930–1938. Trier, Wissenschaftlicher Verlag Trier, 99, 321 p. (bibl., ill.). (Filmgeschichte international, 5).

6578. LUCIANI (Paola). Le passioni e gli affetti. Studi sul teatro tragico del Settecento. Pisa, Pacini, 99, 200 p.

6579. MAC CAFFREY (Donald). Guide to the silent years of American cinema. Westport a. London, Greenwood Press, 99, XV-343 p.

6580. MAC CARTHY (Jin). Political theatre during the Spanish Civil War. Cardiff, University of Wales Press, 99, XIX-251 p.

6581. Mahler (The) companion. Ed. by Donald MITCHELL and Andrew NICHOLSON. Oxford, Oxford U. P., 99, XVIII-633 p.

6582. MELNICK (Jeffrey). A right to sing the blues: African Americans, Jews, and American popular song. Cambridge, Harvard U. P., 99, IX-277 p.

6583. MENARINI (Roy). Il cinema di guerra americano, 1968–1998. Recco, Le Mani, 99, 229 p.

6584. MERKLEY (Paul). Music and patronage in the Sforza court. Turnhout, Brepols, 99, XXX-514 p. (Studi sulla storia della musica in Lombardia, 3).

6585. Mexico's cinema: a century of film and filmmakers. Ed. by Joanne HERSHFIELD and David R. MACIEL. Wilmington, Scholarly Resources, 99, XIV-303 p. (Latin American Silhouettes).

6586. MICHELI (Sergio). Bertolt Brecht e il cinema di Weimar. Firenze, Edizioni Manent, 99, 174 p.

6587. MICKEL (Lesley). Ben Johnson's antimasques: a history of growth and decline. Aldershot, Ashgate, 99, VIII-208 p.

6588. Milano musicale, 1861–1897. A cura di Bianca Maria ANTOLINI. Lucca, LIM, 99, X-428 p. (Quaderni, 5).

6589. MOORE WHITING (Steven). Satie the bohemian. From cabaret to Concert Hall. Oxford, Oxford U. P., 99, 596 p.

6590. NENONEN (Markku). Elokuvatarkastuksen synty Suomessa (1907–1922). (Origins of preventive film control in Finland, 1907–1922). Helsinki, SHS, 99, 231 p. (Bibliotheca historica, 46). [English summary].

6591. Nessuno ci può giudicare. Il lungo viaggio del cinema musicale italiano, 1930–1980. A cura di Renato VENTURELLI. Roma, Edizioni Fahrenheit 451, 99, 159 p.

6592. NICHOLSON (Steve). British theatre and the Red Peril: the portrayal of Communism, 1917–1945. Exeter, University of Exeter Press, 99, XX-195 p. (ill.).

6593. Nordic explorations: film before 1930. Ed. by John FULLERTON and Jon OLSSON. London, John Libbey, 99, 256 p. (ill.).

6594. Orlando di Lasso studies. Ed. by Peter BERGQUIST. Cambridge, Cambridge. U. P., 99, XII-253 p.

6595. Performing America: cultural nationalism in American theatre. Ed. by Jeffrey D. MASON and J. Ellen GAINOR. Ann Arbor, University of Michigan Press, 250 p.

6596. PERKINS (Leeman L.). Music in the age of Renaissance. New York, Norton, 99, 750 p.

6597. PEZZOTTA (Alberto). Tutto il cinema di Hong Kong: stili, caratteri, autori. Milano, Baldini & Castoldi, 99, 442 p.

6598. PORCILE (François). La Belle époque de la musique française, 1871–1940. Paris, Fayard, 99, 477 p. (Que sais-je? 3448).

6599. PRANDONI (Francesco). Anime al cinema: storia del cinema di animazione giapponese, 1917–1995. Milano, Yamato Video, 99, 160 p. (ill.).

6600. RAFFAELLI (Sergio). Pellicole censurate per rispetto della Triplice Alleanza. *Storia e problemi contemporanei*, 99, 12, 23, p. 53-66.

6601. RAVEL (Jeffrey S.). The contested parterre: public theatre and French political culture, 1680–1791. London a. Ithaca, Cornell U. P., 99, XI-256 p. (ill.).

6602. REBELLATO (Dan). 1956 and all that: the making of modern British drama. London, Routledge, 99, XI-265 p.

6603. REDI (Riccardo). Cinema muto italiano (1896–1930). Roma, Edizioni Biblioteca di Bianco e Nero, 99, 255 p.

6604. REEVES (Nicholas). The power of film propaganda: myth and reality? London a. New York, Cassel, 99, VIII-262 p.

6605. Renaissance (The) theatre. Vol. 1. English and Italian theatre. Vol.2. Design, image and acting. Ed. by Christopher CAIRNS. Aldershot, Ashgate, 99, 2 vol., XI-206 p., X-130 p.

6606. REYNAUD (Daniel). Convention and contradiction. Representations of women in Australian war films, 1914–1918. *Australian historical studies*, 99, 30, 113, p. 215-230.

6607. RIMBAU (Esteve). La Escuela de Barcelona: el cine de la "gauche divine". Barcelona, Anagrama, 99, 432 p. (bibl., ill.).(Crónicas Anagrama, 38).

6608. ROBERTS (Philip). The royal court theatre and the modern stage. Cambridge, Cambridge U. P., 99, 254 p.

6609. ROTHWELL (Kenneth S.). A history of Shakespeare on screen: a century of film and television. Cambridge, Cambridge U. P., 99, XIV-352 p. (ill.).

6610. Rouge reels: oppositional film making in Britain, 1945–1990. Ed. by Margaret DICKINSON. London, British Film Institute, 99, 330 p. (ill.).

6611. RUSSELL BROWN (John). New sites for Shakespeare: theatre, the audience and Asia. London a. New York, Routledge, 99, X-211 p.

6612. RUSSO (Vito). Lo schermo velato. L'omosessualità nel cinema. Milano, Baldini & Castoldi, 99, 468 p. (ill.).

6613. SÁNCHEZ-H (José). The art and politics of Bolivian cinema. Lanham, Scarecrow Press, 99, XVIII-267 p.

6614. SANDERS (Eve Rachele). Gender and literacy on stage in early modern England. Cambridge, Cambridge U. P., 99, XVIII-260 p. (Cambridge Studies in Renaissance literature and culture, 28).

6615. SAVAGE (Barbara Dianne). Broadcasting freedom: radio, war, and the politics of race, 1938–1948. Chapell Hill, University of North Carolina Press, 99, XIII-391 p. (John Hope Franklin series in African American history and culture).

6616. SCHROEDER (David). Mozart in revolt. Strategies of resistance, mischief and deception. New Haven a. London, Yale U. P., 99, X-211 p.

6617. SCHWARTZ (Manuela). Wagner-Rezeption und französische Opera des fin de siècle. Untersuchungen zu Vincent d'Indys Fervaal. Sinzig, Studio, 99, XXII-361 p. (Berliner Musik Studien, 18).

6618. SEDERGREN (Jari). Filmi poikki. – Poliittinen elokuvasensuuri Suomessa 1939–1947 (Cut! Political film censorship in Finland, 1939–1947) Helsinki, SHS, 99, 323 p. (Bibliotheca historica, 39). [English summary].

6619. SERVER (Lee). Asian pop cinema: Bombay to Tokyo. San Francisco, Chronicle Books, 99, 132 p. (bibl., ill.).

9. MUSIC, THEATRE, CINEMA AND BROADCASTING

6620. SHELLARD (Dominic). British theatre since the war. New Haven a. London, Yale U. P., 99, 259 p.

6621. SINFIELD (Alan). Out on stage: lesbian and gay theatre in the twentieth century. New Haven, Yale U. P., 99, 407 p.

6622. SOHMER (Steve). Shakespeare's mystery play: the opening of the Globe theatre 1599. Manchester a. New York, Manchester U. P., 99, XII-292 p.

6623. Spectaculum Europaeum. Theatre and spectacle in Europe (1580–1750). Historie du spectacle in Europe (1580–1750). Ed. by Pierre BÉHAR and Helen WATANABE-O'KELLY. Wiesbaden, Harranowitz, 99, X-818 p. (Wolfenbütteler Arbeiten zur Barockforschung, 31).

6624. SPIEKER (Markus). Hollywood unterm Hakenkreuz. Der amerikanische Spielfilm im Dritten Reich. Trier, Wissenschaftlicher Verlag Trier, 99, 394 p. (Filmgeschichte international, 6)

6625. Storia del cinema mondiale. Vol. 1. L'Europa. Miti, luoghi, divi. Vol. 2. Gli Stati Uniti. A cura di Gian Piero BRUNETTA. Torino, Einaudi, 99, 2 vol., 1253 p., XXVI-1015 p.

6626. TAILLIBERT (Christel). L'Institut international du cinématographe éducatif: regards sur le rôle du cinéma éducatif dans la politique internationale du fascisme italien. Paris, L'Harmattan, 99, 401 p. (bibl.). (Champs visuels).

6627. Theater im Kulturwandel des 18. Jahrhunderts. Inszenierung und Wahrnehmung von Körper – Musik – Sprache. Hrsg. v. Erika FISCHER-LICHTE und Jorg SCHÖNER. Göttingen, Wallstein, 99, 568 p. (Das achtzehnte Jahrhundert, Supplementa, 5).

6628. TÖRNQVIST (Egil). Ibsen, Strindberg and the intimate theatre. Studies in television presentation. Amsterdam, Amsterdam U. P., 99, 240 p. (ill.).

6629. TOURNÉS (Ludovic). New Orleans sur Sein, histoire du jazz en France. Paris, Fayard, 99, 501 p.

6630. "Une invention moderne". Baldassarre da Belgioioso e il Balet comique de la Royne. A cura di Mariateresa DELLABORRA. Lucca, LIM, 99, XVI-254 p. (Strumenti della ricerca musicale, 4).

6631. VANDIVER NICASSIO (Susan). Tosca's Rome: the play and the Opera in historical perspective. Chicago, University of Chicago Press, 99, XIX-335 p.

6632. VENDRIX (Philippe). La musique à la Renaissance. Paris, PUF, 99, 128 p.

6633. YOUNGBLOOD (Denise J.). The magic mirror: moviemaking in Russia, 1908–1918. Madison, University of Wisconsin Press, 99, XVII-197 p. (Wisconsin studies in film).

6634. ZIVIN (Joselyn). «Bent»: a colonial subversive and Indian broadcasting. *Past and present*, 99, 162, p. 195-220.

Cf. n°s 914, 4033

N

MODERN ECONOMIC AND SOCIAL HISTORY

§ 1. General. 6635-6670. – § 2. Political economy. 6671-6687.– § 3. Industry, mining and transportation. 6688-6728. – § 4. Trade. 6729-6754. – § 5. Agriculture and agricultural problems. 6755-6781. – § 6. Money and finance. 6782-6820. – § 7. Demography and urban history. 6821-6860. – § 8. Social history. 6861-7035. – § 9. Working-class movement and socialism. 7036-7065.

§ 1. General.

6635. Accumulation and dissolution of large estates of the regular clergy in early modern Europe. Twelfth International Economic History Congress (Madrid, 1998). Ed. by Fiorenzo LANDI. Rimini, Guaraldi, 99, 502 p.

6636. BÄCKLUND (Dan). Befolkningen och regionerna: ett fågelperspektiv på regionalekonomi i Sverige från 1820 och framåt. (La Population et les régions: survol de l'économie régionale en Suède depuis 1820). Östersund, Institutet för regionalforskning, Stockholm, Fritze, 99, 104 p. (Rapport 110).

6637. BÄHR (Johannes). Institutionenordnung und Wirtschaftsentwicklung. Die Wirtschaftsgeschichte der DDR aus der Sicht des zwischendeutschen Vergleichs. *Geschichte und Gesellschaft*, 99, 25, 4, p. 530-555.

6638. CRISTOFFERSEN (Henrik). Danemarks økonomiske historie. (Histoire économique du Danemark). Århus, Systime, 99, 225 p. (ill.).

6639. Décadas (Dos) de investigación en historia económica comparada en América Latina: homenaje a Carlos Sempat Assadourian. Coordinadora Margarita MENEGUS BORNEMANN; colaboradores Antonio IBARRA, Juan Manuel PEREZ ZEVALLOS y Jorge SILVA. México, Colegio de México, Centro de Investigaciones y Estudios Superiores en Antropología Social, Instituto Doctor José María Luis Mora, Centro de Estudios sobre la Universidad/UNAM, 99, 529 p. (ill.).

6640. Economic history (The) of Slovenia (1750–1991). Ed. by Jasna FISCHER, Žarko LAZAREVIĆ, Jože PRINČIČ and Tone KRAŠOVEC. Vrhnika, Razum, 99, 239 p. (ill.).

6641. EKELUND (Robert B., jr.), HEBERT (Robert F.). Secret origins of modern microeconomics: Dupuit and the engineers. Chicago, Chicago U.P., 99, XV-468 p. (figs., tabs.).

6642. Gospodarske krize in Slovenci. (Economic Crises and Slovenes). Ur. Neven BORAK v Žarko LAZAREVIĆ. Ljubljana, Inštitut za novejšo zgodovino, Zveza ekonomistov Slovenije, 99, 280 p. (Zbirka Ekonomska knjižnica).

6643. HABER (Stephen). Cómo se rezagó América Latina. Ensayos sobre las historias económicas de Brasil y México. México, Fondo de Cultura Económica, 99, 363 p.(ill.).

6644. Historia económica de España. Siglos XIX y XX. Ed. por Ponzalo ANES. Barcelona, Galaxia Gutenberg, Circulos de Lectores, 99, 760 p.

6645. HOFFMAN (Philip T.), POSTEL-VINAY (Gilles), ROSENTHAL (Jean-Laurent). Information and economic history: how the credit market in old regime Paris forces us to rethink the transition to capitalism. *American historical review*, 99, 104, 1, p. 69-94.

6646. HYLDTOFT (Ole). Danmarks økonomiske historie 1840–1910. (Histoire économique du Danemark 1840–1910). København, Systime, 99, 320 p. (diagr., tab.).

6647. ILIFFE (John). The South African economy, 1652–1997. *Economic history review*, 99, 52, 1, p. 87-103.

6648. JOHSUA (Isaac). La crise de 1929 et l'émergence américaine. Paris, Presses Universitaires de France, 99, 311 p.

6649. KIMURA (Mitsuhiko). From fascism to communism: continuity and development of collectivist economic policy in North Korea. *Economic history review*, 99, 52, 1, p. 69-86.

6650. Kolize, řevnivost a pragmatismus. Československo-rakouské hospodářské vztahy 1918–1938. [Die Kollision, die Eifesucht und der Pragmatismus. Tschechoslowakisch-österreichische wirtschaftliche Beziehungen, 1918–1938]. Ed. Pavel KLENER. Praha,

Karolinum, 99, 246 p. (Acta Universitatis Carolinae. Philosophica et Historica. Studia historica, 45).

6651. Konkurence i partnerství. Německé a československé hospodářství v letech 1918–1945. (Konkurrenzpartnerschaft. Die deutsche und die tschechoslowakische Wirtschaft in der Zwischenkriegszeit). Hrsg. v. Boris BARTH, Jozef FALTUS, Jan KŘEN und Eduard KUBŮ. Praha, Karolinum, 99. 302 p.

6652. KOROL (Juan Carlos), TANDETER (Enrique). Historia económica de América Latina: problemas y procesos. Buenos Aires, Fondo de Cultura Económica, 99, 117 p. (Sección Obras de historia).

6653. KWOK-CHU (Wong). The Chinese in the Philippine Economy 1898–1941. Quezon City, Ateneo de Manila U. P., 99, XVI-279 p.

6654. MORGAN (Philip). 'The Party is everywhere': the Italian Fascist Party in economic life, 1926–1940. *English historical review*, 99, 114, 455, p. 85-111.

6655. O'ROURKE (Kevin H.), WILLIAMSON (Jeffrey G.). Globalization and history: the evolution of a nineteenth-century Atlantic economy. Cambridge, MIT Press, 99, XII-343 p. (figs, tabs).

6656. PERIČIĆ (Šime). Razvitak gospodarstva Zadra i okolice u prošlosti. (The development of economy of Zadar and its surroundings in the past). Zagreb, Hrvatska akademija znanosti i umjetnosti, 99, 312 p.

6657. POHL (H.). Economic powers and political powers in early modern Europe: theory and history. *Journal of European economic history*, 99, 28, 1, p. 139-170.

6658. RICHARDSON (Philip). Economic change in China, c. 1800-1950. Cambridge, Cambridge U.P. for the Economic History Society, 99, XIII-117 p. (tab., maps).

6659. SCHWARZER (Oskar). Sozialistische Zentralplanwirtschaft in der SBZ/DDR. Ergebnisse eines ordnungspolitischen Experiments (1945–1989). Stuttgart, Steiner, 99, XII-422 p. (Vierteljahrschrift für Sozial- und Wirtschaftsgeschichte, Beihefte, 143).

6660. SEZEN (Seriye). Devletçilikten özelleştirmeye Türkiye'de planlama. (La Planification en Turquie depuis l'étatisme jusqu'à la privatisation). Ankara, Türkiye ve Orta Doğu Amme İdaresi Enstitüsü, 99, 338 p.

6661. SHEAHAN (John). Searching for a better society: the Peruvian economy from 1950. University Park, Penn State U.P., 99, XI-211 p. (tabs., figs.).

6662. SHIMIZU (Hiroshi), HIRAKAWA (Hitoshi). Japan and Singapore in the world economy: Japan's economic advance into Singapore, 1870–1965. London a. New York, Routledge, 99, XXII-279 p. (fig., tab., maps.).

6663. STANZIANI (Alessandro). Istituzioni, informazione e crescita economica: il caso russo, 1861–1930. *Rivista di storia economica*, 99, 15, 1, p. 21-52.

6664. Storia dell'economia mondiale. Vol. 3. L'età della rivoluzione industriale. A cura di Valerio CASTRONOVO. Roma e Bari, Laterza, 99, 650 p.

6665. TOKARSKI (Peter). Die Wahl wirtschaftspolitischer Strategien in Polen nach dem Zweiten Weltkrieg bis 1959. Marburg, Herder-Institut, 99, XV-356 p.

6666. TRENTO (Sandro), FABIANI (Silvia). La crescita economica italiana tra Marx e Kuznets: alcune considerazioni. *Rivista di storia economica*, 99, 15, 3, p. 317-337.

6667. TYRRELL (Ian). True gardens of the gods: Californian-Australian environmental reform, 1860–1930. Berkeley a. Los Angeles, University of California Press, 99, XI-313 p.

6668. UL'JANOVA (Galina N.). Blagotvoritel'nost' moskovskikh predprinimatelej, 1860–1914 gg. (The philanthropy of the businessmen of Moscow, 1860–1914). Mos. gor. ob'ed. arkhivov; RAN, In-t rossijskoj istorii. Moskva, Mosgorarkhiv, 99, 512 p. (bibl., ind.). [Eng. summary].

6669. WEINER (Douglas R.). A little corner of freedom: Russian nature protection from Stalin to Gorbachëv. Berkeley a. Los Angeles, University of California Press, 99, XIV-556 p.

6670. Western Europe. Economic and social change since 1945. Ed. by Max S. SCHULZE. London, Longman, 99, XIV-408 p.

Cf. n°s 183, 4006, 5017, 5512

§ 2. Political economy.

6671. AIMAR (Thierry). Time, coordination and ignorance: a comparison between Hayek and Lachmann. *History of economic ideas*, 99, 7, 1-2, p. 139-165.

6672. AMINEH (Mehdi Parvizi). Die globale kapitalistische Expansion und Iran: eine Studie der iranischen politischen Ökonomie (1500–1980). Münster, Lit, 99, 684 p. (Politikwissenschaft, 62).

6673. ARENA (Richard). The Hayek/Keynes controversy in the light of modern business cycle theory. *History of economic ideas*, 99, 7, 1-2, p. 227-253.

6674. BÜRGIN (Alfred), MAISSEN (Thomas). Zum Begriff der politischen Ökonomie heute. *Geschichte und Gesellschaft*, 99, 25, 2, p. 177-200.

6675. FORTE (F.). Storia del pensiero dell'economia pubblica. 2. Dal Medio Evo al mercantilismo. Milano, Giuffrè, 99, XI-601 p.

6676. GAMBLES (Anna). Protection and politics. Conservative economic discourse 1815–1852. Woodbridge a. Rochester, Boydell Press, 99, XII-291 p.

6677. LAIDLER (David). Fabricating the Keynesian revolution: study of the inter-war literature on money, the cycle and unemployment. Cambridge, Cambridge U.P., 99, XVI-380 p.

6678. Legacy (The) of Friedrich von Hayek. Vol. 1. Politics. Vol. 2. Philosophy. Vol. 3. Economics. Ed. by Peter J. BOETTKE. Cheltentham a. Northampton, Edward Elgar, 99, 3 vol., IV-618 p., VIII-485 p., VII-433 p. (figs).

6679. Liberalismo, nazionalismo, fascismo. Stato e mercato, corporativismo e liberismo, nel pensiero economico del nazionalismo italiano (1900–1923). A cura di Luca MICHELINI. Milano, M&B Publishing, 238 p.

6680. LUMPERDEAN (Ioan). Literatura economică românească din Transilvania la începutul epocii moderne. (Romanian economic literature in Transylvania at the beginning of the Modern Age). Prefaţă de prof. univ. dr. Nicolae EDROIU. Bucureşti, Editura Didactică şi Pedagogică S. A., 99, 380 p.

6681. MAGNUSSON (Lars). Merkantilism: ett ekonomiskt tänkande formuleras. (Le mercantilisme: formulation d'une pensée économique). Stockholm, SNS, 99, 304 p.

6682. MATSUI (Toru). Iwanami koza sekai rekishi 15: Shonin to shijo; Nettowaku no naka no kokka. (Iwanami world history. Vol. 15. Merchants and markets; States in trading network). Tokyo, Iwanami Shoten, 99, 308 p.

6683. MULTAMÄKI (Kustaa). Towards Great Britain. Commerce and conquest in the thought of Algernon Sidney and Charles Davenant. Helsinki, The Finnish Academy of Science and Letters, 99, 233 p. (A. Acad. Scie. Fennicae, Ser. Humaniora, 301).

6684. Present significancy (The) of Thorstein Veblen's contribution in the centennial of The Theory of the Leisure Class. *History of economic Ideas*, 99, 7, 3, p. 81-179.

6685. Reflections on economic development: from the Enlightenment to the classical school. Ed. by Guglielmo FORGES DAVANZATI and Vitantonio GIOIA. Lecce, Milella, 99, 84 p. (Pubblicazioni del Dipartimento di filosofia. Sez. Centro studi economici, 1).

6686. RONCAGLIA (Alessandro). Sraffa: la biografia, l'opera, la scuola. Roma e Bari, Laterza, 99, VI-145 p. (Universale Laterza, 794).

6687. SANDL (Marcus). Ökonomie des Raumes. Der kameralwissenschaftliche Entwurf der Staatswirtschaft im 18. Jahrhundert. Köln, Weimar u. Wien, Böhlau, 99, VIII-518 p. (Norm und Struktur. Studien zum sozialen Wandel im Mittelalter und Früher Neuzeit, 11).

Cf. n°s 1173, 6023

§ 3. Industry, mining and transportation.

6688. ABEILLE (Renato). Storia delle telecomunicazioni italiane e della Sip 1964–1994. Introduzione di Piero BREZZI. Milano, F. Angeli, 99, 153 p.

6689. ANNIBALDI (Cesare), BERTA (Giuseppe). Grande impresa e sviluppo italiano. Studi per i cento anni della Fiat. Bologna, Il Mulino, 99, 2 vol., 428 p., 390 p.

6690. British industrial decline (The). Ed by Jean-Pierre DORMOIS and Michael DINTENFASS. London a. New York, Routledge, 99, XII-234 p. (figs., tabs.).

6691. BRKLJAČA (Seka). Bosanskohercegovački boksit kao strateška sirovina (1981.–1945). (Bosnian-Hercegovinian bauxite as a strategic raw material, 1918–1945). *Časopis za suvremenu povijest*, 99, 31, 2, p. 341-357.

6692. BROMBERG (Joan Lisa). NASA and the Space industry. Baltimore, Johns Hopkins U. P., 99, X-247 p.

6693. CASTRONOVO (Valerio). Fiat 1899–1999. Un secolo di storia italiana. Milano, Rizzoli, 99, XXVIII-2090 p.

6694. FELDENKIRCHEN (Wilfried). Siemens 1918–1945. Columbus, Ohio State U. P., 99, XVI-714 p. (Historical perspectives on business enterprise).

6695. FORBERGER (Rudolf). Die industrielle Revolution in Sachsen 1800–1861. Band 2/1. Die Revolution der Produktivkräfte in Sachsen 1831–1861. Leipzig, Verlag der Sächsischen Akademie der Wissenschaften zu Leipzig u. Stuttgart, Steiner, 99, 612 p. (Quellen und Forschungen zur sächsischen Geschichte, 18).

6696. GARÇON (Anne-Françoise). Mine et métal, 1780–1880. Les non-ferreux et l'industrialisation. Rennes, Presses Universitaires de Rennes, 99, 276 p.

6697. GATTI (Luciana). Navi e cantieri della repubblica di Genova (secoli XVI–XVIII). Genova, Brigati, 99, 421 p.

6698. GESTWA (Klaus). Proto-Industrialisierung in Russland. Wirtschaft, Herrschaft und Kultur in Ivanovo und Pavlovo, 1741–1932. Göttingen, Vandenhoeck & Ruprecht, 99, 680 p. (Veröffentlichungen des Max-Planck-Instituts für Geschichte, 149).

6699. HASEGAWA (Akira). Syoyu jozogyo-shi-kenkyu no aratana doko ni tsuite. (The recent studies in the history of soy sauce manufacture in modern Japan). *In:* Higashi to nishi no shoyu-shi [Cf. n° 6701], p.1-20.

6700. HEYWOOD (Anthony). Modernising Lenin's Russia: economic reconstruction, foreign trade, and the railways. Cambridge, Cambridge U. P., 99, XVIII-328 p. (Cambridge Russian, Soviet, and post-Soviet studies, 105).

6701. Higashi to nishi no shoyu-shi. (The history of soy sauce manufacture in modern Japan). Ed. by Reiko HAYASHI and Masatoshi AMANO. Tokyo, Yoshikawa Kobunkan, 99, 286 p. [Cf. n° <choice> 6699.]

6702. IGOLKIN (Aleksandr A.). Otechestvennaja neftjanaja promyshlennost' v 1917–1920 godakh. (The oil industry of Russia in 1917–1920). With intr. by Ju. P. BOKAREV; Ros. gos. gumanit. un-t, In-t upravlenija i prava. Moskva, [s. n.], 99, 187 p. (bibl.; ind.). – IDEM Sovetskaja neftjanaja promyshlennost' v 1921–1928 godakh. (The oil industry of Soviet Russia in 1921–1928). Ros. gos. gumanit. un-t, In-t upravlenija i prava. Moskva, [s. n.], 99, 183 p. (bibl.; ind.).

6703. Institutions and the transport and communications industries: State and private actors in the making of institutional patterns, 1850–1990. Ed. by Lena ANDERSSON-SKOG and Olle KRANTZ. Nantucket, Science History Publications, 99, XIX-359 p.

6704. JANSEN (Michael). De industriële ontwikkeling in Nederland 1800–1850. Amsterdam, Nederlandsch Economisch-Historisch Archief, 99, 430 p. (Reconstructie Nationale Rekeningen).

6705. KASUYA (Makoto). Kindaiteki koyo no keisei: Meiji zenki no Mitsui Ginko wo chushin ni. (The emergence of modern employment: the case of the Mitsui Bank in the Meiji era). *Mitsui Bunko Ronsô*, 99, 33, p. 109-156.

6706. MAC CRAY (W. Patrick). Glassmaking in Renaissance Venice: the fragile craft. Aldershot, Ashgate, 99, XII-240 p. (ill., fig., tables, bibl.).

6707. MALINEN (Ismo). Laivanvarustus Helsingissä 1700-luvun puolivälissä. Shipowners in Helsinki in the mid 18th century. *Nautica Fennica*, 99, p. 102-137. (ill.).

6708. MARZAGALLI (Silvia). "Les boulevards de la fraude". Le négoce maritime et le Blocus continental, 1806–1813. Bordeaux, Hambourg, Livourne. Villeneuve d'Ascq, Presses Universitaires de Septentrion, 99, 391 p.

6709. MIERZEJEWSKI (Alfred C.). The most valuable asset of the Reich. A history of the German National Railway. Vol. 1. 1920–1932. Chapel Hill a. London, University of North Carolina Press, 99, XX-482 p.

6710. MOHUN (Arwen P.). Steam laundries: gender, technology, and work in the United States and Great Britain, 1880–1940. Baltimore, Johns Hopkins U. P., 99, X-348 p. (Johns Hopkins studies in the history of technology, 25).

6711. MORAGLIO (Massimo). L'autostrada Torino-Milano (1923–1933): i progetti e la costruzione. *Storia urbana*, 99, 86, p. 103-121.

6712. Navi, corsari, pirati e schiavi in Adriatico. Atti del convegno di San Benedetto del Tronto, 21–22 novembre 1998. Introduzione di Renzo PACI. *Proposte e ricerche*, 99, 22, 43, p. 7-252.

6713. NEIERTZ (Nicolas). La coordination des transports en France de 1918 à nos jours. Paris, Imprimerie nationale, Comité pour l'histoire économique et financière de la France, 99, 798 p.

6714. OJALA (Jari). Tehokasta liiketoimintaa Pohjanmaan pikkukaupungeissa. Purjemerenkulun kannattavuus ja tuottavuus 1700–1800-luvulla. (Efficient business activity in small Ostrobothnian towns. Profitability and productivity of shipping by sail during the eighteenth and nineteenth century). Helsinki, SHS, 99, 452 p. (Bibliotheca historica, 40).

6715. PEARCE (Adrian J.). Huancavelica 1700–1759: administrative reform of the mercury Industry in early Bourbon Peru. *Hispanic American historical review*, 99, 79, 4, p. 669-702.

6716. POHL (Manfred). Von Stambul nach Bagdad. Die Geschichte einer berühmten Eisenbahn. Unt. Mitarbeit v. Angelika RAAB-REBENTISCH. München u. Zürich, Piper, 99, 189 p.

6717. RINGMAR (Richard). Gästriklands bergsmän, Kronan och handelskapitalet: aktörer och institutionella spelregler i bergsmansbruket 1650–1870. (Les Mineurs du Gästrikland, la Couronne et le capital commercial: acteurs et règles du jeu institutionnelles dans l'exploitation minière de 1650 à 1870). Uppsala, Acta Universitatis Upsaliensis, Univ. Bibliotek, 99, 274 p. (ill.).

6718. ROY (Tirthankar). Traditional industry in the economy of colonial India. New York, Cambridge U. P., 99, XI-252 p. (Cambridge studies in Indian history and society, 5).

6719. RUGAFIORI (Paride). Imprenditori e manager nella storia d'Italia. Roma e Bari, Laterza, 99, 147 p. (Storia contemporanea. Biblioteca essenziale, 22).

6720. SAGER (Fritz). Spannungsfelder und Leitbilder in der schweizerischen Schwerverkehrspolitik 1932 bis 1998. *Schweizerische Zeitschrift für Geschichte*, 99, 49, 3, p. 307-332.

6721. SMAIL (John). Merchants, markets and manufacture: the English wool textile industry in the eighteenth century. New York, St. Martin's Press, 99, X-198 p.

6722. STEVENSON (David). War by timetable? The railway race before 1914. *Past and present*, 99, 162, p. 163-194.

6723. Storia delle Aziende Elettriche Municipali. A cura di Piero BOLCHINI. Roma e Bari, Laterza, 99, 828 p.

6724. SUGIYAMA (Shinya), YAMADA (Izumi). Seishigyo no hatten to nenryo-mondai: Kindai Suwa no kankyokeizai-shi. (The problem of fuel: an economic history of the environment with reference to the Nagano silk reeling industry). *Shakai Keizai Shigaku*, 99, 65, 2, p. 3-23.

6725. TOMEK (Prokop). Československý uran 1945–1989. Těžba a prodej československého uranu v éře komunismu. (Czechoslovak uranium, 1945–1989. Its mining and sale in the Communist era). Ed. Ladislava KREMLIČKOVÁ. Praha, Úřad dokumentace a vyšetřování zločinů komunismu PČR, 99, 76 p. (Sešity Úřadu dokumentace a vyšetřování zločinů komunismu PČR, 1).

6726. VASTA (Michelangelo). Innovazione tecnologica e capitale umano in Italia (1880–1914). Le traiettorie della seconda rivoluzione industriale. Bologna, Il Mulino, 99, 283 p.

6727. WAGNER (Dieter). Innovation und Standort. Geschichte und Unternehmensstrategien der Chemischen Fabrik Griesheim 1856–1925. Darmstadt, Hessisches

Wirtschaftsarchiv, 99, 383 p. (Schriften zur Hessischen Wirtschafts- und Unternehmensgeschichte, 4).

6728. WIGHTMAN (Clare). More than munitions: women, work and the engineering industries, 1900–1950. London a. New York, Longman, 99, VIII-207 p. (fig., tab.).

Cf. nos 4037, 5047, 6057, 8041

§ 4.Trade.

** 6729. Firma Felix (Die) und Jakob Grimmel zu Konstanz und Menningen. Quellen und Materialen zu einer oberdeutschen Handelsgesellschaft aus der Mitte des 16. Jahrhunderts. Hrsg. v. Frank GÖTTMANN und Andreas NUTZ. Stuttgart, Steiner, 99, 267 p. (Deutsche Handelsakten des Mittelalters und der Neuzeit, 20).

6730. BADEL (Laurence). Un milieu libéral et européen: le grand commerce français, 1925-1948. Préf. de René GIRAULT. Paris, Comité pour l'histoire économique et financière de la France, 99, XVIII-576 p. (Histoire économique et financière de de la France: Etude générales).

6731. BAGHDIANTZ MAC CABE (Ina). The Shah's silk for Europe's silver: the Eurasian trade of the Julfa Armenians in Safavid Iran and India (1530–1750). Georgia, Scholars Press, 99, XXII-414 p. (Armenians texts and studies, 15).

6732. BIENTINESI (Fabrizio). La tariffa del 1921 e le associazioni degli industriali italiani: ricerca della protezione, equilibri interni e rapporti col mondo politico, 1913–1923. *Rivista di storia economica,* 99, 15, 2, p. 167-205.

6733. Business history in Latin America: the experience of seven countries. Ed. by Carlos DÁVILA and Rory MILLER. Liverpool, Liverpool U.P., 99, XIV-241 p. (figs.).

6734. Consumo, condiciones de vida y comercialización. Cataluña y Castilla, siglos XVII–XIX. Ed. por Jaume TORRES y Bartolomé YUN. Valladolid, Junta de Castilla y León, 99, 436 p. (Estudios de Historia).

6735. ERDOĞRU (Akif). Ondokuzuncu yüzyılda Osmanlı İmparatorluğunda hafta pazarları ve panayırlar. (Marchés hebdomadaires et foires dans l'Empire Ottoman au XIXe siècle). İzmir, Ege Üniversitesi Edebiyat Fakültesi, 99, III-174 p.

6736. FERRER (André). Les contrebandiers sur la frontière franco-suisse au XVIIIe siècle. *In*: Mobilitäten = Mobilités [Cf. n° 6962], p. 35-46.

6737. FLEET (Kate). European and Islamic trade in the early Ottoman state: the merchants of Genoa and Turkey. Cambridge, Cambridge U.P., 99, IX-204 p. (tab.).

6738. FODOR (Pál). Málta kalózok, török rabok és francia kereskedõk a Földközi tengeren a XVII. Század elején. (Pirates of Malta, Turkish prisoners and French traders on the Mediterranean Sea in the XVII century). *Történelmi Szemle*, 99, 3-4, p. 369-387.

6739. GRANT (Jonathan A.). Big business in Russia: the Putilov company in late imperial Russia, 1868–1917. Pittsburgh, University of Pittsburgh Press, 99, VIII-203 p. (Pitt series in Russian and East European studies).

6740. HACHEZ-LEROY (Florence). L'Aluminium français. L'invention d'un marché, 1911–1983. Paris, CNRS Ed., 99, 376 p.

6741. HAY (Douglas). The State and the market in 1800: Lord Kenyon and Mr. Waddington. *Past and present*, 99, 162, p. 101-162.

6742. Inventing Nanjing Road: Commercial Culture in Shanghai, 1900–1945. Ed. by Sherman COCHRAN. Ithaca, Cornell University East Asia Program, 99, 252 p. (Cornell East Asia series, 103).

6743. KAURANEN (Kaisa). Rahvas, kauppahuone, esivalta. Katovuodet pohjoisessa Suomessa 1830-luvulla. (The commoners, the authorities and the trading house. The crop failure years in Northern Finland in the 1830's.). Helsinki, SHS, 99, 180 p. (Hist. tutkim., 204). (ill., maps).

6744. KOZLOVA (Natalija V.). Rossijskij absolutizm i kupechestvo v XVIII v. (20-e–nachalo 60-kh godov). (Russian absolutism and the merchants, 1720–the beginning of the 1750es). Moskovskij gos. un-t im. M.V. Lomonosova, Ist. f-t; Ros. gos arkhiv drevnikh aktov. Moskva, Arkheograficheskij tsentr, 99, 382 p. (ind.).

6745. KUWABARA (Kanji). Igirisu kanzei kaikaku undo no shi-teki bunseki. (A historical analysis of the tariff-reform campaign of Chamberlain). Fukuoka, Kyushu U. P., 99, 430 p.

6746. LANARO (Paola). I mercati nella Repubblica veneta: economie cittadine e Stato territoriale, secoli XVI–XVIII. Venezia, Marsilio, 99, 143 p. (Saggi Marsilio. Storia).

6747. MARSH (Peter T.). Bargaining on Europe. Britain and the first common market, 1860–1892. New Haven a. London, Yale U. P., 99, VIII-246 p.

6748. MATTHEE (Rudolph P.). The politics of trade in Safavid Iran: silk for silver, 1600–1730. New York, Cambridge U. P., 99, XXI-290 p. (Cambridge studies in Islamic civilization).

6749. Merchants, companies and trade. Europe and Asia in the early modern era. Ed. by Sushil CHAUDHURY and Michel MORINEAU. Cambridge, Cambridge U. P., 99, XI-330 p. [Cf. n° <choice> 6751.]

6750. MILLER (Judith A.). Mastering the market: the State and the grain trade in Northern France, 1700–1860. New York, Cambridge U. P., 99, XVIII-334 p.

6751. MORINEAU (Michel). Eastern and Western merchants from the sixteenth to the eighteenth centuries. *In*: Merchants, companies and trade [Cf. n° 6749], p. 116-144.

6752. PANZAC (Daniel). Les corsaires barbaresques. La fin d'une épopée (1800–1820). Paris, Ed. du CNRS, 99, 311 p.

6753. PENYAK (Lee M.). Safe harbors and compulsory custody: 'Casas de Depósito' in Mexico, 1750–1865. *Hispanic American historical review*, 99, 79, 1, p. 83-100.

6754. SHIRAKIZAWA (Asahiko). Daikyoko-ki Nihon no tsusho mondai. (The Japanese trade problem during the world depression). Tokyo, Ochanomizu Shobo, 99, 394 p.

Cf. n° 1208

§ 5. Agriculture and agricultural problems.

* 6755. BIARD (Michel), BIANCHI (Serge). La terre et les paysans pendant la Révolution française: une orientation bibliographique. *Annales historiques de la Révolution française*, 99, 315, p. 163-182.

* 6756. Bibliographie rurale 1997–1999. *Ruralia*, 99, 4, p. 183-189; 99, 5, p. 187-206.

6757. ALLEN (Robert C.). Tracking the agricultural revolution in England. *Economic History Review*, 99, 52, 2, p. 209-235.

6758. AYALA (César J.). American sugar kingdom: the plantation economy of the Spanish Caribbean, 1898–1934. Chapel Hill a. London, University of North Carolina Press, 99, XII-321 p. (ill, maps).

6759. BARBERIS (Corrado). Le campagne italiane dall'Ottocento a oggi. Roma e Bari, Laterza, 99, VII-538 p.

6760. BIRTLES (Sara). Common land, poor relief and enclosures: the use of manorial resources in fulfilling parish obligations 1601-1834. *Past and present*, 99, 165, p. 74-106.

6761. BRONSTEIN (Jamie L.). Land reform and working-class experience in Britain and the United States, 1800-1862. Stanford, Stanford U.P., 99, XII-372 p.

6762. BRUSSE (Paul). Overleven door Ondernemen: De agrarische geschiedenis van de Over-Betuwe 1650–1850. Wageningen, Landbouwuniversiteit, 99, 566 p. (A. A. G. Bijdragen, 38).

6763. CIOBOTEA (Dinică). Istoria moşnenilor. (The history of freeholder peasants). Vol. 1. Partea I (1829–1912). Craiova, Editura Universitaria, 99, 228 p.

6764. Confagricoltura (La) nella storia d'Italia: dalle origini dell'associazionismo agricolo nazionale ad oggi. A cura di Sandro ROGARI. Bologna, Il Mulino, 99, 1013 p.

6765. GARAVAGLIA (Juan Carlos). Un siglo de estancias en la campaña de Buenos Aires: 1751–1853. *Hispanic American historical review*, 99, 79, 4, p. 703-734.

6766. KENT (J.). The rural 'middling sort' in early modern England, circa 1640-1740: some economic, political and socio-cultural characteristics. *Rural history*, 99, 10, p. 19-54.

6767. KHUN SONG (Byung). Cuntinuity and change in English rural society: the formation of poor law unions in Oxfordshire. *English historical review*, 99, 114, 456, p. 314-338.

6768. KOTSONIS (Yanni). Making peasants backward: agricultural cooperatives and the Agrarian question in Russia, 1861–1914. Basingstoke, Macmillan, 99, X-245 p.

6769. Landgemeinden im Übergang zum Modernen Staat. Vergleichende Mikrostudien im linksrheinischen Raum. Hrsg. v. Franz NORBERT, Bernd-Stefan GREWE u. Michael KNAUFF. Mainz, von Zabern, 99, [s. p.]. (Trierer Historische Forschungen, 36).

6770. LAURIA-SANTIAGO (Aldo A.). An Agrarian Republic: commercial agriculture and the politics of peasant communities in El Salvador, 1823-1914. Pittsburgh, University of Pittsburgh Press, 99, VIII-326 p. (Pitt Latin American series).

6771. MORICEAU (Jean-Marc). La terre et les paysans aux XVIIe et XVIIIe siècles. Guide d'histoire agraire. Rennes, Presses univ. Rennes, 99, 320 p.

6772. NICHOLAS (Tom). Businessmen and land ownership in the late nineteenth century. *Economic history review*, 99, 52, 1, p. 27-44.

6773. PALLOT (Judith). Land reform in Russia, 1906–1917. Peasant responses to Stolypin's Project of rural transformation. Oxford, Clarendon Press, 99, 280 p.

6774. RAJŠP (Vincenc). Slovenija na vojaškem zemljevidu 1763–1787. Zv. 5, Sekcije 148, 149, 150, 161, 162, 163, 164, 173, 174, 175, 192, 193, 194, 195, 199, 200, 217, 218: karte = Josephinische Landesaufnahme 1763–1787 für das Gebiet der Republik Slowenien. Bd. 5, Sektionen 148, 149, 150, 161, 162, 163, 164, 173, 174, 175, 192, 193, 194, 195, 199, 200, 217, 218: Karten. Ljubljana, Znanstvenoraziskovalni center SAZU, Arhiv Republike Slovenije, 99. 19 vol., [s. p.].

6775. RAVINA (Mark). Land and lordship in early modern Japan. Stanford, Stanford U. P., 99, XX-278 p.

6776. SALVATICI (Silvia). Contadine dell'Italia fascista: preesenze, ruoli, immagini. Presentazione di Renato ZANGHERI. Torino, Rosenberg & Sellier, 99, 253 p. (Storia del lavoro, 6).

6777. SHOJI (Shunsaku). Nihon nochi kaikaku-shi kenkyu. (The history of land reform in Showa Japan). Tokyo, Ochanomizu Shobo, 99, 429 p.

6778. Terre (La) et les paysans, France et Grand-Bretagne, XVIIe–XVIIIe siècles. Actes de la Journée d'études de la S.H.M.C., 7 novembre 1998, Paris. *Bulletin de la Société d'histoire moderne*, 99, 1-2, p. 3-129.

6779. Terre (La) et les paysans. Productions et exploitations agricoles aux XVIIe et XVIIIe siècles en

France et en Angleterre. Actes du Colloque de 1998, Aix-en-Provence. A la mémoire de Jean Jacquart (1928–1998). *Association des historiens modernistes de l'Université*, 99, 24, 195 p.

6780. WADE MARTINS (Susanna), WILLIAMSON (Tom). Roots of change: farming and the landscape in East Anglia, c. 1700-1870. Exeter, British Agricultural History Society, 99, X-214 p. (tabs, figs) (Agricultural History review Supplement, ser. 2).

6781. Zemědělské družstevnictví. Kolektivizace zemědělství – vznik JZD 1951. (Agricultural cooperatives. The collectivization of agriculture and the establishment of the Standard Farming Co-operative (JZD), 1951). Ed. by Jana PŠENIČKOVÁ. Praha, Státní ústřední archiv, 99, 246 p.

Cf. n°s 871, 892

§ 6. Money and finance.

* 6782. NOIRET (Serge). Publications on financial history for 1996. Publications on financial history for 1997. *Financial history review*, 99, 6, 2, p. 223-257.

6783. ALDCROFT (Derek). El problema de la deuda externa desde una perspectiva histórica. *Ciclos*, 99, 9, 1, p. 3-28.

6784. ANDRÈS UCENDO (José Ignacio). La fiscalidad en Castilla en el siglo XVII: los servicios de Millones. Lejona, Universidad del País Vasco, 99, 265 p. (Estudios de historia medieval y moderna).

6785. ARIAS (José Carlos). Reformas financieras en América Latina 1990–1998. *Desarrollo económico*, 99, 39, 155, p. 361-385.

6786. BÄHR (Johannes). Der Goldhandel der Dresdner Bank im Zweiten Weltkrieg. Unter Mitarb. v. Michael C. SCHNEIDER. Ein Bericht des Hannah-Arendt-Instituts. Leipzig u. Weimar, Gustav Kiepenheuer, 99, 232 p.

6787. Banche popolari (Le) nella storia d'Italia: atti della quinta Giurnata di studio Luigi Luzzatti per la storia dell'Italia contemporanea: Venezia, 7 novembre 1997. A cura di Paolo PECORARI. Venezia, Istituto veneto di scienze, lettere ed arti, 99, X-236 p. (Biblioteca luzzattiana, 8).

6788. BNL (La) tra guerre coloniali e guerra mondiale 1937–1945. Saggio di Marcello DE CECCO; documenti a cura di Maria Rosaria OSTUNI. Firenze, Giunti, 99, 742 p. (Collana storica del gruppo BNL, 3).

6789. BONELLI (Franco), CERRITO (Elio). L'emergere di una funzione pubblica di controllo monetario. La Banca d'Italia dal 1894 al 1913. *Rivista di storia economica*, 99, 15, 3, p. 289-315.

6790. BOOT (H. M.). Real incomes of the British middle class, 1760-1850: the experience of clerks at the East India Company. *Economic history review*, 99, 52, 4, p. 638-668.

6791. BUGROV (Aleksandr V.). Moskovskaja kontora Gosudarstvennogo banka Rossijskoj imperii: Razvitie seti uchrezhdenij Gosudarstvennogo banka Rossijskoj imperii: Istoricheskij ocherk. (The Moscow Bureau of the State Bank of the Russian Empire: the development of the network of institutions of the State Bank of the Russan Empire). Moskva, [s. n.], 99, 224 p. (ill., bibl.).

6792. CERRITO (Elio). Cambio, ciclo, efficienza, istituzioni: problemi di politica monetaria nell'Italia di fine Ottocento. Appunti su alcune evidenze empiriche. *Rivista storica italiana*, 99, 111, 2, p. 476-542.

6793. Christian III:s rentemesterregnskaber. (Les Comptes des intendants de finances sous Christian III). Red. par Søren BALLE et Nils Geert BOLWIG. Århus, Selskabet for udgivelse af kilder til dansk historie, 99, 4 vol., 1420 p.

6794. COLZI (Francesco). Il debito pubblico del Campidoglio: finanza comunale e circolazione dei titoli a Roma fra Cinque e Seicento. Napoli, Edizioni scientifiche italiane, 99, 379 p. (Studi e strumenti per la storia di Roma, 1).

6795. Crédit et société: les sources, les techniques et les hommes (XIVe–XVIe siècles). Actes des Rencontres d'Asti-Chambéry, 24–27 septembre 1998. Publié sous la dir. de Jean-Marie CAUCHIES. Neuchâtel, Centre européen d'Etudes bourguignonnes, 99, 270 p.

6796. DE ROSA (Luigi). Le origini del sistema delle Casse di risparmio ordinario in Italia. *Storia economica*, 99, 2, p. 517-572.

6797. DUBUIS (Olivier F.). Le faux monnayage dans le Pays de Vaud (1715–1750): crime et répression. Lausanne, Editions du Zèbre, 99, 216 p. (Etudes d'histoire moderne, 1).

6798. FEIERTAG (O.). Banques centrales et relations internationales au XXe siècle. *In*: Monnaie et relations internationales. 2 [Cf. n° 7277], p. 355-375.

6799. FÉLIX (Joël). Finances et politique au siècle des Lumières. Le ministère L'Averdy, 1763–1768. Paris, Ministère de l'Economie, des Finances et de l'Industrie, 99, XIV-559 p.

6800. GOLDSMITH (Raymond W.), ZECCHINI (Salvatore). The national balance sheet of Italy (1861–1973). *Rivista di storia economica*, 99, 15, 1, p. 3-19.

6801. GRIN (G.). L'évolution du système monétaire international dans les années 1960. *In*: Monnaie et relations internationales. 2 [Cf. n° 7277], p. 377-392.

6802. GÜNEŞ (Mehmet). XIX. Yüzyıl Başlarında Afyon'da Fiyatlar (1806–1830). (Les prix à Afyon aux débuts du XIXe siècle). *Afyon Kocatepe Üniversitesi Sosyal Bilimler Dergisi*, 99, 2, p. 91-106.

6803. HAMON (Philippe). «Messieurs des finances». Les grands officiers de finance dans la France de la Renaissance. Paris, Comité pour l'histoire économique et financière de la France, 99, XXXVII-506 p.

6804. KANÇAL (S.), THOBIE (J.). L'impossible homogénéisation du système monétaire ottoman. *In*: Monnaie et relations internationales. 1 [Cf. n° 7277], p. 251-268.

6805. KARRAS (G.). Taxes and growth in Europe: 1885–1987. *Journal of European economic history*, 99, 28, 2, p. 365-382.

6806. KOKKINANIKS (Gh.). Nomisma kai Politiki stin Ellada 1830–1910. (Currency and politics in Greece 1830–1910). Athena, Ekdoseis Alexandreia, 99, 653 p. (Historikc vivliotheke).

6807. MARICHAL (Carlos). De la banca privada a la gran banca. Antonio Basagorti en México y España, 1880–1911. *Historia mexicana*, 99, 48, 191, p. 767-794.

6808. MARTINAT (Monica). Le blé du pape: système annonaire et logiques économiques à Rome à l'époque moderne. *Annales*, 99, 54, 1, p. 219-244.

6809. MÜLLER (Martin M.). Bausparen in Deutschland zwischen Inflation und Währungsreform 1924–1948. Wohnungsbaufinanzierung im Spannungsfeld zwischen Staat und privaten und öffentlichen Bausparunternehmen. München, Beck, 99, 336 p. (Schriftenreihe zur Zeitschrift für Unternehmensgeschichte, 4).

6810. NAKABAYASHI (Masachi). Kikai seishigyo bokko-ki ni okeru nikawase-tatekae-kin kyokyu seido no keisei. (The institution of advances on documentary bills during the rise of silk reeling industry). *Keiei Shigaku*, 99, 33, 4, p. 52-80.

6811. NOVOTNÝ (Jiří), ŠOUŠA (Jiří). Czechoslovak National Bank (1926–1938) – guardian of fiscal and financial stability of the first Czechoslovak Republic. *Prager wirtschafts- und sozialhistorische Mitteilungen = Prague economic and social history papers*, 99, 5, p. 129-151.

6812. ÖNSOY (Rıfat). Mali tutsaklığa giden yol: Osmanlı borçları (1854–1914). (La voie qui mène à la captivité financière: les dettes ottomans), Ankara, Turhan Kitabevi, 99, 324 p.

6813. OSTUNI (Nicola). Napoli comune, Napoli capitale. Le finanze della città e del Regno delle Due Sicilie. Napoli, Luguori, 99, 272 p.

6814. PEZZOLO (Luciano). Government debts and trust. French kings and Roman popes as borrowers, 1520–1660. *Rivista di storia economica*, 99, 15, 3, p. 233-261.

6815. PILUSO (Giandomenico). L'arte dei banchieri. Moneta e credito a Milano da Napoleone all'Unità. Milano, F. Angeli, 99, 256 p.

6816. Ricerche per la storia della Banca d'Italia. Vol. 7. Stabilità e sviluppo negli anni Cinquanta. 3. Politica bancaria del sistema finanziario. A cura di Franco COTULA. Vol. 8. La Banca d'Italia in Africa: introduzione all'attività dell'istituto di emissione nelle colonie dall'età crispina alla seconda guerra mondiale. A cura di Ercole TUCCIMEI. Roma, Laterza, 99, 2 vol., XXX-VI-951 p., XII-358 p. (Collana storica della Banca d'Italia. Contributi, 8).

6817. State (The), the financial system and economic modernization. Ed. by Richard SYLLA, Richard TILLY and Gabriel TORTELLA. Cambridge, Cambridge U.P., 99, XIV-295 p. (figs, tabs).

6818. UGOCHUKWU UCHE (Chibuike). Foreign banks, Africans, and credit in colonial Nigeria, c. 1890-1912. *Economic history review*, 52, 99, 4, p. 669-691.

6819. WRIGHT (J. F.). British government borrowing in wartime, 1750–1815. *Economic history review*, 99, 52, 2, p. 355-361.

6820. YOSHIOKA (Akihiko). Teikoku shugi to Kokusai tsuka taisei. (Imperialism and international currency system). Nagoya, University of Nagoya Press, 99, 274 p.

Cf. n°s 1039, 4520, 6705, 7277, 7339

§ 7. Demography and urban history.

6821. BENDIKAT (Elfi). Öffentliche Nahverkehrspolitik in Berlin und Paris 1890–1914: Strukturbedingungen, politische Konzeptionen und Realisierungsprobleme. Berlin, W. de Gruyter, 99, XVI-666 p. (ill., maps). (Veröffentlichungen der Historischen Kommission zu Berlin, 96).

6822. Berlin: die Hauptstadt: Vergangenheit und Zukunft einer europäischen Metropole. Hrsg. v. Werner SÜSS und Ralf RYTLEWSKI. Berlin, Nicolai, 99, 911 p.

6823. Bild (Das) der Stadt in der Neuzeit 1400–1800. Hrsg. v. Wolfgang BEHRINGER und Bernd ROECK. München, Beck, 99, 509 p.

6824. BOYD (Robert). The coming of the Spirit of Pestilence: introduced infectious diseases and population decline among Northwest Coast Indians, 1774–1874. Seattle, University of Washington Press a. Vancouver, University of British Columbia Press, 99, XV-403 p.

6825. Buenos Aires 1910. El imaginario para una gran capital. Ed. por Margarita GUTMAN y Thomas REESE. Buenos Aires, EUDEBA, 99, 404 p. (ill.).

6826. BURROWS (Edwin G.), WALLACE (Mike). Gotham: a history of New York City to 1898. Oxford, Oxford U. P., 99, XXIV-1383 p.

6827. CARTOSIO (Bruno). Santa Fe, New Mexico: "un luogo raro al mondo". *Storia urbana*, 99, 87, p. 97-122.

6828. City (The) in central Europe: culture and society from 1800 to the present. Ed. by Malcolm GEE, Tim KIRK and Jill STEWARD. Brookfield, Ashgate, 99, X-276 p.

6829. ĆOSIĆ (Stjepan). Dubrovnik nakon pada Republike (1808–1848). (Dubrovnik after the fall of the Republic, 1808–1848). Dubrovnik, Zavod za povijesne znanosti Hrvatske akademije znanosti i umjetnosti, 99, 404 p.

6830. DAVIS (Diane). El leviatán urbano. La ciudad de México en el siglo XX. México, Fondo de Cultura Económica, 99, 530 p. (ill.).

6831. DAY (Jared N.). Urban castles: tenement housing and urban landlord activism in New York city, 1890–1943. New York, Columbia U. P., 99, X-262 p. (Columbia history of urban life).

6832. Documente privind istoria oraşului Braşov. Vol. 9. Documente de breaslă. 1420–1580. Quellen zur Geschichte der Stadt Kronstadt. Band 9. Zunfturkunden. 1420–1580. Ediţie îngrijită de Gernot NUSSBÄCHER şi Elisabeta MARIN. Braşov, Editura Aldus, 99, 459 p.

6833. FAUVE-CHAMOUX (Antoinette). Comportements démographiques différentiels et statut successoral dans les Pyrénées centrales. In: Alkotas a tarsadalomtudomanyok hataran, Emlekkotet a 80 eves Kovacsics Jozef tiszteletere. (Melanges offerts au Professeur J. Kovacsics). Budapest, ELTE Allam, 99, p. 41-52. – EADEM. La cohabitation des frères et sœurs en France préindustrielle. Miedzy polityka a kultura, 99, p. 211-224.

6834. FRANCHI (Michela). Edilizia popolare a Parma durante il ventennio fascista Storia urbana, 99, 86, p. 75-102

6835. FROIDEVAUX (Yves). Mobilité spatiale, immigration et croissance démographique: le Pays de Neuchâtel, 1750–1914. In: Mobilitäten = Mobilités [Cf. n° 6962], p. 64-86.

6836. GANIAGE (Jean). Beauvais au XVIIIe siècle. Population et cadre urbain. Paris, CNRS Ed., 99, 285 p.

6837. GRESLE-POULIGNY (Dominique). Un plan pour Mexico-Tenochtitlan. Les représentations de la cité et l'imaginaire européen (XVIe–XVIIIe siècles). Paris, L'Harmattan, 99, 361 p.

6838. Habiter la ville (XVIIe–XXe siècles). Ed. par Olivier FARON et Olivier ZELLER. Cahiers d'histoire, 99, 44, 4, p. 509-715.

6839. HEAD-KÖNIG (Anne-Lise). Les apports d'une immigration féminine traditionelle à la croissance des villes de la Suisse. Le personal de maison féminin (XVIIIe–début du XXe siècle). In: Mobilitäten = Mobilités [Cf. n° 6962], p. 47-63.

6840. Histoire des populations de l' Europe. Vol. 3. Les temps incertains 1914–1998. Ed. par J. P. BARDET et J. DUPÂQUIER. Paris, Fayard, 99, 729 p. [Cf. n° <sélection> 6859.]

6841. HOLTFRERICH (Carl-Ludwig). Finanzplatz Frankfurt. Von der mittelalterlichen Messestadt zum europäischen Bankenzentrum. Mit ein. Einl. v. Jürgen JESKE u. ein. Ausblick v. Friederich von METZLER. München, Beck, 99, 372 p.

6842. Juden in der Stadt. Hrsg. v. Fritz MAYRHOFER und Ferdinand OPPL. Linz u. Donau, Österreichischer Arbeitskreis für Stadtgeschichtsforschung, 99, XII-420 p. (Beiträge zur Geschichte der Städte Mitteleuropas, 15).

6843. KAPITSA (Sergej P.). Obshchaja teorija rosta chelovechestva: Skol'ko ljudej zhilo, zhivet i budet zhit' na zemle. (General theory of the growth of the humanity: how many people was, is and will be living on the earth?) Moskva, Nauka, 99, 190 p. (bibl.). [Intr. also in Eng.]

6844. KOMLOS (John), On the nature of the Malthusian threat in the eighteenth century. Economic history review, 52, 99, 4, p. 730-748.

6845. KOROVITSYNA (Natal'ja V.). Srednee pokolenie v sotsiokul'turnoj dinamike Vostochnoj Evropy vtoroj poloviny XX veka. (The generation born in 1950es in Eastern European socio-cultural dynamics of the 2nd half of the 20th century). Ed. Jurij S. NOVOPASHIN. Moskva, Logos, 99, 187 p. (plates; bibl.). [Eng. summary]

6846. Kyodai toshi rondon no bokko. (Rise of a megalopolis: London). Ed. by Kiyoshi SAKAMAKI, Toshio SAKATA [et al.]. Tokyo, Tosui Shobo, 99, 310 p.

6847. LUCASSEN (Leo), VERMEULEN (Floris). Immigranten en lokale arbeidsmarkt. Vreemdelingen in Den Haag, Leiden, Deventer en Alkmaar (1920–1940). CGM-working paper, 99, 1, 62 p.

6848. MASSAIA (Alberto Stefano). Edilizia economica e popolare nella città di Torino dall'Unità d'Italia alla seconda guerra mondiale. Bollettino storico-bibliografico subalpino, 99, 97, p. 315-370.

6849. MATHIEU (Jon). Bevölkerungsdichte, Städtedichte und Migration – die «fabrique d'hommes» neu besichtigt. In: Mobilitäten = Mobilités [Cf. n° 6962], p. 126-131.

6850. MEJÍA PAVONY (Germán Rodrigo). Los años del cambio: historia urbana de Bogotá, 1820–1910. Santa Fé de Bogotá, CEJA, Instituto Colombiano de Cultura Hispanica, 99, 498 p. (ill., maps)

6851. PALMOWSKI (Jan). Urban liberalism in imperial Germany: Frankfurt am Main, 1866–1914. Oxford, Oxford U. P., 99, XIV-391 p. (ill., diagrs., tabs). (Oxford historical monographs).

6852. Paysages urbains (XVIe–XXe siècles). T. 1. Actes du Colloque de Grasse, décembre 1998. Cahiers Méditerranée, 99, 59, p. 1-208

6853. Rivage (D'un) à l'autre. Villes et protestantisme dans l'aire atlantique (XVIe–XVIIe siècles). Sous la dir. de Guy MARTINIÈRE, Didier POTON et François SOUTY. Actes du Colloque de la Rochelle, 13–14 novembre 1998. Paris, Imprimerie nationale, 99, 301 p.

6854. SCHAMBACH (Karin). Von der Identifikation zur Entfremdung. Die Erfahrung städtischer Wirklichkeit im 19. Jahrhundert. Archiv für Kulturgeschichte, 99, 81, 1, p. 133-148.

6855. SCHNEER (Jonathan). London 1900: the imperial metropolis. New Haven a. London, Yale U. P., 99, IX-336 p.

6856. SEPPÄNEN (Maaria). Global scale, local place? The making of the historic centre of Lima into a world heritage site. Helsinki, Helsinki Institute of Development Studies, Univ. of Helsinki, 99, 146 p. (maps).

6857. STOWELL (David O.). Streets, railroads, and the Great Strike of 1877. Chicago, University of Chicago Press, 99, XII-181 p. (Historical studies of urban America).

6858. TANDETER (Enrique). Una villa colonial: Potosí en el siglo XVIII. In: Historias de la vida privada en Argentina. Tomo 1. País antiguo. De la colonia a 1870 [Cf. n° 1216], p.28-53.

6859. VAN POPPEL (F.). Les Pays-Bas. In: Histoire des Populations de l' Europe. Vol. III. Les temps incertains 1914-1998 [Cf. n° 6840], p. 413-424.

6860. VÖGELE (Jörg). Urban mortality change in England and Germany, 1870-1913. Liverpool, Liverpool U. P., 99, XVII-299 p., (fig., tab., pl.).

Cf. n°s 346, 5704, 6042, 6947

§ 8. Social history.

6861. AISENBERG (Andrew R.). Contagion: disease, government, and the "Social Question" in nineteenth-century France. Stanford, Stanford U. P., 99, VII-238 p.

6862. ANDERSON (Olive). State, civil society and separation in Victorian marriage. Past and present, 99, 163, p. 161-201.

6863. ARLETTAZ (Gérald). Ecrire la «question des étrangers» en Suisse. Schweizerische Zeitschrift für Geschichte, 99, 49, 4, p. 541-543.

6864. ASTARITA (Tommaso). Village justice: community, family, and popular culture in early modern Italy. Baltimore, Johns Hopkins U. P., 99, XXIV-305 p. (Johns Hopkins University studies in historical and political science, 3).

6865. BAILY (Samuel L.). Immigrants in the lands of promise: Italians in Buenos Aires and New York City, 1870-1914. Ithaca a. London, Cornell U. P., 99, XVII-308 p. (ill). (Cornell studies in comparative history).

6866. BARTH (Boris). Weder Bürgertum noch Adel. Zwischen Nationalstaat und kosmopolitischem Geschäft. Zur Gesellschaftsgeschichte der deutsch-jüdischen Hochfinanz vor dem Ersten Weltkrieg. Geschichte und Gesellschaft, 99, 25, 1, p. 94-122.

6867. BEAVER (D.). The great deer massacre: animals, honor, and communication in early modern England. Journal of British studies, 99, 38, p. 187-216.

6868. BÉLY (Lucien). La société des princes, XVIe–XVIIIe siècle. Paris, Fayard, 99, 651 p.

6869. BERTRAND (Michel). Grandeur et misère de l'office. Les officiers de finances de Nouvelle-Espagne (XVIIe–XVIIIe siècles). Paris, Publications de la Sorbonne, 99, 458 p.

6870. BJÖRKSTRAND (Carita). Kvinnans ställning i det finländska musiksamhället. Utbildningsmöjligheter och yrkesvillkor för kvinnliga organister, musikpedagoger och solister 1890-1939. (Women's status in the Finnish music life and their ability to pursue a career in the field of music, 1890-1939). Åbo. Åbo akademi 99, 356 p. (ill.). [English summary].

6871. BOLOVAN (Sorina-Paula). Familia în satul românesc din Transilvania în a doua jumătate a secolului al XIX-lea și începutul secolului XX. (The family in the Transylvanian Romanian village in the second half of the 19th–the beginning of the 20th century). Cluj-Napoca, Centrul de Studii Transilvane, 99, 395 p. (Bibliotheca Rerum Transsilvaniae 24).

6872. BONO (Salvatore). Schiavi musulmani nell'Italia moderna. Galeotti, vu' cumpra', domestici. Napoli, Edizioni Scientifiche Italiane, 99, XV-595 p.

6873. BRAGONI (Beatriz). Los hijos de la revolución. Familia, negocios y poder en Mendoza en el siglo XIX. Buenos Aires, Taurus, 99, 328 p.

6874. BRAKENSIEK (Stefan). Fürstendiener, Staatsbeamte, Bürger: Amstführung und Lebenswelt der Ortsbeamten in niederhessischen Kleinstädten, 1750-1830. Göttingen, Vandenhoeck & Ruprecht, 99, IX-538 p. (Bürgertum: Beiträge zur europäischen Gesellschaftsgeschichte, 12).

6875. BRATVOGEL (Friedrich (W.). Landadel und ländliches Bürgertum. Mecklenburg-Strelitz und Oberschwaben 1750-1850. Geschichte und Gesellschaft, 99, 25, 3, p. 404-428.

6876. BREWARD (Christopher). The hidden consumer: masculinities, fashion, and the city life, 1860-1914. Manchester, Manchester U. P., 99, IX-278 p. (Studies in design and material culture).

6877. BROERS (Michael). Sexual politics and political ideology under the Savoyard monarchy, 1814-1821. English historical review, 99, 114, 457, p. 607-635.

6878. BROWN (Michael K.). Race, money, and the American Welfare State. Ithaca, Cornell U. P., 99, XXII-381 p.

6879. BUCHSTEINER (Ilona). Pommerscher Adel im Wandel des 19. Jahrhunderts. Geschichte und Gesellschaft, 99, 25, 3, p. 343-374.

6880. CALDER (Lendol). Financing the American dream: a cultural history of consumer credit. Princeton, Princeton U. P., 99, XV-377 p.

6881. CÂMPEANU (Remus). Elitele românești din Transilvania veacului al XVIII-lea. (Romanian elites in Transylvania in the 18th century). Cluj-Napoca, Editura Presa Universitară Clujeană, 99, 458 p.

6882. CANNADINE (David). The rise and fall of class in Britain. New York, Columbia U. P., 99, XV-293 p.

6883. CAPP (Bernard). The double standard revisited: plebeian women and male sexual reputation in early modern England. *Past and present*, 99, 162, p. 70-100.

6884. CAPUZZO (Ester). Gli ebrei e la società italiana. Comunità e istituzioni tra Ottocento e Novecento. Roma, Carocci, 99, 188 p.

6885. CARDOZA (Anthony L.). Patrizi in un mondo plebeo. La nobiltà piemontese nell'Italia liberale. Roma, Donzelli, 99, XXII-263 p.

6886. CAROLI (Dorena). Socialisme et protection sociale: une tautologie? L'enfance abandonnée en URSS (1917-1931). *Annales*, 99, 54, 6, p. 1291-1316.

6887. CASEY (James). Early modern Spain. A social history. London a. New York, Routledge, 99, VI-305 p.

6888. Charité (La) en pratique: Chrétiens français et allemands sur le terrain social; XIXe-XXe siècles. Ed. par Isabelle von BUELTZINGSLOEWEN et Denis PELLETIER. Strasbourg, Presses Universitaires de Strasbourg, in association with La Mission Historique Française en Allemagne, Centre André Latreille, Université de Lyon 2, and Groupe de recherche E.M.S., Université de Lyon III, 99, 217 p. (Les mondes germaniques).

6889. CHOLVY (Gérard). Histoire des organisations et mouvements chrétiens de jeunesse en France XIXe-XXe siècle. Paris, Ed. du Cerf, 99, 419 p.

6890. CLUNAS (Craig). Modernity global and local: consumption and the rise of the West. [Review essay]. *American historical review*, 99, 104, 5, p. 1497-1511.

6891. Consumers against capitalism? Consumer cooperation in Europe, North America and Japan, 1840-1990. Ed. by Ellen FURLOUGH and Carl STRIKWERDA. Lanham a. Oxford, Rowman & Littlefield, 99, IX-377 p. (tab.).

6892. CONZE (Eckart). Adeliges Familienbewußtsein und Grundbesitz. Die Auflösung des Gräflich Bernstorffschen Fideikomisses Gartow nach 1919. *Geschichte und Gesellschaft*, 99, 25, 3, p. 455-479.

6893. COOK (Noble). El impacto de las enfermedades en el mundo andino del siglo XVI. *Histórica*, 99, 23, 2, p. 54-83.

6894. CREESE (Gillian). Contracting masculinity: gender, class, and race in a White-Collar Union, 1944-1994. New York, Oxford U. P., 99, VII-278 p. (Canadian social history series).

6895. CROWLEY (John E.). The sensibility of comfort. *American historical review*, 99, 104, 3, p. 749-782.

6896. DAM (Hanne). På trods: 100 års kvindehistorie. Danske kvinders Nationalråd 1899-1999. (Par défi: cent ans d'histoire des femmes. Le Conseil national des femmes danoises 1899-1999). København, Danske kvinders Nationalråd, 99, 276 p. (ill.).

6897. DE CLEMENTI (Andreina). Di qua e di là dell' oceano. Emigrazione e mercati nel Meridione (1860-1930). Roma, Carocci, 99, 142 p.

6898. DE REZENDE MARTINS (Estevão). Bürger und Bürgerlichkeit in der brasilianischen Geschichte der Neuzeit – 19. und 20. Jahrhundert. *Geschichte und Gegenwart*, 99, 18, p. 3-12.

6899. DEMİRAY (Emine). Türk sinemasında 1960-1990 yılları arasında çekilmiş filmlerde kentsel aile (Famille urbaine d'après les filmes turcs produits entres les annés 1960-1990). Eskişehir, Anadolu Üniversitesi Açıköğretim Fakültesi, 99, 295 p.

6900. DESAN (Suzanne). Reconstituting the social after the terror: family, property and the law in popular politics. *Past and present*, 99, 164, p. 81-121.

6901. Disorder in the court: trials and sexual conflict at the turn of the century. Ed. by George ROBB and Nancy ERBER. New York, New York U. P., 99, VIII-253 p.

6902. DOĞRU (Halime). "16-17. Yüzyıllarda Şer'iyye Sicilleri ve Kanunnamelere Göre Evlenme, Nişanlanma, Boşanma". (Mariage, fiançailles et divorce d'après les registres du Cadi aux XVIe et XVIIe siècles). *Anadolu Üniversitesi Fen Edebiyat Fakültesi Dergisi*, 99, 1, p. 39-54.

6903. DUCREUX (Marie-Élizabeth). Exil et conversion. Les trajectoires de vie d'émigrants tchèques à Berlin au 18e siècle. *Annales*, 99, 54, 4, p. 915-944.

6904. DUNLAP (Thomas R.). Nature and the English diaspora: environment and history in the United States, Canada, Australia, and New Zealand. Cambridge, Cambridge U. P., 99, XV-350 p. (ill., maps). (Studies in environment and history).

6905. DURUZ (Jean). Food as nostalgia. Eating the fifties and sixties. *Australian historical studies*, 99, 30, 113, p. 231-250.

6906. DÜSELDER (Heike). Der Tod in Oldenbourg. Sozial- und kulturgeschichtliche Untersuchungen zu Lebenswelten im 17. und 18. Jahrhundert. Hannover, Hahn, 99, 390 p. (Veröffentlichungen der Historischen Kommission für Niedersachsen und Bremen, 34. Quellen und Untersuchungen zur Wirtschafts- und Sozialgeschichte Niedersachsens in der Neuzeit, 20).

6907. ESCOBAR (Edward J.). Race, police, and the making of a political identity: Mexican Americans and the Los Angeles Police Department, 1900-1945. Berkeley a. Los Angeles, University of California Press, 99, XIV-358 p. (Latinos in American society and culture, 7).

6908. Exclus (Les) en Europe, 1830-1930. Ed. par André GUESLIN et Dominique KALIFA. Paris, Editions de l'Atelier, 99, 480 p.

6909. Fabrics of feminism. Comparative analysis of XIXth century gender discourse, in Belgium and the Netherlands. Ed. By Hans MOORS. *Revue belge de philologie et d'histoire*, 99, 77, 2, p. 359-472. [Cf. n° <choice> 4097.]

6910. FEDOROVICH (Kent). Reconstruction and resettlement: the politicization of Irish migration to Australia and Canada, 1919–1929. *English historical review*, 99, 114, 459, p., p. 1143-1178.

6911. FONTAINE (Laurence). Confiance et communauté: la réussite des résaux de migrants dans l'Europe moderne. *In*: Mobilitäten = Mobilités [Cf. n° 6962], p. 4-15.

6912. FOUCRIER (Annick). La rêve californien. Migrants français sur la côte Pacifique (XVIIIe–XXe siècle). Paris, Belin, 99, 428 p.

6913. FOYSTER (Elizabeth A.). Manhood in early modern England. Honour, sex and marriage. London a. New York, Longman, 99, XI-247 p.

6914. Französische Frauen der Frühen Neuzeit. Dichterinnen, Malerinnen, Mäzeninnen. Hrsg. v. Margarete ZIMMERMANN und Roswitha BÖHM. Darmstadt, Primus, 99, 288 p.

6915. FRYE JACOBSON (Matthew). Whiteness of a different color: European immigrants and the alchemy of race. Cambridge, Harvard U. P., 99, X-338 p.

6916. GARAVAGLIA (Juan Carlos). Poder, conflicto y relaciones sociales. El Río de la Plata, siglos XVIII–XIX. Rosario, Homo Sapiens, 99, 212 p.

6917. Geglückte Integration? Spezifika und Vergleichbarkeiten der Vertriebenen-Eingliederung in der SBZ/DDR. Hrsg. Dierk HOFFMANN und Michael SCHWARTZ. München, Oldenbourg, 99, 398 p. (Schriftenreihe der Vierteljahrshefte für Zeitgeschichte),

6918. Gendai igirisu shakai seisakushi 1945–1990. (History of British social policies 1945–1990). Ed. by Kenzo MORI. Kyoto, Minerva Shobo, 99, 410 p.

6919. Gender, civic culture and consumerism: middle-class identity in Britain, 1800–1940. Ed. by Alan KIDD and David NICHOLLS. New York, Manchester U. P., 99, XI-223 p.

6920. GERBOD (P.). L'Etat et les activités physiques et sportives des années 1780 aux années 1930. *Revue historique*, 99, 123, 610, p. 307-332.

6921. Girls, boys, books, toys: gender in children's literature and culture. Ed. by Beverly LYON CLARK and Margaret R. HIGONNET. Baltimore, Johns Hopkins U. P., 99, VII-296 p.

6922. GODSEY (William D., jr.). Quarterings and kinship: the social composition of the Habsburg aristocracy in the dualist era. *Journal of modern history*, 99, 71, 1, p. 56-104.

6923. GONZÁLES BERNALDO DE QUIROS (Pilar). Civilité et politique aux origines de la nation argentine. Les sociabilités à Buenos Aires 1829–1862. Paris, Publications de la Sorbonne, 99, 382 p.

6924. GRAY (Marion W.). Productive men, reproductive women. The agrarian household and the emergence of separate spheres during the German enlightenment. New York a. Oxford, Berghahn, 99, XIII-370 p.

6925. GRDINA (Igor). Od rodoljuba z dežele do meščana. (From a countryside patriot to an urban dweller). Ljubljana, Studia humanitatis, 99, 299-16 p. (Apes, 13).

6926. GRENDI (Edoardo). Ipotesi per lo studio della socialità nobiliare genovese in età moderna. *Quaderni storici*, 99, 34, 102, p. 733-748.

6927. GROEBNER (Valentin). «Gemein» und «Geheym». Pensionen, Geschenke und die Sichtbarmachung des Unsichtbaren in Basel am Beginn des 16. Jahrhunderts. *Schweizerische Zeitschrift für Geschichte*, 99, 49, 4, p. 445-469.

6928. HAGIYAMA (Masahiro). Sangyoka no kaishi to kaji-shiyonin: Osakafu seinan-chiho no ichi shoka no jirei wo chushin toshite. (Domestic servants in the early stages of Japan's industrialization 1878–1906). *Shakai Keizai Shigaku*, 99, 64, 5, p. 1-29.

6929. HAMMAR (Inger). Emancipation och religion: Den svenska kvinnorörelsens pionjärer i debatt om kvinnans kallelse ca 1860–1900. (Emancipation and religion: the pioneers of the Swedish movement and the debate over woman's calling, ca. 1860–1900). Stockholm, Carlssons, 99, 318 p.

6930. HAMMERSCHMIDT (Peter). Die Wohlfahrtsverbände im NS-Staat. Die NSV und die konfessionellen Verbände Caritas und Innere Mission im Gefüge der Wohlfahrtspflege des Nationalsozialismus. Opladen, Leske-Budrich, 99, 619 p.

6931. HARRISON (Carol E.). The bourgeois citizen in nineteenth-century France: gender, sociability, and the uses of emulation. Oxford, Oxford U. P., 99, VIII-268 p. (Oxford historical monographs).

6932. Health care and poor relief in Counter-Reformation Europe. Ed. by Ole Peter GRELL, Andrew CUNNINGHAM and Jon ARRIZABALAGA. London a. New York, Routledge, 99, IX-309 p.

6933. HEINEMAN (Elizabeth D.). What difference does a husband make? Women and marital status in Nazi and postwar Germany. Berkeley a. Los Angeles, University of California Press, 99, XVIII-374 p. (Studies on the History of society and culture, 33).

6934. HOCHSTADT (Steve). Mobility and modernity: migration in Germany, 1820–1989. Foreword by Geoff ELEY. Ann Arbor, University of Michigan Press, 99, XVIII-331 p. (Social history, popular culture, and politics in Germany).

6935. HOERDER (Dirk). Individuum, Gesellschaft, Staat: Eine deutsche und eine irische Einwanderin im Kanada der 1920er und 1930er Jahre. *In*: Gesellschaft und Diplomatie im transatlantischen Kontext Festschrift für Reinhard R. Doerries zum 65. Geburtstag. Hrsg. v. Michael WALA. Stuttgart, Steiner, 99, p. 405-421.

6936. HOFFMANN (Frank). Junge Zuwanderer in Westdeutschland. Struktur, Aufnahme und Integration junger Flüchtlinge aus der SBZ und der DDR in Westdeutschland (1945–1961). Frankfurt am Main, Bern, New York, Lang, 99, 791 p. (Schriften zur Europa- und Deutschlandforschung, 7).

6937. HUMM (Antonia Maria). Auf dem Weg zum sozialistischen Dorf? Zum Wandel der dörflichen Lebenswelt in der DDR und der Bundesrepublik Deutschland, 1952–1969. Göttingen, Vandenhoeck & Ruprecht, 99, 352 p. (Kritische Studien zur Geschichtswissenschaft, 131).

6938. ILIJIC (Nikola). Istorija zadruge kod Srba. (Storia delle cooperative presso i serbi). Beograd, Sluzbeni list SRJ, 99, 350 p.

6939. Independence (From) towards freedom: Indian women since 1947. Ed. by Bharati RAY and Aparna BASU. New York, Oxford U. P., 99, XXI-248 p. (Gender Studies).

6940. KALINOVÁ (Lenka). K sociálním dějinám Československa v letech 1969–1989. (Zur Sozialgeschichte der Tschechoslowakei in den Jahren 1969–1989). Praha, Vysoká škola ekonomická, 99, 102 p. (Studie z hospodářských dějin, 12).

6941. KOCKA (Jürgen). Industrial culture and bourgeois society. Business, labor, and bureaucracy in modern Germany. New York a. Oxford Berghahn Books, 99, XVIII-325 p.

6942. Konsumpolitik: Die Regulierung des privaten Verbrauchs im 20. Jahrhundert. Hrsg. v. Hartmut BERGHOFF. Göttingen, Vandenhoeck und Ruprecht, 99, 158 p. (Sammlung Vandenhoeck).

6943. KRIKLER (Jeremy). The commandos: the army of white labour in South Africa. *Past and present*, 99, 163, p. 202-244.

6944. KULAWIK (Teresa). Wohlfahrtsstaat und Mutterschaft: Schweden und Deutschland 1870–1912. New York, Campus, 99, 411 p. (Politik der Geschlechtsverhältnisse, 13)

6945. LAKE (Marilyn). Childbearers as Rights-bearers: feminist discourse on the rights of Aboriginal and non-Aboriginal mothers in Australia, 1920–1950. *Women's history review*, 99, 8, 2, p. 347-363.

6946. LANGUE (Frédérique). Le cercle des alliances. Stratégies d'honneur et de fortune des aristocrates vénézuéliens au 18ᵉ siècle. *Annales*, 99, 54, 2, p. 453-480.

6947. LEBINA (Natalija B.). Povsednevnaja zhizn' sovetskogo goroda: normy i anomalii, 1920–1930 gody. (Everyday life of Soviet town, 1920–1930es). Sankt-Peterburg, Zhurnal "Neva" – Letnij sad, 99, 317 p. (bibl., ind. p.).

6948. LEE DOWNS (Laura). «Boys will be men and girls will be boys»: division sexuelle et travail dans la métallurgie (France et Angleterre, 1914–1939). *Annales*, 99, 54, 3, p. 561-586.

6949. LENNARTSSON (Malin). I säng och säte: relationer mellan kvinnor och män i 1600-talets Småland.

(Corps et biens: les relations entre les femmes et les hommes dans la province suédoise du Småland au 17ᵉ siècle). Lund, Lund U. P., 99, 381 p., tab. (Bibliotheca historica Lundensis, 92). [English summary].

6950. LIND (Vera). Selbstmord in der Frühen Neuzeit. Diskurs, Lebenswelt und kultureller Wandel am Beispiel der Herzogtümer Schleswig und Holstein. Göttingen, Vandenhoeck & Ruprecht, 99, 518 p. (Veröffentlichungen des Max-Planck-Instituts für Geschichte, 146).

6951. LORENZETTI (Luigi). Migration, stratégies économiques et résaux dans une vallée alpine. Le val de Blenio et ses migrants (XIXᵉ–début XXᵉ siècle). *In*: Mobilitäten = Mobilités [Cf. n° 6962], p. 87-104.

6952. MAC HARDY (Karin J.). Cultural capital, family strategies and noble identity in early modern Habsburgh Austria 1579–1620. *Past and present*, 99, 163, p. 36-75.

6953. MAC LAREN (Angus). Twentieth-Century sexuality: a history. Malden, Blackwell, 99, VIII-296 p.

6954. MACHAČOVÁ (Jana), MATĚJČEK (Jiří). Sociální pozice národnostních menšin v českých zemích 1918–1938. (Die soziale Stellung der nationalen Minderheiten in den böhmischen Ländern in den Jahren 1918 bis 1938). Opava, Slezský ústav Slezského zemského muzea, 99, 289 p.

6955. Maids and mistresses, cousins and queens: women's alliances in early modern England. Ed. by Susan FRYE and Karen ROBERTSON. Oxford, Oxford U. P., XVIII-350 p.

6956. MALATESTA (Maria). Le aristocrazie terriere nell'Europa contemporanea. Roma e Bari, Laterza, 99, VI-199 p. (Quadrante Laterza, 101).

6957. MARTINI (Manuela). Fedeli alla terra. Scelte economiche e attività pubbliche di una famiglia nobile bolognese nell'Ottocento. Bologna, Il Mulino, 99, 434 p.

6958. MATZERATH (Josef). Adel in Amt und Landtag. Zur Kontinuität und Diskontinuität der Mitherrschaft des niederen sächsischen Adels nach der Teilung Sachsens 1815. *Geschichte und Gesellschaft*, 99, 25, 3, p. 429-454.

6959. MICHEL (Sonya). Children's interests/mothers' rights: the shaping of America's child care policy. New Haven a. London, Yale U. P., 99, XII-410 p.

6960. MILES (Andrew). Social mobility in Nineteenth- and early Twentieth-Century England. New York, St. Martin's Press, 99, XIV-262 p.

6961. MIRONOV (Boris N.). Sotsial'naja istorija Rossii perioda imperii (XVIII–nachalo XX v.). Genezis lichnosty, demokraticheskoj sem'i, grazhdanskogo obshchestva i pravovogo gosudarstva. (A social history of Russia during the Empire (18ᵗʰ–the beginning of 20ᵗʰ century): the genesis of personality, democratic family, civil society and lawful state). Vols. 1-2. Sankt-Peterburg, Dmitry Bulanin, 99, 548, 566 p.

6962. Mobilitäten = Mobilités. Intr. de Anne RADEFF. *Schweizerische Zeitschrift für Geschichte*, 99, 49, 1, p. 1-147. [Cf. n°s <sélection> 3922, 5499, 6170, 6736, 6835, 6839, 6849, 6911, 6951, 6984, 6994.]

6963. MONZINI (Paola). Gruppi criminali a Napoli e Marsiglia. La delinquenza organizzata nella storia di due città (1820–1990). Catanzaro, Meridiana Libri, 99, XIV-194 p.

6964. MORE (Ellen S.). Restoring the balance: women physicians and the profession of medicine, 1850–1995. Cambridge, Harvard U. P., 99, XI-340 p.

6965. NASH (Mary). Construcció social de la dona estrangera. *In*: Dona i migració a la Mediterrània Occidental. Dir. por M. A. ROQUE. Barcelona, Institut Català de la Mediterrània, 99, [s. p.]. – EADEM. Un/Contested identities: motherhood, sex reform and the modernization of gender identity in early twentieth-century Spain. *In*: Constructing Spanish womanhood: Female identity in modern Spain. Ed. by Victoria Lorée ENDERS and Pamela RADCLIFF. New York, Suny, 99, [s. p.].

6966. NEWMAN (Louise Michelle). White women's rights. The racial origins of feminism in the United States. New York, Oxford U.P., 99, 261 p.

6967. NICCOLI (Ottavia). Rinuncia, pace, perdono. Rituali di pacificazione della prima età moderna. *Studi storici*, 99, 40, p. 219-261.

6968. NITSCH (Meinolf). Private Wohltätigkeitsvereine im Kaiserreich. Die praktische Umsetzung der bürgerlichen Sozialreform in Berlin. Berlin u. New York, de Gruyter, 99, XI-566 p. (Veröffentlichungen der Historischen Kommission zu Berlin, 98).

6969. OERTZEN (Christine von). Teilzeitarbeit und die Lust am Zuverdienen. Göttingen, Vandenhoeck & Ruprecht, 99, 411 p. (Kritische Studien zur Geschichtswissenschaft, 132).

6970. OWENSBY (Brian Philip). Intimate ironies: modernity and the making of middle-class lives in Brazil. Stanford, Stanford U. P., 99, XIII-332 p.

6971. ÖZKARCI (Mehmet). "Niğde-Bor Sokullu Mehmet Paşa Külliyesi. (Etablissements de charité de Sokullu Mehmed Paşa à Niğde-Bor). *Belleten*, 99, 53, 236, p. 95-122.

6972. PÁLFFY (Géza). A bécsi udvar és a magyar rendek a XVI. században. (The court of Vienna and the Hungarian classes in the XVI century). *Történelmi Szemle*, 99, 3-4, p. 331-369.

6973. PAPATHANASSIOU (Maria). Zwische Arbeit, Spiel, und Schule: die ökonomische Funktion der Kinder ärmerer Schichten in Österreich, 1880–1939. Wien, Verlag für Geschichte und Politik, 99, 332 p. (Sozial- und wirtschaftshistorische Studien).

6974. PARTNER (Simon). Assembled in Japan: electrical goods and the making of the Japanese consumer. Berkeley a. Los Angeles, University of California Press, 99, XIV-303 p. (Studies of the East Asian Institute, Columbia University).

6975. Pautas históricas de sociabilidad femenina. Rituales modelos de representación. Ed. por Mary NASH, Maria José DE LA PASCUA y Gloria ESPIGADO. Cádiz, Universidad de Cádiz, 99, 258 p.

6976. PELA (Doriano), SORCINELLI (Paolo). Generazioni del Novecento: guerra famiglia partecipazione consumi. Firenze, La nuova Italia, 99, XII-371 p. (ill.).

6977. PERSSON (Fabian). Servants of Fortune: the Swedish court between 1598 and 1721. Lund, Wallin and Dalholm, 99, VI-278 p.

6978. PIETRW-ENKER (Bianka). Russland "neue Menschen". Die Entwicklung der Frauenbewegung von den Anfängen bis zur Oktoberrevolution. Frankfurt am Main u. New York, Campus, 99, 498 p. (Geschichte und Geschlechter, 27).

6979. PINCHERA (Valeria). Le spese di prestigio di una famiglia della nobiltà fiorentina tra Sei e Settecento. I Salviati. *Cheiron*, 99, 16, 31, p. 99-131.

6980. Polen, Deutsche und Juden in Lodz 1820–1939. Eine Schwierige Nachbarschaft. Hrsg. v. Jürgen HENSEL. Osnabrück, fibre, 99, 370 p. (Einzelveröffentlichungen des Deutschen Historischen Instituts Warschau, 1).

6981. PRICE (Richard). British society, 1680–1880: dynamism, containment, and change. Cambridge, Cambridge U. P., 99, XII-349 p.

6982. PROCACCI (Giovanna). Dalla rassegnazione alla rivolta. Mentalità e comportamenti popolari nella Grande Guerra. Roma, Bulzoni, 99, 391 p.

6983. Profession politique (La). XIXe–XXe siècles. Ed. par Michel OFFERLÉ. Paris, Belin, 99, 363 p.

6984. RADEFF (Anne). Loin des centres. Consommation et mobilités du XVIIIe au XIXe siècle. *In*: Mobilitäten = Mobilités [Cf. n° 6962], p. 115-125.

6985. REIF (Heinz). Adel im 19. und 20. Jahrhundert. München, Oldenbourg, 99, VIII-156 p. (Enzyklopädie deutscher Geschichte, 55).

6986. REITH (Reinhold). Lohn und Leistung. Lohnformen im Gewerbe 1450–1900. Stuttgart, Steiner, 99, 476 p. (Vierteljahrschrift für Sozial- und Wirtschaftsgeschichte, Beihefte, 151).

6987. REITMAYER (Morten). «Bürgerlichkeit» als Habitus. Zur Lebensweise deutscher Großbankiers im Kaiserreich. *Geschichte und Gesellschaft*, 99, 25, 1, p. 66-93.

6988. RHEINHEIMER (Martin). Identität und Kulturkonflikt. Selbstzeugnisse schleswig-holsteinischer Sklaven in den Barbareskenstaaten. *Historische Zeitschrift*, 99, 269, 2, p. 317-370.

6989. RÖSENER (W.). Adelsherrschaft als kulturhistorisches Phänomen. Paternalismus, Herrschafts-

8. SOCIAL HISTORY

symbolik und Adelskritik. *Historische Zeitschrift*, 99, 268, 1, p. 1-34.

6990. ROSENTAL (Paul-André). Les sentiers invisibles. Espace, familles et migrations dans la France du XIXe siècle. Paris, EHESS, 99, 257 p. (Recherches d'histoire et de sciences sociales, 83).

6991. ROTARIU (Traian), SEMENIUC (Maria), MEZEI (Elemer). Recensământul din 1910. Transilvania. (The 1910 census. Transylvania). Bucureşti, Editura Staff, 99, 711 p.

6992. SARTI (Raffaella). Vita di casa. Abitare, mangiare, vestire nell'Europa moderna. Roma e Bari, Laterza, 99, XVI-356 p.

6993. SCHAUB (Jean-Frédéric). Les juifs du roi d'Espagne. Oran, 1509-1669. Paris, Hachette-Littératures, 99, 240 p.

6994. SCHIEDT (Hans-Ulrich). Wegnetze und Mobilität im Ancien Régime. *In*: Mobilitäten = Mobilités [Cf. n° 6962], p. 16-34.

6995. SCHWARZ (Leonard). English servants and their employers during the eighteenth and nineteenth centuries. *Economic history review*, 99, 52, 2, p. 236-256.

6996. Siècle (Un) d'antiféminisme. Ed. par Christine BARD. Paris, Fayard, 99, 481 p. (ill.).

6997. SIGNORELLI (Alfio). Tra ceto e censo. Studi sulle élites urbane nella Sicilia dell'Ottocento. Milano, Franco Angeli, 99, 254 p. (Studi e ricerche storiche).

6998. SIREN (Kirsti). Suuresta suvusta pieneen perheeseen. Itäsuomalainen perhe 1700-luvulla. (From joint family to nuclear family. The family in eastern Finland in the eighteenth century). Helsinki, SHS, 99, 265 p. (Bibliotheca historica, 38). [English summary].

6999. SLACK (Paul). From reformation to improvement: public welfare in early modern England. Oxford, Oxford U. P., 99, VIII-179 p. (Ford lectures delivered in the University of Oxford, 1994–1995).

7000. Sociedade brasileira: uma história através dos movimentos sociais. Rubim Santos Leao DE AQUINO [et al.]. Rio de Janeiro, Editora Record, 99, 599 p.

7001. Società (Le) di mutuo soccorso italiane e i loro archivi: Atti del seminario di studio; Spoleto, 8–10 novembre 1995. Roma, Ministero per i beni culturali e ambientali, 99, 344 p. (Pubblicazioni degli archivi di stato. Saggi, 49).

7002. SÖDERBERG (Johan). Våld och civilisering i Sverige 1750–1870. (Violence et éducation des mœurs en Suède, 1750–1870). Stockholm, Podium, 99, 287 p. [English summary].

7003. SOMMER (Hermann). Zur Kur nach Ems. Ein Beitrag zur Geschichte der Badereise von 1830 bis 1914. Stuttgart, Steiner, 99, XII-786 p. (Geschichtliche Landeskunde, 48).

7004. SPENKUCH (Hartwin). Herrenhaus und Rittergut. Die Erste Kammer des Landtags und der preußische Adel von 1854 bis 1918 aus sozialgeschichtlicher Sicht. *Geschichte und Gesellschaft*, 99, 25, 3, p. 375-403.

7005. State Policy and Gender System in the Two German States and Sweden, 1945–1989. Ed. by Rolf TORSTENDAHL. Uppsala, University of Uppsala, 99, 239 p. (Opuscola historica Upsaliensia, 23).

7006. STUART (Kathy). Defiled trades and social outcasts: honor and ritual pollution in early modern Germany. Cambridge, Cambridge U.P., 99, X-286 p. (ills).

7007. STUURMAN (Siep). Literary Feminism in seventeenth-century southern France: the case of Antoinette de Salvan de Saliez. *Journal of modern history*, 99, 71, 1, p. 1-27.

7008. TAKAHASHI (Motoyasu). Mura no soden kindai eikoku hen. (Inheritance in a village in early modern England: Kinship structure, custom of inheritance and succession over generations). Tokyo, Tosui Shobo, 99, 388 p.

7009. TAYLOR ALLEN (Ann). Feminism, social science, and the meanings of modernity: the debate on the origin of the family in Europe and the United States, 1860–1914. *American historical review*, 99, 104, 4, p. 1085-1113.

7010. Technokracie v českých zemích 1900–1950. (Technocracy in the Bohemian Lands, 1900–1950]. Ed. by Jan JANKO and Emilie TĚŠÍNSKÁ. Praha, Archiv AV ČR, 99, 317 p. (Práce z dějin Akademie věd ČR. Ser. A, 6) (Studie z dějin techniky, 3).

7011. THOMPSON (Peter). Rum punch and revolution. Taverngoing and public life in eighteenth-century Philadelphia. Philadelphia, University of Pennsylvania Press, 99, 265 p.

7012. TONIZZI (M. Elisabetta). Le grandi correnti migratorie del Novecento. Torino, Paravia Scrptorium, 99, 176 p. (Viaggi nella storia del Novecento).

7013. TOSH (John). A man's place: masculinity and the middle-class home in Victorian England. New Haven, Yale U. P., 99, XII-252 p.

7014. TRIVELLATO (Francesca). Salaires et justice dans les corporations vénitiennes au 17e siècle: le cas des manufactures de verre. *Annales*, 99, 54, 1, p. 245-274.

7015. VAN DÜLMEN (Richard). Der ehrlose Mensch. Unehrlichkeit und soziale Ausgrenzung in der frühen Neuzeit. Köln, Weimar u. Wien, Böhlau, 99, 118 p.

7016. VAN POPPEL (F.), BLOOTHOOFD (G.), GERRITZEN (D.), VERDUIN (J.). Naming for kin and the development of modern family structures: an analysis of a rural region in the Netherlands in the nineteenth and early twentieth centuries. *History of the family*, 99, 4, 3, 99, p. 261-296.

7017. VAN POPPEL (Frans), NELISSEN (Jan). The proper age to marry: social norms and behaviour in

19th century Netherlands. *History of the family*, 99, 4, 1, p. 51-76.

7018. VAN POPPEL (Frans). De 'statistieke ontleding van de dooden': een spraakzame bron? Nijmegen, Uitgeverij KU Nijmegen/Nijmegen U. P., 99, 57 p. [Inaugurele rede Katholieke Universiteit Nijmegen].

7019. VEKARIĆ (Nenad). Ubojstva među srodnicima u Dubrovačkoj Republici (1667.–1806). (Homicides committed within the family in the Republic of Dubrovnik, 1667–1806). *Anali zavoda za povijesne znanosti*, 99, 37, p. 95-153.

7020. VENTOURA (Lina). Hellenes metanastes sto Velgio. (Greek migrants in Belgium). Athena, Nephele, 99, 342 p. (ill.). (Nephele-historia).

7021. VENTURELLI (Paola). Vestire e apparire: il sistema vestimentario femminile nella Milano spagnola 1539–1679. Roma, Bulzoni, 99, 203 p. (ill.). (Biblioteca del Cinquecento, 87).

7022. WALKER (Jonathan). Gambling and Venetian noblemen c. 1500–1700. *Past and present*, 99, 162, p. 28-69.

7023. WARIS (Elina). Yksissä leivissä. Ruokolahtelainen perhelaitos ja yhteisöllinen toiminta 1750–1850. (Together as one. Extended families and collective labour in Ruokolahti, 1750–1850). Helsinki, SHS, 99, 248 p. (Bibliotheca historica, 48.) [English summary].

7024. WHELAN (Heide W.). Adapting to modernity. Family, caste and capitalism among the Baltic German nobility. Köln, Weimar u. Wien, Böhlau, 99, XIV-387 p. (Ostmitteleuropa in Vergagenheit und Gegenwart, 22).

7025. Women in the Inquisition: Spain and the New World. Ed. by Mary E. GILES. Baltimore, Johns Hopkins U. P., 99, IX-402 p.

7026. Women in towns: the social position of European urban women in a historical context. Ed. by Marjatta HIETALA and Lars NILSSON. Helsinki, Suomen Historiallinen Seura, 99, 196 p. (Studier i stadsoch kommunhistoria, 18. Studia Historica, 60).

7027. WOOD (Andy). The politics of social conflict: the Peak country, 1520–1770. Cambridge, Cambridge U. P., 99, XVI-354 p. (Cambridge studies in early modern British history).

7028. WOODS (Mary N.). From craft to profession: the practice of architecture in nineteenth-century America. Berkeley a. Los Angeles, University of California Press, 99, XVI-265 p.

7029. YLIKANGAS (Heikki). Klubbekriget: det blodiga bondekriget i Finland 1596–1597. (La guerre des Massues: la jacquerie sanglante de 1596–1597 en Finlande). Stockholm, Atlantis, 99, 420 p., pl. (ill.).

7030. YOUNG (Brigitte). Triumph of the Fatherland: German unification and the marginalization of women. Ann Arbor, University of Michigan Press, 99, XVIII-277 p. (Social history, popular culture, and politics in Germany).

7031. ZAUNSTÖCK (Holger). Sozietätslandschaft und Mitgliedsstrukturen. Die mitteldeutschen Aufklärungsgesellschaften im 18. Jahrhundert. Tübingen, Niemeyer, 99, XI-349 p. (Hallesche Beiträge zur europäischen Aufklärung, 9).

7032. ZOLOTUKHINA (M.V.). Mir amerikanskoj sem'i. (The world of American family, [white middle class, the 1950–1990s]). RAN, In-t etnologii i antropologii im. N.N. Miklukho-Maklaja. Moskva, [s. n.], 99, 319 p. (bibl.). [Eng. summary].

7033. ZÜRCHER (Thomas). «Wo es hinkommt, bringt es Wohlfahrt und Gedeihen». *Das Verhältnis der Schweizer Arbeiter zum Automobil im Diskurs des «Arbeiter-Touring» (1920–1979)*. Schweizerische Zeitschrift für Geschichte, 99, 49, 3, p. 333-350.

7034. Zwischen Alltag und Katastrophe. Der Dreißigjährige Krieg aus der Nähe. Hrsg. v. Benigna von KRUSENSTJERN und Hans MEDICK in Verb. mit Patrice VEIT. Göttingen, Vandenhoeck & Ruprecht, 99, 625 p.

§ 8. Addenda 1998.

7035. TRAVAGLINI (Carlo M.). Dalla corporazione al gruppo professionale: i rigattieri nell'Ottocento pontificio. *Roma moderna e contemporanea*, 98, 6, p. 427-471.

Cf. n°s 165-203, 889, 1208, 4626, 4667, 5005, 6670

§ 9. Working-class movement and socialism.

* 7036. Bibliografia del socialismo e del movimento operaio italiano, 1983–1990. Vol. 1. A–C. A cura di E.S.S.M.O.I., Ente per la storia del socialismo e del movimento operaio italiano, Fondazione Giuseppe Emanuele e Vera Modigliani. Roma, E.S.S.M.O.I., 99, XV-238 p.

** 7037. Rabochee dvizhenie v Rossii, 1895–fevral' 1917 g.: Khronika. (Working-Class Movement in Russia, 1895–February, 1917: a chronicle. Ed. Ju. I. KIR'JANOV. Gos. arkhivnaja s'luzhba RF. Vol. 6: "1900 god". Ed. I.M. PUSHKAREVA. Moskva, IRI RAN, 99, 411 p. (bibl., ind.). [Eng. summary]. [Cf. Bibl. 98, n° 7147.]

7038. ADAM (Thomas). Arbeitermilieu und Arbeiterbewegung in Leipzig 1871–1933. Köln, Weimar u. Wien, Böhlau, 99, 383 p. (Demokratische Bewegungen in Mitteldeutschland, 8).

7039. ANGELICI (Giovanna). L'altro socialismo. L'eredità democratico-risorgimentale da Bignami a Rosselli. Milano, Franco Angeli, 99, 224 p.

7040. ARICÓ (José). La hipótesis de Justo. Escrito sobre el socialismo en América Latina. Buenos Aires, Sudamericana, 99, 203 p.

7041. BAINES (Dudley), JOHNSON (Paul). In search of the 'traditional' working class: social mobility and occupational continuity in interwar London. *Economic history review*, 99, 52, 4, p. 692-713

7042. BELLASSAI (Alessandro). Il caffè dell'Unità. Pubblico e privato nella famiglia comunista degli anni Cinquanta. *Società e storia*, 99, 22, p. 327-358.

7043. BERRINGER (Christian). Sozialpolitik in der Weltwirtschaftskrise: die Arbeitslosenversicherungspolitik in Deutschland und Grossbritannien im Vergleich, 1928-1934. Berlin, Duncker & Humblot, 99, 521 p. (Schriften zur Wirtschafts- und Sozialgeschichte, 54).

7044. DICAPRIO (Lisa). Women workers, state-sponsored work, and the right to subsistence during the French Revolution. *Journal of modern history*, 99, 71, 3, p. 519-551.

7045. FULLER (Linda). Where was the working class? Revolution in Eastern Germany. Urbana, University of Illinois Press, 99, X-242 p.

7046. HIEPEL (Claudia). Arbeiterkatholizismus an der Ruhr. August Brust und der Gewerkverein christlicher Bergarbeiter. Stuttgart, Berlin u. Köln, Kohlhammer, 99, 288 p. (Konfession und Gesellschaft, 18).

7047. Hommes (Les) du pneu. Les ouvriers Michelin à Clermont-Ferrand de 1940 à 1980. Dir. par André GUESLIN. Paris, Ed. de l'Atelier, 99, 338 p.

7048. ILIÈ (Melanie). Women workers in the Soviet interwar economy: from 'protection' to 'equality'. Houndsmill, Macmillan- Centre for Russian and East European Studies, University of Birmingham, 99, IX-241 p. (tab.).

7049. KIMELDORF (Howard). Battling for American Labor: Wobblies, craft workers, and the making of the Union Movement. Berkeley a. Los Angeles, University of California Press, 99, X-244 p.

7050. KNUDSEN (Knud). Arbejdskonflikternes historie i Danmark: arbejdskampe og arbejderbevægelse 1870-1940. (Histoire des conflits du travail au Danemark: luttes ouvrières et mouvement ouvrier de 1870 à 1940). København, SFAH, 99, 384 p., ill., tab. (SFAH skriftserie 41).

7051. POLLARD (Sidney). Labour history and the labour movement in Britain. Aldeshot, Ashgate, 99, XVI-313 p. (figs, tabs).

7052. Pullman Strike (The) and the crisis of the 1890s: essays on labor and politics. Ed. by Richard SCHNEIROV, Shelton STROMQUIST and Nick SALVATORE. Urbana a. Chicago, University of Illinois Press, 99, 258 p. (Working class in American history).

7053. RAPONE (Leonardo). La socialdemocrazia europea tra le due guerre. Dall'organizzazione della pace alla resistenza armata (1923-1936). Roma, Carocci, 431 p.

7054. SANDERS (Elizabeth). Roots of reform: farmers, workers, and the American State, 1877-1917. Chicago, University of Chicago Press, 99, X-532 p. (American politics and political economy).

7055. SCHNEIDER (Michael). Unterm Hakenkreuz: Arbeiter und Arbeiterbewegung 1933 bis 1939. Bonn, Verlag J.H. W. Dietz Nachf., 99, XIII-1184 p. (ill.). (Geschichte der Arbeiter und der Arbeiterbewegung in Deutschland seit dem Ende des 18. Jahrhunderts, 12).

7056. SNELL (K. D. M.). The Sunday-school movement in England and Wales: child labour, denominational control and working-class culture. *Past and present*, 99, 164, p. 122-168.

7057. SOUBIRAN-PAILLET (Franceine). L'invention du syndicat, 1791-1884: itinéraire d'une catégorie juridique. Paris, Maison des Sciences de l'Homme, 99, 189 p. (Droit et société: recherches et travaux, 6).

7058. STEINBERG (Marc W.). Fighting words: working-class formation, collective action, and discourse in early-nineteenth-century England. Ithaca, Cornell U. P., 99, XVIII-286 p.

7059. TANNER (Jakob). Fabrikmahlzeit. Ernährungswissenschaft, Industriearbeit und Volksernährung in der Schweiz 1890-1950. Zürich, Chronos Verlag, 99, 600 p.

7060. Thing (A) of the past? Child labour in Britain in the nineteenth and twentieth centuries. Ed. by Michael LAVALETTE. Liverpool, Liverpool U.P., 99, X-278 p. (tabs., figs).

7061. TÓTH (J.). Rural labor movements in Egypt and their impact on the State, 1961-1992. Gainesville, University Press of Florida, 99, XIII-265 p. (ill.).

7062. Travail (Le) et la nation. Histoire croisée de la France et de l'Allemagne. Sous la dir. de Bénédicte ZIMMERMANN, Claude DIDRY et Peter WAGNER. Paris, Ed. de la Maison des sciences de l'Homme, 99, 402 p.

7063. TURNER (Patricia R.). Hostile participants? Working-class militancy, associational life, and the «distinctiveness» of the prewar French labor movement. *Journal of modern history*, 99, 71, 1, p. 28-55.

7064. WELCH (Cliff). The seed was planted: the Sao Paulo roots of Brazil's rural labor movement, 1924-1964. Liverpool, Liverpool U. P., 99, XXI-412 p. (ill., maps, ports).

7065. WIKANDER (Ulla). Kvinnoarbete i Europa 1789-1950: genus, makt och arbetsdelning. (Le travail féminin en Europe de 1789 à 1950: genre, pouvoir et partage du travail). Stockholm, Atlas, 99, 199 p. 1.

O

MODERN LEGAL AND CONSTITUTIONAL HISTORY

§ 1. General. 7066-7080. – § 2. History of constitutional law. 7081-7107. – § 3. Public law and institutions. 7108-7143. – § 4. Civil and penal law. 7144-7189. – § 5. International law. 7190-7202.

§ 1. General.

** 7066. Deutsche Juristen im Vormärz. Briefe von Savigny, Hugo, Thibaut und anderen an Egid von Löhr. Bearb. u. hg. v. Dieter STRAUCH. Köln, Weimar u. Wien, Böhlau, 99, LXXIII-251 p. (Rechtsgeschichte Schriften 13).

7067. 350 Jahre Westfälischer Friede. Verfassungsgeschichte, Staatskirchenrecht, Völkerrechtsgeschichte. Hrsg. v. Meinhard SCHRÖDER. Berlin, Duncker & Humblot, 99, 193 p. (Schriften zur Europäischen Rechts- und Verfassungsgeschichte, 30).

7068. BADER (Karl S.), DILCHER (Gerhard). Deutsche Rechtsgeschichte. Land und Stadt – Bürger und Bauer im Alten Europa. Berlin, Heidelberg u. New York, Springer, 99, XXVII-853 p.

7069. BERKVENS (A.M.J.A.). Hervorming van bestuur en rechtspraak in Spaans Gelre tijdens de regering van Karel II, Enkele reglementen betreffende de stilus curiae van de Soevereine Raad te Roermond en de bevoegdheden van de Staten van het Overkwartier, 1674–1699. *Bulletin de la Commission royale pour la publication des anciennes lois et ordonnances de Belgique*, 99, 40, p. 7-100.

7070. DELLA TORRE (Giuseppe). L'"Archivio Giuridico" e la cultura giuridica italiana del secondo Ottocento. *Archivio giuridico "Filippo Serafini"*, 99, 219, p. 15-24.

7071. Freiheitlichen sozialen (Zum), Rechtsstaat. Ausgewählte Schriften. Hrsg. v. Thilo RAMM und Rainer SCHRÖDER. Frankfurt am Main, Klostermann, 99, LXIV-687 p. (Studien zur Europäischen Rechtsgeschichte, 112).

7072. FROSINI (Vittorio), RICCOBONO (Francesco). Mortati e Kelsen. *Materiali per una storia della cultura giuridica*, 99, 29, p. 389-406.

7073. Gesellschaftliche Freiheit und vertragliche Bindung in Rechtsgeschichte und Philosophie. Hrsg. v. Jean F. KERVÉGAN und Heinz MOHNHAUPT. Frankfurt am Main, Klostermann, 99, IX-394 p. (Studien zur Europäischen Rechtsgeschichte, 120).

7074. GHISALBERTI (Carlo). Il diritto nel secolo ventesimo: appunti per una riflessione. *Clio*, 99, 35, p. 235-275.

7075. Juristische Zeitschriften. Die neuen Medien des 18.–20. Jahrhunderts. Hrsg. v. Michael STOLLEIS. Frankfurt am Main, 99, XIV-709 p. (Ius Commune. Sonderheft 128).

7076. KOÇ (Yunus). Erken Dönem Osmanlı Hukuku: Yaklaşımlar, Temel Sorunlar. (Le droit ottoman au début de l'Empire). *Hacettepe Üniversitesi Edebiyat Fakültesi Dergisi*, 99, ekim, p. 115-126.

7077. Kontinuitäten und Zäsuren in der europäischen Rechtsgeschichte. Hrsg. v. Andreas THIER, Guido PFEIFER und Philipp GRZIMEK. Frankfurt am Main, Lang, 99, 359 p. (Rechtshistorische Reihe, 196).

7078. PREDIERI (Alberto). Carl Schmitt, un nazista senza coraggio. Firenze, La nuova Italia, 99, 2 vol., VIII-639 p., 626 p. (Biblioteca di cultura, 240).

7079. Privileg (Das) im europäische Vergleich. Band 2. Hrsg. v. Barbara DÖLEMEYER und Heinz MOHNHAUPT. Frankfurt am Main, Klostermann, 99, VIII-362 p. (Ius Commune, 125).

7080. SCHÄFER (Herwig). Juristische Lehre und Forschung an der Reichsuniversität Strassburg 1941–1944. Tübingen, Mohr, 99, XIV-273 p. (Beiträge zur Rechtsgeschichte des 20. Jahrhunderts, 23).

Cf. n°s 1110-1142

§ 2. History of constitutional law.

7081. BASTIDE (David). Notes sur la naissance de la nation moderne: le rapport entre le roi et la nation dans le discours des Constituants, 1789–1791. *Revue d'histoire du Droit français et étranger*, 99, 77, 2, p. 241-256.

7082. BLOMEYER (Peter). Der Notstand in den letzten Jahren von Weimar: die Bedeutung von Recht, Lehre und Praxis der Notstandsgewalt für den Untergang der Weimarer Republik und die Machtübernahme durch die Nationalsozialisten: eine Studie zum Verhältnis von Macht und Recht. Berlin, Duncker & Humblot, 99, 549 p. (Schriften zur Verfassungsgeschichte, 57).

7083. CIOBANU (Veniamin). Statutul juridic al Principatelor Române în viziune europeană (secolul al XVIII-lea). (The legal status of the Romanian principalities in European perspective. The 18th century). Iaşi, Editura Universităţii "Al. I. Cuza", 99, 304 p.

7084. CONRAD (Dieter). Zwischen den Traditionen: Probleme des Verfassungsrechts und der Rechtskultur in Indien und Pakistan. Gesammelte Aufsätze aus den Jahren 1970–1990. Hrsg. v. Jürgen LÜTT und Mahendra P. SINGH. Stuttgart, Franz Steiner, 99, XVIII-499 p. (Beiträge zur Südasienforschung, 184).

7085. Costituzione italiana (La). Atti del convegno, Roma 20–21 febbraio 1998. A cura di Maurizio FIORAVANTI e Sandro GUERRIERI. Roma, Carocci, 99, 425 p. (Fondazione Istituto Gramsci. Annali 1996/VIII).

7086. DATTA (Satya). The enigmatic Republican state of early moderne Venice: an interpretation. *Studi veneziani*, 99, 37, p. 51-109.

7087. Executive and legislative powers in the Constitution of 1848-1849. Ed. by Horst DIPPEL. Berlin, Duncker & Humblot, 99, 286 p. (Schriften zur Verfassungsgeschichte 58).

7088. FOLEY (Michael). The Politics of the British Constitution. Manchester a. New York, Manchester U. P., 99, V-296 p.

7089. FRIEDEBURG (Robert von). Widerstandrecht und Konfessionkonflikt. Notwehr und Gemeiner Mann im deutsch-britischen Vergleich 1530 bis 1669. Berlin, Duncker und Humblot, 99, 190 p. (Schriften zur europäischen Rechts- und Verfassungsgeschichte, 27).

7090. GANCI (Massimo). Costituzionalisti e costituzioni in Sicilia e a Napoli dal 1812 al 1848. *Archivio storico siciliano*, 99, 4, 25, p. 9-179.

7091. GHISALBERTI (Carlo). Nazione liberale e nazione democratica nel '48–'49. *Clio*, 99, 35, p. 559-569.

7092. GRONSKÝ (Ján), HŘEBEJK (Jiří). Dokumenty k ústavnímu vývoji Československa. Tomo 1. 1918–1945. Tomo 2. 1945–1968. (Documents on Czechoslovak constitutional developments). Praha, Karolinum, 99, 244 p.

7093. HUUSSEN JR. (Arend H.). The Dutch constitution of 1798 and the problem of slavery. *Revue d'histoire du droit*, 99, 67, 1-2, p. 99-114.

7094. KIRSCH (Martin). Monarch und Parlament im 19. Jahrhundert: der monarchische Konstitutionalismus als europäischer Verfassungstyp – Frankreich im Vergleich. Göttingen, Vandenhoeck & Ruprecht, 99, 476 p. (Veröffentlichungen des Max-Planck Instituts für Geschichte, 150).

7095. LEGROS (Robert). L'avènement de la démocratie. Paris, Bernard Grasset, 99, 392 p.

7096. MANCUSO (Francesco). Gaetano Mosca e la tradizione del costituzionalismo. Napoli, Edizioni scientifiche italiane, 99, 354 p. (Pubblicazioni dell'Università degli studi di Salerno. Sezione studi giuridici, 22).

7097. OLECHOWSKI (Thomas). Die Einführung der Verwaltungsgerichtsbarkeit in Österreich. Wien, Manz, 99, XXXVI-274 p. (Österreichische Rechtswissenschaftliche Studien 52).

7098. RODOTÀ (Carla). Storia della Corte costituzionale. Roma e Bari, Laterza, 99, VIII-165 p. (Saggi tascabili Laterza, 231).

7099. ROMANELLI (Raffaele). Nazione e costituzione nell'opinione liberale italiana prima del '48. *Passato e presente*, 99, 17, 46, p. 157-171.

7100. RUSCONI (Gian Enrico), WINKLER (Heinrich August). L'eredità di Weimar. Roma, Donzelli, 99, 78 p.

7101. SCIROCCO (Alfonso). Costituzioni e costituenti del 1848: il caso italiano. *Clio*, 99, 35, p. 571-593.

7102. SKACH (Cindy). Semi-presidentialism and democracy: Weimar Germany, the French Fifth Republic and postcommunist Russia in comparative perspective. Oxford, [s. n.], 99, VIII-334 p. [Thesis (D.Phil.) – University of Oxford, Faculty of Social Studies, 1999].

7103. STEIN (Katrin). Parteiverbote in der Weimarer Republik. Berlin, Duncker & Humblot, 99, 226 p. (Schriften zur Verfassungsgeschichte, 56).

7104. THIER (Andreas). Steuergesetzgebung und Verfassung in der Konstitutionellen Monarchie, Staatssteuerreformen in Preußen 1871–1893. Frankfurt a. Main, Klostermann, 99, XXVIII-1047 p. (Ius Commune. Sonderheft 119).

7105. Via (La) alla politica. Lelio Basso, Ugo La Malfa, Meuccio Ruini protagonisti della Costituente. A cura di Giancarlo MONINA. Milano, F. Angeli, 99, 224 p.

7106. Weimar und die deutsche Verfassung: zur Geschichte und Aktualität von 1919. Herausgegeben im Auftrag der Deutschen Nationalstiftung von Andreas RÖDDER; mit Beiträgen von Karl Dietrich BRACHER [et al.]. Stuttgart, Klett-Cotta, 99, 154 p.

7107. WESTERHOLT (Burchard Graf von). Patrimonialismus und Konstitutionalismus in der Rechts- und Staatstheorie Karl Ludwig Haller. Begründung, Legitimation und Kritik des modernes Staates. Berlin, Duncker & Humblot, 99, 112 p. (Schriften zur Verfassungsgeschichte, 59).

Cf. n° 1050-1109, 4600

§ 3. Public law and institutions.

* 7108. Bibliografia di storia delle istituzioni contemporanee. A cura di Carla ABBAMONDI, Rosanna DE LONGIS, Laura LANZA e Fernando VENTURINI. *Le carte e la storia*, 99, 5, 1, p. 63-76.

3. PUBLIC LAW AND INSTITUTIONS

* 7109. VENTURINI (Fernando). Alcune osservazioni critiche (e autocritiche) sulle «Pubblicazioni di storia delle istituzioni contemporanee». *Le carte e la storia*, 99, 5, 1, p. 57-62.

7110. ALIBERTI (G.). Lo stato postfeudale. Burocrazie governanti ed elites locali nel Mezzogiorno prima e dopo l'Unità. Roma, Edizioni Universitarie, 99, 236 p.

7111. Burocrazie non burocratiche. Il lavoro dei tecnici nelle amministrazioni tra Otto e Novecento. A cura di Angelo VARNI e Guido MELIS. Torino, Rosenberg & Sellier e Centro di ricerca e documentazione per la storia del lavoro in Italia in età contemporanea, 99, 255 p.

7112. CASSESE (Sabino). I caratteri originali della storia amministrativa italiana. *Le carte e la storia*, 99, 5, 1, p. 7-15.

7113. CHIMENTI (Anna). Storia dei referendum: dal divorzio alla riforma elettorale, 1974-1999. Roma e Bari, Laterza, XI-237 p. (Saggi tascabili Laterza, 229).

7114. COLOMBO (Paolo). Il Re d'Italia. Prerogative costituzionali e potere politico della Corona (1848-1922). Milano, Franco Angeli, 99, 460 p.

7115. Conseil (Le) d'Etat avant le Conseil d'Etat. 5e Journée d'études, Paris, 16 juin 1999. *Revue administrative*, 99, 52, 3, p. 3-105.

7116. Conseil (Le) d'Etat et la liberté religieuse, deux siècles d'histoire. 4e Journée d'études du 27 novembre 1998 à Paris. *Revue administrative*, 99, 52, p. 3-83.

7117. CZEGUHN (Ignacio). Ursprung und soziale Herkunft der Ständeversammlungen Kastiliens im 15. und Anfang des 16. Jahrhunderts. *Revue d'histoire du droit*, 99, 67, 3-4, p. 313-326.

7118. DEL MAR TIZÓN FERRER (Maria). Audiencias Reales al sur del Tajo, Compilaciones de Ordenanzas en el siglo XVII. *Anuario de historia del derecho español*, 99, 69, p. 519-528.

7119. DI SIMONE (Maria Rosa). Istituzioni e fonti normative in Italia dall'Antico regime all'Unità. Torino, Giappichelli, 99, 300 p.

7120. EMSLEY (Clive). Gendarmes and the states in nineteenth-century Europe. Oxford, Oxford U. P., 99, X-288 p.

7121. Etica pubblica e amministrazione. Per una storia della corruzione nell'Italia contemporanea. A cura di Guido MELIS. Napoli, CUEN, 260 p.

7122. Foundations of democracy in the European Union: from the genesis of parliamentary democracy to the European Parliament. Ed. by John PINDER. Foreword by Princess MARGRIET of the Netherlands. New York, St. Martin's, for the European Cultural Foundation, 99, XII-151 p.

7123. Histoire et perspectives de la juridiction administrative en France et en Amérique latine. Journées d'études internationales, Carthagène, 19-21 novembre 1997. *Revue administrative*, 99, 52, 9, 230 p.

7124. Institutionen, Instrumente und Akteure sozialer Kontrolle und Disziplinierung im frühneuzeitlichen Europa. Hrsg. v. Heinz SCHILLING. Frankfurt am Main, Klostermann, 99, VIII-360 p. (Ius Commune. Sonderheft 127).

7125. KARAMUK (Gümeç). Devşirmelerin Hukuki Durumları Üzerine. (Sur le statut juridique des Janissaires). *Hacettepe Üniversitesi Edebiyat Fakültesi Dergisi*, 99, ekim, p.19-32.

7126. KUNERALP (Sinan). Son dönem Osmanlı erkân ve ricali (1839-1922): prosopografik rehber. (Guide prosopographique: les grand dignitaires de l'Etat Ottoman dans la dernière période de l'Empire). İstanbul, ISIS, 99, XXXV-127 p.

7127. LANG (Sean). Parliamentary reform, 1785-1928. London a. New York, Routledge, 99, 198 p. (Questions and analysis in history).

7128. LONDEI (Luigi). Le magistrature dello Stato della Chiesa nell'età moderna. Qualche nota di sintesi. *Le carte e la storia*, 99, 5, 2, p. 36-54.

7129. MACEK (Pavel), UHLÍŘ (Lubomír). Dějiny policie a četnictva. Tomo 1. Habsburská monarchie (1526-1918). Tomo 2. Československá republika (1918-1939). (Geschichte der Polizei und der Gendarmerie). Praha, Police History, 99, 230 p. (photogr.).

7130. MANNORI (Luca). Le Consulte di Stato. *Rassegna storica toscana*, 99, 45, p. 347-380.

7131. MELIS (Guido). Profilo storico della Pubblica Amministrazione nella prima metà del secolo: i problemi della continuità amministrativa dello Stato. *Storia e memoria*, 99, 8, p. 9-23.

7132. NIFTERRIK (G.P. van). Vorst tussen volk en wet: over volkssoevereiniteit en rechtsstatelijkheid in het werk van Fernando Vàzquez del Menchaca (1512-1569). [S. l.], Sanders Institut, Rotterdam – Gouda Quint, 99, VIII-299 p.

7133. Officiers «moyens». I. Actes de la Table ronde «Présidiaux, élections ...: le travail des institutions», Paris, 28-29 mai 1999. *Cahiers du Centre de Recherches historiques*, 99, 23, 160 p.

7134. Parlamento repubblicano (Il), 1948-1998. A cura di Silvano LABRIOLA. Roma, ISLE e Milano, Giuffrè, 99, XII-656. (Quaderni della Rassegna parlamentare, 3).

7135. PAYEN (Philippe). La physiologie de l'arrêt de réglement du Parlement de Paris au XVIIIe siècle. Avant-propos de Jean IMBERT. Paris, Presses Universitaires de France, 99, 502 p.

7136. Reichshofrat und Reichskammergericht. Ein Konkurrenzverhältnis. Hrsg. v. W. SELLERT. Köln,

Weimar u. Wien, Böhlau, 99. (Quellen und Forschungen zur höchsten Gerichtsbarkeit im Alten Reich, 34).

7137. Reichsständische Libertät und Habsburgisches Kaisertum. Hrsg. v. Heinz DUCHHARDT und Matthias SCHNETTGER. Mainz, Philipp von Zabern, 99, X-362 p. (Veröffentlichungen des Instituts für Europäische Geschichte Mainz, Abteilung Universalgeschichte, 48).

7138. Repertorium der Policeyordnungen der Frühen Neuzeit. Hrsg. v. Karl HÄRTER und Michael STOLLEIS. Band 3. Wittelsbachische Territorien (Kurpfalz, Bayern, Pfalz-Neuburg, Pfalz-Sulzbach, Jülich-Berg, Pfalz-Zweibrücken). Hrsg. v. Lothar SCHILLING und Gerhard SCHUCK. Frankfurt am Main, Klostermann, 99, XIV-XII-1991 p. (Ius Commune, Sonderhefte. Studien zur Europäischen Rechtsgeschichte, 116).

7139. Securitas imperii. Sborník k problematice bezpečnostních služeb. Tomo 5. (Securitas imperii. Articles on the state security forces). Ed. Ladislava KREMLIČKOVÁ. Praha, Themis, 99, 343 p.

7140. STOLLEIS (Michael). Geschichte des öffentlichen Rechts in Deutschland. Band 3. Staats- und Verwaltungsrechtswissenschaft in Republik und Diktatur, 1914-1915. München, Beck, 99, 439 p.

7141. Voter et élire à l'époque contemporaine. Ed. par Annie BLETON-RUGET et Serge WOLIKOW. Dijon, Editions Universitaires de Dijon, 99, 203 p.

7142. YAMAN (Ahmet Emin). Osmanlı İmparatorluğu'nda sadr-ı âzamlık (1876–1922). (Le grand-vizirat dans l'Empire Ottoman). Ankara, Ankara Üniversitesi Dil Tarih Coğrafya Fakültesi, 99, 243 p.

§ 3. Addenda 1996–1998.

7143. LANCHESTER (Fulco). L'innovazione istituzionale e la crisi di regime. Roma, Bulzoni, 96, 164 p. – IDEM. I giuspubblicisti tra storia e politica. Personaggi e problemi nel diritto pubblico del secolo XX. Torino, Giappichelli, 98, [s. p.].

Cf. n°s 1050-1109, 1133, 4986, 4995, 5006

§ 4. Civil and penal law.

** 7144. LORENZO CADARSO (Pedro L.). La documentación judicial en la época de los Austrias: estudio archivístico y diplomático. Caceres, Universidad de Extremadura, 99, 323 p.

7145. ALVAZZI DEL FRATE (Paolo). Il giudice naturale. Prassi e dottrina in Francia dall'Ancien Régime alla Restaurazione. Roma, Viella, 99, p. 293 (Ius nostrum – Studi e testi pubblicati dall'Istituto di storia del diritto italiano dell'Università di Roma «La Sapienza», 9).

7146. APPEL (Hans Henrik). Tinget, magten og æren: studier i sociale processer og magtrelationer i et jysk bondesamfund i 1600-tallet. (Justice, pouvoir et honneur: études sur les litiges et les relations de pouvoir dans une communauté rurale du Jutland au 17e siècle). Odense, Odense Universitetsforlag, 99, 713 p., diagr., cartes, tab.. (Odense University Studies in History and Social Sciences, 219). (rés. anglais).

7147. BAYER (Bernard). Sukzession und Freiheit. Historische Voraussetzungen der rechtstheoretischen und rechtsphilosophischen um das Institut der Familienfideikommisse im 18. und 19. Jahrhundert. Berlin, Duncker & Humblot, 99, 411 p. (Schriften zur Europäischen Rechts- und Verfassungsgeschichte 25).

7148. BECCHI (Paolo). Ideologia della codificazione in Germania. Genova, Compagnia dei librai, 99, 310 p.

7149. BERRINO (Annunziata). L'eredità contesa. Storia di successioni nel Mezzogiorno prenapoleonico. Roma, Carocci, 99, 164 p.

7150. CAZZETTA (G.). Praesumitur seducta. Onestà e consenso femminile nella cultura giuridica moderna. Milano, Giuffrè, 99, 425 p.

7151. CHRIST (Thierry). Les voies de l'intégration confédérale: l'exemple de la législation neuchâteloise en matière de naturalisations (1848–1914). *Schweizerische Zeitschrift für Geschichte*, 99, 49, 2, p. 222-248.

7152. COLAO (Floriana). Progetti di codificazione civile nella Toscana della Restaurazione. Bologna, Monduzzi, 99, 204 p. (Archivio per la storia del diritto medievale e moderno).

7153. DANI (Alessandro). Aspetti e problemi giuridici della sopravvivenza degli usi civici in Toscana in età moderna e contemporanea. *Archivio storico italiano*, 99, 157, 580, p. 285-326.

7154. DAUCHY (Serge). Le dossier de procédure inédit d'une cause d'appel devant le Parlement de Paris entre Nieuport et Ypres (1505–1507). *Bulletin de la Commission royale pour la publication des anciennes lois et ordonnances de Belgique*, 99, 40, p. 101-146. – IDEM. Les recours contre les sentences arbitrales au Parlement de Paris (XIIIe et XIVe siècles). La doctrine et la législation à l'épreuve de la pratique judiciaire. *Revue d'histoire du droit*, 99, 67, 3-4, p. 255-311.

7155. Designs against Charleston: the trial record of the Denmark Vesey Slave Conspiracy of 1822. Ed. by Edward A. PEARSON. Chapell Hill, University of North Carolina Press, 99, XIII-387 p.

7156. Enfermement, prison et châtiments en Afrique: du 19e siècle à nos jours. Sous la direction de Florence BERNAULT. Paris, Karthala, 99, 510 p. (ill.). (Hommes et sociétés). [Cf. n° <sélection> 7187.]

7157. GARLATI GIUGNI (Loredana). Inseguendo la verità. Processo penale e giustizia nel Ristretto della prattica criminale per lo Stato di Milano. Milano, Giuffrè, 99, 376 p. (Università di Milano- Facoltà di Giurisprudenza, Pubblicazioni dell'Istituto di Storia del diritto italiano, 24).

7158. GRILLI (Antonio). Die französische Justizorganisation am linken Rheinufer 1797–1803. Frankfurt am Main, Berlin u. Bern, 99, 287 p. (Rechtshistorische Reihe, Bd. 190).

7159. GSCHWEND (Lukas). Nietzsche und die Kriminalwissenschaften. Eine rechtshistorische Untersuchung der strafrechtsphilosophischen und kriminologischen Aspekte in Nietzsches Werk unter besonderer Berücksichtigung der Nietzsche-Rezeption in der deutschen Rechtswissenschaft. Zürich, Schulthess, 99, LIV-411 p. (Zürcher Studien zur Rechtsgeschichte, 36).

7160. HARMAT (Ulricke). Ehe auf Widerruf? Der Konflikt um das Eherecht in Österreich 1918–1938. Frankfurt am Main, Klostermann, 99, XII-560 p. (Ius Commune. Sonderheft 121).

7161. HARRINGTON (Joel F.). Escape from the great confinement: the genealogy of a German workhouse. *Journal of modern history*, 99, 71, 2, p. 308-345.

7162. HASLIP-VIERA (Gabriel). Crime and punishment in Late colonial Mexico City: 1692–1810. Albuquerque, University of New Mexico Press, 99, XII-193 p.

7163. HOWARD (John R.). The shifting wind: the Supreme Court and civil rights from reconstruction to Brown. Albany, State University of New York Press, 99, VII-393 p. (SUNY Series in Afro-American Studies).

7164. Kriminalität und abweichendes Verhalten. Deutschland in 18. und 19. Jahrhundert. Hrsg. v. Helmut BERDING, Diethelm KIPPEL und Günther LOTTES. Göttingen, Vandenhoeck & Ruprecht, 99, 206 p.

7165. LINDSTEDT (Jukka). Kuolemaan tuomitut. Kuolemanrangaistukset Suomessa toisen maailmansodan aikana. (Under sentence of death. Capital punishment in Finland during World War II.). Helsinki, Suomalainen Lakimiesyhdistys, 99, XCIII-680 p. (Suomal. Lakimiesyhd. julk., 221). [English summary].

7166. LOKIN (J. H. A.), JANSEN (C. J. H.), BRANDSMA (F.). Het Rooms-Friese recht, De civiele rechtpraktijk van het Hof van Friesland in de 17e en 18e eeuw. Leeuwarden. Verloren, Hilversum- Ryksargyf, 99, 240 p.

7167. LOVATO (Andrea). Diritto romano e scuola storica dell'Ottocento napoletano. Roma e Bari, Laterza, 99, 171 p. (Pubblicazioni della Facoltà giuridica dell'Università di Bari, 122).

7168. LUCCHESI (Marzia). Si quis occidit occidetur: l'omicidio doloso nelle fonti consiliari, secoli XIV–XVI. Padova, CEDAM, 99, XXIX-241 p. (Università di Pavia. Studi di scienze giuridiche e sociali, 91).

7169. LUDI (Regula). Die Fabrikation des Verbrechens: zur Geschichte der modernen Kriminalpolitik, 1750–1850. Tübingen, Bibliotheca Academica Verlag, 99, 611 p.

7170. MAC GOWEN (Randall). From pillory to gallows: the punishment of forgery in the age of the financial revolution. *Past and present*, 99, 165, p. 107-140.

7171. MACLEAN (I.). Legal fictions and fictional entities in Renaissance jurisprudence. *Journal of legal history*, 99, 20, p.1-24.

7172. MASCIARI (Francesco), La codificazione napoletana: elaborazione e riforme tra il 1817 ed il 1859. Prime note. *Rivista di storia del diritto italiano*, 99, 72, 72, p. 279-298.

7173. MELIKAN (R.A.). Caging the emperor: the legal basis for deteining Napoleon Bonaparte. *Revue d'histoire du droit*, 99, 67, 3-4, p. 349-362.

7174. NILSSON (Roddy). En välbyggd maskin, en mardröm för själen: Det svenska fängelsesystemet under 1800-talet. (A well-built machine, a nightmare for the soul: the Swedish prison system during the nineteenth century). Lund, Lund U. P., 99, 491 p. (Bibliotheca historica Lundensis, 93).

7175. PETERSEN (Anja). Kvinnliga brottslingar och brottsliga kvinnor: fängelsens berättelse om kön i 1800-talets Sverige. (Criminelles féminines et femmes criminelles: le discours de la prison sur le sexe dans la Suède du 19ᵉ siècle). Lund, Network for Research in Criminology and Deviant Behaviour, Lund university, 99, 93 p.

7176. PEZZINO (Paolo). Le mafie. Firenze, Giunti, 99, 127 p.

7177. PICCIALUTI (Maura). L'immortalità dei beni: fedecommessi e primogeniture a Roma nei secoli XVII e XVIII. Roma, Viella, 99, 229 p.

7178. POLDEN (Patrick). A history of the county court, 1846–1971. Cambridge, Cambridge U. P., 99, XXII-403 p. (Cambridge studies in English legal history).

7179. PRIESTER (Jens M.). Das Ende des Züchtigungsrechts. Eine historische, dogmatische und straftheoretische Untersuchung. Baden-Baden, Nomos Verlag, 99, 339 p. (Strafrechtswissenschaft und Strafrechtspolitik, 2).

7180. Révolutions et justice penale en Europe. Modèles français et traditions nationales (1780–1830). Sous la direction de Xavier ROUSSEAUX, Marie-Sylvie DUPONT-BOUCHAT et Claude VAEL. Paris e. Montréal, L'Harmattan, 99, p. 388.

7181. ROUET (Gilles). Justice et justiciables aux XIXᵉ et XXᵉ siècles. Paris, Belin, 99, 414 p. (Histoire et sociétés-temps présent).

7182. RUBLACK (Ulinka). The Crimes of women in early modern Germany. Oxford, Oxford U.P., 99, X-292 p. (Oxford studies in social history).

7183. RUDISCHHAUSER (Sabine). Vertrag, Tarif, Gesetz. Der politische Liberalismus und die Anfänge des Arbeitsrechts in Frankreich 1890–1902. Berlin, A. Spitz, 99, 291 p. (Studien des Frankreich-Zentrums der Albert-Ludwigs-Universität Freiburg, 4).

7184. SAILER (Rita). Untertanenprozesse vor dem Reichskammergericht. Rechtsschutz gegen die Obrigkeit in der zweite Hälfte des 18. Jahrhunderts. Köln, Weimar u. Wien, Böhlau, 99, XL-497 p. (Quellen und Forschungen zur höchsten Gerichtsbarkeit im Alten Reich, 33).

7185. SCIUMÈ (Alberto). I progetti del codice di commercio del Regno Italico (1806–1808). Milano, Giuffrè, 99, 544 p.

7186. TAEGER (Angela). Intime Machtverhältnisse. Moralstrafrecht und administrative Kontrolle der Sexualität in ausgehenden Ancien Régime. München, Oldenbourg, 99, V-179 p. (Ancien Régime, Aufklärung und Revolution, 31).

7187. THIOUB (Ibrahima). Marginalité juvénile et enfermement à l'époque coloniale: les premières écoles pénitentiaires du Sénégal: 1888–1927. In: Enfermement, prison et châtiments en Afrique. Du 19ᵉ siècle à nos jours [Cf. n° 7156], p. 205-226. – IDEM. Sénégal: la prison à l'époque coloniale. Significations, évitement et évasions. In: Enfermement, prison et châtiments en Afrique. Du 19ᵉ siècle à nos jours [Cf. n° 7156], p. 285-303.

7188. TIXHON (Axel). Contrôler la Justice, construire l'Etat et surveiller le crime au XIXᵉ siècle. Naissance et développement de la statistique judiciaire en Belgique (1795–1901). *Revue belge de philologie et d'histoire*, 99, 77, 4, p. 965-1001.

7189. VERSE (D. A.). Verwendungen im Eigentümer-Besitzer-Verhältnis: eine kritische Betrachtung aus historisch-rechtsvergleichender Sicht. Tübingen, Mohr Siebeck, 99, XXII-192 p. (Max Planck Institut für ausländisches und internationales Privatrecht, Studien zum ausländischen und internationalen Privatrecht, 72).

Cf. n° 4992

§ 5. International law.

** 7190. Hugo Grotius. Le droit de la guerre et de la paix. Traduit par P. PREADIER-FODÉRÉ. Ed. par D. ALLAND et S. GOYARD-FABRE. Paris, Presses Universitaires de France, 99, IV-868 p. (Collection 'Léviathan').

** 7191. PUFENDORF (Samuel). Gesammelte Werke. Hrsg. v. Wilhelm SCHMIDT-BIGGEMAN. Bd. 3. Elementa jurisprudentia universalis. Hrsg. v. Thomas BEHME. Akademie Verlag, 99, 223 p.

7192. BOYLE (Francis Anthony). Foundations of world order: the legalist approach to international relations (1898–1921). Durham, Duke U. P., 99, IX-220 p.

7193. KUSCHNICK (Michael). Integration in Staatenverbindungen. Vom 19. Jahrhundert bis zu EU nach dem Vertrag von Amsterdam. Berlin, de Gruyter, 99, XXXVIII-258 p. (Schriften des Rechtszentrums für europäische und internationale Zusammenarbeit 11).

7194. MANNONI (Stefano). Potenza e ragione. La scienza del diritto internazionale nella crisi dell'equilibrio europeo (1870–1914). Milano, Giuffrè, 99, 276 p. (Per la storia del pensiero giuridico moderno, 54).

7195. Nationalsozialismus (Der) vor Gericht: Die allierten Prozesse gegen Kriegsverbrecher und Soldaten 1943–1952. Hrsg. v. Gerd R. UEBERSCH. Frankfurt am Main, Fischer Taschenbuch, 99, 319 p. (Die Zeit des Nationalsozialismus).

7196. Processo (Il) di Norimberga: scritti inediti e rari. A cura di A. TARANTINO, R. ROCCO e R. SCORRANO. Milano, A. Giuffrè, 99, XX-117 p. (Studi di diritto pubblico e di filosofia del diritto e della politica / Università degli studi di Lecce, 13).

7197. QUAGLIONI (Diego). Pufendorf in Italia. Appunti e notizie sulla prima diffusione della traduzione italiana del De iure naturae et gentium. *Pensiero politico*, 99, 32, p. 235-250.

7198. REPGEN (T.). Grotius redivivus. Die Notwendigkeit einer neuen Übersetzung von De jure belli ac pacis, erläutert am Beispiel der Auswirkung von Willensmängeln und nachträglich veränderten Umständen auf die Verbindlichkeit. *Ius Commune*, 99, 26, p. 299-328.

7199. THOMAS (N.). The intertwining of law and theology in the writings of Grotius. *Journal of the history of international law*, 99, 1, p. 61-100.

7200. TUCK (Richard). The rights of war and peace. Political thought and international order from Grotius to Kant. Oxford, Oxford U. P., 99, 243 p.

7201. WELCH (Steven R.). «Harsh but just?» German military justice in the Second World War: a comparative study of the court-martialling of German and US deserters. *German history*, 99, 17, 3, p. 369-399.

7202. ZEMANEK (K.). Was Hugo Grotius really in favour of the freedom of the seas? *Journal of the history of international law*, 99, 1, p. 48-60.

P

HISTORY OF INTERNATIONAL RELATIONS

§ 1. General. 7203-7300. – § 2. History of colonization and decolonization (*a*. General; *b*. Asia; *c*. Africa; *d*. America; *e*. Oceania). 7301-7386. – § 3. From 1500 to 1789 (*a*. General; *b*. 1500–1648; *c*. 1648–1789). 7387-7451. – § 4. From 1789 to 1815. 7452-7475. – § 5. From 1815 to 1910. 7476-7538. – § 6. From 1910 to 1935. The First World War. 7539-7622. – § 7. From 1935 to 1945. The Second World War (*a*. General; *b*. Diplomacy. Economy; *c*. Military operations; *d*. Resistance). 7623-7800. – § 8. From 1945. 7801-8036.

§ 1. General.

* 7203. HERREN (Madeleine). International History, a view from the top of the Alps [Forschungsbericht]. *Schweizerische Zeitschrift für Geschichte*, 99, 49, 3, p. 375-384.

* 7204. INGRAO (Christian). La violence de guerre. Approches comparées des deux conflits mondiaux: essai de bibliographie introductive. *Bulletin de l'Institut d'histoire du temps présent*, 99, 73, p. 129-138.

** 7205. Albania and Kosovo: political and ethnic boundaries, 1867–1946. Ed. by Beytullah DESTANI. Slough, Archive Editions, 99, XXIV-1039 p.

** 7206. Dokumenti par Latvijas valsts starptautisko atzisanu, neatkaribas atjaunosanu un diplomatiskajiem sakariem 1918–1998. [Recueil de documents sur la reconnaissance internationale, la restauration de l'Indépendance et les relations diplomatiques]. Sastaditajs, Alberts SARKANIS. Riga, Nordik, 99, 541 p. (Latvija starptautiskajas attiecibas).

** 7207. Kanzleiwesen und Kanzleisprachen im östlichen Europa. Hrsg. v. Christian HANNICK. Köln, Böhlau, 99, XIV-232 p. (Archiv für Diplomatik. Beiheft, 6).

** 7208. Policy of occupation powers in Latvia, 1939–1991: a collection of documents. Editor-in-charge E. PELKAUS. Riga, Nordik, 99, 623 p.

** 7209. Relaciones diplomáticas, Paraguay-República Dominicana, República Dominicana-Paraguay: documentos históricos. Compilados por Lucy ARRAYA. Asunción, Editora Paraguaya, 99, 221 p.

** 7210. Rossiia-Marokko: istoriia sviazei dvukh stran v dokumentakh i materialakh, 1777–1916. (Russia and Morocco: documents and materials, 1777–1916). Avtor i sostavitel' N. P. PODGORNOVA. Moskva, In-t Afriki RAN, 99, 623 p.

** 7211. Rossija i Afrika: Dokumenty i materialy, XVIII v.–1960 g. (Russia and Africa: documents and materials, 1701–1960). RAN, In-t vseobshchej istorii. Vol. 1. XVIII v.–1917 g. Vol. 2. 1918–1960. Moskva, [s. n.], 99, 2 vol., 233 p., 397 p.

7212. 120 godini moderna bulgarska diplomacia, 1879–1999. Vstupitelna studija Elena STATELOVA; sustaviteli Petur STOJANOVIČ [et al.] = 120 years modern Bulgarian diplomacy, 1879–1999. Introductory study by Elena STATELOVA; compilers Peter STOYANOWICH [et al.]. Sofija, Izdatelska kushta Anubis, 99, 167 p.

7213. Afrique: partenariat international et conflits régionaux. Intr. par Jean-Claude ALLAIN. *Guerres mondiales et conflits contemporains*, 99, 49, 196, p. 3-150. [Cf. n°s 7226, 7355, 7896, 7899, 7938, 7948, 7973, 7986, 8034.]

7214. Ambiguous Legacy (The): U.S. foreign relations in the "American Century." Ed. by Michael J. HOGAN. New York, Cambridge U. P., 99, XIII-534 p.

7215. American century (The): a roundtable. Part I. Part II. Ed. by M. J. HOGAN. *Diplomatic history*, 99, 23, 2, p. 157-370; 3, p. 391-537. [Cf. n^{os} <choice> 3957, 7224, 7227, 7233, 7250, 7251, 7252, 7256, 7262, 7266, 7267, 7271, 7272, 7292, 8020.]

7216. Anglo-French relations in the twentieth century: rivalry and cooperation. Ed. By Alan SHARP and Glyn STONE. London a. New York, Routledge, 99, 368 p.

7217. ANTONOPOULOS (Elias A.). Hellada, Alvania, Kossyphopedio, 1912–1998: syntome chronologike anaskopese. Athena, Okeanida, 99, 471p. (ill.).

7218. AYDIN (Mustafa). Determinants of Turkish foreign policy: historical framework and traditional inputs. *In*: Seventy-five years of the Turkish Republic [Cf. n° 5175], p. 130-151.

7219. BAGBY (Wesley M.). America's international relations since World War I. New York a. Oxford, Oxford U. P., 99, X-438 p.

7220. BARIÈ (Ottavio). Dal sistema europeo alla comunità mondiale: storia delle relazioni internazionali dal Congresso di Vienna alla fine della Guerra Fredda. Vol. 1. Il sistema europeo. Milano, CELUC, 99, 456 p. (Ricerche, 43).

7221. BARRETT (Thomas M.). At the edge of empire: the Terek Cossacks and the North Caucasus frontier, 1700–1860. Boulder, Westview, 99, XV-243 p.

7222. BECK (Peter J.). Scoring for Britain: international football and international politics, 1900–1939. London a. Portland, F. Cass, 99, XII-306 p. (Cass series, 9).

7223. BELLISA (Marc). La diplomatie et les traités dans la pensée des Lumières: «négociation universelle ou école du mensonge»? *Revue d'histoire diplomatique*, 99, 113, 3, p. 291-318.

7224. BERGHAHN (V. R.). Philanthropy and diplomacy in the «American century». *In*: American century (The): a roundtable. Part II [Cf. n° 7215], p. 393-419.

7225. BLACKWOOD (William Lee). Socialism, Czechoslovakism, and the Munich complex, 1918–1948. *International history review*, 99, 21, 4, p. 4, p. 875-899.

7226. BODIN (Michel). La contribution africaine aux armées européennes, du début du XXe siècle aux années soixante. *In*: Afrique: partenariat international et conflits régionaux [Cf. n° 7213], p. 23-36.

7227. BRANDS (H. W.). The idea of the national interest. *In*: American century (The): a roundtable. Part I [Cf. n° 7215], p. 239-261.

7228. Brésil (Le), l'Europe et les équilibres internationaux: XVIe–XXe siècles. [Colloque Franco-brésilien, tenu en Sorbonne en mars 1998, à l'initiative du Centre d'Etudes sur le Brésil]. Sous la dir. de Katia DE QUEIRÓS MATTOSO. Paris, Presses de l'Univ. de Paris-Sorbonne, 99, 342 p. (Civilisations, 23). [Cf. n° <sélection> 7432.]

7229. CLAYTON (Lawrence A.). Peru and the United States: the condor and the eagle. Athens, University of Georgia Press, 99, XII-363 p. (United States and the Americas).

7230. COERVER (Don M.), HALL (Linda B.). Tangled destinies: Latin America and the United States. Albuquerque, University of New Mexico Press, 99, XII-289 p.

7231. Cuba y España: pasado y presente de una historia común. Bilbao, Universidad del País Vasco, Servicio Editorial, 99, 424 p. (Historia contemporánea, 19).

7232. Cuba y Puerto Rico: a 100 anos del desastre. Coordinador Francisco J. CABALLERO HARRIET. San Sebastián, Departamento de Cultura y Euskera, Diputación Foral de Guipuzkoa, 99, 200 p.

7233. CUMMINGS (B.). The American century and the Third World. *In*: American century (The): a roundtable. Part I [Cf. n° 7215], p. 355-370.

7234. DANESE (Sérgio França). Diplomacia presidencial: história e crítica. Rio de Janeiro, Topbooks, 99, 516 p.

7235. DENT (David W.). The legacy of the Monroe doctrine: a reference guide to U.S. involvement in Latin America and the Caribbean. Westport, Greenwood Press, 99, XI-418 p. (ill., maps).

7236. Deutschland und Großbritannien = Britain and Germany: historische Beziehungen und Vergleich = historical relations and comparisons. Ed. By Adolf M. BIRKE. München, K. G. Saur, 99, XIII-298 p. (Prince Albert research publications, 1).

7237. EPHAISTOS (Panagiotes). Diplomatia & strategike ton megalon Europaikon dynameon: Gallias, Germanias, Megales Vretanias. Athena, Ekdoseis Poioteta, 99, 371 p. (Seira Meleton Diplomatias kai Strategikes, 2).

7238. ESKANDER (Saad Basher). Britain's policy towards the Kurdish question. London, [s. n.], 99, 260 p. [Thesis (Ph. D.) – London, London School of Economics and Political Science. Department of International History, 1999].

7239. European warfare 1453–1815. Ed. by Jeremy BLACK. New York, St. Martin's Press, 99, VII-287 p.

7240. Fabric (The) of modern Europe: studies in social and diplomatic history: essays in honour of Éva Haraszti Taylor on the occasion of her 75th birthday. Ed. by Attila PÓK. Nottingham, É. Haraszti Taylor in association with Astra Press, 99, XIII-252 p.

7241. FISCHER (Alan). A precarious balance: conflict, trade, and diplomacy on the Russian-Ottoman frontier. İstanbul, Isis Press, 99, 191 p. (Analecta Isisiana, 40).

7242. FREY (Linda S.), FREY (Marsha L.). The history of diplomatic immunity. Columbus, Ohio State U. P., 99, XIII-727 p.

7243. Gesellschaft und Diplomatie im transatlantischen Kontext: Festschrift für Reinhard R. Doerries zum 65. Geburtstag. Hrsg. v. Michael WALA. Stuttgart, Steiner, XIII-480 p. (ill.). (USA-Studien, 11).

7244. GILDERHUS (Mark T.). The second century: US-Latin American relations since 1889. Wilmington, SR Books, 99, XVI-282 p.

7245. GIZA (Antoni). Wokół bałtyckiej polityki Rosji od końca XVI do początku XX wieku. Zbiór studiów. (Um die baltische Politik Russlands von dem auslaufenden XVI. bis zum beginnenden XX. Jahrhundert. Studien-Sammlung. Szczecin, Wydaw. Nauk. Uniw. Szczecińskiego, 99, 217 p. (Rozprawy i Studia, 133).

7246. GLENNY (Misha). The Balkans, 1804–1999, nationalism, war and great powers. London, Granta Books, 99, XXVI-726 p.

7247. Great power rivalries. Ed. by Walter THOMPSON. Columbia, University of South Carolina Press, 99, VIII-414 p. (Studies in international relations).

7248. Grossbritannien und Deutschland: gesellschaftliche, kulturelle und politische Beziehungen im 19. und 20. Jahrhundert: Festschrift für Bernd-Jürgen Wendt zu seinem 65. Geburtstag. Hrsg. v. Frank OTTO u. Thilo SCHULZ. Rheinfelden, Schäuble, 99, 210 p. (Historische Forschungen, 44). [Cf. n° <Auswahl> 7700.]

7249. HALLIDAY (Fred). Revolution and world politics: the rise and fall of the sixth great power. Basingstoke, Macmillan, 99, 416 p.

7250. HODGSON (G.). Immigrants and frontiersmen: two traditions in American foreign policy. In: American century (The): a roundtable. Part II [Cf. n° 7215], p. 525-537.

7251. HORNE (G.). Race from power: U.S. foreign policy and the general crisis of «white supremacy». In: American century (The): a roundtable. Part II [Cf. n° 7215], p. 437-461.

7252. HUNT (M. H.). East Asia in Henry Luce's «American century». In: American century (The): a roundtable. Part I [Cf. n° 7215], p. 321-353.

7253. Impact (The) of race on U.S. foreign policy: a reader. Ed. with an introduction by Michael L. KRENN. New York a. London, Garland, 99, XV-334 p. (ill.).

7254. India and Oman: history, state, economy, and foreign policy. Ed. by A. K. PASHA. Delhi, Gyan Sagar Publications, 99, IX-210 p.

7255. Indo-French relations. Ed. by Kuzhippalli Skaria MATHEW and S. Jeyaseela STEPHEN. Delhi, Pragati Publications in association with Indian Council of Historical Research, 99, X-332 p. (Monograph series. Indian Council of Historical Research, 2).

7256. IRIYE (A.). A century of NGOs [non-governmental organizations]. In: American century (The): a roundtable. Part II [Cf. n° 7215], p. 421-435.

7257. İRTEM (Süleyman Kani). Osmanlı Devleti'nin Makedonya meselesi Balkanlar'ın kördüğümü. (Problème macédonien de l'Empire Ottoman en tant que nœud gordien des Balkans). İstanbul, Temel, 99, 304 p.

7258. Israel/Palestine question (The). Ed. by Ilan PAPPE. London, Routledge, 99, IX-278 p. (Re-writing histories).

7259. Istoriï (Z) mizhnarodnykh zv'iazkiv Ukraïny: nauka, osvita: XIX–30-ti roky XX st.: dokumenty i materialy. (Some aspects of the Ukrainian international relations). Redaktsiina kolehiia, M. M. VARVARTSEV [et al.]. Kyïv, In-t istoriï Ukraïny NAN Ukraïny, 99, 200 p.

7260. Italia (L') e le organizzazioni internazionali: diplomazia multilaterale nel Novecento. A cura di Luciano TOSI, prefazione di Francesco Paolo FULCI. Padova, CEDAM, 99, LII-449 p. (Centro interuniversitario per lo studio della storia delle organizzazioni internazionali e dei processi e movimenti di cooperazione internazionale, 1). [Cf. n° <scelta> 8017.]

7261. Japan and New Zealand, 150 years. Ed. by Roger PEREN. Palmerston North, New Zealand Centre for Japanese Studies, 99, 255 p. (ill., maps).

7262. JERVIS (R.). American and the twentieth century: continuity and change. In: American century (The): a roundtable. Part I [Cf. n° 7215], p. 219-238.

7263. JOVER ZAMORA (José M.). España en la política internacional: siglos XVIII–XX. Madrid, Marcial Pons, 99, 279 p.

7264. KALDOR (Mary). New and old wars: organized violence in a global era. Stanford, Stanford U. P., 99, VIII-206 p.

7265. KARSH (Efraim), KARSH (Inari). Empires of the sand: the struggle for mastery in the Middle East 1789–1923. Cambridge, Harvard U. P., 99, X-409 p.

7266. KROES (R.). American empire and cultural imperialism: a view from the receiving end. In: American century (The): a roundtable. Part II [Cf. n° 7215], p. 463-477.

7267. LAFEBER (W.). The tension between democracy and capitalism during the American century. In: American century (The): a roundtable. Part I [Cf. n° 7215], p. 263-284.

7268. LAKE (David A.). Entangling relations: American foreign policy in its century. Princeton, Princeton U. P., 99, XII-332 p. (Princeton studies in international history and politics).

7269. LEHMAN (Kenneth D.). Bolivia and United States: a limited partnership. Athens, University of Georgia Press, 99, XVIII-296 p. (United States and the Americas).

7270. LOREY (David E.). The US-Mexican border in the twentieth century. Wilmington, SR Books, 99, X-195 p.

7271. LUCE (H. R.). The American century. In: American century (The): a roundtable. Part I [Cf. n° 7215], p. 159-171.

7272. LUNDESTAD (G.). «Empire by invitation» in the American century. In: American century (The): a roundtable. Part I [Cf. n° 7215], p. 189-217.

7273. MAC FARLANE (John). Ernest Lapointe and Quebec's influence on Canadian foreign policy. Toronto a. London, University of Toronto Press, 99, 270 p.

7274. Macht und Moral: Beiträge zur Ideologie und Praxis amerikanischer Aussenpolitik im 20. Jahrhundert; Festschrift für Knud Krakau zu seinem 65. Geburtstag. Hrsg. v. Manfred BERG. Münster, Lit, 99, 328 p. (Studien zu Geschichte, Politik und Gesellschaft Nordamerikas, 14).

7275. MATELSKI (Dariusz). Niemcy w Polsce w XX wieku. (Deutsche in Polen im XX. Jahrhundert). Warszawa, Poznań, Wydaw. Nauk PWN, 99, 464 p.

7276. MENDIBLE ZURITA (Alejandro). Venezuela-Brasil: la historia de sus relaciones desde sus inicios hasta el umbral del mercosur, 1500–1997. Caracas, Universidad Central de Venezuela, Facultad de Humanidades y Educación, Escuela de Comunicación Social, 99, 322 p.

7277. Monnaie et relations internationales. 1. 2. Intr. par J.-C. ALLEN (part 1) et R. FRANK (part 2). Relations internationales, 99, 99, p. 239-322; 100, p. 345-424. [Cf. n^{os} <sélection> 6798, 6801, 6804, 7339, 7712.]

7278. MORRIS (Benny). Righteous victims: a history of the Zionist-Arab conflict, 1881–1999. New York, A. A. Knopf, 99, XIV-751 p.

7279. MOSER (John E.). Twisting the Lion's tail: Anglophobia in the United States, 1921–1948. Basingstoke, Macmillan, 99, X-263 p.

7280. NINKOVICH (Frank). The Wilsonian century: U.S. foreign policy since 1900. Chicago, University of Chicago Press, 99, 320 p.

7281. PAGDEN (Andrew). Facing each other: the world's perception of Europe and Europe's perception of the world. Aldershot, Variorum, 99, 2 vol., [s. p.].

7282. PAPAYOANOU (Paul A.). Power ties: economic interdependence, balancing, and war. Ann Arbor, University of Michigan Press, 99, XV-193 p. (ill.).

7283. Politics (The) of strategic adjustment: ideas, institutions, and interests. Ed. by Peter TRUBOWITZ, Emily O. GOLDMAN and Edward RHODES. New York a. Chichester, Columbia U. P., 99, VIII-331 p. (New directions in world politics).

7284. Relaţii româno-ucrainiene. Istorie şi contemporaneitate. (Romanian-Ukrainian relations. History and present). Satu Mare, 99, 578 p.

7285. RENOLIET (Jean-Jacques). L'UNESCO oublié: la Société des Nation et la coopération intellectuelle (1919–1946). Paris, Publication de la Sorbonne, 99, 352 p.

7286. Rivalität und Partnerschaft: Studien zu den deutsch-britischen Beziehungen im 19. und 20. Jahrhundert. Festschrift für Anthony J. Nicholls. Hrsg. v. Gerhard A. RITTER und Peter WENDE. Paderborn, München, Wien u. Zürich, Schöning, 99, 375 p. (Veröffentlichungen des Deutschen Historischen Instituts London, 46).

7287. Rossija i Chernomorskie prolivy (XVIII–XIX stoletija). (Russia and the Black Sea straits, 18th–19th centuries). Eds. Leonid N. NEZHINSKIJ, Anatolij V. IGNAT'EV. RAN, In-t rossijskoj istorii. Moskva, Mezhdunarodnye otnoshenija, 99, 557 p. (bibl.).

7288. RUSCONI (Gian Enrico). Clausewitz, il prussiano: la politica della guerra nell'equilibrio europeo. Torino, Einaudi, 99, IX-394 p. (Biblioteca Einaudi, 67).

7289. RYAN (David). Colonialism and hegemony in Latin America [U.S.A.]. International history review, 99, 21, 2, p. 287-296.

7290. SARAY (Mehmet). Türk-İran İlişkileri. (Relations turco-iraniennes). Ankara, Atatürk Araştırma Merkezi, 99, 344 p.

7291. SCHMITZ (David F.). Thank God they're on our side: the United States and right-wing dictatorships, 1921–1965. Chapel Hill a. London, University of North Carolina Press, 99, XI-383 p.

7292. SMITH (T.). Making the world safe for democracy in the American century. In: American century (The): a roundtable. Part I [Cf. n° 7215], p. 173-188.

7293. SMITH (Thomas W.). History and international relations. London a. New York, Routledge, 99, IX-227 p. (Routledge advances in international relations and politics, 9).

7294. Spain and the great powers in the twentieth century. Ed. by Sebastian BALFOUR and Paul PRESTON. London a. New York, Routledge, 99, VIII-274 p. (Routledge/Canada Blanch studies in contemporary Spain).

7295. Spain and the Mediterranean since 1898. Ed. by Raanan REIN. London, F. Cass, 99, 255 p.

7296. Twentieth-century international history: a reader. Ed. by Stephen CHAN and Jarrod WIENER. London, I. B. Tauris, 99, XI-340 p. (Tauris history readers).

7297. VAN KRIEKEN, (G. S.). Kapers en kooplieden: de betrekkingen tussen Algiers en Nederland, 1604–1830. Amsterdam, De Bataafsche Leeuw, 99, 112 p. (ill.).

7298. VARILLAS (Alberto). Perú y Ecuador: visión actual de un antiguo conflicto. Lima, Pontificia Universidad Católica del Perú, 99, XX-530 p. (ill., maps).

7299. Warlords in international relations. Ed. by Paul B. RICH. Basingstoke, Macmillan, 99, XVI-176 p.

7300. YU-JOSE (Lydia N.). Japan views the Philippines, 1900–1944. Manila, Ateneo De Manila U. P., 99, 209 p. (ill.).

Cf. n°s 866, 3975, 3921-4008, 4599, 5675, 6798

§ 2. History of colonization and decolonization.

a. General

7301. Allemagne (L') et la décolonisation française. Actes du Colloque de l'Université de Paris XII, Créteil, 18–20 mars 1999. Textes réunis et publiés par Klaus-Jürgen MÜLLER et Jean Paul CAHN. Revue d'Allemagne, 99, 31, 3-4, p. 375-648.

7302. Angola e Brasil nas rotas do Atlântico Sul. Organizadores: Selma PANTOJA, José Flávio SOMBRA SARAIVA. Rio de Janeiro, Bertrand Brasil, 99, 254 p.

7303. BOYCE (D. George). Decolonisation and the British Empire, 1775–1997. Basingstoke, Macmillan, IX-317 p.

7304. CHAMBERLAIN (Muriel E.). The Longman companion to European decolonisation in the twentieth century. Harlow, Londgman, 99, 352 p.

7305. DRESCHER (Seymour). From slavery to freedom: comparative studies in the rise and fall of Atlantic slavery. New York, New York U. P., 99, XXV-454 p.

7306. Empire and imperialism: the debate of the 1870s. Ed. and introduced by Peter J. CAIN. Bristol, Thoemmes Press, 99, VI-310 p. (Key issues, 20).

7307. FIELDHOUSE (D. K.). The West and the Third World: trade, colonialism, dependence and development. Oxford, Malden, 99, XII-378 p (History of the contemporary world).

7308. FRADERA (Josep M.). Gobernar colonias. Barcelona, Ediciones Península, 99, 152 p.

7309. Gentlemanly capitalism and British imperialism: the new debate on empire. Ed. by Raymond E. DUMETT. London a. New York, Longman, 99, XIII-234 p. (tab., fig., map).

7310. Guardians of empres: the armed forces of the colonial powers c. 1700–1964. Ed. By David KILLINGRAY and David Enrico OMISSI. Manchester, Manchester U. P., 99, 259 p.

7311. ITTMANN (Karl). The Colonial Office and the population question in the British empire, 1918–1862. *Journal of Imperial and Commonwealth history*, 99, 27, 3, p. 55-81.

7312. KLEIN (Herbert S.). The Atlantic slave trade. Cambridge, Cambridge U. P., 99, XXI-234 p.

7313. LOVEJOY (Paul E.), RICHARDSON (David). Trust, pawnship and Atlantic history: the institutional Foundations of the old Calabar slave trade. *American historical review*, 99, 104, 2, p. 333-355.

7314. MAZENOT (Georges). Evaluer la colonisation. Paris, L'Harmattan, 99, 162 p.

7315. Pacific empires: essays in honour of Glyndwr Williams. Ed. By Alan FROST and Jane SAMSON. Carlton South, Melbourne U. P., 99, XII-334 p.

7316. PARRY (J. H.). Trade and dominion: the European oversea empires in the eighteenth century. London, Phoenix Giant, 99, 432 p. (History of civilization).

7317. PARSONS (Timothy). The British imperial century, 1815–1914: a world history perspective. Lanham a. Oxford, Rowman & Littlefield, 99, XI-153 p.

7318. Statecraft (The) of British imperialism: essays in honour of Wm. Roger Louis. Ed. by Robert D. KING and Robin W. KILSON. *Journal of Imperial and Commonwealth history*, 99, 27, 2, p. 1-260. [Contents: 1. ROBINSON (Ronald). Wm. Roger Louis and the official mind of decolonization. – 2. BELOFF (Max). Empire reconsidered. – 3. HYAM (Ronald). The primacy of geopolitics: the dynamics of British imperial policy, 1763–1963. – 4. MARSHALL (P. J.). Who cared about the thirteen colonies? Some evidence from philanthropy. – 5. BROWN (Judith M.). Gandhi – a Victorian gentleman: an essay in imperial encounter. – 6. GOPAL (Sarvepalli). All Souls and India, 1921–1947. – 7. CELL (John W.). The Indian and African freedom struggles: some comparisons. – 8. FALOLA (Toyin). British imperialism: Roger Louis and the West African case. – 10. DARWIN (John). An undeclared empire: the British in the Middle East, 1918–1939. – 12. MAC INTYRE (W. David). The strange death of dominion status. – 14. MORGAN (Kenneth O.). Imperialists at bay: British Labour and decolonization. – Select bibliography of Wm. Roger Louis]. [Cf. n^{os} <choice> 4881, 7925, 7985.]

7319. WAITES (Bernard). Europe and the Third World: from colonisation to decolonisation, c. 1500–1998. Basingstoke, Macmillan, 99, XVIII-354 p. (Themes in comparative history).

7320. WHITE (Nicholas J.). Decolonisation: the British experience since 1945. London a. New York, 99, XII-153 p. (Seminar studies in history).

Cf. n°s 1008, 4331, 4463, 4821, 7452

b. Asia

** 7321. Independence years: the selected Indian and Commonwealth papers of Sir Nicholas Mansergh. Ed. by Diana MANSERGH; foreword by Sarvepalli GOPAL. Delhi a. Oxford, Oxford U. P., 99, 274 p.

** 7322. KUIPERS (Anske Hielke). In de Indische wateren: Anske Hielke Kuipers, gezaghebber bij de Gouvernementsmarine 1833–1902. Bezorgd door Marietje E. KUIPERS. Zutphen, Walburg, 99, 446 p. (ill., maps, ports.). (Werken uitgegeven door de Linschoten-Vereeniging, 98).

7323. AMES (G. J.). Renascent empire? Pedro II and the quest for stability in Portuguese monsoon Asia ca. 1640–1682. Amsterdam, Amsterdam U. P., 99, 264 p.

7324. BICKERS (Robert A.). Britain in China: community, culture and colonialism, 1900–1949. Manchester, Manchester U. P., 99, XII-276 p. (Studies in imperialism).

7325. BRUGE (Roger). Les hommes de Diên Biên Phû. Paris, Perrin, 99, 615 p.

7326. BUNTON (Martin). Inventing the status quo. Ottoman land-law during the Palestine mandate, 1917–1936. *International history review*, 99, 21, 1, p. 28-56.

7327. CHANDRA (Bipan). Essays on colonialism. New Delhi, Orient Longman, 99, IX-365 p.

7328. Confronting colonialism: resistance and modernization under Haidar Ali and Tipu Sultan. Ed. by Irfan HABIB. New Delhi, Tulika, 99, XLVII-205 p. (ill., map).

7329. Contact colonial franco-vietnamien (Le): Le premier demi-siècle, 1858–1911. Ed. par l'Institut de recherches sur le Sud Est asiatique, l'Ecole française d'Extrême-Orient, Hà Nôi et l'Institut d'histoire comparée des civilisations, Université de Provence. Aix-en-Provence, Publications de l'Université de Provence, 99, 289 p.

7330. COPLAND (Ian). The princes of India in the endgame of empire, 1917–1947. New Delhi a. Cambridge U. P., 99, XIII-302 p. (Cambridge studies in Indian history and society, 2).

7331. CURPUZ (Onofre D.). Saga and triumph: the Filipino revolution against Spain. Manila, Philippine Centennial Commission, 99, XII-363 p. (plates, ill., ports.).

7332. DOS SANTOS ALVES (Jorge Manuel). Um Porto entre dois impérios: Estudos sobre Macau e as relaçoes Luso-Chinesas. Macau, Instituto Português do Oriente, 99, 229 p. (Colecçao Memória do Oriente).

7333. EL-EINI (Roza I. M.). British forestry policy in mandate Palestine, 1929–1948: aims and realities. *Middle Eastern studies*, 99, 35, 3, p. 72-155.

7334. FRADERA (Josep Maria). Filipinas, la colonia más peculiar: la hacienda pública en la definición de la política colonial, 1762–1868. Madrid, Consejo Superior de Investigaciones Científicas, 99, 292 p. (Biblioteca de historia, 38).

7335. Hong Kong's history: state and society under colonial rule. Ed. by Tak-Wing NGO. London, Routledge, 99, XII-205 p. (Routledge studies in Asia's transformations).

7336. KHODARKOVSKY (Michael). Of christianity, Enlightenment, and colonialism: Russia in the North Caucasus, 1550–1800. *Journal of modern history*, 99, 71, 2, p. 395-430.

7337. MARSHALL (P. J.). The making of an imperial icon: the case of Warren Hastings. *Journal of Imperial and Commonwealth history*, 99, 27, 3, p. 1-16.

7338. TALIB (Naimah S.). Administrators and their service: the Sarawak administrative service under the Brooke Rajahs and British colonial rule. New York, Oxford U. P., 99, XXI-274 p. (South-East Asian historical monographs).

7339. TERTRAIS (H.). Indochine 1945–1954: la monnaie au cœur de la guerre. *In*: Monnaie et relations internationales. 1 [Cf. n° 7277], p. 307-322.

7340. VIRMANI (Arundhati). National symbols under colonial domination: the nationalization of the Indian flag, March-August 1923. *Past and present*, 99, 164, p. 169-197.

7341. Yokohama ei futsu chutongun to gaikokujin kyoryuchi. (British and French forces stationed in Yokohama and resident foreigners). Ed. by Yokohama Taigai Kankei-Shi Kenkyukai and Yokohama Kaiko Shiryokan. Tokyo, Tokyodo Shuppan, 99, 407 p.

Cf. n^{os} *4633, 4645, 8037-8329*

c. *Africa*

7342. AYLMER (G. E.). Slavery under Charles II: the Mediterranean and Tangier. *English historical review*, 99, 114, 456, p. 378-388.

7343. BAGNATO (Bruna). Fra Marianna e Maometto. L'Italia e la lotta per l'indipendenza del Marocco e della Tunisia, 1949–1956. *In*: Europe (L') et la Méditerranée [Cf. n° 3951], p. 71-81.

7344. BIRMINGHAM (David). Portugal and Africa. Basingstoke, Macmillan, 99, VIII-203 p.

7345. Branntwein, Bibeln und Bananen: der deutsche Kolonialismus in Afrika: eine Spurensuche. Hrsg. v. Heiko MÖHLE. Hamburg, Libertäre Assoziation, 99, 168 p.

7346. BUSH (Barbara). Imperialism, race and resistance: Africa and Britain, 1919–1945. London a. New York, Routledge, 99, XVIII-394 p. (ill.).

7347. DORE-AUDIBERT (Andrée). Une décolonisation pacifique: chroniques pour l'histoire. Paris, Kartala, 99, 359 p. (ill., maps).

7348. ECKERT (Andreas). Grundbesitz, Landkonflikte und kolonialer Wandel. Douala 1880 bis 1960. Stuttgart, Steiner, 99, X-503 p. (Beiträge zur Kolonial- und Überseegeschichte, 70).

7349. Imperialism, decolonization and Africa: studies presented to John Hargreaves. Ed. by Roy BRIDGES. Basingstoke, Macmillan, 99, 213 p. (Cambridge Commonwealth series).

7350. KIMBLE (Judith Mary). Migrant labour and colonial rule in Basutoland, 1890–1930. Ed. by Helen M. KIMBLE. Grahamstown, Institute of Social and Economic Research, Rhodes University, 99, XV-320 p. (maps).

7351. KIRK-GREENE (Anthony). On crown service: a history of HM colonial and overseas civil services, 1837–1997. London a. New York, I. B. Tauris, 99, XXVIII-276 p.

7352. LORCIN (Patricia M. E.). Imperialism, colonial identity, and race in Algeria, 1830–1870: the role of the French Medical Corps. *Isis*, 99, 90, 4, p. 652-679.

7353. LÜTZELSCHWAB (Claude). Des premiers projets de colonies suisses en Algérie à la «Compagnie genevoise des Colonies suisses de Sétif». Quelques aspects de la question migratoire en Suisse durant les années 1830–1850. *Schweizerische Zeitschrift für Geschichte*, 99, 49, 4, p. 470-495.

7354. MILNE (Malcolm). No telephone to heaven: from apex to nadir: colonial service in Nigeria, Aden, the Cameroons and the Gold Coast, 1938–1961. Stockbridge, Meon Hill Press, 99, XXV-464 p. (ill., ports.).

7355. MOUROU (Max-Williams). Le régime des concessions: une expérience de colonisation du Congo français. *In*: Afrique: partenariat international et conflits régionaux [Cf. n° 7213], p. 125-134.

7356. MUNGAZI (Dickson A.). The last British liberals in Africa: Michael Blundell and Garfield Todd. Westport a. London, Praeger, 99, XVI-285 p. (ill.).

7357. NAGY (László J.). Le bloc socialiste et la décolonisation en Méditerranée. *In*: Europe (L') et la Méditerranée [Cf. n° 3951], p. 155-166.

7358. OERMANN (Nils Ole). Mission, church and state relations in South West Africa under German rule (1884–1915). Stuttgart, Steiner, 99, 267 p. (Missionsgeschichtliches Archiv, 5).

7359. Ports of the Slave Trade (Bights of Benin and Biafra). Ed. by Robin LAW and Silke STRICKRODT. Stirling, Centre of Commonwealth Studies, University of Stirling, 99, VI-189 p.

7360. RIBEIRO (Jorge). Marcas da guerra colonial. Porto, Campo das Letras, 99, 296 p. (ill.). (Colecçao Campo da memória, 2).

7361. ROSS (Robert). Status and respectability in the Cape Colony, 1750–1850: a tragedy of manners. New York, Cambridge U. P., 99, XII-203 p.

7362. SMURTHWAITE (David). The Boer War. London, Hamlyn, 99, 208 p. (ill., map, ports.).

7363. THIOUB (Ibrahima). Combats nationalistes et politique coloniale: le rôle de François Mitterrand, ministre de la France d'Outre-mer, dans le désapparentement du Rassemblement Démocratique Africain. *In*: Mitterrand et l'Afrique. Organisé par Gouvernement du Sénégal/Institut François Mitterrand. Dakar, Médiature de la République, 99, p. 165-177.

7364. VANDERVORT (Bruce). Wars of imperial conquest in Africa, 1830–1914. Bloomington, Indiana U. P., 99, XVIII-274 p.

Cf. n°s 4808, 4857, 4866, 5071, 7211, 8330-8360

d. America

** 7365. British documents on the end of empire. Series B. Vol. 6. The West Indies. Ed. by S.R. ASHTON and David KILLINGRAY. London, The Stationery Office, 99, CIV-750 p.

** 7366. WICKMAN (Patricia Riles). The tree that bends: discourse, power, and the survival of the Maskókî people. Tuscaloosa a. London, University of Alabama Press, 99, XVIII-296 p. (ill., maps).

7367. ANDERSON (Robin L.). Colonization as exploitation in the Amazon rain forest, 1758–1911. Gainesville, University Press of Florida, 99, X-197 p.

7368. BOCCARA (Guillaume). Etnogénesis mapuche: resistencia y reestructuración entre los indígenas del centro-sur de Chile (siglos XVI–XVIII). *Hispanic American historical review*, 99, 79, 3, p. 425-462.

7369. BURNS (Kathryn). Colonial habits. Convents and the spiritual economy of Cuzco, Peru. Durham a. London, Duke U. P., 99, 307 p.

7370. CÉSPEDES (Guillermo). Ensayos sobre los reinos castellanos de Indias. Madrid, Real Academia de la Historia, 99, 398 p. (Clave historial, 26).

7371. CHUST (Manuel). La cuestión nacional americana en las cortes de Cádiz. Mexico City, Instituto de Investigaciones Históricas, Universidad Nacional Autónoma de México y Valencia, Centro Francisco Tomás y Valiente, Fundación Instituto Historia Social, 99, 325 p.

7372. Colonial legacies: the problem of persistence in Latin American history. Ed. by Jeremy ADELMAN. New York a. London, Routledge, 99, XII-318 p.

7373. DIN (Gilbert C.). Spaniards, planters, and slaves: the Spanish regulation of slavery in Louisiana, 1763–1803. College Station, Texas A&M U. P., 99, XIV-356 p.

7374. Istorija russkoj Ameriki (1732–1867). (A history of Russian America, 1732–1867). Ed. N.N. BOLKHOVITINOV. Vol. 2. Dejatel'nost' Roosijsko-amerikanskoj kompanii (The activities of the Russan-American Company), 1799–1825. Vol. 3. Russkaja Amerika: Ot zenita k zakatu (Russian America: from the zenith to the decline). Moskva, Mezhdunarodnye otnoshenija, 99, 2 vol., 472 p., 560 p.

7375. MEEL (Peter). Tussen autonomie en onafhankelijkheid: Nederlands-Surinaamse betrekkingen 1954–1961. Leiden, Koninklijk Instituut voor Taal-, Land- en Volkenkunde Uitgeverij, 99, XIV-450 p. (Caribbean series, 19).

7376. NIZZA DA SILVA (Maria Beatriz). História da colonizaçao portuguesa no Brasil. Lisboa, Ediçoes Colibri, Grupo de Trabalho do Ministério da Educaçao para as Comemoraçoes dos Descobrimentos Portugueses, 99, 127 p. (ill.).

7377. OBERG (Michael Leroy). Dominion and civility: English imperialism and native America, 1585–1685. Ithaca, Cornell U. P., 99, X-239 p.

7378. PINHEIRO MACHADO (Paulo). A política de colonizaçao do Império. Porto Alegre, Editora da Universidade, Universidade Federal do Rio Grande do Sul, 99, 140 p. (ill.). (Síntese rio-grandense, 24-25).

7379. PUNTONI (Pedro). A mísera sorte: a escravidao africana no Brasil holandês e as guerras do tráfico no Atlântico Sul, 1621–1648). Sao Paulo, Editora Hucitec, 99, 207 p. (ill.). (Coleçao Estudos históricos, 35).

7380. TOVAR PINZÓN (Hermes). El imperio y sus colonias: las cajas reales de la Nueva Granada en el siglo XVI. Bogotá, Archivo General de la Nación, 99, 209 p. (ill., charts, maps). (Archivo General de la Nación. Historia, 4).

7381. VELA WITT (María Susana). El departamento del sur en la Gran Colombia, 1822–1830. Quito, Ediciones Abya-Yala, 99, [s. p.]. (Serie Estudios históricos, 2).

7382. WILLIAMS (Caroline A.). Resistance and rebellion on the Spanish frontier: native responses to colonization in the Colombian Chocó, 1670–1690. *Hispanic American historical review*, 99, 79, 3, p. 397-424.

Cf. n^{os} *4591, 8361-8386*

e. *Oceania*

7383. Exiles of empire: convict experience and penal policy, 1788–1852. Selected papers from the annual conference of the Centre for Tasmanian Historical Studies, Hobart, 1998. Hobart, Centre for Tasmanian Historical Studies, 99, 161 p. (Tasmanian historical studies. Special convict issue, 6, 2).

7384. GANTER (Regina). Letters from Mapoon. Colonising aboriginal gender. *Australian historical studies*, 99, 30, 113, p. 267-285.

7385. Quicksands: foundational histories in Australia & Aotearoa New Zealand. Ed. by Klaus NEUMANN, Nicholas THOMAS and Hilary ERICKSEN. Sidney, UNSW Press, 99, XXII-281 p.

7386. WEAVER (John C.). Frontiers into assets. The social construction of property in New Zealand, 1840–1865. *Journal of Imperial and Commonwealth history*, 99, 27, 3, p. 17-54.

Cf. n^{os} *8387-8392*

§ 3. **From 1500 to 1789**

a. *General*

** 7387. Beziehungen (Die) der Herzöge in Preussen zu West- und Südeuropa (1525–1688): Regesten aus dem Herzoglichen Briefarchiv und den Ostpreussischen Folianten. Bearb. v. Dieter HECKMANN. Köln, Böhlau, 99, 605 p. (Veröffentlichungen aus den Archiven Preussischer Kulturbesitz, 47).

7388. CHIRTOAGĂ (Ion). Sud-estul Moldovei şi stânga Nistrului în anii 1484–1699 (expansiunea şi dominaţia turco-tătară). (South-east Moldavia and the left bank of the Dniester between 1484–1699 – the Turkish-Tatar expansion and rule). Bucureşti, Editura Fundaţiei Culturale Române, 99, 208 p.

7389. DUBOIS (Sébastien). Les bornes immuables de l'État: la rationalisation du tracé des frontières au siècle des Lumières (France, Pays-Bas autriciens et Principauté de Liège). Préface de Claude Bruneel. Kortrijk-Heule, UGA, 99, 486 p. (ill.). (Ancien pays et Assemblées d'États = Standen en landen, 102).

7390. GALASSO (Giuseppe). Le relazioni internazionali nell'età moderna (secoli XV–XVIII). *Rivista storica italiana*, 99, 111, 1, p. 5-36.

7391. GOES FILHO (Synesio Sampaio). Navegantes, bandeirantes, diplomatas: um ensaio sobre a formaçao das fronteiras do Brasil. Sao Paulo, Martins Fontes, 99, 332 p. (ill., maps). (Temas brasileiros).

7392. Istorija vneshnej politiki Rossii. Konets XV–XVII vek (Ot sverzhenija ordynskogo iga do Severnoj vojny). (A history of Russian foreign policy, from the late 15th to the end of the 17th century: from the end of the Tatar yoke to the Northern War). Ed. Gennadij A. SANIN. Moskva, Mezhdunarodnye otnoshenija, 99, 448 p. [Cf. Bibl. 98, n° 7391.]

7393. MAXIM (Mihai). L'Empire ottoman au nord du Danube et l'autonomie des Principautés Roumaines au XVIe siècle: études et documents. İstanbul, Isis Press, 99, 273 p. (ill.). (Analecta Isisiana, 36).

7394. MIHNEVA (R.). The Muskovit Tsardom, the Ottoman Empire and the European diplomacy (mid-sixteenth–end of seventeenth century). *Etudes balkaniques*, 99, 3-4, p. 98-129.

7395. Politics and diplomacy in early modern Italy: the structure of diplomatic practice, 1450–1800. Ed. by Daniela FRIGO. New York, Cambridge U. P., 99, [s. p.]. (Cambridge studies in Italian history and culture).

7396. SCHÜLLER (Karin). Die Beziehungen zwischen Spanien und Irland im 16. und 17. Jahrhundert. Diplomatie, Handel und die soziale Integration katholischer Exulanten. Münster, Aschendorff, 99, VII-280 p. (Spanische Forschungen der Görresgesellschaft, Rh. 2, 34).

7397. TISCHER (Anuschka). Französische Diplomatie und Diplomaten auf dem Westfälischen Friedenskongress: Aussenpolitik unter Richelieu und Mazarin. Münster, Aschendorff, 99, XII-493 p. (Schriftenreihe der Vereinigung zur Erforschung der Neueren Geschichte, 29).

7398. WINDLER (C.). De l'idée de croisade à l'acceptation d'un droit spécifique. La diplomatie espagnole et les régences du Maghreb au XVIIIe siècle. *Revue historique*, 99, 123, 612, p. 747-788.

7399. YI (Young). Wako to nichirei kankeishi. (Japanese pirates and the relationship between Japan and the Koryo dynasty). Tokyo, University of Tokyo Press, 99, 296 p.

b. *1500–1648*

** 7400. Acta Pacis Westphalicae. Ser. II, Abt. B. Die französischen Korrespondenzen. Band 3 (in 2 Teilbänden). 1645–1646. Unt. Benutzung der Vorarb. v. Kriemhild GORONZY bearb. v. Elke JARNUT und Rita BOHLEN mit einer Einl. u. einem Anhang v. Franz BOSBACH. Band 4. 1646. Bearb. Clivia KELCH-RADE u. Anuschka TISCHER unt. Benutzung der Vorarb. v. Kriemhild Gorozny u. unt. Mithilfe v. Michael ROHRSCHNEIDER. Münster, Aschendorff, 99, 3 vol., LXXXII-1246 p., LXXI-975 p.

7401. 1648 and European security proceedings: Stockholm, October 15–16, 1998. Ed. by Klaus-Ri chard BÖHME and Jesper HANSSON. Stockholm, Forsvarshogskolan, 99, 227 p.

7402. ANDERSON (Alison D.). On the verge of war: international relations and the Jülich-Kleve succession crises (1609–1614). Boston, Humanities Press, 99, XVIII-276 p. (Studies in Central European histories).

7403. BONNER (Elizabeth). The politique of Henri II: de facto French rule in Scotland, 1550–1554. Sydney, Sydney Society for Scottish History, 99, 107 p. (Journal of the Sydney Society for Scottish History, 7).

7404. CROXTON (Derek). Peacemaking in early modern Europe. Cardinal Mazarin and the Congress of Westphalia, 1643–1648. Selinsgrove, Susquehanna U. P. a. London, Associated University Presses, 99, 397 p. – IDEM. The Peace of Westphalia of 1648 and the origins of sovereignty. *International history review*, 99, 21, 3, p. 569-591.

7405. DORAN (Susan). England and Europe in the sixteenth century. Basingstoke, Macmillan, 99, XVII-145 p. (British history in perspective).

7406. DOS SANTOS ALVES (Jorge Manuel). O Domínio do norte de Samatra: a história dos sultanatos de Samudera-Pacém e de Achém, e das suas relaçoes com os portugueses (1500–1580). Prefácio de Luís Filipe THOMAZ. Lisboa, Sociedade Histórica da Independência de Portugal, 99, 301 p. (Colecçao Memória lusíada, 2).

7407. Frankreich und Hessen-Kassel zur Zeit des Dreissigjährigen Krieges und des Westfälischen Friedens. Hrsg. v. Klaus MALETTKE. Marburg, N. G. Elwert, 99, VI-202 p. (Veröffentlichungen der Historischen Kommission für Hessen, 46, Kleine Schriften, 5).

7408. GATTONI (Maurizio). La spada della croce: la difficile alleanza ispano-veneto-pontificia nella guerra di Cipro. Politica estera e teoresi filosofica nei documenti pontifici. *Ricerche storiche*, 99, 29, p. 611-650.

7409. GIRY-DELOISON (Charles). Elisabeth Ier et le traité d'Arras de 1579. *In*: Arras et la diplomatie européenne XVe–XVIe siècles [Cf. n° 3247], p. 277-297.

7410. HAN (Myong-gi). Imjin Waeran kwa Han-Chung kwangye. (Study on the relations between Korea and China from Japanese invasion of Korea in 1592 to Manchu invasion of Korea in 1636). Soul-si, Yoksa Pip'yongsa, 99, 449 p. (Yokpi Hangukhak yongu ch'ongso, 14).

7411. KAISER (Michael). Politik und Kriegsführung: Maximilian von Bayern, Tilly und die Katholische Liga im Dreissigjährigen Krieg. Münster, Aschendorff, 99, IX-582 p. (Schriftenreihe der Vereinigung zur Erforschung der Neueren Geschichte, 28).

7412. KOLLMANN (Josef). Valdstejn a evropská politika, 1625–1630: historie 1. Generalátu. (Wallenstein e la politica europea, 1625–1630). Praha, Academia, 99, 452 p. (ill., plates).

7413. LUNITZ (Martin). La pratique diplomatique au XVIe siècle: les envoyés permanents de Charles Quint en France. *In*: Arras et la diplomatie européenne XVe–XVIe siècles [Cf. n° 3247], p. 205-217.

7414. PERŁAKOWSKI (Adam). Propaganda cesarska w latach 1635–1648 w świetle pism ulotnych ze "zbiorów berlińskich" Biblioteki Jagiellońskiej. (Die kaiserliche Propaganda in den Jahren 1635–1648 angesichts der Flugblätter aus den "Berliner Sammlungen" der Jagiellonen-Bibliothek). *Studia Historyczne*, 99, 42, 1, p. 23-41.

7415. PHILLIPS (Gervase). The Anglo-Scots wars, 1513–1550: a military history. Woodbridge a. Rochester, Boydell Press, 99, 291 p. (Warfare in history).

7416. PILLORGET (René). «Batterie arrivée entre allemands» à Saint-Germain-des-Prés (1642). *Revue d'histoire diplomatique*, 99, 113, 3, p. 251-260.

7417. POTTER (David). Anglo-French relations 1500: the aftermath of the Hundred Years War. *Franco-British studies*, 99, 28, p. 41-66. – IDEM. The frontiers of Artois in European diplomacy, 1482–1560. *In*: Arras et la diplomatie européenne XVe–XVIe siècles [Cf. n° 3247], p. 261-275.

7418. REPGEN (Konrad). Der Westfälische Friede, Ereignis, Fest und Erinnerung. Opladen u. Wiesbaden, Westdeutscher Verlag, 99, 39 p.

7419. SCHMIDT (Georg). Der Dreissigjährige Krieg. München, Beck, 99, 119 p. (Beck'sche Reihe. Wissen, 2005).

7420. WEGWOOD (C. V.). The Thirty Years War. Introduction by Roy STRONG. London, Folio Society, 99, IX-508 p.

7421. WYCZAŃSKI (Andrzej). Polska w Europie XVI stulecia. (Polen in Europa des XVI. Säkulums). Poznań, Wydaw. Poznańskie, 99, 224 p. (Czas i Myśl).

c. *1648–1789*

** 7422. ABRAHAM, EREWANTS'I. History of the wars (1721–1738): Abraham Erewants'i's, Patmut'iwn paterazmats'n. Annotated translation with introductory notes by George A. BOURNOUTIAN. Costa Mesa, Mazda Publishers, 99, 111 p. (ill., maps). (Armenian studies series, 3).

** 7423. Correspondance consulaire des ambassadeurs de France a Constantinople 1668–1708: inventaire analytique des articles A.E.B1 376 a 385. Par Raia ZAIMOVA; revue pour l'impression par Philippe HENRAT. Paris, Centre historiques des archives nationales, 99, 274 p.

** 7424. Correspondance diplomatique de François II Rákóczi: 1711–1735: choix de documents. Publiée par Béla KÖPECZI. Budapest, Balassi Kiadó, 99, 379 p.

** 7425. DE MASSIAC (Barthélemy d'Espinchal). Plan francés de conquista de Buenos Aires, 1660–1693. Investigación, introducción y traducción de Maud DE RIDDER DE ZEMBORAIN. Buenos Aires, Emecé Editores, 99, 185 p. (ill.). (Memoria argentina).

7426. 1648–1998, 350 años de la paz de Westfalia: del antagonismo a la integración de Europa: ciclo de conferencias celebrado en la Biblioteca Nacional, Madrid, 9 de marzo a 30 de noviembre de 1998. Madrid, Fundación Carlos de Amberes y Biblioteca Nacional, 99, 452 p. (ill.).

7427. BADONEY MARTÍN (Beatriz). Los orígenes del Ministerio de Asuntos Exteriores (1714–1808). Madrid, Ministerio de Asuntos Exteriores, 99, 563 p. (Biblioteca diplomática española. Estudio, 18).

7428. BRAUN (Guido). Frédéric-Charles Moser et les langues de la diplomatie européenne (1648–1750). *Revue d'histoire diplomatique*, 99, 113, 3, p. 261-278.

7429. CHERKASOV (P.P.). Ljudovik XVI i Ekaterina II (1774–1776 gg.). (Louis XVI et Catherine II, 1774–1776). *Novaja i novejshaja istorija*, 99, 47, 5, p. 161-182; 6, p. 35-58.

7430. CIEŚLAK (Edmund). Francuska placówka konsularna w Gdańsku w XVIII wieku. Status prawny – zadania – działalność. (Französische konsularische Dienststelle in Danzig im XVIII. Jahrhundert. Rechtsstatus – Aufgabenbereich – Wirken). Kraków, PAU, 99. 204 p. (Rozprawy Wydz. Hist.-Filoz., 90).

7431. DE LEEUW (Karl). The Black Chamber in the Dutch Republic and the Seven Years' War, 1751–1763. *Diplomacy and statecraft*, 99, 10, 1, p. 1-30.

7432. DE REZENDE MARTINS (Estevão). 1762, le Brésil pour la France: un objet de convoitise. *In*: Brésil (Le), l'Europe et les équilibres internationaux XVIe–XXe siecles [Cf. n° 7228], p. 149-160.

7433. DRAKE (James D.). King Philip's War: Civil War in New England, 1675–1676. Amherst, University of Massachusetts Press, 99, VII-257 p. (Native Americans and the Northeast: culture, history, and the contemporary).

7434. DUCHHARDT (Heinz). «Westphalian System». Zur Problematik einer Denkfigur. *Historische Zeitschrift*, 99, 269, 2, p. 305-316.

7435. DZIEMBOWSKI (Edmond). Un nouveau patriotisme français, 1750–1770: la France face à la puissance anglaise à l'époque de la guerre de Sept Ans. Oxford, Voltaire Foundation, 99, VII-566 p.

7436. GREGORY (Jeremy), STEVENSON (John). The Longman companion to Britain in the eighteenth century, 1688–1820. Harlow, Longman, 99, 568 p.

7437. KAUER (Christiane). Brandenburg-Preussen und Österreich 1705–1711. Bonn, Holos, 318 p. (Philosophie und Gesellschaft, 8).

7438. KLOFT (Matthias Theodor), [et al.]. 1648: Legatus Plenipotentiarius Graf Johann Ludwig von Nassau-Hadamar und der Westfälische Friede. Hrsg. v. der Kulturvereinigung Hadamar. Limburg, Glaukos, 99, 125 p.

7439. KUVAJA (Christer). Försörjning av en ockupationsarmé: den ryska arméns underhållssystem i Finland 1713–1721. (Le Ravitaillement d'une armée d'occupation: le système de subsistance de l'armée russe en Finlande de 1713 à 1721). Åbo, Åbo Akademi, 99, 348 p. (ill., diagr., tab.).

7440. LOVE (Ronald S.). Monarchs, merchants, and missionaries in early modern Asia. The missions étrangeres in Siam, 1662–1684. *International history review*, 99, 21, 1, p. 1-27.

7441. LYNN (John A.). The wars of Louis XIV, 1667–1714. London a. New York, Longman, 99, XIII-421 p. (Modern wars in perspective).

7442. MALETTKE (Klaus). Les traités de Westphalie (24 octobre 1648) et l'idée de «l'ordre européen»: mythe ou realité? *In*: 350e anniversaire du traités de Westphalie, 1648–1998: une genèse de l'Europe, une société à reconstruire [Cf. n° 3924], p.161-173.

7443. Mare nostrum. Om Westfaliska freden och Östersjön som ett svenkt maktcentrum. (Mare nostrum. A propos des traités de Westphalie et de la Baltique comme mer suédoise). Red. par Kerstin ABUKHANFUSA. Stockholm, Riksarkivet, 99, 272 p. (ill.). (Skrifter utgivna av Riksarkivet, 13).

7444. MEYER (Stephan). Vorbote des Untergangs. Die Angst der Schweizer Aristokraten vor Joseph II. Zürich, Chronos, 99, 416 p.

7445. OLIPHANT (John). The Cherokee Embassy to London, 1762. *Journal of Imperial and Commonwealth history*, 99, 27, 1, p. 1-26.

7446. PERINI (Sergio). Venezia e la guerra di Morea (1684–1699). *Archivio veneto*, 99, 130, 153, p. 45-91.

7447. PILLORGET (René). Du traité de Ryswick (septembre–octobre 1697) aux conférences de Francfort (décembre 1698–mai 1701). *In*: 350e anniversaire du traités de Westphalie, 1648–1998: une genèse de l'Europe, une société à reconstruire [Cf. n° 3924], p. 195-202.

7448. PORAZIŃSKI (Jarosław). Epiphania Poloniae. Orientacje i postawy polityczne szlachty polskiej w dobie wielkiej wojny północnej (1702–1710). (Epiphania Poloniae. Orientierungen und politische Haltungen des polnischen Adels während des großen Nordischen Krieges, 1702–1710). Toruń, Wydaw. Uniw. M. Kopernika, 99, 217 p.

7449. STORRS (C.). Diplomacy and the rise of Savoy, 1690–1720. Cambridge, Cambridge U. P., 99, [s. p.].

7450. ŠUNDRICA (Zdravko). Obavještajna služba Dubrovačke Republike u 18. Stoljeću. (The Intelligence Service of the Dubrovnik Republic during the Austro-Turkish War, 1737–1739). *Anali zavoda za povijesne znanosti*, 99, 37, p. 157-204.

7451. TCACI (Vladimir). Moldova în relațiile politice internaționale (1763–1774). (Moldavia in international political relations. 1763–1774). Chișinău, Editura Civitas, 99, 128 p.

Cf. n°s 3924, 4307, 4529, 7464

§ 4. From 1789 to 1815.

* 7452. ROQUINCOURT (Thierry). Bibliographie française sur la marine et les colonies, 1789–1815. Paris, Lettrage Distribution, 99, 498 p.

** 7453. GUYOT (Claude Etienne). Carnets de campagnes (1792–1815). Rec. et ann. par Jean-Hugues DE FONT-RÉAULX. Paris, Librairie historique F. Teissedre, 99, 431 p. (Collection du bicentenaire de l'Épopée impériale).

** 7454. HOCHEDLINGER (Michael). Der Weg in den Krieg: die Berichte des Franz Paul Zigeuner von Blumendorf, k.k. Geschäftsträger in Paris 1790–1792. Wien, Verlag der österreichischen Akademie der Wissenschaften, 99, LXXV-298 p. (Fontes Rerum Austriacarum. 2. Abteilung, Diplomataria et acta, 90).

** 7455. Invasion (L') de 1798: documents d'archives françaises concernant la liquidation de l'Ancien Régime en Suisse par la France. Sous la direction de Derck ENGELBERTS et Jürg STÜSSI-LAUTERBURG; en collaboration avec Alain BERLINCOURT, Hans LUGINBÜHL et Bianca PAULI; avant-propos de Adolf OGI; préface de Philippe HENRY. Auvernier, Editions Le Roset, 99, 307 p. (ill.).

** 7456. KAPODISTRIAS (Ioannes). Aperçu de ma carrière publique depuis 1798 jusqu'à 1822. Précédé de Arthur DE GOBINEAU. Capodistria. Ed. par Thierry ROUILLARD. Paris, La Vouivre, 99, IV-110 p. (Du Directoire à l'Empire, 15).

7457. AMINI (Iradj). Napoleon and Persia: Franco-Persian relations under the First Empire; within the context of the rivalries between France, Britain and Russia. Richmond, Curzon Press, 99, XIX-228 p. (ill.).

7458. DAMAMME (Jean-Claude). La bataille de Waterloo. Paris, Perrin, 99, 414 p.

7459. DEGROS (Maurice). Les consulats français dans l'Europe du nord pendant la révolution. *Revue d'histoire diplomatique*, 99, 113, 4, p. 343-372.

7460. Europa (L') scopre Napoleone, 1793–1804: atti del Congresso internazionale napoleonico, Cittadella di Alessandria, 21–26 giugno 1997. A cura di Vittorio SCOTTI DOUGLAS. Alessandria, Edizioni dell'Orso, 99, 2 vol., XXXVI-VI-1072 p. (ill., maps). (Archivio Marengo, 1).

7461. FLEMING (Katherine Elizabeth). The Muslim Bonaparte: diplomacy and orientalism in Ali Pasha's Greece. Princeton a. Chichester, Princeton U. P., 99, XII-206 p. (ill.).

7462. HOFSCHRÖER (Peter). 1815, the Waterloo campaign: the German victory: from Waterloo to the fall of Napoleon. London, Greenhill, 384 p.

7463. Krig kring Kvarken. Finska kriget 1808–1809 och slaget vid Oravais i ny belysning. (Guerre autour du golfe de Botnie. Nouvel éclairage sur la guerre de Finlande en 1808–1809 et la bataille d'Oravais). Red. par Martin HÅRSTEDT et Göran BACKMAN. Oravais, Oravais historiska förening, 99, 375 p. (ill., cartes).

7464. LUKOWSKI (Jerzy). The partitions of Poland 1772, 1793, 1795. London a. New York, Longman, 99, XV-232 p.

7465. MISCHEVCA (Vladimir). Moldova în politica marilor puteri la începutul secolului al XIX-lea. (Moldavia in the policy of the great powers at the beginning of the 19th century). Chișinău, Editura Civitas, 99, 143 p.

7466. NAWROT (Dariusz). Działania dyplomacji polskiej w Wiedniu w latach 1788–1892. Z dziejów stosunków polsko-austriackich w dobie Sejmu Czteroletniego. (Das Wirken der polnischen Diplomaten in Wien in den Jahren 1788–1892. Zur Geschichte der polnisch-österreichischen Verhältnisse während des Vierjährigen Sejms). Katowice, Wydaw. Uniw. Śląskiego, 99, 200 p. (Prace Uniwersytetu Śląskiego w Katowicach, 1819).

7467. PAWŁOWSKI (Bronisław). Wojna polsko-austriacka 1809 r. (Polnisch-österreichischer Krieg 1809). Warszawa, Volumen, 99, 462 p. (O Wolność i Niepodległość).

7468. RILEY (J. P.). Napoleon and the World War of 1813: lessons in coalition warfighting. Portland, Frank Cass, 99, [s. p.].

7469. SALVEMINI (Raffaella). Gli Spagnoli a Napoli al tempo dei Napoleonidi (1806–1815). Le ragioni di una débâcle economica e politica. *Mélanges de l'École française de Rome. Italie Méditerranée*, 99, 111, p. 683-719.

7470. SCHUR (Nathan). Napoleon in the Holy Land. London, Greenhill Books, 99, 224 p. (ill.).

7471. SPARROW (Elizabeth). Secret service: British agents in France, 1792–1815. Woodgridge, Boydell Press, 99, XVI-459 p.

7472. VAN UYTHOVEN (Geert). Voorwaarts, Bataven! De Engels-Russische invasie van 1799. Zaltbommel, Europese Bibliotheek, 99, 208 p. (ill., maps, ports.).

7473. Wellington studies. Vol. 2. Ed. by C. M. WOOLGAR. Southampton, Hartley Institute, University of Southampton, 99, IX-252 p.

7474. ZEHETBAUER (Ernst). Landwehr gegen Napoleon: Österreichs erste Miliz und der Nationalkrieg von 1809. Wien, Öbv & hpt, 99, 390 p. (Militärgeschichtliche Dissertationen österreichischer Universitäten, 12).

7475. ZEMTSOV (Vladimir N.). Bitva pri Moskvereke: Armija Napoleona v Borodinskom srazhenii. (The Battle of Moskva-river: Napoleon's army in the battle of Borodino). Moskva, Rejtar', 99, 208 p. (bibl.).

Cf. n°s 4307, 4529, 7395, 7427, 7436, 7494

§ 5. From 1815 to 1910.

** 7476. BASENKO (Ju.V.). Rossija i SShA: diplomaticheskie otnoshenija, 1900–1917. (Russia and the USA: the diplomatic relations, 1900–1917). Mezhdunar. fond «Demokratija». Ed. A.N. JAKOVLEV. Moskva, Violanta, 99, 854 p. (bibl.; ind.). [Eng. summary]

** 7477. Documenti diplomatici italiani (I). Ministero degli affari esteri. Commissione per la pubblicazione dei documenti diplomatici. Serie II. 1870–1896. Vol. 26. 15 dicembre 1893–31 marzo 1895. Roma, Istituto poligrafico e Zecca dello Stato, Libreria dello Stato, 99, LXXVII-751 p.

** 7478. Documenti diplomatici italiani sull'Armenia. Serie II. 1891–1916. Commissione per la pubblicazione dei documenti italiani sull'Armenia. Vol. 1. 1 Gennaio 1891–31 Dicembre 1894. A cura di Maurizio RUSSO. Vol. 2. 1 Gennaio–31 Agosto 1895. A cura di Laura LUMINARI. Firenze, Commissione per la pubblicazione dei documenti italiani sull'Armenia, 99, 2 vol., XLI-275 p., XXVIII, 525 p.

** 7479. GIUMANINI (Michelangelo L.). Beni culturali: reciproche restituzioni tra Lombardo Veneto e Stato Pontificio (1816–1818). Presentazione di Giancarlo SANTI. Bologna, CLUEB, 166 p. (ill.).

** 7480. KIŠKILOVA (P.), BELIČKOVA (C.). Rumunski diplomatičeski dokumenti za Suedinenieto na Bulgarija i Srubskobulgarskata vojna prez 1885 g. (Documents diplomatiques roumaines sur l'Union de la Bulgarie et la Guerre serbo-bulgare de l'an 1885). *Voennoistoričeski sbornik*, 99, 3, p. 53-73.

** 7481. Quellen zur Ära Metternich. Hrsg. v. Elisabeth DROSS. Darmstadt, Wissenschaftliche Buchgesellschaft, 99, XX-342 p. (Ausgewählte Quellen zur deutschen Geschichte der Neuzeit, 23a).

7482. Anticipating total war: the German and American experiences, 1871–1914. Ed. by Manfred F. BOEMEKE, Roger CHICKERING and Stig FÖRSTER. Washington, German Historical Institute. Cambridge U. P., New York, 99, IX-496 p. (Publications of the German Historical Institute).

7483. Armenische Frage (Die) und die Schweiz, 1896–1923 = La question arménienne et la Suisse, 1896–1923. Hrsg. v. Hans Lukas KIESER. Zürich, Chronos, 99, 375 p. (ill., maps).

7484. BAUMGART (Winfried). Europäisches Konzert und nationale Bewegung: internationale Beziehungen, 1830–1878. Paderborn, Ferdinand Schöning, 99, XV-600 p. (Handbuch der Geschichte der internationalen Beziehungen, 6). – IDEM. The Crimean war, 1853–1856. London, Arnold, 99, XI-244 p.

7485. BENYON (John). Main show or side-show? Natal and the south African War. *Journal of Imperial and Commonwealth history*, 99, 27, 1, p. 27-58.

7486. BURTON (David H.). British-American diplomacy, 1895–1917: early years of the special relationship. Malabar, Krieger, 99, VI-154 p. (The Anvil series).

7487. CHAMLEY (John). Splendid isolation? Britain and the balance of power 1874–1914. London, Sceptre, 99, X-518 p.

7488. CHIRICA (Codrin-Valentin). Anglia şi "Chestiunea Orientală". 1830–1900. (England and the "Oriental Question". 1830–1900). Iaşi, Editura Helios, 99, 180 p.

7489. CHWALBA (Andrzej). Polacy w służbie Moskali. (Polen im Dienste der Moskowiter). Warszawa, Kraków, Wydaw. Nauk. PWN, 99, 257 p.

7490. Congreso Nacional de Historia Militar: Buenos Aires, 20, 21 y 22 de noviembre de 1996. Buenos Aires, Instituto de Historia Militar Argentina, 99, 2 vol., [s. p.].

7491. CRAM (Robert Gordon). German interests in the Ottoman empire, 1878–1885. London, [s. n.], 99, 392 p. [Thesis (Ph. D.) – London 1999].

7492. Crisis (The) of 1898: colonial redistribution and nationalist mobilization. Ed. by Emma Aurora DÁVILA COX and Angel SMITH. Basingstoke, Macmillan a. New York, St. Martin's Press, 99, IX-221 p. (ill.).

7493. DATSYSHEN (Vladimir Grigor'evich). Russko-Kitaiskaia voina. (Russian-Chinese war). Chast' 2. Pokhod na Pekin. Sankt-Peterburg, Al'manakh "TSitadel'", 99, 157 p. (Malaia seriia).

7494. DAVISON (Roderic H.). Nineteenth century Ottoman diplomacy and reforms. İstanbul, Isis Press, 99, VII-460 p. (Analecta Isisiana, 34).

7495. DE MADARIAGA (Maria Rosa). España y el RIF: crónica de una historia casi olvidada. Melilla, Ciudad Autónoma de Melilla, 99, 535 p. (Colección "La biblioteca de Melilla", 12).

7496. DJULGEROVA (N.). Ruski sčrikhi kum Iztočnija vupros (1894–1904). Ambicii i planove na imperskata diplomacija. [Notes russes à la Question d'Orient (1894–1904). Ambitions et plans de la diplomatie d'empire]. Sofija, [s. n.], 99, 200 p.

7497. DYKSTRA (David L.). The shifting balance of power: American-British diplomacy in North America, 1842–1848. Lanham, University Press of America, 99, XXXIV-247 p.

7498. EDGERTON (Robert B.). Death or glory: the legacy of the Crimean War. Boulder, Westview Press, 99, IX-288 p.

7499. EVANS (John L.). Russian expansion on the Amur 1848–1860: the push to the Pacific. Lampeter, Edwin Mellen Press, 99, III-245 p. (Studies in Russian history, 1).

7500. France (La) et la Serbie du congrès de Berlin à la crise de juillet 1914. Actes du colloque franco-serbe de Strasbourg (décembre 1996). *Revue d'Europe centrale*, 99, 7, 135 p. [Cf. n[os] <sélection> 5244, 7523, 7536.]

7501. Französische Akten zur Geschichte des Krimkriegs. Band 2. 28. März 1854 bis 2. März 1855. Band 3. 3. März 1855 bis 29. Mai 1856. Bearbeitet von Martin SENNER. München, R. Oldenbourg, 99, 2 vol., [s. p.]. (Akten zur Geschichte des Krimkriegs, 4).

7502. GENOV (R.). «Bulgarizacijata» na britanskata vunšna politika. (Preformulirane na bunšnopolitičeskite principi na liberalnata partija prez 70-te godini na XIX v.). [La «bulgarisation» de la politique extérieure britannique. (Réformulation des principes de politique extérieure du parti libéral aux années 70 du XIXe s.)]. *In*: Moderniiat istorik: vuobrazhenie, informiranost, pokoleniia. Sustaviteli Kostadin GROZEV i Todor POPNEDELEV. Sofiia, IK Daniela Ubenova, 99, p. 269-288.

7503. GHIANNOULOPOULOS (Gh.). "I eugenis mas tiphlosis…". Exoterikì politikì kai "ethnicà themata" apo tin itta tou 1897 eos ti Mikroasiatikì Katastrophì. ("Our noble blinding…" foreign policy and "National Issues" since the defeat of 1897 up to the catastrophe in Asia Minor). [S. l.], Bibliorama, 99, [s. p.].

7504. GOODLAD (Graham D.). British foreign and imperial policy, 1865–1919. London a. New York, Routledge, 99, 128 p. (Questions and analysis in history).

7505. HARAKSIM (Ľudovít). Zakladatelia marxizmu o malých slovanských národoch podunajskej monarchie v revolučných rokoch 1848–1849. (Die Gründer des Marxismus über die Rolle der kleinen slawischen Nationen der Donaumonarchie in den Jahren 1848–1849). *Historický časopis*, 99, 47, 1, p. 33-42. [Deutsche Zfassung].

7506. HAREL (Yaron). Le Consul de France et l'affaire de Damas à la lumière de nouveaux documents. *Revue d'histoire diplomatique*, 99, 113, 2, p. 143-170.

7507. HUGHES (Michael). Diplomacy before the Russian Revolution: Britain, Russia, and the old diplomacy, 1894–1917. New York, St. Martins Press, 99, [s. p.]. (Studies in diplomacy).

7508. KHADŽINIKOLOVA (Elena). Srubsko-Turskata vojna, Rusija i Zapadna Evropa prez 1876 g. (La guerre serbo-turque, la Russie et l'Europe Occidentale en 1876). Sofija, FTP, 99, 102 p.

7509. KHEVROLINA (Viktorija M.). Vlast' i obshchestvo: bor'ba v Rossii po voprosam vneshnej politiki, 1878–1894 gg. (Power and society: fighting in Russia apropos of foreign policy, 1878–1894). RAN, In-t rossijskoj istorii. Moskva, [s. n.], 99, 316 p. (bibl.).

7510. KIRCHBERGER (Ulrike). Aspekte deutsch-britischer Expansion. Die Überseeinteressen der deutschen Migranten in Großbritannien in der Mitte des 19. Jahrhunderts. Stuttgart, Steiner, 99, 508 p. (Beiträge zur Kolonial- und Überseegeschichte, 73). – EADEM. The German National League in Britain and ideas of a German overseas empire, 1859–1867. *European history quarterly*, 99, 29, 4, p. 451-483.

7511. KLEJN (Zbigniew). Polskie ślady w budowie nowożytnej Bułgarii 1877–1914. (Polnische Spuren im Bauprozess des neuzeitlichen Bulgariens 1877–1914). Łowicz, Mazowiecka Wyższa Szkoła Humanist.-Pedagog., 99, 449 p.

7512. KOSÁRY (Domokos). Magyarország és a nemzetközi politica 1847–1849. (Hungary and the international politics). Budapest, Historia MTA Tört.tud Int., 99, 348 p.

7513. KUSHNER (David). The district of Jerusalem in the eyes of the three Ottoman governors at the end of the Hamidian period. *Middle Eastern studies*, 99, 35, 2, p. 83-102.

7514. LACAZE (Yvon). La nation Tchèque vue par le premier consul de France à Prague, Alfred-Louis Méroux de Valois (1897–1903). *Revue d'histoire diplomatique*, 99, 113, 1, p. 45-74.

7515. Lincoln Forum (The): Abraham Lincoln, Gettysburg and the Civil War. Ed. by John Y. SIMON, Harold HOLZER and William D. PEDERSON. Mason City, Savas, 99, IX-121 p.

7516. LUNGU (Corneliu Mihail). Transilvania în raporturile româno-austro-ungare. 1876–1886. (Transylvania in the Romanian-Austrian-Hungarian relations. 1876–1886). București, Editura Viitorul Românesc, 99, 469 p.

7517. MARINKOVIC (Miriana). Turska kancelarija Kneza Miloša Obrenovića (1815–1839). (The Turkish Chancellery of Prince Miloš Obrenović, 1815–1839). Urednik Slavenko TERZIC. Beograd, Istorijski institut SANU, 99, 214 p. (ill.). (Posebna izdanja / Istorijski institut Srpske akademije nauka i umetnosti, 31).

7518. MELANCON (Glenn). Honour in opium? The British declaration of war on China, 1839–1840. *International history review*, 99, 21, 4, p. 855-875.

7519. México frente al desenlace del 98: la guerra hispanonorteamericana. Coordinadores, José Alfredo URIBE SALAS, María Teresa CORTÉS ZAVALA y Consuelo NARANJO OROVIO. Morelia, Universidad Michoacana de San Nicolás de Hidalgo y Río Piedras, Universidad de Puerto Rico y Morelia, Instituto Michoacano de Cultura, 99, 194 p. (Colección Estudios de historia mexicana, 6).

7520. MITCHELL (Nancy). The danger of dreams: German and American imperialism in Latin America. Chapel Hill a. London, University of North Carolina Press, 99, XI-312 p.

7521. MONZALI (Luciano). Sidney Sonnino e la politica estera italiana dal 1878 al 1914. *Clio*, 99, 35, p. 397-447.

7522. MÜLLER (Frank Lorenz). A sincere well-wisher of Germany: studies in the British perception of the questions of political reform and national unity in the German Confederation, 1830–1863. Oxford, [s. n.], 99, XI-294 p. [Thesis (D. Phil.) – University of Oxford, 1999].

7523. NOUZILLE (Jean). L'intervention française en Dobroudja (julliet–août 1854). *In*: Révolution (La) de

1848 et ses suites dans les relations franco-roumaines [Cf. n° 7528], p. 49-72. – IDEM. Pierre Ier de Serbie et la France. In: France (La) et la Serbie du congrès de Berlin à la crise de juillet 1914 [Cf. n° 7500], p. 71-87.

7524. OSBORNE (John B.). Wilfred G. Thesiger, Sir Edward Grey, and the British campaign to reform the Congo, 1905–1909. *Journal of Imperial and Commonwealth history*, 99, 27, 1, p. 59-80.

7525. PANTEV (Andrei Lazarov), GENOV (Rumen). Uiliam Gladston i bulgarite: politika na pravedna strast. (William Gladstone and the Bulgarians. A policy of righteous passion). Sofiia, TANGRA TanNakRa-Obshtobulgarska fondatsiia, 99, 199 p. (Bulgarska vechnost, 8).

7526. PÉREZ (Louis A. jr.). Incurring a debt of gratitude: 1898 and the moral sources of United States hegemony in Cuba. *American historical review*, 99, 104, 2, p. 356-398.

7527. RAUCH (Georg von). Conflict in the Southern Cone: the Argentine military and the boundary dispute with Chile, 1870–1902. Westport a. London, Praeger, 99, XII-229 p.

7528. Révolution (La) de 1848 et ses suites dans les relations franco-roumaines. Actes du Colloque francoroumain de Strasbourg, 1998. *Etudes danubiennes*, 99, 15, 2, p. 1-103. [Cf. n° <sélection> 7523.]

7529. RODRÍGUEZ GONZÁLEZ (Agustín Ramón). La Armada Española, la campaña del Pacífico, 1862–1871: España frente a Chile y Perú. Madrid, Agualarga, 99, 141 p. (ill., map).

7530. ROYLE (Trevor). Crimea: the Great Crimean War, 1854–1856. London, Little Brown, 99, XI-564 p.

7531. Russo-Japanese war (The) in cultural perspective, 1904–1905. Ed. by David WELLS and Sandra WILSON. New York, St. Martin's, 99, XIII-213 p.

7532. SÁNCHEZ ANDRÉS (Agustín). La normalización de las relaciones entre España y México durante el Porfiriato (1880–1911). *Historia mexicana*, 99, 48, 191, p. 731-765.

7533. SERGEEV (Evgenij Ju.), ULUNJAN (Artem A.). Voennye agenty Rossijskoj imperii v Evrope, 1900–1914 gg. (Military agents of the Russian Empire in Europe, 1900–1914). RAN, In-t vseobshchej istorii. Moskva, [s. n.], 99, 419 p. (bibl., ind.).

7534. United States-Latin American relations, 1850–1903: establishing a relationship. Ed. by Thomas M. LEONARD. Tuscaloosa, University of Alabama Press, 99, 303 p.

7535. URBACH (Karina). Bismarck's favourite Englishman. Lord Odo Russell's mission to Berlin. London a. New York, I. B. Tauris, 99, VII-279 p.

7536. VOIVODIĆ (Mihailo). Quelques aspects des relations politiques entre la Serbie et la France de 1895 à 1914. In: France (La) et la Serbie du congrès de Berlin à la crise de juillet 1914 [Cf. n° 7500], p. 59-69.

7537. ZAKARIA (Fareed). From wealth to power: the unusual origins of America's world role. Princeton a. Chichester, Princeton U. P., 99, 216 p. (ill., maps). (Princeton studies in international history and politics).

7538. ŻURAWSKI VEL GRAJEWSKI (Radosław Paweł). Działalność księcia Adama Jerzego Czartoryskiego w Wielkiej Brytanii (1831–1832). (Die Tätigkeit des Fürsten Adam Jerzy Czartoryski in Großbritannien, 1831–1832). Warszawa, Semper, 99, 176 p.

Cf. n°s 866, 4806, 4928, 5226, 5244, 7192, 7456, 7555, 7570

§ 6. From 1910 to 1935.
The First World War.

** 7539. Balkanskite vojni po stranitse bulgarskija pechat 1912–1913. Sbornik materiali. (Les guerres balkaniques sur les pages de la presse bulgare des années 1912–1913. Recueil de matériaux). Pod. i sust. P. KICHKILOVA. Sofiia, [s. n.], 99, 250 p.

** 7540. Documents diplomatiques français. 1914. 3 août–31 décembre. Ministère des affaires étrangères. Commission de publication des documents diplomatiques. Paris, Imprimerie nationale, 99, LXXI-763 p.

** 7541. Dokumente për Çamërinë: 1912–1939. Përgatitur nga Kaliopi Naska. Red. Pavli HAXHILLAZI. Tiranë, Dituria, 99, 743 p

** 7542. Mission militaire Française auprés de la République Tchécoslovaque 1919–1939. Edition documentaire. Tomo 1. 1919–1925. Vol. 1. Contracts, accords, statuts. Vol. 2a. 1919–1920, Rapports courants. Ed. par Radko BŘACH et Fréderic GUELTON. Praha, Historický ústav Armády ČR, 99, 2 vol., 120 p., 172 p.

** 7543. Relații româno-sovietice. Documente. (Romanian-Soviet relations. Documents). Vol. I. 1917–1934. Redactor responsabil al ediției române: Dumitru PREDA. București, Editura Enciclopedică, 99, 445 p.

** 7544. ROZENTAL' (Isaak S.), [et al.]. Materialy po istorii Pervoj mirovoj vojny. (Materials on the history of the First World War). Gos. muzej sovremennoj istorii Rossii. Moskva, [s. n.], 99, 309 p. (Sb. nauch. tr. Gos. muzeja sovremennoj istorii Rossii, 24; Golosa istorii, 3).

** 7545. SCURTU (Ioan). România și Marile Puteri: documente. 1. 1918–1933. (Romania and the Great Powers: documents). București, Editura Fundației România de Mâine, 99, [s. p.].

** 7546. VKP(b), Komintern i Kitaj: Dokumenty. (The Communist Party of the Soviet Union, the Comintern and China). Vol. 3. VKP(b), Komintern i sovetskoe dvizhenie v Kitae, 1927–1931. (The C.P.S.U.(B.), the Comintern and the Soviet Movement in China, 1927–1931). Eds. M.L. TITARENKO, M. LEJTNER [et al.]; Ros. tsentr khranenija i izuchenija dokumentov novejshej istorii. Parts 1-2. Moskva, Buklet, 99, 1602 p.

7547. ÁDÁM (Magda). Alliance franco-checoslovaque. *In*: Československo 1918–1938 [Cf. n° 4219], p. 513-522.

7548. BAHOVEC (Tina). Die Kärntner Slowenen 1930–1941: politische, wirtschaftliche und gesellschaftliche Entwicklung. Klagenfurt, ŠT. Bahovecć, 99, 545 p.

7549. BARIÉTY (Jacques). Le projet de pacte franco-britannique, 1920–1922. *In*: France (La) à la recherche de sécurité (1920–1922) [Cf. n° 7566], p. 83-100.

7550. BÁTONYI (Gábor). Britain and Central Europe, 1918–1933. New York, Clarendon Press, 99, 240 p. (Oxford historical monographs).

7551. BELOV (E. A.). Rossiia i Mongoliia: (1911–1919 gg.). Moskva, IV RAN, 99, 237 p.

7552. BLANCPAIN (François). Haïti et les Etats-Unis: 1915–1934. Histoire d'une occupation. Préface de Frédéric MAURO. Paris, Harmattan, 99, 381 p.

7553. BOPPE-VIGNE (Catherine). Lettres inédites d'Alexis Léger, deuxième secrétaire de la légation de France à Pékin (1919–1921). *Revue d'histoire diplomatique*, 99, 113, 1, p. 7-44.

7554. BUDKOVIČ (Tomaž). Bohinj 1914–1918 med fronto in zaledjem. (Bohinj 1914–1918: between the front and the rear). Celovec, Ljubljana v Dunaj, Mohorjeva založba, 99, 229 p. (ill.). (Gorenjski kraji in ljudje, 13).

7555. CABÁN (Pedro A.). Constructing a colonial people: Puerto Rico and the United States, 1898–1932. Boulder, Westview Press, 99, XIV-282 p.

7556. CALLAHAN (Michael D.). Mandates and empire: the League of Nations and Africa, 1914–1931. Brighton, Sussex Academic Press, 99, X-297 p.

7557. ÇELEBİ (Mevlüt). Milli Mücadele döneminde Türk – İtalyan ilişkileri. (Les relations turco-italiennes pendant la guerre de l'indépendance Turque). Ankara, Dışişleri Bakanlığı Stratejik Araştırmalar Merkezi, 99, 447 p.

7558. CŒURÉ (Sophie). La grande lueur à l'Est. Les Français et l'Union Soviétique, 1917–1939. Paris, Ed. du Seuil, 99, 359 p.

7559. DADRIAN (Vahakn N.). Warrant for genocide: key elements of Turko-Armenian conflict. New Brunswick, Transaction Publishers, 99, 214 p.

7560. DREIST (Markus). Die deutsch-italienischen Beziehungen im Spannungsfeld der europäischen Politik 1918–1934. Düsseldorf, [s. n.], 99, 267 p. [Thesis (doctoral) – Universität Düsseldorf, 1999].

7561. DUPRÉ DE BOULOIS (Aude). Les travaillistes, la France et la question allemande (1922–1924). *Revue d'histoire diplomatique*, 99, 113, 1, p. 75-100.

7562. ELVERT (Jürgen). Mitteleuropa! Deutsche Pläne zur europäischen Neuordnung, 1918–1945. Stuttgart, Steiner, 99, 448 p. (Historische Mitteilungen. Beihefte, 35).

7563. FERGUSON (Niall). The pity of war. New York, Basic Books, 99, XLIII-563 p.

7564. FISHER (John). Curzon and British imperialism in the Middle East, 1916–1919. London a. Portland, F. Cass, 99, XVI-342 p. (ill., maps).

7565. FLEURIER (Nicolas). Entre partenariat et alliance: rapports diplomatiques et militaires de la Belgique avec la France en 1920. *In*: France (La) à la recherche de sécurité (1920–1922) [Cf. n° 7566], p. 23-38.

7566. France (La) à la recherche de sécurité (1920–1922). Prés. par Jacques BARIÉTY. *Guerres mondiales et conflits contemporains*, 99, 49, 193, p. 3-130. [Cf. n°s 7549, 7565, 7580, 7597, 7599, 7605, 7613, 7614.]

7567. Francia diplomáciai iratok a Kárpát-medence történetérol, 1918–1919. (Documents diplomatiques français sur l'histoire du bassin des Carpates 1918–1919). Összeállította és szerkesztette ÁDÁM Magda és ORMOS Mária. Budapest, Akadémiai Kiadó, 99, 395 p.

7568. FRIEDMAN (Isaiah). Palestine, a twice-promised land? The British, the Arabs and Zionism 1915–1920. New Beunswick a. London, Transaction Publishers, 99, 411 p.

7569. FUCHS (Friedrich). Die Beziehungen zwischen der Freien Stadt Danzig und dem Deutschen Reich in der Zeit von 1920 bis 1939: unter besonderer Berücksichtigung der Judenfrage in beiden Staaten. Freiburg, HochschulVerl., 99, 202 p. (Hochschulsammlung Philosophie / Geschichte, 11).

7570. GHANAYIM (Zuhayr). Liwa' 'Akka fi 'ahd al-tanzimat al-'Uthmaniyah 1281–1337 H/1864–1918 M. (District of Acre during the Ottoman Tanzimat Period). Bayrut, Mu'assasat al-Dirasat al-Filastiniyah, 99, 565 p. (Silsilat al-mudun al-Filastiniyah, 4).

7571. GODSEY (William D.). Aristocratic redoubt: the Austro-Hungarian Foreign Office on the eve of the First World War. West Lafayette, Purdue U. P., 99, XII-304 p. (Central European studies).

7572. GORGUET (Ilde). Les mouvements pacifistes et la réconciliation franco-allemande dans les années vingt (1919–1931). Bern, P. Lang, 99, XVI-331 p. (Université de Metz. Centre d'étude des périodiques de langue allemande. Convergences, 14).

7573. GORLOV (Sergej A.). Sovershenno sekretno. Moskva-Berlin, 1920–1933. Voenno-politicheskie otnoshenija mezhdu SSSR i Germaniej. (Striktly confidential: Moscow-Berlin, 1920–1933: military and political relations between Soviet Russia and Germany). RAN, In-t vseobshchej istorii. Moskva, [s. n.], 99, 363 p. (bibl., ind.).

7574. Grande Guerra (La) e la pace di Versailles ottant'anni dopo. A cura di G. ORSINA. *Ricerche di storia politica*, 99, 2, 3, 371 p.

7575. GRIŠINA (R.). Formirane na stanovišče po makedonskija vupros v bolševiška Moskva 1912–1924 g. (po dokumenti na ruskite arkhivi). (La formation d'une position sur le problème macédonien à Moscou bolchévique, 1912–1924. Selon les documents des archives russes). *Makedonski pregled*, 99, 4, p. 95-126.

7576. GRUMEL-JACQUIGNON (François). La Yougoslavie dans la stratégie française de l'Entre-deux-Guerres (1918–1935). Aux origines du mythe serbe en France. Bern, Lang, 99, 670 p.

7577. GRZYWACZ (Andrzej). Armia Sowiecka w ocenach polskiego kierownictwa wojskowego 1921–1939. (Die Sowjetische Armee nach der Beurteilung der polnischen Militär-Führungskräfte 1921–1939). *Studia Rzeszowskie*, 99, 6, p. 43-76.

7578. HAIGH (R. H.), MORRIS (D. S.), PETERS (A. R.). The Soviet Union: interventionism and the search for peace 1918–1934. Sheffield, Sheffield Hallam University, 99, 197 p.

7579. HELL (Stefan). Der Manschurei-Konflikt: Japan, China und der Völkerbund 1931 bis 1933. Tübingen, Universitäts Verlag, 99, [s. p.].

7580. HOGENHUIS-SELIVERSTOFF (Anne). La trace ténue d'une alliance ancienne. La France et la Russie, 1920–1922. *In*: France (La) à la recherche de sécurité (1920–1922) [Cf. n° 7566], p. 117-130.

7581. HUGHES (Matthew). Allenby and British strategy in the Middle East, 1917–1919. London, F. Cass, 99, XII-224 p. (ill, maps, ports.). (Cass series: military history and policy, 1).

7582. KARPUS (Zbihniew). Wschodni sojusznicy Polski w wojnie 1920 roku. Oddziały wojskowe ukraińskie, rosyjskie, kozackie i białoruskie w Polsce w latach 1919–1920. (Polens Ost-Alliierten im Krieg 1920. Ukrainische, russische, kosakische und belorussische Truppen in Polen in den Jahren 1919–1920). Toruń, Wydaw. Uniw. M. Kopernika, 99, 230 p.

7583. KELEŞYILMAZ (Vahdet). Teşkilâtı Mahsûsa'nın Hindistan misyonu (1914–1918). [Mission indienne de Teşkilâtı Mahsûsa (organisme ottomane de renseignements)]. Ankara, Atatürk Araştırma Merkezi, 99, 166 p.

7584. KITCHING (Carolyn J.). Britain and the problem of international disarmament 1919–1934. London a. New York, Routledge, 99, VIII-223 p.

7585. KORCZYK (Henryk). Działanie i recepcja Locarna 1927–1936. (Wirken und Rezeption von Locarno 1927–1936). Warszawa, Neriton, Inst. Historii PAN, 308 p.

7586. KRAUSE (Andreas). Scapa Flow. Die Selbstversenkung der wilhelminischen Flotte. Berlin, Ullstein, 99, 431 p.

7587. Kriegsende 1918: Ereignis, Wirkung, Nachwirkung. Hrsg. v. Jörg DUPPLER und Gerhrd P. GROß. München, Oldenbourg, 99, IX-398 p. (Beiträge zur Militärgeschichte, 53).

7588. KUCERA (Jaroslav). Minderheit im Nationalstaat: die Sprachenfrage in den tschechisch-deutschen Beziehungen 1918–1938. München, Oldenbourg, 99, 328 p. (Quellen und Darstellungen zur Zeitgeschichte, 43).

7589. KULA (Mieczysław Henryk). Gdańska "Dziura celna". Polscy inspektorzy celni w Wolnym Mieście Gdańsku 1920–1939. (Danzig – "Zoll-Nest". Polnische Zollbeamte in Freier Stadt Danzig, 1920–1939). Gdańsk, Wydaw. DJ, 99 238 p.

7590. KUZMANOVA (Antonina). Les Balkans dan la stratégie politique de la France et de l'Italie après la Premiere guerre mondiale. *In*: Europe (L') et la Méditerranée [Cf. n° 3951], p. 133-140.

7591. LE PAUTREMAT (Pascal). La commission interministerielle des affaires musulmanes (1911–1936): une institution méconnue. *Revue d'histoire diplomatique*, 99, 113, 4, p. 373-392.

7592. LENTIN (Antony). Lord Cunliffe, Lloyd George, reparations and reputations at the Paris Peace Conference, 1919. *Diplomacy and statecraft*, 99, 10, 1, p. 50-86.

7593. LONGO (Luigi Emilio). L'attività degli addetti militari italiani all'estero fra le due guerre mondiali (1919–1939). Roma, Stato maggiore dell'esercito, Ufficio storico, 763 p. (ill.).

7594. MAC CULLOUGH (Edward E.). How the First World War began: the Triple Entente and the coming of the Great War of 1914–1918. New York, Black Rose Books, 99, XII-346 p.

7595. MACFIE (A. L.). British Intelligence and the causes of unrest in Mesopotamia, 1919–1921. *Middle Eastern studies*, 99, 35, 1, p. 165-177.

7596. MAMAEVA (Natl'ja L.). Komintern i Gomin'dan, 1919–1929. (The Comintern and the Kuomintang, 1919–1929). RAN, In-t Dal'nego Vostoka. Moskva, ROSSPEN, 99, 375 p. (ill., bibl.; ind.). [Eng. summary]

7597. METZGER (Chantal). L'Allemagne: un danger pour la France en 1920. *In*: France (La) à la recherche de sécurité (1920–1922) [Cf. n° 7566], p. 5-22.

7598. MILLER (Karen A. J.). Populist nationalism: Republican insurgency and American foreign policy making, 1918–1925. Westport, Greenwood Press, 99, XVI-198 p. (Contributions to the study of world history, 69).

7599. MOUTON (Marie-Renée). La France et la Société des Nations en 1922. *In*: France (La) à la recherche de sécurité (1920–1922) [Cf. n° 7566], p. 101-116.

7600. NIEDHART (Gottfried). Die Außenpolitik der Weimarer Republik. München, Oldenbourg, 99, X-142 p. (Enzyklopädie deutscher Geschichte, 53).

7601. NIGRO (Louis John, Jr.). The new diplomacy in Italy: American propaganda and U.S.-Italian relations, 1917–1919. New York, P. Lang, 99, XIV-153 p. (Studies in modern European history, 28).

7602. Odrodzona Polska wśród sąsiadów 1918–1921. (Wiederbelebtes Polen unter Anrainer-Staaten 1918–1921). Red. nauk. Andrzej KORYN. Warszawa, Inst. Historii PAN, Mazowiecka Szkoła Humanist.-Pedagog. W Łowiczu, 99 250 p.

7603. ÖZGİRAY (Ahmet). Atatürk'ün dış politikası (1919–1938). (La politique extérieure d'Atatürk), İzmir, 99, 71 p.

7604. PALUSZYŃSKI (Tomasz). Walka o niepodległość Łotwy 1914–1921. (Der Kampf um Lettlands Unabhängigkeit 1914–1921). Warszawa, Bellona, 99, 447 p.

7605. PAVLOVIĆ (Vojislav). Dans l'ombre de Mussolini. Le roi Alexandre et Barthou. *In*: Ere Barthou (L') [Cf. n° 4329], p. 59-80. – IDEM. Une conception traditionaliste de la politique orientale de la France. Le vicomte Joseph de Fontenay, envoyé plénipotentiaire auprés du Roi Pierre Ier Karageorgevitch (1917–1921). *In*: France (La) à la recherche de sécurité (1920–1922) [Cf. n° 7566], p. 69-82.

7606. PHILPOTT (William). Squaring the circle: the higher co-ordination of the Entente in the Winter of 1915–1916. *English historical review*, 99, 114, 458, p. 875-898.

7607. PÖPPINGHAUS (Ernst-Wolfgang). "Moralische Eroberungen"? Kultur und Politik in den deutschspanischen Beziehungen der Jahre 1919 bis 1933. Frankfurt am Main, Vervuert, 99, 522 p. (ill.). (Editionen der Iberoamericana. Serie C, Geschichte und Gesellschaft, 6 = Ediciones de Iberoamericana. Serie C, Historia y Sociedad, 6).

7608. Roma e Pechino: la svolta extraeuropea di Benedetto XV. A cura di Agostino GIOVAGNOLI. Roma, Studium, 99, VII-290 p.

7609. Romania during the World War I era = România în epoca primului război mondial. Papers presented at the Fourth International Conference of the Center for Romanian Studies, 23–27 June 1998, Iași. Ed. by Kurt W. TREPTOW. Iași, Oxford a. Portland, Center for Romanian Studies, 99, 287 p.

7610. ROSE (Inbal). Conservatism and foreign policy during the Lloyd George coalition, 1918–1922. London, Frank Cass, 99, XXIX-289 p.

7611. Rossija i Pervaja mirovaja vojna: Materialy mezhdunar. nauch. kollokviuma. (Russia and the First World War: papers of the Intern. colloquium, 1–5 June, 1998). Ed. Nikolaj N. SMIRNOV. Sankt-Peterburg, Dmitry Bulanin, 99, 563 p. (bibl.).

7612. ROUSSEAU (Frédéric). La guerre censurée. Une histoire des combattants européens de 14–18. Paris, Ed. du Seuil, 99, 416 p.

7613. SANDU (Traian). La Grande Roumanie, alliée de la France. Une péripétie diplomatique des Années Folles? (1919–1933). Paris, L'Harmattan, 99, 279 p. – IDEM. La Roumanie et l'impossible articulation d'un système de sécurité français en Europe centre-orientale,
septembre 1920–décembre 1921. *In*: France (La) à la recherche de sécurité (1920–1922) [Cf. n° 7566], p. 53-68. – IDEM. La Roumanie sur l'axe brisé Paris-Varsovie-Moscou: de la méfiance à la collaboration roumano-soviétique, 1929–1933. *In*: Ere Barthou (L') [Cf. n° 4329], p. 81-88. – IDEM. Le système de sécurité français en Europe centre-orientale, l'exemple roumain, 1919–1933. Paris, L'Harmattan, 99, 495 p.

7614. SCHRAMM (Thomasz), BULHAK (Henryk). La France et la Pologne 1920–1922. Relations bilatérales ou parties d'un système européen de sécurité ? *In*: France (La) à la recherche de sécurité (1920–1922) [Cf. n° 7566], p. 39-52.

7615. SPENSER (Daniela). The impossible triangle: Mexico, Soviet Russia, and the United States in the 1920s. Durham a. London, Duke U. P., 99, XIV-254 p.

7616. STEIGERWALD (D.). The reclamation of Woodrow Wilson. *Diplomatic history*, 99, 23, 1, p. 79-99.

7617. STOUT (Joseph A., Jr.). Border conflict: Villistas, Carrancistas and the punitive expedition, 1915–1920. Fort Worth, Texas Christian U. P., 99, XIV-198 p.

7618. TAFAJ (Afërdita). Diplomacia e Ismail Qemalit. Tiranë, Luarasi, 99, 110 p. (ill.).

7619. WALCZAK (Henryk). Stanowisko polskich ugrupowań politycznych wobec Czechosłowacji w latach 1918–1925. (Der Standpunkt von polnischen Polit-Gruppierungen gegen Tschechoslowakei in den Jahren 1918–1925). Szczecin, Wydaw. Nauk. Uniw. Szczecińskiego, 99, 245 p. (Rozprawy i Studia, 317).

7620. YANIKDAĞ (Yüzel). Ottoman prisoners of war in Russia: 1914–1922. *Journal of contemporary history*, 99, 34, p. 69-85.

7621. ZAUN (Harald). Paul von Hindenburg und die deutsche Aussenpolitik, 1925–1934. Köln, Böhlau, 99, 610 p.

7622. ZBUCHEA (Gheorghe). România și războaiele balcanice 1912–1913: pagini de istorie sud-est europeana. (La Romania e le guerre balcaniche: pagine di storia sudeuropea). București, Albatros, 99, 455 p. (Historia).

Cf. n[os] *866, 4806, 4903, 4987, 7192, 7476, 7476, 7482, 7483, 7486, 7487, 7500, 7503, 7504, 7507, 7520, 7521, 7533, 7536, 7646, 7692, 7724, 7727, 7733, 7738, 7744, 7783*

§ 7. From 1935 to 1945. The Second World War.

a. *General*

* 7623. Philippines (The) in World War II, 1941–1945: a chronology and select annotated bibliography of books and articles in English. Compiled by Walter F. BELL. Westport a. London, Greenwood Press, 99, VIII-276 p. (Bibliographies and indexes in military studies, 12).

** 7624. Akten des Volksgerichtsprozesses gegen Franz A. Basch, Volksgruppenführer der Deutschen in Ungarn, Budapest 1945/46. Hrsg. v. Gerhard SEEWANN und Norbert SPANNENBERGER; unter Berücksichtigung der Arbeiten von Friedrich SPIEGEL-SCHMIDT und Loránt TILKOVSKY. München, Oldenbourg, 99, LXXIV-549 p. (ill.). (Buchreihe der Südostdeutschen Historischen Kommission, 37).

7625. ÁDÁM (Magda). The Munich crisis and Hungary: the fall of the Versailles settlement in Central Europe. In: Munich crisis (The), 1938: prelude to World War II [Cf. n° 7661], p. 81-121.

7626. ARBOIT (Gérald). Le Saint-Siège et la question juive en Europe centrale pendant la Seconde Guerre mondiale (1939–1945). Archivum historiae pontificiae, 99, 37, p. 161-191.

7627. BINGEN (Erik). Indië verloren: Nederland en het ontstaan van de Tweede Wereldoorlog in Azië. Amsterdam, Arch Publishing/Babel Boeken, 99, 124 p. (plates, ill., map, ports.). (Babel Boeken inzichten, 8).

7628. BÖHM (Johann). Die Deutschen in Rumänien und das Dritte Reich, 1933–1940. Frankfurt am Main, P. Lang, 99, VII-411 p.

7629. BOWEN (Elizabeth). "Notes on Eire": espionage reports to Winston Churchill, 1940–1942. Aubane, Aubane Historical Society, 99, 152 p. (ill.).

7630. CARLEY (Michael Jabara). 1939: the alliance that never was and the coming of World War II. Chicago, Ivan R. Dee, 99, XXV-321 p.

7631. ČERNÝ (Bohumil). III. Internacionála a německá emigrace v Československu 1933–1939. (Die Komintern und die deutsche Emigration in der Tschechoslowakei 1933–1939). Paginae historiae, 99, 7, p. 256-276.

7632. CHROBÁK (Tomáš). Jugoslávská opozice a Československo 1935–1938 (Yugoslav opposition and Czechoslovakia in 1935–1938). Slovanský přehled, 99, 85, 3, p. 265-291.

7633. CULL (Nicholas J.). The Munich crisis and British propaganda policy in the United States. In: Munich crisis (The), 1938: prelude to World War II [Cf. n° 7661], p. 216-235.

7634. DENÉCHÈRE (Yves). La politique espagnole de la France de 1931 à 1936: une pratique française de rapports inégaux. Paris, L'Harmattan, 99, 335 p. (Collection Recherches et documents. Espagne).

7635. DIÓSZEGI (István). A Szovjetunió külpolitikája a II. Világháború elsö hónapjaiban. (The foreign policy of the Soviet Union in the first months of the Second World War). Rubicon, 99, 3-4, p. 42-45.

7636. DIRKS (Carl), JANSSEN (Karl-Heinz). Der Krieg der Generäle: Hitler als Werkzeug der Wehrmacht. Berlin, Propyläen, 99, 304 p.

7637. DOCKRILL (Michael). British establishment perspectives on France, 1936–1940. Basingstoke, Macmillan, 99, XIII-212 p. (Studies in military and strategic history).

7638. DURAND (Romain). De Giraud à de Gaulle: les Corps francs d'Afrique. Paris, L'Harmattan, 99, 239 p. (Histoire et perspectives méditerranéennes).

7639. DUTTA (Indrani). The Japanese invasion of India (1944): myth or reality? Delhi, Spectrum, 99, 99 p.

7640. Erzwungene Trennung: Vertreibungen und Aussiedlungen in und aus der Tschechoslowakei 1938–1947 im Vergleich mit Polen, Ungarn und Jugoslawien. Herausgegeben für die Deutsch-Tschechische und Deutsch-Slowakische Historikerkommission von Detlef BRANDES, Edita IVANIČKOVÁ und Jiří PEŠEK. Essen, Klartext, 99, 328 p. (ill.). (Veröffentlichungen des Instituts für Kultur und Geschichte der Deutschen im Östlichen Europa, 15. Veröffentlichungen der Deutsch-Tschechischen und Deutsch-Slowakischen Historikerkommission, 8).

7641. FRY (Michael Graham). The British Dominions and the Munich crisis. In: Munich crisis (The), 1938: prelude to World War II [Cf. n° 7661], p. 293-341.

7642. GALLIN (Isabel). Rechtsetzung ist Machtsetzung: die deutsche Rechtsetzung in den Niederlanden 1940–1945. Frankfurt am Main, Lang, 99, 217 p. (Europäische Hochschulschriften. Reihe II, Rechtswissenschaft, 2736).

7643. GEBEL (Ralf). "Heim ins Reich!" Konrad Henlein und der Reichsgau Sudetenland (1938–1945). München, Oldenbourg, 99, XVI-424 p. (Veröffentlichungen des Collegium Carolinum, 83).

7644. GEIGER (Wolfgang). L'image de la France dans l'Allemagne nazie, 1933–1945. Rennes, Presses Universitaires de Rennes, 99, 412 p. (Histoire).

7645. GOLDSTEIN (Erik). Neville Chamberlain, the British official mind and the Munich crisis. In: Munich crisis (The), 1938: prelude to World War II [Cf. n° 7661], p. 276-292.

7646. GRISHIN (Jakov Ja.). Put' k katastrofe: Pol'sko-chekhoslovatskie otnoshenija, 1932–1939. (A way to a catastrophe: the relations between Poland and Czeckoslovakia, 1932–1939). Kazan', Shkola, 99, 184 p. (bibl., ind.).

7647. HÄUFELE (Günther). Zwangsumsiedlungen in Polen 1939–1941. Zum Vergleich sowjetischer und deutscher Besatzungspolitik. In: Lager, Zwangsarbeit, Vertreibung und Deportation [Cf. n° 7653], p. 515-533.

7648. Historie okupovaného pohraničí 1938–1945. Tomo 3-4. (Die Geschichte des Okkupationsgrenzgebiet 1938–1945). Ed. Zdeněk RADVANOVSKÝ. Ústí nad Labem, Univerzita J. E. Purkyně, 99, 2 vol., 197 p., 209 p.

7649. Internati, prigionieri, reduci. La deportazione militare italiana durante la seconda guerra mondiale. A cura di Angelo BENDOTTI e Anna VALTULINA. Atti del Convegno, Bergamo, 16–17 ottobre 1997 organizzato dall'Istituto bergamasco per la storia della Resistenza e dell'età contemporanea e dall'Assessorato alla Cultura del Comune di Bergamo. *Studi e ricerche di storia contemporanea*, 99, 28, 51, p. 5-311.

7650. JACKSON (Ashley). Botswana 1939–1945: an African country at war. New York, Clarendon Press, 99, XIII-281 p. (Oxford Historical Monographs).

7651. JAROCH (Matthias). Too much wit and not enough warning? Sir Eric Phipps als britischer Botschafter in Berlin von 1933 bis 1937. Frankfurt am Main, P. Lang, 99, 366 p. (Europäische Hochschulschriften. Reihe III, Geschichte und ihre Hilfswissenschaften, 846 = Publications universitaires européennes. Série III, Histoire, sciences auxiliaires de l'histoire, 846 = European university studies. Series III, History and allied studies, 846).

7652. KUHN (Dieter). Der Zweite Weltkrieg in China. Berlin, Duncker und Humblot, 99, 385 p.

7653. Lager, Zwangsarbeit, Vertreibung und Deportation: Dimensionen der Massenverbrechen in der Sowjetunion und in Deutschland 1933 bis 1945. Hrsg. v. Dittmar DAHLMANN und Gerhard HIRSCHFELD. Essen, Klartext, 99, 600 p. (ill.). (Schriften der Bibliothek für Zeitgeschichte, 10). [Cf. n° <Auswahl> 7647.]

7654. LIANG (His-Huey). China, the Sino-Japanese conflict and the Munich crisis. *In*: Munich crisis (The), 1938: prelude to World War II [Cf. n° 7661], p. 342-370.

7655. LUKES (Igor). Stalin and Czechoslovakia in 1938–1939: an autopsy of a myth. *In*: Munich crisis (The), 1938: prelude to World War II [Cf. n° 7661], p. 13-47.

7656. MAC GARRY (Fearghal). Irish politics and the Spanish Civil War. Cork, Cork U. P., 99, X-326 p.

7657. MATESANZ (José Antonio). Las raíces de esilio: México ante la guerra civil española, 1936–1939. Mexico City, Collegio de México, Universidad Nacional Autónoma de México, 99, 490 p.

7658. MERCADER (Antonio). El año del León: Herrera, las bases norteamericanas y el "complot nazi" en el Uruguay de 1940. Montevideo, Aguilar, 293 p. (ill., maps).

7659. Military planning and the origins of the Second World War. Ed. by Brian J. C. MAC KERCHER and Michael HENNESSY. Westport, Greenwood, 99, [s. p.].

7660. MIROVITSKAIA (R. A.). Kitaiskaia gosudarstvennost' i sovetskaia politika v Kitae: gody tikhookeanskoi voiny, 1941–1945. (Chinese statehood and Soviet policy in China). Moskva, "Pamiatniki istoricheskoi mysli", 99, 309 p. (ill.).

7661. Munich crisis (The), 1938: prelude to World War II. Ed. by Igor LUKES and Erik GOLDSTEIN. *Diplomacy and statecraft*, 99, 10, 2-3, p. 1-370. [Cf. n°s <choice> 7625, 7633, 7641, 7645, 7654, 7655, 7665, 7674, 7675, 7679, 7690, 7748.]

7662. MUSIAL (Bogdan). NS-Kriegsverbrecher vor polnischen Gerichten. *Vierteljahrshefte für Zeitgeschichte*, 99, 47, 1, p. 25-56.

7663. Organisierte Chaos (Das): "Ämterdarwinismus" und "Gesinnungsethik": Determinanten nationalsozialistischer Besatzungsherrschaft. Hrsg. v. Gerhard OTTO und Johannes HOUWINK TEN CATE. Berlin, Metropol, 99, 342 p. (Nationalsozialistische Besatzungspolitik in Europa 1939–1945, 7).

7664. OVERMANS (Rüdiger). Deutsche militärische Verluste im Zweiten Weltkrieg. München, Oldenbourg, 99, IX-367 p. (Beiträge zur Militärgeschichte, 46).

7665. OVERY (Richard). Germany and the Munich crisis: a mutilated victory? *In*: Munich crisis (The), 1938: prelude to World War II [Cf. n° 7661], p. 191-215.

7666. PEREIRA FIORILO (Juan). Historia secreta de la Guerra del Chaco: Bolivia frente al Paraguay y Argentina. La Paz, H. Camara de Disputados, Federacion de Entidades Empresariales Privadas de Cochabama, 99, 2 vol., 548 p.

7667. Philippines (The) under Japan: occupation policy and reaction. Ed. by Ikehata SETSUHO and Ricardo Trota JOSE. Quezon City, Ateneo de Manila U. P., 99, XIV-394 p. (ill.). [Contents: SETSUHO (Ikehata). Japanese occupation period in Philippine history. – SATOSHI (Nakano). Appeasement and coercion. – MOTOE (Terami-Wada). The Filipino volunteer armies. – MIDORI (Kawashima). Japanese administrative policy towards the Moros in Lanao. – SETSUHO (Ikehata). Mining industry development and local anti-Japanese rule resistance. – YOSHIKO (Nagano). Cotton production under Japanese rule, 1942–1945. – JOSE (Ricardo Trota). The rice shortage and countermeasures during the occupation. – TAKEFUMI (Terada). The religious propaganda program for Christian churches. – SHINZO (Hayase). The Japanese residents of "Dabaokuo".]

7668. SCHEIL (Stefan). Logik der Mächte. Europas Problem mit der Globalisierung der Politik. Überlegungen zur Vorgeschichte des Zweiten Weltkrieges. Berlin, Duncker & Humblot, 99, 241 p.

7669. SHORE (Zachary). Dictatorship, information, and the limits of power: Hitler and foreign policy decision-making, 1933–1939. Oxford, [s. n.], 99, V-259 p. [Thesis (D.Phil.) – University of Oxford, Faculty of Modern History, 1999]. – IDEM. Hitler, intelligence, and the decision to remilitarize the Rhine. *Journal of contemporary history*, 99, 34, 1, p. 5-18.

7670. SINDING (Richard). Le ralliement de Saint-Pierre-et-Miquelon à la France libre en 1941 et le conflit entre de Gaulle et Muselier. *Guerres mondiales et conflits contemporains*, 99, 49, 194, p. 163-172.

7671. Sovetsko-finskaia voina 1939–1940 gg: khrestomatiia. (Soviet-Finnish war 1939–1940). Redaktorsostaviteľ A.E. TARAS. Minsk, Kharvest, 99, 458 p. (ill., maps). (Biblioteka voennoi istorii).

7672. STEHLÍK (Eduard). Francie a opevňování Československa ve třicátých letech. (The role of France in the fortification of Czechoslovakia in the later 1930s). *Historie a vojenství*, 99, 48, 4, p. 814-847.

7673. STRADLING (Robert). The Irish and the Spanish Civil War 1936–1939. Manchester, Mandolin, 99, XI-288 p.

7674. STRANG (G. Bruce). War and peace: Mussolini's road to Munich. *In*: Munich crisis (The), 1938: prelude to World War II [Cf. n° 7661], p. 160-190.

7675. THOMAS (Martin). France and the Czechoslovak crisis. *In*: Munich crisis (The), 1938: prelude to World War II [Cf. n° 7661], p. 122-159.

7676. UOLA (Mikko). «Suomi sitoutuu hajoittamaan ...» Järjestöjen lakkauttaminen vuoden 1944 välirauhansopimuksen 21. artiklan perusteella. (Article 21 of the 1944 interim peace treaty. The dissolution of organisations during the Finnish «years of danger»). Helsinki, SHS, 99, 288 p. (Hist. tutkim., 205.) (ill.) [English summary].

7677. Vojna i politika, 1939–1941. (War and politics, 1939–1941: [Articles]). Ed. Aleksandr O. CHUBAR'JAN. RAN, In-t vseobshchej istorii; Teľ-Avivskij universitet. Moskva, Nauka, 99, 495 p. (bibl.).

7678. Vostochnaja Evropa mezhdu Gitlerom i Stalinym, 1939–1941 gg. (Eastern Europe between Hitler and Stalin, 1939–1941). Eds. V. K. VOLKOV, L. Ja. GIBIANSKIJ. RAN, In-t slavjanovedenija. Moskva, Indrik, 99, 526 p. (ind.).

7679. WEINBERG (Gerhard). Reflections on Munich after 60 years. *In*: Munich crisis (The), 1938: prelude to World War II [Cf. n° 7661], p. 1-12.

7680. ZIMMERMANN (Volker). Die Sudetendeutschen im NS-Staat: Politik und Stimmung der Bevölkerung im Reichsgau Sudetenland (1938–1945). Essen, Klartext, 99, 515 p. (Veröffentlichungen des Instituts für Kultur und Geschichte der Deutschen im östlichen Europa, 16; Veröffentlichungen der Deutsch-Tschechischen und Deutsch-Slowakischen Historikerkommission, 9).

7681. Zimnjaja vojna 1939–1940. (The Winter War, 1939–1940). RAN, In-t vseobshchej istorii. Part 1. Politicheskaja istorija (Political history). Ed. O.A. RZHESHEVSKIJ, O. VEKHVILJAJNEN. Part 2. I.V. Stalin i finskaja kampanija: stenogramma soveshchanija pri TsK VKP(b). [Stalin and the Finnish Campaign: the shorthand of the meeting at the Central Committee of the C.P.S.U.(B.)]. Ed. E. N. KUĽKOV, O. A. RZHESHEVSKIJ. Moskva, Nauka, 99, 2 vol., 382 p., 295 p. (ill., ind.).

Cf. n°s 866, 4019, 4464, 4903, 5458, 7195, 7541, 7558, 7562, 7569, 7577, 7588, 7822, 7974, 8022, 8098

b. *Diplomacy. Economy*

* 7682. SPOERER (M.). Profitierten Unternehmen von KZ-Arbeit? Eine kritische Analyse der Literatur. *Historische Zeitschrift*, 99, 268, 1, p. 61-96.

** 7683. British documents on Foreign affairs: reports and papers from the Foreign Office confidential print. General editors Paul PRESTON and Michael PARTRIDGE. Part 3. From 1940 through 1945. Series D. Latin America. Vol. 9. South and Central America: July 1944–December 1944. Vol. 10. South and Central America: January 1945–June 1945. Vol. 11. South and Central America: July 1945–December 1945. Ed. by James DUNKERLEY. Bethesda, University Publications of America, 99, 3 vol., XXI-339 p., XXI-522 p., XXI, 546 p.

** 7684. Documenti diplomatici italiani (I). Ministero degli affari esteri. Commissione per la pubblicazione dei documenti diplomatici. Serie VIII. 1935–1939. Vol. 8. 10 gennaio–23 aprile 1938. Roma, Istituto poligrafico e Zecca dello Stato, Libreria dello Stato, 99, LX-695 p.

** 7685. Italian diplomatic documents on the history of the Holocaust in Greece (1941–1943). Ed. by Daniel CARPI. Tel Aviv, Chair for the History and culture of the Jews of Salonika and Greece, The Diaspora Research Institute, Tel Aviv University, 99, 318 p. (Publications of the Diaspora Research Institute, 134. Publication of the Chair for the History and Culture of the Jews of Salonika and Greece, 3).

** 7686. NĚMEČEK (Jan), NOVÁČKOVÁ (Helena), ŠŤOVÍČEK (Ivan). Edvard Beneš v USA v roce 1943. Dokumenty. (Edvard Beneš in the USA in 1943. Documents). *Sborník archivních prací*, 99, 49, 2, p. 469-565.

7687. ABELSHAUSER (Werner). Kriegswirtschaft und Wirtschaftswunder. Deutschlands wirtschaftliche Mobilisierung für den Zweiten Weltkrieg und die Folgen für die Nachkriegszeit. *Vierteljahrshefte für Zeitgeschichte*, 99, 47, 4, p. 503-538.

7688. ALLEN (Michael Thad). Flexible production in Ravensbrück concentration camp. *Past and present*, 99, 165, p. 182-217.

7689. ARCIDIACONO (Bruno). British wartime perception of Soviet intentions in Eastern Europe. *In*: Socialisme, cultures, histoire: itinéraires et représentations: mélanges offerts à Miklós Molnár [Cf. n° 5701], p. 447-464.

7690. BECK (Peter). Searching for peace in Munich, not Geneva: the British government, the League of Nations and the Sudetenland question. *In*: Munich crisis (The), 1938: prelude to World War II [Cf. n° 7661], p. 236-257.

7691. BEHRING (Rainer). Demokratische Aussenpolitik für Deutschland: die aussenpolitischen Vorstellungen deutscher Sozialdemokraten im Exil 1933–

7. FROM 1935 TO 1945. THE SECOND WORLD WAR

1945. Düsseldorf, Droste, 99, 674 p. (Beiträge zur Geschichte des Parlamentarismus und der politischen Parteien, 117).

7692. BERDAH (J.-F.). La politique extérieure de l'Espagne républicaine (1931-1939). *Relations internationales*, 99, 97, p. 5-22.

7693. BOĆKOWSKI (Daniel). Czas nadziei. Obywatele Rzeczypospolitej Polskiej w ZSRR i opieka nad nimi placówek polskich w latach 1940-1943. (Die Zeit der Zuversicht. Bürger der Republik Polen in der UdSSR und deren Betreuung seitens der polnischen Amtsstellen in den Jahren 1940-1943). Warszawa, Neriton; Wydaw. Inst. Historii PAN, 99, 497 p.

7694. BRODY (Kenneth J.). The avoidable war. Vol. 1. Lord Cecil and the policy of principle, 1933-1935. Vol. 2. Pierre Laval and the politics of reality, 1935-1936. New Brunswick, Transaction Publishers, 2 vol., X-389 p., XI-368 p.

7695. CAPUTI (Robert J.). Neville Chamberlain and appeasement. Selinsgrove, Susquehanna U. P., 99, 271 p.

7696. CAROTENUTO (Gennaro). La carta spagnola. Mussolini e la Spagna durante la Seconda Guerra Mondiale (1939-1943). *Spagna contemporanea*, 99, 8, 15, p. 69-92.

7697. CATALA (Michel). Non-belligérance et neutralité de l'Espagne pendant la Deuxième Guerre mondiale. *In*: Neutralité et non-belligérance en Europe pendant la Deuxième Guerre mondiale [Cf. n° 7730], p. 101-116.

7698. CHELYSHEV (Igor' Alekseevich). SSSR - Frantsiia: trudnye gody, 1938-1941. Moskva, In-t rossiiskoi istorii Rossiiskoi akademii nauk, 99, 367 p.

7699. DENKIEWICZ-SZCZEPANIAK (Emilia). Polska siła robocza w Organizacji Todta w Norwegii i Finlandii w latach 1941-1945. (Die Polnische Arbeitskraft in der Todt-Organisation in Norwegen sowie in Finnland in den Jahren 1941-1945). Toruń, Wydaw. Uniw. M. Kopernika, 99, 321 p.

7700. DI NOLFO (Ennio). Le conseguenze diplomatiche dell'accordo navale anglo-tedesco del 16 giugno 1935. *In*: Grossbritannien und Deutschland [Cf. n° 7248], p. 77-87.

7701. DUMITRIU-SNAGOV (Ion). România în diplomatia Vaticanului 1939-1944. Bucureşti, Europa Nova, 99, 237 p.

7702. DYMARSKI (Mirosław). Stosunki wewnętrzne wśród polskiego wychodźstwa politycznego i wojskowego we Francji i w Wielkiej Brytanii 1939-1945. (Innenverhältnisse unter dem politischen und militärischen Polen-Emigrantentum in Frankreich und in Großbritannien 1939-1945). Wrocław, Wydaw. Uniw. Wrocławskiego, 99, 456 p. (Acta Universitatis Wratislaviensis, 2162).

7703. ERICSON (Edward E. III). Feeding the German Eagle: Soviet economic aid to Nazi Germany, 1933-1941. Westport, Praeger, 99, XIII-265 p.

7704. FEIERSTEIN (Daniel), GALANTE (Miguel). Argentina and the Holocaust: the conceptions and policies of Argentine diplomacy, 1933-1945. *Yad Vashem stud.*, 99, 27, p. 157-201.

7705. FIOR (Michel). La Banque nationale suisse et ses achats d'or à l'Allemagne: un débat qui reste ouvert. *Schweizerische Zeitschrift für Geschichte*, 99, 49, 2, p. 253-263.

7706. FLEURY (Antoine). La neutralité suisse à l'épreuve de la Deuxième Guerre mondiale. *In*: Neutralité et non-belligérance en Europe pendant la Deuxième Guerre mondiale [Cf. n° 7730], p. 29-60.

7707. GHISALBERTI (Carlo). Una memoria inedita sulle origini della seconda guerra mondiale e sull'intervento italiano. *Rassegna storica del Risorgimento*, 99, 86, p. 3-18.

7708. GIORDANO (Giancarlo). L'Italia nella seconda guerra mondiale. Aspetti politici e diplomatici. *Clio*, 99, 35, p. 649-663.

7709. GORODETSKY (Gabriel). Grand delusion: Stalin and the German invasion of Russia. New Haven a. London, Yale U. P., 99, XVI-408 p.

7710. GROSS (Jan Tomasz). Studium zniewolenia. Wybory październikowe 22 X 1939. (Ein Studium der Knechtschaft. Oktoberwahlen 22. X. 1939). Kraków, Universitas, 99, 118 p.

7711. GUDERZO (Massimiliano). Madrid and the Mediterranean, 1939-1942: the international system and the ambitions of a minor power, *In*: Seas (The) as Europe's external borders and their role in shaping a European identity [Cf. n° 363], p. 171-181.

7712. HERREN (M.). L'unione monétaire latine, la guerre et la Suisse. *In*: Monnaie et relations internationales. 1 [Cf. n° 7277], p. 269-288.

7713. Historia dyplomacji polskiej. Vol. 5. 1939-1945. Pod redakcja Waldemara MICHOWICZA, Polski Instytut Spraw Miedzynarodowych. Warszawa, Wydawnictwo Naukowe, 99, 844 p. (ill.).

7714. JANČÍK (Drahomír). Třetí říše a rozklad Malé dohody. Hospodářství a diplomacie v Podunají v letech 1936-1939. (Das Dritte Reich und der Zerfall der Kleinen Entente). Praha, Karolinum, 99, 270 p. (photogr.).

7715. JANEIRO PINTO (Helena). Salazar et les trois France (1940-1944). *XXe siècle*, 99, 62, p. 39-51.

7716. KACZMAREK (Ryszard). Pod rządami gauleiterów. Elity i instancje władzy w rejencji katowickiej w latach 1939-1945. (Unter der Regierungsgewalt der Gauleiter. Machteliten und -instanzen in dem Regierungsbezirk Kattowitz in den Jahren 1939-1945). Katowice, Wydaw. Uniw. Śląskiego, 99, 250 p. (Prace Naukowe Uniwersytetu Śląskiego w Katowicach, 1736).

7717. KAZAMIAS (G.). 'The usual Bulgarian stratagems': the Big Three and the end of the Bulgarian occupation of Greek Eastern Macedonia and Thrace,

September–October 1944. *European history quarterly*, 99, 29, 3, p. 323-347.

7718. KOLINSKY (Martin). Britain's war in the Middle East: strategy and diplomacy, 1936–1942. New York, St. Martin's Press, 99, XII-308 p.

7719. Krieg und Wirtschaft. Studien Wirtschaftsgeschichte 1939–1945. Hrsg. v. Dietrich EICHOLTZ. Berlin, Metropol, 99, 352 p. (Nationalsozialistische Besatzungspolitik in Europa 1939–1945, 9).

7720. KRÖGER (Martin), THIMME (Roland). Das Politische Archiv des Auswärtigen Amts im Zweiten Weltkrieg. Sicherung, Flucht, Verlust, Rückführung. *Vierteljahrshefte für Zeitgeschichte*, 99, 47, 2, p. 243-264.

7721. LACROIX-RIZ (Annie). Industriels et banquiers sous l'occupation. La collaboration économique avec le Reich et Vichy. Paris, A. Colin, 99, 662 p.

7722. LEITZ (Christian). Les aspects économiques des relations entre Allemagne nazie et les pays neutres européens pendant la Seconde Guerre mondiale. *In*: Neutralité et non-belligérance en Europe pendant la Deuxième Guerre mondiale [Cf. n° 7730], p. 7-28.

7723. LUKEŠ (Igor). Československo mezi Stalinem a Hitlerem. Benešova cesta k Mnichovu. (Czechoslovakia between Stalin and Hitler. The diplomacy of Edvard Beneš in the 1930s). Praha, Prostor, 99, 374 p. (photogr.). (Obzor, 26).

7724. LYNCH (Cecelia). Beyond appeasement: interpreting interwar peace movements in world politics. Ithaca a. London, Cornell U. P., 99, XI-238 p.

7725. MAIOLO (Joseph A.). Armaments diplomacy and maritime power: the admiralty and the Anglo-German naval agreement of 18 June 1935 *Diplomacy and statecraft*, 99, 10, 1, p. 87-126.

7726. MAISSEN (Thomas). Was motivierte die Nationalbank beim (Raub-)Goldhandel? *Schweizerische Zeitschrift für Geschichte*, 99, 49, 4, p. 530-540.

7727. MAYER (Karl J.). Zwischen Krise und Krieg: Frankreich in der Außenwirtschaftspolitik der USA zwischen Weltwirtschaftskrise und Zweitem Weltkrieg und das Problem der Sicherheit vor Deutschland. Stuttgart, Steiner, 99, XVI-274 p. (Historische Mitteilungen. Beihefte, 33).

7728. MIROVITSKAJA (Raisa A.). Kitajskaja gosudarstvennost' i sovetskaja politika v Kitae. Gody tikhookeanskoj vojny, 1941–1945. (The Chinese State and the Soviet policy in China during the war in the Pacific Ocean, 1941–1945). RAN, In-t Dal'nego Vostoka. Moskva, Pamjatniki istoricheskoj mysli, 99, 311 p. (bibl., ind.). [Eng. summary].

7729. MOUSSON-LESTANG (Jean-Pierre). La neutralité de la Suède pendant la Deuxième Guerre mondiale. *In*: Neutralité et non-belligérance en Europe pendant la Deuxième Guerre mondiale [Cf. n° 7730], p. 61-78.

7730. Neutralité et non-belligérance en Europe pendant la Deuxième Guerre mondiale. Prés. de Michel CATALA. *Guerres mondiales et conflits contemporains*, 99, 49, 194, p. 3-162. [Cf. n°s 7697, 7706, 7722, 7729, 7731, 7732, 7743.]

7731. OSTENC (Michel). La non-belligérance italienne (4 septembre 1939–10 juin 1940). *In*: Neutralité et non-belligérance en Europe pendant la Deuxième Guerre mondiale [Cf. n° 7730], p. 79-100.

7732. PAXTON (Robert O.). Le régime de Vichy était-il neutre? *In*: Neutralité et non-belligérance en Europe pendant la Deuxième Guerre mondiale [Cf. n° 7730], p. 149-162.

7733. QUARTARARO (Rosaria). I rapporti italo-americani durante il fascismo, (1922–1941). Napoli, Edizioni scientifiche italiane, 99, 304 p. (ESI-uni, 116).

7734. RÉTY (György). Le relazioni italo-ungheresi dalla Conferenza di Monaco al primo Arbitrato di Vienna. *Rivista di studi politici internazionali*, 99, 66, p. 207-222.

7735. Români la Hitler. [Rumänen bei Hitler]. Hrsg. v. Ion CALAFETEANU. Bucureşti, Univers Enciclopedic, 99, 289 p. [A collection of documents].

7736. RYCHLÍK (Jan). Politická situácia v Európe a na Slovensku v rokoch 1941–1943 v správach bulharských diplomatov. (The political situation in Europe and Slovakia in the years 1941–1943 in the reports of Bulgarian diplomats). *Historický časopis*, 99, 47, 2, p. 265-305.

7737. Second Quebec conference revisited (The): waging war, formulating peace: Canada, Great Britan, and the United States in 1944–1945. Ed. by David B. WOOLNER. Basingstoke, Macmillan, 99, XIII-210 p. (The Franklin and Eleanor Roosevelt Institute series on diplomatic and economic history).

7738. SHEN (Peijian). The age of appeasement: the evolution of British foreign policy in the 1930s. Stroud, Sutton, 99, XXIX-322 p. (Sutton modern British history, 5).

7739. SLAVINSKII (Boris N.). SSSR i Iaponiia-na puti k voine: diplomaticheskaia istoriia, 1937–1945 gg. (USSR-Japan on the way to war: diplomatic history, 1937–1945). Moskva, ZAO "Iaponiia segodnia", 99, 540 p. (ill., maps).

7740. Spain in international context, 1936–1959. Ed. by Christian LEITZ and David J. DUNTHORN. New York, Berghahn Books, 99, XVII-334 p.

7741. STEINBERG (Jonathan). Die Deutsche Bank und ihre Goldtransaktionen während des Zweiten Weltkrieges. In Verb. mit den Mitgliedern der Historikerkommission zur Erforschung der Geschichte der Deutschen Bank in der NS-Zeit Avraham BARKAI, Gerald D. FELDMANN, Lothar GALL und Harold JAMES. München, Beck, 99, 191 p.

7742. SUŠKO (Ladislav). Miesto autonómneho Slovenska v politike Nemeckej ríše (september 1938–

marec 1939). (Autonome Slowakei in der Politik des deutschen Reiches, September 1938–März 1939). *Historický časopis*, 99, 47, 3, p. 420-431. [Deutsche Zfassung].

7743. TERMINASSIAN (Taline). La neutralité de la Turquie pendant la Seconde Guerre mondiale. *In*: Neutralité et non-belligérance en Europe pendant la Deuxième Guerre mondiale [Cf. n° 7730], p. 117-148.

7744. TOŠKOVA (V.). Izpulnitelnata vlast i vunšnatapolitika na Bulgarija (1919–1945). (Le pouvoir exécutif et la politique extérieure de la Bulgarie, 1919–1945). *In*: 120 godini izpulnitelna vlast v Bulgarija [Cf. n° 4141], p. 162-176.

Cf. n^{os} *7547, 7576, 7593, 7618, 7853*

c. *Military operations*

7745. Armée roumaine (L') dans la deuxième guerre mondiale (1941–1945). Coordonator: Alesandru DUȚU, București, Editura Militară, 99, 260 p.

7746. CABAN (Ireneusz). Na dwa fronty. Obwód AK Tomaszów Lubelski w walce z Niemcami i ukraińskimi nacjonalistami. (Nach zwei Fronten. AK-Landesarmee-Bezirk Tomaszów Lubelski im Kampf gegen Deutsche sowie gegen ukrainische Nationalisten.). Lublin, Oficyna Wydaw. „Czas", 99, 381. (Tomaszowskie Tow. Regionalne).

7747. CHAIX (Bruno). Conception et déroulement de l'intervention des forces franco-britanniques en Belgique en mai 1940. Paris, [s. n.], 99, [s. p.]. [Thèse (Doct. Hist.) – Paris, Univ. Paris-I, 1999).

7748. CIENCIALA (Anna). The Munich crisis of 1938: plans and strategy in Warsaw in the context of the Western appeasement of Germany. *In*: Munich crisis (The), 1938: prelude to World War II [Cf. n° 7661], p. 48-80.

7749. DASSOVICH (Mario). Fronte jugoslavo, 1941–1942: aspetti e momenti della presenza militare italiana sull'opposta sponda adriatica durante la seconda guerra mondiale. Udine, Del Bianco, 99, 242 p. (Civiltà del Risorgimento, 60).

7750. DIMITRIJEVSKI (Marjan). Makedonskata vojska 1944–1945: pregled na Glavniot stab, brigadite, diviziite, korpusite i V jugoslovenska armija. (Die makedonische Armee 1944–1945). Skopje, Institut za nacionalna istorija, 99, 226 p.

7751. FORSEN (Björn), FORSEN (Annette). Tysklands och Finlands hemliga ubåtssamarbete. (La collaboration sous-marine secrète entre l'Allemagne et la Finlande). Helsinki, Söderström, 99, 334 p., pl. (ill.).

7752. FRIEDL (Jiří). Českoslovenští důstojníci v bitvě u El-Alameinu – pozorovatelé u britské 10. tankové divize (Czechoslovak officers in the battle of El Alamein, as Observers with the British 10th Tank Division]. *Historie a vojenství*, 99, 48, 2, p. 306-324.

7753. GARRAUD (Philippe). Une poursuite de la guerre depuis l'AFN était-elle envisageable en juin 1940? Le cas de l'armée de l'air. *Guerres mondiales et conflits contemporains*, 99, 49, 194, p. 173-185.

7754. GAUJAC (P.). La guerre en Provence, 1944–1945. Lyon, Presses Universitaires de Lyon, 99, 192 p.

7755. GAVRILOV (Boris I.). «Dolina smerti»: Tragedija i podvig 2-j udarnoj armii. ('The Valley of Death': the tragedy and the feat of the Second Shock Army, [an attempt to run the blockade of Leningrad, 1942]). RAN, In-t rossijskoj istorii. Moskva, [s. n.], 99, 306 p. (bibl.; ind.).

7756. GLANTZ (David M.), HOUSE (Jonathan H.). The Battle of Kursk. Lawrence, University Press of Kansas, 99, XIII-472 p.

7757. GLANTZ (David M.). Zhukov's greatest defeat: the Red Army's epic disaster in Operation Mars, 1942. Lawrence, University Press of Kansas, 99, X-421 p. (Modern war studies).

7758. GYLLENHAAL (Lars), GEBHARDT (James F.). Slaget om Nordkalotten. Sveriges roll i tyska och allierade operationer i norr. (La bataille pour la Scandinavie septentrionale. Le rôle de la Suède dans les opérations allemandes et alliées dans le Nord). Lund, Historiska Media, 99, 202 p. (ill.).

7759. HARRISON (E. D. R.). British subversion in French East Africa, 1941–1942. SOE's Todd mission. *English historical review*, 99, 114, 456, p. 339-369.

7760. JAKUB (Jay). Spies and saboteurs: Anglo-American collaboration and rivalry in human intelligence collection and special operations, 1940–1945. Foreword by Douglas DODDS-PARKER. New York, St. Martin's, 99, XXIX-280 p.

7761. JERSAK (Tobias). Die Interaktion von Kriegsverlauf und Judenvernichtung. Ein Blick auf Hitlers Strategie im Sommer 1941. *Historische Zeitschrift*, 99, 268, 2, p. 311-374.

7762. KLANJŠČEK (Zdravko). Deveti korpus slovenske narodnoosvobodilne vojske: 1943–1945. (The Ninth Corps of the Slovene National Liberation Army: 1943–1945). Ljubljana, Društvo piscev zgodovine NOB Slovenije, 99, 571 p. (ill.). (Partizanski knjižni klub, 32. Knjižnica NOV in POS, 61).

7763. NEY-KRWAWICZ (Marek). Powstanie powszechne w koncepcjach i pracach sztabu Naczelnego Wodza i Komendy Głównej Armii Krajowej. (Der allgemeine Aufstand in den Auffassungen und Arbeiten des Stabs des Oberbefehlshabers und der Hauptkommandantur der AK-Landesarmee). Warszawa, Semper, 99, 707 p.

7764. OTU (Petre), OZUNU (Mihai Vasile). Înfrânți și uitați. Românii în bătălia de la Stalingrad. (Defeated and forgotten. The Romanians in the battle of Stalingrad). București, Editura Ion Cristoiu, 99, 299 p.

7765. SCHARFF SMITH (Peter), POULSEN (Niels Bo), CHRISTENSEN (Claus Bundgård). The Danish volunteers in the Waffen SS and German warfare at the Eastern Front. *Contemporary European history*, 99, 8, p. 73-96.

7766. UNGVÁRY (Krisztián). Die Schlacht um Budapest: Stalingrad an der Donau 1944/45. München, Herbig, 99, 504 p. (ill.).

7767. Vernichtungskrieg (Der) im Osten: Verbrechen der Wehrmacht in der Sowjetunion aus Sicht russischer Historiker. Hrsg. v. Gabriele GORZKA und Knut STANG. Kassel, Kassel U. P., 99, 154 p. (Reihe Ost West Dialog, 3).

7768. VRESNIK (Drago), JERKIČ (Branko). Zaščita in boj za svobodo: 1944-1945: poveljstvo Vojske državne varnosti – 1. slovenska divizija Narodne obrambe, Prva brigada VDV – NO. (Protection and the fight for freedom: 1944-1945: command of the state security army – 1st Slovene Division of National Defence). Ljubljana, Društvo piscev zgodovine NOB Slovenije, 99, 389 p. (ill.). (Zbirka Partizanski knjižni klub, 35. Knjižnica NOV in POS, 23/5).

7769. WATSON (Bruce Allen). Exit Rommel: the Tunisian campaign, 1942-1943. Westport a. London, Greenwood, 99, XIII-217 p.

d. *Resistance*

** 7770. Latvijas nacionalo partizanu kars: dokumenti un materiali, 1944-1956. Sastadijs un komentejs Heinrihs STRODS. Riga, Preses nams, 99, 654 p.

** 7771. "There is not enough killing": condemned to death, hostages, shot in the Ljubljana province: 1941-1943: documents. Ljubljana, Inštitut za novejšo zgodovino, Društvo piscev zgodovine NOB, 99, 323 p. (ill.).

** 7772. Zalozhniki vermakhta: dokumenty i materialy = Geiseln der Wehrmacht: Dokumente und Belege. Redaktsionnaia kollegiia, Gennadii Ivanovich BARKUN [i dr.]. Minsk, Natsional'nyi arkhiv Respubliki Belarus', 99, 313 p.

7773. AGLAN (Alya). La Résistance sacrifiée. Histoire du mouvement Libération-Nord. Paris, Flammarion, 99, 455 p.

7774. ANDERSON (Truman). Incident at Baranivka: German reprisals and the Soviet partisan movement in Ukraine, October–December 1941. *Journal of modern history*, 99, 71, 3, p. 585-623.

7775. BAUMEL (Jacques). Résister: histoire secrète des années d'Occupation. Paris, A. Michel, 99, 457 p.

7776. BENEŠ (Josef). Život v odboji. Autentické svědectví o osudech čs. vojáků za druhé světové války. (Life in the resistance. Authentic testimony to the fate of Czechoslovak soldiers in WW II). Olomouc, Votobia, 99, 311 p. (photogr.).

7777. BENNETT (Rab). Under the shadow of the Swastika: the moral dilemmas of resistance and collaboration in Hitler's Europe. New York, New York U. P., 99, IX-318 p.

7778. BORODZIEJ (Włodzimierz). Terror und Politik: die deutsche Polizei und die polnische Widerstandsbewegung im Generalgouvernement, 1939–1944. Mainz, Verlag Philipp von Zabern, 99, VIII-302 p. (Veröffentlichungen des Instituts für Europäische Geschichte Mainz, Abteilung Universalgeschichte, 28).

7779. CALEGARI (Manlio). Beyond enemy lines in Italy. Gli OSS tra i partigiani italiani (1944–1945). *Quaderni di storia contemporanea*, 99, 25-26, p. 47-56.

7780. DE FELICE (Renzo). La Resistenza e il Regno del Sud. Con postilla di Rudolf LILL. *Nuova storia contemporanea*, 99, 3, 2, p. 9-24.

7781. GOZZER (Vittorio). OSS and ORI: the Raimondo Craveri and Max Corvo partnership. *Journal of modern Italian studies*, 99, 4, 1, p. 32-36.

7782. HASANI (Proletar). Histori e pashkruar: historia e organizimit të UNÇSH-së 1939–1944. Tiranë, «FLLAD», 99, 198 p.

7783. HOFMAN (Jiří), ŠIRC (Václav), VACULÍK (Jaroslav). Volyňští Češi v prvním a druhém odboji. (Volhynier Tschechen im ersten und zweiten Widerstand). Praha, Český svaz bojovníků za svobodu, 99, 320 p.

7784. HRENKEVIČ (Leanid D.). The Soviet partisan movement: 1941–1945; a critical historiographical analysis. London, Cass, 99, XV-368 p. (Cass series on Soviet military experience, 4).

7785. JESPERSEN (Knud J. V.). Med hjaelp fra England: Special Operations Executive og den danske modstandskamp, 1940–1945. Odense, Odense Universitetsforlag, 99, [s. p.]. (Odense University studies in history and social sciences, 228).

7786. KEDWARD (Harry Roderick). A la recherche du Maquis. La Résistance dans la France du Sud, 1942–1944. Paris, Ed. du Cerf, 99, 474 p. – IDEM. Revisiting French Resistance. *Transactions of the Royal Historical Society*, 99, 6, 9, p. 271-282.

7787. KLINKHAMMER (Lutz). Der Partisanenkrieg der Wehrmacht 1941–1944. *In*: Wehrmacht (Die): Mythos und Realität [Cf. n° 4512], p. 815-836.

7788. KUKLÍK (Jan), NĚMEČEK (Jan). Hodža versus Beneš. Milan Hodža a slovenská otázka v zahraničním odboji za druhé světové války. (Hodža gegen Beneš. Milan Hodža und die slowakische Frage im Auslandswiderstand während des Zweiten Weltkrieges). Praha, Karolinum, 99, 283 p.

7789. Lidice (Von) bis Kalavryta: Widerstand und Besatzungsterror. Studien zur Repressalienpraxis im Zweiten Weltkrieg. Hrsg. v. Loukia DROULIA und Hagen FLEISCHER. Berlin, Metrpol, 99, 295 p. (Nationalsozialistische Besatzungspolitik in Europa 1939–1945

= National Socialist occupation policy in Europe 1939–1945, 8).

7790. MIRABILE (Francesco). La Resistenza tedesca e le responsabilità anglo-americane. *Rivista di studi politici internazionali*, 99, 66, p. 234-244.

7791. NYLANDER (Gert). German resistance movement and England: Carl Goerdeler and Wallenberg brothers. Stockholm, Foundation for Economic History Research within Banking and Enterprise, 99, 100 p. (Banking & enterprise, 2).

7792. PAUCKER (Arnold). Deutsche Juden im Widerstand 1933–1945: Tatsachen und Probleme. Berlin, Gedenkstätte Deutscher Widerstand, 99, 47 p.

7793. PETROVA (Nina K.). Antifashistskie komitety v SSSR: 1941–1945 gg. (The Anti-Fascist committees in the USSR, 1941–1945). RAN, In-t rossijskoj istorii. Moskva, [s. n.], 99, 339 p. (bibl., ind.).

7794. Résistance (La) et les Européens du Sud. Actes du Colloque tenu à Aix-en-Provence, 20–22 mars 1997. Sous la dir. de Jean-Marie GUILLON et Robert MENCHERINI. Paris, L'Harmattan, 99, 401 p.

7795. RICHTER (Timm C.). Die Wehrmacht und der Partisanenkrieg in den besetzten Gebieten der Sowjetunion. *In*: Wehrmacht (Die): Mythos und Realität [Cf. n° 4512], p. 837-857.

7796. ROCHAT (Giorgio). Cefalonia 1943. *Storia e memoria*, 99, 8, p. 295-300.

7797. Rok 1942 v českém odboji. Sborník příspěvků. (The Czech resistance in 1942. Conference proceedings). Praha, Český svaz bojovníků za svobodu, 99, 121 p. (photogr.).

7798. SCHWERIN (Franz). Helmuth James Graf von Moltke: im Widerstand die Zukunft denken: Zielvorstellungen für ein neues Deutschland. Paderborn, Schoningh, 99, 211 p. (Rechts- und staatswissenschaftliche Veröffentlichungen der Görres-Gesellschaft, 86).

7799. TOMASZEWSKI (Longin). Wileńszczyzna lat wojny i okupacji 1939–1945. (Vilniuser Boden während des Krieges und der Okkupation 1939–1945). Warszawa, Rytm, 99, 762 p.

7800. War, resistance and intelligence: collected essays in honour of M. R. D. Foot. Ed. by K. G. ROBERTSON. Barnsley, Cooper, 99, XXV-262 p.

§ 8. From 1945.

* 7801. LEFFLER (Melvyn P.). The Cold War: what do «We Now Know»? *American historical review*, 99, 104, 2, p. 501-524.

** 7802. Akten zur Auswärtigen Politik der Bundesrepublik Deutschland. Hrsg. im Auftrag des auswärtigen Amts von Hans-Peter SCHWARZ. 1951. 1. Januar bis 31. Dezember 1951. Wissenschaftlicher Leiter Rainer A. BLASIUS; Bearbeiter Matthias JAROCH. 1968. Band 1. 1. Januar bis 30. Juni 1968. Band 2. 1. Juli bis 31. Dezember 1968. Wissenschaftlicher Leiter Rainer A. BLASIUS; Bearbeiter Mechthild LINDEMANN und Matthias PETER. München, Oldenbourg, 99, 3 vol., LVIII-816 p., CLVIII-814 p., 958 p.

** 7803. American papers (The): secret and confidential India-Pakistan-Bangladesh documents, 1965–1973. Compiled and selected by Roedad KHAN; introduction by Jamsheed MARKER. Oxford, Oxford U. P., XLIX-997 p.

** 7804. BARIÉTY (J.), DEFRANCE (C.). Naissance et débuts de la RFA, septembre 1949–décembre 1950: récentes publications de documents diplomatiques allemands et français. *Revue d'Allemagne et des pays de langue allemande*, 99, 31, 2, p. 209-233.

** 7805. BARIÉTY (J.). "Deutsche Einheit" – publication de documents de la chancellerie de la RFA sur la réunification (1989–1990). *Revue d'Allemagne et des pays de langue allemande*, 99, 31, 1, p. 155-169.

* 7806. BARIÉTY (Jacques). Die Komplexität der historischen Wahrheit. Akten zur deutschen Außenpolitik 1963/1964. *Historische Zeitschrift*, 99, 269, 1, p. 99-107.

** 7807. British documents on Foreign affairs: reports and papers from the Foreign Office confidential print. General editors Paul PRESTON and Michael PARTRIDGE. Part 4. From 1945 through 1950. Series A. The Soviet Union and Finland. Vol. 1. Northern affairs: January 1946–June 1946. Vol. 2. Northern affairs: July 1946–December 1946. Ed. by Anita PRAZMOWSKIA. Bethesda, University Publications of America, 99, 2 vol. XX-437 p., XX-387 p.

** 7808. British documents on Foreign affairs: reports and papers from the Foreign Office confidential print. General editors Paul PRESTON and Michael PARTRIDGE. Part 4. From 1946 through 1950. Series C. North America. Vol. 1946. Ed. by Richard D.G. CROCKATT. Bethesda, University Publications of America, 99, XXII-393 p.

** 7809. CANTARINO (Geraldo). 1964, a revoluçao para inglês ver: relatórios secretos, documentos confidenciais e mensagens urgentes sobre o golpe militar e o Brasil de 64, seus políticos e governantes, feitos por diplomatas ingleses para o Governo Británico. Rio de Janeiro, MAUAD, 99, 160 p.

** 7810. Chile desclasificado: documentos del Pentágono, Departamento de Estado, Consejo de Seguridad Nacional, FBI & CIA. Ed. por Ernesto CARMONA. Santiago, E.C. Carmona, 99, [s. p.].

** 7811. Documents diplomatiques français. 22. 1962. Tome 2. 1. juillet–31 décembre. Ministère des affaires étrangères. Commission de publication des documents diplomatiques. Paris, Imprimerie nationale, 99, LI-636 p.

** 7812. Documents diplomatiques suisses: 1848–1945. Commission nationale pour la publication de documents diplomatiques suisses. 17. 1. juin 1947–30. juin 1949. Zürich, Chronos, 99, LXXXVI-493 p.

** 7813. Documents relatifs aux relations extérieures du Canada = Documents on Canadian external relations. 21. 1955. Sous la direction de Greg DONAGHY. Ottawa, Canada Communication Group, 99, XLVIII-1703 p.

** 7814. DROOGLEVER (P. J.), SCHOUTEN (M. J. B.), LOHANDA (Mona). Guide to the archives on relations between the Netherlands and Indonesia 1945–1963. The Hague, Institute of Netherlands History, 99, 477 p. (ING research guide, 1).

** 7815. Estados Unidos (Los) y Trujillo: los días finales, 1960–1961: colección de documentos del Departamento de Estado, la CIA y los archivos del Palacio Nacional Dominicano. Ed. por Bernado VEGA. Santo Domingo, Fundación Cultural Dominicana, 99, XX-786 p. (ill., ports).

** 7816. Events and documents of Indo-Pak relations. Ed. by Verinder GROVER and Ranjana ARORA. New Delhi, Deep & Deep Publications, 99, X-538 p. (50 years of Indo-Pak relations, 3).

** 7817. Foreign relations of the United States. 1964–1968. General editor David S. PATTERSON. Vol. 15. Germany and Berlin. Ed. by James E. MILLER. Vol. 22. Iran. Ed. by Nina Davis HOWLAND. Vol. 24. Africa. Ed. by Nina Davis HOWLAND. Vol. 34. Energy diplomacy and global issues. Ed. by Susan K. HOLLY. Washington, United States Government Printing Office, 99, 4 vol., XXX-813 p., XXVIII-592 p., XLVII-1144 p., XXX-606 p.

** 7818. Front lines (On the) of the Cold War: documents on the intelligence war in Berlin, 1946 to 1961. Ed. by Donald P. STEURY. Washington, CIA History Staff, Center for the Study of Intelligence, 99, X-634 p. (ill.).

** 7819. Kennedys (The) and Cuba: the declassified documentary history. Ed. with commentary by Mark J. WHITE. Chicago, I. R. Dee, 99, XVIII-356 p.

** 7820. Psywar on Cuba: the declassified history of U.S. anti-Castro propaganda. Ed. by Jon ELLISTON. Melbourne a. New York, Ocean Press, 99, 320 p. (ill.). (40 years of the Cuban Revolution, 1959–1999).

** 7821. Quellen zu den deutsch-sowjetischen Beziehungen, 1945–1991. Hrsg. v. Horst Günther LINKE. Darmstadt, Wissenschaftliche Buchgesellschaft, 99, XXX-254 p. (Quellen zu den Beziehungen Deutschlands zu seinen Nachbarn im 19. und 20. Jahrhundert, 9).

** 7822. Sovetskij faktor v Vostochnoj Evrope, 1944–1953 gg.: Dokumenty. (Soviet Factor in Eastern Europe, 1944–1953: documents). Ed. T. V. VOLOKITINA. RAN, In-t slavjanovedenija. In 2 vol. Vol. 1. 1944–1948 gg. Moskva, ROSSPEN, 99, 687 p.

** 7823. Soviet deliberations during the Polish crisis, 1980–1981. Edited, translated, annotated, and introduced by Mark KRAMER. Washington, Woodrow Wilson International Center for Scholars, Cold War International History Project, 99, 181 p. (Special working paper, 1).

7824. 1953, Krisenjahr des Kalten Krieges in Europa. Hrsg. v. Bernd STÖVER und Christoph KLESSMANN. Köln, Böhlau, 99, 246 p. (Zeithistorische Studien, 16).

7825. 1960-yondae ui taeoe kwangye in Nam-Puk munje. (Foreign affairs and the North-South problem in 1960's). Ed. by Pyong-yong YU [et al.], Han'guk Chongsin Munhwa Yon'guwon p'yon. Soul, Paeksan Sodang, 99, 266 p. (Han'guk hyondaesa ui chae insik = Rethinking modern Korean history, 11).

7826. 50 Jahre sowjetische und russische Deutschlandpolitik sowie ihre Auswirkungen auf das gegenseitige Verhältnis. Hrsg. v. Boris MEISSNER und Alfred EISFELD. Berlin, Duncker & Humblot, 99, 308 p. (Studien zur Deutschlandfrage, 14).

7827. ABADI (Jacob). Israel and Sudan: the saga of an enigmatic relationship. *Middle Eastern studies*, 99, 35, 3, p. 19-41.

7828. African American voice (The) in U.S. foreign policy since World War II. Ed. with an intr. by Michael L. KRENN. New York a. London, Garland, 99, X-300 p. (ill.).

7829. AKINTERINWA (Bola A.). Nigeria and France, 1960–1995: the dilemma of thirty-five years of relationship. Ibadan, Vantage, 99, XXI-282 p.

7830. AL-ATRASH (Ahmed Ali Salem). Inter-Arab management of regional conflicts: the League of Arab States and the Algeria-Morocco case, 1963–1995. Canterbury, [s. n.], 99, [s. p.]. [PhD thesis, University of Kent at Canterbury].

7831. ALI (S. Mahmud). Cold War in the High Himalayas: The USA, China and South Asia in the 1950s. New York, St. Martin's Press, 99, XXXVIII-286 p.

7832. ALLAN (Pierre) KLÄY (Dieter). Zwischen Bürokratie und Ideologie: Entscheidungsprozesse in Moskaus Afghanistankonflikt. Bern, P. Haupt, 9, 670 p. (ill.).

7833. AMOS (Heike). Die Westpolitik der SED 1948/49–1961: "Arbeit nach Westdeutschland" durch die Nationale Front, das Ministerium für Auswärtige Angelegenheiten und das Ministerium für Staatssicherheit. Berlin, Akademie, 99, 400 p. (ill.).

7834. ANDREW (Christopher), MITROKHIN (Vasili). The Sword and the Shield: the Mitrokhin Archive and the secret history of the KGB. New York, Basic Books, 99, XIV-700 p.

7835. ARMONY (Ariel C.). La Argentina, los Estados Unidos y la cruzada anticomunista en América Central, 1977–1984. Bernal, Universidad Nacional de Quilmes, 99, 296 p.

7836. ASCHMANN (Birgit). "Treue Freunde ..."? Westdeutschland und Spanien 1945–1963. Stuttgart, Steiner, 99, 502 p. (Historische Mitteilungen, 34).

7837. ATHANASSOPOLOU (Ekavi). Turkey: Anglo-American security interests, 1945–1952: the first enlargement of NATO. London, Frank Cass, 99, XIII-274 p.

7838. AYALA MORA (Enrique). Ecuador-Peru: historia del conflicto y de la paz. Quito, Fundación El Comercio, Editorial Planeta del Ecuador, 99, 150 p.

7839. BAGNATO (Bruna). Anciennes élites, nouvelles élites. Le cas du Ministère des Affaires etrangères italien après la deuxième guerre mondiale. In: Europe des élites? Europe des peuples? La construction de l'espace européen, 1945–1960 [Cf. n° 7881], [s. p.].

7840. Balkans (The), nationalism and imperialism. Ed. by Lindsey GERMAN. London, Bookmarks, 99, XVI-189 p. (maps).

7841. BANCHOFF (Thomas). The German problem transformed: institutions, politics, and foreign policy, 1945–1995. Ann Arbor, University of Michigan Press, 99, X-217 p. (Social history, popular culture, and politics in Germany).

7842. BANGE (Oliver). The EEC crisis of 1963: Kennedy, Macmillan, De Gaulle and Adenauer in conflict. Basingstoke, Macmillan, 99, XVI-291 p. (Contemporary history in context series).

7843. BARTOSZEWICZ (Henryk). Polityka Związku Sowieckiego wobec państw Europy Środkowo-Wschodniej w latach 1944–1948. (Die Politik der Sowjetunion gegen Staaten des Mittelost-Europas in den Jahren 1944-1948). Warszawa, Książka i Wiedza, 99, 406 p.

7844. BARUA (Chanda). L'affaire d'Ayodhya et ses répercussion au Bangladesh. In: Conflits (Les) en Asie du Sud (1947–1999) [Cf. n° 7865], p. 189-202.

7845. BENKES (Mihály). Szuperhatalmak kora, 1945–1992. (The era of super powers, 1945–1992). Budapest, Korona Kiadó, 99, 302 p.

7846. BENOCCI (B.). La grande illusione. La questione tedesca dal 1953 al 1963. Manduria, Lacaita, 99, 198 p. (Biblioteca di storia contemporanea).

7847. BEWDLEY-TAYLOR (David). The cost of containment: the Cold War and US international drug control at the UN, 1950–1958. Diplomacy and statecraft, 99, 10, 1, p. 147-171.

7848. BÍLEK (Jiří). Vojenské aspekty čs.-polského sporu o Těšínsko v roce 1945. Vyhrocení situace v červnu 1945. (Military aspects of the Czechoslovak-Polish dispute over the Těšín region in 1945). Historie a vojenství, 99, 48, 2, p. 325-356.

7849. BISCHOF (Günter). Austria in the first Cold War, 1945–1955: the leverage of the weak. Houndsmills, Macmillan Press a. New York, St. Martin's Press, 99, XVII-237 p.

7850. BLACKWELL (Stephen). A desert squall: Anglo-American planning for military intervention in Iraq, July 1958–August 1959. Middle Eastern studies, 99, 35, 3, p. 1-18.

7851. BLANCHARD (Michel). Vietnam-Cambodge, une frontière contestée. Paris, L'Harmattan, 99, 175 p.

7852. BOEHLING (R.). The role of culture in American relations with Europe: the case of the United State's occupation of Germany. Diplomatic history, 99, 23, 1, p. 57-69.

7853. BOLL (Michael M.). Studenata voina na Balkanite: amerikanskata vunshna politika i vuznikvaneto na komunisticheska Bulgariia, 1943–1947. (La guerre froide aux Balcans. La politique extérieure américaine et le surgissement de la Bulgarie communiste 1943–1947). Sofiia, Bulgarska nauka i izkustvo, 99, 399 p.

7854. BOQUÉRAT (Gilles). La nucléarisation de l'Asie du Sud. In: Conflits (Les) en Asie du Sud (1947–1999) [Cf. n° 7865], p. 203-220.

7855. BOUGHERIRA (Mohamed Redha). Algeria's foreign policy 1979–1992: continuity and/or change. [S. l.], [s. n.], 99, [s. p.]. [PhD thesis, University of Salford].

7856. BRADY (Christopher). United States foreign policy towards Cambodia, 1977–1992: a question of realities. Basingstoke, Macmillan, 99, XXVI-227 p. (Contemporary history in context).

7857. BRANCHE (R.). Entre droit humanitaire et intérêts politiques: les missions algériennes du CICR. Revue historique, 99, 123, 609, p. 101-126.

7858. BRIGHAM (Robert K.). Guerrilla diplomacy: the NLF's Foreign relations and the Viet Nam War. Ithaca, Cornell U. P., 99, XVIII-215 p.

7859. BURG (Steven L.), SHOUP (Paul S.). The war in Bosnia-Herzegovina: ethnic conflict and international intervention. Armonk a. London, M.E. Sharpe, 99, XVIII-499 p.

7860. BURR (Millard), COLLINS (Robert O.). Africa's Thirty Years War: Libya, Chad, and the Sudan, 1963–1993. Boulder a. Oxford, Westview Press, 99, XVII-300 p. (maps).

7861. China and Israel, 1948–1998: a fifty year retrospective. Ed. by Jonathan GOLDSTEIN. Westport a. London, 99, XXXIII-215 p.

7862. CLYMER (K. J.). The perils of neutrality: the break in U.S.-Cambodian relations, 1965. Diplomatic history, 99, 23, 4, p. 609-631.

7863. Cold War statesmen confront the bomb: nuclear diplomacy since 1945. Ed. by John Lewis GADDIS. Oxford, Oxford U. P., 99, IX-398 p.

7864. Cold War's end (At): US intelligence on the Soviet Union and Eastern Europe, 1989–1991. Ed. by Benjamin B. FISCHER. Reston, Central Intelligence Agency, 99, LX-378 p.

7865. Conflits (Les) en Asie du Sud (1947–1999). Intr. de Jacques WEBER. Guerres mondiales et conflits contemporains, 99, 49, 195, p. 3-220. [Cf. n°s 7844, 7854, 7872, 7927, 7951, 7975, 8024.]

7866. COTTON (Matthew). Eden, Suez and the lessons of the 1930s. Oxford, [s. n.], 99, 105 p. [Thesis (M.Phil.) – University of Oxford, 1999].

7867. CUESTAS GÓMEZ (Carlos Humberto). Panamá y Costa Rica, entre la diplomacia y la guerra. Panamá, Litho Editorial Chen, 99, 420 p. (ill.).

7868. CULLATHER (Nick). Secret history: the CIA's classified account of its operations in Guatemala, 1952–1954. Stanford, Stanford U. P., 99, XV-142-XL p.

7869. "Dardanele". Delegatura WiN-u za granicą (1946–1949). ("Dardanele". Auslands-Vertretung der Vereinigung "Freiheit und Unabhängigkeit"/WiN, 1946–1949]. Wstęp, dobór tekstów, przypisy Stanisław Jan ROSTWOROWSKI. Wrocław, zarząd Gł. WiN-u, 99, 605 p. (Biblioteka Zeszytów Historycznych WiN-u).

7870. DE MONTCLOS (Christine). Le Vatican et l'éclatement de la Yougoslavie. Paris, Presses universitaires de France, 99, 263 p. (Perspectives internationales).

7871. DEROCHE (A. J.). Standing firm for principles: Jimmy Carter and Zimbabwe. *Diplomatic history*, 99, 23, 4, p. 657-685.

7872. DESHAYES (Laurent). La question tibétaine dans les relations sino-indiennes (1947–1960). *In*: Conflits (Les) en Asie du Sud (1947–1999) [Cf. n° 7865], p. 35-48.

7873. Deutschland unter alliierter Besatzung 1945–1949/55: [ein Handbuch]. Hrsg. v. Wolfgang BENZ. Berlin, Akademie Verlag, 99, 494 p. (maps).

7874. DI NOLFO (Ennio). Der Kalte Krieg: Definitionen und Chronologie. *In*: Macht und Zeitkritik [Cf. n° 4455], p. 465-76. – IDEM. L'Italia alla fine della Seconda guerra mondiale. L'alleato riluttante? *In*: La Fondazione della Repubblica 1946–1966. *Trimestre* (numero speciale), 99, p. 24-42.

7875. DÖRING (Hans-Joachim). "Es geht um unsere Existenz": die Politik der DDR gegenüber der Dritten Welt am Beispiel von Mosambik und Äthiopien. Berlin, Links, 99, 352 p. (Forschungen zur DDR-Gesellschaft).

7876. DORN (Glenn J.). «Bruce plan» and Marshall plan: the United States's disguised intervention against Peronism in Argentina, 1947–1950. *International history review*, 99, 21, 2, p. 331-351.

7877. DUNDOVICH (Elena). Sovietici e Costituente italiana: la rassegna stampa dell'ambasciata italiana a Mosca (1946–1948). *Quaderni del Circolo Rosselli*, 99, 15, [s. p.].

7878. EDWARDS (Jill). Anglo-American relations and the Franco question, 1945–1955. Oxford, Oxford U. P., 99, XVIII-291 p.

7879. EISERMANN (Daniel). Aussenpolitik und Strategiediskussion: die Deutsche Gesellschaft für Auswärtige Politik, 1955 bis 1972. München, R. Oldenbourg, 99, X-334 p. (ill.). (Schriften des Forschungsinstituts der Deutschen Gesellschaft für Auswärtige Politik e. V., Bonn. Internationale Politik und Wirtschaft, 66).

7880. Erobert oder befreit? Deutschland im internationalen Kräftefeld und die Sowjetische Besatzungszone, 1945/46. Hrsg. v. Hartmut MEHRINGER, Michael SCHWARTZ und Hermann WENTKER. München, R. Oldenbourg, 99, VI-382 p. (Schriftenreihe der Vierteljahrshefte für Zeitgeschichte. Sondernummer).

7881. Europe des élites? Europe des peuples? La construction de l'espace européen, 1945–1960. Sous la direction de Elisabeth DU RÉAU. Paris, Presses de la Sorbonne nouvelle, 99, 345 p. [Cf. n° <sélection> 7839.]

7882. Fédéralisme et Union européenne: actes du colloque organisé par l'Institut de science politique, Université de Neuchâtel, 11 décembre 1998. Ed. par Ernest WEIBEL et Cordélia MONNIER. Neuchâtel, Université de Neuchâtel, Institut de science politique, 99, [s. p.].

7883. FIELDING (J.). Coping with decline: US policy toward the British defense. *Diplomatic history*, 99, 23, 4, p. 633-656.

7884. FOGLESONG (David S.). Roots of «liberation». American images of the future of Russia in early Cold War, 1948–1953. *International history review*, 99, 21, 1, p. 57-79.

7885. FOITZIK (Jan). Sowjetische Militäradministration in Deutschland (SMAD) 1945–1949: Struktur und Funktion. Berlin, Akademie Verlag, 99, 544 p. (Quellen und Darstellungen zur Zeitgeschichte, 44).

7886. FREEDMAN (Lawrence). The politics of British defence, 1979–1998. Basingstoke, Macmillan, 99, XI-259 p.

7887. FURSENKO (Aleksandr A.), NAFTALI (Timoti). Adskaja igra [sekretnaja istorija Karibskogo krizisa; 1958–1964]. (One hell of a gamble. The secret history of the Caribian crisis, [1958–1964]). Moskva, Geja It erum, 99, 556 p.

7888. GIESZCZYŃSKI (Witold). Państwowy Urząd Repatriacyjny w osadnictwie na Warmii i Mazurach (1945–1950). (Staatliches Repatriierungs-Amt in dem Siedlungswesen im Ermland und in den Masuren, 1945–1950). Olsztyn, Ośr. Badań Nauk. im. Wojciecha Kętrzyńskiego, 99, 170 p. (Rozprawy i Materiały Ośrodka Badań Naukowych im. Wojciecha Kętrzyńskiego).

7889. GIORDANO (Giancarlo). La politica estera degli Stati Uniti: da Truman a Bush, 1945–1992. Milano, F. Angeli, 99, 330 p. (Politica/studi, 41).

7890. GÖKTEPE (Cihat). The 'Forgotten Alliance'? Anglo-Turkish relations and CENTO, 1959–1965. *In*: Seventy-five years of the Turkish Republic [Cf. n° 5175], p. 103-129.

7891. GOSSEL (Daniel). Briten, Deutsche und Europa. Die Deutsche Frage in der britischen Außenpolitik

1945-1962. Stuttgart, Steiner, 99, 259 p. (Historische Mitteilungen, 32).

7892. GOWLAND (David), TURNER (Arthur). Reluctant Europeans: Britain and European integration, 1945-1998. Kondon, Longman, 99, X-393 p.

7893. GRAHAM-BROWN (Sarah). Sanctioning Saddam: the politics of intervention in Iraq. London, I.B. Tauris, 99, XVII-380 p. (maps).

7894. GREENWOOD (Sean). Britain and the Cold War, 1945-1991. Basingstoke, Macmillan a. New York, St. Martins Press, 99, IX-227 p. (British history in perspective).

7895. GUASCONI (M. E.). L'altra faccia della medaglia. Guerra psicologica e diplomazia sindacale nelle relazioni Italia-Stati Uniti durante la prima fase della guerra fredda (1947-1955). Soveria Mannelli, Rubettino, 99, 251 p.

7896. GUYARD (Murielle). Les puissances occidentales et la crise congolaise: de la sécession du Katanga à l'accord de Kitona (1960-1961). In: Afrique: partenariat international et conflits régionaux [Cf. n° 7213], p. 53-64.

7897. HAHN (Peter L.). Alignment by coincidence. Israel, the United States, and the participation of Jerusalem, 1949-1953. International history review, 99, 21, 3, p. 665-689.

7898. HAYDOCK (Michael D.). City under siege: the Berlin blockade and airlift, 1948-1949. Washington a. London, Brassey's, 99, XIV-321 p.

7899. HEYNDRICKX (Pierre). Lomé démystifiée. Vingt-cinq and de coopération ACP-UE, 1975-2000. In: Afrique: partenariat international et conflits régionaux [Cf. n° 7213], p. 135-150.

7900. HODJATPANAH (Maryam). International relations and social revolution: international aspects of the Iranian 1979 revolution and post-revolutionary state. London, [s. n.], 99, 289 p. [Ph.D. Thesis – London School of Economics and Political Science Department of International Relations]

7901. HOLOBER (Frank). Raiders of the China coast: CIA covert operations during the Korean War. Annapolis, Naval Institute Press, xiii, 253 p. (Naval Institute special warfare series).

7902. HOPPE (Jiří). Od nedůvěry ke spojenectví a zpět. Československo-rumunské vztahy v letech 1967-1970 (From distrust to alliance and back. Czechoslovak-Romanian Relations, 1967–1970). Soudobé dějiny, 99, 6, 4, p. 443-459.

7903. HORVÁTH (István), NÉMETH (István). ... és a falak leomlanak: Magyarország és a német egység 1945-1990: legenda és valóság. (... and the walls fall: Hungary and the German unity 1945-1990: legend and reality). Budapest, Magvető, 99, 455 p. (Lassuló idő).

7904. HUSZÁR (Tibor). Prága-Budapest-Moszkva, 1968. Historia, 99, 1, p. 12-16.

7905. INGIMUNDARSON (Valur). Buttressing the West in the North. The Atlantic Alliance, economic warfare, and the Soviet challenge in Iceland, 1956-1959. International history review, 99, 21, 1, p. 80-103.

7906. Internationale Krisenjahr 1956 (Das): Polen, Ungarn, Suez. Hrsg. v. Winfried HEINEMANN und Norbert WIGGERSHAUS. München, R. Oldenbourg, 99, XXIX-722 p. (Beiträge zur Militärgeschichte, 48).

7907. Jean Monnet, l'Europe et les chemins de la paix: actes du colloque de Paris du 29 au 31 mai 1997. Organisé par l'Institut Pierre Renouvin de l'Université Paris I-Panthéon Sorbonne et l'Institut historique allemand de Paris; sous la direction de Gérard BOSSUAT et de Andreas WILKENS. Paris, Publications de la Sorbonne, 99, 536 p. (Série internationale / Université de Paris-I-Panthéon Sorbonne, 57). [Cf. n° <sélection> 8017.]

7908. JENSEN (Bent). Bjørnen og haren: Sovjetunionen og Danmark 1945-1965. (L'Ours et le lièvre: l'Union soviétique et le Danemark de 1945 à 1965). Odense, Odense Universitetsforlag, 99, 682 p., ill., cartes. (Odense University Slavic Studies 12).

7909. John F. Kennedy and Europe. Ed. by Douglas BRINKLEY and Richard T. GRIFFITHS; with a foreword by Theodore SORENSEN. Baton Rouge, Louisiana State U. P., 99, XVIII-349 p. (Eisenhower Center studies on war and peace). [Cf. n° <choice> 7950.]

7910. JOHNSON (Robert David). Constitutionalism abroad and at home: the United States Senate and the Alliance for Progress, 1961-1967. International history review, 99, 21, 2, p. 414-442.

7911. JONES (Matthew). 'Maximum disavowable aid': Britain, the United States and the Indonesian rebellion, 1957-1958. English historical review, 99, 114, 459, p. 1179-1216.

7912. JONJIĆ (Tomislav). Pitanje priznanja Nezavisne Države Hrvatske od Švicrske Konfederacije. (The question of the recognition of the independent state of Croatia by the Swiss Confederation). Časopis za suvremenu povijest, 99, 31, 2, p. 261-278.

7913. JOST (Hans Ulrich). Europa und die Schweiz 1945-1950: Europarat, Supranationalität und schweizerische Unabhängigkeit. Unter Mitarbeit von Matthieu LEIMGRUBER und Isaline MARCEL. Lausanne, Editions Payot u. Zürich, Chronos, 99, 239 p. (Schweizer Beiträge zur internationalen Geschichte = Contributions suisses a l'histoire internationale, 2).

7914. JULIEN (Elise). Les rapports franco-allemands à Berlin, 1945-1961. Préface de Robert FRANK. Paris, L'Harmattan, 99, 287 p. (Allemagne d'hier et d'aujourd'hui).

7915. KALVODA (Josef). Role Československa v sovětské strategii. (Czechoslovakia's role in Soviet strategy). Kladno, Dílo, 99, 426 p. (photogr.). (Paměť, 2).

7916. KAPLAN (Lawrence S.). The long entanglement: NATO's first fifty years. Westport, Praeger, 99, XII-262 p.

7917. KARABELL (Zachary). Architects of intervention: the United States, the Third World, and the Cold War, 1946-1962. Baton Rouge, Louisiana State U. P., 99, 248 p. (Eisenhower center studies on war and peace).

7918. KHULLAR (Dashan). When generals failed: the Chinese invasion: abdiction from battle, Tawang, Sela, and Bomdila, 1962. Foreword by John CHAPPLE. New Delhi, Manas, 267 p.

7919. KIM (Youngho). The origins of the Korean War: civil war or Stalin's rollback? *Diplomacy and statecraft*, 99, 10, 1, p. 186-214.

7920. KLEIN (Michael B.). Das Institut für Internationale Politik und Wirtschaft der DDR in seiner Gründungsphase 1971 bis 1974. Berlin, Duncker & Humblot, 99, 231 p (Schriftenreihe der Gesellschaft für Deutschlandforschung e.V, 70).

7921. KOFAS (Jon V.). Stabilization and class conflict: the State Department, the IMF, and the IBRD in Chile, 1952-1958. *International history review*, 99, 21, 2, p. 352-385.

7922. KRENN (Michael L.). Black diplomacy: African Americans and the State Department, 1945-1969. Armonk, M. E. Sharp, 99, VIII-223 p.

7923. KÜHNE (Andrea). Entstehung, Aufbau und Funktion der Flüchtlingsverwaltung in Württemberg-Hohenzollern 1945-1952: Flüchtlingspolitik im Spannungsfeld deutscher und französischer Interessen. Sigmaringen, J. Thorbecke, 99, 271 p. (ill., maps). (Schriftenreihe des Instituts für Donauschwäbische Geschichte und Landeskunde, 9).

7924. KUMAMOTO (Robert D.). International terrorism and American foreign relations 1945-1976. Boston, Northeastern U. P., 99, 232 p..

7925. KUNZ (Diane B.). 'Somewhat mixed up together': Anglo-American defence and financial policy during the 1960's. *In*: Statecraft (The) of British imperialism [Cf. n° 7318], p. 213-232.

7926. LABARTA RODRIGUEZ-MARIBONA (Carolina). British foreign policy towards Spain, 1950-1961. Oxford, [s. n.], 99, V-272 p. [Thesis (D.Phil.) – University of Oxford, 1999].

7927. LAMBALLE (Alain). Islamabad-Peshawar-Quetta: un triangle conflictuel au sein du Pakistan. *In*: Conflits (Les) en Asie du Sud (1947-1999) [Cf. n° 7865], p. 169-188.

7928. LEFEBVRE (Jeffrey A.). Kennedy's Algerian dilemma: containment, alliance politics and the 'Rebel Dialogue'. *Middle Eastern studies*, 99, 35, 2, p. 61-82

7929. LEHMKUHL (Ursula). Pax Anglo-Americana: Machtstrukturelle Grundlagen anglo-amerikanischer Asien- und Fernostpolitik in den 1950er Jahren. München, Oldenbourg, 99, 304 p. (Studien zur internationalen Geschichte, 7).

7930. Letzte (Der) macht das Licht aus: wie DDR-Diplomaten das Jahr 1990 im Ausland erlebten. Hrsg. v. Birgit MALCHOW. Berlin, Edition Ost, 99, 308 p. (ill.).

7931. LODEN (Hans). För säkerhets skull: ideologi och säkerhet i svensk aktiv utrikespolitik 1950-1975. (Pour plus de sûreté: idéologie et sécurité dans la politique extérieure de la Suède de 1950 à 1975). Stockholm, Nerenius & Santérus, 99, 341 p. (Göteborg Studies in politics, 63. Sverige under kalla kriget, 6).

7932. LOGEVALL (Fredrik). Choosing war: the lost chance for peace and the escalation of war in Vietnam. Berkeley a. Los Angeles, University of California Press, 99, XXVIII-529 p.

7933. LUCAS (Scott). Freedom's war: the American crusade against the Soviet Union. New York, New York U. P., 99, XII-301 p.

7934. MAC MAHON (Robert J.). The limits of empire: the United States and Southeast Asia since World War II. New York, Columbia U. P., 99, XII-276 p.

7935. MACKENZIE (Hector). An Old Dominion and the new Commonwealth. Canadian policy on the question of India's membership, 1947-1949. *Journal of Imperial and Commonwealth history*, 99, 27, 3, p. 82-113.

7936. MAELSTAF (Geneviève). Que faire de l'Allemagne? Les responsable français, le statut international de l'Allemagne et le problème de l'unité allemande (1945-1955). Paris, Ministère des Affaires étrangères, 99, 740 p.

7937. MAGAGNOLI (Ralf). Italien und die Europäische Verteidigungsgemeinschaft: zwischen europäischem Credo und nationaler Machtpolitik. Frankfurt am Main, P. Lang, 99, 256 p. (Italien in Geschichte und Gegenwart, 12).

7938. MANOKOU (Lucien). L'Afrique et le conseil de sécurité de l'ONU (1946-1990). *In*: Afrique: partenariat international et conflits régionaux [Cf. n° 7213], p. 7-22.

7939. MANTOVANI (Mauro). Another 'special relationship': the British-Swiss early Cold War coordination of defence (1947-1953). *Diplomacy and statecraft*, 99, 10, 1, p. 127-146.

7940. MASTNY (Vojtech). The Soviet non-invasion of Poland in 1980-1981 and the end of the Cold War. *Europe Asia studies*, 99, 51, 2, p. 189-213.

7941. MAWBY (Spencer). Containing Germany: Britain and the arming of the Federal Republic. Basingstoke, Macmillan a. New York, St. Martins Press, 99, XI-244 p. (Contemporary history in context).

7942. MIARD-DELACROIX (Hélène). Ungebrochene Kontinuität. François Mitterrand und die deutschen Kanzler Helmut Schmidt und Helmut Kohl 1981-1984. *Vierteljahrshefte für Zeitgeschichte*, 99, 47, 4, p. 539-558.

7943. MIRČEVA (Kh.). Blizuk Iztok. Interesi, ambicii, konflikti (1948–1988). (Le Proche Orient. Intérêts, ambitions, conflits, 1948–1988). Sofija, [s. n.], 99, 559 p.

7944. MOHR (Antje). Hessen und der Länderrat des amerikanischen Besatzungsgebietes: Möglichkeiten und Grenzen länderübergreifender Kooperation in den Jahren 1945 bis 1949. Frankfurt am Main; New York, P. Lang, 99, 441 p. (Europäische Hochschulschriften. Reihe III, Geschichte und ihre Hilfswissenschaften, 816).

7945. MORALES PÉREZ (Salvador E.), DEL ALIZAL (Laura). Dictadura, exilio e insurrección: Cuba en la perspectiva mexicana, 1952–1958. Mexico City, Secretaría de Relaciones Exteriores, 99, 254 p.

7946. MURRAY (Donette). Kennedy, Macmillan and nuclear weapons. Basingstoke, Macmillan a. New York, St. Martins Press, 99, 220 p. (Cold War history).

7947. NAJDUS (Helena), SMOLAR (Nina). Wejda nie wejda: Polska 1980–1982: wewnetrzny kryzys, miedzynarodowe uwarunkowania: konferencja w Jachrance listopad 1997. (Poland 1980–1982: internal crisis, international dimensions. Organised by Institute of Political Studies, Warsaw). London, Aneks, XXII-342 p.

7948. N'DIMINA MOUGALA (Antoine-Denis). La politique étrangère du Gabon de 1960 à 1967. In: Afrique: partenariat international et conflits régionaux [Cf. n° 7213], p. 65-88.

7949. NITSCHKE (Bernadetta). Wysiedlenie ludności niemieckiej z Polski w latach 1945–1949. (Die Aussiedlung der deutschen Bevölkerung aus Polen in den Jahren 1945–1949). Zielona Góra, Wyższa Szkoła Pedagog. Im. Tadeusza Kotarbińskiego, 99, 310 p.

7950. NUTI (Leopoldo). Gli Stati Uniti e l'apertura a sinistra, 1953–1963. Importanza e limiti della presenza americana in Italia. Roma e Bari, Laterza, 99, XXIII-728 p. (Libri del tempo, 294). – IDEM. Missiles or Socialists? The Italian policy of the Kennedy administration. In: John F. Kennedy and Europe [Cf. n° 7909], [s. p.].

7951. OAUL (Lionel). La question tamoule à Sri Lanka. In: Conflits (Les) en Asie du Sud (1947–1999) [Cf. n° 7865], p. 97-114.

7952. OFFNER (A. A.). «Another Such Victory»: president Truman, American foreign policy, and the Cold War. Diplomatic history, 99, 23, 2, p. 127-155.

7953. OIKARINEN (Jarmo). The Middle East in the American quest for world order. Ideas of power, economics, and social development in United States foreign policy, 1953–1961 Helsinki, SHS, 99, 277 s. (Bibliotheca historica, 47).

7954. ÖZREN (Can). Die Beziehungen der beiden deutschen Staaten zur Türkei: 1945/49–1963; politische und ökonomische Interessen im Zeichen der deutschen Teilung. Münster, Lit, 99, VI-402 p. (Studien zur Zeitgeschichte des Nahen Ostens und Nordafrikas, 5).

7955. Partition of India, Indo-Pak wars and the UNO. Ed. by Verinder GROVER and Ranjana ARORA. New Delhi, Deep & Deep Publications, 99, AXII-565 p.

7956. PASTORI (Gianluca), RADAELLI (Riccardo). L'Italia e l'Islam non arabo. Milano, F. Angeli, 99, 153 p.

7957. Path (The) of a genocide: the Rwanda crisis from Uganda to Zaire. Ed. by Howard ADELMAN and Astri SUHRKE. New Brunswick a. London, Transaction Publishers, 99, XXII-414 p. (ill).

7958. PEROVIĆ (Jeronim). Der Balkanknoten und der sowjetisch-jugoslawische Konflikt von 1948. Osteuropa, 99, 49, p. 55-70.

7959. PIERROS (Filippos), MEUNIER (Jacob), ABRAMS (Stan). Bridges and barriers: the European Union's Mediterranean policy, 1961–1998. Aldershot, Ashgate, 99, IX-336 p.

7960. POGGIOLINI (Ilaria). Post-war international diplomacy over Italy and the origins of the Cold War, 1945–1947. Toronto, Toronto U. P., 99, [s. p.].

7961. PRADOS (John). The blood road: the Ho Chi Minh trail and the Vietnam War. New York, John Wiley and Sons, 99, XVI-432 p.

7962. PREČAN (Vilém). Středoevropský kontext demokratického převratu v Československu roku 1989. (Central-European context of the democratic revolution in Czechoslovakia, 1989). In: November 1989 na Slovensku [Cf. n° 5032], p. 7-23.

7963. PRIEST (Tyler). Banking on development: Brazil in the United States's search for strategic minerals, 1945–1953. International history review, 99, 21, 2, p. 297-330.

7964. PROKŠ (Petr). Americká armáda v Československu. Politicko–diplomatický zápas o střední Evropu v roce 1945. (The American Army in Czechoslovakia. Political and diplomatic struggle over Central Europe in 1945]. Slovanský přehled, 99, 85, 4, p. 457-473.

7965. PSAROUTHAKIS (John), TANTER (Raymond). Balancing in the Balkans. Basingstoke, Macmillan, 99, XIX-188 p.

7966. RABE (Stephen G.). The most dangerous area in the world: John F. Kennedy confronts Communist Revolution in Latin America. Chapell Hill, University of North Carolina Press, 99, 257 p.

7967. RAZOUX (Pierre). La guerre israélo-arabe d'octobre 1973. Paris, Economica, 99, 393 p.

7968. REES (G. Wyn). British strategic thinking and Europe, 1964–1970. Journal of European integration history, 99, 5, 1, p. 57-72.

7969. REITAN (Ruth). The rise and decline of an alliance: Cuba and African American leaders in the 1960s. East Lansing, Michigan State U. P., 99, XVI-155 p.

7970. Renseignement et propagande pendant la Guerre froide (1947–1953). Actes du Colloque international de Caen, 5–7 février 1998. Bruxelles, Ed. Complexe, 99, 320 p.

7971. RIX (Alan). The Australian-Japan political alignment: 1952 to the present. London, Routledge, 99, 195 p. (Routledge studies in the modern history of Asia, 4).

7972. ROBERTS (Geoffrey). The Soviet Union in world politics. Coexistence, revolution and cold war, 1945–1991. London, Routledge, 99, 125 p.

7973. ROZÈS (Antoine). Les Sud-Africains et l'Angola: treize années d'hostilité (1975–1988). In: Afrique: partenariat international et conflits régionaux [Cf. n° 7213], p. 105-124.

7974. SACKER (Richard). A radiant future: the French Communist Party and Eastern Europe, 1944–1956. Edited and with a preface by Michael KELLY. Bern a. New York, Peter Lang, 99, 344 p.

7975. SAKSENA (Jyotsna). Le conflit sino-indien de 1962. In: Conflits (Les) en Asie du Sud (1947–1999) [Cf. n° 7865], p. 49-68.

7976. Saving democracies: U.S. intervention in threatened democratic states. Ed. by Anthony James JOES. Westport a. London, Praeger, 99, IX-233 p.

7977. SCHLESINGER (Stephen), KINZER (Stephen). Bitter fruit: the story of an American coup in Guatemala. Introduction by John COATSWORTH; foreword by Richard A. NUCCIO. Cambridge, Harvard U. P., 99, XXXVIII-331 p. (David Rockfeller Center series on Latin America studies).

7978. SCHNEIDER (Rolf). Europas Einigung und das Problem Deutschland: Vorgeschichte und Anfänge. Frankfurt am Main u. New York, P. Lang, 99, 257 p. (Europäische Hochschulschriften. Reihe III, Geschichte und ihre Hilfswissenschaften, 825).

7979. SCHÖLLGEN (Gregor). Die Außenpolitik der Bundesrepublik Deutschland. Von den Anfangen bis zur Gegenwart. München, Beck, 99, 248 p.

7980. SCHRAFSTETTER (Susanna). Die dritte Atommacht: britische Nichtverbreitungspolitik im Dienst von Statussicherung und Deutschlandpolitik 1952–1968. München, Oldenbourg, 99, 254 p. (Schriftenreihe der Vierteljahrshefte für Zeitgeschichte, 79).

7981. SCHWABE (Ute). Moralische Verpflichtung – Strategischer Vorteil: Amerikanisch-Israelische Beziehungen nach Ende des Yom-Kippur-Krieges (1973) bis zur Unterzeichnung der Declaration of Principles (1993). Münster, Lit, 99, 99, V-302 p.

7982. SCHWARZ (Hans-Peter). Die Regierung Kiesinger und die Krise in der CSSR 1968. Vierteljahrshefte für Zeitgeschichte, 99, 47, 2, p. 159-186.

7983. SCOTT (L. V.). MacMillan, Kennedy and the Cuban missile crisis. London, MacMillan Press, 99, 252 p.

7984. SHALOM (Zakai). The superpowers, Israel and the future of Jordan, 1960–1963: the perils of the pro-Nasser policy. Foreword by Avi SHLAIM. Brighton, Sussex Academic Press, 99, XI-181 p.

7985. SHLAIM (Avi). Israel, the Great Powers and the Middle East crisis of 1958. In: Statecraft (The) of British imperialism [Cf. n° 7318], p. 177-192.

7986. SIBGUET (Ouelguelguet). La France et les Libyens du Tchad pendant la crise du Fezzan (avril 1954–janvier 1955). In: Afrique: partenariat international et conflits régionaux [Cf. n° 7213], p. 37-52.

7987. SIEBS (Benno-Eide). Die Außenpolitik der DDR 1976–1989. Strategien und Grenzen. Paderborn, München u. Wien, Schöning, 99, 461 p.

7988. SIEKMEIER (James F.). Aid, nationalism and inter-American relations: Guatemala, Bolivia, and the United States, 1945–1961. Lewiston, E. Mellen Press, 99, IX-472 p. (Latin American studies, 6).

7989. Slovenci in Makedonci v Jugoslaviji. (Slovenes and Macedonians in Yugoslavia). Ur. Božo REPE, Dušan NEĆAK, Jože PRINČIČ, Novica VELJANOVSKI, Violeta AČKOSKA v Borče DAVITKOVSKI. Ljubljana, Filozofska fakulteta, Oddelek za zgodovino v Skopje, Institut za nacionalna istorija, 99, 187, 163 p.

7990. SMITH (E. Timothy). Opposition beyond the water's edge: liberal internationalists, pacifists and containment, 1945–1953. Westport a. London, Greenwood Press, 99, XII-176 p. (Contributions to the study of world history, 67).

7991. SMITH (Simon C.). Kuwait 1950–1965: Britain, the al-Sabah and Oil. New York, Oxford U. P., 99, 167 p. (British Academy postdoctoral fellowship monograph).

7992. SOGLIAN (Franco). La riunificazione della Germania, 1989–1990. Roma, Carocci, 99, 148 p. (Occasioni).

7993. SOMMER (Karl-Ludwig). Humanitäre Auslandshilfe als Brücke zu atlantischer Partnerschaft: CARE, CRALOG, und die Entwicklung der deutsch-amerikanischen Beziehungen nach Ende des Zweiten Weltkriegs. Bremen, Selbstverlag des Staatsarchivs Bremen, 99, 400 p. (Veröffentlichungen aus dem Staatsarchiv der Freien Hansestadt Bremen, 63).

7994. SONYEL (Salahi R.). New light on the genesis of the conflict [for Cyprus]: British documents 1960–1967. In: Cyprus: the need for new perspectives. Ed. by Clement H. DODD. Huntingdon, Eothen Press, 99, p. 16-82.

7995. SOÓS (Katalin). 1956 és Ausztria. (1956 and Austria). Szeged, József Attila Tudományegyetem Bölcsészettudományi Kara, 99, 147 p.

7996. SORBY (Karol). Bagdadský pakt a problémy arabskej zahraničnej politiky v polovici päťdesiatych rokov. (The Baghdad pact and the problems of the Arab foreign policy in the mid-50s). Historický časopis, 99, 47, 3, p. 466-488.

7997. SOUTOU (George-Henri). Réflexions franco-suisses et modération dans la guerre froide (1945–1955). *Relations internationales*, 99, 98, p. 189-199.

7998. Sowjetisierung und Eigenständigkeit in der SBZ/DDR (1945–1953). Hrsg. v. Michael LEMKE. Köln, Böhlau, 99, 365 p. (Zeithistorische Studien, 13. Herrschaftsstrukturen und Erfahrungsdimensionen der DDR-Geschichte, 2).

7999. Special issue on the clandestine Cold War in Asia, 1945–1965: Western intelligence, propaganda, and special operations. Ed. by Richard J. ALDRICH, Gary D. RAWNSLEY and Ming-Yeh T. RAWNSLEY. London, Frank Cass, 99, 294 p. (Intelligence and national security, 14, 4).

8000. Stalinskoe desiatiletie kholodnoi voiny: fakty i gipotezy. (Stalin's decade of the Cold War. Based on the materials of a conference which took place at the Institut vseobshchei istorii of the Rossiiskaia akademiia nauk in the spring of 1998). Redaktsionnaia kollegiia, I. V. GAIDUK, N. I. EGOROVA, A. O. CHUBAR'IAN. Moskva, Nauka, 99, 251 p.

8001. STEININGER (Rolf). Südtirol zwischen Diplomatie und Terror 1947–1969. Vol. 1. 1947–1959. Vol. 2. 1960–1062. Vol. 3. 1962–1969. Bozen, Athesia, 99, 3 vol., 888 p., 780 p., 872 p. (ill.). (Veröffentlichungen des Südtiroler Landesarchivs, 6-8).

8002. STONE (Glyn). Britain and the Angolan Revolt of 1961. *Journal of Imperial and Commonwealth history*, 99, 27, 1, p. 109-137.

8003. STREETER (Stephen M.). The failure of «liberal developmentalism»: the United States's anti-communist showcase in Guatemala, 1954–1960. *International history review*, 99, 21, 2, p. 386-413.

8004. Streitfall Neutralität: Geschichten, Legenden, Fakten. Hrsg. v. Andreas WEBER. Wien, Czernin, 99, 238 p.

8005. SUBRITZKY (John). Confronting Sukarno: British, American, Australian and New Zealand diplomacy in the Malaysian-Indonesian Confrontation, 1961–1965. Basingstoke, Macmillan, 99, 208 p. (maps).

8006. SUGITA (Yoneyuki). The limits of American hegemony in occupied Japan: Japan-United States relations during the occupation, 1945–1952. Ann Arbor, UMI, 99, IV-388 p.

8007. SZŰCS (László), VIDA (István). A Marshall-terv és Magyarország. (The Marshall plan and Hungary). *Historia*, 99, 3, p. 28-33.

8008. TARDY (Thierry). La France et la gestion des conflits yougoslaves (1991–1995): enjeux et leçons d'une opération de maintien de la paix de l'ONU. Bruxelles, Bruylant, 99, 504 p.

8009. THI DIEU (Nguyen). The Mekong River and the Struggle for Indochina: Water, War, and Peace. Westport, Praeger, 99, XVI-264 p.

8010. THOMAS (Baylis). How Israel was won: a concise history of the Arab-Israeli conflict. Lanham a. Oxford, Lexington Books, 99, XVIII-326 p. (maps).

8011. TODOROVA (R.). Bulgarskata diplomacija ot epokhata na «studenata vojna». (La diplomatie bulgare de l'époque de la «guerre froide»). *In*: 120 godini izpulnitelna vlast v Bulgarija [Cf. n° 4141], p. 259-272.

8012. TONINI (Alberto). Un'equazione a troppe incognite. I Paesi occidentali e il conflitto arabo israeliano, 1950-1967. Milano, Angeli, 99, 264 p. (Politica/studi).

8013. TORCOLI (Francesco). Canada, Italia e Alleanza atlantica 1951–1956: prospettive politiche e sociali. Milano, F. Angeli, 99, 154 p. (Storia diplomatica, 20).

8014. TRACHTENBERG (Marc). A constructed peace: the making of the European settlement, 1945–1963. Princeton, Princeton U. P., 99, XV-424 p.

8015. United States (The) and the European alliance since 1945. Ed. by Kathleen BURK and Melvyn STOKES. Oxford, Berg, 99, VII-324 p.

8016. VALDÉS-UGALDE (José Luis). Intervening in revolution: the US exercise of power in Guatemala, 1954. London, [s. n.], 99, 379 p. [Thesis (Ph.D) – London School of Economics and Political Science. Department of International Relations].

8017. VARSORI (Antonio). Controguerriglia e diplomazia: la Gran Bretagna e il coinvolgimento americano in Viet Nam durante l'amministrazione Kennedy 1961–1963. Firenze, Manent, 99, 123 p. (Il maestrale, 5). – IDEM. Euratom: une organisation qui échappe à Jean Monnet ? *In*: Jean Monnet, l'Europe et les chemins de la paix [Cf. n° 7907], p. 343-356. – IDEM. L'europeismo nella politica estera italiana. *In*: Italia (L') e le organizzazioni internazionali. Diplomazia multilaterale nel Novecento [Cf. n° 7260], p. 391-415. – IDEM. La perception de chefs militaires français en politique par le Foreign Office (1946–1958). *In*: Militaires en République 1870–1962. Les officiers, le pouvoir et la vie politique en France [Cf. n° 4366], p. 181-195. – IDEM. The art of mediation: Italy and Britain's attempt to join the EEC 1960–1963. *In*: Widening, deepening and acceleration. The European Economic Community 1957–1963 [Cf. n° 4006], p. 241-256.

8018. Vatikanische Ostpolitik unter Johannes XXIII und Paul VI, 1958–1978. Hrsg. v. Karl-Joseph HUMMEL. Paderborn, Schöningh, 99, VIII-257 p.

8019. VOLK (Sandi). Ezulski skrbniki: vloga in pomen begunskih organizacij ter urejanje vprašanja istrskih beguncev v Italiji v luči begunskega časopisja 1945–1963. (Esuli guardians: the role and importance of refugee organizations and the settlement of the Istrian refugee question in Italy in the light of refugee newspapers 1945–1963). Koper, Zgodovinsko društvo za južno Primorsko, Znanstveno-raziskovalno središče Republike Slovenije, 99, 290 p. (ill.). (Knjižnica Annales, 20).

8020. WAGNLEITNER (R.). The empire of the fun, or talkin' Soviet Union blues: the sound of freedom and U.S. cultural hegemony in Europe. *In*: American century (The): a roundtable. Part II [Cf. n° 7215], p. 499-524.

8021. WAINSTOCK (Dennis). Truman, MacArthur, and the Korean War. Westport a. London, Greenwood Press, 99, X-186 p. (ill.). (Contributions in military studies, 176).

8022. WANG (David D.). Under the Soviet shadow: the Yining incident: ethnic conflicts and international rivalry in Xinjiang, 1944–1949. Hong Kong, Chinese U. P., 99, VIII-577 p. (maps).

8023. WAPLER (Claire). L'Autriche et l'Europe de 1955 à 1962: le point de vue français. *Revue d'histoire diplomatique*, 99, 113, 1, p. 101-131.

8024. WEBER (Jacques). La guerre de Bangladesh vue de France. *In*: Conflits (Les) en Asie du Sud (1947–1999) [Cf. n° 7865], p. 69-96. – IDEM. La question du Cachemire et les relations indopakistanaises, de la partition à la guerre de 1965. *In*: Conflits (Les) en Asie du Sud (1947–1999) [Cf. n° 7865], p. 9-34.

8025. WERNICKE (Günter), WITTNER (Lawrence S.). Lifting the Iron Curtain: the peace march to Moscow of 1960–1961. *International history review*, 99, 21, 4, p. 900-917.

8026. WETTIG (Gerhard). Bereitschaft zu Einheit in Freiheit? Die sowjetische Deutschland-Politik, 1945–1955. München, Olzog, 330 p.

8027. WHITE (Nicholas Ian). Britain's relations with the United States over policy towards Laos and South Vietnam, 1961–1963: the not-so special relationship. Leeds, [s. n.], 99, 175 p. [Thesis (Ph.D.) – University of Leeds (School of International, Development and European Studies), 1999].

8028. Whitehall and the Suez crisis. Ed. by Saul KELLY and Anthony GORST. London, Frank Cass, 99, 279 p. (*Contemporary British history*, 99, 13, 2 [Special issue]).

8029. WILKENS (Andreas). Ostpolitik allemande et commerce avec l'Est. Objectifs politiques et enjeux économiques d'Adenauer à Brandt (1949–1974). *Revue d'histoire diplomatique*, 99, 113, 2, p. 205-241. – IDEM. Westpolitik, Ostpolitik and the project of the economic and monetary union. Germany's European policy in the Brandt era (1969–1974). *Journal of European integration history*, 99, 5, 1, p. 73-102.

8030. WILLIAMSON (Charles T.). The U.S. Naval mission to Haiti, 1959–1963. Annapolis, Naval Institute Press, 99, XV-394 p. (ill., map).

8031. WOŹNICZKA (Zygmunt). Trzecia wojna światowa w oczekiwaniach emigracji i podziemia w kraju 1944–1953. (Exilpolen und Untergrundbewegungen in der Heimat in der Erwartung des dritten Weltkrieges 1944–1953). Katowice, Wydaw. Uniw. Śląskiego, 99, 371 p. (Prace Naukowe Uniwersytetu Śląskiego w Katowicach, 1808).

8032. YESILBURSA (Behçet K). Turkey's participation in the Middle East Command and its admission to Nato, 1950–1952. *In*: Seventy-five years of the Turkish Republic [Cf. n° 5175], p. 70-102.

8033. YU-JOSE (Lydia N.). The new guidelines for U.S.-Japan defense cooperation: a Filipino point of view. *In*: Philippines and Japan: facets and dimensions. Quezon City, Japanese Studies Program of the Ateneo de Manila University, 99, p. 75-83.

8034. ZERBO (Yacouba). Les relations politiques entre le Mali et le Burkina-Faso de 1983 à 1985: les causes du conflit frontalier de décembre 1985. *In*: Afrique: partenariat international et conflits régionaux [Cf. n° 7213], p. 89-104.

8035. ZIMMERMANN (Hubert). Franz Josef Strauß und der deutsch-amerikanische Währungskonflikt in den sechziger Jahren. *Vierteljahrshefte für Zeitgeschichte*, 99, 47, 1, p. 57-86.

§ 8. Addenda 1998.

8036. HUSZÁR (Tibor). 1968: Prága, Budapest, Moszkva. Kádár János és a csehszlovákiai intervenció. (1968: Prague, Budapest, Moscow. János Kádár and the intervention in Czechoslovakia). Budapest, Szabad Tér, 98, 303 p.

Cf. n°s 866, 4011, 4452, 4903, 5152, 5241, 5243, 7640, 7740, 7770, 8098, 8323

R

ASIA

§ 1. General. 8037-8048. – § 2. Western and central Asia. 8049-8073. – § 3. South Asia and Southeast Asia. 8074-8096. – § 4. China. 8097-8272. – § 5. Japan (before 1868). 8273-8320. – § 6. Korea. 8321-8329.

§ 1. General.

** 8037. Guia de fontes portuguesas para a história da Asia. Vol. 2. Elaborado por Isabel CASTRO PINA, Maria Leonor FERRAZ DE OLIVEIRA SILVA SANTOS, Paulo LEME. Lisboa, Comissao Nacional para as Comemoraçoes dos Descobrimentos Portugueses, 99, 123 p. (Guia da fontes para a história das naçoes / Conselho Internacional de Arquivos).

** 8038. Imperialism & orientalism: a documentary sourcebook. Edited and introduced by Barbara HARLOW and Mia CARTER. Malden a. Oxford, Blackwell, 99, VIII-408 p.

8039. Asie orientale (L') et méridionale aux XIXe et XXe siècles: Chine, Corée, Japon, Asie du Sud-Est, Inde. Sous la dir. de Hartmut O. ROTERMUND; avec la collaboration de Alain DELISSEN [et al.]. Paris, Presses universitaires de France, 99, CCXLIV-546 p. (Nouvelle Clio: l'histoire et ses problèmes).

8040. Buddhism and politics in twentieth-century Asia. Ed. by Ian HARRIS. London, Pinter, 99, XII-300 p.

8041. BÜHLMANN (Elisabeth). La Ligne Siemens: la construction du télégraphe indo-européen, 1867–1870. Bern, P. Lang, 99, XXXII-165 p.

8042. GILLMAN (Ian), KLIMKEIT (Hans-Joachim). Christians in Asia before 1500. Richmond, Curzon, 99, XIV-391 p. (ill.).

8043. IHARA (Takushu). Nihon to chugoku ni okeru seiyo bunka sesshu ron. (Western learning in the nineteenth century about Japan and China). Tokyo, Kyuko Shoin, 99, 422 p.

8044. Istorija Vostoka. (History of the East). Vol. 3. Vostok na rubezhe srednevekov'ja i novogo vremeni, XVI–XVIII vv. (The East between Medieval and Modern time, 16th–18th centuries). Moskva, Vostochnaja literatura, 99, 666 p.

8045. Kindai ajia no ryutsu nettowaku. (Commercial networks in modern Asia). Ed. by Shinya SUGIYAMA and Linda GROVE. Tokyo, Sobun Sha, 99, 349 p.

8046. LIM (Jie-Hyun). Obraz rewolucji 1848 r. w oczach Azji. (The image of 1848 revolution in the eyes of East Asia). *In*: Rok 1848 Wiosna Ludow w Galicji: Zbior Studiow. Ed. Wladyslawa WIC. Kraków: Wydawn. Naukowe AP, 99, [s. p.].

8047. Nation work: Asian elites and national identities. Ed. by Timothy BROOK and Andre SCHMID. Ann Arbor, University of Michigan Press, 99, [s. p.].

8048. VOLKOV (Sergej V.). Sluzhilye sloi na traditsionnom Dal'nem Vostoke. (Service classes in the traditional Far East). Moskovskij gos. un-t im. M.V. Lomonosova. Moskva, Vostochnaja literatura, 99, 312 p. (plates; bibl.).

Cf. n°s 357, 1460, 7321-7341, 8389

§ 2. Western and central Asia.

** 8049. JASTREBOVA (O. M.). Persidskie i tadzhikskie dokumenty v Otdele rukopisej Rossijskoj natsional'noj biblioteki: Sistem. katalog. (Persian and Tadjik documents in the manuscript department of the Russian National Library, [Saint-Petersburg, 16th–20th centuries]: a systematic catalogue). Sankt-Peterburg, Izd. Ros. nats. b-ki, 99, 207 p. (ind.).

** 8050. TSENDINA (A. D.). Istorija Erdeni-dzu: Faksimile rukopisi; per. s mongol'skogo, vved. comment. i pril. ("History of Erdeni-Zuu": [the chronicle of the first Buddistic Monastery of Mongolia, written in the early 19th century]: facsimile of the MS., Russian transl., intr., comment. and app.). Ed. S.Ju. NEKLJUDOV. RAN, In-t vostokovedenija. Moskva, Vostochnaja literatura, 99, 255 p. (bibl., ind.). (Pamjatniki vostochnoj pis'mennosti, 118). [Eng. summary]

8051. Arming the state: military conscription in the Middle East and Central Asia, 1775–1925. Ed. by Erik J. ZÜRCHER. London, I. B. Tauris, 99, 168 p.

8052. BURYAKOV (Y. F.), [et al.]. The cities and routes of the great silk road: on Central Asia documents. Tashkent, Publishing & Printing Concern "Sharq", 99, 126 p.

8053. Central Asia: history, politics and culture: proceedings of the International Conference on Central Asia, November 27–30, 1993. Ed. by Riazul ISLAM, Kazi A. KADIR and Javed HUSAIN. Karachi, Institute of Central and West Asian Studies, University of Karachi, 99, 383 p.

8054. HANEDA (Masashi). Kunshaku-shi Sharudan no shogai: 17seiki Yoroppa to Isuramu sekai. (Sir Chardin's life: Europe and Islamic world in the seventeenth century). Tokyo, Chuo Koron Shinsha, 99, 313 p.

8055. History of civilizations of Central Asia. Vol. 1. The dawn of civilization: earliest times to 700 B.C. Ed. by A. H. DANI and V. M. MASSON. Vol. 2. The development of sedentary and nomadic civilizations: 700 B.C. to A.D. 250. Ed. by János HARMATTA, co-editors: B. N. PURI and G. F. ETEMADI. Vol. 3. The crossroads of civilizations: A.D. 250 to 750. Ed. by B. A. LITVINSKY, co-editors: Zhang GUANG-DA and R. SHABANI SAMGHABADI. Vol. 4. The age of achievement: A.D. 750 to the end of the fifteen century. Pt. 1. The historical, social and economic setting. Ed. by M. S. ASIMOV and C. E. BOSWORTH. Delhi, Motilal Banarsidass Publishers, 99, 4 vol., 535 p., 573 p., 569 p., 485 p.

8056. INABA (Minoru). Goru-cho to 11-12 seiki no Afuganisutan. (The Ghorids and Afghanistan: the eleventh to twelfth centuries). *Middle Eastern studies*, 99, 51, 16-42.

8057. Iwanami koza sekai rekishi 10: Isuramu sekai no hatten. (Iwanami world history. Vol. 10. The development of Islamic World). Ed. by Tsugitaka SATO. Tokyo, Iwanami shoten, 99, 315 p. [Cf. n° <choice> 8065.]

8058. KONOVALOV (Prokopii Batiurovich). Etnicheskie aspekty istorii Tsentral'noi Azii: drevnost' i srednevekov'e (Ethnology and history of Central Asia). Ulan-Ude, Izd-vo Buriatskogo nauchnogo tsentra SO RAN, 99, 213 p.

8059. LAZAREV (Mikhail S.), MGOI (Shakro Kh.), VASIL'EVA (Evgenija I.), [et al.]. Istorija Kurdistana. (A history of Kurdistan, [7th-20th centuries]). Eds. M.S. LAZAREV, Sh.Kh. MGOI. Moskva, [W.p.h.], 519 p. (ill., bibl., ind.).

8060. MAEDA (Hirotake). Safavi cho no "goram": Gurujia kei no baai. (The Gholāms of Safavid dynasty: the case of Georgians). *Journal of the research department of the Toyo Bunko*, 99, 81, 3, p. 1-32 [Eng. summary].

8061. MATSUO (Yuriko). 16 seiki kohan no Osumancho ni okeru kaza no keisei to kadi shoku: "Rumeri Kazasukeri torokubo" no bunseki wo tsujite. (The formation of Kaza and the role of Kadi under the Ottoman empire: Analysis of Rumeli Kazaskerliği Ruznamesi, 1550–1600). *Shigaku Zasshi*, 99, 108, 7, p. 1-42 [Eng. summary].

8062. Naqshbandis in Western and Central Asia: change and continuity: papers read at a conference held at the Swedish Research Institute in Istanbul, June 9–11, 1997. Ed. by Elisabeth ÖZDALGA. İstanbul, Svenska forskningsinstitutet Istanbul, 99, 187 p. (Transactions / Swedish Research Institute in Istanbul, 9).

8063. Patrimoine manuscrit et vie intellectuelle de l'Asie centrale islamique. Sous la dir. de Ashirbek MUMINOV, Francis RICHARD et Maria SZUPPE. Aix-en-Provence, Edisud, 99, 232 p. (Cahiers d'Asie centrale, 7).

8064. Rethinking Central Asia: non-eurocentric studies in history, social structure and identity. Ed. by Korkut A. ERTÜRK. Reading, Ithaca Press, 99, VI-202 p.

8065. SATO (Tsugitaka). Isuramu kokkaron seiritsu no shikumi to tenkai. (The study of the Islamic states: the mechanism of construction and development). *In*: Iwanami koza sekai rekishi 10: Isuramu sekai no hatten [Cf. n° 8057], p. 3-68.

8066. SHITOMI (Yuzo). Myuosu-Horumosu to Reuke-Kome. (Myos Hormos and Leukè Kômè). *Toyo Gakuho*, 99, 81, 3, p. 1-28. [French Summary].

8067. SUEO (Yoshiyuki). Chukinto no suisha, fusha. (The waterwheel and the windmill in the Middle East). Osaka, Kansai U. P., 99, 371 p.

8068. SWIETOSLAWSKI (Witold). Arms and armour of the nomads of the Great Steppe in the times of the Mongol expansion (12th–14th centuries). Lodz, Oficyna Naukowa MS, 99, 144 p. (pl., ill.). (Studies on the history of ancient and medieval art of warfare).

8069. TANIGUCHI (Junichiro). 11–13seiki Harabu no Kadi to shihaisha. (Qādīs and Rulers of Aleppo from the eleventh to the thirteenth centuries). *Toyoshi Kenkyu*, 99, 57, 4, p. 1-37. [Eng. Summary].

8070. VADETSKAJA (El'ga B.). Tashtykskaja epokha v drevnej istorii Sibiri. (The Tashtyk epoch in the ancient history of Siberia). RAN, In-t istorii material'noj kul'tury. Sankt-Peterburg, [s. n.], 99, 440 p. (ill., bibl.). [Eng. summary]

8071. VAJNBERG (Bella I.). Etnografija Turana v drevnosti, VII v. do n.e.–VIII v.n.e. (The ethnology of ancient Turan, c. 700 B.C.–c. 900 A.D.). Moskva, Vostochnaja literatura, 99, 359 p. (ill., bibl.).

8072. YAMAGISHI (Tomoko). Imamu "okakure" sennen-go: 19seiki Iran shakai wo kosatsu suru tame no ichi-shikaku. (Iranian society after a millenary occultation of Imam). *Rekishigaku Kenkyu*, 99, 724, p. 22-30 [Eng. Summary].

8073. YAMAUCHI (Masayuki). Nattoku shinakatta otoko Enveru Pasha: Chuto kara chuo ajia e. (Enver

Paşa, the unsatisfied man: from Middle East to Central Asia). Tokyo, Iwanami Shoten, 99, 638 p.

Cf. n°s 1364, 1462, 1557, 4807

§ 3. South Asia and Southeast Asia.

** 8074. Asia: official British documents, 1945–1965, on CD-ROM: selected documents from the end of World War II to Vietnam. Ed. by Michael David KANDIAH, Gillian STAERCK and Christopher STAERCK. London, Routledge, Public Record Office, 99, 6 computer laser optical discs.

** 8075. Ressources (Les) de l'histoire: tradition, narration et nation en Asie du Sud. Actes du séminaire tenu lors du colloque de Pondichéry, 11–16 janvier 1997. Textes réunis par Jackie ASSAYAG. Paris, Pondicherry, École française d'Extrême-Orient, Institut français de Pondichéry, 99, XIV-374 p. (Études thématiques, 8).

8076. Aryan and non-Aryan in South Asia: evidence, interpretation, and ideology; proceedings of the International Seminar on Aryan and Non-Aryan in South Asia, University of Michigan, Ann Arbor, 25–27 October 1996. Ed. by Johannes BRONKHORST and Madhav M. DESHPANDE. Cambridge, Harvard University, Department of Sanskrit and Indian Studies, 99, II-406 p. (Harvard oriental series. Opera minora, 3).

8077. BOUCHON (Geneviève). Inde découverte, Inde retrouvée 1498–1630: études d'histoire indo-portugaise. Lisbonne, Commission nationale pour les commémorations des découvertes portugaises, 99, 402 p.

8078. Cambridge history of Southeast Asia. Vol. 4. From World War II to the present. Cambridge, Cambridge U. P., 99, 368 p.

8079. DILLER (Stephan). Die Dänen in Indien, Südostasien und China (1620–1845). Wiesbaden, Harrassowitz, 99, X-430 p. (South China and Maritime Asia, 8).

8080. DRAKARD (Jane). A kingdom of words: language and power in Sumatra. New York, Oxford U. P., 99, XXI-322 p. (South-East Asian historical monographs).

8081. GANDHI (Rajmohan). Revenge and reconciliation: understanding South Asian history. New Delhi, Penguin Books India, 99, XXX-463 p.

8082. GOSCHA (Christopher). Thailand and the Southeast Asian networks of the Vietnamese revolution, 1885–1954. Surrey, Curzon, 99, 418 p. (Nordic Institute of Asian Studies).

8083. History and politics: millennial perspectives. Essays in honour of Kingsley de Silva. Ed. by Gerald PEIRIS and S.W.R. de A. SAMARASINGHE. Colombo, Law and Society Trust, 99, XXXVI-542 p.

8084. Invoking the past: the uses of history in South Asia. Ed. by Daud ALI. New Delhi a. Oxford, Oxford U. P., 99, XII-399 p. (SOAS studies on South Asia. Understandings and perpectives series).

8085. IO (Hideyuki). Abu-Ubaido "Zaiseiron" ni miru Sadaka no bunpai kitei (Kouhen). [The distribution of the Sdaqa-Abū 'Ubayd's Kitāb al-Amuāl (a sequel)]. *Bulletin of Tokyo Jogakkan Junior College*, 99, 22, p. 1-29.

8086. Iwanami koza sekai rekishi 20: Ajia no Kindai. (Iwanami world history. Vol. 20. The modern period in Asia). Ed. by Takeshi HAMASHITA. Tokyo, Iwanami Shoten, 99, 290 p. [Cf. n° <choice> 8094.]

8087. JAYAPALAN (N.). History of South-East Asia. New Delhi, Atlantic Publishers and Distributors, 99, VIII-149 p.

8088. LUDDEN (David). The New Cambridge History of India. Vol. 4. Part 4. An agrarian history of South Asia. New York, Cambridge U. P., 99, XIII-261 p.

8089. MISRA (Maria). Business, race and politics in British India, c.1850–1960. Oxford, Clarendon Press, 99, XIII-250 p. (fig., tab.). (Oxford historical monographs).

8090. OGURA (Yasushi). Indo sekai no kukan kozo: Tokyo Daigaku Toyo Bunka Kenkyujo kenkyu houkoku. (The structure of space in the Indian world: a research report of the Institute of Oriental Culture). Tokyo, Shunjusha, 99, 290 p.

8091. OISHI (Takashi). Muslim merchant capital and the relief movement for the Ottoman empire in India, 1876–1924. *Journal of the Japanese association for South Asian studies*, 99, 11, p. 71-103.

8092. REID (Anthony). Charting the shape of early modern Southeast Asia. Chiang Mai, Silkworm Books, 99, 298 p.

8093. ROBINSON (Catherine A.). Tradition and liberation: the Hindu tradition in the Indian women's movement. Richmond, Curzon, 99, X-230 p. (Curzon studies in Asian religions).

8094. SAKURAI (Yumio). 19seiki Tonan-Ajia no sonraku: Betonamu Koka deruta ni okeru sonraku keisei. (Villages in the nineteenth century Southeast Asia: the formation of villages in the Hong Ha delta). *In:* Iwanami koza sekai rekishi 20: Ajia no Kindai [Cf. n° 8086], p. 119-148.

8095. SCHMIDT (Karl J.). An atlas and survey of South Asian history: India, Pakistan, Bangladesh, Sri Lanka, Nepal, Bhutan. New Delhi, Vision Books, 99, XV-168 p. (Sources and studies in world history).

8096. SHAH (Sayed Wiqar Ali). Ethnicity, Islam and nationalism: Muslim politics in the North-West Frontier Province 1937-1947. New York, Oxford U. P., 99, LIV-311 p.

Cf. n°s 896, 647, 3316, 7084

§ 4. China.

** 8097. ABRANTES (M. Luísa Cunha Meneses), INFANTE (Miguel Rui), SINTRA MARTINHEIRA (José).

Macau e o oriente: no Arquivo Histórico Ultramarino 1833–1911. Macau, Instituto Cultural de Macau, 99, 279 p. (Fontes para a história de Macau existentes dentro e fora do território).

** 8098. LEDOVSKIJ (Andrej M.). SSSR i Stalin v sud'bakh Kitaja (Dokumenty i svidetel'stava uchastnika sobytij, 1937–1952). (The USSR and Stalin in the fortunes of China: documents and evidence of an eyewitness). Moskva, Pamjatniki istoricheskoj mysli, 99, 340 p. (bibl.). [Text partly in Eng.].

** 8099. Konfutsieva letopis' "Chun'tsju" ("Vesny i Oseni"). [The Confucius' Spring and Autumn Annals (Ch'un-Ch'iu)]. A Russian transl. and comments by N.I. MONASTYREV; critical studies by D.V. DEOPIK and A.M. KARAPETJANTS, p. 195-350. Moskva, Vostochnaja literatura, 99, 351 p. (bibl.).

** 8100. MAO (Zedong). Mao's road to power. Vol. 5. Toward the Second United Front, January 1935–July 1937: revolutionary writings 1912–1949. Ed. by Stuart R. SCHRAM and Nancy J. HODES. Armonk, M.E. Sharpe, CX-737 p. (maps).

** 8101. Sheng Xuanhuai dang'an mingren shouzha xuan. (Selected letters of famous persons in Sheng Xuanhuai archives). Edited by the Center for historical documentation of the Shanghai Library. Shanghai, Fudan daxue chubanshe, 99, 280 p.

** 8102. SHI (Yuanhua). Yanjiu Wng weizhengfu de xin shiliao - Riben Dongya wenku cang Wang weizhi Ri "dashiguan" dang'an gaishu. (New sources on the collaborationist government of Wang Jingwei – a presentation of the archives of the Wang'government embassy in Japan stored in the Toyo Bunko). Minguo dang'an, 99, 2, p. 57-64.

8103. AN (Jingbo). Lun Liang Qichao de minzu guan. (Liang Qichao's nationalism). Jindai shi yanjiu, 99, 3, p. 281-298.

8104. AO (Wenwei). Wuhan kangzhan shiqi Jiang Jieshi de zhanlüe zhanshu sixiang. (Chiang Kai-shek's strategic and tactical thinking during the Wuhan campaign in 1938). Jindai shi yanjiu, 99, 6, p. 128-156.

8105. BELL (Lynda S.). One industry, two Chinas: silk filatures and peasant-family production in Wuxi County, 1865–1937. Stanford, Stanford U. P., 99, XVI-290 p.

8106. BENTON (Gregor). New Fourth Army: communist resistance along the Yangtze and the Huai, 1938–1941. Richmond, Curzon, 99, XXIV-949 p. (ill., maps, ports). (Chinese worlds).

8107. Cambridge History (The) of Ancient China: From the Origins of Civilization to 221 b.C. Ed. by Michael LOEWE and Edward L. SHAUGHNESSY. New York, Cambridge U. P., 99, XXIX-1148 p.

8108. CAO (Yi). Xin shenghuo yundong yu guomin jingsheng zongdongyuan lunsi. (The new life movement and the activists for the mobilization of the national spirit). Minguo dang'an, 99, 2, p. 97-104.

8109. CHAFFEE (John W.). Branches of heaven: a history of the Imperial Clan of Sung China. Cambridge, Harvard University East Asia Center, 99, XX-441 p. (Harvard East Asian monographs, 183).

8110. CHAN LAU (Kit-ching). From nothing to nothing: the Chinese Communist movement and Hong Kong, 1921–1936. London, Hurst & Co., 99, IX-342 p.

8111. Chinese women in the imperial past: new perspectives. Ed. by Harriet T. ZURNDORFER. Boston, Brill, 99, XII-405 p. (Sinica Leidensia, 44).

8112. CHUEV (Nikolaj I.). Voennaja mysl' v drevnem Kitae: Istorija formirovanija voennykh teorij. (Military thought in ancient China: the formation of military theories). Moskva, Ljubimaja kniga, 99, 218 p. (ill., bibl., ind.). [Chinese and English summaries]

8113. DENG (Cong). Aomen lishi de xin jiegou. (A new structure of Macao's history). Lishi yanjiu, 99, 6, p. 5-22.

8114. DENG (Gang). Maritime sector, institutions, and sea power of premodern China. Westport, Greenwood, 99, XIX-289 p. (Contributions in economics and economic history, 212).

8115. DENG (Kaisong). Putaoya zhanling Aomen de lishi guocheng. (The historical process of Portoguese occupation of Macao). Lishi yanjiu, 99, 6, p. 23-35.

8116. DENG (Yilan). Lu Hua Meiqiao yu 20 niandai zhongqi de Meiguo dui Hua zhengce. (Americans in China and America's policy towards China in 1920s). Jindai shi yanjiu, 99, 6, p. 101-127.

8117. DONG (Changzhi). Song Ziwen, Kong Xiangxi yu Guomin zhangfu de shuizhi gaige. (Song Ziwen, Kong Xiangxi and the fiscal reform of Nationalist government). Minguo dang'an, 99, 3, p. 81-87.

8118. FENG (Min). "Wusi" qianhou de jiaoyu gaige yu Zhongguo jindai xuexiao kaoshi zhidu de jianli yu fazhan. (On Chinese educational reform and the institution and development of a modern examination system before and after the May Fourth period). Minguo dang'an, 99, 2, p. 69-73.

8119. FENG (Tianyu). Riben mufu shituan suojian 1862 nian zhi Shanghai. (Shanghai as seen by the Japanese bakufu embassy in 1862). Jindai shi yanjiu, 99, 3, p. 183-212.

8120. GAO (Jialong) [Sherman Cochran]. Zaoyu Zhongguo jiwang: zai Hua zhi Xifang, Riben yu Zhongguo gongsi 1880–1937. (Encountering Chinese networks: Western, Japanese and Chinese Corporations in China 1880–1937). Minguo yanjiu, 99, p. 75-90.

8121. GAO (Lecai). Riben "baiwanhu yimin" guoce pingsi. (An evaluation of Japan policy on "emigrating one million families"). Lishi yanjiu, 99, 3, p. 114-125.

8122. GAO (Xiaoxing). Zhongguo haijun dui Ri kangzhan he shoujianh shuping. (On Chinese naval forces' resistance against Japan and acceptance of Japanese navy surrender). *Minguo dang'an*, 99, 1, p. 83-89.

8123. GENG (Yunzhi). Lüe lun Liang Qichao mo jiu Guangxu huangdi de huodong 1898 nian 9 yue 1900 nian 9 yue. (A discussion of Liang Qichao's attempt to save Emperor Guangxu's life from september 1898 to september 1900). *Lishi yanjiu*, 99, 4, p. 129-139.

8124. GU (Cheng). Shen Wansan ji jiazu shiji kao. (An investigation of Shen Wansan and his family). *Lishi yanjiu*, 99, 1, p. 66-85.

8125. GUO (Weidong). Yapian zhanzheng qianhou waiguo funü jinru Zhongguo tongshang kou'an wenti. (Problems on the admittance of foreign women in Chinese treaty ports around the Opium War). *Jindai shi yanjiu*, 99, 1, p. 242-267.

8126. GUO (Xuyin). Shilun kangzhan shiqi Feng Yuxiang de lunli guannian. (Feng Yuxiang moral principles during the resistance war). *Minguo dang'an*, 99, 1, p. 70-76.

8127. HARRISON (Henrietta). The making of the Republican citizen: political ceremonies and symbols in China, 1911-1929. Oxford, Oxford U. P., 99, VIII-270 p. (ill). (Studies on contemporary China).

8128. HE (Zhongli). Songdai hubu renkou tongji kaocha. (An investigation of the population statistics of the Ministry of revenue during the Song dynasty). *Lishi yanjiu*, 99, 4, p. 83-98.

8129. HOU (Yijie). Yuan Shikai zaoqi shishi dingwu. (A correction on historical mistakes about Yuan Shikai). *Jindai shi yanjiu*, 99, 1, p. 148-167.

8130. HU (Weiqing). Meiguo jianlihui zai Hua jiaoyu shiye yanjiu 1848-1911 nian. (On American methodist educational enterprise in China 1848-1911). *Jindai shi yanjiu*, 99, 2, p. 224-254.

8131. HUANG (Daoxian). Guanyu Jiang Jieshi diyici xiaye de jige wenti. (Some problems concerning Chiang Kai-shek's first retirement from government). *Jindai shi yanjiu*, 99, 4, p. 138-161.

8132. HUANG (Jianli). The politics of depoliticization in Republican China: Guomindang policy towards student political activism, 1927-1949. Bern a. New York, P. Lang, 99, 242 p.

8133. HUANG (Qinghua). Youguan 1862 nian Zhong Ou tiaoyue de jige wenti. (Some problems concerning the 1862 China-Portugal treaty). *Jindai shi yanjiu*, 99, 1, p. 268-284.

8134. HUANG (Xijia). Zou Linghan yu "Shiwubao" guanxi pian. (An analysis of the relation between Zou Linghan and the "Shiwubao"). *Lishi dang'an*, 99, 2, p. 103-105.

8135. HUANG (Zhenglin). Bianchao yu kangzhan shiqi Shen Gan Ning bianqu de jinrong shiye. (Currency and finance in the Shen Gan Ning border region during the resistance war). *Jindai shi yanjiu*, 99, 2, p. 192-224.

8136. IVANOV (Petr M.). Malye partii Kitaja v bor' be za demokratiju, 1928-1949 gg. (Minor parties of China fighting for democracy, 1928-1949). Moskva, Muravej, 99, 387 p. (bibl.; ind.).

8137. JIA (Kailin). Jianguo chuqi liuxuesheng gui guo jishi. (Records of the Chinese students abroad returning home in the first period of the People's Republic). Beijing, Zhongguo wenshi chubanshe, 99, 502 p.

8138. JIA (Wei). Tan Sitong yu Sheng Xuanhuai. (Tan Sitong and Sheng Xuanhuai). *Jindai shi yanjiu*, 99, 1, p. 100-126.

8139. JING (Shenghong), HUANG (Guowei). Zhang Ji yu diyici Guo Gong hezuo. (Zhang Ji and the first cooperation between the Nationalists and the Communists). *Minguo dang'an*, 99, 1, p. 56-62.

8140. JU (Zhifen). Guanyu Riben zai Huabei de laowu tongzhi ruogan wenti yanjiu. (Some problems concerning the Japanese labour system in Northern China). *Minguo dang'an*, 99, 4, p. 62-69.

8141. Kankan no kisoteki kenkyu. (A basic study on Han Jian). Ed. by Osamu OBA. Kyoto, Shibunkaku Shuppan, 99, 212 p.

8142. KAWAKATSU (Mamoru). Minshin konan shichin shakaisi kenkyu: Kukan to shakai keisei no rekishigaku. (Social history of market towns in the lower Yangtze delta during the Ming and Quing periods: historical science based on space and the social formation). 99, 824 p. [Eng. summary].

8143. KE (Powen) [Parks Coble]. Hezuo yu kangdi: Zhongguo zibenjia he Riben zhaling dangju de guanxi 1937-1945. (Collaboration and resistance: Chinese capitalists and the Japanese 1937-1945). *Minguo yanjiu*, 99, p. 54-64.

8144. KEGASAWA (Yasunori). Fuheisei no kenkyu. (A study of the Fu-bing military system: The Fu-bing soldiers and their society in the Sui-Tang dynasties). Tokyo, Dohosha Shuppan, 99, 492 p. [Eng. summary].

8145. KISHIMOTO (Mio). Minshin kotai to konan shakai: 17seiki chugoku no chitsujo mondai. (The Ming-Qing transition in Jiangnan: the problem of social order in seventeenth-century China). Tokyo, University of Tokyo Press, 99, 289 p.

8146. LAI (Xinxia). Huashengtun huiyi yu Zhongguo minzhong yundong. (The Washington Conference and Chinese mass movements). *Minguo dang'an*, 99, 2, p. 74-78.

8147. LAUWAERT (Françoise). La meurtre en famille. Parricide et infanticide en Chine (XVIIIe-XIXe siècle). Paris, Odile Jacob, 99, 366 p.

8148. LI (Guizhi). Qidan guizu dahui gouchen. (An investigation on the aristocratic assembly of the Qidan). *Lishi yanjiu*, 99, 6, p. 68-88.

8149. LI (Jinming). Shilun Mingchao dui Liuqiu de cefeng. (On the appointment of the kings of Riukyu Islands during Ming dynasty). *Lishi dang'an*, 99, 4, p. 82-87.

8150. LI (Mingshan). 20 shiji chu Zhongguo banquan wenti lunzheng (The quarrels about the copyright in early 20 century China). *Jindai shi yanjiu*, 99, 1, p. 302-310.

8151. LI (Rong), QUAN (Fangmin). Xinhai geming qijian Manzhoutie de qin Hua yinmou. (The Mantetsu secret plan to invade China during the 1911 revolution). *Lishi dang'an*, 99, 2, p. 113-117.

8152. LI (Tingjiang). Wuxu weixin qianhou de Zhong Ri guangxi. (Sino-Japanese relations during the 1898 reform). *Lishi yanjiu*, 99, 2, p. 88-97.

8153. LI (Xueqin). Jiagu xue de qige keti. (Seven research topics on the bone and shell inscriptions). *Lishi yanjiu*, 99, 5, p. 57-62.

8154. LIN (Qiyan) [Lam (Kaiyin)]. Wang Tao de haifang xixiang. (Wang Tao's conception of maritime defense). *Jindai shi yanjiu*, 99, 2, p. 136-150.

8155. LIU (Dingming). Zhongyang Xintuoju gaishu. (An account of the Central Trust Bureau). *Minguo dang'an*, 99, 2, p. 65-68.

8156. LIU (Huiyu). Lun Guomin zhengfu Zhongyang yinghang de zujian ji qi jiaosi dingwei. (The establishment of the Central Bank by the Nationalists and its role). *Minguo dang'an*, 99, 3, p. 76-80.

8157. LIU (Jingyuan). Lun Xianggang zhengfu zaoqi Huaren guanzhi zhengce de xingcheng. (On the formation of the policy to manage Chinese residents by British government in Hong Kong). *Lishi dang'an*, 99, 1, p. 103-109.

8158. LIU (Weidong). Yinzhi tongdao de zhanshi gongneng shulüe. (On the function of the Indo-China Passageway during the war of resistance). *Jindai shi yanjiu*, 99, 2, p. 173-190.

8159. LIU (Yongdai) [Yu Yongtae]. Guomin geming shiqi de gongchan, gongtang wenti – Liang Hu yu Guangdong nongmin yundong zhi bijiao. (The problem of public properties and private courts at the time of the nationalist revolution – a comparison of the peasant movement in Hunan and Hubei and that in Guangdong). *Minguo yanjiu*, 99, p. 5-20.

8160. LIU (Zhangmei). Kangzhan qian Xibei jiaotong jianshe. (The construction of communications in North-Western China before the resistance war). *Minguo dang'an*, 99, 2, p. 90-96.

8161. LU (Fangshang). Geming zhi zaiqi: Zhongguo Guomindang gaizu qian dui xin sichao de huiying 1914–1924. (The resurgence of the revolution: Nationalist Party's reaction towards the new intellectual trends before the party reorganization 1914–1924). Taibei, Zhong yan yuan jinshi suo, 99, 615 p.

8162. LU (Xiqi). Lun Wang Guowei zhi baoshou. (Wang Guoweis' conservatism). *Jindai shi yanjiu*, 99, 4, p. 162-176.

8163. LÜ (Yiran). Minguo shiqi Zhongguo renmin shouhui Aomen de douzheng yu Zhongguo zhengfu de taidu. (Chinese people's fight to recover Macao and Chinese government's attitude in Republican period). *Jindai shi yanjiu*, 99, 6, p. 18-40.

8164. LUO (Zhitian). Cong kexue yu renshengguan zhi zheng kan hou wusi shiqi dui wusi jiben linian de fansi. (Reflections on the basic ideas of the May Fourth Movement: a reassessment of the polemics on science and metaphysics of the May Fourth period). *Lishi yanjiu*, 99, 3, p. 5-23.

8165. LUO (Zhitian). Wudaishi de minguo: yige you guo zhishi fenzi dui beifa qian shunian zhengzhi geju de jishi guancha. (A republic akin to the Five Dynasties period: Chinese political circumstances in the eyes of an elite intellectual in the years before the northern expedition). *Jindai shi yanjiu*, 99, 4, p. 44-87.

8166. MA (Junya). Minguo shiqi Jiangnan xiandai gongye de fazhan yu nongjia jingji jiegou de yanbian. (The development of the Jiangnan modern industry in Republican era and the evolution of the structure of the rural family economy). *Minguo yanjiu*, 99, p. 91-101.

8167. MA (Zhen). Zhongguo diyi lishi dang'anguan cang Qianlongchao chajin tianzhujiao dang'an shulun. (A discussion on the archival documents on prohibiting Catholicism during the Qianlong period stored in the Chinese Archives N. 1). *Lishi dang'an*, 99, 2, p. 79-84.

8168. MA (Zhendu). "Ouran" zhizhongde "biran" – 1926 nian "Zhongshan jian shijian" xingzhi lun. (The Zhongshan gunboat incident in 1926). *Minguo dang'an*, 99, 4, p. 49-56.

8169. MI (Qingyu). Liuqiu piaomin shijian yu Rijun qin Taiwan 1871–1874. (The incident of shipwrecked from Ryukyu islands and the Japanese invasion of Taiwan). *Lishi yanjiu*, 99, 1, p. 22-37.

8170. MI (Rucheng). Geng kuang "tuikuan" ji ji guanli he liyong. (The "refund" of the Boxer indemnity and its charge and use). *Jindai shi yanjiu*, 99, 6, p. 64-100.

8171. MOTE (F. W.). Imperial China: 900–1800. Cambridge, Harvard U. P., 99, XIX-1107 p.

8172. NEPOMNIN (Oleg E.), MEN'SHIKOV (Vladimir B.). Sintez v perekhodnom obshchestve: Kitaj na grani epokh. (Synthesis in a transitional society: China in the 2nd half of the 19th and in the 1st half of the 20th century). RAN, In-t vostokovedenija. Moskva, Vostochnaja literatura, 99, 334 p. (bibl., ind.).

8173. NING (Zhixin). Tangchao shizhi ruogan wenti yanjiu. (Some problems on the title of commissioner during the Tang dynasty). *Lishi yaniu*, 99, 2, p. 53-71.

8174. NIU (Jun). Xin Zhongguo waijiao de xingcheng ji zhuyao tezheng. (The evolution and main characteristics of new China foreign relations). *Lishi yanjiu*, 99, 5, p. 23-42.

8175. OGAWA (Takashi). Meidai chiho kansatsu seido no kenkyu. (A study on supervision system in the Ming dynasty). Tokyo, Kyuko Shoin, 99, 252 p.

8176. OKAMOTO (Takashi). Kindai chugoku to kaiseki. (Modern China and maritime customs system). Nagoya, University of Nagoya Press, 99, 688 p.

8177. OUYANG (Junxi). Wusi xin wenhua yudong yu ruxue: wushi ji qita. (Misunderstandings and other matters about the new culture movement and confucianism during the May Fourth period). *Lishi yanjiu*, 99, 3, p. 42-56.

8178. OWNBY (David). Chinese millenarian traditions: the formative age. [AHR Forum: Millenniums]. *American historical review*, 99, 104, 5, p. 1513-1530.

8179. PENG (Houwen). 19 shiji 80 niandai Shanghai gupiao jiaoyi de xingshuai. (The rising and declining of stock exchange in XIX century 80s Shanghai). *Jindai shi yanjiu*, 99, 1, p. 168-193.

8180. PENG (Houwen). Jiedu Tan Sitong. (An explicative reading of Tan Sitong). *Jindai shi yanjiu*, 99, 1, p. 127-148.

8181. PIAO (Yingji). Shilun Chaoxian Minzu Gemingdang yu Zhongguo Guomindang de guanxi. (On the relationship between the Korean National Revolutionary Party and the Chinese Nationalist Party). *Minguo dang'an*, 99, 2, p. 79-85.

8182. POPOVA (Irina F.). Politicheskaja praktika i ideologija rannetanskogo Kitaja. (Political practice and ideology of the early Tang China, [the 1st half of the 7th century]). RAN, In-t vostokovedenija, Sankt-Peterburgskij filial. Moskva, Vostochnaja literatura, 99, 279 p. (bibl., ind.). [Eng. summary]

8183. PRAZNIAK (Roxann). Of camel kings and other things: rural rebels against modernity in Late Imperial China. Lanham, Rowman and Littlefield, 99, XI-305 p. (State and society in East Asia).

8184. QI (Chunfeng). Kangzhan shiqi Guo tongqu yu lunxianqu jian zousi maoyi shulun. (On smuggling trade between the areas controlled by Nationalists and the occupied areas during the resistance war). *Minguo dang'an*, 99, 1, p. 77-82.

8185. QI (Chunfeng). Kangzhan shiqi Zhong Ri jingji fensuo yu fan fengsuo zheng. (The Sino-Japanese economic blockade during the resistance war and the fight against it). *Lishi dang'an*, 99, 3, p. 123-128.

8186. QIAO (Lingxiao), LIANG (Yandong). Ming Qing shehui de shenshang shentou ji qi yinxiang. (The infiltration of merchants and scholars in Ming and Qing society and its influence). *Lishi dang'an*, 99, 1, p. 78-85.

8187. QIU (Huafei). Lüelun Nanjing zhengfu chuqi Zhong Mei maoyi guanxi. (The Sino-American trade relations in the first periodo of the Nanking government). *Minguo dang'an*, 99, 3, p. 88-95.

8188. QIU (Huafei). Luo Jiesi lai Hua yu Zhong Mei baiyin wenti. (James Harvey Rogers' visit to China and Sino-American silver question). *Minguo yanjiu*, 99, p. 65-74.

8189. QIU (Jin). The culture of power: the Lin Biao incident in the Cultural Revolution. Stanford, Stanford U. P., 99, [s. p.].

8190. SANG (Bing). Chen Jitong shulun. (On Chen Jitong). *Jindai shi yanjiu*, 99, 4, p. 109-137.

8191. SANG (Bing). Hu Shi and guoji hanxue jie. (Hu Shi and international sinology). *Jindai shi yanjiu*, 99, 1, p. 49-99.

8192. SANG (Bing). Jindai Riben liexuesheng. (Chinese students in Japan in modern times). *Jindai shi yanjiu*, 99, 3, p. 155-182.

8193. SANG (Bing). Jindai Zhongguo keshu de diyuan yu liupai. (The academic regionalism and schools in modern China). *Lishi yanjiu*, 99, 3, p. 24-41.

8194. SATO (Fumitoshi). Min dai ofu no kenkyu. (A study on the princely establishment in the Ming dynasty). Tokyo, Kenbun Shuppan, 99, 480 p.

8195. SATO (Kimihiko). Giwadan no kigen to sono undo: Chugoku minshu nashonarizumu no tanjo. (The origin of the Boxer uprising and its movements: the birth of the Chinese popular nationalism). Tokyo, Kenbun Shuppan, 99, 851 p.

8196. SCHMIDT-GLINTZER (Helwig). Geschichte Chinas bis zur mongolischen Eroberung 250 v. Chr.– 1279 n. Chr. München, Oldenbourg, 99, XII-235 p. (Oldenbourg Grundriß der Geschichte, 26).

8197. SHEN (Zhihua). Zhong Su jiemeng yu Sulian dui Xinjiang zhengce de bianhua 1944–1950. (Sino-Soviet Alliance and the change of Soviet policy towards Xinjiang 1944–1950). *Jindai shi yanjiu*, 99, 3, p. 213-242.

8198. SHIGECHIKA (Keiju). Shinkan zeieki taikei no kenkyu. (Tax and service systems of the Quin and Han dynasties). Tokyo, Kyuko Shoin, 99, 352 p.

8199. SLOBODNÍK (Martin). Vzťahy čínskej dynastie Ming a tibetského vládnuceho rodu Phag-mo-gru, 1368–1434). (The relations of the Chinese dynasty Ming and the ruling Tibetan Kin Phag-mo-gru, 1368–1434). *Historický časopis*, 99, 47, 4, p. 655-678.

8200. SONG (Congbing). Taiping tianguo zhaoshuya kaobian. (An investigation on the bureau of royal edicts of the Taiping Heavenly kingdom). *Lishi yanjiu*, 99, 5, p. 90-103.

8201. SONG (Jie). Zhongguo huobi fazhan shi. (A history of the development of currency in China). Beijing, Shoudu shifan daxue chubanshe, 99, 288 p.

8202. SONG (Liming). Youguan Huang Musong fengshi ru Zang de shiliao wenti. (Some problems concerning the documents on Huang Musong's mission to Tibet). *Minguo yanjiu*, 99, p. 126-137.

8203. State and court ritual in China. Ed. by Joseph P. MAC DERMOTT. Cambridge, Cambridge U. P., 99, X-446 p. (Oriental publications, 54).

8204. SU (Xiaodong). Beiyang haijun guandai qunti yu jiawu haizhan. (A study on the group of captains of the Northern Arrmy Fleet and the 1894 naval battle). *Jindai shi yanjiu*, 99, 2, p. 150-172.

8205. TAJIRI (Toru). Shindai nogyo shogyo-ka no kenkyu. (A study on the commercialization of agriculture in the Qing dynasty). Tokyo, Kokyu Shoin, 99, 464 p.

8206. TAN (Wenfeng). Li Hongzhang qianding "Zhong E miyue" zhongde liange wenti. (Two problems on the "Sino-Russian secret treaty" signed by Li Hongzhang). *Lishi dang'an*, 99, 4, p. 119-122.

8207. TANG (Ling). Guanyu kangzhan qijian Guangxi kuangye sunshi de diaocha. (An investigation on the losses of mining industry in Guangxi province during the resistance war). *Lishi dang'an*, 99, 4, p. 128-132.

8208. TANNER (Harold Miles). Strike hard! Anticrime campaigns and Chinese criminal justice 1979–1985. Ithaca, East Asia Program, Cornell University, 99, X-253 p. (Cornell East Asia series, 104).

8209. TSIN (Michael). Nation, Governance, and Modernity in China: Canton, 1900–1927. Stanford, Stanford U. P., 99, 276 p. (Studies of the East Asian Institute, Columbia University).

8210. TWOHEY (Michael). Authority and welfare in China: modern debates in historical perspective. Basingstoke, Macmillan a. New York, St. Martin's Press, 99, XII-227 p. (Studies on the Chinese economy).

8211. WANG (Chaoguang). Jianlun 1946 nian de Guo Gong junshi zhenbian fuyuan. (The military reorganization of Nationalist and Communist troops in 1946). *Mingguo dang'an*, 99, 2, p. 105-110.

8212. WANG (Di). Songdai xiangli liangji zhidu zhiyi. (Questioning the two tiers administrative system of the Song dynasty). *Lishi yanjiu*, 99, 4, p. 99-112.

8213. WANG (Guanghua). Aiguo yundong zhongde "heli" sili: 1905nian dihuo yundong yaosi de yuanyin. ("Reasonable" private interests in a patriotic movement: the reason of the premature end of the 1905 boycott movement). *Lishi yanjiu*, 99, 1, p. 5-21.

8214. WANG (Junyi), HUANG (Aiping). Qingdai xueshu wenhua shilun. (Academic culture in Qing times). Taibei, Wenjin chubanshe, 99, 508 p.

8215. WANG (Kaixi). Majiaerni guiye Qianlong di kaosi. (An investigation on Lord MacCartney kneeling to Emperor Qianlong). *Lishi dang'an*, 99, 2, p. 90-94.

8216. WANG (Qinsheng). Taiwan Ri zhi shiqi de falü gaige. (Legal reforms in Taiwan during the Japanese occupation). Lianjing chubanshe, Taibei, 99, 448 p.

8217. WANG (Qisheng). Minguo shiqi xianzhang de qunti goucheng yu renshi shandi. (The group structure of county magistrates during the Republican period and its evolution). *Lishi yanjiu*, 99, 2, p. 98-116.

8218. WANG (Shanjun). Songdai huangzu pudie kaoshu. (The geneological tree of the imperial clan of the Song dynasty). *Lishi dang'an*, 99, 3, p. 79-85.

8219. WANG (Xianming). Jiedu "Ci Han" – Jianlun Wuzu shiqi Yan Fu yu Li Hongzhang Zhang Zhidong zhi guanxi. (An interpretation of "A critique of Han Yu" – A discussion of the relationship between Yan Fu and Li Hongzhang Zhang Zhidong during the 1898 reforms). *Lishi yanjiu*, 99, 4, p. 113-128.

8220. WANG (Yuhe). Yingguo dui Hua "paojian zhengce" pousi. (British "gunboat diplomacy" towards China). *Jindai shi yanjiu*, 99, 4, p. 1-43.

8221. WANG (Yuhua). Zhang Taifei difang zhengzhi xixiang lun. (Zhang Taifei's conceptions on local politics). *Lishi dang'an*, 99, 2, p. 106-112.

8222. WANG (Yuzhe). Xi Zhou guojia lishi zuoyong. (On the historical function of the State during the Western Zhou). *Lishi yanjiu*, 99, 2, p. 23-29.

8223. WEI (Hongyun). Kangzhan shiqi de Huaqiao juanshu yu jiuwang yundong. (Overseas Chinese's contribution during the resistance war). *Jindai shi yanjiu*, 99, 6, p. 157-221.

8224. Wenzhou Huaqiao shi. (A history of overseas Chinese from Wenzhou). Edited by the Research center for overseas Chinese from Wenzhou. Beijing, Jinri Zhongguo chubanshe, 99, 319 p.

8225. WU (Shanzhong). Lun Gelaohui zhi qiyuan. (On the origins of the Gelao society). *Lishi dang'an*, 99, 3, p. 105-110.

8226. WU (Songdi). Songdai hukou de huizong fabu xitong. (The Song dynasty sistem for collecting and publishing demographic data). *Lishi yanjiu*, 99, 4, p. 66-82.

8227. WU (Zhuo). Xinan sichou zhi lu yanjiu de renshi wuqu. (Misunderstandings in the research on the Silk Road of the southwest). *Lishi yanjiu*, 99, 1, p. 38-50.

8228. Wusi xinlun: jifei wenyi fuxing, yi fei qimeng yundong. Wusi bashi zhounian ji wenlun jianji. (New studies of the May Fourth Movement: neither a cultural renaissance nor an enlightment movement). Edited by YU Yingshi. Taibei, Lianjing chubanshe, 99, 273 p.

8229. XU (Tang). Qingdai qianqi de Jiujiang guan ji qi shanpin liutong. (The customs of Jiujiang and its commodity circulation in the early Qing period). *Lishi dang'an*, 99, 1, p. 86-91.

8230. XU (Tingsheng). Lun Minguo chunian jingji zhengce de fuzhi yu jiangli daoxiang. (On the support and encouragment in economic policy in early Republic). *Jindai shi yanjiu*, 99, 1, p. 194-225.

8231. XUE (Ruili). Shixi Qing ting fenhua Taipingjun de celüe. (A tentative analysis on the Qing court strategy to divide the Taiping army). *Lishi dang'an*, 99, 2, p. 95-102.

8232. YAN (Lixian). Lüelun jindai Zhongguo gongyehua de nongye tiaojian. (On the agricultural conditions for industrialization in modern China). *Jindai shi yanjiu*, 99, 3, p. 125-154.

8233. YANG (Jibo). Ming Qing dang'an wenxian zhon dui Putaoya de chengwei. (The names for Portugal in Ming Qing archival documents). *Lishi dang' an*, 99, 4, p. 88-91.

8234. YANG (Kuisong). Chen Duxiu yu gongchan guoji. (Chen Duxiu and the Communist International). *Jindai shi yanjiu*, 99, 2, p. 69-135.

8235. YANG (Kuisong). Mei Su lengzhan de qiyuan ji dui Zhongguo geming de yingxiang. (The origins of the Cold War between US and Soviet Russia and its influence on the Chinese revolution). *Lishi yanjiu*, 99, 5, p. 5-22.

8236. YANG (Yuqing). Guojia liyi: Su E dui zai Hua hezuozhe de xuanze. (National interest: how Soviet Russia chose partners in China). *Lishi yanjiu*, 99, 4, p. 140-154.

8237. YE (Jiachi) [Ka-che Yip]. Jianshe qiangda de Zhongguo: Minguo shiqi jiankang, shehui yu guojia zhi toushe. (Building a strong China: perspectives on health, society and the State in Republican period). *Minguo yanjiu*, 99, p. 41-53.

8238. YE (Meilan). 1912–1937 nian Jiangsu nongcun dijia de bianqian. (Price change of rural land in Jiangsu from 1912 to 1937). *Mingguo dang'an*, 99, 1, p. 46-55.

8239. YIN (Junli). Xuantong yuannian fankang hukou diaocha fengchao. (The opposition to census registration in the first year of Xuantong emperor). *Lishi dang'an*, 99, 3, p. 110-114.

8240. YU (Jiang). Liangzhong Qingmo xianfa cao' an gaoben de faxian ji chubu yanjiu. (The discovery and preliminary investigation of two drafts for constitution during the late Qing). *Lishi yanjiu*, 99, 6, p. 89-102.

8241. YU (Shanpu). Qinggong guiren. (Qing court nobles). *Lishi dang'an*, 99, 4, p. 99-105.

8242. YU (Songjiang), XUE (Wei). Kangri genjudi de wujia guanli. (Price control in the base area during the resistance war). *Lishi dang'an*, 99, 1, p. 125-130.

8243. YUASA (Kunihiro). Chugoku kodai gunji shisoshi no kenkyu. (A study of the history of military thought in ancient China). Tokyo, Kenbun Shuppan, 99, 381 p.

8244. ZHANG (Beigen). Guonan huiyi zongshu. (A general presentation of the conference on State calamities). *Lishi dang'an*, 99, 4, p. 123-127.

8245. ZHANG (Dianren). Kang Yong shiqi ji ren Jiang Ning zhizao de jieju. (The ending of several Superintendents of the weaving industry in Jiangnan and Ningpo areas). *Lishi dang'an*, 99, 1, p. 86-91.

8246. ZHANG (Guohui). Wan Qing caizheng yu Xianfeng chao tonghuo pengzhang. (Late Qing finance and inflation during Xianfeng reign). *Jindai shi yanjiu*, 99, 2, p. 96-154.

8247. ZHANG (Haipeng). Ju Ao Puren "shuangzhong xiaozhong" shuo pingyi. (The so-called "double loyalty" of Portuguese in Macao). *Jindai shi yanjiu*, 99, 6, p. 1-17.

8248. ZHANG (Hong). Cong Miandian zhangchang kan kangzhan shiqi de Zhong Ying guanxi. (The Sino-British relations during the resistance war viewed from Burma war theatre). *Minguo dang'an*, 99, 3, p. 103-107.

8249. ZHANG (Jin). Minguo shiqi Sichuan junfa zhengzhi de teshu goujia – fangqu zhi. (A special political structure of the Sichuan warlords in Republican period – the defense district system). *Minguo yanjiu*, 99, p. 21-29.

8250. ZHANG (Jinlong). Bei Wei Luoyang lifang zhidu tanwei. (An investigation on the lifang system in Luoyang during the Northern Wei). *Lishi yanjiu*, 99, 6, p. 51-67.

8251. ZHANG (Jishun). Zhongguo zhishifenzi di Meiguo guan 1943–1953. (Chinese intellectual perspectives on USA 1943–1953). Shanghai, Fudan daxue chubanshe, 99, 257 p.

8252. ZHANG (Li). 1937–1941 nian Xianggang huazi gongye de fazhan. (The development of Chinese capital industry in Hong Kong 1937–1941). *Jindai shi yanjiu*, 99, 1, p. 226-241.

8253. ZHANG (Li). Guoji hezuo zai Zhongguo: Guoji lianmeng jiaosi de kaocha 1919–1946. (International cooperation in China: An investigation on the role of the League of Nations 1919–1946). Taibei, Zhong yan yuan jin shi suo, 99, 352 p.

8254. ZHANG (Li). Lun banghui chansheng de shehui tiaojian. (The social conditions for the development of secret societies). *Lishi dang'an*, 99, 4, p. 92-98.

8255. ZHANG (Lianhong). Nanjing Guomin zhengfu de cai li yu ge sheng difang zhengfu de fanying. (The Nanking Nationalist government's elimination of the lijin tax and the response of provincial governments). *Minguo yanjiu*, 99, p. 113-125.

8256. ZHANG (Pengyuan). Liang Qichao yu Qing ji geming. (Liang Qichao and the revolution at the end of the Qing dynasty). Taibei, Zhong yan yuan jinshi suo, 99, 280 p.

8257. ZHANG (Sheng). Nanjing Guomin zhengfu chiqi zhongyang yusuan shulun 1927–1933. (A commentary on the centralized budgeting during the early period of the Nanking Nationalist government 1927–1933). *Minguo yanjiu*, 99, p. 102-112.

8258. ZHANG (Tiancheng). Ma Hongkui yu Ningxia jindai gongye de fushuai. (Ma Hongkui and the rise and decline of modern industry in Ningxia). *Minguo dang'an*, 99, 4, p. 89-104.

8259. ZHANG (Wenyu). "Diaojun pinfu" yu "Xiezhuo pinfu". Cong Kongzi de "chuan bu jun" dato Tangdai de "junping" sixiang. ("Level the difference between the poor and the rich" and "Contribution based on property". From Confucian perception of "inequality as the root of disaster" to Tang dynasty concept of "equalization"). *Lishi yanjiu*, 99, 2, p. 30-41.

8260. ZHANG (Xiaopeng). Meiguo dui Zhong Su tongmeng de renshi yu fanying. (US conception and reaction to the Sino-Soviet alliance). *Lishi yanjiu*, 99, 5, p. 43-56.

8261. ZHAO (Jian). Qing chu cao fu. (Water transportation taxes in early Qing). *Lishi dang'an*, 99, 3, p. 86-92.

8262. ZHAO (Ping'an). Qin Xi Han wushi weishi guanyin kao. (An investigation on the mistakes and lacks in the explications about official seals during the Qin and Western Han dynasties). *Lishi yanjiu*, 99, 1, p. 51-65.

8263. ZHAO (Xianye). Li Wei yu Qingdai qianqi de yanzheng. (Li Wei and the salt policy in early Qing). *Lishi dang'an*, 99, 3, p. 93-99.

8264. ZHAO (Xiude), JIANG (Li). Dageming shiqi Zhonggong beifang quwei ji suoxia zuzhi gaikuang. (A survey on Chinese Communist Party committee for northern areas and its organization in 1923–1927). *Lishi dang'an*, 99, 1, p. 120-124.

8265. ZHAO (Yunkun). Jiansi Zhong Ri guanyu "ershiyi tiao" zhong de tielu jiaoshe. (An analysis of the Sino-Japanese negotiations over the "Twenty-first articles"). *Minguo dang'an*, 99, 3, p. 71-75.

8266. ZHENG (Huixi). Zhongguo Jianshe yingongsi gufen de yanbian. (The evolution of the company shares in the Construction Bank of China). *Lishi yanjiu*, 99, 3, p. 95-113.

8267. Zhongguo kang Ri zhanzheng renwu da cidian. (The great biographical dictionary of the Chinese resistance war against Japan). Edited by LIU Jinquan. Tiajin, Tianjin daxue chubanshe, 99, 618 p.

8268. ZHU (Donghan). Taiping tianguo yu Xian Tong zhengju. (The Taiping Heavenly kingdom and the political situation during the reigns of Xianfeng emperor and Tongzhi emperor). *Jindai shi yanjiu*, 99, 2, p. 1-67.

8269. ZHU (Qingbo). Zhan hou Guomin zhengfu jindu gongzuo shuping. (A critique of the post-war Nationalist government's opium suppression work). *Minguo yanjiu*, 99, p. 30-40.

8270. ZHU (Ying). Wuxu zhi Xinhai difang zizhi de fazhan. (The development of local self-government from 1898 to 1911). *Jindai shi yanjiu*, 99, 4, p. 88-107.

8271. ZHUANG (Jifa). Qingdai Taiwan huidang shi yanjiu. (Historical research on societies and sects in Taiwan during the Qing period). Taibei, Nantian shuju, 99, 314 p.

8272. ZUO (Shuangwen). Kangzhan shengli qianhou Zhongguo shouhui Aomen de mouhua yu liuchan. (Chinese plan to recover Macao and its abortion before and after the resistance war). *Jindai shi yanjiu*, 99, 6, p. 41-63.

Cf. n°s 581, 5240, 7546, 7596

§ 5. Japan (before 1868).

8273. AOKI (Michio). Kinsei-Owari no kai-son to kai-un. (Maritime villages and transportation in early modern Owari). Tokyo, Azekura Shobo, 97, 308 p.

8274. ASAKURA (Yuko). Hoppo-shi to kinsei shakai. (A history of Northern Japan and the early modern society). Osaka, Seibundo Shuppan, 99, 325 p.

8275. Cambridge History (The) of Japan. Vol. 2. Hejan Japan. Ed. by Donald H. SHIVELY and William H. MAC CULLOUGH. New York, Cambridge U. P., 99, XXIII-754 p.

8276. FUJIKI (Hisashi). Sengoku no saho: Mura no funso-kaiketsu. (Manners in medieval Japan: trouble-solution in villages). Tokyo, Heibonsha, 98, 307 p.

8277. FUJITA (Satoru). Kinsei-seiji-shi to Tenno. (The political history and the Emperor in early modern Japan). Tokyo, Yoshikawa Kobunkan, 99, 326 p.

8278. FUJIZANE (Kumiko). Bukan-shuppan to kinsei shakai. (The publication of the books of heraldry and the early modern Japanese society). Tokyo, Toyo Shorin, 99, 325 p.

8279. GOMI (Fumihiko). "Kasuga genki e" to chusei: Emaki wo yomu, aruku. ("Kasuga genki e" and Medieval Japan: reading and walking about picture scrolls). Kyoto, Tankosha, 98, 271 p. – IDEM. Taira no Kiyomori. (Taira Kiyomori). Tokyo, Yoshikawa Kobunkan, 99, 352 p.

8280. HASHIMOTO (Yoshihiko). Nihon kodai no girei to tenseki. (The rituals and books in ancient Japan). Tokyo, Seishi Shuppan, 99, 280 p.

8281. HISANO (Nobuyoshi). Nihon chusei no jiin to shakai. (Buddhist temples and Medieval Japanese society). Tokyo, Hanawa Shobo, 99, 430 p.

8282. HOTATE (Michihisa). Chusei no onna no issho. (Women's lives in Medieval Japan). Tokyo, Yosensha, 99, 183 p.

8283. GRESTI (Maurizio). Riforme economiche e lotte politiche nel Giappone medievale. Il governo delle attività economiche durante le guerre civili del XVI secolo. *Rivista di storia economica*, 99, 15, 1, p. 87-109.

8284. INABA (Tsuguharu). Sengoku jidai no shoensei to sonraku. (Proprietary estates and villages during the Japan's warring states period). Tokyo, Azekura Shobo, 98, 382 p.

8285. IRUMADA (Nobuo). Chusei Bushidan no jikoninshiki. (Identity of warrior groups in Medieval Japan). Tokyo, Miyai Shoten, 98, 318 p.

8286. ISHIGAMI (Eiichi), KATO (Tomoyasu), YAMAGUCHI (Hideo). Kodai monjo ron: Shosoin monjo to mokkan, urushi-gami monjo. (The documents in ancient Japan: Documents preserved in Shosoin, wooden tablets and lacquer paper documents). Tokyo, University of Tokyo Press, 99, 352 p.

8287. ITO (Kiyoshi). Chusei kokka to Tougoku, Ou. (Medieval state of Japan, eastern provinces and Ou). Tokyo, Azekura Shobo, 99, 526 p.

8288. KANDA (Yutsuki). Kinsei no geino-kogyo to chiiki-shakai. (Entrepreneurship and the performing arts in early modern Japan). Tokyo, University of Tokyo Press, 99, 392 p.

8289. Kinsei-chiikishakai-ron: Bakuryo-Amakusa no ôjoya, ji-yakunin to hyakusho-sozoku. (Rural societies in early modern Japan: village grand headman, local officials and peasant inheritance in Shogunate Amakusa). Ed. by Takashi WATANABE. Tokyo, Iwata Shoin, 99, 489 p.

8290. Kinsei-shakai to Chigyo-sei. (The early modern Japanese society and the feudalism). Ed. by John Francis MORRIS, Tatuo SHIRAKAWABE and Nobuharu TAKANO. Kyoto, Shibunkaku Shuppan, 99, 371 p.

8291. LESHCHENKO (Nelli F.). Japonija v epokhu Tokugava. (Japan in the age of Tokugawa). RAN, In-t vostokovedenija. Moskva, [s. n.], 99, 319 p. (ill., bibl.; ind.).

8292. MINAMI (Kazuo). Bakumatsu-toshi-shakai no kenkyu. (A historical study of the urban society in the last days of the Tokugawa government). Tokyo, Hanawa Shobo, 99, 421 p.

8293. MISE (Kazuo). Bakuhan-sei-shijo to Han-zaisei. (The market under the shogunate-domain system and the finance of the feudal clan). Tokyo, Gannando Shoten, 98, 421 p.

8294. MURAI (Shosuke). Chusei nihon no uchi to soto. (Domestic and diplomatic history of Medieval Japan). Tokyo, Chikuma Shobo, 99, 199 p.

8295. NAKAMURA (Hideshige). Kodai saishi ron. (Essays on rituals in ancient Japan). Tokyo, Yoshikawa Kobunkan, 99, 275 p.

8296. NAKAZAWA (Katsuaki). Chusei no buryoku to jokaku. (Military force and forts of Medieval Japan). Tokyo, Yoshikawa Kobunkan, 99, 287 p.

8297. Nihon bukkyo no shiteki tenkai. (The historical process of Buddhism in Japan). Ed. by Koyu SONODA. Tokyo, Haniwa Shobo, 99, 540 p.

8298. Nihon kodai-shakai no shiteki tenkai. (The historical process of the ancient Japanese society). Ed. by Koyu SONODA. Tokyo, Haniwa Shobo, 99, 550 p.

8299. NISHIJIMA (Sadao). Wakoku no shutsugen: Higashi ajia sekai no naka no nihon. (The appearance of Wa: Ancient Japan in eastern Asia). Tokyo, University of Tokyo Press, 99, 312 p.

8300. OKIMORI (Takuya), SATO (Makoto), YAJIMA (Izumi). Toushi-kaden. (The chronicle of the Fujiwara family). Tokyo, Yoshikawa Kobunkan, 99, 528 p.

8301. OTSU (Toru). Kodai no tenno sei. (The imperial system in ancient Japan). Tokyo, Iwanami Shoten, 99, 288 p.

8302. OYAMA (Seiichi). Nihon kodai no gaiko to chiho gyosei. (The diplomacy and the provincial administration in ancient Japan). Tokyo, Yoshikawa Kobunkan, 99, 528 p.

8303. SATO (Makoto). Kodai no iseki to moji shiryo. (The remains and the written materials in ancient Japan). Tokyo, Meicho Kanko Kai, 99, 339 p.

8304. SAWA (Hirokatsu). Kinsei no shukyo-soshiki to chiiki-shakai: kyodan-shinko to minkan-shinko. (Religious organization and local societies: the belief religious order and the popular belief in early modern Japan). Tokyo, Yoshikawa Kobunkan, 99, 352 p.

8305. SHINKAWA (Tokio). Nihon kodai no girei to hyogen: Ajia no naka no seiji bunka. (The relations between rituals and expressions in ancient Japan: The political culture in Asia). Tokyo, Yoshikawa Kobunkan, 99, 416 p. – IDEM. Nihon kodai no taigai kosho to bukkyo: Ajia no naka no seiji bunka. (The relations between diplomatic negotiation and Buddhism in ancient Japan: The political culture in Asia). Tokyo, Yoshikawa Kobunkan, 99, 398 p.

8306. Shozoga wo yomu. (Reading historical portraits). Ed. by Hideo KURODA. Tokyo, Kadokawa Shoten, 98, 270 p.

8307. SUGIMOTO (Fumiko). Ryoiki-shihai no tenkai to kinsei. (The development of the provincial rule and early modern Japan). Tokyo, Yamakawa Shuppansha, 99, 310 p.

8308. TAKAHASHI (Masaaki). Bushi no seiritsu: Bushizo no soshutsu. (The warrior estates in Japanese history: From the emergence of an estate to the creation of the mythical warrior). Tokyo, University of Tokyo Press, 99, 360 p.

8309. TANAKA (Katsuyuki). Chusei no soson to monjo. (Village communities and historical materials in Medieval Japan). Tokyo, Yamakawa Shuppansha, 98, 408 p.

8310. TASHIRO (Kazuo). Edo-jidai Chosen yakuzai chosa no kenkyu. (A historical study of the search for the medicines in Korea in the Edo period). Tokyo, University of Keio Press, 99, 492 p.

8311. TERASAKI (Yasuhiro). Nagaya-o. (Prince Nagaya). Tokyo, Yoshikawa Kobunkan, 99, 282 p.

8312. TOLSTOGUZOV (S.A.). Segunat Tokugava v pervoj polovine XIX v. i reformy godov Tempo. (The Tokugava Shogunate in the 1st half of the 19th century and the reforms of the Tempo era). RAN, Nauch. sovet po istorii sotsial'nykh refom, dvizhenij i revoljutsij. Moskva, [s. n.], 99, 180 p. (plates; bibl.).

8313. TONO (Haruyuki). Kentoshi sen: Higashi ajia no naka de. (The Japanese envoys to Tang China: In the East Asian Sea). Tokyo, Asahi Shimbun Sha, 99, 214 p.

8314. USAMI (Takayuki). Nihon chusei no ryutsu to shogyo. (Distribution and commerce in Medieval Japan). Tokyo, Yoshikawa Kobunkan, 99, 320 p.

8315. WAKITA (Haruko). L'histoire des femmes au Japon. La «maison», l'épouse et la maternité dans la société médiévale. *Annales*, 99, 54, 1, p. 29-54.

8316. WATANABE (Koichi). Kinsei-Nihon no toshi to minshu: Jumin ketsugo to joretsu-ishiki, (Resident groups and rank-order: Consciousness in early modern Japanese towns). Tokyo, Yoshikawa Kobunkan, 99, 350 p.

8317. WATANABE (Takashi). Kinsei-sonraku no tokushitsu to tenkai. (Character and development in the early modern Japanese village). Tokyo, Azekura Shobo, 98, 292 p.

8318. YAMAGUCHI (Toru). Kinsei-gyomin no nariwai to seikatsu. (Work and life of the fishing people in early modern Japan). Tokyo, Yoshikawa Kobunkan, 99, 168 p.

8319. YAMAMOTO (Koji). Yoritomo no seishin-shi. (Images of Minamoto Yoritomo). Tokyo, Kodansha, 98, 254 p.

8320. YAMANAKA (Yutaka). Mido-kampaku-ki zen chushaku: Kanko 2 nen. (The complete commentaries on the diary of Fujiwara Michinaga: 1005 A.D.). Tokyo, Takashina Shoten, 99, 188 p.

Cf. n°s 1115, 4793-4803

§ 6. Korea.

8321. BUZO (Adrian). The guerilla dynasty: politics and leadership in North Korea. London, Tauris, 99, XI-323 p.

8322. Culture and the state in late Choson Korea. Ed. by JaHyun KIM HABOUSH and Martina DEUCHLER. Cambridge, Harvard University Asia Center, 99, X-304 p. (Harvard East Asian monographs, 182. The Harvard-Hallym series on Korean studies).

8323. Foreign affairs (The) and the north-south problem in 1960's. By Yoo BYONG-YONG [et al.]. Seoul, Baiksan-Seodang, 99, 266 p. (Rethinking modern Korean history, 11).

8324. HONG (Yong-pyo). State security and regime security: President Syngman Rhee and the insecurity dilemma in South Korea, 1953–1960. Basingstoke, Macmillan a. New York, St. Martin's Press, 99, 219 p. (St. Antony's series).

8325. Korean war (The) and the change of social structure. By Chung SUNG-HO [et al.]. Seoul, Baiksan-Seodang, 99, 308 p. (Rethinking modern Korean history, 7).

8326. NISHIKAWA (Takao). Chosen ocho kokishi kenkyu. (A study on the late period of Yi dynasty of Korea). Tokyo, Fubai Sha, 99, 369 p.

8327. SIMONS (Geoffrey Leslie). Korea: the search for sovereignty. Foreword by Tony BENN. Basingstoke, Macmillan, 99, XXI-313 p.

8328. Socio-political change (The) of Republic of Korea in the late 1970's. By Kim MYONG-SOB [et al.]. Seoul, Baiksan-Seodang, 99, 322 p. (Rethinking modern Korean history, 13).

8329. Study (The) of the 8 years of North Korea after the liberation. By Suh CHOO-SUK [et al.]. Seoul, Baiksan-Seodang, 99, 163 p. (Rethinking modern Korean history, 15).

Cf. n°s 1017, 7410

S

AFRICA
(To its colonization)

* 8330. WESTLEY (David). The Mfecane: an annotated bibliography. Madison, African Studies Program, University of Wisconsin-Madison, 99, V-60 p.

** 8331. Geste (La) de Nankoman: textes sur la fondation de Naréna (Mali). Ed. par Seydou CAMARA et Jan JANSEN. Leiden, CNWS, 99, 135 p.

** 8332. White slaves, African masters: an anthology of American barbary captivity narratives. Ed. and with an introduction by Paul BAEPLER. Chicago a. London, University of Chicago Press, 99, XIII-310 p.

8333. African diaspora (The): African origins and new world identities. Ed. by Isidore OKPEWHO, Carole BOYCE DAVIES and Ali A. MAZRUI. Bloomington: Indiana U. P., 99, XXVIII-566 p.

8334. ALLEN (Richard B.). Slaves, Freedmen, and Indentured Laborers in Colonial Mauritius. New York, Cambridge U. P., 99, XVII-221 p. (African studies series, 99).

8335. AUSTEN (Ralph A.), DERRICK (Jonathan). Middlemen of the Cameroons Rivers: the Duala and their hinterland, c. 1600–c. 1960. New York, Cambridge U. P., 99, XII-252 p. (African studies series, 96).

8336. BARNES (Teresa A.). "We women worked so hard": gender, urbanization, and social reproduction in colonial Harare, Zimbabwe, 1930–1956. Portsmouth, Heinemann, 99, XLV-204 p. (Social history of Africa).

8337. BAUM (Robert M.). Shrines of the slave trade: Diola Religion and society in precolonial Senegambia. New York, Oxford U. P., 99, XIII-287 p.

8338. BELCHER (Stephen). Epic Traditions of Africa. Bloomington, Indiana U. P., 99, XXII-276 p.

8339. BOELE VAN HENSBROEK (Pieter). Political discourses in African thought: 1860 to the present. Westport, Praeger, 99, VIII-238 p.

8340. Civilisation islamique (La) en Afrique de l'Ouest: communications du symposium international tenu les 27–30 décembre 1996, Dakar, Sénégal. Org. conjointement par le Centre de recherches sur l'histoire, l'art et la culture islamiques (IRCICA), l'Institut fondamental d'Afrique noire (IFAN); édité par Samba DIENG; préface par Ekmeleddin IHSANOĞLU. İstanbul, IRCICA, 99, XXIX-430 p. (Série d'histoire des nations musulmanes, 4).

8341. COQUERY-VIDROVITCH (Catherine). L'Afrique et les Africains au XIXe siècle: mutations, révolutions, crises. Paris, A. Colin, 99, 304 p. (Collection U. Série Histoire contemporaine).

8342. DE VRIES (Joris). Manasse Tjiseseta: chief of Omaruru 1884–1898, Namibia. Köln, R. Köppe Verlag, 99, 146 p. (History, cultural traditions and innovations in Southern Africa, 6).

8343. DOS SANTOS (Joao). Etiópia Oriental e vária história de cousas notáveis do Oriente. Introduçao de Manuel LOBATO; notas de Manuel LOBATO e Eduardo MEDEIROS; fixaçao do texto por Maria DO CARMO GUERREIRO VIEIRA, Célia NUNES CARVALHO, Maria Amélia RODRIGUES COELHO. Lisboa, Comissao Nacional para as Comemoraçoes dos Descobrimentos Portugueses, 99, 759 p. (Outras margens).

8344. DUARTE (José Bento). Senhores do sol e do vento: histórias verídicas de portugueses, angolanos e outros africanos. Lisboa, Editorial Estampa, 99, 314 p.

8345. GILLIS (D. Hugh). The Kingdom of Swaziland: studies in political history. Westport, Greenwood, 99, XV-204 p. (Contributions in comparative colonial studies, 37).

8346. HARDING (Leonhard). Geschichte Afrikas im 19. und 20. Jahrhundert. München, Oldenbourg, 99, XIV-272 p. (Oldenbourg Grundriß der Geschichte, 27).

8347. KRIGER (Colleen E.). Pride of men: ironworking in nineteenth-century West Central Africa. Portsmouth, Heinemann, 99, XIX-261 p. (Social history of Africa).

8348. KUSIMBA (Chapurukha M.). The rise and fall of Swahili states. Walnut Creek, London a. New Delhi, Alta Mira Press, 99, 236 p.

8349. LUNN (Joe). Memoirs of the Maelstrom: a Senegalese oral history of the First World War. Portsmouth, N. H. Heinemann, 99, XIV-264 p. (Social history of Africa).

8350. MACMILLAN (Hugh), SHAPIRO (Frank). Zion in Africa: the Jews of Zambia. London, I. B. Tauris, 99, IX-342 p.

8351. MILLER (Joseph C.). History and Africa / Africa and history. *American historical review*, 99, 104, 1, p. 1-32.

8352. NANTET (Bernard). Dictionnaire d'histoire et civilisations africaines. Paris, Larousse, 99, XII-228 p. (Les référents).

8353. RANGER (Terence). Voices from the rocks: nature, culture, and history in the Matopos Hills of Zimbabwe. Bloomington, Indiana U. P., 99, X-305 p.

8354. RITA-FERREIRA (António). African kingdoms and alien settlements in Central Mozambique: (c. 15th–17th cent.). Coimbra, Departamento de Antropologia, Universidade de Coimbra, 99, 172 p. (Publicaçoes do Centro de Estudos Africanos, 17).

8355. SANNEH (Lamin). Abolitionists abroad: American Blacks and the making of modern West Africa. Cambridge, Harvard U. P., 99, XV-291 p.

8356. Slavery and colonial rule in Africa. Ed. by Suzanne MIERS and Martin KLEIN. Portland a. London, Frank Cass, 99, X-296 p. (Studies in slave and post-slave societies and cultures).

8357. TANADA (Hirofumi). Ejiputo no toshi shakai. (The urban society in Egypt). Tokyo, Waseda University Press, 99, 240 p.

8358. THORNTON (John Kelly). Warfare in Atlantic Africa, 1500–1800. London, University College London Press, 99, 194 p. (Warfare and history).

8359. VILAR (Juan Bautista), VILAR (María José). La emigración española al Norte de Africa (1830–1999). Madrid, Arco/Libros, 99, 78 p. (Cuadernos de historia, 67).

8360. WALKER (Robin.). Classical splendour: roots of black history: a comprehensive guide to the ancient and medieval history of Africa. London, Bogle-L'Ouverture, 99, 167 p.

Cf. n°s 152, 7211, 7342-7364

T

AMERICA
(To its colonization)

---

* 8361. WOODWARD (Ralph Lee). Central America, a nation divided. New York a. Oxford, Oxford U. P., 99, XI-436 p. (Latin American histories).

** 8362. GARCÍA CAMPILLO (José Miguel). Estudio introductorio del léxico de las inscripciones de Chichén Itzá, Yucatán, México. Oxford, Archaeopress, 99, 179 p. (BAR international series, 831).

** 8363. LEÓN PORTILLA (Miguel). Fray Bernardino de Sahagún en Tlatelolco. México, Secretaría de Relaciones Exteriores, 99, 185 p.

** 8364. VARELA (Félix). Xicoténcatl: an anonymous historical novel about the events leading up to the conquest of the Aztec Empire. Translated by Guillermo I. CASTILLO-FELIÚ. Austin, University of Texas Press, 99, VIII-156 p. (Texas Pan American series).

8365. ALMEIDA (Ileana). Historia del pueblo kechua. Quito, Abrapalabra Editores, 99, 381 p.

8366. Amérique (L') du Sud: des chasseurs-cueilleurs à l'Empire Inca: actes des journées d'étude d'archéologie précolombienne, Genève, 10–11 octobre 1997. Oxford, Archaeopress, 99, 138 p. (BAR international series, 746).

8367. Ancient civilizations (The) of Mesoamerica: a reader. Ed. by Michael E. SMITH and Marilyn A. MASSON. Oxford, Blackwell, 99, XV-497 p.

8368. ARNOLD (Philip P.). Eating landscape: Aztec and European occupation of Tlalocan. Niwot, University Press of Colorado, 99, 287 p.

8369. BRILL DE RAMÍREZ (Susan Berry). Contemporary American Indian literatures & the oral tradition. Tucson, University of Arizona Press, 99, X-259 p.

8370. CARRASCO PIZANA (Pedro). The Tenochca Empire of ancient Mexico: the triple alliance of Tenochtitlan, Tetzcoco, and Tlacopan. Norman, University of Oklahoma Press, 99, XVIII-542 p. (The civilization of the American Indian series, 234).

8371. HARRISON (Peter D.). The lords of Tikal: rulers of an ancient Maya city. London, Thames & Hudson, 99, 208 p. (New aspects of antiquity).

8372. HILTUNEN (Juha). Ancient kings of Peru. The reliability of the Chronicle of Fernando de Montesinos. Helsinki, SHS, 99, 511 p. (Bibliotheca historica, 45) (ill., maps).

8373. Historiadores de Indias. Varios autores; estudios preliminar de Germán ARCINIEGAS. Barcelona, Oceano, 99, XXI-441p. (Biblioteca universal).

8374. IBARRA ROJAS (Eugenia). Las manchas del jaguar: huellas indígenas en la historia de Costa Rica (Valle Central siglos XVI–XX). San José, Editorial de la Universidad de Costa Rica, 99, 135 p. (ill., maps).

8375. LAITINEN (Riitta). Lived Land. Identification with places in Navajo society 1800–1930. Turku, author, 99, 270 p. (ill., maps).

8376. LANE (Kris E.). Blood and silver: a history of piracy in the Caribbean and Central Americas. Foreword by Hugh O'SHAUGHNESSY. Oxford, Signal, 99, XX-230 p.

8377. Mayas (The) of the classical period. Por A. Arellano HERNANDEZ [et al.]; editorial advisor, Davide DOMENICI. Milano, Editoriale Jaca Book, 99, 256 p.

8378. Mesoamerica's classic heritage: from Teotihuacan to the Aztecs. Ed. by David CARRASCO, Lindsay JONES and Scott SESSIONS. Boulder, University Press of Colorado, 99, XV-559 p.

8379. NORDENSKIÖLD (Erland). The cultural history of the South American Indians. Edited, and with an introduction by Christer LINDBERG. New York, AMS Press, 99, XXV-223 p. (AMS studies in cultural history, 4).

8380. SAUNT (Claudio). A new order of things: property, power, and the transformation of the Creek Indians, 1733–1816. New York, Cambridge U. P., 99, XIV-298 p. (Cambridge studies in North American history).

8381. SOMEDA (Hidefuji). El imperio de los Incas: imagen del tahuantinsuyu creada por los cronistas. Lima, Pontificia Universidad Católica del Perú, Fondo Editorial, 99, 327 p.

8382. TAYLOR (Gérald). Ritos y tradiciones de huarochirí. Lima, Instituto Francés de Estudios Andinos, Banco Central de Reserva del Perú, Universidad Particular Ricardo Palma, 99, XXXIV-502 p. (Travaux de l'Institut français d'études andines, 116).

8383. VALDÉS (Juan Antonio), FAHSEN (Federico), ESCOBEDO (Héctor L.). Reyes, tumbas y palacios: la historia dinástica de Uaxactun. México, Universidad Nacional Autónoma de México y Guatemala City, Instituto de Antropología e Historia de Guatemala, 99, 123 p. (Cuaderno, 25).

8384. WERTHEIMER (Eric). Imagined empires: Incas, Aztecs, and the New World of American literature, 1771–1876. Cambridge, Cambridge U. P., 99, XII-243 p. (Cambridge studies in American literature and culture, 121).

8385. WHITING (Tomas). Los Mayas. México, Conaculta-INAH, 99, 253 p.

8386. ZUÑIGA (Jean-Paul). La voix du sang. Du métis à l'idée de métissage en Amérique espagnole. *Annales*, 99, 54, 2, p. 425-452.

Cf. n°s 7365-7382

U

OCEANIA
(To its colonization)

** 8387. Journals (The) of Captain Cook. Prepared from the original manuscripts by J. C. BEAGLEHOLE for the Hakluyt Society, 1955–1967; selected and edited by Philip EDWARDS. London, Penguin, 99, XIV-646 p. (Penguin classics).

** 8388. Pacific images: views from Captain Cook's third voyage. Engravings and descriptions from 'A voyage to the Pacific Ocean', volumes 1, 2, and 3, and the Atlas by Captain James Cook and Captain James King, published as the official edition of the Lords Commissioners of the Admirality, in London, 1784. Ed. by Eleanor C. NORDYKE; in collaboration with James A. MATTISON. Honolulu, Hawaiian Historical Society, 99, XXVI-174 p.

8389. Anthropology and colonialism in Asia and Oceania. Ed. by Jan VAN BREMEN and Akitoshoi SHIMIZU. Richmond, Curzon Press, 99, XI-409 p. (Anthropology of Asia series).

8391. BAERT (Annie). Le paradis terrestre, un mythe espagnol en Océanie: les voyages de Mendana et de Quirós, 1567–1606. Préface de Christian HUERTZ DE LEMPS. Paris, L'Harmattan, 99, IV-351 p. (Mondes océaniens).

8392. FLOOD (Josephine). Archaeology of the dreamtime: the story of prehistoric Australia and its people. Sydney, Angus & Robertson, 99, 328 p.

8393. MULVANEY (John), KAMMINGA (Johan). Prehistory of Australia. Washington a. London, Smithsonian Institution Press, 99, XX-480 p.

Cf. n°s 7383-7386

INDEX OF NAMES

A

AALBÆCK-NIELSEN (Kai), 3437.
ABAD (R.), 5359.
ABAD PEREZ (Antolín), 5444.
ABADI (Jacob), 7827.
ABBAMONDI (Carla), 7108.
ABBATE (Janet), 1196.
ABBOTT (Christopher), 3858.
Abdal Musa, 5161.
ABE (Yasunari), 588.
ABED-KOTOB (Sana), 4278.
ABEILLE (Renato), 6688.
Abelardus, Petrus, 3193.
ABELLÁN PÉREZ (Juan), 256.
ABELSHAUSER (Werner), 7687.
ABERDAM (Serge), 4385.
ABÓS (Álvaro), 4040.
ABOU DAOUD, 4897.
Abraham ben Azriel (XIII c.), 3276.
Abraham, 2846.
ABRAHAM, EREWANTS`I, 7422.
ABRAMS (Stan), 7959.
ABRAMSON (Henry), 5180.
ABRANTES (M. Luísa Cunha Meneses), 8097.
Absalon, Archbishop of Lund, 193.
'Abu 'al-Faraj 'al-'Isbahani, 3298.
ABUKHANFUSA (Kerstin), 7443.
ABULAFIA (David), 3206.
Abulkhair, Khan, 4807.
ACCARIE (M.), 638.
ACEVES PASTRANA (Patricia Elena), 6154.
Achilleus, Sanctus, 2767.
ACKOSKA (Violeta), 7989.
ACQUAVIVA (Claudio), 5431.
Acquaviva (Giangirolamo), duca di Atri, 4743.
ÁCS (Gábor), 5544.

ACUN (Fatma), 930.
ACUN (Hakkı), 1273.
ÁDÁM (Magda), 7547, 7567, 7625.
ADAM (Thomas), 7038.
ADAMO (G.), 5978.
ADAMO (Pietro), 4526, 5262.
ADAMS (Alison), 204.
ADAMS (J. N.), 2586, 2590.
ADAMS (Stephen B.), 6036.
ADAMS (Willi Paul), 5184.
ADAMS MAC CORD (Marilyn), 3715.
Adejumobi (Said), 4883.
Adelaida, 5042.
ADELMAN (Howard), 7957.
ADELMAN (Jeremy), 3925, 4041, 7372.
ADEMAR DE CHABANNES, 3162.
Adenauer (Konrad), 7842, 8029.
ADINOLFI (Pierangela), 6293.
ADKIN (Neil), 2849-2851.
ADORNI (Daniela), 4703.
ADORNO (Rolena), 306.
ADREADIS (Y.), 3028.
ADSHEAD (Samuel Adrian Miles), 5891.
Aelfric (Abbot of Eynsham), 280, 3876.
Aelred de Rievaulx, Saint, 3742.
Aeschines, 1898.
Aeschylus, 1877, 2087, 2099, 2118.
Aesopus, 2924.
AFIGENOV (D.), 2996.
AGAMBEN (Giorgio), 4758.
AGAPITOS (Panagiotis A.), 2973, 2997.
Agathias, 3038.
AGLAN (Alya), 7773.
Agnoletto (Attilio), 1380.
AGO (Renata), 1133.

AGOSTI (Aldo), 3926.
ÅGREN (Henrik), 5803.
AGRIMI (Mario), 5953.
Agrippina, 2530.
AGUINAGA (Hélio), 307.
AGUIRRE BELTRÁN (Cristina), 5432.
AHLBÄCK (Tore), 1306.
AHMED (Feroz), 4894.
AIBABIN (A. I.), 885.
AICHHOLZER (Doris), 3522.
AIMAR (Thierry), 6671.
AIRD (Catherine), 1438.
AISENBERG (Andrew R.), 6861.
AJELLO (Raffaele), 1111.
AJMERMAKHER (Karl), 621.
AKA (İsmail), 5159.
AKASAKA (Shunichi), 3358.
AKINBODE (Rahmon O.), *XI*.
AKINTERINWA (Bola A.), 7829.
AKKERMAN (Fokke), 5679.
AKTAN (Ali), 3765.
AKTUĞ-KOLAY (İlknur), 3640.
ALAMEDA OSPINA (Raúl), 4187.
ALANÍS ENCISO (Fernando Saúl), 4822.
AL-ATRASH (Ahmed Ali Salem), 7830.
ALBANESE (Francesco), 785.
Albani (Francesco), 6400.
ALBANO (Lucilla), 6514.
ALBERIGO (Giuseppe), 5339, 5360.
ALBERRO (Solange), 375.
ALBERT (Bat-Sheva), 3859.
ALBERT (Marcel), 5323.
ALBERT (Peter J.), 5211.
Alberti (Leon Battista), 3660, 6229, 6425.
Albertus Magnus, Sanctus, 3698.
ALBES (Andreas), 4399.
ALBORNOZ DE LOPEZ (Teresa), 170.

---

1. The Slavonic and in particular the Russian names are given in their national form translitterated following the usual methods and are classified accordingly. Characters with diacritics, for instance ć, ś, č, š are considered as if ordinary c, s. the German modified vowels ä, ö, ø, ü are considered as if a, o, u. The names of Classical authors, Saints and Popes are indexed in their Latin form. Authors' names are given in capital letters.

ALBRECHT (Clemens), 5570.
ALBRECHT (M. von), 2680.
ALBRECHT (Thomas), 4400.
Alcaeus, 1878.
Alcibiades, 1971, 1985, 2007, 2253.
Alcimus Avitus, 2827.
Alcmaeon, 1980.
Alcmanes, 1879.
ALCOLEA (J. J.), 1488.
ALCOLOUMBRE (Thierry), 3269.
Alcuinus, 3874.
ALDCROFT (Derek), 6783.
ALDRETE (Gregory S.), 2394.
ALDRICH (Richard J.), 7999.
ALEKSEEV (A. N.), 238.
ALEKSEEV (Anatolij A.), 3523.
ALEMANY (Rafael), 3526.
ALENIUS (Kari), 4282.
ALEOTTI (Paolo), 6515.
Alessandro VI (Rodrigo Borgia), 6477.
ALESSANDRONE PERONA (Ersilia), 411.
ALESSIO (Franco), 997.
ALEXANDER (Martin S.), 4333.
ALEXANDER (Robert Jackson), 5074.
Alexander Aetolus, 1880.
Alexander I, Karadjordjević, king of Yugoslavia, 7605.
Alexander Nevskiy , 278.
Alexandr I, emperor of Russia, 4999.
Alexandros III ho Megas, re di Macedonia, 714, 1801, 1970, 1974, 1977, 2022, 2096, 2114, 2127, 2167.
Alfaro (Eloy), 4276.
Alfieri (Vittorio), 6244.
ALFÖLDI (Maria), 237.
ALFÖLDY (Géza), 931, 2308.
ALFONSO FERNANDEZ DE PALENCIA, 3163.
Alfonso V el Magnànimo, rey de Aragona, 3153.
ALFONSO X EL SABIO, rey de Castilla y de León, 3161, 3341, 3605.
ALFONSO-GOLDFARB (Ana Maria), 3697.
Alfred, king of England, 3229, 3355.
ALI (Daud), 8084.
ALI (S. Mahmud), 7831.
Ali Paşa (Tepedelenli), 7461.
ALIBERTI (Giovanni), 710, 7110.
al-Idrisi, 349.
Alighieri (Dante) v. Dante Alighieri.
AL-JUMAILY (Qassam Kh), 4650.

ALLAIN (Jean-Claude), 7213.
ALLAN (Pierre), 7832.
ALLAN (Seán), 6539.
ALLAND (D.), 7190.
ALLEN (J.-C.), 7277.
ALLEN (Michael J. B.), 6125.
ALLEN (Michael Thad), 7688.
ALLEN (Richard B.), 8334.
ALLEN (Robert C.), 6757.
ALLEN (S. H.), 1835.
Allenby (Edmund Henry Hynman, 1st Viscount), 7581.
Allende Gossens (Salvador), 4177.
ALLINSON (Mark), 4401.
ALLISON (J.), 2681.
ALLMAN (Jean), 5445.
ALMEIDA (Ileana), 8365.
ALMOND (Philip C.), 5572.
ALONSO MATHIAS (F.), 1505.
ALONSO TRONCOSO (V.), 1969.
ALPARSLAN (Ali), 1198.
ALRAM (Michael), 240.
ALTAMIRANO (Carlos), 4042.
ALTENBAUGH (Richard J.), 1237.
ALTER (Peter), 5545.
ALTER (Stephen G.), 5573.
ALTERMATT (Urs), 5361.
ALTHAUS (Horst), 5892.
ALTISAPAN (Erol), 3641.
ALTRICHTER (Helmut), 1051.
ALTURO I PERUCHO (Jesús), 4.
ALVAR (Carlos), 3532.
ALVAREZ ALVAREZ (César), 45.
ÁLVAREZ BORGE (Ignacio), 3359.
ALVAREZ CASADO (Ana Isabel), 1270.
ALVAREZ MÁRQUEZ (María del Carmen), 31.
ALVAREZ PALENZUELA (Vicente A.), 3114.
ALVAZZI DEL FRATE (Paolo), 7145.
ALVERED (Zeth), 3100, 3357.
ALVES FILHO (Ivan), 4112.
AMADASI GUZZO (M. G.), 1756.
Amadeo I, rey de España, 5077, 5102.
Amalarius (Archbishop of Lyon), 3757.
AMANN (P.), 790.
AMANN (Wilhelm), 5574.
AMANO (Masatoshi), 6701.
Amanullah Khan, Amir of Afghanistan, 4016.
AMARASINGHE (Y. Ranjith), 5120.
AMATO (E.), 2998.
AMATO (Eugenio), 2682.
AMBROSINI (Federica), 5469.
Ambrosius, Sanctus, 2895.
Amendola (Giovanni), 4745.
AMER (A. A. M. A.), 1611.
AMER (Sahar), 3599.

AMES (G. J.), 7323.
AMIET (P.), 1663.
AMIGÓ I ANGLÈS (Ramon), 257.
AMINEH (Mehdi Parvizi), 6672.
AMINI (Iradj), 7457.
AMMERMANN (A. J.), 1484.
Ammianus Marcellinus, 2334-2337, 2456, 2459, 2796, 2803, 2805, 2809, 2810.
AMOROS (Andrés), 1426.
AMOS (Heike), 7833.
AMOS (Scott), 5777.
AMOURETTI (M. C.), 1815.
AMPARO ALDECOA QUINTANA (M.), 1489.
AMYOT (Éric), 4160.
AN (Jingbo), 8103.
ANAN'ICH (Boris V.), 4991.
ANANIA (Francesca), 6516.
ANASTASIADIS (Vasilis I.), 2395.
ANASTASSIOU (A.), 1915.
Anaxagoras, 2146.
Anaximenes, 2092.
ANDENNA (Giancarlo), 3823.
ANDERSEN (Peter B.), 1329.
ANDERSON (Alison D.), 7402.
ANDERSON (Kirill M.), 1186.
ANDERSON (Olive), 6862.
ANDERSON (Robin L.), 7367.
ANDERSON (S.), 1725.
ANDERSON (Truman), 7774.
ANDERSSON PALM (Lennart), 3210.
ANDERSSON-SKOG (Lena), 6703.
ANDO (Satoshi), 4793.
Andreas I, Hungarian king, 3061.
ANDREATTA (Alberto), 1091.
ANDREAU (Jean), 2527.
ANDREESCU (Mihail M.), 3246.
ANDREN (Åke), 5518.
ANDREOLLI (Bruno), 3334.
ANDREOSE (Alvise), 3178.
ANDRÉS GALLEGO (José), 5265.
ANDRES UCENDO (José Ignacio), 6784.
ANDREUSSI (M.), 2216.
ANDREW (Christopher), 4535, 7834.
ANDREWS (Frances), 3860.
ANDREWS (Malcolm), 6382.
ANDREWS (Peter A.), 1199.
ANDRIVET (Patrick), 806.
Andronicus Callistus, 3031.
ANDROUDIS (P.), 209.
ANDRUKH (Svetlana I.), 1542.
ANDRZEJEWSKI (Marek), 5832.
ANES (Ponzalo), 6644.
ANGEL (Jacques), 4297.
Angela di Foligno, 3861.
ANGELELLI (C.), 2260.
ANGELICI (Giovanna), 7039.

ANGELOPOULOS (Athanasios A.), 258.
ANGELOZZI (Giancarlo), 1019.
ANGIOLILLO (S.), 2217.
ANGIOLINI (Enrico), 3152.
ANGLIVIEL DE LA BEAUMELLE (Laurent), 2335.
ANGREMY (Annie), 41.
Anhalt (Christian von), 779.
ANHEIM (Etienne), 822.
ANISIMOV (Evgenij V.), 4992.
ANKERSMIT (Frank R.), 807.
ANNA (Susanne), 6497.
Anna Paleologina, Byzantine empress, 3017.
ANNIBALDI (Cesare), 6689.
Anonymus Iamblichi, 1927.
ANSARI (Shahabuddin), 143.
ANSTEY (Peter), 5893.
ANTES (Peter), 1332.
ANTIN (Kirsti), *IV*.
Antioche de Syrie, 245.
Antiochus III, king of Syria, 1595.
ANTOHI (Mona), 4984.
ANTOINE (Charles), 5362.
Antoine duc de Brabant, 3250.
ANTOLINI (Bianca Maria), 6588.
ANTON MARTINEZ (Beatriz), 1052.
Antonius, Sanctus, 400.
ANTONMATTEI (Pierre), 4299.
ANTONOPOULOS (Elias A.), 7217.
ANTONOPOULOS (P.), 2977.
Anullinus (proconsul), 2913.
ANZULEWICZ (Henryk), 3698.
AO (Wenwei), 8104.
AOKI (Michio), 8273.
AOKI (Yasushi), 4527.
AOYAMA (Yoshinobu), 3188.
Apollodorus (Carysteus), 2634.
Apollonius Dyscolus, 1881.
Apollonius Pergaeus, 1882.
Apollonius Rhodius, 2122.
APOSTOLOVA MARŠAVELSKI (Magdalena), 3343.
APPEL (Fredrick), 5895.
APPEL (Hans Henrik), 7146.
APPELBAUM (Nancy), 4183.
APPELLÁNÍZ (J. M.), 1491.
Appius Claudius Caecus, 2499.
APPLEGATE (Celia), 3927.
APRILE (Sylvie), 4300.
APTER (Ronnie), 3533.
Apuleius, 2615, 2640, 2658, 2689, 2710.
ARATA (L.), 2118.
ARBEITER (Achim), 3665.
ARBITRIO (Francesco), 5856.
ARBOIT (Gérald), 7626.
ARCA PETRUCCI (Marcella), 339.
ARCE (J.), 2692.
Archaestratus, 2113.

ARCHER (Lucy), 3634.
Archinus, Athenian politician, 2013.
ARCIDIACONO (Bruno), 7689.
ARCINIEGAS (Germán), 8373.
ARDAILLOU (Pierre), 4301.
ARENA (Richard), 6673.
Arendt (Hannah), 5996.
ARETINI (Paola), 2588.
ARGATSKI (Velin Asenov), 933.
ARIAS (José Carlos), 6785.
ARICO (José), 7040.
Ariès (Philippe), 692.
ARIEW (Roger), 5896.
Aristophanes, 1883-1890, 1935, 2036, 2087, 2089, 2105, 2121.
Aristoteles, 430, 1093, 1927, 2045, 2148, 2172, 2173, 3716, 3752.
ARLETTAZ (Gérald), 6863.
ARMANI (Barbara), 5529.
Armburgh (Joan), 3102.
Armburgh (Robert), 3102.
ARMIERO (Marco), 1146.
ARMINJON (Catherine), 6508.
ARMITAGE (David), 3928.
ARMOGATHE (Jean-Robert), 5905.
ARMONY (Ariel C.), 7835.
ARNAL (William E.), 1307.
ARNALDI (Girolamo), 935.
ARNALL (M. Josepa), 3146.
Arnauld (Antoine), 5934.
ARNEŽ (Janez A.), 5058.
Arnim (Achim von), 5703.
Arnobius, 2828.
ARNOLD (Guy), 936.
ARNOLD (M.), 5462.
ARNOLD (Matthieu), 5466.
ARNOLD (Philip P.), 8368.
ARNOT (Madeleine), 5764.
ARNU (Titus), 84.
ARON (Cindy S.), 1200.
ARON (Stephen), 3925.
ARONEN (J.), 2589.
ARORA (Ranjana), 7816, 7955.
ARRAYA (Lucia), 7209.
Arrianus, 1891, 1892, 1901, 2114.
ARRIGONI (G.), 2179.
ARRIVO (Giorgia), 692.
ARRIZABALAGA (Jon), 6932.
Arsaces I, king of the Parthians, 2796.
ARSEN'EV (Aleksej B.), 5242.
ARSLAN (Mehmet), 5578.
ARTEAGA CARVAJAL (Jaime), 4185.
ARTEAGA HERNÁNDEZ (Manuel), 4185.
ARTEM'EVA (Tat'iana Vladimirovna), 5721.
ARTIFONI (Enrico), 1080.
ARTIZOV (Andrej V.), 5566.

ARTOLA GALLEGO (Miguel), 1112.
ARVASTSON (Gösta), 5644.
ARWEILER (A.), 2827.
ARZALIER (Francis), 4819.
ASAKURA (Yuko), 8274.
ASCALONE (E.), 1562.
ASCH (R. G.), 3929.
ASCHERI (Mario), 1113, 1133, 3154.
ASCHMANN (Birgit), 7836.
Asclepiades Bithynicus, 1893.
Asclepiades Samius, 1894.
ASENJO GONZÁLEZ (Maria), 3362.
ASFOUR (Amal), 6038.
ASH (Rh.), 2374.
ASH (Timothy Garton), 4931.
ASHBY (C.), 2078.
ASHERI (David), 636, 1093.
ASHERI (Maia), 1104.
ASHLEY (J. R.), 1970.
ASHLEY (Kathleen M.), 3834.
ASHTON (N.), 1492.
ASHTON (Owen R.), 4533.
ASHTON (S. R.), 7365.
ASIMOV (M. S.), 8055.
Ašnakkum, king of Mari, 1690.
ASPERTI (Stefano), 3532.
Assadourian (Carlos Sempat), 6639.
ASSAYAG (Jackie), 647.
ASSIS YOM (Tov), 3270.
ASSMANN (Aleida), 490.
ASSMANN (Jan), 491, 808, 1384.
ASTARITA (Tommaso), 6864.
ASTELL (Ann W.), 3525.
ASTINGTON (John H.), 6518.
ASTUTO (Giuseppe), 4707.
Atatürk v. Kemal (Mustafa 'Atatürk).
ATHANASSIADI (P.), 2814, 2960.
ATHANASSOPOLOU (Ekavi), 7837.
ATHENS (J. S.), 1485.
ATIF (Mehmed), 5159.
Atticus, 2344, 2432.
Attlee (Clement Richard), 4524.
ATTWOOD (Lynne), 5833.
AUB (Max), 6212.
AUBERT (Alberto), 937, 5346.
Aubert (David), 66.
AUBERT (J.-J.), 2474.
AUBRIOT (D.), 2079.
AUDERHEIDE (A. C.), , 1612.
AUDISIO (G), 5470.
AUERBACH (Jeffrey A.), 452.
AUERBACH (Thomas), 4402.
AUGÉ (Ch.), 1781.
AUGÉ (Marc), 1315.
AUGUSTEIJN (Joost), 4671.
Augustinus (Aurelius), Sanctus, 1407, 2829-2843.

Augustus (C. Iulius Caesar Octavianus), Roman emperor, 1860, 2365, 2408, 2435, 2442, 2517, 2526, 2572, 2694, 2714, 2747, 2777.
AUGUSTYNIAK (Urszula), 4932.
AUHAGEN (Ulrike), 2591.
AULT (B. A.), 2027.
Aurelianus (L. Domitius), Roman emperor, 2468.
AURENCHE (O.), 1514.
Ausonius (Decimus Magnus), 2609.
Austen (Jane), 6375.
AUSTEN (Ralph A.), 1441, 8335.
AUSTIN (C.), 1897.
AUTRAND (Françoise), 3222.
AUZA (Néstor Tomás), 5834.
AVALOS (Hector), 2868.
AVANZINI (Alessandra), 636.
AVARUCCI (Giuseppe), 117.
AVENDANO PAVEZ (Octavio), 4177.
AVGUŠTIN (Cene), 1147.
AVRAM (Alexandru), 2475.
AVRAM (Cezar), 1148.
AYALA (César J.), 6758.
AYALA MORA (Enrique), 7838.
AYALON (David), 3293.
AYDIN (Mustafa), 7218.
AYLLÓN (Fernando), 5363.
AYLMER (G. E.), 7342.
AYMES (Elisabeth), 3792.
AYNSLEY (Jeremy), 609.
AZARI (Shahla), 4655.
AZARPAY (G.), 1782.
Azef (Evno), 5001.
AZHAND (Ya`qub), 4654.
AZIZ (F.), 1500.

B

BABAZADAH (Shahla), 95.
BABBI (Anna-Maria), 1437.
BABELON (Jean-Pierre), 6409.
BABIČKA (Vácslav), 4214.
BABIS (Maria), 4933.
BABIUCH (Jolanta), 5414.
Bacchylides, 1872, 2086.
Bach (Johann Sebastian), 1278.
BACHMANN (Manuel), 6039.
Bachofen (Johann Jakob), 693, 850.
BACHRACH (B. S.), 2999.
BACKE-FORSBERG (Y.), 2287.
BÄCKLUND (Dan), 6636.
BACKMAN (Göran), 7463.
BACZKO (Bronislaw), 492.
BADEL (Laurence), 6730.
BADER (F.), 1783.
BADER (Karl S.), 7068.

BADINTER (Elisabeth), 5579.
BADONEY MARTÍN (Beatriz), 7427.
BADSTÜBNER (Rolf), 4403.
BADURINA (A.), 1213.
BAENA DEL ALCÁZAR (Mariano), 5075.
BAEPLER (Paul), 8332.
BAERT (Annie), 8390.
BAGBY (Wesley M.), 7219.
BAGHDIANTZ MAC CABE (Ina), 6731.
BAGLIVI (Giorgio), 6033.
BAGNASCO GIANNI (Giovanna), 1850, 2280.
BAGNATO (Bruna), 7343, 7839.
BAGNOLI (Paolo), 1054, 1091.
BAHAR (Alexander), 4488.
BAHAR (H.), 1543.
BAHLCKE (Joachim), 5291.
BÄHLER (Ursula), 764.
BAHNERS (Patrick), 684.
BAHOVEC (Tina), 1014, 7548.
BÄHR (Johannes), 6637, 6786.
BAIER (Horst), 802.
BAIER (Thomas), 2363.
BAIGES (Ignasi J.), 3146.
BAILEY (C. R.), 4302.
BAILEY (D. M.), 1613.
BAILEY (Gauvin), 6383.
BAILEY (Matthew), 3509.
BAILY (Samuel L.), 6865.
BAINES (Dudley), 7041.
BAINES (J.), 1614.
BAJOU (Valérie), 6444.
Bak (János M.), 3470.
BAKER (John Hamilton), 1114.
BAKKE (Elisabeth), 5034.
BAKKER (J. A.), 1447.
BAKKER (Jan Theo), 2763.
BAKOS (Miklós), 243.
BAKSHI (Gagan Deep), 4010.
BALBI DE CARO (Silvana), 219.
BALDAROTTA (Donatella), 2261.
Baldassarre da Belgioioso, 6630.
BALDERSTON (Daniel), 1420.
BALDI (Marialuisa), 6081.
BALDINI (Artemio Enzo), 1091, 1096, 5471.
BALDISSIN MOLLI (Giovanna), 69.
BALDO CEOLIN (Massimilla), 6040.
BALDONI (D.), 2219.
BALDWIN (John W.), 3364.
BALDWIN (Peter), 6041.
BALDWIN BOWSKY (M. W.), 2528.
BALFOUR (Sebastian), 7294.
BALL (Stuart), 4524.
BALL (W), 2396.
BALLE (Søren), 6793.
BALMES (François), 5898.
BALOGH (Margit), 5267.

BALSAMO (Luigi), 94.
BALTZER (Klaus), 2866.
BALUEV (Boris P.), 493.
BĂLUȚĂ (Cloșca L.), 2324.
Balzac (Honoré de), 446, 6348.
BALZER (Marjorie Mandelstam), 887.
BAMBACH (Carmen C.), 6445.
BAMFORD (Kenton), 6519.
BANAJI (J.)., 3000.
BANCHOFF (Thomas), 7841.
BANDELLI (G.), 2529.
BANGE (Oliver), 7842.
BANOU (E.), 1836.
BÄR (Jochen), 5899.
BAR (Virginie), 377.
Bar Kokhba, 1752.
BARAHONA (Marvin), 4599.
BÁRÁNDI (Gergely), 4708.
BARANGER (Denis), 4528.
BARASH (Carol), 6100.
BARBAGALLO (Francesco), 709, 4709.
Barbarigo (Gregorio), 5479.
BARBE (Jean-Paul), 5641.
BARBELLION (frère Stéphane-Marie), 3717.
BARBER (James), 5068.
BARBERIS (Corrado), 6759.
BARBERIS (Mauro), 1055.
BARBERIS (Peter), 4665.
BARBICHE (Bernard), 4303.
BARBIER (Frédéric), 427.
BARBIERI (Alvaro), 3178.
BARBIERI (Gabriella), 2281, 2288.
BARBINI (Palmira Maria), 3894.
BARCELÓ (P.), 2877.
BARCHIESI (Alessandro), 2357.
BARCK (Simone), 5864.
BARD (Christine), 6996.
BARDET (J. P.), 6840.
BARDILL (Jonathan), 2729, 3001.
BARDINI (Marco), 6294.
BARDOUT (Jean-Christophe), 5900.
BARDSLEY (Sandy), 3365.
BAREKET (Elinoar), 3271.
BARIÈ (Ottavio), 7220.
BARIÉTY (Jacques), 7549, 7566, 7804, 7805, 7806.
BARIL (Agnès), 3527.
BARIŞTA (Orçun), 6490.
BARITONO (Raffaella), 1091.
BARKAI (Avraham), 7741.
BARKER (Hannah), 5835.
BARKMANN (Udo B.), 4849.
BARKUN (Gennadii Ivanovich), 7772.
BARLES (Sabine), 6042.
BARLOW (Frank), 3506.
BARMAN (Roderick J.), 4113.
BARMANN (L.), 654.

INDEX OF NAMES 345

BARMON (Pascale), 3184.
BARNES (Teresa A.), 8336.
BARNOVSKÝ (Michal), 5035, 5051.
BARONE (Giulia), 3861.
Baronio (Cesare), 694.
Barozzi da Vignola (Jacopo), 6421.
BARRAN (José Pedro), 5226.
BARRAQUE (Jean Pierre), 3335, 3395, 3718.
BARREIRO MARTÍNEZ (D.), 1448.
Barrès (Maurice), 174.
BARRETO DE SOUZA (Adriana), 4114.
BARRETT (Anthony A.), 2530.
BARRETT (Thomas M.), 7221.
BARRINGER (Tim), 6455.
BARRINGTON (Linda), 355.
BARRON (W. R. J.), 3528.
BARROSO BERMEJO (R.), 1488, 1489, 1515.
BARROW (Geoffrey W. S.), 3110.
BARROWMAN (Rachel), 5722.
BARRY (Brian), 509.
BARSBY (J.), 2384.
BÁRTA (M.), 1615.
BARTEČEK (Ivo), 4215.
BARTEL (Gabriele), 4476.
BARTELS (Claudia), 5830.
BARTH (Boris), 6651, 6866.
BARTH (Erwin), 4404.
BARTHÉLEMY (Dominique), 3190.
Barthou (Louis), 4329, 7605.
BARTMAN (E.), 2730.
BARTOCCI (Enzo), 4710.
Bartók (Béla), 6574.
BARTOLI (Roberta), 6446.
Bartolini (Riccardo), 336.
BARTOLOME DE LAS CASAS, 5258.
BARTON (R. N. E.), 1486.
BARTOSZEWICZ (Henryk), 7843.
BARUA (Chanda), 7844.
BARVÍKOVÁ (Hana), 5719.
Basagorti (Antonio), 6807.
BASAÑEZ VILALLUENCA (Maria Blanca), 3105.
BASCAPÈ (Giacomo Carlo), 212.
Basch (Franz Anton), 7624.
BASCH (L.), 2220.
BASDEVANT-GAUDEMET (Brigitte), 5300.
BASENKO (Ju. V.), 7476.
Basile (Giambattista), 6245.
Basilius I Macedonicus, Byzantine emperor, 3058, 3080.
Basilius II, Byzantine emperor, 3024.
BASILOTTA (Nicoletta), 5430.
BASINI (Gian Luigi), 1149.
Baškin (Matvej), 5531.
BASSANI (M. L.), 2727.

BASSIN (Mark), 308.
Basso (Lelio), 7105.
BASTIDE (David), 7081.
BASTYN (Vladimir), 809.
BASU (Aparna), 6939.
BASU (Jyoti), 4620.
Bataille (Georges), 1337.
BATAKOVIC (Dušan), 5244.
BATALLA I GALIMANY (Ramon), 5076.
BÁTHORY (Ludovic), 4967.
BÁTONYI (Gábor), 7550.
BATSCH (C.), 2215.
BATTILOSSI (Stefano), 1188.
BATTISTA (Anna), 5580.
BAUBÉROT (J.), 5280.
BAUD (Michel), 172.
Baudelaire (Charles), 6362.
Baudouin (Jean), 377.
Baudrillard (Jean), 6569.
BAUDRY (G. H.), 1338.
BAUER (F. A.), 2731.
BAUER (Johannes B.), 2871.
BAUER (Volker), 142.
BAUERSCHMIDT (Frederick Christian), 3862.
BAUM (Robert M.), 8337.
BAUMAN (R. A.), 2476.
BAUMEL (Jacques), 7775.
BAUMGART (Winfried), 7484.
BAUMGARTE (Susanne), 3182.
Baumgarten (Alexander Gottlieb), 5978.
BAUMGARTNER (Emannuelle), 3529.
BAUSENHART (Guido), 2878.
BAXANDALL (Michael), 3680.
BAXMANN (Dorothee), 810.
BAXTER (M. J.), 2737.
BAYANI (Manijeh), 96.
BAYAT (Ali Haydar), 6043.
BAYER (Bernard), 7147.
BAYER (Waltraud), 453.
BAYLE (Pierre), 695, 5887, 5994.
BAYLISS (A.), 1549.
BAYLY (Susan), 4623.
BAZELMANS (Jos), 3530.
BAZZANA (André), 3360, 3369.
BAZZOLI (M.), 1093.
BEACHAM (R. C.), 2531.
BEAGLEHOLE (J. C.), 8387.
BEAL (R.), 1664.
BEALE (G. K.), 2879.
BEALE (Marjorie A.), 5581.
BEALEY (Frank), 1056.
BEARD (M.), 2532.
Beato Angelico (Fra Giovanni da Fiesole), 6456.
BEAULIEU (P.-A.), 1665.
BEAUMONT-MAILLET (Laure), 6442.

BEAUNE (C.), 3622.
BEAVER (D.), 6867.
BEBESI (György), 4993.
BECCHI (Paolo), 7148.
BECHTLE (G.), 1939.
BECK (F.), 414.
BECK (Peter J.), 7222.
BECK (Peter), 7690.
BECKER (Ernst Wolfgang), 5582.
BECKER (Jean Jacques), 4354, 4375.
BECKER (Marshall J.), 2282.
BECKER (Michael), 1351.
BECKER (Pia), 6295.
Becket (Thomas), 3906.
BECKMAN (G.), 1721.
BECKMANN (Gustav Adolf), 294.
BECQUET (Jean), 3099.
BEDELL (John), 494.
BEDINI (Silvio A.), 6044.
BEDNÁŘ (Miloslav), 1028.
BEEBEE (Thomas O.), 6184.
BEERTEN (Wilfried),, 4092.
Beethoven (Ludwig van), 1282.
BEGG (Ch.), 1744.
Beham (Barthel), 6469.
BÉHAR (Pierre), 6623.
BEHNE (Frank), 757.
BEHRENDS (O.), 2488.
BEHRENS-ABOUSEIF (Doris), 3294.
BEHRING (Rainer), 7691.
BEHRINGER (Wolfgang), 6823.
BEHRMANN (Günter C.), 5570.
BEHROOZ (Maziar), 4656.
BEIT-ARIEH (I.), 1616, 1745.
BEJOR (G.), 2221.
BEKKER (Balthasar), 5486.
BELARDELLI (Giovanna), 4711.
BELCHER (Stephen), 8338.
BELENGUER CEBRIÀ (Ernest), 5087.
BELGIOIOSO (Giulia), 5905.
BELIČKOVA (C.), 7480.
BELIER (Wouter W.), 1334.
Belinskij (Vissarion G.), 6018.
BELJAEVA (E. V.), 1487.
BELL (A. J. E.), 2592.
BELL (Daniel), 793.
BELL (Lynda S.), 8105.
BELL (Rudolph M.), 1201.
BELL (Walter F.), 7623.
BELLAH (Robert N.), 1335.
BELLASSAI (Alessandro), 7042.
BELLEMORE (Jane), 2693.
BELLER (Maria), 6046.
BELLETTINI (Pierangelo), 94.
BELLI (O.), 1666.
BELLISA (Marc), 7223.
BELLONI (L.), 2080.
BELMONT (Nicole), 888.
BELOFF (Max), 7318.

BELOV (E. A.), 7551.
BELTRAME (Stefano), 4809.
BELUCHE (Olmedo), 4906.
BÉLY (Lucien), 6868.
BENARIO (Herbert W.), 2382.
BENČÍK (Antonín), 4216, 4217.
BENDICK (Rainer), 5766.
BENDIKAT (Elfi), 6821.
BENDOTTI (Angelo), 7649.
BENECKE (Werner), 4934.
BENEDETIČ (Ana), 5752, 5723.
BENEDETTI (Marina), 3890.
BENEDETTO (Robert), 1355.
BENEDICT (Philip), 5511.
Benedictus XIII, antipapa, 3791.
Benedictus XV, Papa, 5352, 5353, 7608.
BENELLI (E.), 2283.
BENERICETTI (Ruggero), 3106.
Beneš (Edvard), 7686, 7723, 7788.
BENEŠ (Josef), 7776.
BENEŠ (Zdeněk), 495.
BENFOUGHAL (T.), 454.
BENGTSSON (Herman), 1279.
BENIGNO (Francesco), 3932, 4712.
Benjamin (Walter), 850.
BENKES (Mihály), 7845.
BENN (Tony), 8327.
BENNET (Andrew), 6296.
Bennett (J. A. W.), 3535.
BENNETT (John M.), 4910.
BENNETT (Judith M.), 3366.
BENNETT (Rab), 7777.
BENOCCI (B.), 7846.
BENOCCI (Carla), 219.
BENRABAH (Mohamed), 4026.
BENREKASSA (Georges), 496.
BENTIVEGNA (Giuseppe), 5583.
BENTLEY (Michael), 497.
BENTON (Gregor), 8106.
BENUCCI (Franco), 2262.
BENVENUTI (Francesco), 4994.
BENYON (John), 7485.
BENZ (Hubert), 5901.
BENZ (Wolfgang), 7873.
BENZI (M.), 1837.
BENZONI (Gino), 4086, 4779, 5324, 5584.
BERBEL (Márcia Regina), 4115.
Berchtold (Abt von Engelberg), 35.
BERCOT (Martine), 1437.
BERDAH (J.-F.), 7692.
BERDING (Helmut), 7164.
BERENGO (Marino), 696, 1150.
BERETTA (Marco), 6183.
BERG (Herbert), 3295.
BERG (Manfred), 7274.
BERG MURRE (H. L.), 5268.
BERGER (A.), 1586.
BERGER (A.), 3002.
BERGER (Albert), 6297.

BERGER (Dieter), 259.
BERGER (Elisabeth), 1099.
BERGER (Gottfried), 309.
BERGER (Jutta Maria), 3795.
BERGER (Stefan), 684, 3983.
BERGES (U.), 2864.
BERGGREN (Lena), 3933.
BERGHAHN (V. R.), 7224.
BERGHOFF (Hartmut), 6942.
BERGIN (Joseph), 498, 5365.
BERGKVAN (Øystein), 4884.
BERGQUIST (Peter), 6594.
BERGSMA (Wiebe), 5777.
Bergson (Henri), 5945.
Berisha (Sali), 4018.
Berkeley (George), 5954.
BERKOWITZ (Peter), 5585.
BERKVENS (A. M. J. A.), 7069.
BERLINCOURT (Alain), 7455.
BERLIOZ (Jacques), 3439.
BERMAN (Constance H.), 3796.
BERMANI (Cesare), 839.
BERNAL CASASOLA (D.), 2327.
BERNAND (André), 1972.
BERNARD (Charles André), 2880.
BERNARD (George), 5777.
BERNARD (Mathias), 499.
BERNARD (Veronika), 6185.
BERNARD-GRIFFITHS (Simone), 770.
BERNARDI (Walter), 6074.
BERNARDIN (Ernst A.), 4592.
BERNARDO (Manuel), 4958.
Bernardus (scholasticus), 3834.
BERNART DE VENTADORN, 3533.
BERNAULT (Florence), 7156.
BERND (Jussen), 491.
BERNDT (Franke), 6298.
BERNECKER (Roland), 5641.
BERNECKER (Walther L.), 939.
BERNET (J.), 4320.
BERNHARD (Nancy E.), 6520.
BERNS (Ch.), 2222.
BERNSTEIN (Serge), 4298, 4304.
BERRINGER (Christian), 7043.
BERRINO (Annunziata), 7149.
BERROCAL (M. C.), 1449.
BERRY (Mary Elizabeth), 3934.
BERRY (Stephan), 811.
BERSCHIN (Walter), 3531.
BERTA (Giuseppe), 6689.
BERTCH GREEN (Louisa), 5209.
BERTÉNYI (István), 940.
BERTI (F.), 2223.
BERTIN-MAGHIT (Jean-Pierre), 4305.
BERTO (L. A.), 3003.
BERTOLONI MELI (Domenico), 5902.
BERTOLUCCI PIZZORUSSO (Valeria), 3532.

BERTONE (Giorgio), 6186.
BERTONHA (Joao Fábio), 4116.
BERTRAND (Michel), 6869.
BERTRAND-DAGENBACH (Cécilie), 2481.
BESALEL (Yusuf), 5530.
BESNIER (M.-F.), 1667.
BESONEN (J.), 1754.
Bessarion, patriarch of Costantinople, 3022.
BESSE (Jean-Marc), 310.
BESSIERE (Jean), 6205.
BESSINGER (M. J.), 2094.
BESSIRE (François), 5903.
BESSMERTNYJ (Jurij L.), 500, 844.
BESSONE (Tânia Maria Tavares), 428.
BEST (R. M.), 1668.
BESTEMAN (J. C.), 3911.
BESTOR (Jane Fair), 889.
BETA (S.), 2081.
Betancourt (Rómulo), 5230.
Bethlen (István), 4615.
BETHOUART (Bruno), 4306.
BETTERIDGE (Thomas), 501.
BETTETINI (M.), 2830.
BETTI (Claudio Maria), 5446.
BETTLES (E.), 1637.
BETZ (Hans Dieter), 1318.
BEUGNOT (Bernard), 6286.
BEULLENS (Pieter), 3716.
BEUTIN (Wolfgang), 3863.
BEVERLEY (Tessa), 3248.
BEVILACQUA (Piero), 1188.
BEWDLEY-TAYLOR (David), 7847.
BEWLEY (Robert), 1483.
BEYER (Robert T.), 6047.
BEZZEL (Irmgard), 5836.
BHATTACHERJE (Satya Bikash), 144.
BIAGIONI (Mario), 5472.
BIANCHI (Lorenzo), 502, 760.
BIANCHI (Luca), 3623.
BIANCHI (Massimo Luigi), 5978.
BIANCHI (Serge), 6755.
BIANCHI (Simona), 34.
BIANCHINI (Marco), 1151, 1168.
BIANCHINI (Paolo), 801.
BIANCHINI (Stefano), 5245.
BIARD (Michel), 6755.
BIBIKOV (Mikhail V.), 3140.
BICKERS (Robert A.), 7324.
BICKERTON (David), 5874.
BICKERTON (James), 4161.
BIDDIS (M.), 674.
BIDEAULT (Marise), 1271.
BIDUSSA (David), 429, 503, 724.
BIEBER (Florian), 4811.
BIEBER (Judy), 4117.
BIEGALSKI (Bogdan), 4936.
BIEGELBAUER (Peter), 6064.

Biel (GABRIEL), 5284.
BIEŃKOWSKI (Wiesław), *XIII*, 697.
BIENTINESI (Fabrizio), 6732.
BIERBRIER (M. L.), 941.
BIESTER (James), 5715.
BIFFI (N.), 1964.
BIGANTI (Tiziana), 6456.
BIGAZZI (Francesco), 4775.
BIGGS (Michael), 311.
BIGSBY (Christopher), 6530.
BIHARI (Péter), 3935.
BIHL (Wolfdieter), *I*.
BIJSTERVELD (Arnoud-Jan A.), 3242.
BIKAI (P. M.), 1753.
BILANDŽIĆ (Dušan), 4199.
BÍLEK (Jiří), 7848.
BILGI (Ö), 1544.
BILIARSKI (Tsocho), 4142.
BILIK (R.), 1973.
BILL (Jan), 3916.
BILLAULT (A.), 1951.
BILLER (Peter), 3772.
BILLERBECK (M.), 2372.
BILLIET (Jaak), 1379.
BILLINGSLEY (William J.), 5186.
BILLOT (Claudine), 3381.
BILLOUET (Pierre), 5904.
BIMAN (Stanislav), 3947.
Bin Barakah (al-Mahdi), 4853.
BINAYÁN (Narciso), 173.
BINDE (Per), 5366.
BINGEN (Erik), 7627.
BINNENKADE (Alexandra), 5142.
Biondo Flavio, 804.
BIRABUZA (André), 4157.
BIRASCHI (A. M.), 1947.
BIRCH (Dinah), 5693.
BIRD (H. W.), 2397.
BIRDWELL (Michael E.), 6521.
BIRELEY (Robert), 5325.
BIRKE (Adolf M.), 7236.
BIRMINGHAM (David), 7344.
BIROCCHI (Italo), 3337.
BIRRICHAGA GARDIDA (Diana), 4847.
BIRTLES (Sara), 6760.
BIRUS (Hendrik), 6321.
BISCHOF (Günter), 7849.
BISHOP (Tom), 5715.
BISK (Izrail' Ja.), 814.
Bismarck (Otto von), 6305, 7535.
BISSCHOPS (Ralph), 1365.
BITELLI (Remo), 526.
BIZCARRONDO (Marta), 5084.
BJÖRKSTRAND (Carita), 6870.
BJØRN (Claus), 4256.
BJÖRNSSON (Anders), 5133.
BLACK (Jeremy), 4307, 4529, 7239.
BLACK (Mechthild), 3853.

BLACKBURN (Bonnie J.), 145.
BLACKMORE (Josiah), 3483.
BLACKWELL (C. W.), 1974.
BLACKWELL (Stephen), 7850.
BLACKWOOD (William Lee), 7225.
BLAIR (Ann), 6125.
BLAISE (F.), 1956.
BLAISE (S.), 174.
BLAKE (Jody), 6384.
Blake (Norman F.), 3542.
Blake (William), 6327, 6378.
BLAME (Christopher B.), 6522.
BLANC (Nicole), 2705.
BLANCHARD (Joël), 3534.
BLANCHARD (Michel), 7851.
BLANCKAERT (Claude), 575.
BLANCPAIN (François), 7552.
BLÄNKNER (Reinhard), 701.
BLANKS (David R.), 678, 3296.
BLANNING (T. C. W.), 1098.
BLASCHKE (Olaf), 5367.
BLASIO (Maria Grazia), 3708.
BLASIUS (Rainer A.), 7802.
BLATTNER (William D.), 5906.
BLAU (Eve), 6410.
BLÁZQUEZ (J. M.), 1563.
BLEANEY (C. H.), 1323.
BLEISTEINER (C. D.), 222.
BLESSER (Stephan), 1431.
BLETON-RUGET (Annie), 7141.
BLICKLE (Peter), 1110.
BLINDOW (Felix), 5907.
BLISS (Katherine), 6048.
BLOCH (Marc), 684, 698.
BLOCHER (F.), 1669.
BLOCKMANS (Willem Pieter), 3415.
BLOCKMANS (Wim), 3249.
BLOEDOW (E. F.), 2224.
BLOM HANSEN (Thomas), 4624.
BLOMEYER (Peter), 7082.
BLONDIAUX (Loïc), 1057.
BLOOTHOOFD (G.), 7016.
BLÖSSNER (N.), 1940.
BLUE (Gregory), 521.
BLUM (D.), 312.
Blumendorf (Franz Paul Zigeuner von), 7454.
Blundell (Michael), 7356.
Bo (Carlo), 711.
BOBB (F. Scott), 942.
Bobbio (Norberto), 1101.
Boccaccio (Giovanni), 3642, 3674.
BOCCARA (Guillaume), 7368.
BOCCARDI STORONI (Paola), 3171.
Bocchi (Achille), 6421.
Bocchoris, king of Egypt, 1646.
BOCHET (I.), 2831.
BOCK (Hans Manfred), 3945.
BOCK (Michael), 5570.
BOCK (Petra), 673.

BOCKHORN (Olaf), 921.
BOĆKOWSKI (Daniel), 7693.
BODEI (Remo), 815.
BÖDEKER (Hans Erich), 5763, 6180.
BODEL (John), 2477.
Bodin (Jean), 5707.
BODIN (Michel), 7226.
BOEHLING (R.), 7852.
BOEHME (Olivier), 4093.
BOEL (G), 3004.
BOËLDIEU-TREVET (J.), 2011.
BOELEVAN HENSBROEK (Pieter), 8339.
BOEMEKE (Manfred F.), 7482.
BOESCH GAJANO (Sofia), 5297.
BOESCHOTEN (R.), 4579.
Boethius (Anicius Manlius Severinus), 2599, 2972, 3054, 3685, 3699.
BOETTKE (Peter J.), 6678.
BOFFA (Serge), 3250.
BOFFO (laura), 636.
BOGAERT (R.), 1617.
BOGLIONE (A.), 313.
Bogucka (Maria), 4937.
BOHÁČ (Zdeněk), 5368.
BOHLEN (Rita), 7400.
Böhm (Johann), 7628.
BÖHM (Roswitha), 6914.
BÖHM (Winfried), 5762.
BÖHME (Klaus-Richard), 7401.
BÖHMER (Peter), 4074.
BOHNSACK (Petra), 5857.
Boiardo (Matteo Maria), 6217.
BOILLET (Danielle), 6248.
BOIS (Jean-Pierre), 3936.
BOIS (Pierre-André), 5876.
BOISSELLIER (Stéphane), 3440.
BOITANI (Piero), 3535, 3606.
BOJTSOV (Mikhail A.), 816, 844.
BOKAREV (Ju. P.), 6702.
BOLANOS MEJIAS (Carmen), 5077.
BOLCHINI (Piero), 6723.
BOLD (Christine), 314.
BOLDRER (Francesca), 2366.
BOLKHOVITINOV (N. N.), 7374.
BOLL (Michael M.), 7853.
BOLLANSÉE (J.), 1905.
BOLLENBECK (Georg), 5586.
BOLLWEG (J.), 1571.
BOLOVAN (Sorina-Paula), 6871.
BOLTANSKI (Ariane), 4308.
Boltzmann (Ludwig), 5967.
BOLWIG (Nils Geert), 6793.
BOLZONI (L.), 1251.
BOM (Klaas), 5908.
BOMMELAER (J.-F.), 2082, 2225.
BOMSDORF (Falk), 621.
BONA (Andrea), 6411.
BONA (Gábor), 4608.

BONAUDO (Marta), 4053.
Bonaventura de Balneoregio, Sanctus, 3412, 3750, 3756.
BONCOMPAGNO DA SIGNA, 3164.
BONDÌ (Sandro Filippo), 735.
BONDIOLI (L.), 1526.
BONECHI (M.), 1722.
BONELLI (Franco), 6789.
BONFANTE (Giuliano), 260.
BONFANTE (Larissa), 260.
BONIFAČIĆ (Vjera), 890.
Bonifácio (José), 4126.
BONIFACIO (R.), 2226.
BONK (Mary), 1161.
BONK (Sigmund), 5909.
BONNAFOUX (Denise), 6447.
BONNANT (Georges), 100.
Bonnassié (Pierre), 3417.
BONNECHER (P.), 2083.
BONNEL (Victoria), 812.
BONNER (Elizabeth), 7403.
Bonnet (Bernard), 4347.
BONNET (C.), 1381.
BONNET (Hans), 1564, 1614.
BONNEY (Margaret), 1153.
BONNEY (Richard), 1153, 1184.
BONO (Salvatore), 6872.
Bontemps-Beaupré (Charles François), 6055.
BONZON (Anne), 5369.
BOOCKMANN (Harmut), 5724.
BOOT (H. M.), 6790.
BOPPE-VIGNE (Catherine), 7553.
BOQUERAT (Gilles), 7854.
BORAK (Neven), 6642.
BORASO (Stefano), 3643.
BORDERS (James M.), 3687.
BORDIER (Jean-Pierre), 6544.
BORDJUGOV (Gennadij A.), 621.
BOREAN (Linda), 455.
BORELLI (Laura), 3797.
BORGEAUD (Philippe), 693, 1370.
Borges (Jorge Luis), 379, 1420.
BORGHESI (Angela), 713.
BORGIA (Luigi), 212.
BORJA DE MEDINA (Francisco), 5370.
BORODIN (Anatolij P.), 4995.
BORODKIN (Leonid I.), 1186.
BORODZIEJ (Włodzimierz), 7778.
BOROS (Zsuzsa), 4601.
BOROVICH (Beatriz), 379.
BOROVSKY (Victor), 6563.
BOROZNJAK (Aleksandr I.), 504.
BORRACCINI VERDUCCI (Rosa Marisa), 117.
BORRI (Gianmario), 117.
Borromeo (Carlo), Santo, 5428.
BORSDORF (Ulrich), 625.
BORZYSZKOWSKI (Józef), 4938.
BOSBACH (Franz), 7400.

Bosch (Robert), 4490.
BOSL (Katharina), 5269.
BOSNA (Ernesto), 5767.
BOSNAKOV (K.), 2227.
BOSOER (Fabian), 4062.
BOSONI (Giampiero), 6491.
BOSSUAT (Gérard), 505, 7907.
Bossuet (Jacques-Bénigne), 699.
BOST (Hubert), 5994.
BOSTOEN (Karel), 5777.
BOSWELL (Laird), 4309.
BOSWORTH (Brian), 2694.
BOSWORTH (C. E.), 8055.
BOSWORTH (R. J. B.), 506, 4753.
BOTER (Gerard), 2845.
BOTEY SOBRADO (Ana María), 4195.
Botta (Carlo), 518.
BOTTIN (Jacques), 1158.
BOTTONI (Luciano), 6523.
BOUCHON (Geneviève), 8077.
BOUCHY (Anne), 1164.
BOUDIN (Hugh Robert), 5463.
BOUET (Alain), 2398.
BOUET (Pierre), 67.
BOUGARD (Françoise), 3425.
BOUGHERIRA (Mohamed Redha), 7855.
BOULBY (Marion), 4804.
BOULLÓN AGRELO (Ana Isabel), 261.
BOULNOIS (Olivier), 3742.
BOULTON BARRY MAC CANN (Maureen), 3536.
Bourdieu (Pierre), 822.
BOUREAU (Alain), 3217, 3719.
BOUREAU (Alain), 786.
BOURGAIN (P.), 3162.
BOURGEOIS (Ginette), 3798.
BOURGON (Jérôme), 1115.
BOURGUET (Marie-Noëlle), 333.
BOURKE (Joanna), 1203.
BOURLET (Caroline), 3151.
BOURNE (M.), 315.
BOURNOUTIAN (George A.), 7422.
BOURQIA (Rahma), 4858.
BOURQUI (Claude), 6524.
BOUTET (Dominique), 3537.
Bouts (Dieric), 3677.
BOUVIER (D.), 2084.
BOUZA (Fernando), 507.
BOVA (Vincenzo), 5371.
BOVESSE (Jean), II.
BOVIE (P.), 1889.
BOWDEN M.), 1482.
BOWEN (Elizabeth), 7629.
BOWEN (Geraint), 5372.
BOWERSOCK (G. W.), 2808.
BOWLIN (John), 3720.
BOWMAN (A. K.), 1144.
BOWMAN (L.), 1957.

BOYCE (D. George), 7303.
BOYCE DAVIES (Carole), 8333.
BOYD (Kelly), 546.
BOYD (Robert), 6824.
BOYLE (A.), 1549.
BOYLE (Francis Anthony), 7192.
BOYLE (Leonard E.), 2, 300, 804, 3639.
Boyle (Robert), 5893.
BOŽIČ (Dragan), 1048.
BOZÓKY (Edina), 3848.
BRAAKHUIS (H. A. G.), 3752.
BRACCESI (L.), 1919.
BRACCHI (Remo), 2593.
BRACEGIRDLE (John), 3699.
BRACEWELL (W.), 3937.
BŘACH (Radko), 7542.
BRACHER (Karl Dietrich), 3922, 7106.
BRACKE (Wouter), 47.
BRACONNIER (Céline), 4310.
BRADEN (Gordon), 6213.
BRADFORD (Churchill J.), 2478.
BRADFORD LANDAU (Sarah), 6412.
BRADLEY (Patricia), 5187.
BRADLEY (R.), 1450.
BRADSHAW (Christopher J.), 5777.
BRADSHER (Henry St. Amant), 4011.
BRADY (Christopher), 7856.
BRADY (Thomas A., jr.), 5464.
BRAGA (G.), 799.
BRAGINA (Lidija M.), 5652.
BRAGONI (Beatriz), 6873.
Brahms (Johannes), 1283.
BRAKENSIEK (Stefan), 6874.
BRAMANTI (Vanni), 5567.
BRAMBILLA (Alberto), 5925.
BRÄMER (Andreas), 62.
BRANCA (Vittore), 3642.
BRANCHE (R.), 7857.
Brand (Adam), 304.
BRAND (John D.), 239.
BRAND (Paul), 3120.
BRANDAO DE BRITO (J. M.), 4962.
BRANDES (Detlef), 4005, 7640.
BRANDES (W), 3005.
BRANDMAIR (Andreas), 84.
BRANDON-JONES (D.), 1625.
BRANDS (H. W.), 7227.
BRANDSMA (F.), 7166.
BRANDT (Harm-Hinrich), 4405.
BRANDT (Hartwin), 561.
BRANDT (Rüdiger), 3538.
Brandt (Willi, Herbert Ernst Karl Frahm), 8029.
BRANDWEIN (Pamela), 508.
BRANGER (Jean-Christophe), 6525.
BRASTER (J. F.), 5083.
BRATE (Tadej), 6429.
BRATVOGEL (Friedrich (W.), 6875.

Brauer (Richard), 6060.
BRAUN (Guido), 7428.
BRAUN (René), 2861.
BRAUNEDER (Wilhelm), 1099.
BRAUNLIN (M.), 213.
BRAVO (B.), 2028.
BRAVO (Manuel J.), 5228.
BRAVO GARCÍA (A.), 3006.
BREAY (Claire), 3108.
BRECHENMACHER (Thomas), 297.
Brecht (Bertolt), 6569, 6586.
BRECHT (Stephanie), 2790.
BRECHTOLD (Jacques), 6006.
BRECKMAN (Warren), 5910.
BREDEKAMP (Horst), 5911.
BREDENKAMP (F.), 3007.
BREDIN (Jean-Denis), 175.
Breitinger (Johann Jakob), 5978.
Breitscheid (Rudolf), 4414.
BRÊME (Dominique), 377.
Brémond (H.), 700.
BRENDECKE (Arndt), 146.
BRENK (Frederick E.), 2881.
BRENK, (Lan), 951.
BRENNECKE (Hanns Christoph), 2882.
BRENNER (Michael), 5553.
BRENTJES (B.), 1723, 1784.
BRESSON (A.), 1565.
BRETSCHER-GISIGER (Charlotte), 998.
BRETT (Michael), 3297.
BRETTELL (Richard), 6385.
BREWARD (Christopher), 609, 6876.
BREWER (John), 1100.
BREY (Hans-Michael), 4406.
BREYMAYER (Ursula), 4517.
BREZZI (Piero), 6688.
BRIAN (Isabelle), 5270.
BRIANDE-PONSART (C.), 2533.
BRIANT (Pierre), 1785.
Brichieri Colombi (G. Domenico), 5568.
BRIDGES (Roy), 7349.
BRIGGS (Charles F.), 1058.
BRIGHAM (Robert K.), 7858.
Brigida, Sancta, 3845.
BRIGNARDELLO (Carlos), 380.
BRILL DE RAMIREZ (Susan Berry), 8369.
BRINDLEY (A. L.), 1463.
BRINGMANN (Klaus), 2479.
BRINKLEY (Douglas), 7909.
BRINKMANN (Reinhold), 6542.
BRIQUEL (D.), 2284.
BRISSON (Luc), 1392, 1817.
BRITNELL (R. H.), 3495.
BRITO (E.), 1303.
BRIZZI (Gian Paolo), 5725.
BRKLJAČA (Seka), 6691.

BROCKMANN (Thomas), 5373.
BRODBECK (Beat), 1255.
BRODERSEN (K.), 1820, 1855.
BRODY (Kenneth J.), 7694.
BROERS (Michael), 6877.
BROGIOLO (G. P.), 2806.
BROISE (Henri), 2732.
BROJAN (Matjaž), 6527.
BROKLOVÁ (Eva), 4218.
BROMBERG (Joan Lisa), 6692.
BROMER (Stephen Eric), 5587.
BRONKHORST (Johannes), 8076.
BRONSTEIN (Jamie L.), 6761.
BRONZINI (Giovanni Battista), 891.
BROOK (Timothy), 521, 8047.
BROOKE (Christopher), 3766.
BROOKS (Jeffrey), 5588.
BROOKSHIRE (J. H.), 4530.
Brost (Erich), 5832.
BROTÓNS NAVARRO (Víctor), 6030.
BROWN (Archie), 509.
BROWN (Cynthia J.), 381.
BROWN (Donald E.), 817.
BROWN (Judith M.), 1008, 7318.
BROWN (Michael K.), 6878.
BROWN (P.), 2808.
Brown (Peter), 2713, 3837.
BROWN (Vivienne), 5912.
BROWN-GRANT (Rosalind), 3539.
BROWNING (Don S.), 1318.
BROWNING (Gary K.), 1059.
BRUBAKER (Leslie), 3008.
BRUCE (Steve), 1103.
BRUCKMULLER (Ernst), 1042.
Bruegel (Pieter), 6465.
BRUGE (Roger), 7325.
BRUGERE (Fabienne), 510.
BRUGUIERE (Marie-Bernadette), 511.
BRUIJN (Jan), 5521.
BRUINS (Clara), 3835.
BRUN (J. P.), 2228.
BRUNA (D.), 214.
BRUNEL (Pierre), 1437.
Brunelleschi (Filippo), 3643, 3655.
BRUNET (Alain), 6349.
BRUNET (Jean-Paul), 4311.
BRUNET (M.), 2229.
BRUNET (Ph.), 2085.
BRUNETTA (Gian Piero), 6625.
Bruni (Leonardo), 3255.
BRUNI (S.), 2263.
BRUNNER (Lance W.), 3687.
BRUNNER (Michael), 6492.
Brunner (Otto), 701.
Bruno (Giordano), 5950.
BRUNO PAGNAMENTA (Roberta), 3540.
BRUSCIA (M.), 711.
BRUSSE (Paul), 6762.
Brust (August), 7046.

BRUTI LIBERATI (Luigi), 4163.
BRUUN (Christer), 262, 2311.
BRYAN (Elizabeth J.), 3541.
BRYCE (T. R.), 1838.
BRYCE (T.), 1724.
BUBEN (Milan), 215.
BUBLITZ (Hannelore), 5913.
Buchelius (Arnoldus), 5508.
BUCHHOLZ (H. G.), 1670.
BUCHHOLZ (Werner), 4417.
BUCHOWSKI (Krzysztof), 4815.
BUCHSTAB (Günter), 4455, 5787.
BUCHSTEINER (Ilona), 6879.
BUCK (Hannsjörg F.), 4467.
BUDAK (Neven), 4200.
BUDANOVA (Vera P.), 1545.
BUDKOVIČ (Tomaž), 7554.
BUDNITSKIJ (Oleg V.), 4998.
BUELTZINGSLOEWEN (Isabelle von), 6888.
BUENO RAMÍREZ (P.), 1488, 1489, 1515.
BUEY (F. Fernandez), 5258.
BUFFET (Cyril), 5708.
BUFON (Milan), 918.
BUGROV (Aleksandr V.), 6791.
BÜHLMANN (Elisabeth), 8041.
BUISEL (M. D.), 2594.
BUISSON (André), 2705.
BUKOWSKA (Krystyna), 3763.
BULATOVA (Angara G.), 892.
BULGARELLI (Sandro), 3328.
BULHAK (Henryk), 7614.
BULHOF (Johannes), 818.
BULL (I. D.), 1451.
BULLICK (Lucie), 4911.
BULLOCK (Alan), 1408.
BULTRIGHINI (U.), 2029.
Bulwer (John), 5715.
BUMBURRY (J.), 1651.
BUNTON (Martin), 7326.
BUONACCORSI (Biagio), 4694.
BUR (Michel), 3191.
BURATTELLI (Claudia), 6528.
Burckhardt (Jacob), 702.
BURCKHARDT (Martin), 1204.
BURDIEL (Isabel), 3960.
BURG (Steven L.), 7859.
BURGALETA (C), 5374.
BURGARD (Friedhelm), 5543.
BURGARELLA (F.), 3009.
BURGDORF (Wolfgang), 5589.
BURGERS (P.), 2399.
BURGESS (Glenn), 4557.
BURGESS (Richard W.), 512, 2962, 3011.
BÜRGIN (Alfred), 6674.
BURGIO (Alberto), 6127.
BÜRGLE (M.), 1581.
BURGUIERE (André), 513.
BURILKOVA (Iva), 4142.

BURK (Kathleen), 8015.
Burke (Edmund), 1077, 5569, 5715, 5918.
BURKE (Peter), 724, 808, 819, 5590.
BURKERT (W.), 2180.
BURKHARDT (Frederick), 6034.
BURKHART (Peter), 38.
BURKI (Shahid Javed), 943.
BÜRKLE (Susanne), 3799.
BURNAND (Yves), 407.
BURNETT (John), 1205.
BURNETT (T. A. J.), 36.
BURNEY (Ch.), 1786.
BURNS (Arthur), 5473.
BURNS (Kathryn), 7369.
BURNS (William E.), 5715.
Burnside (William), 6060.
BURR (Millard), 7860.
BURRIN (Philippe), 4407.
BURROW (J. A.), 3507.
BURROWS (Edwin G.), 6826.
BURSTEIN (S. M.), 1831.
BURTON (Anthony), 456.
BURTON (David H.), 7486.
BURTON (Janet E.), 3800.
BURTON (T. L.), 3518.
BURUCUA (José), 1281.
BURYAKOV (Y. F.), 8052.
BUSCH (Lothar), 39.
BUSH (Barbara), 7346.
BUSH (Jonathan A.), 1244.
BUSH (Rod), 5188.
BUSIN (Valérie), 5375.
BUSINO (Giovanni), 6049.
Busnois (Antoine), 3691.
BUSONERO (Paola), 106.
BUSQUETTE-LABOUÈRIE (Christine), 382.
BUSTARRET (Claire), 5914.
BUTENSCHÖN (Rainer), 4444.
BUTI (I.), 2480.
BUTLER (Orville R.), 6036.
BUTTÒ (Simonetta), 432.
BUTTURINI (Emilio), 5447.
BUTZER (Hermann), 4408.
BUXEDA I GARRIGÓS (J.), 1452.
BUXTON (Julia Dianne), 5229.
BÜYÜKKOLANCI (M.), 1608.
BUZATU (Gh.), 4982.
BUZO (Adrian), 8321.
BYER (Glenn), 3864.
BYNUM WALKER (Caroline), 3770.
BYONG-YONG (Yoo), 8323.
Byrne (F. J.), 3488.
BYSTRICKÝ (Valerián), 5036.

C

CABALLERO HARRIET (Francisco Javier), 7232.
CABAN (Ireneusz), 7746.

CABÁN (Pedro A.), 7555.
CABANES (Bruno), 4018.
CABANES (Pierre), 4018.
CABANI (Maria Cristina), 6243.
CABELLO SARUBBI (Oscar), 4908.
Cabeza de Vaca (Alvar Núñez), 306.
Caboto (Giovanni), 339.
Cabral (Pedro Alvares), 307, 325.
CABRERA (M. A.), 820.
CABRINI (Anna Maria), 749.
CABY (Cécile), 3801.
CACCAMO (Domenico), 5474.
CACCIATORE (Giuseppe), 5944.
CACITTI (Remo), 1380.
CACOUAULT (Marlaine), 5768.
CACUA PRADA (Antonio), 216.
CADILHON (François), 5755.
CADONI (Giorgio), 4713.
Caecilia Metella, 2703.
CAEIRO (José), 5433.
Caesar (C. Iulius), 686, 1250, 2415, 2427, 2721, 2724.
Caetani (famiglia), 3414.
Caetano (Marcelo), 4962.
CAFAGNA (Luciano), 4711.
CAGIANELLI (C.), 2285.
CAGNAZZI (S.), 1787.
CAGNIART (P.), 2595.
CAGNIN (Giampaolo), 3148.
CAHILL (David Patrick), 4912.
CAHN (Jean Paul), 7301.
CAIN (Peter J.), 7306.
CAIN HUNGERFORD (Constance), 6448.
CAIRNS (Christopher), 6605.
CAL PARDO (Enrique), 3112.
CALABI (Donatella), 1158.
CALAFETEANU (Ion), 7735.
CALAME (C.), 2086.
CALATTINI (M.), 1490.
CALBOLI (G.), 2596.
CALDELLI (Maria Letizia), 2312.
CALDER (James D.), 929.
CALDER (Lendol), 6880.
CALDERONI MASETTI (A. R.), 3678.
CALDIRON (Orio), 6517.
CALEGARI (Manlio), 7779.
CALERO PALACIOS (María del Carmen), 29.
Caligula (C. Iulius Caesar Germanicus), Roman emperor, 2702.
CALLAHAN (Michael D.), 7556.
CALLEBAT (Louis), 2391.
Callimachus, 1826, 1895.
CALLOT (Jean-Jacques), 2695.
CALLU (Agnès), 4375.
CALLU (Florence), 41.
CALVANI MARIOTTI (G.), 1934.

Calvert (Frank), 573, 1835.
CALVIN (Jean), 5465, 5517.
CALVINO (André), 316.
Calvino (Jean Cauvin), 6401.
CALVO GÓMEZ (F.), 1491.
CAMARA (Seydou), 8331.
CAMBACERES (Jean-Jacques Régis), 4293.
ÇAMBEL (H.), 1728.
CAMBIANO (G.), 1093.
Cambini (famiglia), 3424.
CAMBRA (José), 4907.
CAMERINO (Giuseppe Antonio), 6244.
CAMERON (Averil), 2349, 2791.
CAMMARANO (Fulvio), 4714.
CAMODECA (Giuseppe), 2313, 2332.
Campana (Dino), 6306.
Campana (Guglielmo), 5388.
Campanella (Tommaso), 5391.
CAMPANINI (Saverio), 74.
CAMPBELL (Alastair), 1284.
CAMPBELL (Mary Baine), 6050.
CAMPBELL (Robert A.), 1337.
CAMPBELL (S.), 1725.
CÂMPEANU (Remus), 6881.
CAMPERO PRUDENCIO (Fernando), 4105.
CAMPIONE (Ada), 2883.
Camus (Jean-Pierre), 6275.
CANCIK (H.), 1827.
CANCIK-KIRSCHBAUM (E.), 1671.
CANDAR (Gilles), 773.
CANDAU (J. M.), 3010.
CANDAUX (Jean-Daniel), 100.
CANDLER HAYES (Julie), 5591.
CANEPA (Nancy), 6245.
CANFORA (Luciano), 430, 449, 514, 792, 1965, 2597.
CANITZ (Auguste Elfriede Christa), 3524.
CANNADINE (David), 515, 6882.
CANNISTRARO (Philip V.), 4715.
CANNON (Joanna), 3836.
CANOSA (Romano), 4716.
CANOVA MARIANI (Giordana), 40, 69.
Cantarella (Raffaele), 1834.
CANTARINO (Geraldo), 7809.
CANTERA CARLAMAGNO (Marcos), 5126.
CANZIANI (Guido), 6081.
CAO (Yi), 8108.
CAPITANI (Lorenzo), 5821.
CAPITANI (Ovidio), 719, 720.
ČAPLOVIČ (Dušan), 3218.
CAPP (Bernard), 6883.
CAPPELLETTI (L.), 2264.
CAPRA (Carlo), 6273.
CAPRARA (M.), 1747.

CAPRILES AYALA (Carlos), 5230.
CAPRINO (Catia), 2733.
CAPSHEW (James H.), 6051.
CAPUTI (Robert J.), 7695.
CAPUZZO (Ester), 4772, 6884.
CARACCIOLO (A.), 516.
CARACI VELA (Maria), 6568.
CARANCINI (G. L.), 1527.
CARANFA (Angelo), 6449.
CARAVALE (Giorgio), 5475.
CARAWAN (E.), 1958.
Carcopino (Jérôme), 703.
Cardano (Girolamo), 6081, 6086.
CÁRDENAS GUTIÉRREZ (Salvador), 4823.
CARDINI (Franco), 821, 945.
CARDON (Dominique), 3367.
Cardoso (Fernando Henrique), 4128.
CARDOZA (Anthony L.), 6885.
CARDUCCI (Nicola), 6300.
CARDÚS (Salvado), 5848.
CAREY (Peter), 3934.
CARFAGNA, 4717.
CARIDI (Giuseppe), 177.
CARILE (A.), 3012.
CARLEY (Michael Jabara), 7630.
CARLIN (Norah), 4531.
Carlo Alberto di Savoia Carignano, re di Sardegna, 4697.
Carlo Emanuele I, duca di Savoia, 4767.
Carlo II d'Angiò, re di Napoli, 3236.
Carlos II, rey de España, 5086.
CARLSEN (J.), 2535.
CARLUER (Jean-Yves), 178.
CARMAGNANI (Marcello), 946.
CARMEL (Alex), 317.
CARMONA (Ernesto), 7810.
CARMONA DE LOS SANTOS (María), 217, 218.
CARMONA RUIZ (María Antonia), 3161.
CARMONT (Pascal), 5165.
CARNIER (Marc), 3854.
CAROCCI (Sandro), 3787.
Carol XII, king of Romania, 4969.
CAROLI (Dorena), 6886.
CARON (Jean-Claude), 5769.
CARON (Vicki), 4312.
CAROTENUTO (Gennaro), 7696.
CAROZZI (Claude), 551, 3442, 3865.
CARPENTER (Christine), 3102.
CARPENTER (Kirsty), 4332.
CARPI (Daniel), 7685.
CARPINELLA (Alessandro), 1116.
Carr (E. H.), 704.
CARR (Raymond), 5710.
Carranza (Venustiano), 7617.
CARRASCO (David), 8378.

CARRASCO (Juan), 3098.
CARRASCO PIZANA (Pedro), 8370.
CARSON (Thomas), 1161.
CARTA (Paolo), 5476.
CARTER (E.), 1725.
Carter (James Earl), 7871.
CARTER (Mia), 8038.
CARTER (Steven D.), 1435.
CARTLEDGE (Paul), 1818.
CARTOSIO (Bruno), 5592, 6827.
CARTWRIGHT (Ken), 6531.
CARUSI (Paolo), 4718.
CARUSO (Barbara), 4763.
CASADIO (G.), 2181.
CASADO MATEOS (A. B.), 1489.
CASAGRANDE (Carla), 3438.
CASAGRANDE MAZZOLI (Maria Antonietta), 106.
CASALI (Luciano), 517.
CASAMASSIMA (Alessandra), 3328.
Casanova (Giovanni Giacomo), 5703.
CASAPULLO (Rosa), 263.
CASARES RODICIO (Emilio), 1286.
CASCIONE (Cosimo), 2482.
CASELLA (M.), 5376.
CASEVITZ (Michel), 484.
CASEY (James), 3960, 6887.
CASINI (Fabio), 5532.
CASINI (Simone), 518.
CASSÁ (Roberto), 4270.
CASSÀ (Rosa M.), 5848.
CASSESE (Sabino), 7112.
CASSINA (cristina), 813.
Cassirer (Ernst), 510, 1345.
Cassius Dio, 705, 2338, 2616.
CÀSSOLA GUIDA (Paola), 2265.
CASSUTO (P.), 5533.
CASTAGNETTI (Andrea), 3368.
CASTELFRANCHI (L.), 4752.
CASTELLANO (Danilo), 6004.
CASTELLI (Alberto), 5837.
CASTELNOVI (Michele), 319.
CASTILLO GÓMEZ (Antonio), 105.
CASTILLO INFANTE (Fernando), 947.
CASTILLO-FELIÚ (Guillermo I.), 8364.
CASTOLDI (M.), 2240.
CASTRO (Daniel), 3994.
CASTRO (P. V.), 1528.
CASTRO (Silvana), 1424.
CASTRO ALFÍN (Demetrio), 1060.
CASTRO LÓPEZ (M.), 1525.
CASTRO PINA (Isabel), 8037.
CASTRONOVO (Valerio), 6664, 6693.
CATALA (Michel), 7697, 7730.
CATANO (Gonzalo), 5593.
CATARSI (Enzo), 5779.
CATENACCI (C.), 1935.

Caterina da Siena, Santa, 3847.
Caterina Fieschi Adorno, Santa, 5396.
Cather (Willa), 6309.
Cato Uticensis (M. Porcius), 2269, 2354, 2388.
CATON (Donald), 6053.
Cattaneo (Carlo), 272, 684.
CATTARUZZA (Marina), 519.
CATTIN (Emmanuel), 5395.
CATTO (Michela), 5377.
CATTON (Philip E.), 5236.
CATTY (Jocelyn), 6215.
Catullus (C. Valerius), 2339, 2340, 2619, 2632, 2634, 2677.
CAU ONTIVEROS (M. A.), 1452.
CAUCHIES (Jean-Marie), 1132.
CAUCHIES (Jean-Marie), 6795.
CAUSSÉ (Jeanne), 4025.
CAVAGLIA (Mario), 3168.
CAVAJONI (G. A.), 2354.
Cavalcanti (Guido), 3555.
CAVALLI (M.), 2087.
CAVALLO (Dominick), 1209.
CAVALLO (Guglielmo), 5, 3166.
CAVANAGH (W. G.), 2256.
CAVE (Richard), 6532.
CAVERA (Giovanni), 4719.
CAZACU (Matei), 320.
CAZANAVE (C.), 741.
CAZORLA-SÁNCHEZ (Antonio), 5078.
CAZZATO (Vincenzo), 6427.
CAZZETTA (G.), 7150.
CEBE (J.-P.), 2386.
CECAMORE (Claudia), 2314.
CECCARELLI (Lucio), 2362.
ÇEÇEN (Kazım), 6054.
Cecil (Robert), 7694.
CEDERNA (Camilla Maria), 6187.
CEDRONIO (Marina), 1061.
ÇELEBİ (Mevlüt), 7557.
CELENZA (Christopher S.), 5594.
CELL (John W.), 7318.
Celsus (Aulus Cornelius), 2341, 2342.
CENTENO (R. M. S.), 248.
CENTINO (Angel M.), 5272.
CENTLIVRES (Pierre), 550, 893.
CENTLIVRES-DEMONT (Micheline), 893.
CEPEDA VILARES (Isabel), 60.
ČEPIČ (Zdenko), 5065.
CERCHIAI (Luca), 2286, 2289.
CERDÀ I JUAN (D.), 1453.
ČERNÝ (Bohumil), 7631.
CERQUEIRA FILHO (Gisáleo), 4119.
CERRI (G.), 2144.
CERRITO (Elio), 6789, 6792.
CERUTTI (Simona), 1133.
Cervantes (Juan de), 31.

Cervantes Saavedra (Miguel de), 1428, 1445, 6209, 6212, 6216, 6219, 6236, 6278.
CESPEDES (Guillermo), 7370.
ÇETINKAYA (İsmail), 5164.
ÇETİNSAYA (Gökhan), 4651.
CEVA (Lucio), 4721.
CEYSSENS (Lucien), 5378.
Chabod (Federico), 756.
CHADWICK (Andrew), 4532.
CHAFER (Tony), 4331.
CHAFFEE (John W.), 8109.
CHAFFEL (Alain), 4313.
CHAIX (Bruno), 7747.
CHALABIAN (Antranig), 4066.
Chamberlain (Arthur Neville), 4563, 4568, 6745, 7645, 7695.
CHAMBERLAIN (Muriel E.), 7304.
CHAMBERS (John Whiteclay), 5182.
CHAMBLAS-PLOTON (Mic), 6409.
CHAMLEY (John), 7487.
Chamorro (Violeta), 4876.
CHAN (Anita), 5240.
CHAN (Stephen), 7296.
CHAN LAU (Kit-ching), 8110.
CHANDLER (David), 4158.
CHANDRA (Bipan), 4625, 7327.
CHANIOTIS (A.), 1726, 1847, 1875.
CHANKOWSKI (A. S.), 2028.
CHANKOWSKI (V.), 1856.
CHAPMAN (R. W.), 1528.
CHAPOT (Frédéric), 2861.
CHAPPLE (John), 7918.
CHAPUIS (Julien), 3680.
CHAPUIS (Olivier), 6055.
CHARD (Chloe), 321.
Chardin (John, sir), 8054.
CHARLE (Christophe), 822, 5595.
Charlemagne v. Karl I der Groβe, rom.-deutscher Kaiser, König der Franken.
CHARLES (Corinne), 6413.
Charles de Gonzaga, duc de Nevers, 4308.
Charles II, king of England, 7342.
Charles II, le Chauve, king of France, 3229.
Charles IV, roy de France, 3256.
Charles le Téméraire, duc de Bourgogne, 3155.
CHARLES-EDWARDS (T. M.), 3336.
CHARNLEY (Joy), 5149.
Chartier (Alain), 381.
CHARTIER (Roger), 11, 101, 3166.
CHARTRAIN (Frédéric), 3348.
CHASSIGNET (Martine), 488.
Chateaubriand (François René de), 6336.
CHATEL DE BRANCION (Laurence), 4293.

CHATELET (Anne-Marie), 5771.
CHATELET (F.), 2152.
CHATTERJEE (Indrani), 4626.
CHATTERJEE (Partha), 4627.
CHATTERJI (Basudev), 4622.
CHATZIOSIPH (Ch.), 4583.
CHAUCER (Geoffrey), 3504, 3542, 3543, 3546, 3559.
CHAUDHURI (Dipak Kumar), 4628.
CHAUDHURY (Sushil), 6749.
CHAUDONNERET (Marie-Claude), 6386.
CHAUMONT (M.-L.), 1788.
CHAUVEAU (Sophie), 6056.
CHAUVOT (Alain), 2481, 2483.
CHAZAN (Mireille), 520.
CHEDEAU (Catherine), 6387.
CHEKIN (Leonid S.), 322.
CHELKOWSKI (Peter J.), 4657.
CHELOTTI (M.), 2315.
CHELYSHEV (Igor' Alekseevich), 7698.
Chen (Duxiu), 8234.
Chen (Jitong), 8190.
CHENEAUX (Philippe), 5379.
CHEPELEVSKAJA (T. I.), 938.
CHERKASOV (P. P.), 7429.
CHEVALIER (Martine), 270.
Chiang (Kai-shek) v. Jiang (Jieshi).
Chiara d'Assisi, Santa, 3835.
CHIARINI (Franco), 5477.
CHICKERING (Roger), 7482.
CHIMENTI (Anna), 7113.
CHIRASSI (I.), 2205.
CHIRICA (Codrin-Valentin), 7488.
CHIRON (P.), 1953.
CHIRTOAGĂ (Ion), 4968, 7388.
CHITTOLINI (Giorgio), 696.
CHOI (Sung-Wan), 4409.
CHOLVY (Gérard), 1263, 6889.
CHOO-SUK (Suh), 8329.
CHOWNING (Margaret), 4824.
Chrétien de Troyes, 3585.
CHRIST (Karl), 522.
CHRIST (Thierry), 7151.
CHRISTADLER (Marieluise), 4355.
CHRISTE (Yves), 3644.
CHRISTENSEN (Claus Bundgård), 7765.
CHRISTENSEN (J.), 2734.
CHRISTENSEN (St. T.), 3252.
Christian III, roi de Danemark, 6793.
Christian VIII, roi de Danemark, roi de Norvège, 4258.
CHRISTIN (Olivier), 5276.
CHRISTINE DE PIZAN, 3534, 3539, 3758.
CHRISTOFFERSON (Michael Scott), 726.
CHRISTOL (M.), 2400, 2792.

Christoph SCHWINGES (Rainer), 1277.
Christus (Petrus), 3677.
CHROBÁK (Tomáš), 7632.
CHRYSOS (Euangelos K.), 2797, 3029.
CHUBAR'IAN (Aleksandr Oganovich), 7677, 8000.
CHUECA INTXUSTA (Josu), 5079.
CHUEV (Nikolaj I.), 8112.
CHUMACHENKO (Tat'jana A.), 5454.
CHUMIŃSKI (Jędrzej), 4939.
Churchill (Winston Leonard Spencer), 4524, 4568.
CHURKINA (Iskra V.), 1319.
CHUST (Manuel), 7371.
CHWALBA (Andrzej), 7489.
CIACHIR (Nicolae), 949.
CIAMPINI (E. M.), 1618.
CIANCAGLINI (C. A.), 2096.
Ciano (Galeazzo), 4762.
CIAPPELLI (G.), 489.
CIARDI (Marco), 5726.
ČIČAJ (Viliam), 5039.
CICCARELLI (Silvia), 5380.
ÇİÇEK (Kemal), 1007.
CICERI (Antonio), 3700.
Cicero (M. Tullius), 2343-2345, 2455, 2513, 2540, 2599, 2613, 2644, 2652, 2674, 2678, 2688, 2782.
CIENCIALA (Anna), 7748.
CIENFUEGOS ÁLVAREZ (Covadonga), 3137.
CIEŚLAK (Edmund), 7430.
CIFRES (A.), 415.
CIGOGNETTI (Luisa), 413.
ÇİLİNGİROĞLU (A.), 1577.
Cimon, 1925.
CINGOLANI (Stefano Maria), 524.
CIOBANU (Veniamin), 4969, 7083.
CIOBOTEA (Dinică), 1148, 6763.
CIOCCA (Pierluigi), 1188.
CIOTTA (Grazia), 4722.
CIOTTI (Laura), 3855.
CIRILLO (O.), 2598.
CIRKOVIC (Sima M.), 3544.
CITTI (V.), 2080.
CIUPKE (Paul), 5804.
CIURTIN (Eugen), 1340.
CIVIL (M.), 1748.
CLAASSEN (Jo-Marie), 2599.
CLACK (J.), 1894.
CLAGETT (M.), 1619.
CLANCHY (M. T.), 3193.
CLARK (Elisabeth A.), 2832, 2884.
Clark (Grahame), 1483.
CLARK (John P. H.), 3109, 3143.
CLARK (Martin), 684.
CLARK (Philip), 3319.

CLARK (T. J.), 5596.
CLARK (William), 1210, 6155.
CLARK HINE (Darlene), 3942.
CLARKE (Aidan), 4666.
CLARKE (Katherine), 323.
CLARKE (M.), 2182.
CLARKE KOSAK (J.), 2088.
CLASSEN (Albrecht), 43.
CLATTERBAUGH (Kenneth C.), 5916.
Claudel (Camille), 6449.
Claudianus (Claudius), 2337, 2346.
Claudius Nero Germanicus (Tiberius), Roman emperor, 2361, 2522.
CLAUSEN (Birthe L.), 3916.
Clausewitz (Carl von), 1049, 5637, 7288.
CLAUSS (M.), 1749.
CLAUSS (Manfred), 2696.
CLAUZEL (Denis), 3247.
CLAYTON (Lawrence A.), 7229.
CLEARY (J. J.), 2169, 2177.
CLEARY (Richard), 6414.
CLEMENS (Detlev), 5597.
CLEMENT (Bruno), 6188.
CLEMENT (Jean-Louis), 5381.
CLEMENTE (José Carlos), 5080.
Cleomenes I, king of Sparta, 2020.
Cleopatra VII, queen of Egypt, 1820.
CLERICI (Luca), 301.
Cliff (Clarice), 6498.
CLIJSTERS (Edi), 4959.
Clisthenes, 1818.
CLOSE (A. E.), 1516.
CLOSE (David), 4875.
CLOUGHLEY (Brian), 4895.
CLOUZOT (Martine), 383.
CLOVER (Frank M.), 2793.
CLUNAS (Craig), 6890.
CLYMER (K. J.), 7862.
COATES (Alan), 44.
COATSWORTH (John), 7977.
COBB (P. M.), 1672.
COBBAN (Alan B.), 3624.
COBDEN (Paul), 5917.
COBETTO CHIGGIA (P.), 2012.
COCCI (A.), 3790.
COCCIA (Michele), 714.
COCHRAN (Sherman), 6742.
COCHRANE (Lydia G.), 3166.
COCKSHAW (Pierre), 3.
CODIGNOLA (Luca), 4163.
COENEN (M.), 1620.
COERVER (Don M.), 7230.
CŒURÉ (Sophie), 7558.
COFRANCESCO (Dino), 5598.
COGLIANO (Francis D.), 5190.
Cohen (Albert), 6381.
COHEN (C.), 1454.

COHEN (Evelyne), 5599.
COHEN (Jeffrey Jerome), 3545.
COHEN (Jeremy), 3273.
COHEN (Paul A.), 147.
COHEN (S. J. D.), 1750.
COHEN (Susan Sarah), 928.
COHN (Ellen R.), 5183.
COHN (S. K.), 5383.
COHN (Samuel Jr.), 3253.
ÇOLAK (Yilmaz), 5167.
COLAO (Floriana), 7152.
COLE (Mary Hill), 4534.
COLE ROOT (M.), 1789.
COLEMAN (E.), 3356.
COLEMAN (K.), 2697.
Coleridge (Samuel Taylor), 846, 6346, 6347.
COLES (J. M.), 1529.
COLES (John), 1483.
COLISH (Marcia L.), 5601.
COLLA (Piero), 527.
COLLADO GIRALDO (H.), 1504.
COLLECOTT (Diana), 6301.
COLLEDGE (Edmund), 3773.
COLLET (Olivier), 3840.
COLLIER (Simon), 6534.
COLLIN BOUFFIER (S.), 2030.
COLLINI (Stefan), 528.
COLLINS (Brian C.), 1033.
COLLINS (James B.), 3934.
COLLINS (Robert O.), 7860.
COLLISON (Patrick), 5273.
COLLOTTI (Enzo), 4771.
COLOMBO (Arrigo), 2885.
Colombo (Cristoforo), 582.
COLOMBO (Paolo), 7114.
COLOMBO (Sylvia), 4923.
Colonna (famiglia), 3263.
COLONNA (G.), 2287.
Colorni (Eugenio), 5629.
COLPE (Carsten), 1341.
COLPO (I.), 2735.
COLTMAN (Vicky), 431.
COLVIN (S.), 2089.
COLVIN (Sarah), 6535.
COLZI (Francesco), 6794.
COMBA (Rinaldo), 3794, 3815.
COMBE (Sonia), 5602.
Comboni (Daniele), Beatus, 5449.
COMI (Anna), 6329.
Commodus (M. Aurelius), Roman emperor, 2526.
COMPANY (Concepción), 3449.
Comte (Auguste), 5656.
CONCA (F.), 1834.
CONCHEIRO COELLO (A.), 1505.
CONDE (Manuel Sílvio), 3444.
CONDIT (Carl W.), 6412.
Condorcet (Marie-Jean-Antoine-Nicolas Caritat Marquis de), 810.

CONDREN (Edward I.), 3546.
CONERMANN (Stephan), 620.
Conforti (Guido Maria), Beatus, 5364.
CONLON (Pierre M.), 5565.
CONNAUGHTON HANLEY (Brian Francis), 4826.
CONNIFF (James), 5918.
CONNIFF (Michael L.), 1094.
CONNOLY (D. K.), 324.
CONNOR (C.), 3013.
CONNORS (C.), 2600.
CONOLLY (J.), 1517.
CONRAD (Dieter), 7084.
CONRAD (Sebastian), 530.
CONRAD-O'BRIAIN (Helen), 3608.
CONSOLO LANGHER (S.), 1976.
Constans (Flavius Iulius Claudius), Roman emperor, 2430.
CONSTANT (Benjamin Henri), 706, 5965.
Constantinus (L. Flavius Valerius), Roman emperor, 2461, 2505, 2777, 2820, 2877, 2962.
Constantinus IX Monomachus, Byzantine emperor, 3061.
Constantinus Pisanus, 3701.
Constantinus VI Porphyrogenetus, Byzantine emperor, 3042.
Constantinus XI Paleologus, Byzantine emperor, 3088.
Constantius II (Flavius Iulius), Roman emperor, 2424, 2962.
CONTADINI (Anna), 96.
CONTAMINE (Geneviève), 3189.
CONTAMINE (Philippe), 3189.
CONTEH-MORGAN (Earl), 5031.
CONTI (Martino), 3709.
CONTI (Simonetta), 339.
CONTINI (Alessandra), 4748.
CONTORBIA (Franco), 6302.
CONTRERAS (Carlos), 4913.
CONWAY (Melissa), 102.
CONZE (Eckart), 6892.
COOK (Harold John), 5919.
Cook (James), 8387, 8388.
COOK (Noble), 6893.
COOK (Paul J.), 4723.
COOK (William R.), 3844.
COOL (H. E. M.), 2737.
COOPER (J. M.), 2031.
COOPER (James F), 5478.
COOPER (Kate), 2795.
COOPER (Laurence D.), 5920.
COOPER (Nicholas), 6415.
COPENHAVER (Brian P.), 6125.
COPLAND (Ian), 7330.
COPPA (Frank J.), 5274.
COPPENS (Yves), 895.
COPPOLA (A.), 1977.
COPPOLA (Giovanna), 2485.

COQUERY-VIDROVITCH (Catherine), 8341.
COQUIO (Catherine), 4469.
Corazzini (Sergio), 6372.
CORBI (Enrico Maria), 5772, 5773.
CORBIER (Mireille), 1143, 2307, 2486.
CORBIN (Alain), 822, 5642.
CORBIN (Annalies), 5603.
Corbulo (Gn. Domitius), 2333.
CORCELLA (Aldo), 739.
CORCORAN (Neil), 6303.
CORDANO (F.), 1850.
CORDERO OLIVERO (Immaculada), 5081.
CORLEY (Brigitte), 3645.
CORN (Wanda M.), 6388.
Corneille (Thomas), 6251.
Cornelia, Iulia Domna, 2554.
CORNELIßEN (Christoph), 775.
CORNELL (Saul), 1062.
CORNIL (P.), 1727.
Cornin (Henry), 1387.
CORNWELL (Neil), 6325.
CORPUZ (Onofre D.), 7331.
CORRE (K.), 3436.
CORRY (Emmet), 5434.
CORSANO (Karen), 21.
CORSI (Mario), 4776.
CORSINI (Carlo A.), 6123.
CORSTEN (Th.), 1978.
CORTÉS ZAVALA (María Teresa), 7519.
CORTESE (Ennio), 3337.
CORTESI (Luigi), 4724.
CORVISIER (J.-N.), 2032.
Corvo (Max), 7781.
CORVOL (André), 424.
COSENTINO (S.), 3014.
COSI (R.), 2401.
ĆOSIĆ (Stjepan), 6829.
Cosimo I de' Medici, granduca di Toscana, 4695.
Cosmas Indicopleustes, 350.
COSSUTTA (Fabio), 6217.
COSTA (Pietro), 1063.
COSTA COUTO (Ronaldo), 4120.
COSTA PINTO (Antonio), 4960.
COSTA RESTAGNO (Josepha), 3251.
COSTA SANTOS TAPAJÓS (Vicente), 4125.
COSTABILE (F.), 2033.
COTTA (Irene), 4695.
COTTON (H. M.), 1751.
COTTON (Matthew), 7866.
COTULA (Franco), 6816.
COUDREUSE (Anne), 5921.
COULIBALY (Abdou Latif), 5030.
COULON (Damien), 3376.
COURRENT (M.), 2684.
COURTENAY (William J.), 3370.

COURTNEY (Edward), 2601.
COURTOIS (Stéphane), 4296.
COUSSEAU (Anne), 6304.
COUTY (Daniel), 954.
COVER (Jan Arthur), 5922.
COWARD (John M.), 5838.
COWDREY (H. E. J.), 3802.
COWELL (Andrew), 3445.
COWGER (Thomas W.), 5191.
COX (Richard A. V.), 6.
COZZI (Gaetano), 4086, 5479.
CRACCO RUGGINI (Lellia), 690, 2951.
CRACROFT (Richard H.), 1444.
CRAIG (Gordon A.), 6305.
CRAIG MELCHERT (G.), 1729.
CRAM (Robert Gordon), 7491.
CRAMER (Gisela), 4043.
CRANACH (Michael von), 6140.
CRARY (Jonathan), 6389.
Cratinus, 1897.
Craveri (Raimondo), 7781.
CRAYCRAFT (Kenneth R.), 5275.
CREASE (Robert P.), 6058.
CREESE (Gillian), 6894.
CRESCI-MARRONE (Giovannella), 2602.
CRESPIN (A.-S.), 1546.
CRESSWELL (Jamie), 1372.
CRESTI (G.), 1490.
CRIADO BOADO (F.), 1448.
CRIBLEZ (Lucien), 5818.
Crijević Tubero (Ludovik), 794.
CRIPPA (S.), 2698.
CRISCIANI (Chiara), 6125.
Crispi (Francesco), 4703, 4707.
Cristina, Santa, 3840.
CRISTOFARI (Mauro), 959.
CRISTOFFERSEN (Henrik), 6638.
CRISTOFOLINI (Paolo), 5923.
CRITCHLEY (Simon), 1399.
CROCE (Benedetto), 707, 823, 891, 1096, 4699, 5924, 5925, 6001.
CROCITTI (John J.), 4118.
CROCKATT (Richard D. G.), 7808.
CROCKETT (Dennis), 6450.
CROIX (Alain), 5780.
CROIZY-NAQUET (Catherine), 531.
CROMARTIE (Alan), 5604.
Cromwell (Oliver), 4569.
CRONE (Patricia), 3298.
CRONIN (Mike), 4667.
Cross (Claire), 3771, 5277.
CROSS (James E.), 3332.
CROSS (Richard), 3721.
CROSSICK (Geoffrey), 1208.
CROSSLEY (Ceri), 684.
CROUZET (François), 532.
CROUZET-PAVAN (Élisabeth), 4725.
CROWLEY (John E.), 6895.

CROWTHER (C. V.), 1857.
CROWTHER (Victor), 6537.
CROXTON (Derek), 7404.
CRUZ SALAS (Luis), 4177.
CSÁKY (Moritz), 3941.
CSÁSZÁR (Gyula), 4602.
CSENDES (Peter), 950.
CSIZMADIA (Ervin), 4603.
CUBITT (Catherine), 23.
CUESTAS GÓMEZ (Carlos Humberto), 7867.
CUETO (Marcos), 4913.
CUHRA (Jaroslav), 4220, 4252, 4254.
CULCLASURE (Scott P.), 824.
CULIOLI (Gabriel Xavier), 4294.
CULL (Nicholas J.), 7633.
CULLATHER (Nick), 7868.
CULTRERA (Giuseppe), 5856.
CUMMINGS (B.), 7233.
Cumont (Franz), 596, 708, 1381.
CUNNALLY (John), 241.
CUNNINGHAM (Andrew), 6932.
CUNNINGHAM (Colin), 451.
CUOCO (Vincenzo), 4696.
CURRANT (A. P.), 1486.
CURRELI (Mario), 6291.
CURRY (John Court), 4535.
CURSENTE (Benoît), 3915.
CURTA (Fl.), 742.
CURTIS (Charles W.), 6060.
CURTIS (Pénélope), 6451.
Curtius Rufus (Quintus), 2347.
CURTY (O.), 2183.
CURZEL (Emanuele), 3869.
Curzon (George Nathaniel Curzon, Marquis of), 7564.
CUSATELLI (Giorgio), 5627.
CUSSET (C.), 2091.
CUTINELLI RÈNDINA (Emanuele), 1064, 4699.
CUYLER YOUNG JR. (T.), 1811.
CVIRN (Janez), 951.
Cyrillus (bishop of Jerusalem), 2891.
Cyrus I, king of Persia, 1697.
Czartoryski (Adam Jerzy), 7538.
CZEGUHN (Ignacio), 7117.
CZICHON (R. M.), 1730.

D

DA COSTA (Avelino de Jesus), 3138.
DA CUNHA BUENO (Antônio Henrique), 179.
DA FONSECA (Luís Adao), 325.
DABAKIS (Melissa), 6452.
DABASHI (Hamid), 4657.
DACOSTA KAUFMANN (Thomas), 6125.

INDEX OF NAMES

D'ACUNTO (Nicolangelo), 3722.
DADRIAN (Vahakn N.), 7559.
DADVAR (Abolghasem), 4629.
DAFINOV (Zdravko), 4143.
D'AGATA (A. L.), 1848.
D'AGOSTINO (Bruno), 2034, 2289.
D'AGOSTINO (Guido), 4746.
DAHAN (Gilbert), 3272, 3274, 3723.
DAHL (Ann-Sofie), 5127.
DAHL (Ottar), 4726.
DAHLBERG (Charles), 3504.
DAHLMANN (Dittmar), 7653.
DAIBER (Andreas), 3547.
DAIBER (Hans), 1393.
DAINOTTO (Roberto M.), 6189.
DAL COVOLO (E.), 2886.
DAL LAGO (Paola), 4727.
dal Pozzo (Cassiano), 6393.
DALARUN (Jacques), 3803, 3861.
DALBERA-STEFANAGGI (Marie José), 264.
D'Alembert (Jean Baptiste Le Ronde), 5960.
D'ALESSIO (Carlo), 6306.
D'ALFONSO (L.), 1673.
DALIMIER (C.), 1881.
DALL'OLIO (Guido), 5384, 5534.
DALLAND (Magnar), 3323.
DALL'ASTA (Mathhias), 5467.
DALLEY (S.), 1674.
DALY (Mary E.), 1103.
DALY (Peter M.), 210.
DAM (Hanne), 6896.
DAMAMME (Jean-Claude), 7458.
Damaratus, king of Sparta, 2020.
Damascius, 2960.
DAMASKOS (D.), 2184.
D'AMATI (L.), 2489.
DAMELL (David), 1154.
DAMIAN-GRINT (Peter), 533.
D'AMICO (Robert), 5926.
DAMIEN (Robert), 760, 5624.
DAMON (Cynthia), 2375, 2490, 2491.
DAN (Joseph), 3290.
DANDAMAYER (M. A.), 1790.
Dandolo (Andrea), doge di Venezia, 3176.
DANDRAU (A.), 1839.
DANELLA (Patrizia), 48.
DANEO (Camillo), 4751.
DANESE (Sérgio França), 7234.
DANESI MARIONI (G.), 2604.
DANFORTH (L. M.), 4580.
DANGEL (J.), 2605.
D'ANGOUR (Armand J.), 2013, 2603.
DANI (A. H.), 8055.
DANI (Alessandro), 7153.
DANIELE (Chiara), 4747.
Danilevsky (Nikolay), 493.

DANKELMANN (Otfried), 334.
Dante Alighieri, 1410, 3726, 3728, 6492.
D'Antonio (Biagio), 6446.
DANY (O.), 1979.
D'ARCY (Anne Marie), 3608.
DARD (Olivier), 4314.
DARDAINE (S.), 2307.
Darius I, king of Persia, 1710, 1788, 1806, 1810.
DARK (K. R.), 3226.
DARMEZIN (L.), 2014.
DARMON (Pierre), 6061.
DAROVEC (Darko), 366.
DAROVEC (Darko), 5999.
DART (Gregory), 5606.
Darwin (Charles), 733, 6034, 6062.
DARWIN (John), 7318.
DASKALOV (Doncho), 4144.
DASSMANN (Ernst), 1375, 2869.
DASSOVICH (Mario), 7749.
DASSOW (E. von), 1675.
DASTON (Lorraine), 5715.
Datis, comandante persiano,1787.
DATSYSHEN (Vladimir Grigor'evich), 7493.
DATTA (Pradip Kumar), 4630.
DATTA (Satya), 7086.
DATTA (Venita), 5607.
DAUCHY (Serge), 1132, 7154.
DAUGEVILLE (Sylvie), 6538.
DAUKS (Klaus-Peter), 4411.
DAULER WILSON (Margaret), 5927.
DAUNTON (Martin), 332.
Davenant (Charles), 6683.
DAVENPORT (Anne Ashley), 3724.
Davers (Charles, sir), 4527.
David (Jacques- Louis), 6468.
DAVID (Miriam), 5764.
David I, king of Scots, 3110.
David, king of Israel, 1744.
DAVIDSDOTTIR (Sigrun), 49.
DAVIDSEN (Leif), 4257.
DAVIDSON (J.), 1959.
DAVIES (Martin), 112.
DAVIES (Norman), 952.
DAVIES (P.), 2606.
DAVIES (Peter), 4315.
DAVIES (Sean), *VII*.
DAVILA (Carlos), 6733.
DÁVILA COX (Emma Aurora), 7492.
DAVIS (Diane), 6830.
DAVIS (John), 4536.
DAVIS (Michael T.), 4559.
DAVIS (P. J.), 2355.
DAVIS (Stephen), 2943.
DAVISON (Roderic H.), 7494.
DAVITKOVSKI (Borče), 7989.
DAVY (Christian), 3646.

DAVYDOVA (S. A.), 3158.
DAWSON (Doyne), 825.
DAWSON (Jane), 5777.
DAY (Jared N.), 6831.
DAY (P. M.), 1853.
DAY JONES (Shirley), 6208.
DAYEN (Daniel), 5761.
DAY-HICKMANN (Barbara Ann), 6390.
de Acosta (José), 5374.
DE AGOSTINI (Daniela), 6204.
DE ALFONSO ALONSO-MUNOYERRO (Belén), 217.
DE ALMEIDA BARATA (Carlos Eduardo), 179.
DE ALMEIDA FERNANDES (A.), 265.
DE ANDRADA E SILVA (Raul), 4125.
DE ANDRADE SILVA (Antenor), 5435.
DE ANGELI (Francesco), 2720.
DE ANGELIS (F.), 2290.
DE AQUINO (Maria Aparecida), 4121.
DE AQUINO (Rubim Santos Leao), 7000.
DE BALBÍN BEHRMANN (R.), 1488, 1489, 1515.
DE BENEDICTIS (Angela), 3351.
DE BLOIS (L.), 2338.
DE BRUYN (Günter), 180.
De Burgh (Elizabeth), 3426.
DE BUSSIERRE (Michèle), 4033.
DE CALLATAŸ (François), 245, 2739.
DE CALLATAŸ-VAN DER MERSCH (Colette), 2740.
DE CECCO (Marcello), 6788.
DE CESSOLE (Bruno), 4025.
DE CHURRUCA (Juan), 2887.
DE CLEMENTI (Andreina), 6897.
DE DIJN (Rosine), 327.
DE DOMINGUEZ SOLER (Susana T. P.), 4039.
DE EPALZA (Miguel), 3870.
De Felice (Franco), 709, 4728.
De Felice (Renzo), 710, 7780.
DE FILIPPIS CAPPAI (Ch.), 2402.
DE FINIS (L.), 2080.
DE FLEURQUIN (L.), 1303.
de Fontenay (Joseph), 7605.
DE FONT-REAULX (Jean-Hugues), 7453.
DE FRANCESCO (Antonino), 534.
DE FREDE (Carlo), 5278.
de Gaulle (Charles), 4160, 4316, 7638, 7670, 7842.
DE GIORGI (Fulvio), 5401, 5774.
DE GOBINEAU (Arthur), 7456.
DE GRAEF (K.), 1676.

DE GREGORI (Giorgio), 432, 433.
De Gregori (Luigi), 433.
de Haro (Don Luis), 5099.
de Heredia (José Maria), 6289.
DE KEUNING (M.), X.
de la Barra (Francisco León), 4834.
DE LA GORCE (Paul Marie), 4316.
DE LA MOTTE (Dean), 5860.
DE LA PASCUA (Maria José), 6975.
DE LA PAZ (J. Augustus Y.), 4927.
de la Riva Aguero y Osma (José), 5632.
DE LANGE (Albert), 5480.
De las Casas (Bartolomé), 5392.
DE LEEUW (Karl), 7431.
DE LI (Andrés), 149.
DE LIGHT (L.), 2316.
DE LONGIS (Rosanna), 7108.
DE LUCA (Giuseppe), 711.
DE MADARIAGA (Maria Rosa), 7495.
DE MADDALENA (A.), 4752.
DE MAFFEI (F.), 3015.
DE MARINIS (R. C.), 2266.
De Martino (Ernesto), 712, 1344, 1346, 1362.
DE MARTINO (S.), 1677.
DE MASSIAC (Barthélemy d'Espinchal), 7425.
DE MATTEI (Roberto), 5481.
de Mena (Juan), 3737.
DE MIN (M.), 1484.
DE MINICIS (Elisabetta), 3121.
DE MIRAMON (Charles), 3871.
DE MIRANDA (Girolamo), 5928.
DE MONTCLOS (Christine), 7870.
DE MONTJOUVENT (Philippe), 181.
de Narváez (Pánfilo), 306.
de Olózaga (Salustiano), 5091.
DE PABLO (Santiago), 5114.
De Palatio (Octavian, Archbishop of Armagh), 3150.
DE QUEIRÓS MATTOSO (Katia), 7228.
DE REYNIES (Nicole), 6508.
DE REZENDE MARTINS (Estevão), 4122, 6898, 7432.
DE RIDDER DE ZEMBORAIN (Maud), 7425.
DE ROBERT (Philippe), 5994.
DE ROMANIS (Federico), 735.
DE ROMANIS (Robero), 6246.
DE ROMILLY (Jacqueline), 1214.
DE ROOVER (Raymond Adrien), 3371.
DE ROSA (Gabriele), 4729, 5358, 5929.
DE ROSA (Luigi), 6796.
de Rossi (Vincenzo), 6481.
de Sade (Donatien Alphonse François, marquis), 6538.

de Sahagún (Bernardino), 8363.
DE SALES (François), 5416.
de Salvan de Saliez (Antoinette), 7007.
De Sanctis (Francesco), 713.
DE SANCTIS (Gaetano), 714.
DE SETA (Cesare), 328.
De Silva (K. M.), 5123.
De Silva (Kingsley), 8083.
DE SILVA Y VERASTEGUI (Soledad), 50.
DE SIMONE (Carlo), 2607.
DE SIMONE (Ennio), 6033.
De Simoni (Juan), 1052.
DE SOLAN (O.), 150.
DE SOTO (Alvaro), 4281.
de Staël (Germaine), 175.
de Tyard (Pontus), 6226.
DE VALOIS (Marguerite), 6210.
DE VERGER (Jean-Claude), 4593.
de Viau (Théophile), 6276.
DE VIDO (S.), 1906.
DE VORKIN (David H.), 6037.
DE VOS (Craig Steven), 2888.
DE VRIES (David), 4898.
DE VRIES (Joris), 8342.
DE VRIES (Kelly), 3233.
DEAN (Carolyn), 5385.
DEAN (Ruth J.), 3536.
DEAN ANDERSON (R.), 2092.
DEANS-SMITH (Susan), 5671.
DEBAX (Hélène), 3417.
DEBIES (Marie-Hélène), 389, 3436.
DEBORD (P.), 1791.
DEBUS (Friedhelm), 287.
DECHARNNEUX (Baudouin), 1343.
Decius (C. Messius Quintus), Roman emperor, 2715.
DECLAIR (Edward G.), 4317.
DECOT (Rolf), 5489.
DÉDEYAN (G.), 3016.
DEFRANCE (C.), 7804.
DEGLER-SPENGLER (Brigitte), 5320.
DEGL'INNOCENTI (Antonella), 3838.
DEGÓRSKI (Bazyli), 2889.
DEGROS (Maurice), 7459.
DEHN-NIELSEN (Henning), 953, 4258.
DEIGHTON (Anne), 4006.
DEITZ (Luc.), 6125.
DEKÓWNA (Maria), 3122.
DEL ALIZAL (Laura), 7945.
DEL COL (Andrea), 5417.
DEL HOYO CALLEJA (J.), 2327.
DEL LITTO (Victor), 6287.
DEL MAR POZO (Andres M.), 5083.
DEL MAR TIZÓN FERRER (Maria), 7118.
DEL MORAL (Rafael), 1426.

DEL NEGRO (Piero), 5930.
DEL PIAZZO (Marcello), 212.
DEL REY FAJARDO (José), 434.
DELACOR (Regina M.), 4414.
DELACROIX (Christian), 535.
DELACROIX (Eugène), 6442.
DELANO-SMITH (Catherine), 329.
DELATOUR (J.), 151.
DELBRUGGE (Laura), 149.
DELCOURT (Thierry), 3517.
DELÉANI (Simone), 2861.
DELETANT (Dennis), 4970.
DELIBES (G.), 1471.
DELIBES DE CASTRO (G.), 1530.
DELISSEN (Alain), 8039.
DELL (Edmund), 4537.
DELLA CASA (Stefano), 6517.
DELLA PERUTA (F.), 4752.
DELLA TORRE (Giuseppe), 7070.
DELLA VALLE (M.), 2978, 3017.
DELLABORRA (Mariateresa), 6630.
DELL'ANNA (Giuseppe), 3725.
DELLE DONNE (Fulvio), 717, 723.
DELMARCEL (Guy), 6495.
DELMAS (Marie-Claire), 220.
DELOGU (Paolo), 536.
DELORIA (Vine), 5279.
DELUMEAU (Jean), 6107.
Delvaux (Laurent), 6462.
DEMANDT (Alexander), 1264.
DEMBOWSKI (Peter F.), 3705.
DEMÉNY (Lajos), 537.
DEMING (James C.), 5482.
DEMIRALP (Yekta), 3299.
DEMİRAY (Emine), 6899.
DEMM (Eberhard), 4415.
DEMOFONTI (Sara), 4729.
Demosthenes, 1898, 2123.
DEMOUGIN (Ségolène), 2403, 2568.
DEN DRIESCH (A. von), 1578, 1607.
DENDLE (Peter), 5931.
DENÉCHÈRE (Yves), 7634.
DENG (Cong), 8113.
DENG (Gang), 8114.
DENG (Kaisong), 8115.
DENG (Yilan), 8116.
DENIAUX (Élizabeth), 2492, 2741.
DENKIEWICZ-SZCZEPANIAK (Emilia), 7699.
DENON (Vivant), 450.
DENSCHER (Barbara), 5655.
DENT (David W.), 7235.
DENTON (Jeffrey), 1181.
DENTZER (J.-M.), 1781.
DENZINGER (Heinrich), 5357.
DEOPIK (D. V.), 8099.
DEPOVERE (Paul), 6063.
DEPREZ (Stanislas), 5932.
DEREMETZ (Alain), 2611.

INDEX OF NAMES 357

DERIN (Z.), 1579.
DEROCHE (A. J.), 7871.
DEROGY (Jacques), 4853.
DEROGY WEITZMANN (Renée), 4853.
DEROLEZ (Albert), 47.
DERRAINE (Pierre-Jacques), 416.
DERRICK (Jonathan), 8335.
DERUETTE (Serge), 4094.
DERVILLE (Alain), 3372.
DERWICH (Marek), 3839.
Des Marez (Guillaume), 765.
DESAN (Suzanne), 6900.
DESANTES FERNANDEZ (Blanca), 217.
Descartes (René), 5880, 5896, 5905, 5933, 5947, 5957, 6007, 6020, 6091.
DESCHENES (Gaston), 4162.
DESCIMON (Robert), 4318.
DESFRAY (S.), 1883.
DESHAYES (Albert), 266.
DESHAYES (Laurent), 7872.
DESHOURS (N.), 2185.
DESHPANDE (Madhav M.), 8076.
DESMULLIEZ (Janine), 2815.
DESPLAND (Michel), 538.
DESTANI (Bejtullah D.), 7205.
DESTREE (P.), 2146.
DESTRO (A.), 2924.
DETTENHOFER (M. H.), 2036.
DETTI (Tommaso), 831.
DETTORI (E.), 1879.
DEUCHLER (Martina), 8322.
DEUTINGER (Roman), 3167.
DEUTSCH (Robert), 221.
Devereux (Robert), 2nd Earl of Essex, 4543.
DEVIJVER (Hubert), 2536, 2568.
DEVINE (Thomas Martin), 4538.
DEVLET (Nadir), 4996.
DEVOS (Isabelle), 1177.
DEVOTI (Luciana), 106.
DEVOTO (Fernando), 1216.
DEWACHTER (Michel), 459.
D'Herelle (Félix), 6160.
DI BERNARDINO (Angelo), 2890.
DI BIASE (Carmine), 6307.
DI DONATO (Riccardo), 1344.
DI FABIO (C.), 3678.
di Lasso (Orlando), 6594.
DI MARCO (Giuseppe Antonio), 5935.
DI MATTIA SPIRITO (S.), 3790.
DI NOLFO (Ennio), 7700, 7874.
DI PAOLA (Lucietta), 2537.
DI RIENZO (Eugenio), 4319.
di Robilant (Maria), 4697.
di Rudinì (Antonio Starabba), 4718.
DI SIMONE (Maria Rosa), 7119.

DI STEFANO MANZELLA (Ivan), 2317.
DI TROCCHIO (Federico), 6033.
DI VASTO (F.), 1899.
Di Vecchi (Girolamo), 5375.
DI VITA (Antonino) , 2404.
DIAKONOFF (Igor M.), 826.
DÍAZ CUEVA (Miguel), 4276.
DIAZ MARTIN (Luis Vicente), 3113.
DIAZ Y DIAZ (Manuel C.), 51, 267.
DICAPRIO (Lisa), 7044.
DICK (E. Michael B.), 1336.
DICK (Wolfgang R.), 6045.
Dickens (Charles), 6357.
DICKIE (M. W.), 540.
DICKINSON (Frederick R.), 4794.
DICKINSON (Margaret), 6610.
Diderot (Denis), 849, 1403, 5936, 5977.
DIDRY (Claude), 7062.
Didymos, 3027.
Diels (Hermann), 757.
DIENEL (Hans-Liudger), 6064.
DIENG (Samba), 8340.
DIERKS (Klaus), 152.
DIESTELKAMP (Bernhard), 1118.
DIETHE (Carol), 1404.
DIETL (Cora), 3550.
DIETRICH (M.), 1731.
DIETZ (Burkhard), 5281.
DIETZSCH (Steffen), 1345.
DILCHER (Gerhard), 1119, 7068.
DILLENBERGER (John), 6391.
DILLER (H.), 1916.
DILLER (Stephan), 8079.
DILLON (John), 4663.
DILLON (M. P. J.), 2037.
Dillon (Myles), 4663.
DIMITRIJEVSKI (Marjan), 7750.
DIMT (Gunter), 921.
DIN (Gilbert C.), 7373.
DINGEL (Irene), 695.
DINTENFASS (Michael), 541, 6690.
DINZELBACHER (Peter), 3872.
Dio Chrysostomus, 2682.
Diocletianus (C. Valerius Diocles), Roman emperor, 2326, 2423, 2811.
Diodorus Pasparos, 2061.
Diodorus Siculus, 1899, 1973.
Diogenes Laertius, 1900.
DION (J.), 1439, 2608.
DION (P.), 1584.
DIONIGI (Ivano), 2659.
Dionisotti (Carlo), 716.
Dionysius Halicarnassensis, 715, 2143, 2348, 2548.
Dioscorus, 1624.
DIÓSZEGI (István), 4604, 7635.
DIOURON (Nicole), 2368.

DIPPEL (Horst), 7087.
DIPPEL (Stewart), 5483.
DIRKS (Carl), 7636.
DIRLMEIER (Ulf), 957.
DITTMER (J.), 1637.
DIXON (Simon M.), 4997.
DIXON-FYLE (Mac), 5031.
DIZDAREVIC (Raif), 5245.
DİZMAN (İbrahim), 5840.
DJALILI (Mohammad-Reza), 4658.
DJEBBAR (Ahmed), 6154.
DJULGEROVA (N.), 7496.
DMITRIEV (Mikhail V.), 3839, 5531.
DMITRIEV (S.), 1580.
DO CARMO GUERREIRO VIEIRA (Maria), 8343.
DOBRANSKI (Stephen B.), 103.
DOBSON (R. Barrie), 3772, 3867.
DOCHERTY (James C.), 960.
DOCHERTY (Thomas), 5727.
DOCKRILL (Michael), 7637.
DOCTER (R. F.), 2248.
DODD (Clement H.), 4210, 7994.
DODDS-PARKER (Douglas), 7760.
DODSON (A.), 1621.
D'OENCH (Ellen), 6494.
DOERING-MANTEUFFEL (Anselm), 1217.
Doerries (Reinhard R.), 6935, 7243.
DOGARU (M.), 934.
DOGARU (Maria), 205.
DOGLIANI (Patrizia), 4730, 4753.
DOGRAMADZHIEVA (E. P.), 3160.
DOĞRU (Halime), 6902.
DOHERTY (Thomas), 6540.
DOHM (Burkhard), 6247.
DOIGNON (J.), 2833.
DOINOV (Stefan), 4148.
DOLBEAU (François), 2834, 2861, 3832.
DOLCI (Fabrizio), 92.
DOLCINI (Carlo), 1091.
DÖLEMEYER (Barbara), 7079.
Dolfin (Lorenzo), 455.
DOLLINGER (Philippe), 3373.
DOMANSKY (Elisabeth), 543.
DOMARADZKA (L.), 1856, 1858.
DOMBECK (Birgit), 182.
DOMENICI (Davide), 8377.
Domenico da Gravina, 717.
DOMÍNGUEZ RODRÍGUEZ (Ana), 3605.
Domitianus (T. Flavius), Roman emperor, 705.
DOMS (Frédéric), 4095.
DONADONI (Sergio), 636.
DONAGHY (Greg), 7813.
DONAT (Helmut), 4471.
DONAT (Peter), 268.

DONAT (Sebastian), 6321.
DONATI (Cl.), 5387.
DONATI (L.), 2230.
DONATO (Maria Pia), 5728.
DONDI (Mirco), 4731.
DONDIN-PAYRE (Monique), 2405, 2484.
DONG (Changzhi), 8117.
Donha (Christoph von), 779.
DONHAM (Donald Lewis), 4284.
DÖNHOFF (Marion), 4418.
Doni (Anton Francesco), 5978.
DONIGER (W.), 1819.
DONLAN (W.), 1831.
DONNELLY (Mark), 4539.
DONNERT (Erich), 5608.
DONOVAN (Josephine), 6190.
DONOVAN (Mark), 684.
DOOLEY (Brendan Maurice), 542, 5609.
Doolittle (Hilda), 6301.
DÖPP (S.), 2587.
DOR (Juliette), 3893.
DOR (Pierre), 3873.
DORAN (Michael Scott), 4277.
DORAN (Susan), 7405.
DORATI (M.), 1884, 1885.
DORE-AUDIBERT (Andrée), 7347.
DORGERLOH (Hartmut), 460.
DORIN (Bernard), 5165.
DÖRING (Detlef), 5628, 5937.
DÖRING (Hans-Joachim), 7875.
DORIVAL (Jérôme), 6541.
DORMOIS (Jean-Pierre), 6690.
DORN (Glenn J.), 7876.
DÖRNER (Gerald), 5467.
D'ORSI (Angelo), 5938.
DOS SANTOS (Joao), 8343.
DOS SANTOS ALVES (Jorge Manuel), 7332, 7406.
DOSDAT (Monique), 67.
DOSSAL (Mariam), 4642.
DOSSE (François), 535, 828.
DOSSENA (Giampaolo), 1218.
Dostoevskij (Fëdor), 6332, 6359.
DOUGLAS (George H.), 5841.
Douglas (Mary), 718.
DOUZINAS (Costas), 394.
DOUZOU (Alain), 3798.
DOVERE (Ugo), 5288.
DOWE (Dieter), 4470.
DOWER (John W.), 4795.
DOWNS (Catherine M.), 6309.
DOWNS (Donald Alexander), 5729.
DOYLE (William), 4377.
Dracontius (Blossius Aemilius), 2844.
DRĂGOESCU (Anton), 4973.
DRAKARD (Jane), 8080.
DRAKE (James D.), 7433.
DRAPALA (Milan), 4222.

DREIST (Markus), 7560.
DRESCHER (Seymour), 7305.
DRESSLER (Wanda), 3998.
DREYER (B.), 1901.
Dreyfus (Alfred), 740, 4350, 5610, 6310, 6335, 6551.
DREYFUS-ARMAND (Geneviève), 4321.
DRIJVERS (Jan Willem), 2796, 2809, 2872, 2891.
DRINKWATER (J. F.), 2609.
DRISCOLL (Michael), 3874.
DROBIN (Ulf), 1376.
DROMMER (Günther), 4396.
DROOGLEVER (P. J.), 4645, 7814.
DROSS (Elisabeth), 7481.
DROSTE (Thomas), 5775.
DROUIN (Michel), 6310.
DROULIA (Loukia), 7789.
Droysen (Johann Gustav), 772.
DROZ (Laurent), 5139.
DRUMMOND (Andrew), 2343, 2406.
Dryden (John), 6253.
DU BOIS (Pierre), 5140.
DU BOIS (Thomas A.), 3320.
DU BRUCK (Edelgard E.), 3448.
DU CHASTEL (Pierre), 4322.
Du Hamel (J. B.), 5978.
DU JONCHAY (Gilles), 4897.
DU REAU (Elisabeth), 7881.
DUARTE (Adriano Luiz), 4123.
DUARTE (José Bento), 8344.
DUARTE (Luís Miguel), 3374.
DUBIEL (Helmut), 4419.
DUBIN (Lois C.), 4075.
DUBOIS (Sébastien), 7389.
DUBOST (Jean-François), 4323.
DUBROW (Heather), 6218.
DUBUIS (Olivier F.), 6797.
DUBUISSON (M.), 1065, 2344.
Duby (Georges), 719.
DUCELLIER (A.), 3018.
DUCEY (Michael T.), 4827.
DUCHHARDT (Heinz), 3946, 7137, 7434.
DÜCKERS (R.), 435.
DUCLERT (Vincent), 410, 417, 740, 773, 797, 3930, 5610.
DUCREUX (Marie-Élizabeth), 6903.
DUCREY (P.), 2038.
DUDEK (J.), 3019.
DUFF (T.), 2093.
DUFFELL (Martin J.), 3552.
DUFOUR (Jean), 3379.
Duguet (Jacques-Joseph), 4777.
Duhalde (Eduardo Luis), 4048.
DUHAMEL (E.), 4366.
DUHAMEL (Morvan), 4324.
DUHAMEL-LACOSTE (Sophie), 384.
Duhem (Pierre), 5967.

Duker (K. A.), 792.
DULAR (Janez), 1048.
DULL (Jonathan Romer), 5183.
DULPHY (Christine), 4360.
DUMAN (Hasan), 87.
DUMETT (Raymond E.), 7309.
DUMITRIU-SNAGOV (Ion), 7701.
DUMONS (Bruno), 4328.
DUMONT (Georges-Henri), 961.
DUMONT (Wouter), 4096.
DUMOUCHEL (Daniel), 5939.
DUMOULIN (Olivier), 829.
DUMVILLE (David), 7.
DUNBABIN (Katherine M. D.), 2742.
DUNDOVICH (Elena), 7877.
DUNI (Matteo), 5388.
DUNKERLEY (James), 7683.
DUNLAP (Thomas R.), 6904.
DUNN (F. M.), 2039.
DUNNAGE (Jonathan), 4704.
DÜNNEBEIL (Sonja), 3155.
Duns Scotus (Johannes), 3721.
DUNTHORN (David J.), 7740.
DUPAQUIER (J.), 6840.
DUPLOUY (A.), 1980.
DUPONT (Jean-Claude), 6065.
DUPONT-BOUCHAT (Marie-Sylvie), 7180.
DUPPLER (Jörg), 7587.
DUPRE (José), 3875.
DUPRE DE BOULOIS (Aude), 7561.
Dupré Theseider (Eugenio), 720.
DUPRET (Baudouin), 3300.
DUPUIS (Anne), 461.
DUPUY (Marie-Anne), 450.
DURĂ (Nicolae), 1121.
DURAND (Isabelle), 5761.
DURAND (Romain), 7638.
DURANTON (Henri), 5843.
Duras (Marguerite), 6304.
Dürer (Albrecht), 6469.
DURISCH (N.), 693.
ĎURIŠKA (Zdenko), 5055.
Durkheim (Emile), 721, 1334, 1345, 5705.
ĎURKOVÁ (Mária), 5037.
ĎUROVČÍKOVÁ (Margita), 5055.
DURUZ (Jean), 6905.
DUSANIC (S.), 1926.
DUSEK (Val), 6066.
DÜSELDER (Heike), 6906.
DUSINBERRE (E. R. M.), 1792.
DUSO (Giuseppe), 5611.
DUTTA (Indrani), 7639.
DUTU (Alesandru), 7745.
DUVAL (Frédéric), 3184, 3762.
DUVAL (Karen), 5183.
DUVAL (Noël), 2892.
DUVAL (Y.-M.), 2835.
DVOŘÁK (Pavel), 3097.

INDEX OF NAMES 359

DWYER (Britta C.), 6453.
DYKSTRA (David L.), 7497.
DYMARSKI (Mirosław), 7702.
DYRVIK (Ståle), 4886.
DYSON (R. H.), 1793.
DZIARNOVICH (Aleh), 4091.
DZIEMBOWSKI (Edmond), 7435.

E

EAKINS (Rex), 3688.
EARNSHAW (Brian), 6432.
EASTERLING (P.), 2798.
EATON-KRASS (M.), 1622.
EBATA (Joanne Michi), 4859.
EBBESEN (Sten), 3741.
EBEL (Edouard), 4325.
EBERSPERGER (Birgit), 3876.
EBRAHIMNEJAD (Hormoz), 4659.
ECHEVARRIA (Ana), 3301.
ECK (Werner), 1752, 2318, 2407, 2428, 2538, 2743.
ECKARD (Michels), 4326.
ECKART (Karl), 4515.
ECKERT (Andreas), 7348.
Eckhart (Meister), 3739.
ECO (U.), 1429.
EDDY (F. W.), 1623.
EDELMAYER (Friedrich), 4076.
Eden (Anthony), 7866.
EDGERTON (Robert B.), 7498.
EDROIU (Nicolae), 8, 932, 3219, 6680.
Edward III, king of England, 3268.
EDWARDS (Catharine), 5690.
EDWARDS (Jill), 7878.
EDWARDS (John), 3767.
EDWARDS (M. J.), 2610.
EDWARDS (Mark), 2867.
EDWARDS (Philip), 8387.
Efeso da Cuma, 722.
EFRATI (Noga), 4652.
EGAN (V.), 1753.
EGELHAAF-GAISER (U.), 2215.
EGGENBERGER (Christoph), 35.
EGGERT (Wolfgang), 3126.
EGGINTON (William), 3726.
Egidio Romano, arcivescovo di Bourges, 1058.
EGORIN (Anatolij Z.), 4814.
EGOROVA (N. I.), 8000.
EHLER (Christine), 3553.
EHRENPREIS (Stefan), 5281.
EHRINGHAUS (H.), 1581.
EICHE (Sabine), 3177.
EICHENHOFER (Eberhard), 4397.
EICHOLTZ (Dietrich), 7719.
EICKHOFF (E.), 3021.
EISENHARDT (Ulrich), 1122.
EISENSTADT (S. N.), 5389.
EISERMANN (Daniel), 7879.

EISFELD (Alfred), 7826.
EISLER (Ejal Jakob), 317.
Ekaterina II, Kaiserin von Rußland, 5608, 7429.
EKELUND (Robert B., jr.), 6641.
EKENGREN (Ann Marie), 5128.
EL GAMMAL (Jean), 4327.
ELAD (Amikam), 3303.
Elagabalus (Varius Avitus), Roman emperor, 2732.
ELEFANTE (Maria), 2387.
EL-EINI (Roza I. M.), 7333.
ELEY (Geoff), 6934.
ELFASSI (J.), 2836.
ELFWENDAHL (Magnus), 1220.
Elia (Leopoldo), 1140.
Eliade (Mircea), 1325, 1373, 1387, 5932.
ELIAS DE TEJADA Y SPINOLA (Francisco), 1066.
Elias Nisibenus, 1594.
ELIASSON (Pär), 331.
ELIODORO (Savino), 2408.
Elizabeth I, queen of England, 4534, 7409.
ELLEMAN (Bruce A.), 4850.
ELLIOTT (Dyan), 3727.
ELLIOTT (J. H.), 787.
ELLISTON (Jon), 7820.
ELLNER (Steve), 5231.
ELLSWORTH (Mary Ellen), 5730.
ELLUL (Jacques), 1123.
ELORZA (Antonio), 5084.
ELOY GUTIÉRREZ (Jesús), 5390.
ELSØE JENSEN (Jørgen), 3375.
ELTON (William R.), 6239.
ELVERT (Jürgen), 7562.
ELWOOD (Christopher), 5485.
EMBREE (Dan), 3175.
EMERY (Anthony), 3648.
EMMERSON (Donald K.), 4646.
EMMERSON (Richard K.), 1221.
EMMETT (Tony), 4862.
Empedocles, 2156, 2159.
EMPTOZ (Gérard), 6154.
EMSLEY (Clive), 7120.
ENDERLE-BURCEL (Gertrude), 4073.
ENDERS (Victoria Lorée), 6965.
ENDREI (Walter), 6064.
Enenn (Edith), 3204.
ENGELBERTS (Derck), 7455.
ENGELMANN (Roger), 4441.
ENGELS (Eve-Marie), 6068.
ENGERMAN (Stanley L.) , 1189.
ENGLISH (Edward D.), 3443.
ENGLISH (Richard), 1103.
Ennius (Q.), 2711.
ENRÍQUEZ FERNÁNDEZ (Javier), 3115ù.
ENSALACO (Mark), 4169.

Enver Paşa, 5177, 8073.
EPHAISTOS (Panagiotes), 7237.
Ephialtes, 1997.
Epicharmus, 2161.
Epictetus, 2845.
EPP (Verena), 3450.
EPPLE (Moritz), 6069.
ERASMUS ROTERODAMUS (Desiderius) , 5259, 5260, 5930.
ERBER (Nancy), 6901.
ERBSE (H.), 2095.
ERDKAMP (P.), 2539.
ERDOĞRU (Akif), 6735.
EREN (Güler), 1007.
Eric Menved de Danemark, 3234.
ERICKSEN (Hilary), 7385.
ERICSON (David F.), 5209.
ERICSON (Edward E. III), 7703.
ERICSON (Lars), 5129.
ERICSSON (Christer), 1154.
Erignac (Claude), 4347.
ERKELENZ (D.), 2540.
ERKENS (Franz R.), 547.
ERLANDE-BRANDENBURG (Alain), 3635.
ERLER (M.), 2817.
ERLINDO (V.), 1251.
ERMINI PANI (L.), 3912.
ERMOLOVA (Irina E.), 1545.
ERNST (Germana), 5391.
ERNST (Waltraud), 6141.
EROFEEVA (I. V.), 4807.
ERTUĞ TARIM (Zeynep), 1222.
ERTÜRK (Korkut A.), 8064.
ERTZDORFF (Xenja von), 3610.
ESAKOV (Vasilii Alekseevich), 335.
ESCH (Arnold), 548, 1288.
ESCOBAR (Edward J.), 6907.
ESCOBEDO (Héctor L.), 8383.
ESCOLAR (Hipólito), 104.
ESCRIBANO (María Victoria), 705, 2893.
ESGUERRA (Jorge Cañizares), 5612.
ESHEL (H.), 1754.
ESIPOV (Valerij V.), 769.
ESKANDER (Saad Basher), 7238.
ESPARZA MARTÍNEZ (Bernardino), 4828.
ESPIGADO (Gloria), 6975.
ESPINO LÓPEZ (Antonio), 5086.
ESPOSITO (P.), 2627.
ESTÉVEZ SOLA (Juan A.), 3180, 3764.
Estienne (H.), 792.
ETEMADI (G. F.), 8055.
ÉTIENNE (Bruno), 4025.
ETIENNE (Sauveur Pierre), 4594.
Euclides, Athenian archon, 2013.
Eudemus Rhodius, 2181.

Eudocia (Aelia Augusta), consort of Theodosius II, 2961.
EUJANIAN (Alejandro), 549.
EULER (Andrea), 921.
Euripides, 2087, 2099, 2116, 2126, 6193.
Eusebius Caesareensis, 2349, 2962.
Eusebius Vercellensis, Sanctus, 2886, 2902, 2932.
Eusthatius Thessalonicensis, 3085.
Eutropius, 2350.
Euw (Anton von), 3679.
EVALET (André), 4283.
EVANS (C. A.), 2894.
EVANS (Dorinda), 6454.
EVANS (Ellen Lovell), 4867.
EVANS (John L.), 7499.
EVANS (Sterling), 4196.
EVENEPOEL (W.), 2895.
EVERGATES (Theodore), 3361.
EVERSHED (R. P.), 1451.
EVERSON (Paul), 3118.
EVLETH (Donna), 5828.
ÉVRARD (É.), 2409.
EVREN (Nazif), 5782.
EWAN (Elizabeth), 3398.
EWERTOWSKI (Jörg), 5940.
Ewoutszoon (Jan), 125.

F

FABIANI (Roberta), 242.
FABIANI (Silvia), 6666.
FABRE (Daniel), 550, 614.
FABRE (Pierre-Antoine), 1310, 5436, 6148.
FABRE (Rémi), 3930, 5315.
FABREGAS VALCARCE (R.), 1450, 1505.
FABRE-SERRIS (Jacqueline), 2611.
FABRE-VASSAS (Claudine), 915.
FABRI (Felix), 3760, 3878.
Fabri (Guglielmo), 6125.
FABRICIUS (Hanne), 3913.
FABRICIUS (J.), 2231.
FAGAN (G. G.), 2040.
FAGGI (Paola), 5392.
FAGGIONATO (Raffaella), 4999.
FAHLBUSCH (Michael), 6070.
FAHRENBACH (Sabine), 5731.
FAHSEN (Federico), 8383.
FAILLER (A.), 2965.
FAIVRE (Alexandre), 2896.
FAIVRE D'ARCIER (Bernard), 3554.
FAIX (Gerhard), 5284.
FAIZER (R. S .), 1582.
FAJNHAUZ (David), 4816.
Falcone di Benevento, 723.
FALES (F. M.), 1755.
FALISOVÁ (Anna), 5038.
FALKNER (C.), 1981.

FALLETTI CRUCIANI (Clelia), 6545.
FALOLA (Toyin), 965, 7318.
FALTUS (Jozef), 6651.
FALZONE (S.), 2260.
FAMERÉE (J.), 1303, 5280.
FANEL (Luis), 4044.
FANO SANTI (Manuela), 458.
FANTHAM (ELAINE), 2612.
Faraday (Michael), 6035.
FARDON (Richard), 718.
FARGE (Arlette), 822.
FARON (Olivier), 4732, 6838.
FASANO (Jacopo), 5393.
FATOUROS (G.), 3022.
FATTORI (Marta), 5978.
FAUBER (C. M.), 1982.
FAULHABER (Charles), 3521.
FAUST (A.), 1547.
Faustina, Roman empress, 2314.
FAUSTO (Boris), 4124.
FAUTH (Wolfgang), 2699.
FAUVE-CHAMOUX (Antoinette), 6833.
Favier (Jean), 1160.
Favorinus, 2998.
FAVREAU (Robert), 3117.
FAVREAUS (R.), 389.
FAYE (Emmanuel), 5933.
FAZIO (Mara), 6546.
Febvre (Lucien), 724.
Federico da Montefeltro, 6499.
FEDERSPIEL (M.), 1882.
FEDOROVICH (Kent), 6910.
FEDOSOVA (El'mira P.), 5616.
FEIERSTEIN (Daniel), 7704.
FEIERTAG (O.), 6798.
FEISSEL (Denis), 2963.
FEJFER (J.), 2745.
FELDENKIRCHEN (Wilfried), 6694.
FELDKAMP (Michael F.), 4392.
FELDMANN (Gerald D.), 7741.
FELDMANN (Reinhardo), 2567.
FELGENTREU (Fritz), 2346.
Felicitas, Sancta, 2957.
Felipe I el Hermoso, rey de Navarra, 3098.
Felipe II, rey de España, 4076, 4739, 4781, 5087.
FELIU (Gaspar), 3146.
FELIX (Joël), 6799.
FÉLIX LÓPEZ (R.), 1515.
FELL (A. London), 1124.
FELLMANN (Dorothea), 5732.
FELLOWS-JENSEN (Gillian), 42.
FELTEN (Franz J.), 3786.
FELTRINELLI (Carlo), 5829.
FENG (Min), 8118.
FENG (Tianyu), 8119.
Feng (Yuxiang), 8126.
FENOALTEA (Stefano), 1159.
FENZI (Enrico), 3512, 3555.

FERENC (Tone), 1000.
Ferenc II Rákóczi, prince of Transylvania, 7424.
FERGUSON (Niall), 183, 878, 7563.
Fernández (Gregorio), 6484.
FERNÁNDEZ CATÓN (José María), 3134.
FERNÁNDEZ DE LA CUESTA (Ismael), 1286.
FERNÁNDEZ FLÓREZ (José Antonio), 3116.
FERNÁNDEZ HIDALGO (María del Carmen), 418.
FERNÁNDEZ MANZANO (J.), 1530.
FERNÁNDEZ VALVERDE (Juan), 3180, 3764.
FERNANDEZ-JALVO (Y.), 1486.
FERNOUX (H.-L.), 2041.
FERRARI (Michele Camillo), 30, 3761.
FERRARI ZUMBINI (Massimo), 5941.
FERRARO VETTORI (Paola), 40.
FERRAZ DE OLIVEIRA SILVA SANTOS Maria (Leonor), 8037.
FERRE I MALLOL (Maria Teresa), 3376.
FERREIRA (Manuel Ennes), 4037.
FERREIRA (Tito Lívio), 4125.
FERREIRA A. S. DUARTE (Teresa), 65.
FERREIRA DOS SANTOS (Estilaque), 4126.
FERREIRA PERAZZO (Priscila), 4127.
FERREIRÓS (José), 6071.
FERRER (Ada), 4205.
FERRER (André), 6736.
FERRER MUNOZ (Manuel), 4841.
FERRERI (Luigi), 756.
FERRONE (Vincenzo), 5673.
FEST (Joachim C.), 4422.
FESTA (Egidio), 6079.
FESTY (M.), 2367.
FEUERSBACH (U.), 1661.
FEYEL (Gilles), 5842.
FICHTE (Johann Gottlieb), 5888, 5955, 6003, 6017.
FICHTNER (Paula S.), 966.
Ficino (Marsilio), 6125.
FIEDEWALD (Michael), 6072.
FIELD (Rosalind), 3556.
FIELDHOUSE (D. K.), 7307.
Fielding (Henry), 6263.
FIELDING (J.), 7883.
FIERRO (Alfred), 269.
FIGAL (Gerald), 5617.
FIJAŁKOWSKI (Paweł), 4940.
Filangieri (Gaetano), 1088.
FILGES (Axel), 2746.
FILOGRASSO (Nando), 5779.

FILORAMO (Giovanni), 1348.
FINCHELSTEIN (Federico), 487.
FINCKH (Ruth), 3557.
FINDLEN (Paula), 6125.
FINE (S.), 1761.
FINK (Eugen), 5889.
FINK (Hilary L.), 5945.
FINK (Troels), 4259.
FINKE (Laurie A.), 3558.
FINLAYSON (J. C.), 1486.
FINLEY-CROSWHITE (S. Annette), 4330.
FINNEGAN (Margaret), 5192.
FINZI (C.), 2897.
FINZSCH (Norbert), 899, 967.
FIOR (Michel), 7705.
FIORANI (Luigi), 3414.
FIORAVANTI (Maurizio), 7084.
FIORE (D.), 2410.
FIORELLO (C. S.), 2789.
FIORENTINI (Erna), 385.
FIORENTINO (Carlo M.), 4733.
Firmicus Maternus (Iulius), 2708.
Firmilianus, 2942.
FIRRO (Kais M.), 4687.
FISCH (Maria), 4863.
FISCHBACH (Frank), 5946.
FISCHEL (Jack R.), 968.
FISCHER (Alan), 7241.
FISCHER (Benjamin B.), 7864.
FISCHER (Bernd Jürgen), 4019.
FISCHER (D.), 6073.
FISCHER (Ernst), 5831.
FISCHER (Heinz), 4084.
FISCHER (Holger), 4617, 6064, 6064.
FISCHER (Jasna), 6640.
FISCHER (Joachim), 4663.
FISCHER (Wilfried Peter A.), 184.
FISCHER-LICHTE (Erika), 6627.
Fishacre (Richard), 3738.
FISHER (John), 7564.
FISHOF (Iris), 62.
FISHWICK (D.), 2747.
FITTSCHEN (Klaus), 2411.
FITZGERALD (Charles M.), 906.
FITZPATRICK (Sheila), 5000.
FIX (Andrew), 5486.
FLACH (Dieter), 2898.
FLADERER (Ludwig), 2854.
FLASHAR (M.), 2042.
Flavius Clemens, Sanctus, 2929.
Flavius Josephus, 743, 1744, 2390, 2693, 2846.
FLEET (Kate), 6737.
FLEGEL (Christoph), 5487.
FLEISCHER (Hagen), 7789.
FLEMING (D.), 1662.
FLEMING (John), 1289.
FLEMING (Katherine Elizabeth), 7461.

FLEMING (Martha H.), 3879.
FLEMMING (Rebecca), 2543.
FLETCHER (Brian H.), 5488.
FLEURIER (Nicolas), 7565.
FLEURY (Antoine), 7706.
FLINT (John E.), 4881.
FLOOD (Josephine), 8391.
FLORES (Marcello), 831.
FLORI (Jean), 3880.
Florus of Lyons, 3757.
FLOWER (Harriet I.), 2493.
FLÜCKIGER-HAWKER (E.), 1678.
FLUSIN (M.), 1794.
FLYNN (William T.), 3689.
FOCARDI (G.), 2361.
FODOR (Pál), 6738.
FOERSTER (G.), 2743.
FÖGEN (Th.), 2613.
FOGLESONG (David S.), 7884.
FOITZIK (Jan), 7885.
FOLCANDO (E.), 2320.
FOLEY (Michael), 7088.
FOLEY (Tadhg), 5747.
FÖLLINGER (S.), 2828.
FOLQUE DE MENDOÇA (Filipe), 207.
FOLTIN (Hans-Friedrich), 5857.
FOLTZ (Richard C.), 1226.
FONKICH (B. L.), 52.
FONKOUA (Romuald), 330.
FONNESBESCH-WULFF (Benedite), 3234.
FONTAINE (Laurence), 6911.
FONTANA (Benedetto), 5619.
FONTANA (Paolo), 5396.
FONTANA (Vincenzo), 6416.
Fontane (Theodore), 6305.
FONTANEDA PÉREZ (E.), 1530.
FONTOLLIET HONORÉ (Micheline), 4283.
FONTUGNE (M.), 1520.
FONYI (Antonia), 6352.
FOOT (John), 6549.
Foot (M. R. D.), 7800.
FOOTE (R. M.), 1583.
FORABOSCHI (Daniele), 2413.
FORBERGER (Rudolf), 6695.
FORCADE (O.), 4366.
FORCE (James E.), 6126.
FORD (Patrick K.), 3508.
FORD (Philip), 6240.
FORD (Robert), 1272.
FORDANT (Laurent), 270.
FORDERER (Christof), 6314.
FORENBAHER (S.), 1496.
FORGES DAVANZATI (Guglielmo), 6685.
FORLIN PATRUCCO (M.), 2899.
FORNARO (Pierpaolo), 2358.
FORNI (Giovanni), 2494.
FORSDYKE (S.), 1983.

FORSEN (Annette), 7751.
FORSEN (Björn), 7751.
FORSSMAN (Erik), 5620.
FÖRSTER (Stig), 7482.
FORSYTHE (GARY), 749.
FORTE (F.), 2043, 6675.
Fortescue (John sir), 3267.
FORTUN (Luis Javier), 3111.
FOSCHI (Enrico), 4735.
FOSSIER (Robert), 3130, 3380.
FOSSO (Mario), 6422.
FOSTER (Edward E.), 3559.
Foucault (Michel), 851, 5904, 5913.
FOUCRIER (Annick), 6912.
FOULON (E.), 767.
FOURNET (J. L.), 1624.
FOURRIER (S.), 2232.
FOWLER (Colin F.), 5947.
FOWLER (William), 4825.
FOX (A.), 552.
FOX (Claire F.), 5621.
FOX (Robert), 1228, 6124.
FOX (Thomas C.), 4423.
FOX-GENOVESE (Elizabeth), 639.
FOYSTER (Elizabeth A.), 6913.
FRACCHIA (Joseph), 830.
FRADERA (Josep Maria), 7308, 7334.
FRÆNKEL (Henry), 168.
FRÆNKEL (Louis), 168.
FRAETERS (Veerle), 3701.
FRAGALÀ DATA (Isabella), 3686.
FRAGNITO (Gigliola), 5397.
FRAME (G.), 1679.
FRAME (Robin), 3495.
FRANCE (J.), 2544.
FRANCE (John), 3194.
FRANCESCHINI (Claudia), 5394.
Francesco II Gonzaga, 315.
FRANCHET D'ESPEREY (Sylvie), 2614.
FRANCHI (Antonino), 3855.
FRANCHI (Michela), 6834.
FRANCIA (Enrico), 4736.
FRANCIOSI (Gennaro), 185.
FRANCIS (James), 1365.
Franciscus Assisiensis, Sanctus, 3412, 3803, 3844, 3852.
FRANCO (Carlo), 1929, 2096.
FRANCO (Paul), 5948.
Franco y Bahamonde (Francisco), 4963, 5088, 5090, 5112, 5118, 7878.
FRANÇOIS (V.), 1795.
François I, roi de France, 4322.
FRANÇOISE DE ROGUIN (C.), 2186.
FRANCOVICH (Riccardo), 3095.
FRANGOULIDIS (Stavros), 2615.
FRANGOULIS (H.), 1930.
FRANK (M.), 2148.

FRANK (R.), 7277.
FRANK (Robert), 7914.
FRANK (Stephen P.), 5622.
FRANK (Tibor), 4605.
FRANKEL (D.), 1541.
Franklin (Benjamin), 5183.
FRANTZ (Pierre), 6550.
FRANZ (M.), 2685.
Franz Joseph I, Kaiser von Österreich, 4085.
FRANZINELLI (Mimmo), 4737.
FRASCADORE (Angela), 9.
FRASER (Russell), 6191.
FRASER (William Hamish), 4540.
FRASSETTO (Michael), 678, 3296.
FRAZIK (Wojciech), *XIII*.
FRECHE (Katharina), 3560.
FREDE (M.), 2799, 2814.
FREDERIKSEN (Peter), 1041.
FREDOUILLE (Jean-Claude), 2861.
FREEDMAN (Joseph S.), 5733.
FREEDMAN (Lawrence), 7886.
FREEDMAN (Paul H.), 3452, 3770.
FREEMAN (Michael), 1129, 3614.
FREEMAN (Peter), *VII*.
FREEMAN (Samuel), 979.
FREESTONE (Robert), 6417.
FREGA (Ana), 5226.
Frege (Friedrich Ludwig Gottlob), 5983.
FREGNI (Euride), 4706.
FREI (Norbert), 553.
Frei Montalva (Eduardo), 4177.
FREIGANG (Christian), 3652.
FREISE (Eckhard), 3853.
FREITAG (Ulrike), 5151.
FRENCH (Roger), 6075.
FRENCH (William E.), 5671.
FRENDO (Henry), 4821.
FRENKEL' (Matvej Ju.), 4813.
FRENKEN (Ralph), 1229.
Freud (Sigmund), 230, 491, 5956.
FREVERT (Ute), 3978.
FREY (Hugo), 684.
FREY (Linda S.), 7242.
FREY (Marsha L.), 7242.
FREYBERGER (Bert), 2412.
FREYBURGER-GALLAND (Marie L.), 2616.
FREYDANK (H.), 1680.
Freymond (Jacques), 7997.
FRICK (Lennart W.), 5130.
Frickenhaus (August), 803.
FRIDENSON (Patrick), 3930.
FRIEDEBURG (Robert von), 7089.
FRIEDL (Jiří), 7752.
FRIEDMAN (Isaiah), 7568.
FRIEDMAN (Russell L.), 3741.
FRIEDMAN MORDECHAI (Akiva), 3275.
FRIEDRICH (J.), 1756.

FRIEDRICH (Margret), 5785.
Friedrich II, röm-deutscher Kaiser, 665, 3244.
FRIELL (G.), 2824.
FRIER (Bruce W.), 554.
FRIGO (Daniela), 7395.
FRIISBERG (Claus), 4260.
FRIIS-HANSEN (Jan), 1518.
FRIMMOVÁ (Eva), 336.
FRIŠ (Darko), 951.
Frischlin (Nicodemus), 6228.
FRITZ (C.), 1456.
FRITZ (V.), 1757.
Frobenius (Ferdinand Georg), 6060.
FRÓES DA FONSECA (María), 4829.
FROIDEVAUX (Yves), 6835.
Froissart (Jean), 3172.
FROLOV (Eduard D.), 555.
Fronto (M. Cornelius), 2351.
FROSINI (Vittorio), 7072.
FROST (Alan), 7315.
Frowin (Abt von Engelberg), 35.
FRUCHTMAN (Maya), 3276.
FRÜH (Dorothee), 186.
FRUTON (Joseph), 6076.
FRY (Michael Graham), 7641.
FRYE (Susan), 6955.
FRYE JACOBSON (Matthew), 6915.
FUBINI (Riccardo), 694, 4720.
FUBINI LEUZZI (Maria), 187.
FUCCARO (Nelida), 4653.
FUCECCHI (Marco), 1955.
FUCHS (Erich), 5888.
FUCHS (Friedrich), 7569.
FUCHS (Konrad), 4425.
FUCIC (Branko), 10.
FUENTES (Jordi), 947.
FUENTES WENDLING (Manuel), 4170.
FUGAZZOLA DELPINO (M. A.), 1531.
FUHRER (Th.), 2817, 2837.
FUHRING (Peter), 6496.
FUHRMANN (Manfred), 5786.
FUJIKI (Hisashi), 8276.
FUJITA (Satoru), 8277.
Fujiwara (Michinaga), 8320.
FUJIZANE (Kumiko), 8278.
Fukuzawa (Yukichi), 5735.
FULBROOK (Mary), 684.
FULCHER (Jane F.), 6551.
FULCI (Francesco Paolo), 7260.
Fulgentius, Sanctus, 2904.
FULLER (Linda), 7045.
FULLERTON (John), 6593.
FULTON (Ann), 5949.
Fumagalli (Vito), 725.
FUMAROLI (Marc), 436, 5623.
FUNARI (R.), 2370.
FURBERTH (Frank), 3592.

Furet (François), 726.
FURLOUGH (Ellen), 6891.
FURRE (Berge), 4887.
FURSENKO (Aleksandr A.), 7887.
FUSI (Juan Pablo), 1230.
FÜSSEL (Stephan), 107.
FUZIER (H.), 2618.
FYSON (Robert), 4533.

G

GABBA (Emilio), 556, 636, 735, 756, 1093, 2413, 4752.
GÄBE (Sabine), 3707.
GABRIEL (C.), 2852.
GADDIS (John Lewis), 7863.
GAGLIANI (Dianella), 4738.
GAGNON (Alain-G.), 4161.
GAIDUK (Ilya V.), 8000.
GAILEY (Harry A.), 981.
GAILLARD-SEUX (P.), 2364.
GAINOR (J. Ellen), 6595.
Gainsborough (Thomas), 6480.
Gaismair (Michael), 4497.
GAL'PERINA (Bella D.), 4987.
GALANTE (Miguel), 7704.
GALASSO (Giuseppe), 776, 4739, 7390.
Galba (L. Livius Ocella Ser. Sulpicius), Roman emperor, 705.
Galenus (Claudius), 1902, 6125.
GALEOTTI (Lorenzo), 2288.
Galilei (Galileo), 6040, 6079, 6091, 6132, 6157, 6182.
GALILI (Ziva), 5015.
GALIMBERTI (Alessandro), 2390.
GALINSKY (K.), 2686.
GALL (Lothar), 637, 7741.
GALLERANO (Nicola), 646, 831.
GALLÍ CEIUDO (R. J.), 2199.
GALLI DELLA LOGGIA (Ernesto), 4711.
GALLICO (C.), 4752.
GALLIN (Isabel), 7642.
GALLINARO (Ilaria), 6192.
GALLO (Gastón), 1420.
GALLO (L.), 557.
GALLORINI (C.), 1660.
GALLOWAY (J.), 2306.
GALLUCCIO (F.), 2291.
GALLUZZI (M.), 4752.
GALOPPE (Raul A.), 6536.
GALPERIN (Charles), 6154.
GALSTERER (H.), 2414.
Gálvez (William), 4190.
GAMAUF (Richard), 2495.
GAMBA (Antonio), 5720.
GAMBERALE (Leopoldo), 2321, 2619.
Gambetta (Léon), 4299.

GAMBINI (Hugo), 4045.
GAMBLES (Anna), 6676.
GAMBONI (Dario), 5276.
GAMES (Alison), 1162.
GAMESON (Richard), 53.
GAMPER-SCHLUND (Rudolf), 54.
GANAPINI (Luigi), 4740.
GANCI (Massimo), 4702, 7090.
Gandhi (Mohandas Karamchand), 4636, 4644, 7318.
GANDHI (Rajmohan), 8081.
GANDINO (Germana), 1080.
GANDOLFO (Francesco), 3649.
GANE (Robert), 3381.
GANELIN (Rafail Sh.), 4991.
GANIAGE (Jean), 6836.
GANS (Evelien), 4868.
GANTER (Regina), 7384.
GANTZ (Ulrike), 2847.
GAO (Jialong), 8120.
GAO (Lecai), 8121.
GAO (Xiaoxing), 8122.
GARAVAGLIA (Juan Carlos), 6765, 6916.
GARBER (Elizabeth), 6077.
GARBINI (Paolo), 282, 3164.
GARBUZOV (V. N.), 5193.
GARCÍA (Hernán David), 5089.
GARCÍA (J. F. F.), 1532.
GARCIA (José Manuel), 337.
GARCIA (Patrick), 535.
GARCÍA CAMPILLO (José Miguel), 8362.
GARCÍA DE CORTÁZAR (Fernando), 971.
GARCIA DE CORTAZAR Y RUIZ DE AGUIRRE (José Angel), 3111.
GARCÌA DELGADO (José Luis), 1163.
GARCÍA DÍAZ (Isabel), 3454.
GARCÍA GUINEA (Miguel Angel), 3451.
GARCÍA I FONTANET (Angel), 5119.
GARCÍA LAGUARDIA (Jorge Mario), 4600.
GARCÍA MARTÍNEZ (Bernardo), 1224.
GARCÍA ORO (José), 437.
GARCIA ROVIRA (Anna M.), 5085.
GARCÍA RUIPÉREZ (Mariano), 418.
GARCÍA SANJUÁN (L.), 1533.
GARCÍA TEIJEIRO (M.), 1966.
GARCÍA VALLE (Adela), 24.
GARCÌA Y GARCÌA (Antonio), 1125.
GARCIA-ARENAL (Mercedes), 558.
GARCÍA-BELLIDO (M. P.), 248.
GARÇON (Anne-Françoise), 6696.
Gardel (Carlos), 6534.
GARDEY (Delphine), 5625.

GARDIKA-ALEXANDROPOULOU (Katerina), 4581.
GARDINER (Ellen), 6249.
GARDT (Andreas), 291.
GARE (Deborah), 4069.
GARFAGNINI (Giancarlo), 390.
GARFINKEL (Simson L.), 6078.
GARGETT (Graham), 5643.
GARIBALDI (Vittoria), 6456.
GARIGLIO (Bartolo), 5271.
Garin (Eugenio), 5558.
GARIPZANOV (I. H.), 244.
GARLAN (Y.), 2044.
GARLAND (L.), 3024.
GARLATI GIUGNI (Loredana), 7157.
GARNIER (Bruno), 6193.
GARNSEY (G), 2545.
GARRAUD (Philippe), 7753.
GARRIDO (Pablo María), 5437.
GARRIDO MORENO (Antonio), 6418.
GARRIDO-HORY (M.), 2546.
GARRISON (M. B.), 1584.
GARSOIAN (Nina G.), 3881.
GARSON (Robert A.), 5194.
GÄRTNER (Th.), 1841.
GARUTI (Adriano), 5398.
GARY (Brett), 5195.
GARZYA (A.), 3025.
GASCOU (Jacques), 2415, 2547.
GASIOROWSKI (Stefan), *XIII*.
GASNAULT (Pierre), 559.
GASRATJAN (Svetlana M.), 5535.
GASSER (Karen M.), 3561.
GASTALDI (V.), 2015.
GASTI (Fabio), 2816.
GASTON COUNT OF FOIX., 3131.
GASTONI (L.), 2900.
GATTAZ (Yvon), 4335.
GATTI (Hilary), 5950.
GATTI (Luciana), 6697.
GATTO (Ludovico), 3455, 3790.
GATTONI (Maurizio), 7408.
GATZ (Erwin), 5329.
GAUCHET (Marcel), 832.
GAUDEMET (Jean), 1087.
GAUJAC (P.), 7754.
GAUTHIER (Christophe), 6552.
GAUTHIER (Ph.), 1859.
GAUTIER DE COINCI, 3840.
GAUVARD (Claude), 3222.
GAVRILOV (Boris I.), 7755.
GAVROLGU (Kostas), 6156.
GAY (Luis), 4046.
GAZIAUX (É.), 1303.
GAZZANO (F.), 1950.
GEARY (Patrick J.), 833.
GEBEL (Ralf), 7643.
GEBHARDT (James F.), 7758.
GEBHARDT (Miriam), 560.

GEDDES (J.), 3650.
GEE (Austin), *VII*.
GEE (Malcolm), 6828.
GEERKEN (John H.), 5626.
Gehry (Frank), 6497.
GEIFMAN (Anna), 5001, 5021.
GEIGER (Wolfgang), 7644.
GEISLER-SZMULEWICZ (Anne), 6316.
GEISS (Imanuel), 972.
GELBER (Steven M.), 1231.
GEL'MAN (E. I.), 3651.
GEMELLI (Giuliana), 545.
GEMIE (Sharif), 4336.
GENET (Jean-Philippe), 3626.
GENG (Yunzhi), 8123.
GENOV (Rumen), 7502, 7525.
GENOVESE (Mario), 2496.
GENTA (Enrico), 188.
GENTILE (Emilio), 4741.
Gentile (Giovanni), 4776.
GENTILE (L.), 2187.
GENTILE (R.), 2964.
Gentileschi (Artemisia), 6486.
GENTILONI SILVERI (Umberto), 4742.
GENTON (Bernard), 5708.
GENTON (François), 6553.
GEOGHEGAN (Patrick M.), 4668.
GEORGELIN (Christine), 3184.
Georgios Gemistos Plethon, 3035.
Georgios Monachos, 2996.
Georgius Pachymeres, 2965.
GÉRARD (Alain), 4337.
GÉRARD (Michèle), 3842.
GÉRARD (Pierre), 3107.
GERARD (Thérèse), 3107.
GERBER (D. E.), 2097.
Gerbert de Montreuil, 3364.
Gerbi (Antonello), 727.
GERBI (Sandro), 727, 5629.
GERBOD (P.), 6920.
GERÇEK (Ferruh), 462.
GERGELY (Jenõ), 5267.
GERHARDT (Volker), 5951.
GERLACH (Stefanie Virginia), 4424.
GERMAIN (René), 3382.
GERMAN (Lindsey), 7840.
Germanicus Caesar, 2322.
GERMINARIO (Francesco), 562.
GERRITZEN (D.), 7016.
Gervasius, Sanctus, 2892.
GESTRICH (Andreas), 189, 957.
GESTWA (Klaus), 6698.
GETTY (J. Arch), 5002.
Geulincx (Arnold), 6007.
GEUS (Armin), 6143.
GEWALD (Jan Bart), 4864.
GHAFFARY (Farrokh), 4661.
GHANAYIM (Zuhayr), 7570.

Gheorghiu-Dej (Gheorghe), 4970.
GHEZZO (Michele Pietro), 3176.
GHIATI (Cl.), V.
GHIANNOULOPOULOS (Gh.), 7503.
GHIOTTO (A. R.), 2727, 2748.
GHISALBERTI (Carlo), 272, 7074, 7091, 7707.
GIACOMONI (A.), 1886.
GIACONE (Franco), 6237.
GIACOVELLI (Enrico), 6554.
GIALLONGO (Angela), 5779.
GIANFRANCESCO PICO DELLA MIRANDOLA, 5322.
GIANFROTTA (Piero A.), 2749.
GIANGRASSO (Giulietta), 3173.
GIANNISI (Phoebé), 2098.
Giannone (Pietro), 728.
GIANSANTE (Massimo), 1080.
GIARDINA (Andrea), 2548, 2800.
GIARRIZZO (Giuseppe), 565, 1093, 4744.
Gibbon (Edward), 729.
Gibbons (Orlando), 6560.
GIBIANSKIJ (L. Ja.), 7678.
GIBSON (Bruce), 2620.
GIBSON (Marion), 5287.
GIBSON (R. K.), 2621.
Gide (André), 6310.
GIENOW-HECHT (J. C. E.), 5845.
GIES (David T.), 1206.
GIESZCZYŃSKI (Witold), 7888.
GIGANTE (Marcello), 2150.
GIGNOUX (Philippe), 1378.
GIJSBERS (Wilhelmina Maria), 1167.
GIL (L.), 2901.
GIL (Thomas), 835.
GIL`ADI (Avner), 3304.
GILBERT (Mark F.), 973.
GILBERT (Scott F.), 6154.
GILDERHUS (Mark T.), 7244.
GILES (Mary E.), 7025.
Giles, of Rome, Archbishop of Bourges, 1081.
GILI (S.), 1528.
GILL (Sam D.), 1311.
GILLESPIE (James), 3264.
GILLET (Patricia), 4375.
GILLI (Patrick), 3625.
GILLIS (Chester), 5327.
GILLIS (D. Hugh), 8345.
GILLMAN (Ian), 8042.
GILLOOLY (Eileen), 6317.
GILMAN (Sander L.), 6080.
GILMONT (Jean-Francois), 5328.
GILMOUR (John), 5090.
GILSON MILLER (Susan), 4858.
GINAT (Joseph), 5152.
GINSBERG (Warren), 3728.
GINZBURG (Carlo), 836.
GIOACCHINO DA FIORE, 3412,

3702, 3756, 3856.
Gioberti (Vincenzo), 6008.
GIOIA (Vitantonio), 6685.
GIORDANO (Giancarlo), 7708, 7889.
GIORDANO (M.), 2188.
Giordano da Pisa, 3731.
GIOVAGNOLI (Agostino), 7608.
Giovanni da Verrazzano, 313, 356.
GIOVANNINI (A.), 1860.
Giovannoni (Gustavo), 6411.
GIOVINI (M.), 2700.
GIPPIUS (Aleksej A.), 3132, 3216.
GIRARDI (E. N.), 4752.
Giraud (Henri), 7638.
GIRAUD (Patrice), 3646.
GIRAULT (René), 6730.
GIRBAL-BLACHA (Noemí), 5839.
Girolamo da Verrazzano, 313.
GIRY-DELOISON (Charles), 3247, 7409.
GISONDI (Francesco Antonio), 5448.
GIUDICE (Franco), 6082.
GIULIANO (F. M.), 2151.
GIUMANINI (Michelangelo L.), 7479.
GIUSTOZZI (Antonio), 4012.
GIZA (Antoni), 7245.
GIZEWSKI (C.), 2045.
GIZIENE (Neder), 4119.
GLAAB (Manuela), 5630.
Gladstone (William Ewart), 7525.
GLANTZ (David M.), 7756, 7757.
GLASCOCK (M. D.), 2250.
GLASSCOE (Marion), 3889.
GLAUSER (Richard), 5954.
GLAZE (Florence Eliza), 3729.
GLEASON (William A.), 6319.
GLENNY (Misha), 7246.
GLICK (Leonard B.), 3277.
GLICK (Thomas F.), 6062.
Glos, 2003.
GNILKA (Joachim), 2870.
GNOLI (Gherardo), 636.
GNOLI (Tommaso), 340.
GÖBEL (Wolfgang), 6064.
Gobi (Jean, le Jeune), 3630.
GOCER (Asli), 1290.
GODARD (Alain), 6248.
GODARD (Henri), 6320.
GODDARD (Jean-Christophe), 5955.
GÖDDE (Günter), 5956.
GODDING (Philippe), 3254.
GODLEWSKA (Anne Marie Claire), 341.
GODSEY (William D.), 6922, 7571.
Godwin (Edward William), 6511.
GODWIN (John), 2339.
Goebbels (Joseph), 4404.

GOEDDE (P.), 4426.
Goerdeler (Carl), 7791.
GOERLITZ (Uta), 766.
GOERTZEL (Ted G.), 4128.
Goes (Hugo van der), 3677.
GOES FILHO (Synesio Sampaio), 7391.
Goethe (Johann Wolfgang), 1417, 5620, 5714, 6284, 6321-6323, 6334, 6336, 6343, 6379.
GOETZ (Hans-Werner), 566.
Goffredo di Monmouth, 524.
GOGA (Mircea), 1232.
GOGA (S.), 2622.
Gogol' (Nikolai Vasil'evich), 1440.
GOHARI (M. J.), 4013.
GOICHOT (E.), 700.
GOICU (Simona), 273.
GOITRE SAMANIEGO (J.), 1449.
GÖKTEPE (Cihat), 7890.
GOLAS (Peter J.), 1233.
GOLD (Daniel), 1352.
GOLDBERG (P.), 1486.
GOLDER (H.), 1960.
Goldhagen (Daniel Jonah), 487, 651.
GOLDIE (Mark), 1097.
GOLDIN (Simha), 3278.
GOLDINA (Irina D.), 974.
GOLDMAN (Emily O.), 7283.
GOLDSMITH (Raymond W.), 6800.
GOLDSTEIN (Erik), 7645, 7661.
GOLDSTEIN (I.), 3026.
GOLDSTEIN (Jonathan), 7861.
GOLDT (Verena), 6083.
Golicyn (Aleksandr), 4999.
GOLINSKI (Jan), 6155.
GOMEZ (B.), 2250.
GÓMEZ (Moreno Angel), 3521.
GOMEZ ACUÑA (Luis), 5632.
Gómez Barroso (Pedro), 31.
GOMEZ DE BENITEZ (Beatriz), 228.
GÓMEZ MOVELLÁN (Antonio), 5400.
GOMEZ PALLARES (Joan), 153.
GOMEZ URDANEZ (Gracia), 5091.
GOMI (Fumihiko), 8279.
GONÇALVES (V. S.), 1493.
GONDICAS (Dimitri), 4587.
GONJO (Yasuo), 4338.
Gonzaga (famiglia), 167.
GONZALBO AIZPURU (Pilar), 5783.
GONZÁLES (Julián), 2322.
GONZÁLES BERNALDO DE QUIROS (Pilar), 6923.
GONZALES DE CLAVIJO (Ruy), 3171.
GONZALEZ (Aurelio), 3449.
GONZALEZ (Raymundo), 4275.
GONZALEZ BERNALDO DE QUIROS (Pilar), 4047.

GONZÁLEZ CALLEJA (Eduardo), 5092.
GONZÁLEZ GAVIOLA (Horacio), 5633.
GONZÁLEZ JÁCOME (Alba), 1224.
GONZALEZ JIMENEZ (Manuel), 3161.
GONZALEZ SANCHEZ (Carlos Alberto), 108.
Gonzàlez-Villar (Rafael), 6418.
GONZALO DE BERCEO, 3759.
GOOD (David F.), 5716.
GOODARE (Julian), 4541.
GOODLAD (Graham D.), 7504.
GOODMAN (Antony), 3264.
GOODMAN (D.), 5093.
GOODMAN (Martin), 2867.
GOOLD (G. P.), 2389.
GOPAL (Sarvepalli), 4621, 7318, 7321.
GOPHNA (R.), 1616.
GÖRANSSON (Eva-Marie Y.), 3321.
GORBACHEV (Mikhail S.), 4389.
GORBATO (Viviana), 4048.
GORDIEJEW (Paul Benjamin), 5536.
GORDILLO Y ORTIZ (Octavio), 975.
GORDON (Bertram M.), 684.
GORDON (Haim), 1401.
Gordon Childe (V.), 1457.
GORDY (Eric D.), 5247.
GÓRECKA (Marzena), 3882.
GORECKI NOWAK (Maria), 927.
Gorgias, 1903, 2111, 2685.
GORGUET (Ilde), 7572.
GORI (Orsola), 4695.
Göring (Hermann), 4446.
GORIZONTOV (Leonid E.), 5003.
GORLOV (Sergej A.), 7573.
GORODETSKY (Gabriel), 7709.
GORONZY (Kriemhild), 7400.
GORRIS (Rosanna), 747.
GORRITI ELLENBOGEN (Gustavo), 4914.
GÖRS (Britta), 6084.
GORSKAJA (Natal'ja A.), 730.
GORSKIJ (Anton A.), 1545.
GORST (Anthony), 8028.
GÖRTEMAKER (Manfred), 4427.
GORUPP (Tiziana), 6324.
GORUPPI (Tiziana), 4339.
GORZKA (Gabriele), 7767.
GOSCHA (Christopher), 8082.
GOSSEL (Daniel), 7891.
GOTTDANG (Andrea), 6457.
GOTTERI (Nicole), 4340.
GOTTHARD (Axel), 4428.
GÖTTMANN (Frank), 6729.
Gottsched (Johann Christoph), 5978.
GØTZ (Heidi Inger), 4261.

GÖTZE (Barbara), 460.
GOUDRIAAN (Aza), 5957.
GOUDSMIT (J.), 1625.
GOUGEROT (Muriel), 3151.
GOUGH (Barry M.), 976.
GOUGUENHEIM (Sylvain), 3456.
GOUK (Penelope), 5634.
GOULD (Eliga H.), 3955.
GOULD (Stephen Jay), 6088.
GOULLET (Monique), 3568.
GOVE (Harry E.), 6085.
GOWARD (B.), 2099.
GOWLAND (David), 7892.
GOYARD-FABRE (S.), 7190.
GOZZER (Vittorio), 7781.
GOZZI (Gustavo), 1069.
Gozzoli (Benozzo), 6456.
GRABAR (O.), 2808.
Gråber (Jakob), 441.
GRACCI (Angiolo), 4746.
GRACH (Nonna L.), 2233.
GRACIA ALONSO (F.), 1452.
GRACIOTTI (Sante), 6221.
GRAFTON (Anthony), 6086, 6125.
GRAHAM (Jenny), 4542.
GRAHAM (M. Patrick), 523.
GRAHAM (T. W.), *VII*.
GRAHAM-BROWN (Sarah), 7893.
GRAHAM-JONES (Jean), 6555.
Gramsci (Antonio), 4747, 4787, 5821, 5894, 5938, 5958, 6024.
GRAN-AYMERICH (J.), 2292.
GRAND (Philippe), 4341.
GRANDA (Stane), 5060, 5063.
GRANDE (Nathalie), 6250.
GRANDE (Troni Y.), 6556.
GRANDOLINI (S.), 3027.
Grandrue (Claude de), 72.
GRANE (Leif), 5489.
GRANINO CECERE (M. G.), 2576.
GRANT (Alexander), *VII*.
GRANT (Jonathan A.), 6739.
GRANT (Judith), 3773.
GRANT (M.), 2801.
GRAßL (Hartmut), 1255.
GRASSO (Christopher), 5196.
GRAUS (Igor), 5040.
GRAVINA (A.), 1446.
GRAY (Edward G.), 5635.
GRAY (Marion W.), 6924.
GRAY (Peter), 4669.
GRAY (Richard T.), 6087.
GRAZIOSI (Andrea), 3956.
GRDINA (Igor), 3383, 6925.
GREATREX (J.), 567.
GREBE (Sabine), 2623.
GREBENAROV (A.), 4145.
GRECO (Emanuele), 2267.
GRECO (Gaetano), 5402.
GRECO (John), 1395.
GRECO (P.), 1732.

GREEN (Richard Firth), 3564.
GREENACRE (R. T.), 5280.
GREENBLATT (Stephen), 5715.
GREENE (K.), 1457.
GREENE (Naomi), 6557.
GREENE (Stephen Lyon Wakeman), 5156.
GREENE (V.), 55.
GREENFILED (Susan C.), 6100.
GREENWALT (W.), 1984.
GREENWAY (Diana E.), 154, 3128.
GREENWOOD (Sean), 7894.
GRÉGOIRE (Emmanuel), 4880.
GRÉGOIRE (R.), 2902.
Gregoras Nicephorus, 2966.
GREGORI (G. L.), 2549.
Gregorius I Magnus, Papa, Sanctus, 2820, 2886, 2932, 2944.
Gregorius Nazianzenus, Sanctus, 3008.
Gregorius Nyssenus, Sanctus, 2847.
Gregorius Palamas, Sanctus, 3755.
Gregorius XVI, Papa, 5471.
GREGORY (Brad), 5289.
GREGORY (Jeremy), 7436.
GREGORY KOHLSTEDT (Sally), 6088.
Grekov (Boris Dmitrievich), 730.
GRELL (Chantal), 201.
GRELL (Ole Peter), 6932.
GRELLE (F.), 2550.
GRELOT (Pierre), 2903.
GRENDI (Edoardo), 342, 731, 6926.
GRESCHAT (MARTIN), 5386.
GRESLE-POULIGNY (Dominique), 6837.
GRESTI (Maurizio), 8283.
GRETSCH (Mechthild), 3805.
GREVET (R.), 5788.
GREW (Raymond), 1227.
GREWE (Astrid), 6251.
GREWE (Bernd-Stefan), 6769.
GREWING (F.), 2624.
Grey (Edward), 7524.
GREY (Jeffrey), 4070.
GREZ TOSO (Sergio), 4174.
GRIBAUDI (Gabriella), 568.
GRIBBLE (D.), 1985.
GRIECO (Allen J.), 3177.
GRIEDER (Peter), 4430.
GRIFFIN (J.), 1962.
GRIFFIN (Leonard), 6498.
GRIFFITHS (Gordon), 3255.
GRIFFITHS (Richard T.), 7909.
Griggs (Frederick Landseer), 6434.
GRIGOR'EVA (Irina V.), 5341.
GRILLI (A.), 2345.
GRILLI (Antonio), 7158.
Grimaldus, 3619.

GRIMES (Ronald L.), 1353.
Grimmel (Jakob), 6729.
GRIMMES (Ole), 4885.
GRIN (G.), 6801.
GRISHIN (Jakov Ja.), 7646.
GRISHINA (R. P.), 999.
GRIŠINA (R.), 7575.
GRISWOLD (Charles L.), 5959.
GRISWOLD (Robert), 190.
GROCE (W. Todd), 5197.
GRODDEK (D.), 1681, 1733.
GROEBNER (Valentin), 5636, 6927.
GROH (Dieter), 4431.
Grolier (Jean), 440.
Gronchi (Giovanni), 4719.
GRÖNLUND (Kimmo), 4287.
GRONSKÝ (Ján), 7092.
GROS (Pierre), 2391.
GROß (Gerhrd P.), 7587.
GROSS (Jan Tomasz), 7710.
GROßE (Jürgen), 702.
GROSSI (V.), 2904.
GROSVENOR (Ian), 1260.
Grotius (Hugo), 7190, 7198, 7199, 7200, 7202.
GROTTANELLI (Cristiano), 1758, 2701.
GROULT (Martine), 5960.
GROVE (Linda), 8045.
GROVER (Verinder), 7816, 7955.
GROZEV (Kostadin), 7502.
GRUAU (Maurice), 901.
GRUCA (Anna), *XIII*, 697.
GRUCHMANN (Lothar), 4432.
GRULLÓN (Sandino), 4271.
GRUMEL-JACQUIGNON (François), 7576.
GRUNCHAROV (Mikhail), 4146.
GRUNCHAROV (Stoicho), 4153.
GRUNDLINGH (Albert), 5069.
Grundtvig (Nicolai Frederik Severin), 877.
GRUNDY (Isobel), 6252.
GRUNEWALD (Michel), 3945.
GRÜNEWALD (Thomas), 2551.
GRÜTTER (Heinrich T.), 625.
GRÜTTNER (Michael), 4447.
GRUZINSKI (Serge), 1248.
GRYSON (R.), 2852.
GRZEGRZÓŁKA (Sabina), 2738.
Grzesinski (Albert), 4400.
GRZIMEK (Philipp), 7077.
GRZYWACZ (Andrzej), 7577.
GSCHNITZER (F.), 1861.
GSCHWEND (Lukas), 7159.
GU (Cheng), 8124.
GUADALAJARA-MEDINA (J.), 2848.
GUAGNINI (Anna), 1228.
GUANG-DA (Zhang), 8055.
Guangxu, emperor of China, 8123.
Guardini (Romano), 5985.

GUARNERIUS IURISPERTISSIMUS, 3330.
GUASCO (Maurilio), 1070, 5403.
GUASCONI (M. E.), 7895.
GUBIN (Eliane), 4097.
GUDEA (Nicolae), 2449.
GUDER (Darrell L.), 1355.
GUDERZO (Massimiliano), 7711.
GUEIT (J.), 5280.
GUELTON (Fréderic), 7542.
GUENÉE (Bernard), 1087, 3222, 3256.
GUÉRAICHE (William), 4342.
GUERRA MANZO (Enrique), 4830.
GUERRERO BARÓN (Javier), 4184.
GUERRIERI (Gabriella), 6033.
GUERRIERI (Sandro), 7085.
GUERRINI (Luigi), 6074.
GUESLIN (André), 6908, 7047.
GUEVARA (Ernesto 'Che'), 4190.
GUEZ (J.-Ph.), 2100.
GUGLIELMINETTI (Marziano), 716.
GUHA (Sumit), 902.
GUICCIARDINI (Francesco), 3172.
GUICCIARDINI (Niccolò), 6089.
GUICHARD (M.), 1682.
GUIDO (Margaret), 3159.
GUIDO D'AREZZO, 3690.
GUIDORIZZI (G.), 2966.
Guignebert (Charles), 750.
GUILAINE (J.), 1466.
Guillaume de Saint-Thierry, 3747.
GUILLELMUS DE CONCHIS, 3703.
GUILLON (Jean-Marie), 7794.
Guilloux (Louis), 6320.
GUINERET (Hervé), 5637.
GUINOT RODRÍGUEZ (Enric), 274.
GULDENTOPS (Guy), 3030, 3716.
GÜLEÇ (E.), 1498.
GULLETTA (M. I.), 1873.
GÜLTLINGEN (Sybille von), 88.
GUNASINGAM (Murugar), 5122.
GÜNAY (Ünver), 5166.
GÜNAY (Vehbi), 5159.
Gundaker von Liechtenstein, 4089.
GUNEL (S.), 1534.
GÜNEL (Sevinç), 2234.
GÜNERGUN (Feza), 6154.
GÜNEŞ (Mehmet), 6802.
GUNST (Péter), 4606.
GÜNTHER (H.-Ch.)3031.
GÜNTHER (W.), 1855.
GUO (L.), 1796.
GUO (Weidong), 8125.
GUO (Xuyin), 8126.
GUOLO (Renzo), 5537.
GUREVICH (Aron J.), 816, 855.
GURTLER (G. M.), 2169.
GURY (F.), 2702.
GUSICK (Barbara I.), 3448.
GUŠTIN (Mitja), 526.

Gutenberg (Johann), 107, 113, 5857.
GUTHKE (Karl S.), 6194.
GUTIÉRREZ (Natividad), 4831.
GUTMAN (Margarita), 6825.
GUTSELL (Rosel), 1417.
GUY (Donna J.), 3953.
GUY OF AMIENS, 3506.
GUYARD (Murielle), 7896.
GUYNN (Noah D.), 3599.
GUYOT (Claude Etienne), 7453.
GUYOTJEANNIN (O.), 155.
GÜZEL (Abdurrahman), 5160, 5161.
Gwathmey (Robert), 6463.
GWENOGVRYN EVANS (J.), 3508.
GYGER (Alison), 6558.
GYLLENHAAL (Lars), 7758.
GYNTHER (Bert), 991.
GYOMLAY (Gyula), 1986.

H

HAALEBOS (J. K.), 2750.
HAAR (Ingo), 569.
HAARLÄNDER (Stephanie), 3786.
HAAS (Aloïs M.), 3604.
HAAS (V.), 1683.
Häber (Herbert), 4390.
HABER (Stephen), 5671, 6643.
HÄBERLEIN (Mark), 1155.
Habermas (Jürgen), 5963.
HABIB (S. Irfan), 761, 7328.
HABICHT (C.), 1585.
Hachette (Louis), 124.
HACHEZ-LEROY (Florence), 6740.
HACHTMANN (Rüdiger), 4447.
HACK (Achim Thomas), 3788.
HACKL (H.), 2497.
HACOHEN (Malachi Haim), 5961.
HADJADJ (Djillali), 4028.
Hadrianus (P. Aelius), Roman emperor, 2510, 2517, 2743.
HADZIHASANOVIC (Aziz), 5245.
HAEFELI (Evan), 3925.
HAEFS (Wilhem), 5831.
HAERS (J.), 1303.
HAESELER (Jens), 5522.
Hagedorn (Friedrich von), 6265.
HAGEDORN (Ludger), 5890.
HAGEMANN (Ludwig), 5538.
HAGENBUCHNER-DRESEL (A.), 1684.
HAGENDORN (Andrea), 2552.
HAGENOW (Elisabeth von), 386.
HÄGG (R.), 2178.
HÄGG (T.), 2952.
HAGHIGHAT (Mamad), 6559.
HAGIYAMA (Masahiro), 6928.
HAGL (H.), 2189.
HAGNER (Michael), 6067.
HAHN (Hans-Henning), 465.

HAHN (Peter L.), 7897.
HÄHNER (Olaf), 570.
Haidar Ali, Nawab of Mysore, 7328.
HAIDER (P. W.), 1581.
HAIGH (R. H.), 7578.
HAIL (Barbara A.), 457.
HAINZMANN (Manfred), 2310.
HAJDU (Tibor), 4607.
HALDON (J.), 2981.
HALDON (John), 3032.
Hale (Charles Adams), 4844.
Halévy (Elie), 732.
HALISI (C. R. D.), 5070.
HALL (Linda B.), 7230.
HALL (Marcia B.), 6458.
HALL (Stuart G.), 2349.
HALLBÄCK (Geert), 1309.
Halldór (Laxness), 4619.
Haller (Karl Ludwig), 7107.
HALLIDAY (Fred), 7249.
HALLOF (K.), 1862, 2046.
HALM-TISSERANT (M.), 2235.
HALPERIN DONGHI (Tulio), 4049.
HALPERN (Rick), 332.
HAMACHER (Elisabeth), 783.
HÄMÄLÄINEN (Pekka), 3925.
HAMASHITA (Takeshi), 8086.
HAMBLY (Gavin R. G.), 3318.
HAMDOUNE (Christine), 2416.
HAMEL (Jürgen), 6045.
HAMER (Andrew), 3332.
HAMESSE (Jacqueline), 300, 804.
HAMILTON (Bernard), 3883.
HAMILTON (Christian), 463.
HAMMAR (Inger), 6929.
HAMMER (Paul E. J.), 4543.
HAMMERSCHMIDT (Peter), 6930.
HAMMERSTEIN (Notker), 6090.
HAMMOND (Jenny), 4285.
HAMMOND (N. G. L.), 1891, 1892, 2016.
HAMMOND (Paul), 6253.
Hammurabi, king of Babylonia, 1685.
HAMNETT (Brian), 4832.
HAMON (P.), 1863.
HAMON (Philippe), 6803.
HAMOU (Philippe), 6091.
HAMPSON (Louise), 3147.
HAN (Myong-gi), 7410.
HANAUSKE (Dieter), 4395.
HANAWALT (Barbara A.), 3397.
HANDOCA (Mircea), 1325.
HANEDA (Masashi), 8054.
HANKE (Christian), 5490.
HANKINS (James), 6125.
HANNAH (Darrell D.), 2905.
HANNEMA (Kiki), 439.
HANNIBALSSON (Arnór), 4619.
HANNICK (Christian), 3033, 7207.

HÄNNINEN (M.-L.), 2703.
HANNOUM (Abdelmajid), 571.
HANSEN (C. K.), 1548.
HANSSON (Jesper), 7401.
HANUS (Jozef), 5033.
HANZAL (Josef), 572.
HAOA (S.), 1476.
HAQUIN (A.), 1303.
HARAKSIM (Ľudovít), 7505.
Haraszti Taylor (Eva), 7240.
HARBISON (Peter), 3653.
HARDIE (Philip), 2357.
HARDIN (Russell), 1126.
HARDING (Leonhard), 8346.
HARDMAN (John), 4334.
HARDT (Nils), 996.
HAREL (Yaron), 7506.
HARF-LANCNER (Laurence), 3529.
Hargreaves (John), 7349.
HÄRKÖNEN (Mirja), 5443.
HARLANG (Christian), 4262.
HARLEY (John), 6560.
HARLOW (Barbara), 8038.
HARMAT (Ulricke), 7160.
HARMATTA (János), 8055.
HARMER (Harry J. P.), 4544.
HARNA (Josef), 4219, 4223.
HAROCHE-BOUZINAC (Geneviève), 1246.
Harpalus, 1974.
HARRAK (Amir), 3165.
HARRAN (Don), 6561.
HARRAUER (Hermann), 229.
HARRIES (Jill), 2498, 2802.
HARRINGTON (Joel F.), 7161.
HARRINGTON (John P.), 4681.
HARRIS (Bernhard), 6141.
HARRIS (Brayton), 5846.
HARRIS (Ian), 8040.
HARRIS (W. V.), 2553.
HARRISON (C. M.), 2047.
HARRISON (Carol E.), 6931.
HARRISON (Dick), 3227, 5638.
HARRISON (E. D. R.), 7759.
HARRISON (Henrietta), 8127.
HARRISON (Mark), 4631.
HARRISON (Peter D.), 8371.
HARRISON (Peter), 5962.
HARRISON (S.), 2838.
HARROD (Tanya), 6500.
Harsdörffer (Georg Philipp), 6026.
HÅRSTEDT (Martin), 7463.
HART (Darryl G.), 5734.
HART (Richard), 4792.
HÄRTER (Karl), 7138.
HARTLEIB-MONNET (Karin), 6326.
HARTMANN (Günther), 6562.
Hartmann (Ludo Moritz), 733.
HARTMANN (Wolfram), 6493.
HARTMANNSGRUBER (Friedrich), 4386.

HARTOG (François), 484, 837.
HARVEY (John), 387.
HARVEY (Margaret), 3385.
HARVEY (Paul B.), 2906.
HARWARDT (H.), 2839.
HASANI (Proletar), 7782.
HASEGAWA (Akira), 6699.
HASELDINE (Julian), 3453.
HASHIMOTO (Yoshihiko), 8280.
Haskell (Francis), 734.
HASLAM (Jonathan), 704.
HASLIP-VIERA (Gabriel), 7162.
HASS (Ludwik), 4941.
HASSAN SHUHAIMI NIK ABDUL RAHMAN (Nik), 963.
HASSIG (Debra), 3457.
HÄSSLER (Hans-Jürgen), 886.
HASSNER (Pierre), 726.
HASS-ZUMKEHR (Ulrike), 291.
Hastings (Warren), 7337.
HATLIE (P.), 3034.
Hatshepsut, king of Egypt, 1647.
HATTE (C.), 1520.
Hattusilis III, king of Hittites, 1737.
HAUDE (R.), 2017.
HÄUFELE (Günther), 7647.
HAUG (Walter), 3203.
HAUNFELDER (Bernd), 4433.
HAUPT (Heinz-Gerhard), 3923, 3978, 4447.
HAUSER (Claude), 4344.
HAUSSIG (H. W.), 1389.
Havel (Václav), 4253.
HAVELANGE (Isabelle), 5761.
HAVERALS (M.), 1305.
HAVERKAMP (Alfred), 3280.
HAWARD (Birkin), 3133.
HAWGOOD (David), 165.
HAWKINS (J. D.), 1728.
HAWTING (G. R.), 3305.
HAWTING (G. R.), 5539.
HAXHILLAZI (Pavli), 7541.
HAY (Douglas), 6741.
HAYA DE LA TORRE DE LA ROSA (Agustin), 4915.
HAYASHI (Reiko), 6701.
HAYCOCK (David), 5750.
HAYDEN (Robert M.), 903.
HAYDOCK (Michael D.), 7898.
HAYDON (Colin), 4377.
HAYE (Thomas), 3565.
Hayek (Friederich August), 6671, 6673.
HAYES (Patricia), 6493.
HAYNES (Roslynn), 6195.
HAYWARD (J. E. S.), 509.
HAYWARD (Paul Antony), 3837.
HAYWOOD (Geoffrey A.), 4749.
HAZAN (Olga), 6392.
HAZAREESINGH (Sudhir), 5789.

HE (Zhongli), 8128.
HEAD-KÖNIG (Anne-Lise), 6839.
Headlam (Cuthbert Morley), 4524.
HEALEY (E.), 1725.
HEALY (J. F.), 2687.
HEAMAN (E. A.), 464.
HEARN (Roger), 4865.
HEATH (J.), 1877.
HEATH (Jonathan), 4833.
HEATHER (P. J.), 3195.
HEATHER (P.), 2803, 2821.
HEBERT (Robert F.), 6641.
Hebrang (Andrija), 4204.
HÉBRARD (Jean), 11.
HECKMANN (Dieter), 7387.
HEDGEPETH (Sonja), 6311.
Hedilla Larrey (Federico Manuel), 5118.
Hedinger (Johann Reinhard), 5514.
HEDRICK (C. W.), 1864.
Heeren (Arnold Herrmann Ludwig), 735.
HEFTNER (H.), 1987.
Hegel (Georg Wilhelm Friedrich), 1059, 2155, 5882, 5892, 5917, 5946, 5948, 5972, 6003, 6025.
Heidegger (Martin), 1406, 5906, 5917, 5970.
HEIDER (Placidus Bernhard), 5963.
HEIJMANS (Marc), 2804.
HEIL (Johannes), 4434.
HEILIG (Walter), 4396.
HEIM (F.), 2907.
Heine (Heinrich), 6361.
HEINEMAN (Elizabeth D.), 6933.
HEINEMAN (Kenneth J.), 5404.
HEINEMANN (Manfred), 5813.
HEINEMANN (Winfried), 7906.
Heinrich, Abt von Engelberg, 35.
HEINRICH (Hans), 6196.
Heinrich der Löwe, Herzog von Bayern und Sachsen, 3232.
Heinrich von Gent, 3735.
Heintze (Helga von), 2778.
HEINZELMANN (M.), 2731.
HEINZLE (Joachim), 3563.
HEIRBAUT (Dirk), 3338.
HEISE (Brigitte), 6459.
HEISER (Lothar), 2908.
HEISER (Richard R.), 3245.
HEITSCH (E.), 1941.
HEITZ (Michael), 5889.
HEITZ (Raymond), 5876.
HEITZMANN (Christian), 3170.
HELAS (Philine), 6460.
HELD (Ursula), 32.
HELD (W.), 1586, 1686.
HELD (Wieland), 745.
HELFT (Nicolás), 1420.
Heliodorus, 1904.
HELL (Stefan), 7579.

HELLE (Andreas), 4670.
HELLEGOUARC'H (Joseph), 2350.
HELLER (Marvin J.), 5540.
HELLIE (Richard), 1234.
HELLINGA (Lotte), 99, 112.
HELLMUTH (Eckhart), 1100.
HELM (Gerd), 660.
HELMER (C.), 5491.
Héloïse, 3432.
HELVETIUS (Anne-Marie), 3848.
HEMECKER (Wilhelm), 3566.
HEMELRIJK (Emily A.), 2554.
HEMMERDINGER (Bertrand), 4345.
HENDERSON (Peter V. N.), 4834.
HENGARTNER (Thomas), 904.
HENGEL (M.), 1759.
HENISCH (Bridget Ann), 156.
HENKE (Klaus-Dietmar), 4003, 4514.
Henlein (Konrad), 7643.
HENNESSY (Michael), 7659.
HENNING (Dirk), 2417.
HENRAT (Philippe), 7423.
Henri de Nunen, 150.
Henri II, roi de France, 7403.
Henri IV, roi de France, 181, 4295, 4330.
Henrich (Dieter), 5963.
HENRY (Philippe), 5138, 7455.
Henry III, king of England, 3120.
Henry VIII, king of England, 5777.
Henry, earl of Notrhumberland, 3110.
HENSEL (Jürgen), 6980.
HENTGES (Gudrun), 5964.
HENTILÄ (Seppo), 4288, 4289.
HEPPNER (Harald), 4151.
Heraclitus, 2161, 2172.
HERB (Karlfriedrich), 5965.
HERBERT (Rosemary), 1438.
HERBORG (Mette), 4263.
HERDA (A.), 1586.
HERDE (Peter), 26.
Herder (Johann Gottfried), 857.
HERGERMÖLLER (Bernd-Ulrich), 3257.
HERHOLT (Volker), 733.
HERKLOTZ (Ingo), 6393.
HERKOMMER (Hubert), 1427, 6470.
HERMAN (Mark), 3533.
HERMANN (Pálsson), 905.
HERMANS (Jos. M. M.), 78.
HERMENEGILDO (Alfredo), 6216.
Hermippus Smyrnaeus, 1905.
HERMON (Ella), 2323.
HERNANDEZ (A. Arellano), 8377.
HERNANDEZ CHAVEZ (Alicia), 946.
HERNANDO (A.), 1458.
HERNOVÁ (Šárka), 4224.

Herodes I, king of Iudaea, 1768.
Herodotus, 636, 816, 1794, 1907, 1908, 1909, 1910, 1983, 1993, 2004, 2119.
HEROLD-SCHMIDT (Hedwig), 5094.
HERREN (Madeleine), 7203, 7712.
Herrera (Luis Alberto de), 7658.
HERRERO DE LA FUENTE (Marta), 3116.
HERRERO MASSARI (José Manuel), 302.
HERRERO SÁNCHEZ (Manuel), 4869.
HERRIN (Judith), 3636.
HERRMANN (Klaus), 3290.
HERRMANN (Ulrich), 957.
HERRMANN-OTTO (Elisabeth), 2487.
HERŠAK (Emil), 897.
HERSANT (Y.), 3035.
HERSHFIELD (Joanne), 6585.
HERSHON (Cyril P.), 3279.
HERVAEUS (Natalis), 3808.
HERVIEU-LEGER (Danièle), 1354.
HERWIG (Holger H.), 4179.
HERY (Evelyne), 838.
HERZ (Dietmar), 5966.
HERZ (Dina), 62.
HERZENBERG (Caroline L.), 6097.
HERZOG (Lawrence Arthur), 6419.
Hesiodus, 1911, 1912, 1913, 1914.
HESS (Daniel), 3119.
HETTLING (Manfred), 5141.
HEUCK-ALLEN (Susan), 573.
HEY (G.), 1549.
HEYDEMANN (Günther), 4480.
HEYNDRICKX (Pierre), 7899.
Heyne (Ch. G.), 2588.
HEYWOOD (Anthony), 6700.
HICKETHIER (Knut), 1235.
HIDALGO DE CISNEROS AMESTOY (Concepción), 3115.
HIDALGO DE PAZ (Ibrahím), 4206.
HIEPEL (Claudia), 7046.
Hieronymus (Sophronius Eusebius), Sanctus, 406, 2849, 2850-2853.
HIETALA (Marjatta), 7026.
HIGGENBOTHAM (C.), 1626.
HIGGINS (Paula), 3691.
HIGHAM (Robin), 683.
HIGMAN (B. W.), 574.
HIGONNET (Margaret R.), 6921.
HIGONNET (Patrice), 1236.
HIGSON (Andrew), 6547.
HILAIRE (Yves-Marie), 643.
Hilbert (David), 6094.
Hildegard von Bingen, Sancta, 3850.
Hilferding (Rudolf), 4414.

HILG (Hardo), 64.
HILL (D. E.), 2356.
HILL (John M.), 3601.
HILLENBRAND (Carole), 3307.
HILLIS (Peter), 5791.
HILLS (Paul A.), 6501.
Hilsner (Leopold), 4225.
HILTUNEN (Juha), 8372.
HIMMEL (Kelly F.), 5199.
Himmler (Heinrich), 4388.
HINARD (F.), 2393.
Hindenburg (Paul von), 4432, 7621.
HINDLEY (Alan), 3551.
HINDLEY (C.), 2048.
HINDRICHS (G.), 746.
HINDS (Stephen), 2357.
HINDSLEY (Leonard P.), 3806.
HINES (John), 3208.
HINRICHS (Ernst), 957, 5763.
HINTERBERGER (M.), 3036.
HINZ (Hans-Martin), 5708.
HINZ (Ulrich), 58.
Hippias, 1973.
Hippocrates, 1915-1918.
Hippolytus, 1591.
HIRAISHI (Naoaki), 5735.
HIRAKAWA (Hitoshi), 6662.
HIRANO (T.), 3037.
HIRSCHBERG (Walter), 925.
HIRSCHFELD (Gerhard), 7653.
HIRST (Derek), 4545.
HIRT (M.), 1760.
HISANO (Nobuyoshi), 8281.
Histieus, 1788.
HITCHINS (Keith), 4971.
Hitler (Adolf), 4386, 4404, 4454, 4490, 4494, 5274, 5597, 7636, 7669, 7678, 7723, 7735, 7761.
HITZEL (Frédéric), 110.
HIZLI (Mefail), 5792.
HLAVOVÁ (Viera), 5032.
HLUŠIČKOVÁ (Růžena), 4226.
HOARE (James), 1017.
Hobbes (Thomas), 1072, 1105, 5646, 5883, 5911, 5935, 5965, 5984, 6082, 6101.
HOBBS (D. R.), 1500.
HOBSON (Anthony), 440.
HOBSON (Christopher Z.), 6327.
HOBSON (Rolf), 4885.
HOCCLEVE (Thomas), 3507.
HOCHEDLINGER (Michael), 4077, 7454.
HOCHKIRCHEN (Thomas), 6094.
HOCHSTADT (Steve), 6934.
HOCKERTS (Hans Günter), 4386.
HOCQUET (Jean-Claude), 3386.
HODES (Nancy Jane), 8100.
HODGES (Donald Clark), 5639.
HODGSON (G.), 7250.

HODJATPANAH (Maryam), 7900.
HÖDL (Günther), *I*.
HÖDL (Uta), *I*.
Hodža (Milan), 4223, 7788.
HOENSCH (Jörg K.), 3947, 4234.
HOEPFNER (W.), 1821.
HOEPFNER (W.), 1166.
HOERDER (Dirk), 6935.
HOFBAUER (Hannes), 5243.
HOFF (J.), 3957.
HOFFELNER (K.), 2236.
HOFFMAN (Philip T.), 6645.
HOFFMAN (Piotr), 1072.
HOFFMAN (Ronald), 5211.
HOFFMANN (Dierk), 6917.
HOFFMANN (Dieter), 6153, 6154.
HOFFMANN (Frank), 6936.
HOFFMANN (Manfred), 2625.
HOFFMANN (Uwe), 4436.
Hoffmann von Hoffmannwaldau (Christian), 6268.
HOFMAN (Jiří), 7783.
HOFMANN (Etienne), 706.
HOFMANN (H.), 1432, 1816, 2190.
HOFMANN (Heinz), 2633.
HOFMEIER (Thomas), 6039.
HOFSCHRÖER (Peter), 7462.
HOGAN (Michael J.), 7214, 7215.
Hogarth (William), 6038.
HOGENHUIS-SELIVERSTOFF (Anne), 7580.
HOHLER BERGENDAHL (Erla), 3654.
HOHLFELD (Rainer), 5740.
HØJ (Dan), 1459.
HÖJELID (Stefan), 5131.
HOLDER (P. A.), 2555.
HOLEC (Roman), 5041.
HOLFORD-STREVENS (Leofranc), 145.
HOLGUÍN (Sandie), 6564.
HÖLKESKAMP (K.-J.), 2556.
HOLLANDER (D. B.), 2557.
HOLLY (Susan K.), 7817.
HOLMBERG (Åke), 5132.
HOLMBERG (Gustav), 6095.
HOLMES (Larry Eugene), 5793.
HOLMES (Megan), 6461.
HOLOBER (Frank), 7901.
HÖLSCHER (Lucian), 1238.
HOLT (F. L.), 2191.
HOLT (Michael F.), 5200.
HOLTFRERICH (Carl-Ludwig), 6841.
HOLTKE (H.-H.), 504.
HOLTSMARK (Sven G.), 4888.
HOLTZ (Sabine), 6228.
HOLZBERG (Niklas), 2359.
HOLZER (Harold), 7515.
HOLZWEISSIG (Gunter), 4467.
HOMANN (Harald), 802, 5570.

Homerus, 1432, 1439, 1820, 1826, 1920, 1921, 2084, 2100, 2112, 2115, 2131, 2139, 2141, 2182, 2213.
HOMMELHOFF (Peter), 4394.
HOMZA (Martin), 5042.
HONG (Yong-pyo), 8324.
HONOLD (Alexander), 1431.
HONOUR (Hugh), 1289.
HOOD (Thomas Samuel), 5226.
HOOGVLIET (Margriet), 78.
HOOKER (Mark T.), 4870.
HOOSE (Jayne), 1342.
HOPKIN (Jonathan), 5095.
HOPKINS (A. G.), 4546.
HOPKINS (Keith), 2704.
HOPKINSON (Michael), 4664.
HOPPA (Robert D.), 906.
HOPPE (Brigitte), 6154.
HOPPE (Jiří), 7902.
HOPWOOD (K.), 2569.
HÖRANDNER (Edith), 921.
Horatius Flaccus (Q.), 2602, 2649.
Hori, priest of Amon, 1639.
HORLACHER (Stefan), 6220.
HORN (Joyce M.), *VII*.
HORN (Michiel), 5736.
HORNE (G.), 7251.
HORNGREN (Myriam), 4272.
HORNOS MATA (F.), 1525.
HORSNELL (Malcolm John Albert), 157.
HORST (Ulrich), 3730.
HORSTBØLL (Henrik), 5847.
HORTON (A. V. M.), 4140.
HORTON (James O.), 967.
HORTON (Lois E.), 967.
HORTON (Lynn), 4877.
HORVÁTH (István), 7903.
HORVÁTH (Pavel), 275.
HÖSCH (E.), 3958.
HOTATE (Michihisa), 8282.
HOU (Yijie), 8129.
HOURS (Henri), 3129.
HOUSE (Jonathan H.), 7756.
HOUSLEY (R.), 1484.
HOUTART (François), 4594.
HOUWINK TEN CATE (Johannes Th. M.), 7663.
HOVANNISIAN (Richard G.), 641, 3312.
HÖVEL (Gerlinde), 6096.
HOWARD (A. J.), 1494.
HOWARD (James), 6565.
HOWARD (John R.), 7163.
HOWARD (Thomas Albert), 702.
HOWARD-HILL (Trevor Howard), 1414.
HOWARD-JOHNSTON (James), 3837.
HOWARTH (Randell S.), 2418.

HOWES (Ruth H.), 6097.
HOWLAND (Nina Davis), 7817.
HOWLAND KENNEY (William), 6566.
HOWLETT (D. R.), 25.
Hoxha (Enver), 4021.
HOXIE (Frederick E.), 5211.
HOYE (Timothy), 4796.
HŘEBEJK (Jiří), 7092.
HRENKEVIČ (Leanid D.), 7784.
HROTSVITA, 3568.
Hu (Shi), 8191.
HU (Weiqing), 8130.
HUANG (Aiping), 8214.
HUANG (Daoxian), 8131.
HUANG (Guowei), 8139.
HUANG (Jianli), 8132.
Huang (Musong), 8202.
HUANG (Qinghua), 8133.
HUANG (Ray), 581.
HUANG (Xijian), 8134.
HUANG (Zhenglin), 8135.
HUBER (K.), 2237.
Huber (Samuel), 5472.
HUBER-REBENICH (Gerlinde), 2626.
HUBERT (Gérard), 388.
HUBERT (Marie-Clotilde), 148.
HÜBINETTE (Staffan), 5134.
HUEBNER (Steven), 6567.
HUERTZ DE LEMPS (Christian), 8390.
HUGHES (Arnold), 981.
HUGHES (Matthew), 7581.
HUGHES (Michael), 7507.
HUGLO (Michel), 3683.
Hugo (Gustav), 7066.
HUGO (Leon), 6328.
Hugo (Victor), 6355.
HUGUET (Josep), 5848.
Huizinga (Johann), 736.
HÜLK (Walburga), 3569.
HÜLSMANN (Jörg Guido), 4476.
HULT (Karin), 2973.
Humboldt (Alexander von), 737.
Humboldt (Wilhelm von), 5826.
Hume (David), 1409, 5931, 5962.
HUMM (Antonia Maria), 6937.
HUMM (M.), 2499.
HUMMEL (Karl-Joseph), 8018.
HUMMEL (P.), 2101.
HUNDT (Michael), 304.
HÜNERMANN (Peter), 5357.
HUNT (Andrew E.), 5201.
HUNT (David), 2805, 2809.
HUNT (Ediwin S.), 3387.
HUNT (Lynn), 812.
HUNT (M. H.), 7252.
HUNTER (R.), 1967.
HUNTZICKER (William), 5849.
HUNZIKER (Hans-Jörg), 32.

HUPPERT (George), 6254.
HUREZAN (George Pascu), 932, 3672.
Hurtado de Mendoza (Diego), 440.
HURTUBISE (Pierre), 5264.
HURWIT (J. M.), 1291.
HUSAIN (Javed), 8053.
HUSAR (Adrian), 2419.
HUSS (B.), 2102.
HUSS (Bernhard), 803.
Hussein (Saddam), 7893.
Husserl (Edmund), 5884, 5970, 5985, 5987.
HUSTON GOODFELLOW (Samuel), 4346.
HUSZÁR (Tibor), 7904, 8036.
HUTCHESON (Gregory S.), 3483.
HUTCHINSON (John F.), 5004.
Hutchinson (Thomas), 5225.
HUTTER (Manfred), 2871.
HUTTNER (Markus), 1073.
HÜTTNER (Martin), 4437.
HUUSSEN JR. (Arend H.), 7093.
HYAM (Ronald), 7318.
HYLAND (Ann), 3618.
HYLDTOFT (Ole), 6646.
HYLSON-SMITH (Kenneth), 3768.

I

IACOBINI (A.), 2978.
IAKOLEVA (L.), 1495.
IANNELLA (Cecilia), 3731.
IBANEZ ROJO (Enrique), 4106.
IBARRA (Antonio), 6639.
IBARRA (Daniel E.), 5232.
IBARRA ROJAS (Eugenia), 582, 8374.
IBHLER GREIFFEN (N. von), 3339.
IBISH (Yusuf), 3302.
Ibn Khaldun (ʿAbd ar-Rahman ibn Muhammad), 3297.
Ibn Saud, King of Saudi Arabia, 5029.
Ibsen (Henrik), 6628.
IÇDUYGU (Ahmet), 5167.
ICKX (Johan), 5319.
IERODIAKONOU (K.), 2176.
Iesus Christus, 762, 1763, 2876, 2877, 2894, 2903, 2905, 2948, 2949.
IGGERS (Georg G.), 684.
IGNAT'EV (Anatolij V.), 7287.
IGOLKIN (Aleksandr A.), 6702.
IGOUNET (Valérie), 583.
IHALAINEN (Pasi), 1074.
IHARA (Takushu), 8043.
IHSANOGLU (Ekmeleddin), 6098, 6099, 6154, 8340.
IKEGAMI (Keiko), 3843.
IKEGAMI (Shunichi), 3196.

ILIÈ (Melanie), 7048.
ILIFFE (John), 6647.
ILIJIC (Nikola), 6938.
ILLADES (Carlos), 4826.
ILLERIS (Sven), 326.
ILLES PAL (Attila), 5285.
IMAMOVIC (Enver), 4109.
IMAMOVIC (Mustafa), 4110.
IMBERT (Jean), 1087, 7135.
INABA (Minoru), 8056.
INABA (Tsuguharu), 8284.
INCERTI (Manuela), 3656.
Indys Fervaal (Vincent d'), 6617.
INFANTE (Miguel Rui), 8097.
INFELISE (Mario), 113.
INGESMAN (Per), 3474.
INGIMUNDARSON (Valur), 7905.
INGRAM (Kenneth E. N.), 4791.
INGRAM MORLEY (Elizabeth), 119.
INGRAO (Christian), 7204.
INGREMEAU (Ch.), 2855.
Ingres (Jean Auguste Dominique), 6443, 6444.
INNOCENTI (Piero), 441.
INSABATO (Elisabetta), 4720.
INVERNIZZI (Antonio), 636.
INWOOD (Michael James), 1406.
Io (Hideyuki), 8085.
IOANNES SCOTUS ERIUGENA, 3704.
Iohannes (Abbé de Gorze), 3822.
Iohannes Doukas, 3077.
Iohannes VI Kantakuzenos, Byzantine emperor, 3037.
IOLY ZORATTINI (Pier Cesare), 5527.
IOPPOLO (A. M.), 2153.
IORDACHE (Anastasie), 4972.
IOSIFOV (Kalin), 4147.
IOTSALD VON SAINT-CLAUDE, 3807.
IOVEVSKA (Mariana), 4078.
Iovianus (Flavius Claudius), Roman emperor, 2803.
IPSEN (Dorothea), 344.
IRACHETA CENECORTA (María del Pilar), 4847.
IRASTORZA (Pascal), 4347.
IRBY-MASSIE (Georgia), 2706.
IRIGOIN (Jean), 1075, 1965.
IRIGOIN (María Alejandra), 4050.
IRIYE (A.), 7256.
IRLAM (Shaun), 6255.
IRMER (D.), 1915.
İRTEM (Süleyman Kani), 7257.
IRUMADA (Nobuo), 8285.
IRVIN (Cynthia L.), 4672.
Isaac (Jules), 738.
ISAAC (Peter), 111.
Isaias, 2852, 2864, 2866, 2921, 2905.
ISAKSSON (Pekka), 1068.

Isbrand Ides (Eberhard), 304.
ISHIDA (Hidetaka), 345.
ISHIGAMI (Eiichi), 8286.
IŞIN (Ekrem), 1170.
ISLAM (Riazul), 8053.
ISLAMOV (Tofik M.), 3931.
ISNENGHI (Mario), 4750.
Isocrates, 1926, 1927.
ISPHORDING (Eduard), 114.
ISSAWI (Charles), 4587.
ITENBERG (Boris S.), 6023.
Ito (Hirobumi), 4797, 4801.
ITO (Kiyoshi), 8287.
ITO (Tadashi), 2049.
ITO (Yukio), 4797.
ITTMANN (Karl), 7311.
Iulianus (Flavius Claudius), Roman emperor, 2459, 2759, 3010.
Iulius Iulianus, 3087.
Iustinianus I (Flavius), Byzantine emperor, 1697, 3052, 3082.
Iuvenalis (Decimus Iunius), 2546, 2668.
IVANIČ (Martin), 983.
IVANIČKOVÁ (Edita), 4005, 7640.
IVANOV (Anatolij E.), 5005.
IVANOV (Petr M.), 8136.
IVANOVA (Evgenija V.), 896.
IVANTCHIK (A. I.), 1627, 1907.
IVKIN (Vladimir I.), 5006.
IZEKI (Tadahisa), 4438.
İZGİ (Cevat), 6098.

J

JACKSON (Alvin), 4673.
JACKSON (Ashley), 7650.
JACKSON (Julian), 684.
JACKSON (Myles), 6031.
JACKSON (Peter), 4632.
JACKSON (Ralph), 234.
JACOB (Christian), 1965.
Jacob (Max), 448.
JACOB-KARAU (Liselotte), 2334.
JACOBS (Alain), 6462.
JACOBS (B.), 1587.
JACOBS (Bruno), 2707.
JACOBSON (David M.), 2751.
JACOBY (F.), 739.
Jacquart (Jean), 6779.
JACQUEMARD (Catherine), 2391.
JACQUEMIN (A.), 1865, 2103.
JACQUES-RIMASSA (P.), 2050.
JACQUET-FRANCILLON (François), 5794.
JAEGER (C. Stephen), 3571.
JAEGER (M.), 2353.
JAEGER (Nils), 4264.
JAFFRO (Laurent), 5395.
JAGANNATHAN (N. S.), 5850.
JAHODA (Gustav), 908.

Jaime II, rey de Aragona, 3105.
JAKIC (Ivan), 1292.
JAKIR (Aleksandar), 5248.
JAKOBS (Hermann), 26.
JAKOVLEV (A. N.), 7476.
JAKUB (Jay), 7760.
JAKUBOWSKI-TIESSEN (Manfred), 158, 3969.
JALIMAM (Salih), 5541.
JAMES (Frank A. J. L.), 6035.
JAMES (Harold), 7741.
JAMES (L.), 1215.
JAMES (P.), 2909.
JAMES (S.), 1461.
JAMESON (R.), 1651.
JANAWAY (Cristopher), 1398.
JANČÍK (Drahomír), 7714.
JANDEROVÁ (Helena), 5719.
JANEIRO PINTO (Helena), 7715.
JANEKOVIĆ ROEMER (Zdenka), 841, 1171.
JAN-EN (Hans-Gerd), 378.
JANIN (Valentin L.), 346, 3333.
JANJATOVIĆ (Bosiljka), 585.
JANKO (Jan), 7010.
JANNENS (E.), 1988.
JANOWSKI (Berndt), 1318.
JANSE (A.), 3415.
JANSEN (C. J. H.), 7166.
JANSEN (Christine), 4439.
JANSEN (Jan), 8331.
JANSEN (Michael), 6704.
JANSEN LUDWIG (Katherine), 3769.
JANSEN-WINKELN (K.), 1628.
JANSON (Henrik), 986.
JANSSEN (Karl-Heinz), 7636.
JANSSEN (Wilhelm), 3204.
JANSSEN-ZIMMERMANN (Antje), 6288.
JANSSON (Sven Bertil), 3572.
JANTING (Jørgen), 1172.
JANUS (Eligiusz), 3921
JAPP (S.), 1588.
JAPP (Uwe), 6330.
JARAUSCH (Konrad Hugo), 4511.
JARDIN (Pierre), 5708.
JARNUT (Elke), 7400.
JAROCH (Matthias), 7651, 7802.
JAROV (Sergej V.), 5007.
JARVA (Eero), 1551.
JÄSCHKE (Kurt-Ulrich), 3259.
JASIEWICZ (Krzysztof), 3949.
JASTREBOVA (O. M.), 8049.
JAUERNIG (Martha), *I*.
JAUMAIN (Serge), 1208.
Jaurès (Jean), 740.
JAVORA (Antonín), 171.
JAYAPALAN (N.), 8087.
JAY-ROBERT (G.), 2104.
JEAN (François), 1180.

JEAN (Jean-Claude), 4595.
Jean de Mirabello dit van Haelen, 3390.
Jean Renart, 3364.
JEAN TINCTOR, 3762.
JEANDILLOU (Jean-François), 5851.
Jeanne d'Arc, 381.
JEANNENEY (Jean-Noël), 4033.
JEANNENEY (Jean-Noël), 6543.
JEAUNEAU (A. E.), 3704.
Jefferson (Thomas), 392.
Jefferson (Thomas), 5224.
JEFFREYS-JONES (Rhodri), 5202.
JEHNE (M.), 1989.
JELASKA (Zdravka), 3388.
JELAVICH (Peter), 1293.
JELEČEK (Leoš), 347.
JELICH (Franz-Josef), 5804.
JENKINS (Everett), 3308.
JENKINS (Keith), 842.
JENKINS (Philip), 5645.
JENNY (Jean), 89.
JENS (Inge), 6343.
Jens Grand, 3234.
JENSEN (Bent), 7908.
JENSEN (Grethe), 1026.
JENSEN (Ola W.), 586.
JENSEN (Robin M.), 2910.
JERÁBEK (Rudolf), 4073.
JERKIČ (Branko), 7768.
JERSAK (Tobias), 7761.
Jerusalem (Wilhelm), 6270.
JERVIS (R.), 7262.
JESKE (Jürgen), 6841.
JESPERSEN (Knud J. V.), 7785.
JESSE (Eckhard), 4515.
JESSEN (Ralph), 5737.
JESSENNE (Jean-Pierre), 4320.
JESSEPH (Douglas M.), 5646, 6101.
JESZENSZKY (Sándor), 6064.
JIA (Kailin), 8137.
JIA (Wei), 8138.
Jiang (Jieshi), 8104, 8131.
JIANG (Li), 8264.
JIMENEZ (Juan Carlos), 1163.
JIMENEZ POLANCO (Jacqueline), 4273.
JIMENEZ ZAMUDIO (R.), 1702.
JIMENEZ-CALVENTE (T.), 2848.
JING (Shenghong), 8139.
JINNAH (Mahomed Ali), 4893, 4896.
JIRÁNEK (Tomáš), 4227.
JOANA (Jean), 4349.
JOAS (Hans), 1356.
JOBERT (Barthélémy), 6442.
JOCELYN (H. D.), 2628.
JOCH (Markus), 1431.
JOES (Anthony James), 7976.
Johann von Würzburg, 3550.

Johannes Paulus II, Papa, 5354.
Johannes Philoponos , 2854.
Johannes, Sanctus (evangelista), 2857, 2924.
Johannes Stobaeus, 1963.
Johannes XXIII, Papa, 5355.
JOHANNOWSKY (W.), 2238.
JOHANSEN (L.), 1475.
JOHANSON (Baber), 5542.
John (Otto), 4501.
JOHNS (Alessa), 1219.
Johnson (Ben), 6532, 6587.
JOHNSON (Dale A.), 5290.
JOHNSON (Eric A.), 4440.
JOHNSON (George M.), 1433.
JOHNSON (Graham Edwin), 987.
JOHNSON (L. Peter), 3563.
JOHNSON (Lesley), 3893.
JOHNSON (M.), 2340.
JOHNSON (Martin Phillip), 4350.
JOHNSON (Maxwell E.), 2911.
JOHNSON (Paul), 7041.
JOHNSON (Robert David), 7910.
JOHNSON (Robert), 5203.
Johnson (Samuel), 6282.
Johnson (Uwe), 6290.
JOHNSON BARKER (Brian), 988.
JOHNSTON (David), 2500.
JOHNSTON (S. I.), 1822.
JOHNSTONE (S.), 1990.
JÖHRENS (Gerhard), 224, 2051.
JOHSUA (Isaac), 6648.
JOIN-LAMBERT (Sophie), 6442.
Joinville (Jean de), 741.
JOITA (Virgil), 1148.
JOKILEHTO (Jukka), 6420.
JOKISALO (Jouko), 1068.
JOLIVET (J.-Ch.), 2629.
JOLLEY (Nicholas), 5968.
JONDORF (Gillian), 6240.
JONES (David Martin), 4548.
JONES (Helen), 343.
JONES (Howard), 5204.
JONES (John D.), 3808.
JONES (Lindsay), 8378.
JONES (Matthew), 7911.
JONES (N. F.), 2052.
JONES (Peter Murray), 3706.
JONES (Robert Alun), 721.
JONES (Ross), 6102.
JONES (Stuart), 684.
JONES (William Jervis), 5647.
JONJIĆ (Tomislav), 7912.
JOOSTEN (Ineke), 2769.
JORDÁ PARDO (J. F.), 1504.
JORDAN (Stefan), 843.
Jordanes, 742.
JÖRDENS (A.), 1866.
JORDI (Jean-Jacques), 5571.
Jørgen af Danmark, 4261.
JØRGENSEN (Torstein), 3789.

JOSE (Ricardo Trota), 7667.
JOSEPH (Gilbert M.), 5671.
Joseph II, röm.-deutscher Kaiser, 7444.
Josephus Flavius v. Flavius Josephus.
JOST (Hans Ulrich), 5144, 7913.
JOST (M.), 1823.
JOUANNA (Arlette), 5484.
JOUANNA (J.), 2192.
JOUBERT (Fabienne), 3637.
JOUET (Valérie), 774.
JOUTSIVUO (Timo), 6103.
JOVER ZAMORA (José M.), 7263.
JOVIC (Dejan), 5249.
Joyce (James), 1432, 6354.
JOYCE (Peter), 4549.
JU (Zhifen), 8140.
JULIÁ (Santos), 990.
Julian of Norwich, 3858, 3862.
JULIEN (Elise), 7914.
JULLIEN (Vincent), 6079.
Jullien de Paris (Marc-Antoine), 4319.
JUNGEL (Eberhard), 1318.
Jünger (Ernst), 5998.
JUNKER (Thomas), 6068, 6143.
JURADO NOBOA (Fernando), 4276.
JURGEIT (F.), 2293.
JUROT (Romain), 54.
JUSCHKA (Darlene M.), 1357.
JUSSEN (Bernhard), 1242.
JUSSILA (Osmo), 4288, 4289.
JUSTER (Susan), 3963.
Jutta von Disibodenberg, Sancta, 3850.
JUUSOLA (Hannu), 276.

K

KABAYAMA (Koichi), 348, 485.
KACIN-WOHINZ (Milica), 1000.
KACZMAREK (Ryszard), 7716.
Kádár (János), 8036.
KADIR (Kazi A.), 8053.
KAELBLE (Hartmut), 3964.
Kafka (Franz), 6381.
KAGAN (Frederick W.), 5008.
KAGAY (Donald J.), 3192.
KAHIN (Audrey R.), 4647.
KAHLCKE (Jan), 5179.
KAHLENBERG (Friedrich P.), 4386.
KAIMIO (M.), 2053.
KAIN (Roger J. P.), 329, 343.
KAISER (Carl-Christian), 4442.
KAISER (Michael), 7411.
KAISER (T.), 1496.
KAL'MINA (Lilija V.), 5009.
KALC (Aleksej), 918.
KALDELLIS (A.), 3038.
KALDOR (Mary), 7264.

KALIFA (Dominique), 6331, 6908.
KALINKE (Marianne E.), 3595.
KALINOVÁ (Lenka), 6940.
KALINOWSKI (Isabelle), 5892.
KALLA (G.), 1687.
KALLENDORF (Craig), 115.
KALLET (L.), 1991.
KALNIKOV (A.), 3965.
KALOEV (Boris A.), 909.
KALUS (Peter), 191.
KALUZA (Zénon), 3713.
KALVODA (Josef), 7915.
KAMENEC (Ivan), 5046.
KAMIL (Ediati), 4649.
KAMMEN (Michael G.), 5648, 6463.
KÄMMER (Harold), 6256.
KAMMERLOHER-LIS (Stephanie), 5406.
KAMMINGA (Johan), 8392.
KAMPPINEN (Matti), 1358.
KAMRIN (J.), 1629.
KANAZAWA (Shusaku), 4550.
KANÇAL (S.), 6804.
KANCEFF (Emanuel), 6287.
KANDA (Yutsuki), 8288.
KANDIAH (Michael David), 8074.
Kangxi, emperor of China, 8245.
KANINSKAJA (Galina N.), 4351.
KANNNICHT (R.), 2193.
Kant (Immanuel), 845, 5715, 5885, 5939, 5952, 5969, 5997, 6003, 6013, 6021, 6029, 6167, 7200.
KANTER (Laurence B.), 3852.
KAPITSA (Sergej P.), 6843.
KAPLAN (Karel), 4228.
KAPLAN (Lawrence S.), 7916.
KAPLAN (Yosef), 3270.
KAPODISTRIAS (Ioannes), 7456.
KARABAŞ (Seyfi), 910.
KARABÉLIAS (Ev.), 2982.
KARABELIAS (Gerassimos), 5168.
KARABELL (Zachary), 7917.
KARAGEORGHIS (J.), 2239.
KARAMUK (Gümeç), 7125.
KARAMUT (I.), 1589.
KARAPETJANTS (A. M.), 8099.
Karg-Elert (Sigfried), 6562.
Karl I der Große, röm.-deutscher Kaiser, König der Franken, 3462, 3864.
Karl IV, röm.-deutscher Kaiser, 3257.
Karl V, röm.-deutscher Kaiser, 327, 397, 4080, 7413.
Karl von Burgund, Graf von Charolais, 3155.
KARNOOUH (Claude), 4984.
KARPANTSCHOF (René), 4265.
KARPOZILU (M.), 2974.
KARPUS (Zbihniew), 7582.

KARRAS (G.), 6805.
KARSH (Efraim), 4688, 7265.
KARSH (Inari), 7265.
KASELOW (Gerhild), 6464.
KASHANI-SABET (Firoozeh), 4660.
Kaspar (Elm), 3786.
KASPER (Elke), 6288.
KASPER (Walter), 1360.
KASPI (André), 738ù.
KASTAN (David Scott), 1425.
KASTEN (Ingrid), 3604.
KASUYA (Makoto), 6705.
KATER (Thomas), 5969.
KATIČIĆ (Radoslav), 3461, 4201.
KATO (Tomoyasu), 8286.
KATZ (D.), 1688.
KATZBURG (Nathaniel), 5544.
KATZER (Nikolaus), 5010.
KAUER (Christiane), 7437.
KAUFMANN (Franz-Xaver), 1173.
KAUFMANN-HEINIMANN (Annemarie) , 2752.
KAUL (Chandrika), 5852.
KAUP (Matthias), 3856.
KAUPEN-HAAS (Heidrun), 924.
KAURANEN (Kaisa), 6743.
KAVALER (Ethan Matt), 6465.
KAWAKATSU (Mamoru), 8142.
KAY (Dennis), 5715.
KAY (Richard), 3491.
Kay (Sarah), 3527.
KAYE (Peter), 6332.
Kaygusuz Abdal, 5160.
KAYLOR (Noel Harold), 3699.
KAZAMIAS (G.), 7717.
KAZGAN (Haydar), 1174.
KAZHDAN (A.), 2983.
KE (Powen), 8143.
KEATING (D.), 1512.
KEATS-ROHAN (K. S. B.), 3096.
KECSKEMÉTI (Judit), 5666.
KEDDIE (Nikki R.), 4661.
KEDOURIE (Sylvia), 5175.
KEDWARD (Harry Roderick), 7786.
KEEGAN (John), 6513.
KEGASAWA (Yasunori), 8144.
KEITEL (Elizabeth), 2376.
KELCH-RADE (Clivia), 7400.
KELEŞYILMAZ (Vahdet), 7583.
KELLEK (Edwige), 6257.
KELLER (Hagen), 3829.
KELLER (Morton), 5222.
KELLER (Pierre), 5970.
KELLEY (Brooks Mather), 5738.
KELLEY (Donald R.), 755.
KELLMAN (Hernbert), 83.
KELLY (Douglas), 3573.
KELLY (Michael), 7974.
KELLY (Saul), 8028.
KELSALL (Malcolm Miles), 392.
Kelsen (Hans), 7072.

Kemal (Ismail Bey), 7618.
Kemal (Mustafa 'Atatürk'), 4650, 5170, 5822, 7603.
KEMP (B.), 1660.
KEMP (Walter A.), 3966.
KEMPSHALL (M. S.), 3732.
KEMP-WELCH (A.), 4952.
KENDALL (Daniel), 2943.
KENDRIC PRITCHETT (W.), 1932.
KENDRICK (Laura), 13.
KENNEDY (A.), 1725.
KENNEDY (David), 5205.
Kennedy (John Fitzgerald), 7819, 7842, 7909, 7928, 7946, 7950, 7966, 7983.
KENNEDY (Liam), 1177.
Kennedy, (Robert Francis), 7819.
KENNELL (N. M.), 2054.
KENNEY (Padraic), 4942.
KENNY (Michael), 791.
KENT (J.), 6766.
KEREC (Darja), 689.
KEREJTOV (Ramazan Kh.), 911.
KERHERVÉ (Jean), 1160.
KÉRIVEN (B.), V.
KERKVLIET (Benedict J.), 5240.
KERNEIS (S.), 2420.
KERNEL (Davor), 5061.
KERR (Berenice M.), 3884.
KERSHAW (Baz), 6569.
KERSHAW (Ian), 4461.
Kersobleptes, king of Thraces Odrysae, 2004.
KERSTING (W.), 2154.
KERVÉGAN (Jean F.), 7073.
KÉRY (Lotte), 3329.
KESSEL (Wolfgang), 4442.
KESSLER (K.), 1699.
KEVAL (Susanna), 4443.
KEY FOWDEN (Elizabeth), 2953.
Keynes (John Maynard), 6673.
KÉZAI (Simon), 3169.
KHACHATUROV (Sergej V.), 6395.
KHADŽINIKOLOVA (Elena), 4817, 7508.
KHAN (Roedad), 7803.
KHAZANOV (Anatolij M.), 4038.
KHELLIL (Mohand), 4034.
KHEVROLINA (Viktorija M.), 7509.
Khnumhotep II, king of Egypt, 1629.
KHODARKOVSKY (Michael), 7336.
KHOROSHEV (A. A.), 3216.
KHOURY (R. G.), 1735, 1743.
KHULLAR (Dashan), 7918.
KHUN SONG (Byung), 6767.
KIBATA (Yoichi), 485.
KICHKILOVA (P.), 7539.
KIDD (Alan), 6919.
KIDD (Colin), 4551.
KIDD (I. G.), 1948.

KIDD (Stuart S.), 5194.
KIEFER (Marcus), 6421.
KIEFNER (Theo), 5492.
KIENZLE (Beverly M.), 3896.
KIERNAN (Kevin S.), 3505.
KIERNAN (Pauline), 6570.
KIESER (Hans-Lukas), 7483.
KIESERITZKY (Wolther von), 4416.
KIESEWETTER (Andreas), 3236.
Kiesinger (Kurt Georg), 7982.
KIJASHKO (Aleksej V.), 1535.
KILIÇ (Davut), 5162.
KILLINGRAY (David), 7310, 7365.
KILSON (Robin W.), 7318.
KIM (S. G.), 587.
KIM (Youngho), 7919.
KIM HABOUSH (JaHyun), 8322.
KIMBLE (Judith Mary), 7350.
KIMELDORF (Howard), 7049.
KIMMELMAN (Burt), 3574.
KIMURA (Mitsuhiko), 6649.
KINDGARD (Adriana), 4051.
KING (Anthony), 2753.
KING (Desmond S.), 5206.
King (James), 8388.
KING (Robert Desmond), 7318.
KING (Sigrid), 6230.
King (William Lyon Mackenzie), 7273.
KINGSLEY (Margery), 5715.
KINGSLEY KENT (Susan), 4552.
KINGSTONE (Peter R.), 4129.
KINLOCH TIJERINO (Frances), 4878.
KINTANAR (Galileo C.), 4927.
KINTZ (Jean-Pierre), 3924.
KINZER (Stephen), 7977.
KIPPEL (Diethelm), 7164.
KIR'JANOV (Ju. I.), 7037.
KIRBY (C. J.), 1660.
KIRCHBERGER (Ulrike), 7510.
KIRJUSHIN (Ju. F.), 1550.
KIRK (Robin), 4914.
KIRK (Tim), 3987, 6828.
KIRK-GREENE (Anthony), 7351.
Kirpichnikov (Anatolij N), 3149.
KIRSCH (Martin), 7094.
KIRSCHBAUM (Stanislav J.), 992.
KISELEV (Aleksandr F.), 4990.
KISHIMOTO (Mio), 8145.
KIŠKILOVA (P.), 7480.
KISLINGER (E.), 2970.
KITCHING (Carolyn J.), 7584.
KITOWSKI (Karin), 5795.
KITTELL (Ellen E.), 3471.
KITTSTEINER (Heinz D.), 845.
KIVELSON (Valerie), 3934.
KLAMT (Johann-Christian), 465.
KLANJŠČEK (Zdravko), 7762.
KLAPISCH-ZUBER (Christiane), 192.

KLAPP-LEHRMANN (Astrid), 1412.
KLARÉN (Peter Flindell), 4916.
KLATCH (Rebecca E.), 5207.
KLAVERSMA (Nel), 439.
KLÄY (Dieter), 7832.
KLEBER (Hermann), 589.
KLEDT (A.), 2708.
KLEIN (Herbert S.), 7312.
KLEIN (Jan Willem), 47.
Klein (Josua), 5407.
KLEIN (Martin), 8356.
KLEIN (Michael B.), 7920.
KLEIN (Richard), 2807.
KLEINGELD (Pauline), 5649.
KLEJN (Zbigniew), 7511.
KLENER (Pavel), 1138.
KLENER (Pavel), 6650.
KLEßMANN (Christoph), 957, 7824.
KLÍMA (Jan), 4229.
KLIMANOV (Lev G.), 225.
KLIMBURG-SALTER (Deborah E.), 240.
KLIMKEIT (Hans-Joachim), 8042.
KLIMÓ (Árpád), 590.
KLINGBEIL (Martin), 393.
KLINGEBIEL (Kathrin), 3503.
KLINKHAMMER (Lutz), 7787.
KLÍPA (Bohumír), 4230.
KLOFT (H.), 1824.
KLOFT (Matthias Theodor), 7438.
KLÖNNE (Arno), 4444.
KLUETING (Harm), 4079.
Klumpke (Anna), 6453.
KLUXEN (Andrea M.), 5739.
KNABE (Hubertus), 4445.
KNAPÍK (Jiří), 5650.
KNAPP (Ulrich), 37.
KNAPPETT (C.), 1842.
KNATZ (Lothar), 5971.
KNAUFF (Michael), 6769.
KNIGHT (Jeremy), 3197.
KNIGHTS (Ben), 6333.
KNIPPENBERG (Hans), 354.
KNJAZEVSKAJA (O. A.), 3160.
KNOEPFLER (D.), 1933.
KNOPF (Volker), 4446.
KNOTTNERUS (J. David), 5796.
KNUDSEN (Knud), 7050.
KNÜTEL (R.), 2488.
KNUTSEN (Torbjørn L.), 993.
KOBIALKA (Michal), 3575.
KÖBLER (Gerhard), 3340.
KOÇ (Bekir), 5164.
KOÇ (Yunus), 7076.
KOCH (G.), 2754.
KOCH (J.), 1689.
KOCH (Matthias), 3389.
KOCH (Walter), 12.
KOCHHAR (R. K.), 6104.
KOCHIN (Michael S.), 3309.
KOCK (Thomas), 442.

KOCKA (Jürgen), 591, 1175, 4393, 4447, 4470, 5740, 6941.
KODALLE (Klaus-M.), 5942.
KODER (J.), 3039.
KOEPPEL (Philippe), 5351.
KOERNER (Lisbet), 6105.
KOFAS (Jon V.), 7921.
KOGMAN-APPEL (Katrin), 63.
Kohl (Helmut), 7942.
KOHL (Ph.), 1797.
KOHLER (Alfred), 4080.
KOHLHEPP (Gerd), 1223.
KOHN (M.), 1519.
KOHUT (Karl), 1223.
KOK (Jan Piet Filedt), 125.
KOKKINANIKS (Gh.), 6806.
KOKOŠKA (Stanislav), 4231.
KOL'TSOV (Lev V.), 1497.
KOLA (Paulin), 4020.
KOLB (Eberhard), 4391.
KOLDE (A.), 693.
KOLENDO (J.), 2558.
KOLIAS (T. G.), 3040.
KOLINSKY (Martin), 7718.
KOLIOPOULOS (John S.), 4584.
KOLLÁROVÁ (Zuzana), 5033.
KOLLER (Guido), 5143.
KOLLER (Walter), 3174.
KOLLMANN (Josef), 7412.
Kolmogoroff (Andrei Nikolaevich), 6094.
KOLOBOV (Aleksandr V.), 2421.
KOLTUKHOV (Sergej G.), 1552.
KÖLZER (Theo), 3198.
KOMLOS (John), 6844.
KONDAKOVA (Irina A.), 4985.
KONDO (Kazuhiko), 984.
Kong (Xiangxi), 8117.
KÖNIG (I.), 2967.
KÖNIG (M.), 5144.
König (René), 847.
KÖNIGSDORF (Helga), 4396.
KONOVALOV (Prokopii Batiurovich), 8058.
KONOVALOVA (Irina G.), 349.
KONRAD (M.), 1590.
KONTLER (László), 994.
KOOPER (Erik), 612.
KOOY (Michael John), 846.
KOPECKÝ (Milan), 3733.
KÖPECZI (Béla), 7424.
Kopernik (Nikolaj), 6157.
KÖPKE (Wulf), 5563.
KORCZYK (Henryk), 7585.
KORDOSIS (M.), 3041.
KORDOSIS (M.), 350.
KOREMAN (Megan), 4352.
KORGUN (Viktor Grigor'evich), 4014.
KOROBENKO (L. A.), 3160.
KOROL (Juan Carlos), 6652.

KOROLKO (Miroslav), 5321.
KOROVITSYNA (Natal'ja V.), 6845.
KORPIOLA (Mia), 3345.
KORTE (Karl-Rudolf), 978.
KORYN (Andrzej), 7602.
KORZO (Margarita A.), 5293.
KOS (Dušan), 3331.
KÓSA (László), 1211.
KOSÁRY (Domokos), 7512.
KOSCH (Wilhelm), 1427.
KOSCHMANN (J. Victor), 1036.
KOSE (A.), 1567.
KOSEKI (Takashi), 588.
KOSELLECK (Reinhart), 995.
KOSEV (Konstantin Dimitrov), 4148.
KOSHI (Koichi), 3658.
KOSINSKAJA (Lubov' L.), 1511.
KOSLOFSKY (Craig), 1242.
KOSLOWSKI (Peter), 5455.
KÖSTER (Burkhard), 4081.
KOSTIS (K.), 1240.
Kot (Stanislaw), 744.
KOTKIN (Stephen), 4850.
KOTLER (E.), 638.
KOTSONIS (Yanni), 6768.
Kottaner (Helene), 3383.
Kötzschke (Rudolf), 745.
KOUDELKA (František), 4232, 4252.
KOULA (Yitzhak), 4191.
KOURVETARIS (Yorgos A.), 4585.
KOUTRAKOU (N.), 277.
KOVÁČ (Dušan), 5044.
Kovacsics (Jozef), 6833.
KOWALSKÁ (Eva), 5043.
Köyden (Bilal), 6499.
Koželuhová (Helena), 4222.
KOZLOV (Vladimir Petrovich), 419, 592.
KOZLOVA (Natalija V.), 6744.
KOZLOWSKI (S. K.), 1514.
KOZU (Kunio), 5972.
KRACIK (Jörg), 4233.
KRÆMMER (Michæl), 193.
KRAGH (Helge), 6106.
KRAHNKE (Holger), 5741.
Krakau (Knud), 7274.
KRAMER (Hilton), 5651.
KRAMER (Mark), 7823.
KRANENPOHL (Uwe), 4448.
KRANTZ (Olle), 6703.
KRAŠOVEC (Tone), 6640.
KRATZSCH (Konrad), 84.
Krauland (Peter), 4074.
KRAUS (Elisabeth), 194.
KRAUS (Hans-Christof), 5564.
KRAUS (K.), 2773.
KRAUSE (Andreas), 7586.
KRAUSE (Thomas), 1127.
KRAUSKOPF (I.), 2294.
KREBS (Roland), 5876.

KRECH (Shepard III), 457.
KREHM (William), 3967.
KREIMENDAHL (Lothar), 5992.
KREIS (Georg), 5144.
Kreisky (Bruno), 4084.
KREJČOVÁ (Helena), 4234.
KREKLER (Ingeborg), 57.
KREMER (Dieter), 283.
KREMLIČKOVÁ (Ladislava), 6725, 7139.
KŘEN (Jan), 3968, 6651.
KRENN (Michael L.), 7253, 7828, 7922.
KRESAL (Franc), 1000.
KŘESŤAN (Jiří), 4235.
KRESTEN (O.), 3020.
KRETSCHMAR (Georg), 5330.
KREUZER (Marcus), 4353.
KRIEGEL (Maurice), 4689.
KRIER (Jean), 30.
KRIGER (Colleen E.), 8347.
KRIKLER (Jeremy), 6943.
KRIKORIAN (Robert O.), 4067.
KRINGS (Ulrich), 3679.
KRINZINGER (F.), 3020.
KRIPPENDORFF (Ekkehart), 6334.
KRISHNA (Sankaran), 5124.
KRISTÓ (Gyula), 3042, 3238.
KROES (R.), 7266.
KRÖGER (Martin), 7720.
KROLL (S.), 1797.
KROLL (Thomas), 4754.
KRUEGER (D.), 2954.
KRUGER (Arnd), 5790.
KRÜGER (Gesine), 4866.
KRÜGER (Klaus), 3135.
KRUIP (Gudrun), 5853.
KRUK (J.), 1447.
KRUMSCHWITZ (P.), 2325.
KRUPP (Michael), 4690.
KRUSE (Britta-Juliane), 3734.
KRUSE (Holger), 3258.
KRUSE (Th.), 1630.
KRUSE (Volker), 847.
KRUSENSTJERN (Benigna von), 7034.
KRUTA PUPPI (L.), 1553.
KRYNEN (Jacques), 1120.
KUBAN (Doğan), 3310.
Kubrick (Stanley), 6565.
KUBŮ (Eduard), 6651.
KUCERA (Jaroslav), 7588.
KUCHERENKO (G. S.), 3939.
KUDRJAVTSEV (Ivan I.), 4988.
KUEHN (Thomas), 3423.
Kues (Nikolaus von), 5901.
KUGEL (Wilfried), 4488.
KÜGLE (Karl), 3686.
KÜHL (Jörgen), 996.
KUHN (Dieter), 7652.
KUHN (S.), 1498.

KÜHNE (Andrea), 7923.
KÜHNL-KINEL (Agnieszka), 6571.
KUHRT (Eberhard), 4467.
KUIPERS (Anske Hielke), 7322.
KUIPERS (Marietje E.), 7322.
KUKLÍK (Jan), 4236, 4251, 7788.
KUL'KOV (E. N.), 7681.
KULA (Mieczysław Henryk), 7589.
KULAWIK (Teresa), 6944.
KÜLZER (Andreas), 3043.
KUMAMOTO (Robert D.), 7924.
KUMANEV (Georgij A.), 4989.
KUMANOV (Milen), 4149.
KUMAR (Anand), 4634.
KUMAR (Ravinder), 4621.
KUNERALP (Sinan), 7126.
KÜNG (Hans), 1359.
KUNST (Christiane), 2559.
KUNZ (Diane B.), 7925.
KUNZE (Gerhard), 4449.
KUNZE (Peter), 4465.
KUPERUS (Tracy), 5493.
KUPIEC (Gabriel), 116.
KUPISCH (B.), 2488.
KUPPER (J.-R.), 1690.
KURAKEEVA (Marija F.), 912.
KURAS (Leonid V.), 5009.
KURATOV (Anatolij A.), 593.
KURGAN-VAN HENTENRYK (Ginette), 4100.
KURKE (L.), 2055.
KURNJEK (Branko), 5059.
KURODA (Hideo), 8306.
KUROKAWA (Tomobumi), 3885.
KURŞUN, 5169.
KURTH (Peter), 802.
KURTZ (Marcus J.), 4172.
KURZAWA (Frédéric), 3809.
KURZMEYER (Roman), 5407.
KURZWEG (Martina), 5854.
KUSCHNICK (Michael), 7193.
KUSHNER (David), 7513.
KUSHNER (Tony), 4560.
KUSIMBA (Chapurukha M.), 8348.
KUSMAN (David), 3390.
KÜSTER (Konrad), 1278.
KÜSTER (Volker), 1280.
KÜSTERS (Hanns Jürgen), 4455.
KUTTIN (Bettina), *I*.
KÜTTLER (Wolfgang), 834.
KUVAJA (Christer), 7439.
KUWABARA (Kanji), 6745.
KUZMANOVA (Antonina), 7590.
Kuznets (Simon), 6666.
KUZNETSOV (Evgenij V.), 3187.
KVÆRNDRUP (Sigurd), 780.
KVISTAD (Gregg Owen), 4450.
KWINT (Marius), 609.
KWOK-CHU (Wong), 6653.
KYLE (Keith), 4808.
KYLE CROSSLEY (Pamela), 594.

L

LA BUA (Giuseppe), 2630.
LA GUARDIA (David), 3463.
La Malfa (Ugo), 4723, 7105.
LA POLLA (Franco), 6572.
LA ROSA (V.), 1840.
LA ROVERE (Luca), 4755.
LA SALVIA (Sergio), 4756.
LAARMANN (Matthias), 3735.
LABAHN (M.), 1763, 2912.
LABARTA RODRIGUEZ-MARIBONA (Carolina), 7926.
Laberthonniére (Lucien), 5413.
LABORDERIE (Noëlle), 3517.
LABRIOLA (Silvano), 7134.
LABRUNA (Luigi), 1128.
Labutina (Inga K.), 3647.
Lacan (Jacques), 5898, 6014.
LACAZE (Yvon), 7514.
Lachmann (Ludwig M.), 6671.
LACINER (Sedat), 5158.
LACKEY (Michael), 5973.
LACROIX-RIZ (Annie), 7721.
Lactantius (Lucius Caelius Firmianus), 2811.
LADA-RICHARDS (I.), 2105.
LAFEBER (W.), 7267.
LAFFAN (Michael), 4674.
LAFFITTE (Marie-Pierre), 128.
LAFFORGUE (Jorge Raúl), 4049.
LAFLEUR (Claude), 3868.
LAFON (X.), 2422.
LAFONT (B.), 1691.
LAFRANCE (David G.), 4848.
LAFUENTE (Gilles), 4854.
LAGERLUND (Henrik), 3736.
LAGREE (Michel), 6107.
LAHAISE (Robert), 4164.
LAHUSEN (G.), 2631.
LAI (Xinxia), 8146.
LAIDLER (David), 6677.
LAIGNEAU (Sylvie), 2632.
LAIRD (Mark), 6423.
LAITINEN (Riitta), 8375.
ŁAJTAR (A.), 1867.
LAKATOS (Pál), 4609.
LAKE (David A.), 7268.
LAKE (Marilyn), 6945.
LAKE PRESCOTT (Anne), 5715.
LAKIC (Goran), 5251.
LALKOV (Milčo), 4151, 5252.
LALOUETTE (J.), 6335.
LALOUETTE (Jacqueline), 595.
LAMARRA (A.), 5978.
LAMBALLE (Alain), 7927.
LAMBERG-KARLOVSKY (C. C.), 1554.
LAMBERIGTS (M.), 1303.
LAMBERT (Gisèle), 6466.
LAMBERT (Peter), 684.

LAMBERT (S. D.), 1868.
LAMBERTI (F.), 2501.
LAMBERTINI (Roberto), 1080.
LAMBIN (G.), 2106.
LAMBOURNE (Lionel), 6467.
LAMOUR (Denis), 743.
Lamprechts (Karl), 746.
LAMPROPOULO (D.), 4586.
LANARO (Paola), 6746.
LANCASTER (Lynne), 2755.
LANCEL (Serge), 1407, 2913.
LANCELLOTTI (M. G.), 1591.
LANCHESTER (Fulco), 7143.
LANDA (V. G.), 4029.
LANDAU (Philippe-E.), 4354.
LANDELS (J. G.), 2056.
LANDI (Fiorenzo), 6635.
LANDOLFI (M.), 2241.
LANDSMAN (Ned C.), 3970.
LANE (Kris E.), 8376.
LANFRANCHI (Giovanni B.), 636.
LANG (Carl Ludwig), 1427.
LANG (F.), 1843.
LANG (Sean), 7127.
LANG-AUINGER (C.), 1592.
LANGBEHN REGULA (Rohland de), 3576.
LANGDON (J.), 3044.
LANGE (Johan), 1243.
LANGER (Ullrich), 6223.
LANGERMANN (Martina), 5864.
LANGERMANN (Y. Tzvi), 3281.
LANGEWIESCHE (Dieter), 3923.
LANGUE (Frédérique), 5233, 6946.
LANTING (A. E.), 1447.
LANTING (J. N.), 1463.
Lanusse (Alejandro Agustín), 4059.
Lanyer (Aemilia), 6241.
LÁNYI (Vera), 243.
LANZA (Federica), 6573.
LANZA (Laura), 7108.
LAPLANCHE (François), 596, 750.
Lapo da Castiglionchio 'il giovane', 5594.
Lapointe (Ernest), 7273.
LAPORTE (Christian), 5408.
LAREMONT (Ricardo René), 4030.
LARFOUILLOUX (J.), 2155.
LARIO (Ángeles), 5096.
LARIZZA LOLLI (Mirella), 3923, 5656.
LARKINS (Jeremy Daniel), 1076.
LARNER (John), 351.
LAROULANDIE (Fabrice), 4356.
LARRÈRE (Catherine), 1050.
LARSEN (Timothy), 5294.
LARSSON (Mats G.), 3322.
LARSSON (Olle), 5409.
LASCH-QUINN (Elisabeth), 639.
Lasker-Schüler (Else), 6311.

LASNER (Mark Samuels), 1415.
LASSEN (Eva Maria), 1176.
LAST (Bärbel), 6064.
LATHAM (Agnes), 4523.
LATHROP (Thomas A.), 1428.
LAUBE (Martin), 5974.
LAUGIER (Sandra), 5975.
LAUNAY (Marcel), 5315.
LAURENS (Henry), 4899.
LAURENT (Franck), 597.
LAURENT (Stéphane), 5797, 6502.
LAURENTI (R.), 2156.
LAURETTA (Enzo), 6350.
LAUREYS (Véronique), 4098.
LAURIA-SANTIAGO (Aldo A.), 4280, 6770.
LAURIDSEN (John T.), 4266.
LAURIE (Ian S.), 1442.
LAURIOLA (R.), 1911.
Lauro (Vincenzo), 5321.
LAURSEN (John Christian), 5309.
LAURSEN (Johnny Nørgaard), 4267.
LAUTH (Reinhard), 5888.
LAUWAERT (Françoise), 8147.
LAUWERS (Michel), 3886.
LAUXTERMANN (Marc D.), 3045.
LAVAGNE (Henri), 407.
Laval (Pierre), 7694.
LAVALETTE (Michael), 7060.
LAVAUD (Jean-Pierre), 4107.
LAVECCHIA (S.), 2107.
L'Averdy (Clément-Charlesrançois de), 6799.
LAW (John E.), 3177.
LAW (Robin), 7359.
LAWALL (M. L.), 2057.
LAWRANCE (Jeremy), 3163.
LAWRIE (Alf), 1408.
LAY (Benny), 5347.
Layamon, 3541.
LAYBOURN (Keith), 4556.
LAYER-BURCHARTH (Ewa), 6468.
LAZAREV (Mikhail S.), 8059.
LAZAREVIC (Žarko), 6640, 6642.
LE BARS (Fabienne), 128.
LE GALL (Jean-Marie), 5270.
LE GOFF (Jacques), 997, 3464.
LE GUILLOU (Louis), 754.
LE JAN (Régine), 3425.
LE MASNE DE CHERMONT (Isabelle), 450.
LE NEVE (John), 3128.
LE PAUTREMAT (Pascal), 7591.
LE PERSON (Xavier), 4295.
Le Picart (François), 5519.
LE RIDER (Georges), 245.
LE RIDER (Jacques), 5976, 6336.
LE RIVEREND (Julio), 4207.
LE ROUX (P.), 2307, 2560.
LEACH (P.), 1529.

LEACH (Robert), 6563.
LEAFSTEDT (Carl S.), 6574.
LEAHY (A.), 1631.
LEAL VALLADARES (J. G.), 1449.
LEBECQ (Stéphane), 3377.
LEBEK (W. D.), 2377.
LEBINA (Natalija B.), 6947.
LECARME (Jacques), 703.
LECA-TSIOMIS (Marie), 5977.
LECLANCHE (Jean-Luc), 3577.
LECLANT (J.), 1632.
LECLERCQ-MARX (J.), 395.
LECOURT (Dominique), 1402.
LECOUTEUX (Claude), 3465.
LECOY (Félix), 3516.
LECUPRE-DESJARDIN (E.), 3466.
LEDOUX-LEBARD (Guy), 388.
LEDOVSKIJ (Andrej M.), 8098.
LEDUC (Christophe), 3247.
LEDUC (Jean), 159.
LEE (Alvin A.), 3578.
LEE (Pamela M.), 6424.
LEE (Paula Young), 466.
LEE (Robert G), 5657.
LEE DOWNS (Laura), 6948.
LEEB (Josef), 4387.
LEES (Clare A.), 3579.
LEFEBVRE (Jeffrey A.), 7928.
LEFEBVRE (R.), 2157.
LEFÈVRE (E.), 2634.
Leff (Gordon), 3772.
LEFF (Gordon), 3887.
LEFFLER (Melvyn P.), 7801.
LEFTOW (B.), 2914.
Léger (Alexis), 7553.
LEGG (Marie-Louise), 5855.
LEGROS (Robert), 7095.
LEGUILLOUX (M.), 2058.
LEHMAN (Kenneth D.), 7269.
LEHMANN (Hartmut), 3954, 3982, 5317.
LEHMANN (Yves), 1377.
LEHMIJORI-GARDNER (Maiju), 3810.
LEHMKUHL (Ursula), 7929.
LEHNERT (Detlef), 4451.
LEHOËRFF (Anne), 2295.
LEHOUCQ (Fabrice), 4197.
LEIBIGER (Stuart), 5208.
LEIBNER (Gerardo), 4917.
Leibniz (Gottfried Wilhelm), 2146, 5311, 5922, 5937, 5978, 6002, 6026.
LEIBY (Richard A.), 4452.
LEICK (G.), 1593.
LEIGHT (Robert L.), 5798.
LEIGHTON (C. D. A.), 5410.
Leighton (Frederic), 6455.
LEIGHTON (R.), 1499.
LEIMGRUBER (Matthieu), 7913.
LEINWAND (Theodore B.), 6575.

LEINWATHER (Thomas), 5799.
Leiris (Michel), 461.
LEITE LINHARES (Maria Yedda), 4130.
LEITZ (Christian), 4504.
LEITZ (Christian), 7722, 7740.
LEJKIND (Oleg L.), 6396.
LEJTNER (M.), 7546.
LEL'CHUK (Vitalij S.), 5017.
LEMAIRE (A.), 1692.
LEME (Paulo), 8037.
LEMESLE (Bruno), 3391.
LEMKE (Michael), 7998.
LEMOINE (Hervé), 420.
LEMUS LOPEZ (Encarnación), 5081.
LENCI (Mauro), 1077.
LENDINARA (Patrizia), 3580.
LENFANT (D.), 1908.
LENGYELOVA (Tünde), 5045.
LENNARTSSON (Malin), 6949.
LENSING (Helmut), 4453.
LENSSEN (J.), 2810.
LENTIN (Antony), 7592.
LENTZ (Thierry), 4357.
Lenz (Jakob Michael Reinhold), 6271.
LENZIN (René), 4521.
LEO (Annette), 4435.
Leo I Magnus, Papa, Sanctus, 2907.
Leo II, Papa, 3905.
Leo III, Papa, 3462.
Leo VI, Byzantine emperor, 3081.
Leo XIII, Papa, 5354.
LEÓN PORTILLA (Miguel), 8363.
LEONARD (Thomas M.), 7534.
LEONARDI (Claudio), 3186, 3702.
Leonardo da Vinci, 6471.
LEONHARDT (Jürgen), 2688.
Leonidas Tarentinus, 1894.
Leopardi (Giacomo), 6337.
LEPELLEY (C.), 2326, 2423.
LEPETIT (Bernard), 598, 848.
LEPPIN (H.), 1992.
LEPPIN (Hartmut), 2424.
LEPPIN (Volker), 5494.
LEPRE (Aurelio), 4757.
LEPRI (Sergio), 5856.
LERNER (J. D.), 1798.
LEROY (Béatrice), 3718.
LÉRTORA MENDOZA (Celina A.), 6154.
LESHCHENKO (Nelli F.), 8291.
LESPAGNOL (André), 5780.
LESSNOFF (Michael Harry), 1078.
LESTER (Geoffrey), 3542.
LESTRINGANT (Frank), 6338.
LESZKA (M. J.), 3046.
LETON (André), 4099.
LETTIERI (Alberto), 4052.

LETTIERI (Gaetano), 5411.
LETTS (John B.), 3136.
LEUTERT (Sebastian), 599.
LEUWERS (Hervé), 4320.
LEV (Yaacov), 3311.
LEVENE (D. S.), 2378.
LEVENSON (Michael), 1207.
Levi (Carlo), 6300.
Levi (Primo), 747.
LEVICK (Barbara), 2425.
LEVINE (Alan), 5282.
LEVINE (Joseph M.), 5658.
LEVINE (Robert M.), 4118, 4131.
LEVRA (Umberto), 4766.
LEVY (Carl), 684.
LEVY (Daniel), 600.
LÉVY (E.), 1993.
LEWENSTEIN (Bruce V.), 6088.
LEWIS (Andrew D. E.), 1129.
LEWIS (John L.), 5742.
LEWIS (John M.), 3659.
LEWIS (Katherine J.), 3472.
LEWIS (Mark Edward), 601.
LEWIS (Milton), 6092.
LEWIS (S. G.), 1492.
LEWIS (Sue), 3737.
LEWIS (Tom), 5605.
LEWISOHN (Leonard), 3306.
LEWONTIN (Richard C.), 830.
LEWUILLON (Serge), 396.
LEYDESDORFF (Selma), 603.
LEYDI (Silvio), 397.
LI (Guizhi), 8148.
Li (Hongzhang), 8206.
Li (Hongzhang), 8219.
LI (Jinming), 8149.
Li (Mingshan), 8150.
LI (Rong), 8151.
Li (Tingjiang), 8152.
Li (Wei), 8263.
LI (Xueqin), 8153.
LIANG (His-Huey), 7654.
Liang (Qichao), 8103, 8123, 8256.
LIANG (Yandong), 8186.
Libanius, 3022.
LIBERMAN (G.), 1878.
Licinius Rufinus (M. Cn.), 2507.
LIDEGAARD (Mads), 1361.
LIDEN (Anna), 3661.
LIEBER (Maria), 5631.
LIEBERG (G.), 2635.
LIEBERMAN (Victor), 3934.
LIEBICH (André), 3971, 5011.
LIEDTKE (Rainer), 3948.
LIEDTKE (Rainer), 5283, 5553.
LIENHARD (Marc), 5466, 5495.
LIEVEN (A. VON), 1633.
Liguori (Alfonso Maria), Sanctus, 5419.
LILIE (Ralph-Johannes), 2984.
LILJENSTOLPE (P.), 2757.

LILL (Rudolf), 7780.
LIM (Jie-Hyun), 1079.
LIM (Jie-Hyun), 3972, 4943, 8046.
LIMONIER (Fabien), 2426.
LIMOUSIN (Eric), 3047.
Lin (Piao), 8189.
LIN (Qiyan), 8154.
Lincoln (Abraham), 5204, 7515.
LIND (Vera), 6950.
LINDBERG (Christer), 8379.
LINDBORG (Rolf), 6108.
LINDEMANN (Mary), 6109.
LINDEMANN (Mechthild), 7802.
LINDENAUER (Leslie J.), 5183.
LINDENBERG (Daniel), 604.
LINDENFELD (David F.), 868.
LINDHARDT (Karsten), 4257.
LINDKVIST (Anna), 5135.
LINDNER (Rainer), 605.
LINDSAY (Lisa A.), 4882.
LINDSTEDT (Jukka), 7165.
LINDSTRÖM (Fredrik), 3950.
LING (Roger), 2758.
LINKE (Horst Günther), 7821.
LINKE (Uli), 913.
Linné (Carl von), 6096.
LINSKY (Bernard), 5979.
LIOGIER (H.), 6576.
LIOTTA (Filippo), 1139.
LIOU-GILLE (Bernadette), 2427.
LIPP (Michael), 5858.
Lippi (Filippo), 6461.
LIPSCHITS (O.), 1764.
LIPTÁK (L'ubomír), 3947, 5046.
LIPTON (Sara), 3282.
LISI (F.), 1942.
LIŠKA (Ondřej), 5412.
LITAVRIN (Gennadij G.), 2993-2995.
LITCHFIELD (R. Burr), 5659.
LITEWSKI (Wieslaw), 2502.
LITTLEWOOD (A. R.), 3048.
LITVINSKII (Boris Anatol'evich), 5546, 8055.
LIU (Dingming), 8155.
LIU (Huiyu), 8156.
LIU (Jingyuan), 8157.
LIU (Jinquan), 8267.
LIU (Tien-lung), 3973.
LIU (Weidong), 8158.
LIU (Yongdai), 8159.
LIU (Zhangmei), 8160.
LIUCCI (Raffaele), 5660.
Liutprand von Cremona, 748.
LIVET (Georges), 3924.
Livia, 2730.
LIVINGSTONE (David N.), 338.
Livius (Titus), 749, 1082, 2195, 2353, 2532, 2563.
LJAMINA (Ekaterina E.), 5012.
LJUBARSKIJ (Jakov N.)., 2969.

LLASERA (Margaret), 5661.
Lleras Restrepo (Carlos), 4186.
LLEWELYN (Morgan), 2636.
LLOYD (Rosemary), 6339.
Lloyd George (David), 7592, 7610.
LLUCH (Ernest), 5662.
LO CASCIO (Elio), 2413, 2561.
LO PORTO (Felice Gino), 2268.
LO SARDO (Eugenio), 1088.
LOACKER (Armin), 6577.
LOBATO (Manuel), 8343.
LOBKOWICZ (František), 171.
LÖCHER (Kurt), 6469.
LOCHRIE (Karma), 3467.
LOCK (F. P.), 5569.
Locke (John), 1072, 1097, 5912, 5968.
LODEN (Hans), 7931.
LOEWE (Michael), 8107.
LÖFFLER (Ulrich), 5496.
LÖFGREN (Orvar), 1247.
LÖFSTEDT (B.), 2637.
LOGEVALL (Fredrik), 7932.
LOGIE (Philippe), 3581.
LOHALM (Uwe), 4388.
LOHANDA (Mona), 7814.
LÖHNEYSEN (Wolfgang von), 3655.
Löhr (Egid Valentin Felix Johann Ferdinand, Ritter von), 7066.
LÖHR (Gebhard), 1312.
Loisy (Alfred), 750.
LOKATIS (Siegfried), 5864.
LOKIN (J. H. A.), 7166.
LOLLI (M.), 2429.
LOLLING (H. G.), 224.
LOMASTRO (Francesca), 3125.
LOMBARD (J.), 2158.
LOMBARDI (M.), 1927.
LOMBARDI (M.), 751.
Lombardo (Guillén), 5429.
LOMNITZ (Claudio), 5671.
LOMONACO (Fabrizio), 5980.
LONDÁK (Miroslav), 5047.
LONDEI (Luigi), 7128.
LONDON (April), 6259.
LONG (A. A.), 1396.
LONG (R. James), 3738.
LONGNON (Auguste), 254.
LONGO (Luigi Emilio), 7593.
LONGO (Nicola), 6224.
LONGO (O.), 2159.
LOOMIS (W. T.), 2059.
LOPATIN (Nancy D.), 4553.
LOPETEGUI (Guadalupe), 3139.
LOPEZ (Claude A.), 5183.
LOPEZ (David Andrew), 2915.
LOPEZ (Frank), 5234.
López Contreras (Eleazar), 5230.
LOPEZ DOMINGUEZ (M.), 1449.
LOPEZ FEREZ (J. A.), 2090.

LÓPEZ JIMENO (Mª del Amor), 1869.
LÓPEZ MARTINEZ (Antonio Luis), 5439.
LOPEZ POZA (S.), 206.
LÓPEZ TOBAR (Mario), 4173.
LÓPEZ-CALO (José), 1286.
LOPEZ-RIOS (Santiago), 3582.
LORA CAM (Jorge), 4918.
LORBLANCHET (M.), 1464.
LORCH (Ingomar), 6425.
LORCIN (Patricia M.), 7352.
LORÈ (Biagio), 5778.
LORENZ (Chris), 529, 606.
LORENZ (Einhart), 4885.
Lorenzetti (Ambrogio), 1136.
LORENZETTI (Luigi), 6951.
Lorenzetti (Pietro), 3836.
LORENZO CADARSO (Pedro L.), 7144.
Lorenzo de' Medici, 3262.
LORENZO GARCÍA (Santiago), 5440.
LORETELLI (Rosamaria), 6246.
LORETO (Luigi), 784.
LOREY (David E.), 7270.
LÖRINCZ (Barnabás), 2567.
LORINSER (Margarete), 4479.
LOSADA ALVAREZ (Abel), 4208.
LOSADA GOYA (José Manuel), 6242.
LÖSCH (Doris), 5663.
LÖSER (Freimut), 3739.
LOSITO (Giacomo), 5413.
LOSONCZI (Terezia), 4974.
LOTTES (Günther), 7164.
LOUD (G. A.), 3239, 3392.
LOUDEN (B.), 2108.
Louis (William Roger), 7318.
LOUIS (Wm. Roger), 1008.
Louis IX [Saint-Louis], roy de France, 741.
Louis XIV, roi de France, 384, 4323, 7441.
Louis XVI, roi de France, 7429.
LOUKOPOULOU (L.), 2060.
LOUREIRO (Rui Manuel), 1248.
LOVATO (Andrea), 2503, 7167.
LOVE (Ronald S.), 7440.
LOVEJOY (Paul E.), 7313.
LOVELL (Stephen), 5859.
LOVEMAN (Brian), 3974.
LOVISI (Claire), 2504.
Low (Alaine), 1008.
Low (Morris), 6110.
Loyd George (David), 7610.
LOYER (François), 6426.
LOYET (M. A.), 1799.
LOZITO (Vito), 2955.
Lu (Fangshang), 8161.
Lu (Xiqi), 8162.

LÜ (Yiran), 8163.
LUBORSKY SAMSON (Ruth), 119.
LUC (Jean-Noel), 5776.
Lucanus (M. Annaeus), 2354, 2627, 2647, 2660.
Lucas (Juan Francisco), 4848.
LUCAS (Scott), 7933.
Lucas, Apostolus, Sanctus, 751.
LUCASSEN (Leo), 6847.
LUCCHESI (Marzia), 7168.
LUCE (H. R.), 7271.
Luce (Henry), 7252.
LÜCHAU (Peter), 1329.
LUCIANI (M.), 1693.
LUCIANI (Paola), 6578.
LUCIFORA (Rosa Maria), 2638.
LÜCKE (Hans-Karl), 1249.
LÜCKE (Susanne), 1249.
Lucretius Carus (Titus), 2664, 2682, 2685, 2691.
LUDDEN (David), 8088.
Ludendorff (Erich), 4432.
Ludgerus, Sanctus, 3853.
LUDI (Regula), 7169.
LUDWIG (Frieder), 5155.
LUDWIG (Roland), 4479.
LUDWIG (Uwe), 3228.
LUEBKE (David M.), 5326.
LUFF (Robert), 3627.
LUGINBÜHL (Hans), 7455.
LUIJTEN (Ger), 125.
Luiken (Caspar), 439.
LUIS (J.-P.), 5097.
LUKACKA (Ján), 3097.
LUKACS (Antal), 3220.
LUKES (Igor), 4237.
LUKES (Igor), 7655, 7661, 7723.
LUKOWSKI (Jerzy), 7464.
Lull (Ramón), 3711.
LULL (V.), 1528.
LUMINARI (Laura), 7478.
LUMPERDEAN (Ioan), 6680.
LUND (J.), 1568.
LUND HANSEN (Ulla), 886.
LUNDESTAD (G.), 7272.
LUNDON (J.), 1920, 1928.
LUNDSTRÖM (S.), 1634.
LUNGU (Corneliu Mihail), 7516.
LUNITZ (Martin), 7413.
LUNN (Joe), 8349.
LUNSINGH SCHEURLEER (R. A.), 1800.
LUNT (James D.), 4805.
LUNTLEY (Michael), 5981.
LUO (Zhitian), 8164.
LUO (Zhitian), 8165.
LUPPINO MANES (E.), 1971.
LUQUE (Guillermo), 5235.
LUQUE TALAVÁN (Miguel), 166.
LUSIGNAN (S.), 1250.
LUSIGNAN (Serge), 3628.

INDEX OF NAMES

LUST (J.), 1303.
LUTERBACH (Jürgen), 1255.
LUTHER (A.), 1594.
LUTHER (Martin), 3857, 5466, 5481, 5489, 5491, 5495, 5501, 5503, 5507, 5516, 5524.
LÜTT (Jürgen), 7084.
LUTTERBACH (Hubertus), 3468.
LUTTRELL (Anthony), 3260.
LUTZ (Annabelle), 4238.
LUTZ (Eckart Conrad), 3778.
LÜTZELSCHWAB (Claude), 7353.
LUXMOORE (Jonathan), 5414.
LUZZATTO (Maria Jagoda), 792.
LVOVICH (Daniel), 4054.
LYNCH (Cecelia), 7724.
LYNCH (Nicolás), 4919.
LYNGE (Aqqaluk), 4262.
LYNN (John A.), 7441.
LYON (Bryce), 765.
LYON (Eileen Groth), 5295.
LYON CLARK (Beverly), 6921.
LYONS (Maryinez), 6092.

M

Ma (Hongkui), 8258.
MA (J.), 1595.
MA (Junya), 8166.
MA (Zhen), 8167.
MA (Zhendu), 8168.
MAC ALEER (Graham), 1081.
MAC ALEER (J. Philip), 3662.
Mac Arthur (Douglas), 8021.
MAC BRIDE (Angus), 3482.
MAC BRIDE (Lawrence W.), 391.
MAC CAFFREY (Donald), 6579.
MAC CALMAN (Iain), 1253.
MAC CANN (Andrew), 6340.
MAC CARTHY (Jin), 6580.
MAC CARTNEY (Donal), 5743.
Mac Cartney (George), 8215.
MAC CLENNEN (C. E.), 1484.
MAC CLURE (L.), 2109.
MAC COOG (Thomas), 5431.
MAC CORMICK EDWARDS (Lee), 6470.
MAC CRAY (W. Patrick), 6706.
MAC CULLOUGH (Edward E.), 7594.
MAC CULLOUGH (Kate), 6341.
MAC CULLOUGH (William H.), 8275.
MAC CUTCHEON (Russell T.), 1313.
MAC DERMOT (B. C.), 1801.
MAC DERMOTT (Joseph P.), 8203.
MAC DERMOTT (Kevin), 5019.
MAC DONOUGH (Christopher James), 3710.
MAC DONOUGH (Frank), 4454.

MAC ELLIGOTT (Anthony), 3987.
MAC EVOY (Carmen), 4920.
MAC FARLAND (E. W.), 4564.
MAC FARLANE (John), 7273.
MAC GARRY (Fearghal), 7656.
MAC GEE DEUTSCH (Sandra), 4055.
MAC GILLIVRAY (J. A.), 1844.
MAC GINN (Thomas A. J.), 2505.
MAC GINNIS (J.), 1569.
MAC GLADE (J.), 1465.
MAC GLEW (J. F.), 1994.
MAC GOWEN (Randall), 7170.
MAC GRATH (Michael), 5800.
MAC GURK (John), 4554.
MAC HARDY (Karin J.), 6952.
MAC HUGH (John), 4665.
MAC INTYRE (W. David), 7318.
MAC IVER (Tom), 1195.
MAC KAY (Barry), 111.
MAC KECHNIE (Paul), 2347.
MAC KEE (Elsie Anne), 5498.
MAC KEE (Sally), 3446.
MAC KENDRICK (S.), 81.
MAC KENNA (Antony), 5522.
MAC KENZIE (Donald Francis), 120.
MAC KENZIE (Steven L.), 523.
MAC KERCHER (Brian J. C.), 3975, 7659.
MAC KIM (Donald K.), 1355.
MAC KIVIGAN (John), 5261.
MAC LAREN (Angus), 6953.
MAC LAREN (Anne N.), 5664.
MAC LEAN (David), 5801.
MAC LEOD (Bruce), 6199.
MAC LEOD (Frederick G.), 2917.
MAC LEOD (Jacqueline), 3942.
MAC MAHON (Robert J.), 7934.
MAC MANNERS (John), 5331.
MAC PHAIL (Eric), 849.
MAC PHAIL (Helen), 4358.
MAC PHAIL (R.), 1486.
Macaulay (Thomas Babington), 6353.
MACCHIARELLI (R.), 1526.
MACDONALD (Aileen Ann), 3510.
MACDONALD (Bradley J.), 5982.
MACDONALD (Catriona M. M.), 4564.
MACEK (Pavel), 7129.
Maček (Vladko), 4204.
MACFIE (A. L.), 7595.
Mach (Ernst), 5967.
MACHAČOVÁ (Jana), 3980, 6954.
Machiavelli (Niccolò), 749, 1064, 1082, 1124, 1134, 5601, 5619, 5626, 5665, 5676, 5677.
MACÍAS GONZÁLEZ (Víctor), 4835.
MACIAS RICHAR (Carlos), 4836.
MACIEL (David R.), 6585.

MACINTYRE (Stuart), 4071.
MACKAY (Ch. S.), 2811.
MACKAY (E. A.), 2133.
MACKAY (Ruth), 5098.
MACKENZIE (Hector), 7935.
MACKIE (C. J.), 1921.
MACKLIN (M. G.), 1494.
MACLEAN (I.), 7171.
MACLEAN (Iain S.), 4132.
Macmillan (Harold), 7842, 7946, 7983.
MACMILLAN (Hugh), 8350.
MACRAKIS (Kristie), 6153.
Macrobius (Ambrosius Aurelius Theodosius), 2924, 3573.
MADDEN (Thomas F.), 3471.
MADERO (Marta), 1216, 3341.
MADIÉGA (Yénouyaga Georges), 4156.
Madison (James), 5208.
MAEDA (Hirotake), 8060.
MAEHLE (Andreas-Holger), 6111.
MAELSTAF (Geneviève), 7936.
MAESSCHALCK (Marc), 4595.
Maffei (Scipione), 649.
MAGAGNOLI (Ralf), 7937.
MAGDELAINE (Michelle), 5499.
MAGEE (P.), 1554.
MAGGI (S.), 2194.
MAGIN (Christine), 3283.
MAGIONCALDA (A.), 2562.
MAGISTRALE (Francesco), 3145.
Magliabechi (Antonio), 5978.
MAGNALDI (I.), 1902.
Magnan (Pierre), 6370.
MAGNANI (Giovanni), 1314.
MAGNANI SOARES-CHRISTEN (Eliana), 3811.
MAGNELLI (E.), 1880.
MAGNESS (J.), 1754.
MAGNIEN (Catherine), 5666.
MAGNIEN (Michel), 5260.
MAGNUSSON (Lars), 6681.
Magovac (Božidar), 4204.
MAGUIRE (Henry), 3049.
MAHAJAN (Sucheta), 4633.
MAHÉ (J.-P.), 1896.
MAHÉ (M.), 2195.
Mahler (Gustav), 6581.
MAI (Gunther), 4480.
MAIER (Barbara), 3235.
MAIER (Lothar), 4975.
MAILLARD (Alain), 4359.
MAILLARD (Jean-François), 5666.
MAILLEFER (Jean-Marie), 3240.
Maimonides (Moses), 3269.
Mainardi (Giovanni), 6125.
MAIOCCHI (Roberto), 6112.
MAIOLO (Joseph A.), 7725.
MAISELS (C. K.), 1570.
MAISSEN (Thomas), 6674, 7726.

MAITRE (Claire), 3684.
MAITRE (Myriam), 6260.
MAIULLARI (F.), 2110.
MAKHROV (Kirill D.), 6396.
MÄKI-PETÄYS (Mari), 278.
MAKOUTA-MBOUKOU (Jean Pierre), 4192.
MALAISE (M.), 1635.
MALASPINA (Saba), 3174.
MALATESTA (Maria), 6956.
MALATO (Enrico), 1413, 3583.
MALCHOW (Birgit), 7930.
MALCOLM (Alistair), 5099.
MALCOLM (Joyce Lee), 4525.
Maldonado de Silva (Francisco), 5316.
Mâle (Emile), 752.
Malebranche (Nicolas), 1397, 5900, 5934.
MALERBA (Jurandir), 4133, 4961.
MALETTKE (Klaus), 7407, 7442.
MALEUVRE (Didier), 468.
MALI (Joseph), 850.
MALINEN (Ismo), 6707.
MALKIN (I.), 1845.
Mallarmé (Stéphane), 6339, 6364.
MALLES (Hans-Jürgen), 1417.
MALLMANN (Klaus-Michael), 4456.
MALLON (Florencia E.), 5671.
MALONI (Ruby), 4642.
MALOSSE (Pierre-Louis), 2430.
Malraux (A.), 1439.
MALTBY (Richard), 6547.
MALTESE (E.-V.), 3050.
MALUQUER DE MOTES (Jordi), 5100.
MALÝ (Karel), 4239.
MALYSHEVA (Svetlana Ju.), 5013.
MAMAEVA (Natl'ja L.), 7596.
MAMINO (Sergio), 4767.
MAMONE CAPRIA (Marco), 1212.
MAN (John), 3201.
MAN CHAN (Joseph), 5869.
MAŇÁK (Jiří), 4240.
MANANCHIKOVA (Nelli P.), 3393.
Manasse Tjiseta, Chief of Omaruru, 8342.
MANCA (Sergio), 758.
MANCINI (Mario), 3606.
MANCINI (S.), 1943.
MANCINI (Silvia), 1362.
MANCUSO (Barbara), 398.
MANCUSO (Francesco), 7096.
MANCUSO (Fulvio), 3342.
MANCUSO (M. A.), 2563.
MANDER (Jenny), 6261.
Mandeville (Bernard), 5919.
MANENT (Albert), 5101.
MANFREDI (Angelo), 5415.
MANGAN (J. A.), 5697.

MANGANELLI (Giorgio), 4758.
MANGANI (E.), 1846.
MANGO (Andrew), 5170.
MANGONI (Luisa), 121.
MANIATIS (George C.), 3051.
MANIGAND (Anne), 4360.
MANIGAND-CHAPLAIN (Catherine), 421.
MANIN (Vitalij S.), 6397.
MANLOVE (Colin), 6200.
Mann (Thomas), 753, 6315, 6381.
Manna (Paolo), 5447.
MANNARINO (Lia), 728.
MANNE (Robert), 4068.
MANNING (J. G.), 1636.
MANNING (John), 210, 223.
MANNONI (Stefano), 7194.
MANNORI (Luca), 1093, 7130.
MANNOVÁ (Elena), 3941.
MANNS (Patricio), 4175.
MANOKOU (Lucien), 7938.
MANSEL (K.), 1765.
MANSELL (Philip), 4332.
MANSERGH (Diana), 7321.
Mansergh (Nicholas), 7321.
MANSUR BARATA (Alexandre), 4134.
MANTOVANI (Dario), 2413.
MANTOVANI (Mauro), 7939.
Manuel I Comnenus, Byzantine emperor, 3075, 3085.
MANUWALD (B.), 1949.
MANUWALD (Gesine), 2385.
Manzalaoui (Mahmoud), 3524.
MAO (Zedong), 1049, 8100.
MA'OZ (Moshe), 5152.
MARANI (Pietro), 6471.
MARASINOVA (Elena N.), 5014.
MARAVAL (Pierre), 3052.
MARBACK (R.), 2160.
MARCACCINI (C.), 2018.
Marceau (Marcel), 6571.
MARCEL (Isaline), 7913.
Marcellus (M. Claudius), 2771.
MARCENARO (M.), 3678.
March (Ausiàs), 3104, 3526.
MARCHAK (M. Patricia), 4056.
MARCHAK (William), 4056.
MARCHESI (G.), 1694.
MARCHESINI (Simona), 2296.
MARCHETTI (P.), 1870.
MARCHETTI (Valerio), 5500.
MARCHIS (Riccardo), 5271.
MARCOCCHI (Massimo), 5401.
MARCONE (Arnaldo), 735, 778.
MARCONI (Diego), 5983.
MARCO-SIMÓN (F.), 2759.
Marcotte (Charles), 6443.
Marcu (Alexandru), 5706.
MARCUS (Sharon), 6342.
Marcus Vinicius, 2387.

MAREK (Doris), 1411.
MAREK (Heidi), 6226.
MAREK (Jaroslav), 607.
MAREK (Pavel), 4236.
MARGADANT (Jo Burr), 4361.
MARGAIRAZ (Michel), 4384.
Margaret of Scotland (consort of Louis XI, King of France), 3189.
MARGETIĆ (Lujo), 3343.
Margherita di Cortona (Sancta), 3836.
MARGRIET, princess of the Netherlands, 7122.
Marguerite d'Oingt, 3589.
MARI (M.), 2019.
Maria (mather of Iesus), 2919.
MARIANO (Marco), 781.
Mariátegui (José Carlos), 4917.
MARICHAL (Carlos), 6807.
MARIN (Brigitte), 6113.
MARIN (Elisabeta), 6832.
MARINCOLA (J.), 556, 2379.
MARINESCU-NICOLAJSEN (Liliana), 2760.
MARINI (A.), 3790.
MARINI CLARELLI (M. V.), 3053.
MARINKOVIC (Miriana), 7517.
MARION (Michel), 443.
MARITAIN (JACQUES), 5379.
MARIUS (R.), 5501.
Marius Maximus, 2397.
Marivaux (Pierre-Carlet de Chamblain de), 6278.
MARK (James A.), 4610.
MARKALE (Jean), 1363.
MARKER (Jamsheed), 7803.
MARKOV (Georgi), 4141, 4150.
MARKOVIĆ (V.), 1213.
MARKUSSE (Jan), 354.
MARLER (J. C.), 3773.
Marlowe (Christopher), 6556.
MARNEF (Guido), 5777.
MAROLT (Janez), 1000.
MAROTTA (Valerio), 2431.
MARQUARDT (Bernd), 1130.
MARQUIS (Bettina), 998.
MARRAPODI (Michele), 6222.
MARRI (Fabio), 5568, 5631.
MARROQUIN (Carlos), 1345.
Marrou (Henri Irénée), 643, 750.
Marseus van Schrieck (Otto), 6483.
MARSH (Jan), 6472.
MARSH (Peter T.), 6747.
MARSHALL (A. M.), 2432.
MARSHALL (Alan), 4555.
MARSHALL (P. J.), 7318, 7337.
MARSHALL (Richard K.), 3394.
MARSINA (Richard), 3097.
MARTEL (Jacinthe), 6286.
MARTELLI (Mario), 1083.
MARTEN-FINNIS (Susanne), 5861.

MARTENS (Stefan), 4446.
MARTÍ GILABERT (Francisco), 5102.
Martialis (M. Valerius), 2546, 2624, 2673.
Martianus Capella, 2623.
MARTIN (Benjamin F.), 4362.
MARTIN (Ch.), 3054.
MARTÍN (Francisco Marcos), 3521.
MARTIN (Henri-Jean), 122.
MARTIN (Ian), 4596.
MARTIN (Jane), 5802.
MARTIN (Jean-Clément), 4363.
MARTIN (L.), 5862.
MARTIN (Xavier), 399.
MARTÍN DE SANTA OLALLA (Aurora), 3521.
MARTIN LE FRANC, 3705.
MARTINA (Giacomo), 5288.
MARTINAT (Monica), 6808.
MARTINELLI (Alberto), 1084.
MARTINELLI (M. C.), 2107.
MARTINELLI TEMPESTA (S.), 1954.
MARTINEZ (Gilles), 4364.
MARTINEZ CARRENO (Aída), 4188.
MARTÍNEZ LAHIDALGA (Adela), 3115.
MARTÍNEZ RIAZA (Ascensión), 4921.
MARTINEZ-PINNA (Jorge), 2269.
MARTINI (Johannes), 3692.
MARTINI (Manuela), 6957.
MARTINICH (Aloysius P.), 5984.
MARTINIÈRE (Guy), 6853.
MARTIN-JACQUEMIER (Myriam), 6227.
MARTIN-KILCHER (S.), 1765.
MARTINUS POLONUS, 3175.
MARTON SZILAGYI (Elizabetha), 2567.
MARTUCCI (Roberto), 4759.
MARWINSKI (Konrad), 438.
MARX (C. William), 3570.
Marx (Karl), 733, 1084, 5910, 6001, 6023, 6666.
MARX-SCOURAS (Danielle), 4027.
MÄRZ (Christoph), 3693.
MARZAGALLI (Silvia), 6708.
MARZATICO (F.), 2297.
MARZOLFF (P.), 2242.
MARZULLO (B.), 1917.
MAS CORNELLÁ (M.), 1504.
MASCH (L.), 1581.
MASCIARI (Francesco), 7172.
MAŠEK (Petr), 171.
MASHKOUR (M.), 1520.
MASI DORIA (C.), 2506.
MASIH (Joseph R.), 4067.
MASO (STEFANO), 2639.
MASOERO (Mariarosa), 4767.
MASON (H. J.), 2640.

MASON (Jeffrey D.), 6595.
MASS (Jeffrey P.), 4799.
MASSABÒ RICCI (Isabella), 4697.
MASSAIA (Alberto Stefano), 6848.
MASSA-PAIRAULT (F.-H.), 2198, 2298.
MASSART (Alexis), 4365.
MASSELLI (G. M.), 2433.
Massenet (Jules), 6525.
MASSENZIO (Marcello), 1315.
MASSON (Marilyn A.), 8367.
MASSON (V. M.), 8055.
MASTELLONE (Salvo), 1085.
MASTERSON (Josephine), 169.
MASTINO (Attilio), 2916, 2932.
MASTNY (Vojtech), 7940.
MASTORÍDIS (Klímis), 5863.
MASTROCINQUE (A.), 1995.
MASTROGREGORI (Massimo), *VIII*, 483, 608.
MASTRUZZO (Antonino), 765.
MASULLO (Aldo), 3328.
MASULLO (Paolo Augusto), 5985.
MATE (Mavis E.), 3396.
MATĚJČEK (Jiří), 3980, 5667, 6954.
MATELSKI (Dariusz), 7275.
MATESANZ (José Antonio), 7657.
MATHEW (Kuzhippalli Skaria), 7255.
MATHIESEN (Thomas J.), 3694.
MATHIESON (I.), 1637.
MATHIEU (Jon), 6849.
MATHIEU (Nicolas), 279.
MATHON (G.), 1338.
MATINUDDIN (Kamal), 4015.
Matisse (Henri), 6474.
MATKOVIĆ (Hrvoje), 610, 4202.
MAŤOVČÍK (Augustín), 5055.
MATSUI (Toru), 6682.
MATSUO (Yuriko), 8061.
MATSUSHITA (Hiroshi), 4062.
Matta-Clark (Gordon), 6424.
MATTER (Michel), 2481.
MATTERN (Susan P.), 2434.
MATTHEE (Rudolph P.), 6748.
MATTILA (Markku), 6114.
MATTIOLI (Aram), 702, 5142.
Mattioli (Raffaele), 5618.
MATTISON (James A.), 8388.
Mattsson (Greger), 3357.
MATURI (Sebastiano), 5924.
MATUŠÍKOVÁ (Lenka), 4213.
MATZERATH (Josef), 6958.
MAUCEC (Marjan), 5059.
MAUGER (Gérard), 5668.
MAUGER-PLICHON (B.), 2641.
MAUME (Patrick), 4675.
MAURER (Armand A.), 3740.
MAURER (Michael), 4458.
MAURICE-CHABARD (Brigitte), 3675.

MAURO (Frédéric), 7552.
MAURO (Marina), 3178.
MAURRAS (CHARLES), 5379.
MAUSE (M.), 2435.
Mauss (Marcel), 889, 1334, 5705.
MAWBY (Spencer), 7941.
MAXIM (Mihai), 7393.
Maximianus (M. Aurelius Valerius), 2641.
Maximilian I von Habsurg, röm.-deutscher Kaiser, 4088.
Maximilian I, elector of Bavaria, 7411.
MAXWELL (Anne), 914.
MAXWELL STUART (P. G.), 5299.
MAYAUD (Jean-Luc), 4292.
MAYER (C.), 1333.
MAYER (Hans), 6343.
MAYER (Johannes G.), 3888.
MAYER (Karl J.), 7727.
MAYER (M.), 2709.
MAYER (R. G.), 2590.
MAYER (W. R.), 1695, 1756.
MAYRHOFER (Fritz), 6842.
MAZAL (Otto), 68.
MAZEK (Dorota), 4944.
MAZENOT (Georges), 7314.
MAZOWER (Mark), 3976.
MAZRUI (Ali A.), 8333.
MAZUR (Eric Michael), 5296.
MAZZA (Mario), 611, 2826.
MAZZANTI (Giuseppe), 3330.
MAZZARA (G.), 2111.
Mazzarino (Giulio Raimondo), 449, 470, 7397, 7404.
MAZZEI (M.), 2255, 2270.
MAZZINI (Innocenzo), 2341.
MAZZOLI (Giancarlo), 2642, 2816.
MAZZOLINI (Renato), 469.
MAZZONI (Vieri), 3261.
MAZZONIS (Filippo), 753.
MAZZOTTA (Giuseppe), 5986.
MÉADEL (Cécile), 4033.
MĚCHÝŘ (Jan), 4241.
MECKELBORG (Christina), 3597.
MEDEIROS (Eduardo), 8343.
MEDEROS MARTÍN (A.), 1536.
MEDICA (Massimo), 3384.
MEDICK (Hans), 7034.
Medina Angarita (Isaías), 5230.
MEDING (Holger M.), 422, 4057.
MEDVEDEV (Aleksandr P.), 1555.
MEDVEDEV (I. P.), 2988, 3055.
MEDVEDSKAYA (I. N.), 1802.
MEE (John), 1253.
MEEL (Peter), 7375.
MEES (Ludger), 5114.
MÉGIER (Elisabeth), 762.
MEHLHAUSEN (Joachim), 2918.
MEHRING (Reinhard), 5951.
MEHRINGER (Hartmut), 7880.

MEIER (Albert), 6258.
MEIER (Christel), 3829.
MEIER (M.), 2020.
MEIER (Martin Gernot), 5502.
MEIER (Thomas), 998.
MEIER (Viktor), 5253.
MEIFFRET (Laurence), 400.
MEIKLE (Maureen M.), 3398.
Meinecke (Friedrich), 1096.
MEIRO (Gerardo), 3521.
MEISSNER (Boris), 7826.
Meissonier (Ernest), 6448.
Meissonnier (Juste-Aurèle), 6496.
MEISTAD (Tore), 5503.
MEISTERSHEM (Anne), 982.
MEJÍA PAVONY (Germán Rodrigo), 6850.
MEJTARCHIJAN (Margarita B.), 1364.
Mel'nikov (Kostantin S.), 6422.
MEL'NIKOVA (Alla S.), 1039.
MEL'NIKOVA (Elena S.), 1043, 3140.
MELAMMED LEVINE (Renée), 3284.
MELANCON (Glenn), 7518.
MELANDER (Veronica), 4589.
MELASUO (Tuomo), 4031.
MELBU (Kari), 1197.
MELCHIORI (Giorgio), 6222.
MELCIC (Dunja), 989.
MELIK (Vasilij), 689.
MELIKAN (R. A.), 7173.
MELIS (Guido), 7111, 7121, 7131.
MELLARS (Paul), 1483.
MELLEY (Timothy), 5669.
MELLIER (Denis), 6202.
MELLINGHOFF-BOURGERIE (Viviane), 5416.
MELLINKOFF (Ruth), 3285.
MELLOR (R.), 2436, 2992.
MELMOUX-MONTAUBIN (Marie-Françoise), 6344.
MELNICK (Jeffrey), 6582.
MELNICK (R. Shep), 5222.
MELVILLE (Gert), 3818.
MELVILLE (Sarah C.), 1696.
MELVILLE-JONES (John R.), 3176.
MELZER (Ralf), 4459.
Memling (Hans), 3677.
Memmius, 2515.
MEN'SHIKOV (Vladimir B.), 8172.
Menander, 1897, 1929.
MENANT (François), 176.
MÉNARD (Philippe), 3585.
MENARINI (Roy), 6583.
MENCACCI (F.), 2564.
MENCHELLI (Simonetta), 2301.
MENCHERINI (Robert), 7794.
Mendana de Neira (Alvaro de), 8390.

MENDE (U.), 444.
MENDEL (Maurice), 805.
MENDIBLE ZURITA (Alejandro), 7276.
MENDUS (Susan), 5306.
MENEGUS BORNEMANN (Margarita), 6639.
Menem (Carlos Saúl), 4048, 4062.
MENICHETTI (M.), 2271.
MENIRAV (J.), 1771.
MENJOT (Denis), 3378.
MENKE (K.-H.), 2919.
MENNITI IPPOLITO (Antonio), 5348.
MENOZZI (Daniele), 5349.
MENUGE (Noël James), 3472.
MENZEL (Josef Joachim), 4425.
MENZER (M. J.), 280.
MERBACK (Mitchell B.), 3664.
MERCADER (Antonio), 7658.
MERCERON (Jacques), 3586.
MERCKX (Kris), 4094.
MERIGGI (Maurizio), 6422.
Mérimée (Prosper), 6352.
MERKL (Peter H.), 4420.
MERKL (Ulrich), 123.
MERKLEY (Paul), 6584.
Merle (Eugène), 5862.
MERLO (Grado Giovanni), 1380, 3794, 3890.
Méroux de Valois (Alfred-Louis), 7514.
MERRIMAN (Nick), 467.
MERT (H.), 2222.
MERTENS (Dieter), 6228.
MERVAUD (Michel), 800.
MESKELL (L.), 1638.
MESSENGER (Ann), 6262.
METHA (Uday Singh), 5670.
METHY (Nicole), 2710.
METZGER (Chantal), 7597.
METZGER (Jan), 1086.
METZLER (Friederich von), 6841.
MEULENGRACHT SØRENSEN (Preben), 1376.
MEUNIER (Jacob), 7959.
MEURANT (A.), 2299.
MEYER (Beate), 4460.
MEYER (Horst), 86.
MEYER (Katharina Eleonore), 2761.
MEYER (Stephan), 7444.
MEYER (W.), 1731.
Meyer-Amden (Otto), 5407.
MEYERSON (Mark D.), 3443.
MEYRAN (Régis), 614.
MEYZIE (Vincent), 353.
MEZEI (Elemer), 6991.
MGOI (Shakro Kh.), 8059.
MI (Qingyu), 8169.
MI (Rucheng), 8170.

MIARD-DELACROIX (Hélène), 7942.
MICCOLI (Giovanni), 5332.
MICHAEL (Jones), 3206.
Michael III, Byzantine emperor, 3058, 3080.
MICHAELSEN (Per), 4263.
MICHÁLEK (Slavomír), 5048.
MICHAUD (Jean), 3117.
MICHEL (Patrick), 470.
MICHEL (Sonya), 6959.
MICHELET (Jules), 754.
MICHELI (G.), 4752.
MICHELI (Sergio), 6586.
MICHELINI (Luca), 6679.
MICHELL (George), 6428.
Michelozzo di Bartolomeo, 3655.
MICHELS (Georg Bernhard), 5459.
MICHELS (Karen), 6398.
MICHELUCCI (Maurizio), 3056.
MICHIE (Allen), 6263.
MICHOWICZ (Waldemar), 7713.
MICKEL (Lesley), 6587.
MICÓ (R.), 1528.
MIDDELL (Matthias), 580.
MIDELFORT (H. C. Eric), 6115.
MIDORI (Kawashima), 7667.
MIERNIK (Grzegorz), 4945.
MIERS (Suzanne), 8356.
MIERSE (W. E.), 2762.
MIERZEJEWSKI (Alfred C.), 6709.
MIETKE (G.), 1596.
MIGDEN SOCOLOW (Susan), 5671.
MIGHALL (Robert), 6345.
MIGLIO (Massimo), 804.
MIHALJCIC (Rade), 3544.
MIHELAČ (Jaro), 1000.
MIHELIČ (Breda), 6429.
MIHELIČ (Darja), 1000.
MIHNEVA (R.), 7394.
MIKA (Sándor), 3241.
MIKHAJLOVA (Tat'jana A.), 3475.
MIKOCKI (Tomasz), 2738.
MIKOLA (Milko), 5062.
MIKULEC (Jiří), 578.
Milani (Lorenzo), 5356.
MILAZZO (Francesco), 2510.
MILES (Andrew), 6960.
MILES (Richard), 2794, 2798.
MILES FOLEY (J.), 2112.
MILHOU (Alain), 5103.
Milíc z Kromeríze (Jan), 3733, 3892.
MILICH (Klaus J.), 5672.
Milieu (Christoph), 755.
MILIN (Gaeël), 1225.
MILISAUSKAS (S.), 1447.
MILITANTE (Pacifico V.), 4927.
Mill (James), 1107.
MILLAR (Fergus), 2507.
Millar (John), 1107.

MILLARES (Carlo Agustín), 51.
MILLER (Daniel E.), 4242.
MILLER (James E.), 7817.
MILLER (Joseph C.), 8351.
MILLER (Judith A.), 6750.
MILLER (Karen A.), 7598.
MILLER (Louis), 851.
MILLER (M. C.), 2243.
MILLER (Nicola), 3979.
MILLER (Randall M.), 5308.
MILLER (Rory), 6733.
MILNE (Malcolm), 7354.
MILNES (Tim), 6346.
Milošević (Slobodan), 5254.
MILSTEIN (Rachel), 3314.
Miltiades, 1871, 1980.
Milton (John), 103, 5307, 5931, 6353.
MILWARD (Alan S.), 4006.
MILZA (Pierre), 4298, 4304, 4760.
MINAMI (Kazuo), 8292.
Minamoto (Yoritomo), 8319.
MINAULT-GOUT (A.), 1632.
MINELLI (Fausto), 711.
MINNA STERN (Alexandra), 4837.
MINNITT (S. C.), 1529.
MINTS (Svetlana S.), 615.
MINTZ (Max M.), 5210.
Minucius Felix (M.), 2855.
MINUTOLO (Ceccarella), 6211.
MIRABILE (Francesco), 7790.
MIRANDA (E.), 1767.
MIRANDA (Maria Adelaide), 60.
MIRANDA GARCÍA (Fermin), 3098.
MIRCEVA (Kh.), 7943.
MIROIR (André), 4099.
MIROLLO (James V.), 5715.
MIRONES LOZANO (Eunate), 3286.
MIRONOV (Boris N.), 6961.
MIROVITSKAJA (Raisa A.), 7660, 7728.
MISCHEVCA (Vladimir), 7465.
MISE (Kazuo), 8293.
MISRA (Maria), 8089.
MISSALLA (Heinrich), 5333.
MITCHELL (Donald), 6581.
MITCHELL (Elizabeth), 4681.
MITCHELL (Linda Elizabeth), 3476.
MITCHELL (Nancy), 7520.
MITCHELL (St.), 2437, 2813.
MITHEN (S.), 1519.
Mithradates VI, king of Pontus, 1995.
MITROKHIN (Vasili), 7834.
Mitterrand (François), 4335, 7363, 7942.
MITZMAN (Arthur), 754.
MIX (York-Gothar), 5831.
MLEZIVA (Štěpán), 281.
MOA (Pío), 5104.

MOAČANIN (Nenad), 4203.
MÓCSY (András), 2438, 2567.
MOCZULSKA (Krystyna), 2738.
MODESTIN (Georg), 3891.
MODICA (Marilena), 5297.
MODZELEWSKI (Karol), 3344.
MOEGLIN (Jean-Marie), 1001, 3222.
MOFFA (Claudio), 5449.
MOFFITT (John F.), 401.
MÖHLE (Heiko), 7345.
MOHNHAUPT (Heinz), 7073, 7079.
MOHR (Antje), 7944.
MOHUN (Arwen P.), 6710.
MOINE (Philippe), 738.
MOÏSE (Claude), 4597.
MOISL (Hermann), 3477.
MOJARES (Resil B.), 4928.
MOKADDEM (Yamina), 4024.
MOKHNACHEVA (Marina P.), 616.
MOKYR (Joel), 3953.
MOLA (Aldo A.), 4773.
Molan (Gerard Wolter), 5311.
MOLAS RIBALTA (Pere), XV.
MOLDOVAN (Ioan), 4974.
MOLENDA (Jan), 4946.
MOLENDIJK (Arie L.), 1317, 1368.
MOLINA (Iván), 4197.
MOLINA VIDAL (J.), 2439.
MÖLK (Ulrich), 5613.
MÖLLENDORFF (Peter von), 803.
MØLLER (Aqigssiaq), 991.
MÖLLER (Hans G.), 617.
MÖLLER (Horst), 486, 3922.
MOLLIER (Jean-Yves), 124.
Molnár (Miklós), 5701.
MOLOD'JAKOV (Valerij E.), 4800.
Moltke (Helmuth James, Graf von), 7798.
MOMIGLIANO (Arnaldo), 756.
MOMIGLIANO LEVI (Paolo), 747.
MOMMSEN (Hans), 4461.
Mommsen (Theodor), 733, 757, 2860.
MOMMSEN (Wolfgang J.), 618.
MOMOH (Abubakar), 4883.
MONASTYREV (N. I.), 8099.
MONCHAMBERT (J.-Y.), 1697.
MONDA (Salvatore), 2643.
MONDOT (Jean), 5755.
Mondrian (Piet), 6497.
MONFASANI (John), 6125.
MONINA (Giancarlo), 7105.
MONMONIER (Mark), 6117.
MONNAIS-ROUSSELOT (Laurence), 6118.
Monnet (Jean), 7907, 8017.
MONNIER (Cordélia), 7882.
MONNIER (Gérard), 6430.
MÖNNINGER (Michael), 1187.

MONOD (Paul K.), 5298.
MONSAGRATI (Giuseppe), 5350.
MONTADON (Alain), 6264.
Montaigne (Michel Eyquem de), 5636, 5715.
Montale (Eugenio), 6302.
MONTANARI (M.), 725.
MONTANARI (Mario), 4761.
MONTANARI (O.), 2113.
MONTANI (Pietro), 6204.
MONTANO DURÁN (Ana María), 4108.
MONTAVONT (Anne), 5987.
MONTEATH (P.), 4462.
Montefeltro (Duchi di Urbino), 3177.
MONTELLA (Luigi), 6203.
MONTENEGRO (Angelo), 6119.
MONTER (William), 5504.
MONTERO (I.), 1471.
MONTERO (Manuel), 971.
MONTERO (S.), 3023.
MONTERO RUIZ (I.), 1521.
MONTES CALA (J. G.), 2199.
MONTESANO (Marina), 3816.
MONTESQUIEU (Charles de Secondat), 805, 1075, 5914.
Montessori (Maria), 5762, 5819.
Monteverdi (Claudio), 6568.
MONTOBBIO (Manuel), 4281.
MONTOYA MARTÍNEZ (Jesús), 3605.
MONZALI (Luciano), 7521.
MONZINI (Paola), 6963.
MOOHAN (Elaine), 3692.
MOOIJ-VALK (S.), 2114.
MOON (David), 1178.
MOON (Paul), 5254.
MOONEY (Catherine M.), 3841.
MOORE (R. I.), 3934.
MOORE WHITING (Steven), 6589.
MOORMAN (E. M.), 2248.
MOORS (Hans), 6909.
MOORTON (R. F.), 2744.
MORA (Bernadette), 3117.
MORA (Clelia), 636, 1755.
MORA (F.), 1825.
MORA (Fabio), 160.
MORA (G.), 248.
MORABITO (Marcel), 4385.
MORABITO (Raffaele), 6211.
MORACCINI (M.), 5356.
MORAGLIO (Massimo), 6711.
MORALEDA (A.), 1488.
MORALES (Humberto), 4825.
MORALES BENÍTEZ (Otto), 4186.
MORALES GORLERI (Claudio), 4176.
MORALES PEREZ (Salvador E.), 7945.
MORAND (Isabelle), 2764.

MORANDI BONACOSSI (D.), 1698.
MORANT (M.-J.), 1865, 2196.
Morante (Elsa), 6294.
MORAVEC (Jan), 4255.
MORDAUNT CROOK (Joseph), 6431.
MORE (Ellen S.), 6964.
MOREAU (A.), 2197.
MOREAU (Denis), 5934.
MOREAU (J.), 1944.
MOREAU (Pierre-François), 6015.
MORÉE (Peter C. A.), 3892.
MOREH (Shmuel), 3298.
MORELLI (M.), 1251.
MORELLO (Giovanni), 3852.
MORENO (Diego), 785.
MORENO (Paolo), 3172.
MORENO FONSERET (Roque), 5088.
MORENZONI (Franco), 3712.
MORETTI (Mauro), 684.
MOREY (James H), 3774.
MORGAN (David), 1295.
MORGAN (Hiram), 4680.
MORGAN (K.), 4290.
MORGAN (Kenneth O.), 7318.
MORGAN (Philip), 684, 6654.
MORGENBROD (Birgitt), 802.
MORGENROTH (U.), 1556.
Morghen (Raffaello), 756.
MORI (Kenzo), 6918.
MORICEAU (Jean-Marc), 6771.
MORIMOTO (Yoshiki), 3399.
MORINEAU (Michel), 6749, 6751.
MORINI (C.), 161.
MORISON (John), 5019.
MORITSCH (Andreas), 1014.
MORITZ (Marina), 6323.
MORLEY (Neville), 852.
MOROSINI (Andrea), 3176.
MOROVICS (Miroslav Tibor), 5054.
MORRIS (Benny), 7278.
MORRIS (Bridget), 3845.
MORRIS (D. S.), 7578.
MORRIS (John Francis), 8290.
MORRIS (Stephen D.), 4838.
Morris (William), 5982.
MORRISON (J. V.), 2115.
Mortati (Costantino), 7072.
MORTELETTE (Yann), 6289.
MORTIER (Roland), 1403.
MORWOOD (M. J.), 1500.
Mosca (Gaetano), 7096.
MOSCA (Joao), 4860.
MOSCATI (Massimo), 6526.
MOSCHOVITIS (Christos J. P.), 6120.
MOSCIATTI (Alessandra), 3763.
MOSCROP (John James), 619.
MOSELEY (Merritt), 6299.
MOSELEY (Ray), 4762.

Moser (Friedrich Karl), 7428.
MOSER (John E.), 7279.
MOSIG-WALBURG (Karin), 2440.
MOSJAKOV (Dmitrij V.), 4159.
MOSS (Christopher Frederick), 3663.
MOSSÉ (C.), 1996.
MOSSE (Werner), 5553.
MOST (G. W.), 2116.
MOSTEIRO LOUZAO (Manuel), 3588.
MOSTERT (Marco), 3434, 3481.
MOSTYN (Trevor), 5547.
MOTE (F. W.), 8171.
MOTOE (Terami-Wada), 7667.
MOTT (Richard), 305.
MOTTA (Giuseppe), 3823.
MOTTE (A.), 1381.
MOUHTADI (Najib), 4855.
MOULIAN (Luis), 4177.
MOULINET (Daniel), 752.
MOULINIER (Pierre), 5674.
MOURAVIEV (S. N.), 2161.
MOUREAU (François), 5865.
Mouriki (Doula), 3663.
MOURITSEN (Henrik), 2441.
MOUROU (Max-Williams), 7355.
MOUSAVY (A.), 1803.
Mousnier (Roland), 758.
MOUSSON-LESTANG (Jean-Pierre), 7729.
MOUTON (Marie-Renée), 7599.
MOWBRAY (Donald), 3363.
MOWL (Timothy), 6432.
MOYA PONS (Frank), 4274.
Mozart (Wolfgang Amadeus), 6616.
MOZETIČ (Iztok), 5059.
MOZZONI (Loretta), 6408.
MROZEWICZ (L.), 2565.
MSELLATI (Henri), 4032.
MUCCCIOLO (John), 6239.
MUCCILLO (M.), 5978.
MUELLER (H. F.), 1997.
MUGNAI CARRARA (Daniela), 6125.
MÜHLSTEDT (Corinna), 2920.
MUKHERJEE (Aditya), 4625.
MUKHERJEE (Mridula), 4625.
MUKHERJEE (Sujit), 1436.
MULCHAHEY (Marian Michèle), 3817.
Mulder (Gerrit Jan), 4875.
MULDOON (James), 1002.
MULFORD (Carla), 1418.
MÜLLER (A. E.), 3057.
MÜLLER (Alfred Lorenz), 4463.
MÜLLER (Bertrand), 698, 724.
MÜLLER (C. W.), 1916.
MÜLLER (Catherine M.), 3589.
MÜLLER (Denis), 5505.

MÜLLER (Frank Lorenz), 7522.
MÜLLER (G.), 1383.
MÜLLER (Inez), 4392.
MÜLLER (Jan-Dirk), 3587.
MÜLLER (Klaus-Jürgen), 7301.
MÜLLER (Martin M.), 6809.
MÜLLER (Rolf-Dieter), 4512.
MÜLLER (U.), 1597.
MÜLLER (Werner), 4480.
MÜLLER-KESSLER (Chr.), 1699.
MÜLLER-LUCKNER (Elisabeth), 1040, 1169, 1762, 2428.
MULLETT (Michael A.), 5334.
MULTAMÄKI (Kustaa), 6683.
MULUZI (Bakili), 4820.
MULVANEY (John), 8392.
MUMINOV (Ashirbek), 8063.
Munatius Plancus, 2602.
MUNGAZI (Dickson A.), 7356.
MUNITA (José Antonio), 3111.
MUÑOZ IBÁÑEZ (F. J.), 1467.
MÜNSTER (Reinhold), 6265.
MUNTEAN (V. V.), 2985.
Müntzer (Thomas), 5507.
MURAI (Shosuke), 8294.
MURASE (Shinichi), 4801.
MURATA (Yasuho), 5548.
Muratori (Ludovico Antonio), 649, 5568.
MUREȘAN (Augustin), 205.
MURISON (C. L.), 705.
MURNAGHAN (S.), 2117.
MURPHEY (Rhoads), 5171.
MURPHY (Brenda), 6529.
MURPHY (Tim), 1369.
MURRAY (Alan), 3185.
MURRAY (Alexander), 3478.
MURRAY (Donette), 7946.
MURRAY (Jacqueline), 3479.
MURRAY (James M.), 3387.
MUSACCHIO (Jacqueline-Marie), 6399.
MUSÄUS (Immanuel), 2574.
MUSCA (Giosuè), 3202.
MUSCATINE (Charles), 3590.
Muselier (Emile Henri), 7670.
MUSGRAVE (Michael), 1283.
MUSGRAVE (William R.), 5715.
MUSIAL (Bogdan), 471, 4464, 7662.
Musset (Alfred de), 6338.
MUSSET (Danielle), 915.
Mussolini (Benito), 686, 4738, 4757, 4760, 4762, 5274, 7605, 7674, 7696.
MUSTAFA HATTI EFENDI, 5163.
MUSTI (Domenico), 1826, 2061, 2272.
MUTH (Susanne), 2720.
MUZZARELLI (Maria Giuseppina), 3480.

MYL'NIKOV (Vladimir P.), 1557.
MYL'NIKOVA (Ljudmila N.), 1522.
MYLLYNTAUS (Timo), 1157.
MYLONAS SHEAR (I.), 2244.
MYNORS (R. A. B.), 3183.
MYONG-SOB (Kim), 8328.
MYRDAL (Janken), 3400.
MYRONE (Martin), 474.
MYŚLIWSKI (Grzegorz), 4947.
MYSSOK (Johannes), 6473.

N

NABERT (Nathalie), 3591.
NACCACHE (Albert F. H.), 6121.
NACIMENTO (Aires Augusto), 60.
NADDEO (Barbara Ann), 6122.
NADEL (D.), 1501.
NADLER (Steven), 1397, 5988.
Naevius (Cn.), 2454.
NAFTALI (Timoti), 7887.
Nagaya-o (Prince Nagaya), 8311.
NAGEL (W.), 1571.
NAGY (Balazs), 3470.
Nagy (Imre), 4612.
NAGY (László J.), 7357.
NAHAYLO (Bohdan), 5181.
NAJDUS (Helena), 7947.
NAJEMY (John M.), 5676.
NAKABAYASHI (Masachi), 6810.
NAKAMURA (Hideshige), 8295.
NAKANO (Takao), 4367.
NAKATA (Ichiro), 1685.
NAKATH (Detlef), 4390.
NAKAYAMA (Shigeru), 6110.
NAKAZAWA (Katsuaki), 8296.
NAMAZOVA (Alla S.), 3991.
Namier (Lewis), 759.
NANTET (Bernard), 8352.
NAO (Oumarou), 4156.
Napoléon Ier, empereur de France, 388, 956, 1016, 4357, 4372, 5274, 6390, 7173, 7457, 7460, 7462, 7468, 7470, 7474, 7475.
Napoléon III (Louis Bonaparte), empereur de France, 4345.
NAPOLI (Paolo), 4758.
NARANJO OROVIO (Consuelo), 3961, 7519.
Nardi (Jacopo), 5567.
Nardi (Piero), 707.
NARDON (Franco), 5417.
NARITA (Ryuichi), 1036.
NASH (Mary), 6965, 6975.
NASH (Susie), 70.
Naska (Kaliopi), 7541.
NASRUDDIN, 1500.
Nassau-Hadamar (Johann Ludwig von, Graf), 7438.
Nasser (Gamal Abdel), 7984.
NASSON (Bill), 5071.

NĂSTASĂ (Lucian), 1030.
NATHAN (Geoffrey S.), 195.
NATIVEL (Colette), 5784.
Naudé (Gabriel), 116, 760, 5624, 5678.
NAUMOV (Oleg V.), 5002, 5566.
NAUTA (L.), 3703.
NAVARRO GARCÍA (Jesús Raúl), 4966.
NAVET-BOURON (Françoise), 4368.
NAVRATIL (Jaromír), 4255.
NAWID (Senzil K.), 4016.
NAWROT (Dariusz), 7466.
NAZZARO (A. V.), 2857.
N'DIMINA MOUGALA (Antoine-Denis), 7948.
NEAD (Lynda), 394.
NEĆAK (Dušan), 7989.
Neckam (Alexander), 3710.
Necker (Jacques), 175.
Necker (Suzanne), 175.
NEDERMAN (Cary J.), 5677.
Needham (Joseph), 761.
NEELY (Mark E., Jr.), 5212.
NEFF (H.), 2250.
NEFONTAINE (Luc), 1343.
NEGRI (Guglielmo), 4763.
NEGRI (M.), 1936.
NEHAMAS (A.), 2162.
NEHRU (Jawaharlal), 4621.
NEIERTZ (Nicolas), 6713.
NEININGER (Falko), 3127.
NEKLJUDOV (S. Ju.), 8050.
NELISSEN (Jan), 7017.
NELLES (Paul), 5678.
NELSON (Janet L.), 3229.
NĚMEČEK (Jan), 4251, 7686, 7788.
NÉMETH (István), 7903.
NENAROKOV (Al'bert Pavlovich), 5015.
NENCI (F.), 2118.
NENCI (Giuseppe), 1814.
NENONEN (Markku), 6590.
NEPOMNIN (Oleg E.), 8172.
NEPOTE-DESMARRES (Fanny), 6266.
NERBØVIK (Jostein), 4889.
Nereus, Sanctus, 2767.
NERLICH (Daniel), 3230.
Nero Claudius Caesar, Roman emperor, 2469.
Nerva (M. Cocceius), Roman emperor, 2721.
NESBITT (J.), 213.
NESSELRATH (H.-G.), 2119.
NESSLER (Bernhard), 5889.
NESTLER (Friedrich), 109.
NETZ (R.), 2163.
NETZER (E.), 1768.
NEU (John), 1194.

NEUBERG (Ehrhart), 4402.
NEUGEBAUER (W.), 4393.
NEUHAUS (Stefan), 6313.
NEUHEUSER (Hanns Peter), 71.
NEUKIRCHEN (Thomas), 6267.
NEUMANN (Florian), 853.
NEUMANN (Klaus), 7385.
NEUMÜLLERS-KLAUSER (Renate), 3205.
NEVAKIVI (Jukka), 4288, 4289.
NEVALA (Arto), 5805.
NEVE (P.), 1736.
NEVEU (Bruno), 622.
NEVILLE (Jennifer), 3593.
NEWMAN (Louise Michelle), 6966.
NEWMAN (William), 6125.
Newmann (Barnett), 6488.
NEWMYER (S. T.), 2164.
NEWTON (Francis), 445.
Newton (Isaac), 6089, 6126.
NEY-KRWAWICZ (Marek), 7763.
NEYZİ (Leyla), 623.
NEZHINSKIJ (Leonid N.), 7287.
NEZU (Yukio), 2986.
NGO (Tak-Wing), 7335.
NIBLO (Stephen R.), 4839.
Nicander, 1918.
NICASTRI (L.), 2627.
NICCOLI (Ottavia), 6967.
Nicetas Heracleensis, 3070.
NICHOLAS (David), 3207, 3401.
NICHOLAS (Tom), 6772.
NICHOLLS (David), 6919.
NICHOLSON (Andrew), 6581.
NICHOLSON (P. T.), 1660.
NICHOLSON (Steve), 6592.
NICKAU (K.), 2644.
NICOLAI (Roberto), 792.
NICOLAÏDIS (Efthymios), 6154.
NICOLAS (Elie), 3272.
Nicolaus Damascenus, 2145.
Nicolaus V, Papa, 3763.
NICOLENCO (Viorica), 4976.
NICOLET (Claude), 2508.
NICOLIELLO (Mónica), 5226.
NICOLINI (Enrico), 4694.
NICOLLE (David), 3482.
NICOLOSO (Paolo), 6433.
Niebuhr (B. G.), 735.
NIEDHART (Gottfried), 7600.
NIELSEN (Henrik Karl), 4262.
NIELSEN (M.), 2300.
NIELSEN HØILUND (Karen), 3208.
NIELSON (Paul-Anthon), 1255.
NIETO-GALAN (Agustí), 6124.
Nietzsche (Friedrich Wilhelm), 851, 1404, 5895, 5941, 5956, 5973, 5976, 6012, 6016, 7159.
NIEWÖHNER (Friedrich), 5266, 5292.
NIFTERRIK (G. P. van), 7132.

NIGHTINGALE (A. W.), 2021.
NIGRO (Louis John, Jr.), 7601.
NIJHOWNE (Jeanne), 226.
Niketas Choniates, 3085.
Nikolaj I, Romanov, emperor of Russia, 5008.
NIKOLOV (S.), 3058.
NIKOLOVA (Tania), 4149.
NILES (John D.), 3594.
NILSSON (Ingmar), 1268.
NILSSON (K. Robert), 973.
NILSSON (Lars), 7026.
NILSSON (Roddy), 7174.
NINCI (Renzo), 3154.
NING (Zhixin), 8173.
NINKOVICH (Frank), 7280.
NIPPEL (Wilfried), 802.
NISHIJIMA (Sadao), 8299.
NISHIKAWA (Takao), 8326.
NITSCH (Meinolf), 6968.
NITSCHKE (August), 3174.
NITSCHKE (Bernadetta), 7949.
NITTI (John J.), 3521.
NIU (Jun), 8174.
NIZZA DA SILVA (Maria Beatriz), 7376.
Nkrumah (Kwame), 4522.
Nnamdi Azikiwe (Benjamin), 4881.
NOACK (Lothar), 6268.
NOACK-HALEY (Sabine), 3665.
NOBIS (G.), 1765.
Nodier (charles), 5851.
NOEL (D.), 2062.
NOËL (M.-P.), 1903.
NOFLATSCHER (Heinz), 4082.
NOIRET (Serge), 6782.
NOIRIEL (Gérard), 4369.
NOLLE (J.), 1765.
NOMURA (Mari), 5549.
NONNIS (D.), 2566.
Nonnus Panopolitanus, 1747, 1930, 1931.
NOONAN (Harold W.), 1409.
NOORDRAVEN (Bert), 2509.
Nopper (Max), 5407.
NORBERG (Dan), 282.
NORBERT (Franz), 6769.
NORBROOK (David), 6269.
NORDENSKIÖLD (Erland), 8379.
NORDMAN (Daniel), 333, 4370.
NORDQUIST (Joan), 5886.
NORDYKE (Eleanor C.), 8388.
NORELLI (Enrico), 2921.
NØRGÅRD JØRGENSEN (Anne), 3917.
NORTH (Michael), 1145.
NORTH (Robert), 1327.
Northcliffe (Alfred Harmsworth, Viscount), 4572.
NORTHROP MOORE (Jerrold), 6434.

NORTON (Glyn P.), 6214.
NOSEK (E. M.), 3122.
NOSOV (E. N.), 3216.
NOTHNAGLE (Alan L.), 4466.
NOTOMI (N.), 2165.
NOURZHANOV (Kirill), 5154.
NOUZILLE (Jean), 7523.
NOUZILLE (Philippe), 3742.
NOVÁČKOVÁ (Helena), 4251, 7686.
NOVATI (Francesco), 5925.
NOVELLO (M.), 2765.
NOVICK (Peter), 5680.
NOVOPASHIN (Jurij S.), 6845.
NOVOTNÝ (Jiří), 6811.
NOWAK (Kurt), 5628.
NUBOLA (Cecilia), 5286.
NUCCIO (Richard A.), 7977.
NULLI (Andrea), 6491.
NUNES (Naidea Nunes), 283.
NUNES CARVALHO (Célia), 8343.
NUÑEZ SEIXAS (Xosé M.), 5105.
NURMI (Ismo), 5049.
NUSSBÄCHER (Gernot), 6832.
NUTI (Leopoldo), 7950.
NUTTON (Vivian), 6125.
NUTZ (Andreas), 6729.
NUZZO (Donatella), 2883.
NYE (David E.), 6162.
NYE (Mary Jo), 6129.
NYHOLM (Peter), 5806.
NYLANDER (C.), 1700.
NYLANDER (Gert), 7791.
NYSTAZOPOULOU-PELEKIDOU (M.), 3059.
NYYSSÖNEN (Heino), 4611.

O

Ó GRÁDA (Cormac), 1179.
Ó SIOCHRU (Michéal), 4676.
OAKLEY (Francis), 1089.
OAKLEY (S. P.), 749.
OAUL (Lionel), 7951.
OBA (Osamu), 8141.
O'BALLANCE (Edgar), 4193.
OBERG (Barbara B.), 5183.
OBERG (Michael Leroy), 7377.
OBERMEIER (Anita), 3596.
OBERSTE (Jörg), 3141, 3818.
OBREGÓN (Clotilde María), 4198.
Obrenović (Miloš), prince of Serbia, 7517.
O'BRIAN (John), 6474.
O'BRIEN (Brendan), 4677.
O'BRIEN (Bruce R.), 3346.
OCAK (Ahmet Yaşar), 5172.
O'CARROLL (Maura), 3738.
Ockham (William of), 1421, 3740.
O'COLLINS (Gerald), 2943.
O'DALY (Gerard James Patrick), 854, 2829.

Odilo von Cluny, 3807.
ODOM (William O.), 5213.
O'DONNELL (James Salibur), 4021.
ODORICO (P.), 2979.
OERMANN (Nils Ole), 7358.
OERTZEN (Christine von), 6969.
OEXLE (Otto G.), 539.
OFFERLÉ (Michel), 6983.
OFFNER (A. A.), 7952.
OGATA (Isamu), 485.
OGAWA (Takashi), 8175.
OGDEN (D.), 2063.
OGI (Adolf), 7455.
OGONOVSZKY-STEFFENS (Judith), 6475.
O'GORMAN (Francis), 6130.
OGUIBENINE (B.), 2120.
OGURA (Yasushi), 8090.
OGUZ (Cem), 1007.
O'HALPIN (Eunan), 4678.
O'HEAR (Anthony), 5952.
O'Higgins (Bernardo), 4180.
OHLMEYER (Jane), 3986.
OHLSSON (Bror-Erik), 1154.
OHNO (Kate), 5183.
OHST (Martin), 5942.
OHTSUKI (Y.), 3060.
OIKARINEN (Jarmo), 7953.
OIKONOMAKOS (K.), 1918.
OIKONOMIDES (Nicolas), 232.
OISHI (Takashi), 8091.
OJA (Linda), 6131.
OJALA (Jari), 6714.
OKAMOTO (Takashi), 8176.
OKHOTIN (N. G.), 5023.
OKIMORI (Takuya), 8300.
OKPEWHO (Isidore), 8333.
ÖKSE (Tuba), 1468.
Okubo (Toshimichi), 4793.
OKUMUŞ (Ejder), 5173.
Olaf, Sanctus, 3661.
OLAJOS (Th.), 3061.
OLÀRIA (C.), 1502.
OLAUSSON (Michael), 1538.
OLD (Hughes Oliphant), 3775.
OLDENZIEL (Ruth), 1252.
OLDONI (M.), 282.
O'LEARY (Cecilia Elizabeth), 5214.
O'LEARY-HAWTHORNE (John), 5922.
OLECH (Lucianus), 5321.
OLECHOWSKI (Thomas), 7097.
OLEKSIW (Susan), 1438.
OLESEN (Thorsten Borring), 4267.
OLIPHANT (John), 7445.
OLIVA (César), 6216.
OLIVEIRA (Luís Filipe), 3403.
OLIVERO (Isabelle), 472.
Olivi (Petrus Johannis), 3700.
OLLILA (Anne), 577.
O'LOUGHLIN Thomas, 19, 3629.

INDEX OF NAMES 387

OLSCHEWSKI (Ursula), 5506.
OLSEN (Olaf), 1004.
OLSEN (Rikke Agnete), 1005.
OLSON (Carl), 1373.
OLSON (James Stuart), 979, 980.
OLSSON (Jon), 6593.
OLUMOROTI (Oluranti), *XI*.
O'MALLEY (John W.), 5438.
O'MARA (V. M.), 3570.
O'MEARA (D. J.), 3743.
O'MEARA (D.), 1946.
OMEZZOLI (Tullio), 4764.
OMISSI (David Enrico), 7310.
O'NEIL (J. L.), 2022.
Onofri (Arturo), 6306.
ÖNSOY (Rıfat), 6812.
OOSTERBOSCH (Michel), 47.
O'PHELAN GODOY (Scarlett), 4922.
OPPENHEIMER (A.), 1762.
OPPL (Ferdinand), 6842.
OPSOMER (J.), 2922.
ORABONA (Domenico), 5418.
ORABONA (Luciano), 5418.
ORAZIO, 2597.
Ordericus Vitalis, 762.
Orellie Antoine I, rey de Araucanía y Patagonia, 4176.
ORGAMBIDE (Pedro), 1424.
ORLANDI (Giuseppe), 5419.
Orlandini (Piero), 2240.
ORLANDO (Francesco), 6318.
ORLOV (Igor' B.), 5017.
ORLOW (D.), 4871.
ORMOS (Mária), 7567.
ORMROD (Mark), 1153.
ORNATO (Ezio), 106.
O'ROURKE (Kevin H.), 6655.
ORQUERA (L. A.), 1469.
ORSELLI (A. M.), 2956.
ORSINA (G.), 7574.
Ørsted (H. C.), 6108.
ØRSTED (Per), 1006.
ORTALLI (Gherardo), 624.
ORTEGA CANADELL (Rosa), *XV*.
ORTH (Karin), 4468.
OSBORNE (John B.), 7524.
OSER-GROTE (C.), 2923.
O'SHAUGHNESSY (Hugh), 8376.
OSIAC (Vladimir), 1148.
OSSA (Manuel), 5420.
OSSOLA (Carlo), 6132.
ÖSTENBERG (I.), 2442.
OSTENC (Michel), 7731.
OSTERHAMMEL (Jürgen), 737.
OSTORERO (Martine), 3460.
OSTRANDER (Gilman M.), 5682.
OSTROWSKI (Janusz A.), 2738.
OSTUNI (Maria Rosaria), 6788.
OSTUNI (Nicola), 6813.
O'SULLIVAN (P.), 1500.
OTÁHAL (Milan), 4243, 4244.

OTERO (Gerardo), 4840.
OTIS (Laura), 5683.
OTLOH VON ST. EMMERAM, 3707.
Otlone di S. Emmerano, 3899.
OTSU (Toru), 8301.
OTT (Thomas), 660.
OTTE (Hans), 5311.
OTTO (Frank), 7248.
OTTO (Gerhard), 7663.
Otto, Sanctus, Bishop of Bamberg, 3179.
Otto III, röm.-deutscher Kaiser, 1080, 3021.
OTTONELLO (Piero), 3821.
OTU (Petre), 7764.
OUY (Gilbert), 72.
OUYANG (Junxi), 8177.
Overbeck (Johann Friedrich), 6459.
OVERMANS (Rüdiger), 977, 7664.
OVERMYER (Daniel L.), 5550.
OVERY (Richard), 7665.
Ovidius Naso (P.), 2355-2360, 2532, 2591, 2606, 2611, 2620, 2626, 2629, 2675, 2679, 2686.
OVIEDO (Luís), 5421.
OWEN (Olwyn), 3323.
OWENSBY (Brian Philip), 6970.
OWNBY (David), 8178.
OWTRAM (Francis Carey), 4892.
OYAMA (Seiichi), 8302.
ÖZ (Mehmet), 1090, 3404.
Ozanam (Federico), 763, 5394.
ÖZDALGA (Elisabeth), 8062.
ÖZGİRAY (Ahmet), 7603.
ÖZKARCI (Mehmet), 6971.
OZOUF (Mona), 726.
ÖZREN (Can), 7954.
ÖZTOPRAK (Izzet), 4650.
ÖZTÜRK (Mustafa), 856.
OZUNU (Mihai Vasile), 7764.

P

PACE (A.), 1140.
PACE (Sergio), 6435.
PACI (Renzo), 6712.
PACKMAN (Z. M.), 2645.
PADOA-SCHIOPPA (A.), 1131, 4752.
PÁEZ (Carlos), 4058.
PAGÁN (V. E.), 2380.
PAGANI (I.), 799.
PAGDEN (Andrew), 7281.
PAGGI (Leonardo), 613, 4728.
PAGLIARA (A.), 2273.
PAHLAVAN (Changiz), 4017.
PAILLET (P.), 1503.
PAINTER (Mark A.), 5990.
PAL'TSEVA (Larisa A.), 1998.
PALACZYK (M.), 2064.
PALAIA (R.), 5978.

Palazzeschi (Aldo), 6308.
PALAZZO (Eric), 402.
PALÉOTHODOROS (D.), 2065.
PALERMO (D.), 1840.
PALESE (Salvatore), 5318.
PALESTRO (Sandra), 4177.
PALEY (Morton D.), 6347.
PÁLFFY (Géza), 6972.
PALLADINI (Fiammetta), 426.
PALLÓ (Gábor), 6064.
PALLOT (Judith), 6773.
PALLUEL-GUILLARD (André), 5145.
PALM (Lodewijk), 6093.
PALMA DI CESNOLA (A.), 1490.
PALMER (Alan), 1009.
PALMER (J. A.), 2166.
PALMER (R. Barton), 3543.
PALMOWSKI (Jan), 6851.
PALOMERO (Esteban J.), 5450.
PALSKY (Gilles), 6133.
PALTI (Elias), 857.
PALUMBO-LIU (David), 1010.
PALUSZYŃSKI (Tomasz), 7604.
PAMMINGER (P.), 1639.
PAMUK (Şevket), 1182.
PANAINO (Antonio), 636.
PANAJIA (Alessandro), 6291.
PANAYI (Panikos), 3988.
PANAYOTOPOULOS (Vassilis), 333.
PANCERA (Carlo), 5778.
PANDOLFI (Dulce Chaves), 4135.
PÁNEK (Jaroslav), 602.
PANERO (Francesco), 3405.
PANESSA (G.), 1814.
PANGRAZIO (Miguel Angel), 4909.
PANI (Mario), 2319, 2443.
PANICO (Guido), 1254.
PANOFSKY (Erwin), 403.
PANTELIĆ (B.), 3062.
PANTEV (Andrei Lazarov), 7525.
PANTOJA (Selma), 7302.
PANZAC (Daniel), 6752.
PAOLETTI (Orazio), 2274.
PAOLI (Andrea), 433.
PAOLI (Michel), 6229.
PAPACOSTEA (Serban), 3221.
PAPAEFTHYMIOU (Eleni), 245.
PAPAGIANNI (E.), 3063.
PAPATHANASSIOU (Maria), 2167, 6973.
PAPATHOMAS (A.), 792.
PAPATHOMOPOULOS (Manolis), 2972.
PAPAYOANOU (Paul A.), 7282.
PAPAZIAN (M. B.), 2168.
PAPAZZONI (Barbara), 5568.
PAPI (Emanuele), 2570.
Papini (Giovanni), 6307.
PAPPE (Ilan), 7258.
PARAPETTI (R.), 2245.

PARAVICINI (Werner), 544, 3258.
PARAVICINI BAGLIANI (Agostino), 3460.
PARELLO (Vincent), 3287.
PARENIČKA (Pavol), 5055.
PARENT-LARDEUR (Françoise), 446.
PARFITT (S.), 1492.
PARINETTO (Luciano), 5507.
Paris (Gaston), 764.
Paris (Matthew), 324.
PARIS (Michael), 6548.
PARISOLI (Luca), 3347.
PARISSE (Michel), 3822.
PARK (Katharine), 6125.
PARK (Seung-Chan), 3744.
PARK POE (J.), 2121.
PARKER (A.), 1598.
PARKER (D.), 5465.
PARKER (K.), 1572.
PARKER (N.), 2444.
PARKER (Noel), 1011.
PARKER (S. T.), 1769.
PARKER (T. H. L.), 5465.
PARKER (V.), 1573, 1737.
PARLATO (Giuseppe), 710.
PARMA (Elena), 6476.
PARMEGGIANI (A.), 3064.
PARMEGGIANI (G.), 722.
Parmenides, 2144, 2166.
PARRI (Maria Grazia), 4748.
PARRY (J. H.), 7316.
PARSHALL (P.), 404.
PARSONS (J.), 2646.
PARSONS (Robert), 5431.
Parsons (Talcott), 1084.
PARSONS (Timothy), 7317.
PARTINGTON (Geoffrey), 5807.
PARTNER (Peter), 3777.
PARTNER (Simon), 6974.
PARTRIDGE (Michael), 7683, 7807, 7808.
PARUSSA (Gabriella), 3758.
PARVIN (Nasir al-Din), 5866.
PASÁK (Tomáš), 4245.
PASÁKOVÁ (Jana), 4245.
PASAMAR LÁZARO (José Enrique), 5422.
Pascal (Blaise), 5411, 5908, 6277.
PASCHOUD (François), 576.
PASCHT (Arno), 916.
PASHA (A. K.), 7254.
Pashuto (Vladimir T.), 1043.
PASQUALINI (Anna) , 2766.
PASQUINO (Gianfranco), 1091.
PASQUINUCCI (Marinella), 2301.
PASSERINI (Luisa), 626, 5684.
PASSMORE (Kevin), 684, 4371.
PASTA (Renato), 627.
PASTOR (Reyna), 3406.
PASTOREAU (Michel), 1257.

PASTORELLI (Sabrina), 5423.
PASTORI (Gianluca), 7956.
PÁSZTOR (Edith), 3790.
Pater (Walter), 131.
PATISSO (Giuseppe), 4743.
PATITIER (Paul), 629.
PATOČKA (Jan), 5889, 5890.
PATON (Derek), 4221.
Patrizi (Francesco), 6125.
PATROIU (Ion), 1148.
PATRON (Sylvie), 5867.
PATTERSON (David S.), 7817.
PATTIE (T. S.), 81.
PATTONI (M. P.), 1961.
PAUCKER (Arnold), 7792.
PAUER (Erich), 4798.
PAULI (Bianca), 7455.
PAULI (Tatjana), 3666.
PAULÍK (Jan), 4216.
PAULIN (Roger), 6270.
Paulinus Nolanus, Sanctus, 2857, 2858.
PAULINY (Ján), 3097.
Paulme (Denise), 461.
PAULSEN (Th.), 1898.
Paulus IV, Papa, 5346.
Paulus Samosatensis, 2949.
Paulus VI, papa, 8018.
Paulus, Apostolus, Sanctus, 2926, 2931, 2940.
Pausanias, 1932, 1933, 2082.
PAUTLER (Stefan), 6271.
PAUTZ (Patrick Charles), 306.
PAVIOT (Jacques), 303.
PAVLAT (Leo), 4225.
PAVLENKO (Mykola), 5050.
PAVLOV (Dmitrii Borisovich), 5015.
PAVLOVIC (Vojislav), 7605.
PAVLOWITCH (Stevan Kosta), 3989.
PAVOLINI (Carlo), 2767.
PAWŁOWSKI (Bronisław), 7467.
PAXTON (Robert O.), 7732.
PAYANE (Annie), *VII.*
PAYEN (Philippe), 7135.
PAYNE (Alina A.), 6436.
Payne (Robert O.), 3601.
PAYNE (Stanley G.), 5106.
PAZZAGLIA (Luciano), 5770.
PEARCE (Adrian J.), 6715.
PEARCE (Edward), 4679.
PEARD (Julian G.), 6134.
PEARL (Jonathan L.), 5685.
PEARLMAN (Michael D.), 5215.
PEARSON (Edward A.), 7155.
PEARSON LYNNE ROPER (Kathy), 3231.
PÉCAUT (Daniel), 4184.
PEČÍNKA (Pavel), 4246.
PECKA (Jindřich), 4216.

Peckham (Jean), 3719.
PECORARI (Paolo), 6787.
PÉCOUT (Gilles), 4765.
PEDERSON (William D.), 7515.
Pedro I, rey de Castilla y León, 3113.
Pedro II, Emperor of Brazil, 4113.
Pedro II, King of Portugal, 7323.
PEDRONI (Matteo), 3562.
PEDROSO (Elizabeth M. K.), 4138.
PEEL (Christine), 3324.
PEIRIS (Gerald H.), 5123, 8083.
PEJOVIC (Cedomir), 4852.
PEKACZ (Jolanta T.), 5991.
PEKÁRY (Irene), 2768.
PELA (Doriano), 6976.
Pelagius (haereticus), 2834, 2835, 2859.
PELINKA (Anton), 4459.
PELKAUS (E.), 7208.
PELLEGRINI (E.), 1531.
PELLEGRINI (Letizia), 3702.
PELLEGRINI (Marco), 3262.
PELLERIN (Denys), 5744.
PELLETIER (Denis), 6888.
PELLICER I BRU (Josep), 247.
PELLINI (Pierluigi), 6348.
PELS (Peter), 894.
PELTZ (Lucy), 474.
PEÑA (Alonso), 858.
PEÑA RODRÍGUEZ (Alberto), 4963.
PENARANDA (Ricardo), 4184.
PENDER (Malcolm), 5149.
PENE VIDARI (Gian Savino), 628, 3328.
PENG (Houwen), 8179.
PENG (Houwen), 8180.
PENIČ (Lojze), 5064.
Penifader (Cecilia), 3366.
Pennac (Daniel), 6370.
PENNELL (C. R.), 4856.
PENSOM (Roger), 3598.
PENTIUC (E.), 1701.
PENUTI (Carla), 1019.
PENYAK (Lee M.), 6753.
PEPE (Alfonso), 5382.
PERANI (Mauro), 74.
PERDICOYIANNI-PALEOLOGU (H.), 1640.
PEREIRA (Michela), 3711.
PEREIRA FIORILO (Juan), 7666.
PEREIRA PAGÁN (Begona), 3791.
PEREN (Roger), 7261.
PERE-NOGUES (S.), 2023.
PEREZ (Louis A. jr.), 4209, 7526.
PÉREZ GARZÓN (Juan-Sisinio), 5091.
PÉREZ GONZÀLEZ (Maurilio), 3511.
Pérez Jiménez (Marcos), 5230.
PÉREZ RIVERA (J. M.), 2327.

PÉREZ TOLEDO (Sonia), 4826.
PEREZ ZEVALLOS (Juan Manuel), 6639.
PERGOLA (Philippe), 3894.
PERICA (Vjekoslav), 5255.
PERIČIĆ (Šime), 6656.
PERIE (Dorin), 4977.
PERINI (Sergio), 7446.
PERKINS (Dorothy), 1012.
PERKINS (Leeman L.), 6596.
PERKINS (Mary Anne), 5302.
PERKOVICH (George), 4635.
PERŁAKOWSKI (Adam), 7414.
PERNES (Jiří), 4247.
PERNLER (Sven Erik), 3783.
Perón (Juan Domingo), 4043, 4045, 4057, 4059, 4065.
PERONI (R.), 1527.
PÉRONNET (Michel), 5484.
PEROVIĆ (Jeronim), 7958.
Perpetua, Sancta, 2957.
PERRETT (Roy W.), 630.
PERRIN-SAMINADAYAR (É.), 1999.
PERRODOT (Mathieu), 798.
PERROIS (Louis), 473.
PERROT (Michelle), 754.
PERRY (Gill), 451.
PERRY LONG (Kathleen), 5715.
PERSSON (Fabian), 6977.
PERSSON (Hans Åke), 3950.
PERTICI (Petra), 3668.
PERTICI (Roberto), 631.
PERUSINO (F.), 1887.
PERUTELLI (Alessandro), 2647.
PERVILLÉ (Guy), 5571.
PESANTE (Maria Luisa), 1080.
PESCE (Dolores), 3690.
PESCE (M.), 2924.
PESCHLOW-BINDOKAT (A.), 1599.
PEŠEK (Jan), 5051, 5052.
PEŠEK (Jiří), 4005, 7640.
PESTALOZZI (K.), 2147.
PETACCIA (R.), 2711.
Pétain (Henri-Philippe), 4160.
PETER (Emanuel), 6272.
PETER (Karen), 5830.
PETER (Matthias), 7802.
Peter I, Karadjordjević, king of Serbia, king of Serbs, Croats and Slovens, 7523.
PETERS (A. R.), 7578.
PETERS (E.), 736.
PETERS (J.), 1578, 1607.
PETERSE (Kees), 2769.
PETERSEN (Anja), 7175.
PETERSOHN (Jürgen), 3179.
PETERSON (Derek), 5445.
PETERSON (Glen D.), 987.
Petiet (Alexandre), 4340.
Petiet (Auguste), 4340.
Petiet (Claude), 4340.

Petiet (Sylvain), 4340.
PETIJEVIC (Tamara), 3695.
PETINOS (Ch.), 2925.
PETITEAU (Natalie), 4372.
PETITFRERE (Claude), 1152.
PETITMENGIN (Pierre), 2861.
PETŐ (Andrea), 4472.
Pëtr I Velikij [le Grand], empereur de Russie, 800.
Petrarca (Francesco), 804, 3512, 3515, 6213.
PETRENCU (Anatol), 4978.
PETRESCU (Ileana), 1148.
PETRICIOLI (Marta), 363.
PETRILLO (Agostino), 1092.
PETRONIO (Ugo), 3337.
Petronius Arbiter, 2361, 2600.
PETROV (Liudmil Kirilov), 4152.
PETROV (Nikita V.), 5023.
PETROVA (Nina K.), 7793.
PETROVIC (Danica), 3695.
PETRUCCI (Armando), 11.
PETRUCCIANI (Alberto), 432.
Petrus Alamire, 83.
Petrus Damianus, sanctus, 3722.
Petrus Lombardus (episcopus Parisiensis), 3738.
Petrus, Apostolus, Sanctus, 2940, 2947.
PETTEGREE (Andrew), 5777.
PETTINATO (G.), 1738.
PETTITT (P. B.), 1486.
PETZOLD (Karl-Ernst), 1829, 2000.
Petzold (Karl-Ernst), 564.
Peuger (Lienhart), 3739.
PEVEAR (R.), 1960.
PEVSNER (Nikolaus), 1289.
PEYRONEL (L.), 1562.
PEZZINO (Paolo), 7176.
PEZZOLO (Luciano), 6814.
PEZZOTTA (Alberto), 6597.
PFAHL-TRAUGHBER (Armin), 4473.
PFEIFER (Guido), 7077.
PFISTER (Christian), 1255.
PFROMMER (M.), 1641.
PFULLMANN (Uwe), 5029.
Pheifer (Joseph Donovan), 3608.
PHILIPPE (Gilles), 6205.
PHILIPPE DE REMI SIRE DE BEAUMANOIR, 3513.
Philippe II le Bon, duc de Bourgogne, 3254.
Philippus II, king of Macedonia, 1970, 1976.
PHILLIPS (Gervase), 6135, 7415.
PHILLIPS (Kevin P.), 5216.
PHILLIPS (Kim M.), 3472.
Philo Alexandrinus, 2161, 2930, 2934.
Philoponus (Johannes), 3054.

PHILPOTT (William), 7606.
Phipps (Eric, sir), 7651.
Photius, 449, 2952, 3058.
Piacentini (Marcello), 6438.
PIANA (E. L.), 1469.
PIAO (Yingji), 8181.
PICARD (Jean-François), 6136.
PICARD (O.), 2066.
PICASSO (Giorgio), 3823, 5318.
PICCIALUTI (Maura), 7177.
PICCINNI (Gabriella), 3209.
PICCIONE (R. M.), 1963.
PICCIONI (Luigi), 1256.
PICCIRILLI (L.), 1900, 1925, 2001.
PICHE (David), 3868.
PICHOIS (Claude), 6349.
PICKERING (O. S.), 3570.
PICKLES (Christopher), 3669.
Pico della Mirandola (Giovanni), 6125.
PICQUET (Théa), 356.
PIEHLER (G. Kurt), 5182.
Pier Paolo Vergerio, il giovane, 5999.
PIERANGELI (Giuseppe), 3328.
PIERI (B.), 2840.
Piero della Francesca, 227, 3666.
Pierre l'Ermite, 3880.
PIERROS (Filippos), 7959.
PIETRI (Charles), 2815.
PIETRI (Luce), 2815.
PIETRINI (S.), 284.
Pietro I Karageorgevic, re di Jugoslavia, 7605.
PIETROSANTI (P.), 2966.
PIETRW-ENKER (Bianka), 6978.
PIETSCH (C.), 2122.
PIGNATELLI (A.), 2511.
PIHLAINEN (Kalle), 859.
PILJEVIC (Đorđe O.), 5250.
PILLER (Gudrun), 599.
PILLINGER (R.), 3020.
PILLORGET (René), 7416, 7447.
PILONE (Rosaria), 3101.
Piłsudski (Józef), 4956.
PILUSO (Giandomenico), 6815.
PIMPINELLA (P.), 5978.
PIN (Corrado), 5995.
PINCH-BROCK (L.), 1642.
PINCHERA (Valeria), 6979.
PINÇON (G.), 1495.
Pindarus, 1934-1938, 2095, 2101, 2107.
PINDER (John), 7122.
Pinel (Philippe), 6176.
PINELLI (Lucia), 3186.
PINHEIRO MACHADO (Paulo), 7378.
PINI (Antonio Ivan), 3895.
Pinochet Ugarte (Augusto), 4169, 4177.

PINTO (António Costa), 4964.
PINTO (Julio), 4171.
PINTO (Pasquale Massimo), 2123.
Pio (Giovanni Battista), 2362.
PIOLETTI (Antonio), 3584.
Piovene (Guido), 5629.
Pirandello (Luigi), 6350, 6351.
PIRARD (Joseph), 4101.
PIREH BABI (Loghman), 5174.
Pirenne (Henri), 765.
PIRJEVEC (Jože), 1013.
PIRSON (Felix), 2770.
PISAPIA (Annamaria), 3351.
Piscator (Hermannus OSB), 766.
Pisistratus, 2065.
Piso (Cn. Calpurnius), 2322, 2330, 2375, 2377, 2383, 2477, 2490, 2491, 2493.
PISO (L.), 2445.
PITSAKIS (C. G.), 3065.
Pittier (Henri), 6116.
Pius IX, Papa, 5350.
PIVATO (Stefano), 285.
PIVOVAR (Efim O.), 871, 5018.
PIWONKA (Gonzalo), 4177.
PIZZOCARO (M.), 1922.
PLAISANCE (Michel), 118.
PLANCHE (Jean-Louis), 5571.
PLANK (Angelika), 5808.
PLANTZOS (D.), 2246.
Planude (M.), 2972.
PLATELLE (Henri), 3379.
PLATINA (Bartolomeo), 3708.
Plato, 1093, 1392, 1939, 1940, 1942-1944, 2021, 2145, 2146, 2151, 2154, 2158, 2160, 2162, 2165, 2166, 2175, 2177, 2681, 3743.
PLATON (Gheorghe), 4979.
PLATT (Peter G.), 5715.
PLATVOET (Jan G.), 1317.
Plautus (T. Maccius), 2362, 2363, 2595, 2645.
PLEHN (Gottfried), 5745.
PLEKET (H. W.), 1875.
PLIN (Frédéric), 1392.
Plinius (Caecilius Secundus Gaius), 2308, 2410, 2674.
Plinius (Secundus Gaius, Senior), 2364, 2365, 2671, 2687.
PLOQUIN (Frédéric), 4853.
PLOSZAJSKA (Teresa), 5809.
Plotinus, 1946.
PLUM (Claus Munk), 5424.
PLUMPE (Werner), 782.
PLUTA (Olaf), 5266.
Plutarchus, 1945, 2093, 2129, 2164, 2199.
POCCETTI (Paolo), 2648.
POCOCK (J. G. A.), 632, 729, 3990.
PODANÝ (Václav), 5719.

PODESTÀ (Gian Luca), 3702.
PODGORNOVA (N. P.), 7210.
PODLES (Leon J.), 5304.
PODOSINOV (Aleksandr V.), 357, 1566, 3140.
PODRIMAVSKÝ (Milan), 5053.
PODVINTSEV (Oleg B.), 4558.
Poe (Edgar Allan), 6377.
POESCHEL (Sabine), 6477.
POGGIOLINI (Ilaria), 7960.
POGLIANO (Claudio), 6137, 6183.
POHL (H.), 6657.
POHL (Karl Heinrich), 4513.
POHL (Manfred), 6716.
Poincaré (Jules-Henri), 5967.
Poirier (Anne), 491.
Poirier (Patrick), 491.
Poirion (Daniel), 3599.
POIRRIER (Philippe), 5560.
POISSON (Georges), 1287.
POJAR (Miloš), 4225.
PÓK (Attila), 7240.
POKORNÝ (Pavel R.), 171.
Pol Pot, 4158.
POLACCO (Marina), 6351.
Polany (Karl), 1084.
POLDEN (Patrick), 7178.
Polemon, 2253.
POLGÁR (László), 5430.
POLI (Diego), 2648.
POLI (S.), 792.
POLIAK (Claude F.), 5668.
POLITO (E.), 1830.
POLITO (R.), 1893.
POLÍVKA (Miloslav), 578.
POLLACK (Marcelo), 4178.
POLLARD (John F.), 5352.
POLLARD (Sidney), 7051.
POLLET (Gilles), 4328.
POLLEX (A.), 1523.
POLLMANN (Judith), 5508.
POLLOCK (S.), 1703.
Polo (Marco), 351, 3178.
POLO DE BEAULIEU (Marie-Anne), 3439, 3630.
POLTORAK (S. N.), 615.
Polybius, 767, 1947.
Polystratus, 1987.
POMEROY (S. B.), 1831.
POMIAN (Krzysztof), 860.
Pompeius Magnus (Cn.), 2460.
POMPER (Philip), 863.
PONCE ALBERCA (Julio), 5108.
PONCE SANGINES (Carlos), 4108.
PONDER (Stephen), 5868.
Ponge (Francis), 6286.
PONGRATZ-LEISTEN (B.), 1704.
PONS (Silvio), 4768.
PONTZEN (Alexandra), 6329.
POOLE (Christine), 5307.
POOLE (Hilary), 6120.

POOLE (Randall Allen), 5997.
POP (Ioan Aurel), 1015.
POPE (Stephen), 1016.
POPKIN (Jeremy D.), 633.
POPKIN (Richard H.), 6126.
POPKO (M.), 1739.
POPNEDELEV (Todor), 7502.
Popov (Nil Aleksandravich), 768.
POPOVA (Irina F.), 8182.
POPOVICI (Mihai), 932.
PÖPPEL (Hubert), 1416.
POPPENBORG (Annette), 3847.
Popper (Karl), 5961.
PÖPPINGHAUS (Ernst-Wolfgang), 7607.
PORAZIŃSKI (Jarosław), 7448.
PORCIANI (Leone), 792, 1832.
PORCILE (François), 6598.
PORETE (Marguerite), 3773.
Porete (Marguerite), 3589.
PORRET (Michel), 6006.
PORTALIER (Monique), 5666.
PORTELA SILVA (Maria José), 437.
PORTELLI (Alessandro), 634.
PORTER (Andrew), 1008.
PORTER (Brian A.), 4948.
PORTER (James I.), 2736.
PORTER (Roy Sydney), 6138.
PORTER (Stanley E.), 2926.
PORTMANN (Werner), 2446.
Posidonius, 1948.
POSNER (David M.), 6231.
PÖSS (Ondrej), 5054.
POST (Jonathan F. S.), 6274.
POSTEL-VINAY (Gilles), 6645.
POSTER (Carol), 3613.
POSTGATE (J. N.), 1548.
POSTLETHWAITE (N.), 2200.
POTAMIUS EPISCOPUS OLISPONENSIS, 3709.
POTMĚŠILOVÁ (Jarmila), 4247.
POTON (Didier), 6853.
PÖTSCHNER (W.), 2124.
POTTER (David Stone), 635, 2447.
POTTER (David), 7417.
POTTHAST (Barbara), 1223.
POTTHOFF (Heinrich), 4474.
POUCET (Bruno), 5810.
POUCHEPADASS (Jacques), 4636.
POULLE (Bruno), 2771.
POULLE (E.), 162.
POULLE (Yvonne), 4373.
POULSEN (Niels Bo), 7765.
POUPENEY-HART (Catherine), 6216.
POUTHIER (P.), 2712.
POUZAR (Vladimír), 171.
POWER (Daniel), 970.
POZHARSKAJA (Svetlana P.), 3991, 4348.
POZNANSKI (Renée), 4374.

INDEX OF NAMES

PRADOS (John), 7961.
PRAKASH (Gyan), 6139.
PRANDI (Stefano), 6232.
PRANDONI (Francesco), 6599.
PRASAD (H. Y. Sharada), 4621.
PRATT (Keith), 1017.
PRAYON (F.), 2302.
PRAZMOWSKA (Anita), 7807.
PRAZNIAK (Roxann), 8183.
Prchlík (V.), 4217.
PREADIER-FODÉRÉ (P.), 7190.
PREBISH (Charles), 1302.
PREČAN (Vilém), 4221, 4248, 7962.
PREDA (Dumitru), 7543.
PREDIERI (Alberto), 5998, 7078.
PREGO (Victoria), 1018.
PREMUDA PEROSA (Maria Luisa), 6371.
PRESCOTT (Andrew), 3505.
PREŠLENOVA (Rumjan), 4151.
PRESSLY (William), 6478.
PREST (Wilfrid), 632.
PRESTEL (P.), 2846.
PRESTON (Jean F.), 15.
PRESTON (Paul), 5109, 7294, 7683, 7807, 7808.
PRESTWICH (Michael), 3495.
PRETO (Paolo), 4769.
PRÊTRE (C.), 2247.
PRETTEJOHN (Elizabeth), 6455.
PREVENIER (Walter), 3249, 3401.
PREVOST (Gary), 4879.
PRICE (John Valdimir), 1400.
PRICE (Richard), 6981.
PRICE (Simon), 2201, 2867.
PRICOCO (Salvatore), 286.
PRIEST (Tyler), 7963.
PRIESTER (Jens M.), 7179.
PRIETO (A.), 2328.
PRIFTI (Peter R.), 4022, 5256.
Primo de Rivera (Miguel), 5108.
Primo de Rivera y Saenz de Heredia (José Antonio), 5118.
PRINČIČ (Jože), 6640, 7989.
PRINCIPE (Angelo), 4165.
PRINZING (G.), 2980, 3066.
PRIOR (Michael), 4691.
PRITCHARD (D. M.), 2067.
PRJAKHIN (A. D.), 1455.
PRO RUIZ (Juan), 358.
PROBST (Veit), 59.
PROCACCI (Giovanna), 6982.
PROCACCI (Giuliano), 3992.
PROCHASSON (Christophe), 822, 5687.
PROCKOVA (Florentína), 5237.
Proclus, 2163, 2211, 2922.
Procopius, 2970.
PRODI (Paolo), 1019.
PRÖGER (Susanne), 1411.

PROKŠ (Petr), 4249, 7964.
PROMEY (Sally), 6479.
Propertius (Sextus), 2366, 2608, 2635, 2638.
PROSPERI (Adriano), 5335, 5425.
PROST (F.), 2249.
PROSTMEIER (Ferdinand R.), 2863.
Protagoras, 1949.
Protasius, Sanctus, 2892.
PROUD (Judith), 5874.
Proust (Marcel), 6295.
PROVOST (Georges), 5780.
Prudentius Clemens (Aurelius), 2909, 2923, 2941.
PRUNERI (fabio), 5811.
PRUNK (Janko), 1000.
PRYSER (Tore), 4890.
Pryzhov Pryzhov (I. G.), 769.
PRZYBLYSKI (Jeannene M.), 5860.
Ps. Andocides, 1950.
Ps. Callisthenes, 2127.
Ps. Lucianus, 1952.
PSAROUTHAKIS (John), 7965.
Psellus (Michael), 3038.
PŠENIČKOVÁ (Jana), 6781.
Pseudo-Aurelius Victor, 2367.
Pseudo-Caesar, 2368.
Pseudo-Chrysostomus, 2971.
Publius Clodius Pulcher, 2462.
Pucci (Francesco), 5471, 5472, 5475, 5476.
PUCCIARELLI (Alfredo R.), 4059.
PUCCINI (Sandra), 359.
PUDAL (Bernard), 5668.
PUFENDORF (Samuel), 426, 7191, 7197.
PUGLIESE (Stanislao G.), 4770.
PUGLIESE CARRATELLI (Giovanni), 2170.
PUGLISI (Catherine R.), 6400.
PUHL (Roland W. L.), 3897.
PUIG-SAMPER (Miguel Angel), 6062.
PUIGSECH FARRÀS (Josep), 5111.
PUNTONI (Pedro), 7379.
PUPPI (Lionello), 196.
PURCELL (Katherine), 6503.
PURDIE (Rhiannon), 3363.
PURI (B. N.), 8055.
PURNELL (Jennie), 4842.
PURVIS SANSON (Jerry), 5217.
PUŞCAŞ (Vasile), 5756.
PUSHKAREVA (I. M.), 7037.
Pushkin (Aleksandr Sergeevich), 1440, 6207.
Pustkuchen (Friedrich), 6284.
PYENSON (Lewis), 5746.
PYLKÄNEN (Anu), 1197.
Pyrrhus, king of Epirus, 2010.
PYTA (Wolfgang), 4475.
Pythagoras, 2195, 2686.

Q

QALB-I-ABID (S.), 4896.
QI (Chunfeng), 8184.
QI (Chunfeng), 8185.
Qianlong, emperor of China, 8167, 8215.
QIAO (Lingxiao), 8186.
QIU (Huafei), 8187.
QIU (Huafei), 8188.
QIU (Jin), 8189.
QUACK (J. F.), 1643.
QUAGLIONI (Diego), 1134, 3148, 7197.
QUAN (Fangmin), 8151.
QUANTIN (F.), 2202.
QUANTIN (Jean-Louis), 5336.
QUARTARARO (Rosaria), 7733.
QUATTROCCHI-WOISSON (Diana), 5839.
QUEEN (Christer S.), 5528.
Queirós (Pedro Fernandes de), 8390.
QUELLER (Donald E.), 3471.
Quéniart (Jean), 5780.
QUEREUIL (Michel), 3534.
QUERUEL (Danielle), 66.
QUETIN (L.), 2448.
QUEYREL (François), 245.
QUILIS (Antonio), 5468.
QUILLIAM (Neil), 5153.
QUIN (Eckehard), 1095.
Quinet (Edgar), 770.
Quintilianus (M. Fabius), 2092, 2369, 2596.

R

RAAB-REBENTISCH (Angelika), 6716.
RAAFLAUB (Kurt), 1045.
Rabano Mauro, 3761.
RABE (Carsten), 5748.
RABE (Stephen G.), 7966.
Rabin (Yitzhak), 4692.
RACINET (Philippe), 3824.
RADAELLI (Riccardo), 7956.
RADAN (George), 376.
RADCLIFF (Pamela), 6965.
RADEFF (Anne), 6962, 6984.
RADELIĆ (Zdenko), 4204.
Radić (Stjepan), 4204.
RADICCHI (Patrizia), 46.
Radishchev (A. N.), 6207.
RÄDLE (Fidel), 5292.
RADNER (K.), 1705, 1706.
RADRIZZANI (Ives), 5888.
RĂDULESCU (Mihai Sorin), 197.
RADVANOVSKÝ (Zdeněk), 7648.
RAECK (Wulf), 2772.
RAEPSAET-CHARLIER (Marie-Thérésé), 2484, 2512.

RAFFAELLI (Sergio), 6600.
Raffaello Sanzio, 6458.
RAFFERTY (Oliver P.), 4682.
RAGGIO (Olga), 6499.
RAGGIO (Osvaldo), 731, 785.
Ragionieri (Ernesto), 771.
RAGONE (Giovanni), 127.
Rahewinus Frisingensis, 3167.
RAHMSDORF (Sabine), 6233.
RAHVEH-KLEMKE (Smadar), 62.
RAICO (Ralph), 4476.
RAIMON VIDAL, 3514.
RAINA (Dhruv), 761.
RAINER (János M.), 4612.
RAINER (Michael J.), 378, 2487.
RAJAN (Balachandra), 6353.
RAJŠP (Vincenc), 1042, 6774.
RAKOB (F.), 1765.
Raleigh (Walter), 4523.
RAMBEAUD (Pascal), 5509.
RAMELLI (Ilaria), 2927.
Ramesses III, king of Egypt, 1626.
Ramesses IX, king of Egypt, 1611.
RAMET (Sabrina P.), 5246.
RAMIERE DE FORTENIER (Armand), 201.
RAMIRES (G.), 1912.
RAMIREZ VAQUERO (Eloisa), 3098.
RAMM (Thilo), 7071.
Ramon Berenguer I el Corb, Comte del Casal de Barcelona, 3146.
Ramon Berenguer I el Vell, Comte del Casal de Barcelona, 3146.
Ramon Borrell, Comte del Casal de Barcelona, 3146.
RAMOS (Carmine), 5761.
RAMOTOWSKA (Franciszka), 4949.
RAMSEY (Ann W.), 5337.
RANDALL (Catherine), 6401.
RANDERS-PEHRSONS (Justine), 4477.
RANDLES (William G. L.), 6142.
RANGER (Terence), 8353.
Ranke (Leopold von), 684, 772.
RANKI (Vera), 4613.
Raoul de Cambrai, 3527, 3529, 3577.
RAOUL-DUVAL (Jacqueline), 4897.
RAPIC (Smail), 6000.
RAPONE (Leonardo), 4705, 7053.
RAPPAPORT (R. A.), 1374.
RAPSAET-CHARLIER (Marie-Thérèse), 2568, 2571.
RAPTOU (E.), 1804.
RASMUSSEN (Leif), 6144.
RATHBONE (Richard), 4522.
Rathenau (Walther), 4484.
Ratti (Achille), 5321.
RATTI (S.), 2853.
RAUCH (Georg von), 7527.
RAULFF (Ulrich), 861.

RAUNER (Erwin), 3515.
RAUSCH (Jane M.), 4189.
RAUSCH (M.), 1871, 2002.
RAUTMAN (M. L.), 2250.
RAVEL (Jeffrey S.), 6601.
RAVENHILL (William), 343.
RAVINA (Mark), 6775.
Rawandi ('Ahmad ibn Yahyá, IX c.), 3315.
RAWCLIFFE (Carole), 3745.
RAWLES (Stephen), 204.
RAWLINGS (L.), 2275.
Rawls (John), 5993.
RAWNSLEY (Gary D.), 5600, 7999.
RAWNSLEY (Ming-Yeh T.), 7999.
RAY (Bharati), 6939.
RAY (J. D.), 1644.
RAY (Raka), 4637.
RAZA (A.), 1500.
RAZDORSKIJ (A. I.), 4986.
Razi ('Abu Bakr Muhammad ibn Zakariya), 3315.
RAZOUX (Pierre), 7967.
READER (C.), 1637.
REAGAN (Patrick D.), 5218.
Reagan (Ronald Wilson), 5193.
REALE (Mario), 6001.
REBELLATO (Dan), 6602.
REBENICH (Stefan), 757.
Rebérioux (Madeleine), 773, 3930, 4376.
REBILLARD (Éric), 2713.
REBUFFAT (R.), 2714.
RECCHIA (V.), 2928.
RECHT (Roland), 3638.
RECHTER (David), 5553.
RECKFORD (Kenneth J.), 2649.
REDEN (Alexander Sixtus von), 4087.
REDFORD (D. B.), 1707.
REDGATE (Anne Elizabeth), 1020.
Redi (Francesco), 6074.
REDI (Riccardo), 6603.
REDISSI (T.), 1765.
REDO (Ferenc), 243.
REDON (Odile), 3407.
REDONDI (Pietro), 6183.
REDONDO (Gonzalo), 5112.
REDOUANE (Najib), 4024.
REDUZZI MEROLA (Francesca), 2542.
RÉE (Jonathan), 791.
REEKEN (Dietmar von), 5338.
REES (G. Wyn), 7968.
REES (Tim), 3962.
REESE (Thomas), 6825.
REEVES (Marjorie), 640.
REEVES (Nicholas), 6604.
REGAN (John M.), 4683.
REGAN WILSON (Charles), 5308.
REGEN (F.), 2689.

REGENER (Susanne), 6504.
REGGI (G.), 2388.
REGIS (Louis), 5157.
REHBERG (Andreas), 3263, 3898.
REHREN (T.), 2773.
REID (Anthony), 8092.
REID (James D.), 3433.
REIF (Heinz), 6985.
REIF-SPIREK (Peter), 4435.
REILL (Peter Hans), 6180.
REILLY (John M.), 1438.
REIMANN (Heike), 268.
REIN (Raanan), 7295.
REINALTER (Helmut), 4459.
REINBOLD (Wolfgang), 4478.
REINER SEPP (Hans), 5890.
REINHARD (Wolfgang), 1021, 1040, 3993.
REINO (Joseph), 376.
REITAN (Ruth), 7969.
Reitel (François), 3952.
REITH (Reinhold), 6986.
REITMAIER (Th.), 1581.
REITMAYER (Morten), 6987.
REITZ (E. J.), 1472.
REIZBAUM (Marilyn), 6354.
Religieux de Saint-Denis, 774.
Rembrandt (Harmenszoon van Rijn), 406, 6482.
REMESAL RODRÍGUEZ (J.), 2572.
REMOND (René), 642, 5310.
Renan (Ernest), 643, 750.
RENARD (J.), 1828.
Renaud IV, duc de Juliers et de Gueldre, 3250.
RENAUT (Alain), 1071.
RENFREW (C.), 1478.
RENGGLI (F.), 4980.
RENNER (Jan), 4250.
Renner (Karl), 4073.
RENOLIET (Jean-Jacques), 7285.
RENOUARD (Alfred), 5812.
RENTON (David), 4561.
RENZ (Reginy), 4935.
RENZI (Lorenzo), 3178.
REPE (Božo), 689, 1000, 7989.
REPGEN (Konrad), 7418.
REPGEN (T.), 7198.
REPINA (Lorina P.), 644, 827, 862.
REQUATE (Jörg), 1258.
RESHETOV (Mikhail), 896.
RESTON (James), 3211.
RETAT (Pierre), 5843.
RÉTY (György), 7734.
REUCHLIN (Johannes), 5467.
REULECKE (Jürgen), 5704.
REULECKE (Jürgen), 957.
REUTER (Timothy), 3206.
Revelli (Nuto), 626.
REVILLA (Federico), 405.
REVILLA CALVO (V.), 2573.

INDEX OF NAMES

REVOL (Thierry), 3600.
REX (Richard), 5777.
REXROTH (Frank), 3408.
REYNAUD (Daniel), 6606.
REYNOLDS (Moira Davison), 6145.
REYNOLDS (Philip Lyndon), 3746.
REYNOLDS (Roger E.), 3779.
REYNOSO (Víctor), 4845.
Reza Pahlavi, Shah of Iran, 4661.
REZAR (Vlado), 794.
Rhee (Syngman), 8324.
RHEIDT (K.), 1600, 2257.
RHEIN (Stefan), 5467.
RHEINBERGER (Hans-Jörg), 6143.
RHEINHEIMER (Martin), 6988.
Rhetorica ad Alexandrum, 1953.
RHODES (Barbara J.), 129.
RHODES (Edward Joseph), 7283.
RHODES (P. J.), 1833.
RHODES (Richard), 6171.
RIALS (Stéphane), 4528.
RIBEIRO (Jorge), 7360.
RIBÉMONT (Bernard), 3435.
RICCARDI (A.), 2276.
RICCI (Aldo G.), 4773.
RICCI (S.), 6146.
RICCOBONO (Francesco), 7072.
RICCOMINI (E.), 4752.
RICE (M.), 1645.
RICE (Tony), 6147.
RICH (Paul B.), 7299.
RICH ABAD (Anna), 3288.
RICHARD (Francis), 8063.
RICHARD (J.), 3067.
RICHARD (Jean), 3243.
Richard I Lionheart, king of England, 3245.
Richard II, king of England, 3264, 3564.
RICHARDS (M.), 5113.
RICHARDS (Sarah), 6505.
RICHARDSON (Brian), 130.
RICHARDSON (David), 7313.
RICHARDSON (Henry S.), 5993.
RICHARDSON (Philip), 6658.
Richardson (Samuel), 6263.
RICHE (Pierre), 763, 3485, 3631.
Richelieu (Armand Jean du Plessis, duc de), 7397.
RICHEMOND (Stéphene), 6506.
RICHTER (H.-F.), 1770.
RICHTER (Karel), 1022.
RICHTER (Ludwig), 4391.
RICHTER (Michael), 3486.
RICHTER (Timm C.), 7795.
Ricoeur (Paul), 5886.
RICOLDUS DE MONTECRUCIS, 3857.
RICUPERATI (Giuseppe), 699, 864.
RIDDELL (Neil), 4562.
RIDGWAY (D.), 1646.

RIDOLFI (Maurizio), 4774.
RIDYARD (Susan J.), 3409, 3849.
RIEDEL (Nicolai), 6290.
RIEDL-DORN (Christa), 6143.
RIEDMAN (N.), 1581.
RIEHL (S.), 1537.
Riemenschneider (Tilman), 3680.
RIEMER (U.), 2929.
RIES (Julien), 1339.
RIESCO TERRERO (Angel), 16.
RIGAUDIÈRE (Albert), 1160.
RIGGSBY (A. M.), 2513.
RIGO (A.), 3068.
RIGONI (Mario Andrea), 6337.
RIHLL (T. E.), 2171.
RIHUETE (C.), 1528.
RIHUETE HERRADA (C.), 1521.
RIIS (Carsten), 648.
RILEY (J. P.), 7468.
RILEY (Patrick), 6002.
RILEY-SMITH (Jonathan), 3825.
Rilke (Rainer Maria), 6356.
RILL (Bernd), 4582.
RIMBAU (Esteve), 6607.
RINALDI (Rinaldo), 1082.
RINDERT (Jona), 5951.
RINEHART (Alice Duffy), 5798.
RINEHART (Michael), 1271.
RINGMAR (Richard), 6717.
RINKLAKE (Hubert), 5832.
RIOUX (Jean-Pierre), 969.
Ripa (Cesare), 377.
RIPOLL (François), 2650.
RIPOLL LÓPEZ (S.), 1504.
RIPOLL PERELLÓ (E.), 1504.
RISCH (R.), 1528.
RITA-FERREIRA (António), 8354.
RITTER (Gerhard A.), 7286.
Ritter (Gerhard), 775.
RIU (X.), 2125.
RIVA (Valerio), 4775.
Riva Palacio (Mariano), 4846.
RIVELLI (Marco Aurelio), 5426.
RIVERA GARCÍA (Antonio), 5441.
RIVERO (Manuel), 358.
RIVES (J. B.), 2715.
RIVES (J. R.), 2381.
RIVET (Daniel), 4857.
RIX (Alan), 7971.
RIZA'I (Insiyah Shaykh), 4655.
RIZZI (Andrea), 3176.
RIZZO (F.), 5924.
RIZZO (Francesco Paolo), 2873.
RIZZO (Giorgio), 2774.
RIZZO NERVO (Francesca), 3584.
RJABOVA (Tat'jana B.), 3410.
ROBB (George), 6901.
Roberto da Sanseverino, 3168.
Roberto d'Altavilla 'Il Guiscardo', duca di Puglia, di Calabria e di Sicilia, 3392.

Roberto di Roberto Pepi, 5659.
ROBERTS (David D.), 4776.
ROBERTS (Geoffrey), 7972.
ROBERTS (J. T.), 1831.
Roberts (Josephine A.), 6230.
ROBERTS (Philip), 6608.
ROBERTS (Stephen), 4533.
ROBERTSHAW (Alan), 3592.
ROBERTSON (K. G.), 7800.
ROBERTSON (Karen), 6955.
Robespierre (Maximilen-François-Isidore de), 532, 4377.
ROBIC (Marie-Claire), 360.
ROBIC-DE BAECQUE (Sylvie), 6275.
ROBIN (L.), 1944.
ROBINS (G.), 1647.
ROBINSON (Catherine A.), 8093.
ROBINSON (Daniel J.), 4166.
Robinson (M.), 1818.
ROBINSON (Ronald), 7318.
ROCCHETTI (L.), 1848.
ROCCO (R.), 7196.
ROCHAT (Giorgio), 7796.
ROCHE (Daniel), 5673, 5749.
ROCHETTE (B.), 299.
Rockwell (George Lincoln), 5219.
RÖDDER (Andreas), 4481, 7106.
RODÉN (Marie-Louise), 3639.
RODERICUS XIMENIUS DE RADA, 3180.
RODGES (Clifford J.), 3268.
Rodin (Auguste), 6451.
RODOTÀ (Carla), 7098.
RODRIGUES (Manuel Augusto), 3138.
RODRIGUES COELHO (Maria Amélia), 8343.
RODRIGUEZ GONZALEZ (Agustín Ramón), 7529.
RODRIGUEZ RANZ (José Antonio), 5114.
ROECK (Bernd), 1296, 6823.
ROELCKE (Thorsten), 291.
RŒSDAHL (Else), 3447.
ROESLER (Jörg), 3996.
ROGAN (E.), 1144.
ROGAN (Eugene L.), 4806.
ROGARI (Sandro), 6764.
Rogers (James Harvey), 8188.
ROGGERO (Marina), 5814.
ROGINSKIJ (A. B.), 5023.
ROHKRÄMER (Thomas), 5689.
ROHRMOSER (Günter), 4482.
ROHRSCHNEIDER (Michael), 7400.
ROISMAN (H. M.), 2126.
ROJAS RODRÍGUEZ-MALO (J. M.), 1515.
Rojas y Spinola (Christoph), 5311.
Rolin (Nicolas), 3675.
ROLLER (L. E.), 1601.
RÖLLIG (W.), 1728, 1756.

ROLLINGER (R.), 1805.
ROLLO GONCALVES (José), 4136.
ROMAGNANI (Gian Paolo), 649.
ROMAN (Andreia), 4981.
ROMAN (Eric), 4614.
ROMAN (Myriam), 6355.
ROMANELLI (Raffaele), 7099.
ROMANELLO (Paola R.), 3899.
ROMANO (Andrea), 5020.
ROMANO (Antonella), 6148.
ROMANO (C. C.), 2450.
ROMANO (R.), 3069.
ROMANO (Ruggiero), 650.
Romanus I Lecapenus, Byzantine emperor, 3057.
Romeo (Rosario), 776.
RÖMER (F.), 788.
ROMERO SALVADÓ (Francisco J.), 5115.
ROMM (J.), 1909.
ROMMEL (Bettina), 2574.
Rommel (Erwin), 7769.
RÖMPP (Georg), 6003.
ROMSICS (Ignác), 4615.
ROMUALDI (A.), 2251.
RONCAGLIA (Alessandro), 6686.
RONCALLI (Marco), 711.
RONCHEY (Silvia), 691.
ROOSENS (Laurent), 6489.
Roosevelt (Franklin Delano), 5194.
ROPER (G. J.), 1323.
RÖPKE (Ian Martin), 1023.
ROQUE (M. A.), 6965.
ROQUINCOURT (Thierry), 7452.
Rörig (Fritz), 684.
ROSA (Mario), 4777, 5312.
ROSADA-GRANADOS (Héctor Roberto), 4590.
ROSANDER (Lars), 5130.
ROSAS (Fernando), 4965.
ROSE (Clifford), 6158.
ROSE (Inbal), 7610.
ROSE (Lynn E.), 163.
ROSE (Peter), 4684.
ROSEN (Wolfgang), 1183.
ROSENBECK (Bente), 1197.
Rosenberg (Arthur), 777.
ROSENBERGER (V.), 2068.
ROSENDORFER (Herbert), 1024.
RÖSENER (W.), 6989.
ROSENFELD (Gavriel D.), 651.
ROSENFELD (Louis), 6149.
ROSENFIELD (B.-Z.), 1771.
ROSENSTEIN (Nathan), 1045.
ROSENTAL (Paul-André), 6990.
ROSENTHAL (Jean-Laurent), 6645.
ROSENTHAL (Michael), 6480.
ROSENTHAL (Sandra B.), 5915.
ROSENWEIN (Barbara H.), 3411.
ROSHCHIN (Sergej K.), 4851.
ROSHWALD (Aviel), 5614.

ROSIVACH (V. J.), 2069.
RÖSKAU-RYDEL (Isabel), 3944.
ROSKIES (David G.), 652.
RÖSLER (Michael), 900.
Rosmini Serbati (Antonio), 5345, 5401, 5929, 6004.
ROSOVSKY (Murray), 3292.
ROSS (Robert), 7361.
ROSS CLUNIES (Margaret), 3325.
ROSSEBASTIANO (Alda), 3168.
Rosselli (Carlo), 1101, 4770, 4787.
Rossetti (Dante Gabriele), 6472.
ROSSETTI (Lucia), 5720.
ROSSI (Aldo), 3602.
ROSSI (C.), 1648.
ROSSI (Elena), 2371.
ROSSI (Leena-Maija), 1297.
ROSSI (Paolo), 6005.
ROSSI (Pietro), 5989.
Rossi (Salomone), 6561.
ROSSIGNOLI (B.), 1919.
ROSSITER (Margaret W.), 6052.
ROSSO (Claudio), 4767.
ROSTISLAVLEVA (Natal'ja V.), 4483.
Rostovtzeff (Mikhail I.), 778.
ROSTWOROWSKI (Stanisław Jan), 7869.
ROTARIU (Traian), 6991.
ROTBERG (Robert I.), 5121.
ROTERMUND (Hartmut O.), 8039.
ROTH (Christoph), 3826.
ROTH (H.), 2990.
ROTH (Hans-Jörg), 2514.
ROTH (J. P.), 2451.
ROTHSCHILD (Jean-Pierre), 3184.
ROTHWELL (Kenneth S.), 6609.
ROTILI (Marcello), 2812.
ROTONDI SECCHI TARUGI (Luisa), 6225.
ROTT (Jean), 5531.
Rotteck (Karl von), 4483.
ROUCHON (Olivier), 198.
ROUET (Gilles), 7181.
ROUGE (Matthieu), 3747.
ROUILLARDThierry), 7456.
ROUSSEAU (Frédéric), 7612.
ROUSSEAU (George S.), 5750.
Rousseau (Jean-Jacques), 1072, 5342, 5920, 6006, 6032, 6280.
ROUSSEAUX (Xavier), 7180.
ROUSSET (Bernard), 6007.
ROUSSO (Henry), 4000.
ROVIRA LLORENS (S.), 1473, 1515, 1530.
ROWE (Peter A.), 3906.
ROWLANDS (Kenneth), 3827.
ROWLANDSON (J.), 1649.
ROWLEY (David G.), 5691.
ROY (J.), 2024.
ROY (Tirthankar), 6718.

ROYLE (Trevor), 7530.
ROYMANS (Nico), 3494.
ROYO (Manuel), 2775.
ROZENTAL' (Isaak S.),, 7544.
ROZES (Antoine), 7973.
ROZMAN (Franc), 689, 1000.
Rubens (Pieter Paul), 6485.
RUBIN (Barry M.), 4900.
RUBIN (Miri), 3289.
RUBIN (P. Lee), 489.
RUBIN (Uri), 3313.
RUBIN LEE (Patricia), 3670.
RUBINOS PÉREZ (A.), 1505.
RUBIO (G.), 1748.
RUBLACK (Ulinka), 7182.
RÜCK (Peter), 14.
RUDHARDT (J.), 2203.
RUDISCHHAUSER (Sabine), 7183.
RUDNITSKAJA (Evgenija L.), 5692.
RUDOLPH (Conrad), 3671.
RÜFFER (Jens), 3828.
RUFFIN (Margit), 5885.
RUFIN (Jean C.), 1180.
RUGAFIORI (Paride), 6719.
Ruggeri (Michele), 5448.
RUGGIERO (John), 4563.
RUGGIERO (R.), 1910.
RUGGLES (C.), 1474.
RÜHRDANZ (Karin), 3314.
Ruini (Meuccio), 7105.
RUIZ (Rosaura), 6062.
RUIZ MORENO (Isidoro J.), 4060.
RUIZ ORTEGA (Manuel), 5815.
RUIZ TABOADA (A.), 1521.
RUMI (Giorgio), 5353, 6008.
RUMPLER (Helmut), 4083.
RUMSCHEID (F.), 1602, 2070.
RUNIA (D. T.), 2930.
RUPPEL (Karl August), 5512.
Rürup (Reinhard), 4447.
RUS RUFINO (Salvador), 5107.
RUSCONI (Gian Enrico), 7100, 7288.
RUSCONI (Roberto), 3900.
RÜSEN (Jörn), 834, 879.
RUSHTON FAIRCLOUGH (H.), 2389.
Ruskin (John), 5693, 6130, 6177.
Russel (Bertrand), 5979.
RUSSEL (Colin Archibald), 6057.
RUSSELL (Gillian), 1253.
RUSSELL (J. M.), 1708.
RUSSELL (J.), 1589.
Russell (Odo), 7535.
RUSSELL BROWN (John), 6611.
RUSSO (Maurizio), 7478.
RUSSO (Vito), 6612.
RUSTICO (Letizia), 2776.
RUSTUM SHEHADEH (Lamia), 4812.
RUSU (Adrian Andrei), 3672.
RUSU (Dorina N.), 5751.
Rutilius Namatianus, 2337.

Rutilius Rufus (P.), 2395.
RUTKOFF (Peter M.), 5696.
RUTLEDGE (Steven H.), 2651.
RUTT (Richard), 1017.
RUZÉ (F.), 1815.
RUZICKA (S.), 2003.
RYAN (David), 7289.
RYAN (F. X.), 2652.
RYAN (Frank), 2515.
RYAN (Judith), 6356.
RYAN (T.), 2340.
RYCHLÍK (Jan), 7736.
RYDEL (Christine A.), 1440.
RYSTEDT (E.), 1558.
RYTLEWSKI (Ralf), 6822.
RZHESHEVSKIJ (O. A.), 7681.

S

SAARELA (T.), 4290.
SAAVEDRA-GUERRERO (M. D.), 2452.
SABA (Guido), 6276.
SABAGH (Georges), 3312.
SABATIER (Gérard), 4378.
SABATO (Hilda), 3940.
SABBAH (Guy), 2335.
SABBATUCCI (Giovanni), 4711, 4784.
SABLAYROLLES (R.), 2453.
SABOURAUD (Frédéric), 6559.
SABROW (Martin), 4429, 4484, 4511.
SABUNCUOĞLU (Şerafeddin), 6150.
SACCHI (Paolo), 636.
SACKER (Richard), 7974.
SACKUR (Amanda), 4331.
SADMON (Zeev W.), 865.
SAENGER (Paul), 98.
SÄFLUND (G.), 2252.
SAFRAN (J. M.), 1603.
SAGE (Lorna), 1422.
SAGER (Fritz), 6720.
SAGONA (A.), 1559.
SAGONA (C.), 1772.
ŞAHIN (M.), 1604.
SAHLINS (Peter), 4323.
SAIKKU (Mikko), 1157.
SAILER (Rita), 7184.
Saint-Evrémond (Charles de Marguetel de Saint-Denis), 806.
Saint-Simon (Claude-Henry de Rouvroy comte de), 5640.
SAJOUS D'ORIA (Michèle), 6550.
SAKAGUCHI (Kokichi), 3412.
SAKAMAKI (Kiyoshi), 6846.
SAKATA (Toshio), 6846.
SAKSENA (Jyotsna), 7975.
SAKURAI (Yumio), 8094.
Saladin, Sultan of Egypt and Syria, 3311.

SALAMAN (C.), 1896.
SALAMITO (Jean-Marie), 2481, 2931.
SALAMON (M.), 2980.
Salazar (António de Oliveira), 4963, 7715.
SALAZAR VERGARA (Gabriel), 4171, 4174.
SALAZAR-PÖPPEL (Amalia), 1416.
SALEM (Elsheikh Mahmoud), 3103.
SALEM (Jean), 5897.
SALEMINK (Oscar), 894.
SALETNICH (Gastone), 3789.
SALGON (Jean-Michel), 4034.
SALICRU I LLUCH (Roser), 3153.
SALIMBENE DE ADAM, 3181.
SALLER (Christian), 924.
Sallustius Crispus (C.), 2370, 2851.
SALMAN (Jeroen), 5870.
SALMERI (Giovanni), 653.
SALMINEN (Esko), 5871.
SALMON (Pierre), 2575.
SALOMON (Frank), 944.
SALRACH I MARÉS (Josep M.), 3146.
SALU (Luc), 6489.
SALVADEI (L.), 1526.
SALVADORI (Massimo), 4778.
SALVADORI (Roberto G.), 5551.
SALVATICI (Silvia), 6776.
SALVATORE (Nick), 7052.
SALVEMINI (Raffaella), 7469.
SALVESTRINI (Francesco), 3261.
SALVIAT (F.), 2004.
SALVIATI (Mariuccia), 4734.
SALVINI (M.), 1577.
SAMARASINGHE (S. W. R. de A.), 5123, 8083.
SAMIR (K.), 2127.
SAMOVER (Nalal'ja V.), 5012.
SAMSON (Jane), 7315.
SAN (Roberto), 5760.
SANAHUJA (M. E.), 1528.
SANCHEZ (Francisco J.), 5605.
SANCHEZ ANDRES (Agustín), 7532.
SANCHEZ DE LA TORRE (Á.), 1135.
SÁNCHEZ DOMINGO (Rafael), 199.
SÁNCHEZ FUERTES (Cayetano), 5444.
SANCHEZ GARCIA (Jesús Angel), 6437.
SÁNCHEZ MARCO (A.), 1506.
SANCHEZ MARTINEZ (Manuel), 3378.
SANCHEZ ORTIZ DE LANDALUCE (M.), 2199.
SÁNCHEZ RECIO (Glicerio), 5110.
SANCHEZ RON (José Manuel), 6151.
SANCHEZ SANCHEZ (Manuel Ambrosio), 3780.

SANCHEZ-H (José), 6613.
SÁNCHEZ-OSTIZ (A.), 2331.
Sancho VI, king of Navarre, 3139.
SANDER (Peter), 4485.
SANDERS (Andrew), 6357.
SANDERS (Elizabeth), 7054.
SANDERS (Eve Rachele), 6614.
SANDERS (Thomas), 579.
SANDERSON (Michael), 5816.
SANDFORD (John), 6539.
SANDL (Marcus), 6687.
SANDRI (Lucia), 6123.
SANDRON (Dany), 3637.
SANDU (Traian), 7613.
SANDY (G. N.), 2653.
SANG (Bing), 8190.
SANG (Bing), 8191.
SANG (Bing), 8192.
SANG (Bing), 8193.
SANGALLI (Maurizio), 4779.
SANGOÏ (Jean-Claude), 288.
SANIN (Gennadij A.), 7392.
SANJIAN, (Avedis Krikor), 75.
SANNA (D.), 2860.
SANNEH (Lamin), 8355.
Sansone (Mario), 6201.
SANSTERRE (Jean-Marie), 3459.
SANTALUCIA (B.), 2454.
SANTAMAITA (Saverio), 5817.
SANTARELLI (Enzo), 4701.
SANTI (Giancarlo), 7479.
SANTINA (Mary Arlene), 3603.
SANTINI (Carlo), 2648.
SANTINI (P.), 2654.
SANTINI (Stefano), 6408.
SANTOMASSIMO (Gianpasquale), 655.
SANTORO (Stefano), 656.
SANTOSUOSSO COLK (Alma), 3685.
Sanzio (Raffaello) v. Raffaello Sanzio.
SAPIN (Christian), 3667.
SAPIRO (Gisèle), 6358.
Sappho, 1954, 2142.
SARACENO (Pietro), 4780.
SARADI (Heleni G.), 27.
SARAY (Mehmet), 7290.
SARGENT-BAUR NELSON (Barbara), 3513.
Sargon II, king of Assyria, 1669, 1679, 1707.
SARKANIS (Alberts), 7206.
SARMANT (Thierry), 420.
SARNELLI (Mauro), 6234.
SARNOWSKY (Jürgen), 3812.
Sarpi (Paolo), 779, 5377, 5995.
SARRACINO (Vincenzo), 5772.
SARRAZIN-CANI (V.), 164.
SARTI (Raffaella), 6992.
Sartre (Jean-Paul), 5949.

SASHI (Akihiro), 4547.
SASSATELLI (G.), 2303.
SASSMANNSHAUSEN (L.), 1709.
SASSO (Gennaro), 707, 712, 756.
SASSOON (Rosemary), 17.
ŠATEJ (Barbara), 5063.
SATER (William F.), 4179.
Satie (Erik), 6589.
SATO (Fumitoshi), 8194.
SATO (Kimihiko), 8195.
SATO (Makoto), 8300.
SATO (Makoto), 8303.
SATO (Tsugitaka), 8057.
SATO (Tsugitaka), 8065.
SATOSHI (Nakano), 7667.
SATTER (Beryl), 5313.
SAUER (Thomas), 5513.
SAUER (V.), 2716.
SAUERTEIG (Lutz), 6152.
SAUNDERS (Alison), 204.
SAUNIER (Annie), 3413.
SAUNIER (Pierre-Yves), 361.
SAUNT (Claudio), 8380.
SAUPINGuy), 5315.
SAUR (Klaus G.), 84.
SAURON (G.), 2717.
SAUTEL (Jacques-Hubert), 2348.
SAUTEL (Jacques-Hubert), 715.
SAUVANET (P.), 2172.
SAVAGE (Barbara Dianne), 6615.
SAVARD (Pierre), 5675.
SAVICKÝ (Ivan), 3997.
SAVIDAN (Patrick), 1071.
Savigny (Friedrich Karl von), 7066.
SAVIO (Giulio), 289.
Savonarola (Girolamo), 3901, 5322, 5397, 5601.
SAVORELLI (Alessandro), 227.
SAVUNEN (L.), 2541.
SAWA (Hirokatsu), 8304.
SAWYER (John F. A.), 2874.
Saxo Grammaticus, 780.
SAYAN (Yüksel), 3673.
SAYERS (Jane E.), 3142.
SAYIGH (Yazid Yusuf), 4901.
SBARBERI (Franco), 1101.
SCAGLIONE GUCCIONE (Rosa), 4702.
SCALABRIN (Carlo), 1390.
SCALERA MAC LINTOCK (G.), 1923.
SCALIA (G.), 3181.
SCALIGER (JulesCésar), 5260.
SCALLEN (C. B.), 406.
SCALVINI (Barbara), 796.
SCANLAN (James Patrick), 6359.
SCARAFFIA (Giuseppe), 6360.
SCARAMELLA (Pierroberto), 5427.
SCARGILL (David Ian), 362.
SCARMONCINI (Franco), 3125.

SCARROCCHIA (Sandro), 6438.
SCARZANELLA (Eugenia), 4061.
SCATTERGOOD (V. J.), 3608.
SCERBINSKIS (Valters), 5872.
SCHACHTER (A.), 2071.
SCHAD (Lothar), 200.
SCHAEBLER (Birgit), 657.
SCHAEFER (Hans-Dieter), 6064.
SCHAEFER (Ursula), 3621.
SCHAER (Frank), 3169.
SCHÄFER (Herwig), 7080.
SCHAFER (Jessica), 4861.
SCHÄFER (Th.), 2777.
SCHAFFER (Simon), 6155.
Schalk (Ellery), 201.
SCHALLERT (Regine), 6481.
SCHAMA (Simon), 6482.
SCHAMBACH (Karin), 6854.
SCHANDEVYL (Eva), 4102.
SCHARFF (Thomas), 3829.
SCHARFF SMITH (Peter), 7765.
SCHAUB (Jean-Frédéric), 6993.
SCHECK (Raffael), 5146.
SCHEFFLER (Wolfgang), 4388.
SCHEIBELREITER (Georg), 3212.
SCHEID (J.), 2576.
SCHEID (John), 2718.
SCHEIDEGGER (Gabriele), 5456.
SCHEIDEL (W.), 2577.
SCHEIDEL (Walter), 658.
SCHEIL (Stefan), 4486, 7668.
Scheler (Max), 5985.
Schelling (Friedrich Wilhelm Joseph), 5940, 5946, 5971, 6003, 6019.
SCHEMANN (M.), 1605.
SCHENK (Peter), 2655.
SCHENKEL (Elmar), 6198.
SCHERBERG (B.), 2656.
SCHERPE (Klaus R.), 1431.
SCHER-ZEMBITSKA (Lydia), 4950.
SCHETTER (Conrad J.), 4009.
SCHEUERMAN (William E.), 6009.
SCHIAPPA (E.), 2128.
SCHIAVONE (Aldo), 1093.
SCHIEDT (Hans-Ulrich), 6994.
SCHIEFFER (Rudolf), 637.
SCHIERA (Pierangelo), 1102, 1136.
SCHIESARO (Alessandro), 2657.
SCHILDT (Axel), 4487, 5694.
Schiller (Iohann Christoph Friedrich von), 5574.
SCHILLING (Heinz), 1025, 7124.
SCHILLING (Lothar), 7138.
SCHINDLER (Peter), 4410.
SCHIPPMAN (K.), 1801.
SCHIRMER (Uwe), 745.
SCHIRMER (W.), 1606.
SCHISTO (E.), 5322.
SCHJØDT (Jens Peter), 1376.
SCHLAPBACH (K.), 2817, 2841.

Schleicher (Kurt von), 4475.
SCHLEIER (Hans), 684.
Schlesinger (Arthur M.), 781.
SCHLESINGER (Stephen), 7977.
Schliemann (Heinrich), 573, 1835, 1846.
SCHLUCHTER (Wolfgang), 802.
SCHLUMBOHM (Jürgen), 6180.
SCHLUSEMANN (Rita), 78.
SCHMÄDEKE (Jürgen), 4488.
SCHMALTZ (Tad M.), 6010.
SCHMALZRIEDT (E.), 1389.
SCHMELZ (Bernd), 5563.
SCHMID (Andre), 8047.
SCHMID (Gerhard), 4084.
SCHMID (Stephan G.), 2778.
SCHMIDLIN (Antonia), 5147.
SCHMIDT (D.), 1872.
SCHMIDT (E. A.), 2204.
SCHMIDT (Georg), 4489, 7419.
SCHMIDT (Hans-Joachim), 3781.
Schmidt (Helmut), 7942.
SCHMIDT (K.), 1607.
SCHMIDT (Karl J.), 8095.
SCHMIDT (S. G.), 2072.
SCHMIDT (Victor M.), 3657.
SCHMIDT THOMAS (S.), 2129.
SCHMIDT-BIGGEMAN (Wilhelm), 7191.
SCHMIDT-GLINTZER (Helwig), 8196.
SCHMIDT-NOWARA (Christopher Ebert), 3925.
SCHMIEDL (Joachim), 5314.
Schmitt (Carl), 5907, 5935, 5998, 6009, 7078.
SCHMITT (H. H.), 1855.
SCHMITT (Hanno), 5780.
SCHMITT (Jean Claude), 997, 3459.
SCHMITT (R.), 1806.
SCHMITZ (Barbara), 3314.
SCHMITZ (David F.), 7291.
SCHMITZ (Th. A.), 1895.
SCHMITZ (W.), 2073.
SCHMITZ (Wolfgang), 3679.
Schmoller (Gustav von), 782.
SCHMUGGE (Ludwig), 3763.
SCHNAUBELT (Joseph C.), 376.
SCHNEEMELCHER (Wilhelm), 2856.
SCHNEER (Jonathan), 6855.
SCHNEIDER (Bernd), 3597.
SCHNEIDER (G.), 1765.
SCHNEIDER (Georg), 109.
SCHNEIDER (H.), 1827.
SCHNEIDER (J.), 3070.
SCHNEIDER (Karin), 18.
SCHNEIDER (Michael C.), 6786.
SCHNEIDER (Michael), 7055.
SCHNEIDER (Norbert), 1298.
SCHNEIDER (Peter K.), 5888.
SCHNEIDER (Rolf), 7978.

SCHNEIDER (Thomas F.), 1241.
SCHNEIDER (Ulrich Johannes), 6011.
SCHNEIDER (W. J.), 2253.
SCHNEIDER (W.), 2455.
SCHNEIDER-SCHMUGGE (Hildegard), 3763.
SCHNEIROV (Richard), 7052.
SCHNETTGER (Matthias), 7137.
SCHNURBEIN (S. von), 1765.
SCHOEP (I.), 1849.
Schoepper (Jacob), 5506.
SCHOFIELD (M.), 2074.
Scholem (Gershom), 783, 1387.
SCHOLL (Sabine), 6235.
SCHÖLLGEN (Gregor), 7979.
SCHÖLLKOPF (Wolfgang), 5514.
SCHOLTYSECK (Joachim), 4490.
SCHOLZ (Sebastian), 3124.
SCHÖNBERGER (O.), 1913.
SCHÖNEGG (Beat), 2690.
SCHÖNER (Jorg), 6627.
SCHÖNERT-GEIß (Edith), 236.
SCHÖNHOVEN (Klaus), 4491.
Schopenhauer (Arthur), 1398, 5956, 6012.
SCHORN-SCHÜTTE (Luise), 701.
SCHÖTTLER (Peter), 684, 698.
SCHOUTEN (M. J. B.), 4645, 7814.
SCHRAFSTETTER (Susanna), 7980.
SCHRAM (Stuart R.), 8100.
SCHRAMM (Thomasz), 7614.
SCHREINER (P.), 2976, 3071.
SCHREURS (Eugeen), 83.
SCHRIJVERS (P. H.), 2691.
SCHRÖDER (Meinhard), 7067.
SCHRÖDER (Rainer), 7071.
SCHRÖDER (S.), 2130.
SCHROEDER (David), 6616.
SCHROEDER (Jean), 30.
SCHROEDER (William R.), 1399.
SCHRÖTER (Bernd), 5227.
SCHUBERT (Dietrich), 6361.
SCHUBERT (Peter), 2310.
SCHUBERT (Werner), 4394.
SCHUCK (G.), 659.
SCHUCK (Gerhard), 7138.
SCHUCKMAN (Christiaan), 125.
SCHULER (Stefan), 3487.
SCHULIN (Ernst), 834.
SCHÜLLER (Karin), 7396.
SCHULZ (Evelyn), 833.
SCHULZ (Günther), 5844.
SCHULZ (Knut), 1169.
SCHULZ (R.), 2005.
SCHULZ (Rudolf), 3610.
Schulz (Thilo), 7248.
SCHULZE (Christian), 2342.
SCHULZE (Max S.), 6670.
SCHULZE (Stefan), 6362.
SCHULZE (Winfried), 539, 660.

SCHUMATE (N.), 2658.
Schumpeter (Josef Alois), 1084.
Schur (Issai), 6060.
SCHUR (Nathan), 7470.
SCHÜRER (Ernst), 6311.
SCHUSTER (Armin), 661.
SCHUSTER (Peter), 662.
SCHUTTE (G. J.), 4872.
SCHUTTE JACOBSON (Anne), 3423.
SCHÜTTE-MAISCHATZ (A.), 1587.
Schütz Zell (Katharina), 5498.
SCHUYLER (Tami), 6120.
SCHVOERER (M.), 2218.
SCHWABE (Ute), 7981.
SCHWAIGER (Georg), 5354.
SCHWALL-HOUMMADY (Christine), 3674.
SCHWANDNER (E. L.), 2257.
SCHWARTZ (Manuela), 6617.
SCHWARTZ (Michael), 6917, 7880.
SCHWARTZ (Stuart B.), 944.
SCHWARZ (Angela), 5695.
SCHWARZ (Hans-Peter), 3922, 4455, 7802, 7982.
SCHWARZ (Leonard), 6995.
SCHWARZENBACH (Alexis), 249.
SCHWARZER (H.), 2254.
SCHWARZER (Oskar), 6659.
SCHWEGMAN (Marjan), 5819.
SCHWEIZER (Katja), 4492.
SCHWEMER (D.), 1773.
SCHWERIN (Franz), 7798.
Sciascia (Leonardo), 6187.
SCIROCCO (Alfonso), 7101.
SCIUMÈ (Alberto), 7185.
SCIUTI RUSSI (Vittorio), 4781.
SCOCOZZA (Benito), 1026.
SCODEL (R.), 2131.
SCORRANO (R.), 7196.
SCOTT (L. V.), 7983.
SCOTT (William B.), 5696.
SCOTT AMOS (N.), 5510.
SCOTT-CHILDRESS (Reynolds J.), 5688.
SCOTTI DOUGLAS (Vittorio), 7460.
SCOTTO DI LUZIO (Adolfo), 5820.
SCURTU (Ioan), 4982, 7545.
SEAGER (R.), 2456.
SEBAÏ (M.), 2719.
SEBASTIAN (Anton), 1193, 1259.
SEBOK (Marcell), 3470.
SECHI (Salvatore), 4782.
SEDERGREN (Jari), 6618.
SEDLIAKOVÁ (Alžbeta), *XIV*, *XVIII*, 5032.
SEDOV (Valentin V.), 3647.
SEE (Klaus von), 3213.
Seeley (J. S), 784.
SEELIGER-ZEISS (Anneliese), 3124.
SEEWANN (Gerhard), 7624.
SEGERS (Rien T.), 5654.

SEGISSEMENT (Marie-José Pernin), 6012.
SEGUENNY (André), 5531.
SEIBERT (Gerhard), 5028.
SEIBERT (H.), 3232.
SEIBT (Ferdinand), 327.
SEIDEL MENCHI (Silvana), 3423.
SEIDL (U.), 1574, 1710.
SEIFERT (Siegfried), 1417.
SEILER (H. H.), 2488.
SEILER (R. M.), 131.
SEIRING (Claudia), 1137.
SELBMANN (Rolf), 6313.
Sella (Quintino), 4698.
SELLERT (W.), 7136.
SELLES (Narcís), 6402.
SELLEVOLD (Berit J.), 3326.
SELLIER (Philippe), 6277.
SELOVUORI (Jorma), 4291.
SELWOOD (Dominic), 3830.
SEMENIUC (Maria), 6991.
SENDLER (Bernhard), 4493.
Seneca (L. Annaeus), 2371, 2372, 2409, 2596, 2639, 2642, 2654, 2657, 2680, 2690.
SENÉN GONZÁLEZ (Santiago), 4062.
SENFT (Theresa M.), 6120.
SENJAVSKAJA (Elena S.), 866.
Sennacherib, king of Assyria, 1674.
SENNER (Martin), 7501.
SENNEWALD (Adolf), 132.
SEPPÄNEN (Maaria), 6856.
SEPPILLI (T.), 2205.
Sereni (Emilio), 785.
SERGEEV (Evgenij Ju.), 7533.
Sergius, Sanctus, 2953.
SERMAIN (Jean-Paul), 6278.
SERMONETA (Hillel M.), 46.
SERNA (Virginie), 364.
SERNETT (Milton C), 5263.
SERRA (Enrico), 5358.
SERRA (G.), 2132.
Serra (Renato), 707.
SERRAI (Alfredo), 133.
SERRANO (Carlos), 884, 3961.
SERROY (Jean), 1434.
SERVER (Lee), 6619.
SERVETTI (Lorenza), 413.
Servius, 1912.
ŞEŞEN (Ramazan), 6098.
Sesostris, king of Egypt, 1627.
SESSIONS (Scott), 8378.
SETÄLÄ (P.), 2541.
SETEL (Philip W.), 6092.
SETH (Sanjay), 4639.
Sethos II, king of Egypt, 1621.
SETSUHO (Ikehata), 7667.
SETTIA (Aldo A.), 3224, 3265.
SEUFERT (Günter), 5552.

SEVCENKO PATTERSON (Nancy), 3072, 3663.
SEVERJUKHIN (Dmitrij Ja.), 6396.
SEVERYNS (Benoît), 6154.
SEVIERI (R.), 1937.
SEVILLANO CALERO (Francisco), 5088.
SEVIN (V.), 1711.
SEYFARTH (Wolfgang), 2334.
SEYS (Pascale), 789.
SEZEN (Seriye), 6660.
SEZER (Ayten), 5822.
SFIKAS (T. D.), 4588.
SGARD (Jean), 126.
SHABANI SAMGHABADI (R.), 8055.
SHAFER (Elizabeth), 6532.
SHAGAN (Ethan H.), 4565.
SHAH (Sayed Wiqar Ali), 8096.
Shakespeare (William), 5307, 6218, 6222, 6239, 6570, 6609, 6611, 6622.
SHALOM (Zakai), 7984.
SHAMIR (Ronen), 4902.
SHAPIRO (Barbara J.), 5698.
SHAPIRO (Frank), 8350.
SHARMA (Arvind), 1347.
SHARP (Alan), 7216.
SHARP (M.), 1650.
SHATZMILLER (Joseph), 3348.
SHAUGHNESSY (Edward L.), 8107.
SHAVER (Robert), 5699.
Shaw (Bernard), 6328.
SHAW (David Gary), 863, 867.
SHAW (I.), 1651.
SHAYESTEH FAR (Mahnaz), 76.
SHEAHAN (John), 6661.
SHEARER (West), 6394.
SHEETS-PYENSON (Susan), 5746.
SHEINGORN (Pamela), 3834.
SHELL (Alison), 6279.
SHELLARD (Dominic), 6620.
SHEN (Peijian), 7738.
Shen (Wansan), 8124.
SHEN (Zhihua), 8197.
SHENCK (David H. J.), 90.
Sheng (Xuanhuai), 8101, 8138.
SHENHAV (E.), 1754.
SHENNAN (S.), 1507.
SHEPARD (J.), 3073.
SHEPARD (Laurie), 3489.
SHEPHERD (Elizabet J.), 2304.
SHEPHERD (Naomi), 4903.
SHERIDAN (Geraldine), 5643.
SHERMAN (Daniel J.), 663.
SHI (Yuanhua), 8102.
SHIBAEV (M. A.), 20.
SHIELDS (C.), 2173.
SHIELDS KOLLMANN (Nancy), 5022.
SHIGECHIKA (Keiju), 8198.
SHIMADA (Makoto), 2457.

SHIMIZU (Akitoshoi), 8389.
SHIMIZU (Hiroshi), 6662.
SHINKAWA (Tokio), 8305.
SHINZO (Hayase), 7667.
SHIRAKAWABE (Tatuo), 8290.
SHIRAKIZAWA (Asahiko), 6754.
SHIRER (William Lawrence), 6513.
SHISHKIN (Valerij A.), 5007.
SHITOMI (Yuzo), 8066.
SHIVELY (Donald H.), 8275.
SHKAROVSKIJ (Mikhail V.), 5457.
SHLAIM (Avi), 7984, 7985.
SHOGIMEN (Takashi), 3748.
SHOJI (Shunsaku), 6777.
SHOJU (Keitaro)., 2989.
SHORE (Zachary), 7669.
SHOUP (Paul S.), 7859.
SHUTTLEWORTH KRAUS (Christina), 2352, 2373.
Siber (Heinrich), 757.
SIBGUET (Ouelguelguet), 7986.
Sibley (Frank), 6013.
SICARD (Patrice), 3184.
SICK (Klaus-Peter), 4416.
SICKER (Martin), 4904.
SICKER-AKMAN (M.), 1740.
SICKINGER (James P.), 423.
Sidney (Algernon), 6683.
SIEBEL (Ernst), 6507.
SIEBS (Benno-Eide), 7987.
SIEGENTHALER (Hansjörg), 1185.
Siegfried (André), 1057.
SIEGMUND (Frank), 3208.
SIEGRIST (Hannes), 1156.
SIEKMEIER (James F.), 7988.
SIEMEN (Hans Ludwig), 6140.
Sigebertus Gemblacensis, 520.
SIGMUND (Anna Maria), 4085.
SIGNORELLI (Alfio), 6997.
SIGURÐSSON (Jón Viðar), 3327.
Sikorski (Wladislaw), 4956.
SILBEY (Joel Henry), 5185.
Silius Italicus (Tiberius Catius Asconius), 2650, 2669.
SILLARS (Stuart), 6363.
SILLETT (Helen Marie), 2933.
SILVA (Jorge), 6639.
Silvanus, 2805.
SILVAS (Anna), 3850.
SILVESTER (Jeremy), 6493.
SILVESTRINI (Maria Teresa), 1133.
SIMA (A.), 1807.
SIMENSEN (Jarle), 4885.
SIMION (Eugen), 5751.
SIMON (Anne), 5562.
SIMON (B.), 1931.
SIMON (Georg), 168.
SIMON (John Y.), 7515.
SIMON (Maria), 182.
SIMONCELLI (Paolo), 937.
SIMONELLI (Frederick J.), 5219.

SIMONITI (Vasko), 951.
SIMONNOT (Philippe), 4335.
SIMONS (Geoffrey Leslie), 8327.
SIMONS (Oliver), 1431.
SIMONS (W. P.), 736.
Simplicius, 3079.
SIMPSON (I. A.), 1451.
SIMPSON (Pamela H.), 6439.
SINAGRA (Augusto), 4211.
SINDING (Richard), 7670.
SINEUX (P.), 2206.
SINFIELD (Alan), 6621.
SINGARAVELOU (Pierre), 664.
Singer Sargent (John), 6479.
SINGER-AVITZ (L.), 1774.
SINGH (Brijraj), 5515.
SINGH (Gurharpal), 4638, 4640.
SINGH (Mahendra Pal), 7084.
SINGH (Sudhir Kumar), 5238.
SINGMAN (Jeffrey L.), 3416.
SINNREICH-LEVI (Deborah M.), 1442.
SINNREICH-LEVI (Deborah M.), 3601.
SINTRA MARTINHEIRA (José), 8097.
Sion (Jules), 365.
SION-JENKIS (Karin), 2458.
SIRAISI (Nancy), 6125.
SIRAT (Renè-Samuel), 3272.
ŠIRC (Václav), 7783.
SIREN (Kirsti), 6998.
SIRINELLI (Jean-François), 954, 969.
SISI (Carlo), 6403.
SIVAN (Emmanuel), 675.
SIVARAMAKRISHNAN (K.), 4641.
SIVIGNON (M.), 365.
SJÖSTEDT (Charlotta), 4891.
SKACH (Cindy), 7102.
SKEEN (C. Edward), 5220.
ŠKEGRO (Ante), 2578.
SKIDMORE (Thomas E.), 4137.
SKINNER (P.), 290.
SKLENÁŘ (R.), 2660.
SKORKIN (Konstantin V.), 5023.
Skubiszewski (Piotr), 389, 3436.
SKUPIŃSKA-LØVSET (Ilona), 2779.
SKYDSBJERG (Henrik), 1027.
SLACK (Paul), 6999.
Slánsky (Rudolf), 4237.
SLAPŠAK (B.), 2075.
SLATER (N. W.), 1888.
SLAVINSKII (Boris N.), 7739.
SLAVITT (D. R.), 1889.
SLIWA (Joachim), 230.
SLIWA (Krzysztof), 6236.
SLOBODNÍK (Martin), 8199.
SLUHOVSKY (Moshe), 4379.
SMADJA (E.), 2516.
ŠMAHEL (František), 607.

SMAIL (John), 6721.
SMARCZYK (B.), 1874.
SMART (Nick), 4566.
SMART (Ninian), 1308.
Smelser (Neil), 1084.
SMETS (An), 3619.
SMEYERS (Maurits), 77.
SMIRNOV (Nikolaj N.), 7611.
SMITH (A. C.), 2006.
SMITH (A. T.), 1712.
Smith (Adam), 5959.
SMITH (Angel), 3983, 7492.
SMITH (Brendan), 3441, 3490.
SMITH (David Edward), 4167.
SMITH (David Lawrence), 4567.
SMITH (David M.), 3867.
SMITH (Denis), 6174.
SMITH (E. Timothy), 7990.
SMITH (Edwin), 3634.
SMITH (Jeremy), 1202, 5024.
Smith (John Raphael), 6494.
Smith (Jonathan Z.), 1353.
SMITH (Michael Ernest), 8367.
SMITH (Patricia Jo), 4398.
SMITH (Patrick J.), 4161.
SMITH (R. R. R.), 2818.
SMITH (R.), 2459.
SMITH (Rebekah M.), 2661.
SMITH (Richard Cándida), 6364.
SMITH (Simon C.), 7991.
SMITH (St. C.), 2662.
SMITH (T.), 7292.
SMITH (Thomas W.), 7293.
SMITH OLE (L.), 2973.
SMITH SHAWN (Michelle), 1299.
SMOLAR (Nina), 7947.
SMOLENSKY (Eleonora M.), 4063.
SMOLIN (Anatolij V.), 5025.
SMURTHWAITE (David), 7362.
SMUTS (Robert Malcolm), 5700.
SMYTH (Alfred P.), 3488.
SNELL (K. D. M.), 7056.
SNICKARE (Mårten), 5136.
SNYDER (Katherine V.), 6365.
SO (Clement Y. K.), 5869.
Soames (Enoch), 1415.
SOARES (Gabriela Pellegrino), 4923.
SOARES (Joseph A.), 5753.
SOARES ROBLES (Laura), 4846.
Socrates, 2102, 2147, 2153, 2155, 2162, 2689.
SÖDERBERG (Johan), 7002.
SOETERMEER (Frank), 3349.
SOFRONOVA (L. A.), 938.
SOGLIAN (Franco), 7992.
SOHMER (Steve), 6622.
SOKAL (Michael M.), 6088.
Sokullu Mehmed Paşa, 6971.
SOLAK (Zbigniew), *XIII.*
SOLDANI (Simonetta), 3923.

SOLIN (H.), 2329.
Solon, 1980, 2076, 2124.
SOMBRA SARAIVA (José Flávio), 7302.
SOMEDA (Hidefuji), 8381.
SOMMER (G.), 693.
SOMMER (Hermann), 7003.
SOMMER (Karl-Ludwig), 7993.
SOMMER (Wolfgang), 5516.
SOMMERFELD (W.), 1713.
SOMMERLECHNER (Andrea), 665.
SOMVILLE (P.), 1924.
SØNDBERG (Olaf), 4268.
SONG (Congbing), 8200.
SONG (Jie), 8201.
SONG (Liming), 8202.
Song (Ziwen), 8117.
SONNABEND (Holger), 352.
SONNE (Wolfgang), 833.
SONNET (M.), V.
Sonnino (Sidney), 4749, 7521.
SONODA (Koyu), 8297, 8298.
SONYEL (Salahi R.), 7994.
SOÓS (Katalin), 7995.
Sophocles, 1935, 1956, 1959-1962, 2088, 2099, 2110, 2137, 2209.
SORANI (Alessandro Vittorio), 4983.
SORBY (Karol), 7996.
SORCINELLI (Paolo), 1261, 6976.
SORDA (Sara), 250.
SORDI (Marta), 2025.
SORGI (Giuseppe), 1105.
SORIN (Antohi), 4984.
SORLIN (Pierre), 413.
SORRENTINO (Tommaso), 3350.
SOSA (Ernest), 1395.
SOSA (Roberto), 4598.
SOSKICE (David), 3999.
SOSSO (Paola), 6280.
SOSSON (Jean-Pierre), 3402.
SOTELO VÁZQUEZ (Adolfo), 5082.
SOTGIU (Giovanna), 2932.
SOUBIRAN-PAILLET (Franceine), 7057.
SOUKEHAL (Rabah), 4035.
ŠOUŠA (Jiří), 6811.
SOUTH (Malcolm H.), 5451.
Southern (Richard), 786.
SOUTO (F.), 2134.
SOUTOU (George-Henri), 7997.
SOUTY (François), 6853.
SOUZA MARTINS (José), 4139.
SOWADA (K. N.), 1652.
SOYARIK (Nalan), 5167.
Sozzini (Fausto), 5500.
SPACCAPELO (Natalina), 2932.
SPADE (Paul Vincent), 1421.
SPAGGIARI (Barbara), 3711.
SPAGNOLETTI (Angelantonio), 4743.

SPAGNUOLO VIGORITA (T.), 2517.
SPANNENBERGER (Norbert), 7624.
SPARROW (Elizabeth), 7471.
SPATH (Thomas), 666.
SPECHTLER (Franz Viktor), 3235.
Speer (Albert), 4422, 6438.
SPENCE (Mark David), 1262.
SPENCER (N. A.), 1653.
Spengler (Oswald), 5941.
SPENKUCH (Hartwin), 4393, 7004.
SPENSER (Daniela), 7615.
Speranskij (Michail), 4999.
SPERLING (Gert), 2780.
SPEYER (Wolfgang), 2875.
SPIEGEL (Gabrielle M.), 667.
SPIEGEL-SCHMIDT (Friedrich), 7624.
SPIEKER (Markus), 6624.
SPIES (Hans-Bernd), 5703.
SPILEERS (Steven), 5884.
SPINA (Luigi), 2135.
SPINETO (Natale), 668, 1380.
SPINOSA (G.), 5978.
Spinoza (Baruch), 5533, 5881, 5988, 6007.
SPIRA (Henry), 5148.
SPIRES (Margaret), 5715.
SPOERER (M.), 7682.
SPOERRI (Bettina), 3607.
SPOO (Eckart), 4444.
SPREMBERG (Heinz), 6013.
SPRINGBORG (Peter), 42.
SPRINGER (Klaus-Bernward), 5442.
SPRINZAK (Ehud), 4692.
Sraffa (Piero), 6024, 6686.
ST. PIERRE (Maurice), 4591.
STABILE (Francesco Michele), 4783.
STABLEFORD (Brian M.), 1443.
STACHORSKI (Stephan), 6315.
STACHURA (Peter D.), 4951.
STACKELBERG (Roderick), 4494.
STAERCK (Christopher), 8074.
STAERCK (Gillian), 8074.
STAFFORD (Pauline), 3902.
STAHL (H.-P.), 2663.
STÄHLI (Marlis), 37.
Stalin (Iosif Visarionovič Džugašvili), 4989, 5000, 5002, 5793, 6487, 7655, 7678, 7681, 7709, 7723, 7919, 8000, 8098.
STALLAERTS (Robert), 1029.
STAMBOLIS (Barbara), 4495.
STANČIČ (Z.), 2075.
STANDEN (Naomi), 970.
STANG (Knut), 7767.
Stanislaw I Leszczynski, King of Poland, 4950.
STANLEY (Glenn), 1282.
STANLEY (P. V.), 2076.

STANLEY (Tim), 96.
STANNARD (Jerry), 3491, 3749.
STANNARD (Katherine E.), 3491.
STANZEL (Franz K.), 898.
STANZIANI (Alessandro), 6663.
STAPERT (D.), 1475.
STARA (Alexandra), 476.
STARKE (D.), 2174.
STATELOVA (Elena), 4153, 7212.
STATHAKOOULOS (D.), 2970.
Statius (P. Papinius), 1955, 2614, 2625, 2697.
STAUB (Iohannes), 3807.
STÄUBLE (Antonio), 3562.
STAUFFACHER (Jack Werner), 134.
STAVIG (Ward), 4924.
STAVRAKAKIS (Yannis), 6014.
STAVRIDU-ZAFRAKA (A.), 3074.
STEEL (C.), 2922.
STEEL (Carlos G.), 3716.
STEENSMA (Susanna), 6483.
STEFANIDIS (Ioannis D.), 4212.
ŠTEFANSKÝ (Michal), 5032.
STEGMANN (Dirk), 4496.
STEHLÍK (Eduard), 7672.
STEIB (Murray), 3692.
STEIGERWALD (D.), 7616.
STEIN (Elisabeth), 3519.
STEIN (Henri), 3155.
STEIN (Katrin), 7103.
STEIN (P.), 2518.
STEINBACH (Peter), 4514.
STEINBAUER (Dieter H.), 2305.
STEINBERG (Jonathan), 7741.
STEINBERG (Marc W.), 7058.
STEINBY (E. M.), 2756.
STEINER (G.), 1714.
STEINHAUF (B.), 669.
STEINHÜBEL (Ján), 3097.
STEININGER (Christine), 12.
STEININGER (Rolf), 8001.
STEINMETZ (Davic C.), 5301.
STEINMETZ (Ralf-Henning), 3567.
STEINSLAND (Gro), 1376.
STELL (Philip Michael), 3147.
STELLA (Aldo), 4497.
STELLA (F.), 2844.
STEMMLER (Theo), 6220.
Stendhal (Henri Beyle), 6287.
STEPANOVA (Veronika V.), 4498.
STEPHAN (Gerd-Rüdiger), 4390.
Stephan von Bourbon, 3182.
Stephanus Hagiocristophorithes, 3024.
STEPHEN (S. Jeyaseela), 7255.
STEPHENS (John), 1400.
STEPHENSON (P.), 3075.
Stepinac (Alojzije), 5426.
STĘPKA (Stanisław), 4953.
STEPPER (R.), 2215, 2721.
STERLING (G. E.), 2934.

STERN (Marianne E.), 2781.
STERNBURG (Wilhelm von), 4499.
STERNHELL (Zeev), 1104.
STETZ (Margaret D.), 1415.
STEUBEN (Hans von), 2728, 2935.
STEURY (Donald P.), 7818.
STEVENSON (C. M.), 1476.
STEVENSON (David), 6722.
STEVENSON (John), 7436.
STEVENSON (William), 5517.
STEWARD (Jill), 6828.
STEWART (Graham), 4568.
STEWART (John), 6159.
STEWART (P.), 2819.
STICHEL (Rudolf H. W.), 2460.
STIEGEMANN (Christoph), 3462.
STIEHLER-ALEGRIA (G.), 1715.
STIELDORF (Andrea), 231.
STIFF (Peter), 5072.
STIGLMAYR (Cristina María), 3652.
ŠTIH (Peter), 951, 3383, 3676.
STINER (M. C.), 1498, 1508.
STITES (Richard), 5614.
STOCKER (David), 3118.
STOCLET (Alain J.), 3352.
STOJANOVA (V.), 4154.
STOJANOVIČ (Petur), 7212.
STOKES (Melvyn), 8015.
STOKES (Raymond G.), 6154.
STOKHOLM BANKE (Cecilie Felicia), 4269.
STOLIAROVA (L. V.), 79.
STOLJAROVA (Lubov' V.), 79.
STOLLBERG-RILINGER (Barbara), 4500.
STOLLEIS (Michael), 7075, 7138, 7140.
STÖLLER (Erich), 1265.
STOLPER (Matthew W.), 1808.
STOLTE (B.), 3076.
Stolypin (Petr Arkad'evich), 6773.
STONE (A. F.), 3077.
STONE (Glyn), 7216, 8002.
Stone (Lawrence), 787.
STONE (T.), 1477.
STONEMAN (William P.), 80.
STORA (Benjamin), 4032.
STORCHI MARINO (Alfredina), 2519, 2542.
STORM (Eric), 5116.
STORRS (C.), 5117, 7449.
STORTI STORCHI (Claudia), 3353.
STOUCK (Mary-Ann), 3851.
STOUT (Joseph A., Jr.), 7617.
STOUTZ (Mahlon L.), 6536.
STÖVER (Bernd), 4501, 7824.
STOVER (T. J.), 2664.
ŠTOVÍČEK (Ivan), 4251, 7686.
STOWELL (David O.), 6857.
Strabo, 1964.
Strada (Famiano), 853.

STRADLING (Robert), 7673.
STRAMAGLIA (Antonio), 2369, 2722.
STRANG (G. Bruce), 7674.
STRANGE (John), 1309.
STRANJ (Pavel), 918.
STRAUCH (Dieter), 7066.
Strauß (Franz Josef), 8035.
STRAUSS (Rafael A.), 919.
STRAUSS CLAY (J.), 1938.
STRAY (Christopher), 525.
STRECK (M. P.), 1575, 1775.
STREED (Jason Edward), 3699.
STREET (M.), 1509.
STREETER (Stephen M.), 8003.
STREETER (William W.), 129.
STRICKRODT (Silke), 7359.
STRID (Jan Paul), 292.
STRID (O.), 2207.
STRIETER (Terry W.), 1300.
STRIKWERDA (Carl), 6891.
Strindberg (Johan August), 6628.
STRINGER (C. B.), 1486.
STRODS (H.), 7770.
STROHM (Klauspeter), 4810.
STROHMAIER-WIEDERANDERS (Gerlinde), 2939.
STROHMEYER (ARNO), 5291.
STROLLO (Maria Rosaria), 5773.
STROMER (Wolfgang von), 3089.
STROMMENGER (E.), 1571.
STROMQUIST (Shelton), 7052.
STRONG (Douglas M.), 5221.
STRONG (Roy), 7420.
STROO (Cyriel), 3677.
STROOMBERG (Harriet), 125.
STROUD (R. S.), 1875.
STROUMSA (Guy G.), 1384, 2936.
STROUMSA (Sarah), 3315.
STRUBBE (J. H. M.), 1875, 1876.
STRUGAR (Vlado), 5250.
Stuart (Gilbert), 6454.
STUART (Kathy), 7006.
STUART-FOX (Martin), 869.
STUCHTEY (Benedikt), 684.
STUDER (Barbara), 1277.
STUNIC (Vesna), 133.
Sturgis (Mark), 4664.
STURZO (Luigi), 5358.
STÜSSI-LAUTERBURG (Jürg), 7455.
STUURMAN (Siep), 7007.
STYKALIN (Aleksandr S.), 3931, 5653.
SU (Xiaodong), 8204.
Suárez (Francisco), 5957.
SUÁREZ (Thomas), 367.
SUBRAHMANYAN (Sanjay), 3934.
SUBRITZKY (John), 8005.
SUCEVEANU (A.), 2208.
SUEO (Yoshiyuki), 8067.
SUERBAUM (Werner), 2330, 2665.

INDEX OF NAMES

SUGARMAN (David), 1156.
SUGHI (Mario Alberto), 3150.
SUGIHARA (Kaoru), 985.
SUGIMOTO (Fumiko), 8307.
SUGITA (Yoneyuki), 8006.
SUGIYAMA (Shinya), 6724, 8045.
SUGIZAKI (Taiichiro), 3831.
Suharto (Mohamad), 4646.
SUHRKE (Astri), 7957.
SUK (Jiří), 4252, 4253.
ŞÜKRÜ BATMAZ (Eftal), 5164.
Sulla Felix (L. Cornelius), 2343, 2448.
SULLIVAN (Denis Joseph), 4278.
SULLIVAN (Henry W.), 6536.
SULTAN (N.), 2136.
SÜMER (Faruk), 293.
SUMMERS (David), 5715.
SUMMERS (William C.), 6160.
SUMNER (W. M.), 1809.
SUMPTION (Jonathan), 3266.
SUNDBERG (Ulf), 3225.
SUNDERMEIER (Theo), 1280.
SUNDHAUSSEN (Holm), 1031.
ŠUNDRICA (Zdravko), 7450.
SUNG-HO (Chung), 8325.
SUOMINEN (Tapani), 5133.
SUPIČIĆ (Ivan), 3484.
SUPICIC (Ivo), 3492.
SURCHAT (P. L.), XVI.
SURET-CANALE (Jean), 4819.
SÜREVEN (Kenan), 6150.
SURYADINATA (Leo), 4648.
SUŠKO (Ladislav), 7742.
SÜSS (Walter), 4502.
SÜSS (Werner), 6822.
SUSTER (Zeljan E.), 1032.
ŠUTAJ (Štefan), 5056.
SUTEAU (Marc), 5823.
SUTER (Andreas), 4001.
SUTHERLAND (Daniel E.), 5198.
SUTHERLAND (Elizabeth), 3419.
SUVOROVA (Anna A.), 3316.
SUYDAM (Mary A.), 3782, 3903.
ŠVAJNCER (Janez J.), 5064.
SVANIDZE (Ada A.), 3914.
Švehla (Antonín), 4242.
SVOBODNÝ (Petr), 6168.
ŠVORC (Peter), 5057.
SWABEY (Fiona), 3420.
SWANSON (Heather), 3421.
SWANSON (R. N.), 3493.
SWEENEY (D.), 1776.
SWEET (Dennis), 6016.
SWEETMAN (David), 3620.
SWIETOCHOWSKI (Tadeusz), 1033.
SWIETOSLAWSKI (Witold), 8068.
Swift (Jonathan), 6256.
SYLLA (Richard), 6817.
Sylvester II, Papa, 1080.
Syme (R.), 784.

Symmachus (Q. Aurelius), 2895.
SYNEK (Eva Maria), 2937.
Synesius (episcopus Cyrenarum), 2189, 2966.
SZABÓ (András), 5405.
SZABÓ (Dániel), 4601.
SZCZUCHI (Lech), 744.
SZEJNMANN (Claus-Christian W.), 4503.
SZILÁGYI (J-G.), 1367.
SZIRMAI (J. A.), 82.
SZLEZÁK (Th. A.), 2209.
SZNAJDER (Mario), 1104.
SZOBRIES (Torsten), 4818.
SZÖGI (László), 6064.
SZUCS (Jeno), 3169.
SZŮCS (László), 8007.
SZUPPE (Maria), 8063.
SZWAGRZYK (Krzysztof), 4954.

T

TABOR (R.), 1529.
TABORELLI (L.), 2579.
TAČEVA (M.), 2580.
Tacitus (Publius Cornelius), 788, 1052, 2322, 2330, 2374-2383, 2473, 2681, 5580, 6283.
TAEGER (Angela), 7186.
TAFAJ (Afërdita), 7618.
TAGLIABUE (Mauro), 3823.
TAGLIAFERRI (Teodoro), 759.
TAGLIENTE (M.), 2277.
TAGUIEFF (Pierre-André), 5577.
TAILLEMITE (Étienne), 368.
TAILLIBERT (Christel), 6626.
Taine (Hippolyte), 684, 789.
Taira (Kiyomori), 8279.
TAJIRI (Toru), 8205.
TAKÁCS (Sarolta), 2490.
TAKAHASHI (Masaaki), 8308.
TAKAHASHI (Motoyasu), 7008.
TAKANO (Nobuharu), 8290.
TAKAO (Yasuo), 4802.
TAKEFUMI (Terada), 7667.
Takiyüddin, 6161.
TALAMANCA (M.), 2520.
TALAR (C.), 654.
TALATTOF (Kamran), 6366.
TALBERT (Richard J. A.), 2383.
TALBOT (Alice-Mary), 3078.
TALBOT (Ian), 4638.
TALIB (Naimah S.), 7338.
Talma (François Joseph), 6546.
TALMAGE (Frank), 3291.
TALVACCHIA (Bette), 6404.
TAMAGNO PERNA (Luisa), 2274.
TAMALIO (Raffaele), 167.
Tambroni Armaroli (Fernando), 4719.
TAMBURRI (Pascual), 3098.

TAMBURRI BARIAIN (Pascual), 3422.
Tamerlano, 3171.
TAMURA (Hideo), 4569.
Tan (Sitong), 8138, 8180.
TAN (Wenfeng), 8206.
TANADA (Hirofumi), 8357.
TANAKA (Katsuyuki), 8309.
TANCK DE ESTRADA (Dorothy), 5824.
TANDETER (Enrique), 6652, 6858.
TANG (Ling), 8207.
TANG (Yanfang), 870.
TANIGUCHI (Junichiro), 8069.
TANNER (Harold Miles), 8208.
TANNER (Jakob), 7059.
TANTER (Raymond), 7965.
TANTILLO (Ignazio), 2461.
TANWAR (Raghuvendra), 4643.
TARANTINO (A.), 7196.
Tarantino (Quentin), 6515.
TARAS (A. E.), 7671.
TARAYRE (Michel), 3904.
TARDAN-MASQUELIER (Ysé), 1382.
TARDIF (A.-I.), 1250.
TARDY (Thierry), 8008.
TAROT (Camille), 5705.
TARPIN (M.), 2581.
Tarsia, (Pablo Antonio de), 4743.
TARTAKOVSKIJ (Andrej G.), 6207.
Tartarotti (Girolamo), 649.
TASHIRO (Kazuo), 8310.
Tassoni (Alessandro), 6243.
TATE (Michael L.), 5223.
TATE (Robert Brian), 3163.
TATEO (Francesco), 4743, 6201, 6238.
TATUM (M. Jeffrey), 2462.
Tauler (Johannes), 3888.
TAUSEND (Klaus), 2463.
TAUTZ (Burkhard), 2365.
TAVANI (Giuseppe), 3759, 3514.
TAVER (Katja V.), 6017.
TAVIANI-CAROZZI (Huguette), 551, 3442.
TAVOILLOT (Pierre-Henri), 1071.
TAVONI (Maria Gioia), 5399.
TAYLOR (Anya), 6367.
TAYLOR (Brandon), 477.
TAYLOR (Craig), 3267.
TAYLOR (Gérald), 8382.
TAYLOR (Jane H. M.), 3614.
TAYLOR (Larissa Juliet), 5519.
TAYLOR (Peter), 4685.
TAYLOR (Philip M.), 4570.
TAYLOR (Sandra C.), 5239.
TAYLOR ALLEN (Ann), 7009.
TCACH (César), 4064.
TCACI (Vladimir), 7451.
TEBIB (Roger), 4034.
TEDDE (Emma), 5355.

TEDOLDI (Fabio Massimo), 3750.
TEGA (Walter), 5681.
TEINONEN (Markku), 907.
TEIXEIRA DA MOTA (José), 207.
TEIXEIRA DA SILVA (Francisco Carlos), 4130.
TEJA (Ramón), 2938.
TEJA LEOPARDI (Teresa), 6291.
TELLI (Cahit), 5159.
TELLINI (Gino), 6308.
Tempier (Etienne), 3868.
TENBRUCK (Friedrich H.), 802, 5570.
TENENTI (Alberto), 1034.
TENTONI (Luca), 4763.
Teobaldo II, rey de Navarra, 3098.
TEODORI (Franco), 5364.
Teodoro di Monferrato, 3265.
TEPPER (Y.), 1777.
TERASAKI (Yasuhiro), 8311.
TERBERGER (TH.), 1509.
Terentius Afer (P.), 2384, 2634, 2656.
TERMINASSIAN (Taline), 7743.
TERPSTRA (N.), 5305.
TERRY (Jennifer), 6163.
TERTRAIS (H.), 7339.
Tertullianus (Q. Septimius Florens), 2849, 2861, 2862.
TERZIC (Slavenko), 7517.
TĚŠÍNSKÁ (Emilie), 7010.
TESSITORE (Fulvio), 565, 872.
TESTA (Fausto), 6405.
TEUNIS (Henk), 3242.
TEXERA ARNAL (Jolanda), 6116.
TEXIER (Yves), 2464.
THADEN (Edward C.), 873.
THAGARD (Paul), 6164.
THALMANN (Rita), 4380.
THÉBERT (Yvon), 2732.
THEIR (Sebastian), 2859.
Themistius, 3030.
Theocritus, 1966, 1967.
Theodora, Byzantine empress, 3088, 3091.
Theodoricus Magnus, Ostrogothic king, 2967.
Theodorus, Sanctus, 2958.
Theodosius I (Flavius Augustus), Roman emperor, 2423, 2729, 2893.
THEON (Erik), 3428.
Theophilus Korydaleus, 2974.
Theopompus of Chios, 790.
Thesiger (Wilfred G.), 7524.
THESLEFF (H.), 2175.
THEUWS (F.), 3494.
THEVENAZ (Clémence), 3156.
THI DIEU (Nguyen), 8009.
Thibaut (Anton Friedrich Justus), 7066.

THIEDE (Simone), 5340.
THIEDEKE (Johnny), 4002.
THIEL (R.), 1890.
THIEL (R.), 3079.
THIER (Andreas), 7077, 7104.
THIHER (Allen), 3751.
THIJSSEN (J. M. M. H.), 3752.
THIMME (Roland), 7720.
THING (Morten), 5873.
THIOUB (Ibrahima), 7187, 7363.
THOBIE (J.), 6804.
THOM (Martin), 684.
THOMAS (Baylis), 8010.
THOMAS (Gordon), 4693.
THOMAS (Jean-Paul), 4381.
THOMÀS (Joan Maria), 5118.
THOMAS (M. L.), 2306.
THOMAS (Martin), 7675.
THOMAS (N.), 7199.
THOMAS (Nicholas), 7385.
THOMAS (Paul), 4571.
THOMAS (R. F.), 2666.
THOMAS (S.), 1654.
Thomas Aquinas, Sanctus, 3717, 3720, 3730, 3744, 3755.
THOMAS DE CHOBHAM, 3712.
THOMAZ (Luís Filipe), 7406.
Thomis (Malcolm I.), 4559.
THOMPSON (Alastair), 684.
THOMPSON (Benjamin), 3814.
THOMPSON (D. J.), 1655.
Thompson (Edward Palmer), 791.
THOMPSON (J. Lee), 4572.
THOMPSON (M.), 1478.
THOMPSON (Mark), 5257.
THOMPSON (Peter), 7011.
THOMPSON (Walter), 7247.
THOMPSON MAC CANDLESS (Amy), 5825.
THOMSON (Alistair), 874.
THOMSON (Francis J.), 3496.
THOMSON (Guy P. C.), 4848.
THOMSON (Rodney M.), 3183.
THORAU (P.), 3244.
THORMÄHLEN (Marianne), 6368.
THORNTON (John Kelly), 8358.
THORPE (Andrew), 3962.
THRANE (H.), 1539.
Thrasybulus, 1983.
THROWER (James), 1320.
Thucydides, 792, 1968, 1988, 1992, 2135.
THUESEN (Peter J.), 5520.
THÜMMEL (Hans Georg), 2940.
TIBALDI (Rodobaldo), 6568.
TIBENSKÝ (Ján), 5054.
Tiberius Claudius Nero, Roman emperor, 1977, 2399, 2473, 2483.
Tibullus (Albius), 2598.
Tieck (Ludwig), 39.

TIKHONOVA (Elena Ju.), 6018.
TILKOVSKY (Loránt), 7624.
TILLIETTE (Xavier), 6019.
TILLY (Charles), 3953.
Tilly (Jean T'Serclaes, Comte de), 7411.
TILLY (Richard), 1035, 6817.
TILMANS (Karin), 5777.
TIMM (Erika), 294.
TIMMERMANN (Heiner), 3923, 3984, 4412, 4413.
TIMMERMANS (Benôit), 6020.
TIMPANARO MORELLI (Maria Augusta), 135.
Tipu Sultan, Fath `Ali, Nawab of Mysore, 7328.
TISCHER (Anuschka), 7397, 7400.
TISHKIN (A. A.), 1550.
TISMANEANU (Vladimir), 3995.
TITARENKO (M. L.), 7546.
TITCHENER (F. B.), 2744.
Tito (Josip Broz), 5245.
TIXHON (Axel), 7188.
TOBER (Holger J.), 4505.
TOBI (Joseph), 3292.
TOCHTERLE (U.), 1581.
TOCK (B.-M.), 155.
Tocqueville (Charles-Alexis Henri Clerel de), 793, 5929.
Todd (Garfield), 7356.
TODESCHINI (Giacomo), 1080.
TODOROV (Tzvetan), 706, 4155.
TODOROVA (R.), 8011.
TOELLE (Heidi), 3317.
TOER (Koesalah Soebagyo), 4649.
TOER (Pramoedya Ananta), 4649.
TOFFOLETTO (Mavis), 425.
Togliatti (Palmiro), 4747.
TOGNETTI (Sergio), 3424.
TOKAREVA (Evgenija S.), 5341.
TOKARSKI (Peter), 6665.
TŐKÉCZKY (László), 4616.
Toller (Ernst), 6313.
TOLSTOGUZOV (S. A.), 8312.
TOLSTRUP (Tor), 1172.
Tomasi di Lampedusa (Giuseppe), 6318.
TOMASONI (Francesco), 6021.
TOMASZEWSKI (Jerzy), 4234.
TOMASZEWSKI (Longin), 7799.
TOMATIS PETERSEN (Aurea), 4138.
TOMBS (Robert), 4382.
TOMEK (Prokop), 6725.
TOMITA (Norimasa), 3214.
TOMITA (Rie), 4573.
Tommaseo (Niccolò), 5393, 5978.
TONDO (S.), 2521.
TONELLI (Natascia), 3609.
Tongzhi, emperor of China, 8268.
TONINI (Alberto), 8012.
TONINI (Carla), 4955.

TONIOLO (Federica), 69.
TONIOLO (Gianni), 1188.
TONIZZI (M. Elisabetta), 7012.
TONO (Haruyuki), 8313.
TOPCHA (Virginie), 270.
TOPDEMİR (Hüseyin Gazi), 6161.
TÖPFER (Bernhard), 3753.
TOPHINKE (Doris), 3157.
TOPOLSKI (Jerzy), 875.
TORBÁGYI (Melinda), 243.
TORCOLI (Francesco), 8013.
TORELLI (Mario), 2255, 2465.
TORGGLER (A.), 1581.
TORKEWITZ (Dieter), 3696.
TÖRNQVIST (Egil), 6628.
TORRE (Juan Carlos), 4046, 4062.
TORRES (Adelino), 4037.
TORRES (Jaume), 6734.
TORRES SEVILLA-QUINONES DE LEON (Margarita), 202.
TORRINI (Maurizio), 6079, 6157.
TORSTENDAHL (Rolf), 7005.
TORTAROLO Edoardo, 795, 6022.
TORTELLA (Gabriel), 6817.
TORTI (Anna), 3535.
TORTORELLI (Gianfranco), 136, 6165.
TOSCANO (A.), 6033.
TOSCH (Frank), 5781.
TOSEL (André), 5936.
TOSH (John), 7013.
TOSHCHEV (Gennadij N.), 1542.
TOSI (Luciano), 7260.
TOŠKOVA (V.), 7744.
TOTARO (P.), 5978.
TOTEV (Totiu), 3681.
TÓTH (J.), 7061.
TOUBERT (Pierre), 369.
TOUBOULIC (A.-I.), 2842.
TOUCHEFEU (Yves), 5342.
TOUGHER (Sh.), 3080.
TOURNES (Ludovic), 6629.
TOURNIKIOTIS (Panayotis), 6440.
TOVAR PINZÓN (Hermes), 7380.
TOWNSHEND (Charles), 1103, 4686.
TOWNSON (D.), 1037.
TRACHTENBERG (Marc), 8014.
TRAHAIR (Richard C. S.), 1266.
Traianus (M. Ulpius), Roman emperor, 1977, 2755, 2777.
TRAINA (G.), 2096.
TRAMONTANA (Salvatore), 370.
TRANFAGLIA (Nicola), 4785.
TRANGBAEK (Else), 5790.
TRANIELLO (Francesco), 813.
TRANIELLO (Paolo), 447.
TRÄNKLE (H.), 2941.
TRANNOY-COLTELLONI (Michèle), 2522.
TRANVOUEZ (Yvon), 1263.

TRAPP (J. B.), 99.
TRAUFFLER (Henri), 30.
TRAVAGLINI (Carlo M.), 7035.
TRAVAINI (Lucia), 246.
TRAVIS (R.), 2137.
TREGGIARI (Susan), 2782.
TREHUB (Aaron), 927.
TREMENT (F.), 1479.
TREMIL (Vladimir Guy), 671.
TREMP (Ernst), 3778.
TRENTER (Cecilia), 672.
TRENTO (Sandro), 6666.
TREPP (Anne-Charlotte), 5317.
TREPTOW (Kurt W.), 7609.
TŘEŠTÍK (Dušan), 876.
TREVETT (Ch.), 2942.
TREVISANATO (A.), 2783.
TRIAS (G.), 1765.
TRIFUNOVSKA (Snezana), 5241.
TRIGG (Roger), 920.
TRINKAUS (Charles), 5259.
TRIPODI (Paolo), 5067.
TRITLE (L.), 2992.
TRIVELLATO (Francesca), 7014.
TROHA (Nevenka), 5066.
TROIANI (Lucio), 636, 2413.
TROIANOS (Sp. N.), 3081.
TROITZSCH (Ulrich), 6128.
TROLESE (F. G.), 3813.
Trombelli (Giovanni Grisostomo), 5399.
TROMBLEY (Stephen), 1408.
TRONCANELLI (Fabio), 5429.
TRONCHET (G.), 2667.
TROPER (Michel), 1141.
TROPPER (J.), 1716, 1717.
TROTTMANN (Christian), 3754.
TROUSSON (Raymond), 1403.
TROUT (D. E.), 2858.
TROUTT POWELL (Eve Marie), 4279.
TRUBOWITZ (Peter), 7283.
TRUDEL (Marcel), 4168.
Trujillo Molina (Rafael Leónidas), 7815.
Truman (Harry S.), 4782, 7952, 8021.
Tryphonus, Sanctus, 2892.
TSENDINA (A. D.), 8050.
TSIMBAEVA (Ekaterina N.), 5343.
TSIN (Michael), 8209.
TSITOU (Anatol'), 233.
TUCCIMEI (Ercole), 6816.
TUCHEL (Johannes), 4514.
TUCK (Richard), 7200.
TUITE (Clara), 1253.
TULARD (Jean), 956, 4293, 4357.
TUMARKIN (Daniil D.), 645.
TUNZI SISTO (A. M.), 1480.
Túpac-Amaru (José Gabriel), 4912, 4924.

TURCAN (Robert), 2705, 2784.
TURCHINI (Angelo), 5286.
TURCUŞ (Şerban), 3905.
TURCUŞ (Veronica), 5706.
TURFAN (Mehmed Naim), 5176.
TURI (Gabriele), 771, 4786, 5754.
TURK (Eleanor L.), 4506.
TURNER (Arthur), 7892.
TURNER (Henry Ashby, jr.), 868.
TURNER (Michael J.), 4574.
TURNER (Patricia R.), 7063.
TURNER (Ralph V.), 3245.
TURPIN (Frédéric), 4036.
TURTAS (R.), 2944.
TURTAS (Raimondo), 1385.
TUSELL (Javier), 5096.
TVARDOVSKAJA (Valentina A.), 6023.
TVOROGOV (O. V.), 3158.
TWARDZIK (Stefano), 4700.
TWOHEY (Michael), 8210.
TYAS (Shaun), 253.
TYLDESLEY (Mike), 4665.
TYLUS (J.), 2094.
TYMOSHYK (Mykola), 137.
TYRRELL (Ian), 6667.
TYRSENKO (Andrej V.), 4383.
Tzetzes (Giovanni), 792.
TZUR (Eli), 4905.

U

UBEROI (J. P. S.), 5554.
Uccello (Paolo), 3668.
UCHITEL (A.), 1741.
UDWIN (Victor Morris), 2138, 3611.
UEBERSCH (Gerd R.), 7195.
UENO (Chizuko), 1164.
UFUK (Esin), 1481.
UGOCHUKWU UCHE (Chibuike), 6818.
UHL (Patrice), 3612.
UHLÍŘ (Lubomír), 7129.
UIMONEN (Minna.), 6166.
UKOLOVA (Viktorija I.), 827.
Ulbricht (Walter), 5737.
ULEWICZ (Tadeusz), 3497.
ULFELDT (Jakob), 305.
ULIANICH (Boris), 779.
ULIČNÝ (Ferdinand), 1386.
ULIVIERI (Simonetta), 5765.
UL'JANOVA (Galina N.), 6668.
ULLMANN (Hans-Peter), 4507.
ULMANN (Ilse), 2334.
ULMANN-MAURIAT (Caroline), 4033.
ULRICH (Bernd), 4517.
ULRICH (Maria Alayde), 4138.
Ulrich von Lichtenstein, 3235.
ULUNJAN (Artem A.), 7533.

UMPHREY (J. H.), 2987.
ÜNAL (Ahmet), 1742.
UNDERHILL (Frances A.), 3426.
Ungaretti (Giuseppe), 6373.
UNGER (Jonathan), 5240.
UNGER (Richard W.), 3427.
UNGER (Thorsten), 6313.
UNGVÁRY (Krisztián), 7766.
UNTERKIRCHER (Franz), 3706.
Untersteiner (M.), 2080.
UNVERRICHT (Hubert), 4425.
UOLA (Mikko), 7676.
URBACH (Karina), 7535.
URBINA (Eduardo), 6209.
URECH (H. J.), 2668.
URIBE SALAS (José Alfredo), 7519.
Urnamma, king of Ur, 1678.
Urquiza (Justo José de), 4039.
URREA (Jesús), 6484.
URRY (William), 3906.
USAMI (Takayuki), 8314.
USHER (M. D.), 2961.
USTINOVA (Y.), 2210.
UTERWEDDE (Henrik), 4355.
UTHEMANN (K.-H.), 3082.
UTZ (Richard J.), 3613.
UTZ TREMP (Katherine), 3460.
UYTTERHOEVEN (Inge), 2785.
UZEL (İlter), 6150.

V

VACCA (Giuseppe), 4747, 5958, 6024.
VACCARINO (Giorgio), 795.
VACULÍK (Jaroslav), 7783.
VADETSKAJA (El'ga B.), 8070.
VAEL (Claude), 7180.
VAGNETTI (L.), 1840.
Vajiravudh, King of Siam, 5156.
VAJNBERG (Bella I.), 8071.
VALAVANIS (P.), 2258.
VALDÉS (Juan Antonio), 8383.
VALDES (Juan de), 5468.
VALDES-UGALDE (José Luis), 8016.
VALENCIA (Heather), 5861.
VALENTA (Jaroslav), 4219, 4234.
VALENTE (Michaela), 5707.
VALENZUELA UGARTE (Renato), 4180.
VALERA (Blas), 5370.
Valerius Asiaticus, 2470.
Valerius Flaccus Setinus Balbus (C.), 2385, 2610, 2650, 2655.
Valerius Maximus, 2672.
Valiani (Leo), 795, 4787.
VALLADA (Paulo), 4958.
VALLÉE (Gérard), 3784.
VALLEJO GIRVÉS (M.), 3083.
VALLELY (Fintan), 1285.

VALLENTIN (Rudolf), 5826.
VALLERAND (Noël), 4164.
VALLERANI (Massimo), 1133.
VALLET (G.), 1814.
VALLONE (Giancarlo), 3354.
VALMAN (Nadia), 4560.
VALTULINA (Anna), 7649.
VÁMOS (Eva), 6064.
VAN ANDRINGA (W.), 2723.
VAN BALBERGHE (Émile), 3762.
VAN BAVEL (B. J. P.), 3428, 3429.
VAN BELLE (G.), 1303.
VAN BERGEN (P. F.), 1451.
VAN BERKEL (Klaas), 6093.
VAN BREMEN (Jan), 8389.
VAN CREVELD (Martin), 4004.
VAN DE MIEROOP (M.), 1576.
VAN DE PLASSE (Jan), 5875.
VAN DE POEL-KNOTTNERUS (Frédérique), 5796.
VAN DEN BERG (Hubert), 6369.
VAN DEN BERG (Johannes), 5521.
VAN DEN HOUT (Michel P. J.), 2351.
VAN DER EIJK (P. J.), 2683.
VAN DER LAAN (Arend Hendrik), 5679.
VAN DER LAARSE (Rob), 4873.
VAN DER PLAAT (G. N.), X.
VAN DER STOCKT (L.), 1945.
VAN DER VEER (Peter), 3982.
VAN DER VLIET (J.), 1656.
VAN DER WAL (N.), 3084.
VAN DEUSEN (Nancy), 3498.
VAN DIETEN (J.-L.), 3085.
VAN DÜLMEN (Richard), 7015.
VAN EENOO (Romain), II.
VAN ELSLANDE (Jean-Pierre), 6281.
VAN FLETEREN (Frederick), 376.
Van Groot (Huig) v. Grotius.
VAN HEESCH (Johan), 2739.
VAN HELDEN (Albert), 6093.
VAN HERWIJNEN (G.), X.
VAN HOUTS (Elisabeth Maria Cornelia), 203, 3499.
VAN HUISSTEDE (Peter), 93.
VAN KAMPEN (Kimberly), 98.
VAN KRIEKEN, (G. S.), 7297.
VAN LAAK (Dirk), 1267.
VAN LIEFFERINGE (C.), 2211.
VAN MELIS (Damian), 4508.
VAN NIEROP (Henk F. K.), 4874, 5777.
VAN NUFFELEN (P.), 2212.
VAN OYEN (D.), 1896.
VAN POPPEL (Frans), 6859, 7016, 7017, 7018.
VAN RAAK (R.), 4875.
VAN UYTHOVEN (Geert), 7472.
VAN VAECK (Marc), 223.

VAN VELTHOVEN (Harry), 4103.
VAN VLIET (C.), X.
VAN WIE (Paul D.), 252.
VAN YOUNG (Eric), 5671.
VANDEN (Harry E.), 4879.
VANDEPUT (L.), 1608.
VANDERHEYDE (C.), 3086.
VANDERJAGT (Arjo J.), 5679.
VANDERSMISSEN (Jan), 6154.
VANDERSPOEL (J.), 3087.
VANDERVORT (Bruce), 7364.
VANDIVER NICASSIO (Susan), 6631.
VANĚK (Miroslav), 4243.
VANIT (Marjorie S.), 2786.
VANOTTI (Gabriella), 2466.
VAQUERO (M.), 1510.
VARANINI (Gian Maria), 3125.
VĂRARU (Ion), 932.
VARELA (Félix), 8364.
VARGAS (P.), 1810.
VARILLAS (Alberto), 7298.
VÁRKONYI (Ágnes), 1038, 4618.
VARNI (Angelo), 7111.
Varro (M. Terentius), 2386, 2388.
VARSORI (Antonio), 363, 8017.
VARTY (Kenneth), 3682.
VÀRVARO (Alberto), 3606.
VARVARTSEV (M. M.), 7259.
VASCONI (Paola), 6167.
VASIL'EV (Mikhail A.), 3215.
VASIL'EVA (Evgenija I.), 8059.
VASIL'EVA (Ol'ga Ju.), 5458.
VASINA (Augusto), 3152.
VASSIS (I.), 3088.
VASTA (Michelangelo), 6726.
VATTIONI (F.), 1765.
VAUCHEZ (André), 3836, 3907.
VAUGHAN (Mary Kay), 5671.
VAUGHAN (S.), 2250.
VAUSSARD (Maurice), 5358.
VAZQUEZ (Josefina Zoraida), 4844.
Vàzquez del Menchaca (Fernando), 7132.
VEBER (Václav), 4254.
Veblen (Thorstein), 6684.
VECCHIO (Silvana), 3438.
VECK (Bernard), 6286.
VEGA (Bernardo), 7815.
VEGAS (M.), 1765, 1778.
VEGAS ARAMBURU (J. I.), 1524.
VEGLIA (Patrick), 416.
VEIT (Patrice), 7034.
VEITL (Philippe), 1057.
VEKARIĆ (Nenad), 7019.
VEKHVILJAJNEN (O.), 7681.
VEKSLER (Aleksandr G.), 1039.
VELA WITT (María Susana), 7381.
VELAY VALLANTIN (Catherine), 922.
VELDMAN (Ilja M.), 5777.

INDEX OF NAMES

VÉLEZ (Pilar), 6509.
VELJANOVSKI (Novica), 7989.
Velleius Paterculus, 2387.
VELLUT (Jean-Luc), 4194.
VELOSO (Júlio Caio), 91.
VELTRI (Patrizia), 2787.
VENARD (Marc), 5369.
VENDRIX (Philippe), 6632.
VENEZIANI (M.), 5978.
VENIT (M. S.), 1657.
VENTOURA (Lina), 7020.
VENTURELLI (Paola), 6510, 7021.
VENTURELLI (Renato), 6591.
VENTURELLI (Roberto), 6406.
Venturi (Franco), 795.
VENTURI BERNARDINI (I.), 2213.
VENTURINI (Fernando), 7108, 7109.
VENTURINO GAMBARI (M.), 1540.
VENTURO (David F.), 6282.
VERA (Domenico), 2035, 2820.
VERA (José Luis), 884.
VERBIJ-SCHILLINGS (Jeanne), 3520.
Vercingetorix, Chief of the Arverni, 396.
VERDAGUER (Pierre), 6370.
VERDON (L.), 295.
VERDUIN (J.), 7016.
VERGA (Marcello), 4788, 5757.
VERGARA (Alexander), 6485.
VERGER (Jacques), 3632, 5755.
Vergilius Maro (P.), 2388, 2389, 2594, 2608, 2618, 2621, 2636, 2662, 2663, 2665, 2666, 2679, 2881.
Verhaeren (Emile), 6312.
VERHEIDEN (J.), 1303.
VERHEYDE (Philippe), 4384.
VERHULST (Adriaan E.), 3918.
Verlaine (Paul), 6371.
VERMEULEN (Floris), 6847.
VERNANT (Jean Pierre), 1214.
VERNIER (Bernard), 923.
Verres, 2496.
Verri (Alessandro), 796.
Verri (Pietro), 6273.
Versace (Gianni), 6497.
VERSCHAVE (François-Xavier), 4191.
VERSE (D. A.), 7189.
VERUCCI (Guido), 4789.
VERVAET (F. J.), 2333.
VERWIEBE (Barbara Katharina Maria), 6283.
Vesey (Denmark), 7155.
Vespasianus (T. Flavius), Roman emperor, 2425.
VESPIGNANI (G.), 3090.
VESTAL (Theodore M.), 4286.
VESZPRÉMY (László), 3169.

VEYNE (Paul), 2467, 2945.
VEYRASSAT (Béatrice), 6170.
VIAL (P.), 4366.
VIANO (Carlo Augusto), 5989.
VICKERS (M.), 2007.
VICKERS (Miranda), 4023.
Vico (Giovanni Battista), 872, 5923, 5928, 5944, 5953, 5986, 6005.
VICTOR (Benjamin), 47.
VIDA (István), 8007.
VIDAL (César), 1445.
VIDAL-NAQUET (Pierre), 773, 797.
VIDIC (Marko), 951.
VIDOTTO (Vittorio), 4784.
VIEHOFF (Reinhold), 5654.
VIENNOT (Eliane), 6206, 6210.
VIEROW (H.), 2957.
VIETTO (Angela), 1418.
VIEWEG (Klaus), 6025.
VIGEVANI JARACH (Vera), 4063.
VIGEZZI (Brunello), 5675.
Viielgorsky (Joseph), 5012.
VILANOVA (Antonio), 5082.
VILANOVA I VILA-ABADAL (Francesc), 5119.
VILAR (Juan Bautista), 8359.
VILAR (María José), 8359.
Vilar (Pierre), 798.
VILLA (Angela Ida), 6372.
VILLA (Dana), 5996.
Villa (Francisco), 7617.
Villa (Pancho), 7617.
VILLA (R.), 1488.
VILLA (Roberto), 5821.
VILLA GONZALEZ (R.), 1515.
VILLABLANCA Z (Hernán), 4181.
VILLALMANZO CAMENO (Jesús), 3104.
VILLALON (L. J. Andrew), 3192.
VILLANI (Pasquale), 4696.
VILLANUEVA (María), 884.
VILLARI (Lucio), 5709.
VILLARROEL (Fidel), 4926.
VILLEDIEU (Françoise), 2774, 2787.
VILLOCH VAZQUEZ (V.), 1448.
Villon (François), 3614.
Vinay (Gustavo), 799.
VINAYO GONZÁLEZ (Antonio), 45.
Vincent (Jean), 5140.
Vincent de Beauvais, 3904.
VINCENTI (U.), 2523.
VINCHESI (M. A.), 2669.
VIND (Ole), 877.
VINOKUROV (Nikolaj I.), 2077.
VINSON (M.), 3091.
VINTI (Carlo), 5905.
VIOLA (Corrado), 5568.
VIOLANTE (Cinzio), 3785.
VIOLANTE PICON (Isabel), 6373.

VIRGILIO (Biagio), 2026.
VIRMANI (Arundhati), 7340.
VIROLI (Maurizio), 1106.
VIRTANEN (Timo J.), 907.
VISA-ONDARÇUHU (V.), 2139.
Visconti (Luchino), 6549.
VISING (Johan), 3536.
VISMARA (Paola), 1380.
VITA (J.-P.), 1716.
VITAL (David), 5555.
VITALE (Luis), 4177.
VITALE (M.), 4752.
VITALE (Maria T.), 2670.
VITALE (Micaela), 2774.
Vitellius (Aulus), Roman emperor, 2470.
Vitellius (L.), 2390.
VITOLO (Giovanni), 3846.
Vitruvius Pollio, 2391, 2684, 2734, 2740, 3487.
Vitte (Sergej Jul'evich), 4991.
VIVARELLI (Roberto), 684, 732.
Vives (Jaume Vicens), 5085.
Vladimir I, grand duke of Kiev, 3215.
VOADEN (Rosalynn), 3908.
VODOFF (V.), 3866.
VODOSEK (Peter), 438.
VOGEL (Sabine), 138.
VÖGELE (Jörg), 6860.
VOGT (Hermann Josef), 2946.
VOGT-SPIRA (Gregor), 2574, 2724.
VOIGT (M. M.), 1811.
VOINOT (Jacques), 234.
VOIVODIC (Mihailo), 7536.
VOLK (K.), 1718.
VOLK (Sandi), 8019.
VOLKMANN (Hans Erich), 4512.
VOLKOV (Sergej V.), 8048.
VOLKOV (V. K.), 7678.
VOLL (John O.), 4804.
VOLLNHALS (Clemens), 4441.
VOLOKITIN (Aleksandr V.), 1511.
VOLOKITINA (T. V.), 7822.
VOLPE (G.), 2822.
Volpe (Gioacchino), 684.
VOLPILHAC-AUGER (Catherine), 126, 1050.
VOLTAIRE (François-Marie Arouet, dit), 800, 1116, 5903.
VONČINA (Dejan), 689.
VONDROVÁ (Jitka), 4255.
VONS (J.), 2671.
VORACEK (Emil), 4219.
VOREL (Petr), 602.
VOROB'EVA (Irina G.), 768.
VOSS (Jürgen), 6322.
VOVELLE (Michel), 801.
VOYÉ (Liliane), 1379.
VRESNIK (Drago), 7768.
VRTEL (Ladislav), 235.

W

WAANDERS (F. M. J.), 1851.
WAARDENBURG (Jacques), 1316.
Wace (Robert), 524.
WACHSMANN (Nikolaus), 4509.
WACHTEL (Nathan), 5316.
Waddington (Samuel Ferrand), 6741.
WADE MARTINS (Susanna), 6780.
WADUD-MUHSIN (Amina), 5556.
WAGNER (Dieter), 6727.
WAGNER (John A.), 1044.
WAGNER (Michæl F.), 6374.
WAGNER (Peter), 7062.
Wagner (Wilhelm Richard), 6567, 6617.
WAGNER (Wolfgang Eric), 3633.
WAGNLEITNER (R.), 8020.
WAHLERT (Glenn), 4072.
WAINSTOCK (Dennis), 8021.
WAITES (Bernard), 7319.
WAKITA (Haruko), 1164, 8315.
WALA (Michael), 6935, 7243.
WALCZAK (Henryk), 7619.
WALDE MOHENO (Lillian, von der), 3449.
WALDMANN (Helmut), 2947.
WALDRON (Mary), 6375.
WALFISH (Barry), 3291.
WALKER (Brett L.), 6172.
WALKER (Charles F.), 4925.
WALKER (Greg), 5777.
WALKER (Jonathan), 7022.
WALKER (Robin.), 8360.
WALKER (S. E. C.), 2256.
WALLACE (Anthony F. C.), 5224.
WALLACE (David), 1423, 3397.
WALLACE (Mike), 6826.
Wallenberg (Jacob), 7791.
Wallenberg (Marcus), 7791.
Wallenstein (Albrecht Wenzel Eusebius von, Herzog von Friedland), 7412.
WALLERFELT (Bengt), 5137.
Wallis (John), 5646.
WALMSLEY (Andrew Stephen), 5225.
WALTER (Christopher), 2958.
WALTER (Dirk), 4510.
WALTER (John), 4575.
WALTER-KARYDI (E.), 2236.
WALTHER (Karl Klaus), 139.
WALTHER (Peter Th.), 5740.
WALZ (Dorothea), 59.
WANDEL (Lee Palmer), 5523.
WANDYCZ (Piotr Stefan), 4956.
WANEGFFELEN (Thierry), 5344.
WANG (Chaoguang), 8211.
WANG (David D.), 8022.
WANG (Di), 8212.

WANG (Guanghua), 8213.
Wang (Guowei), 8162.
WANG (Jessica), 6173.
Wang (Jingwei), 8102.
WANG (Junyi), 8214.
WANG (Kaixi), 8215.
WANG (Qinsheng), 8216.
WANG (Qisheng), 8217.
WANG (Shanjun), 8218.
Wang (Tao), 8154.
WANG (Xianming), 8219.
WANG (Yuhe), 8220.
WANG (Yuhua), 8221.
WANG (Yuzhe), 8222.
WANNER (Heinz), 1255.
WANNING (Frank), 6376.
WAPLER (Claire), 8023.
WARBURG (Margit), 1329.
WARD (J. V.), 1485.
WARD BISSEL (Roger), 6486.
WARDEN (P. G.), 2306.
WARDLE (David), 2672.
WARD-PERKINS (Bryan), 2806.
WAREHAM (Andrew), 3242.
WARIS (Elina), 7023.
WARLAND (D.), 2259.
WARNKE (Ingo), 3615.
WARREN (Frank A.), 5711.
WARTELLE (A.), 2140.
WARTENWEILER (David), 5758.
WASHBOURNE (R.), 1914.
Washington (George), 5208.
WASSERSTROM (Steven M.), 1387.
WASSILIOU (Alexandra-Kyriaki), 229.
WATANABE (Koichi), 8316.
WATANABE (Takashi), 8289, 8317.
WATANABE-O'KELLY (Helen), 5562, 6623.
WATRIN (Christian), 4476.
WATSON (A.), 1512.
WATSON (A.), 2468.
WATSON (A.), 2948.
WATSON (Bruce Allen), 7769.
WATSON (P.), 2673.
WATSON (W. G. E.), 1734.
WATT (J. W.), 2872.
WATTERSON (B.), 1658.
WATTS (Sheldon), 6175.
WAŻNIEWSKI (Władysław), 4957.
WEAVER (John C.), 7386.
WEBB (J. M.), 1541.
WEBB (Ruth), 3092.
Weber (Alfred), 4415.
WEBER (Andreas Otto), 3430.
WEBER (Andreas), 8004.
WEBER (Christoph), 1351.
Weber (Edmund), 1331.
WEBER (Edouard-Henri), 3714.
WEBER (G.), 2008.
WEBER (Gregor), 1269.

WEBER (Jacques), 7865, 8024.
Weber (Max), 802, 847, 1084, 1092, 1335.
WEBER (S.), 1513.
WEBER SOROS (Susan), 6511.
WEBSTER (Jill R.), 3909.
WEGWOOD (C. V.), 7420.
WEHLER (Hans U.), 676.
WEI (Hongyun), 8223.
WEI (Ian), 3363.
WEIBEL (Ernest), 7882.
WEIDENFELD (Werner), 978.
WEIJERS (O.), 300.
WEIL (Françoise), 140.
WEIL (Rachel Judith), 4576.
WEILEMANN (Peter), 4455.
WEILER (Ingomar), 898.
WEINBERG (Gerhard), 7679.
WEINE (Stevan M.), 4111.
WEINER (Amir), 5712.
WEINER (Dora B.), 6176.
WEINER (Douglas R.), 6669.
WEINER (Gaby), 5764.
WEINGARTEN (Michael), 6143.
Weinheber (Josef), 6297.
WEINLICH (Barbara), 2360.
WEIR (R.), 2469.
WEISHAUPT (Arnd), 2524.
WEIß (Pia), 4476.
WEISS (Valentine), 448.
WEITHMAN (Paul J.), 5993.
WEITZMANN (M. P.), 2865.
Weizsäcker (Carl Friedrich von), 5985.
WELCH (Cliff), 7064.
WELCH (Martin G.), 3159.
WELCH (Steven R.), 7201.
WELLENREUTHER (Hermann), 3954.
Wellington, (Arthur Wellesley, first duke of), 7473.
WELLS (David), 7531.
WELLS (Peter S.), 2823.
WELLSTEIN (Matthias), 2862.
WELTMAN (Sharon Aronofsky), 6177.
WELWEI (K. W.), 2009.
WELZ (Stefan), 6198.
WELZER (Harald), 543.
WEMHOFF (Matthias), 3462.
WENDE (Peter), 1098, 7286.
WENDEBOURG (Dorothea von), 5330.
WENDEHORST (Stephan), 3948.
WENDL (Tobias), 900.
WENDLAND (Ulrike), 677.
WENDORF (F.), 1623.
Wendt (Bernd-Jürgen), 7248.
WENGST (Udo), 486.
WENSKUS (O.), 2674.
WENSKY (Margret), 3204.
WENTA (J.), 563.

INDEX OF NAMES

WENTKER (Hermann), 7880.
WENZEL (Horst), 3587.
WERDING (Vera), 772.
WERKER (E.), 1501.
WERMICH (Jürgen), 296.
WERNER (Karl F.), 544.
WERNICKE (Günter), 8025.
WERTHEIMER (Eric), 8384.
Wesley (John), 5503.
WEST (Patricia), 478.
WESTBROOK (Raymond), 2525.
WESTERHOFF (Jan C.), 6025.
WESTERHOLT (Burchard Graf von), 7107.
WESTERMAN (Ingmar), 1107.
WESTERMANN-ANGERHAUSEN (Hiltrud), 3679.
WESTLEY (David), 8330.
WESTPHALEN (S.), 1596.
WETTE (Wolfram), 4471.
WETTIG (Gerhard), 8026.
Wettin (Konrad von), 3237.
WETTLAUFER (Jörg), 303, 3431.
WHALEN (Terence), 6377.
WHARTON (W. D.), 1896.
Whateley Darwall (Mary), 6262.
WHEALE (Nigel), 141.
WHEALEY (A.), 2971.
WHEATLEY (Alan Brent), 2949.
WHEELER (Bonnie), 3432.
WHEELER (Stephen M.), 2675.
WHELAN (Heide W.), 7024.
WHITAKER (Ewen A.), 6178.
WHITCHER (S.), 1725.
WHITCOMB (D.), 1809.
WHITE (Hayden), 880.
WHITE (Mark J.), 7819.
WHITE (Nicholas Ian), 8027.
WHITE (Nicholas J.), 7320.
WHITEHEAD (Barbara J.), 5827.
WHITELEY (Linda), 734.
WHITFIELD (Stephen J.), 5713.
WHITING (Tomas), 8385.
WHITMARSCH (T.), 1952.
WHITMORE (John K.), 3934.
WHITTAKER (J. C.), 1852.
WHITTAKER (Jason), 6378.
WIC (Wladyslawa), 8046.
WICKMAN (Patricia Riles), 7366.
WIDHALM (Sven), 6169.
WIDMER (G.), 1659.
WIEBE (Donald), 1388.
WIEBER-SCARIOT (Anja), 2336.
WIEDEMANN (Peter), 5731.
WIEDEMANN (Th.), 2470.
WIEDEN (Susanne bei der), 5524.
WIELAND (Carls), 3878.
WIELAND (Gernot R.), 3524.
WIELAND (Karin), 4517.
WIELAND (Lothar), 4516.
WIELAND-KARIMI (Almut), 4009.

WIELING (Hans), 2487.
WIENER (Jarrod), 7296.
WIESEHÖFER (J.), 1812.
WIESFLECKER (Hermann), 4088.
WIGET (Josef), 964.
WIGGERSHAUS (Norbert Theodor), 7906.
WIGHTMAN (Clare), 6728.
WIJFFELS (Alain), 1244.
WIKANDER (Ulla), 7065.
Wilamowitz-Moellendorff (Ulrich von), 803.
WILDE (Alexander), 4182.
WILENTZ (Sean), 3500.
Wilhelm II, Dt. Kaiser u. König von Preußen, 317.
WILHELM-SCHAFFER (Irmgard), 3501.
WILK (Stalislauw), 5321.
WILKENS (Andreas), 7907, 8029.
WILLEMS (W. J. H.), 2750.
WILLIAM OF MALMESBURY, 3183.
WILLIAMS (A. N.), 3755.
WILLIAMS (Andrew P.), 6197.
WILLIAMS (Caroline A.), 7382.
WILLIAMS (Craig A.), 2582.
WILLIAMS (David), 1067.
WILLIAMS (David), 3502.
WILLIAMS (Duncan Ryüken), 5528.
Williams (Glyndwr), 7315.
WILLIAMS (John), 61.
WILLIAMS (Peter J.), 5303.
WILLIAMS (R.), 2959.
WILLIAMS (S.), 2824.
WILLIAMS HEDGEPETH (Julie), 5878.
WILLIAMSON (Charles T.), 8030.
WILLIAMSON (Elaine), 450.
WILLIAMSON (Jeffrey G.), 6655.
WILLIAMSON (Tom), 6780.
WILLICH (Cornelia), 268.
WILLIMAN (Daniel), 21.
WILLIS (Michael), 4007.
WILLIS (Sherry L.), 3433.
WILMERING (Antoine), 6499.
WILMETH (Dan B.), 6530.
WILSON (A. S.), 1529.
WILSON (Alfred Jeyaratnam), 5125.
WILSON (Andrew), 2788.
WILSON (Bryan), 1372.
WILSON (D. E.), 1853.
WILSON (Fred), 6027.
WILSON (P.), 1660.
WILSON (Sandra), 7531.
WILSON (W. Daniel), 5714, 6379.
Wilson (Wodrow), 7616.
WILSON JONES (M.), 2751.
WILSON-CHEVALIER (Kathleen), 6206.
WINAND (J.), 1635.
WINANS (Amy E.), 1418.

Winckelmann (Johann Joachim), 6405.
WINCKLER (Onn), 5152.
Windhorst (Ludwig), 4453.
WINDLER (C.), 7398.
WINE (Humphey), 6179.
WING (E. S.), 1472.
WINKELBAUER (Thomas), 4089.
WINKLER (Heinrich August), 4008, 4416, 4470, 4518, 7100.
WINKS (Robin W.), 1008.
WINTER (Jay), 675.
WINTERBOTTOM (Michael), 3183.
WINTERLING (Aloys), 2526.
WINTERS (Jane), *VII*.
WINTLE (Michael), 371.
WINTON (R. I.), 1968.
WIRSCHING (Andreas), 777, 4519.
WIRTH (Jean), 408.
WIRTLER (Lars), 1183.
WIRTY (Emeline), 479.
WISTRICH (Robert S.), 3943.
WITAKOWSKI (Witold), 512, 2962.
WITHERS (Charles W. J.), 338.
WITSCHEL (Christian), 2825.
WITTE (Els), 4103.
WITTE (Peter), 4388.
WITTENBROCK (Rolf), 1165.
WITTER (José Sebastiao), 4139.
Wittgenstein (Ludwig), 6013.
WITTNER (Lawrence S.), 8025.
WIXFORTH (Harald), 1190.
WOBESER (Gisela Von), 5452.
WODAK (Ruth), 5716.
WOFFORD (S.), 2094.
WOGAN-BROWNE (Jocelyn), 3616, 3893.
WOHL (Hellmut), 6407.
WÖHRLE (G.), 2141, 2149.
WOJTYSKA (Henri Damien), 5321.
WOLF (Eric Robert), 1108.
WOLF (Gerhard), 3592.
WOLF (Kurt), 6028.
WOLF (Peter), 3919.
WOLF (Thomas), 6284.
WOLFE (Patrick), 679.
WOLFF (C.), 2214.
WOLFF (Catherine), 2583.
Wolff (Christian), 5944.
WOLFF (Christoph), 6542.
WOLFF (David), 5026.
WOLFF (H.), 2471.
WOLFFSOHN (Michael), 297.
WOLFRUM (Edgar), 673, 680.
WOLFSCHMIDT (Gudrun), 6064.
WOLFZETTEL (Friederich), 6292.
WOLIKOW (Serge), 7141.
WOLLAND (Brian), 6532.
WOLLER (Hans), 4790.
Wollstonecraft (Mary), 5918.
WOLTERS (Reinhard), 2584.

WOMACK (John), 4843.
WOOD (Allen W.), 6029.
WOOD (Andy), 7027.
WOOD (Diana), 3771.
WOOD (I. N.), 2797.
WOOD (Nancy), 681.
WOODHOUSE (C. M.), 4584.
WOODS (Mary N.), 7028.
WOODS (Susanne), 6241.
WOODWARD (Ralph Lee), 8361.
WOOLGAR (C. M.), 3920, 7473.
WOOLNER (David B.), 7737.
WOOTTON (G. E.), 2676.
WORMALD (Patrick), 3355.
WÖRNER (Martin), 480.
WORSTER (Donald), 5189.
Wortley Montagu (Mary), 6252.
WORTZEL (Larry M.), 1046.
WOZNIAK (J.), 1476.
WOŹNICZKA (Zygmunt), 8031.
WRÅKBERG (Urban), 6181.
WRIGHT (Alison), 3670.
WRIGHT (J. F.), 6819.
WRIGHT (R.), 298.
WU (Shanzhong), 8225.
WU (Songdi), 8226.
WU (Zhuo), 8227.
WULF (Rüdiger), 5795.
WULF (U.), 1609.
WULFSTAN (Archbishop of York), 3332.
WUNDER (John R.), 3925.
WURM (A.), 2843.
WYATT (David K.), 3934, 5156.
WYATT (N.), 1734.
WYCKOFF (William), 372.
WYCZAŃSKI (Andrzej), 7421.
WYKE (M.), 674, 686.
WYLIE (G.), 2010.
WYLY (Bryan Weston), 3617.
WYPUSTEK (A.), 2950.

X

XELLA (P.), 1610.
Xenophon, 2048, 2102.
Xianfeng, emperor of China, 8268.
XIMENIUS (Rodericus de Rada), 3764.
XU (Tang), 8229.
XU (Tingsheng), 8230.
Xuantong, emperor of China, 8239.
XUE (Ruili), 8231.
XUE (Wei), 8242.

Y

Yahil (Leni), 865.
YAJIMA (Izumi), 8300.
Yakhontov (A. N.), 4987.
YAKOBSON (Alexander), 2472.

YALÇIN (Ü.), 1560.
YAMADA (Eiko), 4803.
YAMADA (Izumi), 6724.
YAMAGISHI (Tomoko), 8072.
YAMAGUCHI (Hideo), 8286.
YAMAGUCHI (Teruomi), 5557.
YAMAGUCHI (Toru), 8318.
YAMAMOTO (Koji), 8319.
YAMAMOTO (Shintaro), 4577.
YAMAN (Ahmet Emin), 7142.
YAMANAKA (Yutaka), 8320.
YAMANOUCHI (Yasushi), 1036.
YAMAUCHI (Masayuki), 8073.
Yan (Fu), 8219.
YAN (Lixian), 8232.
YANG (Jibo), 8233.
YANG (Kuisong), 8234.
YANG (Kuisong), 8235.
YANG (Yuqing), 8236.
YANIKDAG (Yüzel), 7620.
Yanin (Valentin L.), 3216.
YANNAI (E.), 1779.
YANNI (Carla), 481.
YANNOPOULOS (P. A.), 2975.
YASUR-LANDAU (A.), 1776.
YATES (Margaret), 1192.
YATES (Nigel), 5525.
YATROMANOLAKIS (D.), 2142.
YAVETZ (Zvi), 2473.
YE (Jiachi), 8237.
YE (Meilan), 8238.
YEAGER (Mary A.), 1191.
YEANDLE (Laetitia), 15.
YESILBURSA (Behçet K), 8032.
YEZERSKI (I.), 1561.
YI (Young), 7399.
YILMAZ (Suhnaz), 5177.
YIN (Junli), 8239.
YLI-JOKIPII (Pentti), 373.
YLIKANGAS (Heikki), 1142, 7029.
YOLTON (John), 1400.
YONEYAMA (Lisa), 687.
Yongzheng, emperor of China, 8245.
Yorimoto (Minamoto), 4799.
YOSHIKO (Nagano), 7667.
YOSHIOKA (Akihiko), 6820.
YOSHIOKA (Hitoshi), 6110.
YOUINGS (Joyce), 4523.
YOUNG (Arlene), 6380.
YOUNG (Brigitte), 7030.
YOUNG (Hilary), 6512.
YOUNG (John W.), 1047.
YOUNG (Katherine K.), 1347.
YOUNGBLOOD (Denise J.), 6633.
YU (Jiang), 8240.
YU (Pyong-yong), 7825.
YU (Shanpu), 8241.
YU (Songjiang), 8242.
YU (Yingshi), 8228.
Yuan (Shikai), 8129.

YUASA (Kunihiro), 8243.
YU-JOSE (Lydia N.), 4930, 7300, 8033.
YUN (Bartolomé), 6734.
YUZBASHIAN (Karen), 3093.

Z

ZABBIA (Marino), 688.
ZABORSKA (Urszula), 3921.
ZACARIAS (Agostino), 5073.
ZACHARASIEWICZ (Waldemar), 898.
ZAFRA DE LA TORRE (N.), 1525.
ZAGER (Werner), 2876.
ZAGNI (Luisa), 3144.
ZAGORIN (Perez), 881.
ZAGRA (Giuliana), 432.
ZAGREBIN (Aleksej E.), 926.
ZAHAREAS (A. N.), 3028.
ZAHNER (Paul), 3756.
ZAIDI (Z. H.), 4893.
ZAIMOVA (Raia), 7423.
ZAINA (E.), 2677.
ZAKARIA (Fareed), 7537.
ZAKARIA (Rafiq), 4644.
Zalewski (August), 4956.
ZALI (Anne), 32.
ZALIZNJAK (Andrej A.), 22.
ZAMBON (Francesco), 3910.
ZAMORA BONILLA (Javier), 5107.
ZAMORA VICENTE (Alonso), 5759.
ZANATTA (Loris), 4065.
ZANETTI (Gianfrancesco), 5943.
ZANGHERI (Renato), 5894, 6776.
ZANGHI (Claudio), 4211.
ZANINI (A.), 2278.
ZARD (Philippe), 6381.
ZARINI (V.), 2337.
ZARKA (Yves-Charles), 760, 1053, 5624.
ZARRI (Gabriella), 1245, 5399.
ŽATKULIAK (Jozef), 5032.
ZAUN (Harald), 7621.
ZAUNSTÖCK (Holger), 7031.
ZBUCHEA (Gheorghe), 7622.
ZEBROWSKI (Mark), 6428.
ZECCHINI (G.), 2968, 3094.
ZECCHINI (Salvatore), 6800.
ZECHIEL-ECKES (Klaus), 3757.
ZEHETBAUER (Ernst), 4090, 7474.
ZEITLER (B.), 409.
ZELLER (Olivier), 6838.
ZEMANEK (K.), 7202.
ZEMON DAVIS (Natalie), 882.
ZEMTSOV (Vladimir N.), 7475.
Zeno Tarsensis, 2145.
Zenon, Sanctus, 2907.
ZERBO (Yacouba), 8034.
ZERDOUN BAT-YEHOUDA (Monique), 73.

ZERMEÑO PADILLA (Guillermo), 883.
ZEVI (Fausto), 2143, 2279.
ZEZINA (Marija R.), 5717.
Z'GRAGGEN (Bruno), 5526.
ZHANG (Beigen), 8244.
ZHANG (Dianren), 8245.
ZHANG (Guohui), 8246.
ZHANG (Haipeng), 8247.
ZHANG (Hong), 8248.
Zhang (Ji), 8139.
ZHANG (Jin), 8249.
ZHANG (Jinlong), 8250.
ZHANG (Jishun), 8251.
ZHANG (Li), 8252.
ZHANG (Li), 8253.
ZHANG (Li), 8254.
ZHANG (Lianhong), 8255.
ZHANG (Pengyuan), 8256.
ZHANG (Sheng), 8257.
Zhang (Taifei, Binglin), 8221.
ZHANG (Tiancheng), 8258.
ZHANG (Wenyu), 8259.
ZHANG (Xiaopeng), 8260.
ZHANG (Yingjin), 6533.
ZHANG (Yuanlin), 1049.
Zhang (Zhidong), 8219.
ZHAO (Jian), 8261.
ZHAO (Ping'an), 8262.
ZHAO (Xianye), 8263.
ZHAO (Xiude), 8264.
ZHAO (Yunkun), 8265.
ZHAVORONKOV (Petr I.), 2994.

ZHENG (Huixi), 8266.
ZHILIN (Mikhail G.), 1497.
ZHU (Donghan), 8268.
ZHU (Qingbo), 8269.
ZHU (Ying), 8270.
ZHUANG (Jifa), 8271.
Zhukov (Georgii Konstantinovich), 7757.
Ziegenbalg (Bartholomaeus), 5515.
ZIEGLER (Charles E.), 1109.
ZIEGLER (Dieter), 4520.
ZIEGLER (Joanna E.), 3782, 3903.
ZIEGLER (N.), 1719.
ZIERMANN (M.), 1661.
ZIETHEN (G.), 1904.
ZIK (Yaakov), 6182.
ZILCH (Reinhold), 4393.
ZILYNSKÁ (Blanka), 6168.
ZIMIN (Aleksandr A.), 3333.
ZIMMER (Oliver), 5150.
ZIMMERMANN (B.), 2678.
ZIMMERMANN (Bénédicte), 7062.
ZIMMERMANN (Clemens), 5704.
ZIMMERMANN (Harro), 6285.
ZIMMERMANN (Hubert), 8035.
ZIMMERMANN (Karin), 59.
ZIMMERMANN (Margarete), 6914.
ZIMMERMANN (Martin),564.
ZIMMERMANN (Volker), 7680.
ZIMPEL (Detlef), 748.
ZIOLKOWSKI (Adam), 2585, 2725.
ZISKIN (Rochelle), 6441.
ZITZLSPERGER (Ulrike), 3592.

Ziusudra, king of Sumer, 1668.
ZIVIN (Joselyn), 6634.
ŽNIDARIČ (Marjan), 5064.
Zoffany (Johan), 6478.
ZOGRAFOU (A.), 2726.
ZOLESI (Ilaria), 46.
ZOLETTO (Silvia), 4722.
ZOLL-ADAMIKOWA (Helena), 3122.
ZOLOTONOSOV (Mikhail N.), 6487.
ZOLOTUKHINA (M. V.), 7032.
ZOLYOMI (G.), 1720.
ZONABEND (Françoise), 550.
ZOOK (Melinda S.), 4578.
ZORN (J.), 1780.
Zou (Linghan), 8134.
ZOVATTO (Pietro), 5345.
ZUB (Alexandru), 1030.
ZUBKOVA (Elena), 5027.
ZUÑIGA (Jean-Paul), 8386.
ZUO (Shuangwen), 8272.
ŽUPANCIC (Matej), 526.
ŽUPANOV (Ines G.), 5453.
ŻURAWSKI VEL GRAJEWSKI (Radosław Paweł), 7538.
ZÜRCHER (Erik-Jan), 5178, 8051.
ZÜRCHER (Thomas), 7033.
ZURNDORFER (Harriet T.), 8111.
ŽVANUT (Maja), 1000.
ZWACH (Eva), 482.
ZWEITE (Armin), 6488.
ZWIERLEIN (Otto), 2679.
ZYRJANOV (Pavel N.), 5460.

GEOGRAPHICAL INDEX

A

Abric Romaní (Capellades, Barcelona), 1510.
Acarnania, 1979.
Achaia, 3064.
Achém (sultanato), 7406.
Acre, 7570.
Aden, 7354.
Adriatique (mer), 6712.
Aegaeum (Mare), 3039.
Aegyptus, 941, 1144, 1611-1661.
Aesernia, 2785.
Aethiopia, 1466.
Aezanoi, 1600.
Afghanistan, 893, 4009-4017, 7832, 8056.
Africa proconsularis, 2533, 2719.
Afrique, 330, 936, 1280, 3083, 4761, 4808, 4857, 4866, 5071, 5132, 5263, 5445, 5449, 6506, 6816, 7156, 7211, 7213, 7226, 7319, 7342-7364, 7556, 7638, 7817, 7899, 7938, 8330-8360. – A. centrale, 6092. – A. centrale-occidentale, 8347. – A. occidentale, 8355. – A. orientale, 5446. – A. septentrionale, 8359. – A. sud-occidentale, 7358.
Afyon, 6802.
Ägäis, 1670.
Aigai, 1859.
'Ain Assawir, 1779.
al-Andalus, 1603.
Albania v. Shqiperi.
Albayern, 3430.
Alcántara (Cáceres), 1489.
Aleppo, 1698.
Alexandria, 430, 1641, 1657, 2786.
Alger, 353, 5571.
Algérie, 333, 4024-4036, 7297, 7352, 7353, 7830, 7855, 7928.
Alkmaar, 6847.
Al-Mutawakkil's Damascus, 1672.
Alonia, 1852.
Alsace, 4346.
Altai, 1550, 1557.
Amari (Creta), 1848.

Amarna, 1658.
Amathus, 2220.
Amazon basin, 7367.
Amazonia, 4921.
Ambrona (Soria, España), 1506.
Amérique, 457, 946, 1044, 1212, 3970, 5258, 5261, 5263, 5268, 5279, 5363, 5444, 5635, 5648, 5657, 5688, 5694, 5713, 5734, 5849, 5878, 5975, 6037, 6145, 6173, 7319, 7365-7382, 8361-8386. – A. centrale, 7835, 8361, 8376. – A. latine, 166, 1094, 3940, 3959, 3974, 3979, 3994, 5362, 5612, 6062, 6639, 6652, 6733, 6785, 7040, 7123, 7230, 7235, 7244, 7289, 7372, 7520, 7534, 7683, 7966, 8386. – A. méridionale, 944, 1223, 5783, 5825, 6383, 8366. – A. septentrionale, 3322, 3925.
Amur river valley, 1522, 7499.
Anatolie, 209, 1560, 1598, 1742, 3640.
Ancona, 3164.
Angles-sur-l'Anglin, 1495.
Angola, 4037, 4038, 7302, 7344, 7973, 8002.
Antilles, 330.
Antinoopolis, 1613.
Antiochia, 2925, 2962, 2971, 2999.
Antwerp (Belgique), 47.
Aomen, Macao, 7332, 8097, 8113, 8115, 8163, 8247, 8272.
Aphrodisias (Caria), 2818.
Apollonia, 2741.
Apulia, 2270, 2277, 2439.
'Aqaba, 1769.
Arab countries, 7830, 7967, 8010, 8012.
Arabie Saoudite, Saudi Arabia, 5029.
Arabie, 636, 3294.
Arad, 932, 3672.
Aragona, 3105.
Ardea, 2261.
Arelate, 2804.

Argentina, 173, 1003, 1216, 1224, 1424, 4039-4065, 5272, 5633, 5839, 6555, 7490, 7527, 7666, 7704, 7835, 7876.
Argos, 1992, 2185.
Ariyāramna, 1584.
Arkhangel'skaia oblast', 593.
Armagh (Ireland), 3150.
Armenija, 641, 3881, 4066, 4067, 5162, 5165, 7478, 7483, 7559.
Arras, 3247.
Artois, 3372, 7417.
Ascoli Piceno, 3855.
Asie, 1280, 2437, 2508, 2540, 2975, 3018, 3982, 5132, 5444, 5638, 5657, 6383, 6611, 6619, 6749, 7319, 7321-7341, 7440, 7929, 7999, 8037-8329, 8389. – A. centrale, 8049-8073. – A. du nord-ouest, 238. – A. du sud-est, 367, 896, 7934, 8039, 8074-8096. – A. méridionale, 647, 3316, 7831, 7854, 7865, 8074-8096. – A. minor, 1585, 1595, 1791, 2403, 2746. – A. occidentale, 8049-8073. – Asie orientale, 7252, 8299.
Aşıklı, 1481.
Assur, 1706.
Athenae, 224, 423, 1291, 1804, 1859, 1864, 1871, 1969, 1985, 1987, 1990, 1991, 1994, 1996, 1999, 2002, 2009, 2012, 2013, 2021, 2024, 2052, 2053, 2059, 2069, 2109, 2243, 2244.
Atlantique (ocean), 325, 339, 1466.
Augsburg, 64.
Augusta Traiana, 2461.
Ausones, 2272, 2273.
Australia, 960, 4068-4072, 5488, 6195, 6558, 6606, 6667, 6904, 6910, 6945, 7385, 7971, 8391, 8392.
Austria v. Österreich.
Auxerre, 3667.
Aversa, 5418.
Avilés (España), 3137.
Ayanis, 1577, 1579.

Ayodhya, 7844.
Azerbaijan, 1033.

B

Babylonia, 157, 1683, 1689, 1699, 1709, 1710, 1764.
Bactriana, 1663, 1798, 2191.
Baiae, 2751.
Bajo Zamorano, 4830.
Bǎlgarija, Bulgaria, 648, 933, 3681, 4141-4155, 5329, 7212, 7480, 7502, 7511, 7525, 7717, 7736, 7744, 7853, 8011.
Balkans, 655, 1031, 3958, 3965, 3989, 4078, 7246, 7539, 7590, 7622, 7840, 7965.
Baltique (mer, pays), 907, 3214, 5329, 5616, 7245, 7443.
Bamberg (Deutschland), 139.
Bangladesh, 7803, 7844, 8024, 8095.
Banská Bystrica, 5040.
Baranivka, 7774.
Barcelona, 3146, 3288, 5113, 5815, 6607.
Barcino, 2328.
Basarabia v. Bessarabia.
Basel, 5523, 6927.
Basra (golfe de), 5169.
Bayern, 123, 142, 3231, 3430, 7138.
Beagle, 1469.
Béarn (France), 3335.
Beauvais, 5369, 6836.
Beersheba, 1774.
Bègles (France), 3389.
Beijing, 7553.
Belarus v. Belorussija.
Belgique, 47, 249, 961, 1029, 3854, 4092-4103, 4867, 5463, 6475, 6909, 7020, 7188, 7389, 7565, 7747.
Belorussija, 233, 605, 3949, 4091, 4816, 5293, 7772.
Bengal, 4630, 4638.
Beni Hasan, 1629.
Benin, 7359.
Berg (Herzorgtum), 5281.
Berkshire, 1192.
Berlin, 1592, 1605, 4395, 4449, 5595, 5708, 5740, 5861, 6369, 6821, 6822, 6903, 6968, 6817, 7818, 7898, 7914.
Besançon (France), 3129.
Bessarabia, Basarabia, 949, 4976, 4978.
Beth Shean, 1626, 2743.
Beth Yerah, 1777.
Bhutan, 8095.
Biafra, 7359.
Bilbao, 3115.

Bisitun, 636.
Bithynia, 2308.
Bitonto, 2789.
Black Sea region, 1566.
Black Sea, 7287.
Böblingen (Landkreises), 3124.
Boeotia, 2014.
Bogotá, 6850.
Bohinj, 7554.
Bolivia, 1224, 1416, 4104-4108, 6613, 7269, 7666, 7988.
Bologna, 1080, 3384, 3422, 3895, 5384, 5534, 6421, 6537.
Bombay, 6619.
Bomdila, 7918.
Bordeaux, 3389, 6708.
Borodino, 7475.
Bosna-Hercegovina, 4109-4111, 4811, 5257, 5329, 6691, 7859.
Bosoprian Kingdom, 2077.
Boston, 6479.
Botnie (golfe de), 7463.
Botswana, 7650.
Bourges, 89.
Bourgogne, 3675.
Bramant, 3254.
Brandenburg, 7437.
Brasil, 179, 307, 4112-4139, 4055, 4829, 4961, 5269, 5435, 6134, 6643, 6898, 6970, 7000, 7064, 7228, 7234, 7276, 7302, 7376, 7378, 7379, 7391, 7432, 7809, 7963.
Braşov, 6832.
Breslau, 5748.
Brigstock (England), 3366.
Britannia Minor, 2430.
Britannia, 2310, 2402, 2706.
British Isles, 25, 952.
Brooklyn, 5434.
Bruges, 3371.
Brunei Darussalam, 4140.
Bu Njem, 2586.
Bucovina, Bukowina, 3944.
Budapest, 7624, 7766.
Buenos Aires, 4041, 4050, 4052, 6765, 6825, 6865, 6923, 7425.
Bukowina v. Bucovina.
Bulgaria v. Bǎlgarija.
Burkina Faso, 4156, 8034.
Burma, 8248.
Bursa, 5792.
Burundi, 4157.
Byzantion, Empire byzantin, 225, 232, 277, 409, 691, 1215, 1386, 1795, 2872, 2960-3094.

C

Cachemire, 8024.
Calabar, 7313.

Calabria, 3009.
Callatis, 2475.
Cambodia, 4158, 4159, 7851, 7856, 7862.
Cambrésis, 3372.
Cambridge, 525.
Çamëria (Albania), 7541.
Cameroon, 7354, 8335.
Campania, 3649.
Canada, 464, 976, 4160-4168, 5264, 5736, 6667, 6904, 6910, 6935, 7273, 7737, 7813, 7935, 8013.
Cancho Roano, 1452.
Canton v. Guangzhou.
Cape Colony, 7361.
Caprivi, 4863.
Caria, 1586.
Caribbean area, 3967, 6758, 7235, 8376.
Carinthia, 3676.
Carla-Bayle, 5994.
Carpates (bassin), 7567.
Cartagena (España), 3454.
Carthago Nova, 2439.
Carthago, 1765, 1778, 2426, 2701, 2942.
Castilla, 199, 202, 3284, 3359, 3605, 5098, 6734, 6784.
Çatalhöyük (Türkiye), 1517.
Cataluña, 3376, 3909, 5086, 5119, 5848, 6734.
Cebu, 4928.
Čechy, 171, 281, 3515, 3733, 3892, 4234, 5368, 5667, 5719, 6221, 6954, 7010.
Ceos, 1872.
Cerro Virtud (Cuevas de Almanzora, Almería), 1521.
Československo, Czechoslovak Republik, 602, 1022, 1138, 3947, 3997, 4005, 4213-4255, 5329, 5650, 6650, 6651, 6725, 6811, 6940, 7092, 7129, 7225, 7514, 7542, 7547, 7588, 7619, 7631, 7632, 7640, 7646, 7648, 7655, 7672, 7675, 7686, 7714, 7723, 7752, 7776, 7788, 7797, 7848, 7902, 7904, 7915, 7962, 7964, 7982, 8036.
Ceuta, 2327.
Chaeronea, 1989.
Chalcedon, 2882.
Chalcidica, 1976.
Champagne, 1553.
Chatteris (Abbey), 3108.
Chiapas, 975, 4843.
Chiaravalle della Colomba (abbazie), 3656.
Chicago, 2493.
Chichén Itzá (Yucatán), 8362.

GEOGRAPHICAL INDEX

Chile, 947, 4055, 4169-4182, 5420, 7368, 7527, 7529, 7810, 7921.
China, 304, 350, 521, 594, 601, 617, 1012, 1046, 1115, 1233, 1570, 5447, 5448, 5550, 6658, 7324, 7332, 7410, 7493, 7518, 7546, 7553, 7579, 7596, 7608, 7652, 7654, 7660, 7728, 7831, 7861, 7872, 7901, 7918, 7975, 8039, 8043, 8079, 8097-8272, 8313.
Chocó (Colombia), 7382.
Ciad, 7860, 7986.
Cilicia, 1543, 1546, 1589.
Circesium, 1697.
Città del Vaticano, 7408, 7608.
Ciudad de México, 6830.
Claros, 1859, 2042.
Clermont-Ferrand, 7047.
Cluj, 5756.
Cnidus, 1565.
Cnossus, 1842, 1844, 1853.
Coimbra (Portugal), 3138.
Colle di Val d'Elsa, 3154.
Colombia, 1416, 4183-4189.
Colonia Ulpia Traiana (Xanten), 2773.
Colophon, 2042.
Colorado, 372.
Congo, 942, 4190-4194, 7355, 7524, 7896.
Connecticut, 5196, 5730.
Constantinopolis, 320, 2460, 2729, 2925, 2996, 3002, 3013, 3017, 3034, 3055, 3062.
Copenhagen, 3913.
Cordillera Cantábrica, 1530.
Corinthus, 2181, 2888.
Corse, 264, 982, 4294, 4347.
Costa Rica, 4195-4198, 7867, 8374.
Côte-d'Or (France), 3117.
Cous, 1857, 2037.
Cova Matutano (Villafamés, Castellón), 1502.
Coventry, 4577.
Creta, 1842, 1847, 1849.
Crimean Scythia, 1552.
Crna Gora, Montenegro, 4852, 5251.
Croatia v. Hrvatska.
Cuba, 318, 4205-4209, 7231, 7232, 7526, 7819, 7820, 7887, 7945, 7969, 7983.
Cumae, 1860.
Cuzco, 4925, 7369.
Cyprus v. Kipros.
Cyrenaica, 2695.
Cyzicus, 2385.
Czechoslovak Republik v. Československo.

D

Dacia, 2324.
Dagestan, 892.
Dahshur, 1648.
Dalmacija, Dalmatia, 2578, 3026, 3075, 5248.
Dalmatia v. Dalmacija.
Damas, 6099.
Damascus, 3023.
Danmark, 953, 1004, 1005, 1006, 1026, 1243, 1361, 1459, 3375, 3447, 3474, 4256-4269, 5489, 5847, 5873, 6638, 6646, 6793, 7050, 7785, 7908.
Danuvius (Flumen), 2456.
Darmstadt (Stadt), 3124.
Darmstadt-Dieburg (Landkreises), 3124.
Daunia, 1446, 1480, 2883.
Deccan, 6428.
Decumates agri, 2420.
Delhi, 4632.
Delos, 2071, 2228, 2232, 2247, 2249.
Delphi, 2019, 2082, 2103, 2225, 2469.
Den Haag, 6847.
Detva, 5037.
Deutschland, 97, 114, 132, 231, 259, 438, 471, 504, 519, 530, 539, 543, 553, 587, 591, 600, 618, 657, 660, 676, 677, 680, 684, 698, 868, 913, 957, 1001, 1022, 1024, 1069, 1098, 1100, 1122, 1130, 1217, 1293, 1411, 1434, 3119, 3126, 3214, 3283, 3285, 3563, 3587, 3592, 3615, 3923, 3945, 3947, 3954, 3973, 3999, 4008, 4238, 4373, 4386-4520, 4866, 4867, 4871, 4885, 4888, 5016, 5141, 5333, 5338, 5340, 5367, 5373, 5386, 5405, 5406, 5442, 5480, 5490, 5494, 5500, 5502, 5507, 5545, 5553, 5570, 5580, 5589, 5602, 5627, 5628, 5630, 5631, 5647, 5649, 5680, 5689, 5694, 5695, 5724, 5737, 5763, 5766, 5787, 5795, 5804, 5830, 5831, 5845, 5853, 5858, 5864, 5876, 5899, 6064, 6068, 6070, 6084, 6090, 6115, 6140, 6153, 6256, 6285, 6315, 6329, 6450, 6513, 6535, 6539, 6542, 6553, 6637, 6651, 6659, 6709, 6809, 6851, 6860, 6866, 6888, 6917, 6924, 6930, 6933, 6934, 6936, 6937, 6944, 6987, 7005, 7030, 7031, 7043, 7045, 7055, 7062, 7068, 7082, 7089, 7100, 7102, 7103, 7106, 7140, 7148, 7164, 7182, 7195, 7201, 7236, 7248, 7275, 7286, 7301, 7345, 7482, 7491, 7510, 7520, 7522, 7560, 7561, 7562, 7569, 7572, 7573, 7586, 7588, 7597, 7600, 7607, 7621, 7628, 7636, 7640, 7642, 7644, 7647, 7651, 7653, 7663, 7664, 7665, 7669, 7680, 7682, 7687, 7691, 7700, 7703, 7705, 7709, 7714, 7720, 7721, 7722, 7723, 7725, 7727, 7735, 7741, 7748, 7751, 7758, 7765, 7767, 7778, 7787, 7789, 7790, 7791, 7792, 7795, 7798, 7802, 7804, 7805, 7806, 7817, 7821, 7826, 7833, 7836, 7841, 7846, 7852, 7873, 7875, 7879, 7880, 7885, 7891, 7903, 7914, 7920, 7923, 7930, 7936, 7941, 7942, 7944, 7949, 7954, 7978, 7979, 7980, 7982, 7987, 7992, 7993, 7998, 8026, 8029, 8035. – v. Germaniae.
Deventer, 6847.
Diên Biên Phû, 7325.
Dijon, 6387.
Dniestr, 7388.
Dobrugia, 7523.
Dodona, 2119.
Dominican Republic, 4270-4275.
Don (lower), 1535.
Don forest-steppe region, 1555.
Donauraum, 3430.
Douala, 7348.
Dover (England), 80.
Duala, 8335.
Dublin, 5743.
Dubrovnik, 1171, 3393, 6829, 7019, 7450, 794.
Dyrrachium, 3019.

E

East Anglia, 3648, 6780.
East Asian Sea, 8313.
East Farm (Barnham, Suffolk), 1492.
East Flanders (Belgique), 47.
Easter Island, 1476.
Ebla, 1722, 1738, 1748.
Echternach (Kloster), 30.
Ecuador, 1416, 4276, 7298, 7838.
Edessa, 1594.
Egypt, 163, 229, 333, 1611-1661, 3271, 3311, 4277-4279, 5615, 7061.
El Alamein, 7752.
El Salvador, 4280, 4281.
Ellipi, 1802.
Emar, 1673, 1701.
Emilia Romagna, 4734, 5894.

Engelberg (Kloster), 35.
Engelthal (Deutschland), 3806.
England, 15, 44, 203, 239, 334, 343, 494, 501, 528, 552, 1074, 1114, 1244, 3096, 3102, 3120, 3136, 3142, 3159, 3183, 3187, 3233, 3264, 3268, 3332, 3355, 3365, 3396, 3495, 3528, 3558, 3564, 3579, 3593, 3616, 3624, 3648, 3650, 3669, 3805, 3889, 3902, 3920, 4525, 4526, 4542, 4545, 4576, 4578, 5277, 5287, 5290, 5294, 5295, 5307, 5451, 5473, 5483, 5510, 5604, 5606, 5634, 5658, 5661, 5663, 5664, 5698, 5700, 5715, 5801, 5802, 5807, 5809, 5891, 6000, 6135, 6191, 6196, 6199, 6200, 6215, 6259, 6269, 6274, 6279, 6423, 6432, 6512, 6518, 6531, 6575, 6605, 6614, 6721, 6757, 6779, 6860, 6883, 6913, 6955, 6960, 6995, 6999, 7008, 7056, 7058, 7089, 7405, 7415, 7417, 7435.
Ephesus, 1592, 3012, 3020.
Epidaurus, 2206.
Eretria, 2778.
Eridanus (flumen), 1540.
Ermland, 7888.
Eskilstuna, 1154.
Eskişehir, 3641.
España, Spain, 24, 149, 218, 267, 302, 358, 418, 507, 558, 753, 939, 990, 1095, 1112, 1163, 1206, 1230, 1270, 1426, 3111, 3163, 3180, 3270, 3287, 3301, 3417, 3451, 3532, 3552, 3576, 3582, 3588, 3652, 3665, 3718, 3767, 3870, 4321, 4588, 4672, 4869, 4963, 5074-5119, 5126, 5265, 5378, 5390, 5400, 5422, 5432, 5437, 5439, 5444, 5468, 5605, 5662, 5759, 6030, 6062, 6151, 6242, 6402, 6447, 6536, 6564, 6576, 6580, 6807, 6887, 6965, 7025, 7144, 7231, 7263, 7294, 7295, 7331, 7370, 7371, 7396, 7398, 7408, 7427, 7492, 7495, 7529, 7532, 7607, 7634, 7656, 7657, 7673, 7692, 7696, 7697, 7711, 7740, 7836, 7878, 7926. – v. Hispania.
Essex (England), 3102.
Estland v. Ëstonija.
Estonie v. Ëstonija.
Ëstonija, Estland, Estonie, 4282.
Ethiopia, 4283-4286, 5446, 7875. – v. Aethiopia.
Etruria, 2280, 2292, 2298, 2300.
Euphrates (flumen), 1697, 340.
Eurasie, 357, 970, 1455, 3934.

Europe, 246, 252, 363, 371, 427, 436, 493, 505, 617, 678, 681, 945, 1021, 1025, 1044, 1149, 1150, 1159, 1169, 1518, 2823, 2975, 3059, 3211, 3477, 3812, 3914, 3915, 3923, 3924, 3927, 3932, 3934, 3936, 3945, 3950, 3953, 3965, 3976, 3982, 3984, 3991, 4006, 5283, 5286, 5289, 5298, 5299, 5300, 5302, 5310, 5317, 5360, 5407, 5472, 5555, 5562, 5563, 5589, 5590, 5613, 5614, 5647, 5654, 5672, 5684, 5725, 5727, 5733, 5776, 5786, 5790, 5827, 6004, 6041, 6050, 6075, 6077, 6109, 6124, 6125, 6155, 6156, 6184, 6238, 6264, 6312, 6391, 6394, 6401, 6430, 6435, 6508, 6536, 6544, 6547, 6623, 6625, 6635, 6657, 6749, 6805, 6840, 6911, 6932, 6956, 6992, 7009, 7053, 7065, 7120, 7180, 7220, 7228, 7281, 7304, 7316, 7319, 7405, 7421, 7442, 7460, 7668, 7711, 7730, 7777, 7842, 7881, 7882, 7892, 7907, 7909, 7913, 7959, 7968, 7978, 8014, 8017, 8020, 8023, 8029. – E. centrale, 563, 3218, 3931, 3941, 3952, 3980, 4219, 5285, 5653, 6828, 7550, 7562, 7625, 7626, 7843. – E. centrale-orientale, 7613. – E. du nord-est, 1511. – Europe du sud-est, 3977. – E. méridionale, 7794. – E. occidentale, 684, 1177, 3929, 5874, 6670, 7508. – E. orientale, 322, 349, 618, 927, 1043, 1566, 3140, 3931, 3956, 3966, 5414, 5653, 6845, 7207, 7678, 7689, 7864, 7974, 8018. – E. rhénane, 3952. – E. septentrionale, 3671, 5679, 7459.
Eurymedon (flumen), 2006.

F

Faenza, 3262.
Făgăraş land, 3220.
Faras, 1656.
Fayyum, 1650, 1655.
Felsina (Bononia), 2286.
Fezzan, 7986.
Filipinas, Philippine, 166, 318, 4926-4930, 5440, 6653, 7300, 7331, 7334, 7623, 7667, 8033.
Finland v. Suomi.
Firenze, 135, 187, 441, 489, 3253, 3255, 3261, 3424, 3655, 3670, 5383, 5659, 6123, 4713, 4720.
Flandre wallonne, 3372.

Flandres, 70, 77, 83, 125, 3677, 4093, 6495.
Flores (Indonesia), 1500.
Fontainebleau, 128.
Fontevraud, 3884.
Forlì, 3262.
Fosso Conicchio (Viterbo), 1531.
France, 70, 88, 89, 151, 254, 270, 288, 316, 361, 368, 384, 410, 416, 449, 499, 511, 534, 535, 538, 559, 583, 587, 597, 614, 657, 663, 684, 703, 954, 1001, 1095, 1117, 1412, 1434, 3190, 3361, 3364, 3382, 3413, 3417, 3463, 3537, 3543, 3569, 3586, 3600, 3603, 3646, 3674, 3830, 3873, 3930, 3934, 3951, 4160, 4292-4385, 4518, 4519, 4854, 4857, 5244, 5270, 5310, 5323, 5328, 5331, 5336, 5344, 5379, 5381, 5389, 5393, 5482, 5485, 5504, 5509, 5511, 5519, 5560, 5575, 5580, 5581, 5591, 5607, 5610, 5624, 5636, 5643, 5674, 5685, 5707, 5761, 5766, 5780, 5788, 5789, 5794, 5796, 5797, 5828, 5837, 5842, 5843, 5860, 5991, 6028, 6056, 6193, 6208, 6223, 6240, 6242, 6254, 6260, 6261, 6283, 6293, 6324, 6376, 6386, 6390, 6409, 6426, 6447, 6478, 6541, 6550, 6551, 6553, 6557, 6567, 6598, 6601, 6617, 6629, 6645, 6713, 6730, 6736, 6740, 6750, 6755, 6778, 6779, 6799, 6803, 6833, 6861, 6888, 6889, 6914, 6931, 6948, 6990, 6994, 7062, 7094, 7102, 7123, 7145, 7183, 7216, 7255, 7301, 7329, 7341, 7347, 7389, 7397, 7400, 7403, 7407, 7413, 7417, 7423, 7425, 7429, 7430, 7432, 7435, 7441, 7452, 7455, 7457, 7459, 7471, 7475, 7500, 7506, 7514, 7523, 7528, 7536, 7540, 7542, 7547, 7549, 7553, 7558, 7561, 7566, 7567, 7572, 7576, 7580, 7590, 7597, 7599, 7605, 7613, 7614, 7634, 7637, 7644, 7670, 7672, 7675, 7698, 7702, 7715, 7721, 7727, 7732, 7753, 7773, 7775, 7786, 7811, 7829, 7914, 7923, 7936, 7942, 7974, 7986, 8008, 8017, 8024.
Frankfurt am Main, 3119, 6841, 6851.
French East Africa, 7759.
Friesland, 7166.
Friuli-Venezia Giulia, 918, 5417.

GEOGRAPHICAL INDEX 415

G

Gabon, 7948.
Galicia, 261, 3406, 4946, 4963.
Galizien, 3944.
Gallia Belgica, 2403.
Gallia Cisalpina, 2529.
Gallia Narbonensis, 2400.
Gallia, 2405, 2412, 2484, 2492, 2723.
Galway, 5747.
Gambia, 981.
Gansu, 8135.
Gästrikland, 6717.
Gatas, 1528.
Gattaiola (monastero, Italia), 3797.
Gaule, 407.
Gdańsk, 4938, 7430, 7569, 7589.
Gebel el-Haridi, 1660.
Gèneve, 100, 5145, 6413.
Genova, 5396, 6302, 6697, 6737, 6926.
Gergovia, 2464.
Germania Inferior, 2403, 2555.
Germaniae, 2381, 2382, 2484, 2512, 2723.
Gettysburg, 7515.
Ghana, 4521, 4522.
Gibraltar, 1486.
Göbekli Tepe, 1578, 1607.
Gohram's, 1486.
Gold Coast, 7354.
Göllüdağ, 1606.
Gordium, 1601, 1811.
Gorny, 1473.
Gorze (monastère de), 3822.
Gotland (Sweden), 3324.
Gottingen, 5741.
Graecia, 1558, 1819, 3028, 3029, 365.
Grafschaft Bentheim, 4453.
Gran Colombia, 7381.
Granada, 3153.
Grande-Chartreuse (Monastery), 3109, 3143.
Great Britain, 99, 111, 141, 528, 587, 632, 1008, 1044, 1073, 1098, 1100, 1205, 1244, 1253, 1400, 1414, 1422, 1423, 1474, 1494, 1512, 3187, 3226, 3245, 3421, 3441, 3525, 3608, 3634, 3814, 3827, 3928, 3955, 3970, 3973, 3975, 3985, 3990, 4287, 4290, 4523-4578, 4665, 4669, 4679, 4903, 5206, 5216, 5262, 5273, 5410, 5525, 5553, 5604, 5634, 5658, 5661, 5663, 5664, 5670, 5684, 5695, 5700, 5777, 5816, 5835, 5852, 5891, 5909,
6138, 6158, 6255, 6299, 6317, 6332, 6363, 6367, 6378, 6500, 6519, 6592, 6602, 6620, 6710, 6747, 6761, 6778, 6819, 6862, 6882, 6904, 6918, 6919, 6948, 6981, 7043, 7051, 7088, 7089, 7216, 7222, 7236, 7238, 7248, 7279, 7286, 7303, 7306, 7309, 7311, 7317, 7318, 7320, 7333, 7341, 7346, 7350, 7354, 7356, 7365, 7436, 7471, 7472, 7486, 7487, 7488, 7497, 7502, 7504, 7507, 7510, 7518, 7522, 7524, 7525, 7538, 7549, 7550, 7564, 7581, 7584, 7595, 7610, 7629, 7633, 7637, 7641, 7645, 7651, 7683, 7689, 7690, 7700, 7702, 7718, 7725, 7737, 7738, 7759, 7760, 7785, 7790, 7791, 7807, 7808, 7809, 7837, 7850, 7866, 7878, 7883, 7886, 7890, 7891, 7892, 7894, 7911, 7925, 7926, 7929, 7939, 7941, 7968, 7980, 7991, 8002, 8005, 8017, 8027, 8220, 8248.
Greece v. Hellas.
Grønland, 991, 1027.
Gross-Gerau (Landkreises), 3124.
Guadiana (Portugal), 3440.
Guadyerbas, 1488.
Guangdong, 987, 8159.
Guangxi, 8207.
Guangzhou, Canton, 987, 8209.
Guatemala, 4589, 4590, 7868, 7977, 7988, 8003, 8016.
Guba-Canyon (Kavkaz), 1487.
Gubbio, 6499.
Gürcütepe bei Urfa, 1578.
Guyana, 4591.

H

Haiti, 4592-4597, 7552, 8030.
Halieis, 2027.
Hamburg, 6708.
Hampshire, 3359.
Handaxes, 1519.
Hannover, 4496.
Harare, 8336ù.
Hasanlu, 1793.
Hattuša, 1721, 1730, 1736.
Haut-Maine, 3391.
Havre, 4301.
Heidelberg, 3633.
Hellas, Greece, 245, 258, 344, 511, 522, 1240, 1396, 1813-2259, 4579-4588, 5863, 6806, 7217, 7461, 7503, 7685, 7717. – v. Graecia.
Helsinki, 6707.
Henchir-Mettich, 2316.
Herculaneum, 2770.
Hertfordshire (England), 3102.
Hessen, 661, 7944.
Hierapolis, 1767.
Hierusalem, 2891.
Hilandar (Monastery, Athos, Hellas), 3695.
Hiroshima, 687, 6085.
Hisarlik, 573, 1835.
Hispania Tarraconensis, 2573.
Hispania, 2368, 2560, 2709, 3006, 3028, 3083.
Histria, 2208.
Holland, 5980.
Honduras, 4598-4600.
Hong Ha delta, 8094.
Hong Kong v. Xianggang.
Horom, 1797.
Hrvatska, Croatia, Croatie, 10, 610, 1213, 3343, 3461, 3484, 3492, 4199-4204, 5329, 5426, 5657, 7912.
Hubei, 8159.
Huecas (Toledo), 1515.
Humeima, 1583.
Hunan, 8159.
Hungary v Magyarország.

I

Iasos, 3056.
Iasus (Caria), 1837, 1947, 2216, 2219, 2223, 2226, 2230, 2238, 2241, 2245, 2251.
Iberia, 1556, 2762.
Iceland, 4619.
İkiztepe, 1544.
Ile-de-France, 1287.
Ilium, 2057.
India, 630, 735, 902, 903, 1436, 1570, 1819, 4620-4644, 5124, 5453, 5515, 5850, 5852, 6104, 6139, 6175, 6353, 6634, 6718, 6731, 6939, 7084, 7254, 7255, 7321, 7330, 7340, 7639, 7803, 7872, 7918, 7935, 7955, 7975, 8024, 8077, 8079, 8089, 8091, 8095, 8158.
Indochine, 6118, 7339, 8009.
Indonesia, 4645-4649, 7627, 7814, 7911, 8005.
Indus (flumen), 1513, 1562.
Ingolstadt, 12.
Ino, 2444.
Iolcus, 2242.
Iordanes (flumen), 1501, 1753.
Iran, 95, 240, 636, 1781-1812, 2953, 4654-4662, 5866, 6366, 6559, 6672, 6731, 6748, 7290, 7457, 7817, 7900, 8072.
Iraq, 4650-4653, 7850, 7893.

Ireland, 19, 169, 334, 391, 1044, 1103, 1179, 1285, 1474, 3336, 3441, 3486, 3488, 3490, 3608, 3620, 3634, 3653, 3889, 3986, 4663-4686, 5643, 5800, 5855, 6303, 6432, 7396, 7629, 7656.
Islamabad, 7927.
Island, 49, 3327, 7905.
Ismant el-Kharab, 1612.
Israel, 503, 600, 1501, 1749, 2879, 2919, 4687-4693, 4905, 5535, 7258, 7827, 7861, 7897, 7967, 7984, 7985, 8010, 8012.
İstanbul, 623, 1170, 1174, 6054.
Istria, 366, 8019.
Italia, 92, 118, 127, 130, 136, 246, 250, 285, 290, 301, 328, 385, 447, 506, 518, 562, 613, 646, 656, 684, 688, 709, 853, 889, 958, 973, 1054, 1070, 1188, 1201, 1256, 1261, 1296, 1385, 1390, 1413, 1527, 1814, 2262, 2288, 2295, 2388, 2407, 2443, 2452, 2465, 2535, 2758, 2815, 2978, 3014, 3224, 3239, 3265, 3356, 3405, 3417, 3479, 3657, 3666, 3801, 3810, 3815, 3816, 3821, 3844, 3846, 3951, 4116, 4165, 4230, 4694-4790, 5066, 5067, 5271, 5278, 5341, 5348, 5364, 5366, 5371, 5376, 5377, 5382, 5384, 5387, 5388, 5402, 5403, 5418, 5427, 5448, 5477, 5534, 5551, 5598, 5627, 5629, 5631, 5641, 5660, 5707, 5709, 5754, 5760, 5770, 5779, 5811, 5814, 5856, 5894, 5980, 6112, 6127, 6137, 6192, 6203, 6221, 6222, 6234, 6248, 6294, 6329, 6399, 6408, 6416, 6425, 6427, 6433, 6435, 6436, 6445, 6458, 6460, 6466, 6499, 6517, 6523, 6524, 6545, 6554, 6591, 6603, 6605, 6626, 6654, 6688, 6689, 6693, 6719, 6726, 6732, 6759, 6764, 6776, 6787, 6792, 6796, 6800, 6816, 6864, 6872, 6885, 6897, 7001, 7036, 7042, 7070, 7098, 7099, 7101, 7110, 7112, 7113, 7114, 7119, 7134, 7149, 7185, 7260, 7343, 7395, 7477, 7478, 7521, 7557, 7559, 7590, 7593, 7601, 7605, 7649, 7684, 7696, 7707, 7708, 7731, 7733, 7734, 7749, 7779, 7780, 7781, 7839, 7874, 7877, 7895, 7937, 7950, 7956, 7960, 8001, 8013, 8017, 8019.
Iudaei, 2813, 3043.
Ivanovo, 6698.
İvriz/Konya, 1604.

J

Jamaica, 4791, 4792.
Japan, 345, 530, 1164, 1435, 3934, 4793-4803, 5424, 5548, 5557, 5617, 5735, 6110, 6172, 6599, 6662, 6701, 6754, 6775, 6777, 6891, 6928, 6974, 7261, 7300, 7399, 7531, 7579, 7639, 7654, 7667, 7739, 7971, 8006, 8033, 8039, 8043, 8121, 8122, 8143, 8152, 8169, 8185, 8192, 8265, 8273-8320.
Jerusalem, 7513, 7897.
 – v. Hierusalem.
Jiangnan, 8166, 8245.
Jiangsu, 8238.
Jiujiang, 8229.
Jordan, 4804-4806, 7984.
Jugoslavija, Yugoslavia, 989, 1032, 1319, 3937, 4005, 4852, 5241-5257, 5329, 5536, 7576, 7605, 7632, 7640, 7714, 7749, 7750, 7870, 7958, 7989, 8008.
Julfa, 6731.
Jülich, 7138, 7402.
Jura (Schweitz), 54.
Jutland, 7146.

K

Kadyanda, 1865, 2196.
Kahramanmaras, 1725.
Kaiseraugst, 2752.
Kalavasos-Kopetra, 2250.
Kalavryta, 7789.
Kanlidivane, 1596.
Kanytelis, 1596.
Karatepe-Aslantaş, 1728, 1740.
Kargaly, 1473.
Karnak, 1611, 1622.
Kärnten, 7548.
Kashghar, 5159.
Katanga, 7896.
Katowice, 7716.
Kavkaz, 3012, 7221, 7336.
Kazakhstan, 4807.
Kempen, 71.
Kenya, 4808.
Kephalonia, 7796.
Khabour (flumen), 1697.
Khirbet Yattir (Iudaea), 1754.
Kiev, 137.
Kilise Tepe, 1548.
Kinneret, 1757.
Kitāb al-Maghāzī, 1582.
Kızılırmak, 1468.
Kleve, 7402.
Köln, 1183, 3645, 3679, 5732.
Kondon-Pochta, 1522.
Kongeå, 4259.

Konya, 1543.
Korea, 6649, 7825, 7901, 7919, 8021, 8039, 8181, 8310, 8321-8329.
Korsoté, 1697.
Kosovo, 4018, 4020, 5178, 5254, 5256, 7205, 7217.
Kranj, 1147.
Kremna, 1608.
Kronschtadt, 4988.
Krym, 885, 7484, 7498, 7501, 7530.
Kuban, 912.
Kumtepe, 1537.
Kurdistan, 8059.
Kurpfalz, 5487, 7138.
Kursk, 7756.
Kuwait, 4809, 7991.
Kyoto, 1023.
Kypros, Cyprus, 1541, 1568, 1670, 1804, 1852, 2003, 2220, 2232, 2239, 2250, 2925, 3663, 4210-4212, 7408, 7994.

L

Laconia, 256, 1836.
Lanao, 7667.
Languedoc, 3279, 5482, 5484.
Laos, 8027.
Latmus, 1599.
Latvia, Lettland, Lettonie, 3949, 7206, 7208, 7604, 7770.
Lauenburg, 3135.
Lausanne (Switzerland), 3891.
Lavinium, 2261.
Lebanon, 4811, 4812.
Łęczyca, 4940.
Leiden, 5980, 6847.
Leipzig, 38, 5731, 7038.
Lemnos, 1871.
Leningrad, 7755.
León, 202, 3114, 3605.
Lepreon, 1981.
Lerna, 2179.
Lesotho, 7350.
Lettland v. Latvia.
Lettonie v. Latvia.
Leuctra, 1989.
Liberia, 4813.
Libya, 2404, 4814, 7860, 7986.
Lidar Höyük, 1597.
Lidice, 7789.
Liechtenstein, 142.
Liège, 3893.
Lietuva, Lithuania, 3949, 4815, 4816.
Liguria, 3251, 3678, 6476.
Lima, 6856.
Liman Tepe, 1534.
Limburg (Belgique), 47.

GEOGRAPHICAL INDEX 417

Limoges, 3099.
Lincolnshire (England), 3118.
Lio Maggiore, 3103.
Lisboa, 91.
Lithuania v. Lietuva.
Liuqiu, Riukyu Islands, 8149, 8169.
Livorno, 6708.
Ljubljana, 6429, 7771.
Lodi, 6119.
Łodz, 6980.
Lombardia, 3251, 7479.
London, 477, 3127, 3408, 5861, 6846, 6855, 7041.
Lorraine, 3809.
Loryma, 1586.
Los Angeles, 6907.
Louisiana, 5217, 7373.
Louvain, 5408.
Lübeck, 3135.
Lublin, 4464.
Lucania, 2277.
Lucca (Italia), 3797.
Luceria, 2315.
Luoyang, 8250.
Lyon, 88.

M

Macao v. Aomen.
Macedonia v. Makedonija.
Madagascar, 4819.
Madeira, 283.
Maghreb, 558, 571, 3297, 6573, 7398.
Magnesia apud Maeandrum, 1726.
Magnesia, 2021.
Magyarország, Hungary, 243, 590, 940, 994, 1030, 1211, 3947, 4005, 4087, 4090, 4601-4618, 4151, 5053, 5329, 5405, 5544, 6064, 6972, 7512, 7516, 7571, 7624, 7625, 7640, 7734, 7903, 7904, 7906, 7995, 8007, 8036.
Makedonija, Macedonia, 999, 1830, 1970, 2016, 4142, 4580, 4584, 4817, 4818, 5329, 7575, 7717, 7750, 7989.
Malawi, 4820.
Malaysia, 963, 8005.
Mali, 8034.
Malia-Lasithi, 1842.
Malta, 1772, 4821, 6738.
Maltravieso, 1504.
Mamay-Gora, 1542.
Manchuria (Russian), 5026.
Manchuria, 7579.
Manisa, 1273.
Mantova, 315, 6528, 6561.
Marathona, 1787.
Mari, 1662, 1682, 1691.

Mariñán, 6437.
Maroc, Morocco, 4853-4858, 6442, 7210, 7343, 7830.
Maronaea, 2004.
Marroquís Bajos (Jaén), 1525.
Marsiglia, 6963.
Masada, 1766.
Massa (Italia), 46.
Massachussetts, 5478.
Masseria Tiberio (Gargano), 1490.
Masuren, 7888.
Mataram (India), 3934.
Matopos Hills, 8353.
Mauritius, 8334.
Mecklenburg, 268.
Mecklenburg-Strelitz, 6875.
Mecklenburg-Vorpommern, 4508.
Media, 1802.
Medinet Habu, 1776.
Méditerranée (mer), 890, 948, 3951, 5087, 6738, 7342.
Mekong river, 8009.
Melos, 2007.
Memphis, 1660.
Mendoza, 6873.
Mérida, 170.
Meseta Norte, 1532.
Mesoamerica, 8367.
Mesopotamia, 226, 1662-1720, 7595.
Messenia, 2185.
Messina, 4712.
Metz, 2312.
Mexico City, 7162.
México, 375, 884, 1224, 4822-4848, 5429, 5450, 5452, 5671, 5824, 6419, 6585, 6643, 6807, 6837, 7270, 7519, 7532, 7615, 7617, 7657, 7945, 8370.
Michoacán, 4824, 4842, 4918, 4923, 5621.
Milano, 397, 3890, 4700, 6510, 6549, 6588, 6815, 7021, 7157.
Miletus, 1686.
Minervino Murge, 2268.
Missouri (river), 5603.
Modena, 5388.
Moesia Inferior, 2580.
Moesia, 236.
Moldau v. Moldova.
Moldavia v. Moldova.
Moldova, Moldau, Moldavia, 3246, 3944, 4968, 7388, 7451, 7465.
Monasterio de Sahagún (España), 3134.
Mondoñedo (Galicia, España), 3112.
Mongolia, 3067, 4849-4851, 7551, 8050.
Monsaraz, 1493.

Montecassino (Abbazia), 48.
Montecassino, 445.
Montenegro v. Crna Gora.
Montréal, 4162.
Morano sul Po, 1540.
Moravia, 4234, 5474.
Morea v. Morée.
Morée, Morea, 333, 7446.
Morocco v. Maroc.
Moskva, 1039, 6422, 6668, 6791, 7475.
Mozambique, 4859-4861, 7875, 8354.
München, 1575.
Mureș, 4974.
Mycalessus, 1991.
Mylasa, 1602, 1859, 1929.

N

Nagano, 6724.
Namibia, 152, 4862-4866, 6493, 8342.
Nanjing, 8187, 8255, 8257.
Nantes, 5315, 5823.
Napoli (Regno di), 3236.
Napoli, 568, 4696, 4739, 5773, 5980, 6122, 6813, 6963, 7090, 7167, 7469.
Narna (Mali), 8331.
Natal, 7485.
Navalcán, 1488.
Navarra, 3098, 3139, 3286, 5079.
Nazareth, 1760.
Nederland, Netherlands, Pays-Bas, 93, 125, 2750, 3249, 3427, 3429, 3494, 3520, 3657, 3677, 4645, 4867-4875, 5375, 5486, 5508, 5510, 5511, 5875, 6093, 6704, 6859, 6909, 7016, 7017, 7093, 7297, 7322, 7375, 7389, 7431, 7472, 7627, 7642, 7814.
Negev, 1745.
Nepal, 8095.
Nephelis, 1589.
Netherlands v. Nederland.
Neuchâtel, 5138, 6835, 7151.
Neuva España, 6869.
New England, 7433.
New York, 2777, 5696, 6412, 6826, 6831, 6865.
New Zealand, 6904, 7261, 7385, 7386, 8005.
Nicaragua, 4876-4879.
Niğde-Bor, 6971.
Niger, 4880.
Nigeria, 965, 4881-4883, 6818, 7354, 7829.
Nineveh, 1700, 1708.
Ningpo, 8245.
Ningxia, 8135, 8258.

Nisibis, 3011.
Nogays, 911.
Norge, Norway, 3654, 3789, 4884-4891, 7699.
North Carolina, 5186.
North Sea, 3428.
North West Frontier Province (India and Pakistan), 8096.
Northumberland, 3110.
Norway v. Norge.
Novgorod, 22, 346, 3132, 3216.
Novi Sad, 5242.
Nueva Granada, 7380.
Numidia, 1830.
Nürnberg, 5739, 5836.
Nymphaion, 2233.

O

O Achadizo, 1505.
Oberschwaben, 6875.
Oceania, 7383-7386, 8387-8392.
Odessus, 2317.
Ohalo, 1501.
Oldenbourg, 6906.
Olympia, 1574.
Oman, 4892, 7254.
Oran, 6993.
Orthez (France), 3395.
Osaka, 1023.
Osdroena, 1587, 1594.
Ossets, 909.
Österreich, Austria, 142, 966, 3566, 3947, 4073-4090, 4151, 4867, 5655, 5716, 5785, 5799, 6577, 6650, 6952, 6972, 6973, 7097, 7129, 7137, 7160, 7437, 7450, 7466, 7467, 7474, 7481, 7516, 7571, 7849, 7995, 8004, 8023.
Ostia, 2731.
Ostrobothnia, 6714.
Ou, 8287.
Over-Betuwe, 6762.
Owari, 8273.
Oxford, 5753.
Oxfordshire, 6767.
Oxyrhyncus, 1640.

P

Paderborn (Deutschland), 3462.
Padova, 4722.
País Vasco, 4672, 5114, 971.
Pakistan, 943, 4893-4896, 7084, 7803, 7927, 7955, 8095.
Palaestina, 2908.
Palagruža, 1496.
Palatinus (Mons), 2260, 2732, 2774, 2775, 2787.
Palermo, 5757.
Palestine, 317, 619, 4277, 4897-4905, 7258, 7278, 7326, 7333, 7470, 7568. – v. Palaestina.
Palma de Mallorca, 1453.
Panama, 422, 4906, 4907, 7867.
Panaztepe, 2234.
Pannonia, 2438.
Paraguay, 228, 1224, 4908, 4909, 7209, 7666.
Paris, 269, 446, 1236, 3272, 3370, 3623, 4310, 4318, 4343, 4379, 4382, 5337, 5359, 5595, 5599, 5687, 5749, 5812, 6254, 6384, 6441, 6552, 6821, 7135, 7154.
Parma, 5364, 5415, 6406, 6834.
Parsa, 1803.
Parsu(m)a(š), 1805.
Parthia, 1798.
Pasargadae, 1789.
Pavlovo, 6698.
Pays de Vaud, 6797.
Pays-Bas v. Nederland.
Peak (District), 7027.
Pella, 1984.
Peloponnesus, 1828, 3047.
Península Ibérica, 1450, 1471.
Pennsylvania, 5645.
Pergamum, 1609, 2061, 2254, 2772.
Persepolis, 1801, 1803.
Persicus (sinus), 1562.
Peru, 1416, 4910-4925, 5385, 6661, 6715, 7229, 7298, 7369, 7529, 7838, 8372.
Perugia, 1133, 5376, 6456.
Perusia, 2299.
Peshawar, 7927.
Petersburg, 5721.
Petra, 1781.
Petrograd, 5007.
Peucetia, 2276.
Pfalz-Neuburg, 7138.
Pfalz-Sulzbach, 7138.
Pfalz-Zweibrücken, 7138.
Pharos, 2075.
Philadelphia, 7011.
Philippi, 2888.
Philippine v. Filipinas.
Phocis, 1976.
Phrygia, 1546, 1600, 1601, 1811.
Piemonte, 1133, 3794, 4766, 5726.
Pisa, 198, 2263, 2301, 3353, 5425, 6291.
Pisidia, 1608.
Pistiros, 1856, 1858, 2004, 2028, 2060, 2066, 2227.
Poggio Colla, 2306.
Poland v. Polska.
Polska, Poland, 3122, 3497, 3949, 4005, 4815, 4931-4957, 5003, 5293, 5321, 5329, 5474, 6665, 7275, 7421, 7430, 7448, 7464, 7466, 7467, 7489, 7511, 7577, 7582, 7589, 7602, 7614, 7619, 7640, 7646, 7647, 7662, 7693, 7699, 7702, 7716, 7748, 7763, 7778, 7823, 7848, 7869, 7906, 7940, 7947, 7949, 8031.
Poméranie v. Pommern.
Pommern, Poméranie, 4417, 4938, 6879.
Pompeii, 2332, 2441, 2693, 2769, 2770.
Pontremoli (Italia), 46.
Pontus Euxinus, 2041.
Pontus, 2308.
Populonia, 2304.
Porrentruy (Schweitz), 54.
Porsuk, 1546.
Portugal, 91, 207, 265, 302, 337, 1066, 3111, 3374, 3440, 3444, 3532, 4115, 4958-4965, 5433, 5496, 7323, 7332, 7344, 7360, 7715, 8133, 8233.
Posidonia, 2259.
Potosí, 6858.
Praeneste, 2271.
Praha, 3633.
Prato, 34, 3394.
Preußen, 180, 684, 3921, 4393, 4453, 4498, 5781, 7004, 7104, 7387, 7437.
Propontis, 2041.
Provence, 3251, 3811, 7754.
Pskov, 3647.
Ptuj, 3331.
Puerto Rico, 318, 4966, 7232, 7555.
Puglia, 9, 2789, 2822.
Punjab, 4638, 4640, 4643.
Puteoli, 2313.
Pyrénées, 6833.

Q

Qazvin Plain, 1520.
Quebec, 4160.
Quetta, 7927.
Quintana Roo, 4836.
Quseir, 1796.

R

Raetia, 2297.
Ramat Matred, 1745.
Rapallo, 526.
Ravenna, 2194, 3106.
Ravensbrück, 7688.
Rawa Mazowiecka, 4940.
Regensburg (Deutschland), 3919.
República Dominicana, 7209, 7815.

GEOGRAPHICAL INDEX

Rheinland, 2414.
Rheinland-Westfalen, 5854.
Rhein-Main-Gebiet (Deutschland), 3119.
Rhenus (Flumen), 2456.
Rhine, 7669.
Rhodes, 3260.
Rhodus, 2064.
Rifreddo (moastero di), 3815.
Rio de Janeiro, 428.
Rio Grande do Sul (Brasil), 7378.
Riparo Mochi (Balzi Rossi), 1508.
Riukyu Islands v. Liuqiu.
Rochester, 3662.
Roma, 299, 415, 502, 634, 715, 749, 962, 1118, 1133, 1296, 1933, 2056, 2260-2826, 2940, 2953, 3023, 3263, 3385, 4772, 5347, 5348, 5423, 5609, 5690, 5728, 6372, 6631, 6794, 6808, 7177.
România, 205, 537, 1015, 1030, 1148, 3219, 3221, 4967-4984, 5329, 5706, 5751, 7083, 7284, 7393, 7480, 7516, 7523, 7528, 7545, 7609, 7613, 7622, 7628, 7701, 7714, 7735, 7745, 7764, 7902.
Rossija, Russia, 20, 79, 305, 335, 346, 419, 453, 493, 504, 555, 579, 592, 616, 621, 645, 730, 768, 769, 866, 873, 892, 909, 911, 912, 926, 1039, 1109, 1178, 1202, 1234, 3149, 3215, 3333, 3482, 3496, 3651, 3885, 3934, 4807, 4985-5027, 5242, 5343, 5454, 5455, 5456, 5457, 5458, 5459, 5460, 5566, 5608, 5616, 5622, 5691, 5692, 5693, 5717, 5758, 5859, 6018, 6023, 6207, 6325, 6395, 6396, 6397, 6487, 6563, 6663, 6668, 6669, 6698, 6700, 6702, 6739, 6744, 6768, 6773, 6791, 6947, 6961, 6978, 7037, 7102, 7210, 7211, 7241, 7245, 7287, 7336, 7374, 7392, 7394, 7429, 7472, 7475, 7476, 7489, 7493, 7496, 7499, 7507, 7508, 7509, 7531, 7533, 7544, 7546, 7551, 7573, 7580, 7596, 7611, 7620, 7681, 7755, 7757, 7767, 7822, 7826, 7887, 8098, 8206, 8236. – v. SSSR.
Rouergue (France), 3798.
Roussillon, 295.
Ruhrgebiet, 7046.
Ruokolahti, 7023.
Russia v. Rossija.
Rwanda, 7957.

S

Saarbrücken, 1165.
Saar-Mosel-Raum (Deutschland), 3897.
Sachsen, 886, 4503, 6695, 6958.
Sacromonte (Abadía, Granada), 29.
Saint-Blaise (Bouches-du-Rhône), 1479.
Saint-Denis, 3222.
Saint-Germain-des-Prés, 7416.
Saint-Petersburg, 225, 2988.
Saint-Pierre-et-Miquelon, 7670.
Saint-Sernin (Toulouse), 3107.
Saint-Victor (Abbaye, Paris, France), 72.
Sais, 1660.
Salamina, 1868.
Salento (Italia meridionale), 3354.
Samanud, 1653.
Samarcanda, 3171.
Samudera-Pacém (sultanato), 7406.
Samus, 1862, 2046.
San Giacomo di Ripoli (convento, Firenze), 102.
San Giovanni in Laterano (Roma), 3898.
San Giovenale, 2287.
San Juan Ante Portam Latinam, 1524.
San Millán de la Cogolla (Monasterio, España), 50.
San Miniato, 3261.
San Nicolao, 2281.
San Severino e San Sossio (monastero, Napoli), 3101.
San Silvestro di Nonantola (monastero), 3687.
San Vittore (basilica, Varese), 3144.
Santa Fe, 6827.
Santa María de Otero de las Dueñas (monasterio), 3116.
Santa Maria Maggiore (Roma), 3898.
Sao Paulo, 4116, 4121, 7064.
São Tomé and Principe, 5028.
Saqqara, 1625, 1637.
Sarawak, 7338.
Sardegna (regno di), 6877.
Sardinia, 1385, 2860, 2916, 2944.
Sardis, 1792.
Satricum, 2261.
Saudi Arabia v. Arabie Saoudite.
Savoie, 5145, 6413.
Scamander (flumen), 1921.
Scandinavie, 1197, 1279, 1376, 4002, 7758.
Scapa Flow, 7586.
Scar (Orkney, Scotland), 3323.

Schlesien, 4425.
Schleswig-Holstein, 3135, 6950, 6988.
Schweiz, Suisse, Svizzera, Switzerland, 249, 964, 1110, 1137, 4867, 5138-5150, 5320, 5361, 5407, 5818, 6170, 6720, 6736, 6839, 6863, 7059, 7353, 7444, 7455, 7483, 7705, 7706, 7712, 7726, 7812, 7912, 7913, 7939.
Scotland, 6, 90, 3110, 3398, 3419, 4541, 4564, 4573, 3970, 4540, 5791, 7403, 7415.
Sela pass, 7918.
Senegal, 5030, 7187, 8349.
Senegambia, 8337.
Serbia v. Srbija.
Sermoneta (Italia), 3414.
Sevilla, 31, 5108.
Shanghai, 5140, 6533, 6742, 8119, 8179.
Shenxi, 8135.
Shqiperi, Albania, 2741, 4018-4023, 5329 7205, 7217, 7541, 7618, 7782.
Siam, 7440.
Sibir', 887, 8070.
Sichuan, 8249.
Sicilia, 370, 1499, 1873, 2023, 2793, 2927, 4707, 4781, 4783, 5583, 6187, 6997, 7090.
Siella Leone, 5031.
Siena, 3407, 5380.
Sierra Puebla, 4848.
Sikyon, 2181.
Sina, 3041.
Sinai (mons), 1623.
Singapore, 6662.
Singara, 2440.
Sipontum, 2255.
Sippar, 1687.
Sirkeli Höyük (Adana), 1581.
Sithonii, 2558.
Siwa, 2119.
Slovakia v. Slovensko.
Slovenija, 689, 983, 1048, 1292, 5058-5066, 5329, 5752, 6527, 6640, 6642, 6774, 7762, 7768, 7989.
Slovensko, Slovakia, 191, 235, 275, 992, 1386, 3097, 3515, 3947, 5032-5057, 5329, 7646, 7736, 7742.
Småland, 6949.
Smirna, 1863.
Somalia, 5067.
Somerset, 4565.
Soria (España), 3362.
Sos Höyük, 1559.
Sottland, 4538.

GEOGRAPHICAL INDEX

Soudan, 1632.
South Africa, 988, 5068-5073, 5493, 6647, 6943, 7362, 7485, 7973.
South Cadbury (Somerset), 1529.
Spain v. España.
Sparta, 1833, 1874, 1969, 1981, 1993, 2001, 2020, 2256.
Split, 5255.
Srbija, Serbia, 3544, 5244, 5247, 5256, 5257, 6938, 7480, 7500, 7508, 7517, 7523, 7536.
Sri Lanka, 5120-5125, 7951, 8095.
SSSR, 621, 671, 1047, 3997, 4011, 4518, 4768, 4775, 5006, 5329, 5458, 5588, 5712, 5793, 5833, 6886, 6947, 6961, 7048, 7546, 7558, 7573, 7575, 7577, 7578, 7615, 7635, 7647, 7653, 7660, 7671, 7681, 7689, 7693, 7698, 7703, 7709, 7723, 7728, 7739, 7784, 7793, 7795, 7807, 7821, 7822, 7823, 7826, 7832, 7834, 7843, 7864, 7877, 7880, 7884, 7885, 7904, 7905, 7908, 7915, 7933, 7940, 7958, 7972, 7998, 8000, 8026, 8036, 8098, 8197, 8235, 8260.
St Giles's Hospital (Norwich, England)., 3745.
St. Georgskirche (Oberzell, Reichenau, Baden-Württemberg, Deutschland), 3658.
St. Mang (Benediktinerkloster, Füssen, Deutschland), 3826.
Stalingrad, 7764, 7766.
Stegeborg, 3357.
Strasbourg, 5523, 7080.
Stratonicea, 2222.
Stuttgart, 57.
Sudan, 4279, 7827, 7860.
Sudet v. Sudeten.
Sudeten, Sudet, 7643, 7680, 7690.
Südtirol, 3430, 8001.
Suez, 7866, 7906, 8028.
Sufetula (Tunisia), 2892.
Suffolk, 3133.
Suisse v. Schweiz.
Sumatra, 7406.
Sumatra, 8080.
Suomi, Finland, 926, 1142, 3240, 4287-4291, 5133, 5443, 5805, 5806, 5872, 6114, 6590, 6618, 6743, 6998, 7029, 7165, 7439, 7463, 7671, 7676, 7681, 7699, 7751, 7807.
Suriname, 7375.
Susa, 1562.
Susa, 1801.
Sverige, Sweden, 527, 986, 3100, 3210, 3225, 3240, 3400, 3783, 3933, 4891, 5126-5137, 5518, 5644, 6095, 6131, 6169, 6636, 6929, 6944, 6977, 7002, 7005, 7174, 7175, 7729, 7931.
Svizzera v. Schweiz.
Swaziland, 8345.
Sweden v. Sverige.
Switzerland v. Schweiz.
Sydney, 6417.
Sylvanès (Abbaye de), 3798.
Syria, 657, 1590, 1799, 2779, 2908, 3016, 5151-5153.

T

Tage (Portugal), 3440.
Taiwan, 8169, 8216, 8271.
Tajikistan, 5154.
Tall Šaih Hasan, 1773.
Tanger, 7342.
Tang-I Var, 1679, 1707.
Tanzania, 5155.
Taranto, 3145.
Tarhuntašša, 1673, 1677.
Tarquinia, 2295.
Tarraco, 2747.
Tarsus, 1674.
Tawang, 7918.
Tehran v. Tihran.
Tel Kinrot, 1757.
Tel Ma'ahaz, 1616.
Tel Shalem, 2743.
Tell Chuēra, 1680.
Tell el-Amarna, 1660.
Tell el-Oreimeh, 1757.
Tell en Nasbeh, 1780.
Tell Tuneinir, 1799.
Tennessee, 5197.
Tenochtitlan, 6837, 8370.
Tenus, 2058.
Tepe Guran (Luristan), 1539.
Tepe Yahya, 1554.
Tervakangas (Ostrobothnia), 1551.
Těšín region, 7848.
Tetzcoco, 8370.
Teutoburgiensis (saltus), 2380.
Thailandia, 5156, 8082.
Thasos, 1863, 2004.
Theadelphia, 1650.
Thebe, 1833, 1937, 1989.
Thessalia, 1976, 3068.
Thessalonica, 2888, 3017, 3074.
Thracia, 236, 2227, 2461, 2580, 7717.
Thronos-Kephala, Sybrita, 1848.
Thugga, 2547, 2719.
Thulelandet, 4262.
Tibet, 7872, 8199, 8202.
Tibur, 2733.
Tigray, 4285.
Tihran, Tehran, 4655.
Tikal, 8371.
Tlacopan, 8370.
Tlalocan, 8368.
Toggenburg, 5526.
Tokyo, 6619.
Toledo, 3287.
Toletum, 3023.
Tomaszów Lubelski, 7746.
Torino, 1133, 4785, 6848.
Toscana, 198, 3095, 3407, 4748, 4754, 4786, 4788, 6403, 7152, 7153.
Transbaikalia, 5009.
Transcaucasia, 1712.
Transilvania, 4971, 4973, 5474, 6871, 6881, 6991, 7516.
Transjordan, 4806.
Trebisonda, 3007.
Trebula Suffenatium, 2549.
Trentino, 469, 3869.
Treviso, 3148.
Trieste, Trst, 4075, 5066.
Trinidad and Tobago, 5157.
Tripura, 4628.
Troezen, 2181.
Trogir, 3388.
Troia, 1537, 1835, 1846, 2663.
Trst v. Trieste.
Tunis, 353.
Tunisie, 7343, 7769.
Turan, 8071.
Turkestan, 5546.
Turkey v. Türkiye.
Türkiye, Turkey, 293, 930, 1182, 1498, 3299, 4806, 5158-5178, 5552, 5782, 5822, 5840, 6043, 6054, 6660, 6735, 6737, 6804, 6812, 7076, 7126, 7142, 7218, 7241, 7257, 7287, 7290, 7393, 7394, 7423, 7450, 7491, 7494, 7508, 7517, 7557, 7559, 7603, 7620, 7743, 7837, 7890, 7954, 8032, 8073.
Türkmenistan, 3673.
Tyrrhenum (Mare), 2422.

U

Uaxactun, 8383.
Uganda, 5179, 7957.
Ugarit, 1670, 1716.
Ukraine, 3949, 5180, 5181, 5293, 5329, 7259, 7284, 7774.
Ulster, 4670.
Umma, 1694.
Umma, 1732.
Unelles, 2492.
Uppsala, 1220, 5803.
Ur, 1678, 1686.
Ura, 1677.

GEOGRAPHICAL INDEX

Urbino, 3177.
Urfa, 1594.
Uruguay, 5226, 5227, 7658.
Uruk, 1665.
U.S.A., 309, 314, 508, 587, 772, 1047, 1062, 1161, 1200, 1209, 1252, 3954, 3955, 3999, 4599, 4715, 4837, 4928, 5182-5225, 5275, 5296, 5303, 5304, 5308, 5313, 5327, 5404, 5434, 5528, 5621, 5669, 5672, 5711, 5716, 5729, 5730, 5846, 6051, 6088, 6163, 6170, 6319, 6341, 6377, 6388, 6398, 6419, 6520, 6529, 6530, 6542, 6547, 6566, 6572, 6579, 6583, 6595, 6624, 6625, 6648, 6692, 6710, 6758, 6761, 6878, 6904, 6966, 7009, 7028, 7032, 7049, 7054, 7201, 7214, 7215, 7219, 7224, 7227, 7229, 7230, 7233, 7235, 7244, 7250, 7251, 7252, 7253, 7256, 7262, 7266, 7267, 7268, 7269, 7270, 7271, 7272, 7274, 7279, 7280, 7283, 7289, 7291, 7292, 7374, 7375, 7476, 7482, 7486, 7492, 7497, 7520, 7526, 7534, 7537, 7552, 7555, 7598, 7601, 7615, 7617, 7633, 7658, 7686, 7733, 7737, 7760, 7790, 7808, 7815, 7817, 7820, 7828, 7831, 7835, 7837, 7847, 7850, 7852, 7853, 7856, 7862, 7868, 7871, 7876, 7878, 7883, 7884, 7887, 7889, 7895, 7897, 7901, 7909, 7910, 7911, 7917, 7921, 7922, 7924, 7925, 7929, 7932, 7933, 7934, 7944, 7950, 7952, 7953, 7963, 7964, 7966, 7969, 7976, 7977, 7988, 7993, 8003, 8005, 8006, 8015, 8016, 8017, 8020, 8021, 8027, 8030, 8033, 8035, 8187, 8188, 8235, 8251, 8260.

V

val de Blenio, 6951.
Valachia, 3246.
Valencia, 274.
Valle d'Aosta, 4764.
Van, 1579, 1666.
Van/Karagündüz, 1711.
Veii, 2295.
Vendée, 4337.
Venetia, 2278, 2283, 2303, 3003, 3089.
Veneto, 4769, 5584, 6746, 7479.
Venezia, 115, 455, 1034, 1484, 3176, 3248, 3386, 3471, 4086, 4708, 4725, 4779, 5469, 5479, 5527, 6457, 6501, 6706, 7022, 7086, 7408, 7446.
Venezuela, 434, 5228-5235, 5390, 6116, 6946, 7276.
Venusia, 2315.
Verona, 3368.
Versailles, 4378.
Vicenza, 3125.
Victoria, 6102.
Viducasses, 2492.
Vienna (Gallia Narbonensis), 2415.
Vietnam, 5236-5240, 7329, 7851, 7858, 7932, 7961, 8017, 8027, 8082.
Vigna Barberini, 2314, 2774, 2787.
Villena, 1536.
Villenave-d'Ornon (France), 3389.
Villeneuve, 3156.
Vilnius, 5861. – V. region, 7799.
Visigothae, 2821.
Viterbo, 2281, 2288.
Vivarais, 3820.
Volaterrae, 2291, 2301.
Volga-Oka River Basin, 1497.
Volhynia, 7783.

W

Waadt, 5139.
Wales, 56, 387, 3142, 3187, 3648, 3659, 3889, 5372, 5807, 7056.
Warwickshire (England), 3102.
Waterloo, 7458, 7462.
Weimar, 5714, 6313, 6586.
Wellington, 5722.
Wenzhou, 8224.
West Indies, 4791, 7365.
Westfalia, 58.
Wien, 950, 3633, 5549, 6410.
Wiesbaden-Igstadt, 1509.
Wijnaldum (Netherlands), 3911.
Wuhan, 8104.
Württemberg-Hohenzollern, 7923.
Wuxi County, 8105.

X

Xianggang, Hong Kong, 5869, 6597, 7335, 8110, 8157, 8252.
Xinjiang, 8022, 8197.

Y

Yangtze delta, 8142.
Yangzi valley, 8106.
Yarnton (Oxfordshire), 1549.
Yemen, 3292.
Yokohama, 7341.
York, 3147, 3867.
Yorkshire (England), 3800.
Yugoslavia v. Jugoslavija.

Z

Zadar, 6656.
Zaire, 7957.
Zambia, 8350.
Zimbabwe, 7871, 8336, 8353.
Zürich, 5523, 6369.